Exploring Public Relations

Exploring Public Relations

Third edition

Ralph Tench
Professor of Communications Education,
Leeds Metropolitan University

Liz Yeomans
Principal Lecturer, Public Relations and
Communications,
Leeds Metropolitan University

PEARSON

Harlow, England • London • New York • Boston • San Francisco • Toronto • Sydney • Auckland • Singapore • Hong Kong
Tokyo • Seoul • Taipei • New Delhi • Cape Town • São Paulo • Mexico City • Madrid • Amsterdam • Munich • Paris • Milan

PEARSON EDUCATION LIMITED
Edinburgh Gate
Harlow CM20 2JE
United Kingdom
Tel: +44 (0)1279 623623
Web: www.pearson.com/uk

First published 2006 (print)
Second edition published 2009 (print)
Third edition published 2014 (print and electronic)

© Pearson Education Limited 2006, 2009 (print)
© Pearson Education Limited 2014 (print and electronic)

The screenshots in this book are reprinted by permission of Microsoft Corporation.

Pearson Education is not responsible for the content of third-party internet sites.

ISBN: 978-0-273-75777-1 (print)
       978-0-273-75781-8 (PDF)
       978-0-273-79489-9 (eText)

British Library Cataloguing-in-Publication Data
A catalogue record for the print edition is available from the British Library

Library of Congress Cataloging-in-Publication Data
A catalog record for the print edition is available from the Library of Congress

10 9 8 7 6 5 4 3 2 1
17 16 15 14 13

Print edition typeset in 9.5/12pt Minion Pro by 35
Print edition printed and bound in Great Britain by Butler Tanner & Dennis Ltd

Cover image: Getty Images

NOTE THAT ANY PAGE CROSS REFERENCES REFER TO THE PRINT EDITION

Brief contents

Contents

Lecturer Resources

For password-protected online resources tailored to support the use of this textbook in teaching, please visit **www.pearsoned.co.uk/tench**

Guided tour of book

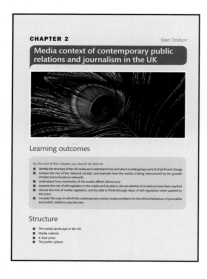

Learning outcomes at the start of each chapter help you to focus on the key points you should understand by the end of the chapter.

The **Structure** section gives you a quick-reference guide to how the chapter will play out.

Explore boxes encourage you to deepen your understanding of the chapter material through exercises that link theory with real-world situations

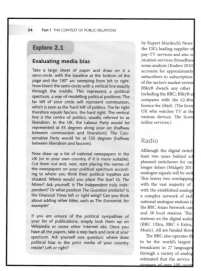

Boxes contain a wealth of additional information and interesting viewpoints on the public relations industry.

Think about boxes suggest exercises and topics for debate around key contemporary PR issues.

Case studies unites chapter themes through a deep exploration of a recent important story

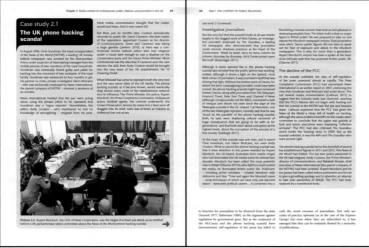

Each chapter ends with a **Summary** that draws together all the chapter topics in a concise overview.

The **Bibliography** offers suggestions for further reading, and can be the ideal starting point if looking for sources for a research paper.

About the authors

Professor Ralph Tench is professor of communication education and acting director of research for the Faculty of Business and Law at Leeds Metropolitan University, with responsibility for the research strategy for over 150 academics representing law, accounting and finance, strategy and economics, marketing and communications and human resource management.

Dr Tench is the former subject head for public relations and communications at Leeds Metropolitan University, where for ten years he oversaw the expansion of the undergraduate, postgraduate and professional course portfolio. As professor he teaches on undergraduate and postgraduate programmes, as well as supervising MA and PhD research students. His current focus is on developing and delivering major research projects in public relations and strategic communication in the UK and worldwide. Current projects include the ECOPSI (European Communications Practitioners Skills and Innovation) programme, the largest EU-funded public relations programme awarded at 360,000 Euro. This project explores the education, skills and competency needs of European communication practitioners (www.leedsmet.ac.uk/ecopsi). The aim is to influence both theory and practice with this project by building knowledge, understanding and practical outputs. This research builds on another international longitudinal research project (since 2007) funded by European bodies and private sector business, the ECM survey. The European Communication Monitor (www.communicationmonitor.eu) is a qualitative and quantitative trend survey of European communications directors using a sample of over 3,000 practitioners from 42 countries. Reflecting the breadth of his research experience and application, Professor Tench has recently directed a research project into communications issues in delivering weight management programmes for young people for the UK NHS, for the Carnegie Weight Management Institute (MoreLife) and a consulting project into CSR in Turkey funded by the EU.

Professor Tench is a past external examiner for many UK and European universities, as well as a visiting professor. His doctoral students are engaged in research on issues of strategic communication related to trust, responsibility, branding and relationship management. He also supervises students on issues of professionalisation and the development of the public relations discipline. He has chaired over 30 PhD examinations and sat on panels for candidates in the UK, Ireland, Australia and Denmark.

Professor Tench is an active member of the European Public Relations Research and Education Association (EUPRERA) and is currently the chair for the annual congress academic papers. He is a member of the International Communication Association (ICA) and sits on the editorial board for the *Journal of Communication Management*, the *Journal of Further and Higher Education, Corporate Communications: An International Journal, Public Relations Review* and the *International Journal of Strategic Communication*.

Ralph is a regular guest and keynote speaker at academic and practitioner conferences and his research has been published and disseminated in books, journals and conferences worldwide. Previous editions of *Exploring Public Relations* have been translated into several European languages. Currently Dr Tench is editing two volumes on his research interests in corporate social responsibility with Emerald – *Corporate Social Irresponsibility: A Challenging Concept* (2013) and *Communicating Corporate Social Responsibility* (2014).

Liz Yeomans is principal lecturer and former subject group head for public relations and communications at Leeds Metropolitan University. Since joining the university in 1994, Liz has helped establish a leading UK centre in public relations education. As well as contributing to the university's BA (Hons) Public Relations course, Liz has led the development of courses for working professionals and established masters programmes in public relations and corporate communications, including, in 2010, a Master in International Communication together with four European institutions that comprise the Geert Hofstede Consortium. Her teaching focuses on the social psychology of communication, research methods, public relations theory, stakeholder relations and employee communication at undergraduate, postgraduate and professional levels. Liz has supervised numerous student dissertations, two of which have gone on to win the annual EUPRERA Jos Willems dissertation prize.

Liz has extensive experience in academic quality systems and processes. She has held external roles at Southampton Solent University, The Robert Gordon University, Aberdeen, the Manchester Metropolitan University and London Metropolitan University. She is a current external examiner at Bournemouth University and Cardiff University.

As a CIPR member, Liz has contributed book reviews to the Institute's *Profile* magazine and was a member of the judging panel for the CIPR's local public service excellence awards in communication. More recently, Liz contributed to a CIPR discussion panel on gender issues in PR.

Liz's research is concerned with the experiences and interactions of individuals inside organisations in relation to their occupational and social contexts. Her doctoral work has involved developing perspectives in PR, drawing on gender and emotional labour theories within the sociology of work. Liz has recently published in the online journal *PRism*, contributed an entry on gender and public relations to *The Encyclopedia of Public Relations* and a chapter to *Gender and Public Relations*, edited by Christine Daymon and Kristin Demetrious, which is part of the Routledge *New Directions in Public Relations and Communication* series. Liz's earlier research has been published in the *Journal of Communication Management*, the *Journal of Public Affairs* and *Corporate Communications: An International Journal*. She has presented research papers at EUPRERA, BledCom and ICA. Liz has acted as reviewer for EUPRERA congresses, the *Journal of Public Relations Research* and the *Journal of Public Relations Inquiry*. Liz is a member of EUPRERA's Women in PR project team.

The contributors

Dr Nilam Ashra-McGrath is a writer and researcher for the non-profit sector. She has extensive experience in communication and training roles for development agencies and charities in the Philippines, India, Republic of Maldives, Sri Lanka and the UK. She has delivered modules in creative work in cultural industries, PR, corporate communications and NGO management for universities in the UK and France (including Leeds Metropolitan University). She runs workshops on the ups and downs of PhD research, qualitative research methods and working for NGOs. Her research interests include media representations of development issues, oral histories, using diaries in research and the sociology of communications work.

Richard Bailey is senior lecturer in public relations at Leeds Metropolitan University and has lectured in universities since 2003. He previously worked as a consultant and trainer.

He edits *Behind the Spin* magazine (www.behindthespin.com) and has contributed to a chapter on the future of public relations education to *Share This: The Social Media Handbook for PR Professionals*, published by Wiley in 2012.

Shirley Beresford is senior lecturer in public relations and marketing at Leeds Metropolitan University, where she teaches on undergraduate, postgraduate and professional courses. She has been an active member of the Chartered Institute of Marketing for 15 years and works as an examiner for their postgraduate courses. Prior to joining Leeds Metropolitan in 1999, Shirley had a 15-year career in arts, leisure, tourism and public sector PR and marketing management. Shirley's research interests lie in the development of arts marketing and PR.

Dr Clea Bourne is a lecturer in promotional media at Goldsmiths, University of London. She completed her PhD at Leeds Metropolitan University, where she also taught before moving to Cardiff and, more recently, Goldsmiths. She worked in corporate communications for more than 20 years, latterly specialising in financial institutions in wholesale and retail markets. Her current research focuses on trust production in financial systems, where she has explored communication strategies used to generate trust by life insurers, institutional investors, hedge funds, credit rating agencies, investment banks and unregulated investment schemes.

Ryan Bowd is the head of active (sports) at IMG Consulting. His client work includes the Abu Dhabi International Triathlon, Adidas Eyewear, Asics, Gatorade, GE, GE Capital, IHG (Holiday Inn brand), Inov-8, NHS (UK National Health Service), Sailfish, Tata Consultancy Services, Virgin Active London Triathlon and Olympic, Commonwealth, Ironman Triathlon and adventure athletes. Prior to joining IMG Consulting, Ryan was an award-winning PR practitioner and until 2009 was a senior lecturer at Leeds Metropolitan University. He has also taught PR and marketing at Leeds University and Manchester Metropolitan University. Ryan started his career at Weber Shandwick, before running his own agency, 1090 Communications, which he sold to Connectpoint PR (now Amaze PR). Ryan's publishing and research background is in corporate and financial communications, PR, CSR and now sports marketing.

Wendy Carthew has worked as a part-time lecturer and associate of the Centre for PR Studies at Leeds Metropolitan University since 2010. She has taught on undergraduate, postgraduate and Chartered Institute of Public Relations (CIPR) professional courses. She is an independent internal communication consultant following a 15-year career in corporate communications, specialising in employee communication and engagement for organisations such as the Department of Health, Aviva and O2. Her research interests lie in the field of internal communication and the role it plays in engaging employees.

Professor W. Timothy Coombs, PhD, is a full professor in the Nicholson School of Communication at the University of Central Florida. His research areas include crisis communication, activist use of the Internet to pressure organisational change and issues management. He is past recipient of the Jackson, Jackson and Wagner Behavioural Research prize from the Public Relations Society of America. His articles have appeared in a variety of international journals and his book chapters have appeared in major works in the field of public relations, including the *Handbook of Public Relations* and *Encyclopedia of Public Relations*. His crisis books include the award-winning *Ongoing Crisis Communication, Code Red in the Boardroom* and he co-edited *The Handbook of Crisis Communication* with Sherry Holladay. His other books include *Public Relations Strategy and Application: Managing Influence, Managing Corporate Social Responsibility: A Communication Approach* and the award-winning *It's Not Just PR* (all co-authored with Sherry Holladay). He has twice been Chair of the Public Relations Division of the National Communication Association in the USA.

Sean Dodson is a senior lecturer and course leader of the undergraduate Journalism course at Leeds Metropolitan University. He has previously worked as a journalist, specialising in the social uses of technology, and has contributed to *The Guardian, Wired, Design Week, The South China Morning Post* and *The Sydney Morning Herald*. Sean has published papers on the subject of emerging network technology for the Institute of Network Cultures in Amsterdam and the Institute for Internet and Society in Berlin. He recently contributed a chapter for *The Phone Hacking Scandal: Journalism on Trial* (2012) and was a judge on *The Orwell Prize 2012*, the UK's most prestigious prize for political writing.

Dr Lee Edwards is lecturer in communications (PR) at the University of Leeds, where she teaches and researches on PR as a socio-cultural occupation. A critical scholar, her primary focus is on the operation of power through PR, both within the occupational field and in wider society. As well as making theoretical contributions to the understanding of PR, she has published on the exercise of symbolic power through PR as a cultural intermediary, and on diversity in PR. Before she became an academic she worked in industry as a technology PR specialist. Lee previously lectured at Leeds Metropolitan University and Manchester Business School.

Dr Johanna Fawkes is senior lecturer in public relations at Charles Sturt University, Australia, and was previously course leader for the BA (Hons) degree at Leeds Metropolitan University. She has devised and delivered PR degrees and professional courses at three UK universities since 1990, following a career in local government and trade union communications. In recent years she has worked as an independent PR and research consultant based in Leeds. Johanna has written numerous papers for leading international journals and conferences, for which she is also often a reviewer, and contributed several chapters to core PR text books. Her specialist areas are professional ethics, Jungian ethics, persuasion and social psychology.

Professor Finn Frandsen is professor of corporate communication and director of the Centre for Corporate Communication at the School of Business and Social Sciences, Aarhus University (Denmark). His primary research interests are crisis communication and crisis management, environmental communication, corporate communication, public relations, marketing communication and organisation and management theories. Finn has been a visiting professor at Copenhagen Business School, BI Norwegian Business School, Lund University, Aalto University, ICN Business School, IULM University and Dakar Business School. He has edited and written numerous books, book chapters and journal articles. He is regional editor (Europe) of *Corporate Communication: An International Journal*. In 2006, he was elected Teacher of the Year at the Aarhus School of Business.

Professor Anne Gregory is director of the Centre for Public Relations Studies at Leeds Metropolitan University and chair of the Global Alliance, the worldwide confederation of over 60 public relations professional associations. Anne leads research and consultancy programmes for public and private sector clients such as the UK Cabinet Office, The Department of Health and Tesco Corporate. She is an advisor to the UK Government having completed three attachments. She has led two global research initiatives being a co-convenor of the Stockholm Accords and the Melbourne Mandate projects and is currently co-leading the Global GAP Survey. Dr Gregory has written and is series editor of 20 books; authored 30 book chapters and over 50 refereed journal articles and conference papers. She is editor-in-chief of the Journal of Communication Management. Anne was president of the Chartered Institute of Public Relations (CIPR) in 2004, leading it to chartered status and was awarded the Sir Stephen Tallents Medal in 2010 for her outstanding contribution to the profession.

Dr Tony Jaques is managing director of the independent consultancy Issue Outcomes Pty Ltd, and was previously issue manager for a major American multinational corporation, with responsibility across the Asia-Pacific region. He is an internationally recognised authority on issue management, with numerous contributions to leading journals and conferences, and is a sessional lecturer in the masters programme at RMIT University in Melbourne, Australia. He is a Fellow of the Public Relations Institute of Australia and received the Howard Chase Award from the Issue Management Council for his work in developing international best practice standards.

Dr Winni Johansen is professor of corporate communication and director of the Executive Master's Programme in Corporate Communication at the School of Business and Social Sciences, Aarhus University (Denmark). Dr Johansen's research interests include crisis communication and crisis management, environmental communication, corporate communication, public relations, marketing communication, visual communication and organisational culture. Winni has been a visiting professor at ICN Business School, BI Norwegian Business School, Copenhagen Business School, IULM University, Lund University, Aalto University and Dakar Business School. Her research has been published in numerous books, book chapters and journal articles. In 2004, she was elected Teacher of the Year at the Aarhus School of Business.

Neil Kelley is a chartered marketer and a senior lecturer responsible for undergraduate marketing and the Chartered Institute of Marketing (CIM) course leadership at Leeds Metropolitan University. He is a senior examiner at the CIM, for the CAM marketing and consumer behaviour and principles of mobile marketing modules, and an examiner at the University of Cambridge. Neil specialises in marketing communications, with a strong focus on digital, and has contributed chapters to a number of print and audio books for the CIM and FT Prentice Hall. As a former marketer, Neil has provided training and services for companies such as Electronic Arts, Toyota, Trading Standards Institute and a number of professional bodies.

Lucy Laville is a senior lecturer and course leader for the undergraduate PR courses at Leeds Metropolitan University. She has 15 years' experience in PR and marketing practice, having worked for American Airlines, KPMG, Epilepsy Action, Northern Profile PR Agency and, more recently, as head of communications at Leeds Metropolitan University, before joining the PR and Communications academic subject group in the Faculty of Business and Law in 2006.

Lucy has experience in a range of areas, including media relations, crisis management, internal communications, community relations, public affairs and marketing. She has spoken at academic and PR professional conferences on crisis communications.

Dr Danny Moss is professor of corporate and public affairs at the University of Chester. Prior to moving to Chester, he was co-director of the Centre for Corporate and Public Affairs at the Manchester Metropolitan University Business School, and programme leader for the University's masters degree in international public relations. He also established and led the first dedicated masters degree in public relations at the University of Stirling in the late 1980s. He is a former external examiner for postgraduate programmes at Leeds Metropolitan University. He is also the co-founder of BledCom, the annual global public relations research symposium that is held at Lake Bled, Slovenia. Danny is co-editor of the *Journal of Public Affairs*, has published articles in a wide range of international journals and has authored and co-authored a number of books, including *Public Relations Research: An International Perspective* (1997), *Perspectives on Public Relations Research* (2000) and *Public Relations Cases: International Perspectives* (2010).

Paul Noble is an independent public relations trainer, consultant, academic, mentor and speaker/facilitator. He is a CIPR-approved trainer, an e-learning specialist and provides management support to growing PR consultancies, as well as mentoring young professionals. He has more than 30 years' experience in senior consultancy, both in-house and in academic environments. Paul is chief examiner of the CIPR's Advanced Certificate and one of the examiners of the Diploma. He is a Fellow of both the CIPR and AMEC, and is a CIPR Chartered Practitioner – as well as an assessor for the scheme. Paul is co-author of *Evaluating Public Relations*.

Elliot Pill is a senior lecturer and director for the MA in International Public Relations and Global Communications Management at the School of Journalism, Media and Cultural Studies at Cardiff University. He is a former newspaper journalist and international public relations consultant who has acted as a publicist for a number of well-known celebrities. The manufacture and maintenance of celebrity status is one of Elliot's current research interests. He is the co-author of *Key Concepts in Public Relations* (2009), published by Sage. Elliot is a former external examiner at Leeds Metropolitan University.

Iain Sheldon is vice president and head of client strategy at IMG Consulting. Iain is a highly experienced sports marketer with over 20 years' experience. Iain has strong rugby experience, currently leading the O2 team, where he was responsible for the recent UK Sports Industry

Association award-winning 'Get Up For England' campaign, as well providing the strategic lead for Gatorade (Premier Rugby Partner). His recent client experience includes developing the European strategy for ASICS, global sports marketing strategies for Hyundai and GE and a global evaluation methodology for Samsung. He also leads the IMG Consulting HSBC business (golf and Wimbledon). Other clients include Coca-Cola (diet Coke, Coca-Cola, Sprite), Cisco Systems, Citroën UK, Guinness, Heinz, Intel, Martell Cognac, Rubicon and Robinsons.

Helen Standing is an accredited practitioner of the Chartered Institute of Public Relations (CIPR) and has an MA in public relations. Helen has worked in a variety of communications roles in consultancy and in-house. She has been named Yorkshire and Lincolnshire's Outstanding Young Communicator by the CIPR, one of *PR Week*'s 'Top 29 under 29' and a finalist for Some Comms' brightest social media communicator under 30. As well as her role as co-director of communications consultancy Engage Comms Ltd, she sits on one of the CIPR's regional committees as treasurer and is a mentor and occasional guest lecturer at Leeds Metropolitan University and Sheffield Hallam University.

Judy Strachan spent over 20 years working in advertising agencies in London and Australia. She started her career as an account manager, progressing to account director, before switching to a creative role. As a copywriter and creative director she worked on varied accounts, including major blue chip companies and international charities. During a career break she completed her MA, and then joined Leeds Metropolitan University as a senior lecturer in marketing. Judy's teaching responsibilities included advertising, marketing communications and branding, as well as course management. Judy took early retirement in 2012 to focus on her writing interests.

Professor Dejan Verčič, PhD, FCIPR, is a founding partner in Pristop, a communication management consultancy based in Ljubljana, Slovenia, and a professor for public relations at the University of Ljubljana. He holds a PhD from the London School of Economics. He has published over 200 articles, books, chapters, papers and reports. Recent books include *Culture and Public Relations* (2012) and *The Global Public Relations Handbook* (2009), both with K. Sriramesh, and *Public Relations Metrics* (2008) with B. van Ruler and A. Tkalac Verčič. Professor Verčič served as the chairman of the research committee of the IABC Research Foundation and as the president of

EUPRERA. Since 1994 he has organised an annual international public relations research symposium – BledCom. He is a member of research teams working with Professor Tench managing the ECM (European Communication Monitor) and the ECOPSI (European Communication Professionals Skills and Innovation Programme). He is also working on TERMIS (Terminology data bank).

Dr Neil Washbourne is senior lecturer in media studies at Leeds Metropolitan University. He teaches and publishes on media, politics, democracy and celebrity. He is the author of *Mediating Politics: Newspaper, Radio, Television and Internet* (McGraw Hill/Open University Press) published in 2010. He also wrote a chapter on 'the media context of PR and journalism' for previous editions of *Exploring Public Relations*. He is currently completing a chapter, 'Mediating Nick Clegg: the celebrity politician, presidentialisation and the UK 2010 leadership debates', for an edited book on *Television Election Debates in the UK, US and Europe* for publication by Palgrave MacMillan in 2013.

Paul Willis is director of the Centre for Public Relations Studies at Leeds Metropolitan University. He was previously board director of a public relations agency and part of the team that won the prestigious *PR Week Consultancy of the Year Award*. He has worked for organisations including ASDA, BT, BMW, the Cabinet Office, Department of Health, Proctor & Gamble and The Football Association. Paul's research has appeared in leading scholarly journals, including *Public Relations Review*, and he is the co-author of *Strategic Public Relations Leadership*. He has also lectured at the National School of Government and been invited to present his research to academic and professional audiences around the world.

Emma Wood is senior lecturer in public relations at Queen Margaret University, Edinburgh, and a coordinator of QMU's Centre for Dialogue. Her research and communications practice focuses on the use of dialogue in communications, particularly in relation to helping young people safely navigate situations involving alcohol (http://www.qmu.ac.uk/mcpa/cdial/AlcoLols.htm). She publishes on corporate identity and corporate communication and is a reviewer for, and former editor of, the *Journal of Communication Management*. She has a background in communication in both the financial and business sectors. Emma is course leader of the CIPR's postgraduate diploma in Scotland and a Fellow of the CIPR; she is also a former external examiner at Leeds Metropolitan University.

Foreword

Like most people in the public relations scholarly community, I have studied numerous books on public relations and on corporate communication, or communication management as the field is often called in other countries. Most books are very technical, 'how to' books, promising that you will be able to do the job as long as you follow the tips of the author. Some books are very theoretical, analysing merely one single theoretical focus, with the promise that you will become a good practitioner as long as you follow this approach. *Exploring Public Relations* is none of these, or, to put it differently, it is all of these books in one. It is theoretical and practical at the same time, it provides an insight in almost all theoretical approaches and different ideas on how to do public relations and it raises unsettled questions about the definition, the tasks of the professional, the debate about professional ethics and the issue of its impact. This is the most open-minded book I know.

Look at the prudent way in which the editors have challenged almost everything that commonly is left undiscussed in the educational and practical fields of public relations: that public relations has to do with persuasion and also with propaganda; that the public relations field has a problem with its legitimacy; and that there is no consensus whatsoever about what public relations is and what its value is for organisations of all kinds. The authors try to avoid taking a stand, leading us through all the discussions, rumours and evidence about these issues. What a book! It is fresh and good, it covers all the current topics and simultaneously opens up a lot of perspectives. And all this in a very user-friendly manner. This book starts with the idea that a textbook should put the student at the centre of the learning experience. And that is exactly what it does.

It is an excellent book for undergraduates who want to know more about the field. But at the same time it is also very practical for associating it with different approaches and models within the discipline of PR, and for interdisciplinary connections with communication studies and the wider context of social sciences. This makes the book also relevant and important for masters programmes in public relations. Leeds Metropolitan University has a history as one of the largest public relations faculties in Europe, and

that breadth of experience pays off in the depth, diversity and range of topics and approaches presented here. Public relations is an evolving discipline, and its growth requires continual questioning to challenge its boundaries and establish its terrain. The authors have succeeded brilliantly in doing that.

The first edition of *Exploring Public Relations* was a milestone. It was both very British and very international. *Exploring Public Relations* not only provided helpful guidelines to practical action, but raised unsettling questions about impact and implications as well. It was diverse, different and consistently thoughtful in departing from the US norm. Instead of simple platitudes about equal exchanges, *Exploring Public Relations* looked at how to actually perform public relations in an ethical manner across very diverse cultures. It was also theoretically inclusive, with a light touch that left students able to make up their own minds at the same time as they learned how to become competent practitioners. It was not uncritical of a field where technical mastery can override moral behaviour, as my colleague Professor David McKie from Waikato Management School, University of Waikato, New Zealand, wrote in his foreword for the second edition.

This third edition is updated in an enviable way, including all kinds of new issues – for example, about the media context of contemporary public relations and journalism (Chapter 2), about the intercultural and multicultural context of public relations (Chapter 5), about corporate image, reputation and identity (Chapter 10) and last, but not least, about research and evaluation (Chapter 9). The book therefore includes reference to almost everything that has been written in the last couple of years. What an effort! It is updated with the newest insights on financial public relations, public affairs, issues management and crisis public relations management.

The European Communication Monitor 2012 describes how social media changes the field of public relations. It is all included in this third edition. Technology, communications and our ever-growing need for credible content were top of mind with business communicators during the International Association of Business Communicators' (IABC) 2012 Annual Conference. These topics are widely discussed in *Exploring Public Relations*, too. In 2010, the Global Alliance of Public Relations and Communication Management engaged more than 1,000 practitioners, academics and PR association leaders from some 30 nations in developing the Stockholm Accords, a bold brief for the role of PR/communications in governance, management, sustainability and internal and external communication, but also a rather idealistic approach to the practice. *Exploring Public Relations* discusses these ideas and challenges the outcome of the Stockholm discussion with daily practice and other codes of conduct.

This is a book every public relations author wishes she or he had written. It will help students to get introduced to the field and it helps teachers to discuss important topics with their students. You will not be disappointed.

Betteke van Ruler
Professor Emerita Corporate Communication and
Communication Management
Department of Communication Science
University of Amsterdam
The Netherlands

Preface

The journey to a third edition

How time flies. It does not seem long ago that we were scoping out the structure and content for the first edition of *Exploring Public Relations*. We first conceived of this book in the early 2000s and it started with the idea that a textbook should put the student at the centre of the learning experience. While it is true that textbooks in general are becoming more student-centred for subjects as varied as biology, law, media and psychology, this was not, and has not been, the case in public relations. *Exploring Public Relations* very much led the way in this approach for our discipline, and the feedback and compliments the book regularly receives are testimony to this. With this approach we wanted students to have an improved learning experience by involving them in a personal journey that brought the subject to life on the page and spurred them on to find out more. And this is what we have tasked ourselves to do with this exciting third edition. Our second edition brought challenges, and so has this version of the book. But we have benefited from the ability to listen to students and academic colleagues in how they read, study with and educate using the first two editions of the book and its supplements. And through this listening we have attempted to answer any questions or gaps in the earlier versions to ensure it is fit for purpose in a challenging, changing world of communication.

The key areas we have addressed are the most obvious ones in contemporary life of how the techniques used in public relations and communication have been influenced by rapid technological change and its integration, particularly in the past five years. To reflect this we have ensured that all chapters consider the implications of technology and change on the theory and practice of the discipline. Clearly, some chapters have integrated these influences more than others. One of the key features of the book is that it is an edited textbook and all chapters are written and reviewed within a consistent framework. This means that the book has a particular style and consistency that we have been keen to preserve. This is partly achieved by only working with senior and experienced academics and practitioners who share a mission to understand and explain the discipline. We are therefore pleased to be able to include contributors from around the world who are closely associated with us individually and collectively at Leeds, and have the same aspirations to improve the subject knowledge and application of public relations in society. Again, we feel this was and continues to be a unique feature and strength of the book as it has evolved.

So, who to write such a comprehensive text? For this we looked to our colleagues – people who are part of the Public Relations and Communications Subject Group at Leeds Metropolitan University who teach on our well-established undergraduate, postgraduate and research programmes. We also looked to our wider network – senior academics and practitioners who have contributed to our subject area and programmes, former colleagues who have moved on to careers elsewhere and past external examiners.

Target audience

Feedback suggests there is a diverse range of readers for *Exploring Public Relations*, from senior practitioners to undergraduate students. It is the preferred textbook for universities around the world, as well as for the professional body and professional courses that adopt it as their core text. Its content is comprehensive, which perhaps explains this broad appeal. That said, the book is written in a way that it can be used and read by someone who is totally new to the discipline as well as a student or practitioner with significantly more depth of understanding. The contents pages of the book demonstrate how it can be used to support more practical and theoretical aspects of the discipline and at different levels. Therefore, it is a perfect accompaniment for undergraduates and postgraduates who are studying public relations as a single subject (i.e. a bachelors or masters in public relations), jointly with another subject, or as a single module or unit within a wider programme.

Book style and structure

The book is divided into four parts. Part 1 provides important background knowledge to help students understand the broad business and societal context in which public relations plays a role. Included here, for example, are chapters on democracy and on the intercultural and multicultural context of public relations. In Part 2 there is a chapter on the related, but often ignored, topic of persuasion and propaganda to help you arrive at your own definitions; while Part 3 includes emerging specialisms such as issues management, community involvement, financial PR and public affairs. Part 4 comprises chapters that are not conventionally included within a public relations textbook. In this section, for example, there are chapters on pressure groups and NGOs, health communication and public relations and celebrity. The final chapter looks to the future and provides some themes and questions that we hope student readers will take up as topics for investigation and research. Public relations is an evolving discipline and its growth requires continual questioning to challenge its boundaries and establish its terrain. As students, teachers, researchers and practitioners we are all responsible for achieving this aim.

Pedagogy and its place

This is an educational textbook for public relations and therefore includes a number of devices that we hope will help both students and tutors to get the most out of the material. First, each chapter begins with a list of the *Learning outcomes* that students should achieve after engaging with the material. We have structured the book to have a range of consistent pedagogy that support the reader in understanding the chapter subject. For example, there are regular *Explore* features that give instructions on where to look for further information or how to engage further with topics. *Think abouts* are included to encourage reflection and for the reader to pause and think a little more deeply about the issues and ideas that are being presented and discussed. We have attempted to define as many terms or phrases as possible that may not be universally understood or that form part of the specialist language related to that topic or area of study, which are included in a glossary at the back of the book. Finally we have included many case studies (*Case studies* and *Mini case studies*), which aim to exemplify and apply the principles under discussion.

Over to you

We have been delighted and occasionally surprised at the warm response to our first two editions. These have been read and used for teaching literally all over the world, and with gratifying endorsements of our original pedagogic strategy of making clear links between theory and practice. However, there are many questions about public relations and its practice that remain under-explored. These we aim to highlight in this book and inspire readers to investigate further, possibly through detailed research for undergraduate and postgraduate projects and dissertations. We hope this revised third edition continues to bridge the divide between theory and practice and, above all, is a thought provoking and enjoyable read for students, practitioners and tutors alike.

Ralph Tench and Liz Yeomans, 2013

Acknowledgements

In addition to the invaluable contributors already mentioned, we would like to thank all those at Pearson Education for making this third edition possible.

Thanks also to Catharine Steers (Acquistions Editor), Joy Cash (Senior Project Editor), Paul Kirkham (Marketing Manager), Emily Anderson (copy editor), Karen McLaren (proofreader), Sasmita Sinha (permissions editor) at Pearson for their encouragement and helping us see through the project to completion.

We would like also to thank our former colleague Naoimh Bohan, who has provided professional support in supporting us in administering and preparing the final manuscript.

Finally, but not least, we would like to thank our families. For Ralph, this dedication goes to my father John and of course to Catherine, Anna and Will. A physical object like the book is some justification for why I spend so much time in a bike-filled home office.

For Liz this third edition is dedicated to my late parents, Peter and Sonia, and to my partner John Faulkner for providing unwavering support during a challenging year. Finally it is dedicated to Daniel and Hannah for their good humour and understanding.

Publisher's acknowledgements

We are grateful to the following for permission to reproduce copyright material:

Figures

Figure 4.5 adapted from The pyramid of corporate social responsibility: toward the moral management of organizational stakeholders, *Business Horizons*, 34 (4), pp. 39–48 (Carroll, A. B. 1991), Copyright (c) 2013. With permission from Elsevier; Figure 4.7 from Paola Sapienza and Luigi Zingales http://financialtrustindex.org/resultswave15.htm, Figure 1: Trust, reproduced with permission; Figure 6.2 after *FT Creative Business*, 13/07/2004, based on research by new2marketing, accessed www.ipr.org.uk, 20 July, The Financial Times, © The Financial Times Limited. All Rights Reserved.; Figure 6.10 from R. Tench and J. Fawkes (2005), 'Mind the gap: exploring attitudes to PR education between academics and employers,' Paper presented at the Alan Rawel, CIPR Academic Conference, University of Lincoln, March, copyright (c) Johanna Fawkes MA MCIPR; Figure 7.3 from *Doing Cultural Studies: The Story of the Sony Walkman*, Vol. 1, Sage/The Open University (Du Gay, P., S. Hall, L. Janes, H. Mackay, and K. Negus 1997) Reproduced by permission of SAGE Publications, London, Los Angeles, New Delhi and Singapore. Copyright (c) Sage Publications 1997; Figure 8.2 from *Strategy: Process, Content, Context*, Thomson (De Wit, R. and Meyer, R. 2010) reproduced with permission; Figure 8.4 from *Effective Public Relations*, 8th ed., Pearson Education, Inc. (Cutlip, Scott M., Center, Allen H. and Broom, Glen M. 2000) p. 244 (c) 2000, Reprinted by permission of Pearson Education, Inc., Upper Saddle River, NJ; Figure 8.6 from *Effective Public Relations*, 8th ed., Pearson Education, Inc. (Cutlip, Scott M., Center, Allen H. and Broom, Glen M. 2000) (c) 2000, Reprinted by permission of Pearson Education, Inc., Upper Saddle River, NJ; Figure 8.7 from *Planning and Managing Public Relations Campaigns*, 3rd ed., Kogan Page (Gregory, A. 2010) reproduced with permission; Figure 8.8 adapted from *Planning and Managing Public Relations Campaigns*, 3rd ed., Kogan Page (Gregory, A. 2010) p. 44, reproduced with permission; Figure 8.11 from Involving stakeholders in developing corporate brands: the communication dimension, *Journal of Marketing Management*, 23, pp. 59–73 (Gregory, A. 2007), reprinted by permission of Taylor & Francis Ltd, http://www.tandf.co.uk/journals; Figure 10.1 from The three virtues and seven deadly sins of corporate brand management *Journal of General Management*, 27 (1), Autumn, pp. 1–17 (Balmer, J.M.T. 2001), reproduced with permission; Figure 10.1a from Shareholding versus stakeholding: a critical review of corporate governance, *Corporate Governance*, 12 (3), pp. 246–262 (Letza, S., X. Sun and J. Kirkbride 2004), Copyright (c) 2004 John Wiley & Sons. Reproduced with permission of John Wiley & Sons Ltd.; Figure 10.2 from Reputation Institute. The RepTrak™ System, http://www.reputationinstitute.com/thought-leadership/the-reptrak-system, reproduced with permission; Figure 11.1 from *Communication and Persuasion: Control and Peripheral Routes to Attitude Change*, Springer-Verlag (Petty, R. E. and J. T. Cacioppo 1986) by kind permission of Springer Science+Business Media, Richard E. Petty and John T. Cacioppo; Figure 13.1 from *Here Comes Everybody: The Power of Organizing without Organizations*, Penguin Books (Shirky, C. 2008); Figure 14.3 from *Making the Connections: Using Internal Communication to Turn Strategy into Action*, Gower Publishers (Quirke, B 2000) p. 12, Copyright (c) 2000 Gower Publishing, reproduced with permission; Figure 15.2 adapted from BITC 2005 Annual Report, accessed 18 February 2005, www.bitc.org.uk, copyright (c) Business in the Community (BITC); Figure 15.3 from 'Co-operative Bank Ethical Policy,' Co-opeartive Bank internal publication, copyright (c) Co-operative Bank; Figure 16.2 from Issue Outcomes P/L, reproduced with permission; Figure 18.1 from Edelman, reproduced with permission; Figure 20.2 adapted from *Public relations: A Managerial Perspective*, Sage (Moss, D.A. and Desanto, B. (Eds) 2011) Reproduced by permission of SAGE Publications, London, Los Angeles, New Delhi and Singapore. Copyright (c) Sage Publications 2011; Figure 21.1 from World Economic Forum, World Scenario Series: The future of the global financial system: a near term outlook and long-term scenarios, fig. 4, http://www3.weforum.org/docs/WEF_Scenario_FutureGlobalFinancialSystem_Report_2010.pdf (c) 2009 World Economic Forum, reproduced with permission; Figure 23.2 from Sport Business International

(2010) (Sport) Sponsorship Revenues by Region published in SportBusiness in Numbers, Vol. 4, SportBusiness Group 2010, reproduced with permission; Figure 24.1 from The organisation of integrated communications: toward flexible integration, *European Journal of Marketing*, 42 (3/4), p. 440 (Christensen, L. T., Firat, A. F., & Torp, S. 2008), reproduced with permission; Figure 24.2 from *Exploring Strategy*, 9th ed., Pearson Education (Johnson, G, Whittington, R. and Scholes, K. 2011) fig. 5.7, reproduced with permission; Figure 24.6 from *Managing Public Relations*, Holt, Rinehart & Winston (Grunig, J. E. and T. E. Hunt 1984) p. 141, reprinted by kind permission of James E. Grunig; Figure 24.7 from *Raising the Corporate Umbrella: Corporate communication in the 21st century*, Palgrave (Kitchen, P. and D. Schultz (eds) 2001) Reproduced with permission of Palgrave Macmillan; Figure 27.1 adapted from *Standing Room Only: Strategies for Marketing the Performing Arts*, Harvard Business School Press, Boston, MA (Kotler, P. and Scheff, J. 1997) Reprinted by permission of Harvard Business School Press. Copyright (c) 1997 by the Harvard Business School Publishing Corporation; all rights reserved; Figure 28.1 from K. Nessmann (2008), 'Personal Communication Management; How to position people effectively,' Paper presented at EUPRERA 2008 Congress, 'Growing PR: Institutionalizing Public Relations and Corporate Communications,' 16–18 October, Milan, Italy, reproduced with permission.

Maps

Map 24.1 from CBI, Offices location map, http://www.cbi.org.uk, reproduced with permission

Screenshots

Screenshot 2.1 from http://www.guardian.co.uk, Copyright Guardian News and Media Ltd 2013; Screenshot 19.2 from Chartered Institute of Public Relations, http://www.cipr.co.uk, copyright (c) Chartered Institute of Public Relations, reproduced with permission; Screenshot on page 441 from http://www.gorkana.com/measurement-matters, reproduced with permission

Tables

Table 4.1 after The pyramid of corporate social responsibility: toward the moral management of organizational stakeholders, *Business Horizons*, 34 (4), pp. 39–48 (Carroll, A. B. 1991), Copyright (c) 2013. With permission from Elsevier; Table 4.3 adapted from *Management learning perspectives on business ethics. In J. Burgoyne and M. Reynolds (eds.),*

Management Learning, Sage (Snell, R. 1997) p. 185, Tab. 10.1, Reproduced by permission of SAGE Publications, London, Los Angeles, New Delhi and Singapore. Copyright (c) Sage Publications 2011; Table 6.1 from *What is public relations? In Theaker, A. (ed.), The Public Relations Handbook,* 3rd ed., Routledge (Fawkes, J. 2008) reproduced with permission; Table 6.2 from J. Fawkes and R. Tench (2004b), 'Public relations education in the UK,' A research report for the Chartered Institute of Public Relations, copyright (c) Johanna Fawkes MA MCIPR and Ralph Tench; Table 6.4 after *Unlocking the Potential of Public Relations*, IPR (DTI/IPR 2003), Contains public sector information licensed under the Open Government Licence (OGL) v1.0. http://www.nationalarchives.gov.uk/doc/open-government-licence/open-government; Tables 16.1, 16.2 from Issue Outcomes P/L, reproduced with permission; Table 19.1 from www.theconstructioncentre.co.uk (www.theconstructioncentre.co.uk/trade-periodicals-and-news/t.html), reproduced with permission; Table 21.1 from Extract from Global Financial Centres 12, published by the Z/Yen Group in September 2012, reproduced with permission; Table 21.2 from Table of press releases from March 2012, with kind permission from Andrew Michael, editor, Headlinemoney.co.uk; Table 22.1 from World Advertising Research Centre (WARC), AA/Warc Expenditure Report, www.warc.com/expenditurereport, reproduced with permission; Table 24.1 from CCI Corporate Communication International at Baruch College/The City University of New York (2011), 'CCI Corporate Communication practices and Trends Study 2011: Final Report,' www.corporatecomm.org/pdf/report2011.pdf [accessed 10th November 2011], reproduced with permission; Table 24.2 from CCI Corporate Communication International at Baruch College/The City University of New York (2011), 'CCI Corporate Communication practices and Trends Study 2011: Final Report,' www.corporatecomm.org/pdf/report2011.pdf [accessed 10th November 2011], reproduced with permission; Table 24.3 from *Organizational identity: linkages between internal and external organizational communication. In F.M. Jablin and L.L. Putnam (eds.), The New Handbook of Organizational Communication,* Sage (Cheney, C.G. and L.T. Christensen 2001) p. 238, Republished with permission of SAGE Publications, Inc. Books; permission conveyed through Copyright Clearance Center, Inc.

Text

Case Study 6.1 after Based on the findings from qualitative case study research conducted in Mexico City between 2004 and 2006 by Dr Caroline Hodges at Bournemouth University, copyright (c) Dr Caroline Hodges and Bournemouth University; Case Study 9.2 adapted from By kind permission of Clare Martin, Pompey in the Community, reproduced with permission; Box 11.4 after *Theoretical foundations of campaigns. In RE Rice and CE Atkin (eds.), Public Communication Campaigns,* 2nd ed., Sage (McGuire, WJ 1989) Republished with permission of SAGE Publications, Inc. Books; permission conveyed through Copyright Clearance Center, Inc.; Box 12.2 from Craig Pearce, http://craigpearce.info/, This blog entry was posted on January 11, 2012 by Australian strategic PR practitioner, Craig Pearce and is reproduced with permission; Case Study 14.1 from By kind permission of Aviva UK; with thanks to Jon Hawkins, Aviva UK; Case Study 14.2 from By kind permission of Corporate Communications and Public Affairs, South Lanarkshire Council; Box 14.2 from CIPD Factsheet: The Psychological Contract, January 2008. The Chartered Institute of Personnel and Development, With the permission of Chartered Institute of Personnel and Development, London (www.cipd.co.uk); Case Study 14.3 from With thanks to Richard Davies, Employee Engagement, eBay Europe; Box 14.5 adapted from www.toyotajobs.com/ENG/Workingat.aspx, Reproduced with permission from Toyota (GB) PLC; Case Study 15.1 from 'BT Community Partnership Programme', copyright (c) Business in the Community (BITC); Case Study 15.2 adapted from 'Leeds Cares: collaborative action', copyright (c) Business in the Community (BITC); Case Study 15.3 from 'American Express', copyright (c) Business in the Community (BITC); Case Study 15.3 from Guide Dogs for the Blind Association and Andrex, copyright (c) Guide Dogs for the Blind Association; Case Study 15.4 from 'HP Sauce', copyright (c) Business in the Community (BITC); Case Study 15.6 from Business in the Community and the Scottish Nappy Company, copyright (c) Business in the Community (BITC); Case Study 15.6 from Used with kind permission of the Co-operative Bank from its Ethical Policy and Strength in Numbers documents, copyright (c) Co-operative Bank; Box 17.2 adapted from *Ongoing Crisis Communication: Planning, Managing, and Responding,* 3rd ed., Sage, Inc. (Coombs, W. T. 2012) Republished with permission of SAGE Publications, Inc. Books; permission conveyed through Copyright Clearance Center, Inc.; Box 17.3 adapted from *Ongoing Crisis Communication: Planning, Managing, and Responding,* 3rd ed., Sage (Coombs, W. T. 2012) Republished with permission of SAGE Publications, Inc. Books; permission conveyed through Copyright Clearance Center, Inc.; Case Study 19.1 from Interview with commerical architect Nigel Jacques BA(Hons) BArch(Hons) RIBA; Box 19.1 from Helen Standing, Director, Engage Comms; Consultant, Trimedia UK; Box 20.5b adapted from http:// webarchive.nationalarchives.gov.uk, Contains public sector information licensed under the Open Government Licence (OGL) v1.0. http://www.nationalarchives.gov.uk/ doc/open-government-licence/open-government; Case Studies 25.1, 25.1 from With thanks to Terrence Higgins Trust; Box 25.6 from With thanks to Terrence Higgins Trust; Case Study 27.1 from imove What's On Guide, www.imoveand.com [Published September 2011], reproduced with permission; Case Study 27.2 from http:// www.leedsmet.ac.uk/festivalvolunteering/index_about. htm [Accessed 18.7.2012], reproduced with permission; Box 27.4 from *The Art Newspaper, no. 223, April 2011,* reproduced with permission.

Photographs

The publisher would like to thank the following for their kind permission to reproduce their photographs:

(Key: b-bottom; c-centre; l-left; r-right; t-top)

5 Getty Images; 6 Alamy Images: Peter Adams; 29 Reuters: Parbul TV; 36 Alamy Images: Mark Sykes; 39 Shutterstock.com: Megastocker; 50 Getty Images: Miguel Vidal; 53 Getty Images: AFP; 66 Evelyn Tambour; 77 from Time Magazine, 26 December 2011 (c) 2001, Time Inc. Used under license. Time Magazine and Time Inc. are not affiliated with, and do not endorse products or services of licensee.; 91 The Kobal Collection; 93 Institute of Communication and Media Studies; 111 Nicola Green; 129 Getty Images; 131 Corbis: Dennis M Sabengan/epa; 135 Alamy Images: Philip Bigg; 163 City Of Darwin Civic Centre; 171 Pompey in the Community; 178 Met Life; 186 Alamy Images: Chris Fredriksson; 192 Alamy Images: PSL Images; 198 Corbis: LLC; 204 Getty Images; 220 Alamy Images: Robert Landau; 225 Getty Images: Hindustan Times; 241 Getty Images; 246 Shutterstock.com: Regien Paassen; 253 Alamy Images: Chris Rout; 285 Alamy Images: Steve Hamblin; 308 Shutterstock.com: Vadim Petrakov; 320 Reuters: Raj Patidar; 331 Cannes Lions; 338 Getty Images: AFP; 347 Timothy Soar; 364 Getty Images: Tim Graham; 375 Shutterstock. com: Elena Elisseeva; 382 Getty Images: Siegfried Layda; 388 Shutterstock.com: FikMik; 393 Getty Images: AFP; 400 Getty Images: Picture Net; 403 Getty Images: Guido Mieth; 407 Getty Images: Gregor Hocevar; 414 Corbis: Red Bull Handout/Redbull content pool; 427 IMG; 430 Ryan Bowd; 431 Ryan Bowd; 433 Getty Images; 435 IHG; 475 Corbis: Ted Spiegal (bl); Eric Nathan/Loop Images (cl); Bob Thomas (br); Bob Sacha (cr); 487 Crown Copyright Courtesy of the Department of Health in association with the Welsh Government, the Scottish Government and the Food Standards Agency in Northern Ireland: Yorks and Humber Strategic Health Authority; 488 MoreLife; 522 Getty Images; 524 Getty Images; 536 Alamy Images: Steven May; 539 Alamy Images: Iain Masterton.

In some instances we have been unable to trace the owners of copyright material, and we would appreciate any information that would enable us to do so.

PART 1

The context of public relations

This first part of the book provides you with the background knowledge you will require to understand the role and purpose of public relations (PR), set against the broader business and societal contexts in which it plays an active role. Chapter 1 discusses how public relations is defined in different ways and how it has evolved as a contemporary practice in the United States, Britain, Germany and Sweden. Chapter 2 discusses the contemporary media environment with specific reference to the UK context, while acknowledging the global reach of news distributed online. Arguably, public relations is essential to modern democratic societies. In Chapter 3 the relationship between democracy and public relations is explored. Chapter 4 examines the societal context of public relations from the organisation's perspective, highlighting the theme of corporate social responsibility. In Chapter 5, the international and multicultural context of public relations is introduced. Finally, we turn to the role of the public relations practitioner in Chapter 6, to focus on what public relations practitioners do.

CHAPTER 1

Lee Edwards

Public relations origins:
definitions and history

Learning outcomes

By the end of this chapter you should be able to:

- identify the key definitions of public relations used in practice today
- recognise the debates around the nature of public relations and what it means
- understand the emerging science of public opinion and its role in the development of public relations
- describe the key features of the history of public relations in the United States, Britain, Sweden and Germany
- understand the social and cultural dynamics that led to the emergence of the profession in these countries.

Structure

- Public relations definitions
- Public opinion: justifying public relations
- Business, politics, society and public relations: country case studies

Introduction

What is public relations? And when did public relations begin? This chapter briefly reviews why it has proved so difficult to define public relations work or reach a universally agreed definition of what the job entails. It outlines what is known about the emergence of public relations as a modern occupation, drawing primarily on the histories of the United States, Britain, Germany and Sweden (but acknowledging developments in other countries). The discussion of both definitions and histories reflects the fact that public relations is a product of the social, cultural, economic and political circumstances of its time and evolves according to the needs of these broader environments. Thus, it has both good and bad consequences, depending on the perspective from which it is viewed.

Public relations is now a global occupation and implemented in many corners of the world in different ways. However, written histories of public relations reflect the dominance of the United States on the academic field of public relations and tend to focus on its origins in the United States rather than in other countries (McKie and Munshi 2007; Wehmeier et al. 2009). Exceptions include the comprehensive history of public relations in Britain by Jacquie L'Etang (L'Etang 2004a), discussed in this chapter, a number of important texts about public relations in Germany (Binder 1983; Bentele 1997; Hein 1998) and *The Global Public Relations Handbook* (Sriramesh and Verčič 2003, 2009), which offers a range of 'potted' histories of public relations in different countries. Here, the limitations of existing histories will be considered and should be taken into account when reading the case studies. There is much still to be said and understood about the emergence of this occupation (see also Chapter 3).

Public relations definitions

Definitions are important because they shape expectations of what public relations (PR) could or should be about. For both academics and practitioners, definitions establish the 'territory' of public relations and therefore help justify budgets, salaries, funding for campaigns, teaching and research. Consequently, debates about definitions are important and ongoing. Agreeing on definitions about PR is, however, a tricky task. One reason for this is that PR is used by organisations of all types for a wide range of purposes. Governments may use it to promote policy decisions and prompt behavioural change among voters, businesses to sell their goods and services or publicise their socially responsible activity, and non-profit organisations to prompt financial or other forms of support among their target audience. A second reason is that the standpoint from which to define PR is a matter of opinion. If one is focused on strategies and tactics, then an organisation-centric definition may be appropriate. However, if one is more interested in its social effects, then a more appropriate starting point may be the organisation's audiences, or the social world in which it operates (Toth 2010; Edwards 2012). As a result, the likelihood is that if you ask three practitioners and three academics to define PR, all six answers will differ. Nonetheless, most will be based on the assumption that PR is something organisations do, which has certain desired effects on the people with whom those organisations wish to have a relationship. The following section outlines some of the most common definitions among academics and practitioners (Cutlip et al. 2006). See Explore 1.1.

Explore 1.1

Defining public relations

With a group of friends, write down your definition of PR. Now think about how you arrived at that definition:

■ Is it based on your experience of PR and what you observe PR practitioners doing?

■ Is it based on what you read about PR in the newspapers?

■ Is it based on what your tutors have told you about PR?

Now compare your definitions:

■ How different are they?

■ What do they have in common?

■ What are the differences and why do you think they exist?

Each of you will have different thoughts about what should and should not be included in the definition. See if you can agree on a common set of ideas, then test them on other friends and see how far they agree or disagree.

Academic definitions of public relations

People have been trying to define PR for over a century. Harlow (1976) found 472 different definitions of PR

Picture 1.1 PR is often a synonym for deception, or 'spin'. The British publicity agent, Mark Borkowski, is associated with high-profile publicity stunts on behalf of his clients. (*source*: Getty Images)

coined between 1900 and 1976, and there have been many more since then. Most have tried to be relatively concise, creating a broad umbrella that can incorporate a wide spectrum of strategies and tactics that focus on organisational needs. Grunig and Hunt (1984: 6), for example, defined PR in one sentence as 'the management of communication between an organisation and its publics', later refined as 'an organisation's managed communications behaviour' (Grunig 1997, cited in Grunig et al. 2006: 23). Grunig (1992) argues that this definition allows for differences in practice between practitioners in different contexts, but still includes important elements, such as the management of communication and the focus on external relationships. Kitchen (1997) is even briefer with his definition, suggesting that PR can be defined as 'communication with various publics', although he does add to this by arguing that PR is an important management function and has a strategic role to play.

Other definitions focus on 'ideal' communications practices: two-way communications and building positive relationships between organisations and their publics (Ledingham 2006). Some include its strategic importance to organisations and recognise its influence on reputation (Hutton 1999; Grunig and Grunig 2000). Cutlip et al.

(2006: 5) combine these aspects and suggest: 'Public relations is the management function that establishes and maintains mutually beneficial relationships between an organisation and the publics on whom its success or failure depends.'

Some scholars suggest that these definitions inaccurately suggest that PR is a neutral communications channel and ignore popular understandings of PR and instead should take social context and costs into account (L'Etang 1996; Coombs and Holladay 2007; Curtin and Gaither 2007; Heath 2010; Edwards and Hodges 2011). Botan and Hazelton (1989), Kitchen (1997) and Cutlip et al. (2006), for example, all emphasise that PR is often a synonym for deception, or 'spin', and that everyday understanding of PR is usually determined by the visible results of PR activity (e.g. media coverage). However, the idea of *persuasion* has been left out of academic definitions, despite recognition of its importance in the profession's history (see also Chapter 11 for further explorations of persuasion).

This approach tends to complicate PR definitions because it recognises the variety of work as well as its wide-ranging effects. Moloney (2006: 165), for example, defines PR as 'competitive communication seeking advantage for its principals and using many promotional techniques,

Explore 1.2

Key debates

Why do you think academics disagree about definitions of PR? Is it because they don't understand PR or because they have different views about its contribution to society? Summarise, in your own words, the key debates between different PR definitions. How would you explain these definitions to your friends and family?

visible and invisible, outside of paid advertising.' Breaking down the concept even more, Heath (2010) suggests a three-dimensional understanding of PR as a 'social and organisational force', as a profession through which the identities of practitioners and their clients are constructed, and as a set of 'complex relationships by which interests and self-interests are enacted through structures, functions and shared meanings' (Heath 2010: 2). See Explore 1.2.

If PR overemphasises the interests of organisations over individuals or the privileged over the less powerful, then people will assume that it can serve only those interests. In fact, while privileged groups may be able to invest more resources in public relations, there are many examples of public relations strategies being applied effectively by 'minority' groups or individuals to challenge governments and corporations (Moloney 2006). Edwards (2012) has tried to address this by following the 'socio-cultural turn' in PR scholarship (Edwards and Hodges 2011) and developing a definition that may encompass both organisationally-driven activity as well as other effects of PR that may be of interest to scholars and practitioners alike. She defines PR as 'the flow of purposive communication produced on behalf of individuals, formally constituted and informally constituted groups, through their continuous trans-actions with other social entities. It has social, cultural, political and economic effects at local, national and global levels' (Edwards 2012: 15). Arguably, any definition of PR should recognise the breadth of possible contexts for activity and the social benefits of PR as a tool to increase discussion about matters that

Picture 1.2 The 1978 'Mexican Statement' has defined public relations as 'the art and social science of analyzing trends, predicting their consequences, counselling organisational leaders, and implementing planned programs of action which will serve both the organisation and the public interest' (*source*: Peter Adams/Alamy Images)

Explore 1.3

Public relations and social awareness raising

The journey of the Olympic Torch to Beijing in 2008 was marked by pro-Tibet protests in every major city, aimed at highlighting China's human rights abuses in Tibet. Look up references to the 'Olympic Torch Relay 2008' on the Internet. How much of the coverage was about the torch's journey and how much comment was made about China's activities in Tibet? Based on this, how successful do you think the protestors were at raising the issue of Tibet's human rights in the context of the Olympics?

Explore 1.4

Developing your own definition of PR

Find five different PR consultancy websites and look at the definitions of PR that they use. How do these definitions differ? How explicit are they about persuasion and manipulation of opinion? How do they measure success? What different services do they provide? Based on your findings, can you develop your own definition of PR that combines all their perspectives?

might otherwise be ignored, as well as the ways in which it can service the interests of some people over others. See Explore 1.3.

Practitioner definitions of public relations

Practitioner definitions of PR tend to be based more in the reality of the day-to-day job, often use the term 'public relations' interchangeably with 'organisational communication' or 'corporate communication' (Grunig 1992; Hutton 1999) and include concepts of persuasion, influence and reputation. Grunig et al. (2006) acknowledge that many practitioners still associate PR with media relations, although some do recognise its potential as a management function guiding interaction with publics. You could argue that this kind of flexibility means simply that practitioners have difficulty explaining exactly what their job entails – and indeed, this seems to be the case.

In 1978, the First World Assembly of Public Relations Associations in Mexico defined PR as 'the art and social science of analyzing trends, predicting their consequences, counselling organisational leaders, and implementing planned programs of action which will serve both the organisation and the public interest' (Newsom et al. 2000: 2). The definition offered by the Public Relations Society of America, coined in 1988, is similarly broad but recognises the assumption of two-way engagement that underpins many understandings of practice: 'Public relations helps an organisation and its publics adapt mutually to each other' (Public Relations Society of America 2011). In the UK, the Chartered Institute of Public Relations (CIPR) defines PR as: 'About reputation – the result of what you do, what you say and what others say about you. Public relations is the

discipline which looks after reputation, with the aim of earning understanding and support and influencing opinion and behaviour. It is the planned and sustained effort to establish and maintain goodwill and mutual understanding between an organisation and its publics' (Chartered Institute of Public Relations 2009). This definition is widely used in the UK and is included in some UK-based text and practitioner books on PR (e.g. Gregory 1996; Harrison 2000; Genasi 2002). In general, consultants will define PR in ways that highlight their own unique approach in a competitive market but emphasise the development of reputation on the basis of goodwill rather than manipulation (see Explore 1.4 and Think about 1.1).

Think about 1.1

Academics vs practitioners

Academics and practitioners have come up with very different definitions of PR. From the summary above, consider the following questions with a group of friends:

■ What are the main differences between the definitions of academics and practitioners?

■ Why do you think such differences exist?

■ Is there a right or wrong definition? If so, why?

■ Which definition do you think is most appropriate for PR and why?

Feedback

Consider the interests of the people creating the definitions. For example, are they trying to build theories about how PR works or are they trying to simply describe what it does? Who is the audience for the definition and how might the audience affect what is included?

Public opinion: justifying public relations

Using communication to influence the public is hundreds of years old, with its roots in ancient civilisations. Throughout history, governments, monarchs and powerful religious and secular institutions have used communication to generate support for their cause among the populace. But it was the emergence of the concept of public opinion that eventually formed the scientific justification for using PR and communications techniques in this way (Grunig and Hunt 1984; Cutlip et al. 2006; Moloney 2006).

Nowadays, the term public opinion is used frequently in the media, by government and by PR practitioners almost without thinking. However, it emerged from the philosophical traditions of the eighteenth and nineteenth centuries. Rousseau, the French philosopher, is generally credited with first coining the term, in 1744, and its use quickly became more extensive in discussions about how democracies should and could incorporate the views of the populations they were supposed to govern (Price 1992). The context in which it is used today only emerged in the early years of the twentieth century, and is based on the seminal book *Public Opinion*, by Walter Lippman, published in 1922.

Two basic conceptions of public opinion have dominated the evolution of the term: public opinion as an abstract, **collective view**, emerging through rational discussion of issues in the population; and public opinion as an **aggregate view**, the sum total of individual opinions of the population governed by the democratic state (Pieczka 1996). There are limitations to both these views – for example, who is included in, and who is excluded from, the term 'public'? To what extent does the rational debate required for the 'collective' view really take place and does everyone have equal access to the debate? If not, then 'public opinion' may only be the view of a select number of individuals who bother to engage in discussions. Alternatively, if public opinion is interpreted as an aggregate of individual opinions, then what happens to minority views that are swamped by majority concerns? Where do they find expression?

In the early twentieth century, there was a prevailing political concern that individuals would be more persuaded by emotional arguments and events than logic in their political decision making. This presented a problem for the political elite, who were concerned that an emotional public would not provide the best guide for governments acting on their behalf. Elite political and economic leaders seriously doubted the ability of the public to understand the complexities of democratic processes and argued that it was the job of communications channels such as the media to simplify politics and government so that the public could understand matters of importance to them (Lippmann 1922; Bernays 1928; Schudson 1984; Ewen 1996; Moloney 2006). Managing public opinion, then, became a matter of controlling an unreliable public so that they are persuaded that what is good for them is that which political elites *think* is good for them.

At the same time, new social research techniques emerged that enabled 'public opinion' on particular issues to be defined and quantified – for example, through surveys. This led to the gradual dominance of the aggregate view of public opinion over the collective view. As a result, public opinion is interpreted today as the view of the majority, and we often see survey statistics in the media that suggest we all think in a particular way about a particular matter (see Explore 1.5).

As literacy levels and the media industry expanded, the ability to quantify public opinion also opened up different routes for it to be influenced. Mass communication methods, such as radio, newspapers and (later) television, offered ready-made channels to communicate messages about complex issues in a manageable format to an increasingly literate population. The formation of public opinion became inseparable from these communication channels (Tedlow 1979) and, as we will see from the case studies outlined below, PR practitioners in business and government were not slow to take advantage of the rapidly growing media industries to put their views across in both logical and emotional forms to individuals who were open to persuasion (Ewen 1996).

More recently, however, attitudes have changed. The advent of Web 2.0, alongside more insightful studies of audience behaviour (Roper 2002; Kahn and Kellner 2004; Breakenridge 2008), have demonstrated that audiences engage with communication on all sorts of levels, are selective about what they do and do not take notice of, and are very 'PR-savvy' in ways they approach communications

Definition: *'Collective view'* of public opinion refers to issues that emerge through rational discussion in the population. One example of such an issue is the general agreement among opinion formers (e.g. health professionals) that obesity in young children is caused through poor nutrition and a lack of exercise.

Definition: *'Aggregate view'* of public opinion refers to the sum total of individual opinions of the population governed by the democratic state. One example of such an issue is banning smoking in public places. In the UK the views of the majority of the population, tested over time through polls, appeared to be in favour of a ban, and this was ultimately introduced in 2007.

Explore 1.5

Surveys and public opinion

PR practitioners often use surveys as a means of making a particular topic newsworthy. For example, you might see an article announcing the latest findings on levels of debt incurred by students taking a degree, or the amount of alcohol drunk each week by men and women in their early twenties. Take a look at the newspapers for the past two weeks and find an example of a survey that has created some 'news' about a particular topic and consider the following questions:

■ To what extent do the views expressed in the survey findings correspond to your own views?

■ How do your views differ and why do you think that might be?

■ Would you support governments or organisations taking action based on these survey findings (for example, making new laws to limit alcohol consumption or reducing student fees)? Why/why not?

■ Has the news story changed your view of the issue being discussed? Why/why not?

Feedback

Consider the motivations of the organisation carrying out the survey (they are usually mentioned in the news article). What motivations might they have for being associated with a particular issue? What kind of influence are they hoping to have on general views of the matter being researched?

from organisations. Consequently, the notion of 'managing' public opinion has largely evolved into 'communicating with' publics, and greater respect for audiences and their thinking has emerged. In PR scholarship, this has been accompanied by arguments that organisation-centric understandings of PR are no longer appropriate, and 'publics' need to be understood and acknowledged in more depth (Leitch and Motion 2010).

Business, politics, society and public relations: country case studies

Histories of public relations are only ever partial, in that they are constructed from a particular perspective and

with a particular purpose in mind (Miller 2000; L'Etang 2004; Hoy et al. 2007). Most often, this perspective puts the development of PR as a business function at the centre of the analysis, but as Miller (2000) points out, there are many ways to examine the evolution of PR, without necessarily prioritising its business-related role. When reading historical accounts of PR, then, it is important to recognise that these accounts are only one of many possible ways of understanding the evolution of PR in a particular context. Different social, economic and political factors come into play, and their effects on PR may be understood differently, depending on the perspective of the past that is being addressed. Importantly, histories are constructed as a means of understanding different aspects of the present: what one wishes to understand about today's PR will therefore shape the information that we select from the past to (re)construct it. They also tend to reflect a male view of the development of PR; the work of successful female practitioners has been neglected (Miller 2000). Hoy et al. (2007) point out that within the field of PR, histories have a way of repeating themselves: texts – and textbooks in particular – tend to reiterate the same basic story as a form of truth rather than as a specific account driven by specific interests.

Historical analyses of PR are still relatively rare, and the four case studies here represent the countries about which most has been written, perhaps because PR as an academic subject is well-established in these locations. PR elsewhere will have been shaped and constrained by different dynamics, and some brief accounts can be seen in, for example, *The Global Public Relations Handbook* (Sriramesh and Verčič 2003, 2009). When reading these cases, you should bear in mind the caveats noted above, as well as noting that inclusion in this chapter is not based on the relative importance of these locations to the field, but on the availability of information. You should also note that these cases are located exclusively in the Northern hemisphere and in 'developed' countries; in this, they reflect the overall bias of PR scholarship towards PR in these contexts, rather than in the Global South (or East). Let us hope that, as scholarship on PR continues to expand, histories from other areas of the world will become more available. See Explore 1.6.

The United States: private interests in public opinion

Many PR textbooks written by US scholars include a brief overview of public relations history in that country (Grunig and Hunt 1984; Wilcox et al. 1992; Cutlip et al. 2000, 2006). For the most part, they focus on the role of key companies and figures, including Ivy Lee, P.T. Barnum and Edward Bernays, in defining the practice and techniques

Explore 1.6

Reading histories

Choose one of the four histories being presented here and ask yourself why the 'story' of PR has been told in a particular way. How are publics conceptualised, and how are organisations presented? After reading the case, what do you still not know about PR? Whose voices are being left out of the accounts? If you were writing it, what other things would you want to research and include?

Feedback

Consider the motivations of those who wrote the original histories – as well as my own motivations in asking you these questions! How does this particular version of PR benefit them, or the people and organisations they portray?

Mini case study 1.1
Early US public relations in practice

During the early nineteenth century, presidential campaigns included a press secretary for the first time and there was general recognition of the need for public support of candidates if they were to be successful. In the commercial world, banks were the first to use PR to influence their publics, while later in the century large conglomerates such as Westinghouse Electric Corporation set up their own PR departments.

of PR during the twentieth century (Cutlip 1994; Miller 2000). Ewen (1996) also provides a useful overview of the broad social context for understanding the emergence of business-related PR in the United States. Hoy et al. (2007; Wehmeier et al. 2009) point out that these histories tend to map the development of PR practice, rather than PR theory, and as such create a narrative of PR developing from a morally suspect to a morally enlightened practice.

Some of these accounts begin with the first widespread use of PR by American Revolutionaries during the War for Independence (1775–1782), and track its development during the early decades of the USA (Cutlip et al. 2000, 2006; Miller 2000). Techniques commonly used today, including symbols, slogans, events, agenda setting (promoting certain topics to influence the themes covered by the media) and long-term campaign development, were deployed successfully (see Mini case study 1.1).

In the late nineteenth century, 'progressive publicists' – individuals and groups arguing through the media for reform of poor business practices – were the first to recognise the need for formal publicity in order to support a cause. They couched their arguments in rational terms, with the intent to appeal to public opinion and generate support. The resulting '**reform journalism**' was regarded by business leaders as '**muckraking**' – overstating the case against business and ignoring much of the social good it provided. The fear was that too much reform journalism might incite social disorder. As a result, businesses tried to counter this tendency and establish social control by proposing and communicating ideas through the media that

would unite the public and stabilise opinions (Ewen 1996). Increasing levels of literacy, the rapidly expanding newspaper industry and new technologies such as the telegraph and wireless all meant that media relations quickly became established as a major tool for both sides of the debate.

At this point, most accounts of PR history in the US begin to focus on the development of PR in the commercial world and note the establishment of a number of individual PR consultancies catering mainly to private sector interests trying to defend themselves against the muckrakers. Clients included railroad companies, telecommunications companies, Standard Oil and companies interested in lobbying state and federal governments (Cutlip et al. 2006). Communications, largely media-based, tended to be practised by organisations in crisis rather than on an ongoing basis, and most businesses hired journalists to combat media on their own terms. As a result, the PR practised was predominantly press agentry (see Chapter 7), using the media to influence public opinion (Grunig and Hunt 1984).

Ivy Lee, one of the most well-known early PR practitioners, made his mark as a publicity agent for the Pennsylvania Railroad. He argued that businesses had to establish understanding and buy in to their practices if they wanted to preserve their legitimacy and autonomy. He put this into

Definition: '*Reform journalism*' refers to journalists who opposed the exploitation of workers for the sake of profit and pressed for social change to curb the negative effects of enterprise.

Definition: '*Muckraking*' is unearthing and publicising misconduct by well-known or high-ranking people or organisations.

practice by opening up communications for the Railroad and being the first to issue press releases to keep journalists up to date with events (Ewen 1996; Cutlip et al. 2006). In 1906 he issued his *Declaration of Principles*, where he stated that accurate, authoritative and factual communications would generate the best arguments for convincing the public. However, corporations were slow to adopt this level of transparency and, while their communications may have been accurate in principle, their practices were still shrouded in secrecy. Indeed, Lee's definition of 'fact' was frequently interpreted by him and his employees as information that could *become* fact in the public's mind as a result of a persuasive argument. As a result, 'muckraking' and the debate over reform continued (Ewen 1996).

In the early years of the twentieth century, increases in disposable income and disposable goods created a new category of public – the consumer. Consumers had a new and very personal interest in the successful functioning of business, and organisations were quick to exploit the potential for uniting their consumer base through advertising and PR; Henry Ford, Samuel Insull and Theodore Vail all implemented impressive public relations strategies for the motor, electricity and telecommunications industries (Cutlip et al. 2000, 2006). At the same time, the discipline of social psychology emerged and gained credibility as the foundation of persuasion. It provided a scientific basis for the arguments in favour of using PR to create a general public 'will' by shaping press coverage of a particular issue. The underlying objective, echoing the original motives behind reform journalism, was to rationalise irrational public opinion through the power of ideas and argument.

Edward Bernays, nephew of Sigmund Freud and regarded by many in the United States as the father of modern PR, was heavily influenced by social psychology and reflected this in his two books: *Crystallizing Public Opinion* (1923) and *Propaganda* (1928). Originally an arts journalist who used his PR career as a publicist for the arts, Bernays ran a highly successful agency with his wife, Doris Fleischman, during the first half of the twentieth century. His books were practitioner-focused, case study-based, backed up by insights from the social sciences into how the public mind could be controlled through persuasive techniques (see Chapter 11). This combination of practical tactics substantiated by scientific argument was extremely powerful, and an increasing number of practitioners, many of whom had gained expertise in propaganda during the war years and subsequently joined the PR profession, were heavily influenced by his ideas (Ewen 1996, Miller 2000).

It might be argued that neither the growth in consumption nor the advent of sophisticated psychological theories were unremittingly positive. Consumption was a privilege most frequently available to White, middle-class Americans; other populations tended to be ignored by practitioners intent on selling goods (Edwards 2010) and were increasingly isolated from the 'American Dream' of material progress. And, as noted above, manipulating public opinion was grounded in a negative view of non-elite publics, who were not capable of making the 'right' decisions for themselves.

The advent of the Depression in the 1930s, when millions of Americans lost their jobs and savings, again called into question the ethics of business and the social good it provided. The myth of a prosperous America full of happy consumers belied the reality experienced by hundreds of thousands of normal American families forced onto the breadline. Perhaps not surprisingly, businesses communicated much less vigorously during this period – but it was not the end of PR. Under the leadership of President Franklin D. Roosevelt, the federal government used communications to promote recovery strategies, combining strategic messages with the power of Roosevelt's charismatic delivery – a highly persuasive technique. Organisations from different ends of the social and political spectrum also adopted PR to lobby the political establishment effectively during this period: the Klu Klux Klan, for example, as well as the National Association for the Advancement of Coloured People (NAACP), who employed Doris Fleishman for their first annual conference (Cutlip 1994; Miller 2000).

As a result of Roosevelt's policies, corporations recognised a shift in public opinion towards an ethos of social good and aligned their messages to this new environment. Business, it was argued, was inherently in the public interest. Perhaps the most obvious demonstration of this was at the World Fair in 1939, which included representatives from all types of businesses, symbolised democracy and forged an idealistic link between business and the greater public good. The advent of the Second World War helped the business sector to recover further from the Depression and reinforce its positive image (Ewen 1996; Miller 2000), while the use of PR in politics became increasingly widespread.

During the Second World War, PR was used widely by the armed forces and emerged as the discipline that could promote American interests and identity overseas. Wartime PR also made extensive use of advertising to generate popular support for the conflict, a combination still used today in marketing and communications strategies.

In the immediate aftermath of war, the overall theme of commercial PR remained welfare capitalism, rather than unfettered free enterprise. However, the origins of PR as an essentially manipulative discipline were never far away, despite this apparent nod to public interest. In 1955, Bernays published *The Engineering of Consent*, underpinning PR as a discipline that could shape and mould

Author	Title	Year
Ivy Lee	*Declaration of Principles*	1906
Edward Bernays	*Crystallizing Public Opinion*	1923
Edward Bernays	*Propaganda*	1928
Rex Harlow	*Public Relations Journal*	1944
Edward Bernays	*The Engineering of Consent*	1955

Table 1.1 Key publications in the early years of American public relations

public opinion for business and political interests, rather than engage and have a dialogue with individual groups. Television, the ultimate visual medium, with a correspondingly large capacity to influence viewers on an emotional level, increased the level of commercial interest in mass media and the manipulation of opinion once more dominated the PR industry.

In subsequent years, the PR industry was characterised by an increasing number of associations promoting sector-based interests, the consolidation of the consultancy industry, the first *Public Relations Journal* (established in 1944), more academic training for the profession and the establishment of the Public Relations Society of America in 1947. Table 1.1 shows key historical publications in American PR.

As consumers have become more sophisticated and technologically literate, and the neo-liberal economic environment has emphasised individual consumerism over collective well-being, PR in the United States has developed increasingly sophisticated communications techniques to reach discerning publics. However, the legacy of Bernays' ethics and morality of PR practice also remain a focus for critique, suggesting that the normative history of PR moving from murky propaganda to enlightened communication (Hoy et al. 2007) is not as clear-cut as it may seem.

Britain: public interest in private opinions

Relatively little has been written about the history of PR in Britain, with the exception of Jacquie L'Etang's (2004b) professional history. Her book forms the basis for much of this discussion.

The roots of PR in the UK go back to the days of the British Empire, when PR was used extensively by the Government to promote British interests abroad, and particularly in its colonies. The focus was on the dissemination of a narrative that promoted Britain as a 'benevolent'

coloniser that brought significant advantages to those nations it was occupying (McClintock 1995). Initially pursued through printed media, the advent of film in the early twentieth century allowed a new way of communicating to develop, and the London-based Empire Marketing Board began producing documentary-style films that focused on particular aspects of British enterprise and the British way of life (L'Etang 2004). These were disseminated abroad, but also shown to domestic audiences to communicate the benefits of running an Empire on such a scale. Such efforts became more important as the Empire began to fragment under pressure from independence movements.

The early twentieth century also saw the first local government authorities set up in the United Kingdom, and these employed the first formally-recognised PR practitioners, whose remit was to persuade their constituents to use the services provided, as well as to assert their role in the face of potential central government cutbacks during the 1920s and 1930s. Local communities and businesses did not understand what the role of local government was and regarded it as a bureaucratic irritant rather than a valuable service. As a result, the focus of much early PR in Britain was on the presentation of facts to persuade the public – genuine truths about what local government contributed to the public good. It was assumed that the power of truth would persuade both the public and central government to be more supportive of local officials and policies. As early as 1922, the local government trade union, the National Association of Local Government Officials (NALGO), recommended that all local councils include a press or publicity division in their makeup (L'Etang 2004b).

The development of PR was also closely linked to the use of propaganda during the two world wars. Truth, here, was not so critical, but its sacrifice was justified in light of the need to win at all costs. Crucial to these efforts was the British Documentary Film Movement, inspired by John Grierson, who focused on using film (one of the most popular media in the days before widespread television ownership) to educate the public on matters of public interest. Visual communications were thus used to present 'truth', in the form of a rational argument, in a compelling fashion (L'Etang 2004b; Moloney 2006). See also Box 1.1.

The success of wartime propaganda was not lost on the commercial sector, which expanded its use of communications after the Second World War and employed many wartime practitioners and journalists, now looking for work. The first UK consultancies were established in the 1950s and in-house practitioners in commercial organisations became much more common (L'Etang 2004b). See Mini case study 1.2.

Perhaps because of the early influence of public sector bureaucracy, PR practitioners were quick to organise themselves as a group in Britain, first under the auspices

Box 1.1

Documentary film in UK public relations

Documentary film was one of the most popular forms of internal and external communication in both the public sector and corporations between the 1930s and the late 1970s. Under the influence of Stephen Tallents, state-sponsored film units were attached to the Empire Marketing Board, the Post Office (GPO), the Ministry of Information during the Second World War and, following the war, the Central Office of Information. One of the most famous documentaries of this early period was *Night Mail* (1936) made for the GPO, scripted by the poet W.H. Auden and with music composed by Benjamin Britten. The nationalisation of key industries after the war led to other public sector film units being set up for internal training and external promotion. Examples of these are British Transport Films (BTF) and the National Coal Board Film Unit.

Corporate film units were connected to Dunlop and ICI, but it is the Shell Oil Film Unit that is regarded as one of the most celebrated of the Documentary Movement. The films were often released into cinemas, and while many were indirectly related to the company's activities (Shell's first film was *Airport* (1934)), the themes were more general, thus exerting a subtle influence on the public. Another group of films made by the Shell Oil Film Unit were educational and unrelated to oil. These films covered topics such as traditional rural crafts, the evolution of paint and the environment. When film was replaced by video in the 1980s, Shell continued as one of the key players in the audio-visual communications industry.

Source: adapted from www.screenonline.org.uk/film/id/964488/index.html (British Film Institute)

Mini case study 1.2

Basil Clarke – Britain's first public relations consultant?

Basil Clarke was a former *Daily Mail* journalist who founded his own consultancy, Editorial Services, in 1926, following a career in several government ministries where he directed public information. Editorial Services was founded jointly with two practising consultants, R.J. Sykes of London Press Exchange (LPE) and James Walker of Winter Thomas. Basil Clarke is credited by some as the 'father' of PR in Britain, partly because of his government track record and partly because he drafted the Institute of Public Relations' first code of practice.

Source: L'Etang (2004a)

the Empire Marketing Board in the 1920s and 1930s, where he used communications to promote the reputation of the British Empire and its products among its trading partners. As the first Public Relations Officer in Britain, he joined the Post Office in 1933 and then moved to the BBC in 1935. Throughout his professional life, he used the widest range of tools at his disposal to promote the interests of his employer to the public, including radio, telegraph, film and, of course, newspapers. He was also a strong advocate for recognition of the publicity role as a profession in itself, with a specific and unique skills base. This was reflected in the Institute's immediate role as a lobbying body to encourage recognition of PR as a legitimate profession and a channel through which practitioners could readily share expertise and establish standards for the field (L'Etang 2004b).

This early institutionalisation of the profession means that the presentation of PR in Britain has been heavily influenced by the efforts of the IPR as the industry body. Key themes emerging from early years of PR practice have permeated the approach taken by the Institute, including: the importance of truth as the 'ideal' PR tool; the conception of PR as a public service; and the potential for PR to be used as a means for promoting freedom, democracy and, in particular, the British way of life – this last being particularly influenced by institutions such as the British Council using PR abroad. As in the US, these developments were not always positive. Using PR to promote the interests of Empire involved promoting a world where Britain was at the centre and other nations peripheral,

of the Institute of Public Administration and subsequently as an independent Institute of Public Relations (now the Chartered Institute of Public Relations, or CIPR). The IPR was established in 1948 under the leadership of Sir Stephen Tallents – a career civil servant and a keen supporter of publicity and propaganda from his tenure as Secretary of

devaluing their cultures and societies by benchmarking them in relation to a superior White British norm (McClintock 1995). Domestically, PR was no stranger to the racism that permeated British society in response to the influx of former colonial citizens from overseas. The Britain they had been told they belonged to was not always welcoming and PR was more often used to promote, rather than challenge, implicit racism in social policies such as housing or employment (Phillips and Phillips 1998).

The emergence of PR consultancies in the 1950s confirmed the existence of PR as a distinct profession, separate from its cousins marketing and propaganda – although these boundaries were often blurred. Indeed, although the IPR was intent on maintaining a broad conception of communications in its definition of the profession, the reality was that the ex-journalists entering the profession could provide a unique, easily identifiable service on the back of their media expertise that did not overlap with advertising or other marketing disciplines and therefore served the profession well.

The IPR, dominated by in-house and public sector practitioners, had difficulty catering to the specific interests of independent consultancies. One particular concern included the maintenance of professional standards and reputation across a wide range of small organisations. In light of this, a specific consultancy association, the Society of Independent Public Relations Consultants (SIPRC), was created in 1960 and worked closely with the IPR. However, the SIPRC itself was poorly defined and eventually folded. Subsequently, in 1969, the Public Relations Consultants Association was set up and still exists alongside the CIPR today (L'Etang 2004b).

By the 1970s, then, the British PR industry had established itself as an identifiable body with a national institute and increasing numbers of practitioners. Standards of practice, areas of competence and the range of services provided were all discussed and developed. With this institutional basis in place, the next phase of development was driven by commercial interests. A rapid expansion, particularly in the consultancy sector, took place in the 1980s and continued in the 1990s. It was driven initially by deregulation and privatisation programmes for state-owned companies under the Conservative government during the 1980s.

Deregulation opened up opportunities for private sector operators in two ways: first, as consultants to lucrative public sector accounts such as the NHS and, second, as professional lobbyists on behalf of the bidding companies (Miller and Dinan 2000). Privatisation during the 1980s and early 1990s of national utilities, including oil, gas, water and telecommunications, prompted extensive use of public relations consultants by government departments. Persuading the public to buy shares in the new companies required more than standard Government Information Service briefings to standard media. Sophisticated techniques were needed to create sound marketing strategies, build public perceptions of the value of the opportunity and then persuade them actually to buy shares in the new companies (Miller and Dinan 2000; Pitcher 2003).

These programmes were highly successful: by the early 1990s and the completion of the privatisation programmes, 12 million members of the British public owned shares (Pitcher 2003). Media headlines were generally positive and company reputations began on a high. The newly privatised companies were the first to recognise the value of PR and continued the use of consultancies after their initial flotation (Miller and Dinan 2000).

The knock-on effects of this for the financial sector were considerable. From now on, listed companies had to communicate with the general public as well as with the privileged few who had previously made up their target audience. Communications had to be simpler and reach a wider range of people. In-house practitioners – if there were any – turned to consultants for support and the new specialism of investor relations was born (Miller and Dinan 2000; Pitcher 2003).

Deregulation of professions such as law and accounting, as well as the financial services industry, also created new opportunities for the PR industry by prompting the companies concerned to market themselves and communicate directly with their customers. For most, the concept of talking to the 'man in the street' was unknown, and the newly expert PR consultancies were able to provide valuable support and advice (Miller and Dinan 2000). Increasing numbers of mergers and acquisitions in these new markets have underpinned the growth of PR during the last two decades, with communications strategies often the deciding factor between success or failure (Davis 2000; Miller and Dinan 2000).

The growth in PR that these processes prompted eased off in the early 1990s, but the social and economic environment continued to encourage PR activity. The 1980s had seen the (right wing) Conservative government consistently emphasise the virtue of individual rights over community responsibilities – home ownership rather than council tenancy, share ownership rather than taxes. By the end of the decade, this mentality had become embedded in Britain; private interests were automatically regarded as superior to social concerns. In this neo-liberal environment, PR was used by groups and individuals to justify their decisions by making their voices heard above the general cacophony of the market (Moloney 2006). Technological change since the advent of the Internet has made this task even more challenging, and consultancies today emphasise their expertise in communicating in a complex environment rather than simple media relations or lobbying capabilities.

Germany: industrialists, politics and critique

The dynamics that shaped the emergence of PR-type activities in Germany were similar to those elsewhere: industrialisation; new forms of technology; changing political environments; increasing levels of literacy; urbanisation; and the emergence of the mass media (Nessmann 2000). Germany is also unique in that the partition between East and West Germany led to the development of two very different industries – and publics – that are recognisable in PR practice in today's unified Germany (Wehmeier 2004).

Nessmann (2000) argues that PR as an activity first emerged in Germany in the early eighteenth century, although it was not formally termed PR until the mid-twentieth century. Practical applications of media relations can be seen with the systematic news office of Frederick the Great (1712–1786), Napoleon's mobile printing press that he used to circulate favourable stories about his military campaigns and his practice of monitoring foreign news coverage to check how his image was developing abroad. State media relations can be traced back to 1807, while in the mid-nineteenth century German industrialists were already recognising the importance of the views of the general public as well as of their own employees as sources of social legitimacy in the rapidly industrialising economy (Kunczik 1996). See Mini case study 1.3.

The German state also cottoned on relatively early to the value of PR, with a press department set up in the Foreign Ministry in 1871 (the year the German Reich was founded). The freedom of the press was first established through the Reichspressegesetz (State Press Law) of 1874, the Navy commissioning its own press officers in 1894 and the first municipal press office set up in Magdeburg in 1906 (Nessmann 2000). Otto von Bismarck, the Chancellor of the German Reich, understood the power of the media and under his rule the press expanded – although he also made efforts to control and influence journalists and editors (Bentele and Wehmeier 2003). In this way, and similar to Britain, ambitions of Empire shaped the development of German PR, although its use in Germany was more to persuade internal audiences of the wisdom of expanding the Reich, rather than promoting German culture to those in the colonised nations (Bentele and Wehmeier 2003).

This early development of PR practice was accompanied from the mid-nineteenth century by an increasingly critical view of PR among academics as an exploitative medium used primarily by political and commercial groups, even as the need for it as a source of legitimacy for such organisations was also acknowledged. At around the same time, a debate emerged in relation to the German media about the separation of clearly labelled advertising materials from unbiased editorial contributions (Baerns 2000). This debate revolved around the need for the press to retain its credibility by separating advertising from journalism, to preserve its legitimacy as a reliable source of information for the general public. This debate continues today and Baerns (2000: 245) points out that, as recently as the 1990s, the German press council issued guidelines that stated: 'The credibility of the press as a source of information demands particular care in dealing with public relations texts.' While Baerns points out that these statements have not necessarily led to a black and white distinction between advertising, PR materials and 'pure' journalism in the modern media, the existence of the debate does highlight the cultural dynamics that frame PR practice in Germany.

As in the United States and Britain, the First World War brought with it new opportunities for press relations and propaganda by the state and businesses. This growth in the practice and understanding of the discipline led to a corresponding flourishing of the profession in the postwar years. During the Third Reich, however, the sophistication of new PR techniques was relegated to the back seat while Adolf Hitler used propaganda techniques and press censorship to cement his regime (Bentele and Wehmeier 2003).

Following the Second World War and the end of the Nazi regime, PR as a profession was revitalised. Two practitioners were particularly instrumental in this. Carl Hundhausen, Director of PR at the German manufacturer Krupp, introduced the term 'PR' in 1937 and published

Mini case study 1.3
The first public relations stunt

In 1851, German steelmaker Krupp executed what was perhaps the first PR 'stunt' when it transported a two-ton block of steel to the Great Exhibition in London, an effort that generated significant publicity and recognition for the company across the world. Krupp remained at the forefront of communicative efforts among German industrialists, along with other conglomerates including Siemens, Henkel, Bahlsen and AEG. Each recognised the value of media relations, circulating reports about their activities to the media on a regular basis, while Krupp established the first formal press office in a German company in 1893.

widely on public relations from the 1950s onwards (Lehming 1997). Albert Oeckl, who was co-founder of the German Public Relations Association in 1958, President of the Association from 1961 to 1967 and Honorary President from 1986 until his death in 2001, worked tirelessly to improve the reputation of public relations and try to reduce the association with propaganda that remained from the Nazi era (Mattke 2006). The term PR finally came into general use in the 1950s, when the influence of the American occupation in West Germany and the desire to distance the profession from its recent past resulted in adoption of the term (alongside the German *Öffentlichkeitsarbeit* and its modern practice). The German Public Relations Association (Deutsche Public Relations Gesellschaft, DPRG) was founded in 1958 and the industry once again expanded rapidly in the newly democratic state. As elsewhere, genuine two-way communications emerged as consumers became more demanding of organ-

isations in the 1970s and 1980s (Bentele and Wehmeier 2003). See Table 1.2.

However, East and West German PR traditions parted ways with the establishment of the German Democratic Republic (GDR) in 1949. The socialist government rejected the term public relations because of its associations with the West, and chose the term *Öffentlichkeitsarbeit* (publicity work) instead, to describe information dissemination by state institutions and (state-run or state-sponsored) economic entities. *Öffentlichkeitsarbeit* was tied to the promotion of the socialist state, both at home and abroad, and the development of a socialist consciousness in GDR citizens (Wehmeier 2004). While PR theory traditionally views propaganda as a relatively simplistic form of one-way communication, Wehmeier's (2004) history shows that the value of communication was in no way under-estimated by the East German government, and many government-run organisations put *Öffentlichkeitsarbeit*

Periods of German public relations	
Pre-history: official press politics, functional public relations, development of instruments	
Period 1 (mid-19th century–1918) Development of the occupational field.	Development of the first press offices in politics and firms, war press releases under the conditions of censorship, first public campaigns.
Period 2 (1918–1933) Consolidation and growth.	Fast and widespread growth of press offices in different social fields: economy, politics, municipal administration.
Period 3 (1933–1945) Media relations and political propaganda and the Nazi regime.	Party-ideological media relations within political propaganda. National and party-related direction and control of journalism, media relations and inner relations.
Period 4 (1945–1958) New beginning and upturn.	Postwar development, upturn and orientation to the American model starting in the early 1950s, development of a new professional self-understanding under the conditions of democratic structures (public relations defined as distinct from propaganda and advertisement), fast development of the professional field predominantly in the economic sphere.
Period 5 (1958–1985) Consolidation of the professional field in the Federal Republic of Germany and establishment of socialist public relations in the German Democratic Republic (GDR).	Development of a professional self-consciousness, 1958 foundation of the professional association DPRG, which initiated private training programmes. Simultaneous with the developments in West Germany, a type of socialist public relations developed in the GDR from the mid-1960s.
Period 6 (1985–present) Boom of the professional field and professionalisation.	Strong development of public relations agencies, professionalisation of the field, beginning and development of academic public relations education improvements in the training system, scientific application and enhancement of the instruments, development of public relations as a science.

Table 1.2 Periods of German public relations (*source*: Bentele and Wehmeier 2003: 200)

at the centre of their efforts to be successful in the communist state. On the other hand, it is true that communication tactics did not invite engagement with the East German citizens; practitioners were not involved in strategic decision making about the organisations' direction, but were there to communicate that direction to the state-run media once it had been agreed. Ultimately, this was a top-down communications process of the type found in many governments, communist or otherwise, that focused on disseminating the prevailing ideology as widely as possible through the country.

The difference between this and the free-market-driven norms of West German PR, which were more open to debate and discussion with both media and the public, became evident. Political PR practices took shape based on the West German model driven by the political and economic dominance of West German states post-reunification (Wehmeier 2004). Commercial PR, however, was very different. The almost total collapse of the East German economy meant that PR practitioners had very little to communicate: their organisations were either failing or had been sold. This imbalance between the economies of the former East and West German states remains, and, as a result, PR as a profession and a practice remains under-developed in the former East Germany, with many organisations controlling their PR from headquarters in the former West German states.

Sweden: consultation in a thriving democracy

As with most other countries apart from the three initially reviewed here, the history of Swedish public relations is somewhat sparse. Nonetheless, the growth of Swedish PR scholarship is based on a thriving industry that deserves attention. A number of authors have reflected on public relations in Sweden, including Larsson (2006), Flodin (2003) and Tyllström (2010). Taken as a whole, these histories show that the shape of PR in Sweden is marked by the consultative democratic environment, developments in the public sector, a strong in-house presence and the rapid modernisation of the economy that marked Sweden in the second half of the twentieth century.

The Swedish economy was largely based on agriculture until the early twentieth century and industrialised relatively late. The increase in wealth that eventually came from mining the country's rich natural resources in the early 1900s was distributed via a welfare state that prioritised high taxation and wide distribution of benefits across the population (Flodin 2003). Alongside this egalitarian emphasis was a focus on maintaining communication with the public on the part of government, which led in turn to

a thriving media sector – perfect conditions for PR to develop. Consequently PR's roots in Sweden lie in state institutions, with early practitioners working in government organisations at local and national level during the first half of the twentieth century. In these early years, media relations and information dissemination was the emphasis of practice, skills that were further honed during wartime as PR and propaganda were used more intensively by the government to manipulate public opinion and behaviour in relation to Sweden's neutral role.

As postwar political and economic circumstances stabilised, Sweden's government structures changed. Municipal authorities merged while, at the same time, the number of local newspapers declined so that the opportunities for direct communication between politicians and citizens via the media were reduced. As a result, the opportunity emerged for PR to fill the gap. Active consultation with the public was pursued by politicians, opening up new and more sophisticated opportunities for PR practitioners to develop their trade (Flodin 2003) and prompting debate about the role of communication in Sweden's democratic society during the 1960s and 1970s. At the same time, Sweden's commercial sector started to grow alongside its European neighbours and PR was increasingly recognised as an important commercial function. The professional association for PR practitioners, the Swedish Public Relations Association (later to become the Swedish Information Association), was set up in the 1950s, a decade that also saw the arrival of the first consultancies on the professional scene (Flodin 2003; Larsson 2006). The 1970s saw significant growth in the industry in both consultancies and in-house contexts.

In the 1980s, Sweden's political and economic climate moved away from an internally-focused, corporatist model where policy was considered within government, to a more pluralist model of engagement with the public. The increased competition for visibility and voice among both policymakers and commercial organisations that accompanied this shift also led to an expansion of PR and lobbying as public support became vital for institutional success. The early understanding of PR as media relations was replaced by increasing recognition of other PR specialities, such as lobbying and longer-term relationship management. In parallel, Sweden's membership of the EU (in 1995) meant that lobbying at an international level was added to the PR skills portfolio (Flodin 2003). Over the past decade, public relations as an occupation has expanded rapidly and, today, work in Sweden is divided between marketing communications (40%), corporate communications (30%), investor relations (20%) and public affairs (10%) (Tyllström 2010). The largest volume of campaigns are executed by government, followed by commercial organisations, while trade associations and third-sector, non-profit organisations of all kinds make up a smaller section of the market (Tyllström 2010).

Unlike in other countries, PR in Sweden remains dominated by in-house practitioners rather than consultancy. The Swedish consultancy industry is also unique in that it is still dominated by Swedish-owned and run companies, rather than multinationals (Tyllström 2010). Nonetheless, all the major international consultancies now have a presence in Sweden, which is testament to the sophistication of PR practice there, as well as to the oppor-

tunities for business that the country continues to offer. The common view among Swedish practitioners today is that PR has a legitimate role to play in the democratic process (Larsson 2006), and evidence suggests that commercial clients have also welcomed the power of PR into their organisations as a means of managing public opinion about their work (Flodin 2003). Indeed, the PR industry is closely linked with political and economic elites in Sweden, not least because of the movement between the sectors that marks practitioner careers (Tyllström 2010).

Summary

The histories presented here highlight the social nature of PR. It is a profession that applies the value of communication to situations where it is required. In the United States, the private sector has been the most active force driving the development of the profession, while in Britain, first the public then the private sector have resulted in the industry we see today. In other countries, such as Germany and Sweden, different cultural and social dynamics affect the practice, popularity and implementation of communications and will shape the PR industry in different ways.

Perhaps because communications techniques can be so widely applied, definitions of PR are various. While the general principles of using relationship management and dialogue in order to exert influence on target audiences are evident in most definitions, controversy exists

about other aspects of the profession – such as reputation management – and whether they are core to its practice. These debates are unlikely to disappear in the near future. Whether they relate to the relative youth of the profession, the fast-changing world in which it operates and the correspondingly rapid changes in the demands made on it, or simply the complexity of the practice itself, the reality is that the social nature of PR will always mean that it differs from one context to the next. Practitioners need to establish the principles that are most appropriate in their personal and professional situation and operate accordingly. The chapters in this book outline some of the issues that they will need to consider: personal and professional ethics, the sector in which they operate, the specialism they choose and the audiences they target.

With acknowledgements to Magnus Fredriksson, Anna Tyllström and Stefan Wehmeier in the development of this chapter.

Bibliography

Baerns, B. (2000). 'Public relations and the development of the principle of separation of advertising and journalistic media programmes in Germany' in *Perspectives on Public Relations Research*. D. Moss, D. Verčič and G. Warnaby (eds). London: Routledge.

Bentele, G. (1997). 'PR-Historiographie und funktional-integrative Schichtung' in *Auf der Suche nach Identität. PR-Geschichte als Theoriebaustein*. P. Szyszka (Hrsg.). Berlin: Vistas.

Bentele, G. and S. Wehmeier (2003). 'From literary bureaus to a modern profession: The development and current structure of public relations in Germany' in *The Global Public Relations Handbook*. K. Sriramesh and D. Verčič (eds). Mahwah, NJ: Lawrence Erlbaum Associates.

Bernays, E. (1923). *Crystallizing Public Opinion*. New York: Boni and Livenight.

Bernays, E. (1928). *Propaganda*. New York: H. Livenight.

Bernays, E. (1955). *The Engineering of Consent*. Norman, OK: University of Oklahoma Press.

Binder, E. (1983). *Die Entstehung unternehmerischer Public Relations in der Bundesrepublik Deutschland*. Münster: Lit.

Botan, C.H. and V. Hazelton (1989). *Public Relations Theory*. Hillsdale, NJ: Lawrence Erlbaum Associates.

Breakenridge, D. (2008). *PR 2.0: New media, new tools, new audiences*. Upper Saddle River, NJ: FT Press.

Chartered Institute of Public Relations (2009). 'About PR'. http://www.cipr.co.uk/content/about-us/about-pr accessed 4 October 2011.

Coombs, W.T. and S. Holladay (2007). *It's Not Just PR: Public relations in society*. Malden, MA: Blackwell.

Curtin, P.A. and T.K. Gaither (2007). *International Public Relations: Negotiating culture, identity and power*. Thousand Oaks, CA: Sage.

Cutlip, S.M. (1994). *Public Relations: The unseen power. A history.* Hillsdale, NJ: Lawrence Erlbaum Associates.

Cutlip, S.M., A.H. Center and G.M. Broom (2000). *Effective Public Relations*, 8th edition. Upper Saddle River, NJ: Prentice Hall.

Cutlip, S.M., A.H. Center and G.M. Broom (2006). *Effective Public Relations*, 9th edition. Upper Saddle River, NJ: Prentice Hall.

Davis, A. (2000). 'Public relations, business news and the reproduction of corporate power'. *Journalism* **1**(3): 282–304.

Department of Trade and Industry and Institute of Public Relations (2003). *Unlocking the Potential of Public Relations: Developing good practice.* London: European Centre for Business Excellence.

Edwards, L. (2012). 'Defining the object of PR'. *Public Relations Inquiry* **1**(1): 1–24.

Edwards, L. and C. Hodges (2011). 'Introduction: Implications of a "radical" socio-cultural turn in public relations scholarship' in *Public Relations, Society and Culture: Theoretical and empirical explorations.* L. Edwards and C. Hodges (eds). London: Routledge.

Ewen, S. (1996). *PR! A Social History of Spin.* New York: Basic Books.

Flodin, B. (2003). 'Public relations in Sweden: A strong presence increasing in importance' in *The Global Public Relations Handbook.* K. Sriramesh and D. Verčič (eds). Mahwah, NJ: Lawrence Erlbaum Associates.

Genasi, C. (2002). *Winning Reputations: How to be your own spin doctor.* Basingstoke: Palgrave.

Gordon, J.C. (1997). 'Interpreting definitions of public relations: Self assessment and a symbolic interactionism-based alternative'. *Public Relations Review* **23**(1): 57–66.

Gregory, A. (1996). *Public Relations in Practice.* London: Kogan Page.

Grunig, J.E. (1992). *Excellence in Public Relations and Communication Management.* Hillsdale, NJ: Lawrence Erlbaum Associates.

Grunig, J.E. and L.A. Grunig (2000). 'Public relations in strategic management and strategic management of public relations: Theory and evidence from the IABC excellence project'. *Journalism Studies* **1**(2): 303–321.

Grunig, J.E. and T. Hunt (1984). *Managing Public Relations.* New York: Holt, Rinehart & Winston.

Grunig, J.E., L. Grunig and D. Dozier (2006). 'The Excellence Theory' in *Rhetorical and Critical Perspectives of Public Relations.* C. Botan and V. Hazelton (eds). Mahwah, NJ: Lawrence Erlbaum Associates.

Harlow, R.F. (1976). 'Building a definition of public relations'. *Public Relations Review* **2**(4).

Harrison, S. (2000). *Public Relations: An introduction.* London: Thomson Learning.

Heath, R. (2010). 'Mind, self, society' in *Sage Handbook of Public Relations.* R. Heath (ed.). Thousand Oaks, CA: Sage.

Hein, S. (1998). *Public Relations und soziale Marktwirtschaft. Eine Geschichte ihrer Abhängigkeiten.* München.

Hoy, P., O. Raaz and S. Wehmeier (2007). 'From facts to stories or from stories to facts? Analyzing public relations history in public relations textbooks'. *Public Relations Review* **33**: 191–200.

Hutton, J.G. (1999). 'The definition, dimensions and domain of public relations'. *Public Relations Review* **25**(2): 199–214.

Kahn, R. and D. Kellner (2004). 'New media and internet activism: From the "Battle of Seattle" to blogging'. *New Media & Society* **6**: 87–95.

Kitchen, P.J. (1997). *Public Relations: Principles and practice.* London: International Thomson Business Press.

Kunczik, M. (1996). *Geschichte der Öffentlichkeitsarbeit in Deutschland.* Köln, Wien und Weimar: Böhlau.

Larsson, L. (2006). 'Public relations and democracy: A Swedish perspective' in *Public Relations: Critical debates and contemporary practice.* J. L'Etang and M. Pieczka (eds). Mahwah, NJ: Lawrence Erlbaum Associates.

Ledingham, J.A. (2006). 'Relationship management: A general theory of public relations' in *Public Relations Theory II.* C.H. Botan and V. Hazelton (eds). Mahwah, NJ: Lawrence Erlbaum Associates.

Leitch, S. and J. Motion (2010). 'Publics and public relations: Effecting change' in *The Sage Handbook of Public Relations.* R.L. Heath (ed.). Thousand Oaks, CA: Sage.

L'Etang, J. (1996). 'Public relations as diplomacy' in *Critical Perspectives in Public Relations.* J. L'Etang and M. Pieczka (eds). London: International Thomson Business Press.

L'Etang, J. (2004a). *Public Relations in Britain: A history of professional practice in the 20th century.* Mahwah, NJ: Lawrence Erlbaum Associates.

L'Etang, J. (2004b). 'Public relations and democracy' in *Handbook of Corporate Communication and Public Relations: Pure and applied.* S.M. Oliver (ed.). London: Routledge.

Lehming, E. (1997). *Carl Hundhausen: Sein Leben, sein Werk, sein Lebenswerk. Public Relations in Deutschland.* Wiesbaden: Deutscher Universitäts-Verlag.

Lippmann, W. (1922). *Public Opinion.* New York: Harcourt Brace Jovanovich.

Mattke, Christian (2006). *Albert Oeckl: sein Leben und Wirken für die deutsche Öffentlichkeitsarbeit.* Wiesbaden: VS.

McClintock, A. (1995). *Imperial Leather: Race, gender and sexuality in the colonial conquest*. New York: Routledge.

McKie, D. and D. Munshi (2007). 'Global public relations: A different perspective', special issue *Public Relations Review* **30**(4).

Miller, D. and W. Dinan (2000). 'The rise of the PR industry in Britain 1979–98'. *European Journal of Communication* **15**(1): 5–35.

Miller, K. (2000). 'Public relations history: Knowledge and limitations.' *Communication Yearbook* **23**: 381–420.

Moloney, K. (2006). *Rethinking Public Relations: PR propaganda and democraacy*. London: Routledge.

Nessmann, K. (2000). 'The origins and development of public relations in Germany and Austria' in *Perspectives on Public Relations Research*. D. Moss, D. Verčič and G. Warnaby (eds). London: Routledge.

Newsom, D., J.V. Turk and A. Scott (2000). *This is PR*. Belmont, CA: Wadsworth.

Phillips, M. and T. Phillips (1998). *Windrush: The irresistible rise of multiracial Britain*. London: Harper Collins.

Pieczka, M. (1996). 'Public opinion and public relations' in *Critical Perspectives in Public Relations*. J. L'Etang and M. Pieczka (eds). London: International Thomson Business Press.

Pitcher, G. (2003). *The Death of Spin*. Chichester: John Wiley & Sons.

Price, V. (1992). *Public Opinion*. Newbury Park, CA: Sage.

Public Relations Consultants Association (2004). 'What is PR?' London: Public Relations Consultants Association.

Public Relations Society of America (2011). 'Public Relations Defined'. http://www.prsa.org/AboutPRSA/Public RelationsDefined/ accessed 4 October 2011.

Roper, J. (2002). 'Government, corporate or social power? The Internet as a tool in the struggle for dominance in public policy.' *Journal of Public Affairs* **2**: 113–124.

Schudson, M. (1984). *Advertising: The uneasy persuasion*. New York: Basic Books.

Sriramesh, K. and D. Verčič (2003). *The Global Public Relations Handbook*. Mahwah, NJ: Lawrence Erlbaum Associates.

Sriramesh, K. and D. Verčič (2009). *The Global Public Relations Handbook: Theory, Research and Practice*. New York: Routledge.

Tedlow, R.S. (1979). *Keeping the Corporate Image: Public Relations and Business 1900–1950*. Greenwich, CT: JAI.

Toth, E. (2010). 'Reflections on the field' in *Sage Handbook of Public Relations*. R. Heath (ed.). Thousand Oaks, CA: Sage.

Tyllström, A. (2010). 'PR-konsultbranschens framväxt i Sverige' in *Företag och medier*. J. Pallas and L. Strannegård (eds). Stockholm: Liber Förlag.

Wehmeier, S. (2004). 'From capitalist public relations to socialist *Oeffentlichkeitsarbeit* and back: Public relations in East Germany' in *Bureaucratic, Societal and Ethical Transformation of the Former East Germany*. J.-C. Garcia-Zamor (ed.). Lanham, MD: University Press of America.

Wehmeier, S., O. Raaz and P. Hoy (2009). 'PR-Geschichten: Ein systematischer Vergleich der PR-Historiografie in Deutschland und den USA' in *Historische und Systematische Kommunikationswissenschaft: Festschrift für Arnulf Kutsch*. S. Averbeck, P. Klein and M. Meyen (eds). Bremen: Edition Lumière.

Wilcox, D.L., P.H. Ault and W.K. Agee (1992). *Public Relations: Strategies and tactics*. New York: Harper-Collins.

Media context of contemporary public relations and journalism in the UK

Learning outcomes

By the end of this chapter you should be able to:

- identify the structure of the UK media and understand how and why it is undergoing a period of profound change
- analyse the rise of the 'network society' and evaluate how the media is being restructured by the growth of telecommunications networks
- understand how ownership of the media effects democracy
- examine the role of self-regulation in the media and be able to discuss whether its limitations have been reached
- discuss the role of media regulators, and be able to think through ideas of self-regulation when applied to the press
- consider the ways in which the contemporary media creates problems for the ethical behaviour of journalists and public relations practitioners.

Structure

- The media landscape in the UK
- Media outlook
- A 'free' press
- The public sphere

Introduction

There is an old Chinese proverb that condemns a man to live in interesting times. For many media observers, such times have now arrived. Old certainties are eroding faster than replacements are appearing. The Internet and a wealth of related technologies are transforming our lives quicker than most of us can keep pace. There is no sign of the rate of change slowing.

The pace of change brought about by the Internet is impacting upon the media faster than almost anywhere else. The age of television is now over, to be replaced by a world much more influenced by the network technology; such as the Internet and mobile phones. If you are reading this book at the start of an undergraduate course, then many of you probably will have grown up in a digital and online world (how many of you can remember a time before the Internet?), which is why sociologists call anyone under the age of 25 the 'Internet generation'. As such, 'digital natives' expect 'anytime, anywhere' media and consume content by often ignoring the schedules their parents stick to religiously. Think of it this way: over the first 60 years, the three main US TV channels produced 1.5m hours of television. YouTube produced the same amount in just six months. Moreover, 88 per cent of that content was new material – a far higher proportion than the TV networks manage today (Branson and Stafford 2010). Now consider that YouTube only

came into being in 2005 (about the time many readers of this book might have been starting high school perhaps), and that it was launched not in the middle of London or Manhattan – the traditional centres of the media – but in a tiny office in a room above a Chinese takea-way in San Francisco. Such is the pace of change the media is experiencing today.

Clearly, YouTube is rewriting the rules of television, Wordpress the printed word, the iPod has more or less done away with your local record shop and soon the Kindle might do the same to the printed book. Certainties that have stayed still for generations, such as the idea that towns and cities in the developed world each have their own morning or evening newspaper, are unravelling quicker than the new technologies can build adequate replacements.

There are two possible responses to this situation. You can either run from it, or run with it. Standing still isn't an option for anybody wanting to enter the media in the second decade of the twenty-first century. This chapter will help you run with it. It will take you through the major critical perspectives shaping the new media landscape. It will introduce you to the key technologies and it will talk you through the most important debates and show you the best texts to read to help you get up to speed.

The interesting times we are living through have quite profound implications

for the liberal democracies of the world. This chapter will think those through too. We will explore how traditional outlets of the media (newspapers, local news stations and so on) are losing readers and viewers, and we will consider what this might mean for our democracy. In other words, *who will continue to hold the powerful to account in the age of the Internet?* We will also look in detail, for example, at the recent phone hacking scandal, which perhaps shows how journalistic practice can become desperate when faced with falling sales, and in doing so, we will thoroughly examine how the media is regulated and ponder whether the current situation is adequate. At the same time we will touch on the growth of public relations: one sector of the media that has so far proved resistant to the great period of uncertainty we have now entered.

This chapter isn't the whole story. Nor is it a guaranteed top grade in an essay asking for you to understand the media in its proper context. The really good students among you will supplement this chapter with your own work – exploring the texts and themes to a greater depth. You will find that it helps you come to terms with the changes the world is going through. Indeed, you might like to think of it as a kind of media survival guide, to help you through these most interesting times.

The media landscape in the UK

The UK has a media network that is broadly similar to its European counterparts in that it has a mix of private and publicly owned media. In the UK, large corporations concentrate ownership of large sections of the press into a handful of companies. Although the broadcast media is more varied, with many more companies owning TV

channels, the broadcast sector is dominated by two organisations: BSkyB, owned by Rupert Murdoch's News Corp, and the British Broadcasting Corporation (BBC), the largest public broadcaster in the world (Lyall and Pfanner 2011).

The media in the United Kingdom has been undergoing a structural transformation since the 1980s. A process of deregulation, begun in earnest by the Thatcher administration but continued by subsequent Labour governments, has remodelled the broadcast and print media, recasting a system that offered a narrow amount of choice (for example, until the 1980s there were just three television channels available in the UK) into one that offers a bewildering array of multi-channel options. There are now hundreds of television channels to choose from, especially if viewers have access to the Sky satellite platform. However, while the quantity of the media options has increased, the quality of media content is often criticised for being poorer. Content for television produced in the UK, for example, was once regarded as the best in the world, but it is now gathering a reputation for being among the most trivial (Rudin 2011).

The rise of the Internet, moreover, has further heightened the liberalisation of the media. This means that the old restrictions placed upon the media (i.e. legislation by government, union agreements that protected media workers' pay and conditions and the cost of media production) have been loosened. This has democratised the media (which means that more people have access to media production) and provided a new means of distribution. More simply put: who needs to own a TV station when YouTube is available to millions?

But, in doing so, the Internet is providing both an opportunity and a challenge to established media companies, particularly the print media who have been losing sales and advertising revenue (which will be explained later in this chapter). The growth in media piracy, moreover, freed from physical distribution by the Internet, is radically altering the viewing habits of millions of people – especially among adolescents, who in a survey in 2011 reported that they would prefer to live without television rather than without the Internet and their mobile phones (Ofcom 2011).

The UK has a privately owned media with control concentrated in a small number of companies, both private and public. Alongside this small group of companies stands the BBC, the world's largest and oldest broadcaster, which is paid for by a licence fee levied on every household in the UK that watches television. The BBC is one of the biggest content producers on the Internet, rated as the most visited traditional media site in the world (Alexa 2011), as well as producing a profusion of radio and television covering everything from light entertainment to investigative journalism. In technical terms, the BBC is an 'autonomous public service' that operates under a Royal Charter. But, in more straightforward terms, this means that the BBC is part of the Government (ie it is a public service), but it is also editorially independent of it. In other words, despite being a state broadcaster, the BBC manages to be very critical of the Government – at times.

The UK also enjoys a diverse and resilient national newspaper scene although, as we will see later, one that is coming increasingly under pressure from declining sales. Despite the rise of the Internet and the downfall of many popular newspapers in the US, and the collapse of many local titles, it is worth considering that a single national newspaper in the UK has yet to fall victim of the move towards online consumption. In other words, the Internet has yet to kill any of the big newspapers. But, in observing this fact we must remember the *News of the World*, which was withdrawn from circulation by the misdeeds of its journalists (see Case study 2.1 later in this chapter). We will now look at each major sector of the UK media in turn.

Newspapers

The UK maintains a vibrant newspaper scene that, although in decline, still attracts the seventh highest newspaper readership per capita in the world (Unesco 2010). The UK publishes, moreover, an impressive array of national daily and Sunday titles. Although it is difficult to produce an exact figure (because several titles publish Scottish and Irish editions, and some Sunday titles, such as *The Sunday Express*, have been folded into a daily title), an acceptable figure would be that the UK produces around 16 'national' titles. This compares with three in the US and four or five in Germany.

Rupert Murdoch, an Australian-born resident of the US, still owns the best-selling tabloid, *The Sun*, as well as the 'broadsheet' sister papers *The Times* and *The Sunday Times*, the book publisher HarperCollins and a controlling 39 per cent stake in the satellite broadcasting network BSkyB, one of the world's largest (Rogers 2011). In July 2011, the Murdoch family closed the *News of the World* – the most popular newspaper in Europe – as a response to the outrage caused by the phone hacking scandal (see Case study 2.1, later in this chapter).

Daily Mail and General Trust (DMGT) owns *The Daily Mail* and *The Mail on Sunday* and the free daily *Metro* (which is now the fourth most-read newspaper in the UK). Richard Desmond owns *The Daily Express* and *The Daily Star* as well as *OK!* magazine and Channel 5. He is also the principal shareholder in two digital 'softcore' pornographic channels: Television X and Red Hot TV (Kjetland 2010; Russell 2010).

The London Evening Standard and *The Independent* (and *i* editions) are owned by Alexander Lebedev, a Russian business magnate. In 2011 Lebedev was embroiled in controversy in his native Russia when he was seen to punch an opponent live on television (Thornhill 2011). *The Guardian* and *Observer* are owned by a charitable organisation, the Scott Trust. *The Daily Telegraph* and *Sunday Telegraph* are owned by the Barclay brothers – reclusive identical twins who live as tax exiles on the island of Brecqhou, the smallest of the Channel Islands.

Evaluating media bias

Take a large sheet of paper and draw on it a semi-circle, with the baseline at the bottom of the page and the 180° arc sweeping from left to right. Now bisect the semi-circle with a vertical line exactly through the middle. This represents a political spectrum, a way of modelling political positions. The far left of your circle will represent communism, which is seen as the 'hard left' of politics. The far right therefore equals fascism, the hard right. The vertical line is the centre of politics, usually referred to as liberalism. In the UK, the Labour Party would be represented at 45 degrees along your arc (halfway between communism and liberalism). The Conservative Party would be at 135 degrees (halfway between liberalism and fascism).

Now draw up a list of national newspapers in the UK (or in your own country, if it is more suitable). Cut them out and, next, start placing the names of the newspapers on your political spectrum according to where you think their political loyalties are situated. Where would you place *The Sun*? Or *The Mirror*? Ask yourself, is *The Independent* truly independent? Or what position *The Guardian* protects? Is the *Financial Times* left or right wing? Can you think about adding other titles, such as *The Economist*, for example?

If you are unsure of the political sympathies of your list of publications, simply look them up on Wikipedia or some other Internet site. Once you have all the papers, take a step back and look at your spectrum. Ask yourself one question: where does political bias in the print media of your country reside? Left or right?

Television

The time when the UK enjoyed a small number of terrestrial channels has now passed. By 2012, the 'digital switchover' meant that the UK had made the transition from 'analogue' to 'digital' (which describes the type of signal media companies use to transmit their message over the airwaves). The old terrestrial stations (BBC1, BBC2, ITV1, Channel 4 and 5) remain, but they now share a platform with several hundred cable and satellite stations. Chief among these, in terms of advertising revenue and audience, is the BSkyB stable of channels, controlled by Rupert Murdoch's News Corp (Rogers 2011). BSkyB is the UK's leading supplier of both residential and business pay-TV services and also supplies residential telecommunication services (broadband and calls) (ibid). This has led some analysts (Enders 2010) to calculate that the company accounts for approximately two-thirds of UK residential subscribers to subscription pay-TV and about four-fifths of the sector's market revenues. In terms of financial clout, BSkyB dwarfs any other supplier in the marketplace, including the BBC; BSkyB enjoys revenue of £5.9bn, which compares with the £2.4bn the BBC receives from the licence fee (ibid). (The licence fee is paid by anyone in the UK who watches TV at the time it is broadcast through various devices. The licence fee covers TV, radio and online services.)

Radio

Although the digital switchover for television arrived at least two years behind schedule in the UK, a similar planned switchover for radio has been dogged by even longer delays (Midgely 2011). It is now doubtful whether analogue signals will be switched off any time before 2020. This leaves two overlapping systems in place in the UK, with the vast majority of listeners choosing to remain with the established analogue signal. The BBC broadcasts a complex network of radio stations based around five national analogue stations (although other stations such as the BBC Asian Network can be considered quasi-national) and 38 local stations. The BBC also broadcasts several stations on the digital audio broadcasting (DAB) network (BBC 1Xtra, BBC 4 Extra, BBC 5 Sports Extra, BBC 6 Music). All are funded through the licence fee.

The BBC also operates the World Service, which is said to be the world's largest international broadcaster. It broadcasts in 27 languages to many parts of the world through a variety of analogue and digital networks. It is estimated that the service reaches 188m people and the airwaves of over 100 countries. Traditionally, the World Service has been paid for by the Foreign and Commonwealth Office, but from 2014 it will be funded by the licence fee (Glanville 2011).

There are, moreover, four national commercial stations on the analogue network (Talksport, Absolute, Classic FM and a Christian broadcaster, Premier) and a patchwork of regional and community radio stations serving smaller locales and niches. One of the trends in recent years has been for small independents to be bought and run by big brands (such as Bauer Radio and UTV Radio), leading to criticism that many local radio stations have begun to sound increasingly similar and have lost their true 'localness' (Stoller 2010).

Magazines

The UK continues to enjoy a diverse magazine market. Nearly 8,000 titles are published in the UK (4,733 trade and 3,212 consumer). In the most recent data available (2006), the Professional Publishers Association estimates that the UK magazine market is worth £8.9bn to the UK economy (PPA 2006). Magazines reach 87 per cent of the population, with 15- to 24-year-olds being the most popular group (NRS Deadtree Media), consuming almost a quarter more titles than the average UK adult. However, the recession of 2009 affected the industry very badly. Advertising revenues have slumped and consumers have cut back on what is often seen as a 'luxury' item. While the magazine industry remains roundly popular, many titles have folded. In the trade sector, for example, the figure of 4,733 titles might sound impressive but five years previously the sector had enjoyed 5,108, which represents a contraction of nearly 20 per cent (ibid).

Part of the problem with magazines, as with other sectors of the 'traditional' media, is that consumers are migrating online. Indeed, big trade magazines, such as *Computer Weekly* and *Accountancy Age*, ceased print editions in 2011 (Dowell 2011).

The Internet

The nebulous nature of the Internet makes an overview of digital media difficult to compress into a few short paragraphs. The picture is diverse and complex thanks to the open-ended structure of the Internet and from the fact that many of the most popular sites are established media providers (such as the BBC) who have crossed over from other media. The BBC is by far the most dominant media presence in the UK, with just under 10m unique visitors (the online equivalent of readers) a month (Alexa 2011). The MailOnline (the website of *The Daily Mail*) enjoys 6.6m (ibid), while *The Guardian* enjoys 4.6m (ibid).

What this means is that traditional media companies have colonised the online media landscape and very few 'new' media companies, ones that have been born on the net, have been able to break through into this established group of content providers; those that have succeeded – such as the Internet Movie Database (imdb.com) and Mashable.com – have had to move to the US to do so. In the UK, the best native performers in terms of traffic (how many people visit their website) are the online portals set up by mobile phone companies (Orange News with 356,000 and TalkTalk News with 268,000 unique visitors a month), but even here much of their content is aggregated from established media providers (Alexa 2011).

Despite the dominance of big media organisations, the UK does enjoy an innovative and increasingly influential new media scene. The political 'blogosphere' (the name given to the blogging community) is alive, with many independent bloggers setting an agenda in parallel with the press and broadcast media. The most notorious of these newcomers is Guido Fawkes, the *nom de plume* of Paul Staines, a libertarian right-wing blogger who seems to despise the political class from which he earns a living. Staines is the biggest seller of UK political advertising on the net (Sherwin 2011). His blog is hugely influential – and controversial – and it has broken some of the most notable political scoops of recent years. In 2006, for example, Staines reported that the former deputy prime minister John Prescott was having an extramarital affair. Then, in 2008, a post by Staines revealed that Peter Hain, the then Secretary for Work and Pensions, had broken rules over party funding. This led to his resignation, representing the first major token of victory by an independent UK blogger (Dale 2008) and, perhaps, a moment when the Internet truly began to rival the press in the UK.

Box 2.1
Liberal pluralism

The UK media practises a system of 'liberal pluralism', meaning that it is free (liberal) and pluralistic (contains many different voices). Liberal pluralism is admittedly a loose theory that perhaps represents an aspiration (as we will examine throughout this chapter) rather than a solid reality. But at its best liberal pluralism allows the media to present a variety of information to its audience. This, in turn, helps form public opinion, which scholars such as Walter Lipmann (1922) cite as being necessary to any functioning democracy. In practice (Mosco 1996; Davies 2008) the diversity of views can be surprisingly narrow and influenced by a range of factors, not least elements that seek to manipulate public opinion to their own ends: namely corporate ownership, advertising and public relations. Furthermore, the temptation to over-simplify complex arguments and to trivialise serious subjects in order to reach the largest possible audience has been a feature of the UK media, to the lament of commentators and scholars alike (Collins 2011).

Media outlook

If you analyse the dominance of old media organisations (for example, the BBC, *The Mail, The Guardian*) on the Internet, it might be tempting to conclude that the transition from old analogue technologies to digital is as smooth and regular as the changing of the tide. Not quite. Although many established media companies have made the transition to digital, the collapse in advertising revenue, from both print and television, is far greater than the revenue they receive from their newer Internet ventures. If it helps, try to imagine a big media company. Nowadays such a company is likely to be losing millions every year because it is losing its customers to content available for free on the Internet. People aren't buying its newspapers as much as they used to, so the big media company is also seeing its revenue gained from advertising fall. At the same time, this big media company has a whizzy Internet department and it is earning money from hosting adverts on the web. But the trouble is that the big media company is losing far more from its old services than it is currently earning from its new services. This imbalance is creating a great deal of uncertainty for people working for big media companies and much change is forecast.

The diminishment of time and space presented by our network society (see Box 2.2) raises both a huge opportunity and a huge threat to media providers. Some, like *The Guardian*, have responded to the challenge by favouring their digital products over print. During the Hugh Cudlipp Lecture of 2010, at the London College of Communication, *The Guardian's* editor, Alan Rusbridger, explained this change in numerical terms. In 1956 the *Manchester Guardian*, as it was then (fixed in time and place), sold a meagre 650 copies outside the UK. Today *The Guardian* (untethered from time and space) is read by 50 million people across the globe, making it one of the eight most-read newspapers in the world (Alexa 2012).

The decline and fall of regional and local newspapers

On the other hand, regional and local newspapers (which are much more fixed in time and space) are under severe pressure and are losing readers and revenue from advertising. The ailing UK newspaper advertising market is set to get even worse next year with national titles forecast to face an almost 9 per cent decline that will see display revenue fall below £1bn for the first time according to Sir Martin Sorrell's Group M.

Picture 2.1 Today *The Guardian* online is read by 50 million people across the globe, making it one of the eight most-read newspapers in the world. (*Source*: http://www.guardian.co.uk, Copyright Guardian News and Media Ltd 2013)

Box 2.2
Network media

Although the national newspaper scene in the UK remains robust, almost all newspapers in the developed world are losing readers. The local press in the UK is collapsing in many parts of the country (Kelner 2011). At the same time, the BBC is having its licence fee cut and is struggling to maintain its influence in the face of a Conservative-led coalition that has in the past been heavily critical of it (Foster 2010). This transformation (some even say revolution) has been characterised by theorists such as Van Dijk (1991) and Castells (1996) as the rise of the 'network society'. The network society is a description of an industrialised world that is being reshaped by globalised telecommunications and computer networks: the web, mobile phones, online gaming and pirate networks (such as bittorrent), to name but a few.

The media is at the centre of this change, not least because its primary commodity is information. One only has to think of a newspaper to understand how this change works in practice. Before the rise of the network society, a newspaper was a consumer item that was fixed in a specific time and a specific place. Think of the three words contained in the title of the *London Evening Standard*. 'Standard' tells you that the product is a newspaper; 'London' fixes the newspaper in a specific space (the regional area of London and its environs); 'Evening' fixes the newspaper in a specific time (actually the mid-afternoon, when the newspaper is published).

In a network society, the constraints of time and place become less certain. Anyone with access to the Internet can read content from the *London Evening Standard* at any time of the day. Indeed, the web editors continue to publish around the clock, which is unlike a print edition that gets published once-per-edition. Nor are readers restricted to reading the *Standard* in or around London. On the Internet the old certainties of time and place are less obvious. Some theorists, such as Cairncross (2001), have even suggested that the rise of such a society means the death of distance altogether. Indeed, Reuters, a leading news agency, has outsourced large divisions of its financial reporters to places such as Dubai and Bangalore, although its primary subject remains the City of London.

Readership, too, is in decline – collapsing in some areas leading to the closing of several titles, the consolidation of others or the loss of daily editions to be replaced by weekly ones. In 2012, several UK towns and cities (including Halifax, Peterborough, Scarborough, Northampton and Kettering) lost their only local daily newspaper, and many more are expected to follow in the coming years. Michael Ellis, a Conservative MP for Northampton North, described the loss of his local daily paper as a 'tragedy for journalism ... but also a tragedy for democracy'. Furthermore, the Newspaper Society estimates that the loss of the daily titles is part of a trend that has seen 200 titles close in the last decade (Halliday 2012) in the UK – a pattern that is reflected right across the developed world.

The growth of the Internet is often cited as the reason for the closing of so many regional papers, although other factors, such as demographics, corporate ownership and 'downsizing' of editorial jobs, are also contributing to the decline of local news. Burgers (1998) has argued that local news is simply no longer relevant or needed to citizens of the network society, whose mores are now more attuned to the mediated reality of soap operas, reality television and big sporting events. Even so, the 'death' of news, particularly at a local level, has enormous ramifications for the Western participatory democracy. According to a few critics, the diminishment of journalism, in particular, coupled with the rise of the public relations industry (Davies 2008), is creating anxiety about the future role of the media (see the section on the public sphere, later in this chapter).

A 'free' press

The UK continues to enjoy a relatively free press (journalism that is not restricted or controlled by government censorship with regard to politics and ideology), but less so than many of its European neighbours. According to Reporters Sans Frontières (Reporters Without Borders), a Paris-based international organisation that advocates freedom of the press, the UK is the nineteenth most-free in the world (behind EU neighbours such as Finland, The Netherlands and Ireland). Why is the UK in such a relatively lowly position? The Official Secrets Act, which is used to protect the military and secret services, is one reason; the UK's rather tame freedom of information legislation is another reason (freedom of information refers to specific laws that allow citizens to have access to public documents, such as hospital data or police numbers). It is also worth noting

Box 2.3

Media regulation in the UK

Like many other Western liberal democracies, the UK media operates under a system of self-regulation for now. This means that the media regulates itself, as opposed to being directly regulated by government. Newspapers in the UK have not been subject to any statutory control on who owns them, aside from some rather weak anti-monopoly laws. This has allowed tycoons and corporations, as mentioned earlier in this chapter, to concentrate ownership in the hands of a few. Instead, the media is regulated in the UK primarily around codes of practice. These codes – which are not legally binding – are drawn up by a variety of bodies, which are either entirely or largely independent.

It is a different picture for TV and radio in the UK, which are subject to some statutory regulation and are policed by Ofcom (the Office of Communication), a government agency. Broadcast laws exist in the UK to regulate who owns TV and radio stations and also on how programmes are broadcast and on programme content itself, including journalism (Banks and Hanna 2009). Ofcom has the power to fine and ultimately close down broadcasters who break the rules. The BBC is further regulated by the BBC Trust – a governing body that remains independent of the corporation's management. Ofcom's Broadcasting Code (its code of conduct) establishes a code of ethics for broadcast journalists, while the BBC is further regulated by the BBC Editorial Guidelines, an enormous list of rules and recommendations that reaches to 75,000 words (about as long as a short novel).

It is worth considering that television is more heavily regulated than the press perhaps because 'politicians have historically regarded it as a medium which, were it to fall into the wrong hands, has a particular power to offend the public or to be harmful, for example the transmission of porn to children' (Banks and Hanna 2009).

---

that the UK media also faces further restrictions from reporting in Northern Ireland, which have yet to be lifted despite an easing of 'the troubles'.

The UK press has long been 'self-regulating' (see Box 2.3). The press was self-regulated by the Press Complaints Commission (PCC) until it disbanded in 2012 after fierce criticism of its handling of the phone hacking scandal (see Case study 2.1); an interim body has been put in its place to be replaced by a new regulator based on recommendations from Lord Leveson. The collapse and failure of the PCC came after many years of heavy criticism – which intensified in the wake of the phone hacking scandal (Bratton 2011). Richard Desmond's Express titles (including *The Daily Express* and *Daily Star*) had already opted out of the PCC, which made a mockery of self-regulation – imagine a burglar opting out of the criminal justice system – because it allowed newspaper owners to take or leave the only form of regulation available.

The PCC did offer a code of practice, until it disbanded, that guided journalistic ethics, just as the National Union of Journalists (NUJ) continues to do. But despite widespread adoption of the PCC code, the UK press has often been guilty of misconduct. The parents of Madeleine McCann (the British child who went missing during a family holiday in Portugal in 2007), for example, received some of the most hostile and negative press in recent years, particularly at the hands of the Express Group, and yet the PCC consistently failed to protect them despite frequent breaches of the code of practice (Alton 2009).

The UK has enjoyed a reputation for press freedom since the late seventeenth century (Habermas 1989). Indeed, it was the growth of a newspaper-reading middle class in London, after the lapse of the licensing act in 1695, that is widely seen as establishing the conditions for the Western liberal democracy we enjoy today. Since then, the UK press has garnered a reputation for being one of the most dogged and vociferous in the world, but also one that is politically partisan and disrespectful of authority. Indeed, during the Leveson Inquiry of 2012, the UK Prime Minister, David Cameron, stated that: 'the volume knob has sometimes been turned really high in our press and I'm not sure that does anyone any favours' (Leveson Inquiry 2012). And yet, despite this, many people in the political classes in the UK seem unwilling to mess with press freedom. In laypersons' terms the press might be a 'beast' but historically it has been a beast that has defended us from perhaps a greater tyranny, and those that have studied the history of the press (as those in the political classes often do) are loath to restrict its freedom.

However, according to many media commentators (Oborne 2011b) and scholars, for the UK to contain a free press it must preserve self-regulation (Harnden 2011). It is taken for granted that it is fundamental for democracy

Case study 2.1
The UK phone hacking scandal

In August 2006, Clive Goodman, the royal correspondent of the *News of the World* (NOTW), a leading UK Sunday tabloid newspaper, was arrested by the Metropolitan Police under suspicion of intercepting messages from the mobile phones of two members of the royal household. Goodman was eventually found guilty and jailed for hacking into the voicemail of two assistants of the royal family. Goodman was sentenced to four months in jail. His partner in crime, private investigator Glenn Mulcaire – who was exclusively employed by News International, the parent company of NOTW – received a sentence of six months.

News International insisted that the pair were acting alone, using the phrase (often to be repeated) that Goodman was a 'rogue reporter'. Nevertheless, the editor, Andy Coulson – who maintained he had no knowledge of wrongdoing – resigned from his post.

Most media commentators thought that the matter would end there. And it very nearly did.

But then, just six months later, Coulson dramatically returned to public life. David Cameron, the then leader of the opposition, appointed Coulson as his director of communications. Some said Cameron was taking a huge gamble (Jenkins 2010), as here was a controversial former tabloid editor who had resigned under a cloud dark enough to cast a shadow on the Conservative party and the future Prime Minister. More controversial was the idea that if Cameron won the next election (he did), then Andy Coulson would be brought into the very heart of the UK establishment: No 10 Downing Street.

What followed has come to represent both the very best and the very worst sides of the UK media. The phone hacking scandal, as it became known, would eventually drag almost every node of the establishment network into its influence. The Prime Minister, the police, Rupert Murdoch, the Press Complaints Commission, Hollywood actors, football agents, the criminal underworld, the Crown Prosecution Service (to name but a few) were all dragged into its orbit; each was at times as helpless as driftwood lost out at sea.

Picture 2.2 Rupert Murdoch, the CEO of News Corporation, was the target of a foam pie attack as he testified before a UK parliamentary select committee about the *News of the World* phone hacking scandal. (*source*: Reuters/Parbul TV)

→

case study 2.1 (continued)

Investigative journalism

But the very fact that the scandal broke at all was thanks largely to the dogged work of Nick Davies, an investigative journalist employed by *The Guardian*, a leading UK newspaper, who demonstrated that journalism could uncover shadowy practices at the heart of the Government. 'Week by week, story by story, column by column, doorstep by doorstep, Nick Davies prised open the truth' (Rusbridger 2011).

Although it rarely seemed like it, the phone hacking scandal also showed that the public sphere was working. Indeed, although it shone a light on the darkest, most fetid corner of journalism, it was journalism itself that was shining that light. Without the tireless work of Davies, for whom the term 'campaigning journalist' could have been coined, the phone hacking scandal might have remained hidden. Davies, along with journalists from *The Telegraph*, *Financial Times*, *New York Times* and Channel 4 News (although conspicuously not the BBC), uncovered a web of intrigue and deceit not seen since the days of the Watergate scandal in the US. Indeed, Carl Bernstein, one of the two Watergate reporters, recently said that he was 'struck by the parallels' of the phone hacking scandal. Both, he said, were 'shattering cultural moments of huge consequence that are going to be with us for generations', and that both were 'about corruption at the highest levels, about the corruption of the process of a free society' (Sabbagh 2011).

At the heart of this scandal was one man, and it wasn't Clive Goodman, nor Glenn Mulcaire, nor even Andy Coulson. What so spiced the phone hacking scandal was that it drew attention to the power wielded by Rupert Murdoch, the US-based, Australian-born media mogul who had dominated the UK media scene for almost four decades. Murdoch has been called 'the most powerful man in Britain' (Oborne 2011b), who didn't so much control the media, he 'dominated British public life'. Politicians – including prime ministers – treated Murdoch with deference and fear. 'Time and again the Murdoch press – using techniques of which we have only just become aware – destroyed political careers...it converted into a flourishing criminal concern that took an evil pleasure in destroying people's lives. The bitter truth is that no major figure in British public life was prepared to take on and expose the Murdoch newspaper empire. Rival proprietors were silent. Senior public figures did not dare to speak out for fear of exposure and attack in the Murdoch newspapers. This is why, for more than a generation, Rupert Murdoch's empire has been a spider at the heart of an intricate web that has poisoned British public life' (Oborne 2011).

The decline of the PCC

As the scandal unfolded, the idea of self-regulation of the press unwound almost as rapidly. The Press Complaints Commission (PCC) had exonerated News International in an earlier report in 2007, endorsing the view that Goodman and Mulcaire had acted alone. This led several media commentators (Cathcart 2011) to suggest that the industry body was 'doomed', asserting that the PCC's failures did not begin with hacking but that the scandal at the NOTW was 'the last and heaviest straw'. Cathcart explained that the PCC had given the *News of the World* a 'clean bill of health on hacking, although the same evidence led MPs on the media select committee to conclude that the paper was gravely at fault and senior executives were displaying "collective amnesia".' The PCC had also criticised *The Guardian*, which broke the hacking story in 2009. But as the scandal unfolded, it was the MPs and *The Guardian* who were proved right.

The phone hacking scandal led to the downfall of several key establishment figures in 2011 and 2012. The *News of the World* had folded. The top two police personnel in the UK had resigned. Andy Coulson, the Prime Minister's director of communications, and Rebekah Brooks, chief executive of News International (the parent company of the NOTW), had been arrested. Rupert Murdoch and his son James had been called before parliament and forced to give a grovelling apology and to abandon an attempt to take sole ownership of BSkyB. The PCC had been replaced by a transitional body.

to function for journalism to be divorced from the state (Sennett 1977; Habermas 1989), so the argument against regulation by government goes. But as the treatment of the McCanns and the phone hacking scandal have demonstrated, self-regulation of the press has failed to curb the worst excesses of journalism. Not only are codes of practice optional (as in the case of the Express Group) but even when they are subscribed to, it has emerged that they can be routinely flouted by a minority of publications.

Think about 2.1

Media regulation in practice

To understand how regulation works in practice, you might want to compare and contrast the output by two news channels owned by Rupert Murdoch – Sky News in the UK and Fox News in the US. Look them up on YouTube if you are unsure. The system of statutory regulation and the BBC's constitution requires that broadcast journalists must be politically impartial in their output, and yet no such restrictions exist in the US. Is this why Sky is so much more sober and neutral than its US cousin?

Source: Sambrook 2012

The public sphere

Journalism's role in the development of Western liberal democracy has given rise to a theory of the public sphere. Defined by the German social theorist Jürgen Habermas, the public sphere is a complex – and frequently contested – theory that explores the media's role in creating and maintaining a space where people can gather freely and discuss problems relating to the functioning of society (societal problems) through the medium of public opinion (Fraser 1990).

At first glance, this might sound as if being able to talk about societal problems (for example, to criticise the Government) is a universal right. But any examination of how many people in the world actually enjoy the benefits of liberal democracy will reveal that the vast majority of the world's inhabitants (Puddington 2012) have yet to experience anything like the public sphere, and its constituent freedoms, that citizens of the West experience today.

In his influential book *The Structural Transformation of the Public Sphere*, Habermas offers an historical-sociological account of the emergence, transformation and eventual decline of the public sphere, tracing its birth in late-seventeenth-century England, through the growth of newspapers in the eighteenth century to the public sphere's zenith in the late nineteenth century, and then its slow decline during the last century. Habermas argues that although the West still enjoys a relatively free press (and a liberal democracy), the contemporary public sphere has been diminished by three factors:

- the commercialisation of the press itself;
- the development of business models that are reliant on the sale of advertising;
- and the growth of public relations.

Habermas argues that the growth of public relations has, to some extent, co-opted the press (and by extension the media at large) and succeeded in managing and even manipulating public opinion. Habermas is critical of the use of PR because it has transformed, he argues, a press that was largely independent (in the nineteenth century) into a 'gate through which privileged private interests invade the public sphere' (Habermas 1989, p. 185), although, arguably, this view doesn't account for the public relations work engaged by, say, charities or trade unions.

This erosion of the public sphere, however, should be of great concern to both journalists and PR practitioners alike. Ian Burrell, media editor of *The Independent*, has put forward the idea that PR is evolving, through the use of social media, into a profession that is increasingly able to further evade what he describes as the 'prism of journalism'. PR practitioners will be able to do this, he argues, in order to 'convey their messages [directly] to a mass audience' (Oliver 2010), citing instances of PR practitioners who are increasingly able to generate their own video- and text-based digital content on behalf of their clients, and describing a future with far more publicists than journalists.

Gatekeeping

The argument being advanced here is that the traditional role of journalists – to be the gatekeepers of society – is being undermined. The concept of gatekeeping, a theory first outlined in the 1950s by David Manning White (1950), accounts for the process in which journalists decide what does and what doesn't make the news. Ideally, journalists use their professional standards and codes of ethics to decide the most newsworthy items of the hour. This further defines their role in the public sphere as mediating between different sections of society (say, big business or the government or the general public). But the growth of the Internet and the development of a new form of public relations that engage *directly* with the public threatens to be altered by the growth of PR and the decline of journalism.

So, while engaging directly with the public might mean a boon for PR companies, we must think about how such a circumvention of journalism could have an effect on democracy. If we accept journalism's central role in the development of democracy (Habermas 1989) then we need to discuss whether the decline of journalism, as discussed earlier in this chapter, could be bad for democracy. In other words, if the messages of big business – those most able to pay the wages of PR practitioners – are communicated directly to the public, who is there to check that the facts are correct, or provide context or commentary that is independent? No concrete answer exists to this quandary, but it needs to be thought through by both journalists and PR practitioners alike, particularly by those entering either profession.

Summary

This chapter has discussed the media context of contemporary public relations and journalism in the UK. It has highlighted that the media landscape is undergoing profound change that has been accelerated by a process of deregulation and liberalisation of media industries, as well as rapid technological developments. Questions were raised about the nature of media ownership and the decline of traditional media outlets and what these factors mean for a democracy in which the role of the journalist is to hold powerful elites to account. The future of the media, including self-regulation of the press, was discussed in the light of the 'phone hacking scandal', as well as the future of the media's role as 'gatekeeper', which is increasingly bypassed due to the growth of the Internet as a means of public engagement.

Bibliography

Alexa (2013). http://www.alexa.com/topsites/global;2, accessed 21 June 2013.

Alton, R. (2009). 'PCC works despite Madeleine McCann case'. www.pressgazette.co.uk/story.asp?storycode=43377 accessed 21 October 2011.

Banks, D. and M. Hanna (2009). *McNae's Essential Law for Journalists.* pp. 16–17. London: Sage.

Branson, G. and R. Stafford (2010). *The Media Student's Book.* London: Taylor & Francis.

Bratton, T. (2011). 'PCC RIP: what next? – the future of press regulation'. www.legalweek.com/legal-week/blog-post/2095507/pcc-rip-future-press-regulation accessed 19 October 2011.

Burger, J. (1988). De Schall van Solidariteit: Eemstudienaar de socialeconstuctie van de omgeving. Leuven: Acco. Cited in Van Dijk, J. (1991). *The Network Society.* pp. 159–160. London: Sage.

Caincross, F. (2001). *The Death of Distance: How the Communications Revolution is Changing our Lives.* Harvard: Harvard Business School Press.

Castells, M. (1996). *The Rise of the Network Society, The Information Age: Economy, Society and Culture* Vol. 1. Oxford, UK: Blackwell.

Cathcart, B. (2011). 'The PCC rearranges the deckchairs; Hacked Off: Campaign for a public enquiry into phone hacking'. http://hackinginquiry.org/comment/the-pcc-rearranges-the-deckchairs/ accessed 26 August 2011.

Collins, R. (2011). 'Content online and the end of public media? The UK, a canary in the coal mine?' *Media, Culture and Society* 33(8): 1202–1219.

Dale, I. (2008). 'Is Hain's resignation the first blogging scalp?' http://iaindale.blogspot.com/2008/01/is-hains-resignation-first-blogging.html accessed 1 October 2011.

Davies, N. (2008). *Flat Earth News: An award-winning reporter exposes falsehood, distortion and propaganda in the global media.* London: Chatto and Windus.

Dowell, B. (2011). 'Have trade magazines got a shelf life?' www.guardian.co.uk/media/2011/apr/25/trade-magazines-online-only accessed 21 October 2011.

Enders, C. (2010). 'News Corporation's proposed takeover of BSkyB: A submission to the Secretary of State by Claire Enders, CEO, Enders Analysis Ltd'. http://image.guardian.co.uk/sys-files/Media/documents/2011/08/24/foi-bskyb-7-enders-letter-31-jtpuly-2010.pdf accessed 27 August 2012.

Foster, P. (2010). 'Tories plan leadership revolution at the BBC'. www.timesonline.co.uk/tol/news/politics/article7012882.ece accessed 11 October 2011.

Fraser, N. (1990). 'Rethinking the public sphere: A contribution to the critique of actually existing democracy'. *Social Text,* **25**(26): 56–80.

Glanville, J. (2011). 'Auntie Mabel doesn't give a toss about Serbia'. www.lrb.co.uk/v33/n16/jo-glanville/auntie-mabel-doesnt-give-a-toss-about-serbia accessed 3 September 2012.

Habermas, J. (1989). *The Structural Transformation of the Public Sphere.* Cambridge: Polity Press.

Halliday, J. (2012). 'Five dailies killed off in latest local paper cull'. www.guardian.co.uk/media/2012/apr/16/johnston-press-dailies-go-weekly accessed 17 April 2012.

Harnden, T. (2011). 'Don't let the politicians turn the British press into an American-style lapdog of the Establishment'. http://blogs.telegraph.co.uk/news/tobyharnden/100096223/dont-let-the-politicians-turn-the-british-press-into-an-american-style-lapdog-of-the-establishment/ accessed 21 October 2011.

Jenkins, S. (2010). 'David Cameron is taking a big gamble with his own party'. The *Guardian.* 4 October. http://www.guardian.co.uk/commentisfree/2010/oct/04/david-cameron-conservative-conference-cuts, accessed 24 June 2013.

Kelner, S. (2011). 'The demise of local papers should be taken seriously'. www.thejournalismfoundation.com/2011/12/the-demise-of-local-papers-is-something-we-should-all-take-seriously/ accessed 15 March 2012.

Kjetland, R. (2010). 'RTL sells UK's Channel 5 to Daily Express owner Desmond for $161m.' www.bloomberg.com/news/2010-07-23/richard-desmond-to-buy-channel-5-from-bertelsman-s-rtl-for-161-million.html accessed 3 September 2012.

Leveson Inquiry (2012). 'Daily transcript of the morning hearing 14 June 2012'. www.levesoninquiry.org.uk/wp-content/uploads/2012/06/Transcript-of-Morning-Hearing-14-June-2012.txt accessed 4 September 2012.

Lyall S. and E. Pfanner (2011). 'BBC, under criticism, struggles to tighten its belt.' www.nytimes.com/2011/04/24/business/media/24bbc.html?pagewanted=all accessed 21 March 2012.

Midgely, A. (2011). 'Digital radio switchover "should be postponed to 2020".' www.telegraph.co.uk/culture/tvandradio/bbc/8487991/Digital-radio-switchover-should-be-postponed-to-2020.html accessed 2 September 2011.

Mosco, V. (1996). *The Political Economy of Communication*. London: Sage.

Oborne, P. (2011a). 'David Cameron is not out of the sewer yet'. www.telegraph.co.uk/news/uknews/phone-hacking/8626421/Phone-hacking-David-Cameron-is-not-out-of-the-sewer-yet.html accessed 21 October 2011.

Oborne, P. (2011b). 'What the papers won't say.' www.spectator.co.uk/essays/7075673/what-the-papers-wont-say.html accessed 21 October 2011.

Ofcom (2011). 'Children and parents media literacy tracking study'. http://stakeholders.ofcom.org.uk/binaries/research/media-literacy/additional-analysis.pdf accessed 15 March 2012.

Oliver, L. (2010). 'Independent: Are PR agencies forging the new journalism?' http://blogs.journalism.co.uk/2010/06/03/independent-are-pr-agencies-forging-the-new-journalism/ accessed 4 September 2012.

Puddington, A. (2012). 'Freedoms in the world: the Arab uprisings and their global repercussions'. www.freedomhouse.org/sites/default/files/inline_images/FIW%202012%20Booklet--Final.pdf accessed 16 March 2012.

Rogers, S. (2011). 'Rupert Murdoch and the BskyB takeover: how powerful will it make him?' www.guardian.co.uk/media/datablog/2011/mar/03/rupert-murdoch-bskyb-takeover#zoomed-picture accessed 3 September 2012.

Rudin, R. (2011). *Broadcasting in the 21st Century*. London: Palgrave.

Rusbridger, R. (2011). 'Q&A with Alan Rusbridger'. www.guardian.co.uk/commentisfree/2011/jul/07/phone-hacking-alan-rusbridger accessed 25 August 2011.

Russell, J. (2010). 'Richard Desmond buys Channel 5'. www.telegraph.co.uk/finance/newsbysector/mediatechnologyandtelecoms/media/7907637/Richard-Desmond-buys-TV-channel-Five.html accessed 3 September 2012.

Sabbagh, D. (2011). 'Phone hacking: Watergate reporter "struck by parallels" with Nixon scandal?' www.guardian.co.uk/media/2011/sep/29/phone-hacking-watergare-reporter-parallels.

Sambrook, R. (2012). 'Delivering trust: Impartiality and objectivity in the digital age'. Reuters Institute for the Study of Journalism. http://reutersinstitute.politics.ox.ac.uk/fileadmin/documents/Publications/Working_Papers/Delivering_Trust_Impartiality_and_Objectivity_in_a_Digital_Age.pdf, accessed 21 June 2013.

Sherwin, A. (2011). 'Paul Staines: "I pummel them until they beg for mercy".' www.guardian.co.uk/media/2011/jan/31/interview-paul-staines-guido-fawkes accessed 15 March 2012.

Stoller, T. (2010). *Sounds of Your Life: A history of independent radio in the UK*. New Barnet: John Libbey.

Sweney, J. (2012). 'UK newspaper advertising facing bleak forecast for 2013'. The *Guardian*. 11 December. http://www.guardian.co.uk/media/2012/dec/11/uk-newspaper-advertising-bleak-forecast-2013, accessed 21 June 2013.

Thornhill, T. (2011). 'When oligarchs attack: Moment Russian media mogul Lebedev "neutralised" fellow billionaire on TV.' www.dailymail.co.uk/news/article-2038778/Alexander-Lebedev-brawl-Russian-TV-Media-mogul-punches-Sergei-Polonsky.html accessed 3 September 2012.

Unesco (2013). Unesco UIS data. Unesco Institute of Statistics. http://www.nationmaster.com/graph/med_new_and_per_cir_dai_percap-periodicals-circulation-daily-per-capita#source, accessed 21 June 2013.

Van Dijk, J. (1991). *The Network Society*. London: Sage.

White, D.M. (1950). 'The gatekeeper: a case study in the selection of news'. *Journalism Quarterly* **27**: 383–391.

Public relations and democracy

Learning outcomes

By the end of this chapter you should be able to:

■ identify and discuss the dilemmas of public relations' role in contemporary democracy
■ understand democracy as an unfinished process, not merely concerned with voting and elections
■ analyse PR's contribution to specific dilemmas around 'fake news', lobbying in secret and the misuse of social media
■ explore PR professional bodies' codes and their relevance to PR's ethical dilemmas and democratic responsibilities
■ understand how PR practitioners' aims to serve client interests and the (material) interest that PR has that its expertise is recognised may be in conflict with democracy.

Structure

■ Democracy, media and expertise
■ PR's relation to democracy since the 1980s
■ PR's contribution to democracy
■ PR versus democracy
■ PR ethics codes and democracy
■ The problem of (PR's) expertise for democracy
■ Futures of PR and democracy

Introduction

This chapter is a critical analysis of the role played in democracy by public relations (PR), focusing on the role of political public relations, public affairs and comprehensive political marketing. This exploration is necessary, firstly, because of the neglect of discussion of democracy in recent and influential PR texts. Secondly, it is necessary because of the ethical dilemmas that face contemporary PR, which relate both to structural problems with its role in the world and well-founded perceptions of the negative consequences of PR for democratic life. The perspective from which this chapter is written is a critical one that recognises problems in the great inequality existing in (the communication channels of) contemporary society. This critical approach argues that there are problems with the liberal pluralist assumption that we should be satisfied with the validity and diversity of information in the current 'marketplace of ideas', which does not take seriously the implications of such inequalities. The existence of such inequalities raises challenging questions about how to reform the institutions and practices of PR to benefit democracy.

Democracy, media and expertise

Democracy is both an ideal, based on the commitment to the political equality of citizens, and a reality. This ideal requires, at a minimum, involving ordinary citizens in debate and making decisions accountable to them (Kelley 1966: 217–218, 225; Washbourne 2010: 19–20). Debate is:

an exchange of opinion in which participants are willing to be persuaded of the truth or justice of something. The idea that such discussion is possible is basic to . . . democracy. (Turner 2003: 48, 69)

In large-scale societies, citizens cannot be involved in every decision and are both physically distant from where decisions are made and mentally distant from the array of expertise necessary to complex contemporary political life. Discussion is organised through *representative* democracy, and media is central to providing publicity of the content and contexts of that discussion. Ordinary citizens elect people to represent their interests, views, opinions and identities. Those elected are meant to make public policies for *all*. Representative democracy should ensure that even though citizens are not actually present at the making of political decisions, their interests, values and concerns *are* properly considered *in* those decisions. Voting institutionalises a degree of power vested in citizens to remove politicians and governments, and elections are special events in which that power is expressed. However, representation means *more* than voting. Representation by elected representatives also goes on between elections. Representation is evident in the content of politicians' speeches as they address 'the people'. It is also evident in the consultation of individuals and interest groups that occurs when proposed legislation and policy are discussed. Further, such representation is present in various forms of media content, as well as in face-to-face meetings (Saward 2009). Contemporary democracy involves a complex attempt at representation, of which the election itself is only an important and highly visible manifestation. Media and expertise are both necessary to contemporary democracy, but may both pose problems for the ideal of democratic equality.

The ideals embedded in representative democracy include political equality, encouragement and support for widespread participation (including space and time to enable deliberation) and the defence of rights, in particular for minorities, in order to forestall the development of tyranny (Davis 2002: 4; Washbourne 2010: 5–6; Fishkin 2011: 65). Democratic ideals also require that media provision supports the needs of citizens for information, and access to debates, and provides an arena through which representatives can be held to account (Washbourne 2010: 6–12, 68–75). However, as we shall see later when considering lobbying – though very far from all important relationships and ideas are made public via media, media are both at the centre of representative democracy and also the activity of PR practitioners. Mediated democracy should do two things. Firstly, it should involve citizens in debates and contribute to their awareness, both of a range of political knowledge and concerning policies, parties, pressure groups and problems. Secondly, it should link citizens' thoughts, perceptions and concerns captured in such debates to those with responsibility for political decisions – governments, ministers and MPs. The activities of PR practitioners involve them in influencing both aspects of mediated democracy.

Democratic ideals are imperfectly realised everywhere in the world. Ideals of the democratic involvement of citizens in debate and decision making appear to fall short even in those countries widely accepted as leading democracies (Washbourne 2010: 7–8, 28–29, 81–85). This suggests that democracy is not so much an end point at which to aim, but, rather, a process potentially without end whose progress is uncertain (see Think about 3.1).

Think about 3.1

Does thinking about democracy as 'representation' rather than as voting make a difference to how PR practitioners might influence it?

What difference might serving or engaging democracy as 'democratic representation' – rather than democracy as merely elections and voting – make to the professional lives and activities of PR practitioners? Is voting in elections really the only role for citizens? Can PR practitioners facilitate debate or is their role likely to impede debate? What roles in democracy do PR practitioners have (should they have)? Can you find (or imagine) contexts when these roles *might* come into conflict with the ideal of political equality of all citizens?

Picture 3.1 Is voting in elections really the only role for citizens in a democracy? Can PR practitioners facilitate debate? (*source*: Mark Sykes/Alamy Images)

PR's relation to democracy since the 1980s

PR has grown in funding and importance since the 1980s in the UK and Western Europe. It has further expanded and intensified its activities in the US, and been spread around the world, by adopting US practices or establishing and developing local ones. These developments have put PR into a relationship of deep significance to democracy everywhere (Banks 2000; Davis 2002: 3, 5; Moloney 2006; Curtin and Gaither 2007; Davis 2007: 213; Morris and Galsworthy 2008). However, PR texts have greatly neglected consideration of democracy (cf. Fitzpatrick and Bronstein 2006; Strömbäck and Kiousis 2011; Guth and Marsh 2012). Famously, Davis (2002) has negatively labelled contemporary political regimes 'Public Relations Democracy', arguing that PR practitioners have great and negative influence on democratic politics. According to Davis, this influence has led to the illicit sidelining of public and political institutions as PR offers to 'listen to' the thoughts and feelings of citizens through polls and surveys on behalf of parties and governments (Davis 2002: 8). This privatises the thinking of citizens rather than allowing it to emerge in, and contribute to, debate. Davis also asserts that the impact of this 'privatisation' of discussion is exacerbated by PR practitioners' support for political policy 'solutions' based on the so-called 'free market' and the denigration of forms of public provision (ibid.). The negative effects of sidelining of specifically political institutions can be seen in PR's contributions to the deficit of political, regulatory oversight of financial institutions before and during the current financial crisis (Davis 2002: 77, 82; Frenken 2010: 39–40, 60). PR practitioners act to limit relevant institutional reform of finance in promoting the interests of corporations and fund managers rather than citizens (Frenken 2010: 60).

PR's contribution to democracy

This section explores PR's positive contribution to democratic debate. Firstly, it investigates criticism of 'bossism' and claims of PR's democratic superiority to it. Secondly, it considers and assesses the information subsidy provided by PR practitioners to newsgathering and provision of the information upon which citizens rely. Thirdly, it explores PR's challenge to radical critiques that assert that PR, necessarily and structurally, forms the opposite of democratic debate.

PR bypasses 'bossism'

Proponents of PR often claim that PR aids democracy by taking it out of the arena of old-style politics, which was deeply unresponsive to citizens and voters. We often forget that contemporary democracies were very undemocratic even in the recent past. In the UK and the US between the 1920s and 1960s, national (prime ministers or presidents) or local (municipal council leaders, US city mayors and state governors) 'bosses' often took the most important decisions in backrooms away from democratic debate. Such 'bosses' thought about their supporters as 'clients' requiring services, *not* citizens to be involved in debate. Though 'bossism' might well have served some of the important material interests of citizen clients, such as finding them a job or a home, it also produced a high-handed attitude towards voters and citizens as potential political *discussants* (Kelley 1966: 206–207, 217; Bloom 1973: 257, 273; Lees-Marshment 2001: 131; Lees-Marshment 2009). Such 'bossism' did not usually acknowledge that it was undemocratic, yet the democratic credentials of such 'bossism' were very much 'a sham' (Kelley 1966: 217). The activity of PR practitioners may be an improvement on this. In its criticism of 'bossism', PR authors have argued that PR's use of surveys and focus groups to capture the thoughts, values and concerns of ordinary citizens means they can be *listened to*, and that political leaders are thus able to know and address their concerns (Leach 2009: 86, 89; Washbourne 2010: 38–40). Thus, the idea is that the use of PR can lead to something significantly closer to democratic ideals than 'bossism' did. PR claims to aid two-way communication between actors – citizens/publics/ stakeholders/politicians – where they may otherwise mutually misunderstand each other (Pimlott 1961: 238; Kelley 1966: 213). PR practitioners are here credited with uncommon expertise in communicational skills and specialist knowledge of media that may benefit others. These claims are also underpinned by the notion that PR *can* both involve ethical acts and function as a neutral mediator and, thereby, play a positive public role (Leach 2009: 86; Washbourne 2009: 78–79).

PR provides information subsidies

PR can aid democracy by providing information subsidies. The argument here is that information (especially news) is central to the functioning of democracy, yet is very expensive to provide. It takes a great deal of work and use of resources to collect and validate (Kelley 1966: 204–205; Gans 2003). PR can aid newsgathering and make us aware of information by collecting and arranging news and providing it to journalists and others in a timely manner

for free (Davis 2002: 32–33; Lieber and Golan 2011: 60; Tedesco 2011: 81). The claim has become more important since news provision is undergoing difficulties in the contemporary world. Newspapers are losing readership, making their task less economically viable and creating a crisis for their business model (Washbourne 2010: 64–65). Television news is losing viewers and may have decreasing amounts of money invested in it by commercial, thus profit-sensitive, broadcasters (Washbourne 2010: 67–68). Though web-based sources may be making some difference in lowering the costs of newsgathering and, for example, expanding the online readership and revenues of 'print' newspapers (Washbourne 2010: 136), the PR information subsidy seems necessary (Lieber and Golan 2011: 61–62). Thus, the claim is that PR benefits democracy by supporting the timely provision of information essential to citizens.

PR can't be too bad since democracy has not disappeared

Moloney (2006: 73) argues, uncommonly among even former PR practitioners, that PR's relation to democracy is *the* most important question concerning PR. He further argues that PR's effect cannot be simply anti-democratic, as some radical theorists assert, since rich Western countries continue to be democracies in spite of massive expansion and intensification of PR in the last thirty years. It is an important argument against reductive accounts that suggests that PR has been an all-powerful and entirely negative influence on the accountability central to democracy (cf. Miller and Dinan 2007).

However, in relation to PR's opposition to 'bossism', its provision of information subsidies and its contemporary happy co-existence with democracy, it is apposite to repeat a claim made first in the 1950s that these activities of PR have 'little to do with the people consulting together' (Kelley 1966: 227). PR's potentially democratically positive activities have nothing directly to do with people's involvement in democratic debate. Furthermore, the positive effects of these activities of PR are typically *assumed* rather than demonstrated in PR texts. Perhaps, at best, where they are realised they may aid the consensual management of society.

PR versus democracy

A larger part of the claims concerning PR and democracy, however, relate to the idea that PR may be harming the fulfilment of democratic ideals. This harm can be seen in two main areas. Firstly, the question of debates that are *not* made public – in short, the role of public *silence* or *invisibility* concerning PR practitioners' relations with journalists ('fake' news) and politicians ('secret' lobbying) – concerns of long-standing in critical analyses of PR (Pimlott 1961: 214; Bloom 1973: 266, 268; Davis 2002: 13, 55–57, 82; Davis 2007: 179). These silences concern not so much the question of manufacturing mass consent but, in a key feature of 'Public Relations Democracy', that of 'excluding both the general public and non-corporate elites' from debate or awareness of significant developments (Davis 2002: 82). Secondly, the role of such expertise as PR practitioners lay a claim to and how democracy should deal, democratically, with (such claims to) special knowledge and skills.

PR and fake news

Fake news is the negative side of 'information subsidy'. The claim is that much news is now dominated by thinly veiled and barely edited publicity releases. This has been asserted since the 1950s and affirmed in detail since then (Davis 2002: 25–27, 172–173; Gans 2003; Davis 2007; Davies 2009; Tedesco 2011: 82). Those publicity releases, while they may sometimes provide useful information, do so in furtherance of the material interests of PR practitioners' clients, and moreover do so without being declared *as* publicity releases. Furthermore, there is more evidence of PR's interference with the provision of a diversity of information, since only some information will serve their clients' interests, and the provision of selective interpretations of information in line with particular interests, than there is that information subsidy benefits democratic media. For instance, Bell Pottinger's plans to enhance the reputation of a human-rights abusing political regime by strategic placement of news stories highlighting positive developments and downplaying criticism could consequentially change attitudes in spite of no changed behaviour of the regime (see Mini case study 3.1). Minimally, PR may contribute to disrupting some of the main normative roles of news media in democracies, which are: providing objective information; playing a watchdog role in relation to the activities of the powerful; and providing an arena for rational debate and an access point both for citizens and a wide range of interest groups to put forward their views (Davis 2002: 4, 55).

PR and lobbying 'in secret'

Lobbying is the attempt to influence the decisions of public authorities; firstly, by building relationships with, and

influence on, local, national or international politicians or administrators (L'Etang 2008: 113). Secondly, lobbyists seek, by the framing of messages in media and society, behind the scenes, to benefit PR practitioners or their clients (Strömbäck and Kiousis 2011). Lobbying is an activity that is very old but that has undergone great change. The most important of recent changes has been the development and intensification of professionalised lobbying, organised in relation to multiple clients as well as in-house. Such lobbying is recognised in the existence of a number of professional bodies (CIPR; APPC; PRCA) that support, and seek to normalise, lobbying's spread around the world.

Open, publicly visible lobbying of public authorities by non-governmental organisations, such as that of Liberty's Shami Chakrabarti in arguing for defence of human rights, is an obviously legitimate pursuit. The very openness allows competing interests and alternative viewpoints and arguments to be raised in public debate (Norman 2011). It is, however, less clear that closed or secretive lobbying is as legitimate an activity as assumed in the PR literature (L'Etang 2008: 113). It has become widely apparent in recent years that lobbying presents significant problems for democracy. Its spread, intensification and professionalisation raises issues of access to politicians for resource-poor individuals and groups (Bernhagen and Mitchell 2009; Miller and Harkins 2010; Kluver 2011). Lobbying also raises broader concerns about sidelining the open debate that is central to democracy (Davis 2002; Davis 2007; Dinan and Miller 2007). The problem is that powerful interests will influence governments to create policy or legislation that serves their interests – but not the public interest – all the while conducting their activity in secret and thereby ensuring that their influence cannot be challenged. Those concerns have led to the creation of organisations to bring to light and criticise the activity of lobbyists in and across countries (for example, Spinwatch and Alliance for Lobbying Transparency – see Think about 3.2).

Think about 3.2

Watchdogs of lobbying: do they serve democratic purposes?

Are lobby watch-style organisations (Spinwatch and Alliance for Lobbying Transparency) necessary to hold PR practitioners to account? Are they of benefit for ethical PR activities and only a problem for unethical ones? What defence, if any, of 'secret' lobbying do you find convincing? Why? What role should it have, if any, in a democracy?

The potentially undemocratic influence of powerful economic actors on public life in this underhand or devious manner has led to the demand for various measures to make such relations transparent. These measures include the registration of lobbyists and clients and accounts of the money spent on lobbying (Public Administration Select Committee 2009: esp. 45–46, 50–51). It seems that, in spite of resistance by PR professional bodies (Public Administration Select Committee 2009: 9–10, 19–20), a system of statutory regulation and transparency concerning lobbyists, clients and money spent is necessary in the United Kingdom. This would bring the UK in line with such systems that have been developed in the United States, Canada and Australia, and which may be in development in the European Union (Public Administration Select Committee 2009: 60). This has been more widely and profoundly recognised in the UK in late 2011 in relation to a major scandal involving Bell Pottinger (see Mini case study 3.1).

Lobbying in representative democracies depends upon silence and invisibility rather than open discussion (Davis 2002: 13). It also depends on the opaqueness of relations of lobbyists to officials, and the claims of expertise that lobbyists make to clients. It is thus in powerful tension with the access of ordinary citizens to political debate.

Picture 3.2 Bell Pottinger's lobbying practices in the UK on behalf of its client, the state of Uzbekistan, reveals certain aspects of contemporary PR that are troubling for democracy. (*source*: Shutterstock.com/Megastocker)

Mini case study 3.1
The Bell Pottinger lobbying scandal

the failure of self-regulation of PR lobbying; and the multinational, cross-jurisdictional organisation and client list of major PR firms raising complex questions concerning the representing of the interests of other countries to domestic politicians and the complexity of PR practice causing increased difficulties bringing such practices to account.

The scandal, revealed by the press in December 2011, concerning the role of PR agency Bell Pottinger (hereafter, BPP) as a lobbyist was highlighted by *The Independent* newspaper and the Bureau for Investigative Reporting (Grice 2011; Newman and Wright 2011a; Newman and Wright 2011b; *The Independent* 2011; Wright 2011; Wright and Duff 2011). BPP agreed to secretly lobby the UK Government and to place stories in the media to downplay the human rights abuses of its client state, Uzbekistan. In addition, BPP offered to secretly edit content of user-generated websites such as Wikipedia to benefit the reputation of its client. Personnel from Bell Pottinger discussed these options with undercover journalists posing as representatives of the human-rights abusing state. This case is invaluable since it reveals certain features of contemporary PR that are troubling for democracy. These include: the use PR firms make of contacts with domestic politicians and senior public servants; BPP's preparedness to secretly edit social media content to benefit its client's interests;

Though BPP was welcomed into PRCA membership, this does not seem to have regulated its behaviour. Further, on 4 April 2012, BPP was cleared by the PRCA Code of Conduct procedure of any wrongdoing, in fact being found '*fully compliant* with the PRCA's Code of Conduct and *best practice* guidelines' (PRCA 2012, author's italics). This makes one suspect either the content of this code or the judiciousness of its application. The fact that BPP is fully prepared to represent states that abuse human rights raises important issues for the ethics of PR. Such questions are also raised by BPP's plans (and ongoing actions) over editing Wikipedia. It is a measure of the fact that some individuals and firms do behave ethically that two PR firms immediately rejected the approach of these dubious (pretend) 'clients'. Ethical behaviour by individual practitioners and PR firms is very important, even if it will check only some aspects of the impact of unethical behaviour – and in relation only to the most flagrantly or obviously unethical clients.

PR ethics codes and democracy

So, what do the ethical codes of professional PR bodies require, how do they attempt to regulate the ethics of their members and what role does democracy play in these codes? Walle (2003) has argued that the PR codes in a range of countries – the US (PRSA), Canada (CPRS), Australia (PRIA), New Zealand (PRINZ) and South Africa (RISA) – have in common neglect of broader responsibilities such as 'practitioners' duties towards the public and to society in general' (Walle 2003: 1, 2–3). Moreover, she also found that ethical commitments are often in tension with these broader duties by being orientated to ease relations with clients. For example, she found that none of the codes imposed obligations to 'truthfulness' of PR practice. The codes may often disavow lying but do not require full and truthful disclosure, therefore making it easy to support clients' requirements but routine to contribute to misleading others. She also noted the absence in codes of directives 'that might help practitioners navigate the complex relations between truthfulness and public interest' (Walle 2003: 3). She also found that the codes did not require PR practitioners' responsibility for client behaviour, even where it might conflict with 'the social good'. None mentioned assessment of social interest in client selection (Walle 2003: 4).

Walle expresses concern over the lack of encouragement of moral reflection. Such moral reflection might be beneficial to PR practitioners in negotiating real-world dilemmas. Such reflection is the central concern of the contemporary PRSA code, which is designed 'to anticipate and accommodate, by precedent, ethical challenges that might arise' (PRSA 2012a: 1). This is surely valuable for PR practitioners. However, this is more *appearance* than achievement. The PRSA's focus on aiding the negotiation of ethical dilemmas actually arises out of its profound failure to sanction practitioners. The PRSA had half-a-century of attempting to enforce a code, yet, 'the meager [sic] results of the effort in relation to the time and resources required, failed to provide a valuable return on investment for the PRSA, its members or the broader profession', from whom they had a 'lack of cooperation' (PRSA 2012b). Other PR professional bodies, such as the UK's CIPR (2012a), do seek to maintain the option of sanctioning their members. The CIPR has also sought to make its guidelines on lobbying more rigorous in response to the Bell Pottinger scandal and public concern over lobbying present in the UK Public Administration Select Committee on lobbying (Public Administration Select Committee 2009; Owens and Luker 2012; CIPR 2012b). However, the CIPR

Explore 3.1

Do PR professional bodies aid ethical behaviour?

Investigate PR professional bodies' ethical codes in your own country by examining their websites. What is the role of PR professional bodies in the regulation of ethical behaviour? Should such ethical codes specifically articulate support for democratic debate in contemporary society? Why do their codes differ (e.g. those of the PRSA, CIPR)? How do the concrete differences in such codes affect or encourage the:

■ Ethical behaviour of PR practitioners?

■ Ethical reflection of PR practitioners?

■ Democratic involvement of citizens in debate?

code can aid its members' ethical behaviour only somewhat since it offers no advice on how to handle *contradictions* between different elements of its code (see Explore 3.1). One important contradiction is conflict between 'public benefit' and serving specific clients' interests. There may be benefit in the existence of the code, however, since it may encourage motivated members to discuss the ethical implications of their (in)actions. Certainly, very many do not wish to behave at all like Bell Pottinger (cf. CIPR 2012c). However, as Bloom (1973: 273) argued four decades ago:

failure to establish a rather rigid code of ethics in political public relations does a disservice not only to the profession but also to the nation.

The CIPR code is also replete with merely worthy clauses, such as those on 'integrity and honesty' that oppose concealment of the practitioner's role as representative of a client (CIPR 2012a, section A.2). That opposition to concealment, however, is violated in much 'routine' PR practitioner activity – particularly, and by definition, in 'secret' lobbying.

There is ongoing debate in the PR industry and in governmental circles about the extent to which lobbying is problematic and not sufficiently or appropriately addressed in the ethics of PR. That debate is also concerned with whether those problems relate primarily to individual ethical behaviour (PR practitioner or PR firm), or more directly to democracy itself (Public Administration Select Committee 2009; Owens and Luker 2012). There are deep concerns among politicians and the public that 'self-regulation' has involved more *self* than *regulation* in areas of PR ethics across the PR professional bodies (Washbourne 2009).

Ethics, democracy and PR's use of Wikipedia

These considerations of PR's ethics and PR practitioners' role in democracy have come to the fore in a particularly stark way in the new information and communication environment provided by social media. PR ethics codes have yet to be updated in order to comprehend the distinctive features of social media and the democratic and broader social questions in which they may involve PR practitioners. Social media are popular new media forms defined by their production by their everyday users (Levinson 2009: 90). The use of social media by PR practitioners raises important ethical concerns and bears democratic implications. Yet, because of the perceived importance of Wikipedia to the public reputation of firms, presently PR practitioners are editing its pages in the *private interests* of their clients (DiStaso 2012: 1, 9–11; CIPR 2012c: 2–3). That form of editing not only raises ethical questions for PR practitioners and violates the community code of Wikipedia (material interests in a topic disqualify editing the relevant page), it also raises important democratic considerations (Levinson 2009: 93; Lievrouw 2011: 177ff.). Edits of Wikipedia pages by Bell Pottinger practitioners were made using fake online identities. This, surely, provides evidence that their activities were considered ethically dubious even by themselves?

However, the key concern here is the role of Wikipedia as a supplementary information source in and for democracy. Since Wikipedia circulates much valid and up-to-date information, PR practitioners editing pages in line with their clients' interests raises the same concerns that 'fake news' and 'secret lobbying' do more generally. If allowed, this will make this user-driven source another space for dominant institutions, including corporations, with the added feature that the activity of the powerful remains invisible to the users of Wikipedia (see Explore 3.2). However, the discussion of these issues, even among ethically inclined PR practitioners, often downplays and confuses the crucial difference between *private interests* (of clients and PR practitioners themselves) and *the (democratic) public interest* in valid and up-to-date information (cf. DiStaso 2012: 4; CIPR 2012c: 2). PR practitioners most often sideline questions of (material) interests, preferring to claim justification to edit on the basis that PR practitioners are especially knowledgeable and, in particular, that they are trustworthy since they are regulated by the ethical codes of their profession. As we have seen above, however, both the content

> ### Explore 3.2
>
> #### Ethics, democracy and PR's use of Wikipedia
>
> What role does Wikipedia play in the democratisation of information? Do you edit Wikipedia? How do PR practitioners, about whom you know, edit it? How do you think PR practitioners' desire to use Wikipedia should be negotiated with Wikipedians' culture and administrative rules? Would you consider editing using a fake identity? Is it ethical to do so? Do you know of colleagues who have felt pressured to do so by the clients' requirements?
>
> Search back copies of *PR Week* (or other trade/industry publications). Can you find examples of the editing of Wikipedia (or other social media) being discussed? What are the democratic and ethical implications for PR practitioners doing so? Are those implications discussed? Are the ethical (or democratic) implications foregrounded as important for PR practitioners to debate? Are you, as a potential future PR practitioner, encouraged to explore those implications? On reflection, what would you do in *their* place if you were asked to edit social media pages?
>
> Perhaps the ethics codes of PR bodies need to be expanded in order to consider the 'ethics of truthfulness' of the profession specifically in relation to social media. How would it be best to do this? How can citizens in a democracy rely upon Wikipedia as a source of reliable information if it is increasingly (and secretly) edited by PR practitioners in the (material) interests of their clients?

of the codes of conduct and the actual regulation of PR practitioners is questionable. The major reason for PR practitioners editing social media is not qualification but competition. PR practitioners' clients pressure them to do it and other, competing, PR practitioners will likely comply with such pressure (Distaso 2012: 1, 4, 5; CIPR 2012c: 2–3). PR needs to have a proper debate about its relationship to Wikipedia and other social media and explore the wider public interest in relation to such activity, rather than allowing its own material interests (satisfying the client, competing with other PR practitioners) to forestall a debate of great importance for democratic societies.

Ordinary citizens, whose role is central to democracy as both practice and ideal, are amateurs who possess, by definition, no special skills, knowledge or contacts in relation to public-political life. The role of PR expertise (or claims to such) itself raises issues of concern to democracy.

The problem of (PR's) expertise for democracy

PR involves a claim to expertise

PR involves a knowledge claim. It is that two-way PR takes a comprehensive approach to understanding and re-forming the relations between political authorities and people (Pieczka 2002: 322). PR aims to fill a lack in other members of society – including citizens themselves (Kelley 1966: 4–5, 7, 142–143). This expertise, it is claimed by PR practitioners, can 'make [political] parties more democratic' and consolidate 'representative democracy' (Lees-Marshment 2001: 225, 226). However, PR expertise is deployed in conditions of inequality often on behalf of powerful groups (Pimlott 1961: 238, 258), which implicates PR in the existence and effects of such inequality (Fischer 2009: 5; Wilkinson and Pickett 2009). Working for the powerful may deflect even ethical PR practitioners from using that expertise on behalf of professional ideals of serving the 'public interest' (Leach 2009: 93, 95; Washbourne 2009).

'Problems of expertise': hiding the (material) interests in knowledge claims

Turner (2003) and Fischer (2009) assert contemporary versions of early twentieth-century focus on the negative relationship between expertise and democracy (Michels 1962; Washbourne 1999; Washbourne 2001). As we have seen, expert knowledge is now increasingly and systematically embedded in everyday practices of politics and administration. It therefore threatens the involvement of people in political decision making (and threatens political equality). Public political discussion in representative democracy is often limited only to those topics *not* delegated to experts. The *legitimacy* that lobbying possesses, and the forms that legitimacy takes in contemporary PR, is limited, however, since, for example, the revelation that lobbying has occurred – the making visible of lobbying – immediately raises doubts about the knowledge claimed. This is somewhat different from cases involving the established expertise of those across an array of arenas of expert decision, such as in environmental policy, law (think of arguments for the end of jury trials because of the need for expert knowledge) and healthcare. Yet, these issues arise, according to Turner (2003: 36), not because of the character of expert knowledge itself and its inaccessibility to the public – not because we citizens don't know enough science, for example – but 'from the *sectarian character*

of the kinds of expert knowledge that bear on...decision making' (ibid., author's italics). Here 'sectarian' means partisan knowledge used in a narrowly confined or limited way. To maintain or expand democracy in conditions of increased expert knowledge requires that such knowledge be validated by public achievements and debate, rather than by mere acceptance of the authoritative advice of experts themselves. It is 'the fact that the public has no effective way of checking the competence of those discretionary decisions that is the source of the problem' (Turner 2003: 42). This highlights that experts don't typically exert their influence by persuasion conducted in public but, rather, by manipulating the conditions of social existence (Turner 2003: 23). This is precisely the case with most examples of PR work – it is carried out behind the scenes in order to influence public opinion by stealth. Yet this fundamentally excludes the debate and persuasion that is central to democratic politics (Turner 2003: 48, 69).

This democratic perspective on expertise implies testing in a public way the acknowledged expert advice. This needn't be impractical. As Fischer (2009: 45, author's italics) argues: 'democracy would *not* require participatory discussion of *every* issue. But it should include open deliberation about *which* decisions should be dealt with democratically and which need not'. As we have seen, routine activities of PR practitioners in 'fake news' and 'secret' lobbying bypass such debate and rational persuasion and require that we investigate more closely.

PR is a practice and discourse emerging in the world of competing expertise trying to establish its value and role (Pimlott 1961: 201; Kelley 1966: 203; Washbourne 2009: 78). And expertise exists in a world where debate over that expertise, once institutionalised, is conducted only among the 'experts' themselves, as we have seen, in silence and in the dark. PR might even have an interest in portraying the citizen in a poor light (Kelley 1966: 231). In short, expertise is, in part, a strategy of 'de-politicisation' – pretending that it is not being used in a sectarian way. Where in the proposed role of PR is the chance for 'the public...[to have a role in] checking the competence of those discretionary decisions' (Turner 2003: 42)? Minimally, transparency is needed about PR and lobbying activities, the interests they serve, the interests they themselves embody and the investments they imply.

Futures of PR and democracy

Public relations is only partially professionalised, which leaves it unable to sanction its members and at best able to give them a little ethical guidance in a complex and competitive role (Washbourne 2009). Many practitioners act ethically and wish to benefit from the support of professional organisations in order to increase the range of that ethical activity. We will all benefit if they are able to do so. Rogue and unethical colleagues cause the most problems and get a great deal of attention. However, the problematic relationship between PR and democracy depends not merely, or even mostly, on those rogue practitioners. It rather depends on the structural role PR plays in contemporary society. PR is the exploitation of a range of tools, knowledge and contacts to present organisations and individuals in the best light. It brings an instrumental approach to the creation of news and events that serve particular interests. It often muddies the meaning of news by creating 'fake news'. It contributes, through secret lobbying, to squeezing many issues of public concern out of the arena of public debate. Furthermore, PR has its own interest in others' belief in its expertise since it needs others' belief to create a market for its skills and tools. The activity of PR does not intrinsically benefit democracy, based as it should be on public discussion of public things via a proper exploration of all relevant alternative policies and information (Bloom 1973: 251). However, ethical PR is better than non-ethical. PR practitioners who give their labours pro bono to worthy but resource-light causes are better than those who do not. Yet, PR does not particularly aid democracy, and through having an elective affinity with market solutions it sidelines politics and democracy, not treating them as crucial procedures whereby decisions are made (Bloom 1973: 246; Davis 2002: 180; Moloney 2006: 32). We need to break with the 'public relations democracy' – not the realisation of democracy, but evidence of its dismemberment. It is strange that PR practitioners rarely consider why there is widespread suspicion of PR – a suspicion that appears to go back more than 60 years (Pimlott 1961: 199). PR textbooks mention but rarely consider this suspicion. If PR addresses this suspicion, it prefers to understand it as related to the reputations of its corporate clients. PR practitioners forget to look at their own activity, they forget that their job is to advance the best claims, create the best images regardless of the exact worth of the client, product or service for which they are working. They forget, too, to look at themselves – yet their foremost PR task is the promotion of a belief in their own expertise. As Moloney concludes about PR's status, even after real ethical reforms (if such prove possible) of the profession, the positive effects of PR on democracy and public life will *only just* outweigh the negative ones (2006: 176). Yet we are nowhere near that reformed place.

Bibliography

Banks, S.P. (2000). *Multicultural Public Relations: A social-interpretive approach*, 2nd ed. Ames, IA: Iowa State University Press.

Bernhagen, P. and N.J. Mitchell (2009). 'The determinants of direct corporate lobbying in the European Union'. *European Union Politics* **10**(2): 155–176.

Bloom, M.H. (1973). *Public Relations and Presidential Campaigns: A crisis in democracy*. New York, NY: Crowell.

CIPR (2012a). 'Code of Conduct'. www.cipr.co.uk/sites/default/files/CIPR%20Code%20of%20Conduct%2008-03-2012.pdf accessed 20 February 2012.

CIPR (2012b). 'Lords report highlights role of CIPR Code of Conduct'. newsroom.cipr.co.uk/lords-report-highlights-role-of-cipr-code-of-conduct accessed 20 March 2012.

CIPR (2012c). 'Defining PR ethically'. conversation.cipr.co.uk/posts/david.phillips/defining-pr-ethically accessed 20 April 2012.

Curtin, P.A. and T.K. Gaither (2007). *International Public Relations: Negotiating culture, identity, and power*. Thousand Oaks, London and New Delhi: Sage.

Davis, A. (2002). *Public Relations Democracy: Public relations, politics and the mass media in Britain*. Manchester: Manchester University Press.

Davis, A. (2007). 'Spinning money: corporate public relations and the London Stock Exchange' in *Thinker, Faker, Spinner, Spy: Corporate PR and the assault on democracy*. W. Dinan and D. Miller (eds). London: Pluto.

Davies, N. (2009). *Flat Earth News: An award-winning reporter exposes falsehood, distortion and propaganda in the global media*. London: Vintage Books.

Dinan, W. and D. Miller (eds) (2007). *Thinker, Faker, Spinner, Spy: Corporate PR and the assault on democracy*. London: Pluto.

DiStaso, M.W. (2012). 'Measuring public relations Wikipedia engagement: how bright is the rule?'. *Public Relations Journal* **6**(2): 1–24.

Fischer, F. (2009). *Democracy and Expertise: Reorienting policy inquiry*. Oxford: Oxford University Press.

Fishkin, J.S. (2009). *When the People Speak: Deliberative democracy and public consultation*. Oxford: Oxford University Press.

Fitzpatrick, K. and C. Bronstein (eds) (2006). *Ethics in Public Relations: Responsible advocacy*. Thousand Oaks, London and New Delhi: Sage.

Frenken, R. (ed.) (2010). *Covering the Crisis: The role of media in the financial crisis*. Maastricht: European Journalism Centre.

Gans, H.J. (2003). *Democracy and the News*. New York, NY: Oxford University Press.

Green, A. (2010). *Creativity in Public Relations*. London: Kogan Page.

Grice, A. (2011). 'Plenty of talk about cracking down on lobbying – but still no action'. *The Independent*, 6 December: 7.

Guth, D.W. and C. Marsh (2012). *Public Relations: A values-driven approach*, 5th ed. Boston, MA: Allyn and Bacon/ Pearson.

Kelley, S. (1966 [1956]). *Professional Public Relations and Political Power*. Baltimore, MD: Johns Hopkins University Press.

Kluver, H. (2011). 'The contextual nature of lobbying: explaining lobbying success in the European union'. *European Union Politics* **12**(4): 483–506.

Leach, R. (2009). 'Public relations and democracy' in *Exploring Public Relations*, 2nd ed. R. Tench and L. Yeomans (eds). Harlow: Financial Times Prentice Hall.

Lees-Marshment, J. (2001). *Political Marketing and British Political Parties*. Manchester and New York: Manchester University Press.

Lees-Marshment, J. (2009). *Political Marketing: Principles and applications*. London and New York: Routledge.

L'Etang, J. (2008). *Public Relations: Concepts, practice and critique*. London, New York, New Delhi and Singapore: Sage.

Levinson, P. (2009). *New New Media*. New York and London: Pearson.

Lieber, P.S. and G.J. Golan (2011). 'Political public relations, new management and agenda indexing' in *Political Public Relations: Principles and applications*. J. Strömbäck and S. Kiousis (eds). London and New York: Routledge.

Lievrouw, L. (2011). *Alternative and Activist New Media*. Cambridge: Polity.

Michels, R. (1962 [1915]). *Political Parties*. New York, NY: Free Press.

Miller, D. and W. Dinan (2007). 'Public relations and the subversion of democracy' in *Thinker, Faker, Spinner, Spy: Corporate PR and the assault on democracy*. W. Dinan and D. Miller (eds). London: Pluto.

Miller, D. and C. Harkins (2010). 'Corporate strategy, corporate capture: food and alcohol industry lobbying and public health'. *Critical Social Policy* **30**(4): 564–589.

Moloney, K. (2006). *Rethinking Public Relations*, 2nd ed. London and New York: Routledge.

Morris, T. and S. Galsworthy (2008). *Public Relations for Asia*. Basingstoke: Palgrave Macmillan.

Newman, M. and O. Wright (2011a). 'Caught on camera: top lobbyists boasting how they influence the PM'. *The Independent*, 6 December: 1–3.

Newman, M. and O. Wright (2011b). 'Exposed: public relations firm's dealings with some of the world's most controversial regimes; we wrote Sri Lankan civil war speech, say lobbyists'. *The Independent*, 6 December: 6.

Norman, M. (2011). 'Do they feel any pain at the dirty, seedy role they play in politics? Unethical lobbyists'. *The Independent*, 7 December: 16.

Owens, J. and S. Luker (2012). 'CIPR moves to stiffen ethics guidelines as lobbying scrutiny intensifies'. www.prweek. com/uk/news/1119649/CIPR-moves-stiffen-ethics-guidlines-lobbying-scrutiny-intensifies accessed 5 April 2012.

Pieczka, M. (2002). 'Public relations expertise deconstructed', *Media, Culture & Society* **24**(3): 201–223.

Pimlott (1961 [1951]). *Public Relations and American Democracy*. Port Washington, NY/London: Kennikat Press.

PRCA (2012). 'PRCA rejects complaint against Bell Pottinger public affairs'. www.prca.org.uk/PRCARejects Complaint againstBellPottingerPublic Affairs accessed 26 April 2012.

PRSA (2012a). 'Code of Ethics'. www.prsa.org/AboutPRSA/ Ethics/documents/Code%20of%Ethics.pdf accessed 15 January 2012.

PRSA (2012b). 'About enforcement'. www.prsa.org/aboutprsa/ ethics/avboutenforcement accessed 30 Janaury 2012.

Public Administration Select Committee (2009). *Lobbying: Access and Influence in Whitehall: First Report of Session 2008–09, Volume I*. London: The Stationary Office Limited.

Saward, M. (2009). *The Representative Claim*. Oxford: Oxford University Press.

Strömbäck, J. and S. Kiousis (2011). *Political Public Relations: Principles and applications*. London and New York: Routledge.

Tedesco, J.C. (2011). 'Political public relations and agenda building', in *Political Public Relations: Principles and applications*. J. Strömbäck and S. Kiousis (eds). London and New York: Routledge.

The Independent (2011). 'Evidence of lobbying industry out of control'. *The Independent*, 6 December: 18.

Turner, S.D. (2003). *Liberal Democracy 3.0*. London and New York: Sage.

Walle, M. (2003). 'Commentary: what happened to public responsibility? The lack of society in public relations codes of ethics'. www.prismjournal.org/fileadmin/Praxis/

Files/Journal_Files/issue1/Commentary-paper1.pdf accessed 15 February 2012.

Washbourne, N. (1999). *Beyond Iron Laws: Information technology and social transformation in the global environmental movement*. Unpublished Doctoral Thesis: University of Surrey.

Washbourne, N. (2001). 'Information technology and new forms of organising? Translocalism and networks in Friends of the Earth' in *Culture and Politics in the Information Age: A New Politics?* F. Webster (ed.). London: Routledge.

Washbourne, N. (2009). 'The media context of public relations and journalism' in *Exploring Public Relations*, 2nd ed. R. Tench and L. Yeomans (eds). Harlow: Financial Times Prentice Hall.

Washbourne, N. (2010). *Mediating Politics: Newspapers, radio, television and the Internet*. Open University Press/McGraw Hill: Maidenhead and New York.

Wilcox, D.L. and Cameron, G.T. (2009). *Public Relations: Strategies and Tactics*. 9th edn. Boston, MA: Pearson/Alyn and Bacon.

Wilkinson, R. and K. Pickett (2009). *The Spirit Level: Why more equal societies almost always do better*. New York/London: Routledge.

Wright, O. (2011). 'Vested interests are entitled to argue their case, but it must be in the open'. *The Independent*, 6 December: 5.

Wright, O. and O. Duff (2011). 'We can help you for a million'. *The Independent*, 6 December: 4–5.

Community and society:
corporate social responsibility (CSR)

Learning outcomes

By the end of this chapter you should be able to:

- critically evaluate the role of organisations in their society(ies)
- define the concept of corporate social responsibility in the context of relevant regulatory frameworks
- define and critically evaluate the role of ethics in business policy and practice
- diagnose ethical problems and identify strategies for making ethical decisions in organisational/cultural contexts
- appreciate the environmental complexities that influence organisational communication and public relations strategies.

Structure

- Social and economic change
- Sustainable business: corporate social responsibility (CSR)
- Business case for corporate social responsibility: why be socially responsible?
- Organisational responsibilities to stakeholders
- Organisational responsibilities to society
- Corporate responsibility and irresponsibility
- Regulatory frameworks
- Ethics and business practice

Introduction

WorldCom, Enron, Shell UK, Union Carbide, BP, Wal-Mart, Lehman Brothers and Exxon Corporation are just a few of the major international corporations that have been under the worldwide media spotlight for their corporate actions and activities. Executives from these companies have, at varying times over the past 20 years, been vilified by the media, attacked by shareholders and customers and in some instances imprisoned. Why? Because the organisations they represent have had a major impact on the social and physical environments in which they operate (e.g. oil and chemical leaks and, more recently, financial mismanagement). This chapter will explore the role of organisations in society and how, irrespective of the profit or not-for-profit imperatives, many are taking a critical view of their roles and responsibilities. In many instances (including some of the companies above), this has involved a radical repositioning of the organisation's **vision and values** that are impacting on the operational as well as the public relations (communication) strategies they employ.

Concern for the environment in which a business operates is not a new phenomenon, but its prevalence in Anglo-American business policy is growing and, due to the internationalisation of markets and business practice, this is influencing corporate strategy for large PLCs and small to medium-sized enterprises (SMEs) throughout the world. These corporate policy changes are encouraging organisations to increase their awareness and concern for the society(ies) in which they operate. An additional development is in the more sophisticated business use of the societal relationship as part of the corporate strategy and as a marketing tool. This has been demonstrated through the expansion of sponsorship programmes (see Chapter 23) and, more recently, with the development of cause-related marketing (CRM) – associating companies or brands with charitable causes (see Chapter 15). This chapter will describe in detail the relationships between an organisation and the community within which it operates. It will explore the complex issue of business ethics, with guidelines on how to promote ethical decision making in practice. There are links from this chapter to Chapter 15, which explores how public relations is responding to an increasingly CSR-conscious business environment through the development of communications programmes (see Case study 4.1).

Social and economic change

All our societies are continually changing and evolving. Factors such as economic and financial performance have a significant influence on our standards of living and manifest themselves in day to day measures such as inflation, taxation, fuel and food prices. These issues are increasingly being highlighted and recognised as the world comes to terms with the significant changes in economic power as North America and Europe move in and out of more regular economic downturns. It is relevant to note the impact worldwide of the US-originated 'credit crunch' in 2008/9, where the ability for banks to lend money to businesses and individuals had a major rippling effect on established economies and even brought down some major companies, such as Lehman Brothers in September 2008. The effect from this credit crunch has reverberated for many years, impacting significantly on other economic regions with the Eurozone suffering severe financial crises in 2012/13. As some national economies have experienced recession or a slowdown in growth, others, such as India, China and parts of South America, continue to expand rapidly. The role of business is therefore put into the spotlight as we witness patterns of change in the climate and the environment more generally. Issues such as global warming have, as a consequence, been brought into sharp focus

> **Definition:** '*Vision and values*' relates to the business practice of identifying an organisation's corporate vision – where it wants to go and how it wants to be perceived through its core values. (Go to the Internet and look up 'value and mission statements for corporations'.)

by a range of campaign and interest groups, as well as by senior public and political figures (Kofi Anan with the United Nations and former US presidential candidate Al Gore).

Al Gore's seminal book and film *An Inconvenient Truth* (2006, 2007, www.climatecrisis.net) focused on and highlighted the environmental damage being caused by modern, consumptive societies/businesses. Although a debated concept, Gore's work did raise the level at which such discussions were being held in nation states. It is not directly as a consequence but in line with this increased awareness that there are now many more powerful organisations asking questions about the role and responsibilities of business in a global society (see the Global Responsible Leadership Initiative, www.grli.org, the UN Global Compact established in 2000, www.unglobalcompact.org, and the UN's recent Millennium Development Goals – MDGs: UN 2011).

Case study 4.1
BBC World Service Trust – international impact

The aim of the BBC's World Service Trust is to help developing countries and countries in transition to build media expertise for the benefit of the population.

Following over 30 years of conflict in Afghanistan, the country is now looking to the future and the Afghan media have a major role to play in uniting the nation, rebuilding its culture and changing the population's mindset from one of war to peace.

The BBC's role has been to help develop the media infrastructure. The work of the BBC World Service Trust has been focused on helping the Afghanistan media to rebuild themselves and ensure they have the necessary broadcasting skills and principles.

The BBC World Service Trust has helped set up a new public service broadcasting body, a strong and independent media network that may reassure the Afghan people that action is being taken to recreate a democratic society. The BBC World Service Trust claims the programme has gone far beyond its remit to rebuild Afghanistan's media infrastructure.

According to the BBC World Service Trust, the impact is as follows:

- increased audience – now estimated at 85 per cent of the population and improved profile for the BBC as a social broadcaster

- staff development opportunities and enhanced motivation for staff from different BBC divisions – including developing skills for BBC journalists working on news gathering

- increased trust – as a result of the BBC's long-term commitment to Afghanistan and production of education programmes, covering human rights, civil society, voter education, women's rights and minority rights

- establishment of an independent media – with a robust infrastructure that allows the reconstruction process to be communicated to even the most isolated communities

- training for Afghan journalists – of whom 20 per cent are women (who were denied employment and education under the Taliban regime)

- media resources and training to use radio and studio equipment.

This example demonstrates how an organisation can get involved with a section of society and make real improvements. In this example, the BBC is using its experience as a broadcaster to help improve the media landscape in a specific country. The engagement with the issues is, however, more than just a practical one; other outputs relate to the communications impact in Afghanistan, staff development, perceptions of the BBC and an ability to meet the corporate objectives/mission of the BBC.

Source: http://www.bbc.co.uk/worldservice/trust/ and www.bitc.org.uk

---

More recently, challenges are being made on the foundations of business principles and how they are 'governed'. Particularly this has relevance following the lack of governance in the finance sector, which has been blamed in large part for the 2008 financial crisis (Sun et al. 2011). Clarke (2009) has argued this system permitted and even encouraged corporations to manipulate share prices and abuse corporate accounting principles in the name of shareholder value (see Enron, WorldCom, Lehman Brothers and others). From this context we have seen a lot of new governance codes in the UK and USA since 2008, but we are still experiencing accusations of excessive bonuses for CEOs and senior managers, as well as banks perceived as 'too big to fail'. From this perspective, Sir Mervyn King, Governor of the Bank of England, claimed Britain was at risk of another financial crisis without reforms to the banks (King 2011; *The Telegraph*, 5 March 2011).

Sustainable business: corporate social responsibility (CSR)

Individual members and groups in the community in which an organisation operates are increasingly being recognised as important **stakeholders** in the long-term security and success of large and small enterprises. Building relationships with these community groups is, therefore,

Definition: A *stakeholder* is someone who has an interest (stake) in the organisation, which may be direct or indirect interest as well as active or passive, known or unknown, recognised or unrecognised.

Definition: *Financial regulation* of donations refers to the legal requirement in the UK that any donation over £200 has to be recorded in a company's end of year annual report and accounts (the financial statement to shareholders).

an important issue in corporate and communications strategy. In order to understand how this can be achieved, it is essential to understand in more detail the complexities of the relationships between a business and its community(ies). It is also important to define some of the business terminology that is frequently used when analysing businesses in their societal contexts.

Corporate social responsibility

A well-used business and management term, corporate social responsibility (CSR) is often associated with the phrase 'enlightened self-interest' – how organisations plan and manage their relationships with key stakeholders. CSR is, therefore, an organisation's defined responsibility to its society(ies) and stakeholders. Although organisations are not a state, country or region, they are part of the infrastructure of society and as such they must consider their impact on it. A simple analogy for the impact organisations have on their community has been presented by

Peach (1987; see Figure 4.1), using the ripples from a stone thrown into a pond to represent the impact of a business on its environment. There are three levels of impact, ranging from the *basic*, in which a company adheres to society's rules and regulations, to the *societal*, where a company makes significant contributions towards improving the society in which it operates. In the middle level, companies are perceived to manage their activities so they adhere to the level and go beyond it. For example, this might be a company obeying legal requirements on employment rights as a foundation and then providing more generous interpretations of these legal rulings. Also, the company may seek to reduce the negative impact of the organisation on its society without necessarily taking positive action to make improvements that would take it to level three. (See also Box 4.1.)

Companies operating at the highest level, *societal*, do exist: companies are increasingly obtaining public recognition and visibility for their positive corporate actions. For example, in the UK, Business in the Community (BITC) has a CommunityMark (launched in 2007 and formerly the Percent Standard/Club, started in 1986, which was awarded as a voluntary benchmark to companies donating at least 1 per cent of pre-tax profits to community/social benefits). The CommunityMark was launched with an initial 21 member companies that met the five principles (see www.bitc.org.uk/communitymark/five_communitymark. html). See also Box 4.2 and Figure 4.2.

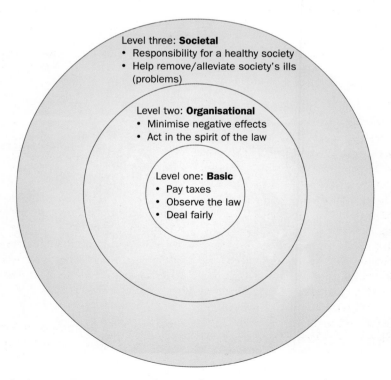

Figure 4.1 Impact of a business on its environment (*source*: after Peach 1987: 191–193)

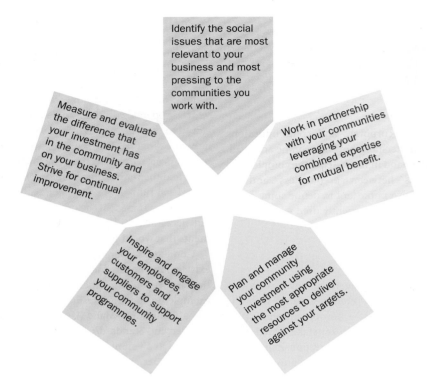

Figure 4.2 BITC CommunityMark five principles (*source*: www.bitc.org.uk)

Picture 4.1 Being corporately responsible should mean taking steps to avoid having a negative impact on the society in which an organisation operates (*source*: Reuters: Miguel Vidal)

Box 4.1

Peach model in action

Some clear examples at the *basic* level might be a company in the supermarket retail sector that is profitable, pays its taxes and maintains minimum terms and conditions for its employees. At the highest, *societal* level you could describe a supermarket retailer that conforms to society's rules and laws but also contributes to its society by funding community initiatives (e.g. holidays for disadvantaged children, investments in school facilities, transport for elderly people, lobbying for improved treatment of waste by local companies in line with its initiatives, contributing to positive legislation change in support of society, surpassing national and international employment rights and conditions, innovation in childcare or part-time mothers' conditions of work, etc.).

Box 4.2

CommunityMark pioneer companies

The 21 initial businesses to achieve the CommunityMark at the launch in September 2008 were:

Axis, Barclays, Blackburn Rovers Football & Athletic Club, BT, Contract Scotland, Deloitte, Design Links, Elementus, Ernst & Young, GlaxoSmithKline, HBOS, Heart of Midlothian Football, KPMG, Marks and Spencer, PricewaterhouseCoopers, Rangers Football Club, RWE npower, Sainsbury's, Tesco, The Town House Collection and Zurich Financial Services (UK).

Source: Business in the Community (www.bitc.org.uk)

When considering CSR it is important to make a distinction between corporate activities that are intended to contribute to the society and charitable acts or philanthropy (see Explore 4.1).

Philanthropy

One simple definition of **philanthropy** is that 'corporations perform charitable actions'. This is very different from CSR, with philanthropy being a charitable act not necessarily linked to the expectations of society. Philanthropy did occur in large industrial firms in the UK during the nineteenth century (such as Joseph Rowntree, Titus Salt) through the donation of money and amenities such as schools, hospitals or housing for employees and their communities. **Corporate philanthropy** can be perceived as a short-term, one-way relationship, which is unpredictable on behalf of the recipient and therefore more difficult to manage and strategically plan for. For example, during the dotcom boom (during the late 1990s when the financial performance and market impact of web-based businesses and technology companies in general were seriously exaggerated), technology company directors commonly gave large sums in charitable donations.

The Slate 60 is an annual list of US charitable gifts and pledges that has reported since 1996; in 2010 the total giving came to $3.36 billion. Interestingly, this is a reduction reflecting economic conditions as previous returns have been significantly higher ($4.29 billion in 2009, $15.78 billion in 2008 and £7.79 billion in 2007 – see www.slate.com).

Explore 4.1

Business impact on society

Identify, name and describe a company or organisation that fits into each of the levels in the 'stone in the pond' analogy.

What would those organisations in levels one and two need to do to move towards the third, *societal* level?

Feedback

You need to consider what changes in ethical business policy or practice would make a difference to society. It is not enough just to make statements of intent.

Definition: *Philanthropy* means 'a love of humankind – practical benevolence, especially charity, on a large scale' (*Concise Oxford Dictionary* 1995).

Definition: *Corporate philanthropy* is 'a way of giving something back into local communities, improving quality of life for employees and practicing corporate citizenship' (Cutlip et al. 2000: 470).

Depending on the general and sector-specific economic performance, individuals go on or off the list, reinforcing the unpredictable nature of this type of activity. For example, Bill Gates (the world's richest man and Microsoft's founder) was on the list in 2001 with $2bn in gifts. In 2005 Gates made the largest ever private donation of £400m ($750m) to the child health charity he set up with his wife, Melinda, the Bill and Melinda Gates Foundation (www.gatesfoundation.org). In 2008 Bill Gates relinquished his management of Microsoft to become non-executive chairman, and his foundation to date has given grants and donations totalling $16.4bn (audited financial accounts for 2008). He has also set up, with fellow businessman Warren Buffet, 'The Giving Pledge' to encourage the super rich to give away their wealth. Buffet is quoted (www.slate.com 2011):

'I've worked in an economy that rewards someone who saves the lives of others on a battlefield with a medal, rewards a great teacher with thank you notes from parents, but rewards, those who can detect the mispricing of securities with sums reaching into the billions', Buffett wrote, reiterating his decision to give away 99 per cent of his wealth. 'That reality sets an obvious course for me and my family: keep all we can conceivably need and distribute the rest to society, for its needs.'

Although gifts can be turned on and off by the donor like a tap, there are some benefactors who donate through trusts, which enable the act to be sustained over longer periods of time (e.g. the Rowntree Foundation or the Wellcome Trust in the UK, the John D. Rockefeller Foundation or the Bill and Melinda Gates Foundation in the US). See Explore 4.2.

In recognition of the interest shown by various stakeholder groups – employees, customers and particularly the financial community and investors – it is now common

---

Explore 4.2

Identifying CSR and philanthropic actions

List examples of what you might consider to be CSR or philanthropic actions by an organisation/company.

Feedback

Can you make distinctions between the two? Think about each organisation's objectives for the action. What was the intended outcome? What did it hope to achieve? Was it long term? Was it pre-planned or in response to an individual's request?

---

business practice for large and small to medium-sized enterprises (SMEs) to publish corporate literature and brochures giving details of their community activities and CSR. Non-financial reporting on corporate responsibility in annual reports became prevalent in the mid-1990s. In the UK, for example, BT's annual review and summary financial statement (1996/7) included a section called 'Why we are helping the community: we're all part of the same team'. Within the report, BT stated that:

It is increasingly clear that businesses cannot regard themselves as in some way separate from the communities in which they operate. Besides, research has shown that the decision to purchase from one company rather than another is not a decision about price alone.

The practice has evolved to such a degree that companies now produce specific corporate responsibility reports. For example, O2 (now owned by Spanish firm Telefonica but was formerly part of BT) is a Europe-wide mobile telephone company that launched its first corporate responsibility report in 2003. It continues this tradition with a current campaign, 'Think Big' (2011), aiming to be agents of positive and sustainable change (www.o2sustainability.co.uk).

Business case for corporate social responsibility: why be socially responsible?

Organisations in developed economies are today influenced by public opinion, shareholders, stakeholders (who can be shareholders, consumers and members of campaign groups) and the political process. Consequently, organisations that ignore their operational environment are susceptible to restrictive legislation and regulation. This is a particular issue in Europe with the increasing power and influence of the European Union, the single currency and the European parliamentary process. Representative bodies for business, such as Business in the Community (BITC), CSR Europe, Institute of Business Ethics, Business for Social Responsibility and the Prince of Wales International Business Leaders Forum (IBLF), have formed to help senior managers deal with the demands of varied stakeholder groups. Outside the EU, influencers such as the United Nations (UN Global Compact) are making an impact on business and political decision making.

Is CSR good business practice? On the one hand, many companies profited from unethical practices in the early part of the twentieth century, as demonstrated by the success of textile and mining industries and, more recently, with companies manufacturing chemical-based products such as asbestos. Furthermore, Milton Friedman has been championed as the consistent (if sometimes misquoted) business voice, stating that the business of business is simply to increase profits and enhance shareholder value. Friedman (1970) wrote key articles arguing these views in the 1960s and 1970s. Although there are few contemporary academic papers supporting his views, they are frequently cited as the opposing arguments to CSR.

On the other hand, in contrast to Friedman's views, there are the examples of both old and new companies benefiting themselves, their stakeholders and employees through more ethically based practice. Worldwide examples include Cadbury, Lever's, IBM, Co-Operative Bank and Coca-Cola. Even before corporate responsibility became a boardroom agenda item around the turn of the millennium, there is evidence of its commercial value. For example, Johnson & Johnson's chief executive officer, James Burke, demonstrates that companies with a reputation for ethics and social responsibility grew at a rate of 11.3 per cent annually from 1959 to 1990, while the growth rate for similar companies without the same ethical approach was 6.2 per cent (Labich 1992). Furthermore, arguments and evidence are put forward to support CSR's contribution to the financial performance of organisations (Little and Little 2000; Moore 2003).

CSR can contribute to corporate image and reputation (Lewis 2003; Sagar and Singla 2004). The importance of a good reputation can include the following:

■ Others are more willing to consider the organisation's point of view.

■ It helps to strengthen the organisation's information structure with society and therefore improve resources in all areas.

■ It makes it easier for the organisation to motivate and recruit employees – and to promote increased employee morale (Lines 2004).

■ It will enhance and add value to the organisation's products and services.

A socially responsible reputation is also a way of differentiating organisations and providing competitive advantage. This is supported by announcements from companies such as McDonald's and BT in the UK that they would be investing more time and resources into socially responsible activities. BT was influenced by a MORI report, which stated that 80 per cent of respondents believed it was important to know about an organisation's socially responsible activities in order to form a positive opinion about them. CEOs worldwide are starting to recognise that CSR is an important agenda item. Research by the India Partnership Forum (2003) claimed that nearly 70 per cent of CEOs stated that CSR was 'vital' to profitability and that, irrespective of economic climate, it would remain a high priority for 60 per cent of CEOs across the globe.

A company with an acknowledged strategy change on corporate responsibility and environmental engagement is oil firm Royal Dutch/Shell. During 1998, Shell had its first meeting with institutional shareholders (major company investors, e.g. on behalf of pension funds) to explain the company's new policies on environmental and social responsibilities. This initiative came following criticism of the company's action in high-profile environmental issues (e.g. when Shell was challenged by campaign groups over its decision to dismantle the Brent Spar oil platform at sea rather than on land owing to the supposed environmental impact) and human rights cases (execution of human rights activist Ken Saro-Wiwa, in Ogoniland, where Shell had a dominant interest).

At the meeting with shareholders, Mark Moody Stuart of Shell Transport and Trading (the company's UK arm) stated that he did not agree with arguments that institutional shareholders were not interested in issues such as social responsibility: 'I don't think there is a fundamental conflict between financial performance and "soft" issues. Many shareholders want outstanding financial returns in a way they can feel proud of or comfortable with.' (See Think abouts 4.1 and 4.2.)

Picture 4.2 Ken Saro-Wiwa was a human rights activist from the Ogoniland, where Shell had a dominant interest (*source*: AFP/Getty Images)

Think about 4.1

Shell Europe

During both the Brent Spar and Ogoniland crises, Shell faced a Europe-wide consumer boycott of its fuel products, as well as significant media criticism (www.shelluk.co.uk, www.greenpeace.org.uk). Why do you think Shell took the potentially risky strategy of reopening debate about environmental and societal issues after such high-profile vilification by the two important stakeholder groups (consumers of their products and the media)?

Feedback

This initiative by Shell clearly demonstrates the company directors' desire to tackle key issues head on, but also to make the company more accountable to its publics and specifically to the communities (and therefore stakeholder groups) in which it operates.

Think about 4.2

Business effects of CSR

Does CSR stretch an organisation's relationship with, and activities of, its supply chains (companies that supply products and services)? Can you think of suppliers for a company that it should not be associated with?

Feedback

Some companies have developed supplier policies that define the requirements for supplier organisations. For example, it would not be socially responsible for a furniture retailer that operates a 'green' purchasing policy to buy its raw materials from suppliers who purchase their wood from unsustainable sources.

The business case for CSR continues to be made, and particularly by communications professionals. Zerfass et al. (2008), in a survey of over 1,500 communications practitioners across Europe, found that three out of four of them are involved directly with CSR activities as part of their job (profit and not-for-profit organisations). Furthermore, they found that the main driver for CSR in the sample (70 per cent) was for reputation management. Again, according to Zerfass et al.'s study, the main focus of communication on CSR is for enhancing the corporate profile (values and strategies of the organisation). Interestingly though, regional differences in Europe were identified, with social

action being a priority in Southern and Eastern Europe whereas corporate ethics plays a more important role for organisations in Northern and Western Europe. Also, through monitoring predictions of the most important disciplines in communication management across Europe, the ECM survey (Zerfass et al. 2007, 2008, 2009, 2010, 2011, 2012, 2013) has found that CSR is predicted to gain in importance for communication practitioners working in profit and not-for-profit organisations (see www.communicationmonitor.eu), although it has stabilised in 2012 and 2013.

Organisational responsibilities to stakeholders

Stakeholder analysis is a clear way of defining those groups and individuals who have a significant relationship with an organisation (see also Chapter 8). Stakeholders can be described as those with a vested interest in the organisation's operations. Figure 4.3 simply demonstrates the most common stakeholders in for-profit organisations.

These are simplified stakeholder groups, which can be expanded and broken down into subgroups. In order for an organisation to act with social responsibility it is necessary to understand the fundamental elements of the organisation's operations and its relationships with stakeholders. To achieve this it can be helpful to ask and analyse the following questions:

■ How is the organisation financed, e.g. shareholders, private ownership, loans, etc.?

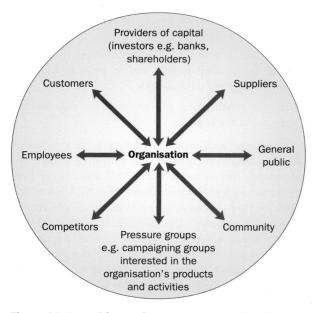

Figure 4.3 Typical for-profit organisational stakeholders

- Who are the customers for the products and services, e.g. agents, distributors, traders, operators, end users, etc.?

- What are the employee conditions and terms, including status, contracts and hierarchical structures?

- Are there community interactions at local, regional, national and international levels?

- Are there governmental, environmental or legislative actions that impact on the organisation?

- What are the competitor influences on the organisation, e.g. markets, agents, distributors, customers, suppliers?

- What are the supplier influences on the organisation, e.g. other creditors, financial supporters, competitors?

- Are there any issues or potential risks that may be affected by local, national or international pressure groups or interests?

CSR from a stakeholder perspective may bring the organisation closer to its stakeholders and importantly improve the two-way flow (Grunig and Hunt 1984) of information and, subsequently, understanding.

Once stakeholders are identified, you need to define the responsibilities you have towards them and then define and develop strategies to manage these relationships (see Explore 4.3).

> ## Explore 4.3
>
> ### Defining organisational stakeholders
>
> - Choose an organisation and define its stakeholders.
>
> - How would you prioritise these stakeholders in terms of their importance to financial performance for the organisation?
>
> ### Feedback
>
> Financial performance is important for all organisations, but this prioritised list may look different if instead it were arranged according to CSR performance towards stakeholders.

Organisational responsibilities to society

Business ethics writer Carroll (1991) argues that there are four kinds of social responsibility – economic, legal, ethical and philanthropic – demonstrated through the CSR pyramid in Figure 4.4.

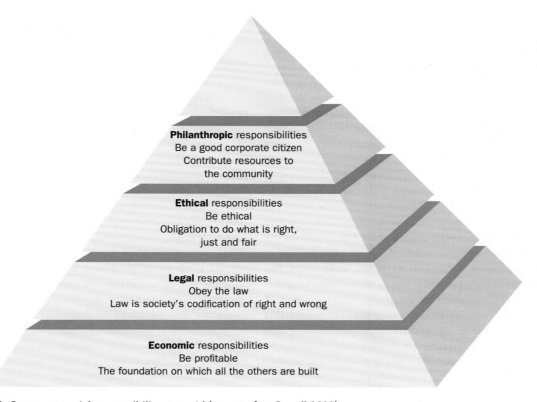

Figure 4.4 Corporate social responsibility pyramid (*source*: after Carroll 1991)

Stakeholders:	Economic	Legal	Ethical	Philanthropic
Providers of capital				
Customers				
Employees				
Community				
Competitors				
Suppliers				
Pressure groups				
General public				

Table 4.1 Stakeholder responsibility matrix (*source*: after Carroll 1991)

To aid managers in the evaluation of an organisation's social responsibilities and to help them plan how to fulfil their legal, ethical, economic and philanthropic obligations, Carroll designed a 'stakeholder responsibility matrix' (see Table 4.1). Carroll makes the clear distinction that social responsibility does not begin with good intentions but with stakeholder actions.

Carroll's matrix is proposed as an analytical tool, or framework, to help company managers make sense of their ideas about what the firm should be doing, economically, legally, ethically and philanthropically, with respect to its defined stakeholder groups. In practice, the matrix is effective as it encourages the manager to record both descriptive (qualitative) and statistical data to manage each stakeholder. This information is then useful when identifying priorities in long- and short-term business decision making that involves the multiple stakeholder groups that influence most organisations. It enables these decisions to be made in the context of the company's or organisation's value systems – what it stands for – as well as accommodating economic, social and environmental factors. To express this simply, the manager is able to make decisions in a more informed way with a clear map of the numerous factors that will impact on these decisions. It is a detailed approach to stakeholder management but is one way of providing informed foundations about stakeholders to enable strategies, actions or decisions to be taken that reflect the complex environment in which most organisations operate (see also Figure 4.5).

Table 4.2 provides an example of the matrix applied to one stakeholder group and the types of recorded data required. The organisation is a small clothing manufacturing business; the stakeholder group used for the analysis is customers. Each social responsibility cell has been considered in the context of this stakeholder group and data input currently available about the responsibility the firm acknowledges towards this group. Clearly, the data included are not exhaustive, and further records could be sought or gaps in information identified and subsequently commissioned by the public relations or communications team. This information will help managers when the organisation is defining corporate strategies for long- and short-term decisions, to ensure they accommodate the multiple stakeholder interests.

Corporate responsibility and irresponsibility

Tench et al. (2007, 2012, 2013) and Jones et al. (2009) build on and critique some of Carroll's early work to discuss alternative interpretations. The main conclusions of this discussion are in the exploration of corporate social irresponsibility (CSI) as a concept in contrast to corporate social responsibility, and the consequences of this dichotomy for corporate communications. The CSI–CSR model is described, explained, analysed and used as a conceptual tool to make the theoretical move from a pyramid or level-based approach (Carroll) to a more dynamic corporate framework for communication.

Figure 4.6 serves to show that internal and external variables, as well as mixing with and affecting each other, also interact and impact on the CSI–CSR continuum. The model is a rotating sphere intersected by its axis, the continuum. The need of business to make profit can, and does at times, coincide as well as conflict with its stated ethical aims and objectives. Competing stakeholders with differing needs, rights and obligations have to be managed to ensure conflict is minimised, the business survives and grows and is able to meet its commitments to CSR.

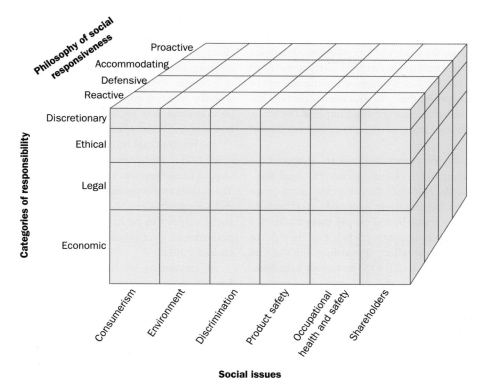

Figure 4.5 Carroll's responsibility matrix (*source*: adapted from Carroll 1991)

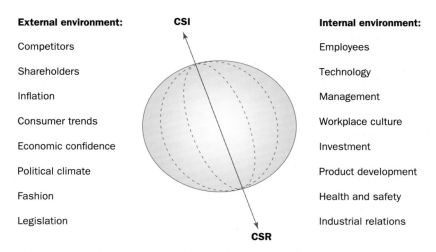

Figure 4.6 CSI–CSR Environmental Dynamic model (*source*: Jones et al. 2009)

The model moves away from a definition, explanation and analysis of CSR as a staged hierarchy, as espoused by Carroll (1991) in his pyramid of corporate social responsibility. Here, an alternative conceptualisation is suggested, based on the notion that CSI should be separated out from CSR to facilitate greater understanding of the terms, their meaning, nature and purpose. Issues interspersed and feeding into the CSI–CSR continuum are affected by internal and external environmental factors. Such factors give shape, form and context to corporate governance and CSR. Placing Carroll's (1991) pyramid of corporate social responsibility metaphorically in the sphere recognises that the levels of responsibility are intrinsic to the way in which CSR is conceived. However, in suggesting that the pyramid and, by implication, the levels can be rotated, the inference is that the levels are neither hierarchical or static but fluid and necessary to each other. By introducing the concept of CSI it counteracts the tendency to treat the concept of CSR as a one-dimensional single entity and unpacks the terms to reveal multi-faceted layers of complexity that are shaped by context.

The majority of companies are keen to embrace CSR issues and, of their own volition, go beyond legal minimum requirements. Not only do companies want to do well by doing good, but also some want to do good because they believe it to be the right and proper thing to do. Not all businesses are communicating what it is they do in regards to CSR to best effect. Regarding their social responsibility practices, a CSI–CSR audit can help businesses identify areas of strength and areas for improvement. In itself such an exercise can act as a useful vehicle of and for communication.

Adding to and supporting this debate in their empirical analysis based on an extensive 15-year panel dataset that covers nearly 3,000 publicly traded companies in the USA, Kotchen and Moon (2011) find that companies actually engaged in CSR in order to offset their CSI. CSI is a rich and challenging alternative concept to CSR and as a conceptual field of enquiry is discussed in detail in an edited volume of essays on the topic by Tench et al. (2013). As discussed, it is increasingly recognised that adopting a CSR approach can be both an ethical and profitable way to manage a business. Ethics and profit are not mutually exclusive terms but have a symbiotic relationship in the form of CSR. Though, nevertheless, at the end of the day, and as Friedman (1970) rightly noted, the purpose of business is to make profit.

Regulatory frameworks

Whilst present public attention is on business and the economy, it is being recognised increasingly that a greater understanding of the role and societal impact of business is essential. This is reflected in a range of transnational initiatives, such as the EU's new sustainability and responsibility policy for business and the launch in 2010 of the ISO CSR standards, which were updated in 2011 to focus explicitly on SMEs (European Commission Enterprise and Industry 2011; ISO 26000 CSR Guidance 2010). The UK CBI (2011) – a business lobby organisation representing UK business and commerce – in its current priorities has recognised this need to focus on the role of business in

society and the important role that business plays in creating and sustaining communities. This 'higher ambition' (Beer et al. 2011) of a responsibility of businesses for creating and balancing both economic and social value is becoming more widely accepted, increasing in parallel with the negative impact of recessionary economic trends on consumer and society confidence as well as trust in business and wider institutions.

The business case is reinforced in 'higher ambition' (Beer et al. 2011), with research showing the positive relationship of these business values with business performance. The success and longevity of brand names such as Cadbury and Kellogg illustrate the way in which both economic and social values can be balanced to deliver strong business performance over generations (Hopper and Hopper 2007; Cadbury 2010).

As consumers we have product choice – do we go for brand, price or even ethical or corporate responsibility performance? Companies such as Shell, Nike and Nestlé have experienced the threat and financial effects of global boycotts and are realising that greater mobility of stakeholders and globalisation of communication mean that reputation management is increasingly important. One manifestation of this is the speed of communication, and in particular news distribution globally via new technology, satellite and the emergence of 24-hour news channels. The process of news gathering has been speeded up, as has the news production cycle – all of which is crucial for public relations when managing reputation and communication for organisations. Research by the World Economic Forum in 2003 revealed that 48 per cent of people express 'little or no trust' in global companies. Consequently, even large and powerful corporations must adopt more ethical working practices in order to reduce risk and maintain favourable reputation. The growth of organisations such as Business in the Community in the UK and CSR Europe is helping to place CSR in the mainstream of business thinking and encourage more organisations to leverage the opportunities of CSR. This has a number of implications, including the increased need for guidance for companies. Subsequently, the past few years have seen the emergence of an increasing number of standards and guidelines in the areas of CSR and sustainable development. These include:

- Dow Jones Sustainability Index

- FTSE 4 Good Index

- Business in the Community's Corporate Responsibility Index

- Global Reporting Initiative's (GRI) Reporting Guidelines.

Stakeholders	Economic	Legal	Ethical	Philanthropic
Customers	Financially well-managed company	Conform to consumer health and safety product guidelines (e.g. quality controls and standards for fire safety of garments, etc.)	Fairly priced products	Give waste products to needy organisations
	Clear financial reporting	Correct labelling	Highest quality	Give unsold products to customers' preferred charities or homeless groups
		National and transnational product labelling, e.g. European standards	Products are designed for and fit for purpose (e.g. if for specialist sector, such as workwear)	Support other employee and customer initiatives
			Provide best products with the highest standards of care for employers and suppliers	
			Transparent sourcing of materials (no use of child labour or low-paid employees)	
			Do not abuse our suppliers or workers	

Table 4.2 An application of the stakeholder responsibility matrix to a small clothing manufacturer

Public and business attitudes have changed over recent years, and in 1999 a global poll of 25,000 citizens (MORI 1999) showed that perceptions of companies was more strongly aligned with corporate citizenship (56 per cent) than either brand quality (40 per cent) or the perception of the business management (34 per cent). Further evidence of the public attitude change was reported in the *Financial Times* (2003), which claimed that in the late 1970s the British agreed by two to one that the profits of large companies benefited their customers. In 2003 the public disagreed by two to one. This attitude change is reiterated by Fombrum and Shanley (1990), who found in earlier studies that a business that demonstrates responsiveness to social concerns and gives proportionately more to charity than other firms receives higher reputation ratings by its publics.

More recently, and mirroring the questions raised by Sir Mervyn King earlier in the chapter, the US Chicago Booth / Kellogg School Financial Trust Index (2011) highlights a decline in trust of financial institutions (see Figure 4.7).

As Luigi Zingales, the Robert R. McCormack Professor of Entrepreneurship and Finance at the University of Chicago Booth School of Business and co-author of the Financial Trust Index, suggests in Marketwatch on 19 October 2011:

only 23 per cent of those surveyed say they trust the country's financial systems, down from 25 per cent in our last report in June 2011. Also, nearly 60 per cent of respondents in our survey said they are angry or very angry about the current economic situation – the highest level of anger we've found since the earliest months of the financial crisis… The findings in this issue reflect what's been reported in the news and demonstrate the fragility of trust many Americans still have in the institutions where they invest their money.

The Edelman Trust Barometer Findings (2011) concludes that high-quality products or services, transparent and honest business practices, trust of the company and employee welfare are the most important elements for corporate reputation. The findings suggest also that there was a strong view by respondents that 'corporations should create shareholder value in a way that aligns with society's interests, even if that means sacrificing shareholder value'. For example, this was 91 per cent in Germany, 89 per cent in the UK, Ireland and China and 85 per cent in the US. Their conclusions include that:

business must align profit and purpose for social benefit; demand for authority and accountability; set new expectations for corporate leadership; trust is a protective

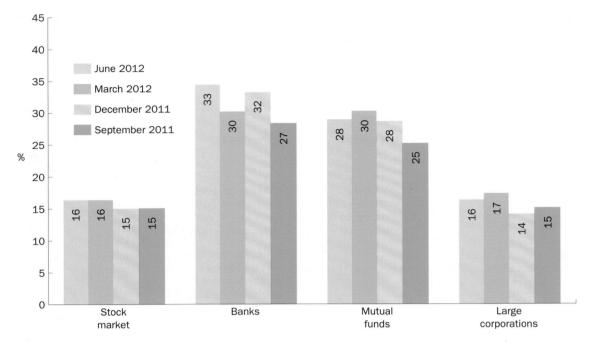

Figure 4.7 Percentage of people trusting various components that comprise the Financial Trust Index (Sapienza and Zingales 2012) (*source*: http//financialtrustindex.org/resultswave15.htm)

agent and leads to tangible benefits; lack of trust is a barrier to change.

There is a range of research that demonstrates consumers' willingness to reward socially responsible companies, with far-reaching effects. One such effect is the changing focus of investment decisions. This has resulted in the emergence of '**triple bottom-line**' reporting, whereby social and environmental performance hold equal importance to financial performance. It can, therefore, be argued that, in the eyes of consumers, the media, legislators and investors, social and environmental responsibilities are increasingly powerful drivers of reputation. (See Case study 4.2.)

Definition: '*Triple bottom-line*' reporting is a phrase increasingly used to describe the economic, environmental and social aspects that are being defined and considered by business. These are sometimes called the three Ps – profit, plant and people!

Case study 4.2

European campaign – GlaxoSmithKline and Barretstown

Therapeutic recreation for children with serious illness

GlaxoSmithKline (GSK) is one of the world's largest pharmaceutical companies. The company's partnership with Barretstown in Ireland began in 1994 to kick-start their European Community Partnership Programme, focusing on children's health.

Barretstown was established as the first 'hole in the wall' camp in Europe, building on the success of the first North American camp to enable children with serious illnesses to experience 'summer camp' by providing first-class medical facilities on the site of the camps. Barretstown Castle was donated by the Irish government to provide a similar facility, and additional facilities were constructed to adapt to the children's special needs.

Through a programme of activities and adventure in a safe and medically supported environment, children meet and develop friendships with other children. Many paediatricians see their patients' participation in Barretstown as an integral part of clinical treatment. As well as helping children feel better through greater confidence and

case study 4.2 (continued)

self-esteem, their experience at Barretstown helps them do more than they ever thought they could. Being involved with the programme helps GSK volunteers learn how to deal sensitively with issues relating to disability.

As Barretstown involves children from countries where GSK has a business operation, it reflects their regional structure and draws different GSK businesses together to work on a shared programme. GSK employees from these countries participate as volunteer carers (helpers) and GSK businesses provide practical support locally – for example, funding children's flights to Ireland. GSK's funding has been focused on establishing the 'European Liaison Network' – an important interface between Barretstown and children's hospitals. The network provides a framework across 19 countries for raising awareness about the camp among doctors, parents and children, as well as recruiting children to participate. More than 110 hospitals across Europe nominate children to participate. According to GlaxoSmithKline, the impact is as follows:

- Barretstown provides volunteers with opportunities for personal development, in particular for developing creativity, teamwork and diversity awareness. GSK

volunteers learn how to deal sensitively with issues relating to disability, especially the way those children feel about their appearance and body image.

- GSK Barretstown has created a model for other GSK businesses to adapt to local programmes. Several of GSK's businesses have adopted 'therapeutic recreation' as a focus in developing their own community programmes. GSK supports smaller-scale programmes with local children's hospitals in Hungary, Portugal and Romania.

- Early data show that the main benefits of the programme are that the children regain self-esteem, develop confidence and have some of their independence restored after what may be long periods of isolation and hospitalisation.

- From serving 124 children in 1994, Barretstown has grown and now supports over 10,000 children drawn from 110 hospitals in 19 European countries.

- The partnership with Barretstown has been key in contributing to building GSK's reputation as a good corporate citizen among internal and external stakeholders.

Source: www.gsk.com, www.bitc.org.uk

Ethics and business practice

Before looking in detail at the techniques for operating a business in society (and for implementing CSR programmes, discussed in Chapter 15), we need to consider the important issue of **ethics** and ethical business practice. **Business ethics** is a substantial issue and an important part of understanding what is called 'corporate governance'. It ranges from high-profile issues about equal opportunities, 'glass ceilings' for women in work, whistleblowing (employees reporting on unethical or illegal activities by their employers) and whether large PLCs pay their SME suppliers or contractor on time, down to whether it is all right for a director or senior manager to take a ream of paper home for a computer printer, when this is a sackable offence for an office junior!

Definition: *Ethics* = extension of good management.

Definition: Trevino and Nelson (1995) define *business ethics* as 'the principles, norms and standards of conduct governing an individual or group'.

Business ethics is therefore about us as individual members of society, as part of the community or as part of organisations (whether these are work or leisure/interest organisations). For example, we may be an employee of a national supermarket chain and a trustee for a local school or scout group. We make decisions within these environments that have ethical implications and societal impact (see Peach 1987: Figure 4.1). Ethics is an important part of business reality, as managers make decisions that affect a large range of stakeholder groups and communities, from the employees of the organisation to the residents who live close to its business sites. (See Think abouts 4.3, 4.4 and 4.5; see also Box 4.3.)

Ethical decision making: theory and practice

Business ethics author Snell (1997) argues that there are two approaches to the teaching and understanding of business ethics by practitioners. One of these is termed 'systematic modernism', which is the more explanatory, conservative voice of business leaders and political leaders on societal issues. The explanations are more functional and seek resolutions in the short to medium term, i.e. through legislation, the use of law and order and reliance

Think about 4.3   Ethical dilemmas

Ethical dilemmas occur when we are faced with decisions that cause dissonance (conflict) in our loyalty (taken from Festinger's theory of cognitive dissonance, see Chapter 11). Take the example of a cheating colleague who is extracting small amounts of money from the organisation through false expenses claims. If we know about their actions, should we show loyalty to them or to our organisation? We are left with an 'ethical decision'. What do you think you would say or do if it were a director or management colleague in this case? How would you manage the ethical dilemma?

Feedback

'Ethical problems are not caused entirely by "bad apples". They're also the product of organisational systems that either encourage unethical behaviour or, at least, allow it to occur' (Trevino and Nelson 1995: 13).

You need to gather all the facts and also consider the impact of your decisions/actions on the organisation as a whole. See the section on ethical decision making.

Think about 4.4

Good apples and bad apples

The 'good and bad apple' analogy is frequently used in the context of ethics. Apply this analogy to your own experience and think of an example of unethical conduct. Was it the responsibility of the individual (apple) or the organisation (barrel), or was it a combination of the two?

Feedback

Arguably, we are born amoral, not moral or immoral. Psychologists have argued that ethics, as such, are not innate. They are culturally bound and influenced by the social environment in which we grow up. We develop and change our personalities throughout our lives – including during our adult life – and research (Rest and Thoma 1986) has found that adults in their 30s who are in moral development programmes develop more than young people.

Box 4.3

Example of ethical guidelines

Unilever has published its ethical guidelines – or ethical principles – as follows: 'Unilever believe that economic growth must go hand in hand with sound environmental management, equal opportunities worldwide and the highest standards of health and safety in factories and offices.'

Its code of business principles covers sensitive issues such as bribery: 'Unilever does not give or receive bribes in order to retain business or financial advantages. Unilever employees are directed that any demand or offer of such a bribe must be immediately rejected.'

Source: www.unilever.com

Think about 4.5

Individual and corporate ethics

Dissonance or conflict is what causes individual problems with corporate ethics, and there are stark examples such as a religious person working for a pharmaceutical company that decides to market an abortion product, or an environmentally conscious employee working for a high-polluting company. What should these individuals do to manage the conflict? What should their management do?

on individual's social responsibility. In contrast, 'critical modernism' is the current 'underdog', yet this has been influenced more by theoretical ethical debates. It is argued, therefore, that the critical approach takes business ethics a stage further than just face-value explanations of why something is right or wrong.

Table 4.3 highlights how the two schools of thought operate and interpret different ethical issues. (See also Explore 4.4.)

Philosophers have studied ethical decision making for centuries and tend to focus on decision-making tools that describe what should be done in particular situations (see also Chapter 12). The most well-known philosophical

Issue	Typical systematic modern narrative	Typical critical modern narrative
Corruption: bribery and extortion	Bad because it dents local or national pride, deters inward investment and is a sign of backwardness	Bad because it is inherently unfair, disadvantaging the politically and economically weak
Protection of the environment	Our sons and daughters will suffer or perish unless we adopt proper controls	Indigenous (native) peoples, rare animal species and future citizens are entitled to a habitable environment
Inflated executive salaries	One should set up systems of corporate governance overseen by non-executive directors to safeguard minority shareholders' interests	One should campaign for wider social justice, including action to help the poor and reduce unemployment
Function of codes of ethics	They are tools for inspiring the confidence of customers and investors, and a means of controlling staff	They are a starting point only; people should be encouraged to develop their own personal moral code
Preferred Kohlberg stages	Conventional reasoning: preserving stability, the rule of law and order and social respectability	Post-conventional reasoning: concern for social welfare, justice and universal ethical principles

Table 4.3 Competing modern narratives on business ethics (*source*: adapted from Snell 1997: 185)

Explore 4.4

Ethics in everyday life

Think about how you act in different situations. How would you react if a college friend started telling jokes about people with physical disabilities? Would you smile in an embarrassed way, laugh and hope they wouldn't carry on, confront the speaker and ask them to stop, or what?

Feedback

It is often useful to reflect on our codes of ethics, what we see as right and wrong, and on whether we act on our beliefs or are more interested in how others perceive or see us.

theories are categorised as consequentialist, regarding the consequences of actions, with utilitarianism being the best known and associated with the 'greatest happiness' principle (i.e. the greatest happiness for the greatest number of people). Trevino and Nelson (1995: 67) state that a utilitarian approach to ethical decision making should 'maximise benefits to society and minimise harms. What matters is the net balance of good consequences over bad.'

Generally, utilitarian ethical decision making is therefore focused on what we do and what are the consequences of our actions, i.e. who will be harmed or affected. In a business context, this means which stakeholders will be affected. One method of testing this approach is to ask if everyone acted in the same way, what sort of environment would be created? Just imagine what the impact would be if each of us dropped our lunch wrappers and leftovers onto the floor every day! Extend this out to all businesses draining their waste water/fluids into the nearest river/ ocean outlet. This theory does underlie a lot of business writing and thinking and people's approaches to ethical decision making.

A second strand of philosophical thinking is categorised under deontological theories, which focus on motives and intentions through duties or the action itself rather than the outcome or results. German philosopher Immanuel Kant wrote about the 'categorical imperative', which asks whether your ethical choice is sound enough to become universally accepted as a law of action that everyone should follow (see Kant 1964). The obvious example is whether telling lies is ever acceptable. Imagine a company context where it was perceived that telling a lie for the good of the company was to its benefit. Kant would argue against this case unless the company is prepared to accept that, from that point forward, all employees were permitted to lie – a 'categorical imperative'. You need only consider the case of Enron in the USA to appreciate where such an ethical management system will lead with regard to telling mistruths and lies to a range of stakeholders.

Another ethical approach that is popular with business ethics academics and fits into the business context is virtue ethics, which is also founded in traditional philosophical theory. It focuses on the integrity of the actor or individual more than on the act itself. Within this approach it is important to consider the relative importance of communities or stakeholder groups. For example, in a professional context you may be bound by community standards or practical codes of conduct. This can help the individual make ethical decisions because it gives them boundaries to work within.

Changing the culture and changing organisational ethics

Any attempt to change ethical practice within an organisation must be based on a simple assumption that all human beings are essentially good and capable of development and change. Changing ethical practice through changing the culture of an organisation is not a quick fix; it takes time as you have to address the formal and informal organisational subcultures. The culture of an organisation clearly affects what is appropriate or inappropriate behaviour. To understand the culture an audit is necessary and can be carried out through surveys, interviews and observations.

Having completed an audit, the next stage is to write a culture change intervention plan that includes targeting the formal and informal systems.

The formal systems are more transparent and easier to change, as follows:

- draw up new codes of conduct
- change structure to encourage individuals to take responsibility for their behaviour

- design reward systems to punish unethical behaviour
- encourage **whistleblowers** and provide them with appropriate communications channels and confidentiality
- change decision-making processes to incorporate attention to ethical issues.

For the informal system, the following may be important:

- re-mythologise the organisation – revive old myths and stories about foundations, etc. that guide organisational behaviour (revived myths must, however, fit with reality).

See Explore 4.5 and Case study 4.3.

Definition: A *whistleblower* is someone who speaks out about an organisation's unethical behaviour or malpractice. Examples are employees who tell the public about financial mismanagement or theft inside an organisation, or government employees who leak evidence of wrongdoing, such as selling arms to particular regimes or government actions that contravene policy or legal frameworks.

Explore 4.5

Ethics in practice

To conclude this chapter on business and its role in communities and society, think about the following.

Managers are the key to ethical business practice as they are potential role models for all employees, customers, suppliers, etc., and also the endorsers of ethical policies. Due to changes in management practice, business process reengineering and the downsizing of Western companies, many modern businesses have fewer managers today – yet each manager has more staff to control:

- How should organisations be ethical? Identify three or four reasons. Divide these reasons into those that are linked to financial gain and those that are societally sympathetic.

- Are employees attracted to ethical employers? Give reasons why you believe they may or may not be.

- List those companies you would be proud to work for and those that you would be ashamed to be employed by or represent. What are the key features of each? What are the similarities and differences?

Case study 4.3
Vattenfall, Sweden

Vattenfall is an international, state-owned Swedish energy company. In 2008 the company conducted a CSR-related campaign, the Climate Signature Campaign, which focused on the global climate change issue. The campaign was just one part of a series of company-wide efforts to combat climate change. With this focus, the campaign reflected a growing interest among international companies to address complex, global, social and environmental issues. Because individual companies cannot expect to provide complete solutions for such complex issues on their own, more and more companies are teaming up with other organisations, such as non-governmental organisations (NGOs), to address them.

Instead of teaming up with another organisation, however, Vattenfall sought to address the climate issue in a joint effort with its customers and the general public. Indeed, this was the primary purpose of the Climate Signature Campaign. To establish this joint effort, the campaign's objectives, messages, media mix and tactics were all characterised by company efforts to actively engage the target groups.

For example, of key importance was the objective of collecting at least 100,000 signatures in support of a company-written manifesto, which encouraged politicians to take necessary actions to:

- Establish a global price on CO_2 emissions
- Support climate-friendly technologies
- Implement climate requirements for products.

This signature collection initiative, besides gathering support for policy changes, was intended to stimulate interest in Vattenfall and its environmental efforts, and positively position the Vattenfall brand with progressive climate initiatives, environmental consciousness and sustainability.

The campaign messages were also designed to engage the target groups in the joint effort to address the climate change issue: 'If we all help out to change the system, global warming can be resolved' (Vattenfall 2008b). In the same way, the media strategy was developed with special attention to the extent to which each media channel could inform or engage the target groups, or stimulate interaction between the company and the target groups. While print advertising in newspapers and news magazines was intended to inform and explain, television, with its high audiovisual impact, was considered the more engaging channel. Finally, interaction was sought through digital media such as social media Internet sites and 'bloggomarketing', in which relevant, seemingly influential bloggers were encouraged to write about the climate manifesto.

Besides the use of these media to reach and engage with the target groups, the most noteworthy campaign tactic was the organisation of public events in several European capitals where decision makers met to discuss the climate issue. At these events, one small, recyclable, bright orange plastic figurine was displayed for each signature collected for the manifesto. With more than 200,000 signatures collected near the end of the campaign, the visual impact of these peaceful demonstrations was indeed impressive.

Due to the progressive nature of several aspects of this campaign, such as the public events, the developers and organisers were of course very keen to map the outcomes. Overall, the campaign:

- exceeded the quantifiable objectives in terms of website traffic, blogging activity and collected signatures
- won advertising and campaign awards
- generated a huge amount of international interest in learning more about Vattenfall and its environmental efforts
- was generally liked and understood (according to respondents in a large post-campaign market survey).

However, the campaign also:

- sparked NGO and activist criticism of the company's operations, which in turn led to demonstrations and negative media coverage
- incited NGOs to accuse Vattenfall of deceptively using NGO tactics by running a collective action campaign rather than a business-centred marketing campaign
- was deemed confusing: many of the post-campaign market survey respondents did not understand why Vattenfall had conducted the campaign.

case study 4.3 (continued)

Despite this criticism and confusion, Vattenfall's CEO has, on the whole, framed the campaign in positive terms:

Our goal with the Climate Manifesto is to give a voice to the strong public opinion that exists with respect to the climate issue, but also to spark a debate. We have succeeded in achieving both objectives, and Vattenfall will continue to invite critics and supporters alike to continued dialogue in this most pressing issue for society (Vattenfall 2008a:1)

The company's internal evaluation has, of course, been more nuanced. While many aspects of the campaign led to positive outcomes, as outlined above, in hindsight several lessons to be learned have emerged that could hinder some of the less desirable outcomes, such as the activist criticism and stakeholder confusion, in future campaigns.

Two lessons stand out:

- In CSR campaigns that address complex, global social and environmental issues, it can be difficult for companies to convince target groups of their genuine interest in bettering the world for the sake of mankind. By explicitly supplementing this sort of normative motive with business-oriented motives, companies can reduce target group confusion and scepticism and thereby boost their own credibility. Another way companies can help stakeholders make sense of a campaign that addresses social or environmental issues would be to collaborate with an NGO, as stakeholders expect NGOs to be concerned with these types of issues.

- Although engaging with target groups and using unconventional tactics, such as public events, can create a lot of 'buzz' for a company, the attention may not necessarily only be positive. To evaluate the risk of sparking criticism and scepticism, companies should establish a clear understanding of their markets and stakeholders before conducting a CSR-related campaign, paying careful attention to the company's reputation.

Picture 4.3 To reach and engage with the target groups, the most noteworthy campaign tactic used by Vattenfall was the organisation of public events in several European capitals, such as Copenhagen in Denmark, where decision makers met to discuss the climate issue

Vattenfall (2008a). 'Corporate Social Responsibility Report'. Vattenfall (2008b). 'Signature Campaign Advertisement'. *The Economist*, 22 November.

Source: Leila Trapp (2012)

Summary

Milton Friedman's perception that the business of business is simply to increase profits and enhance shareholder value has less credibility in the twenty-first century. Also, the public is increasingly sophisticated on environmental and ethical issues such as: global warming; worldwide natural disasters such as the Asian tsunami and earthquakes during 2011 in Turkey and New Zealand, with the related business responses; animal testing; hunting with dogs in the UK; or whale hunting. There is rising power for the consumer in national and international contexts, as demonstrated by Shell (fuel filling station protests), Nestlé (palm oil and deforestation, 2010) and Fruit of the Loom (union rights of workers, 2010). The influence of corporate image and reputation on an organisation's business success (Lehmann Brothers; Andersen; McDonald's/McLibel) is increasingly recognised, as is the use of business ethics to create competitive advantage (Co-Operative Bank; Fairtrade; The Body Shop). Enhanced communication (social media and the Internet) for and with stakeholders and interest groups, media expansion and global influence (24-hour news) and the mobilisation of national and international issue and pressure groups (such as Greenpeace; the 'occupy movement' in 2011 (Occupy London, Occupy Wall Street 2011) or the anti war lobbies; UN Global Compact; or influential figures such as Al Gore) can all separately and together affect any business today.

This chapter has focused on the role organisations play in their society(ies) and how the understanding of business ethics and CSR may improve business performance and enhance reputation through more effective use of public relations and communication to build understanding and awareness. Chapter 15 will build on these principles to discuss how CSR is being incorporated into many organisations' strategic planning and how public relations is being used to support this.

Discussion in this chapter has focused on:

■ responsible and irresponsible business behaviour

■ stakeholder influences

■ ethical decision making

■ changing cultural and organisational ethics.

Bibliography

Beer, M., R.A. Eisenstat, N. Foote, T. Fredberg and F. Norrgren (2011). *Higher Ambition: How great leaders create economic and social value*. Boston, MA: Harvard Business Review Press.

Cadbury, A. (1998). 'The Future for Governance'. Gresham Special Lecture, Gresham College delivered at Mansion House, Tuesday 12 May 1998.

Cadbury, D. (2010). *Chocolate Wars: From Cadbury to Kraft: 200 years of sweet success and bitter rivalry*. London: HarperPress.

Cadbury Report (1992). 'Report on the Committee of The Financial Aspects of Corporate Governance 1 December 1992.' The Committee on the Financial Aspects of Corporate Governance and Gee and Co. Ltd, December.

Carroll, A.B. (1991). 'The pyramid of corporate social responsibility: toward the moral management of organizational stakeholders.' *Business Horizons* **34**(4): 39–48.

CBI (2011). 'CBI website: CBI priorities'. www.cbi.org.uk/campaigns/the-role-of-business-in-society accessed 5 November 2011.

Chicago Booth/Kellogg School Financial Trust Index (2011). www.financialtrustindex.org/resultswave12.htm accessed 5 November 2011.

Clarke, T. (2009). 'A critique of the Anglo-American model of corporate governance'. CLPE Research Paper 15/2009, Vol. 5 No. 3, available at: http://ssrn.com/abstract=1440853.

Concise Oxford English Dictionary, 8th ed (1995). Oxford: Clarendon Press.

Cutlip, S.M., A.H. Center and G.M. Broom (2000). *Effective Public Relations*, 8th ed. Upper Saddle River, NJ: Prentice Hall.

Edelman Trust Barometer Findings (2011) www.edelman.com/trust/2011/uploads/Edelman%20Trust%20Barometer%20Global%20Deck.pdf accessed 5 November 2011.

European Commission Enterprise and Industry (2011). http://ec.europa.eu/enterprise/policies/sustainable-business/corporate-social-responsibility/index_en.htm accessed 7 November 2011.

Fombrum, C. and M. Shanley (1990). 'What's in a name? Reputation building and corporate strategy'. *Academy of Management Journal* **33**: 233–258.

Friedman, M. (1970). 'The social responsibility of business is to increase its profits'. *New York Times Magazine* 13 September: 32.

Gore, A. (2006). *An Inconvenient Truth*. Paramount, director David Guggenheim.

Gore, A. (2007). *An Inconvenient Truth*. New York, NY: Viking Juvenile.

Grunig, J. and T. Hunt (1984). *Managing Public Relations*. New York, NY: Holt, Rinehart & Winston.

Hopper, K. & W. Hopper (2007 and 2009). *The Puritan Gift: Reclaiming the American Dream amidst global financial crisis*. London: I.B. Taurus & Co Ltd.

India Partnership Forum (2003). www.ipfndia.org/home accessed 30 September 2008.

ISO 26000 CSR Guidance (2010). http://www.iisd.org/standards/csr.asp accessed 8 November 2011.

Jones, B., R. Tench and R. Bowd (2009). 'Corporate irresponsibility and corporate social responsibility: competing realities'. *Social Responsibility Journal* 5(3).

Kant, I. (1964). *Groundwork of the Metaphysic of Morals*. London: Harper & Row.

King, M. (2011). Sir Mervyn King, Governor of the Bank of England, 'Speech To the Institute of Directors', St George's Hall, Liverpool, 18 October 2011, Bank of England.

Kotchen, M.J. and J.J. Moon (2011). 'Corporate social responsibility for irresponsibility'. National Bureau of Economic Research Working Paper 17254, available at http://www.nber.org/papers/w17254.

Labich, K. (1992). 'The new crisis in business ethics'. *Fortune* 20 April: 167–176.

Lewis, S. (2003). 'Reputation and corporate social responsibility'. *Journal of Communication Management* 7(4): 356–364.

Lines, V.L. (2004). 'Corporate reputation in Asia: looking beyond the bottom line performance'. *Journal of Communication Management* 8(3): 233–245.

Little, P.L. and B.L. Little (2000). 'Do perceptions of corporate social responsibility contribute to explaining differences in corporate price-earnings ratios? A research note'. *Corporate Reputation Review* 3(2): 137–142.

Moore, G. (2003). 'Hives and horseshoes, Mintzberg or MacIntyre: what future for corporate social responsibility?' *Business Ethics: A European Review* 12(1): 41–53.

MORI (1999). 'Winning with integrity'. London: MORI.

Occupy London (2011). http://occupylondon.org.uk/ accessed 5 November 2011.

Occupy Wall Street (2011). http://occupywallst.org/ accessed 6 November 2011.

Peach, L. (1987). In *Effective Corporate Relations*. N. Hart (ed.). Maidenhead: McGraw-Hill.

Rest, J.R. and S.J. Thoma (1986). 'Educational programs and interventions' in *Moral Development: Advances in research and theory*. J. Rest (ed.). New York, NY: Praeger.

Sagar, P. and A. Singla (2004). 'Trust and corporate social responsibility: lessons from India'. *Journal of Communication Management* 8(3): 282–290.

Sapienza, P. and Zingales, L. (2012). A trust crisis. *International Review of Finance* 12.

Snell, R. (1997). 'Management learning perspectives on business ethics' in *Management Learning*. J. Burgoyne and M. Reynolds (eds). London: Sage.

Sun, W., J. Stewart and D. Pollard (eds) (2011). *Corporate Governance and the Global Financial Crisis: International perspectives*. Cambridge: Cambridge University Press.

Tench, R., R. Bowd and B. Jones (2007). 'Perceptions and perspectives: corporate social responsibility and the media'. *Journal of Communication Management* 11(4): 348–370.

Tench, R., B. Jones and W. Sun (2012) (eds) *Corporate Social Irresponsibility: A challenging concept*, UK: Emerald Publishing.

Tench, R., W. Sun and B. Jones (eds) (2013). *Communicating Corporate Social Responsibility: Lessons from Theory and Practice*. Bingley, UK: Emerald.

Think Big (2011). www.o2sustainability.co.uk/2010 accessed 17 November 2011.

Trevino, L.K. and K.A. Nelson (1995). *Managing Business Ethics: Straight talk about how to do it right*. New York, NY: Wiley & Sons.

UN (2011). 'United Nations Millennium Development Goals 2015'. www.un.org/millenniumgoals/ accessed 17 November 2011.

World Economic Forum (2003). www.weforum.com accessed 26 March 2005.

Zerfass, A., A. Moreno, R. Tench, D. Verčič and P. Verhoeven (2008). 'European Communication Monitor 2008. Trends in Communication Management and Public Relations – Results and Implications'. Brussels, Leipzig: EUPRERA, University of Leipzig. Available at: www.communicationmonitor.eu

Zerfass, A., A. Moreno, R. Tench, D. Verčič and P. Verhoeven (2009). 'European Communication Monitor 2009. Trends in Communication Management and Public Relations – Results of a Survey in 34 Countries'. Brussels: EACD, EUPRERA.

Zerfass, A., R. Tench, P. Verhoeven, D. Verčič and A. Moreno (2010). 'European Communication Monitor 2010. Status Quo and Challenges for Public Relations in Europe. Results of an Empirical Survey in 46 Countries'. Brussels: EACD, EUPRERA. Available at: www.communicationmonitor.eu.

Zerfass, A., B. Van Ruler, A. Rogojinaru, D. Verčič and S. Hamrefors (2007). 'European Communication Monitor 2007. Trends in Communication Management and Public Relations – Results and Implications'. Leipzig, Brussels: University of Leipzig, EUPRERA. Available at: www.communicationmonitor.eu.

Zerfass, A., P. Verhoeven, R. Tench, A. Moreno and D. Verčič (2011). 'European Communication Monitor 2011. Empirical Insights into Strategic Communication in Europe. Results of a Survey in 43 Countries'. Available at: www.communicationmonitor.eu.

Zerfass, A., A. Moreno, R. Tench, D. Verčič. and P. Verhoeven, (2013). 'A Changing Landscape – Managing Crises, Digital Communication and CEO Positioning in Europe. Results of a Survey of 43 Countries'. Brussels: EACD, EUPRERA.

Zerfass, A., D. Verčič, P. Verhoeven, A. Moreno, and R. Tench (2012). 'European Communication Monitor 2012. Challenges and Competencies for Strategic Communication. Results of an Empirical Survey in 42 Countries'. Brussels: EACD, EUPRERA.

Zingales, L. (2011). Citation in *Marketwatch*, 19 October 2011.

Websites

BBC: www.bbc.co.uk

Bill and Melinda Gates Foundation: www.gatesfoundation.org

British Society of Rheology: www.bsr.org.uk

Business in the Community: www.bitc.org.uk

CadburySchweppes: www.CadburySchweppes.com

Chartered Institute of Public Relations: www.cipr.co.uk

Co-Operative Bank: www.co-operativebank.co.uk

ECOPSI: www.ecopsi.org.uk

CSR Europe: www.csreurope.org

The Gap: www.gap.com

GlaxoSmithKline: www.gsk.com

Global Responsible Leadership Initiative (GRLI): www.grli.org

Greenpeace: www.greenpeace.org.uk

Institute of Business Ethics: www.ibe.org.uk

Nike: www.nike.com

02: www.mm02.co.uk

P4ace Portal (ECOPSI): www.p4ace.eu

The Shell Group: www.shell.com

Slate 60: www.slate.com

Unilever: www.unilever.co.uk

United Nations Global Compact: www.unglobalcompact.org

CHAPTER 5

Dejan Verčič

Intercultural and multicultural context of public relations

Learning outcomes

By the end of this chapter you should be able to:

■ identify and discuss relevant key theories, principles and their development up to the present day in relation to the intercultural and multicultural context of public relations
■ review and critique relevant key theories and principles in relation to the intercultural and multicultural context of public relations
■ analyse and apply an intercultural and multicultural context of public relations theories/principles to practice
■ evaluate your learning about the intercultural and multicultural context of public relations and pursue further sources for investigation.

Structure

■ The context of culture
■ Public relations and culture
■ Between universalism and relativism
■ Global principles and specific applications
■ Social media and activists in the global village
■ How to prepare for international and global public relations
■ Key principles in intercultural and multicultural public relations
■ Public diplomacy

Introduction

Culture is a noun with many meanings. Each of us carries her or his own individual combination of cultural traits that we have acquired as members of several collectives – class, ethnic, gender, national, professional, racial, voluntary and other organisations and communities. All these can be described as having certain qualities we recognise as cultures. They exist in larger collective systems denoted as societies, having their own societal cultures. Because we are born into our cultures, they exist as our 'true' nature and we are rarely aware of them. It is when we geographically or socially move and meet (or even collide with) cultures different from ours that we become conscious of others and/or our differentness. In recognition of us being different from others we develop our sameness, i.e. identity (Sha et al. 2012). Public relations as management of communication and relationships between an organisation (with its culture) and its stakeholders (with their cultures) is always an intercultural practice, and public relations practitioners are intercultural interpreters (Banks 1995).

Explore 5.1

The nature/nurture debate

Everybody has an opinion about how much of what we are is given to us biologically (in genes) and how much culturally (through learning). It is a centuries-old debate. Westernist scientists and philosophers prefer culture over nature (or anything else larger than us) as an explanatory variable of our behaviour. A recent book on the topic summarising arguments is Prinz's (2012) book, *Beyond Human Nature: How culture and experience shape our lives.*

Feedback

Where do you stand on the nature/nurture debate? How much of what you are is in your genes (or anything else permanent and directly passed on from your parents) and how much in how you were brought up?

Can we transcend our nature?

The context of culture

Culture entered the language of management to alert leaders that social organisations (like companies) are not as easily engineered as machines. The latter follow rules of Newtonian causality: providing resources, you can make or break them at your will and if designed and produced properly, they will automatically follow an author's instructions. Companies and other human organisations behave more like plants than machines: you have to nurture (cultivate) them, for certain processes they take their own time and they behave as if following their own will, which is different from the will of their constructors and/or members. In this sense, managers talk of 'corporate cultures' they would like to manage. Dominant cultures can be further broken into sub-cultures and often contra-cultures that defy the ruling interpretation of the right order of a system (organisation or society). Culture is also about power and dominance (Dutta 2012).

Throughout history, travellers have encountered a different sense of culture: that of other countries and peoples. With the emergence first of empires and then of multinational companies, national cultures gained prominence in helping people understand why others behave differently than us. Today, international and global operations of all kinds of organisations – companies, non-governmental organisations, governments, international governmental and non-governmental organisations – depend on intercultural and multicultural knowledge. Public relations, as it is presented throughout this book, is an occupation that is continuing to gain in importance as an essential carrier of that knowledge.

You don't have to travel to be exposed to other cultures. Some major towns are themselves multicultural – London has 7 million inhabitants who speak around 300 languages (www.multicultural.co.uk). You may live in Sub-Saharan Africa and be influenced by foreign interests searching for minerals. In Asia you may be employed by a multinational company from the West, or by an Asian company expanding its operations worldwide. There is no place to hide from other cultures and there is no alternative but to learn how to live with and in them. All of us share several cultures – not only ethnic/national, but also professional, racial, gender, class or caste, organisational, associational or gang. Humans are multicultural beings.

Think about 5.1

Cultures, nations, countries and states

What in English language is commonly referred to as a country or a nation, international law defines as a sovereign state. Although there seems to be a correspondence between ethnic cultures and sovereign states – sometimes refered to as nation-states (i.e., France is a sovereign state of French, China of Chinese and Nigeria of Nigerians), the real world is far more complicated (even when discounted for international migrations). Even in France, as a highly centralised state, there are different populations that are French by citizenship but not ethically – Basques on the border with Spain or Corsicans on the island of Corsica in the Mediterranian Sea. In Switzerland they speak three major languages – French, German and Italian, and one minor – Retroroman. England is a country in the United Kingdom (Scotland, Wales and Nothern Ireland being other constitutive entities of the monarchy). Although over 90 per cent of Chinese citizens belong to the largest ethnic group – Han – the Government recognises 55 other distinct ethnic groups. In India, currently the second largest country in the world and projected by 2025 to surpass China and become the most populated country in the world, where four of the world's major religions originated – Hinduism, Buddhism, Jainism and Sikhism – there are 30 languages spoken by more than a million, and 122 languages spoken by more than 10,000 speakers. In Indonesia there are around 300 different ethnicities living in that country and speaking 742 different languages and dialects. Nigeria, the most populous country in Africa and with one of the fastest growing populations in the world, has more than 250 ethnic groups. South Africa has eleven languages recognised in its constitution. In the United States of America, some federal States (Arizona, New Mexico and Texas) have Spanish next to English as their *de jure* or/and *de facto* official language.

At the beginning of 2012 there were 193 member states of the United Nations, and there are at least a dozen more states that are not included in the UN system and whose sovereignity is disputed.

Feedback

Try to list as many countries per continent as you can.

For selected countries, try to see how many ethnic cultures and major religions you can identify.

Picture 5.1 This T-shirt illustrates the need for knowledge and sensitivity for the world beyond our backyard (*source*: Evelyn Tambour/Photographers Direct)

Public relations and culture

If we think of public relations as purposeful, persuasive communication, then it is as old as the human race. But as a contemporary practice of strategic communication, responsible for management of mutually beneficial relations between organisations and their publics, it is of a much more recent origin (Sriramesh 2008). We can think of public relations as a social technology that exploits developments in social sciences to influence human behaviour. To flourish, it needs educational and institutional infrastructure to enable training and funding for practitioners and their activities (Edwards 2012). It emerged in the second half of the nineteenth century in Europe and in the United States and its birth was closely related to developments in information and communication technology, specifically the mass media.

Investments in the practice of public relations are unequally distributed around the world (Sriramesh and Verčič 2007). Societies provide resources that are needed for public relations to work: practitioners, equipment, funding. Societies also provide institutional environments that are more or less hospitable to public relations practices.

Generally, public relations requires open democratic social environments with free speech and rights to communication and association; dictatorships and autocratic regimes don't use communication and relationships to rule – they rely on physical force. (But they may use public relations in other countries to try to polish their image abroad, e.g. agency Bell Pottinger was criticised for its work on behalf of Egypt's Hosni Mubarak, Quorvis Communications for Equatorial Guinea's Teodoro Obiang, Brwon Lloyd James for Libya's Muammar Gaddafi, Hill and Knowlton for Uganda's Yoweri Musaveni and Shanwick for its work for Columbia.) Social, political and media cultures of a country in that respect determine ways in which public relations can be practiced in a country, and in that context we can say that culture operates as an antecedent to public relations (Sriramesh 2012).

But as on one side social (and political) cultures determine ways in which public relations can be practised in a country, so does public relations co-create these very societal (and political) cultures (Mickey 2003; Ławniczak 2005; McKie and Munshi 2007; Heath 2012). The ways in which we see ourselves, objects around us, other people and nations is today presented to us with the help and support of public relations work. Public relations is a great force in creating meaningful social environments for us. In that context we can say that culture not only operates as an antecedent to public relations, but it is also a consequence of these very public relations practices.

Not only that, we can extend the metaphor of culture further, also to organisations practicing public relations and to the very occupation of public relations. We can describe organisations as having different cultures, more or less open (or closed), more mechanical, machine-like, or organic, like biological organisms. Organisational or corporate (similarly as societal) cultures are environments promoting or hindering the use of public relations (Sriramesh and Verčič 2012). Therefore the usefulness of public relations is dependent not only on the skills of practitioners, but also on the expectations and support of their clients (see also Chapter 24).

Even public relations as an occupation can be observed as having a culture of its own (Edwards 2012), and it is different from cultures of managers (Verčič and White 2012): while managers are usually focused, goal- and numbers-orientated, public relations practitioners are often seen to be much 'softer', creative and not so results-orientated. Verčič (2012) also analysed public relations firms using differences in their cultures as a criterion. He found that there are public relations agencies that specialise in producing publicity and that sell mainly journalistic skills of practitioners who are often ex-journalists. Then there are public relations services operating as outsourcing posts for communication departments of corporate clients – their

rationale is often critiqued as buy cheap (young, mainly female workers or interns) and sell expensive. And there are public relations consultancies, some of which are really in the business of providing research-based advice, with the best being founded on public relations theoretical knowledge.

It is not only products, services and organisations as whole corporate bodies, but countries also that use public relations tools to build (Taylor and Kent 2006) and to present themselves (Kunczik 1997; Taylor 2001).

Think about 5.2

Public relations around the world

It is easy to forget that both management and public relations are concepts of a Western origin, and therefore culturally loaded. Furthermore, in their current dominant interpretation they are very North American. It is impossible to translate the term 'public relations' in many languages, and there are differences in popular understanding of the term even between British and American English. While public relations in American English commonly stands for 'management of relationships with publics', in British English it often means 'relations with the media' (with 'public affairs' in British English standing for American English 'public relations' – while 'public affairs' in American English stands for 'government relations'). The term 'public relations' was translated in German as *Öffentlichkeitsarbeit* (literally meaning 'public work' and in German often described as 'work in public for the public'), referring to work in general public or the public sphere. Similar problems exist in other Germanic and Slavonic languages (generally, translating 'public relations' into 'relations' or 'contacts with the public' in the singular). Other language groups and cultures have even more approximate and vague translations.

Feedback

How many different meanings of the term 'public relations' do you know in your language?

How many similar terms used as synonyms for 'public relations' do you know?

Discuss denotations and connotations of these different terms. ('Denotation' stands for 'literal', 'vocabulary', or explicit and primary meaning of a term and 'connotation' for 'subjective', 'emotional', implicit or secondary meaning of the term, usually implying valuation and related positive and negative associations.)

The notion of culture has recently become so important for contemporary life that an anthropologist, Grant McCracken, wrote a book proposing for each company to employ its own *Chief Culture Officer* (2009).

Between universalism and relativism

The current public relations theory and practice are founded in the West, predominantly Western Europe and the US. Only recently have researchers addressed the issue of differences in thinking and doing public relations around the world. In the past 15 years, several key books were published on the subject: Culbertson and Chen (1996) – *International Public Relations: A comparative analysis*, Curtin and Gaither (2007) – *International Public Relations: Negotiating culture, identity, and power*, Ruler and Verčič (2004) – *Public Relations and Communication Management*

in Europe: A nation-by-nation introduction to public relations theory and practice, Sriramesh (2004) – *Public relations in Asia: An anthology*, Sriramesh and Verčič (2009) – *The Global Public Relations Handbook: Theory, research and practice*, Sriramesh and Verčič (2012) – *Culture and Public Relations: Links and implications* and Tilson and Alozie (2004) – *Toward the Common Good: Perspectives in international public relations*.

Research shows that public relations practitioners are more numerous in the most developed parts of the world, although their services might be more needed elsewhere (Sriramesh and Verčič 2007). Observations of large multinationals headquartered in the UK have found that their offices in different parts of the world vary significantly, from one to ten practitioners, without any consistency in size or the scope of their work in relation to their responsibilities. Moss et al. (2012) found that the UK headquarters and their closest offices in Europe had numerically more and more qualified staff than more distant offices, even if these were covering much larger territories.

Mini case study 5.1

Others are different: the bribery scandal at Siemens AG

Siemens AG is the largest Europe-based electronics and electrical engineering company, operating in the industry, energy and healthcare sectors. Headquartered in Munich, Germany, it is 160 years old and, together with its subsidiaries, it employs over 400,000 people in practically all countries in the world. Its global revenue in 2010 was €76 billion and net income €4.1 billion. 'For decades, Munich-based Siemens paid kickbacks and bribes to win contracts in places including Russia, Bangladesh, Venezuela and Nigeria, according to investigations in more than a dozen countries' (www.bloomberg.com/news/2011-01-27/siemens-bribery-scandal-leaves-von-pierer-unbowed-in-his-ceo-memoir-books.html). After being investigated in several countries, including the US and Germany, in 2008 Siemens agreed to settle cases of bribery, corruption and trying to falsify corporate books. The total fine for Siemens was more than US$2.6 billion to clear its name: US$1.6 billion in fines and fees in Germany and the United States and more than

US$1 billion for internal investigations and reforms. Top management has been replaced. The new management has put compliance with new rules, values and principles at the centre of its business (Pohlman 2008). Siemens is today one of the promoters of the United Nations Global Compact, which 'is a strategic policy initiative for businesses that are committed to aligning their operations and strategies with **ten universally accepted principles** in the areas of **human rights**, **labour**, **environment** and **anti-corruption**. By doing so, business, as a primary driver of globalisation, can help ensure that markets, commerce, technology and finance advance in ways that benefit economies and societies everywhere' (http://www.unglobalcompact.org/).

The UN Global Compact's Ten Principles

Human rights
Principle 1: Businesses should support and respect the protection of internationally proclaimed human rights; and

Principle 2: make sure that they are not complicit in human rights abuses.

Labour
Principle 3: Businesses should uphold the freedom of association and the effective recognition of the right to collective bargaining;

→

mini case study 5.1 (continued)

Principle 4: the elimination of all forms of forced and compulsory labour;

Principle 5: the effective abolition of child labour; and

Principle 6: the elimination of discrimination in respect of employment and occupation.

Environment
Principle 7: Businesses should support a precautionary approach to environmental challenges;

Principle 8: undertake initiatives to promote greater environmental responsibility; and

Principle 9: encourage the development and diffusion of environmentally friendly technologies.

Anti-corruption
Principle 10: Businesses should work against corruption in all its forms, including extortion and bribery.

Companies such as Siemens before 2008 are victims of cultural myopia (short-sightedness): rules in other coun-tries seem to them different than those at home and so they believe that they can do things abroad they wouldn't dare do at home.

Transparency International is the global civil society organisation leading the fight against corruption (http://www.transparency.org/). In its reports on corruption around the world, Finland always comes out as one of the least corrupt countries. Yet Patria, a defence company that is majority-owned by the Finnish government, is suspected of exporting corruption by paying bribery in places such as Egypt, Slovenia and Croatia (*Helsingin Sanomat* 2008; Rubenfeld 2011).

Feedback

Do you think that corruption is a cultural phenomenon, being more acceptable in some rather than in other countries?

Do you think that international initiatives such as the Global Compact to promote human rights, fair labour practices, respect for the natural environment and to fight corruption make a difference to the world in which we live?

Certain principles, like those inscribed in the Ten Principles of the Global Compact, seem to be universal and need to be followed worldwide. Respect for local cultures, localisation of organisational practices and communications is responsible only if it adheres to the highest ethical standards. But somehow many people believe that when abroad, they can lower their moral guard and do things they would never do at home. This is a problem of double standards that many multinational companies (MNCs) are accused of: Jahansoozi et al. (2012) provided a thorough and vivid description of the double standards that Shell and other MNC oil companies use in Nigeria as compared to their behaviour in, for example, Canada.

It seems that humans have evolutionarily developed a tendency to categorise other humans between 'us' and 'them'. 'We' belong to the same culture, while 'they' think, decide and behave differently. This goes symmetrically in all directions: 'they' are always different from 'us', and 'we' are different from 'them'. And it is 'we' who know what is right, and if they do it differently, it is 'wrong'. Every civilisation in history wanted to 'civilise' others. The very term 'barbarian', which nowadays stands for describing uncivilised behaviour or individuals, originated in Old Greek and it described anybody who was not Greek.

Global principles and specific applications

A general explanation of how public relations adds value to organisations is proposed in the *Excellence Theory* (Grunig et al. 2002). It is a result of a decade-long research project aimed at the development of a general theory of public relations and it is generally credited to be the mainstream theory in public relations in American academia and around the world (see also Chapter 7 for a discussion and critique). This theory proposes nine general principles, or characteristics, that public relations needs to contribute to organisational effectiveness: (1) involvement of public relations in strategic management; (2) empowerment of public relations in the dominant coalition or a direct reporting relationship to senior management; (3) integrated public relations function; (4) public relations as a management function separate from other functions; (5) the role of the public relations practitioner; (6) two-way symmetrical model of public relations; (7) a symmetrical system of internal communication; (8) knowledge potential for managerial role and symmetrical public relations; and (9) diversity embodied in all roles (Grunig 1992; Dozier et al. 1995; Grunig et al. 2002).

Explore 5.2 — Worldviews

At the beginning of the new millennium, Western scholars were full of optimism in seeing their way of life and their worldview as a model for the whole world. Francis Fukuyama, an American political scientist, had even declared *The End of History* (1992). In the twenty years since the publication of his book (which is an expanded version of the argument first presented three years earlier in a journal article) everything changed, and not only did history not stop, it seems to be accelerating. Cultural presuppositions implicit in the mainstream public relations theories (individual human rights, political liberalism and market economy) have recently been challenged from Asia, but also Africa. Huang (2012) presents her arguments from a Chinese perspective: 'The difference between Chinese and Western worldviews, respectively, can be succinctly summarised: (1) emphasis on whole-ness versus parts, (2) complex interpersonal relationships versus individuals, (3) emphasis on emotional/spiritual versus cognitive outcomes, and (4) nature of communication being intuitively and directly experienced versus language-centered.' (p.96). She notes two reasons for a shortage of cultural sensitivity in research: deliberate avoidance that favours context-free research to contextualised knowledge, and careless oversight due to ethnocentric insensitivity.

Feedback

Can you explain differences in worldviews from a Western, a Confucian, a Buddhist and a Taoist perspective? Use the Internet to learn more about them, adding also other non-Western worldviews you can find.

In 1989, Anderson proposed to distinguish between international public relations and global public relations. International public relations denotes practices when organisations develop distinctive programmes for different markets in different locations. Global public relations, however, denotes an overall perspective, an approach to work in two or more countries, recognising similarities while adapting to differences (Anderson 1989).

Verčič et al. (1996) adopted the nine excellence principles of public relations as global principles and adjusted their use around the world using specific (localised) applications determined by five environmental variables:

- political ideology,

- economic system (including the level of development of the country's economy),

- degree of activism (the extent of pressure that organisations face from activists),

- culture, and

- media system (the nature of the media environment in a country).

Sriramesh and Verčič (2009) collapsed these five variables into three factors:

- a country's infrastructure (composed of political system, economic system and level of development, legal system and social activism),

- media environment (with media control, media diffusion and media access being critical), and

- societal culture.

The notion of culture and public relations has been taken further by Sriramesh and Verčič (2012).

Social media and activists in the global village

When Marshal McLuhan, in his book *The Guttenberg Galaxy: The making of typographic man* (1962), put forward an idea that the world has been contracted into a village by electronic technology and the instantaneous movement of information from one continent to another, social media were not yet invented. Fifty years later we really do live on a contracted planet, in what Manuel Castells calls *The Rise of the Network Society* (Castells 2007, 2009 and 2010).

The emergence of social media and mobile technologies in the first decade of the twenty-first century enabled a mushrooming of activism, demonstrations and social movements at the beginning of the second decade. Time's *Person of the Year* 2011 was 'The Protester' – from 26-year-old street vendor Mohhamed Bouazizi, who set himself on fire in the Tunisian town of Sidi Bouzid, to millions protesting in Greece, Egypt, Myanmar, Nigeria, Russia, Spain, USA – all around the globe (Andersen 2011) (See Picture 5.2).

Box 5.1

Eyes and ears of God

Nuba peoples live in Southern Kordofan, a territory in the centre of the Sudan (about 30,000 square miles, about the size of Scotland). According to some of their sources, there may be up to two million of them. They represent a wealth of cultures, speaking more than 50 languages. For at least 20 years they have been victims of cultural and often physical cleansing. Their suffering has gained the attention of many celebrities, including George Clooney and Mia Farrow. In 2008, Slovenian peace activists Tomo Križnar and Klemen Mihelič started distributing small cameras (over 400 hundred so far), together with satellite modems, laptops and instructions about how to upload the shots, to enable locals to raise the awareness of the international community about the crimes against these indigenous peoples. In 2012, Tomo Križnar and filmmaker Maja Weiss produced a documentary about ethnic Nuba civilians defending themselves in one of the most remote and inaccessible places in all of Sudan with this modern technology.

See the whole documentary, *Eyes and Ears of God*, on http://www.youtube.com/playlist?list=PL61773FC2FF46F738

Picture 5.2 The cover page of The Time magazine – Person of the Year, The Protester (*source*: From *Time* Magazine, 26 December 2011 © 2011, Time Inc. Used under license. *Time* Magazine and Time Inc. are not affiliated with, and do not endorse products or services of Licensee.

How to prepare for international and global public relations

Technology has enabled globalisation, and together they have changed our lives forever. We travel for education, business or fun to other countries, we meet people coming to our towns and villages from around the world. We can try (in vain) to stop the world going round, or we can prepare for living in a multicultural global society. If planning to work internationally, one should consider enlisting on an *intercultural training programme*. Browsing on the Internet produces long lists of public and commercial providers of seminars and other educational formats for acquiring intercultural competence for different parts of the world. (In general, the vast majority of these programmes are for Westerners moving to other parts of the world.) Such programmes have four goals. First, they are preparing people to '*enjoy and benefit* from their experiences with people from other cultures'. Second, they try to make 'these positive feelings *reciprocated by host nationals* with whom sojourners work'. Third, 'sojourners should be able to *manage the stress* that is inherent in overseas assignments'. And fourth, sojourners should be able to '*accomplish the tasks* called for in their work assignments' (Brislin 2008: 2331–2332).

Intercultural public relations is more than just practicing public relations geographically away from home – it doesn't even need to be a question of physical distance. Intercultural public relations is interesting because it is a matter of social distance that is invisible to the eye and, more often than not, can be experienced only in one's heart.

Mini case study 5.2

When operating procedures and cultures collide

With 3.2 million employees, the US Department of Defence is the largest employer in the world. It is also one of the most multicultural organisations in the world. Its personnel are of different races, ethnic origin, gender, occupational and military specialities, and deployed all around the globe. The US Department of Defence is investing in research, education and training of its public relations function, which it calls 'public affairs'.

Allen and Dozier (2012) present a case study on relations between the US military public affairs officers

(PAOs) and Arab journalists in the Middle East. The US military are Western-trained professionals favouring personal responsibility and exchange relations enabling expediency, while Arab journalists belong to a culture founded on family, community and giving importance to honour. The PAOs have relatively short deployments in a foreign country, so they can't develop long-term, communal relations with the Arab media. This experience is shared by expatriates working in multinational companies or international organisations: they are responsible for 'establishing and maintaining symbiotic relationships with relevant publics', but they are limited in their opportunity(ies) to do so, because they are called back home or moved to another position somewhere else. While in host cultures it could take years to develop trusted relationships and become an accepted member of a community. Operating procedures of many organisations prevent their employees 'going local' by moving them before they can 'localise'.

Explore 5.3

Understanding 'the other'

In a chapter proposing a framework for indigenous engagement based on examples related to New Zealand Maori, Motion et al. (2012) concluded that we need to develop a culturally contextualised public relations practice that is open, adaptable and flexible in relations with groups that are different from us in one or another respect.

Feedback

How often do you engage in communication with people that you perceive as different from you, because they belong to another ethnicity, have a different legal status (illegal or temporary immigrants), or maybe simply belong to another class, caste or any other groups characteristic that is meaningful to you? What are your experiences from such encounters?

Key principles in intercultural and multicultural public relations

Intercultural and multicultural public relations is the management of diverse public relations practices: there is a multitude of people and worldviews around us and we

must learn to embrace the rainbow. This, however, is far from easy and there are no quick recipes for the management of successful multicultural programmes. Instead of searching for short-cuts, it is better to face the practical challenges and attempt to resolve what may appear to be paradoxes in the delivery of public relations programmes.

■ *Increase the complexity and focus on simplicity*: if an organisation operates in a culturally rich environment (and it is practically impossible to operate differently), it must work towards increasing its own cultural richness internally. Only that way can it understand and communicate with various publics. But cultural multitude is not the same as chaos. Common values should provide guiding principles that bring simplicity to the multitude. Communication is instrumental in co-production of common foundations.

■ *Communication belongs to the top and can only work at the bottom*: public relations is more than a set of tools to broadcast messages from the top of an organisation downwards and outwards. Public relations can best serve organisations by performing a role of ears and eyes of management, through which it is tuned to the larger society. To be influential at the top, public relations needs to have its top person positioned at the top of an organisation. But it is impossible to communicate to everybody everywhere from there, so local teams are needed to have local experiences, and relationships need to perform well.

■ *Good external communication is founded in good internal communication*: organisations can be trusted only if they communicate what they mean, and in that respect internal communication provides a foundation for authenticity of expressions for organisational members when they engage with others. Even before social media penetrated organisational borders, they were anything but firm. In today's information environments, all organisations leak all the time. Engaging insiders is a prerequisite for successful engagement with anybody else.

■ *The science of communication is universal, but the art of communication is always cultural = local*: modern science based on empirical research is a powerful force that has transformed humanity in the past three to four hundred years. Social sciences are with us a half of that period, and public relations as an applied communication and management science has only been exten-

sively studied since the 1980s. But scientific research in public relations offers powerful technological solutions that easily travel around the globe. However, human communication can never be only scientifically programmed and there is always an artistic, creative side to human intercourse, closely linked to cultures as small universes of meanings.

Public diplomacy

When watching international news on television, one can see that we live in a violent world. But '[v]iolence has declined by dramatic degrees all over the world in many spheres of behaviour: genocide, war, human sacrifice,

---

Think about 5.3   Can('t) buy me love

In 1953, the US President Dwight Eisenhower established the United States Information Agency 'to understand, inform, and influence foreign publics in the promotion of the US national interest, and to broaden the dialogue between Americans and US institutions, and their counterparts abroad' (USIA 1998). In 1961, John F. Kennedy appointed Edward R. Murrow the director of the USIA. Murrow was previously a prominent US broadcast journalist who had made his name first during his wartime reporting from Europe from 1938 to 1945, and then by producing a series of TV news reports that were instrumental in censuring Senator Joseph McCarthy, an infamous fighter against Red Scare (communism) in 1950s USA. Murrow resigned as the director of the USIA due to illness in 1964 and died in 1965 from the lung cancer he developed as a chain-smoker. In 1965, the Edward R. Murrow Centre of Public Diplomacy was established at the Fletcher School of Law and Diplomacy at Tufts University – its Dean, Edmund Gullion, is credited with inventing the term 'public diplomacy' in its present usage. The same activities were previously known, and are still referred to by critics, as 'international propaganda'. The USIA is known for being effective in influencing public opinion behind the Iron Curtain during the Cold War, but was in the mid-1990s downsized as part of a budget-cutting 'peace dividend'. In 1999, the Clinton administration merged the USIA into the State Department. Before being abolished, the USIA had a budget of US$1,109 billion and was employing 6,352 employees.

Inside the US State Department, public diplomacy is now run by the Under Secretary for Public Diplomacy and Public Affairs, who defines its mission as follows:

The mission of American public diplomacy is to support the achievement of US foreign policy goals and objectives, advance national interests, and enhance

national security by informing and influencing foreign publics and by expanding and strengthening the relationship between the people and government of the United States and citizens of the rest of the world.

The Under Secretary for Public Diplomacy and Public Affairs leads America's public diplomacy outreach, which includes communications with international audiences, cultural programming, academic grants, educational exchanges, international visitor programs, and US Government efforts to confront ideological support for terrorism. The Under Secretary oversees the bureaus of Educational and Cultural Affairs, Public Affairs, and International Information Programs, and participates in foreign policy development. (US Department of State 2012)

Currently, the US budget for public diplomacy is around US$1.5 billion, which is comparable in size to sums spent by France or Britain (Armitage and Nye 2007). Comparing sizes and international responsibilities, one could say that the US Government is seriously underinvesting in public diplomacy. Many still believe that dismantling of the USIA was a strategic mistake. However, US$1.5 billion per year is still a respectable sum of money. It is interesting to see how it reflected in public opinion in Western Europe, the closest ally of the US in the world.

Feedback

What are the similarities and differences between propaganda, public relations and public diplomacy?

How would you answer a question posed by US diplomat Richard Holbroke: 'How can a man in a cave outcommunicate the world's leading communications society?' (Where 'a man in a cave' denotes Osama bin Laden and 'the world's leading communication society' the USA.)

torture, slavery, and the treatment of racial minorities, women, children, and animals' (Pinker 2012b; see also Pinker 2011a). And notwithstanding the current depressive economic and political climate in the Western world, there is a good chance that our lives will continue to get better (Diamandis and Kotler 2012) – but progress is not an automatic ride, it is a human-made condition. And at the centre of that condition is communication.

International relations, relations between states or countries, can be conducted by war, trade or diplomacy, i.e. force, money or communication. Traditional diplomacy covers communication between representatives of governments. It is possible to talk about cultural diplomacy that has been practiced for centuries between traders and scholars travelling to other countries in search of profit, knowledge or simple adventure. 'Public diplomacy' meant only civility when it first emerged in the English language in the mid nineteenth century. In the mid twentieth century it stepped into political language to replace the term 'international propaganda' that was largely discredited during the Second World War. Defined simply, public diplomacy means communication of governments with peoples of other countries. McClellan (2004) defines it as 'the strategic planning and execution of informational, cultural and educational programming by an advocate country to create a public opinion environment in a target country or countries that will enable target country political leaders to make decisions that are supportive of advocate country's foreign policy objectives.'

Related to public diplomacy is the notion of soft power:

The basic concept of power is the ability to influence others to get what you want. There are three major ways to that: one is to threaten them with sticks; the second is to pay them with carrots; the third is to attract them or co-opt them, so that they want what you want. If you can get others to be attracted, to want what you want, it costs you much less in carrots and sticks. (Nye and Myers 2004)

For Nye (2004), soft power is founded in a nation's 'culture (in places where it is attractive to others), its political values (when it lives up to them at home and abroad) and its foreign policies (when they are seen as legitimate and having moral authority)' (p.11). Soft power, therefore, comes from a nation's behaviour and not from symbols it uses to present itself to others.

Today, practically all countries use public diplomacy with varying degrees of success.

Summary

We live in a multicultural world, and public relations practitioners are in the business of intercultural mediation. Wherever we live, we are exposed to other cultures. Cultures as mental programming of our minds are reflecting not only our ethnic or national background, but also class, professional, racial, gender and other differences. We trust our cultural views to be 'natural' because we are born in them – but so are others in theirs. Public relations as management of communication and relationships is directly concerned with the management of cultural differences. To provide an alternative image and comparison we can also say that public relations practitioners are required to perform like intercultural interpreters.

Bibliography

Allen, M.R. and D.M. Dozier (2012). 'When cultures collide: theoretical issues in global public relations' in *Culture and Public Relations: Links and implications.* K. Sriramesh and D. Verčič (eds). New York/London: Routledge.

Andersen, K. (2011). 'The protester'. *Time Person of the Year.* www.time.com/time/specials/packages/article/0,28804,2101745_2102132,00.html

Anderson, G. (1989). 'A local look at public relations' in *Experts in Action: Inside public relations*, 2nd ed., B. Cantor (ed.). New York, NY: Longman.

Armitage, R.L. and J.S. Nye (2007). 'CSIS Commission on Smart Power: A smarter, more secure America'. http://csis.org/files/media/csis/pubs/071106_csissmartpowerreport.pdf accessed 19 June 2012.

Banks, S.P. (1995). *Multicultural Public Relations: A social-interpretive approach.* Thousand Oaks, CA: Sage.

Brislin, R.W. (2008). 'Intercultural communication training' in *International Encyclopedia of Communication, Vol. VI.* W. Donsbach (ed.). Malden, MA: Blackwell.

Castells, M. (2007). 'Communication, power and counter-power in the network society'. *International Journal of Communication* 1: 238–266.

Castells, M. (2009). *Communication Power.* Oxford/New York: Oxford University Press.

Castells, M. (2010). *The Rise of the Network Society*, 2nd ed. Chichester, UK: Willey-Blackwell.

Center for Strategic and International Studies (2008). 'Appendix to Armitage-Nye Joint Testimony before US Senate Foreign Relations Committee, April 24'. http://csis.org/files/media/csis/congress/ts0804024Armitage-Nye_Appendix.pdf accessed 26 June 2012.

Culbertson, H.M. and N. Chen (eds) (1996). *International Public Relations: A comparative analysis.* Mahwah, NJ: Lawrence Erlbaum.

Curtin, P.A. and T. Gaither (2007). *International Public Relations: Negotiating culture, identity, and power.* Thousand Oaks, CA: Sage.

Debeljak, A. (2012). 'In praise of hybridity: globalization and the modern Western paradigm' in *Culture and Public Relations: Links and implications.* K. Sriramesh and D. Verčič (eds). New York, NY: Routledge.

Diamandis, P.H. and S. Kotler (2012). *Abundance: The future is better than you think.* New York, NY: Free Press.

Dozier, D.M., L.A. Grunig and J.E. Grunig (1995). *Manager's Guide to Excellence in Public Relations and Communication Management.* Mahwah, NJ: Lawrence Erlbaum Associates.

Dutta, M.J. (2012). 'Critical interrogations of global public relations' in *Culture and Public Relations: Links and implications.* K. Sriramesh and D. Verčič (eds). New York/London: Routledge.

Edwards, L. (2012). 'Public relations' occupational culture: habitus, exclusion and resistance in the UK context' in *Culture and Public Relations: Links and implications.* K. Sriramesh and D. Verčič (eds). New York/London: Routledge.

Fukuyama, F. (1992). *The End of History and the Last Man.* New York, NY: The Free Press.

Grunig, J.E. (ed.) (1992a). *Excellence in Public Relations and Communication Management.* Hillsdale, NJ: Lawrence Erlbaum Associates.

Grunig, L.A., J.E. Grunig and D.M. Dozier (2002). *Excellent Public Relations and Effective Organizations: A study of communication management in three countries.* Mahwah, NJ: Lawrence Erlbaum Associates.

Heath, R.L. (2012). 'Western classical rhetorical tradition and modern public relations: culture of citizenship' in *Culture and Public Relations: Links and implications.* K. Sriramesh and D. Verčič (eds). New York/London: Routledge.

Helsingin Sanomat (2008). 'Finland's central criminal police to investigate Patria deals in Slovenia and Egypt'. *Helsingin Sanomat: International Edition*, 15 May www.hs.fi/english/article/1135236367677 accessed 19 June 2012.

Huang, Y.H.C. (2012). 'Culture and Chinese public relations research' in *Culture and Public Relations: Links and implications.* K. Sriramesh and D. Verčič (eds). New York/London: Routledge.

Jahansoozi, J., K. Eyita and N. Izidor (2012). 'Mago Mago: Nigeria, petroleum and a history of mismanaged community relations' in *Culture and Public Relations: Links and implications.* K. Sriramesh and D. Verčič (eds). New York/London: Routledge.

Kunczik, M. (1997). *Images of Nations and International Public Relations.* Mahwah, NJ: Lawrence Erlbaum.

Ławniczak, R. (2005). *Introducing Market Economy Institutions and Instruments: The role of public relations in transition economies.* Poznań: Piar.pl.

McClellan, M. (2004). 'Public diplomacy in the context of traditional diplomacy'. Presented to Vienna Diplomatic Academy on 14 October 2004. www.publicdiplomacy.org/45.htm accessed 13 June 2012.

McCracken, G. (2009). *Chief Culture Officer: How to create a living, breathing corporation.* New York, NY: Basic Books.

McKie, D. and D. Munshi (2007). *Reconfiguring Public Relations: Ecology, equity, and enterprise.* London/New York: Routledge.

McLuhan, M. (1962). *The Guttenberg Galaxy: The Making of typographic man.* Toronto: University of Toronto Press.

Mickey, T.J. (2003). *Deconstructing Public Relations: Public relations criticism.* Mahwah, NJ: Lawrence Erlbaum Associates.

Moss, D., C. McGrath, J. Tonge and P. Harris (2012). 'Exploring the management of the corporate public affairs function in a dynamic global environment'. *Journal of Public Affairs* **12**: 47–60.

Motion, J., J. Haar and S. Leitch (2012). 'A public relations framework for indigenous engagement' in *Culture and Public Relations: Links and implications.* K. Sriramesh and D. Verčič (eds). New York/London: Routledge.

Nye, J. (2004). *Soft Power: The means to success in world politics.* New York, NY: Public Affairs.

Nye, J.S. and J.J. Myers (2004). *Soft power: The means to success in world politics.* (Carnegie Council for Ethics in International Affairs, audio transcript.) http://www.carnegiecouncil.org/studio/multimedia/20040413/index.html

Pinker, S. (2011a). 'A history of violence: *Edge* master class 2011'. http://edge.org/conversation/mc2011-history-violence-pinker accessed 13 June 2012.

Pinker, S. (2011b). *The Better Angels of our Nature: The decline of violence in history and its causes.* London: Penguin.

Pohlman, A. (2008). 'A new direction for Siemens: improving preventive systems'. *Compact Quarterly.* www.enewsbuilder.net/globalcompact/e_article001149152.cfm?x=bd2Hd2m accessed 18 June 2012.

Prinz, J.J. (2012). *Beyond Human Nature: How culture and experience shape our lives.* London: Allen Lane.

Rubenfeld, S. (2011). 'Finland expands Patria bribery investigation into Croatia sales'. http://blogs.wsj.com/corruption-currents/2011/01/04/finland-expands-patria-bribery-investigation-into-croatia-sales/ accessed 19 June 2012.

Ruler, B. van and D. Verčič (eds) (2004). *Public Relations and Communication Management in Europe: A nation-by-nation introduction to public relations theory and practice.* Berlin/New York: Mouton de Gruyter.

Sha, B.-L., N.T.J. Tindall and T.-L. Sha (2012). 'Identity and culture: implications for public relations' in *Culture and Public Relations: Links and implications.* K. Sriramesh and D. Verčič (eds). New York/London: Routledge.

Shweder, R.A., J.J. Goodnow, G. Hatano, R.A. LeVine, H.R. Markus and P.J. Miller (1998). 'The cultural psychology of development: one mind, many mentalities' in *Handbook of Child Psychology: Vol. 1. Theoretical models of human development*, 5th ed. W. Damon (series ed.) and R.M. Lerner (vol. ed.). New York, NY: Wiley.

Signitzer, B. and C. Wamser (2006). 'Public diplomacy: a specific governmental public relations function' in *Public Relations Theory II.* C.H. Botan and V. Hazleton (eds). Mahwah, NJ: Lawrence Erlbaum.

Sriramesh, K. (ed.) (2004). *Public Relations in Asia: An anthology.* Singapore: Thomson Learning.

Sriramesh, K. (2008). 'Public relations, intercultural' in *International Encyclopedia of Communication, Vol. IX.* W. Donsbach (ed.). Malden, MA: Blackwell.

Sriramesh, K. (2012). 'Culture and public relations: formulating the relationship and its relevance to the practice' in *Culture and Public Relations: Links and implications.* K. Sriramesh and D. Verčič (eds). New York/London: Routledge.

Sriramesh, K. and D. Verčič (2007). 'Introduction to this special section: the impact of globalization on public relations'. *Public Relations Review* **33**: 355–359.

Sriramesh, K. and D. Verčič (eds) (2009). *The Global Public Relations Handbook: Theory, research, and practice,* expanded and revised edition. New York, NY: Routledge.

Sriramesh, K. and D. Verčič (eds) (2012). *Culture and Public Relations: Links and implications.* New York, NY: Routledge.

Taylor, M. (2001). 'International public relations: opportunities and challenges for the 21st century' in *Handbook of Public Relations.* R.L. Heath (ed.). Thousand Oaks, CA: Sage.

Taylor, M. and M.L. Kent (2006). 'Public relations theory and practice in nation building' in *Public Relations Theory II.* C.H. Botan and V. Hazleton (eds). Mahwah, NJ: Lawrence Erlbaum.

Tilson, D.J. and E.C. Alozie (eds) (2004). *Toward the Common Good: Perspectives in international public relations.* Boston, MA: Pearson.

US Department of State (2012). 'Under Secretary for Public Diplomacy and Public Affairs'. www.state.gov/r/ accessed 17 June 2012.

USIA (1998). 'United States Information Agency'. http://dosfan.lib.uic.edu/usia/usiahome/overview.pdf accessed 13 June 2012.

Verčič, D. (2012). 'Public relations firms and their three occupational cultures' in *Culture and Public Relations: Links and implications.* K. Sriramesh and D. Verčič (eds). New York/London: Routledge.

Verčič, D. and J. White (2012). 'Corporate public relations as a professional culture: between management and journalism' in *Culture and Public Relations: Links and implications.* K. Sriramesh and D. Verčič (eds). New York/London: Routledge.

Verčič, D., L.A. Grunig and J.E. Grunig (1996). 'Global and specific principles of public relations: evidence from Slovenia' in *International Public Relations: A comparative analysis.* H.M. Culbertson and N. Chen (eds). Mahwah, NJ: Lawrence Erlbaum Associates.

Websites

The European Public Relations Education and Research Association: www.euprera.org

The Global Alliance for Public Relations and Communication Management: www.globalalliancepr.org

Human Development Index: http://hdr.undp.org/en/statistics/hdi/

The International Association of Business Communicators: www.iabc.com

The International Public Relations Association: www.ipra.org

Transparency International: www.transparency.org/

Role of the public relations practitioner

Learning outcomes

By the end of this chapter you should be able to:

- describe issues and debates surrounding the role of the public relations practitioner
- consider the role of public relations in society
- recognise the range of activities undertaken by practitioners
- evaluate the skills needed by individual practitioners
- recognise the issues around the education and training of the public relations practitioner
- apply the above to real-life contexts.

Structure

- Who are the public relations practitioners?
- Who does what: the bigger picture
- Role of the communicator
- What public relations people do: individual practitioners
- Skills for the ideal practitioner
- Role of theory in practice
- Professionalism
- Education and research

Introduction

Working out exactly what a PR practitioner does can be confusing. Many people assume it's all about hanging out with celebrities, selling kiss 'n' tell stories to the Sunday newspapers, tweeting endlessly about clients and social events or whispering in politicians' ears and 'spinning' the entire national media. Isn't it?

A glance at the contents page of this book will suggest otherwise. Each chapter addresses a particular area of public relations theory or practice, and while there are chapters on media relations and public affairs, PR is about so much more than these two areas and is used by a wide variety of organisations, governments and individuals for a whole range of purposes.

This chapter aims to show where people work in public relations and what they do in their jobs. It explores the problems caused by difficulties in defining the field, but also the opportunities for individual and professional development. Public relations practice is linked to public relations theory, and the need for individuals to undertake lifelong learning is stressed. The role of education and the question of professionalism are also discussed, along with the role of professional and trade bodies.

This chapter aims to bridge the divide between detailed academic books and 'how to' textbooks by setting practice clearly in a theoretical context and including examples of practice from different countries. It also reflects a range of experiences, through case studies and diaries, of being a practitioner in the twenty-first century. Throughout the chapter you will be able to read mini case histories and diaries of public relations practitioners who are working in different types of settings, to help you appreciate the diversity of the practice and gain an insight into what people actually do.

Explore 6.1 — What is public relations all about?

If you've ever asked your friends and family what they think PR is all about and/or which PR practitioners they have heard of, you will get a variety of answers.

Feedback

Chances are that the responses will not be flattering and that the individuals named may be high-profile themselves, such as Max Clifford – who wouldn't consider himself to be anything other than a publicist, rather than a PR practitioner. Many will describe activities or individuals with a significant media interest in areas such as sport, music or politics. Yet the bona fide public relations practitioner will not be seeking exposure for themselves, but for the client or the organisation for whom they work.

You may also find that media relations is the function or activity most closely associated with these high-profile individuals or sectors. However, the breadth and range of subject matter covered in this book will dispel the misunderstanding that most people will have of the practice.

Who are the public relations practitioners?

There is a lot of confusion about who does what in public relations (PR) – see Explore 6.1. It may be helpful to look at some facts about the industry in Britain and in Spain as two country examples (see Boxes 6.1 and 6.2 and then complete Explore 6.2).

Explore 6.2

Comparing public relations in two countries

Look at the information in Boxes 6.1 and 6.2. What are the key differences? How does each country's PR association define PR? Look at each of their websites (the Spanish site has an English translation).

Feedback

Check out other websites – how do their ideas and statistics vary? How many have English translations? Does the UK site have other languages available? If not, why not? (See also Chapter 5.)

Box 6.1

Key facts about public relations in Britain

According to the UK's Chartered Institute of Public Relations (CIPR):

- On a global scale, the UK PR market is second only to that of the United States.

- Private and public sector organisations in Britain will spend about £6bn on PR services this year.

- The UK Graduate Careers Survey reported that the media including PR (attracting 12.4 per cent of finalists), teaching (11.9 per cent), investment banking (11.1 per cent), marketing (11 per cent) and accountancy (10.8 per cent) were the top five career destinations for the class of 2006.

- According to the VSS Communications Industry Forecast 2004–2014, total communications-industry spending will increase 3.5 per cent in 2010 and post a compound annual growth rate of 6.1 per cent in the 2009–2014 period, to $1.416 trillion, driven by a gradual economic recovery, advances in digital technology and other trends.

- PR is seen as a vibrant, attractive industry, consistently ranking among new graduates' top three career choices.

- A survey of 300 marketing professionals by the Marketing Society showed that nine out of every 10 believed that PR will become more important (over the next five years) than TV/radio advertising, sponsorship, email marketing and events/exhibitions (source: *Financial Times*, Creative Business 21 October 2003). Note since this data there has been a worldwide economic recession, which has affected growth; as such, in 2012, by sector the main media budgets were revised up for the first time since Q3 2007. Internet budgets were adjusted up for the third quarter in succession; this upgrade was the most pronounced since Q1 2008 and the fastest of all categories. Sales promotion and direct marketing budgets were unchanged, while 'all other' (below-the-line such as PR, events) was the only sector to record a downward revision to spend (see IPA Bellwether Report 2012).

- All listed FTSE100 companies have a PR department communicating on their behalf.

In November 2005 the CIPR launched the results of the first major study into the size, nature and composition of the PR industry. The research was carried out by the Centre for Economics and Business Research (CEBR) and showed that:

- On a global scale, the UK PR market is second only to that of the US.

- The UK PR industry has a turnover of £6.5bn; the profession contributes £3.4billion to the UK's economic activity and generates £1.1 billion in corporate profits.

- The annual turnover of PR consultancies is £1.2billion.

- 82 per cent of practitioners work in-house and 18 per cent work in PR consultancy.

- The UK PR industry employs around 48,000 people.

- The health, public and not-for-profit sectors are the biggest employers of PR, together accounting for 36 per cent of turnover for PR consultancies and employing 51 per cent of in-house practitioners.

- 25 per cent of PR practitioners work in London.

- 6.5 per cent of the profession comes from an ethic minority and 2 per cent describe themselves as disabled.

- The majority of employees are graduates.

In December 2011 the CIPR launched the results of its annual 'State of the Profession' survey:

- In the current economic landscape, company performance and reputation management remain increasingly important to client organisations.

- Sponsorship and event management are seeing the greatest area of decline.

- Nearly two-thirds of PR practitioners are female.

- Male practitioners employed in the profession are more likely to be in a senior position, with a higher salary, and to have a position on the board of their organisation.

- CIPR estimates that its membership as a whole is made up of 55 per cent in-house PR practitioners and 45 per cent consultancy PR practitioners.

- The largest percentage of consultancy practitioners is involved in strategic planning (88 per cent). This is closely followed by media relations (85 per cent). There is also significant consultancy PR involvement in communication strategy development (74 per cent).

- The smallest percentage of respondents were involved in financial PR.

- Areas of growth for the next five years: online reputation management (72 per cent), strategic planning (50 per cent) and crisis management (42 per cent).

box 6.1 (continued)

The CIPR's 'PR 2020: The Future of Public Relations' report by Dr Jon White (2011) highlighted the following expectations on the profession by current practitioners in 2020:

■ The practice will be clear on what public relations is, and the benefits it can deliver.

■ The profession will be strongly led, respected and established as a senior management discipline.

■ PR practitioners will be confident, committed to professional development and working to well-developed codes of conduct.

■ The Chartered Institute of Public Relations will provide strong leadership to the practice, and there will be recognised and credible role models speaking out for the practice.

Source: www.cipr.co.uk

Box 6.2

Country profiles from the Global Alliance – a sample

The following is not an exhaustive list of member states or associations, but a sample from different continents to indicate the range and variety of PR education, with a brief history of the development of the field or the professional organisation to indicate the relationship between the two. For further, more current details on the status of PR in a range of countries, see the Global Alliance website: www.globalpr.org/knowledge/landscapes.asp

Europe

United Kingdom

According to L'Etang (1999, 2002) the origins of British PR lie in the public rather than private sector: during and after the Second World War, the number of PR consultants appointed in government departments increased greatly to enable the handling of information and intelligence, propaganda and psychological warfare and persuasion and public relations. The UK professional body, the Chartered Institute of Public Relations (CIPR), has been involved in education since its inception, though these were closer to training than academic courses. PR education in Britain in the past 10 years has seen an expansion in public relations courses, often influenced by the location of the course in either a business or media school. Tench and Fawkes (2005) suggest there are two types of courses: a business school curriculum and a media school curriculum. Most PR education has moved from technical training in skills required by public relations practitioners, embodied in the Public Relations Education Trust (PRET) Matrix, to a broader, more academic approach. While most PR educators have practitioner backgrounds, many have over a decade of teaching and research experience. However, according to Tench and Fawkes (2005) 'the pressure on the post-1992 sector to manage large cohorts and prioritise teaching over research' has left a gap in UK research into PR.

The Netherlands

Van Ruler and Verčič (2004) argue that the rebuilding of Dutch society after the Second World War involved the promotion of business and social goods, although society had a new, powerful repugnance towards propaganda. In 1945, the first professional association to ease the exchange of knowledge between journalists and PR officers representing government, businesses and agencies was established, leading to the Association for Public Contact, later renamed the Association for Public Relations in the Netherlands, and now the Dutch Association of Communication.

The first course in PR in the Netherlands was in 1940 and this was offered as optional in universities under 'mass communication' and 'journalism'. Current PR education in the Netherlands is very well developed, with about 30 full Bachelor of Arts (BA) programmes in organisational communication or communication management. They further state that all 13 research universities offer BA streams in the area of organisational communication or communication management. The Netherlands School of Communication Research (NESCoR) offers a Doctorate in Philosophy (PhD) programme in communication science.

France

The communicational paradigm in France that emerged during the early 1980s was the 'Communicational Director model' due to the emergence of the concept of corporate image, management requirements,

box 6.2 (continued)

institutional advertising and that of consultancy agencies in 'overall communications'. The term 'PR' is rarely used, even though it is popular in consultancies. In the PR educational field, van Ruler and Verčič (2004) state that 'the number of professional university training courses is extremely high', as a result of which the private sector plays a minor role in education. France has undergraduate BA programmes as well as postgraduate education and doctoral programmes, with some doctorates in information and communication science.

Germany

Public relations development in Germany has been related to political, economic and social conditions (van Ruler and Verčič, 2004). Six periods of German public relations history, including Nazi-era propaganda, have been defined. After 1945, PR did redefine its tenets of practice under a democratic government, but PR and research in PR are in their initial stages, with purpose-free research undertaken in universities, and applied research, which aims to solve concrete practical problems, privately financed.

In the 1980s PR entered the universities and polytechnics and, in the 1990s, several universities established PR courses within their communication programmes. Most universities in Germany today offer BA, Masters and PhD programmes. In some polytechnics PR Diploma courses are offered.

Bulgaria

The term 'public relations' was first mentioned in Bulgaria in 1972 in an article by Svetozar Krastev as a component of marketing. Bulgaria discovered the real PR profession after the changes to democracy in 1989. In 1996 the first Bulgarian professional association – the Bulgarian Public Relations Society – was founded. It constitutes practitioners and teachers in the sphere of PR, marketing, communication and advertising.

Attempts to teach PR as an academic subject were made by the first private university in Bulgaria – New Bulgarian University Sofia. In March 1991, the Department of Mass Communication of the new private university opened its first three-year experimental course in PR as a separate speciality. Bulgarian universities now offer a three-year degree, and postgraduate education and PhD courses, in PR.

Romania

In Romania, multinational companies were the first to introduce public relations at the beginning of the 1990s. Today there are PR agencies, PR departments within companies and advertising agencies and officers and specialists within government institutions. Non-governmental organisations (NGOs) also employ public relations specialists. There have been several institutions trying to represent PR practitioners and promote PR in Romania, including the Romanian Public Relations Association (ARRP), the Club of the Romanian Public Relations Agencies and the Forum for International Communications.

The first recognised college-level course in public relations was not taught in Romania until 1993 and was at the University of Bucharest. This PR course was added to undergraduate programmes for The Faculty of Journalism and Communication Studies and, according to the Global Alliance, was a milestone in the development of PR practice in the country, which was followed by a couple of other state and private universities.

Italy

The Federazione Relazione Pubbliche Italiana (FERPI) and Associazione Comunicazione Pubblica since the mid-1950s have helped in the development of PR in Italy. The history of PR has gone through many phases from the late 1940s through to the 1990s. FERPI currently has about 70,000 practitioners who operate professional PR in the private, public and not-for-profit organisations, according to Global Alliance.

In the last 10 years, with a focus on university reorganisation, the Italian academy has seen an expansion in degree programmes in Communication Science in PR, with postgraduate specialisation in the fields of communication, public relations and organisation. According to van Ruler and Verčič (2004), many in Italian universities question the scope of PR and its roots in sociological, psychological, historic-geographic, legal and economic disciplines.

The Americas

Canada

The professional body Canadian Public Relations Society (CPRS) was founded in 1948 in two original groups, first in Montreal and second in Toronto. The CPRS has about 2,000 members; it is estimated that 10 per cent of practitioners become members. Owing to the dual culture of the country, national public relations includes special considerations for communication with the Francophone market. Public relations education in Canada is a vital area, with many students graduating in majors and minors in public relations; in addition to the formal education, colleges and other adult education courses offer certificates in public relations.

→

box 6.2 (continued)

United States of America

The subject of public relations has been taught in universities for more than 70 years and there are now reported to be over 3,000 degrees in the discipline. The US public relations education is associated with schools and departments of journalism or mass communications; with the first practitioners being trained journalists, priority was given to the ability to write well.

In 1975 the first commission for public relations education recommended that public relations programmes should consist of a minimum of 12 hours per semester, which was upgraded in 1978. A model curriculum consisting of a minimum of five courses in public relations was later introduced (Grunig and Grunig 2002). It has been argued that, while several practitioners emphasised the increase in international public relations, the fact that public relations education in the USA focused on technical skills rather than on theory and research resulted in this area being overlooked to a large degree in public relations programmes.

'A Port of Entry' (1999) and 'The Professional Bond' (2006), research-based reports by the Public Relations Society of America (PRSA), demonstrated a congruity between what practitioners and scholars believe is vital to the public relations curriculum. 'A Port of Entry' recommended undergraduate and graduate education in which curricular models are grounded in the liberal arts, theory-based across the curriculum and with the emphasis on courses rather than departments where these courses are undertaken.

It has been suggested that in the US, PR education can be seen as technical training, in contrast to Europe where strategic communication is the focus of public relations education. This has led some to question whether the public relations profession will be able to handle the challenges to be faced in the twenty-first century. However, an area of strength that American public relations has is the issue of ethics. Verwey (2000) suggests the practice of ethical public relations may become a force to reckon with in the twenty-first century for public relations professionals. This will invariably demarcate the lines that the post-modern public relations practitioner will need to serve as the agent for change to an organisation, and also being the conscience of the organisation.

Argentina

The growth of public relations was affected by Argentina's military rule, but when the country emerged as an independent and democratic nation, PR played a more prominent part in society. Argentina has two professional councils of public relations, the first founded in 1997 to represent public relations professionals with university and other tertiary education degrees in public relations or related communication fields. There are two professional associations active in the province of Buenos Aires: The Professional Council of Public Relations of the Buenos Aires Province and the Professional Council of Public Relations.

Public relations education is still developing; there are also specialised educational courses offered by universities and institutions, including three- to five-year programmes in PR.

Puerto Rico

Public relations in Puerto Rico follows US practice closely, but adapted to the cultural implications of the Puerto Rican society. The driving force of PR in Puerto Rico is the Asociación de Relacionistas Profesionales de Puerto Rico (ARPPR). The ARPPR was founded in 1970 and now has more than 200 members.

Communication programmes can now be found in various educational institutions in Puerto Rico, offering bachelors degrees in communications or journalism, or related curriculum as part of social science programmes.

Africa

It has been suggested that the concept of PR was practiced in Africa long before colonialism, if one sees the similarity between the task of a PR practitioner and that of a chief's spokesperson in traditional African villages. The move towards democracy on a broad front has promoted the development of public relations in Africa. As regards education, courses in public relations in Africa are varied, and range from in-service training by employers and within government ministries (Ferreira 2003) to formal tertiary diplomas, degrees and post-degree courses. A variety of short courses are offered in different countries by development agencies, professional institutes and private colleges, and at tertiary level, many public relations programmes are taught as part of a bachelors degree in communication, mass communication or journalism (Ferreira 2003). Some universities also teach public relations to complement other disciplines, such as marketing and business management. A number of distance learning programmes in public relations are also available in Africa.

box 6.2 (continued)

However, Ferreira (2003) states that one cannot pin down or make a generalisation of the state of public relations education in Africa. He is of the view that some public relations officers have entered the career through journalism, as in the UK and the US – indeed some of these officers have been trained abroad. In some countries the training is informal and is undertaken by other external bodies, such as banks and private institutions, private companies and sometimes by the public relations institute or societies in that country.

Asia and the Middle East

India

Public relations began to increase in India in the early 1990s when the government opened the economy and multinational corporations began to enter the country. Public relations companies emerged offering strategic advice and integrated communication solutions. Specialisation has become increasingly important and firms are demanding higher qualifications and skill sets from workers.

The Public Relations Consultants Association of India (PRCAI) was established in 2001 to develop standards, ethics, expertise and knowledge in the public relations industry in India. In each of these areas, the primary objective is to align the public relations industry in India with international practices.

Sriramesh (1996) argues that almost all of India's big companies have separate public relations departments, working in marketing, social welfare or consumer affairs.

China

According to Culbertson and Chen (1996) the development of public relations in China began 20 years ago, with much emphasis on interpersonal communication. About 150 public relations societies exist throughout China at the local and provincial as well as national levels. The China International Public Relations Association (CIPRA) seeks to enhance professionalism, according to Culbertson and Chen (1996). The CIPRA sets standards for PR education, not the national Ministry of Education. CIPRA and Shanghai Public Relations Association (SPRA) both encourage and support academic research and theory development. According to CIPRA, there are only two PR master's degree programmes in China.

Culbertson and Chen (1996) suggest that Chinese public relations education has undergone many challenges, that public relations in China is diverse, and is offered in interdisciplinary programmes, mass communication or in departments of journalism, and units that offer speech and interpersonal communication. Public relations education is offered in four-year baccalaureate degree programmes, in two-year technical colleges and through television and distance learning targeted at older and non-traditional PR students. In 2001, the CIPRA introduced the first accreditation examination for public relations practitioners (www.cipra.org.cn/english/memo/memo1.htm).

Culbertson and Chen (1996) describe public relations professors in China treating theory and practice equally, using Confucius and other classic Chinese philosophers, in addition to Western ideas.

Australasia

Although there are historical, cultural and economic differences between Australia and New Zealand, public relations has evolved in similar ways. The development of public relations in New Zealand has been described as following a meeting in the Auckland Star Hotel in 1954, which led to the creation of the Public Relations Institute of New Zealand (PRINZ). Singh and Smyth (2001) state that public relations practitioners in New South Wales formed a professional body in Australia, five years ahead of practitioners in New Zealand, which led to the national Public Relations Institute of Australia (PRIA), which has divisions in all states. The PRIA currently has over 3,000 members.

Australia has developed an approach to public relations education, which bridges and cooperates between educators and practitioners. Formal education in public relations began in New Zealand in the latter part of the 1960s.

Summary

The pattern that emerges from this brief survey of the development of professional organisations and PR education in a range of countries is that most of the former were founded in the post-war period, with exceptions where democracy (or, in the case of China, capitalism) was not established until later.

Most early practitioners in the countries covered were originally journalists, a fact that influenced the content of early PR education. This largely consisted of technical training for many years, with a growth of theoretical and reflective approaches at undergraduate and postgraduate levels in the 1990s. Some countries are still in the technical stage, with PR officers envisaged as little more than 'errand boys' (Deflagbe 2004). Most have found a correlation between the development of under- and postgraduate courses and the status of the profession as a whole (see also Case Study 6.1).

Who does what: the bigger picture

Definitions of field

Early on in the text we explored the historical evolution of PR and discussed the various definitions that are provided from a range of sources, including academics, practitioners, national and international professional bodies.

This lack of an agreed definition is, however, still a problem for the practice. Deciding what it is and what people do has evidently caused much distraction and expenditure of individual and collective energies. Some of the long-winded definitions still do not easily convey what the discipline stands for and what people do. Fawkes (2008) argues that the synthesised UK CIPR definition of PR, below, is one that at least simplifies the discussion and helps students and practitioners understand what it is they do or should be doing: 'Public relations is about reputation – the result of what you do, what you say and what others say about you' (Chartered Institute of Public Relations 2005).

Tench and Deflagbe (2008) state that public relations (PR) education is responding to the challenges of the globalisation of communication and economies – but slowly and unevenly. They identify that problems defining the field are multiplied when the different cultural perspectives on public relations itself come into play. Even within Europe the term has varying connotations reflecting cultural associations with 'the public sphere'. Several scholars express concern that the lack of a central concept for PR is weakening its hold in the marketplace. These debates in the literature reflect tensions between academics and between academics and practitioners, and illustrate some of the problems facing the project of a global curriculum (see also Chapter 5 for a discussion on intercultural and multicultural issues for public relations).

Professional bodies, academics and most practitioners are keen to ensure that education continues to play its crucial role in improving the professional standards of public relations, producing reflective and engaged practitioners and enhancing, rather than limiting, public relations' important role in the changing global environment.

However, modern ideas about PR are moving away from reputation management as the key concept, to relationship building, so the CIPR definition may be revised or fade from use. The Public Relations Society of America adopted a new definition of public relations in March 2012. It reads:

> *Public relations is a strategic communication process that builds mutually beneficial relationships between organizations and their publics.*

Note also the rather different description by the Spanish public relations association (www.adecec.com) and also the varied country profiles of public relations in Box 6.2. In fact, it is worth pointing out that the problem with definitions extends to problems with language. As Verčič et al. (2001) point out, the term 'public relations' is founded wholly on US references and does not translate across the Atlantic. Their own three-year research programme on PR in Europe (European Body of Knowledge (EBOK)) showed that all except English speakers had problems with the term 'public relations'. For example, the German *Öffentlichkeitsarbeit* carries associations with the public sphere and public opinion, perhaps rooted in the origins of European PR through public bodies, such as central and local government, rather than the corporate work of early PR in the United States.

So, shall we abandon the search for a decent description? It could be said that it encourages ringfencing and competition and works against integrated communication approaches to problem solving. Other disciplines, such as marketing, share these challenges.

However, Hutton (2001) says that PR has lost the battle for supremacy with marketing and is terminally threatened by its failure 'to define itself and to develop sophisticated and progressive theory' or develop its central tenet or core concept. He comments that 'there remains a critical need for public relations to define its intellectual and practical domain . . . to regain control of its own destiny' (2001: 205). See Explore 6.3.

The debate continues to unfold in journals and textbooks and at conferences, and will do so for years to come. In the meantime, students and practitioners still need to be able to describe their jobs in terms meaningful to their

---

Explore 6.3

Job descriptions

One way of gathering information about what PR practitioners do is to look at the job ads. Find a publication or look online at *PR Week* or *The Guardian* for PR jobs (see www.prweek.com or jobs.guardian.co.uk/job/marketing-and-pr). Read the adverts and make a note of what the employers are looking for. What job titles are advertised? What skills do they mention? How many ask for relevant qualifications? What specific knowledge (e.g. social media)? What personal qualities?

Feedback

Some of the job titles will vary, even for similar positions. The duties described may not vary so much. The differences and similarities in these ads offer real insight into what people do in PR.

Picture 6.1 Malcolm Tucker (actor Peter Capaldi), is a fictional UK Government 'spin doctor' in the BBC's acclaimed satirical TV programme, *The Thick of It*, which was also made into a feature film, *In the Loop* (*source*: The Kobal Collection)

friends and family. This chapter aims to provide information and insight to assist in that goal.

Of course, the answers to many of the questions raised by Explore 6.3 will depend on the type of role, its level and whether it is in-house or consultancy. The next section looks at how organisations see the role of the PR practitioner, before going on to look at what individuals do on a daily basis.

Case study 6.1
Public relations in Mexico

The closest Latin American neighbour to the United States, Mexico, is the focus of much interest from the international business community, particularly following the signing of the North American Free Trade Agreement between the United States, Canada and Mexico in 1994. Despite rapid economic development, Mexico continues to be recognised as one of the countries with significant socioeconomic inequality in the region. The country has experienced significant political transition within the last decade, as the system has moved away from a 70-year one-party rule to a more 'democratically inspired' government. The democratic imperative is thematic to Mexican development and building the foundations for trust is significant in a society that is seeking to overcome deep and longstanding sentiments of '*desconfianza*' (a lack of trust) in the political system and institutions of power. In these times of change, a new condition of dialogue has emerged in Mexico creating a wealth of opportunity for public relations (PR) practitioners.

As social agents, PR practitioners are open to certain socio-cultural and globally influenced conditions and situations. Public relations is an industry that is regarded as constantly changing, but in regions such as Latin America these changes are much quicker in instance due to a series of socioeconomic factors. PR professionals are exposed to harsh realities, both professionally and personally, and, as a consequence, practice in Latin America has developed by shaping its own profile based on the political, economic and social conditions present in the area. Public relations in Mexico developed after the Second World War under the influence of larger international companies – primarily those of US origin – and state development programmes. The 'professional' practice was reborn as a result of free trade agreements, particularly the NAFTA agreement, which came into force in 1994. The absence of indigenous research and a dependence on concepts and theories from elsewhere has meant that, at first glance, the PR industry in Mexico appears to have taken on a distinctly American 'look'. When we begin to explore beneath the surface, however, it becomes clear that the Mexican paradigm of public relations is not the same as that of the United States. Public relations in Mexico is reflective of the Latin American '*Corriente*' (or 'School') of public relations, which Molleda and Connolly-Ahern (2002)

case study 6.1 (continued)

suggests has a more humanist focus and is based on acceptable social behaviour and harmony. Public relations in Latin America, according to Molleda, is about integrating the organisation in its environment and, therefore, contributing to the development of the community and the organisation.

The nature of professional public relations practice in Mexico is immersed in capitalism, competition and globalisation. The practice tends to be concentrated in a handful of wealthy cities and economic inequality and high levels of illiteracy continue to affect the implementation of PR efforts throughout the country. A Mexican phrase that best describes the activity of public relations and the role of the PR practitioner in Mexico is *'un chile de todos los moles'* – a bit of everything. Some practitioners regard themselves as *'publirelacionistas'* (public relations practitioners), while others, particularly those working in social communication within the government or public institutions, refer to themselves as *'comunicologos'* (communicologists). Those who regard themselves as *'communicologos'* are more typically practitioners who have entered public relations from a journalism background and whose PR responsibility is focused on press/media relations.

The professional values relevant to PR practitioners in Mexico include transparency and access to information, solidarity, symmetry, strategic vision and social responsibility. Practitioners believe that in order for their country to progress, it needs to have a global vision and to 'participate' in global affairs. This would require a public relations practitioner to not only be an effective communicator but to have a degree, be able to speak English almost perfectly (and possibly more languages), and to understand their own culture as well as others and how to adapt to different cultural needs. Practitioners in Mexico, therefore, would require a close understanding and analysis of the social, political and economic environments that organisations and clients face.

The true effectiveness of public relations in Mexico City is established in the possibility of developing interpersonal means of communicating messages to build bridges and forge links in order to overcome obstacles. Interactions with other people play a significant role in shaping practitioner behaviour. The PR practitioner in Mexico would communicate a particular sense of 'character', a Mexican *'Don de gente'* – someone who combines a natural flair for communication with an interest in people, and would use interpersonal strategies to achieve their aims. While using *'palanca'* (a form of patronage) to build influential personal relationships between business leaders and politicians is rapidly becoming a thing of the past, practitioners seek to

develop a rapport with networks of people and use opinion formers and personal influencers to communicate key messages, either face to face or via television.

PR practitioners in Mexico share a sense of responsibility to participate proactively in the transition toward more participative and ethical democratic systems. They regard their work as a source of social integration that facilitates community participation. RELAPO (Profesionales en Relaciones Publicas del Occidente), a professional association for public relations, uses the term 'Huehuetlatolli' to describe their approach to public relations. The term refers to the patron of community interaction (or mediator) in Aztec society who held the responsibility for passing on ethical values and wisdom to the public. RELAPO believes that this model of communication might inspire public relations activity today – encouraging Mexicans to live in order and peace, while at the same time encouraging prosperity and cultural growth.

It is difficult for the PR practitioner to always maintain his or her personal and professional ethics in a country that has suffered so many brisk political and social changes, and it often calls for 'improvisation'. Practitioner ethics, therefore, are culturally mediated visions of right and wrong, a combination of internal morality, group cohesion and professional and societal influence. They are grounded in trust, or *'confianza'*. One way of helping to reshape society is through transparency of practice and access to information. Practitioners regard public relations as a public service that facilitates and encourages knowledge and understanding and are conscious of the need to avoid any direct or indirect association with political parties, politicians or political issues as the media and publics could interpret this association as corruption.

Mexican people have traditionally put family before the community and there has been marginal interest in, or encouragement to become involved with, volunteer or community issues. Private organisations are slowly increasing their contribution to community development, however. While there has been a tendency for the Mexican people to believe that the main direction of social welfare should be guided by governments, ever increasing numbers regard such social responsibility as a positively shared activity among the private, public and not-for-profit sectors. Corporate social responsibility, therefore, represents a significant potential area for growth within the public relations industry in Mexico.

Source: based on the findings from qualitative case study research conducted in Mexico City between 2004 and 2006 by Dr Caroline Hodges at Bournemouth University.

Role of the communicator

Elsewhere in the text we discuss the division between managers and technicians in PR practice. However, the dichotomy is not always clear-cut. Most PR practitioners are involved in both manager and technician work, but it is generally accepted that one role may dominate. On entry into the practice, and at the start of their career, most recruits are given technical tasks. Through experience and after time this generally means they move on to fulfilling the more managerial role (see Mini case studies on practitioner roles and responsibilities and Figure 6.1).

The emphasis on these roles of the communicator has also had an effect on the advancement of women in PR, as is explored more fully later in the text. Another issue about the roles of communicators is that so many of the texts are US-based.

In many ways, the struggle to define the role of the communicator has an edge to it: this is not just an academic debate; PR practitioners need to demonstrate their value to the employing organisations – whether it is reputation management or relationship building that they are offering. Neither is the comparison with financial or legal aspects of an organisation misplaced. As Hutton (2001: 214) points out, the failure to have a clear rationale for PR has led to erosion of its base:

> *Many corporate public relations departments have lost responsibility for crisis communications to management consulting firms and marketing departments, some have lost responsibility for corporate identity programmes to marketing departments, some have lost government relations to legal departments, and some have lost internal/employee communications to human resources departments.*

These debates are supported by European research (Zerfass et al. 2008) in a survey of 1,500 communications professionals across 37 countries. The detailed survey revealed that 75 per cent of practitioners believe they are taken seriously by senior management but only 64 per cent are actually involved in decision making and planning. This research has been conducted every year since 2007 as

Picture 6.2 The European Communication Monitor (ECM) is a longitudinal research project looking into communication trends. The ECM has been running since 2007 and is the largest transnational research project in public relations (www.communicationmonitor.eu) (*source*: Institute of Communication and Media Studies)

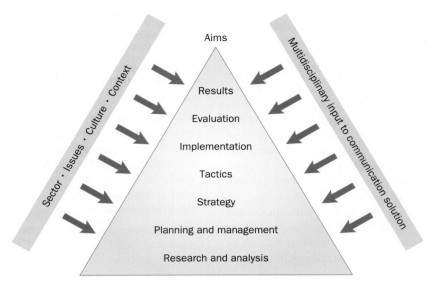

Figure 6.1 The PR practitioner as 'communicator'

a longitudinal study to enable annual comparisons of trends in public relations across Europe. For 2012, the number of countries expanded to 42 countries with 2,295 senior communicators responding to an in-depth, online survey (see www.communictionmonitor.eu). From the 2012 data there were some interesting findings on the evolving complexity of communication, which affects the role of the modern practitioner. For example, from the sample, 82 per cent of practitioners believe their organisations have more 'touchpoints' with their publics (stakeholders) compared with five years earlier. Also, 74 per cent believe the 'organisational voice' is created by all organisational members interacting with stakeholders, supporting the notion that all employees are part of the public relations team.

The drive to get on the board of directors is also connected to the desire to be taken seriously. There is some success in this area: as Box 6.1 shows, all the top 100 companies in Britain have PR departments. The question is, how much authority do they have within those companies? A survey by Watson Helsby Consultancy of PR directors at 28 of Britain's top companies, including BP, Vodafone and HSBC, found that while most reported directly to the chief executive, many failed to get the attention of the board. The survey found that only 30 per cent of PR people sat on their company executive committees and none on the board (*Financial Times* 22 October 2003).

Other evidence suggests a flourishing time ahead for PR. For example, PR was considered the best return on investment by entrepreneurs in a survey for the *Financial Times* in 2004, as shown in Figure 6.2.

Mini case study 6.1 illustrates the kind of career available in PR and the richness (and challenge) of the PR role

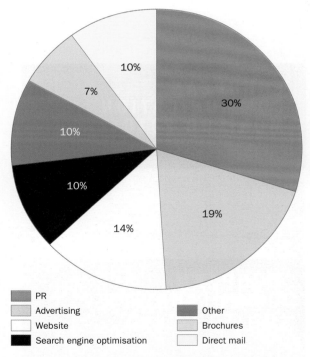

PR
Advertising   Other
Website   Brochures
Search engine optimisation   Direct mail

Figure 6.2 What type of marketing activity gives the best return on investment for startup SMEs? (*source*: after *FT Creative Business* 13 July 2004, based on research by new2marketing accessed www.ipr.org.uk, 20 July *Financial Times*)

at a senior level. The communicator is often expected to play a wide range of roles.

The PR practitioner must be adaptable, energetic, versatile, diplomatic and resilient to get along with a mixed

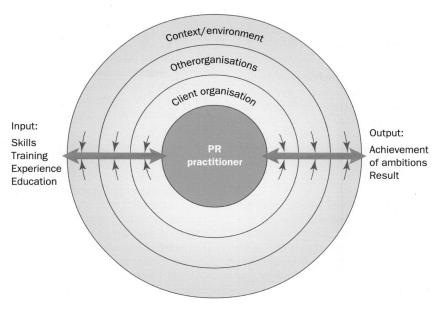

Figure 6.3 PR practitioner role within systems theory

group of clients and stakeholder groups. Pieczka refers to the existence of 'an expertise which is distinctive yet flexible enough to be applicable across a wide field', and suggests that public relations expertise is a complex interactive structure organised through past experience and current exigencies (demands), which modifies itself through action (Pieczka 2002: 321–322).

This perspective would suggest that there is no one paradigm or template for the role, but that it is a dynamic process created through the interface of our past and our interactions with the present. Figure 6.3, presents a model that uses systems theory as the basis for the concept of this role as a dynamic, interactive and open system.

Mini case study 6.1

Katherine Bennett OBE – UK Director of Communications and Government Affairs, Airbus SAS UK

Role at Airbus

Katherine joined Airbus in August 2004 and became UK Director of Communications and Government Affairs in 2007. She commenced the role of Vice President, Head of Political Affairs for Airbus SAS in October 2010. Her government affairs role encompassed managing relationships between Airbus and national, regional and local government. She takes the lead on all public policy issues affecting the company and ensures that key government and interested stakeholders are kept informed and aware of company developments. Her time is split between Bristol, where Airbus SAS UK's HQ is based, and an office in Westminster, London. The Government Affairs Department has a direct reporting function to the managing director in the UK.

In the public affairs industry, the managing director's direct involvement is a prerequisite for the function. Government affairs need to be integral in company strategy and direction. This integration can take a number of forms, whether in considerations over avoidance of risk, ensuring there is a supportive legislative background for the company's forward plans and product development or indeed issues surrounding sustainability and CSR.

Airbus's Communications Team is a sister department to Government Affairs and the two functions are closely aligned, which allows joint allocation of resources when required and the necessary coordination of messages to Airbus's key audiences.

mini case study 6.1 (continued)

Issue management

Airbus is the market leader in aircraft manufacturing and sales, employing over 50,000 people worldwide, of whom 13,000 are in the UK and represent highly skilled research and development (R&D) and manufacturing jobs. The UK business is the Airbus 'Centre of Excellence' for wing design and manufacture and also heads up the integration of landing gear and fuel systems for Airbus aircraft.

One of Katherine's first challenges was to ensure the UK business was fully represented and involved in the unveiling of the new A380 aircraft. With the capacity of seating 555 passengers, this is the largest civil airliner ever launched and brought a completely new dimension to the aircraft market in terms of customer offering and innovative systems technology.

The unveiling ceremony took place in Toulouse, France, in front of over 5,000 assembled media, government representatives and customer representatives. Katherine undertook the coordination of the logistics, media activity and protocol surrounding the participation of UK Prime Minister Tony Blair. The key part of this activity was to ensure the smooth running of a two-way satellite link between Blair and Airbus employees back in the UK.

The event was probably one of the largest product unveilings ever seen and the media coverage reflected this. Over 500 media representatives with 60 film crews attended the ceremony. In the UK, the event attracted 650 separate items of media coverage, including BBC/ITV main TV news slots of more than two minutes. The Airbus website had live coverage, and received 3,419,398 hits that day.

Background

Katherine is a member of the Chartered Institute of Public Relations and graduated in history and politics from Leicester University. She has a postgraduate diploma in marketing from the Chartered Institute of Marketing. Katherine's previous employment was with Vauxhall/GM UK, where for nearly nine years she also headed up their government affairs function. Her time at Vauxhall involved managing numerous public policy lobbying campaigns and issues management such as major industrial restructuring programmes and CSR. Her time with GM included several months based in the USA. Before joining Vauxhall, Katherine was an account manager in the Public Affairs Department of Hill and Knowlton (an international PR company), working on behalf of energy, charity and automotive clients. While at Hill and Knowlton she undertook several in-house training courses. Katherine was awarded the Order of the British Empire in June 2004 for services to the motor industry and charity.

Source: based on interview with author and information supplied by Katherine Bennett

Systems theory works on the basis that everything in the social world is part of a system that interacts with other systems, in that the whole equals more than the sum of its parts (von Bertalanffy 1969). Building on the work of Katz and Kahn (1978), PR scholars (e.g. Cutlip et al. 2000, 2008) use systems theory to explain the interactions between organisations and their environments, interactions between organisations and interactions within organisations. (Systems theory is fully explained in Chapter 7.)

This model assumes that the PR practitioner is part of an open system interacting with other systems, and therefore the nature of the role will not be fixed but depend on the influences both in and out of the system, from early experiences and education through to ongoing **continuing professional development (CPD)**. Key to this model is that the system does not exist in isolation, but only exists insofar as it relates to other systems. This model also reaffirms that the PR practitioner as counsel must be aware of the context of their own role, and the context of the organisation or client they are representing, and acting as the 'boundary spanner'. That requires an interest in, and understanding of, the wider community, whether it is political, economic, sociological or any number of other ways to frame the narrative of the twenty-first century.

There is an increasing body of research, with enormous potential for further development, for looking at the role of the practitioner and using a number of methodologies to explain and measure the role. Moss et al. (2004) have

Definition: *CPD (continuing professional development)* acknowledges in all professions (law, medicine, accountancy, PR, etc.) the role of continued learning and updating throughout the career.

identified a number of common themes in both the UK and USA among senior practitioners, such as their part in the dominant coalition and their contribution to strategic decision making.

Wilkin (2001) provides an interesting and controversial perspective on the implications of global communication; Allan (2000) on the social divisions and hierarchies reproduced by the news media. Research among employers' needs in graduates tends to highlight the requirement for employees who can manage change and understand the context the organisation is functioning in, and can evidence the more abstract cognitive powers.

The argument supports the idea that the role of the PR practitioner is a very wide-ranging one, far wider than many PR exponents might feel happy with, but worth considering if we want to move PR onto a higher plane. Those with a background in corporate communications will already recognise the role. It is often with the introduction of a corporate communicator and the playing out of territorial and functional wars that the true potential of a role, which both oversees and connects, is appreciated, not only by senior management but also by the organisation as a whole and significantly by other functions within the organisation (such as marketing). This is a role which, with the right training and development, can become synonymous with the PR role (see Figure 6.4). (See also Chapter 8 on the management and planning of PR activities.) See Think about 6.1.

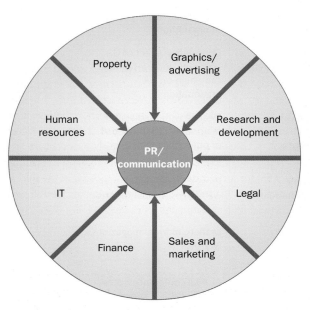

Figure 6.4 Public relations/communication role within an organisation

Think about 6.1

Public relations and its influence within organisations

Is there anywhere in the organisation where public relations does not have a role to play?

What public relations people do: individual practitioners

Lots of people work in PR and in a range of roles. As Explore 6.3 showed, there is a huge variety of job titles in trade or national newspapers, including public relations/corporate communications *consultant, executive, manager, director, officer, advisor, counsellor*, etc. To help us understand in more detail what these individuals are actually doing, it is necessary to simplify and classify the locations in which they are working. So, there are three simple categories of where people work in public relations:

1. In-house (employed by an organisation, whether a public or private company or a public body, charity or non-governmental organisation, NGO).

2. Consultancy (agency where practitioners work for one or more different clients for a fee).

3. Freelance practitioner (where an individual works for himself and is employed by in-house departments or consultancies on a short-term contract basis, either for a specific project or to fill in during peaks in demand or because staff absence requires additional resource).

While much of the work is the same across these categories, there are key differences:

■ In-house: get to know one organisation in depth; work across wide range of PR activities, from writing/editing house journal to arranging visits by or to MPs/opinion-formers, etc.; get to know a sector or industry well, e.g. music, motoring.

■ Consultancy: work across many accounts; variety of clients; changing environment; may work in specialist area such as technology, finance or public affairs.

Fawkes (2008) argues that understanding the practice is helped by analysing how people engage in different activities. She does this by describing the common PR areas, with examples of what practitioners will do in each area (see Table 6.1, Box 6.3 and Explore 6.4).

Public relations activity	Explanation	Examples
Internal communication	Communicating with employees	In-house newsletter, suggestion boxes
Corporate PR	Communicating on behalf of whole organisation, not goods or services	Annual reports, conferences, ethical statements, visual identity, images
Media relations	Communicating with journalists, specialists, editors from local, national, international and trade media, including newspapers, magazines, radio, TV and web-based communication	Press releases, photocalls, video news releases, off-the-record briefings, press events
Business to business	Communicating with other organisations, e.g. suppliers, retailers	Exhibitions, trade events, newsletters
Public affairs	Communicating with opinion-formers, e.g. local/national politicians, monitoring political environment	Presentations, briefings, private meetings, public speeches
Community relations/ corporate social responsibility	Communicating with local community, elected representatives, headteachers, etc.	Exhibitions, presentations, letters, meetings, sports activities and other sponsorship
Investor relations	Communicating with financial organisations/ individuals	Newsletters, briefings, events
Strategic communication	Identification and analysis of situation, problem and solutions to further organisational goals	Researching, planning and executing a campaign to improve ethical reputation of organisation
Issues management	Monitoring political, social, economic and technological environment	Considering effect of US economy and presidential campaign on UK organisation
Crisis management	Communicating clear messages in fast-changing situation or emergency	Dealing with media after major rail crash on behalf of police, hospital or local authority
Copywriting	Writing for different audiences to high standards of literacy	Press releases, newsletters, web pages, annual reports
Publications management	Overseeing print/media processes, often using new technology	Leaflets, internal magazines, websites
Events management, exhibitions	Organisation of complex events, exhibitions	Annual conferences, press launches, trade shows

Table 6.1 Examples of what public relations people do (*source*: Fawkes 2004)

Box 6.3

Public relations competency debate – some definitions

Knowledge: can be defined as what practitioners are required to know in order to do their job/role effectively (see PRSA 1999, 2006; Gregory 2008).

Skills: these are the things practitioners are able to do to perform their job/role effectively (PRSA 1999, 2006; Goodman 2006; Gregory 2008). Identifying 'skill' will be

a complex process, but a useful definition by Proctor and Dutta (1995) will help us: 'goal-directed, well-organized behaviour that is acquired through practice and performed with economy of effort' (p.18).

Personal attributes: are defined in the literature as separate from competencies, the distinction being that personal attributes can determine how well a competency is performed and secondly competencies can be taught, while personal attributes are modelled or fostered (Jeffrey and Brunton 2011: 69).

Competencies: are the sets of behaviours the person can perform. These behaviours are based on the application, combination and potential integration of knowledge and skills (see Boyzatis 1982; Gregory 2008; Jeffrey and Brunton 2011; Tench et al. 2013b).

Explore 6.4

In-house and consultancy jobs

Look at the job ads you gathered in Explore 6.3. How many of them are for in-house, how many are for consultancy jobs? What differences are there in the skills, qualifications and interests they require?

Feedback

It may be easier to find in-house jobs, especially for public sector jobs, as they are more likely to advertise in national newspapers. Consultancies often advertise in *PR Week* in the UK, or recruit informally through word of mouth and 'headhunting' (asking an individual to change agencies). You can find out about some of these jobs by looking at a PR agency's website.

Skills for the ideal practitioner

So what skills are needed to work in PR? It would probably be quicker to identify those that are not required, although that is not easy either. Because there are so many kinds of work and so many kinds of employer, there is room in PR for everyone, from the extrovert party person to the researcher glued to the PC.

However, some indication of what employers are looking for can be gleaned by their responses to questions posed by Fawkes and Tench (2004b) (see Table 6.2). This research shows that there was agreement from employers that literacy was the primary skill required by PR graduates. Both in-house and consultancy employers also ranked teamwork as the next most important attribute, followed by problem solving, analytical thinking, research skills, IT skills and numeracy. There were some variations between the employer groups, with in-house employers giving

Table 6.2 Key graduate skills (*source*: Fawkes and Tench 2004b)

Employers – combined evaluation of skills	Not important	%	Fairly important	%	Very important	%
Numeracy	7	7	65	63	28	27
Literacy	0	0	0	0	101	98
IT skills	2	2	49	47.5	49	47.5
Problem solving	1	1	21	20	77	75
Analytical thinking	0	0	26	25	73	70
Teamwork	0	0	11	10	87	84
Research skills	0	0	56	54	45	44

greater weighting to IT skills over research skills – the opposite of consultants' priorities.

Another insight into skills required by PR practitioners can be found in the results of the major research-based investigations into PR education in the United States, presented in the Public Relations Society of America (PRSA) 'Port of Entry' report (1999) and the follow up report, 'The Professional Bond' (2006) (see Table 6.3). This surveyed employers and debated with other academics before concluding that the range of knowledge and skills listed in Table 6.3 were desirable in PR practitioners.

More interesting work on the skills and capabilities of practitioners has been developed through the largest EU-funded public relations research project into practitioner skills and competencies – the European Communication Skills and Innovation Programme (ECOPSI, Tench et al. 2012, 2013a, b and c).

While the DTI/IPR report (2003) is not about education but practice and the future of the sector, it is notable that the practitioner requirements shown in Table 6.4 are very much more limited than those suggested by practitioners and educators in the United States.

Table 6.3 'Port of Entry' and 'Professional Bond' recommendations on knowledge and skills (*source*: PRSA 1999, 2006)

Necessary knowledge includes	Necessary skills include
Communication and public relations theories	Research methods and analysis
Societal trends	Management of information
Legal requirements and issues	Problem solving and negotiation
Public relations history	Management of communication
Multicultural and global issues	Strategic planning
Participation in the professional PR community	Issues management
Working with a current issue	Audience segmentation
Applying cross-cultural and cross-gender sensitivity	Informative and persuasive writing
Communication and persuasion concepts and strategies	Community relations, consumer relations, employee relations, other practice areas
Relationships and relationship building	Technological and visual literacy
Ethical issues	Managing people, programmes and resources
Marketing and finance	Sensitive interpersonal communication
Use of research and forecasting	Fluency in a foreign language
Organisational change and development	Ethical decision making
Message production	
Public speaking and presentation	

Table 6.4 DTI/IPR recommendations on knowledge and skills (*source*: based on DTI/IPR 2003)

Necessary knowledge includes	Necessary skills include
Understanding of business	Written and verbal communication
Corporate strategy	Creativity
Finance and corporate governance	Media relations
Data analysis	Crisis management
Audience research	Issues management
Management of resources and people	Interpersonal skills
	Credibility and integrity
	Flexibility

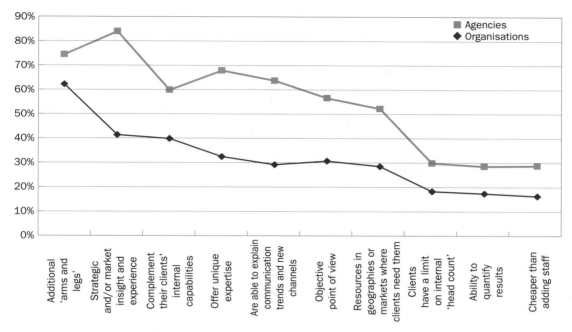

Figure 6.5 Reasons for cooporation: different perceptions between PR agencies and their clients (*source*: Zerfass et al. (2008), European Communication Monitor 2008, Trends in Communication Management and Public Relations – Results and Implications Brussels, Leipzig: Euprera/University of Leipzig Nov. 2008. Available as a free pdf at www.communicationmonitor.eu)

Furthermore, research suggests that some practitioners may exaggerate their contribution, particularly consultants. Zerfass et al. (2008), for example, showed that 83 per cent of respondents working in agencies (consultancies) thought that they were used for strategic and/or market insight/experience. However, only 42 per cent of their clients agreed (see Figure 6.5). Further to the 2008 survey, the 2012 European Monitor research found that both advisory and executive influence were down in Europe. Advisory influence is the perception of how seriously senior managers take the recommendations of communication professionals, and executive influence is the perception of how likely it is that communication representatives will be invited to senior-level meetings dealing with organisational strategic planning. The perception of advisory influence went down from nearly 78 per cent in 2011 to less than 70 per cent in 2012. Executive influence went down from almost 77 per cent to 72 per cent (Zerfass et al. 2011, 2012). 2012 was the first year since the monitor started that these figures have dropped. A comparison shows that communication functions in the United States are better in these dimensions on average – however, all Scandinavian states, as well as Germany, the United Kingdom and The Netherlands, report a stronger and partially much stronger executive influence (see Figure 6.6).

From the 2008 European ECM study, when results were compared with data from a US study, it was apparent that clients in Europe are less dependent on agencies than their counterparts in the US. See Figure 6.7.

Before turning to the academic debates about skills, it is worth looking at Mini case study 6.2, which lists the kind of skills required by one particular sector – financial and investor relations (IR). (See also Chapter 21.)

Mini case study 6.2
Financial investor relations skills

- Understand in depth how the markets work
- Count top opinion-formers among contacts
- Able to talk to top broadsheet financial journalists
- Have the ear of the board members, if not on the board
- Understand the financial calendar and rules/regulations of the Stock Exchange
- Overview of all communication activity related to financial and investor relations
- Oversee production of annual report, etc.
- Effective proofreading skills/on-press checking
- Manage media events
- Train senior management in media interviews
- Produce media and other stakeholder information

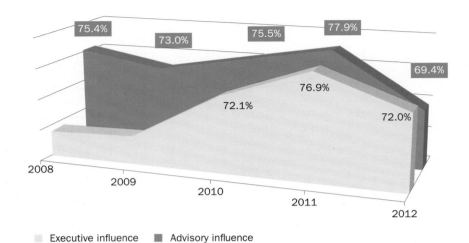

www.communicationmonitor.eu / Zerfass et al. 2012 / n = 1,712 PR professionals working in communication departments. Advisory influence, Q 26: In your organisation, how seriously do senior managers take the recommendations of the communication function? / Executive influence, Q 27: How likely is it, within your organisation, that communication would be invited to senior-level meetings dealing with organisational strategic planning?; Zerfass et al. 2011 / n = 1,449, Q7; Zerfass et al. 2010 / n = 1,511; Q4; Zerfass et al. 2009 / n = 1,267; Q3 / Zerfass et al. 2008 / n = 1,027; Q1. Executive influence: wording in the questionnaire was changed 2010 in line with the US GAP surveys (Swerling et al. 2012). Scale 1 (never) – 7 (always). Considered scale points 5–7.

Figure 6.6 Decline in influence across Europe? (*source*: Zerfass et al. (2012). European Communication Monitor 2012. Challenges and Competencies for Strategic Communication. Results of an Empirical Survey in 42 countries. Brussels: EACD/EUPRERA, p. 46)

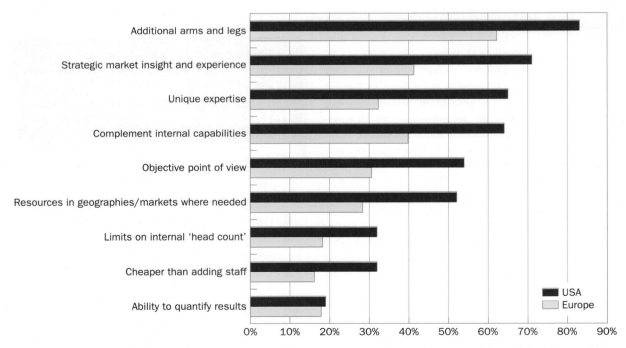

Figure 6.7 Clients in Europe are less dependent on agencies than those in the US (*source*: Zerfass et al. (2008), European Communication Monitor 2008. Trends in Communication Management and Public Relations – Results and Implications Brussels, Leipzig: Euprera/University of Leipzig, Nov. 2008. Available as a free pdf at www.communicationmonitor.eu)

The skills debate

What skills do PR practitioners need in order to deliver results effectively and how do they acquire these skills? The wider UK contextual framework for education and training puts skills centre stage. In some ways this has worked in favour of PR education and training. No one will argue with the need for 'skills' in one form or another. In many areas, the creative industries (which include public relations consultancies) are seen as a growth sector. The debate over skills has been muddied by the different terminologies employed and by the fact that, whereas some skills may be transferable and portable, others are very subject specific. Undergraduates may lack basic literacy skills; for example, something we might (and practitioners do, according to Fawkes and Tench (2004a)) see as essential for the PR role. A look at the job specs for PR positions today reveals an increasing trend for online media skills, especially at executive level.

Skills have become an integral component of benchmarking (setting achievement and quality levels), and are therefore now part of the curriculum. There has been a trend in the last decade towards generic skills and towards the involvement of employers and educationalists in defining those skills. This has led to new concepts, such as 'employability' and 'externality'. These have translated in the UK into the requirement for all students to have a personal progress file, which records and reflects on their individual achievements, and which follows on from school-based records of achievement. This sits well with the portfolio-based work of many PR-related HE courses. As discussed earlier, skills is also an important agenda item for practitioners in the training, development and continuing evolution of the practice (see Tench et al. 2012, 2013a, b and c).

This at least provides us with a potential paradigm for the PR practitioner where they become a lifelong learner and are able to reflect on their own learning and development throughout their career (and beyond). Education and training does not end with the last day of term or the last exam. From school, through education and training (where learning logs or portfolios are used to evidence and assess certain skills, including reflection), through to CPD responsibility for our own learning, we never stop learning (see Mini case study 6.3).

Mini case study 6.3
A student placement with MINI (Emma Knight)

I realised my interest in the PR profession as the UK government's 'spin doctors' were frantically 'burying bad news' in the wake of September 11th. I wondered who dealt with crisis management, image preservation and damage limitation.

Having worked for two years, I decided my first step was to get a good educational foundation. Navigating a diagonal career path from my current position (sales) to where I wanted to be (PR), seemed like the slow-track approach.

I opted for a university degree to give me the fundamental underpinning theory and practice required to kick-start my career. University also offered support from practising lecturers who encouraged me to take my industrial year placement.

This was how I came to work as a PR year-placement student for MINI in 2004 – an international brand and part of an international organisation, the BMW Group.

The environment in which I worked was fast-paced and continually changing. MINI was, and still is, one of the most exciting and fun brands in the motor industry, which provided lots of scope for PR. As a student, I was fortunate to be involved in projects at the strategic planning stages as well as implementation.

A typical day? There wasn't one. But that is the beauty of most PR roles, I think. Obviously there were some routine tasks, such as preparing press kits and collating daily press coverage, but the majority of my role was spent working on projects to support the brand. I would arrange logistics for events, book flights and hotels for journalists, compile itineraries for press trips and host journalists at events.

In order to get the information I required for a press release, make an event work or obtain permission for a certain activity, occasionally my 'typical day' would be spent on the phone or writing emails to nobody other than MINI and BMW Group employees.

I believe building internal relations is among the most challenging issues that an in-house PR practitioner must deal with. Cynical though it may seem, everyone needs a favour once in a while. If you haven't any favours to cash in on, a potentially simple job can become quite time-consuming.

PR as an industry is not always given the credibility it warrants. Fortunately, PR for MINI is considered a fundamental part of the brand's presentation. As a sector I believe practitioners will continue to face the ongoing challenge of being taken seriously. It is the responsibility of each practitioner to promote PR as an indispensable function that adds value to an organisation. Do it, if not for the sector, then for the sake of your budget!

Source: Emma Knight

Hargie (2000) suggests that competence in a profession involves three sets of skills:

1. cognitive (the knowledge base)
2. technical or manipulative skills inherent in a profession
3. social or communication skills.

He points out that education and training have usually focused on the first at the expense of interpersonal skills. For the PR practitioner, interpersonal skills must surely be as important as any other, and perhaps even a given.

This is a confusing situation, but the graduate in disciplines related to PR has the advantage that the sector already encompasses skills and employability as a key component, even intrinsic to the subject matter. Therefore, a portfolio that may evidence skills the student has mastered, illustrated in outcomes such as strategic campaign planning, online social media and activities, press release writing or event management, may also be valuable for taking around to interviews to show employers what the student can actually do and has done.

The Hargie approach to the skills debate, outlined above, mirrors the earlier suggestion that PR practitioners must have a wide range of skills to move up the continuum. The UK-based perspective is supported by evidence from the United States. The PRSA studies (1999, 2006) provide a wide perspective on addressing the 'next PR crisis', which is ensuring appropriate education and training. The emphasis here is on the complementary approach of knowledge that graduates are expected to have and skills specific to the profession (see Figure 6.8).

The model of the PR practitioner is now someone who encompasses both higher level and 'how to' skills, and is still (and always will be) learning. This provides a continuum with, at one end, someone ready to learn and, at the other, no end point as there is always room to learn more. What point they are at on that continuum will depend on background and experiences and the context in which they function. The school leaver who joins an agency on a trial period will be at one end of the continuum. If the employer provides in-house training, supports them through further education and training and the student wants to learn and develop, then they are as likely to get to the boardroom position in due course as someone who has come up a different route. They will be moving up the continuum. Their ability to succeed will be a combination of their own abilities and experiences and the expectations and input of others around them. This links well with the model of the practitioner as a system.

Competencies of public relations practitioners

What is clear from studies of skills, knowledge and personal attributes is that they overlap in terminology and that there is a pattern forming about how skills, knowledge and personal attributes lead to broader competencies (Tench et al. 2013a). Gregory (2008) uses the following definition of competencies in a study of senior communication managers in the UK: 'behavioural sets or sets of behaviours that support the attainment of organisational objectives. How knowledge and skills are used in performance' (p.216). This distinguishes competencies from skills, knowledge and personal attributes (see Table 6.5 and Figure 6.9).

Jeffrey and Brunton (2011) highlight the advantage of studying competencies over roles 'as . . . roles outline tasks and responsibilities in the job description, in today's dynamic workplace these same roles are likely to change frequently. In contrast, competencies are the underlying foundational abilities that are integral to successfully carrying out the tasks and responsibilities, and thus remain a stable blueprint for practice over time' (p.60).

The difficulty in establishing a workable definition of competencies has been discussed in work for the European Centre for the Development of Vocational training (CEDEFOP), which aimed to clarify the concepts of knowledge, skills and competences (Winterton et al. 2005). This highlights the usefulness of competences as providing a link between education (and skills) and job requirements (roles). For example, there is

- 'conceptual competence', which refers to knowledge about an entire domain;
- 'procedural competence', which refers to the application of conceptual competence in a particular situation; and

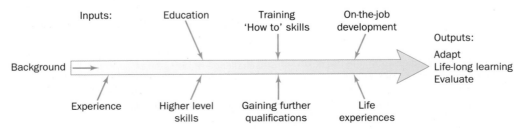

Figure 6.8 Public relations practitioner life cycle

Skills	Knowledge	Personal attributes
Writing and oral communication	Business knowledge/literacy	Handling pressure
Project planning and management	Current awareness	Leadership
Critical thinking	Theoretical knowledge	Integrity/honesty/ethical
Problem solving	Knowledge of PR history	Objectivity
Media skills	Knowledge of other cultures	Listening
Persuasion	Knowledge of communication models	Confidence/ambition
Strategic thinking	Knowledge of how to apply PR theory	Team player
Mentoring and coaching		Energy/motivation
Advanced communication skills		Discipline
IT skills (including new media channels)		Intelligence
Crisis management		Ability to get on with others/ interpersonal skills
Research		Wide interests
Reading comprehension		Intellectual curiosity
Community relations		Creativity
Consumer relations		Flexibility
Employee relations		Judgement and decision making
Professional service skills		Time management
Social responsibility		Respect for hierarchy
PR ethics		Follows organisational 'rules'
		Honesty
		Adaptability
		Integrity
		Ambition
		Reliable attendance
		Willingness to accept assignments
		Completes work on time

Table 6.5 Range of skills, knowledge and personal attributes identified in public relations literature (*sources*: Tench et al., 2012 and 2013b, adapted from Pieczka 2002; Oughton 2004; Brown and Fall 2005; Goodman 2006; McCleneghan 2006; Gregory 2008; Jeffrey and Brunton 2011; Sha 2011a)

■ 'performance competence', which is required to assess problems and select a suitable strategy for solving them (p.15).

In the context of public relations, Oughton (2004) suggests that there is a difficulty with defining competency because it can refer either to the ability to perform a task or how people should behave in order to carry out the role. Szyszka (1995) subdivides two categories of competencies of PR practitioners:

1. specific qualifications – those qualifications that are directly connected to the topic 'public relations'; and

2. unspecific qualifications – those qualifications, like leadership, that can be seen as a core competence for PR practitioners.

Although some studies have focused on the skills, knowledge and personal attributes of practitioners, there was no definitive research that brought these elements together in a single study until the EU-funded ECOPSI project (Tench et al. 2013a, b and c). Given the focus of roles and labelling practitioners according to the tasks they undertake, or where they are in the organisational hierarchy, specialisms are difficult to define. There is also a lack of research on social media practice within the PR sector, and the skills, knowledge and personal attributes needed to fulfil this role efficiently.

The ECOPSI programme has taken the broad labels provided by prior research and used them to examine four roles: internal communications, social media, crisis communication and communication director. This research fills a gap in knowledge about how these roles are enacted across Europe, and the skills, knowledge and personal attributes required, which subsequently contribute to the competencies needed by practitioners to fulfil these roles

efficiently. Figures 6.9 and 6.10 illustrates how ECOPSI views skills, knowledge and personal attributes.

Role of theory in practice

The value of theory as underpinning practice is up for discussion. Some practitioners will have managed very well for many years without theory, or rather they will have relied on their own version of common sense theory. Others have taken postgraduate courses, like a masters degree or professional postgraduate qualification (such as those from the CIPR) and been exposed to theory through education. Increasingly, public relations graduates who have studied theoretical modules in their degree courses are joining the profession and shaping the expectations of the next generation. The theory that practitioners have been exposed to will inform the role they play.

Relevant to this discussion is research conducted by Tench and Fawkes (2005) into PR education in Britain. Research was conducted with employers of PR students who were asked about different aspects of the curriculum and its value. In relation to theory, the practitioners were asked about the dissertation and how important it was as a core part of a public relations curriculum. The research found there was more enthusiasm for dissertations among in-house employers than consultancies, with over three-quarters (78 per cent) of the former supporting dissertations, as against 56 per cent of consultancies (see Figure 6.10).

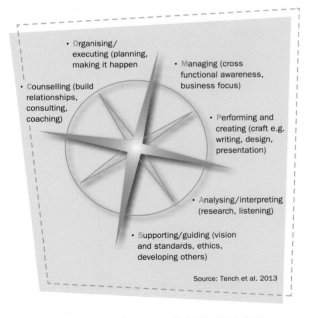

Source: Tench et al. 2013

Figure 6.10 COMPAS (Tench et al. 2012, 2013c). This acronym defines the competencies in the Communication Riles Matrix developed from the largest EU funded research project into communication in Europe, www.ecopsi.org.eu

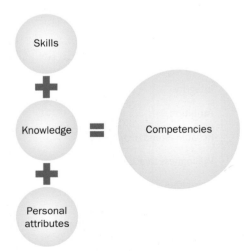

Figure 6.9 Skills, knowledge and personal attributes contributing to competencies (Tench et al. 2012, www.ecopsi.org.uk)

Qualitative comments help explain these responses. Support for the dissertation was expressed as: '[proves] the student's understanding and application of theory and practice, assuming that the topic of the dissertation is relevant'; 'closest thing to thinking through a situation from start to finish, which is what is required to handle PR campaigns for clients'; 'a dissertation shows an ability to think and analyse, takes planning and writing skills and hopefully places demands on a student'. It should be noted that a minority of employers were extremely dismissive of all theory, and dissertations in particular: 'PR is concise; dissertations are long', said one.

Tench and Fawkes argue that the supporters seem to appreciate what a dissertation involves, unlike the detractors who clearly place no value at all on abstract thought. They argue that there are serious implications 'for the intellectual health of the industry. There is also evidence of a "shopping list" approach to education, with [a number of] employers mentioning the lack of benefit to them of a dissertation.'

The range of theory relevant to PR is explored later in the text, but it is worth pointing out here that the majority of employers do value the role of theory in educating practitioners, albeit not so much as they value actual practical experience. Moreover, it is not only the views of employers that count in this debate. See Think about 6.2, as Cheney and Christensen (2001: 167) point out:

Still, it is important that a discipline's theoretical agenda not simply be beholden to trends already present or incipient in the larger society. Otherwise, a discipline can fail to exercise its own capacity for leadership on both practical and moral grounds.

Professionalism

The issue of defining PR to protect its jurisdiction (or borders), discussed at the beginning of this section, has an impact not only on practice, as described earlier, but also on issues concerning the professionalisation of PR (L'Etang and Pieczka 2006).

There are a number of different approaches (called 'trait' and 'process') to what defines a profession and some controversy over whether PR qualifies for the term. For example, practitioners are not licensed, as doctors or lawyers are – indeed, even the UK CIPR's 8,000 membership represent perhaps one-third, maybe less, of all eligible practitioners.

The 2000 Global Alliance of PR Associations, however, declared its guiding principles of professionalism to be characterised by:

1. mastery of a particular intellectual skill through education and training

2. acceptance of duties to a broader society than merely one's clients or employers

3. objectivity and high standards of conduct and performance.

The problematic nature of some of these concepts, such as defining or measuring 'objectivity' or the difficulties in controlling members' standards of behaviour, is not examined.

However, everyone agrees with the first point: that education plays a key part in establishing any profession.

Think about 6.2

Disciplines that inform public relations

Which subject disciplines could inform the PR role (apart from PR itself)?

Feedback

There are lots of disciplines that are relevant to the education and training of the PR practitioner:

- business and management/human resource management
- communication subject areas: marketing/marketing communication/advertising
- psychology
- cultural studies
- politics/sociology/social psychology
- media
- human geography.

The list is, in fact, endless. Are there any that are not in some way relevant?

Think about 6.3

Professions

Is PR a profession? Throughout this text we do use the term 'profession' and associate it clearly with PR. However, it is important to acknowledge that, according to sociological definitions of professions, there is debate about whether PR meets the criteria. This is a useful topic for future discussion, research and student dissertations.

L'Etang (2002) called education the 'crucial plank in PR's quest for professional status', and this view is shared by the PRSA 'Port of Entry' (1999), which quotes Kerr (1995) as saying 'a profession gains its identity by making the university the port of entry'.

The development of PR education is discussed in more detail below. However, to set the context, there has always been a tension between education as training for the profession and as an end in itself. Research (Chan 2000, cited in Rawel 2002) continues to show that practitioners want PR education to be primarily of service to the industry. The focus for many academics, including Neff and Grunig, is also employability and the perspective of the profession: 'Research must address problems faced by working professionals and be directed toward improvement of the profession' (Grunig and Grunig 2002: 36).

Research on the legitimacy of PRs to operate in 2008 identified that a revolution of the sector had been enhanced by developments in the digital generation, global integration and stakeholder empowerment (Johansson and Ottestig 2011: 146). However, despite the consequential communications needs generated by the Internet for business and organisations, PR's opportunity to gain 'internal status and legitimacy appear to be dependent on the attitudes of other executives' (ibid).

For PR, the route to professionalisation seems to be linked to boardroom acceptance, 'empowerment legitimacy is dependent on attitudes of senior executives' (Johansson and Ottestig 2011: 164). This view appears to be embedded in PR theory: 'degrees of influence are also leading factors in CEO's decision to grant a role within dominant coalition' (Berger 2005, quoted in Valentini 2010: 158).

Merkelson argues that 'theoretical development is a precondition to professionalisation'. It would seem that PR's role is less to do with legislation and established practice and more to do with social capital of the individual. 'Having extended personalised networks of influence is an asset for a career-conscious PR practitioner' (Valentini 2010: 160).

The 2012 ECM survey (Zerfass et al. 2012) focused on the issue of professionalism and ethics in practice. A large majority of the respondents stated that a lack of understanding of communication practice within the top management (84 per cent) and difficulties of the profession itself to prove the impact of communication activities on organisational goals (75 per cent) are the main barriers for further professionalisation of the practice. So, the key challenges for European communication professionals were reported as the need to explain the communication function to top management and to prove the value of communication for organisations. Other barriers are, in decreasing order, a shortage of up-to-date communication

training (54 per cent), a poor reputation of professional communication and public relations in society (52 per cent), the phenomenon that experience is valued more highly than formal qualifications in communication or public relations (52 per cent), and the status of PR and communication associations and professional bodies (40 per cent).

Although a lack of formal accreditation systems for the profession is only seen as a barrier by every fourth respondent, most practitioners did see advantages of such systems, which are already in place in the United Kingdom, Brazil and other countries. Seventy per cent of the respondents replied that national or international accreditation could help to improve the recognition and the reputation of the field. But only 58 per cent thought that a global accreditation system will help to standardise the practice of public relations, and 54 per cent agreed that accreditation ensures that practitioners will have proper knowledge of recent communication tools and trends.

The skills and attributes that chief executive officers (CEOs) are looking for in their top communications executives have expanded. Experience in communications is taken for granted, and not considered enough anymore. 'CEOs want communications executives who are business "savvy", with a deep understanding of their companies from top to bottom. CEOs also want communications chiefs to be proficient in three key modes of operation – reactive, proactive and interactive. CEOs see their communications chief as a critical part of their team, and across the board. There are categories of decision making in which CEOs would consider it grossly negligent not to have that individual at the table' (Arthur Page Society, Authentic Enterprise White Paper 2008). The European Communications Monitor (ECM) 2011 reports that 59.9 per cent of senior communicators in Europe report to the CEO and 17.8 per cent have a seat on the board, compared to 45 per cent of communications practitioners reporting to the CEO in the US (Arthur Page Society 2008), and close to 80 per cent of practitioners being a member of the senior management group in Sweden in 2009 (Johansson et al. 2011: 143).

This compares more favourably towards recognition of PR in the boardroom than a UK study, which recorded 6 per cent of senior practitioners were members of the management team, and 51 per cent of practitioners reported directly to CEO (Hogg and Doolan 1999).

From these four different research projects, spanning nearly ten years, it is clear that European PR practitioners are better represented in the boardroom than their US colleagues, and more of them report directly to the CEO. The ECM 2011 also shows a better representation at board level by PR practitioners in northern Europe than their colleagues working in southern Europe. 'Often the degree of influence and power held by PR practitioners are leading factors in determining CEOs' decisions of granting a role within the dominant coalition' (Berger 2005, cited in Valentini 2010: 158). It could therefore be argued that the legitimacy of the PR industry has been granted by this influential group of publics.

Research into CEOs' views on PR in the UK indicated that a valued practitioner understands the organisational context, stakeholder requirements, the business model and organisational drivers and has the confidence to challenge. However, CEOs recognise they 'under-invest in PR and that if there were the right measures to evaluate its contribution, they would spend more' (Gregory and Edwards 2011: 99).

While the profession has come a long way in ten years, it is still considered a soft discipline, rather than a core discipline, for many organisations (see Think about 6.3).

Representative bodies

Another requirement for a profession is the existence of a body that represents and, in some cases (although not for PR), licenses its members to practise. The UK's professional body is the Chartered Institute of Public Relations (CIPR). The industry also has a trade body called the Public Relations Consultants Association.

Key facts about the UK's Chartered Institute of Public Relations (CIPR)

- The CIPR was founded in 1948 and awarded charter status in 2005.
- The Institute has over 9,000 members, with a turnover of £3m.
- The CIPR is the largest professional body for PR practitioners in Europe.
- The CIPR is a founding member of the Global Alliance for Public Relations and Communication Management.
- CIPR membership has more than doubled in the last ten years.
- Approximately 60 per cent of its members are female – this has grown from only 20 per cent in 1987.
- Of its members, 45 per cent work in PR consultancy and 55 per cent work in-house.
- Two-thirds of CIPR members are based outside London.
- The CIPR has a strict code of conduct that all members must abide by.

Membership grades range from the following:

Affiliate: for those who are not currently working in PR but are interested in the public relations profession.

Associate ACIPR: for those who are currently working in or teaching PR (or temporarily unemployed) and have some (up to two years') PR experience, or who have graduated from the CIPR Advanced Certificate, or who have not yet gained any PR experience but have graduated from a CIPR-recognised course or have been a student member of the CIPR.

Member MCIPR: for those who are currently working in or teaching PR (or temporarily unemployed) and have more than two years' PR experience or have graduated from the CIPR Diploma.

Fellow FCIPR: open to UK and overseas practitioners and awarded by the Institute in recognition of significant contribution to the Institute or the industry.

Student: open to those studying on a UK higher education course lasting more than 12 months.

Global Affiliate: open to non-UK residents only.

The Institute represents and serves the interests of people working in PR, offering access to information, advice and support and providing networking and training opportunities through a wide variety of events, conferences and workshops.

The CIPR is represented throughout the UK by 14 regional groups and has groups for the following sectors:

Construction & Property: the group supports in-house and agency PR professionals within construction, residential and commercial property, architecture, building services, housebuilding, structural and civil engineering and other associated sectors. It organises events on industry-related best practice, site visits and useful networking opportunities.

Corporate & Financial: this group aims to improve the understanding of the role and value of corporate and financial public relations, both within the City and industry in general. It has regular meetings, with senior speakers from business, government and the media, and a full social programme offering excellent networking opportunities.

Education & Skills: this newly established group will emphasise the professional role and credibility of PR professionals in the education sector by providing a forum for serious debate, and sharing of knowledge and experience.

Fifth Estate – Voluntary Sector: the group supports anyone working with PR in the not-for-profit sector. It holds regular meetings with top-rank speakers from the media and not-for-profit organisations, runs a mentoring scheme and provides a membership directory.

Public Affairs (CIPR PA): CIPR PA group members are communication and public affairs professionals who interact with governments, the EU and the devolved Parliament and Assemblies. The group regularly organises speaker meetings and lunches and offers a free members' handbook.

Box 6.4

European public relations associations

PRVA – Public Relations Verband (Austria)
BPRCA – Belgian Public Relations Consultants Association
APRA – Czech Association of Public Relations Agencies
DKF – Dansk Kommunikationsfrening (Denmark)
STiL – Finnish Association of Communicators
Information, Presse & Communication (France)
DPRG – Deutsche Public Relations Gesellschaft EV (Germany)
HPRCA – Hellenic Public Relations Consultancies Association (Greece)
PRII – Public Relations Institute of Ireland
FERPI – Federazione Relazioni Pubbliche Italiana (Italy)
Beroepsvereniging voor Communicatie (Netherlands)
Kommunikasjonsfreningen (Norway)
NIR – Norwegian Public Relations Consultants Association
APECOM – Association of Public Relations Consultancies in Portugal
PACO – Russian Public Relations Association
APRSR – Public Relations Association of the Slovak Republic
PRSS – Public Relations Society of Slovenia
ADECEC – Assoc de Empresas Consultoras en Relaciones Publicas (Spain)
SPRA – Swedish Public Relations Association
BPRA – Bund der Public Relations Agenturen der Schweiz (Switzerland)
PRCI – Public Relations Consultancies Inc. of Turkey
PRCA – Public Relations Consultants Association (UK)

Source: www.cipr.co.uk

Health & Medical: the CIPR Health and Medical Group aims to unite PR professionals from across the healthcare and medical sectors. PR in this sector is particularly wide-ranging, covering the NHS, private healthcare, health insurance and the pharmaceutical industry. The meetings are designed to appeal to communications professionals from agency and in-house, including those who specialise in general healthcare, patient groups, government, health charities and medical research.

CIPR Inside: CIPR Inside's objective is to provide a forum for internal communication professionals where they can share ideas and practices and agree professional standards.

CIPR International: for members working in-house or in consultancy in an international context, or who wish to develop their careers in an international direction. It is an opportunity for both networking and training.

Local Public Services: the group's members work in or with local public services, such as local government, health, housing and education. It promotes professional development, runs awards schemes and workshops and publishes *PR News*.

Marketing Communications: this sectoral group represents all of the PR professionals who operate or have an interest in the wider marketing communications arena, giving access to the latest information and best practice to stimulate a business through a number of events each year. These normally include case studies of best practice in marketing communications.

Science, Technology, Engineering and Mathematics Group (STEM): with this group, technology communicators have the opportunity to meet and exchange information and extend contacts.

The aims of the CIPR are:

- To provide a professional structure for the practice of public relations.
- To enhance the ability and status of our members as professional practitioners.
- To represent and serve the professional interests of our members.
- To provide opportunities for members to meet and exchange views and ideas.
- To raise standards within the profession through the promotion of best practice – including the production of best practice guides, case studies, training events and a continuous professional development scheme, 'Developing Excellence'.

Source: www.cipr.co.uk

The following statements and comments are from the press release (February 2005) from the CIPR to announce the Charter status approval for the Institute:

This marks the 'coming of age' of the PR profession and is official recognition of the important and influential role that public relations plays in business, government and democratic society.

The award of a Charter by the Privy Council is affirmation of the role the Institute plays in the public relations industry – providing leadership, developing policy, raising standards through training and education, and making members accountable through the Code of Conduct.

Chris Genasi, 2005 President of the Chartered Institute of Public Relations, said:

> This is a milestone for the Institute and the PR industry. The CIPR can now implement its strategy to further improve and support the industry with the formal stamp of approval from Government.
>
> The IPR has been acknowledged as the official body to strengthen and lead the profession. The Government has recognised the PR industry as a leading player in public and corporate life and PR practitioners as professionals with specialist skills, knowledge and qualifications.'

Colin Farrington, then Director General of the CIPR, said:

> Chartered status will make it easier for employers, clients and the general public to distinguish between PR practitioners who are prepared to commit to the industry code of conduct and to be accountable, and those who aren't. Membership of the Institute has always been about professionalism, commitment and standards and now Chartered status gives CIPR members external, third-party approval and endorsement. Membership of CIPR is a clear demonstration of professionalism.
>
> *Source*: www.cipr.co.uk

Box 6.4 details other European associations. All their websites contain much relevant information for further investigation (see Explore 6.5).

Explore 6.5

Join an institute

Find the web address of the national institute where you are studying or working. Search the website for details about the national association. How many people are members? What benefits does membership bring? Could you be an associate or student member? Talk to a friend or colleague about the benefits of membership. If it is possible for you to be a member, why not think about joining?

Box 6.5

Practitioner diary: 'A week in the life of Nicola Green', Director of Communication and Reputation at Telefónica UK

Picture 6.3 Nicola Green

Monday

I'll leave home at around 7am for the 35-minute drive to O2's offices in Slough. Sometimes I'll drive myself and sometimes a colleague will pick me up. O2 encourages car sharing and I like it because it gives me a chance to chat with colleagues more informally than a busy day normally allows.

I've taken advantage of O2's flexible working policies so I arrive early and leave early (although my day doesn't end when I leave Slough) so a day at O2's head office begins at 8am with a quick scan of my emails. Then I check what meetings I have and work out my priorities for the day. I usually focus on three key things that I have to achieve before I go home.

At 9am every Monday I meet with my four direct reports for a weekly update. They make sure I'm aware of any issues and that I know what's going on. It's really important to me that people are clear about their roles and responsibilities, and I give them responsibility to drive their own teams without much intervention from me unless they want it. I've created a team who know when to bring me in and when to just get on with things.

box 6.5 (continued)

At 10am I attend the Leadership team meeting, which is the company's CEO and his direct reports. It's an opportunity to catch up with what's going on around the company and get clear about my priorities for the week. I update the board on the comms activity we've planned and explain what it's intended to achieve.

This meeting demonstrates more than ever the value that comms is bringing to the organisation. Every board member will have something they want to discuss with me or ask for my team's help on. They trust that I can get on and do the job well for them. They see the value of PR; for example we've launched products without above-the-line marketing support and seen increased sales driven entirely by PR, and motivated teams.

O2 is a brand built on collaborative working. We're interdependent and they know what PR can deliver, both in terms of positive results and in reducing the impact of any negative issues.

Sometimes we have to think carefully about how we position a product within the press, as in some cases we may not be the first to market, or even the last, or we have to think about things that may be unpopular but are better for us and our customers in the long term, such as data monetisation whereby we've stopped offering 'unlimited data' tariffs for mobile data.

After that, I meet with the CEO and the Chief Finance Officer to discuss key messages for our forthcoming Q1 financial results.

I'm one of a tiny handful of people who are allowed to know the company's financial results in advance. We discuss the results and how they are likely to be received by the press, the public and the financial markets. Together we talk through our messaging, both for people within the company and what we want them to take away.

We review the press from the last quarter's financial results, as well as our competitors' results and the coverage they received. This shapes our message and helps us decide how we will steer internal opinion. Every single person in the company is at some point responsible for how we occur to the public so we need to be clear and consistent. One of the actions is to engage the senior leadership team so that they can share this information to their teams and help explain it powerfully.

At noon I have a weekly status meeting to update my whole team. That's around 12 people with me in the Slough office, and another 26 or so in other O2 locations, working from home or out and about.

I download points from the board meeting to the team so they can have the information straight away and start implementing anything new. Clear direction and transparency are vitally important in motivating my team and making sure they know what they are responsible for. The meeting is also an opportunity for my team to ask questions so I allow time for that and the meeting wraps up at around 12.30pm.

I'm diabetic, so I try hard to eat healthily at lunchtime. We have a good canteen with plenty of choice, but sometimes I'll pop to Marks & Spencer partly for the walk in the fresh air and partly to get something different, such as a prawn salad.

After lunch, I have a meeting with our Group Director of Communications (O2 is part of the Telefónica Europe group). Although I have no direct reporting line to him, we meet regularly as I greatly value his advice and the perspective he brings. He's very experienced and a great resource. It's always good to talk things through and see things from a different side. He's also very good at going back to our parent company and getting agreement and support for any of our activities that may affect Telefónica's share price. Telefónica in the UK isn't listed but we're a key part of the Telefónica Group.

At 2pm I catch up with my PA. I get around 250 emails a day and each of them needs to be assigned or answered. We sort out those that my team can respond to and those that I need to handle myself.

Sadly I don't have the time to meet with every person who asks to meet me, and I don't want to waste people's time talking about a service or idea that we'll never be able to develop. So my PA and I look at the months ahead and try to plan it so that I have time to focus on what's important as well as having meetings that are useful both for me and the other person.

Next I have a meeting with a director of an artist management company. He's come to see if we have a need to work with the fashion industry to help promote various products and services. We talk about whether we could work with the fashion world to drive positive association for O2. It's good to connect with people like him, even if we can't do business immediately, because I now know who to call in the future.

In my view, relationship building is one of the most important aspects of my job. It's important to meet people and talk about their ideas, whether or not you

box 6.5 (continued)

'need' them right now or they can sell you something, or vice versa. It's important to know people, to help them where you can and take an interest in them so that when and if you do need them, you've already established your own credentials.

At 4pm I have 'travel time' blocked out in my diary. I usually drive home, sometimes taking and making a few calls on the way. O2 is an advocate of flexible working and, as the comms role is 24/7, it works out well for me to go home at 4. I have a family and it's really important to balance that with work without either one eating into the other's time. I always make sure I get home for bathtime – I'll perhaps watch Peppa Pig with my BlackBerry by my side – and spend a quality couple of hours with my daughter before she goes to bed.

I'll log on again after that and do any serious writing that requires concentration. I'll spend two or three hours writing, reading and checking up on emails and generally preparing for the next day. It's a corny but accurate saying 'fail to prepare, prepare to fail'.

Tuesday

On Tuesday I meet with my four direct reports, to talk about embedding our brand strategy in all our comms. We need to ensure that it's woven into our internal messaging as well as externally, to ensure that all our people are talking naturally about who we are and what we are trying to achieve.

I have lunch with the Editor of *Marketing* magazine and Telefónica's Marketing Director. The lunch is an opportunity for relationship building – I firmly believe that it's important to keep in touch with people, whether you have something to 'sell' or not. It builds a positive foundation of opinion that will help, whether we have bad news to manage or good news to announce one day in the future. News people want news but, if you time it right, the slow approach produces better coverage in the end.

On this occasion we are taking the opportunity to brief the magazine's editor on O2 Wallet, which we plan to launch the following day.

Next it's on to a final meeting to talk to my team about the launch. We have a full run-through of the press briefing with the spokespeople, and make sure that we've thought about the questions we'll be asked and how we will respond. I ask as many questions as I can to test the messages and test our Q&A document, to make sure we have everything covered.

At 4pm I head for home. In the car I'll make a few calls to catch up on the launch of a new app that Telefónica Digital is launching, called TU ME.

After my daughter's in bed I'll log on and have a look at my emails and review my day tomorrow.

Wednesday

The first meeting I have is to talk to someone who's leaving us to go to Sky. I wanted to say goodbye and also make sure I stay in touch with him after he leaves O2. It's also useful to hear his honest views about the company.

At 11am I meet with our Head of Public Affairs about a forthcoming visit to No 10 Downing Street by our CEO. He briefs me on the agenda and we talk about the key points we want our CEO to raise. It's important that all our messages are joined up and that we are saying the same thing across every channel.

In the afternoon I have a meeting with our Events Manager to talk about internal conferences. We've decided to cut back on costs for these and do every department's conference all in one week at the same venue. The coordination of logistics is going to be pretty tricky but it's important we do it well so that people get behind the initiative to be more cost-effective, as well as having a productive conference of course.

At 4pm I attend the launch of O2 Wallet. My team has been working hard for weeks on this and I'm pleased with the way the event goes and with the press attendance.

I love these events and the opportunity they give me to talk to the press, help brief the spokespeople and generally be supportive of my team, who pulled it all together.

Thursday

First thing today I'm attending a creative agency's presentation on research they've carried out on 'fan culture' and how companies can go about generating fans. They tell me that the response to their research has been unprecedented, with enquiries from across the globe. The subject of fan culture is much-discussed at the moment and I think PR has an important role to play in influencing how a company interacts with its customers and non-customers alike at every point of contact.

At 10am it's on to Shoreditch to visit Telefónica's new Wayra Academy. Wayra is a Telefónica Digital initiative designed to promote innovation and identify talent in Latin America and Europe and help entrepreneurs in the fields of Internet and new information and communication technologies (ICT).

→

box 6.5 (continued)

We're briefed by the Wayra team to make sure we're engaged and up-to-date on their plans, as comms will be an integral part of helping them drive registrations.

That evening, I attend an event called 'The language of leaders', led by Kevin Murray, the Chairman of Bell Pottinger. It's important to attend these events, both to understand the wider business of PR and to network with people in a similar role to mine.

Friday

I'm meeting with my direct reports all day at the offices of our advertising agency, VCCP. I'm very keen on the

integration of disciplines and I firmly believe that someone who only limits themselves to, say, PR shuts down opportunities as well as reduces their effectiveness day to day. At the beginning of my career I had the opportunity to step out of PR and become brand manager for Dr Pepper. It gave me valuable insight into each element of the marketing mix.

And, finally, Friday evening arrives. I check who's on press duty for the weekend and head home.

Source: Nicola Green

Education and research

The first UK undergraduate degree in PR was launched at Bournemouth in 1989, followed by Leeds Metropolitan University and the College of St Mark and St John, Plymouth in 1990. The pioneer postgraduate courses were launched at Stirling University in 1989 and Manchester Metropolitan University shortly after. Research conducted in 2003 found 22 PR or similar undergraduate degrees in Britain, of which 13 were then approved by the CIPR. With the addition of non- or recently approved CIPR courses, it is estimated that approximately 500 PR undergraduates enrolled on UK PR courses in 2004 (Tench and Fawkes 2005).

PR education continues to evolve (Fawkes and Tench 2004a), and while most PR educators have practitioner backgrounds, many in Britain now have over a decade of teaching and research experience (L'Etang 1999). Teaching academics in the UK institutions are also increasingly acquiring doctorates and other research qualifications. New ideas, drawing on critical theory and other cultural and political approaches (see below), are being developed and taught as academics seek to expand the theoretical frameworks with which to critique PR and its role in society.

There has been a worldwide growth in courses at higher education (HE) level that aim to feed the profession, including general degrees covering PR as one part of a wider remit and the specialist CIPR-approved PR degrees that focus on PR and its related context, with a commensurate growth in academics and academic publishing. According to Fawkes and Tench (2004b) even here the emphases in the programmes differ, from PR as a management discipline with an emphasis on strategy (in the business schools) to PR as an aspect of media activity with an

emphasis on communication (media schools) and PR as a social science.

For many years the United States was the main repository of PR research; now Britain and Europe have developed an impressive research base. The term 'public relations' may not be familiar in other European countries, but the roles are similar. Van Ruler and Verčič (2004) highlight both the common underlying themes, such as professionalisation and the influence of communication technologies, set against the 'similar yet idiosyncratic' national backdrops, where differences are more obvious, from a study of PR within national contexts.

In addition, there are many other academic and functional disciplines, such as the social sciences, business and management, cultural studies, linguistics, media studies and psychology, that also input into the research underpinning for the sector. This interdisciplinary approach is a strength; it provides a wide range of methodological options, such as a cultural studies approach to deconstruct PR case studies (Mickey 2003) rather than sticking to the traditional PR methodologies. This is known as theoretical pluralism (Cobley 1996). A number of academics discount the term interdisciplinary now, preferring post-disciplinary, and the implication that outdated structures have given way to more fluid fields of study.

Drawing on a wide range of references, such as those outlined later in the text, should increase the credibility in terms of knowledge and expertise of the practitioner who is pursuing a PR qualification.

Another backdrop to the role are the national initiatives within Britain at secondary and HE levels to encourage more vocational and skills-based programmes as a complement to the traditional academic route. This trend, which also attracts funding, means that a discipline such as PR, which successfully links academic, skills and employ-ability, is well-positioned for growth. So PR can be taught as a new-style foundation degree in the way that other subjects might not, given the inherent employer input prerequisite. Again, this may prove to be both a strength and a weakness: a strength because this offers a way forward where funding in more traditional programmes has been curtailed; a weakness because PR may lose academic credibility and become just another vocational training ground (see Boxes 6.6 and 6.7).

Box 6.6

Practitioner diary: 'A day in the life of Helen Standing', Director at Engage Communications

Friday 20th January

I get up at 7.30am. I've got a meeting in central Leeds at 12pm so am working from home this morning and getting the train straight there.

I check my phone for urgent emails, tweets, LinkedIn updates, etc. before getting up. I also have a quick scan of the BBC news app for headlines. There's an email from my boss with the notes for her presentation at today's Northern Lights marketing network meeting, which I have a quick read of. It is the second of a new series of meetings we are holding for clients and contacts in in-house marketing roles to get together and share ideas. Today's meeting is on internal communications and I'm leading a segment on how to get the best from your Intranet.

I get showered and ready for the day then eat a bowl of cereal while watching BBC Breakfast. I sit down at my laptop to log on to my remote desktop at around 8.30am. My first task for the day is to finish writing up a blog for a professional services client. I interviewed the managing director of the consultancy firm a couple of days before for her thoughts on a topical issue in HR. She gave me a lot of detailed advice for SMEs and I'm just shaping it into a blog that can be used on her website and sent out to online media and other business blogs. Then I chase up some leads for a journalist writing a feature for *Yorkshire Business Insider* for a university client.

In the background, I'm checking my own and a client's Twitter and Facebook accounts and responding to group discussions on LinkedIn. I'm quite selective about what I post, share, respond to and take part in, both for myself and clients. You could spend all day on social media – you have to just look at and do the things that are relevant and ultimately contribute towards your goals. I tend not to use tools to monitor everything; I prefer to check and search for things manually on the separate platforms so that I know I'm not missing anything. I also never use automated updates.

I catch up with a client on the phone to arrange a meeting to input into their marketing strategy for 2012. I'm also working on a project for a client, reviewing their marketing communications materials and providing recommendations on how to engage a business audience to achieve their goals. I take a call from a journalist looking for a case study.

Then I've just got time to re-read my notes for today's meeting before going for the train.

I read the *Metro* newspaper on the train and check emails before pulling in to Leeds, then walk to Leeds City College's new Food Academy restaurant, which has kindly offered to host the event. I arrive 15 minutes before the start, talk over final arrangements with the staff and my boss and then start greeting attendees – ten senior marketing people from law firms, colleges, universities, schools and arts organisations. Most of them attended the last meeting and they are all really keen to talk to their peers about internal comms issues.

The meeting and lunch goes really well and there's lots of lively debate and discussion. It's 'Chatham House rules', so people talk quite candidly about the issues they are facing. I stay behind after the meeting to catch up with a former client about a potential project and then get the train home.

I get home at around 4pm, catch up on emails, Twitter, LinkedIn and Facebook, give the team back at the office a de-brief and read through a new tender that has just come in. I then start writing up the notes from the meeting and an outline for a blog or two out of what was discussed.

I finalise some arrangements for a client event and edit some copy for their website before logging off at around 6.15pm.

Source: Helen Standing

Box 6.7

Practitioner diary: 'A day in the life of Jack Adlam', Communications Officer at Nottingham University Hospitals NHS Trust (NUH)

I am woken by my alarm and, after a quick shower, I drive to work listening to Radio 5 Live. There is a particularly interesting interview with the chairwoman of the Royal College of GPs, setting out her opposition to the proposed NHS reforms.

On my way into the office I pick up a copy of the *Nottingham Post*, scanning Twitter and Facebook as I work my way through the many corridors of the hospital.

At my desk I log on and scan the newspaper for anything that might be of interest. I work through my emails and take a couple of media calls, including one from a local radio station who want to know if the adverse weather has resulted in more admissions to our Emergency Department.

We have organised some press conference training for our executive team this morning and a local media training company come in to run the session. The training consists of splitting the executive team into three groups and each member of the communications team taking a group, preparing them for the press conference. Our scenario is about some deaths in our Neonatal Unit. The training proves to be a very useful exercise.

After the training and a quick sandwich, I go to the main entrance of the hospital and meet a journalist from the *Nottingham Post*. I have managed to sell in a feature about our complementary therapy service that we offer to children and young people at the hospital.

The reporter speaks to our complementary therapy nurse specialist and a patient who has agreed to talk about her experience. The story will feature in next week's 'Health and Wellbeing' section.

After I have said goodbye to the reporter I go back to my desk to catch up on my emails and make some calls. I need to chase up on some media enquiries we had this morning.

I finish the day by updating our Intranet with a story about the introduction of e-payslips and tweet about an upcoming members' event at the Nottingham Children's Hospital.

I leave work and drive home, listening to the drive time show on Radio 5 Live, with the NHS reforms debate still going strong.

Source: Jack Adlam

Summary

This chapter has demonstrated the range of skills demanded of PR practitioners and, it is hoped, dispelled the false images of celebrity or spin presented in the introduction. It has shown the different ways in which PR is organised and delivered in various countries and examined the issue of professionalism, as well as highlighting information about professional bodies in Britain and elsewhere. Finally, it has addressed the evolving role of education in shaping the future of PR by providing the PR practitioner of the future.

This 'ideal' practitioner will be able to manage the complex, dynamic context and functions of their organisation as they will possess the cognitive, technical, social and communication skills to gain the confidence of colleagues from other sectors and functions. They will facilitate communication within their organisation, as well as with external publics; they will be able to advise senior management using their higher-level skills, as well as oversee more detailed hands-on activity (not least because they will have a clear understanding of relevant theories and their value to practice); they will be committed to lifelong learning and continual professional development, as well as being active in the professional body; and they will also educate others about the value of PR and in this way help reinforce the position of PR as a profession.

Is this too much to ask? Perhaps, but it is not impossible that practitioners of the future, who will achieve these kinds of standard, are, even now, reading this chapter.

Bibliography

Allan, S. (2000). *News Culture*. Milton Keynes: Open University Press.

Arthur Page Society (2008) http://www.awpagesociety.com/insights/authentic-enterprise-report/ accessed 31 May 2013

Bernstein, D. (1986). *Company Image and Reality*. London: Cassell.

Brody, E.W. (1992). 'We must act now to redeem PR's reputation'. *Public Relations Quarterly* **37**(3) in F. Cropp and J.D. Pincus (2001). 'The mystery of public relations' in *Handbook of Public Relations*. R.L. Heath (ed.). Thousand Oaks, CA: Sage.

Brown, A. and L.T. Fall (2005). 'Using the port of entry report as a benchmark: survey results of on-the-job training among public relations internship site managers'. *Public Relations Review* **31**(2): 301–304.

Boyzatis, R.E. (1982). *The Competent Manager*. New York: Riley.

BVC, Dutch Professional Association for Communication (2002). *Job Profile Descriptions in Communication Management*, third revised edition. The Hague: BVC & VVO.

Chan, G. (2000). 'Priorities old and new, for the research of public relations practice in the UK and their implications for academic debate'. Internal paper cited in 'How far do professional associations influence the direction of public relations education?'. A. Rawel. *Journal of Communication Management* **7**(1): 71–78.

Cheney, G. and L.T. Christensen (2001). 'Public relations as contested terrain' in *Handbook of Public Relations*. R.L. Heath (ed.). Thousand Oaks, CA: Sage.

Cobley, P. (ed.) (1996). *The Communication Theory Reader*. London: Routledge.

Culbertson, H.M. and N. Chen (1996). *International Public Relations: A comparative analysis*. Mahwah, NJ: Lawrence Erlbaum Associates.

Cutlip, S.M., A.H. Center and G.M. Broom (2000). *Effective Public Relations*, 8th edition. Upper Saddle River, NJ: Prentice Hall.

Cutlip, S.M., A.H. Center and G.M. Broom (2008). *Effective Public Relations*, 9th edition. Upper Saddle River, NJ: Prentice Hall.

Dearing Report (1997). 'Higher Education in the Learning Society: Report of the National Committee'. The National Committee of Inquiry into Higher Education. London: HMSO.

Deflagbe, D. (2004). 'How The Internet Is Modifying The Day-To-Day Practice of Public Relations (PR) In Ghana'. Unpublished MA dissertation.

DeSanto, B. and D. Moss (2004). 'Defining and refining the core elements in public relations/corporate communications context: what do communication managers do?'. Paper presented at the 11th International Public Relations Symposium, Lake Bled, Slovenia.

DiStaso, M.W., D.W. Stacks and C.H. Botan (2009). 'State of public relations education in the United States: 2006 report on a national survey of executives and academics'. *Public Relations Review* **35**(3): 254–269.

Dowling, G. (2001). *Creating Corporate Reputations*. Oxford: Oxford University Press.

Dozier, D.M. and G.M. Broom (2006). 'The centrality of practitioner roles to public relations theory' in *Public Relations Theory II*. C.H. Botan and V. Hazleton (eds). London: Lawrence Erlbaum.

DTI/IPR (Department of Trade and Industry/Institute of Public Relations) (2003). 'Unlocking the Potential of Public Relations: Developing Best Practice'. London: DTI/IPR.

Fawkes, J. (2004). 'What is public relations?' in A. Theaker (2004). *The Public Relations Handbook*. London: Routledge.

Fawkes, J. (2008). 'What is public relations?' in *Handbook of Public Relations*, 3rd edition. A. Theaker (ed.). London: Routledge.

Fawkes, J. and R. Tench (2004a). 'Does practitioner resistance to theory jeopardise the future of public relations in the UK?'. Paper presented at the 11th International Public Relations Research Symposium, Lake Bled, Slovenia.

Fawkes, J. and R. Tench (2004b). 'Public Relations Education in the UK'. A research report for the Chartered Institute of Public Relations.

Ferreira, E.M. (2003). 'Vocationally-oriented Public Relations Education in Globalised Contexts: An analysis of technikon-level public relations education'. Johannesburg: RAU. Dissertation – D.Litt. et Phil.

Garnham, N. (2000). 'Information society as theory or ideology'. *Information, Communication and Society* **3**: 139–152.

Goodman, M.B. (2006). 'Corporate communication practice and pedagogy at the dawn of the new millennium'. *Corporate Communications: An International Journal* **11**(3): 196–213.

Green, L. (2002). *Communication Technology and Society*. Thousand Oaks, CA: Sage.

Gregory, A. (2005). 'Research into Competency Characteristics of Senior Communicators for the UK Communications Directors' Forum'. Research seminar presented at Leeds Metropolitan University, February.

Gregory, A. (2008). 'Competencies of senior communication practitioners in the UK: an initial study'. *Public Relations Review* **34**(3): 215–223.

Gregory, A. (2011). 'The state of the public relations profession in the UK: A review of the first decade of the twenty-first century', *Corporate Communications: An International Journal*, **16**(2): 89–104.

Grunig, J.E. & L.A. Grunig (2002). 'Implications of the IABC Excellence Study for PR education'. *Journal of Communication Management* **7**(1): 34–42.

Hague, P. (1998). *Questionnaire Design*, 3rd edition. London: Kogan Page.

Hardin, M.C. and D. Pompper (2004). 'Writing in the public relations curriculum: practitioner perception versus pedagogy'. *Public Relations Review* **30**(3): 357–364.

Hargie, O. (2000). *The Handbook of Communication Skills*, 2nd edition. London: Routledge.

Heath, R.L. (2001). 'Shifting foundations: public relations as relationship building' in *Handbook of Public Relations*. R.L. Heath (ed.). Thousand Oaks, CA: Sage.

Hogg, G. and D. Doolan (1999). Playing the part: practitioner roles in public relations. *European Journal of Marketing*, **33**(5/6): 597–611.

Holtzhausen, D. (2002). 'Towards a post-modern research agenda for public relations'. *Public Relations Review* **28**(3): 251–264.

Hutton, J.G. (1999). 'The definition, dimensions and domain of public relations'. *Public Relations Review* **25**(2): 199–214.

Hutton, J.G. (2001). 'Defining the relationship between public relations and marketing' in *Handbook of Public Relations*. R.L. Heath (ed.). Thousand Oaks, CA: Sage.

Hutton, J.G., M.B. Goodman, J.B. Alexander and C.M. Genest (2001). 'Reputation management: the new face of corporate public relations?' *Public Relations Review* **27**(3): 247–261.

Institute of Public Relations (2004). *Profile* **42**, April: 7.

IPA Bellwether Report (2012). www.ipa.co.uk/page/IPA-Bellwether-Report?menu=open accessed 14 June 2012.

Jeffrey, L.M. and M.A. Brunton (2011). 'Developing a framework for communication management competencies'. *Journal of Vocational Education and Training* **63**(1): 57–75.

Johansson, C. and A.T. Ottestig (2011). 'Communication executives in a changing world: Legitimacy beyond organizational borders'. *Journal of Communication Management* **15**(2): 144–164.

Katz, D. and R.L. Kahn (1978). *The Social Psychology of Organizations*, 2nd edition. New York, NY: John Wiley & Sons.

Kerr, C. (1995). *The Use of the University*, 4th edition. Cambridge, MA and London: Harvard University Press.

Kim, E. and T.L. Johnson (2009). 'Sailing through the port: does PR education prepare students for the profession?'. 12th Annual International Public Relations Research Conference.

L'Etang, J. (1999). 'Public relations education in Britain: an historical review in the context of professionalisation'. *Public Relations Review* **25**(3): 261–289.

L'Etang, J. (2002). 'Public relations education in Britain: a review at the outset of the millennium and thoughts for a different research agenda'. *Journal of Communication Management* **7**(1): 43–53.

L'Etang, J. and M. Pieczka (eds) (1996). *Critical Perspectives in Public Relations*. London: ITBP.

L'Etang, J. and M. Pieczka (eds) (2006). *Public Relations: Critical debates and contemporary problems*. Hillsdale, NJ: Lawrence Erlbaum Associates.

Liu, B.F., S. Horsley and A.B. Levenshus (2010). 'Government and corporate communication practices: do the differences matter?' *Journal of Applied Communication Research* **38**(2): 189–213.

Logeion (2012). 'Beroepsniveauprofielen' [Job level profiles]. www.logeion.nl/beroepsniveauprofielen

McCleneghan, J.S. (2006). 'PR executives rank 11 communication skills'. *Public Relations Quarterly* **51**(4): 42–46.

McQuail, D. (2002). *Mass Communication Theory*. London: Sage.

Mickey, T. (2003). *Deconstructing Public Relations*. Hillsdale, NJ: Lawrence Erlbaum Associates.

Miles, S. (2001). *Social Theory in the Real World*. London: Sage.

Molleda, J.C. and C. Connolly-Ahern (2002). 'Cross-national conflict shifting: a conceptualization and expansion in an international public relations context'. Paper presented to the convention of the Association for Education in Journalism and Communication. Miami: Florida.

Molleda, J.C. & A. Moreno (2006). 'The transitional socio-economic and political environments of public relations in Mexico'. *Public Relations Review* **32**: 104–109.

Moss, D., A. Newman and B. DeSanto (2004). 'Defining and redefining the core elements of management in public relations/corporate communications context: what do communication managers do?'. Paper presented at the 11th International Public Relations Research Symposium, Lake Bled, Slovenia.

Neff, B.D., G. Walker, M.F. Smith and P.J. Creedon (1999). 'Outcomes desired by practitioners and academics'. *Public Relations Review* **25**(1): 29–44.

Oughton, L. (2004). 'Do we need core competences for local government communications?' in Local Government Communication Leaders Development Programme, *Ideas in Communication Leadership*. London: Improvement and Development Agency, pp. 65–72.

Pieczka, M. (2002). 'Public relations expertise deconstructed'. *Media Culture and Society* **24**(3): 301–323.

Pieczka, M. and J. L'Etang (2001). 'Public relations and the question of professionalism' in *Handbook of Public Relations*. R.L. Heath (ed.). Thousand Oaks, CA: Sage.

Proctor, R.W. and A. Dutta (1995). *Skill Acquisition and Human Performance*. London: Sage.

PRSA (Public Relations Society of America) (1999). (National Commission on Public Relations Education). 'A Port of Entry – Public relations education for the 21st century'. New York: PRSA.

PRSA (Public Relations Society of America) (2006). 'Education for the 21st Century. The Professional Bond'. *Public Relation Education and the Practice*, www.compred.org/report/2006. Report of the Commission edited by J. VanSlyke Turk, November 2006.

Rawel, A. (2002). 'How far do professional associations influence the direction of public relations education?' *Journal of Communication Management* **7**(1): 71–78.

Riedel, J. (2011). 'Was sind die Kompetenzen für Social Media?' [Which competencies are required in social media?]. http://social-media-experten.de/2011/03/16/was-sind-die-kompetenzen-fur-social-media/

Schirato, T. and S. Yell (2000). *Communication and Culture*. London: Sage.

Sha, B-L. (2011a). '2010 practice analysis: professional competencies and work categories in public relations today'. *Public Relations Review* **37**(3): 187–196.

Sha, B-L. (2011b). 'Does accreditation really matter in public relations practice? How age and experience compare to accreditation'. *Public Relations Review* **37**(1): 1–11.

Sha, B-L. (2011c). 'Accredited vs. non-accredited: the polarization of practitioners in the public relations profession'. *Public Relations Review* **37**(2): 121–128.

Singh, R. and R. Smyth (2001). 'Australian public relations: Status at the turn of the 21st century'. *Public Relations Review*, **26**(4): 387–401.

Sriramesh, K. (1996). 'Power distance and public relations: An ethnographic study of Southern Indian organizations'. *International Public Relations: A comparative analysis*. 171–190.

Szyszka, P. (1995). Öffentlichkeitsarbeit und Kompetenz: Probleme und Perspektiven künftiger Bildungsarbeit. In *PR-Ausbildung in Deutschland* (pp. 317–342). VS Verlag für Sozialwissenschaften.

Tench, R. (2003). 'Stakeholder influences on the writing skills debate: a reflective evaluation in the context of vocational business education'. *Journal of Further and Higher Education* **27**(4), November.

Tench, R. and D. Deflagbe (2008). 'Towards a Global Curriculum: A summary of literature concerning public relations education, professionalism and globalisation'. Report for the Global Alliance of Public Relations and Communication Management, Leeds Metropolitan University, UK.

Tench, R. and J. Fawkes (2005). 'Mind the gap – exploring attitudes to PR education between academics and employers'. Paper presented at the Alan Rawel CIPR Academic Conference, University of Lincoln, March.

Tench, R., A. Zerfass, A.M. Moreno, D. Vercic, P. Verhoeven and A. Okay (2012). European Communication Professionals Skills and Innovation Programme, see www.ecopsi.org.uk

Tench, R., A. Moreno, A. Okay, D. Vercic, P. Verhoeven and A. Zerfass (2013a). ECOPSI (European Communication Practitioner Skills and Innovation programme). www.ecopsi.org.uk

Tench, R., A. Zerfass, P. Verhoeven, A. Moreno, A. Okay and D. Vercic (2013b). ECOPSI Benchmarking Report (Full). May 2013. Leeds, UK: Leeds Metropolitan University.

Tench, R., A. Zerfass, P. Verhoeven, D. Verčič, A. Moreno and A. Okay (2013c). Communication Management Competencies for European Practitioners. (Book). Leeds, UK: Leeds Metropolitan University.

Theaker, A. (2004). 'Professionalism and regulation' in *Handbook of Public Relations*. A. Theaker (ed.). London: Routledge.

Turk, J.V., C. Botan and S.P. Morreale (1999). 'Meeting education challenges in the information age': Strategic resources for achieving successful professional outcomes. *Public Relation Review* **25**(1): 1–4.

Valentini, C. (2010). 'Personalised networks of influence in public relations: Strategic resources for achieving successful professional outcomes'. *Journal of Communication Management* **14**(2): 153–166.

Van Ruler, B., D. Verčič, G. Bütschi and B. Flodin (2000). *The European Body of Knowledge on Public Relations/Communication Management: The Report of the Delphi Research Project 2000*. Ghent/Ljubljana: European Association for Public Relations Education and Research.

Van Ruler, B. and D. Verčič (2004). Overview of public relations and communication management in Europe. *Public Relations and Communications Management in Europe*. 1–11.

Varey, R. (1997). 'Public relations in a new context: a corporate community of cooperation'. Paper presented at the 3rd Annual Conference of the Public Relations Educators' Forum.

Verčič, D., B. van Ruler, G. Butzchi and B. Flodin (2001). 'On the definition of public relations: a European view'. *Public Relations Review* **27**(4): 373–387.

Verwey, S. (2000). 'Public relations: a new professionalism for a new millennium?' *Communicare* **19**(2): 51–68, December.

von Bertalanffy, L. (1969). *General Systems Theory: Foundations, development, applications*, 2nd edition. New York, NY: Braziller.

Wilcox, D.L., P.H. Ault and W.K. Agee (2003). *Public Relations: Strategies and tactics*, 5th edition. New York, NY: Addison–Wesley.

Wilkin, P. (2001). *The Political Economy of Global Communication: An introduction*. London: Pluto Press.

Windahl, S., B. Signitzer and J. Olson (1992). *Using Communication Theory*. London: Sage.

Winterton, J., F. Delamare-Le Deist and E. Stringfellow (2005). *Typology of Knowledge, Skills and Competences: Clarification of the concept and prototype*. Thessaloniki: CEDEFOP.

Zerfass, A. (1998). 'Management-Knowhow für Public Relations' [Management know how in public relations]. *Medien Journal 3/1998* – Public Relations: Qualifikation & Kompetenzen, pp.3–15.

Zerfass, A., A. Moreno, R. Tench, D. Verčič and P. Verhoeven (2008). '*European Communication Monitor 2008*. Trends in Communication Management and Public Relations – Results and Implications'. Brussels, Leipzig: EUPRERA/University of Leipzig. Available at: www.communication-monitor.eu

Zerfass, A., A. Moreno, R. Tench, D. Verčič and P. Verhoeven (2009). '*European Communication Monitor 2009*. Trends in Communication Management and Public Relations – Results of a Survey in 34 Countries'. Brussels, Leipzig: EUPRERA/University of Leipzig. Available at: www.communicationmonitor.eu.

Zerfass, A., A. Moreno, R. Tench, D. Verčič and P. Verhoeven (2010). '*European Communication Monitor 2010*. Status Quo and Challenges for Communication Management in Europe. Results of an Empirical Study in 46 Countries'. Brussels, Leipzig: EUPRERA/University of Leipzig. Available at: www.communicationmonitor.eu.

Zerfass, A., P. Verhoeven, R. Tench, A. Moreno and D. Verčič (2011). '*European Communication Monitor 2011*. Empirical Insights into Strategic Communication in Europe. Results of an Empirical Survey in 43 Countries'. Brussels: EACD, EUPRERA.

Zerfass, A., D. Vercic, P. Verhoeven, A. Moreno and R. Tench (2012). European Communication Monitor 2012. Challenges and Competencies for Strategic Communication. Results of an Empirical Survey in 42 Countries. Brussels: EACD, EUPRERA.

Websites

ECOPSI: www.ecopsi.org.uk

European Communication Professionals Skills and Innovation Programme: www.leedsmet.ac.uk/ecopsi

'The Authentic Enterprise' White Paper 2008: www.awpagesociety.com

P4ace Portal (ECOPSI): www.p4ace.eu

PART 2

Public relations theories and concepts

There is no one unifying 'public relations theory'. This section will demonstrate that public relations is multifaceted and can be interpreted through a number of relevant theoretical perspectives. The key theoretical discussions in Chapter 7 take us from theories that describe how a profession ought to behave (normative theories) through to alternative theoretical approaches drawn from critical theory, socio-cultural theories, rhetorical and feminist perspectives, among others. Chapter 8 introduces our first 'concept': public relations as planned communication, in which public relations is presented as a process for achieving organisational objectives. Continuing the planning theme, Chapter 9 discusses the role of programme research and evaluation in the public relations process. There is sometimes confusion around the concepts of image, reputation and identity. Chapter 10 attempts to unpack this confusion, as well as firmly identifying these concepts as important to understanding public relations within a corporate context. Drawing mainly on theories of social psychology, Chapter 11 aims to demonstrate that the concepts of persuasion and propaganda must be defined and applied in helping us to recognise when public relations is used responsibly and when it is not. Finally, the ethical issues raised by public relations and its role in society inevitably leads to a discussion of public relations' professionalism and ethics, which is found in Chapter 12.

Public relations theories:
an overview

Learning outcomes

By the end of this chapter you will be able to:

- identify and discuss public relations theories that shape the field
- discuss the different understandings of public relations that these theories produce
- use this chapter as a backdrop for further study into other specialist areas in this book.

Structure

- Systems theory of public relations and related approaches
- Internationalising systems theory
- Shortcomings of systems theory
- Postmodernism and PR
- Rhetorical theory and PR
- Feminist analyses of PR
- Diversity and 'race' in PR
- Critical approaches to PR
- Socio-cultural approaches to PR

Introduction

Public relations research and practice traditionally have been closely linked. Systems theory, which emerged in the second half of the twentieth century, was initially the dominant approach to public relations and took the view that theory development should improve practice, first and foremost. More recently, the assumptions underpinning the systems theory approach have been criticised as the technological, social and cultural environments for PR have evolved. A wider range of theoretical approaches to public relations has emerged, with the growth of critical, sociological and cultural approaches in particular. As the body of knowledge about public relations increases, this theoretical diversity will continue to grow and improve our understandings of the profession. This chapter examines a range of theoretical approaches to public relations, beginning with a brief summary of findings in the systems tradition and continuing with an examination of alternative approaches.

Systems theory of public relations and related approaches

For systems theorists, research begins with the practitioner working for the organisation, the organisation carrying out PR or the situation in which the PR activity takes place. The main objective of PR is to develop and execute strategies and tactics that will benefit an organisation in a given context. In 1984, two of the earliest systems theorists, James E. Grunig and Todd Hunt, published *Managing Public Relations*, in which they presented a set of PR **typologies** based on observations of practice in the United States: press agentry/publicist; public information; two-way asymmetric; and two-way symmetric communications (Grunig and Hunt 1984).

Press agentry is one-way communication: no dialogue with the intended audience is required and the main objective is to put forward one particular view of the world through the media and other channels. Public information is related to press agentry in its focus on one-way information dissemination, but it differs in that the information has to be accurate, true and specific – the main aim is to inform rather than persuade. Two-way asymmetric communication is rooted in persuasive communications (see Chapter 11) and should generate agreement between the organisation and its publics by bringing them around to the organisation's way of thinking. Feedback from publics is used to adapt communications strategies to be more persuasive, not to alter the organisation's position. Finally, in two-way symmetric communication the aim is to generate mutual understanding – the two-way communications process should lead to changes in the position of both the public *and* the organisation. Grunig and his colleagues,

> **Definition:** '*Typology*' means identifying the different types of something, usually by working out the key elements that distinguish one kind of PR practitioner or activity, in this case, from another.

supported by the International Association of Business Communicators (IABC), subsequently conducted a three-country, ten-year study of PR practice to establish what might be defined as 'excellence' in PR (Grunig 1992; Grunig et al. 2002) and produced a four-level framework for 'excellent' PR:

1. *Programme level* (why, when and how individual communications programmes are implemented).

2. *Departmental level* (how the PR department operates and fits in with other departments and the organisation as a whole).

3. *Organisational level* (understanding of, and respect given to, communications processes and audience feedback by the organisation and its staff).

4. *Economic level* (the tangible value provided by excellent PR to the organisation, in terms of happy external and internal publics).

At the heart of the theory is the following proposition from Grunig (1992: 6) about PR effectiveness:

> *Public relations contributes to organisational effectiveness when it helps reconcile the organisation's goals with the expectations of its strategic constituencies. This contribution has monetary value to the organisation. Public relations contributes to effectiveness by building quality, long-term relationships with strategic constituencies. Public relations is most likely to contribute to effectiveness when the senior public relations manager is a member of the dominant coalition, where he or she is able to shape the organisation's goals and to help determine which external publics are most strategic.*

According to the study, two-way symmetric communication practices are a keystone for excellent PR, although in practice a mix of asymmetric and symmetric approaches is often used. The symmetric and asymmetric communication models, in particular, have stimulated a large body of research into how PR is practiced, and evidence suggests that symmetric communication is associated with ethical and effective communication (Brown 2010).

Cutlip et al. (2000), for example, suggest that PR should view itself as part of an open system, helping the organisation to monitor and adapt to relevant environmental influences, as well as encouraging changes in the external environment that will help the organisation. In this model, two-way symmetric communications and strategic monitoring of the environment are also fundamental to good PR practice (see Chapter 8 and Mini case studies 7.1 and 7.2).

Mini case study 7.1

Symmetric and asymmetric communication practices on the web: Oxfam GB

Non-governmental organisations have to communicate effectively with their stakeholders and take their views into account if they want to ensure long-term support for their causes. Symmetric communications are, therefore, particularly important for them. However, websites are not always ideal spaces for symmetric communication because of their technological make up. Social media, on the other hand, are designed with 'conversation' in mind. Oxfam offers a good example of how these media can be combined in a holistic online communications strategy that allows the organisation to 'display and inform' using web pages, but engage in a 'conversation' with those same people using social media.

The website is asymmetric, delivering as much information as possible about the organisation and its activities, but offering only limited opportunity for feedback and contact. It includes: the aims and objectives of the organisation; annual reports and evaluations of its activities; a summary of the different processes used by Oxfam to evaluate its activities in light of its objectives; frequently asked questions and answers; headline articles and videos on current and long-term activities; success stories and a rolling update of individual members' actions taken on Oxfam's behalf; a shop selling Oxfam products; an opportunity to sign up to Oxfam's email newsletter; press releases and other communications, reports and reviews released by Oxfam; educational materials relating to Oxfam's aims and objectives; policy and practices; and further opportunities to contact the organisation by post, email or telephone.

The site also links viewers to Oxfam's social media sites (Facebook, Twitter, YouTube). Here, 'fans' of the organisation can be much more interactive, commenting on posts, 'liking' certain stories and clicking through to further links in a way that engages them actively in Oxfam's wider network. These sites allow for rich engagement and enable Oxfam to pursue a longer-term and more personal relationship with its supporters. Taken as a whole, then, 'old' web technology combined with 'new' social media creates more realistic opportunities for a holistic relationship to develop, which allows enough information to be distributed by the organisation and enough opportunities for feedback from supporters who wish to engage.

Mini case study 7.2

Greenpeace – an open system

For environmental activists, clear communication with the right people at the right time is essential for getting their message across. An organisation such as Greenpeace is a classic example of an open-system organisation. Campaign planners have to take into account views from external parties in order to ensure that they develop appropriate and effective communications for the cause they serve. These are just some of the people whose views Greenpeace needs to take into account when deciding which campaigns to execute and how to execute them:

■ biologists and environmental scientists – to determine which plants, animals or environmental features are in most need of help, as well as to gather useful facts and figures for campaigns;

■ its membership – to determine which causes will generate most support, based on audience interests, as well as which causes would alienate members and therefore need to be avoided;

■ public opinion polls – in order to establish what the public already knows about current or planned Greenpeace campaigns and where more education is required;

■ government and policy makers – to understand what kind of information, in terms of content and presentation, they need to take into account on Greenpeace's position when making policy;

■ people who are directly affected by Greenpeace campaigns – for example, whaling communities that might lose their livelihoods if whaling were completely banned. The strongest campaigns need to present alternative options for such people to survive and maintain their living standards.

Definition: *'Game theory'* is based on observations about negotiation and compromise that demonstrate that many conflicts are based on the zero-sum principle, whereby for someone to win, their opponent has to lose. Win–win outcomes are the result of compromise and mutually satisfactory negotiation.

Following critiques focusing on the idealistic nature of symmetrical communication, Grunig and his colleagues reformulated the model (Grunig 2001) using game theory, originally developed to study situations of conflict and cooperation. **Game theory** allows us to understand how PR strategies balance the interests of the organisation with those of the public in ways that allow a compromise to be reached (Murphy 1991).

Practitioners often develop strategies and define goals based on the need to reach a compromise with audiences – for example, persuading 18–30-year-olds of the value of an iPod. These are non-zero-sum games, where opportunities exist for all parties to benefit (in this case, the seller gets the money, while the buyer gets a portable music collection). Grunig and his colleagues extended this idea of non-zero-sum situations to construct a new model of communications as a continuum (see Figure 7.1).

At each extreme of the continuum, asymmetric communications are practised either in the interests of the organisation or of the public. In the central win–win zone, mixed motive communications is practised. Here the organisation and its publics enter into a dialogue of enlightened self-interest, characterised by negotiation,

Think about 7.1

Negotiating an evening out

When you and your friends are discussing where to spend your Friday night, how do you decide?

- Does one person dominate the decision and everyone else has to go along with it?
- Do you try and meet everyone's interests, perhaps by splitting up initially and then meeting up later?
- Does it get too complicated so you give up all trying to go out together and go your separate ways instead?
- Do some people happily give up their ideas and go along with the others?
- Do some people give up their ideas for now and instead do them at a later date?
- Do you either all go out together or not go out at all?

How does the option you chose fit with the mixed motive model? Could you negotiate things differently? What stops you doing so? Is there one person who tends to be the 'peacemaker' and finds a compromise? How much do you all rely on that person? What would happen if they were not there?

persuasion and compromise (see Figure 7.1 and Think about 7.1). Grunig argues that this continuum of communication more accurately reflects the contingencies that dictate organisational communications practice – where,

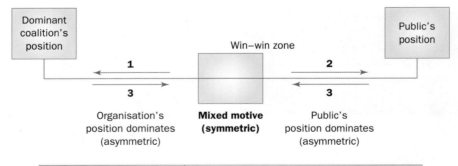

Type of practice	Explanation
1 Pure asymmetry model	Communication used to dominate public, accept dominant coalition's position
2 Pure cooperation model	Communication used to convince dominant coalition to cave in to public's position
3 Two-way model	Communication used to move public, dominant coalition or both to acceptable 'win–win' zone

Figure 7.1 New model of symmetry as two-way practices (*source*: Dozier et al. 1995)

for example, asymmetric communication may be the norm for some issues, but mixed motive models may be practised for those less critical to the organisation's survival (see also Plowman 1998 for an elaboration of this model).

Systems theory has prompted a focus on the objectives, processes and practices of PR and an emphasis on research associated with these areas. While there are too many to detail here, some are worth noting because of the volume of research they have prompted.

The notion of publics, for example, has long been debated by PR academics. One of the most important models in the systems theory tradition is that of the situational theory of publics (Grunig 1983; Grunig and Hunt 1984). In this theory, publics are segmented based on a typology of problem recognition. Latent publics are people who face a similar problem but do not recognise it; aware publics recognise a common issue; and active publics are those who recognise the problem and organise to do something about it. Underpinning this is a divide between active publics, who are proactive and have the potential to affect the organisation, and passive publics, who are less engaged with issues and unlikely to agitate. The theory of situational publics has been criticised for being ethnocentric and ignoring cultural contexts (Sriramesh et al. 2007), as well as for its limited acknowledgement of audience diversity and of power asymmetries between audiences and organisations (Leitch and Neilson 2001). Some have also argued that it is too one-dimensional in its portrayal of audience–organisation relationships (Moffitt 1994; Hallahan 2000; Cozier and Witmer 2001). (See Think about 7.2.) At the time of writing, the theory has been further developed as a 'situational theory of problem solving', emphasising the behaviour of publics in relation to organisations as a way of solving issues in their own lives, and moving away from what might be called 'organisational determinism' in the relationship (Kim and Grunig 2011).

Elsewhere, research into public relations specialisms, including issues and crisis management, PR using social media and consumer PR, recognises the multidimensional nature of audiences' lives and has moved away from conceptualising them purely in terms of their relevance to the organisation. In an attempt to integrate this more deeply into theorisations of PR, Vardeman-Winter and Tindall (2010) argue that intersectionality – the ways in which multiple markers of individual identity, such as gender, class, ethnicity and sexuality, shape social engagement and interaction – can act as a lens for understanding publics that is more fine-tuned to the complexity of their lives.

A second significant area of research has theorised PR as relationship management. This approach argues that maintaining and improving relationships between

---

Think about 7.2

Multiple images of organisations

If you work part time, what is your image of the company you work for from the point of view of an employee? How do you feel about the company as a customer? And what do your friends say about the company? Does their opinion affect the way you feel about the company when you are talking to them? Now think about how your company thinks about its audiences. Does it treat them as one group or does it differentiate between smaller groups or individuals? What criteria does it use to do that? How effective is that differentiation?

Feedback

How do you reconcile contradictions in the way you think about your company? Do you expect to have a different relationship with it once you are 'in the door', as compared to when you are not working? If so, why? If not, why not?

---

organisations and their audiences is the objective of PR (Ledingham and Bruning 2000). In Ledingham's view (Ledingham 2003: 190), PR is about:

Effectively managing organisational–public relationships around common interests and shared goals, over time, [which] results in mutual understanding and benefit for interacting organisations and publics.

This approach means that PR strategies and tactics should always be assessed in terms of their effect on the relationship between an organisation and its publics, rather than, for example, the benefits they provide for the organisation. Factors that affect all relationships, such as their history, the background of the people or organisations involved and the social context of the relationship, need to be considered in any PR campaign. In this way, the focus on relationships broadens the perspectives used to formulate and evaluate PR strategies and tactics, but also requires greater involvement from organisations. This is not as simple as it sounds – involvement means genuine dialogue, which in itself can be challenging. Kent and Taylor (2002) point out that dialogue in practice frequently fails to meet the expectations of those taking part and dialogue itself requires disclosure of information that may make the owner of that information vulnerable. Practitioners pressing for greater interaction with publics must recognise, explain and manage these potential risks for organisations, as well as for the publics they interact with. See Box 7.1.

Box 7.1

Theory in practice

Putting relationships first

The relationship perspective of PR does not require an organisation to give up its interests when deciding how to conduct its PR. But it does mean that wider thinking is required about how those objectives might be achieved. For example, if a computer manufacturer is faced with price increases from its suppliers, it will have to pass on some of those costs to its customers. Without a relationship perspective of communications, the company might decide to increase the cost of its products at short notice, announce it in a press release on the day of the increase and explain little about the conditions that led to the need to raise prices. This could alienate customers, who might feel that their needs and interests are being ignored – after all, they might also be facing a tough economic climate. A relationship perspective would prompt practitioners to moderate the impact of the price rise on customer opinions by developing a communication strategy that ensures they do not feel aggrieved. They might give six months' notice of the price rise, a full explanation of the reasons behind it and offer a senior member of staff for interviews on the topic. Customers would then have more complete information and better understand the company's position. They could assess and plan for the change and would feel that the company has taken their situation into account.

Broom et al. (2000) proposed the following principles for a relationship management approach to PR:

- Relationships are characterised by *interdependence*: parties to the relationship adapt in order to pursue a particular function in the relationship.

- Relationships represent *exchanges or transfers of information*, energy or resources; the attributes of these exchanges represent and define the relationship.

- Relationships have *antecedents and consequences* that must be taken into account when analysing them; organisation–public relationships therefore have specific antecedents (histories) and consequences (effects or results).

Because communication is so central to relationship management, the communication process should, therefore, be the starting point for an analysis of organisation–public relationships. Importantly, this means that the cultural norms that underpin communication will also affect the success of PR. To support practitioners trying to measure the health of their relationships, Huang (2001) developed a cross-cultural scale for measuring public perceptions of organisations, based on five dimensions of relationships:

1. control mutuality
2. trust
3. relational satisfaction and relational commitment
4. **renqing** ('favour')
5. **mianzi** ('face').

A third major focus of research in the systems tradition is on practitioner roles. Broom and Dozier (1986) defined two basic roles that are still valid today: the communications technician, who focuses on tactical matters such as writing, event management and media management, and the communications manager, who has a more strategic perspective and will normally create overall strategy, take and analyse client briefings and deal with issues and crises.

Researchers have explored the factors that lead to a managerial or technical emphasis in roles. Lauzen and Dozier (1992, 1994), for example, found that variability in the communications environment and an open systems-orientated organisation made it more likely that practitioners had a managerial role, while close links to marketing made a technical role more likely. Moss et al. (2000) also found that a managerial role was more likely if the organisation valued its stakeholders, the PR function could demonstrate its value to the organisation and if PR staff had a strong understanding of the general business principles that shaped their input. They found that senior managers divided up their roles into five main areas (Moss et al. 2004):

1. *monitor and evaluator* – organising and tracking PR work
2. *trouble shooting/problem solver* – handling a range of internal and external challenges to the organisation

> **Definition:** *'Renqing'* (favour) refers to a set of social norms based on the exchange of gifts and support, by which one must abide to get along well with others in Chinese society.
>
> **Definition:** *'Mianzi'* (face) refers to face, or face work – the process of impression management, or presenting oneself in an advantageous light, in order to expand or enhance human networks (Huang 2001: 69).

Picture 7.1 Mass movements were all influenced by communication techniques, including the 'Arab Spring' pro-democracy uprisings of 2011, which led to the overthrow of authoritarian regimes in the Middle East (*source*: Getty Images)

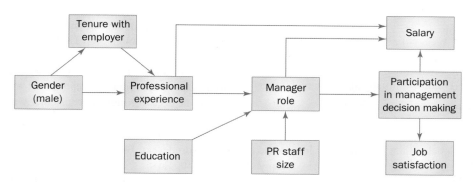

Figure 7.2 Interaction between gender, experience, education and managerial role (*source*: Dozier and Broom 1995: 16)

3. *key policy and strategy advisor* – contributing to top management, including contributions to and advice given in regular briefings and senior management meetings

4. *issues management expert* – intelligence gathering and analysis, monitoring external trends and recommending responses

5. *communication technician* – executing technical tasks associated with the PR role (e.g. writing press releases for financial reporting periods).

There is evidence of a gendered hierarchy between these two roles, with managerial roles more frequently occupied by male practitioners and generally enjoying greater perceived value and status (Grunig 1992; Grunig et al. 2002). Dozier and Broom (1995) showed that gender indirectly affected the role of practitioners and subsequent career success (see Figure 7.2). Men are more likely to have been longer with the organisation (tenure) and have more professional experience. The longer the tenure, the greater the professional experience; the greater the professional experience, the more likely it is that a practitioner has a managerial rather than a technician role, and the higher the salary. Women, then, tend to be associated with the technician role and, as a consequence, feminist researchers argue that this role has become devalued because of social stereotypes associated with 'women's work', even though it holds significant value in itself (Creedon 1991; Fröhlich and Peters 2007).

Internationalising systems theory

Researchers outside North America have tested Grunig and Hunt's typologies and found that country culture has a significant impact on the practice of PR (see Chapter 5). Practitioners use cultural norms and expectations to shape their approach to communication and these play a large part in determining the effectiveness of tactics and strategies (see, for example, Holtzhausen et al. 2003; Sriramesh et al. 2007). Sriramesh (2002, 2010) argues that recognition of this variety is essential if the body of knowledge about public relations is to remain relevant in a rapidly globalising world; remaining ethnocentric in pedagogy and practice is not an option. *The Global Public Relations Handbook* (Sriramesh and Verčič 2003, 2009) offers a summary of PR practice in a wide range of countries, elaborating on cultural, social, economic and political contexts and their implications for PR practice.

Sriramesh and Verčič (1995) outlined factors to consider when researching international public relations (IPR) practices, and Sriramesh (2010) has evolved this into generic principles for PR practice. These include:

- Culture (societal and organisational)
- Political system
- Economic system
- Political economy (defined as the ways in which politics and the economy mutually influence each other)
- The media system
- Forms of activism.

Most international studies have taken at least some of these variables into account (see, for example, Sriramesh 1992; Grunig et al. 1995; Sriramesh et al. 1999; Rhee 2002; Bardhan 2003; Holtzhausen et al. 2003).

Other studies have found region-specific characteristics associated with practice. Molleda (2000) found that economic, social and political circumstances in Latin America resulted in expectations that organisations would contribute to the development of society; consequently, the PR practitioner has a strong role as both change agent and conscience of the organisation (see Chapter 6 for further discussion). These findings are echoed by Hodges' (2011) ethnographic study of Mexican public relations practitioners, who contextualised their work in the unique social and cultural environment of Mexico City. In Europe, van Ruler et al. (2004) identified four characteristics of European PR: managerial, operational, reflective and educational, of which the reflective and educational characteristics were specific to Europe. Reflective characteristics are concerned with 'organisational standards, values and views and aimed at the development of mission and organisational strategies' and developed in light of relevant societal values, views and standpoints. Educational characteristics are concerned with work focused on 'the mentality and behaviour of the members of the organisation by facilitating them to communicate, and aimed at internal public groups' (van Ruler et al. 2004: 54).

Shortcomings of systems theory

Shortcomings of the systems theory approach to PR relate to the fundamental conceptualisation of PR, the privileging of organisational issues over socio-cultural contexts, the neglect of power-related issues that shape its effects and the theory's relevance to non-US contexts (Brown 2010).

Two of the earliest critics of systems theory, L'Etang and Piezcka (1996), argued that symmetrical communication is an idealistic model that misrepresents the reality of communications processes, where vested interests dictate the nature of PR practice and rarely encourage a truly balanced communications process. Leitch and Neilson (2001) critiqued the lack of context and power in systems theory and Vardeman-Winter and Tindall (2010) suggest that public relations work should recognise the importance of social background in its interaction with publics. Others argue that traditional conceptions of stakeholder and publics neglect the interactive, discursive and competitive processes that characterise PR activities in the public sphere, and therefore omit important aspects of the operation and effect of PR activities (Jensen 2001; Ihlen 2004; Raupp 2004).

Gilpin and Murphy (2008, 2010) critique the modernist assumptions of control and stability that underpin systems theory, instead using complexity theory to formulate new understandings of crisis situations and PR more generally. Complexity theory can be defined as the study of 'the (simple) interactions of many things (often repeated) leading to higher level patterns' (Goldberg and Markozy 1998: 4, cited in Gilpin and Murphy 2006: 380). A complexity-based approach emphasises the reality of unpredictable and unknowable events that the organisation must absorb and react to in the manner of Weick's *enacting organisations*, which actively engage with an indeterminate world, rather than simply passively reacting to it (Gilpin and Murphy 2006: 386). Skills such as improvisation, information gathering, ongoing reflective practice, situation awareness, risk assessment and problem solving all become crucial to effective PR in this context.

Witmer (2006; Cozier and Witmer 2001) argues that systems theory sidesteps the mutual influence of organisations and practitioners with their environments over time and uses structuration theory (Giddens 1984) to explain this influence in more detail. Structuration theory focuses on the ways in which social life and social structures emerge through patterns of interaction over time. It informs how public relations practitioners both shape and are constrained by their environments, as well as how 'organisational publics' operate as multifaceted, fluid discursive communities – an analysis that presents new challenges for organisations seeking to connect and communicate with their stakeholders (Witmer 2006). Falkheimer (2007) draws on this work and suggests that structuration prompts a focus on shared meanings, sensemaking and ideology in public relations work that influences symbolic spaces in society, builds relationships and generates trust.

Others have called for a stronger focus on the influence of PR over audiences, societies and cultures, and consideration of the power dynamics that underpin communication and its effects beyond the organisation (Motion 1999; Edwards 2006; Moloney 2006; McKie and Munshi 2007; Edwards 2010a; Bardhan and Weaver 2011).

> *Public relations scholars no longer can pretend that dialogue, symmetry and responsiveness are values and practices that concern only the actors involved in the resolution of specific corporate issues. Not only do we need to ask, on an ongoing basis, who is representing whose interests, we also need to look at the broader implications for conflict resolutions between organisations and their stakeholders.*
> (Cheney and Christensen 2001: 181)

These critiques have resulted in greater engagement with sociological and critical theories originating outside the PR field. At the same time, momentum has gathered behind a second tradition of PR theorising: the rhetorical approach. The application to PR of these theoretical understandings of society, culture and communication has generated a more multifaceted and nuanced understanding of the profession. In the next section of this chapter, we explore the main strands of research that have emerged as a result.

Picture 7.2 Worldwide protest against alleged human rights abuses in China was led by Amnesty International in the run-up to the 2008 Beijing Olympics. Critical theorists argue that PR practitioners perpetuate the ability of both corporations and governments to maintain a privileged position in society, usually by dominating the news agenda and excluding minority voices, such as campaigning groups, from public debate (*source*: Dennis M. Sabengan/epa/Corbis)

Postmodernism and PR

Postmodernist views of public relations challenge the very foundations of theory building in the field. PR originates in the **modernist** paradigm, in that most frameworks attempt to create single explanations, or metanarratives, that define the social environment. In contrast, **postmodernists** acknowledge variability, welcome fragmentation and engage with the multiplicity of voices, meanings and 'realities' that exist in society (Boyd and Vanslette 2009). Postmodernists argue that **metanarratives** have no inherent claim to superiority over other views. Instead, they should be acknowledged as one of many possible perspectives.

Holtzhausen (2002) argues that the profession is facing a future characterised by ever greater fluidity and diversity in its audiences; if practitioners continue to try and present metanarratives to a fragmented world, they will simply fail. A *postmodern* approach to PR can accommodate differences in culture, gender, ethnicity and society more effectively. Like critical theorists, postmodernists recognise that PR can perpetuate the existing system of power relations by creating and sustaining 'realities' for its audiences, indirectly communicating principles that support the organisations for which PR works via the media and other channels. Postmodernists also argue that, because of the existing power of businesses and government, they will always enjoy a more profitable outcome than their publics

> **Definition:** *'Modernist'*, in PR, means an approach that legitimises the discourse of management and organisations as given and superior. Modernist PR attempts to reduce or eliminate crises, control publics and contribute to organisational effectiveness, usually measured in financial terms.
>
> **Definition:** *'Postmodernism'*, in PR, is an approach that understands PR to generate perceived truths among publics through its role as a creator of organisational discourse. Postmodernist PR recognises that the language used in PR also generates, sustains and shapes power relations in society.
>
> **Definition:** *'Metanarrative'* means an attempt to make sense of the larger picture, or the wider social environment. Critical theorists and postmodernists (see below) suggest organisations and individuals use metanarratives as overarching explanations of the way the world works. They believe reliance on these 'stories' can prevent closer examination of reality.
>
> **Definition:** *'Discourse'* here refers to particular ways of making sense of the world, communicated, sustained and justified through language and social institutions.

when the two are in dialogue. This has specific ethical implications for PR practice (Mickey 1997; Holtzhausen 2002). For example, PR practitioners have a duty to work reflexively and act ethically in acknowledging other voices and pointing them out to the organisation when the need arises. In light of this, Holtzhausen and Voto (2002) explored the possibilities inherent in the PR role as a form of organisational activism, and Holtzhausen (2011) extended this to PR in the context of globalisation. She suggests practitioners can adopt a critical stance to their work in order to enable and respect resistance to organisational goals; can ensure that stakeholders' voices have space to be heard in debates; and can acknowledge the importance of change by generating opportunities for dissent, through which change will emerge. In this sense, Holtzhausen frames public relations activities themselves as a form of activism, when strategies are designed to instigate change in societal norms or dominant policies.

Boyd and Vanslette (2009) adopt a postmodern approach for their discussion of 'outlaw' **discourses**, disseminated through campaigns employing tactics that lie outside the normal canon of accepted practice. They suggest that studies of these discourses will help PR reveal alternative voices 'that fall outside society's norms and assumptions about what is good, fair and sometimes even lawful' (2009: 333). This can help practitioners and scholars understand how marginalised groups deploy communications in ways that ensure their views and voices are heard, but without adhering to normative expectations of argument and debate. Ultimately, such debates are a legitimate part of the picture that makes up a 'fully functioning society' (see below), significant in the implications they have for social and cultural change and evolution.

In summary, postmodernists recognise that PR practitioners face significant challenges from fragmented audiences, greater access to uncontrolled media, a more aggressive media, frequent challenges to government policies and to the principles of capitalism and globalisation and a greater number of active publics. A postmodern perspective integrates this fragmentation and diversity into approaches to PR.

Rhetorical theory and PR

Rhetorical approaches to PR have evolved significantly as a result of the efforts of the main protagonist of theory in this area, Robert L. Heath, and rhetorical approaches are arguably one of the main schools of thought in PR today. They underpin a range of approaches to PR centring on the quality, ethics and effectiveness of discourse (see Boyd and Waymer 2011; Heath 2011; Ihlen 2011; Taylor 2011).

Rhetoric in the context of PR may be defined as 'persuasive strategies and argumentative discourse' (L'Etang 1996: 106) – a two-way discussion between parties that has a particular end goal in mind. It takes place, as Heath (2009) puts it, as part of a 'wrangle' of voices and not in isolation. Heath (2006) argued that rhetorical theory applied to PR focuses on the importance of this debate and discussion to generate a 'fully-functioning society' in which all voices are heard, and this concept has been used widely as a principle for research on PR since its introduction. Public relations is crucial as a means of generating debate between parties, but must operate responsibly, ethically and take a wide range of perspectives into account rather than only operating in the interests of one organisation. Meaning is developed through the interactions of organisations with audiences through discourse and relationships (Taylor 2009, 2010) and debate and disagreement is assumed to be part of this process (Heath 2009). Genuine dialogue will result in a meeting of minds, while a failure to communicate effectively is ethically irresponsible. As Heath (1992: 19) puts it:

> [The] ability to create opinions that influence how people live is the focal aspect of the rhetoric of public relations. In the process of establishing product, service or organizational identity . . . public relations practitioners help establish key terms – especially slogans, **axioms** and metaphors – by which people think about their society and organizations. These terms shape the way people view themselves as consumers, members of a community, contributors to the arts, and myriad other ways.

Rhetorical analyses of PR focus on ethics, power, influence and access to communication and recognise that the success of PR rests on agreement between parties; rhetorical practice ensures that this is achieved through responsible discursive engagement (Ihlen 2011). Rhetorical analyses include both text-based and symbolic aspects of PR (Heath 2009), including non-verbal and visual cues used by organisations in the process of persuasion (Cheney and Dionisopoulos 1989). (See also Chapter 11 for discussion of symbols and persuasive communication.)

A number of researchers have adopted a rhetorical approach to analyses of PR narratives, content, evaluation, underlying assumptions about the relationship between organisations and publics and the enactment (or not) of social exchange in the communications process (e.g., Crable and Vibbert 1983; Cheney and Dionisopoulos 1989; Livesey 2001; Heath 2006, 2009; Ihlen 2011). Cheney

---

Definition: An 'axiom' is a statement, proposition or idea that people accept as self-evidently true, even though the proposition itself may be unproven.

---

et al. (2004), for example, argue that rhetoric can be used to analyse the ways organisations anticipate, respond to and shape rhetorical situations in which they find themselves, in the process also developing their own identity. Taylor (2009, 2010) argues that rhetorical principles fit well with theorising PR as a mechanism for the effective enactment of civil society, based on cooperative relationships between all participants. Finally, L'Etang (1996) urges a focus on organisations, rather than just PR practitioners, as rhetoricians in society in order to detect structural influences on the power of the rhetorical process (see also Skerlep 2001; Boyd and Waymer 2011).

Feminist analyses of PR

Feminist analyses of PR emerged in the late 1980s and are grounded in the practical reality of the profession: women outnumber men in PR but are still under-represented at managerial level, and studies have repeatedly found gender inequalities in salaries, salary expectations, hiring perceptions and representation at management level (Grunig et al. 2001; Aldoory and Toth 2002; Aldoory 2009).

Feminist analyses of the profession have emphasised the ways that stereotypes shape perceptions of male and female practitioners, of PR as a feminised profession, of the relatively low-status technician role frequently occupied by women and of the more limited support for women in the form of mentors and access to informal organisational networks (Creedon 1991; Grunig et al. 2001; Choi and Hon 2002; O'Neil 2003; Fröhlich 2004; Wrigley 2010). (See Mini case study 7.3.) Evidence of a glass ceiling is clear: women are more often overlooked for promotion by men making senior appointments, they take on a wide range of unrewarded responsibilities, including managerial ones, they have lower salaries (PRCA/*PRWeek* 2011) and slower career progression (see Wrigley 2010 for a useful overview of these findings).

Some researchers have focused on the specific ways in which women conduct PR. For example, Aldoory (2009) reviewed studies of PR-related work from a feminist perspective and revealed the ways in which both the content of campaigns and PR practice and process can perpetuate women's disadvantage in relation to men in that they fail to acknowledge the complexity and specificity of their lives, both locally and in the context of global campaigns. On the other hand, Grunig et al. (2000) argue that the feminist values of inclusivity, respect, caring, cooperation, equity, self-determination and interconnection could enhance the ethical and effective practice of PR.

However, Fröhlich (2004) points out that such values might be seen as disadvantages rather than advantages at

Mini case study 7.3
A female public relations manager

To put these findings into context, take the example of a female PR manager with four staff in her team, managing a budget of £100,000. She might develop and manage PR campaigns primarily linked to marketing and product launches. When the volume of work gets too much for her team she might 'muck in' and help them with day-to-day tactical jobs, such as ringing the media or writing press releases. This doubling up of tasks (alongside family commitments) may prevent her from taking part in informal networking activities (such as drinks after work or sporting activities). She therefore has fewer opportunities to influence or impress senior managers and may find it hard to move up the management hierarchy as a result. As a manager, she might be on the management team alongside marketing, HR, finance and other business functions, but if she is the only woman – and working in an area that is seen to be subordinate to marketing – her opinions might not be valued as much as the other managers' and decisions are unlikely to reflect her input.

senior management level. Fitch and Third (2010) argue that the industry is still patriarchal in its structure, while Yeomans (2010) suggests that organisations may be characterised by an 'emotional ecology', with different 'feeling rules' for men and women affecting the ways their roles are enacted. Fröhlich and Peters (2007) suggest that differences between men's and women's roles in public relations may be a function of preferences for different types of organisational culture. This, combined with the social barriers to promotion for women (such as work/home conflict), results in women choosing not to pursue managerial roles and selecting certain work environments over others. They also found that organisational preferences for men at managerial level, combined with individual practitioner characteristics, affected career progression, and that women's incorporation of the 'PR bunny' stereotype into their own self-image and their descriptions of other practitioners was potentially a significant threat to both their own career and the regard for the profession as a whole. Perhaps more sympathetically, Wrigley (2002) noted the tendency of both women and men to deny the scale of discrimination that research had revealed and suggested the concept of negotiated resignation to describe how women practitioners come to terms with workplace discrimination in a way that enables them to validate both their own position and the structures and processes that perpetuate that discrimination. Yeomans (2010) finds similar dynamics in her research, where women PR consultants engaged enthusiastically with the 'feminine' role of 'trusted advisor', but balanced this with a strong notion of professionalism, ultimately generating a gender-neutral professional self-identity for themselves.

Overall, this body of work recognises the roots of discrimination in PR as located in pervasive divisions at societal level, rather than solely within the profession. For example, Hon (1995) acknowledges the effects of institutionalised sexism and organisational stereotypes on

Explore 7.1

Women in public relations

Why do you think so many women work in PR? Ask fellow students and any practitioners you know:

- What attracted them to the profession?
- What might make them leave?
- Where do they see themselves in 5, 10 and 20 years' time?
- Does being female affect their career opportunities?

women in PR and argues for change at four levels: society, organisation, profession and individual. Aldoory (2009) argues strongly for more research grounded in feminist critique to address gender as an instrument of power and explore ways in which it may be challenged. Finally, Daymon and Demetrious (2010: 1) suggest a starting point for more critical feminist research that recognises gender is 'about the negotiation, construction and performance of masculine and feminine identities'. The new ways of thinking they advocate affect all aspects of research, from question formulation to methodological directions, to data collection and analysis (see Explore 7.1).

Diversity and 'race' in PR

There are two main diversity-related strands of thought in public relations scholarship. The first relates to the increasing variety of audiences that PR practitioners are trying to reach. This has resulted in calls for greater diversity within the profession, using the logic of 'requisite variety' (matching the diversity in audiences with diversity in the practitioner body, in order to communicate effectively). This approach has been criticised for ultimately generating an impossible logic, where the 'requisite' variety becomes unmanageable (Sha and Ford 2007), and for prioritising the organisation's needs over those of diverse groups and individuals (e.g. Munshi and McKie 2001; McKie and Munshi 2007). In contrast, post-colonial and critical race scholars have highlighted the need to integrate a wide variety of values and approaches to communication because they have the potential to change and enrich communications practice in ways that extend beyond simple economic benefit (e.g. Dutta and Pal 2011). Bardhan (2011) and Kent and Taylor (2011), for example, propose public relations as a means of 'third culture building', engaging with the dialogue and relationship building that is central to intercultural communication. They suggest that PR practitioners may be understood as 'transcultural', in the sense that they can structure and communicate shared meanings that overcome 'us/them' divisions between global communities.

Some work has analysed the 'raced' nature of public relations itself, focusing on practitioner diversity and the difficult experience of being a minority in an overwhelmingly white environment. Different forms of systemic discrimination based on racial identity have been found in the US and the UK professions: Black and other minority ethnic PR practitioners are under-represented and experience significant difficulty as minority professionals in the field (Pompper 2007; Ford and Appelbaum 2009; Edwards 2010b). Barriers include stereotyping, pigeonholing, positive and negative discrimination on the basis of race or colour and having a role as 'the minority representative'. Participants emphasised the need to attract more minorities into the profession by increasing the visibility of existing minority practitioners and educating career advisors in schools and universities about PR and the opportunities it offers. Retaining staff by providing mentors and ensuring fair promotion processes was also vital (for an understanding of the persistence of these dynamics, see early research by Zerbinos and Clanton 1993; Kern-Foxworth et al. 1994; Len Rios 1998).

These discussions frequently address the racialised nature of PR discourses that work against the interests of minority groups, and reveal how 'whiteness' – the systemic association of white embodiment and identities with privileged social categories and superior personal skills and attributes – has been recognised as an implicit to practitioner cultures, 'othering' those who do not have the advantage of this identity (Aldoory 2005; Edwards 2010b; Logan 2011; Munshi and Edwards 2011; Vardeman-Winter 2011). Others have argued that whiteness and western-centric perspectives mark PR research and pedagogy, and need to be explicitly acknowledged in order to

avoid perpetuating discrimination through this channel (Waymer 2010; Weaver 2010; Vardeman-Winter 2011). Munshi and Edwards (2011) draw on post-colonial, critical race and sociological theories to go further and propose a research agenda for 'race' in/and public relations based on four dialectics: racialised elites/racialised non-elites; visibility/invisibility; race-as-process/race-as-category; and general/particular.

Vardeman-Winter and Tindall (2010; Vardeman-Winter 2011) called for greater use of intersectionality to explore these experiences, in order to avoid essentialising individuals as 'only' black, or female, or working class, for example. Certainly, as the range of ethnic groups entering the profession increases and diversity among audiences also becomes greater, a better understanding of the lives of both practitioners and publics in relation to PR will be necessary. Such research will also facilitate recognition of the new perspectives that diversity brings to communication, and enrich the body of knowledge both in this area and in the field of PR as a whole.

Picture 7.3 PR practitioners in the UK are trying to reach an increasingly diverse range of publics. See Think about 7.3 (*source*: Philip Bigg/Alamy Images)

Think about 7.3

Connecting with publics

What problems do you think there might be in conducting a PR campaign to encourage Asian women to use the public swimming baths if no one in the office understands the cultural factors that might prevent some of them from taking part in mixed events? What about language problems? How would you approach these issues?

Critical approaches to PR

Critical approaches to PR are based on a very wide range of theoretical approaches connected by their focus on the interrogation of power dynamics produced by and through public relations. Critical theorists make a vital contribution to the field in that they examine the effect of PR practice on its social and economic context, and particularly the potential for PR to privilege the interests of dominant groups – usually corporations and government.

An important strand of critical work focuses on the ways in which PR sources dominate the news agenda and exclude other voices from public debate (Davis 2000; Miller and Dinan 2000; Mickey 2002; L'Etang and Pieczka 2006). The 'resource imbalance' perspective emphasises the pressure on journalists to manage decreasing amounts of resource with increasing demands for copy. Such pressures, combined with the improved skills of PR practitioners and the resource invested in PR, lead to journalists becoming more dependent on PR sources (Stauber and Rampton 1995; Moloney 2000; Pitcher 2003). The 'structural' argument demonstrates that corporate patterns of media ownership result in internal censorship of news stories within media organisations and a news agenda that hesitates to challenge received wisdom, for fear of stepping on owners' and advertisers' toes (McChesney 1999; Croteau and Hoynes 2001; Davies 2008; Lewis et al. 2008).

Other critical scholars explore the discursive and symbolic work executed through PR. Here, Bourdieu, Foucault and Habermas have been an important source of inspiration for many researchers.

Habermasian scholars focus in particular on his conceptualisation of the public sphere (Habermas 1989), a social space that mediates between the political sphere and the private sphere by providing space for discussion and negotiation. Jensen (2001) suggests that the public sphere can refer to 'the discursive processes in a complex network of persons, institutionalised associations and organisa-

tions' (2001: 136), and is therefore characterised by disagreement rather than agreement. She suggests that PR is particularly relevant to public sphere discussions about organisational legitimacy and identity, since it promotes and justifies particular organisational identities and 'ways of being'. On the other hand, PR strategies and tactics must adjust to the changing social expectations of organisations that emerge from discussions in the public sphere. For example, the ways in which organisations attempt to legitimise their activities (such as through corporate social responsibility arguments) will shape expectations of organisational behaviour, and may also affect regulation of company activities through legislation. Taking a slightly different tack, Hove (2009) argues that communication in the public sphere takes two forms: the first acts as a warning of potential issues, where (sometimes irrational and illogical) communication generates interest and attention; and the second as critical engagement, based on Habermas' ideal of communicative action, and through which agreement between different actors may be achieved. Clearly, PR is implicated in both these forms of communication.

Moloney (2006), in contrast, suggests a redefinition of the public sphere, suggesting we now live in a persuasive sphere where citizens must make sense of myriad messages about the merits of a vast range of products, policies and issues. He argues that PR practitioners who set out to persuade should do so ethically, in a way that ensures balance between the views that they represent and those of others. Relatedly, some scholars have attempted to apply Habermas' principles of communicative action as a source of ethical guidance for public relations practice (Leeper 1996; Meisenach 2006). This would prioritise understanding as the ultimate public relations goal, ensure practitioners stood by their claims of comprehensibility, truth, rightness and sincerity and target equal participation in the discursive process for all stakeholders, in line with Habermas' conceptualisation of the ideal speech situation (Leeper 1996). More practically, Burkart (2007) proposes a model of Consensus-Oriented Public Relations (COPR) for planning and evaluating public relations based on Habermas' analysis of the ideal type of communication process (Burkart 2007: 250–251). The COPR model prompts practitioners to modify their practice in order to eliminate doubts about its sincerity, veracity or other sources of validity.

Edwards (2006, 2008, 2009) and Ihlen (2007) have adopted Pierre Bourdieu's framework of fields, capital and habitus to examine public relations practice in organisational contexts. Bourdieu argues that individuals and groups compete for power by acquiring four types of resources: economic capital, social capital, cultural capital and symbolic capital (Bourdieu and Wacquant 1992). The volume and composition of the capital obtained determines whether they dominate or are dominated in a particular field (Bourdieu 1991). Ihlen (2007) argues that PR practitioners help organisations in this power struggle. He suggests that a key role of PR is to develop organisational networks and thereby extend the organisation's social capital – the resources associated with the networks that they are part of. Edwards (2008, 2009) takes a more critical approach, using Bourdieu's ideas to investigate practitioners and the profession. Her exploratory survey of UK practitioners (Edwards 2008) revealed a homogenous group of individuals with high levels of cultural and economic capital, similar to other powerful groups in society and in a position to use those connections in order to make their clients' voices heard, whether they are corporate, government or third-sector organisations. She also applied Bourdieu's ideas to PR practitioners' activities within organisations and concluded that they act as symbolically violent cultural intermediaries, who communicate particular cultural and social values and attitudes through discourses that shore up the interests of those for whom they work (Edwards 2012).

Discourse theory, and particularly the work of Michel Foucault and Norman Fairclough, has also been used fruitfully to deconstruct public relations work and reveal the more complex effects of this work on society (Motion and Leitch 2007; Leitch and Motion 2010). From this perspective, PR practitioners develop and transform discourses and socio-cultural practices because they affect the normalisation of 'truths' and the distribution of power and knowledge in society. Motion and Leitch (2007) argue that PR practitioners may be thought of as 'discourse technologists', who 'seek to achieve change by transforming discourses, which involves changing established ways of thinking about particular objects, concepts, subjects and strategies (Foucault 1969/1972) or introducing new language and, therefore, new ways of thinking' (Leitch and Motion 2010: 103). In so doing, they (re)shape discourses by altering their boundaries, changing the identities and roles for people affected by them, changing the ways that language is used and the forms of that language, and altering the ways in which discourses circulate across society (Leitch and Motion 2010: 104). They have applied this thinking to public relations work on personal and organisational identities (Motion 1999; Motion and Leitch 2002), to government consultation processes (Motion 2005) and, theoretically, to the conceptualisation of organisations, publics, truth and context in public relations (Motion and Leitch 2007). In the twenty-first century, they suggest that this approach to PR is more productive in considering dynamics of power, the multiplicity and complexity of communications environments, the nature of resistance to PR discourses and the ways in which PR can engage its audiences (Leitch and Motion 2010).

Taken as a whole, these and other critical analyses explicitly counter the apparent neutrality of PR presented in systems theory, and instead highlight the *interested* nature of PR as a profession that exists to serve those who use it. (See Think about 7.3 and Explore 7.2)

Think about 7.4

External pressures on journalists

If you were a journalist working for a TV news channel owned by Company A, and one of its main advertisers is Company B, how would you handle a report that criticised Company A's treatment of employees or problems with Company B's new product launch?

Feedback

Critical theorists would argue that you would be under pressure to downplay the story, with some suggesting that self-censorship means the story never even goes to the news editor. (See also Herman and Chomsky's propaganda model in Chapter 11.)

Explore 7.2

What's the real story?

Examine a party political press conference or broadcast. (Examples, including videos, from the 2010 UK election can be found at http://news.bbc.co.uk/1/hi/uk_politics/election_2010/parties_and_issues/8593869.stm)

What message is the speaker communicating about their party's activities and what 'picture' are they presenting of their organisation? What symbols are they using to tell the story (e.g. positive stories about technology, schoolchildren, nurses, or negative stories about wasted resources, irresponsible management or national security)? How do they want you to react to their 'story'? What perspectives could have been included in the story but are not mentioned? What issues is the person refusing to answer, or avoiding? Why?

Feedback

Consider what ideological perspective the party is presenting – is it one that questions the principles of business or political process, or assumes they are inherently correct? Does it assume we all think the same way? Does it present 'families' or 'immigration' in a different way from other parties?

Think about 7.5

Your university or college

Do you passively accept what your university says to you about your course? Or do your experience, opinions, the views of other students and other sources of information all act on their message to create a specific interpretation that is yours alone?

Feedback

Only you can create meaning in light of your own experience. What you tell other people about the university and the course you are on reflects this process of dialogue between what the university says and what you actually experience.

Socio-cultural approaches to PR

A significant body of work to emerge over the past few years focuses on the interaction between society, culture and public relations, positioning the profession as both a determining force in culture and determined by culture (Curtin and Gaither 2007; Edwards and Hodges 2011; Hodges 2011). Included in this are examinations of the history of public relations in different countries, where socio-cultural dynamics are understood to have actively shaped the profession. Toledano and McKie (2007), for example, situate their analysis of Israeli public relations in the cultural context of social integration as an unequivocal political and social goal.

Curtin and Gaither (2007) emphasise the importance of culture as a defining element in professional practice, industry structures and social expectations of the PR profession. In the context of international public relations, they argue that PR practice is never neutral, because it implicitly or explicitly promotes specific cultural values and assumptions. They use the model of the circuit of culture (Du Gay et al. 1997) to create an understanding of how PR as a cultural practice also generates meaning and power in society. The model (see Figure 7.3) illustrates how five different 'moments' of meaning construction interact and overlap to create points of 'articulation', where meanings are renegotiated.

Curtin and Gaither (2007) explain public relations as a practice of socio-cultural representation (primarily discursive), of meaning production (in the practice of producing messages, stories, releases or images for a particular purpose) and of identity in its specific presentations of organisations and audiences in particular socio-cultural roles. Public relations also shapes consumption practices and is in turn shaped by them, as products and services are consumed in particular ways, while it is also a source of regulation in that it attempts to define what is and is not acceptable in specific cultural contexts. In all these moments, the public relations profession and its practitioners can either enhance existing power structures or liberate subordinate voices; its effects fluctuate, but power is always implicated in its practice. The model positions

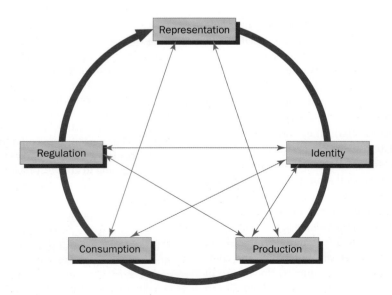

Figure 7.3 The circuit of culture (*source*: Du Gay et al. 1997: 3)

practitioners as 'cultural intermediaries' (Curtin and Gaither 2005: 107) – conduits for cultural norms and values that are constantly renegotiated between organisations, individuals and social institutions through the articulations of the five moments of the circuit. Hodges (2006) echoes this understanding of public relations practitioners as cultural intermediaries, 'an occupational group which mediates between organisations and groups within wider society, seeking to communicate meanings through influential communicative practice' (2006: 88). This leads to a focus on practitioner cultures (formal and informal rules, professional and cultural knowledge, norms, values and attitudes, socio-cultural influences), political, economic and legal structures and historical contexts as a means of understanding the profession in society (Hodges 2011).

On a different tack, but also positioning public relations as an active force in the socio-cultural environment, Merten (2004) offers a constructivist interpretation of PR, suggesting that it constructs 'realities' through the promotion of particular discourses (for example, consumerism), particularly in the media. Merten points out that journalists used to present a version of reality that could be trusted because journalists were usually present at the event being described. However, the growth of news outlets means that journalists can no longer be present for each and every news story, leaving space for PR to act as a news intermediary. Yet these third-hand stories are never differentiated; they carry the same kudos as original news stories and are treated as equally real. From the constructivist perspective, then, reality has in fact become a combination of authentic reality (observed first hand) and the representations produced by PR practitioners, among others, that appear in the news. Obviously, the power of PR is significant since it is now in a position to both provide a selection of realities from which journalists can choose to create a story, and/or define which events are in the public interest by providing representations and discourses that are only relevant to these events.

From a more pragmatic perspective, McKie and Munshi (2007; McKie 2010) argue that PR should play a key role in helping businesses meet their social responsibilities to the communities in which they operate, but suggest it is poorly equipped to meet 'the demand for a learning orientation, for experimentation, for discovery, for acknowledging uncertainty and for embracing ambiguity' (McKie and Munshi 2007: 21). In their view, public relations is uniquely placed to address three major challenges faced by businesses in the twenty-first century. These are: environmental and climate change; the decline of western dominance and the increasing importance of non-western cultural, social and economic contexts; and the need for enterprise to be used responsibly to make commerce more socially and ecologically sustainable. They suggest that, by accepting ambiguity and uncertainty, embracing a constant search for understanding and integrating insights from other understandings of enterprise and organisations, public relations can be a force for the public good.

Summary

PR sits at the intersection of a wide range of both academic and practical disciplines. It is therefore appropriate that we learn more about our own area by integrating other understandings into our body of knowledge. By developing theory in this way, it can and will be of genuine help to PR practice.

Bibliography

Aldoory, L. (2005). 'A (re)conceived feminist paradigm for public relations: a case for substantial improvement'. *Journal of Communication* **55**(4): 668–684.

Aldoory, L. (2009). 'Feminist criticism in public relations: how gender can impact public relations texts and contexts' in *Rhetorical and Critical Approaches to Public Relations II*. R.L. Heath, E. Toth and D. Waymer (eds). New York, NY: Routledge.

Aldoory, L. and E. Toth (2002). 'Gender discrepancies in a gendered profession: a developing theory for public relations'. *Journal of Public Relations Research* **14**(2): 103–126.

Bardhan, N. (2003). 'Rupturing public relations metanarratives: the example of India.' *Journal of Public Relations Research* **15**(3): 225–248.

Bardhan, N. (2011). 'Culture, communication and third culture building in public relations within global flux' in *Public Relations in Global Cultural Contexts: Multiparadigmatic perspectives*. N. Bardhan and C.K. Weaver (eds). New York, NY: Routledge.

Bardhan, N. and C.K. Weaver (2011). *Public Relations in Global Cultural Contexts: Multi-paradigmatic perspectives*. New York, NY: Routledge.

Bourdieu, P. (1991). *Language and Symbolic Power* (G. Raymond and M. Adamson, trans). Cambridge, UK: Polity Press.

Bourdieu, P. and L. Wacquant (1992). *An Invitation to Reflexive Sociology*. Chicago, IL: Polity Press.

Boyd, J. and S.H. Vanslette (2009). 'Outlaw discourse as postmodern public relations' in *Rhetorical and Critical Approaches to Public Relations II*. R.L. Heath, E. Toth and D. Waymer (eds). New York, NY: Routledge.

Boyd, J. and D. Waymer (2011). 'Organizational rhetoric: a subject of interest(s)'. *Management Communication Quarterly* **25**: 474–493.

Broom, G.M. and D.M. Dozier (1986). 'Advancement for public relations role models.' *Public Relations Review* **12**(1): 37–56.

Broom, G.M., S. Casey and J. Ritchey (2000). 'Concept and theory of organization-public relationships' in *Public Relations as Relationship Management*. L.A. Ledingham and S.D. Bruning (eds). Mahwah, NJ: Lawrence Erlbaum Associates.

Brown, R. (2010). 'Symmetry and its critics: antecedents, prospects and implications for symmetry in a postsymmetry era' in *The Sage Handbook of Public Relations*. R.L. Heath (ed.). Thousand Oaks, CA: Sage.

Burkart, R. (2007). 'On Jurgen Habermas and public relations'. *Public Relations Review* **33**(3): 249–254.

Cheney, G. and L.T. Christensen (2001). 'Public relations as contested terrain: a critical response' in *Handbook of Public Relations*. R. Heath (ed.). Thousand Oaks, CA: Sage.

Cheney, G. and G.N. Dionisopoulos (1989). 'Public relations? No, relations with publics: a rhetorical-organizational approach to contemporary corporate communications' in *Public Relations Theory*. C.H. Botan and V. Hazelton. Hillsdale, NJ: Lawrence Erlbaum Associates.

Cheney, G., L.T. Christiansen, C. Conrad and D.J. Lair (2004). 'Corporate rhetoric as organizational discourse' in *The Sage Handbook of Organizational Discourse*. D. Grant, C. Hardy, C. Oswick and L. Putnam (eds). London: Sage.

Choi, Y. and L.C. Hon (2002). 'The influence of gender composition in powerful positions on public relations practitioners' gender-related perceptions'. *Journal of Public Relations Research* **14**(3): 229–263.

Cozier, Z.R. and D.F. Witmer (2001). 'The development of a structuration analysis of new publics in an electronic environment' in *Handbook of Public Relations*. R. Heath (ed.). Thousand Oaks, CA: Sage.

Crable, R.L. and S.L. Vibbert (1983). 'Mobil's epideictic advocacy: "observations" of Prometheus-bound'. *Communication Monographs* **50**: 380–394.

Creedon, P. (1991). 'Public relations and "women's work": toward a feminist analysis of public relations roles.' *Public Relations Research Annual* **3**: 67–84.

Croteau, D. and W. Hoynes (2001). *The Business of Media: Corporate media and the public interest*. Thousand Oaks, CA: Pine Forge Press.

Curtin, P.A. and T.K. Gaither (2005). 'Privileging identity, difference and power: the circuit of culture as a basis for public relations theory'. *Journal of Public Relations Research* **17**(2): 91–115.

Curtin, P.A. and T.K. Gaither (2007). *International Public Relations: Negotiating culture, identity and power*. London: Sage.

Cutlip, S.M., A.H. Center and G.M. Broom (2000). *Effective Public Relations*, 8th edition. Upper Saddle River, NJ: Prentice Hall.

Davis, A. (2000). 'Public relations, business news and the reproduction of corporate power'. *Journalism* **1**(3): 282–304.

Davies, N. (2008). *Flat Earth News: An award-winning reporter exposes falsehood, distortion and propaganda in the global media*. London: Chatto and Windus.

Daymon, C. and K. Demetrious (2010). 'Gender and public relations: perspectives, applications and questions'. *PRism* 7.

Dozier, D.M. and G.M. Broom (1995). 'Evolution of the manager role in public relations practice'. *Journal of Public Relations Research* **7**(1): 3–26.

Dozier, D.M., J.E. Grunig and L.A. Gruning (1995). *Manager's Guide to Excellence in Public Relations and Communication Management*. Mahwah, NJ: Lawrence Erlbaum Associates.

Du Gay, P., S. Hall, L. Janes, H. Mackay and K. Negus (1997). *Doing Cultural Studies: The story of the Sony Walkman (Vol. 1)*. London: Sage/The Open University.

Dutta, M.J. and M. Pal (2011). 'Public relations and marginalization in a global context: A postcolonial critique' in *Public Relations in Global Cultural Contexts: Multi-Paradigmatic Perspectives*. N. Bardhan and C.K. Weaver (eds). New York, NY: Routledge.

Edwards, L. (2006). 'Rethinking power in public relations'. *Public Relations Review* **32**: 229–231.

Edwards, L. (2008). 'PR practitioners' cultural capital: an initial study and implications for research and practice'. *Public Relations Review* **34**(4): 367–372.

Edwards, L. (2009). 'Symbolic power and public relations practice: locating individual practitioners in their social context'. *Journal of Public Relations Research* **21**(3): 251–272.

Edwards, L. (2010a). 'Critical perspectives in global public relations: theorizing power' in *Public Relations in Global Cultural Contexts: Multi-paradigmatic perspectives*. N. Bardhan and C.K. Weaver (eds). New York, NY: Routledge.

Edwards, L. (2010b). 'An exploratory study of the experiences of "BAME" PR practitioners in the UK industry: industry report.' Manchester: Manchester Business School, University of Manchester.

Edwards, L. (2012). 'Exploring the role of public relations as a cultural intermediary.' *Cultural Sociology* **6**(4).

Edwards, L. and C.E.M. Hodges (eds) (2011). *Public Relations, Society and Culture: Theoretical and empirical explorations*. London: Routledge.

Falkheimer, J. (2007). 'Anthony Giddens and public relations: a third way perspective'. *Public Relations Review* **33**(3): 287–293.

Fitch, K. and A. Third (2010). 'Working girls: revisiting the gendering of public relations'. *PRism 7*.

Ford, R. and L. Appelbaum (2009). 'Multicultural survey of PR practitioners'. www.ccny.cuny.edu/prsurvey accessed 22 September 2009.

Foucault, M. (1969/1972). *The Archaeology of Knowledge*. London: Routledge.

Fröhlich, R. (2004). 'Feminine and feminist values in communication professions: exceptional skills and expertise or "friendliness trap"?' in *Gender and Newsroom Cultures: Identities at work*. M. de Bruin and K. Ross (eds). Cresskill, NJ: Hampton.

Fröhlich, R. and S. Peters (2007). 'PR bunnies caught in the agency ghetto? Gender stereotypes, organisational factors, and women's careers in PR agencies'. *Journal of Public Relations Research* **19**(3): 229–254.

Giddens, A. (1984). *The Constitution of Society*. Princeton, NJ: University of California Press.

Gilpin, D. and P. Murphy (2006). 'Reframing crisis management through complexity' in *Public Relations Theory II*. C.H. Botan and V. Hazelton (eds). Mahwah, NJ: Lawrence Erlbaum Associates.

Gilpin, D. and P. Murphy (2008). *Crisis Management in a Complex World*. New York, NY: Oxford University Press.

Gilpin, D. and P. Murphy (2010). 'Implications of complexity theory for public relations: beyond crisis' in *The Sage Handbook of Public Relations*. R.L. Heath (ed.). Thousand Oaks, CA: Sage.

Grunig, J.E. (1983). 'Communications behaviors and attitudes of environmental publics: two studies'. *Journalism Monographs 81*.

Grunig, J.E. (1992). *Excellence in Public Relations and Communication Management*. Hillsdale, NJ: Lawrence Erlbaum Associates.

Grunig, J.E. (2001). 'Two-way symmetrical public relations: past, present and future' in *Handbook of Public Relations*. R. Heath (ed.). Thousand Oaks, CA: Sage.

Grunig, J.E. and T. Hunt (1984). *Managing Public Relations*. New York, NY: Holt, Rinehart and Winston.

Grunig, J.E., L. Grunig, K. Sriramesh, Y.H. Huang and A. Lyra (1995). 'Models of public relations in an international setting'. *Journal of Public Relations Research* **7**(3): 163–186.

Grunig, L.A., E.L. Toth and L.C. Hon (2000). 'Feminist values in public relations'. *Journal of Public Relations Research* **12**(1): 49–68.

Grunig, L.A., E.L. Toth and L.C. Hon (2001). *Women in Public Relations*. New York, NY: Guilford Press.

Grunig, L.A., J.E. Grunig and D.M. Dozier (2002). *Excellent Public Relations and Effective Organizations*. Mahwah, NJ: Lawrence Erlbaum Associates.

Habermas, J. (1989). *The Structural Transformation of the Public Sphere: An inquiry into a category of bourgeois society*. Cambridge: Polity.

Hallahan, K. (2000). 'Inactive publics: the forgotten publics in public relations'. *Public Relations Review* **26**(4): 499–515.

Heath, R. (1992). 'The wrangle in the marketplace: a rhetorical perspective of public relations' in *Rhetorical and Critical Approaches to Public Relations*. E. Toth and R. Heath (eds). Hillsdale, NJ: Lawrence Erlbaum Associates.

Heath, R. (2006). 'A rhetorical theory approach to issues management' in *Public Relations Theory II*. C.H. Botan and V. Hazelton (eds). Mahwah, NJ: Lawrence Erlbaum Associates.

Heath, R.L. (2009). 'The rhetorical tradition: wrangle in the marketplace' in *Rhetorical and Critical Approaches to Public Relations II*. R.L. Heath, E. Toth and D. Waymer (eds). New York, NY: Routledge.

Heath, R.L. (2011). 'External organizational rhetoric: bridging management and sociopolitical discourse.' *Management Communication Quarterly* **25**: 415–435.

Hodges, C. (2006). 'PRP culture: a framework for exploring public relations practitioners as cultural intermediaries'. *Journal of Communication Management* **10**(1): 80–93.

Hodges, C. (2011). 'Public relations in the postmodern city: an ethnographic account of PR occupational culture in Mexico City' in *Public Relations, Society and Culture: Theoretical and empirical explorations*. L. Edwards and C. Hodges (eds). London: Routledge.

Holtzhausen, D.R. (2002). 'Towards a postmodern research agenda for public relations.' *Public Relations Review* **28**: 251–264.

Holtzhausen, D.R. (2011). 'The need for a postmodern turn in global public relations' in *Public Relations in Global Cultural Contexts*. N. Bardhan and C.K. Weaver (eds). New York, NY: Routledge.

Holtzhausen, D.R. and R. Voto (2002). 'Resistance from the margins: the postmodern public relations practitioner as organizational activist.' *Journal of Public Relations Research* **14**(1): 57–82.

Holtzhausen, D.R., B.K. Petersen and N.J. Tindall (2003). 'Exploding the myth of the symmetrical/asymmetrical dichotomy: public relations models in the new South Africa.' *Journal of Public Relations Research* **15**(4): 305–341.

Hon, L.C. (1995). 'Toward a feminist theory of public relations.' *Journal of Public Relations Research* **7**(1): 27–88.

Hove, T. (2009). 'The filter, the alarm system, and the sounding board: critical and warning functions of the public sphere.' *Communication and Critical/Cultural Studies* **6**: 19–38.

Huang, Y-H. (2001). 'OPRA: a cross-cultural, multiple-item scale for measuring organization-public relationships.' *Journal of Public Relations Research* **13**(1): 61–90.

Ihlen, O. (2004). 'Mapping the environment for corporate social responsibility: stakeholders, publics and the public sphere.' Paper presented at the EUPRERA International Conference on Public Relations and the Public Sphere: (New) Theoretical Approaches and Empirical Studies, Leipzig.

Ihlen, O. (2007). 'Building on Bourdieu: a sociological grasp of public relations.' *Public Relations Review* **33**(4): 269–274.

Ihlen, O. (2011). 'On barnyard scrambles: towards a rhetoric of public relations.' *Management Communication Quarterly* **24**: 423–441.

Jensen, I. (2001). 'Public relations and emerging functions of the public sphere: an analytical framework'. *Journal of Communication Management* **6**(2): 133–147.

Kent, M.L. and M. Taylor (2002). 'Toward a dialogic theory of public relations.' *Public Relations Review* **28**: 21–37.

Kent, M.L. and M. Taylor (2011). 'How intercultural communication theory informs public relations practice in global settings' in *Public Relations in Global Cultural Contexts: Multi-paradigmatic perspectives*. N. Bardhan and C.K. Weaver (eds). New York, NY: Routledge.

Kern-Foxworth, M., O. Gandy, B. Hines and D. Miller (1994). 'Assessing the managerial roles of black female public relations practitioners using individual and organizational discriminants.' *Journal of Black Studies* **24**(4): 416–434.

Kim, J.N. and J.E. Grunig (2011). 'Problem solving and communicative action: a situational theory of problem solving.' *Journal of Communication* **61**: 120–149.

Lauzen, M.M. and D.M. Dozier (1992). 'The missing link: the public relations manager role as mediator of organisational environments and power consequences for the function.' *Journal of Public Relations Research* **4**(4): 205–220.

Lauzen, M.M. and D.M. Dozier (1994). 'Issues management mediation of linkages between environmental complexity and management of the public relations function.' *Journal of Public Relations Research* **6**(3): 163–184.

Ledingham, J.A. (2003). 'Explicating relationship management as a general theory of public relations.' *Journal of Public Relations Research* **15**(2): 181–198.

Ledingham, J.A. and S.D. Bruning (2000). *Public Relations as Relationship Management: A relational approach to the study and practice of public relations*. Mahwah, NJ: Lawrence Erlbaum Associates.

Leeper, R.V. (1996). 'Moral objectivity, Jurgen Habermas' discourse ethics and public relations.' *Public Relations Review* **22**(2): 133–150.

Leitch, S. and J. Motion (2010). 'Publics and public relations: effecting change' in *The Sage Handbook of Public Relations*. R.L. Heath (ed.). Thousand Oaks, CA: Sage.

Leitch, S. and D. Neilson (2001). 'Bringing publics into public relations: new theoretical frameworks for practice' in *Handbook of Public Relations*. R. Heath (ed.). Thousand Oaks, CA: Sage.

Len-Rios, M. (1998). 'Minority public relations practitioner perceptions'. *Public Relations Review* **24**(4): 535–555.

L'Etang, J. (1996). 'Public relations and rhetoric' in *Critical Perspectives in Public Relations*. J. L'Etang and M. Pieczka (eds). London: International Thomson Business Press.

L'Etang, J. and M. Pieczka (1996). *Critical Perspectives in Public Relations*. London: International Thomson Business Press.

L'Etang, J. and M. Pieczka (2006). *Public Relations: Critical Debates and Contemporary Practice*. Mahwah, NJ: Lawrence Erlbaum Associates.

Lewis, J., A. Williams and B. Franklin (2008). 'A compromised fourth estate?: UK news journalism, public relations and news sources.' *Journalism Studies* **9**: 1–20.

Livesey, S.M. (2001). 'Eco-identity as discursive struggle: Royal Dutch/Shell, Brent Spar, and Nigeria.' *Journal of Business Communication* **38**(1): 58–91.

Logan, N. (2011). 'The white leader prototype: a critical analysis of race in public relations'. *Journal of Public Relations Research* **23**(4): 442–457.

McChesney, R.W. (1999). *Rich Media, Poor Democracy: Communication politics in dubious times*. Chicago, IL: University of Illinois Press.

McKie, D. (2010). 'Signs of the times: economic sciences, futures and public relations' in *The Sage Handbook of Public Relations*. R.L. Heath (ed.). Thousand Oaks, CA: Sage.

McKie, D. and D. Munshi (2007). *Reconfiguring Public Relations: Ecology, equity and enterprise*. Abingdon, Oxon: Routledge.

Meisenach, R.J. (2006). 'Habermas' discourse ethics and principle of universalization as a moral framework for organizational communication.' *Management Communication Quarterly* **20**(1): 39–62.

Merten, K. (2004). 'A constructivist approach to public relations' in *Public Relations and Communication Management in Europe*. B. van Ruler and D. Verčič (eds). Berlin: Mouton de Gruyter.

Mickey, T.J. (1997). 'A postmodern view of public relations: sign and reality.' *Public Relations Review* 23: 271–285.

Mickey, T.J. (2002). *Deconstructing Public Relations: Public relations criticism*. Mahwah, NJ: Lawrence Erlbaum Associates.

Miller, D. and W. Dinan (2000). 'The rise of the PR industry in Britain 1979–98'. *European Journal of Communication* **15**(1): 5–35.

Moffitt, M.A. (1994). 'Collapsing and integrating concepts of public and image into a new theory.' *Public Relations Review* **20**(2): 159–170.

Molleda, J.C. (2000). 'International paradigms: the Latin American school of public relations.' *Journalism Studies* 2(4): 513–530.

Moloney, K. (2006). *Rethinking Public Relations: PR propaganda and democracy*, 2nd edition. Oxon: Routledge.

Moss, D., G. Warnaby and A. Newman (2000). 'Public relations practitioner role enactment at the senior management level within UK companies.' *Journal of Public Relations Research* **12**(4): 277–307.

Moss, D., A. Newman and B. DeSanto (2004). 'Defining and redefining the core elements of management in public relations/corporate communications context: what do communication managers do?' Paper presented at the 11th International Public Relations Research Symposium, Lake Bled, Slovenia.

Motion, J. (1999). 'Personal public relations: identity as a public relations commodity.' *Public Relations Review* **25**(4): 465–479.

Motion, J. (2005). 'Participative public relations: power to the people or legitimacy for government discourse?' *Public Relations Review* **31**: 505–512.

Motion, J. and S. Leitch (2002). 'The technologies of corporate identity'. *International Studies of Management and Organization* 32(3): 45–64.

Motion, J. and S. Leitch (2007). 'A toolbox for public relations: the oeuvre of Michel Foucault.' *Public Relations Review* **33**(3): 263–268.

Munshi, D. and L. Edwards (2011). Understanding 'race' in/ and public relations: where do we start from and where should we go? *Journal of Public Relations Research* **23**(4): 349–367.

Munshi, D. and D. McKie (2001). 'Different bodies of knowledge: diversity and diversification in public relations.' *Australian Journal of Communication* 28(3): 11–22.

Murphy, P. (1991). 'The limits of symmetry: a game theory approach to symmetric and asymmetric public relations' in *Public Relations Research Annual*. J.E. Grunig and L.A. Grunig (eds). Hillsdale, NJ: Lawrence Erlbaum Associates.

O'Neil, J. (2003). 'An analysis of the relationships among structure, influence and gender: helping to build a feminist theory of public relations practice.' *Journal of Public Relations Research* **15**(2): 151–179.

Pitcher, G. (2003). *The Death of Spin*. Chichester: John Wiley and Sons.

Plowman, K.D. (1998). 'Power in conflict for public relations'. *Journal of Public Relations Research* **10**(4): 237–261.

Pompper, D. (2007). 'The gender-ethnicity construct in public relations organizations: using feminist standpoint theory to discover Latinas' realities'. *The Howard Journal of Communications* 18: 291–311.

Raupp, J. (2004). 'Public sphere as a central concept of public relations' in *Public Relations and Communication Management in Europe*. B. van Ruler and D. Verčič (eds). Berlin: Mouton de Gruyter.

Rhee, Y. (2002). 'Global public relations: a cross-cultural study of the excellence theory in South Korea.' *Journal of Public Relations Research* **14**(3): 159–184.

Sha, B.L. and R. Ford (2007). 'Redefining "requisite variety": the challenge of multiple diversities for the future of public relations excellence' in *Future of Excellence in Public Relations and Communication Management*. E. Toth (ed.). Mahwah, NJ: Lawrence Erlbaum Associates.

Skerlep, A. (2001). 'Re-evaluating the role of rhetoric in public relations theory and in strategies of corporate discourse.' *Journal of Communication Management* 6(2): 176–187.

Sriramesh, K. (1992). 'Societal culture and public relations: ethnographic evidence from India.' *Public Relations Review* **18**(2): 201–211.

Sriramesh, K. (2002). 'The dire need for multiculturalism in public relations education: an Asian perspective.' *Journal of Communication Management* **7**(1): 54–70.

Sriramesh, K. (2010). 'Globalization and public relations: opportunities for growth and reformulation' in *The Sage Handbook of Public Relations*. R.L. Heath (ed.). Thousand Oaks, CA: Sage.

Sriramesh, K. and D. Verčič (1995). 'International public relations: a framework for future research.' *Journal of Communication Management* 6(2): 103–117.

Sriramesh, K. and D. Verčič (2003). *The Global Public Relations Handbook: Theory, research and practice*. New York, NY: Routledge.

Sriramesh, K. and D. Verčič (2009). *The Global Public Relations Handbook: Theory, research and practice*, 2nd edition. New York, NY: Routledge.

Sriramesh, K., Y. Kim and M. Takasaki (1999). 'Public relations in three Asian cultures: an analysis'. *Journal of Public Relations Research* **11**(4): 271–292.

Sriramesh, K., S. Moghan and D. Wei (2007). 'The situational theory of publics in a different cultural setting: consumer publics in Singapore.' *Journal of Public Relations Research* **19**(4): 307–332.

Stauber, J. and S. Rampton (1995). *Toxic Sludge is Good for You: Lies, damn lies and the public relations industry.* Monroe, ME: Common Courage.

Taylor, M. (2009). 'Civil society as a rhetorical public relations process' in *Rhetorical and Critical Approaches to Public Relations II*. R.L. Heath, E. Toth and D. Waymer (eds). New York, NY: Routledge.

Taylor, M. (2010). 'Public relations in the enactment of civil society' in *The Sage Handbook of Public Relations*. R.L. Heath (ed.). Thousand Oaks, CA: Sage.

Taylor, M. (2011). 'Building social capital through rhetoric and public relations.' *Management Communication Quarterly* **25**(3): 436–454.

Toledano, M. and D. McKie (2007). 'Social integration and public relations: global lessons from an Israeli experience.' *Public Relations Review* **33**(4): 387–397.

van Ruler, B., D. Verčič, G. Butschi and B. Flodin (2004). 'A first look for parameters of public relations in Europe.' *Journal of Public Relations Research* **16**(1): 35–63.

Vardeman-Winter, J. (2011). 'Confronting whiteness in public relations campaigns and research with women.' *Journal of Public Relations Research* **23**(4): 412–441.

Vardeman-Winter, J. and N. Tindall (2010). 'Toward an intersectionality theory of public relations' in *The Sage Handbook of Public Relations*. R.L. Heath (ed.). Thousand Oaks, CA: Sage.

Waymer, D. (2010). 'Does public relations scholarship have a place in race?' in *The Sage Handbook of Public Relations*. R.L. Heath (ed.). Thousand Oaks, CA: Sage.

Weaver, C.K. (2010). 'Public relations, globalization and culture: framing methodological debates and future directions' in *Public Relations in Global Cultural Contexts: Multi-paradigmatic perspectives*. N. Bardhan and C.K. Weaver (eds). New York, NY: Routledge.

Witmer, D.F. (2006). 'Overcoming system and culture boundaries: public relations from a structuration perspective' in *Public Relations Theory II*. C. Botan and V. Hazleton (eds). Mahwah, NJ: Lawrence Erlbaum.

Wrigley, B. (2002). 'Glass ceiling? What glass ceiling? A qualitative study of how women view the glass ceiling in public relations and communications management.' *Journal of Public Relations Research* **14**(1): 27–55.

Wrigley, B. (2010). 'Feminist scholarship and its contributions to public relations' in *The Sage Handbook of Public Relations*. R.L. Heath (ed.). Thousand Oaks, CA: Sage.

Yeomans, L. (2010). 'Soft sell? Gendered experience of emotional labour in UK public relations firms.' *PRism 7.* www.prismjournal.org/fileadmin/Praxis/Files/Gender/Yeomans.pdf

Zerbinos, E. and G.A. Clanton (1993). 'Minority practitioners: career influences, job satisfaction, and discrimination.' *Public Relations Review* **19**(1): 75–91.

CHAPTER 8

Anne Gregory

Strategic public relations planning and management

Learning outcomes

By the end of this chapter you should be able to:

- describe and discuss the principal external influences and the organisational context in which public relations planning and management is undertaken
- use strategic tools to analyse the external and organisational context
- plan a research-based strategic campaign or programme
- critique and apply relevant underlying theories
- effectively manage and evaluate the impact of campaigns and programmes.

Structure

- The importance of context
- External environment
- Internal environment
- Strategic public relations programmes and campaigns
- Systems context of planning
- A planning template

Introduction

Every organisation manages and undertakes its public relations campaigns and programmes in different ways. That is because there are significant differences in the context in which they operate, the way the organisation is structured and managed and their specific public relations needs. A single-issue pressure group will have a very focused purpose and its publics and stakeholders are often very specific. A large government department – for example, the UK's Department of Health – will touch the lives of every citizen in a variety of ways, from prenatal care to childhood and adult illnesses, through to end-of-life care. Some business enterprises operate in tiny niche markets in one country, while others operate in several markets on a global scale.

The first part of this chapter examines a range of factors that influence the way public relations campaigns and programmes are planned within organisations. It will be seen that understanding and analysing organisational context is vitally important. Public relations campaigns and programmes do not stand in isolation: they are both 'buffers and bridges' (Mezner and Nigh 1995) to the world that is external to the organisation and therefore a profound understanding of this world is imperative. Furthermore, public relations campaigns and programmes are often directed at or involve staff within the organisation, and they too have lives outside work, thus any formal communication with them has to make sense within the broader context of their lives.

The importance of context

Business history is littered with companies that have not been able to adapt to changing industry trends, or have struggled. Olivetti made excellent typewriters, but were unable to make the transition to keyboards successfully. Polaroid makes cameras that develop instant photographs; however, with the advent of digital cameras the industry has been transformed and Polaroid has had to adjust to a reduced market and extreme competition.

Public relations describes exactly the formal management function that organisations employ to handle the relationships they have with their numerous publics and stakeholder groups, both internally and externally. Box 8.1 provides definitions of stakeholders and publics.

These groups comprise people who are, in turn, affected by developments, trends and issues in society. The environment in which modern organisations operate is dynamic: rapidly changing and complex. The forces at play are difficult to understand and their consequences hard to predict. Society is changing: new issues and trends arise, some of them very rapidly. For example, the issues created by the instability of the Euro, the predominant currency in the European Union, arose quickly after the global financial crisis in 2009. This has had far-reaching effects, not only on organisations in the Euro zone, but on all organisations who trade with Europe. Investors are anxious about those organisations that have substantial holdings in Europe; European financial regulations will be tightened, many employees are losing their jobs and organisations have less money to invest in charitable giving and community activities.

Organisations themselves are changing. For example, there are more women and part-time workers and, in many countries in the world, more immigrants. Furthermore, attitudes are changing. In the Western world, because people have more choices about where they live, their lifestyles and what they will spend their income on, they are no longer willing to be disempowered at work (Smyth 2007). In addition, organisations now find themselves much more accountable to external groups who want to know what they stand for and how they conduct themselves.

'Context' is, of course, different for each organisation and depends critically on, for example, what sector the organisation operates in, where it is based geographically, its size, areas of operation and culture.

Box 8.1

Stakeholders and publics

The words 'stakeholder' and 'publics' are often used interchangeably. In this chapter, stakeholders are those groups that have a 'stake' in an organisation – i.e. those who are affected by or can affect it (Freeman 1984). Stakeholders can have very loose or intermittent relationships with an organisation and can be passive. Publics, on the other hand, are active: they have an issue, a problem, or see opportunities and are supportive of the organisation. They have much closer engagement with it (Grunig and Hunt 1984). Any stakeholder has the potential to become a public.

External environment

The external context is vitally important for organisations because, ultimately, it determines their future. Smart organisations constantly scan the external environment to identify emerging trends and issues. Having spotted these issues early, precious time is bought for the organisation to adjust itself to them, to engage with them and, where appropriate, to influence their development. The public relations function is a natural organisational 'boundary spanner' (White and Dozier 1992), because building relationships requires it to have one foot inside and one foot outside. It is perfectly placed to do this 'environmental scanning'.

The external environment can be divided into two categories: the 'macro' and the 'task' environment (Grant 2005).

Macro environment

The macro environment can be described as the 'big picture' over which the organisation has no control, but could well impact on it. These are the issues that emerge from the actions of governments, economic and social trends and from scientific and technological developments. Sometimes called the 'remote' or 'societal' environment, the macro environment develops beyond and independent of any organisation's operating situation (de Wit and Meyer 2010).

To make sense of the macro environment, analysts use frameworks that help them systematically examine environmental influences. The most well-known analytical tool is PEST, which divides the overall environment into four categories – **P**olitical, **E**conomic, **S**ocial and **T**echnological. Figure 8.1 provides some examples of topics that fall under each of these headings. What is important is the impact they may have on an existing relationship, or what they reveal about the need to develop a relationship. For example, a potential change in trade legislation may indicate the need to deepen relationships with the trade organisation and develop contact with government departments for lobbying purposes. In addition, the identification of certain topics could present potential issues for the organisation (see Chapter 16 for further discussion).

Given the increasing complexity of the macro environment, PEST is beginning to be regarded as a rather limited tool. A development of PEST is EPISTLE, which includes the four elements of PEST, but also forces consideration of **I**nformation, **L**egal and the green **E**nvironment. The 'information' heading invites special consideration of the fact that empowerment comes to groups and individuals through new technologies, although it must be remembered that people who are deprived of relevant technology will become increasingly disenfranchised and unable to engage in debate effectively. The legal environment is becoming more complex. Organisations not only have to be aware of national regulations, but also of transnational legislation, such as EU law, and of non-binding but moral undertakings agreed to by nations, such as the agreements reached at the United Nation's Climate Summit held in Durban, December 2011. As this agreement indicates, the green environment is the cause of increasing concern and no analysis of the macro environment would be complete without reference to it (see Think about 8.1).

Clearly, different organisations will be affected in different ways by these macro issues. A car manufacturer will be very

Political	Economic
Change of government New political alliances within and between nations Employment legislation Industry regulation Environmental legislation	Value of the currency International trade agreements Interest rates Skills level in workforce Levels of employment Inflation
Social	**Technological**
Social attitudes Demographic changes Lifestyle developments Purchasing habits Levels of education	Impact of technology on work practices Developments in IT Access to technology Cost of research and development Speed of change

Figure 8.1 Example of a PEST analysis

Think about 8.1

Macro trends

What macro or global trends do you think are important? What are their possible implications for public relations professionals? How might you communicate with rural communities in developing countries that do not have access to the Internet or mobile technology?

Feedback

For further information about global trends, read Patricia Aburdene (2007). *Megatrends 2010*. Charlottesville, VA: Hampton Roads Publishing. Also, look at http://www.youtube.com/watch?v=IAP0b1_S4gA

susceptible to political, technological, environmental and social pressures to design engines that are carbon efficient. A fashion manufacturer needs to be acutely aware of social trends and how consumer preferences and changing life-styles will impact on their business. However, a careful eye needs to be kept on all these macro trends because issues arising from them are often interrelated – technological developments can drive social change, and vice versa. Also, some issues could be placed in more than one category – for example, educational achievement not only has social consequences, but economic and technological relevance too. While there are dozens of issues and trends in the wider environment it is worth picking out a few for special mention.

Globalisation

Public relations people working for global organisations will understand the need to communicate across time zones, cultures, languages and different communication delivery systems. But, even if the organisation is local, what it does may have global implications and attract global attention. A local baker's shop may buy flour from an intermediary who is supplied by a global grower who damages the environment in developing countries. Organisations also need to be sensitive about what they put on their websites and social media platforms for national audiences, as these may be accessed by people from other cultures who may take exception. For example, encouragement to drink alcohol may be offensive in cultures where alcohol is frowned on. (See Explore 8.1.)

Information technology

When linked to the theme of globalisation this is a very powerful force. The fact that information can be sent and accessed immediately across time and geographical boundaries brings great opportunities, but can also introduce threats for the public relations professional. Activists can organise quickly and globally and spread news of malpractice, or disseminate misinformation worldwide instantly. Contrariwise, organisations can connect and converse with stakeholders in new, enriching and innovative

ways. This capability brings opportunities and pressures for organisations and public relations practitioners who need to be geared for action 24 hours a day, seven days a week, 365 days a year.

Pluralism and activism

In an era of mass migration and easy travel, society is becoming more plural. The merging of values and ideals, together with an understanding and acceptance of different cultures and alternative views, is taken as a sign of advancing civilisation. But at the same time it increases uncertainty and insecurity as people question formerly accepted religious beliefs and authority norms. Some say (Ritzer 2008) that in an attempt to replace the old certainties people in developed societies are seeking out like-minded others who share their tastes and values. The number of pressure groups, non-governmental organisations (NGOs) and special interest groups is burgeoning (Jaques 2006). Counter to this, the rise of nationalism, fundamentalism and activism poses a threat to these liberalising forces (Herriot and Scott-Jackson 2002). Stepping around the tensions involved is a great challenge for public relations professionals. They find themselves having to assert or defend a particular position while trying not to offend anyone.

News media

The traditional news media, comprising newspapers and broadcast channels, have been revolutionised over the last few years (see also Chapter 2). Global news businesses owned by powerful groups and individuals, often with their own political agendas, were, up until the mid-2000s, setting the political backdrop and leading public opinion (Hargreaves 2005). However, more recently they themselves have become threatened as online sources of information become more ubiquitous. According to the American Pew Research Center's Project for Excellence in Journalism report on 'The State of the News Media 2011' (Pew Center 2011), online news consumption now outstrips that of the traditional media, and the structural threats posed by digital media are creating ongoing problems. According to Pew, traditional newsroom staff have been cut by 30 per cent since the year 2000, and online advertising revenues have overtaken those off-line. The impact of this is that the traditional media, rather than researching their own stories, are becoming increasingly dependent on other sources including citizen-generated content and content that cannot be guaranteed to be free of bias – for example that provided by public relations professionals. While this provides openings and opportunities to public relations, there are dangers in the 'PRisation of the media' (Moloney 2006). A free press

Explore 8.1

Globalisation issues

Go to the World Economic Forum website at http://www.weforum.org/ and look at the latest 'Outlook on the Global Agenda' report. What other issues can you identify that are specifically related to globalisation?

Box 8.2

Campaigns and programmes

A campaign: a planned set of public relations activities, normally over a limited period of time and with specific objectives addressing a particular issue and involving an identified group. For example, a local pharmacy may wish to inform customers in its neighbourhood of extended opening hours or the tax authorities may run a campaign to increase the number of tax returns from people over 65.

A programme: ongoing, planned activities over an extended period of time that call for continuing relationships with groups of publics and stakeholders, often including complex and interlinked objectives. For example, corporate social responsibility programmes and relationships with regulatory authorities.

requires resources to operate independently and challenge vested interests. There should be a distance between public relations practitioners and journalists because they have very different jobs to do (see Chapter 2 for more on the role of the media).

Task environment

The task environment consists of those forces and organisations that the organisation interacts with regularly and that can affect its performance. The task environment is normally categorised into groups of influential stakeholders with identifiable characteristics, such as customers, suppliers, regulators, competitors and pressure groups.

A useful categorisation of stakeholders is that provided by de Wit and Meyer (2010), who identify the web of relational actors that an organisation interacts with (Figure 8.2).

■ *Upstream vertical (supplier) relations* are relatively self-explanatory. Suppliers include providers of raw materials and business services, but also include labour and

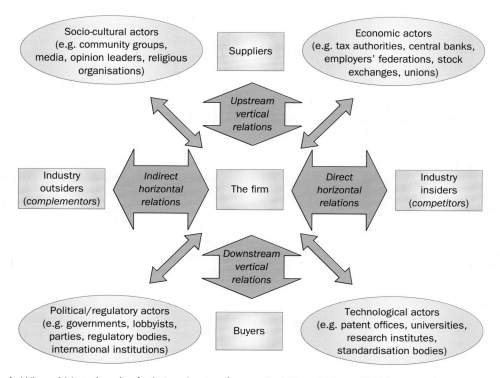

Figure 8.2 de Wit and Meyer's web of relational actors (*source*: De Wit and Meyer 2010.)

information that is external to the organisation and upon which it draws.

- *Downstream vertical (buyer) relations.* These can be clients, customers or intermediaries who sell the products of the organisation.

- *Direct horizontal (industry insider) relations.* This includes relationships between the organisation and others in their industry – they are at the same level.

- *Indirect (industry outsider) relations.* This is where an organisation has relationships with others outside its industry, for example those who will provide complementary goods or services, such as a bedroom furniture manufacturer working with an interior design organisation.

- *Socio-cultural actors.* Those individuals or organisations that have an impact on societal values, beliefs and behaviours. These may include community groups, the media, religious organisations, NGOs and opinion leaders.

- *Economic actors.* Those organisations who influence the general economic context, such as central banks, stock exchanges, taxation authorities and trade organisations.

- *Political/legal actors.* These are organisations that set or influence the regulatory regime and include government, regulatory bodies, international institutions and special interest groups.

- *Technological actors.* Given the importance of technology to modern life, those who influence the pace and direction of technological developments and the development of new knowledge are critical. Organisations such as universities, research bodies, government agencies and patent offices play a role here.

It is worth making the point here that the notion of organisations as stakeholding communities is important because it is stakeholder groups who ultimately give an organisation 'permission' to exist (or not) by supporting its 'licence to operate' or removing it. Now go to Explore 8.2.

Analysis of the macro and task environments may seem more appropriate to the identification of strategic business issues rather than public relations. However, practitioners need to be alert to the wider environmental issues because they will force some sort of action from the organisation and action always has communication dimensions. Early warning of issues allows organisations to manage future and potential risks and this is a strategic input that public relations can make at senior management level. Given the speed at which activists can galvanise action, even the most astute practitioner may get only the briefest or even no warning of an issue that could develop into a crisis. However, most issues gestate more slowly, and forward-thinking and diligent intelligence gathering can help predict many of them.

The main questions to be asked when undertaking this kind of environmental analysis are:

1. What are the environmental factors that affect this organisation?

2. Which ones are of most importance now?

3. Which ones will become the most important in the next four years?

From this it will be possible to derive a prioritised list of the main issues that will affect the organisation over a reasonable time horizon.

Internal environment

Having identified the broader environmental issues that affect the organisation, it is now appropriate to look at the organisation itself and those things over which it has greater control.

A classic way to undertake this internal analysis is to use a technique called SWOT. The first two elements, **s**trengths and **w**eaknesses, are particular to the organisation and are usually within the organisation's power to address. The third and fourth, **o**pportunities and **t**hreats, are generally external to the organisation and can be derived from the wider analysis of the macro and task environment and the selection of those issues most relevant to it. An example of SWOT analysis is given in Figure 8.3.

There are a number of other issues that affect the internal environment of an organisation and its public relations activities. For example:

Explore 8.2

Stakeholding

Who are the stakeholders of a university? How would you describe the relation linkages between the university and its:

- students
- lecturers
- governors
- local residents
- local business community
- central government's education departments?

Strengths	Weaknesses
Financially strong Leading edge products Innovative Good leadership Loyal workforce	Risk averse investment Limited product line Lack of investment in R&D Traditional and hierarchical Limited skills base
Opportunities	**Threats**
Cheap supplies from Asia New market opportunities in China Potential to acquire competitors Favourable tax breaks if offices relocated	Reputational issues re labour exploitation Danger of being overstretched Danger of being taken over by larger conglomerate Loss of loyal workforce

Figure 8.3 Example of SWOT analysis

1. **The sector in which the organisation is located**. If this is well established and stable, this will allow for significant preplanning. Fast-growing and turbulent sectors, such as IT, will require quick, reactive public relations as well as proactive programmes.

2. **Size and stage of organisational development**. Small organisations usually have a small, multifunctional public relations department or are serviced by a consultancy. Large ones may well have substantial public relations departments with a number of specialisms, also complemented by consultancy support. When the organisation is at start-up stage, most suppliers, customers and employees will be well known. Thus public relations effort is often face to face and online and focused on 'growing the business' – that is, marketing public relations. When companies reach maturity, it is probable that they will undertake the full range of public relations activity, including investor relations, public affairs, CSR programmes and sophisticated internal communication programmes.

3. **Culture**. This topic is discussed in Chapter 14, but briefly culture can be defined as the way people think and behave within an organisation, and the tone of the organisation is set by its leaders. A hierarchical, non-involving culture will often see public relations as a way of enforcing the management will. More open and involving cultures will see public relations and communication as integral to the fabric of the organisation, both shaped by and shaping the way 'things' are done.

An analysis of external and internal influences is critical to understanding the context in which public relations programmes will be undertaken. However, equally important is the fact that strategic public relations programmes address the issues that organisations face – the most impactful programmes are issues-based. They can be seen

to contribute directly to solving organisational problems and that is why they are of strategic importance. Furthermore, the ability to undertake that vital systematic internal and external environmental monitoring (Lerbinger 1972) and analysis again positions public relations as a strategic management function.

Against this backcloth, strategic public relations programmes and campaigns are planned. The second half of this chapter will provide an overview of the planning process.

Strategic public relations programmes and campaigns

According to Thompson and Martin (2010: 790), strategy is 'the means by which organisations achieve (and seek to achieve) their objectives and purpose' and strategic management is 'the process by which an organisation establishes its objectives, formulates actions (strategies) designed to meet these objectives in the desired timescale, implements the actions and assesses progress and results' (p. 790). Strategic public relations programmes and campaigns are those, therefore, that are proactive, planned, have a purpose and contribute towards organisational objectives. (See Box 8.2)

Research among Europe's public relations community (Zerfass et al. 2011) indicates that 91 per cent of them focus on supporting business goals by planning and executing communication programmes. Planning will not make a poorly conceived programme successful, but careful planning means that a programme is likely to be well conceived in the first place.

Box 8.3
Ways to segment publics

- geographics – where they live, work
- demographics – age, gender, income
- psychographics – attitudes, opinions
- group membership – e.g. clubs, societies, parents
- media consumption – e.g. newspapers, TV, websites, bloggers
- overt and covert power – e.g. religious leader, information gatekeeper, level of connectedness
- role in decision process – e.g. financial manager, CEO, parent

Box 8.2 explains the difference between programmes and campaigns, but in the rest of this chapter the word 'programme' is used to embrace both types of activity.

Why planning is important

There are a number of practical reasons for planning public relations programmes; it:

- focuses effort by eliminating unnecessary and low-priority work

- improves effectiveness by ensuring the plan works to achieve agreed objectives from the outset

- encourages forward-thinking by requiring the planner to look to the organisation's future needs, preparing it for change and helping it manage future risks; it also helps to identify any potential difficulties and conflicts, which can then be thought through at an early stage

- minimises mishaps; thinking through potential scenarios means that most eventualities can be covered and contingency plans put in place

- demonstrates value for money; planners can show they have achieved programme objectives within budget.

While strategic planning takes the practitioner through a systematic process, they must be mindful that a level of flexibility and pragmatic adjustment is required along the way. Indeed, unseen events, such as a takeover or major natural disaster, may require a radical departure from the best-laid plans.

Systems context of planning

Public relations planning is located within the positivist framework and maps across well to the systems view of organisations (see Chapter 7 for more discussion of systems thinking in public relations). The 'open system' is an important concept for public relations planning because it assumes that an organisation is an organism or 'living entity with boundaries, inputs, outputs, "throughputs", and enough feedback from both the internal and external environments so that it can make appropriate adjustments in time to keep on living' (McElreath 1997).

Cutlip et al. (2006) provide an open systems model of public relations that identifies how these systems characteristics map onto the planning process (see Figure 8.4).

So, for example, 'input' refers to actions taken by, or information about, publics. These inputs in turn are transformed into goals (aims) and objectives, which underpin the desired relationships with publics. By contrast, a 'closed' approach might neglect to take into account information about publics and thus the planner might formulate aims and objectives in isolation.

Scope of public relations planning

Systematic planning can be applied to long-term activity, such as the ongoing work by governments to prevent drivers from drinking or taking drugs. It can also be applied to short-term campaigns, such as the launch of a new service, or even to single projects such as fundraising for a celebration event.

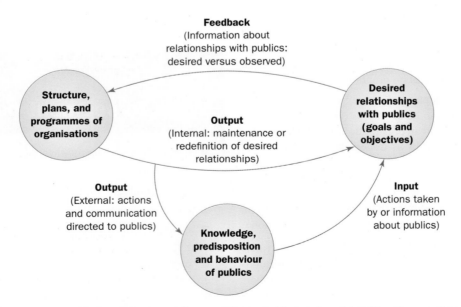

Figure 8.4 Open systems model of public relations (*source*: *Effective Public Relations*, 8th Edition, Pearson Education Inc. (Cutlip, Scott M., Center, Allen H. and Broom, Glen M.) p. 244 © 2000, Reprinted by permission of Pearson Education, Inc., Upper Saddle River, NJ)

When discussing the role of the communication planner, Windahl et al. (2009) embrace a wider interpretation for planning. Informal communication can be intended to begin a dialogue for its own sake and it may be planned, in that it will have a purpose. For example, opinion-formers may be invited to a university hospitality event that may not have a specific planned outcome other than an appreciation that this dialogue helps build relationships and a sense of community around the university.

Windahl et al. (2009) also point out that communication initiatives can start at the bottom of an organisation as well as the top. For example, a small department may begin raising money for a local charity to build goodwill in the community, which eventually widens out to the whole company supporting it and, by popular demand, it being adopted as a formal charitable partner.

Approaches to the planning process

The planning process is ordered and takes the practitioner through a number of key steps. It is helpful to see it as answering six basic questions:

1. What is the problem? (Researching the issue.)

2. What does the plan seek to achieve? (What are the aims and objectives?)

3. Who should be communicated with? (With whom should a relationship be developed?)

4. What should be said? (What is the content?)

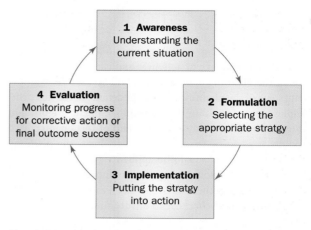

Figure 8.5 Basic business planning model

5. How should the content be communicated? (What channels should be used?)

6. How can success be measured? (How will the work be evaluated against the objectives?)

All planning processes follow a basic sequence, whether they are for the strategic management of the organisation or for public relations, and this is provided in Figure 8.5.

Marston (1979) provided one of the best-known planning sequences for public relations, which is encapsulated in the mnemonic RACE – **R**esearch, **A**ction, **C**ommunication and **E**valuation. American academics Cutlip et al. (2006) articulate the planning process, as depicted in Figure 8.6.

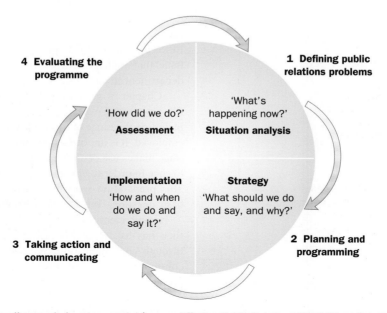

Figure 8.6 Cutlip and colleagues' planning model (*source*: *Effective Public Relations*, 8th Edition, Pearson Education Inc. (Cutlip, Scott M., Center, Allen H. and Broom, Glen M.) © 2000, Reprinted by permission of Pearson Education, Inc., Upper Saddle River, NJ)

A planning template

Gregory's planning template, or model, in Figure 8.7 provides a sequence of activities and captures the essence of all the planning approaches. It will be used to examine the steps of the planning process in detail. All the key principles, or steps, within this planning template are brought together in Case study 8.1 at the end of this chapter. Two points need to be made at this stage. First, the planning template is not meant to be applied rigidly. Practitioners have to move rapidly in response to unpredictable events; however, even in these circumstances, the template can be used as a mental checklist to ensure that all the essential elements have been covered. Second, the degree to which any element of the planning process is applied will vary according to the task in hand. For example, an analysis of the organisation's external environment will not be required to run an effective open day for families.

It is important to understand the structure of the first part of the diagram. Ideally, the public relations practitioner would undertake analysis of the situation before determining aims and objectives. In practice, they are often given aims and objectives by their managers. In these circumstances it is still vital that the objectives themselves are scrutinised to see if they are appropriate. For example, an organisation may wish to resist the introduction of a piece of legislation because it will be expensive to implement. However, on investigation the public relations practitioner may discover that a lobbying campaign against it is fruitless because stakeholders are very much in favour.

The 'aim' element can, on occasion, be omitted because sometimes a project or campaign has a single, simple objective that does not need an overarching aim. If the programme is particularly large, it may be necessary to break down the whole into a series of projects that follow the same basic steps. Each project will have its own specific objectives, publics and content. This then needs to be incorporated into the larger plan, which provides a coordinating framework with overall aims objectives and consistent content guidance to ensure that the individual projects do not conflict. See Figure 8.8.

Analysis

Analysis is the first step in the process and this will identify the issues or specific problems on which to base the programme.

Analysis can include a thorough investigation of both the external and internal environments that have already been covered. However, a key component of analysis entails a careful examination of publics and stakeholders to discover what their attitudes are towards the organisation itself, to the wider issue as identified by the EPISTLE and SWOT processes or to the particular issue that management have asked the public relations department to address.

Chapter 9 goes into detail about how to conduct PR programme research with stakeholders and publics, including the range of social scientific methods that can be employed. It is important to mention here that the analysis stage makes use of all the available information and intelligence in order to ensure the programme is well founded. This preparation work is critical to answering the first basic question, 'What is the problem?'.

Having identified the issue or problem, the planner then has to decide whether it can be remedied purely through communication. Windahl et al. (2009) define a communication-based problem in two ways: first, a problem may arise from the *lack of* or *wrong* sort of communication. For example, a new child vaccination is not being requested by parents because it has only been publicised to doctors (lack of information) and because it

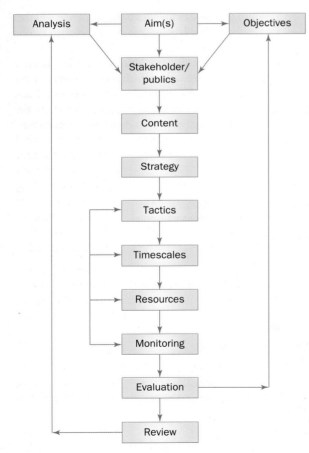

Figure 8.7 Gregory's planning model (*source*: Gregory 2010)

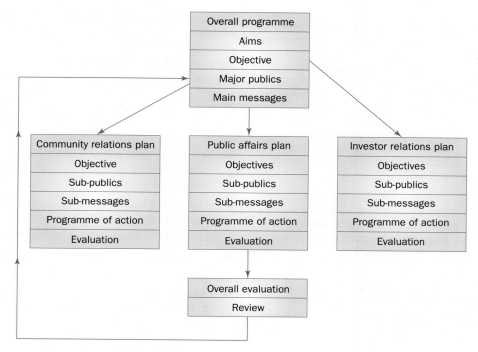

Figure 8.8 Framework for multi-project public relations plans (*source*: adapted from Gregory 2010: 44)

has been described by its technical name, not its popular name (wrong sort of information) – this problem can easily be solved by good communication. Second, the problem is a communication problem if it can be solved by communication alone. For example, if the uptake of child vaccinations has also been affected by suspicions about side-effects, or if there are a limited number of clinics where it is available, then this is more than just a communication problem. Some other measures, such as independent opinion to confirm the vaccine is safe or wider distribution, may be needed to stimulate use. In this case the public relations professional needs to bring these problems to management attention and, once they are addressed, communication can step in. Thus it can be seen that analysis not only identifies the issues, but also what needs to be done and the precise contribution that public relations can make.

Setting aims and objectives

Setting realistic aims and objectives is complicated, but through analysis public relations planners can scope the size and nature of the communication task. The aim or aims will state what the programme seeks to achieve in overall terms. Aims must be agreed before implementation and must be linked to organisational aims. If the corporate objective is to improve what have been poor community

relations, then public relations activity must be focused on that. A good aim should be able to be evaluated at the end of the programme by turning it into a question. Thus, the aim 'to improve community relations' becomes the evaluative question, 'Were community relations improved?'.

Objectives are the specific, measurable steps that break the aims into what are effectively milestones for the programme. Research on publics will have uncovered their position on any particular topic that provides a starting point, or benchmark. The planner then needs to decide what movement, if any, is required; a legitimate objective may be to confirm existing attitudes or actions. Smith (2009) provides a hierarchy of three levels of objectives:

- *Awareness objectives* deal with information and knowledge, focusing on providing the *cognitive*, or thinking, element of the content and on what information publics should be exposed to, know, understand and remember.

- *Acceptance objectives* deal with how people react to information, focusing on the *affective*, or feeling, elements of the content and on what emotional response is generated and how this affect's interests and attitudes.

- *Action objectives* deal with the hoped-for response, focusing on the *conative*, or behavioural, outcomes that might be generated when people are exposed to the content of the programme.

Cognitive (means related to thoughts, reflection, awareness)	Encouraging the target public to *think* about something or to create awareness. For example, local government might want the local community to be aware that it is holding a housing information day. The whole community will not need the service, but part of local government's reason for making them aware is so that they know what a proactive and interested local council they have
Affective (means related to feelings, emotional reaction)	Encouraging the target public to form a particular attitude, opinion or feeling about a subject. For example, a pressure group may want moral support for or against gun ownership
Conative (means related to behaviour, actions or change)	Encouraging the target public to *behave* in a certain way. For example, the local hospital may use social media to ask for emergency blood donors following a major incident

Table 8.1 Objectives set at one of three levels

Table 8.1 shows how objectives can be set at these levels.

Generally speaking, it is much more difficult to get someone to *behave* in a certain way than it is to prompt them to *think* about something, the notable exception being over 'hot' issues. According to Grunig and Hunt (1984), three things should be borne in mind that will make the achievement of objectives easier:

1. The level of effect (or outcome) should be chosen with care. If the public relations planner wants to induce radical change, it will be sensible to set cognitive objectives first, rather than hoping for conative effects from the start.

2. Choose target publics with advocacy in mind. Research should have identified those who already support the position of the organisation; they can then act as advocates on its behalf.

3. Organisations can change too. Sometimes minor adjustments in the organisation's stance can elicit a major, positive response from publics.

Cutlip et al. (2006) warn that public relations programme objectives all too often describe the tactic instead of the desired outcome for a particular public. In the 'employee' public example, below, a tactical objective would be to issue the corporate plan. However, the objective that focuses on

the desired outcome for employees is 'to ensure awareness of the new corporate plan', and is highlighted in italics.

All objectives should be SMART: specific, measurable, achievable (within the planner's ability to deliver), resourced and time-bound. Examples of SMART objectives follow.

- Employees: *Ensure every employee is aware* of new corporate plan by 10 November and, three weeks later, can list three priorities for next year.

- Community: Use sponsorship of 20 local junior football teams to *promote more positive opinion* about the company among parents.

- Corporate: Change legislation on taxation of charity giving within two years by *influencing voting behaviour of government ministers* via a lobbying campaign.

- Trade: Double amount of coverage in trade media in one year to *overcome lack of awareness* among key suppliers.

- Consumer: Increase face-to-face contact with consumers by 20 per cent in 18 months to *counter perception of company being remote*.

To show how issues flow through to the framing of aims and one exemplar objective, Table 8.2 provides a number of examples. Note how the objectives do not go into the detail of the tactics.

Setting sound aims and objectives is fundamental to public relations planning. They define what the outcomes of the programme will be, they provide the rationale for the strategy, set the agenda for tactical actions and are the benchmark against which the programme will be evaluated. Their importance cannot be overstated. This section on objectives has answered the second basic question in planning programmes, 'What does the plan seek to achieve?'

Issue	Aim	Objective
Company viewed as environmentally irresponsible	Demonstrate environmental credentials	Promote company recycling scheme in local media
After-sales service perceived as slow and unresponsive	Create awareness of customer service facilities	Publicise guaranteed repair service and 24-hour customer helpline
Proposed legislation will damage environmentally sensitive areas	Change proposed legislation by lobbying government	Galvanise local pressure groups into action

Table 8.2 Examples of the link between issue, aim and objective

Identifying publics

This next section answers the third question, 'Who should we talk to?'.

Research for the proposed programme will have identified the significant stakeholders and publics. Sometimes these two terms are used interchangeably; however, stakeholders may be defined as those who have a stake or interest in an organisation, while publics may be defined as stakeholders that have an issue with the organisation. If the programme is to support a product launch, then existing and potential customers will be a priority. However, groups that can be easily defined often are not homogenous. It is incorrect to assume that all-embracing categorisations, such as the 'local community', comprise individuals who are similar or who will act in the same way. Within these groups there will be the 'active', 'aware', 'latent' and 'apathetic' publics that Grunig and Repper (1992) discuss. They will have very different interests and concerns. It is likely that many individuals will belong to more than one stakeholding group. Employees of an organisation may well be partners in a community relations campaign, or consume their organisation's products or services; they may be shareholders.

There are many ways in which stakeholders and publics can be segmented (placed into groups with a defined range of characteristics) and the type of campaign will determine the best way to do that. For example, if a government wants to introduce a new benefit targeted at lower-income families, it makes sense to segment stakeholders by income and where they live. A charity wanting to start up a counselling service for refugees may wish to segment by ethnicity and political affiliation; a leisure company wanting to set up Saturday morning clubs for children will segment by age and locality. (See back to Box 8.3 on p. 151.)

The practitioner has to decide the most appropriate ways to undertake the segmentation of stakeholders. This could be done on the basis of selecting the two most important variables for the situation being addressed and then making a matrix out of them.

The power/interest matrix (see Figure 8.9) is a popular combination used in strategic planning (Johnson et al. 2008) and can be readily transferred to the communication context. It categorises stakeholders depending on the amount of power they have to influence others and the level of interest they may have in a particular issue. Clearly, the more power and interest they have, the more likely their actions are to impact on the organisation, so the support of this group is crucial.

It is possible, even desirable at times, that stakeholders in one segment should move to another. For example, powerful, institutional investors often reside in segment C. It may be in times of crisis that the communicator will want to move them to segment D so that they can use

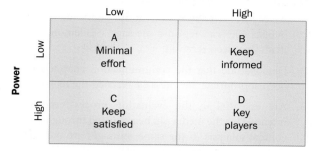

Figure 8.9 Power/interest matrix (*source*: adapted from Mendelow 1991, cited in Johnson, Scholes and Whittington 2008: 156)

their power and influence with others to support the organisation.

Similarly, just because a stakeholding group appears not to have much interest or power does not mean that it is not important.

It is informative to map stakeholders in a number of ways. For example, not only can current position and desired position be mapped, but a useful exercise is to map how stakeholders might move in relation to a developing issue and whether or not this is desirable, preventable or inevitable. Communication strategies can then be devised that accommodate these movements.

Once categorised according to a suitable method, the groups need to be prioritised and the amount of communication effort devoted to them apportioned.

The number of publics that are communicated with and the depth of that communication is likely to be limited by either a financial or time budget. However, it is important that all the key 'gatekeepers' or leaders of active groups are identified. They may well interpret information for others, act as advocates on the organisation's behalf and catalyse action.

Messages or content

The fourth basic question is, 'What should be said?'. Traditionally, public relations people have focused on messages. Heath (2001) says this could be explained partly because many practitioners have come from a journalistic background, where 'getting the story out' is seen as important. This has led to a focus on 'message design and dissemination to achieve awareness, to inform, to persuade – even manipulate' (Heath 2001: 2).

There are many kinds of campaign where messages are critically important, especially in public information campaigns. Road safety messages are encapsulated in slogans such as 'Don't drink and drive'.

Messages are important for four main reasons. They:

1. Assist the awareness and attitude-forming process: publics who can repeat a message are demonstrating that it has been received.

2. Demonstrate that the communication channels have been appropriate: the message reached the recipient.

3. Are essential in the evaluation process: messages intended for the media can be evaluated through media content analysis. If the same messages are picked up and repeated by the target public (e.g. through survey research), it demonstrates that the communication has been, at least in part, effective.

4. Help focus management minds: summarising an argument down to its essentials and encapsulated in a message imposes discipline on woolly thinking.

However, messages have limitations. They indicate one-way communication: the originator simply checks to see if their communication has been received. If an organisation genuinely wants to enter into a dialogue with publics where the outcome will be mutually determined, messaging is not appropriate. For example, if a new organisation wants to discuss with its employees what its values and goals should be, dialogue is required.

As indicated earlier, organisations are now seen more as communities of stakeholders and there is growing acceptance that collaboration with stakeholders to solve problems and to gain their input and support is a better way of working (Agerwal and Helfat 2009; de Wit and Meyer 2010). Collaboration and cooperation require consultation and involvement – in other words, dialogue. Furthermore, the developments in social media and mobile technologies are forcing even the most reluctant organisations into having

---

Box 8.4

Deliberative engagement

Deliberative engagement brings together a representative cross-section of the stakeholding group to deliberate on an issue. The process provides the time for participants to truly understand the issues.

By being involved, participants take part in the decision-making process. They are given access to information and experts, can ask questions, seek clarification, learn about and consider complex issues, make compromises and gradually move towards a consensus.

---

conversations. Particularly in the public sector, there is a growing move towards coproduction of solutions to problems and consensus-building, where conflict is avoided and the public 'own' the solutions that are arrived at because they have contributed to them directly through dialogue-based activities. Techniques such as deliberative engagement (see Box 8.4), which requires time, effort and resources, are becoming increasingly prevalent.

There is also evidence that the private sector is doing similar things with their supply chain partners (Johnson et al. 2007; De Wit and Meyer 2010; Thompson and Martin 2010). An example of this dialogic way of working is given in Mini case study 8.1.

How, then, can programmes that involve dialogue be evaluated if messages are one of the ways to measure communication effectiveness? The answer is: by the quality of

---

Mini case study 8.1

Your Health, Your Care, Your Say

The Your Health, Your Care, Your Say initiative (YHYCYS) for the Department of Health created one of the largest and most ambitious public engagement exercises ever mounted in the UK. The aims were complex and ambitious: to ensure that the public (especially the 'seldom heard') were actively involved in deliberative debates on contentious issues, including 'trading off' public investment in different types of health and social care services, alongside creating a high public profile to encourage wide public involvement (including through open access questionnaires) and professional stakeholder involvement.

Over 41,000 responses were received through the various methods used over the course of the three months that the main work took place (September to December 2005), with 1,240 people attending deliberative events in Gateshead, Leicester, London, Plymouth and Birmingham. The process also included a unique 'report back' event in London in March 2006 (after the publication of the 'White Paper' in January 2006). At this event, 110 people who had been at previous deliberative events heard the Secretary of State for Health, alongside two ministers from health and social care, report back to them on what had been taken forward from the YHYCYS exercise into the 'White Paper', and ask for feedback on the participants' satisfaction with what had been done with their input.

Source: taken from the Department of Health website: http://www.dh.gov.uk/prod_consum_dh/groups/dh_digitalassets/@dh/@en/documents/digitalasset/dh_4138597.pdf

	Example 1	**Example 2**	**Example 3**
Objective	Publicise new product	Establish organisation as thought leader	Encourage people to exercise
Strategy	Mount media relations campaign	Position as industry-leading think-tank	Drive home health policy through memorable message
Tactics	Press conference, press releases, exclusives, features, competition	Research reports, speaker platforms, information resource facility, online helpline, sponsorship of awards, etc.	Media campaign, posters, competitions, bus adverts, website, schools programme, social media, etc.

Figure 8.10 Different types of strategy

Explore 8.3

Message design

Devise an overarching message or slogan for a 'grass roots' or community-led campaign aimed at stopping children dropping litter outside the school premises. What would be a suitable sub-message for children? For parents? For teachers?

the relationship that results from the dialogue and the level of mutual cooperation, support and advocacy (see Chapter 9 on PR programme research and evaluation).

The importance of content cannot be overemphasised. It is the point of contact, providing the meaning between an organisation and its publics. It is 'given' by the organisation and 'received' by its publics, and vice versa. Once mutually understood and internalised it can be said that the meaning is mutually 'owned'. If content is poorly conceived and the way it is conveyed poorly executed, it can be the end of the communication process. (See Explore 8.3).

Strategy and tactics

Strategy

The fifth basic question, 'How should the message be communicated?', falls into two parts: strategy and tactics. The temptation for the public relations planner is to move immediately to tactics because, in many ways, it is easier to think of a raft of ideas than to think about the rationale behind them. An underpinning strategy provides coherence and focus and is a driving force. Strategy is the guiding principle (sometimes called the 'big idea') that determines the menu of activities, that gives it purpose. Strategy is the 'how' of the programme, not the detailed 'what'. It is

described as: the 'overall concept, approach or general plan' by Broom (2009). Strategy is the bridge between the aims of the programme (what is to be achieved) and the foundation on which tactics are built (what is going to be done). Tactics are the 'events, media and methods used to implement the strategy' (Broom 2009). In the three examples in Figure 8.10, the first shows how strategy can describe the nature of, and summarise the tactical campaign for, a simple, single-objective campaign. The second example is for a conceptual proposition, the third for a slogan-driven campaign encapsulating a key theme. All are equally valid.

Tactics

It is obvious that tactics should be linked to, and flow from, strategy. Strategy should guide brainstorming and be used to reject activities that do not support the strategic intent or the programme objectives. There should be a clear link between aim, objectives, strategy and tactics.

A level of caution is required when planning the tactics of a programme. The aim is to build a programme that reaches the right people in sufficient numbers and that has the right level of impact to do the job required, all within acceptable costs and timescales. Sometimes that can be done with a single activity – for example, the international Live 8 concerts on 2 July 2008 stimulated global awareness of developing countries' indebtedness overnight.

More usually, a raft of complementary tactics over a period of time is required. These will vary depending on the nature of the programme, so the practitioner will need to draw from a palette of tactics as appropriate. For example, if a company wants to launch new and highly visual products, such as a range of expensive household accessories, it is important that tactics are selected that will show how these products look and feel. In this case, a range of tactics might include displays at exhibitions and in-store, product samples provided, YouTube clips showing the products in use, a Twitter campaign led by satisfied customers, brochures and high-quality posters.

In a different situation – for example, if the campaign involves lobbying over some aspect of financial legislation – quite different tactics, such as research reports, seminars, opinion-former briefings, one-to-one meetings with politicians and websites, would be more appropriate.

When designing the tactical elements of a campaign, two areas should be addressed:

- Is the tactic appropriate? Will it reach the target publics? Will it have the right impact? Is it credible and influential? Does it suit the content in terms of creative treatment and compatibility with other techniques used?

- Is the tactic deliverable? Can it be implemented successfully? Is there sufficient budget? Are the timescales correct? Are there the right people and expertise to implement it?

Figure 8.11 shows the power/interest matrix again, this time showing the COI's strategic approach towards those groups in each quadrant, along with some tactics.

Timescales and resources

Time

Time is a finite commodity and the life of a public relations practitioner is notoriously busy. Furthermore, public relations often involves the cooperation of others, and getting them to observe deadlines requires firmness and tact.

Deadlines can be externally imposed or internally driven by the organisation. Internal events may include the announcement of annual results, launching a new service or the appointment of a senior executive. External events may be major calendar dates, such as the Olympic Games, Chinese New Year or Thanksgiving.

To ensure deadlines are met, all the key elements of a project must be broken down into their individual parts and a timeline put against them. Box 8.5 contains a list of the main elements of a press facility visit.

Box 8.5

Checklist for a press facility visit

1. Draw up invitation list
2. Alert relevant departments
3. Select visit hosts
4. Book catering
5. Issue invitations
6. Prepare display materials
7. Write speeches
8. Prepare media packs
9. Brief visit hosts
10. Follow up invitations
11. Prepare visit areas
12. Collate final attendance list
13. Rehearse with visit hosts
14. Facilitate visit
15. Follow up

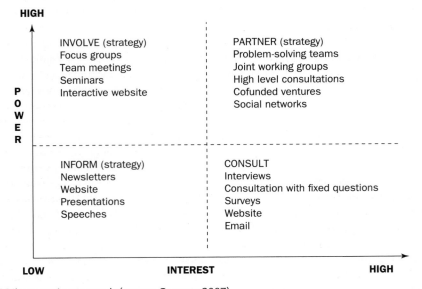

Figure 8.11 The COI's strategic approach (*source*: Gregory 2007)

Each of these elements will need its own action plan and timescale. Thus, preparing the visit areas may include commissioning display boards with photographs and text and a DVD player with commissioned DVD. That, in turn, will mean briefing photographers and printers, producers and film crew and getting content text approved by senior management, and so on. It may also involve liaising with the marketing department for product literature, organising cleaners and arranging for porters to move furniture and erect the displays.

Having split the project down into its individual tasks, it is then useful to use techniques such as critical path analysis (CPA) and other project management tools to ensure the project is managed and delivered on time (see http://www.mindtools.com/critpath.html for more information). If tasks have to be done to a short timescale, time-saving measures will have to be implemented, such as employing a specialist agency to help or using existing display material.

An annual activity plan that collates everything into one accessible and visible place allows the peaks and troughs of activity to be identified so that they can be resourced accordingly. The times when activity is less intense can be used for reviewing or implementing other proactive plans.

Resources

There are three areas of resourcing that underpin public relations work: human resources, implementation costs and equipment (Gregory 2010). Having the right staff skills and competencies, as well as an adequate budget, are critical to success. Skilled investor relations personnel, for example, are rarer and more expensive than public relations generalists. Usually, a single practitioner with a few years' experience can handle a broad-ranging programme of limited depth or a focused in-depth specialism, such as internal communication.

Ideally, the organisation decides its optimum public relations programme and resources it accordingly. The reality is usually a compromise between the ideal and the actual budget allocated. However, it has to be borne in mind that public relations is relationship-driven and therefore people are more valuable than materials. Sponsorship work may survive without expensive sponsor packs, but it cannot survive without people.

When considering the implementation costs of a programme, public relations practitioners have a duty to be effective and efficient. So, for example, if an investor magazine is an appropriate medium, choices have to be made on the number of colours, quality of paper, frequency of publication and so on. A full-colour, glossy, monthly magazine may be desirable, but would it be effective and efficient? On the other hand, a single-colour publication on cheap paper, issued once a quarter, may fail to make investors feel important or be frequent enough to be meaningful.

If budgets are restricted, it is important to think creatively about how a similar result can be obtained at a fraction of the cost. Joint ventures with complementary organisations, sponsorship and piggyback mailings (i.e., when one mailing such as an annual statement from a bank is used to include other information) should be considered.

Sometimes it can be more effective and efficient to spend slightly more money. Holding an employee conference off-site may cost more, but may guarantee their attention. Sending an analyst's briefing to other key shareholders may cost a little extra, but it may retain their support.

While not requiring excessive amounts of equipment to support their work, it is important that practitioners have the right technology to ensure quick and easy access to key stakeholders in a manner that is appropriate.

Evaluation and review

Monitoring and evaluation

Chapter 9 goes into detail about evaluation, but it is important to cover some basic principles here. Monitoring and evaluation answers the sixth key question: 'How can success be measured?'. Public relations is like any other business function. It is vital to know whether the planned programme has done what it set out to do and if not why not.

All the planning approaches emphasise the importance of ongoing monitoring. Throughout its duration, practitioners will be regularly checking to see if the programme is on track. So, for example, media coverage will be monitored monthly to see if the selected media are using the material supplied (e.g., feature articles or press releases) and to judge how they are using it.

Sometimes evaluation is relatively easy – for example, if the aim was to achieve a change in legislation and that has happened, then clearly it was successful. Sometimes the situation is rather more complicated. If the plan is to change societal attitudes towards people who have mental health problems it will take a long time: different publics will require different amounts and types of communicative effort; as a result the evaluation programme will need to be much more sophisticated and long term, employing formal social scientific research methods (see Chapter 9 for more detail).

Building in evaluation focuses effort, demonstrates effectiveness and efficiency and encourages good management and accountability. However, research shows that there is still a limited amount of evaluation done in the public relations industry and it is fraught with debate and difference (Gregory and White 2008).

There are a number of principles that can help to make evaluation easier:

- Building in evaluation from the start: if aims and objectives are set with evaluation in mind, the task is simpler.

- Setting smart objectives: if objectives are clear and measurable, then judging whether they have been achieved is relatively easy.

- Agreeing measurement criteria with whoever will be judging success.

- Monitoring as the programme progresses: using ongoing monitoring as a management information tool.

- Taking an objective and a scientific approach: the requirement to provide facts and figures about the programme means that the planner may need training in research methods or to employ specialists.

- Evaluating processes: the planner needs to make sure they are managing the programme well, within budget and to timescales.

- Establishing open and transparent monitoring processes, through, for example, monthly review reports.

Evaluation is a contentious issue among public relations practitioners. Few believe that public relations should not be evaluated, but there is significant debate about how, and whether, there should be standard measures (Michaelson and Stacks 2011).

Review

While evaluation is both an ongoing and end-of-campaign process, a thorough review of all public relations activity should be undertaken regularly, but on a less frequent basis, every 12 months or so. As part of this, the external and internal environment should be surveyed systematically to ensure that all issues have been captured and any new ones accommodated. Campaign strategies should be tested to see if they are still entirely appropriate. Certainly tactics should be reviewed to see if they need refreshing with any new creative input, and to ensure that they are addressing the needs of the target publics.

Where a major review is required, it is important to take a holistic approach. Programmes always need to be dynamic and flexible enough to embrace opportunities and challenges, but sometimes a fundamental reappraisal has to take place. If that is the case, all the steps in the planning process outlined in this chapter need to be taken again.

Case study 8.1
'Prove You Love Me'

This case study illustrates how even a relatively modest public relations campaign with limited budget can be well researched, have clear objectives, a strategy and tactics that are linked and can demonstrate success. The 'Prove You Love Me' campaign was created by Creative Territory for Darwin City Council.

Darwin is the capital city of the Northern Territory, Australia. It has a population of 127,500, making it by far the largest and most populated city in the sparsely populated Northern Territory, but the least populous of all Australia's capital cities. It is the most northerly of the Australian capital cities, and is situated on the Timor Sea.

Situation analysis

After a spate of serious dog attacks, Darwin City Council decided to implement new animal control by-laws in the city in 2008. While there was a small groundswell of support for tough action, a large proportion of the community was 'weary' of new laws they felt 'eroded the Territory way of life'. The fiercely independent residents of northern Australia are strongly resistant to new rules and regulations governing their behaviour. They traditionally shun nationally-imposed road rules, pool-fencing laws, fireworks bans, boat licensing, fishing permits and animal regulations.

When a new Labour Government came to power they immediately began imposing new laws on the residents of the north. Pool laws, speed limits, red light cameras; one by one the freedoms of the old Darwin were being taken away. Consequently, any new law was met with fierce resistance. When Darwin City Council briefed Creative Territory on this project, they were well aware of the challenges. Darwin residents would need to be convinced to accept and take responsibility for dog and cat control laws that many regarded as draconian and a threat to their 'Territorian way of life'.

Aims and objectives

Darwin City Council introduced the new Animal Management By-laws from 1 July 2008.

The campaign aim was for Darwin dog and cat owners to take responsibility for the effective management and control of their pets.

Primary objectives were to:

1. Reduce reported dog attacks within Darwin City Council by 30 per cent.

2. Microchip 5 per cent of all Darwin's 11,000 registered dogs between June and September.

case study 8.1 (continued)

Woof woof!

You are now a Darwin registered dog owner!

Don't forget to renew your dog's registration 1 year from now. If your dog forgets to remind you, the enclosed fridge magnet will help.

Your dog should always wear its registration tag so we can find you quickly if it's lost.

Enclosed is a booklet, 'The woof in your dog'. It's full of helpful information about looking after your dog and will help you to prevent problems like excessive barking. It also tells you about things like cleaning up if your best friend has an 'accident' while running around at the park or beach.

Our Pet Care Help Line number is (08) 8930 0606 for questions about registration or advice about looking after your dog.

Animal Education Officer

Darwin City Council

Prove that you love me

Picture 8.1 Dog ownership registration poster
(*source*: Darwin City Council)

If you don't let me have one I'm going to scream

Dogs have always had all the attention from humans. Collars, microchips and those little rego tags that hang around their necks ....well I want one too!

From 1 July, all cats in the Darwin City Council area have to be registered and microchipped just like dogs.

And, like dogs, cats have to be kept in our own home and yard where the temptation to get in trouble is far less.

The new cat By-laws will make it better for humans, and safer for me.

Find out about the new Darwin City Council By-laws for cat and dog owners.

Pick up a pamphlet from Council or your local vet or pet shop. Can you pick me up a treat at the same time?

Or go to the human website www.darwin.nt.gov.au

Darwin City Council

Prove that you love me
Register and microchip me

Picture 8.2 Cat ownership registration poster
(*source*: Darwin City Council)

3. Microchip 100 Darwin cats between June and September.

These objectives would be physical indicators of Darwin residents changing their behaviours to abide by the new by-laws.

Secondary objectives were to:

1. Reduce negative animal management opinion pieces in Darwin news media by 30 per cent.

2. Ensure take-up of at least one key message in all Darwin media coverage of the new by-laws between June and September.

These objectives would be indicators that the Darwin population was embracing the laws in a positive way.

Research

Understanding the target public, where its thinking was on this and other regulatory issues and appreciating the size of the pet issue itself was crucial in informing the campaign.

Research included:

1. Numerical data on dog attacks from February to the end of May 2008; this helped establish a target for fewer dog attacks.

2. Numerical data on the number of pets in the target area; this established the size of audience and

case study 8.1 (continued)

helped establish targets for microchipping dogs. This also revealed one of the biggest challenges: that there was no information available on the number of cats or cat owners in the Darwin area.

3. Review of the media climate and public sentiment on the introduction of previous regulatory issues, including changes to schooling, introduction of speed limits on open roads and pool safety laws. This confirmed what was already suspected – that the fiercely independent residents of northern Australia are resistant to new regulation.

4. Review of the media climate and public sentiment on recent dog attacks, from February to May 2008. This helped set targets for changing public attitudes, as reflected by Darwin media. It also helped understand the attitudes, fears and concerns of the audience.

5. Review of existing sources of information for Darwin pet owners; this involved looking at what Darwin City Council was already offering pet owners. How could the most be made of services that already existed? Where were target publics already going for their information?

6. Review of common pet owner behaviours and frequented services; this involved qualitative research with Darwin City Council Animal Management staff, local veterinarians and pet groomers, as well as reviewing research papers investigating pet and owner behaviour. This helped to develop a clear picture of the target public, their behaviours, their similarities and their differences.

Target publics

Primary targets:

- Darwin City Council dog owners
- Darwin City Council cat owners.

On paper, the primary targets look obvious. Look a little further and it is evident that a wide range of people needed to be spoken with – there's a significant difference between owners of Pit Bull Terriers and Chihuahuas. During the planning phase, research was used to develop profiles of common pet owner characteristics to further break down publics.

Secondary targets:

- Victims of dog attacks
- Darwin City Council rate payers concerned about rising dog attacks
- Residents living in the vicinity of nuisance animals
- People thinking of buying a pet.

These targets were chosen because they needed to be aware of the new by-laws, either for peace of mind, to make complaints about nuisance animals, or to ensure they adhered to the laws in the future.

Stakeholders:

- Darwin City Council veterinarians, animal shelters and pet care workers
- Darwin City Council Animal Management staff
- Animal associations
- Northern Territories print and radio media.

Strategy

'Don't beat them over the head with a stick.' Given the background, this was the starting point. Darwin people were not impressed by being told what to do. The threat of legal action would not achieve the aim of *making pet owners take responsibility for the effective management and control of their pets.*

'Prove That You Love Me'

These five simple words turned the campaign on its head. Research insights showed one thing all pet owners had in common: dog owners might hate cats and cat owners might hate dogs, but they all love their pets. The strategy was an appeal from the pets of Darwin directly to their owners.

The creative direction for the campaign featured a fun, personal appeal from the pet begging the human to 'prove that you love me'. The combination of images, colours and fonts established a strong campaign brand. Comical and bold photos were used, featuring pets in humourous positions appealing to their owners to 'pleeease let me have my microchip' or ashamedly admitting 'oops, just couldn't hold on till we got home.'

Campaign strategy had four enabling elements:

1. **Appeal to pet owners' love for their animals** – through cheeky, fun, creative and clear but informal key messages.

2. **Make it easy for pet owners to find out information about the laws** – by developing information resources and distributing them to pet owners as widely as possible.

3. **Make it easy for pet owners to register and microchip their pets** – by holding a series of public microchipping events.

4. **Reach pet owners at a time when they are thinking about their pets** – by making information about the new by-laws available in places pet owners frequent.

case study 8.1 (continued)

Implementation

Element 1. Appeal to pet owners' love for their animals

- Launch the campaign with a teaser campaign featuring a paw print and the words 'prove that you love me', placed with high frequency to generate curiosity among the target audience.
- Build on the creative concept by developing a series of cheeky taglines and key messages that could be used in all campaign materials.

Element 2. Make it easy for pet owners to find out information about the laws

- Write and produce a series of fact cards, DL brochures and posters.
- Review, update and reformat Council's existing fact sheets to fit the brand.
- Write to all registered dog owners.
- Write and produce press, radio and TV advertisements.
- Provide website content.
- Establish a 'Pet Care Hotline' for residents.
- Host a media launch at local supermarket.
- Distribute media releases at key campaign milestones and coordinate media liaison.

Element 3: Make it easy for pet owners to register and microchip their pets

- Work with animal associations to sponsor and provide microchipping at existing events.
- Host specific microchipping events within the amnesty period.
- Coordinate live radio broadcasts from the main public event.
- Coordinate media coverage and photo opportunities at the main public event.
- Coordinate, produce and distribute pre-event promotional signage and advertising.

Element 4: Reach pet owners at a time when they are thinking about their pets

- Develop in-store floor stickers, signage and collateral for placement in the pet food aisle of supermarkets, at veterinary surgery front counters and animal grooming salons.
- Coordinate display of ambient materials in supermarkets, veterinary surgeries and pet grooming salons.
- Prepare letters, re-registration reminder fridge magnets and promotional collateral for direct mail outs to registered dog owners.

Budget

Category	Description	Expenditure
Strategy	Development of communication strategy	$3,500
Creative development	Development of creative concept	$5,000
Collateral	Includes: ■ Promotional collateral design ■ Promotional collateral production ■ Event signage and materials	$27,000
In-store and ambient	Includes: ■ Distribution management ■ Display hardware ■ Display materials design and production	$19,000
Media and issues management	Includes: ■ Issues management planning ■ Media planning and management ■ Spokesperson training	$14,000

case study 8.1 (continued)

Category	Description	Expenditure
Events	Includes: ■ Event management	$11,000
Advertising	Including: ■ Teaser campaign ■ Press ■ Radio ■ TV	$35,500
Online	Website	$2,500
TOTAL		$117,500

Notes:

■ Large components of the budget were allocated to producing and displaying ambient media including posters, floor stickers, brochure display units and signage because this fulfilled two of the strategies – reaching pet owners at a time when they were thinking about their pets and making it easy for pet owners to find out information about the new laws. This allowed the allocation of lesser amounts to paid advertising.

■ Large components of the budget were allocated to designing, developing and producing brochures and other promotional material with a view to creating an information resource for Darwin City Council that would live beyond the designated campaign period.

Results

Aim:

Darwin dog and cat owners would take responsibility for the effective management and control of their pets.

Outcomes:

■ Dog attacks in Darwin were reduced by 62 per cent when comparing the pre- and post-campaign periods.

■ All registered dog owners were notified about the new laws using direct mail.

■ Three highly successful and well-attended public microchipping events were held.

■ Ambient promotional material was displayed in areas frequented by pet owners. Reprints of certain brochures were required as information was very popular.

■ Media launch and releases at key campaign milestones led to a significant positive uptake of key messages in Darwin print and radio news media.

Evaluation

The success of the campaign proved that Darwin pet owners really *do* love their cats and dogs. Most importantly, there was a 62 per cent reduction in the number of reported dog attacks in pre- and post-campaign evaluation periods.

Objective	Outcome
■ Reduce reported dog attacks within Darwin City Council by 30 per cent.	■ Dog attacks were reduced by 62 per cent.
■ Microchip 5 per cent of all Darwin's 11,000 registered dogs at public events.	■ 7.9 per cent of Darwin's dogs were microchipped.
■ Microchip 100 Darwin cats at public events.	■ 134 cats were microchipped.
■ Reduce negative animal management opinion pieces in Darwin news media by 30 per cent.	■ Negative opinion pieces were reduced by 52 per cent.
■ Reduce negative animal management media pieces in Darwin news media by 30 per cent.	■ Negative media pieces were reduced by 45 per cent.
■ Ensure take-up of at least one key message in all Darwin media coverage of the new by-laws.	■ 100 per cent of stories in local media included at least one key message.

Summary

This chapter has sought to show that planning public relations is critical to success. Successful public relations programmes do not just happen: professionals plan. Planning helps to put them in control. It puts order and purpose into a busy and potentially chaotic and reactive working life. Seeing a planned public relations programme come to life is exciting and rewarding. It also clearly demonstrates to organisational peers and employers that public relations can make a real, measurable difference.

To bring together all the principles given in the second half of this chapter, a longer case study has been presented.

Bibliography

Agerwal, R. and C. Helfat (2009). 'Strategic renewal of organizations'. *Organization Science* **20**(2): 281–293.

Broom, G.M. (2009). *Cutlip and Center's Effective Public Relations*, 8th edition. Upper Saddle River, NJ: Prentice-Hall, Inc.

CIPR. (2011). 'What is PR? www.cipr.co.uk/content/careers-cpd/careers-pr/what-pr accessed 1 December 2011.

Cutlip, S.M., A.H. Center and G.M. Broom (2000). *Effective Public Relations*, 8th edition. Upper Saddle River, NJ: Pearson Education, Inc.

de Wit, R. and R. Meyer (2010). *Strategy: Process, content, context*. London: Thomson.

Freeman, R.E. (1984). *Strategic Management: A stakeholder approach*. Boston, MA: Pitman.

Grant, R.M. (2005). *Contemporary strategy analysis*. Malden: Blackwell Publishing.

Gregory, A. (2007). 'Involving stakeholders in developing corporate brands: the communication dimension.' *Journal of Marketing Management* **23**: 59–73.

Gregory, A. (2010). *Planning and Managing Public Relations Campaigns*, 3rd edition. London: Kogan Page.

Gregory, A. and J. White (2008). 'Introducing the Chartered Institute of Public Relations work on research and evaluation. in *Public Relations Metrics*. B. Van Ruler, D. Vercic and A. Veraz (eds). New York, NY: Routledge.

Grunig, J.E. and F.C. Repper (1992). 'Strategic management, publics and issues' in *Excellence in Public Relations and Communication Management*. J.E. Grunig (ed.). Hillsdale NJ: Lawrence Erlbaum Associates.

Hargreaves, I. (2005). *Journalism: A very short introduction*. Oxford: Oxford University Press.

Heath, R.L. (2001). 'Shifting foundations: public relations as relationship building' in *Handbook of Public Relations*. R.L. Heath (ed.). Thousand Oaks, CA: Sage.

Herriot, P. and W. Scott-Jackson (2002). 'Globalisation, social identities and employment.' *British Journal of Management* **13**(2): 249–257.

Jaques, T. (2006). 'Activist "rules" and the convergence with issue management.' *Journal of Communication Management* **10**(4): 407–420.

Johnson, G., K. Scholes and R. Whittington (2008). *Exploring Corporate Strategy*, 8th edition. London: Pearson Education.

Lerbinger, O. (1972). *Designs for Persuasive Communication*. Englewood Cliffs, NJ: Prentice Hall.

Marston, J.E. (1979). *Modern Public Relations*. New York: McGraw Hill.

McElreath, M.P. (1997). *Managing Systematic and Ethical Public Relations Campaigns*, 2nd edition. Madison, WI: Brown and Benchmark.

Meznar, M.B. and D. Nigh (1995). 'Buffer or bridge: environmental determinants of public affairs activities in American firms.' *Academy of Management Journal* **38**(4): 975–996.

Michaelson, D. and D.W. Stacks (2011). 'Standardization in public relations measurement and evaluation.' *Public Relations Journal* **5**(2): 1–22.

Moloney, K. (2006). *Rethinking Public Relations*. Abingdon: Routledge.

Pew Center (2011). 'The state of the media 2011.' http://stateofthemedia.org/2011/overview-2/ accessed 4 December 2011.

Ritzer, G.F. (2008). *The McDonaldisation of Society*, 5th edition. Thousand Oaks, CA: Pine Forge Press.

Smith, R.D. (2009). *Strategic Planning for Public Relations*, 3rd edition. Mahwah, NJ: Lawrence Erlbaum Associates.

Smythe, J. (2007). *The Chief Engagement Officer*. Aldershot: Gower.

Thompson, J. and F. Martin (2010). *Strategic Management: Awareness and change*. Andover: Cengage Learning EMEA.

White, J. and D.M. Dozier (1992). 'Public relations and management decision making' in *Excellence in Public Relations and Communication Management*. J.E. Grunig (ed.). Hillsdown, NJ: Lawrence Erlbaum Associates.

Windahl, S. and B. Signitzer (with J.E. Olson) (2009). *Using Communication Theory*, 2nd edition. London: Sage.

Zerfass, A., P. Verhoeven, R. Tench, A. Moreno and D. Verčič (2011). 'European Communication Monitor 2011. Empirical Insights into Strategic Communication in Europe'. Results of an Empirical Survey in 43 Countries (Chart Version). Brussels: EACD, EUPRERA. Available at: www.communicationmonitor.eu

CHAPTER 9

Paul Noble

Public relations programme research and evaluation

Learning outcomes

By the end of this chapter you should be able to:

- understand the thinking behind the Barcelona Principles
- appreciate the role of quantification and objective setting in the evaluation of public relations
- define and distinguish output and outcome evaluation
- define qualitative and quantitative research and their application to outcome evaluation
- understand content analysis and its role in output evaluation
- recognise the challenge that social media offers to evaluation.

Structure

- Barcelona Principles
- Valid metrics guidelines
- Quantification of public relations
- Objective setting
- Research
- Outcome evaluation
- Output evaluation
- Content analysis
- Social media

Introduction

For many years, public relations has been under pressure to prove its worth. As PR has sought to gain management approval to be taken more seriously, this pressure has increased. The need to compete for budgets and demonstrate a business case to justify corporate survival has only served to further ratchet up this pressure.

We have now reached a point where the rhetoric surrounding the need for public relations to justify itself is beginning to be backed up by some practical steps to put that rhetoric into practice. First, there has been some clear thinking about the pivotal role that objective setting plays in planning in general, and in evaluation in particular. Objectives are the specific end points that a PR pro-

gramme seeks to achieve. Consequently, at its simplest, evaluation is checking that the objectives set have been met. So, effective objective setting is key to effective evaluation – as well as being one of the first things to consider when putting together a PR programme or campaign.

It is also important to realise that public relations is a multi-step activity. For example, in step one a press release is issued and gains media coverage. In step two, members of the public 'consume' that coverage and some sort of change is achieved – in awareness, attitude, or even behaviour. The first step is an example of an output, the immediate result of PR activity, and is equated to exposure. Stage two is an example of an

outcome, a change in the 'targeted audiences to whom the messages were directed' (Lindenmann 2003: 5/7).

Outputs concern the process of public relations and outcomes the impact. And we need to evaluate both because outcomes relate to the programme objectives, the end result; but the better the outputs the more likely we are to achieve the outcomes we seek.

Finally, there is an increasing realisation that evaluation is a research-based activity. This implies rigour, underpins credible practice and generates confidence among practitioners. So, PR practitioners need to be 'research aware': to have the background knowledge to commission and manage researchers, as well as use the data they generate.

Barcelona Principles

These challenges, and others, are addressed by the Barcelona Principles. These seven principles were adopted in June 2010 at the second European Summit on Measurement. This summit was organised by the international Association for the Measurement and Evaluation of Communication (AMEC) and the Institute for Public Relations (IPR), as well as being supported by most of the leading PR bodies across the globe. These principles represent the first internationally agreed set of standards on the measurement of PR campaigns and now progress is being made on developing the means of implementing them – see the discussion below on valid metrics guidelines. The Barcelona Principles state (AMEC 2010):

■ The importance of goal setting and measurement.

■ Measuring the effect on outcomes is preferred to measuring outputs.

■ The effect on business results can and should be measured, where possible.

■ Media measurement requires quantity and quality.

■ AVEs (Advertising Value Equivalents) are not the value of public relations.

■ Social media can and should be measured.

■ Transparency and replicability are paramount to sound measurement.

These principles will be referred to throughout this chapter, but two notes of caution need to be sounded. The thinking behind the second principle has some justification. It resonates with what Cutlip et al. (2006: 367/8) have long referred to as the 'substitution game': this is where – for example – an output measure such as volume of media coverage is substituted for the outcomes spelled out in the objectives, such as changes in awareness, opinion or behaviour. Together with a lack of linkage between objectives set

---

Think about 9.1   **The substitution game**

Look at published public relations case studies (in *PRWeek* and award entries, for example). Can you find examples of the substitution game? That is, process (output) evaluation – most often press coverage – masquerading as impact (outcome) evaluation. Have you any ideas how the evaluation could be more impact-orientated?

Feedback

Why do people play the substitution game? Reasons could include using data that is easily available rather than useful, and lack of confidence that the programme will have a measurable effect.

and evaluation evidence presented, this forms the two most common errors in programme evaluation.

While the substitution game is to be avoided, outcome and output evaluation are not alternatives in the sense that one is better, or worse, than the other is. It is not a question of 'either/or' but rather 'both': the more efficient the process, the more likely the impact sought will be achieved.

Singling out AVEs is also a concern. As far back as the late 1940s they were established and were being criticised (Watson 2011), and yet continue to be employed. Their drawbacks are well documented and they should be left to wither on the vine in peace rather than continually being brought to the attention of new generations of PR practitioners. (See Think about 19.1 on the 'substitution' game?)

Valid metrics guidelines

To support the Barcelona Principles, guidelines for a set of valid metrics have been established (AMEC 2011). The aim is to relate the five communications stages from awareness to action, to a simplified model of how the public relations process operates. The template is the basis for a series of grids according to types of PR programmes involved: from product marketing, through investor relations, to community engagement. The focus of these grids is the bottom-right-hand corner, where the action taken by the target audience demonstrates the organisational results achieved by the public relations effort.

It is possible to criticise this template/matrix for repetition and the use of marketing terminology. But much more

---

Explore 9.1

Studying the metrics in more detail

Go to this link and look at slide numbers 14 and 15 ('How to use the matrix'):
http://ameceuropeansummit.org/amecorgdocs/ValidMetricsFramework7June2011PrintVersion.pdf

Identify the grids and activities that are relevant to the type of public relations you are involved in. Are there any activities you can add?

To see an example of a completed grid, look at page 20 of this online document: http://www3.westminster.gov.uk/Newdocstores/publications_store/communications/evaluating_your_comms_aw_lr-1319206316.pdf

---

important is the effort to develop a standard approach, which suits the diversity of public relations practice and makes progress towards balancing completeness and simplicity.

Quantification of public relations

There is a lot of interest in the quantification of the effects of public relations programmes. This has some validity because it translates what public relations people do into terms and language that others – inside and outside the organisations and clients they serve – can easily relate to. Mini case study 9.1 gives examples of using financial indicators to evaluate public relations campaigns.

Mini case study 9.1

Calculating the financial impact of public sector campaigns

Her Majesty's Revenue and Customs (HMRC) is the body responsible for collecting taxes in the UK. A 2008 campaign encouraged submission of tax returns online and on time. The numbers responding could be tracked, and HMRC knew the administrative savings that resulted. The cost of the campaign was £6.1m; the number of people filing returns online due to the campaign was 183,000, and on time was 328,749.

The Government Communication Network (GCN) evaluates the financial impact of campaigns through two respects: return on investment and cost per result. Return on marketing investment (ROMI) is calculated by dividing net payback

(admin savings achieved less cost of campaign) by campaign cost. For the HMRC campaign, the return – after the campaign had paid for itself – was £2.04 for every £1 spent.

For the HMRC, a 'result' is one person filing online or on time. The cost per result (dividing campaign cost by number of results) is £11.92. This figure has limited meaning in isolation but could act as a benchmark for other and/or future campaigns.

When it is not possible to calculate the exact financial value of a campaign's outcomes, an alternative is a financial proxy. For example, in 2010, if the number of smokers in the UK is divided into the treatment cost of smoking to the health service, the cost per smoker was £342 pa. This approach could be used to calculate the savings resulting from a stop smoking campaign.

Source: This mini case study has been developed from 'Evaluating the financial impact of public sector marketing communication, GCN/COI, January 2011' and IPA Effectiveness papers, with additional input from Kevin Traverse-Healy and Matthew Taylor

The use of quantification is also important to enable both baselines and benchmarks that underpin the principle of comparativeness in public relations evaluation: comparing programmes and campaigns against themselves (or rather previous iterations) and other, similar, organisations or campaigns.

So establishing a baseline is an essential first step to effective evaluation. That means knowing what the current position is before you apply the public relations input. This will do two things: first, establish a basis on which objectives can be developed and, second, provide a reference point for calculating whether any effect has been achieved. For example, Portsmouth FC uses a baseline to judge the success of a community affairs initiative that is measured by the take up of a voucher scheme (see Mini case study 9.2).

In contrast to the internal focus of baselines, benchmarking looks externally to compare a particular programme with similar programmes undertaken in similar circumstances by similar organisations, to provide some sort of external reference point. Mini case study 9.1 has an example of establishing a benchmark for future campaigns. (Explore 9.1 asks you to look at PR metrics in more detail.)

Picture 9.1 Portsmouth FC player Hermann Hreidarsson dressed as Henry VIII on Southsea Castle where Henry stood and watched the Mary Rose sink (*source*: Pompey in the Community)

Mini case study 9.2
Community relations at Portsmouth FC

In early 2010, financial pressures forced the English Premier League football club, Portsmouth FC (known as 'Pompey'), into administration. This contributed to the club's relegation at the end of the 2009/10 football season.

These straitened circumstances forced the club to review how it operated. Focus shifted to local supporters and the local community in Portsmouth. There was an opportunity to help the local community engage in the city's rich heritage. Heritage was in tune with Pompey's long history – the club was formed at the end of the nineteenth century.

So the community relations programme included 'Get on Board', linking the club with a local icon: the Mary Rose, Tudor King Henry VIII's flagship and the centrepiece of Portsmouth's historic naval dockyard. It drew parallels between the club and the ship. For example, nutrition was important to both (human bones found on board indicated the sailors had suffered from rickets). Similarly, participants were introduced to Futsal, a form of five-a-side football with a heavy leather ball similar to that used in Tudor times.

Successful participants were eligible for vouchers for free family visits to the four museums linked with 'Get on Board'. Of the children participating in the scheme, 32 per cent took up the offer, compared with a baseline of 3 per cent visiting local museums before the scheme started.

Source: By kind permission of Clare Martin, Pompey in the Community

One concept that has been introduced to quantify editorial coverage is opportunities to see (OTS) – referred to as impressions (or media impressions) in North America. OTS/impressions are used to illustrate the reach of media coverage. Particularly when public relations operates in a marketing context, the concept can be seductive because all marketing communications channels (both print and poster sites, for example) have an OTS figure, although the methodologies behind their calculation vary.

Smith (2005: 344) defines media impressions as 'potential total audience of people who could have been exposed to a message presented in a particular medium'. According to this definition, the OTS of a print publication is its readership. Other authorities suggest the lower figure of circulation – probably preferable as OTS figures can frequently appear inflated. With broadcast media, the concept becomes slightly more complex as reach varies according to time of day and programme, and with online media an equivalent figure for 'readers' is challenging.

The concern with OTS lies in the words 'opportunity', reinforced by Smith's use of the word 'potential'. The fact that an individual has spent a few minutes reading a newspaper or website does not mean they have read every item, let alone attended to, remembered, absorbed and digested that item's content.

Another commonplace piece of management jargon that has been imported to at least imply that the effect of public relations efforts can be quantified in a monetary fashion is ROI (return on investment). Likely et al. (2006) explain that ROI is an established means of calculating the value of an investment by dividing the return on that investment by the cost. So if £1,000 is invested for a return of £10,000, then the ROI is 10:1.

Strictly speaking, ROI is an inappropriate term as it is rare that it can be applied to PR in its generally accepted financial definition. However, in spite of efforts over the years to resist its use in PR measurement and evaluation, it has now become an established, if ill-defined, phrase, meaning something along the lines of 'results of public relations activities based on some evidence gathered with some degree of rigour'.

There are approaches that combine ROI and OTS, such as the UK Government's 'cost per impact' metric (COI 2009). This is calculated by dividing the cost of the programme by the OTS figure. For the reasons already outlined, the use of the word 'impact' when discussing OTS is optimistic, given there is no guarantee that any contact takes place between media vehicle and media consumer. In fairness to the COI, it does recommend using qualitative measures (such as key message penetration and favourability) alongside its quantitative metric of cost per impact.

Objective setting

The Barcelona Principles state that 'goal-setting and measurement are fundamental aspects of any public relations program'.[1] Smith (2005: 72) is more specific, adding that objectives 'give the planner a reference point for evaluation'. Probably the most common term associated with objectives is 'SMART' (see Chapter 8) – **s**pecific, **m**easurable, **a**chievable, **r**esourced and **t**ime-bound.

However, objective setting is not simple in public relations, and this contributes significantly to the complexity of evaluating public relations programmes. The reason can vary. For example, in an integrated or marketing communications context there may be a range of communications tools deployed (PR, sales promotion and advertising, for instance) and the effect sought may be achieved, but it might be difficult to isolate the contribution each tool made.

In another context, there might be significant environmental factors at play, such as a country with a strong currency trying to attract inbound tourists. An effective PR programme might well be cancelled out by the high costs for visitors.

So SMART objectives should be regarded as an ideal to aspire to. Frequently, when public relations is the only or lead communications discipline and there is not an unfavourable environment to operate in then PR can commit to ensuring that specific outcomes can be achieved. When there is a range of communications activities in play, PR's role might be to create a change in attitudes as a necessary precursor to other activities changing behaviour. Finally, when PR is operating in an unfavourable environment, informed assumptions might have to be made. An example could be that in the scenario of promoting tourism in a country with a strong currency, an assumption is made that without any PR input, tourist numbers would fall by 10 per cent so the PR objective (and therefore success) might be to maintain tourism at current levels.

Another key concept associated with public relations objective setting is the concept of a hierarchy of objectives: cognitive, affective and conative (see Chapter 8). Importantly, these levels are hierarchical; that is, the second cannot be achieved without first achieving the first, and the third cannot be achieved without first achieving the second. So the role of PR *might* be to change attitudes in pursuance of a broader communications or organisational objective to change behaviour.

Stacks and Bowen (2011: 3) make the same point but with slightly different terminology: there are three PR objectives found in any campaign – informational, motivational and behavioural. They occur in a logical order. First, communication must occur; that is, the information must be sent, received and understood. Second, the public, stakeholders or audience must be motivated by that communication toward the intended action. And, third, the target should adopt the desired behaviour.

The final point about objective setting is the crucial connection between outcome/impact evaluation and objectives set. Evaluation falls at the first fence if it is not taken into account at the beginning of the programme when objectives are set. Quite simply, output evaluation links directly back to the objectives set at the beginning of the programme. (See Think about 9.2.)

Research

Watson and Noble (2007: 237) stress the intimacy of research and evaluation: 'evaluation is a research-based discipline. All public relations practitioners need to need to have some understanding of research methods.' A research orientation is in tune with the Barcelona Principles (AMEC 2010), which stress that 'PR measurement should be done in a manner that is transparent and replicable for all steps in the process . . .'

All types of research, however informal and anecdotal, can be useful. All too often, practitioners ignore the 'free' research available within many (particularly large) organisations. Two related topics are the use of 'piggyback' research (e.g., adding questions to an existing survey), or an 'omnibus' survey where questions – and therefore costs – are shared with others.

So, 'a basic understanding of research methods is part of the professional practitioner's toolkit' (Watson and Noble 2007: 53). Anyone managing public relations campaigns and activities needs to be an effective commissioner and user of research. 'Even though it cannot answer all the questions or sway all decisions, methodical, systematic research is the foundation of effective public relations' (Cutlip et al. 2006: 284).

Research has five roles in public relations practice:

1. Research to plan programmes, analysing the PR 'problem'.
2. Research to monitor the effectiveness of PR programmes.
3. Research to assess the impact of the PR programme.
4. Research as a tool: the survey or visibility study.
5. Research and professionalism.

The first role is the province of situational analysis, while the next two are the process/output and impact/outcome guises of programme evaluation. The fourth role is pseudo-research, where research acts as a tactical activity generating newsworthy stories – sometimes referred to as a visibility study. Finally, a reminder that a body of knowledge obtained through academic research is an essential prerequisite of being regarded as a profession.

'Research begins with informal and often simple methods of gathering relevant information' (Smith 2005: 16). This is an important point: at any stage of a public relations programme, casual information, however unsystematically gathered, can be useful *provided no more weight is placed on the data than it deserves*. A couple of random anecdotes prove nothing but may suggest more careful investigation or even start to validate input from other sources (see discussion of triangulation below).

More formal research is divided into primary and secondary. Secondary research (also known as desk research) refers to information that has already been published in some form, ranging from information on the Internet to internal reports. Secondary research is frequently quick to obtain and is usually – but not always – free. However, frequently it is not specific enough to meet planners' needs. In contrast, primary research (also known as field research) is undertaken to meet a specific need. Primary research can be time-consuming, technical and resource intensive.

Primary research strategies are frequently described as either quantitative or qualitative. The former is associated with statistics/numbers and tends to answer the question 'what is happening?'. Associated with questionnaires and surveys, quantitative research normally involves relatively large numbers and is regarded as relatively objective. Sampling and piloting are issues that quantitative research needs to address. The Barcelona Principles (AMEC 2010) state: 'Standard best practices in survey research include sample design, question wording and order, and statistical analysis should be applied in total transparency.'

Surveys are usually based on questionnaires and involve relatively large numbers so have a quantitative feel:

- You should use a survey **when you can easily define your questions** (perhaps after some initial semi-structured interviews or focus groups), and the range of answers are limited. They are helpful when you want to collect information from a large number of people.

- Consider whether to administer a survey using a **self-completion questionnaire** (web surveys, postal surveys and feedback forms) or **a structured interview** (face to face or via telephone).

One slight variant is known as a tracking survey. It is applicable to PR evaluation because it is used at intervals to track changes in the views of a particular group of people over a period of time. Importantly, the survey needs to be designed and applied in the same way on each occasion, although it does not have to be applied to the same people, provided sampling is consistent. If some changes are made, then it is important to keep at least a core set of questions unchanged.

In contrast to quantitative, qualitative research is usually associated with words as the unit of analysis and answers the question 'why is it happening?'. Interviews and focus groups are the main methods associated with qualitative research, the numbers involved are relatively small, and it is regarded as subjective owing to researcher involvement.

These two strategies are not mutually exclusive and can be combined: undertaking a wide-ranging, questionnaire-based survey, followed by a limited number of qualitative interviews to understand and interpret the results of the survey in more detail, for example. Indeed the second Barcelona Principle suggests (AMEC 2010) – in the context of measuring the effect on outcomes – that it is often preferable to employ quantitative approaches, but they can be complemented by qualitative measures. Mini case study 9.3 demonstrates the role of research and benchmarking in PR planning and evaluation.

Denscombe (2010) talks about a mixed methods approach in some detail. He states that it has three characteristics: in addition to using both qualitative and quantitative approaches, it is a pragmatic approach and is associated with triangulation.

Triangulation is a useful concept for public relations research and evaluation, where we may rely on a number of sources of data at least some of which are, at best, based on informal or casual research. It involves the practice of viewing things from more than one perspective. This can mean the use of different methods, different sources of data or even different researchers within the study. The principle behind this is that the researcher can get a better understanding of the thing that is being investigated if he/she views it from different perspectives (Denscombe 2010: 346).

Outcome evaluation

The Barcelona Principles discuss examples of outcome evaluation (AMEC 2010):

> . . . shifts in awareness, comprehension, attitude and behaviour related to purchase, donations, brand equity, corporate reputation, employee engagement, public policy, investment decisions, and other shifts in stakeholders regarding a company, NGO, government or entity, as well as the stakeholder's own beliefs and behaviours.

These examples indicate that a large proportion of outcomes are evaluated through direct measurement – the type of research that has already been discussed. However, there are parallel issues to consider.

There is something close to a holy grail or magic bullet for the evaluation of public relations campaigns. This is econometrics: a statistical technique that can separate out the different influences on an outcome (e.g., sales) and quantify the effects of each. In PR, it is most associated with marketing communications. 'With the right data, econometrics can measure the impact your communications

---

Mini case study 9.3
Research underpins member relations

Nationwide is the UK's third largest mortgage lender and savings provider; as a mutual, it is owned by and run for the benefit of its members. By 2005, member participation in voting at its Annual General Meeting (AGM) had fallen to 730,000 out of an electorate of 6.5 million.

Since that date, voter participation has been increased by 50 per cent and maintained at that level. This success is based on a research strategy that has three foundations: member communications, external benchmarking and improvements to the voting process.

Quantitative research identified which groups of members were most likely to vote, and what incentives would persuade them to do so. Qualitative interviews were conducted with senior staff and branch managers. Benchmarking research was carried out with other building societies and the Electoral Reform Society.

The member research also led directly to key revisions to the AGM process. These included simpler voting, incentivising voting through charitable donations, more voting channels (e.g., in-branch and online), and buy-in from branch staff. The success was confirmed by both the significant increase in voting turnout and its maintenance at high levels. And post-AGM research shows the effectiveness of improvements to the process – over 90 per cent of voters used a new 'quick vote' option, for example.

Source: By kind permission of Alan Oliver, Nationwide

have on sales and profit. It can even forecast the effects of future campaigns' (Cook and Holmes 2004: 2).

In essence, what econometrics can do is to tell you what would have happened without your PR/communications input. However, it does require large budgets, technical expertise and historical data. Consequently, it tends to be restricted to large consumer campaigns where significant resources and details of past campaigns are available. But we can use the spirit of econometrics. For example, the evaluation of a teacher recruitment campaign in the UK was based on extrapolating recruitment levels from historical trends, and making informed guesses about environmental influences, such as the state of the economy.

The Barcelona Principles argue that there are occasions where it is possible to measure the effect of public relations activity on business results; see Box 9.1, which is based on the third principle and discusses market mix modelling (MMM) and survey research. Survey research is a form of direct measurement and MMM is linked to econometrics.

Rockland (2011: 2) explains that the role of MMM is to show the degree to which PR outputs, such as media coverage, drive business results, such as sales. It is much more than noticing a correlation between improving media coverage and increasing sales, and assuming that there is a connection between the two. 'The reality is that most PR practitioners are not going to be doing MMM any time soon. This truly is the domain of statistical professional [sic], and an econometrician with a doctorate is the person who does the actual modelling.' So, market mix modelling and econometrics are not techniques that public relations practitioners are likely to employ themselves. However, they do need to have enough of a basic understanding to commission and manage relevant experts, as well as to collect data in the format that research suppliers need.

Output evaluation

In contrast to outcomes, the nature of outputs (and therefore their evaluation) varies according to the tactics employed. The evaluation of media coverage will employ different techniques to the evaluation of an event, for example.

The Barcelona Principles (AMEC 2010) stress that media measurement 'requires both quantity and quality'. Counting general impressions (OTS) is rejected in favour of targeting: only counting impressions relating to relevant stakeholders or audiences. Quality of media coverage is categorised as tone, credibility and relevance, message delivery, third party or spokesperson quote, prominence and bna (beneficial, neutral, adverse).

The establishment of media evaluation was indeed prompted by a desire for media coverage to be analysed in a rather more sophisticated manner than the thickness of a clippings book. While a wide range of criteria can be employed, the most common are probably the following:

- Some indication of volume, such as clippings, mentions or column centimetres.

- Some indication of success in delivering key messages (this starts to link forward to organisational objectives).

- Some indication of the relevance of the media where coverage has been obtained (one common approach is to divide media into tiers one, two and three).

- Some indication of the reach of the coverage (frequently opportunity to see, known in North America as impressions, is used).

- Some indication of tonality – whether the tone of coverage is positive, negative or neutral.

At its simplest, media evaluation can be undertaken manually or with the deployment of some basic spreadsheet expertise. At this level, media evaluation probably does not tell the PR practitioner anything they are not aware of from reading press clippings. But presenting it in a systematic and graphical manner makes it more credible to clients and colleagues.

Box 9.1

The effect on business results can and should be measured, where possible

To measure business results from consumer or brand marketing, models that determine the effects of the quantity and quality of PR outputs on sales or other business metrics (while accounting for other variables) are a preferred choice. Related points are:

- Clients are creating demand for market mix models to evaluate the effect on consumer marketing.

- The PR industry needs to understand the value and implications of market mix models for accurate evaluation of consumer marketing PR, in contrast to other measurement approaches.

- The PR industry needs to develop PR measures that can provide reliable input into market mix models.

- Survey research can also be used to isolate the change in purchasing, purchase preference or attitude shift resulting from exposure to PR initiatives.

Mini case study 9.4
The 'Best Job in the World'

In January 2009, Queensland Tourism announced that applications had opened for the 'Best Job in the World': to be the caretaker of the islands of Australia's Great Barrier Reef. The job was real but it also involved promoting the islands, as did the process of applying for the role. The successful applicant was to receive a six-month contract paying 150,000 Australian dollars and free accommodation, with duties ranging from feeding fish to producing a weekly video blog.

Online recruitment listings and display advertising directed traffic to a website, islandreefjob.com. The website encouraged users to generate their own content through one-minute video job applications. The campaign was supported by a YouTube channel, branded presence on Facebook and Twitter, as well as viral videos, online banner advertising and worldwide media relations.

With a brief to 'create international awareness of the islands of the Great Barrier Reef', the coverage and reach achieved were impressive:

■ More than 6,000 news stories in broadcast and print media worldwide, reaching a global audience of approximately three billion.

■ Web statistics of nearly 8.7 million unique visits, more than 58 million page views and an average of 8.25 minutes spent on-site.

■ 34,684 one-minute video applications from 197 countries.

Two major US travel companies launched campaigns promoting the islands of the Great Barrier Reef as stand-alone destinations; they were the first US travel sellers to do this and their decision to do so related to the 'Best Job in the World'. The true value of this campaign is more likely to be seen in years to come as opposed to the immediate sales return. Queensland's Whitsundays received great growth in international visitors, particularly from Asian countries following the 'Best Job in the World' campaign. As Queensland emerges from the global financial crisis, many of the state's core international markets are returning, some are even booming and the outlook for the future is extremely positive. (See also Mini case study 14.2).

Sources (with additional input from Queensland Tourism):
http://www.ourawardentry.com.au/bestjob/
http://www.tq.com.au
http://youtu.be/SI-rsong4xs

It is important to recognise that media coverage is a means towards an end, not an end in itself. It remains the prime candidate for Cutlip et al.'s substitution game (2006). Finally, the term 'media evaluation' is a misnomer. We are not evaluating media but looking at our media coverage. Media content analysis is a more accurate term. And content analysis is recognised as a reputable research term, thus providing media evaluation with a credible underpinning.

Mini case study 9.4 illustrates a combination output and outcome evaluation. One point the case makes is that outputs are frequently available quickly, while outcomes can take longer to become apparent.

Content analysis

Denscombe (2010) explains that content analysis quantifies the qualitative content of textual material, and that it does so in a fashion that is clear and repeatable. Stacks (2002) confirms that it is not a research method but rather a means of analysing research data, and Smith (2005: 295) adds that: '. . . content analysis has been used for years to study mass media'.

Content analysis involves identifying the content to be analysed (e.g., key messages), what is to be analysed (e.g., media coverage), the approach to categorisation (e.g., positive, negative and neutral), and then the coding, counting and recording. In some circumstances, sampling may be employed so that not every artefact needs to be examined.

Cutlip et al. (2006: 302) confirm the definition of content analysis, reinforce its role in analysing media coverage and outline its limitations. 'Content analysis is the application of systematic procedures for objectively determining what is being reported in the media. Press clippings and broadcast monitor reports, all available from commercial services, have long been used as the bases for content analysis. They indicate only what is being printed or broadcast, *not* what is read or heard. And they *do not* measure whether or not the audiences learned or believed message content.'

Content analysis is a widely recognised research methodology, accepted well beyond the public relations community. So, content analysis can both underpin more effective process evaluation and provide much-needed enhancement to the credibility of public relations evaluation in general.

Case study 9.1 illustrates the use of content analysis as output evaluation. The main lesson is that output evaluation acts, in part at least, as a learning activity to input directly into campaign planning.

Case study 9.1
A novel approach to content analysis

MetLife is a leading life insurance and employee benefits company that has been operating for more than 140 years. With the help of Echo Research, MetLife has developed a novel application of content analysis to support its US public relations effort. This fresh approach was based on analysing how messages had been reported in the past before determining which messages needed to be communicated differently: establishing a benchmark to inform media relations planning.

The identification of key messages is fundamental to effective media relations. Public relations professionals take great care to determine those messages that should be communicated to the media. And many regard their presence in coverage as an important indicator of effective media relations.

Anecdotally, MetLife felt that not all coverage of financial products and services was accurate, leading to the possibility of the public being misinformed. To underpin its media relations strategy, MetLife decided to identify the specific product features and related issues that journalists were either reporting incorrectly, or omitting to mention at all. This would enable MetLife's media relations efforts to focus on key information and increase the accuracy of reporting on financial services.

Echo designed a new content analysis methodology known as Media Reality Check. This analyses published articles in three respects: basic facts, misstatements and omissions. The aim was to determine the degree to which the reported information was correct, partially correct, incorrect, or that key information was omitted.

The value of this new approach to content analysis has been demonstrated in a number examples, two of which are outlined below.

1. Media Reality Check: income annuities.[2] Clearly, saving for retirement is very (and increasingly) important. But there also needs to be a focus on guaranteed incomes in retirement so that people do not outlive their nest egg. MetLife felt that there was not enough information on this second aspect that can only be delivered by income annuities. Indeed, income annuities were unfairly compared in the media to other investment materials. Annuities were being reported as inflexible and expensive, and therefore being overlooked.

The media analysis examined all articles on income annuities in the top 25 dailies, plus personal finance publications and personal finance columns, over a period of more than two years between January 2001 and March 2003. It concluded that:

- 74 per cent of articles had at least one error or omission.
- A typical article with errors and omissions contained up to five misstatements, incomplete truths or omissions.
- The omission of basic facts about income annuities was more common than the inclusion of misstatements or incomplete information.

The results of this benchmarking study were shared with journalists and informed MetLife's continuing media relations strategy. MetLife appreciated there was a need to educate the media on all areas of financial services so they would be comfortable reporting all the facts.

A 12-month follow-up study in 2004 showed that the accuracy of coverage had increased: the number of articles containing errors reduced to 53 per cent from over 60 per cent. In addition, coverage of annuities in major consumer media increased by 45 per cent during the year; probably a result of MetLife's educative approach making journalists more comfortable reporting financial services issues.

2. Media Reality Check: life insurance. The most recent Media Reality Check analysed all articles on life insurance that appeared in the major US dailies, as well as leading personal finance publications and websites, newswires and high-circulation consumer magazines. Undertaken over the 12-month period from October 2007 to September 2008, it concluded that:

- 90 per cent of articles had at least one error or omission in its reporting on life insurance.
- A typical article contained up to three omissions and one misstatement of basic facts.
- The most frequent writers on life insurance were not always the most accurate.
- Only 20 per cent of articles featured life assurance in any detail, most only gave it a passing mention.

MetLife developed a media relations strategy to close the gaps identified in the research. For example, journalists may omit key information because they overestimate consumer knowledge, or they themselves may need additional education on the topic.

MetLife's efforts to understand the nature of personal finance reporting has been well received. Independent

case study 9.1 (continued)

qualitative research among the media and influencers has returned comments such as, 'MetLife stands out as actively speaking out on issues that are important . . .' and 'MetLife makes it easy to work with them and makes my job easier'.

The key conclusion drawn from these studies is that moving the focus of media content analysis to determining the accuracy of reporting can offer significant benefits. Conventionally, content analysis tends to concentrate on tonality of an article (whether an organisation is positioned favourably, unfavourably, or neutrally on key issues), rather than the fundamental correctness of the reporting that can be the primary barrier to achieving a programme's communications goals. This concentration on tonality fails to provide the evidence that can underpin a corrective strategy.

In contrast, the research undertaken on behalf of MetLife is one of the few examples where content analysis has concentrated on accuracy of coverage. Using this initial analysis as a benchmark, and then focusing efforts where these errors and omissions in reporting occur, results in improved accuracy – as well as an overall increase in volume of coverage.

Source: This case study has been developed from the winning entry of the 2009 Golden Ruler Award, available at http://www.instituteforpr.org/wp-content/uploads/JFGRAMetLifeandEchoResearch.pdf, with additional input from Dan Soulas, Managing Director, Echo Research USA

Picture 9.2 Met Life's New York headquarters (*source*: MetLife)

Social media

The evaluation of social media 'coverage' is still developing its first stage: monitoring the conversation so a decision can be made as to when and how to intervene. There are a range of online monitoring tools, which range from free, basic tools to much more sophisticated paid-for variants. The main difference is that the former allow the monitoring of current conversations, while the latter provide some sort of historical analysis, as well as drilling down into detail.

The CIPR (2011: 31) outlines what these social monitoring tools can deliver:

■ Track blogs, forums, comments, tweets, online news, social networks and video for mentions of your organisation or client and competitors.

■ Analyse these mentions and produce reports that summarise the number of Twitter followers, comment counts, tweet counts, retweets, @replies, DMs, comments and ratings.

■ YouTube comments/ratings, media type and sentiment (positive, neutral, negative).

■ Segment this data by geography, media type and language and identify links and sources, or segment by keywords.

■ Present this information in various reporting formats, including 'dashboards' that summarise key data points.

Sentiment (attitudes displayed online) or tone is an increasingly common analysis that these types of tools make available. This analysis can be performed automatically but accuracy is poor (irony, sarcasm and humour are typical problems, while manual analysis clearly attracts a significant price premium).

This hints at the big challenge associated with monitoring and evaluation online: the volume of material to track and analyse. The challenge is to keep any effort in proportion so that it is manageable.

Box 9.2 summarises the thinking on social media from the Barcelona Principles (AMEC 2010). The striking point about this thinking is the extent to which it echoes with

Online, much of the terminology employed results in quantitative measures being veiled in qualitative clothing – going in the opposite direction to content analysis. Take, for example, the 'authority' rating allocated to blogs. The dictionary definition of the word is 'the power to influence others' (*Oxford Dictionary*). However, leading blog search engine Technorati defines authority as the number of blogs linking to a website in the last six months. The higher the number, the more Technorati Authority the blog has. The suggestion is that this quantitative measure is more an indicator of popularity than authority.

New media has the potential to harness technology to establish linkages between cause and effect. But, nonetheless, most of the evaluative effort of new media is focused on quantification. The difference seems to be that, rather than being overtly quantitative in the way that AVEs and impressions are, online terminology adds a qualitative feel: terms such as authority and engagement are used as a cloak to give quantitative measures additional weight. (See Explore 9.2.)

considerations that apply to the measurement of public relations in general:

- There is no single solution.
- Defining clear objectives is essential.
- Draw on data from a variety of sources.
- Examine both quality and quantity.
- Measuring exposure needs to be developed to the effect of that exposure.

Perhaps there are two points that are 'new': that social media is about prompting conversations in communities, and that the reliability of the tools to evaluate social media still needs to be developed.

Summary

Effective evaluation starts with objective setting. Objectives need to be specific and measurable, and as impact-orientated as possible. Evaluation then looks at both the process of public relations (outputs) and its impact (outcomes). The former provides feedback to improve effectiveness while the latter demonstrates the contribution that PR makes to meeting organisational goals. There are good reasons to quantify public relations results, but this needs to be complemented with some qualitative analysis and placed in the context of wider thinking about metrics. Public relations practitioners have to be research aware, and to consider the particular challenges that social media poses for programme research and evaluation.

Bibliography

AMEC (2010). *Barcelona Declaration of Measurement Principles.* www.amecorg.com/amec/Barcelona%20Principles%20for%20PR%20Measurement.pdf

AMEC (2011). *Valid Metrics for PR Measurement.* http://ameceuropeansummit.org/amecorgdocs/ValidMetrics Framework7June2011PresentationVersion.ppsm

CIPR (2011). *Research, Planning and Measurement Toolkit.* www.cipr.co.uk/sites/default/files/Measurement%20March%202011_members.pdf

COI (2009). *Standardisation of PR Evaluation Metrics.* www.coi.gov.uk/guidance.php?page=330

Cook, L. and M. Holmes (2004). *Econometrics Explained.* London: Institute of Practitioners in Advertising.

Cutlip, S., A. Center and G. Broom (2006). *Effective Public Relations,* 9th edition. Upper Saddle River, NJ: Pearson Education.

Denscombe, M. (2010). *The Good Research Guide for Small-Scale Social Research Projects,* 4th edition. Maidenhead: Open University Press.

Likely, D.F., D. Rockland and M. Weiner (2006). *Perspectives on ROI of Media Relations Publicity Efforts.* http://www.instituteforpr.org.

Lindenmann, W. (2003). *Guidelines for Measuring the Effectiveness of PR Programs and Activities.* www.instituteforpr.org.

Oxford Dictionary. http://oxforddictionaries.com

Rockland, D. (2011). *Market Mix Modelling.* London: CIPR. http://www.cipr.co.uk/sites/default/files/MMM.pdf

Smith, R. (2005). *Strategic Planning for Public Relations,* 2nd edition. Mahwah, NJ: Lawrence Erlbaum.

Stacks, D. (2002). *Primer of Public Relations Research.* New York, NY: Guilford Press.

Stacks, D. and S. Bowen (2011). 'The strategic approach: writing measurable objectives' in *Charting Your PR Measurement Strategy.* www.instituteforpr.org

Watson, T. (2011). 'The evolution of evaluation – public relations' erratic path to the measurement of effectiveness'. www.bournemouth.ac.uk/lectures/professor/tom-watson.html

Watson, T. and P. Noble (2007). *Evaluating Public Relations,* 2nd edition. London: Kogan Page.

Notes

1. Note that goals are frequently a broader and higher level term than objectives and without measures. However, the Barcelona Principles use the two terms as synonyms so this chapter does the same, reserving the term 'aims' for what others may refer to as goals.

2. Usually in retirement, an annuity pays a steady income (normally for life) and is 'purchased' using a lump sum.

Corporate image, reputation and identity

Learning outcomes

By the end of this chapter you should be able to:

■ understand the importance and implications of living in a 'brand society'

■ define the key concepts of corporate image, reputation and identity

■ describe and understand the process of reputation management (corporate branding).

Structure

■ The controversy of image in public relations

■ Corporate image and reputation

■ Corporate identity

■ Reputation management and corporate branding

■ Measuring image and reputation

■ A critical point of view

Introduction

According to many scholars, we are living in a 'brand society' where product brands as well as corporate brands transform the way we manage organisations and live our lives (Kornberger 2010). Since the early 1990s, the idea that persons and organisations operate in a 'symbolic marketplace', where they are forced to build up a symbolic capital, that is, to create a favourable image or reputation (Schultz et al. 2000), has spread to more and more areas of society.

Private companies not only brand their products and services (product branding), but also the organisation behind these products and services (corporate branding). The driving force behind this branding effort is a search for strategic differentiation. As the 'corporatisation' of public organisations has become more evident, public authorities, regions and municipalities have also started branding themselves in front of their citizens. City branding and nation branding have established themselves as new disciplines and practices in an attempt to attract more inhabitants, tourists and firms. Personal (and personality) branding has also seen the light of day and is frequently observable in international print, broadcast, magazine and online media.

In all the cases mentioned above, three concepts are pivotal: image, reputation and identity. Persons and organisations must communicate who they are, and what they stand for, in order to create a favourable image or reputation among their stakeholders.

To possess a strong symbolic capital seems to be an advantage for organisations in many ways. A good product or corporate brand is instrumental to differentiating a company and its products from its competitors and their products. A good corporate brand makes it easier for the company to attract new investors (investor branding) and facilitates the process of attracting and maintaining valuable employees (employer branding). Finally, a good corporate brand also makes it easier for the company to recover from a severe organisational crisis.

The controversy of image in public relations

Let's start out by emphasising that the concept of image has been subject to a major controversy within the field of public relations. Already Edward Bernays declared: 'Down with image, up with reality' (Bernays 1977). At the beginning of the 1990s, James E. Grunig introduced an important distinction between two types of relationships between an organisation and its publics: *symbolic relationships* versus *behavioural relationships*; a distinction that Grunig at that moment considered part of 'perhaps the most important paradigm struggle in the field today' (Grunig 1993). Grunig defined the symbolic relationships as based on superficial and short-term activities (communication), whereas he saw the behavioural relationships as based on substantive and long-term activities (actions). However, he also admitted that the two types of relationships are closely related:

> *Although I consider long-term behavioral relationships to be the essence of public relations, I do not dismiss symbolic relationships. Symbolic and behavioral relationships are intertwined like strands of a rope.* (Grunig 1993: 123)

Think about 10.1   Image, communication and behaviour

Think of a private company that you know reasonably well. It may be a production company, such as the Coca Cola Company, an airline, such as Ryanair, a chain of supermarkets, such as Carrefour, or a retail bank, such as Barclays. How has the actual *image* that you have created of the company and its products or services come to existence? Is it because of the behaviour of the company (product, service encounter, etc.)? Is it because of the words and pictures used by the company in its external communication (advertising campaigns, corporate website, etc.)? Or is it because of a completely different source of information (family, friends, the media)?

What is communication, and what is not communication? Is it only words and pictures (what we say) that communicate a message? Or can behaviour (what we do) also communicate? Is it possible to distinguish between communication and actions?

Today, 20 years later, Grunig's distinction between communication and behaviour appears a little too narrow. Instead of defining image as the production of organisationally controlled messages for the purpose of manipulating media images, academics and practitioners have started defining and working with image as the dynamic result of interactions or negotiations between an organisation and its publics. Words, pictures and actions form part of this process. Instead of viewing image as a sender-determined construct, academics and practitioners now understand image as a receiver-determined construct (Wan and Schell 2007).

During the last two decades, corporate communication and strategic communication, two areas that are closely related to public relations in many aspects, have been institutionalised as professional practices and academic disciplines. According to the European Communication Monitor, a survey conducted by EUPRERA on an annual basis among communication professionals in private and public organisations in more than 40 European countries, public relations is no longer seen as a suitable label for the profession compared to other concepts. Thus, almost 70 per cent prefer to call their professional practice as 'corporate communications' (in particular respondents working for private companies), more than 60 per cent prefer 'strategic communication' (in particular respondents from non-profit or public organisations) and 55 per cent prefer 'communication management' (Zerfass et al. 2011).

Corporate communication and strategic communication build on two basic assumptions, between which there is a certain tension, and which are summarised in the concepts of *integration* and *relation*.

Integration (because the proponents of corporate communication and strategic communication assume that the communication activities of an organisation will be most effective and efficient) works when an organisation's external communication activities (public relations and marketing communication) and its internal communication activities (organisational communication) are coordinated to a certain extent. This mind set has given birth to the idea of integrated corporate branding focusing on coherence, not only between the external and internal dimensions of the communication activities, but also between what an organisation says (brand promise) and what it does (brand experience).

Relation (because the proponents of corporate communication and strategic communication assume that the complex and dynamic relationships between an organisation and its stakeholders is of vital importance) states that an organisation in many cases will benefit from differentiating its corporate branding depending on which stakeholder group(s) it is interacting with. Investors expect something different from the organisation than employees;

although they can of course be the same individual wearing different hats. Both integration and relation are expected to contribute to the creation of a favourable image or reputation.

With the rise of corporate communication and strategic communication there is a new focus on the *ideational* dimensions of organisations, including the crucial role played by corporate image, reputation and identity (Atvesson 1990). In accordance with this mind set and practice, Cornelissen (2011) defines corporate communication in the following way:

> *Corporate communication is a management function that offers a framework for the effective coordination of all internal and external communication with the overall purpose of establishing and maintaining favourable reputation with stakeholder groups upon which the organization is dependent.* (Cornelissen 2011: 5)

Corporate image and reputation

The first key concept is the concept of *image*, that is, how a person or an organisation is perceived by people (stakeholders). Corporate image studies were conducted already in the 1950s, and it is not until the 1990s that the concept of corporate image is joined by its close relative, the concept of corporate reputation. Referring to Aaker and Meyers (1982), Australian professor of marketing, Grahame Dowling defines image as:

> *An image is the set of meanings by which an object is known and through which people describe, remember and relate to it. That is the result of the interaction of a person's beliefs, ideas, feelings and impressions about an object.* (Dowling 1986: 110)

Dowling adds that the word 'object' can be replaced with either 'brand', 'product' or 'company', etc. to gain a definition of the image one is interested in studying.

Organisations are concerned about how they are perceived by others – that is, the image that various types of key stakeholders produce of the organisations. An image is not something that belongs to the organisation – stakeholders hold an *image* of the organisation. Very often organisations mirror themselves in the global evaluation made by their stakeholders, creating a more or less realistic self-image (Christensen and Cheney 2000).

However, an image is not a unitary, monolithic phenomenon. Each group of stakeholders perceives the company, its employees and/or its products depending on their stakes, the context and their relationship with the organisation over a shorter or longer period of time. If you are a consumer of products and services, you will most probably be interested in the quality and price of products and services, sustainability, animal welfare, or the 'brand promise' made by the company. But even consumers form a very heterogeneous group of stakeholders, producing many different images of the same company. If you are an investor, you will probably first of all be interested in the profitability and overall economic performance of the company, but also in its overall reputation and legitimacy. If you are a citizen, and let's say the neighbour of a large company, you are probably interested in how the organisation in question contributes to the local community. Does it create new jobs for the members of the local community? Are the products or the production processes harming the environment or the climate?

Another important question: 'Where do the stakeholders get the information from?' Are they in direct contact with a company – that is, they work for the company or they buy and consume its products? Or are they only indirectly in contact with the company – that is, they get the information from members of their social and professional networks (family, friends, colleagues), or they get the information from the press (stakeholder by proxy)?

But if corporate image is 'the global evaluation (comprised of a set of beliefs and feelings) a person has about an organization' (Dowling 2001: 19), what, then, is corporate *reputation*? In the early days of corporate communication, people did not highlight the difference. The two concepts were considered synonyms and accordingly used at random. Today, most researchers and practitioners make a clear distinction, based on a variety of dimensions, between the concept of image and the concept of reputation.

A first dimension concerns time – that is, reputation as *a time-based construct*. A corporate image can be viewed as a momentary snapshot based on a short-term, emotional evaluation of the company, whereas a corporate reputation can be viewed as a kind of background set based on a long-term and more rational evaluation of the company. Schultz (2005) defines corporate reputation as

the longitudinal judgement of who the company is and what it stands for among multiple stakeholders. (Schultz 2005: 43)

According to crisis communication researcher W. Timothy Coombs and his situational crisis communication theory, the reputation of an organisation builds upon the relationship between the organisation and its stakeholders, which has developed *over time* (Coombs 2012; see also Ledingham's (2005) relationship management theory). Thus, an organisational crisis can be defined as a 'relational damage'.

A second dimension concerns reputation as *a value-based construct*. In his book entitled *Reputation: Realizing value from the corporate image* (1996), Charles J. Fombrun from the Reputation Institute defines corporate reputation as 'the overall estimation in which a company is held by its constituents' (Fombrun 1996: 37). This estimation is based on the perceptions of a series of values such as reliability, credibility, social responsibility and trustworthiness. Dowling also sees corporate reputation as a value-based construct. He defines the notion in the following way:

Corporate reputation: the attributed values (such as authenticity, honesty, responsibility and integrity) evoked from the person's corporate image. (Dowling 2001: 19)

Values are about beliefs and ideals, used by human beings to give preference of something over something else. They reflect a person's sense of what is important, desirable, good, right, etc. Thus, whether an organisation has a good or bad reputation is connected to the degree of accordance between the way an organisation acts and the values that a stakeholder or stakeholder group considers to be personally or socially preferable for an appropriate behaviour of an organisation. Basic assumptions of human beings are thought to be relatively stable, whereas values, societal or personal, develop faster and in a more dynamic way over time, influenced by internal as well as external circumstances. A good example of this is the debate about climate changes and the possibilities of citizens and organisations to influence the evolution in the right way. This development of society has clearly influenced the attitude of consumers to sustainability and the use of climate- and environmentally-friendly products.

Today, organisations are very engaged in the creation of a strong and good reputation because this is a way to make them stand out from their competitors, whether it is about growth and turnover, attracting the best workforce, or

Think about 10.2

Favourable and not so favourable reputations

Think of persons and organisations that have either a very good or a very bad reputation. It may be a private company or a public organisation. It may be a political party or an NGO. It may be a football player or a golf player. Try to explain why. What kind of factors has an impact on the reputation of persons and organisations?

gaining political influence. For the very same reason, the symbolic capital plays a central role on a par with financial capital, human capital and social capital.

Corporate identity

The third key concept is the concept of identity (from the Latin *idem*, 'same'), referring to what an organisation is and what it stands for. It is a complex concept – a so-called macro-concept – covering different understandings and developments of what the identity of an organisation is.

According to Hatch and Schultz (2000) the concept of identity within management, organisation and communication studies has emerged simultaneously, but along different paths.

First, the concept of corporate identity was coined within a research tradition, which is rooted in marketing management (brand management). The concept refers to how an organisation expresses and differentiates itself in relation to its external stakeholders. Cees van Riel defines corporate identity in the following way:

> Corporate identity is the self-presentation of an organisation; it consists in the cues which an organisation offers about itself via the behaviour, communication, and symbolism which are its forms of expression. (van Riel 1995: 36)

Scholars often make a distinction between two different approaches to corporate identity (Balmer 1995). The first approach is the *visual school of identity*, emphasising the visual or tangible manifestations of what an organisation is, and what it stands for (such as the name, logo, architecture or design of the organisation, e.g. Apple and Coca Cola). Today, many organisations also include, for example, sound (sound logo, jingle, brand music and brand theme, e.g. Nokia and Intel) as an integrated part of their corporate identity mix. The second approach is the *strategic school of identity*, focusing on the ideas behind the organisation including its mission and vision statements, philosophy and values. From this perspective, corporate identity is viewed as part of a planned process linking the strategy of the organisation with its image or reputation (see the 'Reputation management and corporate branding' section of this chapter).

Second, the concept of organisational identity was established within a research tradition, which is rooted in organisation studies. The concept refers to how the members of an organisation perceive and understand 'who we are' and 'what we stand for'. Many interpretations of organisational identity are based on a version of social identity theory examining how people identify themselves by referring to the social group to which they (do not) belong (Jenkins 2008). Contrary to the concept of corporate identity, which applies an organisation-external perspective, the concept of organisational identity applies an organisation-internal perspective (all the members of the organisation). In this sense, there is affinity to the concept of organisational culture. Albert and Whetten define organisational identity as a particular kind of question:

> The question, 'What kind of organization is this?' refers to the features that are arguably core, distinctive, and enduring and reveal the identity of the organization. (Albert and Whetten 1985: 292)

Also, here, scholars often make a distinction between two different approaches to organisational identity (Whetten 1997). The first approach highlights the employee's 'identification with' the organisation. To what extent do employees define themselves by the same attributes that they believe define the organisation? To what extent is there congruence between the goals and values of the employees and the goal and values of the organisation? To what extent do they demonstrate a sense of belonging? The second approach focuses on 'the identity of' the organisation. How do the employees of an organisation see themselves as an organisation? Where the afore-mentioned approach is interested in the personal level, the latter conducts analyses at the organisational level.

Some scholars, such as Hatch and Schultz (2000), have suggested that we combine the concepts of corporate identity and organisational identity, turning them into a single concept of identity, whereas other scholars, such as Cornelissen (2011), insist on maintaining the difference between the two concepts. In the concept of corporate identity, the focus is on creating identity with the explicit purpose of differentiating the organisation in relation to its external stakeholders, whereas in the concept of organisational identity, the focus is on patterns of meaning and sense making, leading to common values, identification and belonging among members of an organisation.

The debate on postmodernity, which started in the 1980s and which took place across many academic disciplines, has also had an impact on research conducted within identity studies. In the modern society, some sociologists claim, the individual saw it as an important existential task to construct an identity and to maintain it as a stable 'core' throughout his or her life. However, in the postmodern society, nobody any longer believes that identity has such an essence. An identity is and will always remain a social construction – that is, a preliminary product of the social and cultural contexts in which we live and

Box 10.1

Managing the multiple identities of an organisation

An organisation has not only one, but multiple identities. Balmer and Greyser (2003) have established a model, or framework, the AC³ID test, allowing us to identify and to manage the various identities of an organisation. According to this model, it is possible to identify no less than six different types of identities:

A: Actual identity = What we really are (ownership, organisational structure, type of product, markets, business performance, etc.)

C: Communicated identity = Who we say we are (part of corporate branding)

C: Conceived identity = Who people think we are (corporate image and reputation)

C: Covenanted identity = What we promise to be

I: Ideal identity = Who we should be (the optimum positioning of the organisation in its market in a given time frame)

D: Desired identity = Who we want to be (the vision for the organisation as defined by the CEO or top management)

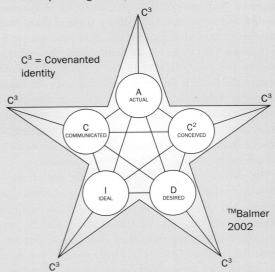

C^3 = Covenanted identity

™Balmer 2002

Figure 10.1 The AC³ID test (*source*: J.M.T. Balmer 'The three virtues and seven deadly sins of corporate brand management', *Journal of general Management*. Autumn 2001 **27**(1): 1–17)

interact with other people over time. In such a society, the task of the individual is to avoid fixation and to keep the options open (Bauman 1996). This debate has recently been revitalised by the concept of the *authentic* company – an organisation that is 'true to itself' (Gilmore and Pine 2007).

Corporations, places, and offerings have actual identities (the selves to which they must be true to be perceived as authentic), not just articulations of those identities (the representations that must accurately reflect those selves to be perceived as authentic). There's an old saw in advertising circles: nothing makes a bad product fail faster than good advertising. There should be a new one in branding circles: nothing makes a real branding effort fail faster than a phony product. Such phoniness results from representations detached from the reality of a company's actual identity. (Gilmore and Pine 2007: 129)

Picture 10.1 The Carlsberg elephants – the main entrance to the corporate headquarters of the Carlsberg Group (*source*: Chris Fredriksson/Alamy Images)

Case study 10.1
Re-branding Carlsberg

Perched on Valby hill in Copenhagen, the Carlsberg brewery was founded in 1847 by J.C. Jacobsen, a young man interested in natural science, industrial innovation and high-quality yeast. In 1882, J.C. Jacobsen carved his now famous 'golden words' into the stonework of the original Carlsberg Brewery: 'In working the brewery it should be a constant purpose, regardless of immediate gain, to develop the art of making beer to the greatest possible degree of perfection so that this brewery as well as its products may ever stand out as a model, and through their example, assist in keeping beer brewing in this country at a high and honourable level.'

More than a hundred years later, Carlsberg started implementing an ambitious and aggressive growth strategy. In 1999, Carlsberg was still primarily a regional brewer in Scandinavia and the UK. However, only a few years later Carlsberg saw itself as the market leader in Northern Europe and parts of Eastern Europe and Asia. In 2008, Carlsberg acquired Scottish & Newcastle, the biggest acquisition ever made in Denmark.

Today, Carlsberg has become the Carlsberg Group – the fourth largest brewery in the world. The Group has more than 40,000 employees, it is present in more than 150 countries and it represents more than 500 different product brands.

As the Carlsberg Group grew bigger and bigger, President and CEO Jørgen Buhl Rasmussen and his team of managers became aware that it was becoming crucial to unify all these companies, while at the same time acknowledging that each of these companies represented its own corporate culture, nationality and point of market differentiation. The top management of the Carlsberg Group decided to re-brand the corporate brand, communicating an authentic and inspiring Group story, while at the same time maintaining a 'GloCal' (Global and Local) approach, and retaining regional and local brand value.

First, the Carlsberg Group defined its ambition: *to be the fastest growing global beer company*. In 2010, it adopted a new global vision expressing the corporate identity of the Group across cultures. It was called the Carlsberg Group Stand:

Thirst for Great
Great people. Great brands. Great moments.
Founded on the motto, Semper Ardens – Always Burning – we never settle, but always thirst for the better.
We are stronger together because we share best practices, ideas, and successes. We brand as many, but stand as one.

With the courage to dare, to try, to take risks, we constantly raise the bar. We don't stop at brewing great beer.
We brew a greater future – for our consumers and customers, our communities, and our people.
This passion will continue to burn and forever keep us thirsty.

Carlsberg Group

At the same time, the Carlsberg Group established what they call the five 'Winning Behaviours' – that is, a set of values or action-orientated principles of best behaviours that provide employees across the Group guidance on how to work with colleagues and customers and how to drive a 'performance culture':

The Carlsberg Group Winning Behaviours
Together we are stronger.
We want to win.
Our consumers and customers are at the heart of every decision we make.
We are each empowered to make a difference.
We are engaged with society.

In 2011, the Carlsberg Group finally launched a new brand proposition for its flagship beer *Carlsberg*. The old tagline of the beer, 'Probably the best beer in the world', infused with Danish irony, was replaced with a new, modernised proposition – 'That calls for a Carlsberg' – encouraging consumers to 'step up and do the right thing' and subsequently gratifying themselves with a Carlsberg for their good deeds.

Questions to consider

Which challenges does the Carlsberg Group face in its re-branding strategy?

'We brand as many, but stand as one'. What kind of corporate identity does this statement presume?

Consider the corporate vision (the Carlsberg Group Stand) and values (the Winning Behaviours) of the Carlsberg Group. Are the vision and the values authentic, unique and distinctive viewed from the perspective of the customers and the employees?

Will the local brand heritage (an old Danish brewery) cause any problems? And what about intercultural differences? To what extent will the image and reputation vary from market to market, from country to country?

Sources: www.carlsberg.com and *Global Challenges on Sustainable Corporate Communications for Carlsberg Group*, ComCaseCompetition 2012 organised by Danish Association of Communication Professionals in cooperation with Young Communicators, Copenhagen Business School and Carlsberg Group.

Reputation management and corporate branding

To work strategically with reputation management involves a number of disciplines or fields of practice, such as corporate strategy, stakeholder management, issues management and crisis management (see Chapters 8, 16 and 17). However, corporate branding constitutes one of the cornerstones if an organisation wants to strengthen its reputation among its internal and/or external stakeholders.

Branding is a universal phenomenon. All human beings are able to create mental pictures of themselves and the phenomena that they meet in the outside world. What we call branding today is the strategic and goal-orientated exploitation of this human ability, in order to build up relationships between people and the products of a company or the company itself. Corporate branding can be defined as:

The process of creating, nurturing, and sustaining a mutually rewarding relationship between a company, its employees and external stakeholders. (Schultz in Schultz et al. 2005: 48)

As it appears from Box 10.2, corporate branding has undergone a rapid development since its appearance in the 1990s. It has moved from the first wave, where the emphasis

Box 10.2

Corporate branding: towards the third wave

First wave (mid-1990s) Marketing mind-set	Second wave (2005–present) Corporate mind-set	Towards the third wave Enterprise mind-set
Grounded in a marketing and campaign approach (uni-functional and myopic)	Grounded in a strategic cross-functional approach (multifunctional and fragmented)	Grounded in a strategic holistic approach (inter-functional and integrated)
Product-orientated, short-sighted, tactical and narrow focus on visual identity and aesthetics	Branding as a part of the continuous adaptation and development of the company Long-term-orientated development of culture, vision and image based on 'who we are' Integration across disciplines	The brand as the voice, not just of the company, but of the entire enterprise, encompassing the interests and expectations of the full range of a company's stakeholders To gain the perspective of the whole enterprise and develop the awareness of the symbolism involved
Internally anchored understanding of 'who we are' and 'what we stand for'	Involvement of employees and customers (employer brands)	Stakeholder capitalism: thinking in terms of network relations
Communication: sender-orientated, transmission	Communication: receiver-orientated, interaction, co-creation of brand meaning	Communication: many voices will participate in the shaping and informing of the corporate brand
The corporate brand as a sense giver	The corporate brand as a facilitator of relations between sense giving and sense making	The corporate brand as conversant (as initiator of conversations)
A linear process	A dynamic process *Five principles:* Know thyself Be facilitator Lead through interaction Embrace paradoxes Think dynamic	A co-creational process *Five principles:* Corporate branding is dynamic Anticipate the future by celebrating the past Listen and you will speak volumes Serve your customers by delighting your employees Think like an enterprise

Sources: Schultz et al. (2005) and Hatch and Schultz (2008)

was on a short-term, marketing-orientated and campaign-driven approach with a main focus on visual identity, to the second wave – and very recently even to a third wave. Today, corporate branding is viewed as a strategic asset of increasing importance for the entire organisation, and the brand is viewed as something that is constantly being co-created in dynamic interaction between stakeholders, their networks and the organisation.

According to Hatch and Schultz (2008), the second wave of corporate branding emerges in the first decade of 2000. At this moment corporate branding has developed into a discipline with a more strategic and long-term way of thinking about the corporate brand. It is no longer just anchored in the department of marketing or public relations, but is embedded in a long series of functions and disciplines across the organisation, with a focus on the interaction between the vision of management, the organisational culture and the images of the stakeholders.

However, in 2008 Hatch and Schultz start talking about the rise of a third wave of corporate branding. Even though there is a certain accordance between the understanding of the second and the third wave of corporate branding, they want to emphasise that a paradigm shift has occurred when it comes to the new stakeholder focus. There has been a shift from primarily thinking separately and with a few stakeholder groups, such as customers or employees, to having a broader stakeholder perspective and thinking in stakeholder networks. Local communities, NGOs and politicians all contribute to the co-creation and brand meaning of the corporate brand. For that reason, reputation management is not only the duty of one or two departments but must penetrate all functions of an organisation in an integrated, holistic way. Thus, reputation management is demonstrated in practice by the tension between an organisation and its promises and relations to its (networks of) stakeholders.

Corporate branding is a strategic management discipline with the scope to make the organisation attractive to current and potential stakeholders in order to strengthen its image and reputation and to make its vision come through.

Typically a corporate branding process is initiated by doing a *situational analysis* to find out about the identity, beliefs, positions, core competencies and performances of an organisation (see Box 10.3). Thus, it is important to carry out analyses of possible gaps between what you are, what you want to be and the way you are perceived by your key stakeholders. If the gaps have grown too big, you often as an organisation want to strengthen or to change the image and reputation of the company in relation to various key stakeholders.

Box 10.3

The corporate branding process

T H E C O R P O R A T E B R A N D	Situational analysis	*Who are we? What are our main challenges? How are we perceived by our key stakeholders? Any gaps?* Stakeholder analysis, gap analysis, market analysis, etc. => adaptation or development of new position
	Strategic decisions	*Who do we want to be, and how will we become what we want to be? What are the vision, the goals and the new strategies? How do we differentiate ourselves from others?* Branding platform (brand-architecture, CSPs, organisational stories, behaviour, symbols, visual and verbal communication) Organisational changes (structure, culture, etc.)
	Implementation	*How to put the decisions into action? Execution of plans (how to communicate internally and to the outside world)* Planning and execution of communication strategies: goals, stakeholder groups, content, tactical organising of CSPs and key stories, choice of media, budget and resources
	Evaluation	*What images and what reputation do we have at the moment? What kind of dynamics? New gaps? How far have we come?* Alignment between vision/strategy, culture/identity and images/reputation Measuring our corporate/organisational identity, images and reputation as viewed by our key stakeholders

(right margin vertical text: S T A K E H O L D E R S)

The next step is to make *strategic decisions*. It has to be decided what should be the branding platform and how to live up to the new visions and goals. It includes questions about key values, common starting points (CSPs) and stories the organisation lives that have to be taken into account in an integrated, holistic communications perspective. It also deals with the choice of branding architecture. Should you go for a monolithic structure (single, all-embracing identity, e.g. Virgin and Heinz), an endorsed structure (identity badged with parent company name, e.g. Sony – Sony Electronics, Sony PlayStation, etc.) or a branded identity structure (each business, unit or product has its own name, e.g. Proctor and Gamble – Always, Ariel, Duracell, etc. Inditex – Zara, Massimo Dutti, etc. and Unilever – Becel, Lipton, etc.)?

The third step is to *develop and implement* the strategic decisions. The decisions must be put into action. Plans must be elaborated and implemented, for instance about the brand architecture, the role of communication and the communication tactics.

However, it is not just about implementing new strategies. It is also about a dynamic, on-going process during which the corporate brand is constantly negotiated between an organisation and its stakeholders. This is the reason why it is important as the fourth step to continuously make *evaluations* of the development of the brand and of the achievements of the strategic goals.

The corporate branding process

According to Hatch and Schultz (2001) and Schultz et al. (2005), the ideal branding process takes its point of departure in the *corporate brand identity*. It constitutes the core aligning of the three strategic stars: (1) the strategic vision, i.e. the central idea that expresses top management's aspiration for the achievements of the company in the future; (2) the organisational culture, i.e. values, beliefs and basic assumptions that reflect the heritage of the company as well as the (emotional) relations of the employees to the company; and (3) stakeholder images, i.e. views of the organisation developed by its external stakeholders.

To be able to evaluate to what extent the three strategic stars are aligned, Hatch and Schultz (2001) have developed *the corporate branding tool kit* (Box 10.4). By means of three sets of diagnostic questions the organisation can find out whether gaps have opened between the three interfaces of: (1) vision and culture (a gap opens when employees do not understand or support the strategy); (2) culture and image (a gap opens when the organisation does not live up to its promises); and (3) vision and image (a gap opens when there is a conflict between the vision and the views of the stakeholders).

Box 10.4

The corporate branding toolkit (Hatch and Schultz 2001)

Diagnostic questions for analysing gaps between:

Vision and culture

- Does the organisation practise the values it promotes?
- Does the organisation's vision inspire all its subcultures?
- Are the organisation's vision and culture sufficiently differentiated from those of its competitors?

Culture and image

- What images do stakeholders associate with the organisation?
- In what ways do its employees and stakeholders interact?
- Do employees care what stakeholders think of the organisation?

Image and vision

- Who are the organisation's stakeholders?
- What do the stakeholders want from the organisation?
- Is the organisation effectively communicating its vision to its stakeholders?

Measuring corporate image and reputation

The image and reputation of private companies are measured and evaluated on a regular basis by various organisations. These evaluations are followed closely by the companies themselves and by many of their key stakeholders (first of all competitors, investors, employees and the media). It is one of the characteristics of the new 'audit society' (Power 1997) or 'evaluation society' (Dahler-Larsen 2011).

Rankings in business magazines and newspapers, such as *Fortune* magazine's 'Most Admired Companies' survey or *Financial Times*' 'World's Most Respected Companies', are among the most well-known and respected rankings.

Explore 10.1

The reputation of universities

Is your university or business school represented on one or more academic ranking lists, such as that in *Times Higher Education*? If yes, on which list(s) is it represented? What are the criteria applied by the ranking list(s) in question? How good or bad are the selected criteria? Is it the university or business school as a whole that is ranked, or is it a specific faculty or department? What is the position of your university or business school?

Who will be affected by such rankings (if anybody)? And how?

What made you choose your university or business school? Geographical location, recommendations made by your parents or friends (including students who already studied at the university or business school), or an official university or business school ranking?

Go to *Times Higher Education*'s website and see how this ranking list has been made.

Fortune magazine evaluates the image and reputation of a company based on criteria such as quality of management, quality of products and services, innovativeness, long-term investment value, financial soundness, ability to attract, develop and retain talent and community and environmental responsibility. The *Financial Times* also includes criteria such as successful change management, business leadership and robust and human corporate culture.

An organisation of particular interest when it comes to measuring the images and reputations of companies, cities and nations is the Reputation Institute in New York. It is a private consultancy and research firm with a global network of local offices, which has specialised in corporate reputation management. The work of the Reputation Institute is based on a reputation quotient model launched as the Global RepTrack™ Pulse in 2006. Not only are the images and reputations of large companies assessed, but also the symbolic capital of public authorities such as municipalities and taxation authorities, cities such as London, Geneva, Sydney and Vienna (the top four of the City Reptrak™ in 2011) and countries such as Canada, Sweden, Australia and Switzerland (the top four of the Country RepTrak™ in 2011) are being evaluated (see Explore 10.2).

Explore 10.2   Reputation Institute and the Global RepTrak™ Pulse

The Reputation Institute (RI) was founded in 1997 by Charles J. Fombrun, Professor of Management at Stern School of Business, New York University, and Cees B.M. van Riel, Professor of Corporate Communication at the Business School at Erasmus University. The Reputation Institute first of all evaluates the reputation of large private companies based on a measuring tool formerly known as the Reputation Quotient model, and which was relaunched in 2006 as the Global RepTrak™ Pulse. The model is based on the assumption that the reputation of a company is based on the emotional attachment between a company and its stakeholders (admiration, trust, good feeling and general esteem). Seven key dimensions are the drivers behind the reputation of a company: products/services, innovation, workplace, governance, citizenship, leadership and performance. Each of these key dimensions comprises a series of attributes.

The Reputation Institute also evaluates city and country reputations. Go to the website of the Reputation Institute and examine how the Global RepTrak™ Pulse, the City RepTrak™ and the Country RepTrak™ are structured and how these measurement tools are applied.

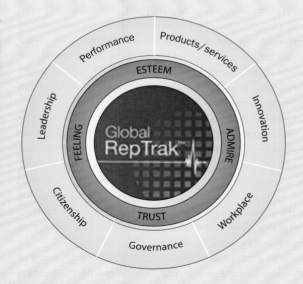

Figure 10.2 The RepTrak™ Pulse measures the degree of admiration, trust, good feeling and overall esteem that stakeholders hold about organisations (see http://www.reputationinstitute.com/thought-leadership/the-reptrak-system)

Picture 10.2 The *Financial Times*'s 'World's Most Respected Companies' (*source*: PSL Images/Alamy Images)

A critical point of view

Brands are pervasive and ubiquitous. We take them for granted – from pop art to McDonald's, from Starbucks to Greenpeace, brands are the mechanism that connects organizations and people. (Kornberger 2010: 263–264)

During the last two decades, the concepts of image, reputation and identity have conquered the mind and soul of many a communication executive or manager, not only in the business world but also in many public organisations (see the introduction of this chapter). However, the popularity of corporate communication is counterbalanced by a growing number of critical voices coming from within the academic community. One of these voices belongs to two Danish communication researchers, Lars Thøger Christensen and Mette Morsing, joined by their American colleague, Georges Cheney.

Christensen et al. define corporate communication as 'a management ideal with wide-ranging organisational implications' (2008: 168). At the heart of their critique lies the concept of *integration* – that is, the idea that in order for an organisation to be effective and efficient there must be a high degree of coherence between the strategic vision of the organisation, its culture, its internal and external communication activities and its image and reputation among external stakeholders.

One of the organisational implications of applying an integrated perspective in practice, according to the three scholars, is that this approach easily transforms the organisation into a tightly coupled system – that is, a system where input and output are closely connected, and where even the slightest change in principle will prompt a

response (action) in all parts of the system. To put it differently, in such a system, integrated corporate branding will be enforced as a global solution turning all the members of the organisation (top management, employees) into the same type of 'brand evangelists' (Ind 2001).

The idea may seem very promising, especially if you adopt a traditional leadership style based on control and predictability. However, Christensen et al. (2008) claim an integrated perspective will also make the organisation vulnerable. Today, both private and public organisations are faced with many expectations and demands from their stakeholders. At the same time, organisations are operating in socio-cultural contexts, which have become much more complex and dynamic due to globalisation and new information and communication technologies. They have to demonstrate 'strategic readiness'; they have to prepare for change.

Flexibility is the solution to this new situation. But how flexible is an organisation whose communication activities are based on the idea of integration? If we return to the Carlsberg case: how, on the one hand, can the Carlsberg Group integrate the local (national) brand heritage of the Danish brewery with all the new brands and, on the other, be flexible enough to be able to meet the expectations and demands from both internal and external stakeholders working and living in more than 150 different markets, cultures and societies all over the world?

Summary

This chapter has sought to show how the field of corporate communication and the concepts of corporate image, reputation and identity have become important in a society obsessed by brands and the idea of a 'symbolic capital'. Image is the global evaluation (comprised of a set of beliefs, ideas, feelings and impressions) that a person has about a product and/or an organisation. Compared to image, reputation is a time-based and value-based construct. It is built up over time and based on the relationship between the organisation and its multiple stakeholders. Identity refers to who an organisation is, and what it stands for. An organisation very often has multiple identities and images. In a complex, dynamic and ever-changing society, organisations have to balance the need for both integration (global control) and flexibility (local responsiveness).

Bibliography

Aaker, D. and J.C. Myers (1982). *Advertising Management*. New Delhi: Prentice Hall.

Albert, S. and D.A. Whetten (1985). 'Organizational identity' in *Research in Organizational Behavior* Vol. 7. L.L. Cummings and M.M. Staw (eds). Greenwich, CT: JAI Press.

Atvesson, M. (1990). 'Organization: from substance to image?'. *Organization Studies* **11**(3): 373–394.

Balmer, J.M.T. (1995). 'Corporate branding and connoisseurship.' *Journal of Grand Management* **21**(1): 22–46.

Balmer, J.M.T. and S.A. Greyser (eds) (2003). *Revealing the Corporation: Perspectives on identity, image, reputation, corporate branding and corporate-level marketing*. London: Routledge.

Bauman, Z. (1996). 'From pilgrim to tourist – or a short history of identity' in *Questions of Cultural Identity*. S. Hall and P. du Gay (eds). London: Sage.

Bernays, E.L. (1977). 'Down with image, up with reality.' *Public Relations Quarterly* **22**(1): 12–14.

Christensen, L.T. and G. Cheney (2000). 'Self-absorption and self-seduction in the corporate identity game' in *The Expressive Organization: Linking identity, reputation and the corporate brand*. M. Schultz, M.J. Hatch and M. Holten Larsen (eds). Oxford: Oxford University Press.

Christensen, L.T., M. Morsing and G. Cheney (2008). *Corporate Communications: Convention, complexity, and critique*. Los Angeles, CA: Sage.

Coombs, W.T. (2012). *On-going Crisis Communication: Planning, managing, and responding*. Los Angeles, CA: Sage.

Cornelissen, J. (2011). *Corporate Communication: A guide to theory and practice*. London: Sage.

Dahler-Larsen, P. (2011). *The Evaluation Society*. Stanford, CT: Stanford University Press.

Dowling, G. (1986). 'Managing your corporate image.' *Industrial Marketing Management* **15**: 109–115.

Dowling, G. (2001). *Creating Corporate Reputations: Identity, image and performance*. Oxford: Oxford University Press.

Fombrun, C.J. (1996). *Reputation: Realizing value from the corporate image*. Boston, MA: Harvard Business School Press.

Gilmore, J.H. and B.J. Pine II (2007). *Authenticity: What consumers really want*. Boston, MA: Harvard Business School Press.

Grunig, J.E. (1993). 'Image and substance: from symbolic to behavioral relationships.' *Public Relations Review* **19**(2): 121–139.

Hatch, M.J. and M. Schultz (2000). 'Scaling the Tower of Babel: relational differences between identity, image, and culture in organizations' in *The Expressive Organization: Linking identity, reputation, and the corporate brand*. M. Schultz, M.J. Hatch and M. Holten Larsen (eds). Oxford: Oxford University Press.

Hatch, M.J. and M. Schultz (2001). 'Are the strategic stars aligned for your corporate brand?' *Harvard Business Review*. February.

Hatch, M.J. and M. Schultz (2008). *Taking Brand Initiative*. San Francisco, CA: Jossey-Bass.

Ind, N. (2001). *Living the Brand: How to transform every member of your organization into a brand champion*. London: Kogan Page.

Jenkins, R. (2008). *Social Identity*. Oxon: Routledge.

Kornberger, M. (2010). *Brand Society: How brands transform management and lifestyle*. Cambridge: Cambridge University Press.

Larkin, J. (2003). *Strategic Reputation Risk Management*. New York, NY: Palgrave Macmillan.

Ledingham, J.A. (2005). 'Relationship management theory' in *Encyclopedia of Public Relations* Vol. 2. R.L. Heath (ed.). Thousand Oaks, CA: Sage.

Power, M. (1997). *The Audit Society: Rituals of verification*. Oxford: Oxford University Press.

Schultz, M., M.J. Hatch and M. Holten Larsen (2000). 'Introduction: why the expressive organization?' in *The Expressive Organization: Linking identity, reputation, and the corporate brand*. M. Schultz, M.J. Hatch and M. Holten Larsen (eds). Oxford: Oxford University Press.

Schultz, M. (2005). 'A cross-disciplinary perspective on corporate branding' in *Corporate Branding: Purpose, people, process*. M. Schultz, Y.M. Antorini and F.F. Csaba (eds). Copenhagen: Copenhagen Business School Press.

Schultz, M., Y.M. Antorini and F.F. Csaba (eds) (2005). *Corporate Branding: Purpose, people, process*. Copenhagen: Copenhagen Business School Press.

van Riel, C.B.M. (1995). *Principles of Corporate Communication*. London: Prentice Hall.

Wan, H.-H. and R. Schell (2007). 'Reassessing corporate image: an examination of how image bridges symbolic relationships with behavioral relationships.' *Journal of Public Relations Research* **19**(1): 25–45.

Whetten, D.A. (1997). 'Theory development and the study of corporate reputation.' *Corporate Reputation Review* **1**(1): 26–34.

Zerfass, A., P. Verhoeven, R. Tench, A. Morena and D. Verčič (2011). 'European Communication Monitor 2011. Empirical Insights into Strategic Communication in Europe. Results of an Empirical Survey in 43 Countries.' Brussels: EACD, EUPRERA.

Websites

Carlsberg Breweries: www.carlsberg.com
Financial Times: www.ft.com
Fortune: www.money.cnn.com/magazines/fortune
Reputation Institute: www.reputationinstitute.com
Times Higher Education: www.timeshighereducation.co.uk

CHAPTER 11

Johanna Fawkes

Public relations, propaganda and the psychology of persuasion

Learning outcomes

By the end of this chapter you should be able to:

- describe and evaluate the components of propaganda and persuasive communication
- describe and distinguish between attitudes and their effect on behaviour
- describe and evaluate theories of attitude learning and change
- apply these concepts to a communication campaign.

Structure

- Public relations and propaganda
- Public relations and persuasion
- Who says: the question of credibility
- Says what: the nature of the message
- To whom: the audience perspective
- To what effect: forming and changing attitudes and beliefs

Introduction

In November 2011 YouGov research suggested that over 60 per cent thought PR agencies were not to be trusted (prmoment.com/809). Journalists often see public relations as just propaganda, an accusation that PR practitioners – and some academics – treat as outrageous. Students and those wishing to practise responsible public relations may prefer a more rigorous response, based on examination of the issues rather than simple rejection of all charges. This chapter examines the connections between propaganda and public relations, particularly in their shared history. This is then linked to persuasion and the processes involved in trying to persuade others. It uses a simple communication model to describe the stages of persuasion in some detail, drawing on theories from social psychology to understand concepts such as attitudes and their effect on behaviour. The perspective is largely that of the public relations practitioner seeking to influence others. Examples are given from the history of public relations and from recent world events.

Public relations and propaganda

See Think about 11.1. Critics of public relations say that much of public relations *is* propaganda; its practitioners insist public relations is only practised for the public good. Both agree that propaganda is harmful; the latter deny it has anything to do with them. These views are very simplistic and have a strong 'either/or', 'good/bad' approach to the subject. One group assumes all public relations is propaganda, the other that none is. It is also much easier to accuse others of propaganda than to examine one's own practices – you do propaganda, I do public relations. The realities are more complex and take some unravelling. Let's start with trying to explain the differences.

The word 'propaganda' has its origins in the seventeenth-century Catholic Church, where it meant to 'propagate the faith'. It played a major part in recruiting support for the First World War, when the key Committee on Public Information (CPI) was established in the USA. (See Box 11.1 for the impact this committee had on the development of public relations in the UK and USA.) L'Etang (2004) notes that propaganda was a neutral term at the start of the twentieth century, when theorists such as Bernays (1923), Lippman (1925) and Lasswell (1934) saw no problem with trying to organise the responses of mass audiences. Indeed, they saw it as 'democratic leadership' in Lippman's phrase, and Bernays, sometimes called the father of public relations, called his second book *Propaganda* (1928). Bernays opens *Propaganda* (1928/2005: 38) with the sentence: 'The conscious and intelligent manipulation of the organised habits and opinions of the masses is an important element in democratic society.' According to Weaver et al. (2006: 9), 'the real value of propaganda lies *not* in its dissemination and promotion of *ideas* but in its ability to orchestrate public opinion and social action that supported the ruling elite'.

Grunig and Hunt (1984: 21) locate propaganda in the press agentry model, the first of their four models: 'Public relations serves a propaganda function in the press agentry/publicity model. Practitioners spread the faith of the organisation involved, often through incomplete, distorted, or half-true information'. This links (some) public relations activity to propaganda, but later makes clear this is often unethical in content and tends to associate it with historical examples.

Think about 11.1

Are these examples of propaganda or public relations?

- In September 2011, a US PR company set up a fake news website and posted positive articles about clients, written by fake journalists (prdaily/10021).

- The *British Medical Journal* reported (September 2011) that the majority of UK schools were receiving free teaching aids to help children understand and 'think critically' about advertising. This material is produced by an organisation, Media Smart, set up by leading advertisers of children's products (Cookson 2011).

- The UK *Guardian* newspaper reported that the Taliban in Afghanistan had started using Twitter to keep in touch with their followers (Boone 2011).

- Campaign group Breast Cancer Action has complained about 'pinkwashing', where companies associate themselves with such health campaigns for PR purposes but actually contribute very little. For example: BMW and Ford both ran car promotions with 'fight cancer' themes; and Rimmel sold a lipstick with the strapline 'Pucker up and kiss breast cancer goodbye' (Landman 2008).

Box 11.1

Public relations – a little history

Edward Bernays (1891–1995) is widely described as the 'father of public relations', and his life and career sheds some interesting light on current dilemmas regarding public relations, persuasion and propaganda.

Born in Vienna, Bernays was the nephew of the pioneering psychologist Sigmund Freud. He developed the notion of applying his uncle's theories of mass psychology to the practice of corporate and political persuasion. He started the first educational course in the subject at New York University in the 1920s and introduced the term 'public relations counsel' in his 1923 book, *Crystallizing Public Opinion*, which was the first text on the subject. His next book was called *Propaganda* (1928) because he believed that public relations was about engineering social responses to organisational needs (he also wrote *The Engineering of Consent*, 1955). His influence on the twentieth century is described in a fascinating BBC documentary, *The Century of the Self* (Curtis 2002), which looked at the impact of persuasion techniques and psychology on commercial and political communication throughout the twentieth century.

In the 1920s, when the American Tobacco Company asked for his help in promoting cigarette smoking among women, Bernays persuaded a group of young women's rights campaigners to light cigarettes on the New York Easter Parade as 'Torches of Freedom' (a slogan that he ensured was the caption to all the media photographs of the event), thus combining the image of the cigarette with women's independence – a powerful image that affected consumer behaviour for the rest of the twentieth century (Wilcox et al. 2003). He had learned some of these techniques during the First World

War when he served on the US Committee on Public Information (CPI).

The CPI included many of the leading public relations practitioners in the post-war period. As Bernays said in *Propaganda* (1928): 'It was, of course, the astounding success of propaganda during the war that opened the eyes of the intelligent few in all departments of life to the possibilities of regimenting the public mind. It was only natural, after the war ended, that intelligent persons should ask themselves whether it was not possible to apply a similar technique to the problems of peace.' (Cited in Delwiche 2002.)

More information about Bernays and his contemporaries can be found at www.prmuseum.com/bernays. There is an interesting account of Stuart Ewen's interview with the 90-year-old Bernays (Ewen 1996), which also has a website at www.bway.net/~drstu/chapter.

The history of UK public relations also demonstrates its origins in propaganda. Unlike the growth of the field in the USA, European public relations is rooted in public service information traditions, with the emphasis on local and central government supply of information (L'Etang 2004). This was also the source of persuasion campaigns, such as the 1924 campaign (including films and posters) to promote the British Empire to the rest of the world, led by Sir Stephen Tallents who went on to found the Institute of Public Relations (IPR) in 1948. He also wrote *The Projection of England* (1932), which was influential in 'persuading British policy makers of the benefits of a cultural propaganda policy' (L'Etang 2004). Tallents was active in producing propaganda for both world wars, as were the founders of several major public relations companies in the interwar period, many of which survive to this day. A more negative response came from George Orwell, who resigned from the BBC 'sickened by the propaganda he had had to do' (Ewen 1996) and proceeded to write *Nineteen Eighty-Four* (published in 1949) 'as a response to the experience' (L'Etang 2004).

Propaganda was not seen as a pejorative (negative or disparaging) concept until after the Second World War. When everyone saw the power of Nazi propaganda, especially their use of film, to promote anti-Semitism and the horrific consequences of that message, it is hardly surprising that communicators distanced themselves from the concept of propaganda. Nevertheless, propaganda is part of our everyday lives, not just something from history. As Pratkanis and Aronson (2001: 7) point out: 'Every day we are bombarded with one persuasive communication after another. These appeals persuade not through the give-and-take of argument and debate, but through the manipula-

tion of symbols and of our most basic human emotions. For better or worse, ours is an age of propaganda.'

Many scholars who study propaganda concentrate on its wartime application. However, there are increasing numbers of academics, journalists and campaigners who are examining the role of public relations in civil and corporate propaganda. There are websites dedicated to monitoring public relations activity, such as the US-based Center for Media and Democracy (www.prwatch.org), which contains extremely interesting and disturbing examples of unethical corporate public relations, and the UK-based www.ethicalconsumer.org/, which is particularly concerned with environmental aspects of corporate behaviour. The most interesting – and sometimes challenging – site for public relations students is probably the UK-based Spinwatch (www.spinwatch.org.uk), which describes itself as: 'An independent organisation set up to monitor the PR and lobbying industry in the UK and Europe and the spin and lobbying activities of corporations.' Some of its contributors have also written books, such as Miller and Dinan's *A Century of Spin: How public relations became the cutting edge of corporate power* (2008), which outlines the historical and contemporary involvement of public relations companies in both wartime and current corporate messages and activities, which they describe as propaganda. See Explore 11.1.

Explore 11.1

Defining different forms of practice

Look at the definitions in Table 11.1. How easy is it to put them in the right column? Try and come up with a definition for propaganda, persuasion and public relations that makes the differences clear.

Defining propaganda

Much academic attention has focused on the role of propaganda during wartime. Jowett and O'Donnell (1992), with backgrounds in communications and rhetoric, categorise propaganda as either black (use of false information and sources), white (selected to advance the communicator's interests) or grey (distorting rather than inventing situations). They use wartime examples to illustrate their points and do not discuss the role of public relations then or now, although, as Table 11.1 demonstrates, their definition encompasses a great deal of modern practice. In contrast, Taylor (2001), a historian and communications academic, suggests that propaganda is a 'practical process of persuasion', neither good nor bad, and that the issue of intent is important – not just who says what to whom, but *why*. The removal of value judgements from the communication act is useful and allows a much cooler appraisal of the place of propaganda in the post 9/11 world. This seems a useful insight to bring to the debate between those who claim PR is propagandist and those who seek to create a more ethical practice.

The political economy approach developed by Herman and Chomsky (1988) and Chomsky (2002) proposes a model in which propaganda is not neutral but designed to give the appearance of a 'free press' while actually producing messages that favour the views of government and business above other voices. The role of public relations in

shaping political, military and corporate communications, not just publicity, is seen as propagandist, an argument repeatedly made by public relations' greatest critics, Stauber and Rampton (2004) in the US and Miller and Dinan (2008) in the UK. They particularly highlight the distortions to the democratic process caused by PR firms' fake grass roots campaigns (astroturfing), or planting questions in press conferences by PR people masquerading as journalists. However, they provide little insight into what might constitute legitimate public relations, and they tend to conflate corporate business interests with communication without considering the promotional activities of voluntary, charity or trade union groups, for example.

More useful discussions of the relationship between public relations and propaganda can be found in the work of PR scholars such as Moloney (2006), Fawkes and Moloney (2008) and Weaver et al. (2006), who explore the connections between these topics in the past and present practice of the field. Most find the issue of persuasion lies at the heart of this debate.

Picture 11.1 James Montgomery Flagg's memorable recruiting poster (produced under the direction of the Division of Pictorial Publicity of the Committee on Public Information) was successful in stimulating American public opinion in favour of US involvement in the European conflict during the Second World War (*source*: LLC/Corbis)

Propaganda	Persuasion	Public relations
The deliberate and systematic attempt to shape perceptions, manipulate cognitions and direct behaviour to achieve a response that furthers the desired intent of the propagandist *Jowett and O'Donnell 1992: 4*	A successful intentional effort at influencing another's mental state through communication in a circumstance in which the persuadee has some measure of freedom *O'Keefe 2002: 5*	The planned and sustained effort to establish and maintain goodwill and understanding between an organisation and its publics *UK Institute of Public Relations (IPR) 1987; Fawkes 2006*
A propaganda model . . . traces the routes by which money and power are able to filter out the news fit to print, marginalise dissent and allow the government and dominant private interests to get their messages across to the public *Herman and Chomsky 1988: 2*	A symbolic process in which communicators try to convince other people to change their attitudes or behavior regarding an issue through the transmission of a message, in an atmosphere of free choice *Perloff 2012: 8*	The art and social science of analysing trends, predicting their consequences, counselling organisation leaders and implementing planned programmes of action which will serve both the organisation's and the public interest *Mexican statement, Wilcox et al. 2003: 6*
Public relations serves a propaganda function in the press agent/publicity model. Practitioners spread the faith of the organisation involved, often through incomplete, distorted or half-true information *Grunig and Hunt 1984: 21*	Ethos (the credibility or charisma of the speaker) + logos (the nature of the message) + pathos (the response of the audience) *Aristotle*	. . . the planned persuasion to change adverse public opinion or reinforce public opinion and the evaluation of results for future use *Peake 1980, cited in Grunig and Hunt 1984: 7*
A practical process of persuasion . . . it is an inherently neutral concept . . . We should discard any notions of propaganda being 'good' or 'bad', and use those terms merely to describe effective or ineffective propaganda *Taylor 2003: 8–11*	Because both persuader and persuadee stand to have their needs fulfilled, persuasion is regarded as more mutually satisfying than propaganda *Jowett and O'Donnell 1992: 21*	The discipline concerned with the reputation of organisations (or products, services or individuals) with the aim of earning understanding and support *CIPR 2004; Fawkes 2006*
	Situations where attempts are made to modify [attitudes and/or] behavior by symbolic transactions (messages) that are sometimes, but not always, linked with coercive force (indirectly coercive) and that appeal to the reason and emotions of the intended persuadee(s) *Miller 1989*	. . . the process of attempting to exert symbolic control over the evaluative predispositions ('attitudes', 'images' etc.) and subsequent behaviours of relevant publics or clienteles *Miller, 1989: 47*

Table 11.1 Comparison of definitions (*source*: Fawkes 2006)

Public relations and persuasion

As already stated, early public relations theorists had no problem with acknowledging the centrality of persuasion to public relations; indeed, Bernays considered public relations to be about 'engineering public consent'. However, more recent public relations theory has tended to move away from this aspect of communication and concentrate on the more acceptable images of negotiation and adaptation. Very few public relations textbooks really explore persuasion. This is largely because the Grunig and Hunt (1984) models stress the positive aspects of excellent public relations and relegate persuasion to 'second best', the two-way asymmetric model (see Chapter 7 for details of systems theory and Grunig's approach). Moloney (2006) notes that they treat persuasion as an inferior or less ethical activity than negotiation or compromise, but argues that one often involves the other.

Grunig (2001) has accepted that the two-way asymmetric model describes the majority of PR communication. He also recognises that persuasion is relevant to symmetrical public relations – as long as it includes the public persuading the organisation to change its attitudes and behaviour and not just vice versa. The emphasis in his approach is still on encouraging excellence and symmetry rather than exploring persuasion in more depth. But, as Jaksa and Pritchard (1994: 128) argue, 'it cannot be seriously maintained that all persuasion is bad or undesirable'.

Pfau and Wan (2006) suggest that public relations has problems with the concept of persuasion because it confuses means and ends: the Grunig approach mentioned earlier concentrates on means, or *processes* – whether they are symmetrical or not – and deems persuasion unethical because it is asymmetrical (a view shared by Porter 2010, see below). But, if we look at the ends or *outcomes* of communication then it is clear how prevalent persuasion is in PR activity. 'Public relations is best viewed as a form of strategic communication, in which persuasion plays an integral role . . . Many of the core functions of public relations, such as community relations, media relations, crisis communication and others, manifest an implicit if not explicit goal of cultivating or maintaining a positive organizational image' (Pfau and Wan 2006: 102). Rhetorical approaches to public relations (e.g. Toth and Heath 1992; Heath 2001; Porter 2010) address the role of persuasion in communication, drawing on the work of Aristotle and strong links to concepts of democracy. In this view, the communicator uses words and symbols to influence the perceptions of others, with varying outcomes. The roles of speaker, audience, the choice of message and the dynamics and characteristics of each provides the focus of study.

Curtin and Gaither (2005) look at persuasion as part of a 'circuit of culture', which sees communication as a dynamic process of constructing meaning in a social and cultural context:

> The dominant normative paradigm has removed propaganda and persuasion from the ranks of legitimate public relations practices, but the circuit demonstrates the need to recognize them as part of the repertoire of legitimate practices . . . (p.109)

More recently, Porter (2010) has revisited the issue of persuasion in public relations, arguing that the dominance of the Grunig models and their distaste for persuasion has 'vilified' one of the key aspects of modern PR strategy:

> . . . the ultimate outcome of public relations efforts will always remain influencing attitudes and, ultimately, behavior. Public relations professionals are paid to advocate ideas and to influence behaviour (p.132)

Pfau and Wan (2006) think one of the reasons PR texts don't engage with persuasion is because they don't have a good enough understanding of the complex and challenging theories of persuasive communication that have emerged from social psychology. So, instead of trying to convince ourselves and others that public relations doesn't get involved with the dirty business of persuasion, let's agree with those scholars who say it's central to PR and look more closely at the psychology of persuasion.

Persuasion and psychology

Promotional campaigns, including advertising and public relations, have made use of psychological insights since the 1950s' consumer boom. A recent example of a psychological theory that has influenced political and economic leaders is nudge theory, developed by Thaler in 2008; it suggests that people are more easily influenced by statements about what other people are doing than by direct messages about changing their behaviour. The most effective campaign on cutting fuel bills, for example, simply mentioned what most of the neighbours paid. Not surprisingly, this idea has been embraced first by Obama's White House, then in 2010 by the policy unit at Downing Street. Governments spend millions on persuading citizens to drive safely, eat wisely, claim benefits and so on, so a strategy for improving the effectiveness of these campaigns was bound to be welcome. Messages on issues from hygiene in urinals to pension rights have all shown to be more powerful using nudge theory (McSmith 2010).

Another example of how psychology can be used in promotion is called neuromarketing, where scientists identify which parts of the brain are stimulated by different tastes, sounds and images, and help manufacturers test the response to their products. For example, research (reported in *The Guardian* on 29 July 2004) showed that while people liked the taste of Pepsi better than Coca-Cola in blind tests, they preferred Coke when they knew which brand they were drinking. Brain scans showed that while one (rewards) section of the brain was activated by the tasting, a different (thinking) centre responded to the brand names, suggesting that we call on memories and impressions associated with a name, rather than just the direct experience.

This chapter will not be probing anyone's brains, but draws on more theoretical models of how people make decisions and what influences them.

Propaganda, persuasion and public relations all involve communication, although they have other aspects, and it is worth examining the communication process to understand what is involved. Rogers (2007: 12) offers a detailed and thorough communication model that describes the various stages of intention, selection, preparation, presentation of messages by senders and selection, comprehension and response (or not) of attitude and behaviour in receivers. This chapter will use a much simpler, but rather old-fashioned transmission model of communication, summarised by Harold Lasswell (1948) as 'Who (1) says What (2) in Which channel (3) to Whom (4), with What effect (5)'. While this view of the powerful sender and the passive receiver is rightly discredited, these elements provide useful 'hooks' for looking at the communication process – as long as it is remembered that the receiver is usually the key player in making sense of the message. The second half of this chapter analyses persuasive communication and the role of the sender (1), the message (2) and the receiver (4) in achieving (or failing to achieve) an effect (5). It does not analyse the use of different media in constructing persuasive messages, as the chapter focuses more on psychology than media relations. It draws on social psychology theories to illustrate the personality variables of sender and receiver, the effectiveness of different message strategies and, finally, how the elements all fit into a persuasive campaign.

Who says: the question of credibility

This element concerns the nature of the sender or sender variables. Aristotle said that communication consisted of: *Ethos* – the character of the speaker; *Logos* – the nature of the message; and *Pathos* – the attitude of the audience. He placed most emphasis on the speaker's (orators tended to be male, then) character: 'We believe good men more fully and more readily than others . . . his character may almost be called the most effective means of persuasion he possesses' (cited in Perloff 1993: 138).

Credibility has been an important – but hard to define – element of persuasive communication ever since. Look at today's newspapers and concerns about the credibility of politicians to see how relevant it is today. A great deal of public relations activity is designed to enhance the credibility of the organisation or individual. Many politicians and business leaders today make credibility their central platform for election or boardroom support – 'trust me' is their key message. However, surveys in recent years (Arthur W. Page Society 2007, 2009; Edelman Trust Barometer 2009) have identified the loss of public trust in institutions as a major priority. The 2012 Edelman Trust Barometer reports 'The 2012 Edelman Trust Barometer sees an unprecedented nine-point global decline in trust in government. In twelve countries, it trails business, media, and non-governmental organizations as the least trusted institution. This has pushed more countries into the distruster category' (Edelman 2012).

Many scholars in the USA in the 1950s, especially at Yale and Harvard, concentrated on attributes of speakers – how attractive are they, how expert, how similar/dissimilar to audiences – to try and measure credibility. But later scholars, such as McCroskey (1966), said that 'credibility is the attitude toward a speaker held by a listener'. In other words, it is something that is given by the audience and cannot be demanded by the speaker. Another fascinating discovery from the Yale school was the 'sleeper effect' (Hovland et al. 1953), which showed that however much effort was put into providing a credible source, when audiences were tested several weeks after exposure to the message, they remembered the message but forgot the source!

Perloff (1993) summarises the four key elements by which audiences evaluate speakers as:

1. *expertise* – how competent the speaker is on this issue

2. *trustworthiness* – this includes confidence and likeability

3. *similarity* – credible speakers should be like the receiver (**homophily**), unless the subject concerns different experiences or expertise, in which case they should be dissimilar (**heterophily**)

4. *physical attractiveness* – people tend to trust attractive speakers – which may reflect the social value attached to appearance, as in celebrity public relations, unless the speaker is so attractive that their looks distract from the message (adapted from Perloff 1993).

Other theorists (Raven 1983) added 'power' to the list, saying that the kind of authority the speaker has over the listener can influence the persuasion process. Bettinghaus and Cody (1994: 123–145) summarise Raven's types of power as:

■ *informational influence* – access to restricted information gives authority to a speaker

■ *referent influence* – membership of key social groups can confer power

> **Definition:** *'Homophily'* means similarity between speaker and audience.
>
> **Definition:** *'Heterophily'* means difference between speaker and audience.

Explore 11.2

Speaker credibility

Which speaker or presenter would you choose for the following events:

1. Launch of new bio-fuel engine to audience of motoring journalists: (a) TV motoring correspondent; (b) lead engineer from motor company; (c) learner driver?

2. Promotional posters for new phone app aimed at youth market should feature: (a) app designer; (b) presenter of popular music site; (c) CEO of phone company?

3. Short film about safe sex for showing in schools: (a) minister for education; (b) doctor working in genito-urinary health unit; (c) young person?

Feedback

These choices involve considerations about expertise and trustworthiness, and illustrate that there are times when you want a speaker who resembles the audience (homophily) and other occasions when the differences will increase credibility (heterophily).

- *expert influence* – knowledge of the field
- *legitimate influence* – authorised by law or other agreement (e.g. traffic warden, safety officer)
- *reward/coercive influence* – are there rewards for being persuaded, or punishments for resisting?

The role of power in persuasion is also important to critical approaches to public relations theory (see Chapter 7 for details). Explore 11.2 illustrates the sorts of decision public relations practitioners need to make that require knowledge or insight into credibility.

Says what: the nature of the message

This element of persuasion looks at which kinds of messages are most convincing and the ways in which messages are absorbed and used by people. Message research includes investigating whether messages using fear or humour are more persuasive and whether it's more effective to appeal to the audience's reason or emotion. At first it was thought that fear made a message more powerful, but a later theory, fear protection motivation schema (Rogers 1983), suggested that if a message is too frightening, receivers tend to block the message to protect themselves from being alarmed. This is borne out by experience of early AIDS campaigns in the 1980s, when ads showing tombstones with the message 'Don't Die of Ignorance' were subsequently seen as counterproductive (Miller et al. 1998). Scholars do not agree on this issue – what do you think?

One of the most interesting theories concerning how messages are processed is the elaboration likelihood model (Petty and Cacioppo 1986), which suggested that there are two routes to persuasion: the central and peripheral routes (see Figure 11.1). The central route involves processing (or elaborating) the arguments contained in a message, using reason and evaluation. The peripheral route involves reacting emotionally to a message that appeals to a range of responses – such as humour, or feelings towards the person giving the message (such as a celebrity) – without having to weigh up the arguments for and against the message. The central route is more likely to lead to long-lasting attitude change; the peripheral route, often used by advertisers, works for short-term messages.

Use of arguments to persuade

If the message aims to involve the receiver in internal reasoning or elaboration, then it has to ensure that there is a good range of arguments to support the message. The communicator also has to decide whether to present all the arguments in favour of their position or whether to deal with the counterarguments as well. Research suggested that more educated or hostile audiences often prefer to be given both points of view, even if the message concludes with the preferred position of the communicator. People who already support the point of view – fans of a band, members of a political party, for example – are more receptive to messages reinforcing just that one point of view. Petty and Cacioppo also suggest that some people have a 'need for cognition' – that is, a motive to find out things and a preference for making choices based on thought and reflection rather than impulse. Of course, if the messages are unclear, or irrelevant to the receiver, then they will not be motivated to elaborate further.

Toulmin (1958) suggested that effective messages use evidence (data, opinions, case studies, etc.) to make a claim (the message the communicator wants the receiver to agree with), which is then backed by a warrant (reason to agree). An example might be the anti-smoking adverts shown regularly on television. These tend to show a terminally ill person (evidence) talking about their life expectancy (claim) and close with statements about the effectiveness

Central route	Peripheral route
Simon is considering a new life insurance policy	Rowena has a plane to catch but needs to pick up travel insurance on the way
The decisions he makes will affect the financial well-being of his family after his death	The policy will only last for the duration of her holiday
He wants to take his time comparing options, and will talk to his advisors	She scans the web to compare prices
Simon chooses the policy that balances the cost of the premiums with the benefits to his loved ones	A link comes up with bright graphics and a link to holiday cover. A celebrity from a TV travel show is shown giving the thumbs up. The price is about right for one-off cover. She doesn't check the small print
He visits the insurance offices to sign the forms	She buys it online
Simon is persuaded by the quality of the policy, its costs and benefits, despite the time taken to choose	Rowena is persuaded by images and ease of purchase, regardless of the actual policy benefits

Figure 11.1 Elaboration likelihood model (*source*: adapted from Petty and Cacioppo 1986)

of support lines (warrant). There is an excellent website explaining current UK campaigns, key messages and target groups, with examples of TV, press and poster ads, at http://smokefree.nhs.uk/ (see Picture 11.2).

In the increasingly visual environment of modern communication, messages are more likely to appeal to the emotions of the receiver than their reason. There is some evidence that making people feel good is more effective than making them feel bad. Pratt (2008) analyses health communication campaigns (in the US) specifically concerning obesity and suggests six key phrases for crafting such communication: (1) Be attentive; (2) Be personal; (3) Be selective; (4) Be casual; (5) Be active; (6) Be sparing.

However, research into the use of fear in US presidential elections campaigns has revealed that suggesting to voters that they will be less safe with an opponent in charge can be very effective. (See Explore 11.3.)

Approaches to persuasion

Another angle to studying persuasive messages is the rhetorical approach, which looks in detail at the language used by communicators and the exchange of information, or discourse, between parties seeking to influence each other through the use of words and symbols. This viewpoint does not see persuasion as inherently good or bad, but as the stuff of human interaction: 'Through statement and counterstatement, people test each other's views of reality, value, and choices relevant to products, services

Picture 11.2 Giving up smoking. With many countries now banning smoking in public places, such as offices, bars and restaurants, determined smokers are forced to find some unusual places to smoke their tobacco (*source*: Getty Images)

Explore 11.3

Message appeals

Look at the messages around you – can you find examples of appeals to your feelings? What about engaging your reason? Can you see 'feel good' messages? What about fear campaigns? Do you prefer a message that makes you laugh?

Feedback

Look at the posters produced by candidates in elections – whether for local, general, EU or student elections. Are they creating positive images of themselves or negative images of their opponents? Which campaigns do you think are more effective?

Content or discourse analysis examines the words and images in messages, whether from corporations, politicians or mass media, looking below surface meanings for deeper associations. Political speeches are increasingly analysed to decode their underlying meanings. Leaders' speeches are run through computer programs to reveal how often they use the word 'freedom' or 'democracy', or notice when the Australian Prime Minister, Julia Gillard, name checks all her predecessors except the one trying to get his old job back (Coorey 2011).

These approaches offer useful insights to the public relations practitioner because they remind us that messages *received* are often very different from those *sent*. Failure to understand the different values and attitudes that people might bring to understanding a communication can destroy an organisation's reputation. Senders who use their own terms of reference or value systems will not create understanding or 'shared meaning', as rhetoric puts it. Sometimes this involves literal mistranslations, as when a leading pen manufacturer translated the line 'our pen

and public policies' (Heath 2001: 31). Public relations is seen as the search for shared meaning and emphasis is placed on the importance of relationship in achieving such understanding. (See Chapter 8 for more about **rhetoric** and public relations.)

> **Definition:** '*Rhetoric*' means the study of language and how it is used to create shared meanings.

will not leak in your pocket and embarrass you' for its Mexican launch, but used the word *embrazar* . . . meaning to make pregnant. Many websites list PR gaffes; for examples of PR blunders from the US not-for-profit sector, see Kennedy (2011).

As social media facilitate detailed analysis of user patterns and preferences, communicators have access to vast data about audiences. For example, see the composite findings of Research Matters and MastersDegreeOnline.org (prdaily/10212). But facts don't always improve understanding: the next section looks at the 'to whom' part of Lasswell's saying and, in particular, the role of the receiver's psychology in creating successful communication.

To whom: the audience perspective

Receivers can be grouped in many ways. There is a range of media theories showing how publics come together to use a particular medium to gain information or entertainment, for example. They can be categorised by age, geography, occupation, gender, marital status, etc. This is called **demographics**. Then there are the theories that look at **psychographics**, or differences in personality.

Psychologists have investigated a number of theories that might explain why some people are easier to persuade than others and the internal process by which persuasion takes place. Aspects of personality, such as self-esteem, are examined, as are the internal structures of personality, such as attitudes and behaviour. This section looks at the psychology of persuasion from the individual receiver's perspective.

Self-esteem was felt to be an important component of persuasion, and research showed that people with lower self-esteem were much easier to persuade. However, it was not entirely simple, as people with low self-esteem were more easily influenced by superficial aspects of the message, whereas people with higher self-esteem tended to engage with relevant thinking on the issue before deciding whether to agree or disagree with the message. As a result, those who were most easily persuaded by peripheral cues (colour, music, celebrity) tended not to internalise the

message and were therefore equally easily persuaded by the next message to use the same tactics. There was also evidence (Cohen 1959) that people with high self-esteem avoided or deflected unwelcome or challenging messages – a bit like smokers leaving the room when anti-smoking ads come on. This is called ego-defensive behaviour, as it allows the person to maintain self-belief by avoiding contradictory evidence. These findings suggest that different tactics are needed for different audiences – with reasons to agree provided to those who prefer to process messages, and simple, non-threatening messages to those who do not. There are echoes here of the elaboration likelihood model outlined above.

Another personality variable that affected how easily an individual could be persuaded was discovered by Snyder and DeBono (1985), who showed that some people are more likely to look outside themselves for clues about how to respond (high self-monitors), while others look inwards (low self-monitors). The former are influenced by the reactions of those around them, especially people they would like to be accepted by (sometimes called the referent group). The latter consult their own values and beliefs before responding to messages. (See Explore 11.4 and Think about 11.2.)

This theory also raises the issue of the influence of groups on the persuasiveness of the individual. There are a number of theories that look at how individuals behave in group situations, of which the most relevant here is social comparison theory (Festinger 1954). This applies when

> **Definition:** '*Demographics*' means external differences between people – e.g. race, age, gender, location, occupational status, group membership.
>
> **Definition:** '*Psychographics*' describes internal differences between personalities – e.g. anxious, approval-seeking, high self-esteem, etc.

Explore 11.4

Are you a high self-monitor?

Bettinghaus and Cody (1994: 165) provide the following statements as tests for self-monitoring:

- ■ 'I have considered being an entertainer.'
- ■ 'I'm not always the person I appear to be.'
- ■ 'I may deceive people by being friendly when I really dislike them.'
- ■ 'I guess I put on a show to impress or entertain others.'
- ■ 'I can make impromptu speeches even on topics about which I have almost no information.'

The authors suggest that people who agree with most of these statements are likely to be high self-monitors. They go on to identify key areas of difference that are important to understand if one wishes to construct relevant messages. (To work out which group you belong to, see Table 11.2.)

Table 11.2
Personality types
(*source*: based on
Bettinghaus and
Cody 1994)

High self-monitors (HSM)	Low self-monitors (LSM)
Concentrate on the actual and potential reactions of others in social situations	Refer to their core values
Adaptable and flexible, presenting aspects of themselves most suitable for each occasion	More consistent in any given situation
Actively contribute to the smooth flow of conversation and bind participants together by using 'we', 'our' words, humour and exchanging self-disclosures, as appropriate	Less able to facilitate conversation
More likely to have different friends for different activities	Are more likely to do different things with the same people
Have other HSMs as friends	Have other LSMs as friends
Males are more concerned with the physical appearance of a potential date, have more and briefer relationships	Males are more concerned with date's personality, more likely to make a commitment
More responsive to messages that emphasise image, status, public approval, glamour or sex appeal	More interested in the quality and good value of a product

Think about 11.2

Personality and public relations practitioners

It is interesting to note that the HSM attributes are quite common among public relations practitioners – are they all high self-monitors? If so, is this good because they are sensitive to people around them, or bad because they fit in with others' expectations rather than develop values of their own?

Box 11.2

Theory in practice – social comparison theory

Student X might be asked whether they think dissertations are a valuable element in a degree programme. As X has not yet done one, they have no direct experience. In these circumstances, individuals are likely to compare their responses to those around them – by waiting, perhaps, to see what others have to say first. The individual is more likely to agree with someone with whom they already have things in common than someone with very different attitudes. To continue the example, if X enjoys working hard and has friends who share this approach, they are likely to agree about the value of dissertations. X is less likely to be influenced by someone who has said they don't care what kind of a degree they get. This process explains how groups often come to hold strong common beliefs, but also how there is a pressure to conform within groups. If X was really unsure, but their friends all strongly supported dissertations, X is more likely to say nothing than risk the disapproval of the group. This theory is similar in some ways to nudge theory, mentioned at the start of this chapter.

individuals have to evaluate an opinion or ability and cannot test it directly. (See Box 11.2.)

This, and similar theories, show how important it is to understand the group dynamics when communicating important messages. Just think about how hard it is to persuade people to stop drink driving if all their friends think it is a brilliant thing to do. Messages that conflict with group beliefs, or norms, are most likely to be rejected by the group.

So, is it even possible to persuade people to stop drink driving? Why not just use legal powers and stop trying to persuade these hard-to-reach groups? But what if the message is to encourage people to take more exercise, use less energy, join this organisation, visit that country?

The law cannot help here. Threats will not work. Persuasion is the only tool. After all, it is said that the objective of most public relations campaigns is either 'to change or neutralise hostile opinion, crystallize unformed or latent opinion or conserve favourable opinions by reinforcing them' (Cutlip et al. 1985: 152). These are all acts of persuasion. The question for practitioners is – what works?

In order to understand whether or not persuasion has any effect, we need to understand what attitudes consist of, how they are acquired and then how they can be changed.

To what effect: forming and changing attitudes and beliefs

Before examining attitudes, let us look at some related aspects of thoughts and feelings that affect the way we see the world, such as beliefs and values. **Belief** is seen as a function of mind, assembling thoughts to create a system of reference for understanding.

We can all make many thousands of belief statements (sentences beginning 'I believe that . . .') (Rokeach 1960), which can be sorted into *descriptive*, *evaluative* and *prescriptive*: *descriptive* beliefs describe the world around us ('I believe the sky is blue', 'this is a good university', etc.); *evaluative* beliefs weigh up the consequences of actions

> **Definition:** *'Belief'* is 'commitment to something, involving intellectual assent' (Columbia 2003).

('I believe this course is right for me'); and *prescriptive* beliefs suggest how things ought to be ('I believe men and women should share housework').

Another approach is to divide beliefs into central and peripheral beliefs, where central beliefs are close to values and describe what we hold most important ('I believe in equality, justice', etc.). These may then underpin peripheral beliefs ('I believe in the secret ballot, jury trials', etc.). It is also possible to have peripheral-only beliefs ('I believe this shampoo will clean my hair'). Rokeach (1960) suggests there are two types of central beliefs – those that are agreed by everyone, such as 'rocks fall when dropped', and those that are personal, such as 'I believe in horoscopes'. Bettinghaus and Cody (1994) also talk about authority-derived beliefs, where we adopt ideas proposed by those in authority, although recent social developments suggest reduced trust in traditional authority figures such as politicians or even doctors.

Persuasion attempts often target peripheral beliefs because they are most easily changed ('I believe *this* shampoo is even better'), whereas authority-based beliefs, such as family values or childhood religion, change more slowly, and central beliefs hardly at all. Central beliefs are very close to values, as are prescriptive beliefs. Values are the core ideals that we use as guides and that express ourselves – they concern issues such as justice or the environment or freedom. How we treat each other reflects our central values – whether 'you've got to look out for yourself first' or 'we have to sink or swim together'. (See Figure 11.2 for examples of how values affect beliefs, attitudes and opinions.)

Dave

Sarah

	Dave	Sarah
Opinion, peripheral beliefs	This is expensive so it must be better quality	I like own-brand products – they're just as good
Attitudes	Poor people are losers. They're all scroungers. My worth is my bank balance	It could be me in trouble. I like to help. Money isn't everything
Central beliefs	Competition is good – as long as I win. You make your own luck	If we work together we can improve life for everyone
Values	Fair reward for fair effort. Self-reliance	Equality for all. Cooperation

Figure 11.2 Opinions, attitudes and values

This is a blurred area: many of the definitions for beliefs overlap with opinions and values. The simplest way to note the difference is that beliefs and opinions usually involve thoughts, values and attitudes also involve feelings. It is also worth remembering that, while psychology scholars need to divide us into smaller and smaller boxes to examine the contents, we actually use all of these aspects in combination to negotiate our way through the world.

Now, let's turn to attitudes, where our beliefs about what is right and wrong meet our feelings about right and wrong.

Attitudes

Allport (1935), an early researcher in this field, said that *attitudes* underpin our reactions to people and events, creating a filter or system against which we measure our responses to messages and events. We said, above, that values affect our attitudes. These attitudes may, in turn, affect our behaviour by causing the GM protester to buy organic goods, for example (although, being human, they may drive to the health food shop). Attitudes do not predict behaviour but they do provide a reasonable guide and so are well worth further investigation by communicators wishing to understand their audiences. (See Explore 11.5 and Think about 11.3.)

> When we talk about attitudes, we are talking about what a person has learned in the process of becoming a member of a family, a member of a group, and of society that makes him react to his social world in a consistent and characteristic way, instead of a transitory and haphazard

---

Explore 11.5

Attitudes towards television

1. 'Reality TV (where "ordinary" people are followed by camera crews) is a fascinating experiment.'
2. 'Reality TV is cheap entertainment at others' expense.'
3. 'TV is dumbing down.'
4. 'TV has always been a mix of good and bad.'
5. 'Programme makers only produce what audiences want to watch.'
6. 'I don't care about TV.'

Which of these statements reflects your own views? How far does the selected statement connect with other attitudes – to television, to entertainment, to society at large?

Think about 11.3

Your attitudes

Have you ever boycotted a product or service, signed a petition, voted for or against something or someone or got into an argument with friends or family? Do you have strong attitudes on a range of subjects? If so, can you identify the core values that underpin them? Or do you feel fairly neutral about most things and avoid disagreement on such subjects?

---

way. We are talking about the fact that he is no longer neutral in sizing up the world around him: he is attracted or repelled, for or against, favourable or unfavourable. (Sherif 1967: 2)

Attitudes are also more likely to affect behaviour if you are in a position to act on them (*individuated*). You are less likely to act out your attitudes if you are in a group (*de-individuated*) whose members hold different views, or if you are in a formal situation such as a lecture theatre where the range of available behaviours is restricted (*scripted*). These are called situational factors.

So where do attitudes come from? How are they acquired? Social psychology suggests a number of paths to explain how we learn attitudes.

1. Classic conditioning, which was made famous by Pavlov (1849–1936), who showed the difference between unconditioned and conditioned responses. The former refers to physiological reactions to certain stimuli – to blink at bright lights, flinch from pain, or in the case of Pavlov's dogs (and humans) salivate at the smell and sight of food.

2. Instrumental or operant conditioning, which means using rewards and/or punishment to encourage/discourage behaviours and attitudes. Most parents will use these techniques to instil attitudes towards road safety, table manners, etc.

3. Social learning theory, which says that we acquire our attitudes either by direct experience, by playing out roles that mimic experience and/or by modelling, that is watching how others behave in a range of situations. For example, we might learn how to react by watching characters in soap operas deal with betrayal, disappointment, bereavement or crisis.

4. Genetic determinism disputes all these explanations and looks for the roots of our motives in our genes. There has always been a conflict between scientists who believe human psychology is determined by biology

Think about 11.4

Changing attitudes

Geneticists suggest much of our behaviour is hard wired in our bodies, so it should be impossible to change someone's attitude. And yet, they can be changed – think of changing social attitudes to drink driving over the past 20 years, for example.

Have you ever changed an attitude – to education, religion or even career choices? What made you change your mind? Was it a long, slow process or a sudden flash?

and social psychologists who believe how we are raised and life experiences contribute more to our personality. The new discoveries in gene science have given strength to the former group, but the dispute is certainly not over. (See Think about 11.4.)

Social psychologists have a number of theories about how to change attitudes, and these are all interesting and relevant to the public relations practitioner. Two particularly interesting theories are the theory of reasoned action and the theory of cognitive dissonance.

The theory of reasoned action (Fishbein and Azjen 1980) looks at the links between attitude and behaviour and the points where change might be possible. It draws on expectancy value theory (Fishbein and Azjen 1975), which describes how attitudes are the results of having expectations met or disappointed. The theory of reasoned action suggests that individuals conduct complicated evaluations of different influences, such as the opinions of family, friends or teachers, giving them different weightings depending on how important their views are to the individual, who then compares these opinions to their own views and forms attitudes based on the results. It also suggests attitudes can be changed by altering one of the key components in the equation.

Understanding this process can be helpful if you are a communicator seeking to influence behaviour. It suggests that you can address the attitude towards the behaviour, for example by introducing new *beliefs* about the risks of smoking or by persuading audiences to *re-evaluate* the outcome of smoking by convincing them that their own health is in danger. Alternatively, a campaign might seek to change the *subjective norm* by suggesting that key groups of people think that smoking is uncool, anti-social, etc. It is also relevant for any persuasion campaign where the subjective norm plays a part in the behaviour, such as football hooligans where violence is approved by the group's leaders.

However, this theory is somewhat mechanistic and suggests a rather linear approach to persuasion and attitude change. An alternative, more intuitive approach was developed by Leon Festinger in 1957 – the theory of cognitive dissonance. This proposes that thoughts generate emotional responses and that people prefer to have harmony (*consonance*) between their thoughts and feelings, rather than disharmony (*dissonance*): 'The existence of dissonance, being psychologically uncomfortable, will motivate the person to try to reduce the dissonance and achieve consonance' (Festinger 1957). Aronson (1968) later stressed that the dissonance needed to be psychological, not merely logically inconsistent. (See Box 11.3.)

Cognitive dissonance describes how we rationalise internal conflicts to ourselves. We are usually most reluctant to change our behaviour, and prefer to alter our thinking to make our behaviour fit our ideas rather than vice versa. Sound familiar?

So how does this relate to persuasion? Because the theory not only describes how we avoid changing our behaviour but also suggests pressure points for undermining our rationalisations. Creating cognitive dissonance in an audience can be a powerful tool for disrupting habits of thought and consequently increasing the chances of altering their behaviour. Campaigns that use shock tactics, such as the anti-fur ads, can jolt an audience out of a complacent attitude.

Another essential element of a persuasion campaign is that people must believe that they are capable of making the change required by the campaign, such as giving up smoking, exercising more or whatever the objective is. This is called *self-efficacy*. Campaigns that expect more of the audience than people are able to achieve will fail. For example, many people who have positive attitudes towards recycling are not sure how to divide their materials or what to do with them – and may be overwhelmed by the sense that saving the planet is down to them. So they give up and do nothing. Recent campaigns concentrate on encouraging people to do small, achievable acts of recycling. This is more likely to be successful. (See Think about 11.5.)

Whatever tactics a campaign uses, there are a number of barriers it has to overcome in order for persuasion to occur. Research is continually undertaken to measure the effectiveness of persuasion campaigns, and while commercial campaigns tend to keep their research findings to themselves, public health campaigns are often analysed and the findings published widely. For example, Schiavo (2007) combines several marketing and communication models to produce an analytical tool (similar to a PEST analysis) for health communication, with four interlocking variables: Audience (beliefs, attitudes, cultural factors, literacy, risk, socioeconomic factors, etc); Political environment

Box 11.3

Cognitive dissonance in action – making choices when what you think and what you do clash

We suggested earlier that someone who values the environment is more likely to have negative attitudes towards genetically modified (GM) foods and positive attitudes towards organic produce. If these attitudes are weakly held, the person may not find any problems with driving to the health food store for their goods. If they are held strongly, the person may feel some distress that they are burning fossil fuel and contributing to global warming. How can cognitive dissonance predict their responses? The theory suggests that if they do hold the views strongly and experience dissonance they will have three choices:

1. They can change their behaviour – for example, cycle to the shop or give up buying organic foods.

2. They can alter their cognitions (thoughts) – perhaps tell themselves that there is no point worrying about one car journey when so much damage is being done by others.

3. They can alter the importance of their cognitions – that is, downgrade the importance they place on the whole set of ideas and convince themselves that they had been taking it all too seriously.

(legal, political support and priority); Social environment (stakeholder beliefs, social norms, structures and existing programmes); and Recommended health behaviour, service or product (e.g. benefits, risks, costs and access).

Whatever the desired effects, the key audience must actually see or hear the message, or the effort is obviously wasted. They must also understand it, and remember it and undertake more actions before their behaviour is likely to be altered. McGuire (1989) created a matrix to illustrate the barriers that a message must overcome to persuade any individual (see Box 11.4). The input section describes all the communications decisions the persuader must take; the output section describes the processes involved in having an effect on any individual, and the stages in the persuasion process where messages may need to be reinforced or repeated. (See Explore 11.6.)

Think about 11.5

Health campaigns

Take a look at current health campaigns, such as an anti-obesity drive in your area/country. They usually try and persuade people to change their behaviour – eat less, do more. What else are they saying? Do they target the guilt of parents, for example, or stress the health dangers? Are they trying to shock? Do they suggest that people have the skills and ability required to diet? Do you think the campaigns succeed?

Picture 11.3 This poster – featuring singer Sophie Ellis-Bextor and with the slogan 'Here's the rest of your fur coat' – aimed to shock viewers into changing attitudes to wearing fur. (*source*: Mary McCartney/PETA)

Box 11.4

McGuire's input/output matrix

Input variables

These are the choices the communicator makes when designing a persuasion campaign:

- *Sources:* who is the speaker; how credible/expert/ attractive are they?

- *Messages:* what kind of appeal is made; how is infor- mation presented?

- *Channels:* mass media or mail shots; TV ads or text messages; context in which channel is consumed?

- *Receivers:* who is the message aimed at; what is the age group/education level/personality structure?

- *Intent:* what is the desired aim; does it require a behaviour or attitude change?

Output variables

These describe the stages through which a message must pass to achieve a persuasive outcome:

- *Exposure:* did the intended receiver even get the message; do they watch or read the chosen channels?

- *Attention:* if they *were* exposed, were they paying attention or were they doing something else as well?

- *Liking:* did they like the message – not in the sense of finding it 'nice' but in appreciating the design, appearance, music, etc?

- *Comprehension:* did they understand the message – or was the stuff about polyunsaturated fats, for example, too confusing?

- *Acquiring skills:* do they need to change a behaviour/ learn how to cook/put on a seatbelt – and do any of these changes require new skills?

- *Changing attitudes:* did they like the campaign but vote for the other party; have they decided that they do want to change their approach to a topic or product?

- *Remembering:* did they remember the key message at the point where it was most likely to influence their response, such as the supermarket or voting booth?

- *Deciding to act:* having seen, liked, understood and remembered the messages, having changed atti- tudes towards the intent of the campaign, did the audience make the next step and actually decide to do something about it – whether that's stopping smoking, eating more fruit or going to Thailand?

- *Behaviour change:* having decided to act, did they actually make the effort and alter their behaviour in line with the desired intent, or, perhaps, in a different way?

- *Reinforcing the decision:* having behaved as sug- gested once, will they repeat the action or forget the message?

- *Consolidating the results:* does the campaign make the most of its own successes by telling the audience how they'd responded, perhaps through individual case studies or release of relevant statistics?

Source: based on McGuire 1989

Explore 11.6

Case study

Apply the McGuire input/output matrix to one of the campaigns you can find at the following websites:

http://smokefree.nhs.uk/ways-to-quit/motivational- messages-at-home/ www.farenet.org http://www. influenceatwork.com/

http://www.more-life.co.uk/

Think about 11.6

Dissertation/research ideas

1. Compare the views of Bernays to those of current public relations practitioners.

2. Contrast the Hovland and McCroskey appro- aches to credibility, using current public relations campaigns.

3. Apply the theory of reasoned action to a public health campaign.

Think about 11.7   Resisting persuasion

This chapter has looked at how communicators can more effectively persuade others regarding the merits of a particular point of view or action. This knowledge can also be used to improve one's own defences against being persuaded. The following suggests how you could use the theories outlined in this chapter to increase your awareness when others are trying to persuade you:

■ Know yourself – are you a high or low self-monitor? Are you strongly influenced by the views of those around you? Do you fit in or stand out?

■ Know your own ethics – what are your core values, your moral boundaries?

■ Know the source – who are they? What are their interests? Is the Sugar Information Bureau actually the sugar industry in a white coat? Does the celebrity really use/wear/believe it?

■ Know the intentions of the message – what do they want you to do? Is this what you want? Is it consistent with your core values?

■ Know the methods of the message – are they appealing to your reason or emotion? Are they trying to catch you in a hurry? Are they suggesting if you don't do it right now, the chance is gone?

■ Take your time, check the facts, make up your own mind.

Summary

This chapter has shown that propaganda is not always easy to distinguish from persuasion or public relations, possibly due to the fact that public relations has its origins in propaganda, with many pioneers of public relations learning the craft in wartime. However, it concluded that this should not condemn all persuasive communication and that persuasion deserves further study as an aspect of public relations.

Clearly, communicators can learn from a range of social psychology theories about the means by which people process messages and the different emphasis they place on the source of the message and its content, depending on their personality types. The section also described the links between attitudes and behaviour and the theories that suggest ways of influencing attitudes and, possibly, behaviour in public relations and communication campaigns.

It has also talked about the personality of the communicator and the importance of reaching beyond one's own assumptions and experience to create an effective communication between sender and receiver. Having demonstrated how persuasion can work, it emphasised the importance of applying the highest ethical standards to such work.

It can be concluded that persuasion is, actually, a difficult thing to achieve – there are so many different personality types and so many barriers to messages actually reaching the desired audience at the correct level, let alone the difficulties of translating altered attitudes into altered behaviour. And yet, public relations and advertising and, increasingly, political and commercial life are all dedicated to making us rethink prior assumptions, to change our minds about butter, or political parties, or recycling. Wernick (1991) called this a 'promotional culture', and evidence since then confirms his description. We are bombarded with persuasive messages every day as consumers, and public relations campaigns are part of that assault. PR practitioners play a key role in shaping the persuasive messages that pervade society; whether that is always an ethical role is explored in the next section.

Bibliography

Allport, G.W. (1935). 'Attitudes' in *A Handbook of Social Psychology Vol. 2*. C. Murchison (ed.). Worcester, MA: Clark University Press.

Aronson, E. (1968). 'Dissonance theory: progress and problems' in *Theories of Cognitive Consistency: A sourcebook*. R.P. Abelson, E. Aronson, W.J. McGuire, T.M. Newcomb, M.J. Rosenberg and P.H. Tannenbaum (eds). Chicago, IL: Rand McNally.

Arthur W. Page Society (2007). 'The authentic enterprise: relationships, values and corporate communications'. Arthur W. Page Society.

Arthur W. Page Society (2009). 'The dynamics of public trust in business – emerging opportunities for leaders'. Arthur W. Page Society.

Bernays, E. (1923). *Crystallizing Public Opinion*, New York, NY: Boni and Liveright.

Bernays, E. (1928). *Propaganda*. New York, NY: Liveright (2005 edition New York, NY: Ig Publishing).

Bernays, E. (1955). *The Engineering of Consent*. Norman, OK: University of Oklahoma Press.

Bettinghaus, E.P. and M.J. Cody (1994). *Persuasive Communication*, 5th edition. Orando, FL: Harcourt Brace.

Boone, J. (2011). 'Taliban join the Twitter revolution'. *The Guardian*, 12 May.

Campbell, D. (2009). 'Trust in politicians hits an all-time low'. *The Observer*, 27 September.

Chomsky, N. (2002). *Media Control*. New York, NY: Seven Stories Press.

Cohen, A.R. (1959). 'Some implications of self-esteem for social influence' in *Personality and Persuasability*. C.I. Hovland and I.L. Janis (eds). Yale: Yale University Press.

Columbia (2003). *The Columbia Electronic Encyclopedia*, 6th Edition. New York, NY: Columbia University Press.

Cookson, R. (2011). 'Media smart.' *British Medical Journal*, www.bmj.com/content/343/bmj.d5415 accessed 13 December 2011.

Coorey, P. (2011). http://www.smh.com.au/national/titfortat-draws-plea-for-rudd-and-gillard-to-cool-it-20111205-1ofjy.html accessed 13 December 2011.

Curtin, P.A. and T.K. Gaither (2005). 'Privileging identity, difference and power: the circuit of culture as a basis for public relations theory'. *Journal of Public Relations Research* 17: 91–115.

Curtis, A. (2002). *The Century of the Self*. BBC, clips available on YouTube.

Cutlip, S.M. (1994). *The Unseen Power: Public relations, a history*. Hillsdale, NJ: Lawrence Erlbaum Associates.

Cutlip, S.M., A.H. Center and G.M. Broom (1985). *Effective Public Relations*, 6th edition. Upper Saddle River, NJ: Prentice Hall.

Delwiche, A. (2002). 'Post-war propaganda.' www.propagandacritic.com/articles/ww1.postwar.html

Edelman Trust Barometer (2009). *The Global State of Trust*. New York: Edelman.

Edelman, R. (2012). 'Edelman Trust Barometer, Executive Summary'. www.scribd.com/doc/79026497/2012-Edelman-Trust-Barometer-Executive-Summary 3 July 2012.

Ewen, S. (1996). *PR! A Social History of Spin*. New York, NY: Basic Books.

Fawkes, J. (2006). 'Can ethics save public relations from the charge of propaganda'. *Ethical Space. Journal of the Institute of Communication Ethics* 3(1): 32–42.

Fawkes, J. and K. Moloney (2008). 'Does the European Union (EU) need a propaganda watchdog like the US Institute of Propaganda Analysis to strengthen its democratic civil society and free markets?' *Public Relations Review* 34: 207–214.

Festinger, L. (1954). 'A theory of social comparison processes'. *Human Relations* 7.

Festinger, L. (1957). *The Theory of Cognitive Dissonance*. New York, NY: Harper & Row.

Fishbein, M. and I. Azjen (1975). *Belief, Attitude, Intention, and Behavior: An introduction to theory and research*. Reading, MA: Addison-Wesley.

Fishbein, M. and I. Azjen (1980). 'Predicting and understanding consumer behavior: attitude-behavior correspondence' in *Understanding Attitudes and Predicting Social Behavior*. I. Azjen and M. Fishbein (eds). Upper Saddle River, NJ: Prentice-Hall.

Grunig, J. (2001). 'Two-way symmetrical public relations: past, present and future' in *Handbook of Public Relations*. R.L. Heath (ed.). Thousand Oaks, CA: Sage.

Grunig, J. and T. Hunt (1984). *Managing Public Relations*. New York, NY: Holt, Rinehart & Winston.

Heath, R.L. (2001). 'A rhetorical enactment rationale for public relations: the good organisation communicating well' in *Handbook of Public Relations*. R.L. Heath (ed.). Thousand Oaks, CA: Sage.

Herman, E.S. and N. Chomsky (1988). *Manufacturing Consent: The political economy of the mass media*. New York, NY: Pantheon Books.

Hovland, C.I., I.L. Janis and H. Kelley (1953). *Communication and Persuasion*. Yale: Yale University Press.

Jaksa, J.A. and M.S. Pritchard (1994). *Communicator Ethics: Methods of analysis*, 2nd edition. Belmont, CA: Wadsworth.

Jowett, G.S. and V. O'Donnell (1992). *Propaganda and Persuasion*, 2nd edition. Thousand Oaks, CA: Sage.

Kennedy, M. (2011). www.ereleases.com/prfuel/top-5-non-profit-pr-blunders/

Landman, A. (2008). 'Pinkwashing: can shopping cure breast cancer?' www.prwatch.org/node/7436 accessed 22 September 2008.

Lasswell, H.D. (1934). 'Propaganda' in *Propaganda*. R.A. Jackall (ed.). New York, NY: New York University Press.

Lasswell, H.D. (1948). 'The structure and function of communication in society' in *The Communication of Ideas*. L. Bryson (ed.). New York, NY: Harper.

L'Etang, J. (2004). *Public Relations in Britain: A history of professional practice in the twentieth century*. Mahwah, NJ: Lawrence Erlbaum.

L'Etang, J. and M. Pieczka (eds) (2006). *Public Relations, Critical Debates and Contemporary Practice*. Mahwah, NJ: Lawrence Erlbaum Associates.

Lippman, W. (1925). 'The phantom public' in *Propaganda*. R.A. Jackall (ed.). New York, NY: New York University Press.

McCroskey, J.C. (1966). 'Scales for the measurement of ethos' *Speech Monographs* 33: 65–72.

McGuire, W.J. (1989). 'Theoretical foundations of campaigns' in *Public Communication Campaigns*, 2nd edition. R.E. Rice and C.E. Atkin (eds). Thousand Oaks, CA: Sage.

McSmith, A. (2010). www.independent.co.uk/news/uk/politics/first-obama-now-cameron-embraces-nudge-theory-2050127.html accessed 28 November 2011.

Miller, D. (2004). 'The propaganda machine' in *Tell Me No Lies*. London: Pluto Press.

Miller D. and W. Dinan (2008). *A Century of Spin: How public relations became the cutting edge of corporate power*. London: Pluto Press.

Miller, D., J. Kitzinger, K. Williams and P. Beharrell (1998). *The Circuit of Mass Communication*. London: Sage.

Miller, G. (1989). 'Persuasion and public relations: 2 Ps in a pod?' in *Public Relations Theory*. C.H. Botan and V. Hazleton (2006). *Public Relations Theory II*. Mahwah, NJ: Lawrence Erlbaum.

Moloney, K. (2006). *Rethinking Public Relations: PR, propaganda and democracy*, 2nd edition. London: Routledge.

O'Keefe, D.J. (2002). *Persuasion: Theory and research*, 2nd edition. Newbury Park, CA: Sage.

Peake, J. (1980). *Public Relations in Business*. New York, NY: Harper & Row.

Perloff, R.M. (1993). *The Dynamics of Persuasion*. Hillsdale, NJ: Lawrence Erlbaum Associates.

Perloff, R.M. (2012). *The Dynamics of Persuasion: Communication and attitudes in the twenty-first century*. Abingdon: Routledge.

Petty, R.E. and J.T. Cacioppo (1986). *Communication and Persuasion: Control and peripheral routes to attitude change*. New York, NY: Springer-Verlag.

Pfau, M. & H. Wan (2006). 'Persuasion: an intrinsic function of public relations' in *Public Relations Theory II*. C.H. Botan and V. Hazleton (eds). Mahwah, NJ: Lawrence Erlbaum Associates.

Porter, L. (2010). 'Communicating for the good of the state: a post-symmetrical polemic on persuasion in ethical public relations.' *Public Relations Review* 36: 127–133.

Pratkanis, A. and E. Aronson (2001). *Age of Propaganda*. New York, NY: Freeman/Owl Books.

Pratt, C.B. (2008). 'Crafting campaign themes (and slogans) for preventing overweight and obesity'. *Public Relations Quarterly* 52(2): 2.

Prdaily/10021. www.prdaily.com/Main/articles/10021.aspx accessed 28 November 2011.

Prdaily/100212. www.prdaily.com/Main/Articles/10212.aspx accessed 13 December 2011.

Prmoment. www.prmoment.com/809/over-60-per-cent-of-journalists-think-pragencies-cannot-be-trusted.aspx accessed 28 November 2011.

Rampton, S. and J. Stauber (2002). *Trust Us, We're Experts: How industry manipulates science and gambles with your future*. Tarcher: Penguin.

Raven, B.H. (1983). 'Interpersonal influence and social power' in *Social Psychology*. B.H. Raven and J.Z. Rubin (eds). New York, NY: John Wiley & Sons.

Rogers, R. (1983). 'Cognitive and physiological processes in fear appeals and attitude change: a revised theory of protection motivation' in *Social Psychophysiology*. J.T. Cacioppo and R.E. Petty (eds). New York, NY: Guilford Press.

Rogers, W. (2007). *Persuasion – Messages, receivers and contexts*. Lanham, ML: Rowman and Littlefield Publishers Inc.

Rokeach, M. (1960). *The Open and Closed Mind*. New York, NY: Basic Books.

Schiavo, R. (2007). *Health Communication: From theory to practice*. San Francisco, CA: Jossey-Bass.

Sherif, M. (1967). 'Introduction' in *Attitude, Ego-involvement, and Change*. C.W. Sherif and M. Sherif (eds). New York, NY: John Wiley & Sons.

Snyder, M. and K.G. DeBono (1985). 'Appeals to image and claims about quality: understanding the psychology of advertising.' *Journal of Personality and Social Psychology* **49**.

Stauber, J.C. and S. Rampton (2004). *Toxic Sludge is Good for You: Lies, damn lies and the public relations industry*. London, Robinson.

Tallents, S. (1932). *The Projection of England*. London: Olen Press.

Taylor, P. (2001). 'What is propaganda?' www.ics.leeds.ac.uk/pmt-terrorism/what-propaganda.pdf

Taylor, P.M. (2003). *Munitions of the Mind: A history of propaganda from the ancient world to the present day*. Manchester: Manchester University Press.

Toth, E.L. and R.L. Heath (1992). *Rhetorical and Critical Approaches to Public Relations*. Hillsdale, NJ: Lawrence Erlbaum Associates.

Toulmin, S. (1958). *The Uses of Argument*. Cambridge: Cambridge University Press.

Weaver, C.K., J. Motion and J. Reaper (2006). 'From propaganda to discourse (and back again): truth, power, the public interest and public relations' in *Public Relations, Critical Debates and Contemporary Practice*. J. L'Etang and M. Pieczka (eds). Mahwah, NJ: Lawrence Erlbaum Associates.

Wernick, A. (1991). *Promotional Culture*. London: Sage.

Wilcox, D.L., G.T. Cameron, P.H. Ault and W.K. Agee (2003). *Public Relations, Strategies and Tactics*, 7th edition. London: Allyn & Bacon.

Websites

Centre for Media Democracy: www.prwatch.org/spin
Influence at Work: www.influenceatwork.com
Institute of Communications Studies, University of Leeds: http://ics.leeds.ac.uk/
NHS – Giving up Smoking: http://smokefree.nhs.uk/
Propaganda: www.propagandacritic.com
Spin Watch: www.spinwatch.org.uk

CHAPTER 12

Johanna Fawkes

Public relations' professionalism and ethics

Learning outcomes

By the end of this chapter you should be able to:

- discuss whether or not public relations is a profession
- describe a variety of approaches to professional ethics
- compare and critique views of public relations ethics
- identify different ways of imagining public relations
- evaluate the effect of PR images on PR ethics
- reflect on the way you make ethical decisions.

Structure

- Defining professions
- Is PR a profession?
- Professional ethics: an overview
- The ethics of codes
- Approaches to public relations ethics
- The practitioner perspective

Introduction

This chapter deals with two key concepts in public relations – professionalism and ethics. The first idea is usually taken for granted, as everyone assumes PR is a profession, but the second is often avoided because it leads to serious confusion and discomfort. Most writers will try and solve this unease by giving you a box for decision making or a list of 'Dos and Don'ts'. This text takes a different approach and encourages the reader to understand – not avoid – their own confusion on ethical issues.

But first, it explores ideas about professions and professionalism, and whether or not they contribute to society. Most professions base their claims for making such a contribution at least partially on their ethical stance, so this is a crucial aspect of being professional. The text looks at different kinds of professional ethics, and discusses some of the philosophical issues behind codes and ethical policies. It also asks whether ethical claims are truer in theory than in practice.

Having looked at various ethical approaches, the chapter then considers which of these are found in discussions of public relations ethics. It suggests that each view of PR has its own 'take' on PR ethics, and the strengths and weakness of these approaches are assessed. Finally, there is a discussion about the gap between the ethical ideals of academics and untrained views of practitioners, and suggestions for PR practitioners to reflect inwardly for guidance.

Let's start with some examples of the kind of ethical conflict that can confront PR practitioners and students (see Think about 12.1).

Think about 12.1   Ethical communication dilemmas

- There are problems with a new detergent you're launching next week – with nationwide TV ads – nothing dangerous, but it might be less effective than tests first showed. Do you pull the ads and delay the launch?

- Membership of the sports club you represent has fallen drastically in the past year. The client asks you to come up with a press release that minimises the impact and blames a new computer system.

- You're on work placement and the public relations agency asks you to say you're doing student research for the university/college rather than for the agency.

- You're pitching for a new account that will save the agency. You see that the previous team left their pitch details in the waiting room. Do you use this information?

- A tobacco company asks you to launch a fitness campaign for schools with free footballs – covered in its logo.

- A major US coffee chain that's been getting protests over its treatment of staff and suppliers asks you to do an ethical makeover – in its image, not its employment or trade activities.

- You organise meetings between the local authority and community groups to explain new council policies. Do you make it clear that the authority is interested in their views but unlikely to make major changes?

Feedback

We'll come back to these examples at the end of the chapter, so you can compare how you think about them now and later.

Mini case study 12.1

'Whispergate': PR in Facebook vs Google ethics crisis

In May 2011 it was revealed that Facebook had hired leading public relations consultancy Burson-Marsteller (B-M) to spread rumours about an aspect of Google's Gmail (called Social Circle), alleging it represents a serious invasion of privacy. Two high-profile B-M executives (both recently employed from the media, interestingly) encouraged journalists to write negative copy, without revealing their client, until some of the targeted journalists made the pressure (and the emails offering to place the stories in high-profile media outlets) public, leading to outcry. B-M made the situation worse by deleting hostile comments from its own Facebook page. (The full gory details can be found at http://www.usatoday.com/money/media/2011-05-06-google_n.htm?loc=interstitialskip.)

mini case study 12.1 (continued)

Two contrasting responses come from Steve Earl, of UK agency Speed Communications, who said 'What PRs need to admit, rather than getting all high and mighty about the Burston-Marsteller incident, is that smearing is an integral part of PR' (Earl 2011) and, more thoughtfully, from Keith Trivitt, a senior member of the Public Relations Society of America (PRSA):

> Will our profession use this as a teachable moment – an opportunity to reassess our commitment to serving the public interest and being ethical counselors to our clients? Or will we just brush it aside as yet another instance of an ethical lapse taking center stage for a couple of news cycles? (Trivitt 2011).

Both blogs, and the heated comments that follow them, are well worth reading as background to the issues raised in this chapter. As one outcome of the huge online discussion of this fiasco, B-M has offered to 're-train' the employees who led the campaign and redistributed its ethics codes to all. Do you think that will be enough to make a difference? Is this a story about 'bad apples' or what Zimbardo (2007) calls 'bad barrels'? What do you think the professional body (PRSA) will do?

Professions and a crisis of trust

The story described in this Mini case study made mainstream coverage. But every day, websites such as spinwatch.com and corporatewatch.com provide examples of PR ethical lapses, from creating false front organisations to PR people masquerading as journalists, which fail to attract such attention, either inside or outside public relations circles. Of course, public relations is not alone in its scandals: professions that have been exposed in recent years as falling below their own self-proclaimed standards include banking, accounting, the clergy, the medical and caring professions, athletes, sports institutions (look at the mess at FIFA) . . . the list goes on. During 2011–12, the UK Leveson Inquiry received detailed testimonials from those who have been abused by the unethical behaviour of journalists (with similar accusations and responsibility targeted towards their employers, such as Rupert Murdoch's News International). The '12th Edelman Trust Barometer' (an annual international survey of trust and credibility based on a sample of 25,000 'informed' people across 25 countries) found a massive drop in trust in governments, together with a desire from nearly half the respondents for greater government regulation of business which also experienced a drop in trust levels, compared to non-government organisations and, interestingly, media (Edelman 2012).

It is not surprising, then, that many groups are having to think again about what makes them professional and how to regain lost trust. So, what *is* a profession?

Defining professions

The history of professions in the UK is usefully summarised as:

- pre-industrial (1500): divinity, medicine, law;
- industrial (1800) (agricultural to industrial revolutions): engineers, chemists, accountants;
- welfare state (1900–1948): teachers, social workers;
- enterprise (1980s): business and management specialists;
- knowledge workers (1990s): information, communications and media specialists.

(Watkins et al. 1992, cited by
Broadbent et al. 1997: 51).

Similar developments can be found in European countries, with differences beyond the region. It is interesting to note that the older professions, particularly medicine and law, continue to earn respect and have not lost professional status, despite being joined by so many new occupations. Freidson (1994) distinguishes between the older professions that have legally protected licences to practice and those less prestigious occupations that are protected by professional bodies. Some of the issues of professionalism and professional ethics are particularly relevant to the newer disciplines, which of course includes public relations.

Whatever their origins, most professions possess the following qualities:

- esoteric knowledge – theoretical or technical – not available to the general population;
- commitment to social values, such as health or justice;
- national organisation to set standards, control membership, liaise with wider society;
- extra-strong moral commitment to support professional values (Cooper 2004: 61–63).

Dent and Whitehead (2002) also stress the importance of ethics, suggesting professions must have (among other attributes), 'independence and discretion within the working context showing allegiance to an ethical framework and often to specific codes of practice which govern relationships between the profession, the professional, his/her clients and the wider society' (2002: 51). So, a profession's role in society is expressed in its codes of practice.

The role of professions in society is an area of sharp disagreement between scholars – a dispute that has repercussions for professional ethics. Some scholars (such as Durkheim 1933 and Parsons 1951) argue that professions play a supportive role in maintaining social order; others (such as Weber et al. 1964 and Larson 1977) see the label as an empty claim to social standing, won as the result of conflicts with competing occupations. Sciulli (2005) terms these groups functionalists and revisionists in his overview of professionalism studies. Most professional associations and groups who write and observe codes belong to the first group; most critics of professions and their ethics belong in the second camp. We'll come back to ethics – the next question is: does public relations count as a profession?

Is PR a profession?

Public relations meets some but not all of the criteria of a profession outlined earlier: some scholars (Bivins 1992; Pieczka and L'Etang 2001) have questioned whether public relations can be considered a profession, given the open entry to this work and the difficulty of imposing ethical and other standards on the membership. Unlike medicine or law, anyone can practise PR and it is impossible to guess what percentage of PR practitioners belongs to professional bodies. But, as Sriramesh and Hornaman (2006: 156) point out:

> *all agree that it is important for public relations to gain professional status because that would give credibility and reputation to the industry, increase the accountability and credibility of practitioners, enhance the quality of work produced by practitioners, and give practitioners greater opportunities to contribute organizational decision making.*

They summarise the literature as indicating that for public relations to be accepted as a profession (which the majority of their sources say has not yet happened) it must satisfy the following criteria:

1. Maintaining a code of ethics and professional values and norms.

2. Commitment to serve in the public interest and be socially responsible.

3. Having a body of esoteric, scholarly knowledge.

4. Having specialised and standardised education, including graduate study.

5. Having technical and research skills.

6. Providing a unique service to an organisation and the community.

7. Membership in professional organisations.

8. Having autonomy in organisations to make communication-related decisions (Sriramesh and Hornaman 2006: 157).

It's not clear which of these hurdles PR fails to leap, though Pieczka and L'Etang (2001) believe open access to practice and unenforceable ethics provide obstacles to professional status. They think most approaches to professionalism in public relations rely on a very optimistic view of the profession in society, based on Durkheim and using concepts abandoned by the sociology of professionalism in the 1970s. They note a tendency to describe what PR professionals *do* (the *trait* approach), rather than reflect on their wider role, which, they say, results 'from professionalisation efforts that necessarily rely on an idealistic understanding of the profession' (Pieczka and L'Etang 2001: 229). Breit and Demetrios (2010) investigate claims made by public relations bodies in New Zealand and Australia against a trait approach to professions and find PR fails to meet the criteria for a profession. For example, they find thin evidence of a body of knowledge underpinning public relations practice in New Zealand and Australia, a view supported by research into UK practitioner attitudes (Tench and Fawkes 2005), which revealed a resistance to theory. Heath (2001) argues that practitioners and academics need to establish an international body of knowledge, standards for entry into the field, shared ethical values, professional competencies and a foundation of knowledge to provide practitioners with a reason to depend on universities for education, as in traditional professions such as law and medicine. This debate is contextualised by van Ruler (2005: 161), who outlines models of professions applicable to public relations:

- *knowledge model*, in which professionalisation develops from expertise, with a commitment to both the client and society;

- *status model*, whereby an organised elite secure power and autonomy;

- *competition model*, which focuses on the client's demands and evaluation in competition with other professionals; and

- *personality model*, which is suggested as the development of experts who build a reputation with clients by virtue of expertise and personal charisma.

She finds that the knowledge model is strongly represented in US literature, with the competition model endorsed by others, though she points out that the first is over-reliant on the 'body of knowledge', while the second leads to confused identity – she argues that public relations needs a professional 'brand'. None of this discussion has prevented PR practitioners and some academics referring throughout to 'the profession', whether it technically qualifies or not. It might be suggested, then, that the term doesn't really matter much, if everyone uses it anyway. On the one hand, Hutton (1999, 2001) considers that public relations' failure to identify its core concept threatens its very survival, especially as its closest rival, marketing, is much clearer about what it is as a discipline. On the other, public relations continues to flourish, according to industry statistics (CIPR 2011) with only 20 per cent of practitioners surveyed expressing concern about redundancy and indications of growth, particularly in agencies and consultancies. What do you think?

The argument for exploring the term 'professional' more deeply, not just using it as shorthand, is that the older meaning emphasises ethics. There is a danger that this gets lost when 'professional' merely comes to mean well-dressed, or carrying a briefcase. So, what are professional ethics?

Professional ethics: an overview

For the first half of the twentieth century, professional ethics focused on the specific conflicts facing particular professions, such as patient confidentiality or accounting procedures – following the trait approach discussed earlier (Cooper 2004). Then wider reading of classical philosophy introduced ethics that focus on the consequences of actions or the duty of professionals to clients, patients or society generally or, more often, an ad-hoc combination

Picture 12.1 Ethical dilemmas for public relations practitioners include deciding whether to represent controversial companies, brands or sectors, such as the tobacco industry (*source*: Robert Landau/Alamy Images)

of both. Most discussion of professional ethics concentrates on the relative merits of consequentialist and deontological approaches, as developed by Bentham and Kant respectively (Lefkowitz 2003), which are discussed below. Cooper (2004) distinguishes between *justification discourse*, the reasons offered to support ethical principles at a philosophical level, and *application discourse*, the attempt to implement ethical principles in action. The next section is about the first of these, digging a bit deeper than is common in PR ethics to find where the ethical ideas we use (or ignore) spring from. It is also worth pointing out that some commentators dismiss the whole concept of professional ethics, stating that they exist simply to promote professional organisations, not to improve standards.

Utilitarianism/consequentialism

This approach was developed by Bentham and Mill in the nineteenth century and concerns making ethical choices that will maximise the 'good' for the majority. Bentham (1748–1832) stated that happiness was the highest human goal and that decisions that enhanced general, rather than individual, human happiness must be ethical. This approach underpins many modern business practices but can be used to justify deception ('if the truth were known, we'd go out of business and then everyone would be unhappy') or the victimisation of smaller or less powerful groups ('the customers prefer being served by men, so we don't employ women'). And, on an individual basis, how often have you told a friend he/she has a great figure/haircut/partner just to keep them happy?

It concentrates on the effects or outcomes of ethical decisions – should you abandon a sick member of a group when escaping danger if that improves the survival chances for the rest? Should you immunise all babies against measles because the chances of a reaction to the jab are tiny compared to the health risks of measles? There are dangers that minority interests will get squashed by the needs of the majority, and also that ethical decisions will be reduced to mathematical calculus. Lucas (2005: 41) suggests that 'utilitarian thinking has infiltrated all levels of public decision making, through the widespread use of economic methods such as cost benefit analysis'.

Deontology

The eighteenth-century philosopher Immanuel Kant (1724–1804) argued that members of society have a range of duties (deontology) that we are all obliged to carry out, regardless of consequences. He also suggested we should behave as if our actions were subject to a universal law, and not make rules that apply only to us. He called this duty the *categorical imperative*, so that if it's OK for you to copy something from a friend's assignment, then it's OK for everyone. He also says that we should treat others as 'ends in themselves' – that is, not as a means of getting something we want. This approach places a high value on honesty and respect and resembles the fundamental laws of many faiths, including the Golden Rule to 'Do Unto Others as You would be Done By' (Cooper 2004: 221). The difficulty with this approach is that it assumes high ideals beat in the breasts of all and offers no help when confronted with two conflicting duties. For example, a friend tells you, in absolute confidence, that she/he is cheating on their partner, who later asks you to tell him/her the truth. Do you break a promise or tell a lie?

Situationist ethics

This approach combines consequentialist and deontological approaches by starting from the specifics of the ethical dilemma, before evaluating both principle and likely outcomes. This is sometimes called contingency ethics (Curtin and Boynton 2001), and a series of social psychological experiments have demonstrated the degree to which individual ethical behaviour is influenced by circumstances, such as a pleasant aroma (Appiah 2008). However, as Day et al. (2001) point out, it is often confused with *situational ethics*, which is a kind of 'anything goes' approach, suggesting a reluctance to engage with underlying ethical principles.

Discourse ethics

Discourse ethics is based in the idea of equal access to ethical debate and decision making, founded in Habermas' (1989) theory of dialogic communication. These principles have been summarised as:

- participants must have an equal chance to initiate and maintain discourse;

- participants must have an equal chance to make challenges, explanations or interpretations;

- interaction among participants must be free of manipulations, domination or control; and

- participants must be equal with respect to power.

(Burleson and Kline 1979, cited in Day et al. 2001: 408.)

Like the earlier descriptions, discourse ethics requires a process of reasoning and argument to ensure equality of access for all parties – a requirement not often found in contemporary professional practice (Curtin and Boynton 2001).

Virtue ethics

In recent years, virtue ethics, as described by MacIntyre (1984) and others, has had a considerable impact on the field of professional ethics. The virtue approach is particularly useful in its lack of reliance on external rules or codes to prescribe acceptable ethical behaviour, relying instead on character and reflection and making it an agent-based ethics. The main ideas are summarised as:

- an action is right if, and only if, it is what an agent with a virtuous character would do in the circumstances (this is sometimes turned into a game of 'what would Madonna/Ghandi/Jesus/Obama/Jay-Z do?');

- goodness is prior to rightness (trying to be good is a better moral guide than trying to do the right thing);

- the virtues are irreducibly plural intrinsic goods (there isn't a 'best' virtue);

- the virtues are objectively good (that is, honesty and justice are not subjective);

- some intrinsic goods are agent-relative (but some people will value some virtues more highly than others); and

- acting rightly does not require that we maximise the good (we aim to do the best possible in the circumstances, not to be perfect).

(Based on Oakley and Cocking 2001)

Aristotle uses the term *phronesis* to describe practical wisdom, which results not from being right but from finding a midpoint between extremes, so that courage lies somewhere between cowardice and recklessness, for example. The influence of virtue ethics on professional ethics has led to much examination of concepts such as integrity, transparency and authenticity in contemporary professional practice, with different authors championing particular virtues. For example, Kultgen (1988: 352) decides that care and justice are the most salient virtues to professions and he describes the ideal professional as 'a moral person [who] refuses to be an agent in an immoral enterprise or to use immoral means in a legitimate one'.

Explore 12.1

For a fascinating and lively introduction to ethics, see Michael Sandel's videos at http://www.justiceharvard.org/. He is Professor of Ethics at Harvard University, and these films show him engaging with students on ethical dilemmas.

Other approaches

There are other approaches to professional ethics, drawing on Confucianism, social identity theory, post-modern and feminist approaches. Many of these seek to move away from Anglo-American approaches and find some universal, globally applicable approach. For example, Benhabib (1992) takes a post-modern approach and rejects universal claims to truth, arguing that concepts of reality are socially constructed. Feminist scholars particularly challenge the reliance on rationality as the ground for ethical decision making and the absence of emotional bases for moral judgement. Cooper (2004: 34) outlines six possible principles of universal morality, which he summarises as:

1. Ethical egoism: 'Everyone ought to act to promote his or her own best interest'.

2. Utilitarianism: 'Everyone ought to act to promote the greatest amount of happiness for everyone'.

3. Natural Rights Theory: 'Everyone ought to act in accordance with everyone's inalienable, indefeasible natural rights'.

4. Social Contract Theory: 'Everyone ought to act in accordance with the principles that would be chosen if free and equal rational people were to enter a social contract to establish a moral community'.

5. Kantian Duty Ethics: 'Everyone ought to always treat people as ends unto themselves and never use them as a means only'.

6. Discourse Ethics: 'Just those action norms are valid to which all possible affected persons could agree as participants in rational discourses'.

Increasingly, new voices in professional ethics are challenging the traditional reliance – still present in Cooper's list – on rational decision making and procedural systems for ethics, calling for greater reliance on internal values rather than external codes.

The ethics of codes

The primary tool upholding and enhancing social mores for most professional bodies is their code of conduct – as Abbott (1983: 856) says, 'ethics codes are the most concrete cultural form in which professions acknowledge their societal obligations', but it is questionable whether they also play a part in determining the ethical behaviour of those they govern. Friedson (2001) suggests that professional codes fall into three types of obligation: (a) obey law/regulations; (b) practice competently; and (c) reflect values in behaviour, such as care and trust. Generally, codes involve seeking to do good, reducing harm, being fair to individuals, respecting their autonomy and behaving with integrity in line with the profession's aims and values (Rowson 2006). However, despite these laudable claims, some say that the main function of codes of practice is to improve the reputation of the professional organisation rather than change the behaviour of members. Kultgen (1988: 120) suggests that this may be because 'the *Urmythos* from which all of the myths in the professional mythology spring is that professions are oriented to the service of humanity'. Many codes reflect this sense of duty but, as Rowson (2006: 52) comments:

> *Portraying ethics in the professions as obedience to rules can have undesirable effects . . . As regulatory codes have proliferated in recent years, and as examples of unethical behaviour in professions have increasingly made the headlines, the cry has gone up that what is needed is fewer rules and a greater sense of individual moral responsibility among professionals.*

Explore 12.2

Codes of ethics

Compare the codes of ethics that you can find at the following locations:

■ CIPR (www.cipr.org)

■ Global PR (www.globalalliancepr.org)

■ PRIA (www.pria.com.au)

■ PRSA (www.prsa.org)

Feedback

Now compare the codes under the following headings:

■ *Language* – do the same terms keep cropping up?

■ *Do's and Dont's* – what differences are there between what they advise against? For example, do some codes mention refusing bribes?

■ *Best practice* – do they describe 'ideal' behaviour?

■ *Culture/nationality* – are there differences that stem from the culture of the code-writers? If so, how does that affect global codes?

■ *Moral claims* – do the codes claim the profession makes a moral contribution to society?

Explore 12.3

Philosophical approaches to ethical dilemmas

How do you think a consequentialist and a deontologist would respond to the following scenario?

You work for a large pharmaceutical company that has been developing a new male contraceptive. But the latest laboratory results suggest some cases of cancer in rats. Do you:

- Deny the results, because the company's bound to get it right eventually
- Deny the results, because the company could go bust if word gets out
- Prepare to answer questions from the media, but only for use if word leaks out
- Prepare a press release announcing the setback
- Resign
- Leak the information to the media.

Feedback

How do you make ethical decisions? By thinking or feeling? Who do you discuss them with, if anyone? What influences your decisions?

Approaches to public relations ethics

In previous writing (Fawkes 2007, 2010), public relations theory has been summarised as falling into the following loose groupings: (a) 'Excellence'; (b) advocacy; (c) relationship management; and (d) critical theory. This is not a perfect way of organising the field (Macnamara 2012 points out that it omits the information role), but it allows us to see how different approaches to public relations ethics are based in competing ways of looking at PR.

Excellence

The 'Excellence' project, based in systems theory and developed in quantitative longitudinal studies (Grunig et al. 1992, 2007), seeks to measure the dimensions of best practice both in its country of origin (USA) and worldwide. Here the practitioner is mainly described as a *boundary spanner*, linking external publics to organisational

strategic communications. This role achieves its highest level in two-way symmetric communication when the full range of negotiating and diplomatic skills is used to secure positive outcomes for all parties: 'In the two-way symmetric model . . . practitioners serve as mediators between organisations and their publics. Their goal is mutual understanding between practitioners and their publics.' (Grunig and Hunt 1984: 22). This level is the only one that is seen as inherently ethical, meaning that the 'Excellence' approach to ethics relies on structural issues. 'It is difficult, if not impossible, to practice public relations in a way that is ethical and socially responsible using an asymmetrical model' (Grunig et al. 1992: 175). Other scholars disagree; for example, Porter (2010: 127) suggests the Grunigian approach limits discussion of public relations to output rather than outcome, and that a post-symmetrical theory 'requires a reorientation towards audiences rather than organisations'.

Although there are writers who tackle ethics within this school, overall the project tends to focus on codes and idealised or excellent behaviour, particularly regarding duty to client and society. For example, Bowen (2007: 275) writes about Kant and the 'Excellence' approach, finding that 'ethics is a single excellent factor and the common underpinning of all factors that predict excellent public relations'. She concludes that 'public relations is serving a larger and more ethically responsible role by communicating for the good of society, both for the benefit of specific groups and for the maintenance of society itself' (p.279). The tone throughout promotes the ethical contribution of public relations without addressing issues of propaganda and persuasion discussed earlier in the text. This view is explicitly founded in the Durkheim view of professions as maintaining social order.

Parkinson (2001) notes that the Public Relations Society of America (PRSA) code of ethics is based on the 'Excellence' model and has influenced codes around the world. However, he concludes that such codes are designed more to improve the reputation of the profession than to control its standards of behaviour, echoing other critics of professional claims to ethical standards. Breit and Demetrios (2010) also report that practitioners in New Zealand support the existence of a code of conduct but rarely consult it for guidance in ethical issues.

Advocacy

This model recognises that public relations often plays a more asymmetrical or persuasive role than is covered by the boundary spanner. Here the PR person is seen as similar to a lawyer (known as 'advocate' in the US). Some writers, such as Fitzpatrick and Bronstein (2006), argue that all organisations are entitled to have a voice.

Marketplace theory is predicated, first on the existence of an objective 'truth' that will emerge from a cacophony of voices promoting various interests, second on a marketplace in which all citizens have the right, and perhaps the means, to be both heard and informed, and third, on the rational ability of people to discern 'truth' (Fitzpatrick 2006: 4). It is strongly USA-based, claiming the First Amendment (Freedom of Speech) as inspiration. The question of whether debate always leads to 'truth' is not addressed. Indeed, this approach is fairly uncritical of the free market, but does recognise the need for awareness of factors such as access, process, truth and disclosure. This is where debates about the ethics of withholding damaging information from the media are often located.

A deeper approach to advocacy is based on rhetorical theory (Toth and Heath 1992; Heath 2001; Porter 2010), which addresses the role of persuasion in communication, dating back to Aristotle and strongly linked to concepts of democracy. Here the image is of the speechmaker seeking to persuade fellow citizens to a point of view. The communicator uses words and symbols to influence the perceptions of others, with varying outcomes. The roles of speaker, audience, the choice of message and the dynamics and characteristics of each provides the focus of study. These writers have examined the ethics of public relations at depth; for example, Heath (2007) compares ethics in the 'Excellence' and advocacy approaches, noting Grunig's (2001) acceptance that not all ethical dialogue can be symmetrical or there would be no room for debate. Rather, argues Heath, ethical advocacy requires equal access to the structures and platforms of debate. Porter (2010: 128–9) goes further, suggesting that public relations *is* rhetoric and that 'rhetoric provides a framework for ethical public relations', illustrating the earlier point that each theory of PR has its own ethical approach.

Virtue ethics has made a considerable impact on rhetorical public relations, which is not surprising as they both stem from the work of Aristotle. For example, Harrison and Galloway's (2005: 14) analysis of the public relations practitioner's roles found that 'virtue ethics can explain, in a way that codes-based approaches do not, how "good" people can be led into acting badly because they care for the wrong person or organisation'. Edgett (2002) proposes ten principles for ethical advocacy, while Baker and Martinson (2002) suggest five principles, which they call the TARES test (Truthfulness, Authenticity, Respect, Equity and Social Responsibility), both drawing on virtue ethics (see Think about 12.1). As outlined earlier, this approach addresses the personality of the communicator and asks them to reflect on their own motives and behaviours, shifting the focus from action to agent.

Relationship management

Audiences move to centre-stage in relationship theory, which conceptualises public relations professionals as negotiating a complex set of relationships inside and outside client or employer organisations (Ledingham and Bruning 2001). It identifies the elements that make up a positive relationship, such as control mutuality, trust, satisfaction, commitment, exchange relationship and communal relationship (Hon and Grunig 1999). Unlike the organisation-centred perspective of systems theory approaches to public relations, it takes the standpoint of the publics (Leitch and Neilson 2001), which may be due partially to cultural and technological shifts that have empowered publics and facilitated international dialogue and/or coalitions (Jahansoozi 2006). The ethics of relationship management seem underexplored, particularly in the lack of a developed theory of relationship dialogue. An emerging theme in PR ethics is ethical dialogue (Day et al. 2001; Kent and Taylor 2002), though Pieczka (2010) suggests that while many public relations scholars have stressed the centrality of dialogue to the field, there has only been superficial engagement with dialogic theory – unlike related disciplines such as political science and organisational communication, which have developed a range of techniques and applications that have changed their practice. In contrast, she says, 'there is very little in public relations scholarship to help the discipline think about how dialogue can become an expert communication skill' (p. 117).

Interestingly, while discourse ethics is applied to public relations (Day et al. 2001), this is not located in the context of relationship management, which might appear a natural 'home'. Discourse ethics rests on the notion of equal access to ethical debate and decision making, as discussed earlier in this chapter. Curtin and Boynton (2001) explore how Habermas' discourse ethics has been applied to public relations by Pearson (1989) and Leeper (1996), particularly in attempts to construct procedures that will allow everyone taking part to communicate equally. However, as they point out, this rules out advocacy approaches and requires rational application of procedural rules, which are more likely to be observed in theory than practice.

Critical theory

Critical approaches, including post-modernism, political economy and, at the outer reaches, propaganda studies, are sceptical of the PR role. L'Etang summarises this grouping as 'an interdisciplinary approach that seeks to define assumptions that are taken-for-granted with a view to challenging their source and legitimacy' (2005: 521). Critical writers scrutinise the power dynamics of organisations and their

Picture 12.2 Some writers challenge public relations for distorting the democratic process. This accusation has been levelled at PR firms, who have been accused of developing fake grass roots campaigns (astroturfing), or planting questions in press conferences by PR people masquerading as journalists (*source*: Hindustan Times/Getty Images)

publics and often reveal persistent involvement of PR practitioners in propaganda and deception, past and present. While the previously covered models share an optimistic view of public relations' contribution to democracy and tend to minimise the role of propaganda in the formation of the field (Moloney 2000; Fawkes 2006), critical scholars are more sceptical (L'Etang 2004; Moloney 2006; Weaver et al. 2006; Fawkes and Moloney 2008). Public relations' greatest critics, Stauber and Rampton (2004) in the US and Miller and Dinan (2008) in the UK, continually highlight how PR firms distort the democratic process, by fake grass roots campaigns (astroturfing) or planting questions in press conferences masquerading as journalists. However, they provide little insight into what might constitute legitimate public relations, and they tend to conflate 'bad' corporate business interests with communication, without considering the PR activities of 'good' voluntary, charity or trade union groups.

Critical scholars have written about ethics from a broad perspective, looking at how PR functions in society: for example Curtin and Boynton (2001) provide a critical overview of PR ethics and L'Etang (2003) raises serious reservations about the public relations function as the 'ethical conscience' of the organisation, given the lack of moral philosophy in the educational or training backgrounds of most practitioners. Many others have written about PR's origins in propaganda and the challenges this presents for ethics, especially those who see corporate PR as a kind

of abuse of power. Yet, overall, critical scholars tend to talk more about social, political or economic theory than ethical issues, which may be explained by Kersten's (1994) comment that 'a critical perspective on the ethics of PR maintains that the question of ethics cannot be examined without exploring the social context in which PR practice takes place' (cited in Bowen et al. 2006: 126). Curtin and Gaither (2005) do, however, move from critique to construction, with a proposal for the 'circuit of culture' as a new framework for public relations scholarship. This borrows concepts from cultural and sociological writers and shows how a circuit of 'moments' (made up of representation, identity, production, consumption and regulation) offers a powerful model of interrelated, continuing, process-based communication with strong foundations in and implications for public relations. This model places ethics under the regulatory heading, encouraging PR ethics to move away from focusing on codes and reflect on 'what meanings codes have as cultural artefacts . . . for example, ethics codes may play quite different roles in different cultures . . . [and] in constructing the identities of public relations practitioners and the profession' (Curtin and Gaither 2005: 104).

This comment highlights the impact different ways of looking at PR might have on PR ethics, as this chapter has illustrated. Interestingly, Tilley (2005: 313–315) combines the above approaches to ethical PR as follows:

Think about 12.2

Practitioners' ethical roles

How do you see PR people – as bridge builders, negotiating between groups, or like lawyers, arguing for their clients?

Do you think these images imply different ethical approaches?

What if practitioners play both (and other) roles? Does it matter if their ethical approach changes in different situations?

Feedback

Many core textbooks portray PR people as ethical guardians with strong commitment to social values; practitioners often describe themselves as 'hacks for hire', with primary loyalty to the client. The next section (Practitioner Perspective) explores this tension further.

■ *Ethical intent* (input) concerns the planning stages and draws on virtue ethics in its intention to do good;

■ *Ethical means* in the enactment/outputs of the communication takes place within a deontological frame (as legal, obeying codes etc.); and

■ *Ethical outcomes* can be viewed in their consequences.

This is appealingly neat but suggests that ethical approaches are partial and can be swapped for other frameworks mid-activity, as if ethics are a set of interchangeable decision-making tools, rather than springing from philosophical questions such as how to be in the world. In contrast, Holtzhausen (2012: 33) takes a post-modern approach to ethics, whereby 'there can never be a justification for moral codes or sets of ethical rules because they are all socially constructed and therefore serve some hidden purpose in society'. This new book is an important contribution to PR ethics and brings overdue ideas from philosophy and culture into PR scholarship.

The practitioner perspective

Most of the ideas described so far have come from philosophers and public relations academics. So what do PR people think about ethics? These comments are taken from a debate in the UK in 2007 (see Box 12.1), worldwide research in 2006 and a 2011 blog post from a UK PR practitioner. (For an even more recent blog post from an Australian practitioner, see Box 12.2.)

Box 12.1

'PR does NOT have a duty to tell the truth'

In 2007, the University of Westminster organised a debate on PR ethics. The motion 'PR has a duty to tell the truth' was defeated by 138 to 124 votes, and, according to commentators, the winning arguments (put forward by PR academic Goldsworthy and leading publicist Max Clifford) were that public relations professionals have a primary duty to clients not the truth, and that media hostility made it impossible for clients to tell the truth. The debate was covered in the UK PR trade magazine, *PRWeek*, the Chartered Institute of Public Relations (CIPR) newsletter and various other blogs from the UK and USA (kindly supplied by Simon Goldsworthy). Their comments illustrate the tension referred to earlier between the advocate and 'Excellence' roles:

■ 'Are you telling the truth by creating a campaign that highlights the amazing focus of customer care and philanthropic nature of a client . . . and leaving out pending lawsuits by upset clients, former employees and product defects?' (Comment on blog, Jarvis, n.d. 2007.)

■ 'I was dismayed. Truth and integrity have to be the cornerstones of our profession if we are to have any credibility with the media and the wider world.' (Peter Crumpler, Director of Communication, Church of England, *PRWeek*, 21 February 2007.)

■ 'The victorious Clifford insisted that lying was sometimes necessary to achieve the greater good.' (*PRWeek*, 21 February 2007.)

■ 'I hope any CIPR members in the audience were aware of the requirements of the Code and that they had voted accordingly.' (CIPR President, Lionel Zetter, from his blog, cited in Goldsworthy 2007: p.5.)

■ 'To survive as a useful marketing tool, it is a necessity that PR should be seen as a truthful medium: if we cannot rescue our reputation for honesty, we have no commercial future.' (John Mounsey, Director, Trail Communications, Letter, *PRWeek*, 9 March 2007.)

■ 'The fact that PR people admit they need to lie occasionally is a sign of growing honesty and confidence in what they do.' (Daniel Rogers, Opinion, *PRWeek*, 21 February 2007.)

■ Industry maxim: 'ethical PR consultancy = small PR consultancy' (Goldsworthy 2007: 5.)

Box 12.2

A practitioner's view of PR ethics

The following blog entry was posted on 11 January 2012 by Australian Strategic PR Practitioner Craig Pearce and is reproduced with permission.

The primary code of ethics I refer to is my own moral compass. In most cases there is a clear right or wrong way to go about business activity. But, of course, that is subjective and dependant on each individual's own moral perspectives, which will of course (and thankfully) vary.

PR as an industry is not legally bound to a code of ethics, though industry associations such as the Public Relations Institute of Australia (of which I am both a member and supporter) has one and requires its members to apply its principles. The PRIA can't do much about practitioners that don't apply it, however, except boot them out of the association.

The ethics of balancing organisational and stakeholder interests

In regard to balancing the interests of all organisational stakeholders, in the real world of business and PR, sometimes there are times when it is appropriate (and there is an opportunity) to look at stakeholders' interests and sometimes there isn't.

I always, however, consider if there is, or is likely to be, a need to consider stakeholder needs and wants. And if there is, I definitely counsel an organisation on what these perspectives might be, potentially **recommend proactive engagement or market research** and, dependent on the results, design appropriate communication and engagement strategies.

This includes prompting the organisation to change the way it goes about its business and/or operations, as well as the way it communicates and engages with its stakeholders.

But getting organisations to **consider the interests of others** is a long-term game. It doesn't happen overnight and it almost always involves short-term pain. Motivating organisations to embrace multiple perspectives is one of our profession's greatest challenges and, as a result, one of our greatest rewards.

PR has a responsibility, and the ability, to incorporate the views of all relevant stakeholders into the way an organisation operates. And as **corporations run the world, not governments**, it is imperative they take on the broadest possible modes of operating that benefit society as a whole, not just narrowly segmented elements of it.

Where does PR's loyalty lie?

Because a communicator is employed by an organisation, he or she has first and, arguably, overriding responsibility to them. However, we all live in society and have a broader responsibility, as well. So it's not a simplistic equation.

Truth and honesty are values I hold in high esteem.

I don't support the transmission of false messages, though often it is not black and white. **If you focus on the positives and not the negatives, to a large degree that is acceptable**. But approach life-threatening areas such as cigarette smoking and speeding cars with a gung ho focus on positive messaging and the woods get very murky indeed.

I once worked for an organisation that, whilst it didn't support cigarettes per se, supported the sale of them because they are a legal product. Now, in many ways this is fair enough. If they are legal, why shouldn't you be allowed to sell them (bearing in mind the issue of under-age smokers etc.)?

But, as someone with strong anti-smoking industry views, I never felt comfortable about this specific moral positioning, so I was relieved to stop working for the client. I've also refused to work for a gambling organisation and have knocked back opportunities to work directly for a cigarette manufacturer.

I've not been asked by an employer to work on an account I considered to be ethically dubious, thank goodness. I have found my personal stances on issues such as gambling to be respected.

On the other hand, I have proudly worked for a **nuclear science and technology organisation** that, yes, produced nuclear waste that is a danger to the environment. And I've worked with organisations that **produce coal-fired electricity** and have found that morally justifiable as well.

Like I said, we each have our own moral compass and perspectives.

Whether it's PR or any other industry, if you are asked to work in a field you are not ethically comfortable with,

box 12.2 (continued)

then you really need to **get out of there ASAP**, financial considerations notwithstanding. If it comes to a choice of earning money whilst detesting yourself for the choice you have made, or the opposite, to me the correct choice is clear.

I have actually left an organisation where I felt the **culture was wrong** and the reason I felt the culture was wrong was based on ethical issues. I just didn't like the way the owner of the company treated people and as that person wasn't going to change, I felt I had no choice

but to move on as, by staying there, I would have been implicitly supporting a way of dealing with people I found unacceptable.

What have been your ethical challenges as a public relations professional? Have you been in situations similar to the ones I recount above? Do you consider the ethics of an organisation before and whilst you work for it? Have you had any successes or frustrations in influencing what you consider the ethical dimensions for organisations you have worked for?

The IABC report, '*The Business of Truth: A guide to ethical communication*' (Bowen et al. 2006), surveyed just under 2,000 mostly senior practitioners in North America, New Zealand, Israel and Australia, as well as qualitative interviews and focus groups. The research found a sizeable proportion of respondents rejected the 'ethical counsellor' role, feeling that was the province of the legal department or the board itself – particularly where communications were not represented at board level. The research also found that, while many wished to be considered as ethical counsellors, there was very little training in ethical theory or practice. One respondent is quoted as saying: 'It's simple stuff. Fundamentally you're either a good person or you're not' (p.8). On the other hand, another respondent commented, 'My job is filled with ethical issues. Who we are, what we've done, what we'd like to do, and what do we want to do in the future', which is echoed by another, 'I do ethics stuff all the time – they just don't call it that' (p.9). The report stresses that ethics matters because of its relationship to communication credibility, organisational reputation and

relationships to publics (p.13), but that practitioners are ill-equipped to participate fully in such roles due to inadequate training and lack of discussion on such issues by employers. Paul Seaman is an experienced practitioner who writes regular articles on issues of practice and theory; in his essay 'A new moral agenda for PR' (Seaman 2011) he attacks the concept of ethical guardian, suggesting that the idea of PRs as 'moral keepers of their organisation' (p.6) is rather grand. Indeed, he says that 'Grunig, in common with many PR thinkers, mistakenly believes that PR is about establishing mutual understanding between publics and clients. Actually, PR is about advocacy on behalf of clients.' (p.8). He also notes the export of Grunigian views of the world to the development of stakeholder doctrine, CSR, sustainability and as embedded in the Stockholm Accords – all of which he sees as falsely claiming to serve social rather than corporate or shareholder interests. These views echo Milton Friedman's approach to corporate responsibility, but also raise interesting questions about the role and image of the practitioner.

Think about 12.3   Feedback – solving ethical dilemmas

To help the practitioner facing dilemmas such as those in Explore 12.1, Baker and Martinson (2002) have put together five principles to act as guiding principles for ethical persuasive public relations, which they call the TARES test:

1. **t**ruthfulness – the commitment to honesty in communication

2. **a**uthenticity – relates to personal and professional integrity

3. **r**espect – for the rights of your audience

4. **e**quity – relates to fairness, not manipulation

5. **s**ocial responsibility – awareness of the effects of communication on the wider society.

Feedback

Are these still rather idealistic ways of describing PR practice? How do they relate to what Craig Pearse says in Box 12.2?

Summary

This chapter has explored some of the confusion surrounding professional ethics in general, and public relations ethics in particular. It suggests that the confusion is made worse because different ways of looking at PR imply different ethics, but that these differences are hidden rather than explored. The chapter has shown that the gap between the idealistic 'ethical guardian' image contained in some 'Excellence' writing and the views of practitioners is very wide. It has also demonstrated that there are ways of considering professional ethics, such as post-modernist approaches, which are only just coming into PR debates (Holtzhausen 2012). Most PR ethics is still reliant on procedural, structural and rational approaches, with little discussion of where an individual might look for internal guidance, rather than more rules. Virtue ethics does open this debate to a certain extent, but can still end up as a competition for best practice. Codes have been shown to be empty – not only in PR, but in professions generally. There is an argument in the field for encouraging greater reflection in individual professionals and in professional associations. Instead of looking for rules or accepting situations that 'feel' wrong but are legal, perhaps practitioners need to learn to trust their discomfort. It takes courage to listen to one's own unease, to say 'are we sure about this action/policy?'. Without such reflection, it is hard to see how PR can earn back lost trust. It is new practitioners, graduates from educational and professional qualifications, who will shape this future.

Bibliography

Abbott, A. (1983). 'Professional ethics'. *The American Journal of Sociology* **88**(5): 855–885.

Appiah, A. (2008). *Experiments in Ethics*. Cambridge, London: Harvard University Press.

Baker, S. & D.L. Martinson (2002). 'Out of the red-light district: five principles for ethically proactive public relations'. *Public Relations Quarterly* **47**(3): 15–19.

Benhabib, S. (1992). *Situating the Self: Gender, community, and postmodernism in contemporary ethics*. New York, NY: Routledge.

Bivins, T.H. (1992). 'Public relations, professionalism, and the public interest'. *Journal of Business Ethics* **12**(2): 117–126.

Bowen, S.A. (2007). 'The extent of ethics' in *The Future of Excellence in Public Relations and Communication Management*. E.L. Toth (ed.). Mahwah, NJ: Lawrence Erlbaum.

Bowen, S.A., R.L. Heath, J. Lee, G. Painter, F.J. Agraz, D. McKie and M. Toledano (2006). *The Business of Truth: A guide to ethical communication*. San Francisco, CA: International Association of Business Communicators.

Breit, R. and K. Demetrios (2010). 'Professionalisation and public relations: an ethical mismatch'. *Ethical Space* **7**(4): 20–29.

Broadbent, J., M. Dietrich and J. Roberts (1997). *The End of the Professions? The restructuring of professional work*. London: Routledge.

CIPR (2011). 'State of the PR profession: benchmarking survey' www.cipr.co.uk/sites/default/files/CIPR%20Membership%20Survey%20Report%20Nov11%20with%20foreword.pdf July 2012.

Cooper, D.E. (2004). *Ethics for Professionals in a Multicultural World*. Upper Saddle River, NJ: Prentice Hall.

Curtin, P.A. and L.A. Boynton (2001). 'Ethics in public relations: theory and practice' in *The Handbook of Public Relations*. R.L. Heath (ed.). Thousand Oaks, CA: Sage.

Curtin, P.A. and T.K. Gaither (2005). 'Privileging identity, difference and power: The circuit of culture as a basis for public relations theory'. *Journal of Public Relations Research* **17**(2): 91–115.

Day, K.D., Q. Dong and C. Robins (2001). 'Public relations ethics: an overview and discussion of issues for the 21st century' in *The Handbook of Public Relations*. R.L. Heath (ed.). Thousand Oaks, CA: Sage.

Dent, M. and S. Whitehead (2002). *Managing Professional Identities: Knowledge, performativity and the 'new' professional*. London: Routledge.

Durkheim, E. (1933). *The Division of Labour in Society*. Glencoe, IL: Free Press.

Earl, S. (2011). 'Smear all in it together'. www.speedcommunications.com/blogs/earl/2011/05/13/smear-all-in-it-together/ 4 July 2012.

Edelman, R. (2012). 'Edelman Trust Barometer, Executive Summary'. www.scribd.com/doc/79026497/2012-Edelman-Trust-Barometer-Executive-Summary 3 July 2012.

Edgett, R. (2002). 'Toward an ethical framework for advocacy'. *Journal of Public Relations Research* **14**(1): 1–26.

Fawkes, J. (2006). 'Can ethics save public relations from the charge of propaganda?' *Ethical Space* **3**(1): 38–42.

Fawkes, J. (2007). 'Public relations models and persuasion ethics: a new approach'. *Journal of Communication Management* **11**(4): 313–331.

Fawkes, J. (2010). 'The shadow of excellence: a Jungian approach to public relations ethics'. *Review of Communication* **10**(3): 211–227.

Fawkes, J. and K. Moloney (2008). 'Does the European Union (EU) need a propaganda watchdog like the US Institute of Propaganda Analysis to strengthen its democratic civil society and free markets?' *Public Relations Review* **34**: 207–214.

Fitzpatrick, K. (2006). 'Baselines for ethical advocacy in the "marketplace of ideas"' in *Ethics in Public Relations: Responsible advocacy*. K. Fitzpatrick and C. Bronstein (eds). Thousand Oaks, CA: Sage.

Fitzpatrick, K. and C. Bronstein (2006). *Ethics in Public Relations: Responsible advocacy*. Thousand Oaks, CA: Sage.

Freidson, E. (1994). *Professionalism Reborn: Theory, prophecy, and policy*. Cambridge: Polity.

Freidson, E. (2001). *Professionalism: The third logic*. Cambridge: Polity.

Grunig, J.E. (2001). 'Two-way symmetrical public relations: past, present and future' in *The Handbook of Public Relations*. R.L. Heath (ed.). Thousand Oaks, CA: Sage.

Grunig, J.E. and T. Hunt (1984). *Managing Public Relations*. New York, NY; London: Holt, Rinehart and Winston.

Grunig, J.E., D.M. Dozier, W.P. Ehling, L.A. Grunig, F.C. Repper and J. White (1992). *Excellence in Public Relations and Communication Management*. Hillsdale, NJ: Lawrence Erlbaum.

Grunig, J.E., L.A. Grunig and E.L. Toth (2007). *The Future of Excellence in Public Relations and Communication Management: Challenges for the next generation*. London: Lawrence Erlbaum.

Habermas, J. (1989). *The Structural Transformation of the Public Sphere: An inquiry into a category of bourgeois society*. Cambridge, MA: MIT Press.

Harrison, K. and C. Galloway (2005). 'Public relations ethics: a simpler (but not simplistic) approach to the complexities'. *Prism* **3**.

Heath, R.L. (2001). 'A rhetorical enactment rationale for public relations: the good organisation communicating well' in *The Handbook of Public Relations*. R.L. Heath and G. Vasquez (eds). Thousand Oaks, CA: Sage.

Heath, R.L. (2007). 'Management through advocacy: reflection rather than domination' in *The Future of Excellence in Public Relations and Communications Management*. J.E. Grunig, E.L. Toth and L.A. Grunig (eds). Mahwah, NJ: Lawrence Erlbaum Associates.

Holtzhausen, D. (2012). *Public Relations as Activisim: Postmodern approaches to theory and practice*. New York, NY: Routledge.

Hon, L.C. and J.E. Grunig (1999). 'Guidelines for measuring relationships in public relations'. http://www.instituteforpr.com

Hutton, J.G. (1999). 'The definition, dimensions and domain of public relations'. *Public Relations Review* **25**(2): 199–214.

Hutton, J.G. (2001). 'Defining the relationship between public relations and marketing' in *The Handbook of Public Relations*. R.L. Heath (ed.). Thousand Oaks, CA: Sage.

Jahansoozi, J. (2006). 'Relationships, transparency and evaluation: the implications for public relations' in *Public Relations, Critical Debates and Contemporary Practice*. J. L'Etang and M. Pieczka (eds). Mahwah, NJ: Lawrence Erlbaum.

Kent, M.L. and M. Taylor (2002). 'Toward a dialogic theory of public relations'. *Public Relations Review* **14**(28): 21–37.

Kersten, A. (1994). 'The ethics and ideology of of public relations: a critical examination of American theory and practice' in *Normative aspekte der public relations*. W. Armbrecht and U. Zabel (eds). Opladen, Germany: Westdeucher Verlag.

Kultgen, J. (1988). *Ethics and Professionalism*. Philadelphia, PA: University of Philadelphia Press.

Larson, M.S. (1977). *The Rise of Professionalism: A sociological analysis*. Berkeley, CA: University of California Press.

Ledingham, J.A. and S.D. Bruning (2001). *Public Relations as Relationship Management: A relational approach to the study and practice of public relations*, 2nd edition. Mahwah, NJ; London: Lawrence Erlbaum.

Leeper, K.A. (1996). 'Public relations ethics and communitarianism, a preliminary investigation'. *Public Relations Review* **22**: 163–179.

Lefkowitz, J. (2003). *Ethics and Values in Industrial-organisational Psychology*. Mahwah, NJ: Lawrence Erlbaum Associates.

Leitch, S. and D. Nielson (2001). 'Bringing publics into public relations: new theoretical frameworks for practice' in *The Handbook of Public Relations*. R.L. Heath (ed.). Thousand Oaks, CA: Sage.

L'Etang, J. (2003). 'The myth of the "ethical guardian": an examination of its origins, potency and illusions'. *Journal of Communication Management* **8**(1): 53–67.

L'Etang, J. (2004). *Public Relations in Britain: A history of professional practice in the twentieth century*. Mahwah, NJ; London: Lawrence Erlbaum.

L'Etang, J. (2005). 'Critical public relations: some reflections'. *Public Relations Review* **31**(4): 521–526.

Lucas, P. (2005). 'Humanising professional ethics' in *The Teaching and Practice of Professional Ethics*. J. Strain and S. Robinson (eds). Leicester: Troubador.

MacIntyre, A. (1984). *After Virtue: A study in moral theory*, 2nd edition. Notre Dame, IN: University of Notre Dame Press.

Macnamara, J. (2012). *Public Relations, Theories, Practices, Critiques*. Frenchs Forest, NSW: Pearson Australia.

Miller, D. and W. Dinan (2008). *A Century of Spin: How public relations became the cutting edge of corporate power*. London: Pluto.

Moloney, K. (2000). *Rethinking Public Relations: The spin and the substance*. London: Routledge.

Moloney, K. (2006). *Rethinking Public Relations: PR propaganda and democracy*, 2nd edition. London: Routledge.

Oakley, J. and D. Cocking (2001). *Virtue Ethics and Professional Roles*. Cambridge: Cambridge University Press.

Parkinson, M. (2001). 'The PRSA Code of Professional Standards and Member Code of Ethics: why they are neither professional nor ethical'. *Public Relations Quarterly* **46**(3): 27–31.

Parsons, T. (1951). *The Social System*. London: Routledge and Kegan Paul.

Pearson, R. (1989). 'Beyond ethical relativism in public relations: co-orientation, rules and the ideal of communication symmetry' in *Public Relations Research Annual*, Vol. 1. J.E. Grunig and L.A. Grunig (eds). Hillside, NJ: Lawrence Erlbaum Associates.

Pieczka, M. (2010). 'Public relations as dialogic expertise?' *Journal of Communication Management* **15**(2): 108–124.

Pieczka, M. and J. L'Etang (2001). 'Public relations and the question of professionalism' in *The Handbook of Public Relations*. R.L. Heath (ed.). Thousand Oaks, CA: Sage.

Porter, L. (2010). 'Communicating for the good of the state: a post-symmetrical polemic on persuasion in ethical public relations'. *Public Relations Review* **36**: 127–133.

Rowson, R. (2006). *Working Ethics: How to be fair in a culturally complex world*. London: Jessica Kingsley Publishers.

Sciulli, D. (2005). 'Continental sociology of professions today: conceptual contributions'. *Current Sociology* **53**(6): 915–942.

Seaman, P. (2011). 'A new moral agenda for PR'. *21st Century PR Issues*, http://paulseaman.eu/wp-content/uploads/2011/04/a-new-moral-agenda-for-PR1.pdf accessed July 2012.

Sriramesh, K. and L. Hornaman (2006). 'Public relations as a profession an analysis of curricular content in the United States'. *Journal of Creative Communications* **1**(2): 155–172.

Stauber, J.C. and S. Rampton (2004). *Toxic Sludge is Good for You: Lies, damn lies and the public relations industry*. London: Robinson.

Tench, R. and J. Fawkes (2005). 'Mind the gap, exploring different attitudes to public relations education from employers, academics and alumni'. Paper presented at the Alan Rawel/CIPR conference, Lincoln, UK.

Tilley, E. (2005). 'The ethics pyramid: making ethics unavoidable in the public relations process'. *Mass Media Ethics* **20**(4): 305–320.

Toth, E.L. and R.L. Heath (1992). *Rhetorical and Critical Approaches to Public Relations*. Hillsdale, NJ: Lawrence Erlbaum Associates.

Trivitt, K. (2011). 'PRSA official: smear campaigns have no part in PR'. *Ragan's Daily*, www.prdaily.com/Main/Articles/8288.aspx 4 July 2012.

van Ruler, B. (2005). 'Professionals are from Venus, scholars are from Mars'. *Public Relations Review* **31**: 159–173.

Weaver, C.K., J. Motion and J. Reaper (2006). 'From propaganda to discourse (and back again): truth, power the public interrest and public relations' in *Public Relations, Critical Debates and Contemporary Practice*. J. L'Etang and M. Pieczka (eds). Mahwah NJ: Lawrence Erlbaum.

Weber, M., A.M. Henderson and T. Parsons (1964). *The Theory of Social and Economic Organization* (Translated by A.M. Henderson and Talcott Parsons. Edited with an introduction by Talcott Parsons). New York, NY: Free Press of Glencoe; London: Collier-Macmillan.

Zimbardo, P.G. (2007). *The Lucifer Effect: How good people turn evil*. London: Rider.

PART 3

Public relations specialisms

This part of the book focuses on the practice of public relations. We have divided it into 11 distinct chapters in recognition of the increasingly specialist knowledge, experience and skills required to achieve an effective programme or campaign on behalf of an organisation or client. Each chapter, therefore: examines the broad context of the specialism; discusses the main theories and principles of building effective relationships with key publics; and identifies some of the methods of achieving successful results. Extensive use is made of Mini case studies and long Case studies to illustrate the theories, principles and methods described.

CHAPTER 13

Richard Bailey

Media relations

Learning outcomes

By the end of this chapter you should be able to:

- discuss media relations from historical and professional/ethical perspectives
- discuss and explain the distinction between editorial and advertising approaches to media placement
- critique media relations from media and political perspectives
- analyse and apply theories to media relations practice
- evaluate your learning about media relations and pursue further sources for investigation.

Structure

- Media relations or public relations?
- Media publicity and media relations
- Origins and history
- Media and political perspectives
- Practical media relations
- Theories for media relations
- Digital public relations: beyond media relations

Introduction

Putting the Public Back in Public Relations is the expressive title of a 2009 book on public relations and social media by two consultants from the US. Its subtitle is: *'How social media is reinventing the aging [sic] business of PR'* (Solis and Breakenridge 2009).

The title implies that PR practitioners have been focused on something other than public relations – and this other thing is media relations. The subtitle asserts that public relations is no longer a young industry. In its media relations guise, the industry is over 100 years old.

This chapter reviews the century-old business of media relations and discusses whether it has a future in the digital age. We will review media relations from practical, ethical/professional and theoretical perspectives and argue that there is a distinction between media publicity and media relations.

Media relations or public relations?

Media relations is the most visible part of public relations. According to the 2011 'PR Census', 85 per cent of PR practitioners said they were involved in 'general media relations', with 21 per cent saying that media relations was the main function of their role (*PRWeek*, 15 July 2011: 21). Research by Tench and Fawkes (2005) showed that writing skills and media relations expertise were the two most highly-ranked PR qualities sought by employers.

High-profile publicity stunts and celebrity events bring a supposed allure to the role that attracts many young people onto public relations courses. Perhaps the most widely-known name among some 60,000 PR practitioners in the UK is the publicist Max Clifford, associated with many 'kiss and tell' stories in the media over several decades.

Yet the same visibility attracts scorn and criticism from the media (who sometimes describe public relations as 'the dark side' and PR practitioners as 'flacks') and from critics concerned about PR's ability to distort debate in favour of the rich and powerful through its supposed control of the media.

In the public imagination, media relations *is* public relations. Yet it is very hard to find an academic definition of public relations that even mentions media relations. We know of only one:

> *PR is the planned persuasion of people to behave in ways that further its sponsor's objectives. It works primarily through the use of media relations and other forms of third party endorsement.* (Morris and Goldsworthy 2008: 102)

This definition is a challenge to much academic thinking that has tried to distance publicity and media relations from professional public relations practice. Most famously, the 'Four Models of Public Relations' (Grunig and Hunt 1984) can be seen as a conscious attempt to assert the difference between professional, 'two-way symmetric' public relations and one-way 'press agentry/publicity', as practised by early masters of manipulation such as circus impresario P.T. Barnum.

Publicity may have been developed in the nineteenth century by P.T. Barnum, but it certainly did not die with him. Media publicity and media relations continued growing throughout the twentieth century, even as editorial jobs in the media began to decline. As *The Economist* newspaper reported: 'For each American journalist there are now, on average, six flacks hassling him [sic] to run crummy stories' (*The Economist*, 21 May 2011: 76).

This article in *The Economist* identified the trend away from traditional media relations towards the targeting of social media influencers in certain industries. 'Some in PR see new opportunities in the cacophony of voices in online social media. Bombarded with all that blogging, tweeting and Facebooking, consumers will surely, more than ever, be looking to a few trusted "influencers" to tell them what to think, an idea foreshadowed in '*Propaganda*', a 1928 spinner's bible by Edward Bernays, PR's founding father' (op cit pp.76–77). (See Think about 13.1.)

This raises two questions. Can media relations be reconciled with professional public relations; and is a new approach needed for social media?

Media relations can be viewed as a key part of an organisation's stakeholder relationship management. The media (reporters, editors and producers of print, broadcast and online channels and publications) are both a trusted channel to other stakeholder groups (internal and external) and a stakeholder group in their own right with a legitimate right to question those in power and authority.

US consultant and author Shel Holtz describes this well: 'Contrary to the apparent belief of many observers, the role of an organizational media relations department is not to make the company look good in the press, nor is it to keep the company out of the newspapers . . . Ideally, the

Think about 13.1   The 'dark side', 'spin' and 'flacks'

What do journalists mean when they describe PR as the 'dark side' and when they call public relations 'spin' and PR practitioners 'flacks'? What does *The Economist* mean when describing 'flacks hassling [reporters] to run crummy stories'?

What defence can be made for media relations as a legitimate, professional activity?

Here's Stefan Stern, a former management writer on the *Financial Times*, describing his new role at Edelman, a public relations consultancy, for the Public Relations Society of America (PRSA) in May 2011:

'As far as I can see, this famous "dark side" really isn't quite as dark as all that. Sure: clients sometimes make difficult and demanding requests. PR pros are asked to put the best possible gloss or, if you must, "spin" on the facts. But that, I think, is not really very different from

what a good lawyer (or advocate) would do. Are lawyers all working on the "dark side" too? I don't think so.'

'And then there is the world of journalism as it is currently practiced. Is that a shining beacon of light? The shocking behaviour of the UK's *News of the World*, exposed by *The New York Times* and *The Guardian*, is hardly a picture of moral rectitude. Tapping celebrities' phone calls to produce scandalous headlines – now that really is dark.'

Source: http://prsay.prsa.org/index.php/2011/03/16/
life-on-the-dark-side-stefan-stern/

Feedback

There are legitimate questions and concerns about media relations practice, and you need to be aware of these questions before contacting the media with your stories. Have you thought this through, as Ivy Lee did in 1906 (see Chapter 1)?

---

job of the media relations department is to help reporters and editors do their jobs. That objective is entirely consistent with the broader goal of public relations, which is to manage the relationship between the organization and its various constituent audiences.' (Holtz 2002: 157)

Coombs and Holladay make the logical argument that media relations has a narrower focus than public relations since it is concerned with just one public, the news media. 'Media relations is the relationship between the organization and members of the media' (Coombs and Holladay 2010: 108).

Media publicity and media relations

Students often begin their public relations courses convinced that the only technique available to make people aware of something is advertising (paid-for messages in the media). Yet in practice, media relations is often deployed as a means of generating free publicity and so is often used as an alternative to advertising.

Advertising and public relations share similar goals. Lord Bell, who has worked at senior levels in both the advertising and public relations industries, distinguishes them in this way: 'Advertising is the use of paid-for media

space to inform and persuade. Public relations is the use of third-party endorsement to inform and persuade' (cited in White and Mazur 1995: 259). In other words, the distinction is the medium (paid or unpaid), not the message.

US brand marketing consultants Al Ries and Laura Ries called their 2002 book *The Fall of Advertising and the Rise of PR*. The provocative title can easily be misinterpreted: they were not proclaiming the death of advertising but were making the case that in certain industries, and in certain sectors, publicity is a more credible tool for raising brand awareness than advertising.

'You can't launch new brands with advertising because advertising has no credibility. It's the self-serving voice of a company anxious to make a sale. You can launch new brands only with publicity or public relations (PR). PR allows you to tell your story indirectly through third-party outlets, primarily the media.' (Ries and Ries 2002: xi)

The key point here is credibility, not money. We mistrust advertising because we know the advertiser is trying to persuade us, whereas public relations messages gain credibility because they are carried by independent sources (media and other influencers) and are not labelled as PR messages. This is what is meant by third-party endorsement, a phrase used by Morris and Goldsworthy (2008) and by Lord Bell, above.

Public relations scholars view the Ries and Ries book as a mixed blessing: while it heralds the arrival of public relations as a major force within the 'marketing mix', it also

Think about 13.2   Publicity stunts and the truth

'Freddie Starr Ate My Hamster' was a notorious front page headline from 13 March 1986 in *The Sun* newspaper. Freddie Starr, a comedian, had pretended to eat a hamster in a sandwich as a joke two years earlier (the hamster was not harmed). So how did it come to be front page news? It's an invented story created by publicist Max Clifford and *Sun* editor Kelvin Mackenzie. The story was not 'true'. Should it be condemned, or is this form of public entertainment hamless fun? (Cited in Hargreaves 2003: 114–115.)

'Bring back Wispa' was reported as a newsworthy example of a grassroots campaign on Facebook that caused a large business (Cadbury) to change its mind over its plans for a confectionery product ('Web campaign prompts Wispa return', BBC News, 18 August 2007), yet it later won Borkowski PR a *PRWeek* award for digital innovation. This was less an example of genuine groundswell than another example of a spectacular PR stunt.

(Mark Borkowski's blog: http://www.markborkowski.com/winning-with-wispa/)

These two examples raise questions about media publicity and the truth. Do public relations practitioners have a duty to tell the truth in all circumstances, or can a defence be made of publicity-as-entertainment? Is this an acceptable deceit as long as the media understand where the story has come from?

Feedback

Truth is a problematic concept for public relations practitioners. Journalists will sometimes make a distinction between a PR practitioner's duty to be accurate and a journalist's duty to tell the whole truth. The distinction is that PR promotes the view of an organisation or client, whereas the news media can, and should, report a range of perspectives on a story (Davies 2008).

limits public relations by confusing it with publicity (Coombs and Holladay 2007).

So what is the relationship between publicity and public relations? It's the difference between a 'one-night stand' (a brief sexual encounter) and a committed relationship. The publicist's goal is to make something known: at one extreme, they have no responsibility to the media or to the public and may not even care to ensure the truthfulness of what they're saying. This is the 'Freddie Starr Ate My Hamster' school of PR publicity (see Think about 13.2) and it did not die with P.T. Barnum. Max Clifford has already been named as a skilful and prominent publicist; Mark Borkowski views himself as a 'son of Barnum' and has written a history of Hollywood publicity (Borkowski 2009). At the other extreme, public relations is concerned with developing long-term relationships, so should see no advantage in fooling the media or the public for short-term publicity gains.

The distinction between media publicity and media relations can be shown through an example. Imagine a company has commissioned some research in order to publicise its product or service (a standard public relations approach). If the research is mentioned in the media, but the company or the brand is omitted from the news report, then is this a success or a failure in terms of media relations? It's clearly a failure as an exercise in media publicity, but it's arguably a media relations success as it shows the technique works and it opens the door to future stories through the same journalist or media outlet. The client will

not see it this way, but the PR adviser should be willing to put long-term relationship building ahead of short-term publicity advantage.

Publicity is a part of public relations, but it is usually performed by junior members of the team or only forms part of a job description. Exceptions to this are in the world of arts and sports, where the role of the publicist is primarily to promote upcoming performances or events in order to sell tickets.

Origins and history

In its media relations guise, the industry is just over 100 years old. A 1906 press release written by Ivy Lee following a fatal accident on the Pennsylvania Railroad was printed, word for word, by the *New York Times* on 30 October in that year. This is now acclaimed as the first of many press releases.

Following this success, Ivy Lee was contracted to more clients and more press releases followed. He was forced to defend the ethics of this activity in his famous 'Declaration of Principles'. His statement opened: 'This is not a secret press bureau. All our work is done in the open. We aim to supply news. This is not an advertising agency' (Ewen 1996)

Media relations is a creation of the mass media age. Mass-circulation newspapers did not arrive until the late nineteenth century as they could only exist once there was mass adult literacy, some disposable income, leisure time and a means of distributing the newspapers quickly. The mass media age was born from education, industrialisation and the railways.

The mid twentieth century was the high point of the mass media age. Broadcast media (radio then television) were added to mass-circulation newspapers, and limited spectrum and government control meant that a few broadcasters could reach large sections of the population.

By the end of the twentieth century, the move to a digital spectrum and liberalisation from government control led to a proliferation of TV and radio channels. Rather than mass media, we had entered an era of 'masses of media'. As John Naughton argues (2012: 138–139): 'One of the laws of communications technology is that new media are generally additive rather than substitutive, which is a fancy way of saying that new technologies generally don't wipe out older ones . . . New media don't wipe out old media. But their arrival does change the ecosystem.'

Early in the twenty-first century, the Internet had begun to challenge the broadcasters. Young people now turn to YouTube for entertainment, and when watching popular television programmes such as *The X Factor* are likely to be sharing their thoughts on Twitter. We still have the mass media, but it's now commonplace to say that every organisation (even every individual) is now a media channel, with our lives streamed on Facebook. Mass media has become masses of media and now 'me media'.

Media and political perspectives

How successful is public relations in terms of getting its messages in the media? Research conducted by the journalism department at Cardiff University for Nick Davies's *Flat Earth News* (2008) found that 60 per cent of home news stories in the quality UK daily newspapers (*Daily Mail, The Times, The Guardian, The Independent* and the *Daily Telegraph*) 'consisted wholly or mainly of wire copy and/or PR material and a further 20 per cent contained clear elements of wire copy and/or PR' (Davies 2008: 52).

By 'wire copy' Davies is referring to stories from news agencies such as Reuters and the Press Association, so the 60 per cent figure does not necessarily reflect the true power of PR over the news media. Yet the news agencies, which pride themselves on the speed and accuracy of their reporting, have to rely on sources for their stories – and public relations is clearly one such source.

The imbalance between the numbers of people working in public relations and the numbers working in media newsrooms suggests an increasing reliance by the media on public relations sources. Davies describes this as 'churnalism': 'Journalists who are no longer out gathering news but who are reduced instead to passive processors of whatever material comes their way, churning out stories, whether real event or PR artifice, important or trivial, true or false' (Davies 2008: 59).

Half a century earlier, US historian Daniel Boorstin revealed the power of the then much smaller public relations industry to dominate the news agenda through creating what he called 'pseudo-events'. These are fake events designed solely to gain media attention (Boorstin 1961).

Today, almost every press release leads with the language of a pseudo-event ('Today, X announced Y' or 'A launched B'), in the sense that there was no announcement other than the press release itself and it is ships, not products, that are literally launched. This is the language of the pseudo-event, made legitimate by the usefulness of many of these press releases to the news media.

The Cluetrain Manifesto (Levine et al. 1999/2009) also attacked bad practice from the PR industry: 'Everyone – including many PR people – senses that something is deeply phony about the profession. And it's not hard to see what it is. Take the standard computer industry press release. With few exceptions, it describes an 'announcement' that was not made, for a product that was not available, quoting people who never said anything, for distribution to a list of people who mostly consider it trash.'

'Dishonesty in PR is *pro forma*. A press release is written as a plainly fake news story, with headline, dateline, quotes and all the dramatic tension of a phone number. The idea, of course, is to make the story easy for editors to 'insert' in their publications.' (Searls and Weinberger in Levine et al. 2009: 160)

We have a paradox here that needs explaining. Public relations is being condemned for being ineffectual at the same time as it is being criticised for being over-influential in the media. Though these two perspectives appear contradictory, they arise from the same concern: that public relations is an unaccountable force and that its influence is not good for society.

To address this concern, we need to take a broader view of the role of media in society.

Beyond its role in entertainment, the media plays an important function through its mediating role between those in power (producers) and citizens (consumers). One of the pillars of liberal democracy is a free media (that the media should be independent of government or commercial control). For example, free speech and freedom of the press is enshrined in the First Amendment to the United States Constitution.

Think about 13.3   PR versus the media

BBC *Newsnight* presenter Jeremy Paxman has outlined the role of journalism as follows:

'Essentially journalism is a matter of instinct, the expression of primitive curiosity and an instinctive urge to cause trouble, to be difficult, coupled with an atavistic distrust of anyone in authority' (*Media Guardian*, 8 May 2000: 11).

Now consider how public relations practioners can develop good working relationships with the media.

Feedback

At a professional level, you should always respect that journalists have a different job to do, and you should avoid seeing them merely as a channel for your messages.

One of the first jobs of the PR practitioner embarking on a media relations programme is to give key spokespeople media training. You should expose them to difficult questions and awkward journalists. It is better for the training to be difficult and for the reality to be a much easier relationship than the other way around.

In a 'liberal pluralist' society (one with a free press, free elections and wide choice of consumer products; see earlier in the text for further discussion of liberal pluralism) the media play an important role in enabling citizens to make informed choices. Does the public relations industry assist the media in performing this role, or does PR seek to distort the debate in favour of commercial interests?

Your answer to this question may depend on your political perspective. Media sociologists Miller and Dinan are in no doubt that 'public relations . . . has aided and abetted the rise to power of the global corporations and the consequent withering of democracy' (Miller and Dinan 2008: 1). If globalised corporations are too powerful, then public relations must be condemned as being (in their words) 'the cutting edge of corporate power'.

Others, and especially those from new and emerging democracies, may take a different view, noting the correlation between liberal democracy and a flourishing public relations industry. As Morris and Goldsworthy argue: 'Much of the negative talk about PR is western and insular: a luxurious by-product of wealth and assured freedom. In many parts of the world, including most emerging democracies, PR not only surges ahead but is inseparably linked to rising prosperity, increased choice, and freedom of expression' (Morris and Goldsworthy 2008: 174).

Public relations scholar Kevin Moloney finds a middle way between these two perspectives. While he 'is critical of many PR practices and consequences (e.g. impact on democracy; unequal spread of resources; invisibility in the media)', he 'does not deny the right of others to do PR in societies such as the UK and USA. It is futile to "lament" the presence of PR, because public relations is expressive of foundational features of liberal democracy in its representative variety – its pluralism and promotional culture' (Moloney 2006: 2).

In other words, public relations is a part of society – and it can be a force for good, though we need better and more accountable PR. (His point about invisibility in the media is not that public relations does not get its messages in the media but that these messages do not carry a health warning that they are from a PR source.)

Coombs and Holladay make a similar argument in defending PR as part of the 'marketplace of ideas' (Coombs and Holladay 2007). In a liberal democracy and in a consumer society, people are presented with competing ideas, ideologies and products. The process of public debate and interrogation should produce better outcomes for individuals and for society (just as a competitive free market should produce better value products for consumers). Public relations has a role in facilitating this debate and providing arguments and information for scrutiny in the public sphere.

Moloney provides an academic perspective on the 'dark side' taunt mentioned earlier by citing what Jensen calls 'hemispheric communicators': 'people who because of their defined role in society such as lawyers, advertisers, lobbyists and public relations practitioners express messages that speak to only half the landscape. Like the shining moon, they present only the bright side and leave the dark side hidden' (Jensen 1997: 68, cited in Moloney 2006: 106). (See Think about 13.3.)

Practical media relations

Despite the 'dark side' taunts of some journalists, the problem with media relations is that it is too focused on the 'sunny side'. The instinct is to tell 'good news' and to try to 'bury bad news'.

This leads to the use of soft language in news releases: 'We are proud to announce' and 'We are delighted . . .'. This soft language is a clue to a journalist that the announcement is puffery rather than hard news.

Picture 13.1 Large set-piece press conferences like this one at the start of the Euro 2012 football tournament are now much less common than the public might imagine from watching television news (*source*: Getty Images)

Here are some tips for avoiding puffery and focusing on hard news:

- Does the announcement pass the 'so what?' test. If it's only of interest to the organisation itself, then it should not be made public.

- Write news objectively (except for the quotations). 'X has today announced Y' is better than 'We are pleased to announce Y'.

- A news release is rarely sufficient, and it's too late to do anything with it once it's already been issued. You should develop your media relations skills and pre-brief key contacts before the news has been issued (though you should limit the use of formal embargoes, see below).

Let's review some well-established media relations tools and techniques:

Press releases: These are still necessary and important as a formal document of record, particularly for stock market-listed companies. But they have become overused

and discredited as a marketing and promotional tool. Earl and Waddington summarise the problem: 'Here's the reality; the majority of news releases do not contain news content. The press release has become a general purpose document that an organisation publishes on its website and issues via a wire service, not to inform the media of a news event, but typically to reach broader audiences and to satisfy an internal audience . . . We call them wire fodder or public relations spam' (Earl and Waddington 2012: 100).

Practitioners should be aware of the problem of 'public relations spam' (unsolicited email). The best ways to do this are to ensure that each news release contains news (as distinct from promotional messages) and is narrowly targeted at those who are most likely to value this news. Another approach is to drop the archaic term 'press release' in favour of 'news release'. This should help you argue that point to bosses or clients that 'no news' should mean 'no release'.

There is much talk about the press release/news release becoming the 'social media news release' – targeted not just at news journalists but also at bloggers and designed for social media sharing (Bruce 2012). The goal of traditional media 'coverage' now becomes searchable content, resulting in higher 'organic' placement in searches, reflecting the primacy of Google among media companies.

Press conferences: Outside crisis management situations, large set-piece press conferences are now much less common than the public might imagine from watching television news. The key question with press conferences is 'who benefits from holding one?' If it's being arranged to satisfy the vanity of a boss or client, this may lead to problems. If it's being arranged to suit the demands of the media, then this is the right approach. There are (rare) times when the media demand for timely information is so overwhelming that a press conference is the best way to make this access possible. With a few notable exceptions (such as Apple's new product launches), the circumstances of a well-attended press conference will usually involve a crisis situation (i.e. bad news rather than good news).

A good alternative to set-piece press conferences is to arrange briefing meetings with individual reporters. If these can be detached from specific news announcements, then they are a good means of developing two-way relationships with key members of the media and developing your media relations beyond a tool for one-way publicity.

Embargoes: Public relations news is often worked on for weeks or months before the agreed launch date. An embargo is a media relations technique for giving journalists the story in advance, to help them prepare their reports or packages, on the understanding that publication or broadcast will be held until the agreed launch date. This approach requires a high level of trust on both sides and should be used sparingly. You need to think through your response when someone breaks your embargo (in the competitive news industry, this is highly likely): will you sue the journalist or the publication or programme? Unlikely, and not good media relations. Will you withhold future embargoes from this individual, or this publication/programme? Again, this could be self-defeating. The best approach to embargoes is to use them sparingly, and preferably only when they are offered as a way of helping journalists to do their job.

Exclusives: This is when a 'story' is offered first to one media outlet, while others are excluded from access to the story. They are popular and effective with the tabloid press, which especially values stories that it gets ahead of its competitors. An exclusive does not usually require a news blackout but is usually a question of timing. One outlet could be offered the story early – with all others being offered the story a day later. An exclusive is a useful tool for adding value to a PR-led story, but there are problems with using them. While one publication might welcome being offered your exclusive, you risk annoying or alienating the others. And all publications will be irritated if they find they've all been offered the same exclusive on the same story (in other words, it wasn't an exclusive at all, but a dishonest attempt at PR manipulation).

Non-attributable: Most often used in political communication, a non-attributable briefing is given on the understanding that the source's name will be kept out of the story. This enables a journalist to write an informed piece of speculation using phrases such as 'sources close to the prime minister confirmed . . .'. It benefits the public relations practitioner by enabling them to preserve their good relationship with key members of the media while keeping their job and avoiding becoming the story. That said, there would be few credible 'sources close to the prime minister' who could have discussed the story with that reporter, and suspicion will inevitably fall on the chief press secretary or equivalent. So non-attributable briefing has a place in public relations practice, but should only be used by senior practitioners with good relationships with equally senior reporters.

Bernard Ingham, a government communicator who went on to become chief press secretary to Margaret Thatcher, had earlier (13 April 1976) argued that 'non-attributable briefing has an honourable place in open government . . . It is not necessarily the antithesis of openness' (INGH 1/8).

Off-the-record: It is possible to mount a defence of off-the-record briefing as ethical and professional, but the simple rule should be to avoid using this technique. Only discuss those things with a journalist that you would be prepared to see made public. Never use a phrase like 'strictly off the record' merely to gain a journalist's attention, on the Pandora's Box principle that things that are concealed are more interesting than those that are revealed.

The exceptions usually involve matters of national security, when editors have sometimes been asked to withhold publishing details of military operations or terrorist atrocities to protect lives, to withhold the oxygen or publicity or to preserve public morale. When he was prime minister, Tony Blair gave an off-the-record briefing to editors on the then controversial subject of the MMR vaccine (thought by some to be linked to autism in children). The subject was important because public resistance to the vaccine was causing concern among senior medical practitioners. Tony Blair chose to speak 'off the record' because he faced the conflicting demands of doing the right thing for public health and doing the right thing as a parent keen to protect his children's privacy.

Mini case study 13.1
Risk and public relations

The 2010 Deepwater Horizon accident was 'the first major [oil] spill of the digital age', making BP 'public enemy number one'. Oil companies are better than most at assessing and managing risk, yet the company was seemingly unprepared for this event.

'As the crisis unfolded, the PR industry watched with a mixture of despair and alarm as tried and tested tactics failed to stem the criticism. TV appearances, town hall meetings, press conference apologies – nothing reduced the clamour.' (Burt 2012: 6)

By the time the oil well was sealed, 'more than $100 billion had been wiped off BP's market capitalisation, and the company had set aside $40 billion for compensation. For BP, it was a near-death experience' (Burt 2012: 4–5).

Clearly, this was a major crisis involving much more than media relations, but if a well-managed business such as BP could fall so heavily, who would be immune from media and public criticism?

Commentator Tim Burt believes it's time for PR practitioners to become more proficient in risk management. 'Agencies now have an opportunity to exploit the business world's increased appetite for reputation risk management. They may succeed in this emerging business area only if they establish a credible niche, connecting their media expertise and communication skills to proven risk analysis.' (Burt 2012: 173)

Theories for media relations

Communication theory

Public relations communication necessarily involves the use of some form of media. Meetings, emails, posters are all means of communicating (i.e. media), though mass media communication differs by being mediated by independent parties (journalists and editors). It is this mediation by a third party that explains the strength and the weakness of a media relations approach to communication.

The strength of the traditional approach is that the message is received through a trusted source; the weakness is that the sender loses control of the message and cannot know if or when it will appear, and whether it will be presented favourably or negatively.

Yet, as Yaxley (2012: 423) argues, 'the multi-directional nature of online communications challenges the traditional idea of public relations involving straightforward distribution of a message to a passive audience (though a compliant mediator)'. So we need to review our understanding of how communication works.

Communication theory explains the gatekeeper role of the mass media (Westley and McLean 1957); it explains that people are not solely influenced by the mass media but also by opinion leaders (Katz and Lazersfeld 1955). These and other communication theories remain relevant in the digital age. So what's new?

Authors and commentators are exploring the laws governing online influence: Clay Shirky has explored 'power law distribution' and Jakob Nielsen 'participation inequality'. In essence, despite the democratic appearance of online discussions in which many people have equal access to information, a few people always gain disproportionate attention and influence. We can read almost any website in the world (with some help from tools such as Google Translate), yet we prefer to return again and again to the same, few, trusted sources.

Shirky explains this through the concept of 'publish then filter' (Shirky 2008). There is so much information available since anyone can publish, that we need reliable filters to bring information to our attention (to tell us what to think about). (See Figure 13.1.)

'Publish then filter' has important implications for media relations. In the earlier model ('filter then publish') the skill was to get information published through the many filters provided by professional gatekeepers: news wires, news desks and editors. The skill is no longer in getting something published – anyone can do that. The public relations skill is to make something more widely known by being shared and spread ('going viral').

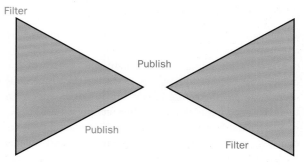

Figure 13.1 'Filter then publish' becomes 'publish then filter' (*source*: adapted from Shirky 2008)

Yet 'publish then filter' reminds us of the continuing influence of the mass media in the social media age. There is so much information, so much rumour, so much opinion that we need the traditional editorial skills of selecting and presenting news and analysis more than ever. I may now hear the news first on Twitter, say, but I will turn to a trusted site such as BBC News before believing and spreading this information. We may all be the media, but we are not all investigative journalists: in *Mediactive* (2010), Dan Gillmor shows how onerous the task of checking facts is, even for experienced reporters. We are all media – yet we are not all investigative journalists – meaning that misinformation can spread faster than the truth.

Media theory

News values: The essential skill for effective media relations is to gain a 'nose for news'. This involves identifying news stories and presenting them in a format that a journalist or editor can understand. So-called 'news values' have been listed by journalists (Hetherington 1985) and academics (Galtung and Ruge 1965). In summary, the most important measure of headline news is that it is something that *affects everyone*. Wars, disease, natural disasters can all meet this criterion, though public relations news rarely does (short of the discovery of a cure for cancer).

Agenda setting: The news media set the public agenda by telling us what to think about (Zoch and Molleda 2006). This theory explains the primacy of media relations in public relations and corporate communication. Which companies are regularly mentioned in the media; and what are they most often associated with? For example, Apple is frequently mentioned, and most often in connection with innovation and product design, conferring competitive advantage over its competitors.

Framing: News is as much a matter of opinion as of objective fact. The capture of a ship by Somali pirates may not make headlines in the UK (since it doesn't affect everyone) – unless a British citizen was harmed or kidnapped. Suddenly the news seems more immediate and important to us when framed in this way. Just as you can crop a photograph to highlight one aspect of the image and exclude others, so news can be framed. If agenda setting theory describes which stories appear in the news, framing is about how they are presented.

Experienced public relations practitioners and political communicators use framing for communicative advantage. Nick Davies cites a striking example in *Flat Earth News*. Following the financial collapse of 2008, bankers are so criticised that it is notable that, as recently as 2004, a public relations practitioner was able to sway public opinion in support of three British bankers charged with fraud in the US over the collapsed energy company Enron.

How did she do this (the PR adviser was Melanie Riley of Bell Yard Communications)? She turned the debate away from a discussion of guilt or innocence into one about the new Extradition Treaty between the US and UK. These discredited bankers became, as the 'NatWest Three', heroes in a struggle for national autonomy (Davies 2008).

Framing has academic respectability (Cornelissen 2011), yet can be seen as a different way to frame the old charge of 'spin'.

Davies outlines the problem: 'Journalists who no longer have the time to go out and find their own stories and to check the material which they are handling, are consistently vulnerable to ingesting and reproducing the packages of information which are provided for them by this PR industry. At the very least, this involves their being directed into accepting stories and angles which have been chosen for them in order to satisfy someone else's commercial or political interests. At the worst, this embroils them in the dissemination of serious distortion and falsehood.' (Davies 2008: 203)

Information subsidy: What Davies has described is information subsidy (Gandy 1982): the way in which public relations provides packaged stories to the news media enabling them to save on the time and expense of investigative journalism. Depending on your perspective, this is either a gift to the media or an attempt to distort debate (for more discussion on information subsidy see Chapter 3). But it helpfully suggests that the news production side of public relations does have a cost, so the description of media placement as 'free advertising' is misleading.

Digital public relations: beyond media relations

It is now possible to see, in retrospect, that media relations played such an important role within public relations during the twentieth century because this was the mass media age. But what is the role of media relations in the more complex media ecosystem (Naughton 2012) of the twenty-first century?

Industry insider Daryl Willcox observes a two-paced industry. 'Those who are not offering a wide, digitally-inclusive consultancy service are making less money because they are trapped in a fiercely competitive and shrinking world of traditional PR.'

Put simply, and this really is a simplification, a fast lane PR professional will understand the fundamental concepts behind search, be good at using lots of different online tools to identify audiences and influencers, identify relevant social media channels and focus on doing them well and be able to adjust their tone when speaking to social media authors rather than just treating [them] in the same way as journalists. (Wilcox 2011)

In this argument, media relations is no longer the primary PR tactic. Practitioners need to broaden their skills into the digital realm and learn to develop relationships with influencers other than journalists. (Some practitioners will argue that they have always focused on the end, not the means to the end; most academics will point out that public relations has never been conceptualised as only media relations.)

In the last century, the decision on media was in effect a choice between '*paid media*' (advertising) and '*earned media*' (via media relations/media publicity). Consultants also describe a third category: '*owned media*'. (http://blogs.forrester.com/interactive_marketing/2009/12/defining-earned-owned-and-paid-media.html)

Owned media has always existed as an expensive option, in the form of sponsored publications and corporate videos, but has become much more credible and much less expensive with the rise of digital broadcasting, the Internet and social media.

Consultant Philip Sheldrake has reconceptualised public relations as being 'the business of influence' (Sheldrake 2011) – a concept echoed by Realwire CEO Adam Parker. 'Media relations are [sic] also likely to remain a major element of a PR practitioner's responsibilities for some time yet. Given the blurring of media boundaries and the importance of key bloggers and other online content producers, perhaps influencer relations may be a more appropriate term these days.' (Parker 2012: 130)

Consultants Steve Earl and Stephen Waddington (2012) argue the need to move beyond media relations: 'Shedding the shackle of media relations will be critical to the future success of the public relations industry. It is inevitable that as traditional media continues to fragment because of technological change, and consumer behaviour becomes increasingly participatory, organisations must change how they communicate.' (Earl and Waddington 2012: 202)

These authors suggest a list of eight key skills and qualities required of practitioners in the new environment:

1. **Branded media:** 'Creativity and editorial skills are required to develop compelling content that engages the target audience.'

2. **Engagement and conversation:** 'Good interpersonal and social skills are essential to represent a brand and be its voice online.'

3. **Speed:** 'Interaction and communication on the web requires a level-headed attitude. Individuals must be calm and considered.'

4. **Planning:** 'Rudimentary mathematics and a familiarity with analytics are increasingly important for practitioners in the development, implementation and measurement of campaigns.'

5. **Monitoring:** 'The Internet doesn't have an "off" button. Business online is relentless. Attention to detail and quick-wittedness are required.'

6. **Integration:** 'Practitioners must be familiar with all aspects of the business and be able to work across functional departments within an organisation.'

7. **Measurement:** 'As with planning, rudimentary mathematics and a familiarity with analytics is increasingly important in the measurement of campaigns.'

8. **Technology:** 'Fearless [sic] and a willingness to test new products and applications are critical to anyone wanting to stay ahead.' (Earl and Waddington 2012: 227–230)

Is this not a case of 'back to the future'? With a few technical exceptions, an experienced practitioner of a century ago (an Ivy Lee or an Edward Bernays) would recognise these demands. Public relations has always been this broad activity, at least in theory. In practice, for much of the twentieth century it became a far narrower media relations function, only to broaden out again at the start of the twenty-first century in response to the changing media landscape.

Yet there are reasons to argue for a continued mix of traditional and digital techniques. In the crowded online space, in which anyone can be a publisher, it is becoming more important than ever to filter out what's important from what's of passing interest. In an age of instant electronic communication, there is still a place for relationships built on face-to-face interaction.

The traditional media act as an important filter to help with information overload. Twitter is not a new channel for news, as some argue, but rather a powerful echo chamber that amplifies the news from the major media and other sources. (See Case study 13.1 and Explore 13.1.)

Picture 13.2 The Great Barrier Reef, Australia – location of 'The Best Job in the World' (see Mini case study 13.2) (*source*: Shutterstock.com/Regien Paassen)

Mini case study 13.2
Functional convergence

As discussed in Chapter 22 marketers are not slow to recognise the power of public relations and media relations. When the Cannes Lions Advertising Industry Awards created a new category for public relations, the first winner (in 2009) was the celebrated 'The Best Job in the World' campaign for Queensland Tourism.

This memorable campaign created a dream role of island caretaker on the Great Barrier Reef, perfectly timed for the Northern Hemisphere winter, and solicited video applications from those wanting to land this a dream job with a large salary. The winner, a British man, had few duties other than to write blog posts about his experiences. The result was a brilliant viral campaign across traditional and social media and more than a year's 'free' publicity for Queensland in Australia.

The campaign is a good example of how public relations can be used to get people talking, without the huge expense of a global advertising campaign. But there's one problem with this narrative: the winning team behind the campaign was Brisbane-based advertising agency, Nitro (now SapientNitro). (See also Mini case study 9.4.)

The heralded 'fall of advertising' need not necessarily result in the 'rise of PR' (Ries and Ries 2002). It may result in a new breed of creative ideas agency capable of implementing their ideas across an appropriate mix of paid, earned and owned media (Bailey 2012).

Case study 13.1

first direct: integrating social media with media relations

first direct is a UK-based retail bank that operates entirely online and via telephone. It is headquartered in Leeds and is a division of HSBC Bank plc. It currently has more than 1.16 million customers and is commonly known as 'the UK's most recommended bank', with more than one in four customers joining because of personal recommendation.

first direct is also known as the UK's 'social media bank' for its range of digital innovations, including: a social media newsroom; a public relations Twitter stream; a Facebook page; a customer service discussion forum, Talking Point; a lifestyle recommendation forum for anything other than banking, Little Black Book; a crowdsourcing customer engagement platform, lab; and a social media aggregation tool, live, that sources and displays every social media mention of first direct on the main site.

In October 2010, first direct had been in operation for 21 years and to champion the bank's position as a financial services innovator during this period, the in-house public relations team, supported by Leeds-based digital public relations agency Wolfstar PR, undertook a media relations campaign around the 'future of banking' – what the financial sector might look like over the next two decades.

The campaign was created in the context of consumer distrust in banks around the recent collapses of financial institutions such as Northern Rock and the Lehman Brothers. The activity was designed to position first direct as sector pioneer and thought leader, in terms of its approach to both customer service and marketing.

For years the process of media relations in the financial sector has remained largely unchanged; traditional media relations is, by its nature, one-way. Client messaging and campaigns are created, then media coverage is sought, but ultimately PR teams are never sure how many people see the messages, or how they consume them.

The thinking behind first direct's 21st birthday campaign recognised that the media and consumer landscape has changed irrevocably, with online media becoming interactive and media titles valuing search-optimised content that now drives almost 50 per cent of all traffic to media sites. The focus was on doing media relations differently – recognising, analysing and understanding the effects social media and search has had on the media landscape, and the willingness to adapt internal processes and established procedures to embrace this change.

Elements of the campaign involved:

- Q & A sessions with first direct CEO Matt Colebrook in *The Times* and Reuters, supplemented with video and a feature in *The Independent*, driven by a series of guest posts and videos from financial analysts. This was hosted within a dedicated 'Banking Future' channel on the Independent.co.uk website.

- Syndicated webchat between Matt Colebrook and three leading banking bloggers who were gauged the most influential in the banking and social media space.

As a result of the activity, Matt Colebrook was quoted heavily in *The Independent* feature on the 'future of banking'. The dedicated channel received around 30,000 hits and the content generated further posts and discussions on web 2.0 and financial blogs, with first direct perspectives on social media and the 'future of banking' becoming the featured top stories on sites including Finextra and Reuters' 'Great Debate'.

The webchat set up with Matt Colebrook and three influential banking innovation bloggers, Chris Skinner, Christophe Langlois and Brett King, transformed first direct's CEO's executive availability in conversing live with 'modern' influencers, as opposed to traditional Q & A media briefings with mainstream journalists. The chat was promoted and embedded on each of the bloggers' sites, reached more than 90,000 people on Twitter and the bloggers' positive comments around first direct's social media strategy prompted a 300 per cent increase in conversation around the bank on financial forums.

Campaign content ranked against key, high-value search terms, with Google recognising 'Matt Colebrook' and 'first direct' as being connected to 'social media bank' and 'future of banking'. This resulted in campaign

case study 13.1 (continued)

content featuring on Google's first pages against these terms, exposing first direct's perspectives and position as the 'future of banking' to more than 55,000 people every month.

According to Amanda Brown, PR Manager, first direct:

> The campaign is representative of the way first direct approaches all public relations activity. We're constantly looking to respond to the changing needs of journalists, influencers and their audiences in order to build productive relationships and generate high-value coverage. Our social media newsroom is first direct's communications mouthpiece and it enables us to provide rich, accessible media content for journalists and bloggers, while allowing us to monitor and refine which content is most useful and effective.
>
> In the future, this willingness to adapt will be no different – at first direct we aim to be present and ready for transparent engagement with our audiences in places of their choosing – whether this be customers on the phone or online 24/7, the media on social channels, or anyone with a general interest in the brand and our products on Facebook and lab.

Case study questions:

1. Can you identify the traditional media relations elements in the case study?

2. How does social media complement this traditional approach?

3. What effects has social media had on the media landscape?

4. How can an in-house team work well with an external consultancy?

5. Is finding a 'big idea' for a campaign becoming more or less important?

Case study answers:

1. Targeting of national media and use of a senior spokesperson in pursuit of 'thought leadership' position.

2. Content for owned media as well as for earned media; greater ability to monitor and evaluate the campaign.

3. Growth in importance of search producing a virtuous circle between social media and traditional media.

4. Each should bring complementary roles and skills. The consultants should bring new ideas and insights to support the in-house team, who take responsibility for – and gain credit for – the campaign.

5. It was always important in a world of 'filter then publish', but is arguably even more important in the 'publish then filter' world of short attention spans and information overload.

Explore 13.1

Publicity: The launch of a new book, film or record is often accompanied by multiple media appearances by the author, leading actor or musician.

Gather recent examples of these appearances from a recent launch and draw your conclusions about the effectiveness of the media strategy. Why would the media channel agree to be a vehicle for this promotional campaign? Is this exposure only available to 'A-list' celebrities?

Social media: Companies and brands monitor their mentions on social media, and you can watch this in action on channels such as Twitter by the use of keyword searches and by following appropriate hashtags (#). Next time you are delighted with a product or a service, why not send a tweet describing your experience. Is the company listening? How do they respond?

Media relations: Journalists are people, and it's never been easier to learn about their social and professional interests. Follow on Twitter some journalists writing about a sector you're interested in. What can you learn about them? Can you find a way to engage them in conversation, and perhaps help them to do their job?

Summary

The media has an important role in a democratic society holding the rich and powerful to account. Bloggers can't and don't do this. Without a formal media relations function, who within an organisation would respond in a timely fashion to legitimate media enquiries? And who would make the case that the media should be given priority access to the diaries of busy chief executives?

Media relations will remain important as long as the media retains its significance in society. But media relations (two-way) should be seen as distinct from media publicity (one-way), and those practitioners whose roles and job titles reflect the primacy of print media (e.g. 'press officer') should be looking to develop their skills in broadcast and online media to reflect the twenty-first century media ecosystem.

The good news for public relations practitioners is that the skills needed for media relations and media publicity should be adaptable to the demand for digital storytelling suitable for the online and mobile environments.

Bibliography

Bailey, R. (2012). 'The future of PR education' in *Share This: The social media handbook for PR professionals*. S. Waddington (ed.). Chichester: Wiley.

Bernays, E. (1928). *Propaganda*. New York, NY: Liveright.

Boorstin, D. (1961). *The Image: Or what happened to the American dream?* London: Weidenfeld & Nicolson.

Borkowski, M. (2006). *The Fame Formula: How Hollywood's fakers, fixers and star makers created the celebrity industry*. Basingstoke: Sidgwick & Jackson.

Bruce, S. (2012). 'Modern media relations and social media newsrooms' in *Share This: The social media handbook for PR professionals*. S. Waddington (ed.). Chichester: Wiley.

Burt, T. (2012). *Dark Art: The changing face of public relations*. London: Elliott and Thompson.

Coombs, W.T. and S. Holladay (2007). *It's Not Just PR: Public relations in society*. Oxford: Wiley-Blackwell.

Coombs, W.T. and S. Holladay (2010). *PR: Strategy and application*. Oxford: Wiley-Blackwell.

Cornelissen, J. (2011). *Corporate Communication: A guide to theory and practice*, 3rd edition. London: Sage.

Davies, N. (2008). *Flat Earth News*. London: Chatto & Windus.

Earl, S. and S. Waddington (2012). *Brand Anarchy: Managing corporate reputation*. London: Bloomsbury.

Ewen, S. (1996). *PR! A social history of spin*. New York, NY: Basic Books.

Fawkes, J. (2012). 'Public relations and communications' in *The Public Relations Handbook*, 4th edition. A. Theaker (ed.). Abingdon: Routledge.

Galtung, J. and M. Ruge (1965). 'The structure of foreign news'. *Journal of Peace Research* (1): 64–90.

Gandy, O. (1982). *Beyond Agenda Setting: Information subsidies and public policy*. Norwood, NJ: Ablex Publishing.

Gillmor, D. (2010). *Mediactive*. www.Lulu.com

Grunig, J. and T. Hunt (1984). *Managing Public Relations*. New York, NY: Holt, Rinehart and Winston.

Hargreaves, I. (2003). *Journalism: Truth or dare?* Oxford: Oxford University Press.

Hetherington, A. (1985). *News, Newspapers and Television*. London: Macmillan.

Hobsbawm, J. (2010). *Where the Truth Lies: Trust and morality in the business of PR, journalism and communications*, 2nd edition. London: Atlantic Books.

Holtz, S. (2002). *Public Relations on the Net*, 2nd edition. New York, NY: Amacom.

Ingham, B. (ND). Personal papers in the Churchill Archives Centre, Cambridge.

Katz, E. and P. Lazersfeld (1955). *Personal Influence*. New York, NY: The Free Press.

L'Etang, J. (2008). *Public Relations: Concepts, practice and critique*. London: Sage.

Levine, R., C. Locke, D. Searls and D. Weinberger (2009). *The Cluetrain Manifesto*, 10th anniversary edition. New York, NY: Basic Books.

Macnamara, J. (2010). *The 21st Century Media (R)EVOLUTION: Emergent communication practices*. New York, NY: Peter Lang.

Miller, D. and W. Dinan (2008). *A Century of Spin: How public relations became the cutting edge of corporate power*. London: Pluto Press.

Moloney, K. (2006). *Rethinking Public Relations: PR propaganda and democracy*, 2nd edition. Abingdon: Routledge.

Morris, T. and S. Goldsworthy (2008). *PR – A Persuasive Industry? Spin, public relations and the shaping of the modern media*. Basingstoke: Palgrave Macmillan.

Naughton, J. (2012). *From Gutenberg to Zuckerberg: What you really need to know about the internet*. London: Quercus.

Parker, A. (2012). 'Media relations modernised' in *Share This: The social media handbook for PR professionals*. S. Waddington (ed.). Chichester: Wiley.

Ries, A. and L. Ries (2002). *The Fall of Advertising and the Rise of PR*. New York, NY: HarperCollins.

Sheldrake, P. (2011). *The Business of Influence: Reframing marketing and PR for the digital age*. Chichester: Wiley.

Shirky, C. (2008). *Here Comes Everybody: The power of organizing without organizations*. London: Penguin Books.

Solis, B. and D. Breakenridge (2009). *Putting the Public Back in Public Relations: How social media is reinventing the aging business of PR*. New Jersey: Pearson Education.

Tench, R. and J. Fawkes (2005). 'Mind the gap, exploring different attitudes to public relations education from employers, academics and alumni.' Paper presented at the Alan Rawel/CIPR Academic Conference, Lincoln.

Westley, B. and M. Maclean (1957). 'A conceptual model for communications research'. *Journalism and Mass Communication Quarterly* **34**(1): 31–38.

White, J. and L. Mazur (1995). *Strategic Communications Management: Making public relations work*. Harlow: Addison-Wesley.

Wilcox, D. (2011). 'PR – a two-speed industry'. www.behindthespin.com/features/two-speed-industry accessed 28 August 2012.

Yaxley, H. (2012). 'Digital public relations – revolution or evolution?' in *The Public Relations Handbook*, 4th edition. A. Theaker (ed.). Abingdon: Routledge.

Young, P. (2012). 'Media relations in the social media age.' *The Public Relations Handbook*, 4th edition. A. Theaker (ed.). Abingdon: Routledge.

Zoch, L. and J. Molleda (2006). 'Building a theoretical model of media relations using framing, information subsidies, and agenda building' in *Public Relations Theory II*. C. Botan and V. Hazleton (eds). Mahwah, NJ: Lawrence Erlbaum Associates.

Website

www.churnalism.com

CHAPTER 14

Liz Yeomans and Wendy Carthew

Internal communication

Learning outcomes

By the end of this chapter you should be able to:

- define internal communication and recognise it in practice
- critically analyse the employee/employer relationship within contemporary organisations and their environments
- describe, analyse and critically evaluate communication roles for effective leadership and management
- describe, analyse and critically evaluate corporate strategies, tactics and evaluation methods for communicating with employees.

Structure

- Definition and purpose of internal communication
- Changes in the external environment affecting an organisation's internal communication
- The changing employee/employer relationship
- Communication roles of leaders and managers
- Organisational culture and values statements
- Developing an internal communication strategy

Introduction

Communication happens inside organisations, whether it is managed or not. Daily interactions between colleagues are a necessary part of getting the job done. But as organisations grow larger and more complex, so do the everyday interactions between colleagues who may be spread across different countries, regions and time zones. For management, engaging staff in the 'bigger picture' – the many challenges, threats and opportunities faced by the organisation as a whole – often requires a formal system of communication.

Internal communication (IC) is a growing specialism inside the broader field of strategic public relations or corporate communication. While public relations has traditionally communicated news and information to an organisation's employees through a house magazine or staff newsletter, this internal communication role has expanded alongside the need for organisations to communicate in a more coordinated way with all their external stakeholders.

Internal communication is not just a concern for multinational or large organisations that need to communicate with thousands of employees. While it is essential for an international company such as Sony or BT to have a sophisticated communication system in order to engage with their employees worldwide, a small, family-owned printing firm also benefits from information sharing and feedback to help the business perform better. Internal communication is also essential where an organisation is re-branding; management has to develop a clear understanding of what employees think – as well as understanding external perceptions.

Public organisations also use internal communication. Hospitals need to tell staff about organisational changes, but also to involve staff in improving the services to patients. In the UK, public organisations regularly survey staff attitudes to determine communication effectiveness.

This chapter discusses the growth of internal communication as a management function; analyses the external factors driving change in organisations; explores the employee and employer perspectives including the concept of engagement and the psychological contract; discusses the importance of organisational culture and leadership as the context for effective internal communication; and identifies the key communication methods and measures of success.

Definition and purpose of internal communication

Internal communication is the term used in the UK and elsewhere to describe an organisation's managed communication system, where employees are regarded as a public or stakeholder group. (See Chapter 8 for further discussion of publics and stakeholders.) In the US, the term most often used is 'employee communication', and another term is 'organisational communication'. Employees are communicated with through a variety of activities, including newsletters, noticeboards, staff briefings and Intranets, to name just a few. But how can internal communication be defined and what is the purpose behind these activities? One definition of internal communication is 'the planned use of communication actions to systematically influence the knowledge, attitudes and behaviours of current employees' (Stauss and Hoffmann 2000: 143). Internal communication is also 'a way to describe and explain organizations' (Deetz 2001, cited in Berger 2008). The former definition sees internal communication as a management activity whereas the latter definition sees internal communication as synonymous with the interactions that make up an organisation. (For other definitions and extensive literature reviews on internal communication, see Welch and Jackson 2007 and Berger 2008.)

With some exceptions, internal communication receives relatively little attention from public relations theorists. Among the PR theorists, Grunig asserts that if a system of two-way symmetrical communications is adopted then 'open, trusting, and credible relationships with strategic employee constituencies [groups] will follow' (Grunig 1992: 559). Kennan and Hazleton (2006) take a relational perspective that places emphasis on trust (between management and employees) and identification or connectedness among employees as the key features of internal relationship building. (Box 14.1 looks at these themes.) And, as we see later in the text, the corporate communication school of thought regards employees as important stakeholders whose behaviour and communication contribute to corporate identity and project it to external stakeholders.

The strategic purpose of internal communication can perhaps best be summarised as one that is concerned with building two-way, trusting relationships with internal publics, with the goal of improving organisational effectiveness.

From the early days of internal communication, some organisations made audiovisual presentations to induct new staff, organised events such as long-service awards and created foyer displays to explain company policy to

Box 14.1

Communication and social media: the issue of trust and connectedness

Social media channels such as Facebook and Twitter are not just creating new opportunities for people to connect with others but are also a risk for employees who post critical comments about their employer, its products or services, or even colleagues. The case of the Apple employee sacked from his job from the Norwich, UK, Apple Store in November 2011 for criticising his iPhone and job (Smith 2011) shows how employers are monitoring social media channels and will take action to protect

their brand's reputation. It also means that trust and connectedness between employers and employees explicitly extends beyond the boundaries of the working day or environment. According to Smith's (2011) news report on the Apple employee's claim for unfair dismissal, the tribunal panel upheld the dismissal because 'Apple had a clear social media policy that banned critical remarks about the brand and the criticisms were particularly damaging because "image is so central to its success"'.

Now consider:

■ How far should an employee's 'brand ambassador' role extend into their life outside of work?

■ What role does trust and employee engagement play in reducing the risk posed by social media to both employees and employers?

■ What are the implications for an individual's right to freedom of expression versus an organisation's right to protect its brand reputation?

Picture 14.1 Social media channels such as Facebook and Twitter are not just creating new opportunities for people to connect with others but are also a risk for employees who post critical comments about their employer, its products or services, or even colleagues (*source*: Chris Rout/Alamy Images)

employees. Today, technology has provided a wealth of new media channels and formats – so that continuous internal news, information and feedback opportunities can be delivered direct to the PC and smartphone. Much of this communication is generated by specialist staff working in PR or corporate communications departments. (See Think about 14.1 on p. 254.)

Skills to strategy

While it is true that organisations need people with writing and editing skills to create internal news content for e-newsletters, factsheets, and so on, there has emerged a more strategic internal communication role that has broadened the scope and complexity of the discipline. Kernaghan et al. noted in 2001 that the internal communication function had 'grown in size, status and access to resources' (Kernaghan

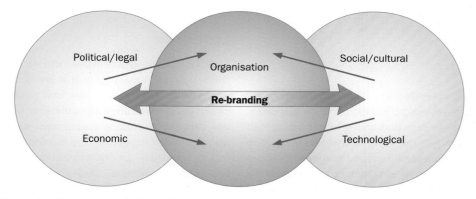

Figure 14.1 Factors leading to strategic internal communication

Think about 14.1   Learning about the organisation

Think about an organisation you have worked for – perhaps as a part-time employee. How were you made aware of the business, its products or services and other activities? Was it through your line manager, colleagues or other methods? List the methods of communication that helped you to understand your employer's business.

Now list the methods of communication that you have used to communicate with a line manager and colleagues. Why did you choose these methods? Consider which methods were likely to be the most effective.

Feedback

It is likely that you will have learned about the organisation from your line manager, more formally, and from your colleagues on an informal basis. Other methods, such as e-newsletters, provide the 'bigger picture' on what the business is about.

However, you may prefer to communicate with people, including your line manager, face to face.

et al. 2001: viii). A decade later, the discipline of 'internal communication and change management' was ranked as fourth in importance by communication practitioners across Europe. This ranking was predicted to rise to second place (equal with marketing/brand and consumer communication) by 2014, which suggests even greater emphasis is being placed on communication with employees to support organisational change and employee engagement (Zerfass et al. 2010). There are a number of factors that influence this 'strategic' approach to internal communication, not least the rapidly changing external environment. (See Figure 14.1 on previous page.)

Changes in the external environment affecting an organisation's internal communication

Hardly any organisation is untouched by political, economic, social and technological (PEST) change. The following PEST analysis (see Chapter 8 for a fuller discussion of environmental analysis) identifies a wide variety of factors affecting organisations and employees in particular.

Political

Trends in the political environment relate to *new legislation, government policy, national politics* and *international politics.* Organisations have to be in tune with governments at both a national and international level – sometimes in order to survive. What happens in national and European elections will shape the direction of government and whether its policies are favourable towards business enterprises and public services.

In recent years, UK organisations of all types have had to become more *accountable* and *transparent* to their stakeholders. Social and environmental reporting have become a requirement within the private sector, whereas in the public sector, government-led quality audits and league tables (for example, for local councils, schools and hospitals) have become the norm. The drive for improved business performance through better management and employee involvement is encouraged by a number of organisations in the UK, such as Investors in People (www.investorsinpeople.co.uk/Pages/Home.aspx), The Work Foundation (www.theworkfoundation.com/) ACAS (www.acas.org.uk/index.aspx?articleid=1461) and the UK Department for Business Innovation and Skills (www.bis.gov.uk).

Since the 2002 European directive on information and consultation, employees in Europe have information rights: a right to be informed about a business's economic situation; a right to be informed and consulted about employment prospects; and a right to be informed about decisions that are likely to lead to major changes in their workplace. All this presents a challenging role for internal communication management during a period of economic turbulence and change.

Economic

Trends in the economic environment are often tied in with political decision making, such as *world trade agreements* or *legislation* surrounding how many companies can be owned by one enterprise. Then there are the laws of *supply and demand*: markets and consumer spending patterns fluctuate. What happens at the macroeconomic level will in turn affect how an organisation conducts its business. For many organisations, it is a matter of keeping costs down while driving up quality to the customer, or end user, resulting in the following:

1. *outsourcing and 'offshoring'*, where services are contracted to an outside organisation or located overseas to reduce costs;

2. *acquisitions*, where a company buys another company (also known as a 'takeover' – see later in the text for a more detailed discussion of company takeovers); and

3. *mergers*, where an organisation merges with another organisation to provide a more cost-effective service.

There is a need for effective, timely communication during these changes because employees may be affected by the consequences. Organisational restructures, relocations, redundancies and contractual changes could mean difficult times ahead for employees. A bank relocating its head office to another part of the country will need to manage communication very clearly and sensitively so that rumour and speculation (for example, about which staff groups are required to move and which are not) do not become 'official' information.

Social (and cultural)

Organisations need to monitor trends in the social and cultural environment because they determine not only which markets are likely to emerge, but also the future availability of skills and knowledge among the population. Global, as well as local, social factors that are likely to have an impact on organisations' recruitment and retention policies include: *demographic structure* of the population (especially *education and qualifications*, skills and competencies); workforce *mobility*; workforce *diversity*; and *career/lifestyle* choices and aspirations. As we identify later in this chapter (see 'Psychological contract'), the nature of employment is changing. Because there is less job security, people (especially the under-35s) have different aspirations and expectations. Moving from job to job to gain experience is increasingly seen as the norm. With increased opportunities for mobility across the globe, more people are seeking job fulfilment elsewhere.

Also, as we shift towards a knowledge-based economy, large numbers of graduates and professional workers are entering the knowledge-based industries, including high tech, financial services, market knowledge services and other services including health, education, recreation and culture. More than 40 per cent of the European workforce was employed in knowledge-based industries in 2005; the UK and Scandinavian countries were among those in Europe having the largest share of employment in the knowledge economy (Brinkley and Lee 2007; Levy et al. 2011). Well-qualified knowledge workers need less supervision, but at the same time they have a higher level of need for involvement and consultation within an organisation.

Technological

Trends in the technological environment are, arguably, one of the most significant shapers of organisations, changing both the nature of work and the nature of jobs. Technology plays a major role in how employees behave – redefining expectations of work turnaround, privacy and politeness norms in an online environment (Eisenberg and Riley 2001).

The widespread use of information and communication technologies has opened up many new, interactive channels for internal communication – email, Intranets and online networking – with the benefits of speed and efficiency of communication and improved access to information.

However, there are drawbacks: the main disadvantages of electronic communication to employee relationships are communication overload and the replacement of face-to-face communication. And as we enter an age where risk and security are a concern for many organisations, there is also the reality of surveillance online (for example, monitoring of external emails and, increasingly, social networking sites) as well as closed-circuit television cameras monitoring behaviour. Such trends threaten rather than encourage good employee relationships, yet in those same organisations 'excellent' two-way internal communication will often be emphasised.

Internal marketing, or 'branding from the inside, out'

Another factor that has led to the rise in strategic internal communication is the adoption of internal marketing techniques. Many organisations are defining brand values that consumers can emotionally identify with (for example, iPhone equals 'cool'). The concept of internal marketing positions employees as internal customers who are the target of marketing campaigns designed to enthuse them to become brand 'champions' or 'ambassadors' for their organisations (Thomson and Hecker 2000). Internally marketing to and through employees can be viewed as controversial; however, many organisations, especially in the service sector, have combined human resource management strategies with internal marketing strategies to leverage the 'emotional capital' of employees (Gould 1998; Thomson 2000) to provide increased external customer satisfaction and loyalty. However, as noted in Box 14.3 later in this chapter, authentic and trusting relationships between organisations and their employees are the key underpinnings of employee commitment.

Location of the IC function

In theory, at least, internal communication viewed as part of the overall communication function may seem fairly straightforward, but who 'owns' the IC function will vary from organisation to organisation. This chapter is placed within a text about public relations, but it would be no surprise to find it in one about strategic marketing or human resources, because both functions have a claim on the IC role. Yet another school of thought sees internal communication as a new management discipline that should ideally report directly to the CEO.

However, throughout this text we have discussed many examples of where internal communication has proven to be a vital component within a broader communication programme in:

■ responding to issues and crises

■ promoting brand values to consumers

■ managing relationships with the community

■ communicating with employees as shareholders.

Wherever the IC function is located, there is still a need for good internal communication management.

Where does internal communication fit into the organisation?

What we call the 'internal communication function' may comprise just one full-time individual, or a team of five or more in a large corporation. In some organisations, the internal communication function may be a 'stand-alone' department reporting directly to the chief executive and in others, to the head of a functional department, such as human resources. A survey of 596 internal communication professionals in the UK found that reporting lines varied across different types and sizes of organisations. The overall picture showed that 38 per cent reported to corporate affairs or corporate communications; 32 per cent reported to human resources; 30 per cent reported to the CEO; and 25 per cent reported to marketing, which demonstrates that in some organisations, IC is accountable to more than one department (Mahdon and Bevan 2007).

For many practitioners working in organisations with small budgets, internal communication and external communication roles will be combined (see also Chapter 6 on the role of the practitioner). Table 14.1 illustrates the most common types of internal communication activities or methods that are undertaken under the 'internal communication' heading. Not all of these activities will be undertaken by a dedicated internal communication professional;

Communication method: number (%) of organisations using method (based on 596 respondents)	% using method
Employee Intranet	92
Regular email announcements	91
Newsletters/magazines	91
Team briefing	91
Face-to-face events	89
Employee consultation	88
Information cascades	87
Upward communication and feedback channels	84
Employee surveys	77
Exit interviews	72
Recognition schemes	66

Table 14.1 Most common methods used in internal communication across all organisations in the UK (*source*: adapted from Mahdon and Bevan 2007: 35)

some, such as recognition schemes, will be the responsibility of human resources, while holding team briefings will be the responsibility of line managers. Figure 14.2 shows a hypothetical reporting structure for internal communication.

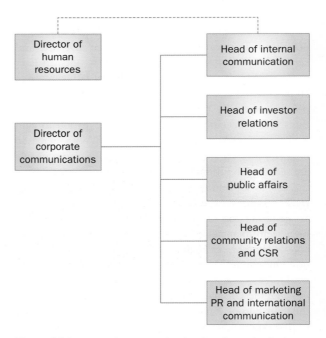

Figure 14.2 Internal communication in a hypothetical organisation

To carry out the internal communication activities shown in Table 14.1, budget size will play an important role. In 2007, the budgets for internal communication in the UK had increased in 42 per cent of organisations surveyed, especially in the voluntary sector, with the majority of organisations dedicating more than £50,000 to internal communication activities. A key finding of the Work Foundation study was that internal communication professionals believed that their main role was to help staff understand the business (Mahdon and Bevan 2007).

The changing employee/ employer relationship

Employee perspective: the 'psychological contract'

Even before the global financial crisis of 2008 affected organisations across all sectors, not just financial, the world of work was evolving and changing the relationship between employees and employers. The last two decades has seen a significant increase in mergers and acquisitions alongside the restructuring and downsizing of many organisations. Such changes inevitably have a negative impact on employees in the form of job losses, job uncertainty, ambiguity and heightened anxiety (Cartwright and Holmes 2006).

Against a backdrop of rapid social, demographic and technological change, the increasing demands on organisations has without doubt increased demands on employees. In Western society, we also see a breakdown of community and a growing culture of consumerism where commercial values and corporate scandals challenge the confidence and trust that shareholders, employees and customers have in business leaders (Cartwright and Holmes 2006).

For employees, in particular, the nature of the *psychological contract* with their employer is also challenged. When it emerged in the 1960s, the psychological contract referred to an employee offering commitment to an employer in exchange for job security. But, since then, as employers cannot offer job security, a new contract has emerged.

'Employee value proposition'

Towers Watson's 2010 report into communications return on investment defines the new employment deal in terms of the 'employee value proposition (EVP)'. Similarly to the psychological contract, the EVP broadly refers to what employees can expect from the company and what the company expects from its employees. The 'new deal' means employees are expected to commit to working harder, longer hours and take on more responsibility in exchange for training and development to increase future employability, fair pay and treatment. (See Think about 14.2.)

All this is changing the relationship between employers and employees. As employers need to deliver more for customers, stakeholders and shareholders through their employees, employees themselves are becoming more demanding about what they want from their working life.

Today, the psychological contract emphasises that employment is a *relationship* in which the mutual obligations of employer and employees may not be precise but have to be respected (CIPD 2011). It is based on the beliefs, values, expectations and aspirations of both the employee and employer, and, as such, *trust* underpins the nature of the contract and its maintenance (Middlemiss 2011).

Atkinson (2007) explored trust and the psychological contract concluding that *cognitive* trust – defined as being rational and calculative, focusing on an individual's gains, such as pay – needs to develop before *affective* (emotional) trust can be possible. While breaches of both types of trust undermine the relationship between employers and employees, it is *affective* trust that is linked to employees enhancing their contribution to an organisation (Atkinson 2006).

Mini case study 14.1
Public sector employees and the issue of 'trust'

Industrial action in November 2011 by public sector union members in the UK over proposed changes to pension arrangements can be considered the result of a perceived breach of cognitive trust between the Government and public sector employees. If, as shown by Atkinson (2006), cognitive trust appears to operate as a 'hygiene factor' that must be adequate before a relationship can move to a more relational/affective level, the current economic and political climate presents organisations with additional challenges in engaging employees. But she also shows that breaches of cognitive trust do not necessarily reduce affective trust – where it already exists.

*Note: Hygiene factors were first identified in a 1959 study of motivation and job satisfaction by Frederick Hertzberg (1959), which led to his two-factor theory of motivation.

Think about 14.2

Trust and the psychological contract

How might understanding the nature of *trust* and the *psychological contract, or EVP,* help internal communicators to build two-way, trusting relationships with internal publics to improve organisational effectiveness?

Feedback

Guest and Conway (2001: 19) concluded that a wide range of approaches to communication helps to set and reinforce the psychological contract. But it is those closest to day-to-day performance and to the job that are most effective. This supports the view that the manager–worker relationship lies at the heart of the psychological contract or EVP.

It is not news that managers are key to effectively delivering messages and engaging employees. When leaders and managers convey confidence to employees, they build trust, which can help stoke employee engagement. In many ways, managers are the face of the organisation for employees – translating mission, values and strategy into behaviour and words (Towers Watson 2011: 19). Supporting and coaching managers to develop their communication skills is one of the roles of the internal communicator (see communication roles later in the section.)

We can see that temporary contracts, part-time working, irregular shift patterns, as well as professional, social and cultural factors, may give rise to an employee's 'disconnectedness' from the organisation and a resistance to corporate messages. Quarterly research by the CIPD on job satisfaction, trust and fairness shows that the recession has had an increasingly negative impact on UK employees' attitudes. It suggests that managers face a serious challenge to restore and maintain employees' commitment in both private and public sectors (CIPD 2011). (See Mini case study 14.1 and Box 14.2 for more discussion about the employee/employer relationship.)

It is not just managers and leaders who are challenged, but also internal communicators. Later in the chapter, we discuss communication effectiveness. Towers Watson's 2010 study concludes that high-performing companies do not shy away from tough messages, and acknowledge when the new deal is different. It also emphasises that discipline in communication is needed – establishing metrics and holding the communication function accountable for results tied to the business strategy. As Quirke (2008: 327) says: 'The bottom line for internal communication is its contribution to the bottom line'.

Employer perspective: employee engagement

In recent years, the notion of *employee engagement* has become increasingly important to organisations, particularly as they fight to survive and remain competitive during the unprecedented global economic downturn fuelled by the financial crisis of 2008. (Box 14.3 defines employee engagement.)

Box 14.2

The psychological contract

The psychological contract may have implications for organisational strategy in a number of areas, for example:

■ **Process fairness**: people want to know that their interests will be taken into account when important decisions are made; they would like to be treated with respect; they are more likely to be satisfied with their job if they are consulted about change.

■ **Communications**: an effective two-way dialogue between employer and employees is a necessary means of giving expression to employee 'voice'.

■ **Management style**: in many organisations managers can no longer control the business 'top down' –

they have to adopt a more 'bottom up' style. Crucial information, which management need, is known by employees from their interactions with customers and suppliers.

■ **Managing expectations**: employers need to make clear to new recruits what they can expect from the job. Managing expectations, particularly when bad news is anticipated, will increase the chances of establishing a realistic psychological contract.

■ **Measuring employee attitudes**: employers should monitor employee attitudes on a regular basis as a means of identifying where action may be needed in order to improve performance.

Source: CIPD Factsheet: The Psychological Contract, January 2008. The Chartered Institute of Personnel and Development, with the permission of Chartered Institute of Personnel and Development, London (www.cipd.co.uk)

Think about 14.3   Enhancing dialogue

How could internal communication be used to enhance the psychological contract, or EVP, by employees and employers? To what extent should internal communication give expression to the employee 'voice' in comparison to the employer's?

Feedback

Up until recently, internal communication has controlled and managed corporate messages using mainly one-way channels with a subsequent degree of distrust and resistance from employees who may view it as management propaganda. While face-to-face communication remains the most highly valued channel by employees (Haas 2007, cited in White et al. 2010), due to its ability to facilitate dialogue, social media is opening new channels that have potential to give expression to the employee voice and support conversations across all levels within organisations. Embracing the opportunity that social media presents is a new challenge for internal communicators and leadership teams, with some doing so more successfully than others.

Organisations' enthusiasm for creating and building employee engagement is not surprising given the credit attributed to it for improving performance. In 2008, the UK Government commissioned an in-depth report on its potential benefits for companies, organisations and individual employees. 'Engaging for Success: enhancing performance through employee engagement' made a strong case for engagement with its authors MacLeod and Clarke (2009: 5) stating:

We believe the evidence we cite of a positive correlation between an engaged workforce and improving performance is convincing.

Box 14.3

Defining employee engagement

'We believe it is most helpful to see employee engagement as a workplace approach designed to ensure that employees are committed to their organisation's goals and values, motivated to contribute to organisational success and are able at the same time to enhance their own sense of well-being.

'Engaged organisations have strong authentic values, with clear evidence of trust and fairness based on mutual respect, where two-way promises and commitments – between employers and staff – are understood, and are fulfilled.'

Source: MacLeod and Clarke 2009: 9

While the evidence for pursuing engagement as an organisational/strategic goal seems clear, defining employee engagement is not easy and raises questions about whether it is 'old wine in a new bottle' (Fawkes 2007; MacLeod and Clarke 2009).

In broad terms, employees are engaged when they are thinking about work, feeling involved in work and are willing to 'go the extra mile' to deliver beyond their contract (Truss et al. 2006; Quirke 2008). But, as we have seen from the psychological contract, employers are facing the challenge of rising employee cynicism and need to take care that approaches to engagement are genuine. Differing views of what engagement is, how it feels and what it results in means it is likely to be problematic, even for the most highly competent leader. Despite this, the business benefit means that interest in improving engagement is rising. (See Think about 14.3 and Box 14.4 overleaf.)

Drivers of employee engagement

A variety of researchers have attempted to identify key drivers, but exactly what influences engagement is dependent on a wide variety of factors such as the culture and leadership of an organisation, as well as employee demographics (Melcrum 2005).

In their research on employee attitudes and engagement, Truss et al. (2006: 45) found the main factors influencing employee engagement are:

- Having opportunities to feed your views upwards

- Feeling well informed about what is happening in the organisation

- Thinking your manager is committed to the organisation.

However, Smythe (2007: 80) contends that organisations should identify the drivers of engagement that are

Box 14.4

Benefits of employee engagement

■ Research suggests a positive relationship between engaged employees and customer engagement, expressed in customer loyalty and recommendations to others.

■ Engaged employees are more likely to stay with the organisation, perform 20 per cent better than their colleagues, and act as advocates of the organisation.

■ Engagement can have a significant impact on the performance of the organisation, driving bottom-line profit and enabling organisational agility and improved efficiency in driving change initiatives.

■ Engagement may enable individuals to invest themselves fully in their work, with increased self-efficacy and a positive impact on the employee's health and well-being, which in turn evokes increased employee support for the organisation.

Source: Adapted from Robertson-Smith and Markwick 2009

Think about 14.4

Leader's style and personality in engaging employees

How might a leader's style and personality impact on their ability to engage employees?

Richard Branson of Virgin and the late Steve Jobs of Apple are well-known leaders of highly successful, global businesses. Both are known as 'charismatic' (see discussion below on the styles of leadership). But while Jobs was considered autocratic, managing detail and controlling the company rigorously, Branson is seen to be more relaxed and interested in people, keen to listen and engage. What's your perception of them as leaders? What impact have they had on their organisations?

peculiar to them and trust their instincts by shaping the experience of work around them. What is clear is the influence of an organisation's leadership and the effectiveness of communication within it. Smythe (2007) emphasises the challenges and opportunities for leaders and internal communicators that engaging employees presents. Smythe (2007) and Tourish (2008) challenge the traditional view of a 'good' leader being a charismatic figurehead whose personality pervades the organisation by dominance rather than through engagement, and suggest a different style is needed to engage – a communicative leader with a collaborative and inclusive approach to engaging employees.

Coaching and advising leaders and managers on communication to develop their capabilities, as well as providing insight into what employees are thinking and feeling, are, arguably, the roles of the internal communication manager. The variety of factors influencing engagement and employee motivation, including career development and reward and recognition, means that human resources professionals often lead employee engagement strategies. With the knowledge and expertise that HR and internal communication professionals offer, it makes sense that the functions collaborate with an organisation's leaders to develop and implement engagement strategies successfully. (See Think about 14.4.)

Communication roles of leaders and managers

Leadership role: from monologue to dialogue

Although the chief executive officer (CEO), or the equivalent leader, of an organisation is 'automatically the designated chief communication officer' (White et al. 2010: 4), it does not follow that leaders have the natural aptitude to communicate effectively with their employees. Indeed, as Tourish (2008) points out, 'charismatic' or 'transformational' leaders tend towards an autocratic style of leadership, which, in turn, means a top-down, one-way style of communication is adopted and upward feedback from employees is resisted.

We are all shaped by our experience and environment, including our national culture. And organisations' leaders are no exception.

A key researcher in the field of national cultures and their impact on leadership is Hofstede (1991), who identified four dimensions of national cultures:

Table 14.2 Four styles of leadership in strategic change (*source*: adapted from Smythe 2004: 34–35 and reproduced with kind permission of John Smythe and McKinsey & Company)

Approach to strategic change	Methods used
Telling (traditional information campaign)	Fragmented 'drip-feeding' news; cascade briefings; executive roadshows; profiles and interviews in internal newsletters; corporate videos; feedback/dialogue to check with compliance of targets; change agents' network as a channel to deliver the message Role of leader: 'Gaining compliance'
Selling (internal marketing or persuasive approach)	Spectator events; entertainment; some attempts to collect ideas to influence change or create 'a sense of involvement'; 'back to the floor' communication by bosses; employee suggestion schemes and staff attitude surveys that do not lead to change; customers illustrating their experiences/issues; role play to understand behavioural challenges; change agents' network offering workshops for people to explore the rationale for change; celebration of milestones of achievement Role of leader: 'Enabling other people to discover what you have already discovered/decided by giving them a taste of the experience'
Individual accountability (on-the-job change involving individual self-evaluation; learning and problem solving)	Web-based consultation and learning; problem solving by small task groups or teams; clear definitions of expected behaviours; coaching to support individual change; opportunity for staff to explore evidence for change and propose solutions and targets; corporate 'university' to equip people with skills needed; change agents' network to facilitate opportunities for people to discover, learn and adapt; leadership development programme Role of leader: 'Driving ownership down to individuals'
Co-creation (participative decision making)	Business simulation games; giving people the actual business challenge; shopfloor participation in designing engagement experiences; employee involvement that visibly influences the agenda; job swapping internally or externally; engagement workshops or local teams to identify a small number of high-priority symbols/habits to change/develop Role of leader: 'More guide than god'

1. *Power distance* – the distribution of power in organisations (i.e., between leaders and subordinates).

2. *Uncertainty avoidance* – how far a society feels threatened by uncertain situations and the rules it establishes to avoid uncertainty.

3. *Individualism* versus *collectivism* – whether people see themselves as needing to look after their own and their family's interests above societal concerns, or as loyal to a community that, in turn, will look after them.

4. *Masculinity* versus *femininity* – the dominant values in a society (e.g., assertiveness, competition as masculine values).

Sadler (2001) argues that leaders are more likely to be able to enact the role as 'change agents' in cultures where power distance is low and tolerance of uncertainty is high. In Scandinavian countries, for example, employees are more likely to participate in decision making (see 'co-creation' in Table 14.2), because such a leadership style is culturally more acceptable.

In an age when symbolic acts help us make sense of the world, leaders have to 'show the way' to employees through 'symbolic acts of leadership and the rituals used to engage and enrol them' (Smythe 2004: 20). Leaders engage employees strategically through monologue (transmission of messages) or dialogue (conversations). As we can see in Table 15.2, Smythe identifies four different approaches to leading employees in strategic change:

1. telling

2. selling

3. individual accountability

4. co-creation.

Mini case study 14.2

Council engages employees to make 'Smarter Choices for Harder Times'

The global financial crisis has led to deep and protracted cuts to funding the UK's public sector. In response, South Lanarkshire Council, Scotland, chose to engage its employees in working out how to manage reductions while maintaining quality service delivery. Internal communication with its 16,000 employees was vital to involving people in finding innovative solutions.

The Council launched an internal campaign, 'Hard Choices for Hard Times', in September 2009 to explain the difficult choices it faced, with an overall strategy of 'Explanation, reassurance, action'.

The campaign included:

■ A leaflet with a personal message from the Chief Executive asking for input to tackle the unprecedented financial challenge

■ Team briefings, Intranet information and discussions with trades unions

■ A promise to keep in touch with employees, sharing financial information and examples of good practice to show employees how savings could be achieved.

In February 2010, following conversations with employees, the campaign became 'Smarter Choices for Harder Times'. This included an hour-long budget 'Question Time' with the Chief Executive and 100 of the Council's staff representing a cross-section of their colleagues. An edited DVD recording of the session was then shown at a series of facilitated workshops, to which every employee was invited and involved answering questions such as 'What role do I play?'. Employees also received an updated 'Smarter Choices' leaflet and were assured that the Chief Executive would respond personally to every question asked or suggestion made.

Evaluation showed that direct consultation with every employee generated a genuine sense of involvement, with employees feeling that their input was valued. The campaign cost less than £10,000, while the Council identified more than £6m potential savings from ideas submitted and received a total of 5,603 responses from employees. 'Smarter Choices' is now part of the Council's culture and was reflected in its 2010 employee survey results: 72 per cent agreed they were involved in decisions that affect their work, 78 per cent agreed they were encouraged to express their ideas and new ways of working, 83 per cent agreed that overall information about the Council was communicated well, 85 per cent believed they were able to make a positive difference to the organisation's performance and 88 per cent agreed that they were proud to work for South Lanarkshire Council.

Source: By kind permission of Corporate Communications and Public Affairs, South Lanarkshire Council

---

Table 14.2 suggests that a particular strategic approach is consciously chosen by the organisational leader. However, in reality such choices are often instinctive, reflecting the leader's experiences. It is also likely that more than one of the approaches will be adopted (Smythe 2004). Mini case study 14.2 demonstrates how a local council successfully engaged its employees, through consultation, in finding ways to save money.

Line manager role: listening and interpreting

Throughout this chapter we have stressed the importance of the line manager's role in communicating with their staff. However, line managers (who are part of middle management) may not always be the best communicators. Middle managers have traditionally been viewed as 'blockers' of information because they may perceive sharing information as a threat to their own status.

Good communication skills can sometimes be confused with good presentation skills, when in reality a wide variety of communication skills are needed to deal with large and small groups and one-to-one situations. It is increasingly recognised that line managers need well-developed listening skills to interpret messages from staff and well-developed judgement to interpret the messages cascaded through senior management from the board.

Studies show that line managers are the most trusted source of information among employees, with one of the most common channels used being team briefing. Team briefing is a method of communication whereby a line manager briefs their team – usually on a regular basis – about company policy and on day-to-day issues related to the completion of team tasks. Team briefings are often structured to allow for staff feedback and questions. While

Think about 14.5   Segmentation

Can you think of other ways of segmenting employees?

How could segmenting employees and increasing understanding of who works for an organisation help to build a culture of trust and engagement?

Feedback

There are many other ways of segmenting internal publics. Some organisations tune in to groups of employees' lifestyles as a way of connecting with them; others have to consider 'hard-to-reach' internal publics, such as 'remote' (people working at home or on maternity/paternity leave) or mobile workers (for example, sales staff who are mainly on the road or nurses working in the community). Employees may also be shareholders and members of the local community, which is why it is important to have a coordinated communication approach to avoid misunderstandings. Understanding the opportunities for contact with some groups of employees is a key challenge but one that employees value. As discussed earlier, key drivers to engagement may be different for each organisation, but knowing your employees, appreciating and recognising what they know and what they contribute to the organisation will create a more engaged workforce.

elements of team briefings may be prepared by the internal communication function, it is the line manager who shares the corporate messages with his or her team.

In developing an internal communication strategy (see below), the ability to build strong networks and relationships with line managers as well as senior managers is a key competence of the internal communication manager (Chalmers 2008). As discussed earlier, internal communication practitioners may be called upon to provide advice and coaching to line managers to develop their communication competencies.

Segmenting internal publics

When employees are discussed, there is sometimes an assumption that they are a single, homogenous group who share the same worldview; as we have seen already, this is not the case. Employees can be segmented (broken down into categories) as follows:

- demographics – age, gender, income, educational/skill level

- psychographics – personality, attitudes, values, behaviours

- staff groups – top management (or the board), senior/middle managers, frontline employees, supervisors and junior managers, specialist professional employees, overseas employees, pensioners

- contract with the organisation – full time, part time or temporary

- geographical location – head office, regional office, manufacturing plant.

Attitudes are a conventional way of segmenting employees, particularly in relation to the psychological

contract (discussed earlier), the organisation's strategic direction and communication. We identified earlier that the rise of internal communication as a discipline is largely due to factors driving the organisational environment and organisational change. In discussing employees' attitudes to organisational change, Quirke categorises employees as shown in Figure 14.3.

'*Unguided missiles*' refers to employees who are willing to help but unclear about the direction their organisation is taking. Quirke asserts that 50 per cent of employees do not know what the strategy is and these are often the people who are on the frontline dealing with customers. Their notion of strategy may be based on past practice rather than current thinking. An MCA/MORI study conducted in 1998 labelled this group 'loose cannons', claiming that 14 per cent of the UK workforce fit this category (Thomson and Hecker 2000).

'*Hot shots*' refers to the group of enthusiastic employees who are totally in tune with their organisation's direction and their own role within it. The MCA/MORI research identified this group (37 per cent) as '*champions*' or '*advocates*'.

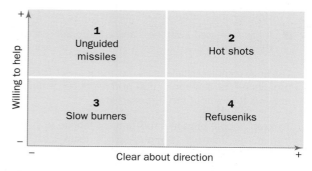

Figure 14.3 Different degrees of employee clarity and willingness (*source*: Quirke 2000: 12)

Think about 14.6   Employee attitudes research

Does it help the communication function to label groups of employees, as in Figure 14.3? What are the implications of this segmentation for the IC practitioner in devising a communication plan?

Feedback

For the IC practitioner, it is important to understand not just who the 'hot shots' and 'champions' are who will be committed to a change initiative, but to understand how the 'refuseniks' or 'saboteurs' communicate. While

the two last groups may never support a change programme, and indeed could actively disrupt it, they should not be ignored completely as they could present management with issues for the future. The danger in labelling groups of employees is that we can forget they are human beings who expect to be treated as such.

However, it is the informal side of the organisation where we find clues on how employees communicate – and connect – with each other.

Mini case study 14.3

eBay connects its European employees

In January 2009, faced with a need to engage employees following a regional restructure, eBay Europe launched its European Team Brief (ETB) – an interactive video conference to deliver its weekly business updates to employees.

Since the launch of the ETB, eBay's European communication and leadership team report that:

- The channel cuts through the noise that a fast-moving Internet-based organisation generates and is their lead channel.

- It reaches 700 employees weekly in 15 locations and 12 countries.

- High levels of participation are enhanced by not recording it, so employees who do not attend feel like they are missing out.

- It has broken down hierarchies by generating high levels of interaction between leaders and employees – it's a two-way, not a top-down channel.

- Participants feel better informed about business strategy and performance than they have ever been.

- It has increased awareness and collaboration across the region.

The huge technical challenge is met using a user-friendly, broadband hi-definition and hi-fi videoconferencing network throughout the European sites.

To keep people engaged and prevent fatigue with the format, the internal communications team treat the channel like a live TV show with all the discipline needed to run one, including constantly looking for small improvements.

In 2011, eBay added a new audience voting feature, ETB Live, which allows employees to connect using mobile devices and internal wi-fi to take part in instant surveys, submit questions and provide feedback to presenters.

Another addition is the use of roving reporters at each location to get employees talking. Each reporter has access to ETB Live so they can pose attendees' questions to the presenters, helping to manage the gap between presenter and audience.

So what do eBay's employees think of the ETB? The numbers revealed by the 2011 annual survey speak volumes:

Keeps me in touch with eBay Europe business strategy	99%
Keeps me in touch with eBay Europe leadership	85%
Informs me about what's happening in the business	97%
Keeps me in touch with other teams and functions in eBay Europe	82%
An important part of the culture in eBay Europe	81%
Provides content at a level I can understand	93%
Helps me understand how eBay is moving in the right direction as a business	92%
Keeps me informed about partner businesses within eBay	82%

Figure 14.4 Feedback on eBay's European Team Brief (ETB)

Find out more on: http://www.youtube.com/watch?v=T9cLbQyRHeg&feature=player_embedded. This case study summarises ETB practice at eBay until the beginning of 2012.

Source: adapted from http://www.simply-communicate.com/case-studies/company-profile/ebay-europe-enhances-its-popular-virtual-team-meetings. With thanks to Richard Davies, Employee Engagement, eBay Europe

'*Slow burners*' describes employees who are 'not knowing and not caring' (Thomson and Hecker 2000: 13). In reality, this is a mix of people who feel unmotivated through a lack of direction and those who prefer to follow their own priorities. This group roughly corresponds to the MCA/MORI study, which calls this group '*weak links*', typically 'switched off' and representing 39 per cent.

'**Refuseniks**' refers to employees who understand the organisation's direction but are most resistant to organisational change. Such groups may actively disagree with proposed changes and feel that their professionalism is under threat. The MCA/MORI study identified this group (deemed to be one in five employees in the UK) as '*saboteurs*' (Thomson and Hecker 2000). (Now read Think about 14.5 and 14.6.)

Networks

Places where people gather inside organisations, such as by watercoolers, in corridors and in post rooms, tend to be where the latest information, rumours and gossip can be shared. Informal networks play an important role in organisational communication, but traditionally they have been downplayed or frowned on in management handbooks because they are outside management's control. And yet, informal networks often provide employees with meaningful interpersonal relationships, self-respect, greater job satisfaction and knowledge about their organisation (Conrad and Poole 1998). For example, an active networker who regularly attends management meetings – perhaps to take the minutes – might be regarded as the 'official' source of information by their informal network and so will enact the role of informant about 'what really goes on'.

As organisations become more fluid and their boundaries more permeable across time zones and cultures, it is clear that networks have become increasingly important. Most internal communication practitioners play a role in creating and enabling networks, such as 'Intranets, cross-functional teams, knowledge management databases, and even informal grapevines' (Kernaghan et al. 2001: 58). In a Web 2.0 environment, enabling and supporting networks takes on even greater importance, as illustrated in Mini case study 14.3 which discusses eBay's European team brief (ETB).

Now consider:

■ What are the strengths and weaknesses of the ETB as a communication channel?

■ What conditions do you think might need to exist in an organisation for it to adopt a similar approach to team briefings?

■ What roles do eBay's European leadership and internal communications team play in ensuring the success of this channel?

Organisational culture and values statements

Corporate culture

Broadly speaking, there are two views of organisational culture: the first sees culture as something that can be influenced, shaped and managed to the liking of top management ('**corporate culture**'); the second sees organisation *as* a culture that is, in turn, made up of subcultures formed from different networks and groups that make up the organisation ('**organisational culture**').

The 'corporate culture' view is attractive to ambitious chief executives who believe that their organisation can be completely changed – if influenced, shaped and managed in the right way. An infamous example of this is the 'corporate culture' imposed by Enron, for example, whose chief executive insisted on the recruitment of 'high flyers' – well-educated, tough-dealing, competitive people with high-level career aspirations who were willing to sacrifice personal relationships and family life for the benefit of

> **Definition:** A '*refusenik*' was a citizen of the former Soviet Union, especially a Jewish person, who was not allowed by the government to emigrate. Now the term refers to somebody who refuses to cooperate with something.

> **Definition:** *Corporate culture* means 'values or practices that account for an organisation's success and that can be managed to produce better business outcomes' (Eisenberg and Riley 2001: 209).
>
> **Definition:** '*Organisational culture*' is . . . a pattern of shared basic assumptions that was learned by a group as it solved its problems of external adaptation and internal integration, that has worked well enough to be considered valid, and therefore, to be taught to new members as the correct way to perceive, think, and feel in relation to those problems' (Schein 2004: 15).

Box 14.5

Values statements of leading organisations

Example 1: Toyota

'Globalisation has led Toyota to create a remarkably **multicultural environment,** with 63 nationalities in our Brussels Head Office alone. This environment is reflected in the diversity of our ideas and concepts, making for a rich and unique working atmosphere.

Toyota believes that an effective workplace is one that allows people of different ages, genders, ethnic groups and cultural backgrounds to work together as a team. We believe in **challenges** and the importance of decisions based on personal investigation, efficient fact-finding and in-depth analysis. Working at Toyota is also an exercise in **long-term thinking**.

Toyota Way
Toyota has a very strong culture called the **Toyota Way**. The Toyota Way is supported by two main pillars. They are "Continuous Improvement" and "Respect for People". We are never satisfied with where we are and always improve our business by putting forth our best ideas and efforts. We respect people, and believe the success of our business is created by individual efforts and good teamwork. All Toyota team members, at every level, are expected to use these principles in their daily work and interactions.

Our future is your future. Our commitment to improvement and development applies not just to our products and work ethics but also to our staff. We encourage training at all levels, along with structured management support and extensive growth opportunities within Toyota Motor Europe.'

Source: www.toyotajobs.com/ENG/Workingat.aspx

Example 2: The Co-operative Group

'At The Co-operative we encourage new ideas to tackle issues that are important to our members – from helping the community to changing the world. Membership is open to everyone as long as they share our values and principles. Our members show these values by working together for everyone's benefit, and are encouraged to play a full part in the community. Here are our underlying values and principles which influence The Co-operative Membership and the way we run all of our businesses:

Our co-operative values

■ Self-help – we help people to help themselves

■ Self-responsibility – we take responsibility for, and answer to, our actions

■ Democracy – we give our members a say in the way we run our businesses

■ Equality – no matter how much money a member invests in their share account, they still have one vote

■ Equity – we carry out our business in a way that is fair and unbiased

■ Solidarity – we share interests and common purposes with our members and other co-operatives.

Our ethical values

■ Openness – nobody's perfect, and we won't hide it when we're not

■ Honesty – we are honest about what we do and the way we do it

■ Social responsibility – we encourage people to take responsibility for their own community, and work together to improve it

■ Caring for others – we regularly fund charities and local community groups from the profits of our businesses.'

Source: www.co-operative.coop/corporate/aboutus/our-democracy/The-Co-operative-Group-Values-and-Principles/

Think about 14.7   Values statements

Drawing on your own experience, perhaps as a part-time employee, critique the two statements in Box 15.5 in terms of helpfulness to employer and employee. In doing so, think about:

■ how far organisations consult/engage employees when devising their values; and

■ the role of an organisation's leaders in visibly upholding its values internally and externally in terms of reputation management.

Think about 14.8

Organisational culture

Think about an organisation with which you are familiar (this may be a college, university or an organisation where you work part time). Can you identify aspects of its culture? For example, do people tend to communicate in a particular way (e.g., emails in preference to face-to-face meetings)? Why? Does their dress code reflect a preferred style? Do people in general like or dislike their work? Why? Does the work environment encourage or suppress self-expression and ideas? Why?

Feedback

From this exercise you will probably see how difficult it can be to be precise about culture. As Eisenberg and Riley (2001) suggest, a starting point for research might be the 'psychological contract' that we referred to earlier. Within a global economy that has encouraged workforce mobility, how and to what extent do employees identify with an organisation? Scholars such as Banks (2000) believe that we need to have a better understanding of subcultures and diversity across industries in order to conduct more meaningful and culturally aware public relations and internal communication. (For more discussion on cross-cultural communication, see Chapter 5.)

Indeed, a cultural perspective recognises that organisations comprise a collection of subcultures, where some employees 'choose not to participate in an organisation's key rituals or may participate for different reasons' (Conrad and Poole 1998: 117). Nevertheless, the management of culture, through the circulation of mission, vision and values statements, often forms the basis of a culture change and engagement programmes in which the communication function will play a significant role. But it is important that the internal communicator recognises that not all employees want to be uniformly engaged, and resistance may result from internal communication programmes that are not carefully thought through. (See Think about 14.7.)

Organisational culture

Conrad and Poole (1998: 116) argue that organisational cultures are 'communicative creations'. This refers to the idea that employees produce and sustain culture by communicating with each other; culture is not created by senior management. Organisational culture may, therefore, be defined as 'taken for granted shared meanings that people assign to their surroundings' (Conrad and Poole 1998: 116). Drawing on his extensive research in organisations, Schein defines organisational culture as 'a pattern of shared basic assumptions' (2004: 15). These shared assumptions are taught to new members as the correct way to perceive, think and feel in relation to a problem. (See Think about 14.8.)

the company (Boje et al. 2004). Other commentators have pointed to successful brands such as Disney, McDonald's and Pepsi for their conscious focus on corporate culture, as these companies have striven for the correct alignment of shared values and practices – in other words, employees are required to share the espoused values and practices of the company. Box 14.5 contains the values statements from leading global brand Toyota and from The Co-operative Group, one of the UK's top 50 best places to work in 2011. The internal communication function will often be involved in the process of helping to develop (perhaps through employee consultation) as well as promote values statements for an organisation.

There is a certain amount of controversy as to whether so-called 'strong' cultures can lead to organisational effectiveness. Alvesson (1993), for example, argues that corporate culture is better termed as 'management ideology', in that the preferred norms and values are the ideals of a particular group and as such cannot be uniformly imposed on an organisation that employs a wide range of people.

Developing an internal communication strategy

Communication strategy

Clampitt (2010: 260) defines a communication strategy as 'the macro-level communication choices we make based on organisational goals and judgments about others' reactions, which serves as a basis for action'. 'Strategy' is a grand-sounding word, but in practice it means prioritising the issues that need to be communicated about, and then developing the key messages and communication objectives, or goals, that can be measured. The communication objectives will aim to influence employees to think, feel or do something in response to key messages. The relevant tactics, methods or channels of communication are then selected to deliver the messages. (See also Chapter 8 for a more detailed discussion of objectives, messages and tactics.)

Box 14.6

Communication audits and 'pulse reports'

Communication audits were established by the International Communication Association (ICA) in the 1970s. They are typically used to assess an organisation's communication system and provide the organisation with valuable information about its communicative strengths and weaknesses. They often measure employees' satisfaction with communication – for example, whether there is too much or too little information or whether upward feedback channels are effective. A communication audit involves a wide variety of data-collection techniques such as questionnaires, interviews, communication logs or diary studies, network analysis and the critical incident technique (CIT).

A criticism of communication audits is that although they provide valuable data for management, they are often time-consuming and are not responded to quickly enough. More commonly used methods of employee satisfaction measurement nowadays are 'temperature checks' or 'pulse reports' that provide 'a timely and accurate record of the current working climate' (Clampitt 2010: 260). Such processes may take advantage of new technologies that identify employees' concerns through online surveys as well as what they are saying on company or public blogs.

Think about 14.9   Communication channels

Consider the key differences in channel use between public and private sector organisations in Table 15.3.

Why do you think these differences exist? What is the likely purpose of each channel of communication?

Feedback

1. A key observation is that public sector organisations are more likely to adopt (although not exclusively) collective mechanisms of communication, involving dialogue. Many public sector staff groups are represented by a trade union member who will act as a point of contact in regard to consultation and negotiation on important issues of pay and conditions of service.

2. Four methods in the public sector list in Table 15.3 involve face-to-face communication, while only 'upwards communication' is a clearly identifiable face-to-face method in the private sector. Upwards communication is a system of communication that allows employees to feed back their views to their team leaders or line managers, and where line managers in turn feed back these views to senior management.

Communication channels or methods

The channels or methods for communicating with employees have proliferated in recent years in line with technological innovation. But newer channels are not necessarily better. An employee-centric communication strategy will build on employees' preferences for message content combined with communication flow (e.g., one-way, two-way, face-to-face), ideally identified through formative research.

Research tools may include a communications audit or staff survey. (See Box 14.6 for a brief discussion of communication audits. See also Chapter 9 on PR programme research and evaluation.) The insight gained from research will, in turn, help the internal communicator to develop the most effective communication plan. The communication plan will involve a combination of channels and messages to reach specific groups of employees. This means that the appropriate channels of communication will differ from organisation to organisation and a 'one size fits all' approach is unlikely to work. Table 14.3 shows a contrast in methods between 'high-performing' public and private sector organisations. (See Think about 14.9.)

Internal communication effectiveness

Internal communication practitioners need to demonstrate the value of managed communication to their bosses. Having a separate budget for internal communication leads to expectations that IC people can show a return on investment (ROI) for their work; however, an organisation's overall communication effectiveness will depend (especially during times of change) as much on strong leadership and good line management as on a solid system of communication processes to ensure that employees feel engaged (Ipsos MORI 2006).

A key finding from a global survey of 328 organisations by the consulting firm Towers Watson (2010) is that

Private sector	Public sector
Individual mechanisms	**Collective mechanisms**
Extranets	Work councils
Employee Intranet	Partnerships with unions
Regular employee surveys	
Ezines	**Individual mechanisms**
Upwards communication	Upwards communication
Knowledge management initiatives	Knowledge management initiatives
Recognition schemes	Video streaming
Podcasting	Exit interviews

Table 14.3 Internal communication methods more likely to be used by higher performing organisations (*source*: Mahdon and Bevan 2007: 43)

effective employee communication is a leading indicator of financial performance. The survey reported that companies with highly effective communication had 45 per cent higher total returns to shareholders over the five-year period between mid-2004 to mid-2009 compared to companies with less effective communication practices. In organisations where shareholder value is not a key measure of performance, internal communicators will need to ensure that they are contributing directly to their organisation's own performance measures to enable a meaningful evaluation of communication effectiveness. In the public and voluntary sectors, performance measures may include an organisa-

tion receiving excellent ratings from external auditors; using its resources efficiently; and delivering an excellent service to target populations (Mahdon and Bevan 2007). Measuring effectiveness is critical for building the case for resources and being valued as a strategic business function that contributes to the bottom line (Towers Watson 2010). (ROI is examined in Box 14.7.)

Box 14.7

What is ROI in internal communication?

As discussed earlier in the text, 'return on investment', or ROI, is a financial term that is not easy to apply to public relations activities and their impacts, including internal communication. But it remains important that internal communication effectiveness is measured and, where possible, in financial terms – its contribution to the 'bottom line'. If IC is a support function, then it should measure its support role in terms of helping to foster good internal relations – by facilitating upward feedback channels and multiple output channels for communicating organisational messages. If well-designed, culturally sensitive and based on feedback, these outputs will result in effective and financially measurable outcomes, such as improved productivity or employee retention, for the organisation as well as for internal stakeholders.

Case study 14.1

Communicating strategic priorities at Aviva UK through 'Our Plan' to employees

One of the challenges facing today's internal communicator is how to support their organisation's leadership team in communicating its business strategy in an engaging way that helps all employees understand how they contribute to business success.

Aviva is largest insurer in the UK with strong businesses in selected international markets. It is the leading provider of life, general insurance, healthcare and financial services in the United Kingdom.

In 2010, Aviva UK had 24,000 employees in roles ranging from customer contact representatives to financial advisors, marketers to actuaries, HR professionals to roadside recovery officers in the RAC. Its employees were a diverse mix: half female, half male, most aged between 26–40, and coming from a range of cultural and ethnic backgrounds. Spread across nine major office sites and thousands on the road, they provide services to customers all over the country.

The communication challenge

In July 2010, the UK leadership team asked the internal communication team to help them articulate the strategic priorities that would help them achieve their ambition to be the most recommended company in the market.

case study 14.1 (continued)

Never before had Aviva UK had a region-wide plan aligning its life insurance, general insurance (GI), health and roadside protection businesses. Nor had it tried to communicate such a joined-up plan across its historically disparate businesses through diverse teams, channels and tools.

Employees, like consumers, were concerned by the economic climate and the impact on the business, and their own investments and pensions. The challenge was to share Aviva's story in an engaging way to a large and diverse audience with different needs, wants and interests.

Project planning and research

A UK project team was galvanised into action, incorporating members of the two in-house internal communications teams (Life and GI), human resources and front-line operational managers. All agreed the solution must emerge from rigorous research and be based on detailed insight on the UK-wide, cross-business audience.

The research took a detailed look at employee demographics such as age, lifestyle and length of service. The aim was to fully understand the people who work for Aviva UK and challenge senior-level ideas about the type of people in different roles, their issues and interests.

During the summer of 2010, extensive research was conducted with more than 2,000 employees at all levels, disciplines and departments to find out if different employee segments had different communication needs. Using focus groups, face-to-face and telephone interviews and an online survey asking both qualitative and quantitative questions, employees were asked how, when and what they wanted to hear about Aviva UK's business strategy and plan. Aviva UK had never got to know its employees in this way before.

The research and rigorous approach to employee segmentation revealed that one solution would not meet everyone's needs (Figure 14.5), even within groups of employees such as contact centre associates or

actuaries. The solution would have to be flexible. Not only did people want different amounts of information but they wanted to receive it in different ways.

Communication objectives

Using the research, the internal communications team developed and implemented 'Our Plan 2011' – an employee engagement programme to be launched in the final quarter of 2010 to help Aviva UK's employees:

- understand Aviva UK's strategy and plan
- see how they contribute to the plan
- feel a connection with its purpose
- understand the external context
- recommend Aviva products, services and as a place to work.

The programme – 'Our Plan 2011'

Aviva UK's leadership team have a long-term goal to bring the inherent strengths of its life and general insurance operations, which are currently separate businesses, under one brand in one group.

The messages were:

- We're a UK company now with one clear UK strategy. No matter where you work in the organisation, you contribute to one of our eight key areas of focus.
- We have a common purpose in the UK – to provide prosperity and peace of mind to our customers. No matter where you work you contribute to that.
- We make a difference in customers' lives.
- We want everyone to understand and think about the part they play in this.

Programme design

The employee research was clear, everyone wanted something different. So flexibility and involvement were the focus of the UK project team's approach to developing the programme.

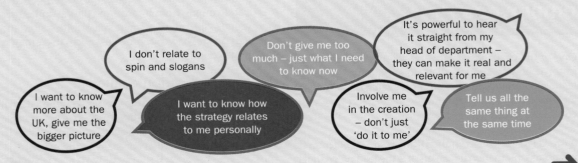

Figure 14.5 What Aviva's employees said in focus groups

case study 14.1 (continued)

Because of the complexity of the audience and their diverse needs, the project team decided to involve employees in creating the programme by setting up several co-creation teams:

- A solution design group made up of managers and strategy experts from across the business to challenge the design of the solution from their employees' perspective.

- A test-bed team of more than 75 employees to try out the solution design group's ideas and give feedback, candidly and constructively, every step of the way.

- A communications group made up of all the communication managers across the UK region who played an active role during the design phase, and when launching and embedding the plan into the business.

Working together, these teams developed an interactive experience based around facilitating content-rich conversations with employee teams listening to, understanding, debating and working through the plan with their head of department – not just their line manager. While line managers are a key internal communication channel, and would normally be the focus of internal communications support, the research showed that employees wanted to hear from their heads of departments.

Tools were developed to support 'Our Plan 2011' sessions:

- CD-ROM disk with a film of customers, employees and senior executives

- Workbook and card-based discussion questions and exercises

- A plan-on-a-page template for completion by each team

- Supporting material on the Aviva World Intranet.

These tools had to be flexible. For example, the CD-ROM presentation could be accessed by employees, even sales or RAC teams who were out on the road, through the disk or the Aviva World Intranet. The information was given in modular chunks. This meant that if there was not enough time to view all the material at once, or if employees had a preference to not do so, they could view it at a time and place convenient to them. It also helped managers to involve their teams in deciding how and when they wanted the information.

Programme governance

Senior stakeholders were updated using the engaging and innovative ideas similar to those used in the final programme to make sure they were fully supportive of the approach.

Implementation

It was launched in November 2010 at the UK director and 'heads of' conference, where 99 per cent of attendees said they understood their role in leading communication on the 2011 plan in their area. Each head of department was fully supported throughout the implementation with workshops, facilitator guides, top tips and dial-in and face-to-face surgeries.

The internal communications team monitored the programme's implementation by asking heads of departments to confirm when they had completed their conversations with their teams and their own business plans to support Aviva UK's strategy. The programme was successfully delivered to more than 90 per cent of Aviva UK's 24,000 employees by the end of February 2011.

Results/evaluation

A post-implementation survey revealed how well the programme had met its objectives and overcome the challenges of its audience's diversity to help them understand Aviva UK's strategic priorities:

- Understand Aviva UK's strategy and plan – 95 per cent of respondents understood the UK plan and 94 per cent understood the plan for their part of the business.

- See how they contribute to the plan – 90 per cent felt motivated by the session and 93 per cent understood how their area contributes to the plan.

- Feel a connection with its purpose – 97 per cent felt motivated to go the extra mile to make it work and 81 per cent felt excited and inspired by the plan.

- Understand the external context – 95 per cent found it useful and informative and 78 per cent believe the plan is the right approach to achieve Aviva UK's vision.

- Recommend Aviva products, services and as a place to work – 65 per cent are proud to work for Aviva UK, 58 per cent are 'extremely' satisfied with Aviva as a place to work and 63 per cent would recommend its products and services.

The programme's success is summed up in an employee comment: '. . . the consensus was that the materials enabled a clear link to be drawn between Aviva strategy and what we need to do at a local level. By the end of the session we had completed a first draft of the plan . . . where everybody had a chance to input. "The most painless business plan I have ever put together", as one member of the team put it.'

Aviva's innovative approach to internal communication achieved a Gold Award from the UK's Institute of Internal Communication.

Source: By kind permission of Aviva UK.
With thanks to Jon Hawkins, Aviva UK

Think about 14.10   **Aviva's communication plan**

How would you describe Aviva UK's approach to employee segmentation?

How important was the research to the success of this programme?

How were the issues highlighted by the research addressed?

What were the roles of the leadership team and internal communication managers in this case study?

Picture 14.2 Aviva 'Our Plan' logo was used to brand the 2011 employee engagement programme (*source*: Reproduced with permission of Aviva (www.aviva.com))

Picture 14.3 Aviva 'Our Plan 2011, CD-ROM was one of the tools used to support interactive sessions with heads of department

Summary

This chapter has examined the key issues for organisations in building relationships with employees or internal publics. We have identified the main external and internal factors driving organisations today and interpreted these from a communication perspective. We have argued that the changing nature of work and jobs is presenting many challenges for the IC function, including that of employee engagement. We have emphasised the importance of organisational culture and leadership in providing the context for the internal communication strategy and demonstrated these through case studies.

Throughout this section we have evidenced the essential role of face-to-face communication and, in particular, the role of the line manager in providing the link between the top of the organisation and small teams of employees. We have discussed communication strategy development, examined effective communication channels and discussed key evaluation issues for internal communication.

Bibliography

Alvesson, M. (1993). *Cultural Perspectives on Organizations.* New York, NY: Cambridge University Press.

Atkinson, C. (2007). 'Trust and the psychological contract'. *Employee Relations* **29**(3): 227–246.

Banks, S.P. (2000). *Multicultural Public Relations: A social-interpretive approach*, 2nd edition. Ames, IA: Iowa State University Press.

Berger, B.K. (2008). Employee/Organizational Communications. www.instituteforpr.org/topics/employee-organizational-communications/ accessed 12 January 2012.

Boje, D.M., G.A. Rosile, R.A. Durant and J.T. Luhman (2004). 'Enron spectacles: a critical dramaturgical analysis.' *Organization Studies* **25**(5): 751–774.

Brinkley, I. and N. Lee (2007). *The Knowledge Economy in Europe: A report prepared for the 2007 EU Spring Council.* London: The Work Foundation.

Cartwright, S. and N. Holmes (2006). 'The meaning of work: the challenge of regaining employee engagement and reducing cynicism.' *Human Resource Management Review* **16**: 199–208.

Chalmers, S. (2008). 'The changing role of internal communications. Are required practitioner competencies keeping pace with the opportunities and challenges?' Paper presented at Euprera (European Public Relations Education and Research Association) 2008 conference, Milan, 16th–18th October 2008, unpublished.

CIPD (Chartered Institute of Personnel and Development) (2011). 'The psychological contract'. Factsheet July 2011.

Clampitt, P.G. (2010). *Communicating for Managerial Effectiveness: Problems, strategies and solutions*, 4th edition. Los Angeles, London, New Delhi, Singapore, Washington DC: Sage.

Conrad, C. and M.S. Poole (1998). *Strategic Organizational Communication: Into the twenty-first century*, 4th edition. Fort Worth, TX: Harcourt Brace.

Deetz, S. (2001). 'Conceptual foundations' in *The New Handbook of Organizational Communication: Advances in theory, research and methods.* F.M. Jablin and L.L. Putnam (eds). Thousand Oaks, CA: Sage.

Eisenberg, E.M. and P. Riley (2001). 'Organizational culture' in *The New Handbook of Organizational Communication: Advances in theory, research and methods.* F.M. Jablin and L.L. Putnam (eds). Thousand Oaks, CA: Sage.

Fawkes, J. (2007). 'Employee engagement: a review of the literature' in *The CEO Chief Engagement Officer: Turning hierarchy upside down to drive performance.* J. Smythe (ed.). Aldershot: Gower.

Gould, B. (1998). 'Emotional capital and internal marketing.' *The Antidote* **3**(8): 34–37.

Grunig, J.E. (1992). 'Symmetrical systems of internal communication' in *Excellence in Public Relations and Communication Management.* J.E. Grunig (ed.). Hillsdale, NJ: Lawrence Erlbaum Associates.

Guest, D.E. and N. Conway (2001). *Employer Perceptions of the Psychological Contract.* London: CIPD.

Guest, D.E. and N. Conway (2002). *Pressure at Work and the Psychological Contract.* London: CIPD.

Haas, J.W. (2007). 'A communication meta-myth revisited: is more communication in the workplace better?' Presented to the International Communication Association, San Francisco.

Hertzberg, F., B. Mausner and B.B. Snyderman (1959). *Motivation to Work.* New York, NY: John Wiley & Sons, Inc.

Hofstede, G.H. (1991). *Cultures and Organizations.* New York, NY: McGraw-Hill.

Ipsos/MORI (2006). 'Common sense in a changing world.' Ipsos MORI 'White Paper' on employee relationship management by S. Lydon. London: Ipsos MORI.

Kennan, W.R. and V. Hazleton (2006). 'Internal public relations, social capital, and the role of effective organizational communication' in *Public Relations Theory II.* C.H. Botan and V. Hazleton (eds). Mahwah, NJ and London: Lawrence Erlbaum Associates.

Kernaghan, S., D. Clutterbuck and S. Cage (2001). *Transforming Internal Communication.* London: Business Intelligence.

Levy, C., A. Sissons and C. Holloway (2011). 'A plan for growth in the knowledge economy'. www.theworkfoundation.com/Reports/290/A-Plan-for-Growth-in-the-Knowledge-Economy-A-Knowledge-Economy-paper accessed 13 January 2011.

MacLeod, D. and N. Clarke (2009). *Engaging for Success: Enhancing performance through employee engagement.* London: Department for Business, Innovation and Skills.

Mahdon, L. and S. Bevan (2007). 'IC UK 2006/7: the definitive analysis of current internal communication practice'. www.theworkfoundation.com/Reports/195/IC-UK-20067 accessed 13 January 2011.

MCA/MORI (1998). 'The buy-in benchmark: a survey of staff understanding and commitment and the impact on business performance'. www.mori.com/polls/1998/mca98.shtml accessed 14 April 2004.

Middlemiss, S. (2011). 'The psychological contract and implied contractual terms: synchronous or asynchronous models?' *International Journal of Law and Management* **53**(1): 32–50.

Mudie, P. (2000). 'Internal marketing: a step too far' in *Internal Marketing: Directions for management*. R.J. Varey and B.R. Lewis (eds). London: Routledge.

Quirke, B. (2000). *Making the Connections: Using internal communication to turn strategy into action*. London: Gower.

Quirke, B. (2008). *Making the Connections: Using internal communication to turn strategy into action*, 2nd edition. London: Gower Publishing.

Robertson-Smith, G. and C. Markwick (2009). *Employee Engagement: A review of current thinking*. London: Institute for Employment Studies.

Sadler, P. (2001). 'Leadership and organizational learning' in *Handbook of Organizational Learning and Knowledge*. M. Dierkes, A. Berthoin Antal, J. Child and I. Nonaka (eds). Oxford: Oxford University Press.

Schein, E. (2004). *Organizational Culture and Leadership*, 3rd edition. San Francisco, CA: Jossey-Bass.

Smith, H. (2011). 'Apple fires employee over iPhone Facebook rants.' http://www.metro.co.uk/tech/883333-apple-sacks-worker-for-ranting-about-iphone-on-facebook accessed 23 April 2012.

Smythe, J. (2004). *Engaging People at Work to Drive Strategy and Change*. London: McKinsey & Company.

Smythe, J. (2007). *The CEO Chief Engagement Officer*. Aldershot: Gower Publishing Ltd.

Stauss, B. and F. Hoffmann (2000). 'Minimizing internal communication gaps by using business television' in *Internal Marketing: Directions for management*. R.J. Varey and B.R. Lewis (eds). London: Routledge.

Thomson, K. (2000). *Emotional Capital: Maximising the intangible assets at the heart of the brand and business success*. London: Capstone.

Thomson, K. and L.A. Hecker (2000). 'The business value of buy-in: how staff understanding and commitment impact on brand and business performance' in *Internal Marketing: Directions for management*. R.J. Varey and B.R. Lewis (eds). London: Routledge.

Towers Watson (2010). 'Capitalizing on effective communication. 2009/2010 ROI study report.' http://www.zeroriskhr.com/pdfs/articles/towers-watson-roi.pdf accessed 19 August 2013.

Towers Watson (2011). 'Clear direction in a complex world: 2011–2012 change and communication ROI study report.' www.towerswatson.com/united-kingdom/research/6639 accessed 19 August 2012.

Tourish, D. (2008). 'Challenging the transformational agenda: leadership theory in transition?' *Management Communication Quarterly* online 19 March 2008 accessed 12 January 2012.

Truss, C., E. Soane, C.Y.L. Edwards, K. Wisdom, A. Croll and J. Burnett (2006). *Working Life: Employee attitudes and engagement 2006*. London: Chartered Institute of Personnel and Development.

Welch, M. (2011). 'The evolution of the employee engagement concept: Communication implications'. *Corporate Communications: An International Journal* 16(4): 328–346.

Welch, M. and P.R. Jackson (2007). 'Rethinking internal communication: a stakeholder approach.' *Corporate Communications: An International Journal* 12(2): 177–198.

White, C., A. Vanc and G. Stafford (2010). 'Internal communication, information satisfaction, and sense of community: the effect of personal influence.' *Journal of Public Relations Research* 22(1): 65–84.

Zerfass, A., R. Tench, P. Verhoeven, D. Verčič and A. Moreno (2010). 'European Communication Monitor 2010. Status quo and challenges for public relations in Europe.' Results of an Empirical Survey in 46 Countries (chart version). Brussels: EACD, EUPRERA. Available at: www.communicationmonitor.eu

Managing community involvement programmes

Learning outcomes

By the end of this chapter you should be able to:

■ define, describe and compare the concepts of community involvement, corporate social responsibility and cause-related marketing

■ identify the key principles of community relationship building and apply this understanding to simple, meaningful scenarios

■ evaluate the issues arising from an organisation's community involvement

■ critically evaluate corporate strategies for integrating corporate social responsibility and community programmes into the business plan from a stakeholder perspective.

Structure

■ Corporate community involvement (CCI) programmes

■ Employees and community programmes

■ Cause-related marketing (CRM)

■ Developing community programmes

■ Evaluating community programmes

Introduction

If you saw a child helping an elderly citizen cross the road or giving up a seat for them on the train, you would probably think it was a mature and generous act by someone with a considered view of their place in society. If the child then went home and wrote about it in their private diary it may still be viewed as a positive action being considered and reflected on to inform the child's future behaviour in similar situations. The child could then share the experience over dinner with family members to elicit praise, credit or a reward of a coveted sweet or drink. What if they then went to their school headteacher (principal) soliciting further praise, even a headteacher's award, which may attract interest from outside the school through a parental contact with the local paper? And the accolades pour in.

A little far fetched perhaps, but is this analogous with organisations and their involvement in society through corporate social responsibility? It may be for some. Certainly criticisms have been levelled at some companies for over-promoting their acts of corporate giving, particularly around major incidents such as 11 September in the USA and the Asian tsunami in December 2004. We have also been forced to reflect on major corporations' responsibilities and responsible behaviour in the aftermath of the 2008 economic crises. What are organisations' motivations and interests in their communities? How much are they interested in doing something 'good' and how much in being acknowledged, recognised and rewarded for this act? Earlier in the text we discussed the role of organisations in their communities and in this chapter we will explore the different ways in which organisations apply their individual interpretations of community involvement and how this can have various outcomes, outputs, benefits and rewards for them and the communities they are involved with.

The chapter will therefore evaluate community involvement programmes that can range from the philanthropic (donations) through to campaigns that have much more tangible returns for the organisation, such as initiatives like cause-related marketing (CRM).

Corporate community involvement (CCI) programmes

These are the tactical approaches organisations plan in order to discharge their corporate social responsibility policy. CCI may be viewed as the organisational recognition that businesses cannot survive unless there is a prosperous community or wider society from which to draw both employees and trade. Building relationships with stakeholders and community groups is important for many organisations when there are changing patterns of employment and recruitment, with increasing use of short-term contracts and part-time work, particularly in the retail and service sectors. Other influences include the continuing increase in the number of women in full- and part-time work and the worldwide issue of **downsizing**. It is important to recognise that not all organisations take an enlightened view of their role in society and, in fact, many are content to work at the basic level of responsibility to

> **Definition:** *'Downsizing'* is a term used to describe the reduction in the number of employees working for an organisation in either full- or part-time positions.

society – i.e., to pay taxes and obey corporate and societal laws (see Chapter 4). Some also, as Jones et al. (2009) have discussed, find themselves behaving irresponsibly while not necessarily breaking society's rules or laws. So how do organisations obtain guidance on the best ways to proceed in the modern business world? There are many groups and non-governmental organisations giving advice on the issue globally and nationally. One of the principal drivers in this is the United Nations through the UN Global Compact (www.unglobalcompact.org). The Global Compact is a framework for businesses that are committed to aligning their operations and strategies, with ten principles that fall within the areas of human rights, labour, the environment and anti-corruption. The ten principles are outlined in Table 15.1.

All these factors are influential in the increasing drive by organisations to build links with communities and stakeholders in order to enhance public understanding of the organisation's function and its business objectives and subsequently impact on the environment in which it operates. In recognition of many of these changes, businesses are attempting to forge direct links with communities, either individually or collectively, through organisations such as Business in the Community (BITC) in the UK.

BITC is a non-political UK organisation founded in 1995 whose aim is to work in partnership with businesses to build their relationships and involvement with the

Table 15.1 The Global Compact's ten principles (*source*: www. unglobalcompact.org)

Human rights	Principle 1: Businesses should support and respect the protection of internationally proclaimed human rights; and
	Principle 2: make sure that they are not complicit in human rights abuses.
Labour standards	Principle 3: Businesses should uphold the freedom of association and the effective recognition of the right to collective bargaining;
	Principle 4: the elimination of all forms of forced and compulsory labour;
	Principle 5: the effective abolition of child labour; and
	Principle 6: the elimination of discrimination in respect of employment and occupation.
Environment	Principle 7: Businesses should support a precautionary approach to environmental challenges;
	Principle 8: undertake initiatives to promote greater environmental responsibility; and
	Principle 9: encourage the development and diffusion of environmentally friendly technologies.
Anti-corruption	Principle 10: Businesses should work against corruption in all its forms, including extortion and bribery.

communities in which they operate. BITC defines its aims as 'supporting the social and economic regeneration of communities by raising the quality and extent of business involvement and by making that involvement a natural part of successful business practice'.

The organisation represents over 400 member companies in the UK and this includes 75 of the UK's top-performing stock exchange-listed companies, the FTSE 100. Member companies are encouraged to provide their skills, expertise, influence, products and profits to assist in building a prosperous society that is attractive to investors, in which businesses can thrive and where all stakeholders in the community can have access to opportunities. The organisation is run through 11 regional offices throughout the UK. BITC claims the benefits to the members are as follows:

- employee development
- increased staff morale
- enhanced relations with local decision makers
- motivated, high-quality recruits
- improved corporate image.

BITC is a member of CSR Europe, a network of national affiliation organisations interested in CSR. CSR Europe describes itself as a business-to-business network that aims to help companies achieve profitability by placing CSR in the mainstream of business practice (CSR Europe 2012). In the USA, Business for Social Responsibility (BSR) is the coordinating organisation (www.bsr.org). (See Case study 15.1.)

Sponsorship and the community

Today, sponsorship is an important area of business policy and a large proportion of it is highly visible to an organisation's stakeholders. Examples include sponsorship of major sporting events, such as FIFA's football World Cup or the summer and winter Olympic Games (see Chapter 23 for more on sponsorship). A further area of popular sponsorship is of specific, high-profile television programmes, such as soap operas and drama series. It is therefore clear that not all sponsorship fits into the CCI category – for example, tobacco sponsorship of Formula 1 motor racing came in for ethical and political debate for many years. During 2004 the Breakthrough breast cancer charity rejected £1m of sponsorship from Nestlé because of the company's past policy of promoting formula milk products for newborn babies in developing countries. Similar issues have arisen for companies accused of 'greenwashing' when they support major sporting events such as the 2012 London Olympics (Gibson 2012). Corporate sponsorship can be planned, well managed and fit into corporate strategies within ethical guidelines, but it can also challenge ethical rules if the organisation is not clear about its aims, objectives and criteria for sponsoring.

It is important, therefore, for the organisation to clarify its aims and objectives when embarking on a sponsorship programme. For commercial sponsorship the organisation may have one of the following reasons for sponsoring:

- To raise awareness of the organisation or its products.
- To build organisational image by association with worthwhile causes, e.g. charities or the arts, or to

Case study 15.1
BT Community Partnership Programme

BT is a founder member of BITC's Per Cent Standard (formerly the Per Cent Club) – a group of top companies in the UK that donate a percentage of their annual profits to community-based projects and organisations.

BT has a long history of working in the community. In the 1990s the guiding principle of BT's Community Partnership Programme was access and communication. The aim was to help people to communicate better by providing organisations with resources, expertise and the technology to improve the quality of life and well-being of the community. BT's mission statement pledged the company to 'make a fitting contribution' to the community in which it conducts its business. The recipients of BT's membership of the Per Cent Club have been charitable causes such as the Samaritans, which has received over £1m in five years. The company has also supported the Royal National Institute for the Deaf's Communications Support Unit. This enabled 15 people to be trained to professional sign language interpreter standard and provided support during their first year of employment. BT has also supported people with disabilities: BT Swimming, for example, together with the disabled swimming organisation, BSAD, organised national competitions. BT Swimathon, a nationwide charity swim, raised millions for a number of different charities including ChildLine (see Case study 15.6).

This demonstrates the long-term commitment BT has had to the community in which it conducts its business, and allows the company to see the links into its corporate strategy and goals and particularly the connections with the company's industry, communications. This is a common theme with many corporate community initiatives and it is clearly one way that makes the technique acceptable to directors in the boardroom (see also Case study 15.6).

Source: used with kind permission of BT and BITC

enhance image in particular geographical locations by sponsoring regional or national sports teams.

- To overcome legislation, such as gaining exposure on television for products banned from advertising (e.g. contraceptives and tobacco in the UK).

- To provide corporate hospitality opportunities for stakeholders, such as customers and investors, to attend.

However, there are other forms of sponsorship that fit into the CCI category more closely, such as charitable donations given to an activity that is not commercial but helps the community or members of that community and from which no commercial return is sought. This form of sponsorship does frequently provide significant public relations benefits but this is not always of importance to organisations, nor is it always exploited. There are significant differences between corporate sponsorship and charitable donations, not least in the classification of tax. Sponsorship is liable to value added tax (VAT) in the UK, whereas charitable donations are not. This situation is similar in many other countries. Having looked at the definitions of sponsorship it is therefore wrong and potentially illegal for organisations to redefine their sponsorship activity as charitable donations to avoid paying tax.

It is possible for CCI initiatives to be either sponsorship that benefits both parties or to be clearly examples of charitable donation by the organisation. Sponsorship can, therefore, be seen as part of the armoury used in corporate community relations. Community relations programmes are often defined as mutually beneficial partnerships with one or more stakeholders to enhance the organisation's reputation as a good corporate citizen. The stakeholders are, therefore, usually the target audiences for the company and include customers, suppliers, media, employers, trade unions, politicians, local government representatives, community organisations, key opinion formers, shareholders, educationalists, environmentalists, etc. Community relations can have an influence on the corporate reputation and this is increasingly an important measure for individual and institutional investors for the quality of an organisation. As such, the link between good corporate citizenship, good reputation and share value/price can be identified (see Figure 15.1, Think about 15.1 and Explore 15.1).

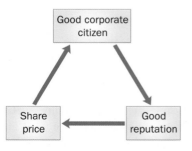

Figure 15.1 Link between community relations, financial performance and reputation

Think about 15.1

Why companies get involved in community relations

Company stock valuation is one reason for being involved in community relations. What others can you think of that might benefit the organisation?

Feedback

Some businesses are increasingly concerned with educational development of the community, in what is termed 'cradle to grave'. Community relations can influence this process by education-based sponsorship. This creates awareness in local schools and establishes the company as a desirable employer. This may, in turn, influence future recruitment or create a positive image around products/services/outputs. Also, the community initiatives can provide employees with opportunities to develop further skills by working with local schools and organisations. The benefits of such education are a properly trained and developed workforce, which is crucial to the company's future success.

Think about 15.2

Sponsoring

What do you think are the implications for a sponsee of a high-profile event (for example, sponsoring a world-famous horse race or established annual charity walk and collection fund) if the sponsor withdraws their support?

Feedback

The event may be put into jeopardy. Think about contracts and the following:

1. What if no suitable sponsor comes to take their place?

2. What about negative publicity if the event is no longer able to run?

(See also Chapter 23.)

The bigger picture

Community initiatives can have benefits beyond links with specific community-based stakeholders (such as schools or community-based groups). Through involvement in

Explore 15.1

Finding examples of community relations

Think about an organisation you know well or are interested in and research its website and external activities. Make a list of those activities you believe might be regarded as community relations. Note down what you believe the organisation and the recipient got out of the relationship.

Feedback

Community relations are diverse and the involvement need not be significant. Typically, community relations programmes involve one or more of the following techniques or tactics:

1. sponsorships

2. targeted donations

3. awards

4. hospitality

5. employee volunteering

6. use of facilities (loan of equipment)

7. training/seminars

8. secondments (staff).

Links between organisations and community groups are normally made with organisations in areas such as sports, arts, education, the environment, occupational health and safety, charities, youth/young people's groups, senior citizens, the disadvantaged, disability, heritage and many other groupings.

community relations an organisation is often complementing other objectives (such as its corporate strategy). This can have an impact on share value, as discussed, but also on media relations, investor relations, shareholder communications strategies and even, in the event of crisis, communication. For example, establishing a relationship with specialist or local journalists during positive news stories connected to community initiatives may help during a crisis. A well-disposed journalist is more likely to give the organisation the opportunity to respond or give the organisational view of the negative situation. This can prevent more damaging news stories escalating into a crisis (see Mini case study 15.1 and Think abouts 15.2 and 15.3).

Mini case study 15.1
The M&S and Oxfam Clothes Exchange

The UK clothes retailer Marks and Spencer (M&S) and Oxfam Clothes Exchange aim to encourage customers to recycle more and to help to reduce the amount of clothing going to landfill. The campaign attracted a lot of interest and comment and was supported with national television adverts in April and May 2012. The campaign used the actress Joanna Lumley, with the aim of changing clothes shopping habits towards greater recycling. During the campaign, M&S completely covered a street – including trees and a dog – with clothes in East London's Brick Lane fashion district to highlight the amount thrown into UK landfill every five minutes. In the initiative customers are encouraged to return their used M&S clothes to Oxfam and receive a £5 voucher, which can be redeemed when they spend £35 or more in an M&S store.

Reported in the *Huffington Post* in April 2012, M&S chief executive Marc Bolland said: 'We're leading a change in the way we all shop for clothing, forever. This is the right, responsible move for the UK's biggest clothing retailer and the ultimate goal is simple – to put a complete stop to clothes ending up in landfill. We want to get back one garment for every one we sell. For us that's 350 million a year. It is a big number, but with our customers' help, we will do it.'

Impact
The campaign is claimed to have:

- Raised over £1.8 million for Oxfam projects so far through re-selling the clothes that customers return.
- Diverted over 3 million garments from going to landfill.
- Saved millions of pounds for M&S customers through the redemption of the £5 vouchers.

Think about 15.3 — Sponsoring and corporate giving

The concept of corporate philanthropy was discussed earlier in the text. This relates to the process of providing money or gifts in kind to organisations on behalf of a company or organisation. Here are some issues for you to think about related to the process of giving and sponsoring on behalf of an organisation:

- Does sponsorship and corporate giving discourage the state and government agencies from fulfiling their duties to society?
- Consider a company that sponsors local schools and supplies them with computers. Does this discourage state provision of information technology to schools? What happens when the hardware dates and the software become obsolete and the organisation moves on to other causes or stops giving?

- Will giving to one group in society disadvantage others if the state withdraws or reduces support?
- Might some groups be more attractive to sponsors and donors than others? Is it easier to support babies orphaned in a disaster than disturbed teenagers?

Feedback
Think about the impact of initiatives such as national lotteries (which exist in many countries) on charity donations. Do they provide much-needed support while at the same time take away the responsibility of individuals or the state to support parts of society? Some charities in the UK claim to have lost out because of the National Lottery. They believe that because people are buying lottery tickets they feel they are 'doing their bit' and no longer need to make the kinds of contribution they used to.

Employees and community programmes

Increasingly, employers are encouraging their employees to become involved in the local communities in which they and often their families live. This is true of public as well as private organisations. For example, Leeds Metropolitan University supports the Leeds Cares initiative, which includes employees working on voluntary projects in and around Leeds (see Case study 15.2 and Explore 15.2).

To achieve practically the increased involvement of employees, the following techniques should be considered:

- *preferential treatment* given to requests supported by employees of the organisation (the Leeds Cares Case study 15.2 is an example);

Case study 15.2

Leeds Cares – collaborative action

Leeds Cares is the leading programme for engaging business support in the northern UK city of Leeds. Through the collaboration of its 33 supporting businesses working closely with public sector and community partners, it has a real social impact in the most deprived areas of Leeds.

Leeds Cares began in 1999, with 11 founder companies providing action days for teams and calendar opportunities for individuals. It has grown to include 33 companies and offers a range of employee involvement activities, including team challenges, brokering business mentors who support prisoners due for release and seeking work, and helping homeless people into permanent employment.

The social impact of the programme is achieved through planning and consultation with stakeholders. Leeds Cares' vision is based on the Vision for Leeds – a community strategy for the city prepared through consultation with the people of Leeds by the Leeds Initiative, the city's local strategic partnership, bringing together the public, private and voluntary sectors.

Leeds Cares recognises that education is the primary social issue of concern to business. Its programmes provide: one-to-one literacy support to primary schoolchildren; individual mentors to work with selected secondary schoolchildren; and management support to head-teachers through Partners in Leadership.

Leeds Cares states its aim is to continue helping businesses to engage in wider corporate social responsibility issues through community involvement. By addressing hard social issues, such as ex-offender re-offending rates, getting homeless people into jobs and developing reading and numeracy in schools, the programme has the potential to be at the heart of the city's regeneration movement.

According to Leeds Cares, the impact of the programme has been:

- over 8,000 volunteers giving over 100,000 hours of time; of these, 90 per cent were volunteering for the first time
- support for over 350 community partners and 50 companies
- human resources benefits for supporting companies, through employee development, communications, project management, teambuilding and motivation, as well as reputation building through public relations around action days
- development of new training packages based around the staff development benefits of Leeds Cares, while others used it to support their business objectives around social diversity.

Source: adapted from http://www.bitc.org.uk/

Explore 15.2

Employee involvement

List the benefits you think involving employees with the local community might bring to:

- the individual
- the organisation.

Feedback

Individual benefits might include:

- personal development
- learning new skills
- developing communication skills.

Organisational benefits might include learning from working in partnership with your employees and sharing their professional skills, time and experience.

- *launching a reward and recognition programme* that highlights and supports the achievements of employees in out-of-hours activities (e.g. sporting honours); leadership initiatives; commitment to an organisation (e.g. school governor); academic support (e.g. encourage employees to give lectures at local schools and colleges);
- *awards presentations* where employees volunteer to represent the organisation as an 'ambassador' at presentation events;
- *employee volunteering* that actively encourages employees to gain personal development experience by volunteering their time and skills to a willing community organisation;
- *committee membership* that develops employees by encouraging involvement with external committees; this will help their networking and understanding of how other organisations work.

Involving employees in community programmes can offer numerous benefits to both parties. For employees,

Picture 15.1 The UK clothes retailers Marks and Spencer (M&S) and Oxfam Clothes Exchange aim to encourage customers to recycle more and to help to reduce the amount of clothing going to landfill. The 'Plan A' campaign attracted a lot of interest and comment and was supported with national television adverts (*source*: Marks and Spencer)

it improves motivation and pride in the organisation, which can improve productivity, reduce sickness absence, increase innovation, develop communication skills, improve understanding of corporate strategy/policy objectives and offer a measure/comparison against competitor organisations. If it is so good, however, why are so few organisations doing it? Perhaps some individuals and companies are, but they do not make a big deal out of it. Alternatively, it may be just too costly and not worth the effort. This may be influenced by the business area, range of employee profiles (age, gender, education), corporate interest in the region or local society or, more importantly, the organisation's size or profitability – it just might not be able to afford the time or the money.

Cause-related marketing (CRM)

Cause-related marketing (CRM) is when 'companies invest in social causes that complement their brands' (Blowfield and Murray 2008: 26), or 'where a company associates a marketing promotion with a charitable cause' (Hart 1995: 219), or 'a strategy designed to promote the achievement of marketing objectives (e.g. brand sales) via company support of social causes' (Barone et al. 2000).

BITC defines CRM as 'a commercial activity by which a company with an image, product or service to market, builds a relationship with a "cause" or a number of "causes" for mutual benefit' (BITC 2012).

CRM has become a popular practice for Anglo-American organisations in recent years and a number of leading UK companies have forged particularly close partnerships with charities and good causes. For example, Tesco, one of the UK's largest supermarket retailers, runs a well-known CRM programme in conjunction with local schools called 'Tesco Computers for Schools'. The scheme involves consumers collecting tokens with their shopping that can be exchanged by schools for computer equipment.

BITC in the UK carries out regular research into CRM and its use. For example, in October 2008, Business in the Community published research showing that FTSE 350 companies that consistently managed and measured their corporate responsibility outperformed their FTSE 350 peers on total shareholder return 2002–2007 by between 3.3 per cent and 7.7 per cent per year. Also, earlier studies such as BITC's Profitable Partnerships research (2000) revealed that the vast majority of the population (88 per cent) are aware of cause-related marketing; that 76 per cent of consumers who had heard of CRM associations have participated in these programmes; and 80 per cent of consumers who had participated in a CRM programme said that it would positively impact on their future behaviour and attitudes.

BITC has been researching company and consumer attitudes in the UK since the 1990s. For example, Research International (1995) surveyed over 450 major companies operating in the UK, including 81 of the top 100 FTSE companies. The results demonstrated that CRM was already established and 93 per cent indicated some level of CRM spend. The survey also found that marketing directors, community affairs directors and chief executives all believed CRM held 'obvious benefits for businesses and causes', including:

- enhancing corporate reputation
- achieving press coverage and public relations
- raising brand awareness
- increasing customer loyalty
- building and increasing sales (Research International 1995).

The 'Winning Game' was a large-scale consumer survey carried out among 1,053 UK consumers (Research International 1997). The purpose of the study was to understand consumer attitudes towards CRM. It found that consumers had a high expectation that large businesses and corporations should demonstrate an active social responsibility. It also found that consumers felt CRM is a 'means by which businesses can become involved

in the community'. The most significant finding of the research was that 'when price and quality are equal, consumers will discriminate in favour of the company that espouses a good cause. Furthermore, consumers believe that companies should support a good cause' (Research International 1997). According to the IEG Sponsorship Report (Chipps 2011), US spending on cause marketing was up 3.1 per cent to $1.68 billion in 2011. IEG claims this reflects significant growth in the US, where in 1990 cause sponsorship spending was only $120 million. The 2012 report breaks down cause spending over the past four years as follows:

- 2011 – $1.68 billion, 3.1 per cent growth
- 2010 – $1.62 billion, 6.7 per cent growth
- 2009 – $1.51 billion, 0.3 per cent decline
- 2008 – $1.52 million, 5.5 per cent growth

The attraction of CRM for organisations is that these programmes generate direct, measurable benefits for the company. Further benefits of this approach include:

- those needing help receive it
- the public feels good about buying/supporting the product
- the donor organisation gains reputation and sometimes sales
- it is a win–win situation for both parties.

Talking about CRM in the mid 1990s, Cadbury Schweppes' chairman, Dominic Cadbury (1996: 25), one of the biggest proponents in the UK, enthused about CRM's 'ability to enhance corporate image, to differentiate products, and to increase sales and loyalty. It is enlightened self-interest [see Chapter 4], a win–win situation'. (See Mini case studies 15.2–15.4, then look at the examples provided in Boxes 15.1 and 15.2 and Case study 15.3.)

Mini case study 15.2
Procter & Gamble: Podaruj dzieciom słońce (Bring sunshine to children)

About the company

Procter & Gamble (P&G) is one of the world's leading companies in the household and personal products industry. P&G's product line includes over 23 brands. The company owns 60 factories worldwide, employs just under 110,000 people and is ranked in the top 100 global companies (Global 500 CNNMoney.com accessed 18 September 2008).

In Poland, P&G has been active since 1991, when Procter & Gamble Poll was established. After 20 years of activity on the Polish market the company employs over 1,000 people and has been one of the leading providers of home care and beauty care products.

mini case study 15.2 (continued)

About the programme

Podaruj dzieciom słońce ('Bring sunshine to children') is the biggest cause-related marketing initiative in Poland. The campaign has been run by P&G since 1999, together with the 'Polsat' Foundation. The essence of the campaign is to raise funds for specialist medical equipment for children.

The campaign is based on a simple mechanism that is always the same. Consumers buy particular products, with a yellow sun sign on them, and support the action at the same time (products include Vizir, Pampers, Blend-a-med, Gillette, Ariel, Bonux, Lenor, Always, Naturella, Pantene and Head & Shoulders). Part of the profit from the sale of these products goes to the Polsat Foundation's account. Decisions on how to distribute the funds are made by the Polsat Foundation, P&G company and medical advisors.

Rationale and results

In 1995, P&G defined its global cause-related strategy by implementing the 'Live, Learn and Thrive' programme as a part of its CSR. P&G's head office encouraged all departments to focus their activities on children in greatest need, especially those aged 0–13. When the programme was being implemented worldwide, the Polish department of P&G was already experienced in this subject. According to Małgorzata Wadzińska, Director of Procter & Gamble Poland's External Cooperation Department, coming onto the Polish market the company looked for a group that would need the most help. 'We believed that children are our future and by investing in their development we can bring the best benefit to society. We also took into account the fact that mothers and children are our prime customers so we do have detailed knowledge about their needs and delivering proper solutions.'

As a result of this project, many of the company's goals/aims have been realised. First of all, it has developed the company's image with consumers. Furthermore, the campaign is organised on a large scale and is recognisable all over Poland. This has affected sales so that the company can gather even more funds to support health care and treatment programmes for ill children. So far the campaign has covered 260 hospitals in Poland and 11 million Euros have been raised. Due to accompanying advertising campaigns the action has also brought educational value, as it has broadened the awareness of the social issues that P&G has chosen to tackle.

Box 15.1

Other CRM examples from the UK

Norwich Union (financial services):	St John Ambulance
Nivea (cosmetics):	Fashion Targets Breast Cancer
Lloyds TSB (financial services):	'Visible Women' (ethnic minority women one-off magazine)
Nike (sports goods):	Kick Racism out of Football
Andrex (toiletries):	Guide Dogs for the Blind (see Case study 16.3)
HP Foods 'Daddies' Sauce' (food):	NSPCC (see Mini case study 16.4)

Box 15.2

Other examples from around the world

Toyota:	Leukaemia Society of America
American Express:	Elizabeth Taylor AIDS Foundation
	Magic Johnson Foundation
Florida Citrus:	American Cancer Society
Kellogg's:	Race For The Cure (breast cancer)
Zachodni WBK Bank (Polish bank):	Puppet Clown Action (*Akcja Pajack*)

Mini case study 15.3
American Express

Picture 15.2 American Express developed a CRM strategy to help restore the Statue of Liberty

An often-cited example of early CRM dates back to 1983 when American Express was invited to make a donation to restore one of the USA's most famous symbols, the Statue of Liberty. The company's response was not just to write a cheque but to propose a more imaginative solution, which was that every time one of its cardholders used their card they would help towards the appeal. Within a few months American Express had contributed $1.5m. Most importantly for the company, however, was that the use of its card had increased by 27 per cent. Today many companies have adopted CRM tactics to merge corporate social responsibility and commercial aims.

Source: BITC
(*Picture source*: Steve Hamblin/Alamy Images)

Mini case study 15.4
HP sauce

In the mid-1990s, food producer HP's packaging highlighted the company's involvement with the child protection charity, NSPCC. One penny from every purchase of Daddies' Brown Sauce was donated to the NSPCC, which resulted in a minimum donation of £80,000. (See Think about 15.4 and Explore 15.3.)

Source: BITC

Explore 15.3

CRM

■ CRM in the Mini case study examples is obviously very successful. Why would an organisation involve itself in any other type of corporate support if it were not going to bring direct commercial benefits?

■ Think about an organisation you know well, research it and consider whether it involves itself in any CRM. If not, how might it build a relationship with a charity or cause, and which one(s) should it choose?

Feedback

Reasons for more straightforward sponsorship might include goodwill, community involvement, stakeholder interest and good citizenship.

Think about 15.4   HP sauce

■ In the HP example, are both parties equal in the relationship?

■ Is it acceptable for one partner to have the balance of power and potentially benefit more from the arrangement?

■ What are the corporate communication dangers of this type of contract?

■ Could HP not simply give a sum of money to the NSPCC?

Feedback

Both parties may not always be equal. In the HP example, they may both benefit financially but the reputational benefits are clearer for HP. Power is not always equal due to the financial influence of the sponsoring organisation. Some of the dangers of the relationship include: crisis management for both parties (something goes wrong that is unrelated to the contract); and contract length and withdrawal from it. HP stood to gain more ongoing publicity from the special packaging than from the short-term effects of announcing a corporate donation to the NSPCC.

Case study 15.3
Guide Dogs for the Blind Association and Andrex

Picture 15.3 Guide Dogs for the Blind Association and Andrex have long enjoyed a mutually beneficial association (*source*: Kimberly-Clark)

Guide Dogs for the Blind Association (GDBA) and Andrex (the toilet paper brand owned by Kimberly-Clark) have an association that stretches back over 15 years. Back in 1997 the Andrex toilet tissue brand celebrated the 25th anniversary of the Andrex puppy famously used in its on-pack promotions and television commercials. To celebrate the event, both parties decided to launch a cause-related marketing programme. The scheme was a significant one that raised £275,000 in donations for the GDBA.

The promotional packs of Andrex tissue were on display for three months and each pack contained tokens that could be sent back to GDBA or Andrex, which resulted in a donation being made to the charity.

Kimberly-Clark maximised the public relations opportunities of this venture by creating local news stories involving the GDBA training centres and the Girl Guides Association regional prize winners. The company claimed to achieve five times the amount of press coverage during the programme than before it started.

Both parties believed the CRM programme to be a success because it brought benefits to both sides and to the consumer. From the charity's perspective, the campaign was financially beneficial and provided it with opportunities to improve awareness of its name and to inform the public about the range of services it provides as an organisation. From the company's perspective, the scheme led to an increase in the level of local and national press coverage, increased the level of sales of the product and improved the company's corporate reputation. It could also be argued that consumers benefited from the association as they continued to receive the same product at the same price while being able to feel they were financially supporting a service that helps disadvantaged members of society. (See also Explore 15.4.)

Source: used with kind permission of Kimberly-Clark and GDBA

Mini case study 15.5
Danone Poland: *Podziel się posiłkiem* (Share a meal)

About the company

Danone Sp. Z o.o. is part of the Danone Group – one of the leading companies in the global food industry. The company employs over 86,000 people in 150 countries worldwide. Danone Sp. Z o.o. started activities in Poland 15 years ago. It currently employs 1,353 people in two factories (in Warsaw and Bieruń), at the head office in Warsaw and sales departments all over Poland. Its major brands include: Actimel, Activia, Danonki, Danio, Fantasia and others.

About the programme

'Share a meal' is a cause-related marketing programme that is a part of Danone's corporate social responsibility strategy. Its aim is to provide meals for primary (elementary) and high-school pupils in parts of Poland where children are undernourished. This type of activity was suggested by consumers who took part in focus research before launching the campaign.

The research carried out by Danone and consultations with humanitarian organisations in Poland indicated that the issue of malnutrition was a significant national problem. Research demonstrated that 30 per cent of school-age children in Poland are undernourished. However, 'unofficial statistics', provided by numerous organisations dealing with the issue of malnutrition

mini case study 15.5 (continued)

among children, suggest this problem may affect much greater numbers of children.

The 'Share a meal' campaign, organised in association with the Polish Humanitarian Organisation (PHO), gathers funds to support the *Pajacyk* ('Puppet Clown') programme, which aims to provide at least one hot meal, every day of the school year, to children in need. Each year, in September and October, consumers can purchase Danone's products with a 'Share a meal' sign on them. Part of the profit from selling those products goes to support the programme.

The 'Share a meal' programme is also supported by a promotion campaign in media and shops all over Poland. Information about the programme and its logo are placed on the product packaging and promotion materials in shops. Additionally, adverts are broadcast in the media carrying the campaign messages.

During four cycles of the 'Share a meal' programme, the Danone Company donated over 1 million Euros to fight the problem of malnutrition in Poland. This has equated to the distribution of 3,877,044 meals to undernourished children across Poland since 2006.

Consumers and CRM

Research from the USA in the early days of CRM demonstrated a significant return and reflected the importance of CRM with consumers as follows:

- CRM increasingly becoming the 'tiebreaker' in a purchase decision.

- 76 per cent of Americans say that when price and quality are equal they are more likely to switch to brands associated with a good cause.

- Consumers are less cynical about CRM (than about standard marketing campaigns).

- CRM has long-term strategic benefits rather than being a short-term promotional device.

- Being socially responsible can create good 'word of mouth' (Cone Roper 1997; Cone Inc. 2011).

Cone Inc.'s (2011) 'Cause Evolution Survey' claims more than two-thirds of Americans say they consider a company's business practices when deciding what to buy.

Developing community programmes

Planning and implementing corporate social responsibility

Having defined techniques for determining to whom an organisation is responsible, what responsibilities there are and a framework for identifying stakeholder responsibilities, we need to consider how this process works in practice. Endorsement of the CSR concept by senior management

is important if it is to be successful and Carroll (1991) recommends seven key questions to ask management when planning CSR strategies:

1. Who are our stakeholders?

2. What are their stakes?

3. What do we need from each of our stakeholders?

4. What corporate social responsibilities (economic, legal, ethical and philanthropic) do we have to our stakeholders?

5. What opportunities and challenges do our stakeholders present?

6. How important and/or influential are different stakeholders?

7. What strategies, actions or decisions should we take to best deal with these responsibilities?

(See also Box 15.3.)

The fourth of the strategies outlined in Box 15.3 is the ideal. The strategy should forecast the anticipated benefits for the business as a result of the organisation changing its approach to CSR. The strategy should also indicate:

- necessary levels of investment

- how to monitor the strategy

- evaluation of the strategy

- benefits communicated to management, employees and stakeholders.

Some companies claim to meet the ideal interactive strategy, such as the UK-based Co-operative Bank, which has ethical policies dating back to the organisation's foundation in 1872 as part of the cooperative movement. The bank publishes its ethical policy annually, detailing its performance and track record (see Case study 15.6 at the end of this section).

Box 15.3

Four strategies of CSR response

Four strategies of response to stakeholder perspectives on CSR have been identified, as follows:

1. An *inactive* strategy: resisting societal expectations and sometimes government regulation.

2. A *reactive* strategy: responding to unanticipated change after the significant change has occurred.

3. A *proactive* strategy: attempting to 'get ahead' of a societal expectation or government regulation (often coupled with efforts to influence the outcome).

4. An *interactive* strategy: anticipating change and blending corporate goals with those of stake-holders and societal expectations. An organisation employing an interactive strategy consciously reduces the gap between its performance and society's expectations. An interactive strategy is often accomplished by management's commitment to a serious dialogue with stakeholders.

Explore 15.4

The Andrex case study

1. From the GDBA and Andrex case study, do you think all parties were equal?

2. List the strategic objectives of this CRM campaign for Andrex – what was the company trying to achieve? How might these objectives be measured?

Feedback

Consider longer-term issues for the company, such as: corporate image; media exposure; building closer links with key stakeholders, i.e. the customer, regional and national media; brand reinforcement; increased revenue; and corporate social responsibility. All these factors are encapsulated in one marketing-led initiative.

Another example of a company meeting these commitments in a transparent way is the Scottish Nappy Company. Mini case study 15.6 demonstrates how a small company can develop a strategic business plan that helps solve a societal issue and contributes to environmental sustainability. (See also Case study 15.6.)

Mini case study 15.6

Scottish Nappy Company Limited

The Scottish Nappy Company is a small company, employing nine staff and based in west central Scotland. The company's main commitment is to its environmental aim of reducing landfill through minimising the 'disposable' nappy mountain. The operation was established with environmental considerations being key, including the selection of operational site, choice of chemicals, energy, vehicle, machinery, packaging materials and marketing.

The Scottish Nappy Company provides local people in the region with a weekly home delivery of fresh cotton nappies, the collection of soiled ones and their subsequent laundering. It embraces the environmental benefits of the laundering process itself, with significant benefits to the environment and health of its customers and the community at large within the area serviced.

The impact of the business has been a significant reduction in 'disposable' nappies going to landfill. Also, the rural base for the company's operation has minimised airborne pollutions affecting clean nappies. Furthermore, the selection of computer-controlled washing machines has ensured optimum cleanliness while minimising the use of water, gas and electricity. In addition, non-biological detergent and oxygen-based bleach are used in the laundry process and deliveries are made by a LPG/petrol dual fuel van to reduce harmful emissions.

Further interesting evidence for the company and in support of its strategy is that babies in cotton nappies are generally trained out of them 6 to 12 months earlier than if they had been in 'disposables'.

Source: BITC and Scottish Nappy Company

Case study 15.4
Everton Football Club in the community

Disability Football Development Programme

The Disability Football Development Programme offers the same opportunities to disabled people as those open to people without disabilities and aims to lead the way in the provision of disabled footballing opportunities at all levels. By using the powerful brand of Everton Football Club, with a structured development plan, Everton is making significant progress in bringing the game to this previously excluded group.

The programme started in the late 1990s with a small group of just six enthusiastic disabled footballers and one coach. It has now evolved into a totally inclusive project, incorporating annual contact with over 10,000 disabled recreational players per year, eight competitive official Everton teams (amputee, deaf, partially sighted and five pan-disability teams, including junior, adult and female groups) with 100 registered disabled players, eight coaching staff and many trophies.

The programme is delivered by three full-time Everton Football in the Community (EFITC) staff and includes the country's first disabled FITC coach, Steve Johnson, who is also the captain of England's amputee football team.

This complete integration of the Football in the Community programme into the new commercial planning structure cements the club's belief in the impact and measurable benefits of community relationships and engagement. It also helps the club with its aim to be 'every supporter's second favourite team' by actively promoting accessibility and transparency, and emotionally engaging all football fans.

EFITC was a key participant in the consultation with Liverpool City Council during the application for the Capital of Culture 2008. It was invited to contribute to the delivery plan for the Year of Sport and to celebrate the inclusive nature of the EFITC disabled football programme.

According to Everton Football Club, the impact of the programme is as follows:

- Employees are proud to be associated with a company that not only engages disabled people, but also allows them to excel in a sport they all feel passionately about.

- Staff retention within EFITC is almost 100 per cent over 10 years and days off through illness are rare.

- Through the programme the disabled community has access not only to fitness, health, discipline and the social benefits of football, but also to employment, training and mentoring opportunities.

In 2010 Everton's Disability Programme achieved several honours, including the FA Community Club Charter Standard Award, which recognises the commitment to player and coach development. Also, in 2011, the Disability Programme won a 'sporting Oscar' at the Sports Industry Awards for 'Best Community Programme' and was named 'Best Community Scheme in Europe'.

Source: used with kind permission of BITC and Everton Football Club

How to develop community relations programmes

Community relations is not just about being good or 'nice to people', although this may be one of its results. Instead, the concept is based on sound commercial principles of:

- research
- vision (corporate need for one)
- strategic objectives
- tactical programme
- measurement and evaluation
- dissemination (how the results will be communicated to key audience/stakeholders, particularly employees).

Research

The company needs to be aware of its reputation in the community and this can be measured through research, mainly with employees, their families and the local community. Additional stakeholder views are important from investors, suppliers, competitors, etc. Further understanding is required of the local environment and the needs of the community(ies). These attitudes and opinions can be collected through internal and external communications audits using both qualitative and quantitative techniques. Research should also include an investigation into competitors' involvement in community activities and desk research into best community relations theory and practice. Demetrius and Hughes (2004) argue for the inclusion of stakeholder analysis software (planning, implementing and evaluating campaigns) to save time and support students and practitioners in developing CSR strategies and programmes. Their argument is that equivalent software is used by accountants and other professional groups to provide information and support the administration process so that practitioners can provide creativity in the non-routine aspects of the planning process to develop strategic solutions to problems.

Vision

The programme needs a vision that links into the corporate philosophy and strategy. BT in the UK, for example, has used the title and strapline 'Community Partnership Programme', which links its corporate strategy for improving company communication with customers on the ground in order to increase its customer base. BT's expertise lies in the communications industries (initially telecommunica-

Box 15.4

Strategic objectives for a community programme

Typical objectives for a community programme are:

- to create and develop a positive view of the company as a socially responsible, good corporate citizen among its key stakeholders
- to capitalise on this positive perception in terms of employee motivation, recruitment of new personnel, supplier development and community goodwill
- to support other initiatives aimed at creating an understanding of the company's aims and policies (an example might be the use of community displays at the company's annual general meeting)
- to develop opportunities that encourage employee participation in the community, through increased communication initiatives
- to support the needs of the local community with innovative, role-model initiatives, which position the company as a centre of excellence for community involvement
- to brand the programme clearly so that it is easily recognised and remembered.

tions and increasingly mobile and electronic communications) and it utilises its corporate skills in communications and technology to underpin its community programmes. The company clearly links its corporate objectives with its community vision.

It is not always necessary to make such clear links between the corporate strategy and the community, but it is vital that the programme has a vision and therefore a purpose for all those involved with it. (See Box 15.4.)

Tactics

Some of these have already been discussed in the earlier section on 'corporate community involvement programmes' and are listed as follows: sponsorships; targeted donations; awards; hospitality; employee volunteering; use of facilities (loan of equipment); training/seminars; and secondments (staff). (See Case study 15.5.)

Case study 15.5

BT 'Am I Listening?' and ChildLine campaigns – a lesson in long-term relationships

In 2011 the British telecommunications company BT celebrated a 25-year relationship with Childline – a charity to support young people. This case study demonstrates the value and returns for a business of developing long-lasting relationships with charities and other social organisations. ChildLine (0800 1111) is a confidential telephone service dedicated to children and young people and has helped over three million young people since it was set up in 1986.

Over the years, BT's 'Am I Listening?' campaign aimed to ensure that the voice of every young person in the UK is heard. It starts with ChildLine – because every day around 4,000 young people call the helpline, but lack of funds means only 1,800 get through.

BT's research in 2001 revealed that BT's CSR reputation had plateaued. To improve its reputation, an unprecedented (in terms of scope and scale) process of consultation with stakeholders was undertaken, beginning with an assessment of CSR perceptions. This resulted in focusing on young people as a key social issue. Further research undertaken by BT in May 2002, 'Are Young People Being Heard?', provided evidence of where communication gaps were greatest. The key finding was that only 47 per cent of UK children and young people felt their voices were being listened to and acted on. Findings went to over 500 key influencers – receiving overwhelming interest from MPs, peers, statutory and voluntary agencies – forming the basis of an opinion-former strategy. The research determined the direction of the campaign, providing benchmarks to measure success.

BT's most ambitious social campaign was launched in October 2002. The first two years concentrated on helping ChildLine reach its goal of answering every call.

Aims and objectives

BT's vision
BT believes that when young people are heard, it will release untapped potential, making a positive contribution to a better world.

Overall objectives
- Raise money for ChildLine and provide operational support.
- Help ChildLine move closer to its goal of answering every call.
- Raise awareness of the need to listen to young people and demonstrate the positive results when young people are heard.

Specific public relations objectives
- Improve BT's CSR reputation.
- Ensure at least 75 per cent of BT's 100,000 employees are aware of the campaign within two years.
- Accrue tangible business benefits from the campaign.

Implementation

The public relations campaign created and supported fundraising platforms for ChildLine. The cause-related marketing initiatives were highly visible, raised significant funds and were core to the overall campaign strategy.

BT Answer 1571
To start the fundraising drive, BT Retail donated £1 for every person who signed up to its free answering service, 1571. This was delivered via an intense media relations programme and an internal communications plan, with call-centre staff briefed to highlight the scheme to inbound callers.

Customer survey
BT Retail sent surveys to each of its 19 million residential customers – the largest customer survey ever undertaken in Europe. For every survey returned, £1 was donated to ChildLine. Designed to take advantage of milestones and extend the news value of the initiative, the public relations programme involved three phases: survey launch; £500k reached; and £1m reached.

Speaking Clock
As part of the BIG Listen week, BT ran a national competition with BBC children's news programme *Newsround* to find a young person's voice to be the Speaking Clock for one week. The winner was a 12-year-old Scottish girl.

case study 15.5 (continued)

Seen & Heard

In partnership with the UK youth parliament, the campaign undertook a nationwide search for examples of young people who had succeeded in making their voices heard. Fifteen case studies were used in the 'Seen & Heard' report. These were presented to government, leading to a meeting with Margaret Hodge, Minister of the UK Parliament for Children and Young People.

BIG Listen

The BIG Listen week was the focal point of the campaign's calendar. The aim during the week was to raise funds and awareness of the need to listen to young people. Activities and events during 2003 included:

- Speaking Clock initiative
- launch of the Listening Guide; based on the unique way that ChildLine trains its volunteers, the guide is for adults who want to communicate better with young people
- launch of the How To Make Yourself Heard Toolkit, which highlights easy and effective ways young people can make themselves heard
- BT Tower sponsored dash, reflecting the urgency to raise cash; led by world-record holder Colin Jackson, over 100 people took part in a timed sponsored dash up the 900 steps of BT Tower
- Seen & Heard case study subjects met Margaret Hodge MP and demonstrated how government can better engage young people in society.

Evaluation and measurement

Fundraising

With 99 per cent of BT employees aware of the company's support for ChildLine, the partnership has made quite an impact. Since the end of 2002, BT and its people have raised more than £7.5 million for the charity and BT has provided a further £5.5 million of in-kind support.

Business benefits

BT Answer 1571 initiative: In one month, take-up increased by 25 per cent, raising over £203,000 for ChildLine. The service encourages callers to stay on the line and there is a retrieval cost, so revenue is increased.

Customer survey: Over 1.3 million customers responded, representing the views of 3.25 million individual BT customers (approximately 2.5 people per household that uses BT), a response rate of nearly 7 per cent (three times the normal response). Findings allowed the company to target its marketing accurately, particularly for its Internet broadband service. Twenty-two per cent of interviewees identified the association with ChildLine as a 'very strong

positive influence' in persuading them to return the survey (GfK NOP Media (NOP)).

Speaking Clock: There were over 2,000 entries to be the speaking clock and the scheme raised £200,000. The theme 'it's time to listen to young people' secured coverage on every terrestrial TV channel, seven pieces of national radio, over 175 regional radio stations, 16 items of national print and a further 100 items in regional publications. Pieces even appeared in the *Seattle Times* and on National Public Radio (USA).

Creativity, what makes the campaign stand out?

Fundraising ideas focused on listening (e.g., customer survey/Speaking Clock) to raise funds for a listening campaign.

The initiative stands out because it is truly holistic in nature: as well as communication and public relations, BT helped ChildLine with fundraising, research activity, volunteering, training, advising on use of communications technology and development of the charity's long-term strategy. ChildLine is answering more calls as a result of the fundraising activity and strategic support. Through the public relations campaign, more children are being heard, particularly by government. The campaign also demonstrates how a company as large as BT, through a hard-hitting public relations campaign, can galvanise support behind a single cause, internally and externally.

Quotes from BITC

Mervyn Pedelty, Chief Executive, Co-operative Financial Services, last year's winner and sponsor of this year's award, said: 'The BT "Am I Listening?" campaign is a really good example of "joined up thinking". BT has mobilised its staff (including the personal enthusiasm of its chairman), its customers, its financial resources and, importantly, its technical know-how to transform the operations of a charity that is all about what BT does best – communications. The BT "Am I Listening?" campaign with ChildLine is a truly inspirational example of excellence and a worthy winner of this prestigious Award.'

Sue Adkins, Director, Business in the Community, said: 'BT is a worthy winner of this year's Business in the Community Award for Excellence. The "Am I Listening?" campaign is an holistic programme that has successfully been integrated into the whole of the organisation, engaging new and different aspects of the business as it

case study 15.5 (continued)

Picture 15.4 Aerial picture of the ChildLine launch at the London Eye (*source*: Beth Courtier/BT)

develops. This strategic cause-related marketing partnership has achieved considerable impact on many levels for both BT and ChildLine and is an inspirational example.'

Other supportive quotes
Dr Carole Easton, Chief Executive Officer, ChildLine: 'BT's support for ChildLine has never been stronger and we're delighted with the results so far. The BT "Am I Listening?" campaign has raised awareness for ChildLine's need for funds, has raised a significant amount through fundraising and provided fantastic strategic support. By helping Child-Line move closer to its goal of answering every child's call, "Am I Listening?" is certainly making an impact – enabling more children's voices to be heard in the UK.'

Beth Courtier, Head of Charity Programmes, BT: 'This campaign is delivering on every level, especially PR, where awareness internally and externally has exceeded expectation – recall levels are already nine months ahead of schedule. The PR has been crucial in ensuring the success of the fundraising.
   'The alignment between these two organisations is perfect; ChildLine is about communication and commu-nication is BT's business. It is a great example of how CSR partnerships create mutual benefits as well as improving the society and communities that each operates in.'

Source: used with kind permission of BT and Tri Media

Evaluating community programmes

Community involvement programmes can be difficult to measure in terms of quantifiable data, however this does not mean that the activities are unmeasurable. The following performance indicators can be used as means of measuring the programme's achievements:

- publicity achieved
- employee feedback
- value for money
- creativity
- comparable external benchmark
- 'thank you' letters and appreciation
- measured opinion-former perceptions
- internal and external communications audit results
- social media engagement, response and comment.

The BT 'Am I Listening?' campaign (Case study 15.5) illustrates some evaluation and measurement techniques in practice.

Measuring community involvement

Social reporting is a relatively new practice and differs from the financial reporting that is the established, legal requirement for all companies and organisations. Social reporting has been around since the mid 1980s and Blowfield and Murray (2008) cite Gray et al. (1987) who provide an early definition:

> . . . the process of communicating the social and environ-mental effects of the organisations' economic actions to particular interest groups within society, and society at large . . . Such an extension is predicated upon the assumption that companies do have wider responsibilities than simply to make money for their shareholders. (Gray et al. 1987)

David Davies, Chairman of Johnson Matthey plc, said in that company's 1995 annual statement:

Good corporate citizenship provides tangible benefits in many ways. It provides links with the community in which we operate and community projects can provide important training and experience to employees. The application of management skills to community projects and wider environmental initiatives is beneficial to the business and community alike.

Since the 1990s there has been significant growth in the interest and activity of social reporting. Figures produced by KPMG (2005) show an increase from 13 per cent in 1993 for the top 100 companies to 64 per cent in 2005.

In the USA it is estimated that 10 per cent of stock market investments are graded on ethical grounds and as such a positive ethical image is important to managers. A study by Alperson (1996) for the Conference Board of America into 463 US companies identified four new trends in corporate-giving strategies that demonstrate their integration into mainstream business policy:

1. programmes narrowly focused and aligned to business goals

2. giving is moving towards investment yielding a measurable return

3. image enhancement and employee loyalty are emerging as the value added elements of programmes

4. link between corporate-giving strategies and customer concerns is strengthening.

An increasingly popular method of measuring ethical performance is through social audits, which assess business policy on issues ranging from whether suppliers worked in a manner consistent with the firm's ethical policy to employee and customer attitudes. Allied Dunbar and the Body Shop in the UK have both recently gone through the audit process using outside auditors and published the results. Other companies interested in this approach are Ben and Jerry's, the US ice-cream firm, and BT in the UK.

Key factors to success of community involvement programmes

There a number of key factors that determine the success of a programme, the key one of which is the acceptance of the strategy by board directors and senior management. Without their endorsement the programme and individual initiatives will suffer from unnecessary scrutiny beyond the stated measurement criteria that should be put in place. Factors that may influence the success of such a programme include:

■ top management support

■ line management understanding and support

■ successful internal and external communication

■ central coordinator of activities

■ resources to meet necessary costs

■ employee-owned

■ recognition

■ partnership with community organisations

■ modest beginnings

■ monitoring and evaluation.

Figure 15.2 highlights the interlinking of three key areas for a successful community involvement programme. The three areas are the company, the community and the employees. (See Case study 15.6 and Explore 15.5.)

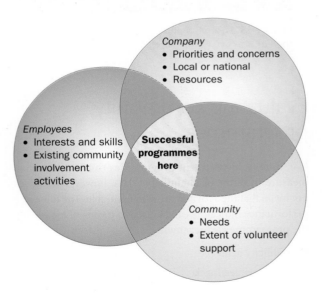

Figure 15.2 Elements of a successful community involvement programme (*source*: adapted from BITC 2012)

Case study 15.6
The Co-operative Bank

The Co-operative Bank was founded in 1872 to support the aims of the cooperative movement in the UK, which first started in Rochdale, in the north of England, in the middle of the nineteenth century. The cooperative movement's strength in the UK has traditionally been in grocery retailing and wholesaling but the bank has also been successful. One could argue that this success has been supported by the bank's strategic decision to re-affirm its commitment to cooperative values and to define its ethical position with regard to its customers and wider stakeholders.

Evolution of the corporate strategy

Mission statement

In 1988 the company first published its mission statement, which, at the time, could have been perceived as a commercial risk due to the strong right-of-centre political power balance of Margaret Thatcher's Conservative government. This government was also a great influence on business policy and practice, and at the time the economy was going through a boom. Business focus was on maintaining and enhancing shareholder value during an era of aggressive takeovers, mergers and acquisitions, together with privatisation of national utilities. Consequently, in business, there was no significant focus on ethical and societal issues. The Co-operative Bank's decision did prove to be significant and helped differentiate it from most of its competitors. (Harvard business professor, Michael Porter, has written about the significance of such difficult 'choices' in developing business strategies but also emphasises how they can be key to business success.)

Ethical policy

A second significant date for the bank was 1992, when it published its first ethical policy, developed in consultation with its customers. The policy aims to set out when and whether the bank will invest its money and where it will not.

Co-operative Bank's ethical policy

'Following extensive consultation with our customers, with regard to how their money should and should not be invested, the bank's position is that:

It will not invest in or supply financial services to any regime or organisation that oppresses the human spirit, takes away the rights of individuals or manufacturers any instrument of torture.

It will not finance or in any way facilitate the manufacture or sale of weapons to any country that has an oppressive regime.

It will actively seek and support the business of organisations that promote the concept of "Fair Trade" – i.e. trade that regards the welfare and interest of local communities.

It will encourage business customers to take a proactive stance on the environmental impact of their own activities, and will invest in companies and organisations that avoid repeated damage of the environment.

It will actively seek out individuals, commercial enterprises and non-commercial organisations that have a complementary ethical stance.

It will welcome suppliers whose activities are compatible with its ethical policy.

It will not speculate against the pound, using either its own money or that of its customers. It believes it is inappropriate for a British clearing bank to speculate against the British currency and the British economy using deposits provided by their British customers and at the expense of the British taxpayer.

It will try to ensure, by the continued application and development of its successful internal monitoring and control procedures that its financial services are not exploited for the purposes of money laundering, drug trafficking or tax evasion.

It will not provide financial services to tobacco product manufacturers.

It will not invest in any business involved in animal experimentation for cosmetic purposes.

It will not support any person or company using exploitative factory farming methods.

It will not engage in business with any farm or other organisation engaged in the production of animal fur.

It will not support any organisation involved in blood sports, which involve the use of animals or birds to catch, fight or kill each other – for example, fox hunting and hare coursing.

In addition, there may be occasions when the bank makes decisions on specific business involving ethical issues not included in this policy. We will regularly reappraise customers' views on these and other issues and develop our ethical stance accordingly.'

Ecological mission statement

This statement was followed in 1996 by an ecological mission statement, which acknowledges that all areas of human activity, including business, are dependent on the natural world for their well-being.

case study 15.6 (continued)

Co-operative Bank's ecological mission statement

'We, The Co-operative Bank, will continue to develop our business, taking into account the impact our activities have on the environment and society at large. The nature of our activities are such that our indirect impact, by being selective in terms of the provision of finance and banking arrangements, is more ecologically significant than the direct impact of our trading operations.

However, we undertake to continually assess all our activities and implement a programme of ecological improvement based on the pursuit of the following four scientific principles:

1. Nature cannot withstand a progressive build-up of waste derived from the Earth's crust.

2. Nature cannot withstand a progressive build-up of society's waste, particularly artificial persistent substances that it cannot degrade into harmless materials.

3. The productive area of nature must not be diminished in quality (diversity) or quantity (volume) and must be enabled to grow.

4. Society must utilise energy and resources in a sustainable, equitable and efficient manner.

We consider that the pursuit of these principles constitutes a path of ecological excellence and will secure future prosperity for society by sustainable economic activity.

The Co-operative Bank will not only pursue the above path itself, but endeavour to help and encourage all its partners to do likewise.

We will aim to achieve this by:

Financial services
Encouraging business customers to take a proactive stance on the environmental impact of their own activities, and investing in companies and organisations that avoid repeated damage of the environment (as stated in our ethical policy).

Management systems
Assessing our ecological impact, setting ourselves clear targets, formulating an action plan and monitoring how we meet them, and publishing the results.

Purchasing and outsourcing
Welcoming suppliers whose activities are compatible with both our ethical policy and ecological mission statement, and working in partnership with them to improve our collective performance.

Support
Supporting ecological projects and developing partnerships with businesses and organisations whose direct and indirect output contributes to a sustainable society.

Legislation
Adhering to environmental laws, directives and guidelines while continually improving upon our own contribution to a sustainable society.'

Partnerships (stakeholders)

The bank also developed a partnership framework, which is similar to the stakeholder concept discussed earlier in the text and is based on the writings of one of the Rochdale Pioneers of the cooperative movement, Robert Owen. The Co-operative Bank believes, as did Owen, that balanced, long-term relationships with these partners is key to the longevity and business success of the bank. The key partnership framework for the Co-operative Bank is detailed in Figure 15.3.

On its launch in 1996 the bank's partnership approach described its interaction and support for these groups as follows.

Society
From the ecological mission statement came an initiative by the bank to develop the Co-operative Bank National Centre for Business and Ecology. The centre draws on the expertise of four Greater Manchester-based universities. Affinity cards contribute to charities including the RSPB (Royal Society for the Protection of Birds), Oxfam, Amnesty International, Help the Aged and Children's Aid Direct.

Community
Investments are wide ranging, including support for public, private and voluntary initiatives in the Manchester area where the bank's head office is based, as well as supporting community groups in disadvantaged areas.

Suppliers and partners
The bank is a member of the Confederation of British Industry's (CBI) prompt payment scheme. It also cites examples of successful long-term contracts between itself and suppliers such as UNISYS Payment Services Limited, IBM and other smaller contractors involved in maintenance, cleaning and design services.

case study 15.6 (continued)

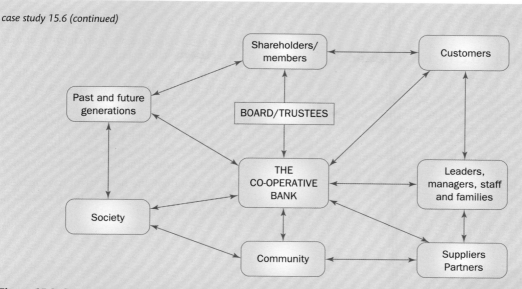

Figure 15.3 Seven partnership networks for the Co-operative Bank (*source*: Co-operative Bank Ethical Policy, Co-operative Bank internal publication)

Staff and families

Homeworking initiatives have been explored, with equipment installed at the employee's home; career breaks are supported; staff training is encouraged, including NVQs (national vocational qualifications); Investors in People has been achieved by the bank – an award for organisations that are judged to provide their staff with excellent training and development opportunities.

Customers

Progression and use of technology, such as 24-hour banking; interactive home banking; mobile phone banking; Internet access; as well as service developments such as affinity Visa cards, available to support individual schools and hospices.

Shareholders

The sole equity shareholder of the bank is the Co-operative Group. This society shares the bank's commitments on ethical and environmental issues.

Past and future generations

Links the bank back into its cooperative movement roots. The movement has been going for over 150 years and has always focused on the community in which a business operates.

Business benefits

The Co-operative Bank has seen its customer base grow in both the personal and business banking sectors. In the five years between 1992 and 1996 the bank saw profits before taxation rise from approximately £9m to £54.5m. At the end of 1996 the bank had total assets worth £4.5bn. Satisfaction levels of customers, when compared with other banks' customers in the UK, were also positive, with 94 per cent of Co-operative Bank customers satisfied with service compared with other banks at 89 per cent, and this compared with 73 per cent of the Co-operative's customers being very satisfied, with 51 per cent as an average for other banks (MORI 1996).

See also Explore 15.5.

Source: used with kind permission of the Co-operative Bank from its 'Ethical Policy' and 'Strength in Numbers' documents

Explore 15.5

Responding to criticism of ethical policy

As an executive for the Co-operative Bank, how would you respond to criticism that your ethical policy was described as a 'marketing initiative'?

How would you reply to critics who claim that the bank's initiatives are trivialising ethical debates in business practice?

Feedback

1. Write down the reasons why the bank may or may not replace the ethical policy 'initiative' next year.

2. Can you name other banks with an ethical banking policy? How do they compare to the Co-operative Bank?

3. In 1996 the Co-operative Bank stated its ecological mission statement. Think about contemporary issues that might affect the corporate strategy of an organisation involved in the banking sector today.

4. Why do you think the bank might have made a risky strategic decision in 1988 when it decided to publish its mission statement?

Summary

This chapter has attempted to bring to life some of the principles about the role organisations play in their society(ies) introduced earlier in the text by interpreting and applying them through current or recent case studies. A range of different examples has demonstrated that organisations worldwide are questioning and addressing their role in the societies in which they operate. This is being done in a variety of different ways – sometimes through actions that have clear links to corporate philosophies and strategies (the Co-operative Bank, Case study 15.6) and in other examples where the action has a clear business benefit and provides rewards for both parties. Community involvement is today a key component of many organisations' strategic thinking. Corporate social responsibility and the other terms used to describe this type of activity are boardroom buzzwords. Yet debate still rages (Crook 2005) on its role and purpose. Your role as students and practitioners is to understand why organisations get involved with their stakeholder communities and to continue to develop the debate.

Bibliography

Alperson, M. (1996). 'Conference Board of America'. In *Business in the Community Annual Report*: 5. London: Business in the Community.

Barone, M.J., A.D. Miyazaki and K.A. Taylor (2000). 'The influence of cause related marketing on consumer choice: does one good turn deserve another?' *Journal of the Academy of Marketing Science* 28(2): 248–262.

BITC (Business in the Community) (1996). 'Annual Report'. London: Business in the Community.

BITC (Business in the Community) (2000). 'Profitable Partnership Report'. London: Business in the Community.

BITC (Business in the Community) (2012). 'Annual Report'. www.bitc.org.uk accessed 1 May 2012.

Blowfield, M. and A. Murray (2008). *Corporate Responsibility: A critical introduction*. Oxford: Oxford University Press.

BT (1996). 'Community Partnership Programme: Annual review'. London: BT.

Cadbury, D. (1996). cited in *Business in the Community Annual Report*: 25. London: Business in the Community.

Carroll, A. (1991). 'The pyramid of corporate social responsibility'. *Business Horizons* July–August.

Chipps, W. (2011). Sponsorship spending: 2010 proves better than expected: Bigger gains set for 2011. IEG Sponsorship Report, 2011.

Cone Inc. (2011). 'Cause Evolution Survey Cone Inc'. www.coneinc.com accessed 10 May 2012.

Cone Roper (1997). *Cause-Related Marketing Trends Report*. London: Cone Roper.

Crook, C. (2005). 'The good company: a survey of corporate social responsibility'. *The Economist*: 22 January.

CSR Europe (Corporate Social Responsibility Europe) (2012). 'About us'. www.csreurope.org accessed 1 May 2012.

Davies, D. (1995). *First Forum*. 59. London: First Magazine Ltd.

Demetrius, K. and P. Hughes (2004). 'Publics or stakeholders? Performing social responsibility through stakeholder software'. *Asia Pacific Public Relations Journal* **5**(2).

Gibson, O. (2012). 'Protest groups target Olympics sponsors with new campaign'. *The Guardian*: 15 April.

Gray, R.H., D. Owen and K.T. Maunders (1987). *Corporate Social Reporting: Accounting and accountability*. Hemel Hempstead: Prentice Hall.

Hart, N. (1995). *Effective Corporate Relations*. Maidenhead: McGraw-Hill.

Ihlen, O., J. Bartlett and S. May (eds) (2011). *The Handbook of Communication and Corporate Social Responsibility*. Chichester: Wiley and Sons Limited.

Jones, B., R. Bowd and R. Tench (2009). 'Corporate irresponsibility and corporate social responsibility: competing realities.' *Social Resposibility Journal* **5**(3): 300–310.

Klein, N. (2000). *No Logo: Taking aim at the brand bullies*. London: Flamingo.

KPMG (2008). 'KPMG International Survey of Corporate Responsibility Reporting 2005' cited in M. Blowfield and A. Murray. *Corporate Responsibility: A critical introduction*. Oxford: Oxford University Press.

MORI (1996). 'Financial Services Survey'. London: MORI.

Research International (1995). 'Business in the Community'. www.bitc.org.uk accessed 8 May 2012.

Research International (1997). 'Consumer Survey: The Winning Game'. London: Business in the Community.

Schwartz, P. and B. Gibb (1999). *When Good Companies Do Bad Things: Responsibility and risk in an age of globalization*. New York, NY: John Wiley & Sons.

Smith, A. (1997). 'BT seeks to reassure caring consumers'. *Financial Times*: 13 January.

Thomson, S. (2000). *The Social Democratic Dilemma: Ideology, governance and globalization*. London: Macmillan.

UN Global Compact. www.unglobalcompact.org accessed 2 May 2012.

Websites

Business in the Community: www.bitc.org.uk
Business for Social Responsibility: www.bsr.org
Cause-Related Business Campaign: www.crm.org.uk
CSR Europe: www.csreurope.org
CSR Watch: www.csrwatch.com

Issue management

Learning outcomes

By the end of the chapter you should be able to:

■ characterise an issue and understand the difference between issues and other management problems
■ recognise that issues progress through a life cycle and identify what stage an issue has reached
■ identify the original and emerging theories and principles of issue management
■ analyse the characteristics of issues and identify the different driving forces of corporate and activist issues
■ understand issue management as both a communication discipline and as a component of broader strategic thinking
■ develop a basic issue management strategy using a four-step plan.

Structure

■ Birth of the discipline
■ What's an issue, and why is it important?
■ The rise of issue management
■ Tools and processes
■ Developing an issue strategy
■ Evolution of issue management

Introduction

In the Hollywood movie *Pretty Woman*, the unsophisticated heroine Vivian Ward (Julia Roberts) is taken to the upmarket Voltaire restaurant in Los Angeles where she is served a plateful of snails. When she tries to extract one from its shell, the expensively cooked *escargot* slips out of the clamp and flies through the air, provoking Vivian's famous quote: 'Slippery little sucker!'

That's a good description of issues, too. They are the slippery little suckers of public relations – the challenging problems where there is no black and white answer; where emotion often prevails over facts; where opponents may hate you and everything you stand for; where the risks of failure can be substantial; and where many senior executives would much prefer not to get involved.

Imagine your organisation being accused of using prison labour in third world countries; allegations that your product contributes to childhood obesity; critics who oppose your involvement with genetically modified material; the impact of global warming; opposition to new social legislation; a local community fighting against your new industrial facility; claims that your operations are destroying rain forest and killing endangered species.

Issues are constantly threatening the reputation and success of organisations, and this chapter will explore the nature and life cycle of issues, where they come from, how to identify them, and the stakeholders who play a role in managing issues.

We will also touch on the evolution of issue management as a formal discipline that provides proven tools and processes for responding to issues and working towards planned outcomes that are positive and aligned with strategic goals and objectives.

It draws on many other public relations activities, including risk communication, government relations, community outreach, media relations, stakeholder management, investor relations, corporate communication, litigation public relations and reputation management, among others. But, most importantly, it provides a structured framework for applying these various skills so that the organisation can participate in the issue in a focused way and, hopefully, reduce the chance that the issue will develop into a fully-fledged crisis. In this way, issue management is a vital concept that adds real value to society and to the business bottom line.

Birth of the discipline

Issue management began in the 1970s when a small group of American public relations practitioners determined to do something about what they saw as the lack of corporate capacity to respond to the influence of activists and other non-government organisations in the formation of public policy.

The leading advocate was Howard Chase, who believed that what was needed to help corporations fully participate in public policy, rather than just respond to it, went far beyond traditional government lobbying. What emerged was a formal discipline that was the new concept of issue management.

Chase, who became known as the 'father' of issue management, described the new discipline as 'the capacity to understand, mobilise, coordinate and direct all strategic and policy planning functions, and all public affairs/public relations skills towards achievement of one objective: meaningful participation in creation of public policy that affects personal and institutional destiny . . . Issue management is the systems process that maximises self-expression and action programming for most effective participation in public policy formation. Thus, issue management is the highest form of sound management applied to institutional survival' (Chase 1982: 1).

The purpose, he said, was to enable private business to be 'co-equal with the government and citizens in the formation of public policy rather than being the tail of a policy kite flown by others' (Chase 1984: 10).

By the time Chase died in 2003, at a remarkably active 93 years old, issue management was firmly established as an important business activity and as an acknowledged academic pursuit for both scholars and students.

Definition: 'Issue or issues?' 'Issue management' is sometimes referred to as 'issues management'. Asked about this question, Howard Chase, the 'father' of the discipline, is reported to have said it should always be 'issue management', not 'issues management', for the same reason that it is 'brain surgery', not 'brains surgery'.

What's an issue, and why is it important?

Before exploring issue management in detail, it is important to fully understand exactly what issues are, and how are they are different from day-to-day management problems.

There is no universally accepted single definition of an issue. In fact, this lack of agreement is reflected in the emergence of three different approaches to understanding issues. The distinction between these three approaches, or themes, was originally developed in Wartick and Mahon (1994) and subsequently updated in Jaques (2010).

Early on, Howard Chase defined an issue as 'a contested matter which is ready for decision', and this approach developed into what is called the 'disputation theme' that an issue arises where there is a social or political dispute. This theme was well captured by Heath and Coombs (2006: 262), who said 'an issue is a contestable difference of opinion, a matter of fact, evaluation or policy that is important to the parties concerned'.

Picture 16.1 High-profile demonstrations or media stunts to generate awareness are a standard element of many issue management strategies (*source*: Greenpeace UK)

Explore 16.1

Stakeholder analysis

Stakeholders are not just people or organisations who can affect or be affected by an issue, but also people or organisations who *think* they are a stakeholder. Consider the issue of fast food and the alleged link to childhood obesity and identify as many real or perceived stakeholders as you can think of. Remember that effective stakeholder analysis is not simply a list, but also a brief description of *why* each person or organisation may be a stakeholder and what is their stake in the issue.

The second approach is called the 'expectation gap theme', which basically arises when there is a gap – real or perceived – between how an organisation acts as opposed to how its key stakeholders believe it *should* act. This approach is popular with NGOs and community groups, which often have very definite opinions about what they see as shortcomings in the performance of business, especially 'big business'. (See Explore 16.1.)

The third approach is called the 'impact theme', which focuses attention on potential issues that are categorised by their capacity to seriously impact the organisation concerned. This is captured in the definition: 'An issue is any development – usually at least partly external to the organisation – which, if it continues, could have a significant impact on the organisation's financial position, operation, reputation or future interests, and requires a structured response.'

From all three of these approaches it can be seen that issue management is a sophisticated problem-solving tool. But it is not a general, all-purpose tool for dealing with the full range of day-to-day management problems. Instead, it is specifically intended to respond to a particular type of challenge, called issues. Table 16.1 compares problems with issues.

Whether seen as based on a dispute, or an expectation gap, or organisational impact, issues have particular qualities that separate them from other problems. These qualities include the following:

- **Ambiguous** – No black and white answer or 'right' solution; often relies on opinion and perspective.

- **External** – At least partly external to the organisation, involving outside people or entities.

- **Emotive** – Emotions rather than facts and figures often prevail.

- **High risk** – Risks of failure are substantial; high potential to become a crisis.

- **Policy** – May involve public policy or regulation or litigation.
- **Ongoing** – No obvious conclusion; may continue over a prolonged period of weeks, months or even years.
- **Media** – Intense media attention or potential for high media interest.

- **Contentious** – Involves committed, contending parties, often with uncompromising or confrontational positions.
- **Controversial** – May concern matters that are publicly controversial, often with a moral or ethical element.

Think about 16.1

Communicating risk and science

Many high-profile issues revolve around risk, science and technology. Competing parties involved in the issue may interpret risk in very different ways and may disagree completely about what is presented as an indisputable 'fact'. A good example would be whether mobile phone towers affect the health of the nearby community. Think about the factors that make science-based issues more difficult to manage. Why do scientists and experts sometimes find it hard to communicate and persuade? Why do experts and non-experts often reach different conclusions about risk?

Feedback

Scientists and other experts are usually trained to focus on facts and data that can be proven. Their training encourages them to find the 'right answer'. But many issues also involve emotions and opinions, and many risks are judged by concepts such as degree of control, trust, dread, fairness, familiarity and whether it is voluntary or enforced. Organisations should never ignore or misrepresent the facts, but they must recognise that many issues cannot be resolved by facts alone.

Think about 16.2

Confrontation or negotiation?

Think about the issues or situations where a confrontational strategy might be appropriate. How do those issues or situations differ from when negotiation may be best?

Imagine yourself as a senior executive of a 'target' organisation facing a significant issue. Would you prefer to face a high-profile assault, which you might be able to dismiss as a one-off stunt, or would you rather commit time and resources to prolonged negotiation that might require you to compromise your position on the issue?

Feedback

In dealing with an issue, choosing confrontation or negotiation is not necessarily right or wrong, but just different. Activists who prefer confrontation sometimes claim that negotiators are 'getting into bed with the enemy', while groups who prefer to negotiate may say the direct action people are only interested in headlines, and that stunts 'trivialise' the issue. These are two very different roles, and they enable big corporates and big government to divide and conquer, or pick and choose who they deal with. Either course of action could lead to a quick or easy resolution to the issue but it may not always be the best outcome.

The property developer must design his proposed building to optimise natural light on site that is shaded much of the year. **This is a problem**	The proposed development is opposed by the local residents association as being ugly, inappropriate and unsympathetic to the local environoment. **This is an issue**
Technical	Emotional
Based on demonstrable fact	Depends heavily on opinion
Recognised technical solutions	Solution must be negotiated
Results can be measured	Values harder to measure
Impersonal	Committed contending parties
Resolved in private	Argued in public

Table 16.1 A practical example to compare how a problem can become an issue (*source*: Issue Outcomes P/L)

The rise of issue management

Although the term 'issue management' was first coined in 1976, it was not until the 1980s that the discipline began to gain full momentum, reinforced by the publication in 1984 of Chase's seminal book, *Issue Management – Origins of the future*. Since that time it has become a core public relations and management activity, at the academic level in scholarly publications and university courses throughout the world, and as a central skill for consultants and practitioners. However, the concept of issue management also has its critics. (See Explore 16.2.)

While issue management was initially introduced to help corporations compete with governments and NGOs in the development of public policy, governments soon began to recognise the value of issue management to promote and implement those very policies.

As a result, issue management was quickly adopted by governments and government agencies to assist in gaining public or corporate support for new laws, policies and programmes. This might be as simple as a local government programme to build a highway bypass through a popular park, or to implement new parking restrictions that are opposed by local residents, or to introduce new regulations affecting Sunday shopping hours. Or, at the other end of the spectrum, it might be as major as introducing a new national education or health system, or working with international governments to ban nuclear weapons.

At the same time, issue management was also quickly adopted by activists, community groups and NGOs to help drive their particular agendas. This might be seen at a local level, with residents opposed to a corporation building a new shopping complex that will take business from high-street shops, right through to multinational activist NGOs, Greenpeace and Amnesty, or quasi-official international NGOs such as UNICEF and other agencies of the United Nations.

Mini case study 16.1
People power to ban landmines

In the late 1980s and early 1990s many activists became concerned about the terrible effects of anti-personnel landmines that devastated lives and communities long after a war was over. Most people at the time thought a few concerned individuals and some disconnected non-government organisations had no hope of success against the power of governments and militaries around the world. But in 1992 American teacher Jody Williams launched the International Campaign to Ban Landmines (ICBL), which eventually grew to a coalition of over 1,200 organisations working in 90 countries (www.icbl.org). This was before the rise of the Internet and social media, but Williams made brilliant use of the fax and email to drive the issue, and recruited high-profile supporters such as Diana, Princess of Wales (see Explore 16.3. In 1997 Williams and ICBL shared the Nobel Peace Prize, and the Mine Ban Treaty became a binding international law – the first time in history that a conventional weapon in widespread use had been comprehensively banned.

Explore 16.2

Critics of issue management

The modern development of issue management has seen the emergence of some outspoken critics, including some who believe it is a cloak for 'corporate spin' and gives an unfair or improper advantage to big business. These critics, from academia or journalism, include Dinan and Miller (2007), Miller and Dinan (2008), Lubbers (2002), Beder (2002, 2006) and the classic book by Stauber and Rampton (1995), *Toxic Sludge is Good For You: Lies, damn lies and the public relations industry*. What are their main criticisms? Are they mainly concerned about issue management itself or about the way it is used or misused?

Explore 16.3

Using celebrity power to influence issues

In 2009 British actress Joanna Lumley (famous for starring in *Absolutely Fabulous*, a television comedy that satirised the public relations industry) was acclaimed for her decisive role in the five-year campaign to secure rights of residence in Britain for Ghurkha soldiers from Nepal who had served in the British army.

Identify and investigate other cases where celebrities became associated with high-profile issue campaigns. Did they simply lend their names to the cause or were they actively involved in implementing an issue strategy?

Not all organisations use the same language – in fact some NGOs specifically try to avoid what they see as 'corporate terminology'. But for all these organisations, at every level, the same principal ideas behind issue management are now seen as essential to achievement of their purposes – namely, identifying a problem or opportunity early, attempting to frame the issue in a favourable way and using proven tools to develop and implement an effective strategy. (See Mini case study 16.1 and Explore 16.3.)

Tools and processes

Issue management has a dual identity. On one hand it is a strategic management approach to dealing with issues in a planned way, utilising cross-functional resources across the whole organisation. At the same time it is also a practical activity that utilises a variety of tools and processes to ensure consistency and delivery of intended outcomes.

These include, but are not confined to: a formal mechanism for recognising and identifying potential issues; an objective process for prioritising issues to determine allocation of resources; a way to recognise how developed any issue is; and a formal issue strategy process that can be objectively assessed and benchmarked against best practice.

The issue readiness checklist (Table 16.2) helps assess an organisation's progress in establishing an effective system.

Two of the most important tools used to help facilitate real progress are the issue life cycle and the strategy process model. We will look first at the life cycle model and then consider the process model under the section called 'Developing an issue strategy'.

Issue life cycle models were an early development, and their purpose is to convey in a graphic form the concept that issues are not static, but progress along a fairly predictable path. However, the pace at which they move along that path can vary enormously. Issues can progress through the cycle extremely rapidly, sometimes moving from concern to crisis in a matter of days, while other issues develop

---

Box 16.1

Where do issues come from?

One of the commonest questions in issue management is: 'Where do issues come from and how do you recognise them?' Simply maintaining a very close watch on news and current affairs is the obvious answer. As the American issue expert George McGrath (1998: 74) said: 'For most organizations, key issues will be found from reading headlines rather than tea leaves'. But there are many other sources that are obvious but are often overlooked, including:

- industry and political conferences
- trade publications
- industry association meetings and newsletters
- client and customer surveys
- industry and business allies
- websites and information from organisations that oppose you
- analysis by experts
- feedback from your own staff who deal with external people.

Most of these sources are inexpensive, yet can yield priceless intelligence.

Table 16.2 An issue-readiness checklist helps assess an organisation's progress in establishing an effective system (*source*: Issue Outcomes P/L)

How it sometimes is	How it should be
Focus mainly on updating issue briefs, positioning statements, contact lists	Focus is on specific issue strategies to deliver planned, positive outcomes
Reactive mode – getting prepared in case the news media phone	Proactive mode – willing and able to take action
Business units assign issue responsibility to public affairs department	Business units take ownership of issues with public affairs as a resource and centre of expertise
Focus is on getting the process right	Focus is on making a difference
Management regard issue management as low-priority activity	Issue management is an integral part of business planning

Mini case study 16.2

When asthma inhalers became an issue battleground

At the beginning of the global warming debate, countries around the world got together in Montreal and agreed to ban chlorofluorocarbons (CFCs) – a group of chemicals widely used in applications such as refrigeration, air conditioning and as an aerosol propellant, but were proved to damage the atmosphere. In order to enforce the ban, governments and special interest groups believed there should be a policy of 'no exemptions'. However, it was not widely known that CFCs were used as the propellant in asthma inhalers, and this became a classic challenge for issue management.

Without a replacement propellant, millions of asthma sufferers worldwide would be denied life-saving medication, and finding and testing a replacement could take up to ten years. Delaying the CFC ban was deemed impossible, so nine major manufacturers formed a coalition to persuade the international community that health risk should be balanced against environmental damage and that big drug companies should get special treatment. It was a tall task, but proved a triumph for coordinated issue management. The UN and EU eventually agreed on a ten-year extension to allow a replacement propellant to be introduced, and asthma inhalers are still available today – CFC-free.

Source: Regester and Larkin 2005

very slowly and can take months or years to gain a foothold in public awareness, and may never move beyond the awareness phase.

Typical of these early models is the work of Max Meng (1992), who characterised issues moving over time through five phases of a life cycle – Potential, Emerging, Current, Crisis and Dormant. Other models don't include a crisis phase on the basis that not all issues develop into a crisis. It is argued that many issues have the potential to become a crisis if not properly managed, but that issue management and crisis management are distinctly different processes, even though they can sometimes be very closely linked (see Chapter 17).

The life cycle model shown in Figure 16.1 includes two parallel elements. The first is the basic evolution of the issue itself, from origin or potential through emergence and organisational response to resolution or dormancy. The other element shows the parallel evolution of an issue through the political process, from expectation expressed by some sections of society, through recognition as a political issue, then on to the introduction of legislation and eventually to enforcement and litigation.

Explore 16.4

Issue life cycles

The concept of the issue life cycle is central to the development and implementation of issue management. Use the Internet to search for alternative issue life cycle models. What is common about them? What is different? How does the terminology change? What makes some models more effective than others?

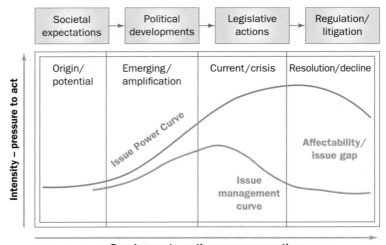

Figure 16.1 Life cycle of a strategic issue

The key to most life cycle representations, including this version, are two fundamental truths about issue management. One of these fundamental truths is that the majority of issues, if left unmanaged, tend to deteriorate and become worse. This may seem obvious, but is often ignored or not understood by executives who would prefer not to deal with the issue and say: 'Let's leave it alone and it might go away', or maybe: 'Let's just watch it and decide later whether we need to take action'. Issue management is about recognising a problem early and taking planned action.

The second fundamental truth illustrated by life cycle models is that as time passes issues get harder to deal with, the options available become fewer and the cost of dealing with the issue increases. As the American commentator James Lukaszewski says: 'The cheque you write today will always be the smallest cheque you will ever write' (2002: 68).

Understanding this process and the status of any particular issue as it moves through the cycle is critical to developing the strategy and assigning resources. (See Mini case study 16.2 and Explore 16.4.)

Developing an issue strategy

The basis of effective issue management is translating information and data and good intentions into practical actions. This means not just making a plan but making a difference. Developing an issue strategy demands a systematic approach, and over the years this has led to the development of many different process models. Some issue management models are complex work-flows that produce thick, three-ring binders with pages of analysis and appendices. And sometimes their focus is on meetings and minutes rather than delivering progress.

The essence of effective issue strategy planning is that the plan must be easy to understand and communicate, easy to implement and focused on getting things done. A good example is the five steps of issue management supported by the Issue Management Council (n.d.):

1. Issue **identification**
2. Issue **analysis**
3. Issue **change strategy options**
4. Issue **action programme**
5. **Evaluation** of results

While there are also many similar examples, one proven detailed model is the 'Do-it Plan'™, which takes its name from four progressive steps – Definition, Objective, Intended Outcomes, Tactics (see Figure 16.2). Inexperienced practitioners tend to think quickly about an issue then immediately start brainstorming tactics. But the 'Do-it Plan' provides a framework to focus on what you are trying to achieve, before focusing on the tactics to achieve it.

Step one – definition

Before you can do anything about an issue you have to define exactly what the issue is. It is only natural that different people will see any issue in different ways. A lawyer,

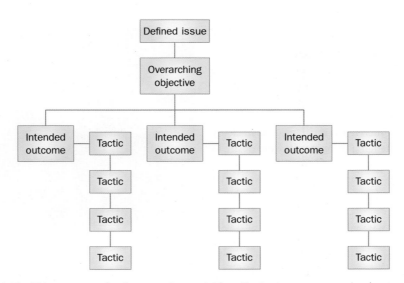

Figure 16.2 The 'Do-it Plan'™ is one example of a step-wise model for effective issue management (*source*: Issue Outcomes P/L)

for example, will tend to see the issue in legal terms, an engineer will see it as a technical problem, an accountant will see it in financial terms and a public relations person may see it primarily as a communication problem. All these perspectives may be valid, but for the organisation as a whole there needs to be a single definition that everyone agrees about and that forms the foundation for the whole strategic plan. Experience shows there is real value in having the issue defined in writing, preferably in a single sentence, to capture the problem and its impact on the organisation, which may be financial, reputational or affecting the organisation's ability to do business. An unambiguous definition helps keep focus on what really is the problem rather than peripheral matters, and helps keep all the key participants in full alignment.

Step two – objective

The greatest barriers to effective issue management are (a) failure to agree on a clear objective and (b) unwillingness or inability to take action. But it is objective-setting where issue management most often comes undone. Successful implementation of issue management is basically achieving an agreed overarching objective by determining and carrying out practical and agreed actions designed to deliver that objective. There often seem to be several possible objectives and these can easily demand conflicting or even contradictory actions. The key to this step is to make sure – even in complex issues – that there is only one overarching objective. Not having an agreed objective results in duplication, waste, frustration and failure.

Step three – intended outcomes

Intended outcomes are the 'bite-sized pieces' that it is agreed will deliver the objective. In some models these are described as sub-objectives or desired outcomes. But the terminology 'intended outcomes' has a particular significance. Desired outcomes are 'what we would like to SEE happen'. Intended outcomes, by contrast, are 'what we plan to MAKE happen'. The difference is much more than clever semantics. It is about changing the mind-set from desire to intent. It moves the thinking forward from 'I am a victim of this issue and things are happening TO me', to 'I am a player in developing this issue and I intend to make things happen FOR me'.

For example, a desired outcome might be 'wouldn't it be good if the news media stopped criticising our consumer products division'. The equivalent intended outcome would be 'that we work with the news media to help them better understand the contribution of the consumer products

division within the overall business strategy'. While the end result might be similar, the way it is presented highlights the difference between talking about it and doing it.

Step four – tactics

Once the intended outcomes have been agreed, the tactics usually follow reasonably easily. Experience shows that the intended outcomes capture the main themes of any issue management plan, and the tactics tend to group together naturally under each of these themes. Alongside each tactic, of course, comes the name of the individual or individuals who will implement that tactic, and the proposed timeline. The four steps of the plan are then drawn up in a single document and together comprise a logical and targeted issue management plan or strategy.

Evaluation

Evaluation in public relations is often regarded as difficult, and may seem particularly elusive in the discipline of issue management. A step-wise approach helps address this question, as evaluation is carried out, not against a broad issue, and not even against the over-arching objective, but against the intended outcomes and the plan itself. It is important to occasionally revisit the definition and the objective, because the issue may change over time. By working through an agreed plan, not only is it possible to objectively and accurately evaluate impact against the plan, but the process itself facilitates progressive evaluation partway through the project and enables easy adjustment to meet changing needs. (See Explore 16.5.)

Picture 16.2 Global warming is the emblematic issue of the twenty-first century, with organisations at every level, from global to local, relying on issue management to stake out the position (*source*: Shutterstock.com/Vadim Petrakov)

Explore 16.5

Evaluating best practice

While every organisation faces different issues and manages them in different ways, a standard of 'Best Practice Indicators' has been developed by the Issue Management Council in Leesburg, Virginia. Access this document on the IMC website (www.issuemanagement.org) and review their recommendations against an organisation you know. Which indicators are relevant to an organisation beginning the issue management journey, and which would be regarded as advanced practice?

Evolution of issue management

Issue management has evolved very substantially over the last 40 years. Indeed, it is still evolving in response to our changing environment, which makes it a particularly vibrant and contemporary public relations activity.

One of the most important changes to issue management has already been discussed in this chapter, namely the migration from being a corporate activity to one that is now utilised by governments and government agencies, as well as activists, community groups and NGOs. This change is extremely important, although it is not always obvious because of the fact that these groups don't necessarily use the same issue management language and terminology. (This convergence between the activist and corporate perspective is explored in detail in Jaques 2006.)

Another major change that occurred, and is still occurring, is the impact of technology on issue management, especially as it applies to activists, community groups and NGOs.

Not many years ago a small local group concerned about an issue had to use limited tools such as word of mouth, public meetings and brochures to create awareness, and relied on traditional news outlets to spread the word further. Now these small groups can instantly access a national or international audience to promote their issue, drive fundraising, encourage feedback and recruit participation.

Social media and other new technology has also facilitated sharing of information about issues and issue management techniques, online publication of books on the issue, and has provided blogs, discussion groups and other platforms to develop and disseminate ideas.

As British practitioner Simon Titley (2003: 86) has noted: 'Resources that were once the preserve of governments and large corporations, such as access to intelligence and an ability to communicate and mobilise (both globally and instantaneously), are now available to anyone for the price of a cup of coffee in a cybercafé.'

Not only do these technology tools help small groups communicate, but they also mean 'resource-poor' organisations and individuals have a more level playing field to help frame issues – which means the ability to set the language that is used to position and define the issue (see Mini case study 16.3 and Explore 16.6).

From the perspective of organisations responding to issues, new technology has created fresh challenges, especially in terms of dramatically increasing scrutiny by stakeholders and the speed at which information spreads. For a multinational business, for example, its activities in response to an issue in one country will almost instantly

Mini case study 16.3

When social media helped win the 'bra war'

British woman Beckie Williams was no hardened activist. But she got really angry in mid-2008 when the clothing chain Marks and Spencer introduced a £2 surcharge for larger women's bras. She wrote to complain but got an unsatisfactory reply, and received no reply at all when she wrote again. So Ms Williams launched a Facebook page, 'Busts4Justice', to raise awareness of what she portrayed as discriminatory pricing. Within weeks the Facebook page had over 5,000 followers, while the company argued publicly that larger bras needed more material and 'additional engineering'. The Facebook followers increased to over 18,000 and the issue gained massive Internet support and mainstream media coverage around the world. Ms Williams then purchased one M&S share and vowed to take the issue to the company AGM in July 2009. The company still persisted it was 'impossible for us to reduce price without cutting quality'. But they had completely misjudged the situation and misread their customers. Two days later M&S Chairman Stuart Rose said they had got it wrong and he announced an immediate withdrawal of the surcharge. The so-called 'bra war' ended in victory for the protesters and failure by M&S to manage what should have been a straightforward issue.

Explore 16.6

Naming and framing issues

How an issue is named and defined can be critical in the way that issue is perceived. For example, censorship can be portrayed as protecting society's values or restricting free speech; a new industrial facility can be described as a secure landfill or as a toxic waste dump; the abortion debate is rarely referred to these days as pro-abortion and anti-abortion but as pro-choice or pro-life. What are some other examples of how language is used to create a positive or a negative frame for an issue?

become known to critics in another part of the world.

Moreover, the rise of technology and social media has had a direct effect on one of the core aspects of issue management mentioned earlier, namely the so-called 'expectation gap'. Social media has fostered a major change in the community's expectation of what is acceptable corporate behaviour, which, in turn, is opening new areas of debate and raising the bar for corporations and executives.

In this respect, not only have these technology changes enabled organisations to respond much more rapidly to emerging issues, but there is now an expectation about that response, which can sometimes be measured in hours rather than days. For example, companies are now often criticised not just because of what they did or said, but why they didn't do it or say it quicker, or why they didn't communicate it to a wider audience.

So social media has dramatically changed what is expected of an organisation in response to issues, and it has also dramatically increased the community's capacity and willingness to express those expectations and demand improved performance.

Issue management began as a purely corporate concept 40 years ago, but development and evolution mean its basic strengths and ideas are still as relevant today to new generations of students, managers and practitioners.

Case study 16.1
How an iconic brand was humbled by two schoolgirls

When two 14-year-old New Zealand schoolgirls at Pakuranga College in Auckland set out to test the vitamin C content of various fruit drinks for a classroom chemistry project, they had no idea that their findings and the subsequent mismanagement of a local issue would lead to a corporate prosecution, as well as public humiliation and international damage for an iconic global brand.

Ribena blackcurrant drink was launched in Britain in the 1930s and won lasting fame during the Second World War as a source of vitamin C for British children denied fresh fruit such as oranges. It subsequently became established as an iconic 'healthy food', served by mothers in many countries around the world, especially British Commonwealth nations such as Australia and New Zealand with strong post-war British migration. Today, Ribena generates massive worldwide sales for its brand owner, the giant global manufacturer GlaxoSmithKline.

So when teenagers Anna Devathasan and Jenny Suo wanted to test fruit drinks in 2004, it was only natural that they included the ready-to-drink (RTD) version of Ribena, which is packaged in a form ideally suited for the school lunch box. But to their surprise they found that the ready-to-drink Ribena did not contain four times the vitamin C of oranges, despite wording used in product advertising.

The schoolgirls wrote to GSK New Zealand complaining that the television advertising statement 'the blackcurrants in Ribena contain four times the vitamin C of oranges' was 'intentionally misleading and quite inappropriate' in that it misled people to believe that Ribena fruit drink itself contained four times the vitamin C, which is untrue. They also reported that they telephoned the company and were dismissed with the response: 'It's the blackcurrants which have it.'

Now, an important element of issue management is to act on early warning signs about potential problems, and just a few years earlier GSK in the United Kingdom had been severely embarrassed over Ribena Toothkind – a reduced-sugar formula of Ribena with added calcium, which it was claimed did not encourage decay in children's teeth. In that case the advertising was found to be misleading and the company had to withdraw the tooth decay claim from its packaging.

Notwithstanding that bruising recent experience, the company in New Zealand seemingly chose not to

case study 16.1 (continued)

respond to the written approach from the two schoolgirls. So the intrepid teenagers took their case to top-rating New Zealand television consumer programme 'Fair Go,' which broadcast the story nationally in October 2004.

GSK did not appear on 'Fair Go' but issued the TV producers a written statement, which was summarised on air:

The claim 'blackcurrants in Ribena contain four times the vitamin C of oranges' is correct and relates to blackcurrants and oranges in their natural fruit state. This is a claim applicable to all Ribena products, not just concentrate. We make no comparison to juices, fruit drinks or any other pre-packaged drink product. The advertising statement has appeared as part of Ribena advertising worldwide for more than a decade. All Ribena products boldly highlight the actual and correct vitamin C content as required by law. We sincerely apologise for the way in which Anna and Jenny's complaint was dealt with.

Despite the UK experience, and this negative exposure on New Zealand national television providing early indications of an impending serious issue, the TV commercial with the 'four times' claim remained in use for another 18 months. Meanwhile, the two girls took their complaint directly to the government consumer watchdog, the New Zealand Commerce Commission.

In subsequent statements the company tried to separate the vitamin C content in the concentrated Ribena syrup from the level in the RTD version, but in 2007 both products were the subject of prosecution for misleading advertising. Appearing before the Auckland District Court, GSK pleaded guilty to ten representative charges arising from the 'four times' advertising claim. They also pleaded guilty to five other charges relating to false labelling of the RTD Ribena, which was advertised as containing 7 mg of vitamin C per 100 ml when subsequent testing showed it contained no measurable vitamin C at all. Judge Phil Gitos described the labelling statement as 'not just incorrect but wholly false' and fined the company $NZ 227,500 (then equivalent to about £81,750 or $US 163,400). In addition, the second-largest global pharmaceutical company was forced to take out apology advertising in both Australia and New Zealand.

Over this period, the New Zealand story received disproportionate publicity around the world, undoubtedly amplified by the involvement of the two photogenic schoolgirls, now aged 17, who gave extensive interviews before and after the court hearing. As New Zealand's largest circulation newspaper quipped: 'Seldom has a case of commercial chicanery been exposed as delightfully as that of the sugar drink Ribena' (*NZ Herald* 28 March).

The impact of this news angle alone can be gauged from just a brief sampling of international mainstream media headlines – 'Ribena shamed by New Zealand schoolgirls' (*The Australian* 27 March); 'Schoolgirls expose firm's claim of vitamin C in drink' (*Times of India* 27 March); 'School project trips up Ribena' (BBC online 27 March); 'Drinks giant faces court after girls' Ribena test' (*The Scotsman* 27 March); 'Schoolgirls rumble vitamin claims' (*The Guardian* 27 March); 'The schoolgirls who cost Ribena £80k for its vitamin fib' (*Daily Mail* online 27 March); 'Ribena maker squashed after NZ schoolgirl exposé' (Reuters 27 March); 'Ribena caught out by schoolgirls' (CNN online 27 March); 'Sweet victory for NZ schoolgirls' (*Daily Telegraph* 28 March); 'Schoolgirls expose drink scandal' (*Bangkok Post* 3 April).

Among the fundamental principles of issue and crisis management are to recognise the problem early, to promptly institute a strategic response plan and corrective action and, if necessary, to apologise genuinely and without delay.

This case study highlights the manufacturer's lack of success against each of these principles and demonstrates how the giant corporation that owns Ribena mismanaged a seemingly simple local problem and suffered unnecessarily severe consequential damage to its brand and international reputation.

Source: adapted from Jaques 2008b

Summary

This chapter explored issue management both as a management approach to dealing with potential threats and as a system of proven tools and processes for achieving planned, positive outcomes aligned with strategic objectives.

Discussion highlighted the historical context of issue management and its migration from being a mainly corporate discipline to also become a key public relations activity for government agencies as well as activist, community and NGO groups.

The chapter introduced the concept of the issue life cycle, which characterises the important phases of issue management. It also set out a simple four-step process that provides a practical framework to develop and implement a strategic issue management plan.

Bibliography

Argenti, P.A. (2004). 'Collaborating with activists: how Starbucks works with NGOs'. *California Management Review* **47**(1): 91–116.

Beder, S. (2002). *Global Spin: The corporate assault on environmentalism.* Totnes, Devon: Green Books.

Beder, S. (2006). *Suiting Themselves: How corporations drive the global agenda.* London: Earthscan.

Chase, W.H. (1982). 'Issue Management Conference – A special report'. *Corporate Public Issues and their Management* **7**(23): 1–2.

Chase, W.H. (1984). *Issue Management – Origins of the future.* Stamford, CT: Issue Action Publications.

Coombs, W.T. and S.J. Holladay (2007). *It's Not just PR: Public relations in society.* Malden, MA: Blackwell.

Dinan, W. and D. Miller (eds) (2007). *Thinker, Faker, Spinner, Spy: Corporate PR and the assault on democracy.* London: Pluto Press.

Gregory, A. (1999). 'Issues management: the case of Rhone-Poulenc Agriculture'. *Corporate Communications: An International Journal* **4**(3): 129–135.

Hallahan, K. (2001). 'The Dynamics of Issue Activation: An Issues Processes Model'. *Journal of Public Relations Research* **13**(1): 27–59.

Heath, R.L. (1997). *Strategic Issues Management – Organisations and public policy Challenges.* Thousand Oaks, CA: Sage.

Heath, R.L. and W.T. Coombs (2006). *Today's public relations: An introduction.* Thousand Oaks, CA: Sage.

Heath, R.L. and M.J. Palenchar (2008). *Strategic Issues Management: Organizations and Public Policy Challenges.* 2nd Edition. Thousand Oaks, CA: Sage.

Heugens, P.P.M.A.R. (2005). 'Issues Management: Core understandings and Scholarly Development'. In P. Harris & C.S. Fleischer (eds). *The Handbook of Public Affairs* (pp. 481–500). Thousand Oaks, CA: Sage.

Issue Management Council (n.d.). *Origins of Issue Management.* http://issuemanagement.org/learnmore/origins-of-issue-management/

Jaques, T. (2006). 'Activist "rules" and the convergence with issue management'. *Journal of Communication Management* **10**(4): 407–420.

Jaques, T. (2007). 'Issue or problem? Managing the difference and averting crises'. *Journal of Business Strategy* **28**(6): 25–28.

Jaques, T. (2008a). 'Howard Chase: the man who invented issue management'. *Journal of Communication Management* **12**(4): 336–343.

Jaques, T. (2008b). 'When an icon stumbles – the Ribena issue mismanaged'. *Corporate Communications: An International Journal* **13**(4): 394–406.

Jaques, T. (2010). 'Embedding issue management: from process to policy' in *The Sage Handbook of Public Relations*, 2nd edition. R.L. Heath (ed.). Newbury Park, CA: Sage.

Lubbers, E. (ed.) (2002). *Battling Big Business: Countering greenwash, infiltration and other forms of corporate bullying.* Totnes, Devon: Green Books.

Lukaszewski, J.E. (2002). 'How to build your reputation during litigation to avoid crummy trial visibility' in *Crisis Management.* J.A. Gottschalk (ed.). Oxford: Capstone.

McGrath, G. (1998). *Issues Management – Anticipation and influence.* San Francisco, CA: IABC.

McGrath, G. (2006). 'Issues management: linking business and communication planning' in *The IABC Handbook of Organizational Communication.* T.L. Gillis (ed.). San Francisco, CA: Jossey-Bass.

Meng, M. (1992). 'Early identification aids issue management'. *Public Relations Journal* **48**(3): 22–24.

Miller, D. and W. Dinan (2008). *A Century of Spin: How public relations became the cutting edge of corporate power.* London: Pluto.

Regester, M. and J. Larkin (2005). 'CFC's – finding an essential breathing space' in *Risk Issues and Crisis Management: A case book of best practice*, 3rd edition. London: Kogan Page.

Stauber, J. and S. Rampton (1995). *Toxic Sludge is Good for You: Lies, damn lies and the public relations industry.* Monroe, ME: Common Courage Press.

Titley, S. (2003). 'How political and social change will transform the EU public affairs industry'. *Journal of Public Affairs* **3**(1): 83–89.

Wartick, S.L. and J.F. Mahon (1994). 'Toward a substantive definition of the corporate issue construct: a review and synthesis of the literature'. *Business and Society* **33**(3): 293–311.

Websites

www.issuemanagement.org

www.icbl.org

www.issueoutcomes.com.au

www.bbc.co.uk/news/

www.huffingtonpost.com/

www.globalalliancepr.org/content/1/3/about

CHAPTER 17

Tim Coombs

Crisis public relations management

Learning outcomes

By the end of this chapter you should be able to:

- define and describe the concepts of crisis and crisis management
- recognise the value of communication to crisis public relations management
- understand the different crisis types and how the crisis type affects crisis communication
- identify the key principles in crisis public relations management
- apply principles of crisis public relations management to actual crisis cases
- understand the effects of the Internet on crisis public relations management.

Structure

- Crisis public relations management: the context
- Where do crises come from?
- How to prepare for a crisis
- Communicating during a crisis
- The Internet and crisis public relations management

Introduction

In 2005, a political cartoon in a Danish newspaper sparked international protests and a boycott of Danish goods in the Middle East. Arla Foods, a company with strong ties to Denmark, lost millions of dollars in sales as a result of the boycott. Crisis public relations management was one of the tools Arla management relied upon to repair the damage inflicted by the cartoon affair (Frandsen and Johansen 2010). In 2010, BP faced a crisis as crude oil poured from a ruptured well into the Gulf of Mexico. At times, crisis messages coming from then BP CEO Tony Hayward made the crisis worse for BP. Effective crisis public relations management can make a crisis better but will make the situation worse when it is ineffective. An extended example will help to illustrate the value of crisis public relations management.

On 4 July 2011, media giant News Corp began to dominate international news coverage because of their phone hacking scandal highlighted by the Milly Dowler case. *News of the World*, a News Corp publication, was collecting information for stories by hiring people to hack into mobile phones. On 14 July, Rupert Murdoch, head of News Corp, said the crisis was being handled 'extremely well' (Estes 2011). Mr Murdoch was one of the few to take that position. News Corp was in a crisis and handling it badly as media attention intensified, News Corp's stock price began to drop and the company had to abandon its bid to buy BSkyB. The day Mr Murdoch's crisis appraisal was published, News Corp hired public relations titan Edelman to guide the crisis management effort. On 16 and 17 July an apology from News Corp, signed by Rupert Murdoch, appeared in major UK newspapers with the headline 'We are sorry' (Timeline 2011). The apology marked a new and improved direction in News Corp's crisis public relations management. News Corp became more cooperative with government officials and news coverage began to soften. The News Corp example reflects the dangers of ineffective crisis

public relations management and benefits it can provide when it is effective.

Effective crisis public relations management protects stakeholders from harm, helps stakeholders recover from the crisis and works to repair the damage the crisis has inflicted on the organisation in crisis. The key difference between effective and ineffective crisis public relations management is strategic thinking. Effective crisis public relations management is built on a foundation of preparation that is informed by research. When a crisis hits, managers have practised handling similar situations and understand what actions should help and which could hurt in their crisis situation.

Crisis public relations management is a rapidly developing field, with new knowledge being added regularly. This chapter presents the key points of crisis public relations management that can help guide managers toward an effective crisis management effort.

Crisis public relations management: the context

Crisis public relations management is an applied field. Like most applied fields, understanding the field began by analysing what managers were already doing then trying to develop ways to improve on the practice. The early literature on crisis public relations management were simply lists of 'what to do' and 'what not to do' in a crisis. Box 17.1 presents a list of the common recommendations found in the early crisis writings. These lists were based upon case studies of what crisis managers had done in the past. The lists are a type of 'accepted wisdom'. Some accepted wisdom really is wisdom and some is simply urban myth. As the field matures, researchers have begun exploring crisis public relations management in a more systematic fashion, to separate the wisdom from the urban myths and to begin building crisis public relations management theory. Theory improves the practice by developing and testing reasons for why certain actions are effective and others are ineffective.

Box 17.1

Early crisis communication recommendations

What to do

- Speak with one voice/consistent message (Carney and Jorden 1993)
- Respond quickly (Caruba 1994)
- Be open and disclose information about the crisis (Twardy 1994)

What not to do

- Speculate on the cause of the crisis
- Say 'no comment' (In a Crisis 1993)

The accepted wisdom is replaced with evidence based on theory and empirical tests. Crisis public relations management is in a transitional phase from accepted wisdom to evidence-based approaches. Researchers in contingency theory (e.g., Jin et al. 2007) and situational crisis communication theory (e.g., Coombs and Holladay 2001) are at the forefront of evidence-based crisis communication. The evidence-based approaches use experiments to test how people react to crises and to the crisis response strategies used in a crisis. The experiments test speculation about how people will react to a crisis or react to a crisis response strategy. Speculation is then replaced with evidence.

Defining key concepts

We should begin the exploration of crisis public relations management by defining the key terms 'crisis' and 'crisis public relations management'. A crisis can be defined as 'the perception of an unpredictable event that threatens important expectancies of stakeholders and can seriously impact an organisation's performance and generate negative outcomes' (Coombs 2012: 2). Crises are perceptual. If an organisation's stakeholders believe it is in a crisis, the organisation is in a crisis unless it can prove otherwise to its stakeholders. Crises violate stakeholder expectations for how an organisation should behave. Products should not harm customers and aeroplanes should not lose their engine power during a flight. By violating expectations an organisation risks damage to its performance through loss of sales or a drop in share price. A crisis can create a range of negative outcomes beyond diminished performance, including physical damage to facilities and organisational reputation, while stakeholders can suffer physical, psychological and/or economic harm. The actual damage inflicted by a crisis is determined, in part, by the effectiveness of the crisis public relations management.

Crisis public relations management is a collection of factors that are used to address the crisis and to lessen the damage a crisis might inflict on the organisation and its stakeholders. Crisis public relations management involves interventions that occur throughout the life cycle of a crisis. Box 17.2 outlines the commonly used three-stage crisis life cycle.

Box 17.2

Three-stage crisis life cycle

1. Pre-crisis: actions taken prior to occurrence of the crisis

   ■ Signal detection: search for warning signs that a crisis may occur

   ■ Prevention: take steps to lessen the likelihood that a crisis risk becomes a crisis

   ■ Preparation: take steps to prepare for handling a crisis

2. Crisis event: a trigger event indicates a crisis has begun

   ■ Crisis recognition: define the situation as a crisis

   ■ Crisis containment: words and actions used to address the crisis

3. Post-crisis: actions taken after a crisis is considered to be over

   ■ Learning: discover lessons from the crisis management effort

   ■ Follow-up: provide any information or actions promised during the crisis

   ■ Healing: address lingering psychological issues created by the crisis

Odwalla's 1996 recall: an illustration of the three-stage crisis life cycle

In 1996, US juice manufacturer Odwalla had an *E. coli* outbreak that sickened over 70 people and killed 16-month-old Anna Gimmestad. A review of the Odwalla case demonstrates the stages of the crisis life cycle. Odwalla sold unpasteurised juice. The idea was that the juice retained more vitamins and better taste when it was not pasteurised. However, pasteurisation is used to kill bacteria so unpasteurised juice must be carefully controlled or you have a food-borne illness outbreak, as Odwalla did.

There was a belief, in the unpasteurised juice industry, that the high acid content of juice helped to kill bacteria. To add extra protection, Odwalla used an acid wash on its fruit. A previous bacteria outbreak at another juice maker raised questions about the acid wash prior to 1996. Dave Stevenson, head of Odwalla's quality assurance, had recommended a shift to a chlorine wash.

box 17.2 (continued)

Acid wash was rated as only 8 per cent effective and the chlorine wash would have improved bacteria control. Signal detection was working. Stevenson had seen the problems in the industry and that Odwalla had had 300 reports of bacteria in juice prior to 1996. Other executives rejected Stevenson's proposal and the acid wash remained in place. Prevention was a failure because Odwalla did nothing to reduce the threat identified in signal detection. Little is known about Odwalla's state of preparation prior to the 1996 crisis (Entine 1998, 1999).

When the crisis hit, Odwalla was quick to recognise and to contain a crisis. Odwalla quickly issued a recall of its product and was among the first companies to utilise the Internet as part of the crisis response. The quick action reflected crisis recognition, while the recall demonstrated containment efforts (Thomas 1999). In fact, Odwalla is frequently praised in crisis case studies for its response. Unfortunately, those who praise Odwalla fail to examine how its own prevention failure helped to create the deadly recall (Coombs 2012). Odwalla did learn, as it began pasteurising its juices in order to kill bacteria. The Internet helped provide follow-up information to stakeholders, thereby keeping them informed. As part of the healing, Odwalla paid for the medical expenses of anyone who became ill from their juice (Baker n.d.).

Source: adapted from Coombs 2012

The value of strategic communication

From a public relations perspective, it is important to realise a crisis creates an information vacuum. Something negative has occurred and potentially threatens an organisation and its stakeholders. People immediately want to know more about the crisis event. Who was involved? What happened? Why did it happen? What risks will it create? A key to effective crisis public relations management is locating the desired information and relaying it to the interested stakeholders. The need to address the information vacuum created by a crisis places a premium on effective communication (Barton 2001). Public relations people do not simply throw information at stakeholders during a crisis. To be effective, crisis communication must be strategic. Those engaged in crisis public relations management must determine what information particular stakeholders need and the best way to deliver that information. When hazardous chemicals are released, for example, crisis communicators must determine who is at risk, if those at risk should evacuate or shelter where they are and how best to deliver the public safety message to the targeted stakeholders.

Where do crises come from?

There is no one type of crisis that crisis public relations managers will face. There are a variety of crises and each presents its own unique demands on the public relations people attempting to manage it. Situational crisis communication theory (SCCT) has used empirical research to create three general categories of crises, based upon evaluations of crisis responsibility (Coombs 2007). The crises in each category create similar attributions of organisational responsibility for a crisis. Crisis responsibility, stakeholder perceptions of how much an organisation is responsible for the crisis, is critical in assessing the threat posed by a crisis. Research (e.g., Mowen 1980; Jorgensen 1996; Coombs and Holladay 2001) consistently has shown that the greater the attribution of crisis responsibility, the greater the threat posed by the crisis to the organisation. Increases in crisis responsibility lead to greater reputational loss, decreases in purchase intention, decreases in supportive behaviours and increases in likelihood to engage in negative word of mouth (Coombs 2007; Coombs and Holladay 2007b). Box 17.3 presents the crisis categories of crisis types developed by SCCT.

What should become clear by looking at the list of crises is that crises come from a variety of sources. In other words, organisations have a wide array of potential crisis risks. Essential stakeholders can be risks for an organisation and the operation of a facility creates crisis risk as well. For instance, employees can cause crises by not performing tasks properly (accidentally or purposefully), by violating laws, or by engaging in violence against co-workers. Customers can cause crises by misusing products or by protesting at how an organisation behaves. Assailants can attack an organisation through product tampering, physical attacks, or computer hacking. Geography can cause crises through the acts of nature that can occur at that locale, such as tornadoes or floods. Products can cause crises by being manufactured improperly and harming customers. The manufacturing process can cause crises through technical failure, poor quality raw materials, or the release of toxic chemicals. Potential crises can develop within the organisation and from its environment. Organisations are swimming in a sea of crisis risks. So where do crises come from? The answer is, almost anywhere.

Box 17.3

Crisis types and categories from SCCT

Victim: minimal attributions of crisis responsibility. The organisation is considered a victim of the crisis along with the stakeholders:

Natural disasters: damage from weather or 'acts of God'. An example is the 2011 tsunami and earthquakes in Japan.

Rumours: damage from false information being circulated about the organisation. An example is the 2010 'report' that Pampers disposal nappies (diapers) would burn babies.

Workplace violence: damage from employee or former employee attacking current employees. An example is the 2001 shootings at a furniture manufacturing facility in Goshen, in the US.

Malevolence: damage from outside actors attacking the organisation. An example would be the 1986 tampering of Tylenol capsules in the US.

Accidental: moderate attributions of crisis responsibility. The organisation is involved in the crisis but had limited control over the events that precipitated the crisis:

Challenges: threat of damage from stakeholder claims that the organisation is acting in a manner that is inappropriate or irresponsible. An example would be the 2005 claim by the American Family Association that

Ford Motor Company was harming families by offering same-sex partner benefits and advertising in gay and lesbian publications.

Technical-error accidents: damage when technology fails, creating an accident. An example would be the 2003 explosion of the West Pharmaceutical facility in Kinston, NC, USA, from rubber dust particles.

Technical-error product harm: damage when technology fails, resulting in a defective product. An example would be the 2010 HP recall of laptop batteries due to potential fire hazard from dendrite fibre build up in the lithium batteries.

Intentional: very strong attributions of crisis responsibility. The organisation knowingly placed stakeholders at risk and/or wilfully violated laws or regulations:

Human-error accident: damage when human error causes an accident. An example is the 1999 Tosco Refinery fire in Martinez, CA, USA, that was a result of poor supervision of safety.

Human-error product harm: damage when human error causes a defect product. An example is the 1990 Perrier water recall because of high benzene levels caused by an employee not changing a filter at the spring designed to trap the benzene.

Organisational misdeed: damage when managers knowingly place stakeholders at risk or knowingly violate laws or regulations. An example is when, in 2007, melamine, which is poisonous to dogs and cats, was purposefully added to pet food so it would test with a higher protein level.

Source: adapted from Coombs 2012

How to prepare for a crisis

Managers need to recognise that no matter how well they run the organisation, a crisis can still occur. Marconi's (1992) book title sums it up best: *When bad things happen to good companies*. Unfortunately for managers, experiencing a crisis is a matter of when, not if. All organisations should prepare for the eventuality of a crisis. Preparing for a crisis is part prevention and part preparation.

Preventative actions

Steven Fink (1986), an influential crisis expert, argued that all crises have warning signs or what he calls 'prodomes'.

The skilful crisis manager discovers the warning and takes actions to prevent the crisis from occurring. The best way to manage a crisis is to prevent one. Prevention means no stakeholders are harmed and the organisation suffers no damage. Crisis managers find warning signs by monitoring sources related to specific types of crisis risks. Typical sources to monitor for warning signs would be safety data, consumer complaints, insurance audits, environmental audits, employee complaints and activist activities.

Each organisation needs to design its own early warning system for crises. That involves identifying the most likely crises the organisation will have and working backwards to determine what sources of information would provide the most reliable warning signs for each crisis. The best starting point is to assemble top management from

Box 17.4

Sample crisis risk score calculations

1. Airline crash

   $1 \times 10 \times 10 = 100$

   Likelihood is very low.

   Impact on stakeholders and the organisation is very high.

2. Product recall for *E. coli* in beef

   $5 \times 10 \times 10 = 500$

   Likelihood is moderate as *E. coli* in beef does happen on a regular basis.

   Impact on stakeholders and the organisation is high because *E. coli* can cause death.

Think about 17.1

Pick two organisations from two different industries. For instance, use a retail store and a university or a restaurant and coal mining company. Now create a list of potential crises each organisation might encounter. From that list, select what you feel are the top five crises an organisation in that industry should be prepared to manage. How are the lists similar and different?

Feedback

There should be some overlap in the lists because organisations share some basic crisis risks, but there is a problem if the lists are exactly the same. Different industries have slightly different crisis risks. However, these slight differences can be very important when trying to identify what potential crises should be considered the most important to a particular organisation.

the various divisions in the organisation. This group should brainstorm all the possible crises that might befall the organisation. Once the list is created, the managers go back and assign each crisis a 'crisis risk score'. The crisis risk score is an assessment of likelihood of the crisis occurring and the impact such a crisis would have on both stakeholders and the organisation. The managers would generate three scores: (1) crisis likelihood (L), (2) impact on stakeholders (IS) and (3) impact on the organisation (IO). The scores would be based on a scale, with '1' being unlikely or little impact and '10' being very likely and serious impact. Admittedly, the scores will be rather subjective but it is a fairly effective system. The scores are then placed in the following formula: crisis risk score = L × IS × OI. Box 17.4 presents examples of calculating a crisis risk score.

Once all the crises have scores, the managers review the data to create a list of the most prominent crises. The list of the most prominent crises would serve as the foundation for creating the crisis early warning system. Managers need to determine what would be the early warning signs for each crisis and what information sources could be monitored to find those warning signs. For instance, an organisation that is at risk from industrial accidents would monitor safety data. Lapses in safety practices could indicate the potential for an industrial accident. Or, an organisation that sells consumer goods would monitor consumer complaints. The consumer complaints could indicate a potential for product harm. Once a warning sign is located, actions would be taken to reduce the likelihood of the crisis occurring.

Value of preparation

While prevention is ideal, the reality is crises will still occur. Managers cannot locate all warning signs, and preventative actions are not guaranteed to be effective. Note how the last sentence in the previous paragraph said reducing the likelihood of a crisis happening, not eliminating it. There are limits to crisis prevention. That is why organisations need to develop an insurance policy in the form of crisis preparation. Crisis preparation is built around three points: (1) a crisis management plan (CMP), (2) a crisis team and (3) training.

The CMP is a rough guide for managing a crisis, not a step-by-step formula. Each crisis is a little different, so the crisis team needs to adapt the CMP to the current situation. CMPs should be short and easy to use. The basic elements of a CMP are contact information (people you might need to reach during a crisis) and key reminders, such as the need to document what the crisis team has done and record requests for information the crisis team received but could not answer immediately. Most CMPs are now digital and the crisis team can access them from mobile devices during a crisis. It is essential that CMPs are updated regularly, at least every six months. Personnel and procedures change in organisations. If the CMP is inaccurate, it is of little value. Mini case study 17.1 provides an example of the need to test CMPs.

CMPs provide an organised approach to crisis management that helps to save time during a crisis. One way a CMP saves time is by making some decisions before the crisis hits. Team members will have pre-assigned tasks so they know what to do when they receive word a crisis has

Mini case study 17.1
The need to test crisis management plans (CMPs)

The value of testing the crisis management plan (CMP) is demonstrated by its application at a US airport. The airport was running a crisis simulation of a plane crash. The simulation involved airport personnel and emergency personnel from the community, including fire, police and ambulance. When the simulation began, the emergency personnel tuned their radios to the frequency recommended in the CMP. The emergency responders found they could not talk with the airport personnel, resulting in chaos rather than coordination. The problem was that the wrong radio frequency was listed in the CMP for emergency responders. Testing the CMP discovered a serious flaw that could have been disastrous in a real crisis.

occurred. The Crisis Appendix is a separate set of materials that is linked to the CMP. The Crisis Appendix stores information that might be needed during a crisis, such as past safety data and templates for messages. The templates are drafts of sample messages the organisation might use in the crisis. Essentially, a template is a message with key points left blank, such as the date, time and people involved. The legal department should approve the templates before the crisis. Time is saved because the complete message does not have to be written from scratch during a crisis and it has already been approved by the legal department.

The crisis management team are those people in the organisation that have been selected to administer the crisis response. The crisis management team is composed of personnel from a variety of departments in the organisation. The exact composition will vary according to the nature of the crisis. For instance, IT is involved when the crisis involves computer systems or the Internet, and human resources is included when the crisis involves personnel issues. The core of the crisis team includes: public relations, legal, operations, security, safety and quality assurance (Barton 2001).

Ideally, the crisis team begins its work by developing the CMP. However, not all crisis teams are used to create CMPs. The primary task of the crisis team is managing the crisis. The crisis team must be able to apply the CMP to a crisis – they must know how to use the CMP. If the crisis team cannot use the CMP, the CMP has no value and has

failed to save time. More important than using the CMP is the ability of the crisis team to cope with factors not covered in the CMP. Remember, a CMP is a rough guide so there are many details and specifics about a crisis that the crisis team must address on their own. The CMP provides extra time by addressing the routine aspects of a crisis; everything else must be handled by the crisis team (Regester 1989; Barton 2001; Regester and Larkin 2008).

Training is the last of the three elements of preparation, but is the most critical. Without training, any CMP or crisis team is of unknown value. Crisis management training involves practice with handling a crisis. The crisis management team, armed with its CMP, confronts a simulated crisis. Training assesses the value of the CMP and the abilities of the crisis management team. Was the CMP useful during the training or does it require extensive revision? It is better to discover flaws in the CMP during training rather than during an actual crisis. Can the crisis team members perform their tasks effectively? Weak team members will either need additional training or may need to be replaced. Crises are time-sensitive and ambiguous. Not everyone responds well to ambiguity and to time pressure. Some people should not be on crisis teams, and training will indicate if the person is right for a crisis team (Coombs 2012). Again, better to learn a person is not suited for a crisis team during a simulated rather than an actual crisis.

Without training, an organisation has no idea if its CMP or crisis team is any good. Both the CMP and crisis team should be tested on a regular basis, at least once per year. Training does not have to be a complete simulation of a crisis but can be in the form of simple simulated interactive exercises that test a part of the crisis management effort. To be effective in a crisis, organisations must use training to establish the value of their CMPs and crisis management teams.

Explore 17.1

Universities and crisis public relations management

Universities face crises, just like any other organisation. Look around your university's website to see what information you can find about its preparation for crises. Do you know what you should do if a particular crisis occurred at your university? How do you learn about that information? What channels will your university use to inform you about a crisis? What can you do to be better prepared for a crisis at your university?

Communicating during a crisis

Effective crisis communication is vital to a successful crisis management effort. Crisis public relations management research brings important insights to understanding what makes crisis communication effective and ineffective (Coombs 2010). Crisis communication involves managing information and managing meaning. Managing information reflects the information processing aspect of crisis communication. Crisis managers need to collect information, process it into knowledge and share it with their stakeholders. Managing meaning emphasises the strategic aspect of crisis communication. Crisis managers use crisis messages to influence how stakeholders perceive the crisis and the organisation in crisis. Managing meaning recognises that stakeholders have emotional reactions to crises (e.g., Jin and Pang 2010). The type and strength of emotions created by a crisis depend upon how people perceive the crisis. If an organisation is a victim, stakeholders are likely to feel sympathy. If the organisation is responsible for the crisis, stakeholders are likely to feel anger. Those different

emotions affect how the stakeholders then perceive the organisation and behave towards that organisation (Jorgensen 1996).

The focus of crisis public relations management research has been on effective communication during the crisis event. The crisis communication research can be divided by its focus: (1) tactical and (2) strategic. The tactical focus crisis communication research examines how messages are sent during the crisis and the general characteristics of those messages. The emphasis is crisis communication as information management. The strategic focus crisis communication research examines the content of the messages sent during a crisis and the effects of those messages. The strategic focus considers the goals crisis managers are pursuing through their crisis communication.

Crisis communication: tactical focus

Early writings about crisis communication focused on the tactical aspects. Experts advised that an initial crisis response should be quick, accurate and consistent. A crisis

Picture 17.1 Protests against Union Carbide following the Bhopal chemical plant disaster (*source*: © Raj Patidar/Reuters)

response needs to be quick so that the organisation is part of the information used to fill the vacuum created by the crisis. Many writers note the need for the organisation to tell its side of the story (e.g., Holladay 2009). If an organisation is slow in responding, it allows other actors to define and to control the crisis (Coombs 2012). Research has confirmed the value of responding quickly. Arpan and Pompper (2003) found that an organisation suffers less reputational damage when it announces that a crisis has occurred than when someone other than the organisation makes the same announcement. They called this effect 'stealing thunder'.

Speed does not always fit with accuracy, but crisis managers need both. If crisis messages are shown to be inaccurate, the organisation loses credibility and risks suffering additional reputational damage. We must remember that ineffective crisis communication does hurt an organisation. Part of accuracy is avoiding speculation. It is common for the news media to ask crisis managers to speculate on the cause of the crisis. A common piece of advice for crisis managers is to never speculate. If your speculation is wrong, your messages are judged as inaccurate. Inaccuracy implies that the organisation is either incompetent or hiding something from its stakeholders.

Finally, crisis messages need to be consistent. Many crisis experts talk about speaking with one voice, but that phrase is often misinterpreted. It does not mean only one person speaks for the organisation during a crisis. Multiple experts may be needed to explain a crisis, or a crisis can go on for days. In either situation would it be effective to have just one person speak for the organisation? Consistency is a better term. Consistency does not mean everyone using the same exact talking points. Instead, consistency means sharing information with all spokespersons so they work from a common knowledge base. You want consistency in the information your spokespersons are providing about the crisis, not consistency in phrasing of the message (Coombs 2012).

Crisis communication: strategic focus

Researchers have examined the strategic aspect of crisis communication by attempting to determine how crisis communication can be used most effectively to protect the organisation's reputation. The strategic crisis communication research began by trying to understand why people react favourably or unfavourably to a crisis spokesperson. Box 17.5 provides a summary of the proven advice for crisis spokespersons.

More advanced strategic crisis communication research has explored the various crisis response strategies (what an

---

Box 17.5

Advice for crisis spokespersons

- Never say 'no comment' – people hear 'I am guilty' or 'I am hiding something' when a crisis manager says 'no comment'.

- Make eye contact, avoid vocal fillers ('urhs' and 'uhms') and avoid nervous gestures – they create the impression the spokesperson is being deceptive.

- Provide answers to the question that was asked, not the question you want to answer.

- If you do not know the answer, say so and promise to deliver the necessary information when you receive it.

- Avoid using jargon because it is confusing, and the spokesperson will appear to be hiding something.

Sources: Carney and Jorden 1993; Feeley and de Turck 1995; Levick 2005; Mackinnon 1996; Nicholas 1995; Pines 1985

---

organisation says and does after a crisis hits) and how strategy choices affect the way stakeholders react to the crisis and the organisation in crisis (Coombs 2010). William Benoit (1995) was instrumental in identifying a wide range of crisis response strategies. Benoit's list of crisis response strategies was combined with works of other experts to form the crisis response strategies presented in Box 17.6. While having a list is useful, crisis managers still need to understand when certain strategies would be more effective than others and why. Let us explore the strategic use of crisis response strategies further.

Crisis managers should start any crisis response with instructing and adjusting information. Instructing information tells stakeholders how to protect themselves physically from a crisis; examples would be product recalls and evacuation warnings. Adjusting information helps people to cope psychologically with a crisis; this would include expressions of regret, steps taken to prevent a repeat of the crisis and explanations of what happened during the crisis (Sturges 1994). Public safety should be the top priority in a crisis. Failure to address public safety first is an ethical as well as a strategic failure in crisis communication.

Perceptions of crisis responsibility are critical to crisis communication. Crisis response strategies can be used to shape those perceptions. Denial strategies argue that there is no crisis (crucial in the case of a rumour) or that the

Box 17.6

Crisis response strategies

Denial strategies

Attacking the accuser: crisis manager challenges the person or group that says a crisis exists

Denial: crisis manager claims there is no crisis

Scapegoating: crisis manager blames the crisis on some person or group outside of the organisation

Diminish strategies

Excusing: crisis manager argues the organisation has minimal responsibility for the crisis

Justification: crisis manager attempts to reduce perceptions of the seriousness of the crisis

Rebuild strategies

Compensation: crisis manager offers money and/or gifts to people affected by the crisis

Apology: crisis manager acknowledges responsibility of the crisis and requests forgiveness

Bolstering strategies

Ingratiation: crisis manager praises the stakeholders

Reminding: crisis manager informs people about the organisation's past good works

Victim: crisis manager notes it is a victim of the crisis too

Examples of crisis response strategies used in crises

Attacking the accuser

The crisis: The news show *Dateline NBC* accused GM of selling unsafe pick-up trucks.

The response: GM provided evidence that the news show was deceptive with its report of how the gas tanks on GM pick-up trucks would explode. Harry Pearce of GM said: 'The 11 million households that viewed the program were never told that NBC used remotely controlled incendiary devices to try to ensure that a fire would erupt, seemingly due to the collision. We cannot allow the men and women of GM, the thousands of independent businesses that sell GM products, and the owners of these pick-up trucks, to suffer the consequences of NBC's irresponsible conduct and deliberate deception' (Pelfrey n.d.).

Denial

The crisis: Firestone tyres were associated with blowouts that caused a number of Ford Explorers (an SUV) to role over.

The response: Firestone denied their tyres were unsafe. Johan Lampe of Firestone said: 'Let me state categorically: tyres supplied to Ford Motor Company and other customers are safe, and the tyres are not defective' (Bradsher 2001: 2).

Scapegoating

The crisis: The Union Carbide Bhopal explosion in India that killed thousands of people.

The response: Jackson Browning, a former safety employee at Union Carbide, wrote: 'Late in 1986, Union Carbide filed a lengthy court document in India detailing the findings of its scientific and legal investigations: the cause of the disaster was undeniably sabotage. The evidence showed that an employee at the Bhopal plant had deliberately introduced water into a methyl isocyanate storage tank. Union Carbide claimed it had witnesses, evidence, and documents to prove it and that the explosion was sabotage by a group of workers' (Weisman and Hazarika 1987).

Excusing

The crisis: People were protesting Abercrombie & Fitch's use of semi-nude photographs in its catalogues because children under 18 were bringing the catalogues into schools.

The response: Abercrombie & Fitch denied any intention to do wrong and that they could not control the misuse of their catalogues. Hampton Carney from Abercrombie & Fitch said: 'It's never been intended for anyone under 18. We're very sensitive to that matter' (Pickler 1999).

Justification

The crisis: In 2007 a number of toys made in China had been recalled in the US due to lead in their paint.

The response: Carter Keithley, president of the US Toy Industry Association, noted that recalls of toys due to hazardous material involved 0.03 per cent of the three billion toys the US imported from China in 2007 (Greenless 2008).

Compensation

The crisis: Seven people died from cyanide in Johnson & Johnson's Tylenol crisis.

The response: In addition to a recall, Johnson & Johnson paid for psychological counselling for the

box 17.6 (continued)

families of the victims and provided other assistance (Berg and Robb 1992).

Apology

The crisis: *News of the World*, owned by News Corp, had private investigators hack into mobile phones to get information for stories.

The response: News Corp CEO Rupert Murdoch placed advertisements in major newspapers with an apology that included the statement: 'The *News of the World* was in the business of holding others to account. It failed when it came to itself. We are sorry for the serious wrongdoing that occurred. We are deeply sorry for the hurt suffered by the individuals affected. We regret not acting faster to sort things out. I realize that simply apologizing is not enough' (Ambrogi 2011).

Ingratiation

The crisis: In 2009 and 2010, Toyota recalled vehicles over problems with the accelerator (gas) pedal and braking.

The response: Chief Executive Akio Toyoda said: 'I am sincerely grateful to our dealers and suppliers who remained fully committed to providing as many cars as possible to customers, and to our employees as well as our overseas business operations for their efforts in working together so that the company will return to its normal state as soon as possible. And finally, above all, I am sincerely grateful to our customers of more than 7 million people around the world who newly purchased Toyota vehicles' (Ruddick 2010).

Reminding

The crisis: Nestlé 2010 accused of irresponsible palm oil sourcing.

The response: In a news release Nestlé stated: 'As a part of this commitment, we have accelerated the investigation of our palm oil supply chain to identify any palm oil source that does not meet our high standards for sustainability. Given our uncompromising food safety standards, we have done this in a deliberate manner as we use palm oil for food products rather than for soap or other personal care products' (Anderson 2010).

Victim

The crisis: In 1986, one person died from potassium cyanide in Johnson & Johnson's Tylenol.

The response: Johnson & Johnson noted how it was a victim of the attack as well. Johnson & Johnson CEO James Burke said: 'But we cannot control random tampering with capsules after they leave our plant' (McFadden 1986).

Source: adapted from Benoit 1995 and Coombs 2012

---

organisation is uninvolved in a crisis. If there is no crisis or the organisation is not responsible for the crisis, there should be no threat to the organisation. As Benoit (1995) noted, crisis communication is only needed when there has been a crisis and the organisation is held responsible for the event. Denial should only be used when an organisation has no involvement in the crisis and can support that claim. If the organisation is later shown to be involved in the crisis, much greater damaged is inflicted on the organisation than if they had not denied involvement (Ferrin et al. 2007). The dangers in using denial are evidence to support effective communication helping and ineffective communication hurting during a crisis.

Diminish strategies seek to reduce the perceptions of crisis responsibility. The organisation recognises that a crisis has occurred and it is involved to some degree with the crisis. However, communication is used in an attempt to reduce the organisation's perceived responsibility for the crisis. If the organisation had moderate responsibility for the crisis, the potential damage from the crisis is reduced. As with denial, there are limits to when diminish strategies can be used. An organisation must have a legitimate claim of limited responsibility or the diminish strategies can cause more harm than good.

As noted in the discussion of crisis types, there are times when an organisation is perceived as highly responsible for the crisis and that perception is accurate. Denial and diminish strategies would be ineffective, so crisis managers must use the rebuild strategies. The rebuild strategies are compensation and apology. Organisations are perceived as clearly taking responsibility for a crisis when they use either of these two strategies. Rebuild strategies are the most appropriate response for a crisis in the 'preventable' cluster from Box 17.3. A general piece of strategic crisis communication advice is that as perceptions of crisis responsibility increase, crisis managers should utilise strategies that are perceived to take responsibility for the crisis. There should be a match between perceived acceptance

Picture 17.2 The front page of the last ever edition of one of the UK's oldest newspapers, the *News of the World*. The paper, which was owned by Rupert Murdoch's News Corp, was forced to close as a result of the phone hacking crisis involving employees of the media group (*source*: John Frost Historical Newspapers)

of responsibility for the crisis by the organisation and stakeholder attributions of crisis responsibility. It should be noted that crises in the 'Accidental' cluster can generate strong attributions of crisis responsibility if the organisation has a history of similar crises and/or a negative prior reputation (is known to treat stakeholders badly, for example) (Coombs 2007). Crisis managers should consider these two intensifying factors (crisis history and prior reputation) when selecting their crisis response strategies.

Finally, the bolster strategies are a secondary strategy that can be used in combination with denial, diminish or rebuild. Bolster strategies seek to create positive pieces of information to associate with an organisation in the hope of countering some of the negative information generated by the crisis. The Cadbury Chocolate case (Case study 17.1) is used to illustrate various crisis communication responses and the importance of matching the response to the level of crisis responsibility. Box 17.6 includes examples of how organisations have actually used each of the crisis response strategies.

Case study 17.1
Cadbury chocolate recall

Cadbury is consistently the most trusted brand of chocolate in the UK. In 2006, Cadbury recalled eight of its products (over 1 million items) for salmonella contamination that caused sickness in about 40 people. This is proof that crises happen even to the best of companies. Cadbury estimates the recall cost it £20 million and resulted in a 14 per cent drop in sales for 2006 (Walsh 2006). A BrandIndex poll taken after the recall showed a sharp drop in Cadbury's reputation (salmonellablog 2006). The lost revenue, lost sales and reputation damage reflect the negative effects a crisis can have on an organisation.

The British Government determined that Cadbury's standards for assessing the risk of salmonella was unreliable and needed to be changed (Booth 2006). Cadbury was not properly executing part of its food safety tasks. The crisis was caused by poor job performance, making this at best human-error product harm crisis. Cadbury's management admitted (pleaded guilty) to breaching food and hygiene regulations. Cadbury was fined £1m for its violations (Cadbury 2007). The crisis could be considered management misconduct because there was violation of regulations. Either categorisation places the Cadbury chocolate recall in the 'Preventable' crisis cluster.

Cadbury did recall the product and informed customers about the recall (instructing information). Here is a sample of Cadbury's statement following its government fine: 'Quality has always been at the heart of our business, but the process we followed in the UK in this instance has been shown to be unacceptable. We have apologised for this and do so again today. In particular, we offer our sincere regrets and apologies to anyone who was made ill as a result of this failure. We have spent over £20 million in changing our procedures to prevent this ever happening again' (Reuters 2007). The crisis response notes the corrective action taken and offers regret (adjusting information). More importantly, Cadbury's apology indicates that it accepts responsibility for the crisis. The response fits nicely with recommendations for a 'Preventable' cluster crisis. Instructing and adjusting information were provided, coupled with an apology (acceptance of responsibility). In 2007, Cadbury was again named the most trusted chocolate brand in Britain. Marketing analysis argued the poll results showed Cadbury had rebounded from the salmonella crisis (Rano 2008). We can argue that the crisis communication utilised by Cadbury is part of the reason its reputation was able to rebound so quickly from the crisis.

The Internet and crisis public relations management

If you believe the hype, the Internet has revolutionised crisis public relations management, rendering all previous knowledge on the subject obsolete. A word of advice, do not believe the hype. Yes, the Internet has changed crisis public relations management, just as it has changed all other aspects of public relations. But we are witnessing evolution rather than a revolution. The key points are reviewed thus far and the research evidence is still valid. The question is what new challenges and opportunities does the Internet bring to crisis public relations management? We shall explore the challenges and opportunities in this section.

Challenges

The Internet is fast and has the potential to increase the transparency of an organisation by exposing previously private practices/information. The Internet has changed people's perceptions of time. More specifically, people expect organisations to act much more quickly than they did in the past. As discussed earlier, organisations need to respond fast in a crisis – ideally being the first one to release information about the crisis. The Internet makes it more difficult for organisations to be the ones to release information about a crisis first because anyone with access to a smart phone or keyboard can post information about a crisis. Moreover, when the crisis appears online, people expect the organisation to respond in 'Internet time' – very fast. A common criticism of crisis communication in the Internet age is that an organisation acted too slowly. The Internet has resulted in less time to formulate a crisis response and less opportunity for the organisation to be the one breaking the news about a crisis.

The pre-crisis phase of crisis management typically was not seen by most stakeholders. Even today, many internal crisis prevention activities are unseen, but not for challenge and rumour crises. When stakeholders challenge the responsibility of an organisation's actions or a rumour appears, the warning signs are now public – as are the organisation's efforts to prevent the crisis from developing. Let's use a challenge crisis to illustrate this point. Prior to the Internet, stakeholders would challenge an organisation in private. They would contact management and explain why they were upset with how the organisation was operating. Occasionally these activist stakeholders could attract media attention, but most challenges were unknown to other stakeholders (Ryan 1991). The recent development of managing crisis risks publicly has been called 'para-crises'. Para-crises draw from the proactive nature of issue management. Issue management seeks to locate threats and opportunities that exist in an organisation's environment. Typically, issues are related to public policy concerns (Heath 2005). Para-crises broaden the scope of crisis risks by expanding beyond issues to social concerns and reputational threats (Coombs 2012). The process of managing para-crises resembles crisis management but crisis managers are addressing crisis risks and the dynamics are significantly different from traditional crisis management (Coombs 2012).

Today, activist stakeholders take their messages to the Internet. Other stakeholders may still miss the challenge but the challenge is public – people have the potential to see. In fact, the Internet is an important tool when activist stakeholders are trying to change an organisation's behaviour (Coombs and Holladay 2009). How the organisation responds publicly to the challenge matters as well. Other stakeholders have the opportunity to watch and to evaluate both the challenge and the response. Ineffective challenge responses can change how stakeholders feel about and interact with an organisation (Coombs 2012). The once private crisis prevention activities are becoming more public. With this transparency comes greater scrutiny of crisis public relations management and increased pressure to respond effectively.

An example of the increased scrutiny of crisis public relations management is the 2008 backlash against the Motrin brand for a 50-second online advertisement. The advertisement was intended to be humorous. The focus of the humour was on mothers who carry their babies in slings. Motrin is a pain reliever and the advertisements claimed the slings can cause back pain. Many mothers were vocal online about being insulted. Twitter was popular for complaining about the advertisement, resulting in a 'Twitterstorm' and a potential crisis for Motrin. When you offend your target audience, that has the potential to become a crisis. The criticisms began on a Friday. Motrin removed the online advertisement and placed an apology on its website the following Monday. The actions by the Motrin managers were dissected and criticised. Some critics argued Motrin acted too slowly in removing the advertisement, while others claimed the criticism would blow over and the removal was an overreaction (Tsouderos 2008). Prior to social media, the Motrin complaints would have been sent to the company. Neither the complaints nor the company's response would have been in public view and subjected to such close inspection.

Opportunities

Speed is an opportunity as well as a threat. The Internet provides a number of channels a crisis communicator can use to send information rapidly to stakeholders. Many organisations prepare dark sites prior to a crisis – a site that has content but no active links to it. Each dark site is designed for a specific type of crisis and includes information stakeholders will want to know about the crisis, along with templates for crisis messages. Once a crisis hits, the dark site becomes active and information is quickly sent to stakeholders. Various social media channels (Internet content created by users), including blogs, microblogs and social networking sites, can be used to deliver crisis messages too. In 2011, Southwest Airlines in the US used its popular blog to explain a crisis that involved grounding a large number of planes for government inspections. The inspections were necessary because one of their planes had its roof tear open during a flight.

The Internet is invaluable for detecting potential crises. Social media is a rich source of warning signs. For instance, customers might post complaints and concerns online that suggest a product defect and potential product harm crisis. When Greenpeace challenged Nestlé over unethical sourcing of palm oil in 2010, YouTube and the popular social networking site Facebook were the first places the challenge (a form of warning sign) emerged. Of course, the challenge is to determine which of the messages really matter and which are just background noise most stakeholders will ignore (Coombs and Holladay 2007b).

The Internet also provides a gauge of how people are reacting to the organisation's crisis management efforts. Crisis managers evaluate news media coverage of crises in part to determine how their crisis management efforts are being reported. The Internet provides a natural environment for people to comment on the organisation's crisis management effort.

The Internet is frequently used to create online memorials for people who have passed away; the online memorials help facilitate grieving and recovering from a loss (Explore 17.2). Some crises tragically do result in the loss of life. The sinking of the Deepwater Horizon oil rig in the Gulf of Mexico claimed the lives of 11 people. An online memorial quickly emerged to remember the fallen. The site allowed people to post pictures, messages and videos of those who were lost. Transocean, the company that staffed the oil rig, chose to support this online memorial by linking to it and placing its own comments on the site. Crisis managers need to decide how their organisation will relate to any online memorials and whether or not they should create their own online memorial.

Explore 17.2   Online memorials

Online memorials are becoming fairly common. Most are created by individuals to remember a lost family member or friend and have nothing to do with crises. If you do a search online for memorials you are likely to find one of these individual memorials. Again, these are like plaques or memorials you find in the physical world. An example of a physical memorial would be the London Bombing Memorial in Hyde Park. The 52 pillars represent each of the individuals who lost their lives in the 7 July 2005 bombings. A quick overview of the memorial can be found at http://www.viewlondon.co. uk/whatson/london-bombing-memorial-feature-3100. html. An online memorial for the 7 July bombings can be found at http://londonbombvictims.gonetoosoon.org/. For an example of how an organisation handles an online memorial, visit http://www.cantorfamilies.com/ cantor/jsp/index.jsp. The site was created by Cantor Fitzgerald to commemorate the people the organisation lost in the 11 September attacks on the World Trade Center. By visiting these memorial sites you will gain a better appreciation of the role memorials can play in a crisis.

Summary

Unfortunately, crises are a natural part of society. Organisations must accept the fact that they are not immune to crises. Effective crisis public relations management involves factors such as preventing, preparing, reacting, learning and healing. The key is preparation. If organisations think about crises and how they will respond to crises before a crisis hits, crisis public relations management will be much more effective. Being ready for a crisis improves reaction time, can save lives and allows crisis communication to be more strategic and effective. Effective crisis public relations management is good because it benefits anyone touched by a crisis.

Bibliography

Ambrogi, S. (2011). 'Full text of Rupert Murdoch apology in UK newspapers'. www.reuters.com/article/2011/07/15/us-text-murdoch-apology-idUSTRE76E48320110715 accessed 13 August 2011.

Anderson, A. (2010). 'Nestlé ditches palm oil supplier'. www.supplymanagement.com/news/2010/nestl-ditches-palm-oil-supplier/ accessed 13 August 2011.

Arpan, L.M. and D. Pompper (2003). 'Stormy weather: testing "stealing thunder" as a crisis communication strategy to improve communication flow between organizations and journalists'. *Public Relations Review* **29**: 291–308.

Baker, M. (n.d.). 'Odwalla and the E. coli outbreak'. www.mallenbaker.net/csr/CSRfiles/crisis05.html accessed 6 September 2006.

Barton, L. (2001). *Crisis in Organizations II*, 2nd edition. Cincinnati, OH: College Divisions South-Western.

BBC News Cadbury fined £1m over salmonella. http://news.bbc.co.uk/2/hi/uk_news/england/6900467.stm Accessed 16 July 2007.

Benoit, W.L. (1995). *Accounts, Excuses, and Apologies: A theory of image restoration.* Albany, NY: State University of New York Press.

Berg, D. and S. Robb (1992). 'Crisis management and the "paradigm case"' in *Rhetorical and Critical Approaches to Public Relations.* E.L. Toth and R.L. Heath (eds). Hillsdale, NJ: Lawrence Erlbaum Associates.

Booth, J. (2006). 'Cadbury's salmonella testing procedures "inadequate"' www.timesonline.co.uk/tol/news/uk/article682877.ece accessed 9 April 2011.

Bradsher, K. (2001). 'Bridgestone disputes need for bigger Firestone recall'. *The New York Times*: C2.

Carney, A. and A. Jorden (1993). 'Prepare for business-related crises'. *Public Relations Journal* **49**: 34–35.

Caruba, A. (1994). 'Crisis PR: most are unprepared'. *Occupational Hazards* **56**(9): 85.

Coombs, W.T. (2007). 'Attribution theory as a guide for post-crisis communication research'. *Public Relations Review* **33**: 135–139.

Coombs, W.T. (2010). 'Parameters for crisis communication' in *Handbook of Crisis Communication.* W.T. Coombs and S.J. Holladay (eds). Malden, MA: Blackwell Publishing.

Coombs, W.T. (2012). *Ongoing Crisis Communication: Planning, managing, and responding*, 3rd edition. Los Angeles, CA: Sage.

Coombs, W.T. and S.J. Holladay (2001). 'An extended examination of the crisis situation: a fusion of the relational management and symbolic approaches'. *Journal of Public Relations Research* **13**: 321–340.

Coombs, W.T. and S.J. Holladay (2006). 'Unpacking the halo effect: reputation and crisis management'. *Journal of Communication Management* **10**(2): 123–137.

Coombs, W.T. and S.J. Holladay (2007a). 'Consumer empowerment through the web: how internet contagions can increase stakeholder power' in *New Media and Public Relations.* S.C. Duhe (ed.). New York, NY: Peter Lang Publishing.

Coombs, W.T. and S.J. Holladay (2007b). 'The negative communication dynamic: exploring the impact of stakeholder affect on behavioural intentions'. *Journal of Communication Management* **11**: 300–312.

Coombs, W.T. and S.J. Holladay (2009). 'Cooperation, co-optation or capitulation: factors shaping activist-corporate partnerships'. *Ethical Space: The International Journal of Communication Ethics* **6**(2): 23–29.

Entine, J. (1998). 'Intoxicated by success: how to protect your company from inevitable corporate screw-ups'. www.jonentine.com/ethical_edge/corp_screwups.htm accessed 7 October 2010.

Entine, J. (1999). 'The Odwalla affair: reassessing corporate social responsibility'. www.jonentine.com/articles/odwalla.htm accessed 13 September 2006.

Estes, A.C. (2011). 'Rupert Murdoch admits to "minor mistakes"'. www.theatlanticwire.com/global/2011/07/rupert-murdoch-admits-minor-mistakes/39999/ accessed 4 August 2011.

Feeley, T.H. and M.A. de Turck (1995). 'Global cue usage in behavioral lie detection.' *Communication Quarterly* **43**(4): 420–430.

Ferrin, D.L., P.H. Kim, C.D. Cooper and K.T. Dirks (2007). 'Silence speaks volumes: the effectiveness of reticence in comparison to apology and denial for responding to integrity- and competence-based trust violations'. *Journal of Applied Psychology* **92**(4): 893–908.

Fink, S. (1986). *Crisis Management: Planning for the inevitable.* New York, NY: AMACOM.

Frandsen, F. and W. Johansen (2010). 'Crisis communication, complexity, and the cartoon affairs: a case study' in *Handbook of Crisis Communication.* W.T. Coombs and S.J. Holladay (eds). Malden, MA: Blackwell Publishing.

Greenless, D. (2008). 'Toy makers mount drive to salvage China's safety reputation'. www.nytimes.com/2008/01/10/business/worldbusiness/10toys.html accessed 13 August 2011.

Heath, R.L. (2005). 'Issues management' in *Encyclopedia of Public Relations*, Volume 1. R.L. Heath (ed.). Thousand Oaks, CA: Sage.

Holladay, S.J. (2009). 'Crisis communication strategies in the media coverage of chemical accidents'. *Journal of Public Relations Research* **21**: 208–217.

In a Crisis (1993). *Public Relations Journal* **49**(9): 10–11.

Jin, Y. and A. Pang (2010). 'Future directions of crisis communication research: Emotions in crisis – The next frontier' in *Handbook of Crisis Communication*. W.T. Coombs and S.J. Holladay (eds). Malden, MA: Blackwell.

Jin, Y., A. Pang and G.T. Cameron (2007). 'Integrated crisis mapping: towards a public-based, emotion-driven conceptualization in crisis communication'. *Sphera Publica* 7: 81–96.

Jorgensen, B.K. (1996). 'Components of consumer reaction to company-related mishaps: a structural equation model approach'. *Advances in Consumer Research* **23**: 346–351.

Levick, R. (2005). 'In staging responses to crises, complacency plays a big role'. *PR News*. http://web.lexis-nexis.com/universe accessed 20 April 2006.

Mackinnon, P. (1996). 'When silence isn't golden'. *Financial Executive* **12**(4): 45–48.

Marconi, J. (1992). *Crisis Marketing: When bad things happen to good companies*. Chicago, IL: Probus Publishing Company.

McFadden, R. (1986). 'Maker of Tylenol discontinuing all over-counter capsules'. *New York Times*: 18 February, A-1.

Mowen, J.C. (1980). 'Further information on consumer perceptions of product recalls'. *Advances in Consumer Research* **8**: 519–523.

Nicholas, R. (1995). 'Know comment'. *Marketing* 23 November: 41–43.

Pelfery, W. (1993). 'GM vs NBC, a new wave of employee pride' http://history.gmheritagecenter.com/wiki/index.php/GM_vs._NBC,_a_New_Wave_of_Employee_Pride accessed 13 August 2001.

Pickler, N. (1999). 'Abercrombie & Fitch agree to card young catalogue buyers'. Retrieved from Lexis/Nexis database 13 August 2011.

Pines, W.L. (1985). 'How to handle a PR crisis: five dos and five don'ts.' *Public Relations Quarterly* **30**(2): 16–19.

Rano, L. (2008). 'Cadbury's sweet brand success despite apology'. www.foodanddrinkeurope.com/Consumer-Trends/Cadbury-s-sweet-brand-success-despite-apology accessed 9 April 2011.

Regester, M. (1989). *Crisis Management: How to turns a crisis into an opportunity*. London: Hutchinson.

Regester, M. and J. Larkin (2008). *Risk Issues and Crisis Management: A casebook of best practice*, 4th edition. London: Kogan Page.

Reuters (2007). 'Cadbury fined in salmonella case'. http://uk.reuters.com/article/2007/07/16/cadbury-salmonella-idUKL1619895820070716 accessed 9 April 2011.

Ruddick, G. (2010). 'Toyota "sincerely grateful" as it returns to profit despite crisis'. www.telegraph.co.uk/finance/newsbysector/transport/7710225/Toyota-Akio-Toyoda-sincerely-grateful-profit-recall-crisis.html accessed 13 August 2011.

Ryan, C. (1991). *Prime Time Activism: Media strategies for grassroots organizing*. Boston, MA: South End Press.

Salmonellablog (2006). 'Cadbury Schweppes reputation suffers following salmonella scare' www.salmonellablog.com/salmonella-watch/cadbury-schweppes-reputation-suffers-following-salmonella-scare/ accessed 9 April 2011.

Sturges, D.L. (1994). 'Communicating through crisis: a strategy for organizational survival'. *Management Communication Quarterly* **7**(3): 297–316.

Thomas, E.J. (1999). Odwalla. *Public Relations Quarterly*. http://findarticles.com/p/articles/mi_qa5515/is_199907/ai_21442792.

Timeline (2011). 'Phone hacking scandal hits News Corp'. http://news.yahoo.com/timeline-phone-hacking-scandal-hits-news-corp-152313299.html accessed 4 August 2011.

Tsouderos, T. (2008). 'Company caves to moms' Motrin as backlash'. http://articles.chicagotribune.com/keyword/cave-in/recent/3 accessed 13 August 2011.

Twardy, S.A. (1994). 'Attorneys and public relations professionals must work hand-in-hand when responding to an environmental investigation'. *Public Relations Quarterly* **39**(2): 15–16.

Walsh, F. (2006). 'Salmonella outbreak costs Cadbury £20 million'. www.guardian.co.uk/business/2006/aug/03/food.foodanddrink accessed 9 April 2011.

Weisman, S.R. and S. Hazarika (1987). 'Theory of Bhopal sabotage is offered'. www.nytimes.com/1987/06/23/world/theory-of-bhopal-sabotage-is-offered.html accessed 13 August 2011.

Public relations and the consumer

Learning outcomes

By the end of this chapter you should be able to:

■ understand the term consumer public relations

■ describe different types of consumer public relations activity

■ appreciate the critical factors that drive successful consumer public relations campaigns

■ appreciate the benefits that can be generated by a successful consumer public relations campaign

■ understand some of the issues and challenges facing practice.

Structure

■ Why is consumer public relations important?

■ What does it involve?

■ Tools and techniques

■ An expanded strategic role

■ Issues that afflict practice

Introduction

This chapter explores the role public relations plays in helping a company to promote its products and services to consumers. It therefore has a commercial focus and is concerned with how PR interacts with marketing activities, such as advertising, to win customers and generate profits. Recent research on consumer PR has pursued various lines of inquiry. It has included practical overviews of what it involves (Willis 2009; Harrison 2011); explorations of the relationship between PR and marketing (Hutton 2010; McKie and Willis 2012); as well as a range of critical reflections relating to practice (L'Etang 2008; Tench and Willis 2009). This chapter will touch on all of these areas and the discussion is framed by some contemporary issues that have been selected for their potential to generate debate and reflection. These are the fragmented nature of modern practice; the challenges generated by a complex media environment; the opportunity for PR to play an expanded strategic role in consumer engagement; and ongoing, endemic problems that continue to damage the reputation of public relations practice.

The section begins by highlighting the significant role that consumer PR plays in the working lives of many practitioners and why it is an important but problematic area of study. It then provides an overview of what consumer PR involves and the activities it incorporates. This includes a discussion of its place in the marketing mix, its role in brand building, as well as the impact of the new media landscape on this field of practice. A discussion follows that highlights marketing's quest for cultural insights and the role that PR can play in this process by helping a brand remain in tune with the times. The chapter ends by flagging up two issues that continue to dog and damage the discipline.

Why is consumer public relations important?

Consumer PR is an important area of study given that marketing communication plays a big part in the working lives of the majority of today's public relations practitioners (Kitchen 2006; Zerfass et al. 2008). It is carried out in the public relations departments of companies and in PR agencies working for private sector clients. Some practitioners will focus exclusively on this type of work, while others will juggle marketing-driven PR campaigns alongside a host of activities involving a range of stakeholders who stretch beyond the company's customers.

An investigation of consumer PR is also worthwhile given the contribution it can make to a company's sales and financial viability. This is especially important during a time of economic recession, when many businesses are struggling to survive. A report on the PR consultancy sector by *The Economist* (2010) noted that since the credit crunch in 2008 PR revenues have increased at the expense of other forms of marketing. Growth has not been uniform but services linked to social media and word-of-mouth campaigns are increasingly popular with organisations investing in this type of marketing support during a time of economic hardship (Public Relations Society of America 2012).

The price of success

This situation generates threats as well as opportunities for the PR industry. Hutton (2010: 509) notes that 'the marketing field is reinventing itself to include or subsume much or all of public relations' and 'marketing thought is evolving towards a public relations perspective' to such an extent that marketing is essentially redefining itself as public relations' (2010: 515) Given the blurring of boundaries between different communication disciplines and the convergence of media channels and platforms, this development looks set to continue.

McKie and Willis (2012) note that the same trend emerges in recent award entries to the Cannes Lions International Festival of Creativity. Cannes positions itself (www.canneslions.com) as the world's largest and most prestigious advertising awards event. In 2011 it received more than 28,000 award entries and hosted 9,000 delegates from 90 countries. An examination of its winning campaigns confirms Hutton's thesis that traditional PR skills are now so mainstream across marketing that the distinct nature of the discipline, and the ownership of many of its core activities, are under threat. This is illustrated by the Grand Prix Winner for Creative Effectiveness in 2011 from Abbot Mead Vickers BBDO (AMVBBDO) for its client PepsiCo – the international food and drinks company whose portfolio of brands includes Walkers Crisps. To promote the snack's benefits when eaten in conjunction with a sandwich the agency planned a day of surprise events 'to make the village of Sandwich national news' (Cannes Lions 2012). Media coverage was generated through the use of celebrities and famous sporting figures engaging in a range of community activities. This was supported by online media activity, such as films that showcased the celebrity appearances.

Picture 18.1 The Cannes Lions International Festival of Creativity positions itself as the world's largest and most prestigious advertising awards event and yet some of the prize-winning entries are using traditional public relations techniques. In 2011 the Grand Prix Winner for Creative Effectiveness was from Abbot Mead Vickers BBDO (AMVBBDO) for its client PepsiCo, the international food and drinks company whose portfolio of brands includes Walkers Crisps. To promote the snack's benefits traditional PR skills were used, for example, 'to make the village of Sandwich national news' (*source*: Cannes Lions 2012, http://www.canneslions.com/inspiration/past_grands_prix_advert.cfm?sub_channel_id=301&award_year=2011)

The campaign illustrates how tools and techniques that have traditionally been associated with public relations have been subsumed seamlessly into a wider commercial offer provided by agencies strongly associated with the advertising industry. Indeed, the Cannes Lions Festival, despite showcasing the hybrid beast of modern marketing communication, cannot entirely shake off its historic label as an advertising awards event. In the AMVBBDO award entry PepsiCo is even referred to as an advertiser, despite a campaign with all the hallmarks of classic PR execution. To muddy the water still further, Cannes Lions also introduced a separate PR Award category in 2009 but the winner of this in 2011 was an advertising agency rather than a PR outfit (Foster 2011). (see Think about 18.1.)

Think about 18.1

Who does consumer PR?

- Take a look at the campaigns featured on the Cannes Lions website.

- Can you neatly categorise the campaign activity that is being described? For example, is it advertising, public relations, digital marketing or a combination of several different elements?

- What sort of agencies are behind the campaigns? How do they position themselves to potential clients?

A guilty secret

Consumer PR is practised in a range of commercial settings and often by people who do not refer to themselves as PR practitioners. Similarly, senior figures from the PR sector refer to themselves as marketers (Brown 2009). This creates a messy arena for those interested in the study of public relations and generates some interesting questions. For example, do we just ignore those people who do not correspond to neatly packaged conceptualisations of practice? Or, do we recognise that protracted debates that seek to stake out the borders between public relations and marketing can neuter discussion and reflection about the real challenges that confront practitioners at the coalface?

This chapter is sympathetic to the second perspective because the alternative course runs the risk of disconnecting theory from practice at a time when the field is witnessing significant change. It is important that discussions do not become stuck in arguments over academic terrain, ownership and idealised notions of practice. The aim must be to get beyond the real and false boundaries and territorial disputes to focus on the issues facing professionals in the field. These include ethics, what it is that practitioners are doing and how well these activities are understood by the academic community, clients and practitioners themselves.

Despite this need for pragmatic reflection there has been a tendency to relegate this aspect of practice to a pew at the back of public relations' broad church. Consumer PR's output has been framed traditionally in the academic literature as little more than publicity, its adherents denied access to PR's top table and its ethical intentions questioned (Grunig 1992). This view fails to recognise that practitioners often find themselves shuttling between a variety of roles and tasks that are defined largely by their organisation. (see Think about 18.2.)

What does it involve?

The world we are concerned with in this chapter is where PR interfaces with **marketing** activities, such as **advertising**, to stimulate the sale of products and services in the free market economy. Although the endgame of PR activities in this context is to drive sales, its role is often more subtle than other forms of communication. By looking to change consumer attitudes towards a particular product or company, PR seeks to create a more favourable commercial environment for the company rather than generating outcomes that can be linked directly to an immediate increase in sales. However, as later case studies will show, it can also be a powerful sales generator in its own right.

Public relations has become a valuable part of what is known as the '**marketing mix**', an often quoted term that refers to the set of tools that a company has at its disposal to influence sales. The traditional formulation is popularly known as the '4Ps': product, price, place and promotion (Kotler 2003). Promotion is the area that encompasses public relations, as it is this part of the marketing equation that focuses on the content that is designed to stimulate awareness, interest and purchase. To attract interest and awareness in their products and services, companies use a combination of disciplines – including advertising, **sales promotion**, **direct mail** and public relations – to

---

Think about 18.2

What is legitimate PR activity?

- Can publicity generation be a bona fide goal in a consumer PR campaign?

- Does a PR campaign have to involve conversation and dialogue with the consumer?

Feedback

Public relations activity is best viewed as a continuum, with one-way communication at one end (such as publicity generation) and mutual dialogue at the other. Providing any activity associated with publicity is conducted ethically there is no reason why it should not be recognised as a legitimate, value-added part of public relations. Indeed, PR's promotional capacity can assist a range of organisations, groups and individuals. For many small enterprises, publicity generation through PR is essential to their survival as a business.

Definition: '*Marketing*' is the management process responsible for identifying, anticipating and satisfying customer requirements profitably.

Definition: '*Advertising*' is a form of promotional activity that uses a totally controllable message to inform and persuade a large number of people with a single communication.

Definition: '*Marketing mix*' is the term used to define the four key elements of an organisation's marketing programme: product, price, place and promotion.

> **Definition:** '*Sales promotion*' means short-term or temporary inducements, such as price cuts or two-for-one offers, designed to encourage consumers to use a product or service.
>
> **Definition:** '*Direct mail*' is electronic and posted communications sent to individuals' mobile phones, email and work and home postal addresses.

reach their desired audiences. When used in this way, public relations should become a planned and sustained element of the wider promotional mix, working in tandem with other marketing activities to achieve maximum impact and with the potential to meet a range of objectives, such as:

- raising a company's profile
- redefining its image
- helping to promote its credibility in a new or existing market
- demonstrating empathy with a target audience
- launching a new product or service
- reinvigorating an existing product or service
- stimulating trial and purchase.

It's personal

PR campaigns are often driven by the need to communicate a company's personality and set of values to consumers. If a company can communicate these qualities it may succeed in differentiating itself from the competition. (See Think about 18.4.)

By helping to project human qualities on to a company, product or service, public relations can play an active role in the world of **brand** development. It is necessary to understand the role and power of effective branding more fully to appreciate the benefits that public relations can generate within the context of a successfully executed consumer strategy.

Our societies appear to be overflowing with brands. In popular culture everything and everybody seems to be referred to as a brand: pop and film stars, sportsmen, royalty, airlines, places, politicians – never mind the products

> **Definition:** A '*brand*' is a label that seeks to add perceived value to a consumer product by generating loyalty or preference.

that line the shelves in supermarkets or fill the shops on the high street. In one sense, everything can be legitimately called a brand because the term does apply to any label that carries some meaning or association. However, for the purposes of this chapter, it is necessary to apply a more structured definition in order to fully appreciate the role that public relations can play in brand development.

Morgan (1999) defines a brand as an entity that satisfies all the following four conditions:

1. Something that has a buyer and a seller (e.g., David Beckham and Lady GaGa but not the Queen). Morgan also makes the distinction that 'buying and selling' does not have to be a financial transaction to be of value to both sides.

2. Something that has a differentiating name, symbol or trademark (e.g., easyJet but not aeroplanes). Morever, it is differentiated from other similar products around it for reasons other than its name or trademark, (e.g., an iPod rather than an MP3 player).

3. Something that has positive or negative associations in consumers' minds for reasons other than its literal product characteristics (e.g., Coca-Cola but not tap-water).

4. Something that has been created, rather than is naturally occurring (e.g., the Eiffel Tower, Taj Mahal or Nou Camp (Barcelona), but not Niagara Falls or the Amazon River).

(See also Think about 18.3.)

By studying different brand definitions, such as the one put forward by Morgan, it begins to become apparent how brands can add resonance to a product or service. Successful brands offer consumers tangible and emotional benefits over other products, which consumers not only recognise but also desire, at both a conscious and subconscious level. Furthermore, great brands usually take this appeal a stage further by focusing more on emotional than rational benefits and this ultimately manifests itself in a distinct and consistent personality running through all their marketing activities. (See Think about 18.4.)

Think about 18.3

Brands

- Can you think of any other examples that fit each of Morgan's four criteria?

- How do these brands communicate with consumers?

Think about 18.4

Brands and their personalities

Think of five brands and the personalities they try to project.

- Do you admire these brands?

- What attracts or repels you about each brand?

Think about different brands of the same product – e.g., mobile phones or record companies.

- Do they carry different personalities?

- How is that personality conveyed?

Heart versus head

It is not surprising that brand owners are increasingly turning to image and emotional marketing to win over consumers. In today's fast-paced marketplace, companies tend to copy any competitor's advantage until it is nullified, which is why emotional appeal assumes such importance and why companies such as Nike try to sell an attitude: 'Just Do It'.

The power of brands is also linked to an increasingly strong desire to express individuality through the ownership of goods and services that are perceived to be innovative, different and original. Indeed, Lewis and Bridger (2003) go as far as to say that:

> For many New Consumers the purchase of products and services has largely replaced religious faith as a source of inspiration and solace. For an even larger group, their buying decisions are driven by a deep rooted psychological desire to enhance and develop their sense of self.

Given the emotional capital that is invested in some, if not all, purchasing decisions, public relations can be used to demonstrate that a brand empathises with the worries, needs and aspirations of particular groups of people. This allows it to connect and align itself with consumers in an indirect but powerful association. From an implementation perspective, this is one of the reasons why many public relations campaigns hook into lifestyle issues and popular culture, using celebrity association, the services of psychologists, anthropologists, fashion gurus, chefs, interior designers and a range of other experts to add bite and relevance to the campaigns.

Tools and techniques

Before discussing the individual tools and techniques that can make up a public relations programme, it is important to stress that the key characteristics of the target audience play a big part in defining and shaping the strategy and tactics that are deployed in a campaign. Who do we need to talk to? How can we reach them? What are they interested in? What do we want them to do? By posing a series of simple questions it is possible to refine and sharpen the scope of the planned activity, ensuring a clinical rather than a wasteful, scattergun approach to the tools and techniques that are at the practitioner's disposal.

If the purpose of the campaign is to get young mothers to visit their local supermarket, a national media relations campaign might not have the same impact as activity targeted at a local newspaper. Or, if research shows that the same audience is concerned about their children walking to school, then a road safety sponsorship executed at local level may strike a chord and help to establish a positive relationship with the store. One of public relations' great attributes is its flexibility, as campaigns can be tailored to appeal to many audiences and modified to accommodate the requirements of different delivery channels, such as the media, events or sponsorship.

Media relations

Public relations practitioners confront a diverse and fast-moving media environment. Gilpin and Murphy (2010) note that today's media landscape can be best viewed as 'a single **complex system** that encompasses a vast range of digital, non-digital, mass and personal communication'. They highlight that this generates a number of issues for practitioners. For example, information, rumour and emotional responses can spread like a forest fire across media more quickly than ever before. Gilpin and Murphy (2010) also note that it is increasingly difficult to draw neat boundaries between traditional media and digital channels. They cite Qvortrup's (2006) observation that digital media 'integrate all known media into one converged multimedia system (with) an unlimited system of features'. Even traditional media, from print to broadcast, are migrating to digital formats: 'multiple strands of message and dialogue intertwine, disconnect, and recombine to form patterns across platforms and social contexts'.

Definition: According to Gilpin and Murphy (2010), *'complex systems'* are made up of multiple interacting agents. These might be individuals, organisations or media sources. It is the interactions between these agents that bring about fundamental changes to the system itself. The unpredictable nature of these interactions also creates a dynamic and unstable system.

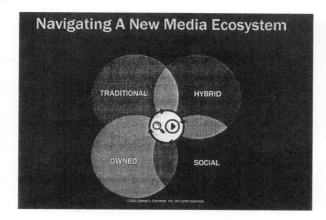

Picture 18.2 The Edelman Media cloverleaf ™

Edelman, the global PR consultancy, has tried to make sense of this world for their clients and employees by conceptualising the modern media environment as a cloverleaf consisting of four, overlapping elements:

- **Traditional media** encompasses radio, TV and print media outlets. This sector includes established media brands such as the BBC, CNN, Le Figaro and El Pais.

- **Hybrid media** includes media companies that have emerged in the digital age. These are largely blogs, some of which focus on niche audiences and issues while others have a more mainstream appeal. One of the most well known examples of hybrid media is the Huffington Post.

- **Owned media** refers to the media channels that the organisation controls, such as its own website, blogs, podcasts and apps. Companies now have the capacity to cost-effectively create content that can be instantaneously communicated to a wide range of external and internal stakeholders.

- **Social media** platforms such as Facebook and Twitter mean that content about a business is not just produced and distributed globally by the company's communication team but also by consumers, employees, partners, suppliers, communities and competitors. As The Arthur W. Page Society (2007) memorably noted, 'it is literally the case that any literate person today can become a global publisher for free in five minutes, drawing on a richer array of communications capabilities than William Randolph Hearst . . . ever dared to imagine'.

When considering the implications of Edelman's model it is important to keep in mind the potential for overlap between each category. To illustrate this point, consider two issues regarding the role of social media in a consumer context. First, stories that are featured in the traditional media increasingly break first in social media. (see Think about 18.5.)

Now reflect on the fact that the Twitter and Facebook platforms that a company creates and controls might also be categorised as owned media. In this context they are often used as an important customer service channel, where grievances are aired and disputes resolved. In these online spaces companies are seen to have a legitimate right to interact with consumers who post comments and messages about them. In contrast, social media that is not owned by the company is more problematic. A consumer might post unfavourable comments about a company's products on their personal Facebook page. Their friends may join in the chorus of disapproval online. The company may then detect this dissatisfaction as part of its online monitoring activities. However, how will it be received if it tries to engage with consumers in a place where they usually only interact with friends and family? Understanding the social mores and norms of this new media landscape is crucial. It is a complex picture, particularly as Gilpin and Murphy's (2010) insights suggest consumers increasingly view all of these media channels as one entity, rather than as four distinct categories.

Back to basics

In this dynamic media landscape, getting a journalist to write or talk on air about a company, product or service is still the primary objective of many consumer public relations campaigns. The persuasive power of editorial is much greater than paid-for advertising as the stories and features that appear in newspapers and magazines (as well as on radio and television) tend to be viewed by consumers as unbiased and objective. In contrast, advertising in the same media channels relies on paid-for space and therefore lacks the same credibility as coverage that has been created by an independent third party, such as a journalist. Influencing this editorial process is a key task for the public relations practitioner. No advertisement or sales person can convince you about the virtues of a product as effectively as an independent expert, such as a journalist, and if this opinion is then repeated to you by a friend, family member or colleague it has an even greater resonance. Indeed, most of us got to hear about Apple, Amazon and Google not through advertising but from news stories in the press, radio, TV and online, or through personal recommendation.

Definition: *'Company propaganda'* is a negative term used by some journalists to describe positive statements presented by an organisation about its beliefs, practices and products.

While the benefits of a successful media relations campaign are obvious, achieving the desired result is not so easy. As editorial coverage, by definition, cannot be bought and because someone else produces the finished article, the public relations practitioner has no direct control over it (unlike an advertisement). In addition, although there are opportunities to write straightforward product press releases that achieve positive coverage (a glance at the 'best buy' features in lifestyle magazines or an examination of the motoring press will highlight good examples of product-focused editorial), most journalists tend to shy away from commercially driven stories and are certainly not receptive to what they see as **company propaganda**.

Furthermore, to reach many consumers a company needs to be featured in the general news sections of the media rather than in specialist editorial. In this environment, media relations campaigns have to incorporate an additional news hook to motivate a journalist to cover a story and this might involve independent research, a celebrity association, an anniversary, a great photograph or a new and surprising angle on a traditional theme. (See Explore 18.1.)

Explore 18.1

Media stories

Take two daily newspapers – one quality paper and one popular or tabloid paper. Identify stories that you believe have been generated by an in-house public relations department or agency to promote a product or service.

Feedback

Clues to stories with a public relations source include: staged photographs accompanying the news item; results of research published on the date of the news item; anniversary of an event; book/film/CD published on the date of the news item.

Events

It is a common misconception that public relations is only concerned with the generation of positive media coverage. Open days, workshops, roadshows, exhibitions, conferences and AGMs are all events that can provide a company with the opportunity to interact directly with consumers, either on its home turf or out and about in the community, generating enhanced presence for the business and a forum for face-to-face, two-way communication. (see Mini case study 18.1 and Think about 18.7.)

Mini case study 18.1
Stimulating word-of-mouth promotion through events

Diageo GB, part of the world's second largest drinks company, used social media to help seed its Venezuelan golden rum, Pampero. The campaign was targeted at independently-minded young males in the city of Leeds – the drink's first test market in the United Kingdom.

In the planning and research phase Diageo's public relations consultancy researched the independent bar and lifestyle culture within the city and concluded that the target audience adopted brands quickest if they were also recommended by friends and opinion formers. The agency also discovered that the target group were Internet savvy and enjoyed new entertainment experiences. Consequently, a key element of the communications strategy was that the brand should be promoted to consumers through what would appear to be a series of independent events. With this in mind, the public relations consultancy created an event company called Rumba Caracas, which became the public vehicle for the delivery of specific campaign activity. Its website (www.rumbacaracas.co.uk) included a forward events calendar, a community exchange and blog space, as well as an interactive picture galley.

As part of a wider word-of-mouth campaign, and to help bring Venezuela's vibrant and colourful art scene to life, a free graffiti jam was organised in Leeds, showcasing the skills of 25 artists. Working closely with some of the city's key lifestyle influencers, the event was promoted by Rumba Caracas through its own website and social media. It was held in a series of disused dark arches under Leeds railway station, and local film students were hired to document the graffiti jam and their productions were set to Venezuelan music and seeded onto YouTube, under the auspices of Rumba Caracas and as part of an online viral campaign.

As a result of the campaign, Pampero's outlet listings in the city increased from 10 to 80, while its rate of sale rose by 160 per cent in six months and, after a year, it had exceeded its target rate of sale in each outlet by an average of 25 per cent. (see Think about 18.6.)

Sponsorship

Whether in sport, the arts or in support of a worthy cause, sponsorship is fundamentally about third-party endorsement and as such sits neatly under the public relations umbrella. If successfully managed to maximise opportunities – and this is where advertising and direct mail also play a role – sponsorship can provide a powerful platform from which to increase the relevance of a company and its products among key target audiences. By harnessing the emotions, qualities and values associated with the sponsorship property and perhaps providing some form of added-value experience, a business can successfully stand out in a cluttered consumer market. (See Think about 18.8 and Mini case study 18.2.)

By discussing the different tools a practitioner has at their disposal, it soon becomes clear that a consumer public relations campaign can have many dimensions, with media relations, event or sponsorship initiatives supporting one another in an integrated programme of activity. Figure 18.1 seeks to show the components that

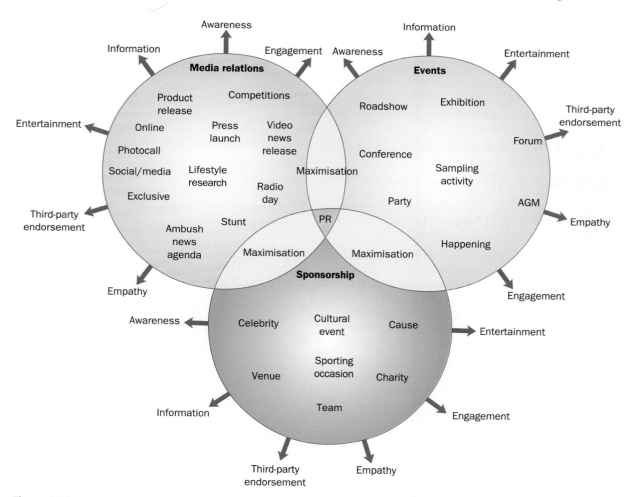

Figure 18.1 Universe of consumer PR

Mini case study 18.2

Maximising a sponsorship: Thomas Cook Sport

Thomas Cook Sport (TCS) is the UK's leading sports tour operator, selling consumer and corporate packages to sporting events globally. One of the company's sponsorship assets is its status as Official Travel Partner to eight Premier League clubs: Arsenal, Chelsea, Everton, Liverpool FC, Manchester City, Manchester United, Newcastle United and Tottenham Hotspur.

TCS tasked PR agency Hatch Communications with the job of managing its contractual rights with football clubs, maximising the sponsorship and coordinating the overall marketing strategy to promote its sport packages to fans. This included the management of the company's social media platforms to ensure a consistent and integrated approach to the campaign.

Picture 18.3 Sport sponsorship in action
(*source*: AFP/Getty Images)

The agency's strategy and tactics were framed by a number of key objectives:

■ to increase sales by 10 per cent

■ to develop campaigns that engage directly with a minimum of 10,000 fans in a single year

■ to deliver 15 favourable national media outcomes during the same time

■ to use this and other media coverage to drive traffic to www.thomascooksport.com

■ to use the sponsorship assets to support the Thomas Cook Children's Charity.

The agency developed a campaign that featured four key initiatives:

1. **Celebrate with TCS**: January and February is a key sales period for Thomas Cook. This is when many consumers book their summer holiday. To capitalise on this interest, Hatch created events at six partner football club stadiums. These sought to inject the vibrancy, colour and celebration of exotic holiday destinations into the football stadiums at a peak booking time.

2. **What Would You Do?**: To integrate TCS' social media channels with some of the more lucrative contractual rights, Hatch created the 'What Would You Do?' concept, whereby fans sent in entries via social media to win the chance to play on their team's home pitch. The competition received over 1,500 entries in total

and included ideas such as cleaning Anfield with a toothbrush and dressing up like Michael Jackson at Old Trafford.

3. **Charity pitch days**: This provided an opportunity for the Thomas Cook Children's Charity to provide underprivileged children from local schools the chance to play on the same pitch as their heroes. The partner clubs involved were Celtic, Rangers, Aston Villa and Newcastle.

4. **Player appearances**: This element of the campaign used the contractual player appearances to create branded media coverage, engage with fans via store appearances and integrate with social media and sales incentives.

Campaign results

■ An annual sales increase of 30 per cent

■ 85 national media hits

■ 28,455 fans directly engaged through the four main campaign themes

■ Traffic to the TCS website increased by 65 per cent in 2011 and online bookings now account for 80 per cent of sales

■ An increase in followers to TCS' Twitter feed from 1,538 to 10,284

■ An increase in the company's Facebook friends from 927 to 5,713

Think about 18.8

Sponsorship

For a sponsorship to be truly effective, does the sponsoring company need to have an obvious link with the property (for example, Adidas and football)?

Can you think of an example of a successful sponsorship where there is no obvious connection between the core activities of the business and the sponsored property, such as Mastercard and football?

If you were public relations director of Coca-Cola, how would you justify its sponsorship of the Olympics? Is it about sporting performance, a particular lifestyle statement, credibility by association or none of these?

can make up a campaign; the different audience outtakes that can be generated; and the great potential for overlap and maximisation. For example, a sponsorship might be promoted through a media relations campaign and a series of events. Integrating the different elements of a consumer PR campaign requires a strategic approach to planning. (see Think about 18.8.)

An expanded strategic role

The attributes public relations can bring to consumer campaigns is growing in importance. The expansion of social media places a greater emphasis on conversation rather than the one-way transmission of messages. PR's focus on third-party endorsement is also highly prized for its ability to work through many different media channels. The rise of the marketing refusenik and a focus on person-to-person, word-of-mouth channels also contribute to its growing influence (Willis 2009). As a result, a public relations approach infuses the strategy of many consumer marketing programmes. This is illustrated by the Cannes Lions campaigns that were discussed earlier. In this context, public relations ceases to be just a technical activity and instead becomes a strategic mindset that shapes a campaign's direction of travel. This moves the focus from tactics and implementation to the campaign's guiding theme and rationale.

New thinking in marketing provides an opportunity for consumer PR practitioners to further enhance the scope of their strategic input. Rather than just participating in campaign planning they have the potential to guide a brand's positioning. For example, McKie and Willis (2012) argue that the publication in 2004 of Douglas Holt's book, *How Brands Become Icons: The principles of cultural branding*, served to popularise the idea in marketing of a cultural approach to brand strategy. Holt adopted a socio-cultural perspective to the marketing strategies adopted by brands such as Coca-Cola, Volkswagen and Corona and argued that they become powerful cultural symbols by responding to historical changes in society. In *Cultural Strategy: Using innovative ideologies to build breakthrough brands* (2010), Holt and Cameron built on this work to address the issue of how organisations identify the opportunities generated by these historical shifts and what should then be done to maximise this through a specific product or service offering. In doing so, they argue that previous literature on brand innovation adopts an economists' way of thinking – that is, the view that innovation is about breakthrough functionality in terms of a product or service offer. Holt and Cameron instead argue that for some of the most successful brands innovation is cultural rather than functional and seek to provide a model that allows organisations to forge new strategies designed to generate commercial advantage from these changes in society.

At the heart of their analysis is the idea of social disruption. It is this, according to Holt and Cameron, that produces the necessary ideological opportunities for organisations. If these are significant enough, the conditions will destabilise the product category's cultural orthodoxy, 'creating latent demand for new cultural expressions . . . moments when once-dominant brands lose their resonance and when innovative brands take off because they deliver the right expression' (p.185). They claim that consumers yearn for brands that champion new ideology, brought to life by new myth and cultural codes, and to illustrate the point discuss how Jack Daniel's (JD) went from a small and unprofitable brand in 1955 to the leading premium whiskey in the United States ten years later. They argue that this success was due to the fact that JD took advantage of an ideological opportunity that gained significant traction in post-war America, namely a rejection of an association of masculinity with the new, slick, middle-class company man and 'the pent-up desire for rekindling the masculine ideology of the American frontier' (Holt and Cameron 2010: 48). To respond to this, JD went against marketing norms in the category to begin a campaign that used homespun parables featuring its rural Tennessee distillery that evoked the frontier of the rural South and Appalachia. Holt and Cameron also discuss other examples of so-called ideological opportunism through a series of further case studies featuring brands such as Nike, Ben & Jerry's, Starbucks and Patagonia.

At a time of turbulence and social disruption, the ideas linked to cultural strategy might be said to have a particular resonance as organisations seek to gain competitive advantage in the demanding and volatile commercial environment that has followed in the wake of the 2008–2009 global financial crisis. At the heart of this debate is the notion of contextual intelligence. It is about creating, developing and nurturing brands that remain in tune with the times. Indeed, Holt's focus on cultural strategy requires marketers to be more concerned with context than they have ever been. Rather than a preoccupation with market research that explores the attitudes of consumers with regard to particular products and services, marketing practitioners need a much broader appreciation of the forces that are shaping society and are required to look beyond the limited commercial horizons of their own category or sector. This, in turn, brings the marketing professional firmly into the realm of public relations.

As MacManus (2003) notes in his study of the cultural dimension of public relations, context has an obvious importance and centrality for PR 'because of the high degree of interpersonal skills needed in forming relationships with clients, stakeholders and other strategic publics'. Accordingly, public relations practitioners are required to exhibit an acute cultural sensitivity as part of their strategic environmental scanning role, and culture for the public relations practitioner, as L'Etang (2008) notes, 'shapes our understanding and sense making facilities and determines what is taken for granted or assumed in a particular environment'.

These strategic preoccupations also complement the research of other management scholars. For example, Mayo and Nohria (2005) concluded that the best leaders not only have 'an almost uncanny ability to understand the context they live in – and to seize the opportunities their times present' (p. 45), but 'can sense the mindset of change and adapt to the times'. As a result, they conclude that the 'ability to understand the zeitgeist and pursue the unique opportunities it presents for each company is what separates the truly great from the merely competent' (p. 60). The chief limitation of Mayo and Nohria's analysis is that it focuses on the intuitive gifts and zeitgeist sensitivities of individual business leaders. Beyond calling for the recruitment of leaders with a commercial outlook that is compatible with the prevailing context, they do not discuss how organisations should be structured and organised to systematically scan the cultural horizon, interpret its most important attributes and plan effectively. However, public relations' strategic environmental scanning role and the emergence of a cultural strategy perspective in marketing can be viewed as separate attempts to address this challenge by drawing on the

strengths of each discipline: sustained and systematic engagement with the stakeholder environment to inform organisational strategy in public relations and an attempt in marketing to identify key societal trends from a consumer perspective.

This common ground suggests that the two disciplines should work together strategically to pool the insights and expertise that each brings to the organisation. Such an approach is necessary if a genuine attempt is to be made to interpret and maximise the opportunities generated by a complex external environment, requiring marketing to assimilate public relations perspectives into its planning lexicon and similarly for PR with regard to the consumer insights generated by marketing. This should also help to enhance the strategic reputation of public relations practitioners within organisations as it will also link the discipline with commercial success as its insights and intelligence will have a direct and pivotal role on marketing strategy. Public relations wider strategic perspective should also assist marketers to identify long-term shifts in the external environment rather than falling prey to short-term fads and trends. Indeed, given the broad role that public relations should play in analysing an organisation's external environment, it is suggested that the PR team, among their other responsibilities and tasks, should take on a zeitgeist leadership role within the organisation and ultimately be responsible for gathering together the intelligence that is crucial to the success of marketing's cultural strategy project.

Issues that afflict practice

It is now appropriate to balance the picture of strategic opportunity that has just been painted with two cautionary tales. Each is related to a common issue that blights public relations practice in a consumer context. The first is about the limits of PR's power. The second relates to an approach to public relations campaign activity that damages the discipline's reputation. Both link public relations to spin and the glossy communication of products and services rather than the activities associated with a responsible, strategic discipline.

Putting lipstick on a pig

'Putting lipstick on a pig' is a colloquial phrase. It is linked to the idea that making a cosmetic change to a product or service cannot obscure its real character and nature. In short, it is related to the notion of style over substance. In the consumer context we are concerned with the phrase refers to the practice of using PR tools and techniques to obscure the fact that a product or service is flawed or problematic in some way. For example, it might be that the offer the company is providing to consumers is inferior to the competition in terms of price, range, availability or ease of use. A spectacular celebrity launch does not make such issues disappear. Indeed, it is dangerous to underestimate the ability of stakeholders, such as consumers and journalists, to see through such hype. Given this situation it is therefore important for PR practitioners to understand the fine detail of the products they are promoting and to provide appropriate advice. For example, the excessive promotion of a lacklustre product can be counter-productive as it might antagonise consumers and bring the organisation's credibility into question. This is also the case if the communication campaign downgrades key issues such as excessive charges and penalty clauses. Examples of this sort of practice can be found in the United Kingdom financial sector, particularly among companies providing cheque cashing services, short-term loans and prepaid credit cards. (See Think about 18.9.)

The act whose name they dare not speak

The requirement to maintain brand awareness in a highly competitive market place can also lead practitioners into other territory that can tarnish public relations' reputation. An example of this is when organisations engage in media relations activity that has no foundation in fact or solid research. The BBC focused memorably on this dubious practice as the global financial crisis began to unravel in 2008/2009. It established what it called a 'Crunch Creep

Monitor' to record 'the unlikely, sometimes highly doubtful, reported effects of the credit crunch' (BBC, n.d.). The spurious claims attributed to the impact of the financial crisis in company press releases included the rise in sales of pasties and sausage rolls, heightened insurance fraud and the success of musical theatre in London's West End. None of these examples provided any evidence for the claims made in the press release and instead relied on such unsubstantiated statements as: 'the firm might be benefiting from the shoppers looking for a cheaper lunch'; 'wonders whether credit crunch-inspired fraud could be to blame'; and 'when times are hard, people are more likely to spend what little money they have on being cheered up by a musical'.

A serious point lies behind the BBC's light-hearted exposé that has implications for consumer PR. Ethical reflections on public relations practice consider issues such as propaganda, where this is defined as lying as opposed to telling the truth (L'Etang 2008). What we are examining is not lying but something that should also trouble those concerned with PR's reputation. Harry Frankfurt, Emeritus Professor of Philosophy at Princeton and an influential moral commentator, labels the phenomenon under discussion here as 'bullshit'. Frankfurt (2005) argues that the increase in communication in society is contributing to what he calls a 'culture of bullshit' and that this has become one of the most salient features of modern culture. He notes that bullshit is a form of representation that does not necessarily involve lying. While the liar and truth teller each knows what the truth is, the bullshitter is indifferent to it. The liar must remember the truth if only to ensure that it does not come out. In contrast, the bullshitter is involved in a 'kind of bluff' (Frankfurt 2005) and 'does not care whether the things he says describe reality correctly (he) just picks them up, or makes them up, to suit his purpose'. (See Think about 18.10.)

Think about 18.10   PR 'bullshit'

Can you identify any consumer PR campaigns using news hooks that contain unsubstantiated views and opinions? Do you have a problem with this? How does it make you feel about the brand being promoted? How does it make you feel about PR practice?

Feedback

Bullshit is prevalent whenever circumstances require someone to communicate without knowing what they are communicating about. Good consumer PR should be based upon solid research and transparency rather than unsubstantiated opportunism. Otherwise, the reputation of PR practice is damaged and its strategic and professional aspirations are undermined.

Summary

This chapter has explored the role of public relations in a consumer marketing context. It discusses a number of perspectives. These include the nature of contemporary practice, the constituent elements of a consumer PR campaign, current challenges in implementation, its future strategic role, as well as issues that damage the reputation of practice. The aim of this wide-ranging discussion has been to try and chart some of the tides that are shaping the development of consumer PR. These are not intended as an exhaustive list, but provide a set of different lenses through which to view an important, intriguing and contentious aspect of PR practice.

Bibliography

Arthur W. Page Society (2007). 'The authentic enterprise'. www.awpagesociety.com/images/uploads/2007Authentic-Enterprise.pdf accessed 28 January 2012.

BBC (n.d.). www.bbc.co.uk/blogs/magazinemonitor/2008/09/crunch_creep_5.shtml accessed 30 January 2012.

Brown, R. (2009). *Public Relations and the Social Web: How to use social media and web 2.0 in communication*. London: Kogan Page.

Cannes Lions (2012). 'Walkers, Sandwich'. www.canneslions.com/inspiration/past_grands_prix_advert.cfm?sub.channel_id=301 accessed 12 January 2012.

Foster, S. (2011). 'Aussie ad agency Clemenger BBDO Melbourne wins Cannes PR Grand Prix'. www.moreaboutadvertising.com/2011/06/aussie-ad-agency-clemenger-bbdo-melbourne-wins-cannes-pr-grand-prix accessed 15 January 2012.

Frankfurt, H. (2005). *On Bullshit*. Princeton, NJ: Princeton University Press.

Gilpin, D.R. and P.J. Murphy (2010). 'Implications of complexity theory for public relations: beyond crisis' in *The Sage Handbook of Public Relations*. R.L. Heath (ed.). Thousand Oaks, CA: Sage.

Grunig, J. (ed.) (1992). *Excellence in Public Relations and Communication Management*. Hillsdale, NJ: Lawrence Erlbaum Associates.

Harrison, K. (2011). *Strategic Public Relations: A practical guide to success*. South Yarra, Australia: Palgrave Macmillan.

Holt, D.B. (2004). *How Brands Become Icons: The principles of cultural branding*. Boston, MA: Harvard Business School Press.

Holt, D.B. and D. Cameron (2010). *Cultural Strategy: Using innovative ideologies to build breakthrough brands*. Oxford: Oxford University Press.

Hutton, J. (2010). 'Defining the relationship between public relations and marketing: public relations' most important challenge' in *The Sage Handbook of Public Relations*. R.L. Heath (ed.). Thousand Oaks, CA: Sage.

Kitchen, P. (2006). *A Marketing Communications Scenario for 2010*. London: Chartered Institute of Public Relations Marketing Communications Group.

Kotler, P. (2003). *Marketing Insights from A to Z: 80 concepts every manager needs to know*. New York, NY: John Wiley.

L'Etang, J. (2008). *Public Relations: Concepts, practice and critique*. London: Sage.

Lewis, D. and D. Bridger (2003). *The Soul of the New Consumer*. London: Nicholas Brealey.

MacManus, T. (2003). 'Public relations: the cultural dimension' in *Perspectives on Public Relations Research*. D. Moss, D. Vercic and G. Warnaby (eds). London: Routledge.

Mayo, A.J. and N. Nohria (2005). 'Zeitgeist leadership'. *Harvard Business Review* **83**(10): 46–60.

McKie, D. and P. Willis (2012). Renegotiating the terms of engagement: public relations, marketing and contemporary challenges. *Public Relations Review* doi:10.1016/j.pubrev.2012.03.008.

Morgan, A. (1999). *Eating the Big Fish: How challenger brands can compete against brand leaders*. New York, NY: John Wiley.

Moss, D. and G. Warnaby (2003). 'Strategy and public relations' in *Perspectives on Public Relations Research*. D. Moss, D. Vercic and G. Warnaby (eds). London: Routledge.

Public Relations Society of America (2012). 'Industry facts and figures/PRSA newsroom'. http://media.prsa.org/prsa+overview/industry+facts+figures accessed 8 July 2012.

Qvortrup, L. (2006). 'Understanding new digital media'. *European Journal of Communication* **21**(3): 345–356.

Tench, R. and P. Willis (2009). 'Creativity, deception or ethical malpractice: a critique of the Trumanization of marketing public relations through guerrilla campaigns'. *Ethical Space: The International Journal of Communication Ethics* **6**(2): 47–55.

The Economist (2010). 'Public relations in the recession: good news'. www.economist.com/node/15276746 accessed 22 December 2011.

The Guardian (2010). 'Steve Jobs solves iPhone 4 reception problems: "Don't hold it that way".' www.guardian.co.uk/technology/blog/2010/jun/25/iphone-reception-problems-solved accessed 11 January 2012.

Willis, P. (2009). 'Public relations and the consumer' in *Exploring Public Relations*. R. Tench and L. Yeomans (eds). Harlow, England: Pearson.

Zerfass, A., A. Moreno, R. Tench, D. Verčič and P. Verhoeven (2008). *European Communication Monitor 2008. Trends in Communication Management and Public Relations – Results and Implications*. Brussels, Leipzig: Euprera/University of Leipzig. Available at: www.communicationmonitor.eu.

CHAPTER 19

Dennis Kelly and Helen Standing

Business-to-business public relations

Learning outcomes

By the end of this chapter you should be able to:

- define and describe business-to-business public relations
- distinguish business-to-business public relations from consumer PR
- recognise the key role of the business and trade media in shaping perceptions
- understand the evolving role of social media in business-to-business reputation and relationship building
- identify the key principles of business-to-business public relations
- apply this understanding to simple, relevant scenarios
- recognise business-to-business activity through case examples
- apply the principles to real-life scenarios.

Structure

- Core principles of business-to-business (B2B) public relations
- Business or trade media and journalists
- B2B social media
- Coordinating the communications disciplines
- Building corporate reputation

Introduction

The concept of business-to-business (B2B) public relations (PR) is based on the recognition that most organisations, businesses and individual professionals sell to other businesses rather than directly to the consumer. The scope of such business transactions is enormous and incorporates products and services as diverse as aircraft and microchips, law and web design. Each sector of the marketplace has its own operating environment but the fundamental need for PR and communications activity that is aligned with business goals is a key part of the selling process.

The traditional focus of B2B PR has been the use of **editorial** in trade magazines as a direct method of building awareness and reputation and generating new business leads with a niche regional, national or international audience.

However, contemporary B2B PR uses the full spectrum of PR techniques as the business-to-business marketplace becomes increasingly sophisticated. An examination of entries into B2B categories in the UK Chartered Institute of Public Relations Excellence Awards and the PRCA Frontline Awards shows how PR is being successfully used to manage corporate reputations and build relationships, as well as providing vital support for sales and marketing programmes. Social media – blogging, Twitter, LinkedIn, Facebook (to a lesser extent) and other platforms – are also increasingly being used by B2B professionals and organisations to communicate directly with target customers, clients and stakeholders.

Core principles of business-to-business (B2B) public relations

The starting point for **business-to-business (B2B)** PR is a detailed understanding of the business goals, specific marketplace, the application of the products or services in question and an appreciation of the dynamics of the buying process. This reflects the traditional emphasis on supporting sales and the very real need for PR activity to present the benefits of particular products, services or experts.

Advocates of B2B PR as a specialism say that the depth of marketplace understanding is a point of differentiation with consumer PR (see Chapter 18), where practitioner knowledge of consumer behaviour outweighs the need for product and marketplace familiarity. Simply put, B2B PR is usually about complex messages to a niche audience, while consumer PR is usually about simple messages to a mass audience. (See Explore 19.1.)

The characteristics of a business-to-business marketplace include:

- a relatively small number of 'buying' publics – it may even be that potential customers can be named as individuals (e.g., manufacturers in the building trade will know of the specific builders' merchants who could stock their products: there may only be three or four);

- a specific application/end user for products and services (e.g., a producer of thermal insulation boards for house building);

- defined product and service terms of technical specifications and any legal/trading restrictions (e.g., controls on building products such as insulation requirements

> ## Explore 19.1
>
> ### Finding B2B examples
>
> Go into a large newsagent or magazine shop and see how many magazine/journal titles you can see that are non-consumer and are targeting the trade/specialist business-to-business marketplace. Also do a Google search for influential business websites and blogs for specific sectors. Cision's Social Media Index has a library of top 10 UK blogs in different specialist areas, including architecture and law.
>
> ### Feedback
>
> Examples might include *PRWeek* in the UK or a regional business magazine such as *Yorkshire Business Insider*. Other examples could be *Accountancy Age, Architecture Today, The Stage, People Management,* etc. Influential business-to-business websites include online versions of key trade publications and online-only business media, such as thebusinessdesk.com.

of windows or insulation boards, as in the previous example);

- purchasing decision often negotiated individually and subject to finite contract periods.

This list indicates the depth of company and marketplace knowledge required by successful practitioners of B2B PR. The traditional use of media relations techniques in trade and specialist magazines also requires a detailed understanding of the workings and requirements of these journals and their editors.

Business or trade media and journalists

The business and trade press is an important and integral part of the B2B marketplace. The UK is unusually well served by specialist publications covering all sectors, from aerospace to waste management. The pan-European marketplace is not dissimilar, with prominent titles addressing all market sectors (see also the website of Cision, formerly Romeike, at www.uk.cision.com, or PR Newswire at www.prnewswire.com). Table 20.1 provides a select list of trade publications in the UK.

Managers and professionals tend to read the titles specific to their trade or industry as part of their working lives. And it is this special linkage that attributes particular influence to trade and specialist magazines.

Publication	Purpose
Thatched Living	The official publication of the Thatched Property Association, helping you to buy a thatched home, find a local thatcher or get thatch insurance.
The Architects' Journal	The voice of architecture in Britain brings you news, comment, analysis, building projects, design guidance and reviews.
The Architectural Review	A colourful global subscription magazine offering forums, jobs, competitions and reader enquiries, with a useful professional directory.
The Builder	Here you will find *The Builder* and *Building News*, two free trade journals, as well as a product locator service.
The Builder and Architect Series	For the latest news on building products and construction services, making life even easier for architects, specifiers, building services engineers and facility managers.
The Designer	Get all the latest news from the design world with this monthly magazine, in print, on subscription, or online.
The English Home	*The English Home* showcases the best in homes, fabrics, furniture, accessories and design. It also advises you about property news and places to stay.
The Georgian	Published three times a year, it plays an important role in providing communication to members. It contains vital information, with regular features on buildings at risk, practical tips for owners of Georgian properties, restoration projects (both exterior and interior), casework, art, news, reviews, events and activities.
The Glazine	A weekly email site, giving you all the latest from the glazing and fenestration industries, covering issues such as energy efficiency.
The Global Cement Report	This is a subscriber site for the magazine *Cement Review*, with all the latest issues to do with cement and related industries.
The Haywood Handbook for Flooring	A once-yearly spring publication, the *Handbook* lists suppliers and manufacturers, technical information about all flooring products, training opportunities and forthcoming exhibitions.
The Installer	This is the link to *The Installer* and *The Fabricator*, both available to read online. There is also a product finder service.
The Interior Design Handbook	
The Landscaper	*The Landscaper* is an online magazine keeping you up-to-date with current news in landscaping, jobs, advertising and features.
The Really Useful Directory	This comprehensive directory will guide you through the minefield of product sourcing, with help on bathrooms, bedrooms, furniture and technology.
The Structural Engineer	This is the international journal of The Institute of Structural Engineers, providing you with the latest news, advertising and recruitment in the industry.

Table 19.1 Select list under 'T' of trade publications in the UK construction industry
(*source*: www.theconstructioncentre.co.uk (www.theconstructioncentre.co.uk/trade-periodicals-and-news/t.html)

Circulation and **readership** relate to the size of the sector and the existence or otherwise of competitive titles. Thus a key trade publication such as *The Grocer* in the UK, which serves the food and drink industries, has a circulation of 54,000 and a readership of over 200,000. This dwarfs *The Architects' Journal*, one of the 64 titles covering the building sector in the UK. But both publications have the unique advantage of the trade press (see Case study 19.1). They are read by decision makers in their sector. The loyalty of trade press readerships creates a strong role for their titles in the B2B cycle of influence and persuasion.

Case study 19.1

How trade publications are used

Picture 19.1 *The Architects' Journal* is one of 64 titles in the UK covering the construction industry. This particular cover features an Adjaye/Associates scheme (*source*: photograph Timothy Soar)

The following case study shows how a practising architect uses B2B titles such as *The Architects' Journal* in his everyday working life. Nigel Jacques is an award-winning commercial architect who discusses the role of specialist media for his profession:

'As an architectural practice we use *The Architects' Journal* and other similar trade magazines at varying levels and for different reasons. *The Architects' Journal* is used in our practice as an important technical and visual resource. It keeps us up-to-date with new design concepts, regulations and innovative materials and also with the legal and professional aspects of architecture.

'The more senior you are within the practice the more in-depth you tend to read *The Architects' Journal*. At director level it is used as a resource for keeping up-to-date on a weekly basis with the market as it evolves and with new materials and design concepts. To a young design architect, *The Architects' Journal* is used more as a visual resource. When you read through an architectural trade magazine it is a media experience in which you are constantly absorbing knowledge and picking up ideas and inspiration on an often subliminal level. Architecture is an art, which means that we are constantly looking at visual stimuli first and foremost and then looking in more detail and noticing aspects of design, such as products or innovative use of materials.

'*The Architects' Journal* can influence buying and design decisions in as much as an architect might notice a particular material and/or form used in a building on an image and start thinking how it may influence one of our schemes. Technical articles within *The Architects' Journal*, for instance, indicate in detail how the material is used effectively in the design and who the supplier is.

'The journal also contributes to sector understanding as it provides an up-to-date and informative source of current trends, regulations and changes in legislation that could impact on the practice. As well as an architectural resource, it is therefore also a useful trend predictor. In growing and developing your business you are constantly monitoring the performance of other practices (*The Architects' Journal* top 100 architects, for instance), watching the political environment and organisations with whom you may wish to collaborate or who may directly impact upon your business. *The Architects' Journal* can be used as a tool for all these things.

case study 19.1 (continued)

'In terms of alternative thinking and inspiring creativity, *The Architects' Journal* contributes in as much that it features the commercial conformists, the individuals and the mavericks of the trade. The visual illustrations can inspire architects with ideas for their own work and often promote healthy debate.

'Our PR consultants also target *The Architects' Journal* as a means of raising our profile as a national practice and we are frequently approached by journalists for comment on national and project-specific issues. However, publications of this nature can also be responsible for negative comment and it can be somewhat frustrating when publications are predictable and frequently one-sided. A good relationship with journalists, though, can help to offset this and allow you the opportunity to respond to potential negative coverage. Regular positive editorial coverage within national trade publications adds equity to the architect and their practice's brand, acts as an efficient business development tool when read by key decision makers, contributes to the 'feel good' factor within the practice as an excellent motivator and attracts high calibre staff to our practice.

'*The Architects' Journal* is a key resource for our practice, without which we would be working within a vacuum with regard to current trends. Every design practice needs to monitor the macro environment within which it operates, and without national trade publications such as *The Architects' Journal* this would prove extremely difficult.'

Source: Interview with commerical architect
Nigel Jacques BA(Hons) BArch(Hons) RIBA

This accounts for the traditional B2B PR focus on gaining editorial coverage in trade magazines. This role remains important, and editorial staff on trade magazines are worthy of special attention for the B2B PR practitioner. However, due to declining advertising revenues and increasing competition from online media, many long-established trade publications in the UK (such as *Accountancy Age*) have been discontinued and those that are still in existence have fewer editorial staff on tighter deadlines, with greater pressures to contribute to selling advertising space (Dowell 2011).

Those trade publications that remain tend to be the one or two key opinion-forming titles in each sector (building, health, retail, finance, etc.). These are the journals/periodicals that influence the business/sector and they are the ones organisations will look to for editorial coverage and discussion about their organisation. It's important when working in the B2B sector that you research and understand which publications are key to your organisation/client organisation. It is important to note, therefore, that some publications have high 'news value' and others very low. You need to be able to discern and make use of the difference.

and potentially responsive audience. But you will need to be knowledgeable and show your competence when dealing with trade journalists. However, also remember that we all have to start our careers somewhere, so you may be dealing with a **cub reporter** or a journalist who has moved recently to a particular title. The big media groups have a raft of trade titles, and journalists move frequently between titles and specialist areas. They may still be learning about their new subject area, perhaps at the same time as you.

As a rule of thumb, when dealing with trade press journalists assume expertise. This is usually the case and it is common for editors of relatively small circulation magazines to be frequent commentators on television news programmes and in the national dailies. This is simply because such individuals do become genuine experts through their professional concentration on a subject area. For example, the editor of *The Grocer* is often used on national business broadcasts on radio and television as an expert commentator on supermarket trends and prices. Also *Jane's Defence Weekly* editors are frequently called on to supply expert knowledge during armed conflicts around the world. (See Explore 19.2.)

Business or trade media and journalists

As a PR practitioner, you will routinely find that trade press journalists have a thorough understanding of their subject area. This fact creates both an opportunity and a challenge for the practitioner. You will have an informed

Story ideas

The news values of trade publications obviously have a sector-specific focus, and regular reading of key magazines will readily identify the news angles adopted. Practitioners working in a B2B marketplace should be avid readers of the sector's periodicals and know which ones are most

Box 19.1

B2B media relations in practice

Securing coverage in specialist trade media for a regional law firm

'The legal sector is highly competitive and getting a voice on topical issues for legal clients can be difficult. A small regional law firm I used to work with tasked us with raising their profile both on a regional level but also in specific sectors to promote their expertise in specialist areas.

'For example, the firm's insurance division is highly specialist and has a national reputation, working on behalf of organisations on disputes related to insurance claims, including public sector bodies and contractors. There is little mileage for the team to get coverage in regional media and, besides, their work is rarely relevant to a general regional audience. They are therefore only interested in appearing in key insurance trade titles, such as *Post Magazine* and *Insurance Times*.

'These titles are esteemed industry publications and it is a great challenge securing a voice for a regional law firm. They are not interested in news items about the firm's work and rarely take proactively pitched viewpoint comment. Targeting their "forward features" is also a challenge because any that are relevant are targeted by every insurance law specialist in the UK, and often the bigger, more high-profile firms and lawyers are chosen to provide comment. Our strategy was to find out how to make the features editors' lives easier and thus have a better chance of getting coverage.

'We made the time to talk to them about how they put features together and discovered that they usually took comment from whoever put an expert forward first, and preferred to set up telephone interviews rather than receiving written comment so that they didn't have to go back and forth through PR contacts for more information. We therefore asked to be added to their mailing lists to receive features synopses as soon as they were available and, instead of targeting every remotely relevant feature, we selected very specific features that we knew we could source a specialist expert on. This also made things easier for the client and demonstrated that we understood their expertise in this complex area.

'For example, when we received a synopsis on a feature about noise-induced hearing loss, we got straight in contact with a partner at the firm who specialised in these cases and asked if he would be prepared to do an interview should the journalist be interested. We then went straight back to the features editor and offered a telephone interview with the partner at specific times at which he was available. As a result, our client was quoted heavily throughout a double-page feature in *Post Magazine*, the leading insurance industry publication. Following that, we managed to secure face-to-face meetings for the head of the firm's insurance division with the features editor at both *Post Magazine* and *Insurance Times* and secured increasing amounts of coverage in the insurance trade media.

'In order to be able to achieve this, we had to immerse ourselves in the firm's complex areas of expertise and keep on top of what individual partners were working on so that we could proactively spot relevant features and confidently pitch comment to sector journalists.'

Source: Helen Standing, Director, Engage Comms; Consultant, Trimedia UK

Explore 19.2

Trade magazines in your country

Do you know just how many trade magazines are published in your country? Use the Internet or media databases such as PIMS or Cision (www.uk.cision.com) to search the number of titles.

Feedback

You may be surprised by the results. In the UK there are titles relevant to a wide variety of sectors, from the railway industries to animal health, chemical processing and embalming.

influential and credible (see Box 19.1). Do also be aware of the prevalence of advertising-style editorial, which is driven by revenue from charging companies to include a picture/image of the product (a colour separation fee/charge is made for this). Box 19.2 provides some examples of typical B2B news angles for gaining editorial coverage.

News will usually be presented to the media through a press release, but other techniques of regular use to B2B PR practitioners include:

- one-to-one briefings and interviews
- full feature articles
- comment to be included in wider features
- case studies

Box 19.2

Typical news angles for B2B editorial

Typical news angles for B2B editorial would include:

- comment on latest industry developments, innovations, trends and legislation
- insights from major industry conferences and events
- new senior technical and managerial appointments
- new technology and new processes
- new contracts
- unusual or problem-solving contracts and applications
- market diversification or convergence
- partnerships, associations, mergers, takeovers.

- press conferences
- conferences, workshops, roundtable discussions and other events.

These techniques are covered in Chapter 13, but here are some other techniques that are available to the PR practitioner.

Advertorials

The advertorial is also used frequently in B2B promotional campaigns. Advertorials are paid-for advertisements designed to look like editorial. However, journals will always indicate clearly the sponsoring company in order to differentiate from editorial. So, although advertorials may look like editorial, they do not have the credibility of news or features material written and/or edited by journalists. As advertising revenues and circulation figures decline, advertorials are becoming a key source of revenue for trade publications and journalists will often try and sell them as an alternative to sub-standard editorial content pitched by PRs.

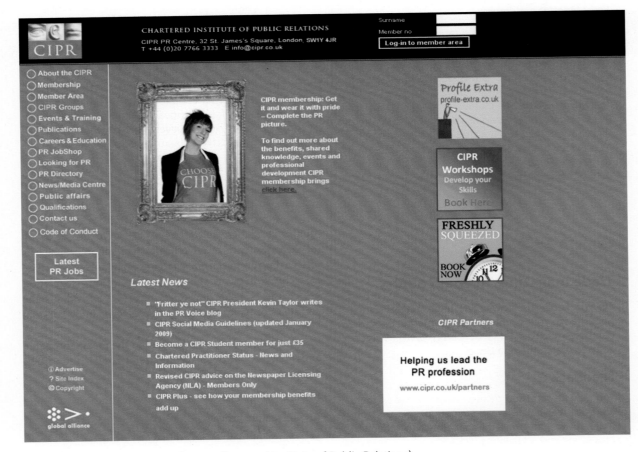

Picture 19.2 CIPR home page (*source*: Chartered Institute of Public Relations)

From the practitioner's perspective, an advertorial is often regarded as promotional material and treated much like a newsletter or a company publication.

Websites and blogs

Particular note must also be taken of the specialist websites gaining common currency in most industry sectors. Many specialist and trade publications maintain their own websites to complement their printed publications. Equally, the trade associations operating in each sector often have websites. Major industry events such as conferences, seminars and exhibitions are also frequently supported by websites. Such websites are both a vital source of information for practitioners and offer an additional source of target outlets for placing product and corporate news and information. In the UK, a good starting point for seeking industry-sector websites is via the Chartered Institute of Public Relations (CIPR) website (www.cipr.co.uk).

Beyond the specific product or company-related news items, trade magazines offer a particularly good opportunity to place commentary on marketplace, technology and product developments. In-depth material available through your client company may be highly valued by the editor of trade magazines. In practice, this creates the opportunity for a client or company to be seen as a source of authoritative industry information. (See Think about 19.1 and Think about 19.2.)

B2B social media

In his book *Engage! The complete guide for brands and businesses to build, cultivate and measure success in the new web* (2010), Brian Solis describes social media as 'a matter of digital Darwinism that affects all forms of marketing and service'. By this he means that communications are evolving with technology and that social media is more than just a 'fad' – its use will very soon become fundamental to business. Although the use of social media in B2B public relations is still developing, it is now widely accepted among B2B professionals that it cannot be ignored as a business tool.

While the B2B market has been much slower than the B2C (business-to-consumer) market to embrace social media, in *The B2B Social Media Book* (2012), Bodner and Cohen argue that there are five reasons why B2B companies are actually better suited to using social media to generate business:

1. Clear understanding of customers
2. Depth of subject matter expertise
3. Need for generating higher revenue with lower marketing budgets

Think about 19.2

Creating business-to-business conversations online

How could you help an organisation or client get into dialogue with potential clients and customers?

Feedback

B2B sales are often relationship based. B2B organisations, such as law firms, often have to 'sell' the expertise of individuals within the business. Using social media such as Twitter and LinkedIn it is possible to give these individual experts a voice and the ability to engage directly with target customers. However, their complex messages need to be translated into accessible content that acts as a talking point – and can be distilled into concise statements (e.g., tweets that are no longer than 140 characters, or 500-word blogs broken down into useful points).

This is often where B2B PR practitioners can use their expertise to advise, train and create content that enables organisations and individuals to communicate and engage more effectively and strategically using social media.

Think about 19.1

Becoming an expert

How would you, as a PR practitioner, become an expert on your company/client, its products, experts and unique selling points?

Feedback

To build understanding, we often need to spend a lot of time researching the company and its products, services and people. For PR practitioners, this can mean taking time to work with the company, spending time in different departments and perhaps learning to use the products and services they offer. It also involves closely monitoring what competitors are doing and what the latest developments in the wider marketplace are. Regularly reading the trade media is important and you can also use social media for research (see 'B2B social media').

4. Relationship-based sales

5. Already have practise using social media principles of telling business-focused stories and educating customers with content.

All five of these reasons relate to key elements of B2B PR and communications and demonstrate why B2B social media belongs within the PR discipline – as opposed to marketing, advertising or web development.

The use of social media as part of B2B PR can work in conjunction with trade media relations. Many trade and business journalists now use Twitter (a popular microblogging platform) for most of their news and feature leads, and most trade journals use social media platforms to share their content with a wider specialist audience.

Social media tools used by B2B PR practitioners include blogs, Twitter, LinkedIn and, to a lesser extent, Facebook, YouTube and Flickr. Other platforms are emerging and evolving all the time. These platforms give B2B companies and professionals the opportunity to engage directly with potential and existing customers and clients to demonstrate expertise, raise awareness, build reputation and sell their products and services.

However, as Brian Solis (2010) says: 'The use of [social media] tools does not guarantee that people will listen. Engagement is shaped by the interpretation of its intentions. In order for social media to mutually benefit you and your customers, you must engage them in meaningful and advantageous conversations, empowering them as true participants in your marketing and service efforts.'

The etiquette of social media – informality, sharing, collaboration, freedom of speech – is often at odds with the way B2B professionals are used to working. As such, there is an important role for B2B PR practitioners to advise and train colleagues and clients in adapting their communications style and techniques. In many cases, PR practitioners are responsible for managing and monitoring social media channels on behalf of B2B organisations and creating tailored content that makes their specialist areas of expertise more accessible and engaging to a wider audience. Case study 19.2 provides a practitioner's account of using social media in B2B PR.

Case study 19.2

B2B social media as part of a wider marketing communications strategy

The following case study shows how an organisation with a niche audience experimented with and then embraced social media as a key part of their marketing communications strategy. Ruth Wilson was New Media and Web Manager at the UK Resource Centre for Women in Science, Engineering and Technology at the time of this interview, which was carried out by Helen Standing and featured in Victoria Tomlinson's 2011 ebook *Why You Can't Ignore Social Media in Business*.

What were your first experiences with social media?

'I was working in the Communications team at the UKRC, an organisation that is building gender equality in science, engineering and technology. We started experimenting with social media tools and techniques when we realised how beneficial it would be for engaging with our members and stakeholders. Our client groups include computing and IT companies and professionals, and young adults who are growing up with social media, so we needed to demonstrate our awareness of emerging communications channels. Our first step was setting up a blog on our website, where every fortnight we host a different woman SET professional.

'We built a Facebook presence and found it a useful way of creating links and disseminating news – one Facebook campaign was run with an external PR company and gained us international media coverage. Then, at our annual conference a few years ago, we were aware that some of the speakers and attendees were tweeting about the event – including a government minister – and we realised we needed to be part of the conversation. At the same time we started looking at LinkedIn. Again, the approach was experimental at first and we made use of the enthusiasm and knowledge of particular members of staff who were keen that we make use of these tools.

'Over time, we began to join the dots with all of our different activities and I was given responsibility for managing the overall approach. A brand refresh and launch of a new website gave us the perfect opportunity to assess what we were doing and what more we could do to get the full potential out of social media and integrate it with our overall communications strategy

case study 19.2 (continued)

and activity. In particular, we built RSS feeds into the new site, and this enables us to drive out core information across different platforms. We are more efficient at sharing news in a way that creates dialogue and engagement, and we are also able to pick up on issues and events relevant to our work through tracking social media activity.'

How do you now use social media in your current role?

'I am now responsible for all of our social media activity. We don't claim to be experts but we have come on a hugely valuable journey. Social media is a very reciprocal, conversational environment, which has allowed us to expand our offering to women in science, engineering and technology as well as strengthen our links with a wide range of audiences. And we have been able to do this at very little cost.

'One of our key roles is to help these women to raise their professional profile and we can now give them training on how to do this using social media channels. We have started using YouTube and Flickr to share content and have occasional sessions in Second Life (a virtual reality platform that has now declined in popularity).'

What is your advice to others venturing into using social media to achieve their business goals?

'We took it one step at a time – you don't have to have an instant presence on every platform. Talk to people already making good use of social media, and involve members of staff who are already enthusiasts and have useful experience. If appropriate, provide in-house training and information sessions, so you keep people up-to-date on what you are doing and bring the whole organisation with you.

'At the UKRC, senior management have been able to see the successes each step of the way, and it has been important for us to have one person managing the process. We have a corporate approach: we have to balance the personal and conversational tone of much new media with making sure we are always promoting the UKRC and its key messages and services, and it is my role to make sure this happens.

'Social media activity is now an integrated part of our overall organisational objectives and is a highly valued marketing tool.'

Source: By kind permission from Ruth Wilson

Coordinating the communications disciplines

The use of PR techniques to support the marketing and sales environment is well understood and is often the motivation for appointing a PR manager or using a PR consultancy. Practitioners can demonstrate that insightful and creative PR can both indirectly and directly generate business leads, opportunities and sales. However, as corporate reputation management grows in importance, B2B PR is gaining credibility and being seen as an overarching discipline within which other marketing communication disciplines sit. Many PR practitioners argue that they should be responsible for the communications strategy at board level and marketers should carry out tactical activities to support the strategy. In reality, though, most in-house teams are still led by marketing directors.

In B2B PR, an understanding of the role of other marketing communication disciplines is essential, as is the timing and coordinated application of the right techniques. PR practitioners working in B2B often display an in-depth understanding of advertising, direct mail and sales promotion and of how PR can act as a unifying mechanism as part of the wider business strategy.

The marketing mix, originally defined by Borden (1964), is the combination of the major tools of marketing, otherwise known as the 4Ps – product, price, promotion and place (see Table 19.2).

Figure 19.1 shows some of the promotional disciplines typically employed in B2B marketing. All are aimed at supporting the sales effort, and their application reflects views on the best way to reach decision makers. It is often not enough to rely on one channel, hence most promotional campaigns use a combination of techniques to make up the promotion aspect of the 4Ps in the marketing mix.

Role of advertising

Advertising has the very particular job of placing a proposition in front of the target audience. The strength of advertising is in the control of message delivery. Your message is placed in front of a known audience at an

Price	Product
Cost	Product management
Profitability	New development
Value for money	Product features and benefits
Competitiveness	Branding
Incentives	Packaging
	After-sales service
Place	Promotion
Access to target market	Promotional mix
Channels to market	Public relations
Retailers and distributors	Advertising
Logistics	Sales promotion
	Sales management
	Direct marketing
	Social media

Table 19.2 The marketing mix

agreed point in time. This precise control of the message, audience and timing can make advertising very effective. And in the B2B arena, results can usually be measured and analysed.

The very best advertisements offer a single proposition in a highly creative way. In the B2B marketplace, there should always be a 'call to action', making it clear what we are asking interested readers to do – phone this number, send in this coupon, visit this website.

Some sales and marketing managers may believe that the importance of advertising revenue to trade magazines means that big advertisers can expect an editorial quid pro quo (obtain editorial coverage if they have paid for advertising space). This is not the case. Editorial staff cherish their independence and this should be respected. The promise of advertising spend should not be used in an attempt to influence editorial decisions. Editorial decisions should be based on the news value of '**copy**' submitted in the form of press releases and news features.

Advertising has a defined role in placing repetitive messages in front of buying audiences, hence its value in B2B marketing. PR can be used in a complementary way to expand on a necessarily simple advertising message and to broaden audience reach. It is also worth noting that news value is usually enhanced if editorial is offered before an advertising campaign. Something that is already being advertised cannot really be regarded as 'news'.

Role of direct marketing

Direct marketing is appropriately named as a promotional technique. The proposition is put directly to the

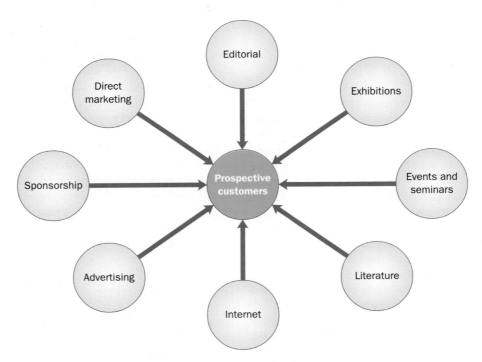

Figure 19.1 Promotional disciplines used in business-to-business (B2B) marketing

prospective buyer, for example in an email, leaflet or brochure, without an intermediary such as a distributor, agent or salesperson. This creates its major advantage in many B2B marketplaces where there are an identifiable and discrete number of buyers and/or influencers. Direct marketers work from target lists (databases) that they either buy from a list brokerage or compile themselves. Responses are tracked and measured with precision.

Direct marketing is becoming increasingly sophisticated as a promotional technique as communication channels, message content and response rates can be tracked and refined. PR supports direct marketing by building the credibility and reputation of the organisation. It is able to do this by placing key messages in front of target audiences.

Role of sales promotion

Sales promotion techniques, such as special offers, '**bogofs**' (buy one, get one free), vouchers, redeemable gifts, competitions, etc. are well established in consumer marketing and are being used increasingly in B2B. This is simply because a well-thought-through sales promotion can work and has a single objective – to increase sales. Sales promotions can also be popular with sales teams as they give them something specific to offer their customers.

Sales promotion is very distinct from PR but the disciplines do have much in common. When they run in tandem their effectiveness in creating sales opportunities can be enhanced. The linkage between sales promotion and PR is strong because sales promotions can offer benefits that supplement the basic product, price, place and offer.

Role of public relations

PR can support the other promotional disciplines and be a promotional technique in its own right. Undoubtedly, the most effective use of the promotional disciplines is shown when there is clear coordination in the planning stage. Common themes can be developed that 'work' in all channels, albeit with content and messages presented in different ways to different audiences at different times.

Creative routes can be developed jointly through '**brainstorming**', and practitioners in all the disciplines can work to a shared timetable. Cost savings will be demonstrated through minimising the time input of contributing professionals and through shared creative work (branding, design, photography, etc.).

The special role of PR is in taking the proposition to a broader range of influencers through the use of media relations and other PR techniques. Of course, PR as defined in marketing terms, as one element of the marketing mix (see

---

Box 19.3

Activities used in B2B public relations campaigns

Most frequently, editorial will be the lead PR tool. Other activities used in B2B PR campaigns include:

- newsletters
- literature
- seminars
- briefings
- conferences
- roadshows
- awards and competitions
- presentations
- sponsorship and endorsements
- blogging
- social media platforms, e.g. LinkedIn and Twitter.

Table 19.2), is a more limited concept than you will find elsewhere in this book. For a fuller discussion of PR and marketing see Chapter 22. PR in its larger sense is also of value to B2B communications, as discussed in the next section. (See Box 19.3.)

The best B2B campaigns invariably use the appropriate promotional techniques in a parallel and supportive way. (See Think about 19.3, Think about 19.4 and Case study 19.3.)

Think about 19.3

Business-to-business as a public relations specialism

PR practitioners regard B2B as a specialism. This is primarily because of the special emphasis placed on supporting the business goals and sales effort and understanding the marketplace and specialist area of expertise. Think again about how B2B PR has been defined and how this differs from consumer PR (see also Chapter 18).

Case study 19.3
CPP Group

Building corporate reputation

This campaign by PR consultancy Financial Dynamics on behalf of its client, the CPP Group, provides an example of creative PR that aims to build corporate reputation. The methodology is more typical of consumer PR but is here applied with outstanding results in a B2B environment. (This campaign was a finalist in the UK CIPR Excellence Awards, see www.cipr.co.uk.)

The CPP Group is an international provider of everyday consumer assistance products, with 11.3 million customers worldwide. It offers a number of services including:

- credit card protection
- retrieval service for lost or stolen keys
- emergency service for everyday domestic problems
- mobile phone insurance
- insurance, advice and support for people with debt worries.

CPP works with many partners, including high-street banks, which re-brand CPP products as their own, leading to virtual anonymity for CPP among end consumers.

Public relations objectives

The PR objectives of this 12-month communication programme were to build greater awareness of the company among corporate audiences, to profile new and existing products in trade and specialist publications and to increase the 'share of voice' for CPP and its products.

Implementation

Rather than simply promote CPP's range and products, the campaign focused on product-related issues of concern to the customer, both to raise CPP's profile and to position it as a consumer champion. Robust, topical research formed the backbone of the campaign, with each topic carefully considered for impact in terms of delivering optimum news value and boosting CPP's sales figures. Research was undertaken on a quarterly basis, enabling CPP to examine trends and become more central to industry debate – achieving results such as the lead story on the front page of UK national newspaper the *Daily Express* (circulation 748,664 in August 2008, source Audit Bureau of Circulation – www.guardian.co.uk/media/table/2008/sep/08/abcs.pressandpublishing?gusrc=rss&feed=media accessed 10 October 2008).

Announcements linked to other products, such as home emergency and mobile phone insurance, worked in synergy with CPP's product marketing activity so that different issues were prioritised at different points in the year. Finance Dynamics carried out an aggressive media programme, based on regular consumer omnibus research, to provide contemporary news angles.

Proactive news releases generated for CPP included:

15 February – 'Fear of debt soars by 44 per cent in three months'

28 February – 'Mobile phones top the league of most useful modern inventions'

12 March – 'Consumers display lax attitude toward plastic card fraud'

3 May – 'Young Britons crippled by financial commitments'

13 June – 'It may be good to talk . . . but it's clearly better to text'

20 August – 'Obsession with home improvement TV puts Britons at risk of injury and expense'

17 September – '1 in 10 only alarmed by debt when they lose their home or partner'

2 October – 'Britons ill-prepared for rollout of chip and pin'

12 November – 'Brits' patriotic tendencies revealed in mobile phone tune hate list'

5 December – 'CPP Group plc promotes improved financial awareness with new product launch'

10 December – 'Credit card spending cut back this Christmas'

Financial Dynamics also undertook a number of additional PR initiatives throughout the year. These included the launch of CPP's new financial advice and support service, Financial Health, which capitalised on the strong relationships with journalists from the debt index stories. A programme of media briefings was organised between target business writers and CPP's chief executive to help build the company's corporate profile. A weekly 'Box of Tricks' was created to allow opportunistic CPP comment 'piggybacking' (working alongside or aligned to) the news agenda, to help maintain CPP's position at the cutting edge of industry issues.

Evaluation and measurement of the campaign

The campaign generated 373 pieces of news coverage – 19 per cent of which appeared in the national media. CPP's average share of voice in the market against

case study 19.3 (continued)

competitors – including Barclaycard, RBS, Egg, National Debtline and Citizens Advice Bureau – was 18 per cent.

Seventy per cent of all coverage included at least one of CPP's key messages: 'Fear of debt soars by 44 per cent in three months' generated the greatest media interest, with 51 positive news hits, including national dailies and trade publications, and the 'Elderly set for a winter of debt and discontent as tax hikes hit hard' press release led to the lead, front-page story in UK national paper the *Daily Express*.

Presence in home news, rather than just the money pages, suggests that the campaign succeeded in positioning CPP with consumers as well as with trade audiences.

Coverage for CPP achieved a potential audience reach of more than 146 million people. Based on flat-rate card figures, coverage was valued at over £583,000 – five times greater than PR fees and expenses.

The campaign was vigorously evaluated every quarter, enabling Financial Dynamics to present the value of PR as a discipline to CPP's internal audiences and offer quarterly recommendations for continuous improvement to the programme. The positive results shown through evaluation correlate with coverage volumes rising by an average of 20 per cent per quarter.

Rob Miatt, Marketing Manager for CPP, commented: 'The targeted media relations approach via regular, thought-provoking and hard-hitting research led by the news agenda gave us a strong media following, raised our profile amongst an important consumer audience, forged our position as an industry leader, and even made us front-page news.'

Observations

This case study offers an example of contemporary public relations activity that is able to encompass the traditional B2B role with the substantial 'added value' of developing a simultaneous consumer-facing campaign. The regular use of research provides both the trade and consumer media with the relevant material while positioning CPP as the major industry commentator. The annual PR programme is acting as a major platform for building the corporate reputation of CPP that can be supported subsequently by other activities.

Source: www.cipr.co.uk

Building corporate reputation

The use of editorial and social media to support the sales environment is an essential element of most B2B PR campaigns. However, there is a fundamental difference between media relations and online engagement as a promotional technique and the comprehensive application of PR methodology to analyse trends, counsel organisational leaders and to plan and deliver reputation-building communications programmes. Media relations and social media can be used as part of the marketing mix alongside the other promotional disciplines, such as advertising and direct mail, to great effect. But the true impact of PR is seen when applied as a strategic planning tool in support of top-line corporate objectives.

An examination of award-winning B2B public relations campaigns shows a clear trend. The support for sales and marketing efforts, usually through a thoroughly planned approach to trade media relations, is undiminished. But senior practitioners are imposing their professionalism on client organisations to use PR methodology to plan strategically, to integrate and unify communications around wider business goals and to build reputation with key stakeholders before the sales process is engaged. Good

Think about 19.4

B2B in action

Can you think of an exhibition/sponsorship campaign in your country or internationally that is targeted at B2B audiences?

Feedback

Think about big trade shows – for example, motor shows where cars are launched to the 'trade', i.e. the people who then go on to sell them to us, the consumers. There are many other big specialist shows/exhibitions, such as for the print industry (do a search for 'printing exhibitions' in Germany on the Internet), building and even the conference/exhibition industry! To see the range of international trade exhibitions held at one site, look at the Barcelona 'Fira' Exhibition and Trade Fair venue at www.firabcn.es.

examples can be found on the websites of national PR organisations such as the UK's CIPR and PRCA.

The most effective use of PR from an organisational perspective is to build a favourable reputation with key

Explore 19.3

Managing reputation

Do an Internet search to find an example of a B2B company that actively uses a wide range of communications techniques to manage its reputation.

stakeholders. And this process is critical to B2B communications, where 'reputation' is the essential element in the buying process. No one wants to do business with an organisation or individual without a reputation, and certainly not those with a poor reputation. Thus the PR function in a B2B organisation has the same remit as that applied in a consumer or public sector organisation – to establish and maintain mutual understanding between the organisation and its publics. (see Explore 19.3)

This reputation-building role will become increasingly important as external stakeholders, including customers and activist groups, start to look at the organisation behind the brand (which they can now do much more easily using social media) and make purchasing decisions based on wider judgements including social responsibility considerations and corporate ethics (see also Chapters 4, 6 and 12).

Organisational leaders with an understanding of PR are using PR in two interconnected ways, regardless of the size of the operation. PR works as a promotional tool with the other marketing disciplines such as advertising and sales promotion. But PR is also being used to manage the organisational reputation at board level, with audiences beyond the marketing remit, such as shareholders, the local community, staff, suppliers and government at all levels. (See Case study 19.3.)

Summary

B2B PR will always concentrate on supporting the commercial performance and business goals of an organisation. The mainstay of this support has been well-placed editorial, especially in the trade media, read by influencers and decision makers in the buying process (the buying chain). This 'works', and there are good examples showing just how the craft skills of PR can be applied with outstanding results. This core activity is fundamental to B2B PR, and B2B practitioners are able to demonstrate in-depth knowledge of their client organisations, of products, services and applications, and of the mechanisms of the marketplace. However, the trade media landscape is developing and online/social media is becoming an increasingly important B2B PR tool for demonstrating expertise and engaging with and selling directly to clients and customers.

The understanding that buying decisions are not solely based on promotion, price, place and product (the marketing mix: Brassington and Pettitt 2006) but also on *reputation* offers scope for PR practitioners to adopt a holistic approach to B2B communications. The concept of the influence of the 'brand' is established in consumer PR. We are now recognising that the brand – and all it stands for – is also relevant to B2B. This is an evolving area of B2B practice, with increased opportunity for creativity in supporting communications in the field.

It is also the case that buying decisions are no longer left to individuals in an organisation; their decisions may have to withstand the scrutiny of a range of internal and external stakeholders. Thus an integrated communications strategy is essential, with consistent messages being communicated to diverse audiences.

B2B campaigns will always focus on the bottom line to support sales and marketing targets. The very best work is planned strategically to help enhance corporate reputation and show clear and consistent linkage through to all internal and external communications.

Bibliography

Black, C. (2001). *The PR Practitioner's Desktop Guide*. London: Hawksmere.

Bodner, K. and J.L. Cohen (2012). *The B2B Social Media Book*. New Jersey: John Wiley & Sons.

Borden, N. (1964). 'The concept of the marketing mix'. *Journal of Advertising Research* June: 2–7.

Brassington, F. and S. Pettitt (2006). *Principles of Marketing*. London: Pearson.

Cornelissen, J. (2004). *Corporate Communications: Theory and practice*. London: Sage.

Cornelissen, J. (2008). *Corporate Communications: Theory and practice*, 2nd edition. London: Sage.

Davis, A. (2004). *Mastering Public Relations*. Basingstoke: Palgrave Macmillan.

Dowell, B. (2011). 'Have trade magazines got a shelf life?' *The Guardian*. 25 April. www.guardian.co.uk/media/2011/apr/25/trade-magazines-online-only accessed 28 August 2012.

Fill, C. and K. Fill (2004). *Business to Business Marketing: Relationships, Systems and Communications*, 4th edition. London: Prentice Hall.

Gregory, A. (ed.) (2004). *Public Relations in Practice*. London: Kogan Page.

Hart, N. (1998). *Business to Business Marketing*. London: Kogan Page.

Haywood, R. (1998). *Public Relations for Marketing Professionals*. Basingstoke: Macmillan.

Howard, W. (ed.) (1988). *The Practice of Public Relations*. London: Heinemann.

Robinson, R. and N. Kovac (2011). 'Business-to-business public relations agency practice'. In D. Moss and B. DeSanto (eds) *Public Relations: A managerial perspective*. London: Sage.

Solis, B. (2010). *Engage! The complete guide for brands and businesses to build, cultivate, and measure success in the new web*. New Jersey: John Wiley & Sons.

Tomlinson, V. (2011). *Why You Can't Ignore Social Media in Business*. Free ebook available at www.northern-lightspr.com

Websites

Chartered Institute of Public Relations (CIPR): www.cipr.co.uk
Cision (formerly Romeike): www.uk.cision.com
Public Relations Consultants Association (PRCA): www.prca.org.uk
PR Newswire: www.prnewswire.com
Twitter: www.twitter.com
LinkedIn: www.linkedin.com
Facebook: www.facebook.com
YouTube: www.youtube.com
Flickr: www.flickr.com

Public affairs

Learning outcomes

By the end of this chapter you should be able to:

■ identify and critically discuss the nature, role and scope of the public affairs function and its relationship with public relations
■ identify and critically review key theories, principles and their development and application in contemporary public affairs
■ appreciate the potential contribution that public affairs can make to organisational strategies and goal attainment
■ identify and critically review the knowledge, skills and competencies required of today's public affairs professionals
■ analyse and apply public affairs theories/principles to practice
■ evaluate your learning about public affairs and pursue further sources for investigation.

Structure

Introduction: why public affairs?

As business, and, particularly, larger corporations have become increasingly conscious of the changing expectations held of them not only by their customers, but also by a wide array of stakeholders including governments, regulators, community groups and employees, they have come to recognise the value of having a well-organised and professional communications and public affairs function, capable of handling any contingencies that may arise that might threaten the stability and reputation of the organisation (van Riel 1995; Argenti 2009). Indeed, in many societies, including the UK and many EU countries, regulations and legislative intervention has become a significant potential constraint on the operations and expansion plans of many businesses. Thus, for example, one might expect that BP may find it increasingly difficult to secure further oil exploration licences, particularly in US-controlled territorial waters, following the recent Deepwater Horizon oil rig disaster in the Gulf of Mexico. On a lesser scale, many companies seeking to expand the development of offshore and on-land wind farms around the UK have come up against strong local opposition to their plans, which has held up their progress.

Locating the role of public affairs within the organisation

These are just two examples of situations where businesses face the challenge of managing their interface with regulators, planners, pressure groups and others with a vested interest in a particular issue or situation that requires careful management to advance the business's interests in the face of what may be quite vociferous opposition (whether legitimate or not). It is in such situations that senior management may turn to the corporate public affairs function to act both as the 'corporate voice' and advocate of the business's interests (Heath 1994; Cornelissen 2008), while also seeking to assuage the concerns of opposing parties. This potentially difficult 'balancing act' of representing business and stakeholder interests is likely to become all the more complicated and challenging when corporations are operating across many international or global markets, and hence across a range of governmental and regulatory regimes. Thus, an understanding of the role and scope of contemporary public affairs needs to be set against the particular environmental context or background in which the organisation(s) in question operates. Clearly, where organisations face an increasingly politicised business environment, as is the case in most Western economies, the need for an effectively resourced public affairs function is more likely to be evident. Yet even here there may be quite wide variations found in the extent to which public affairs is recognised and supported across sectors of industry or even within particular sectors, which may reflect management attitudes and prejudices towards public affairs rather than any inherent differences in the need for public affairs support between organisations or across sectors. This tendency will often be exacerbated when looking at the management of public affairs within organisations operating on an international or global scale.

Defining public affairs: a confused professional identity

Despite the significant growth of professional interest in (corporate) public affairs over the past decade or more, and a growing body of academic and professional literature about public affairs (Hillman 2002; Griffin and Dunn 2004; Showalter and Fleisher 2005), there is still considerable confusion about what public affairs is, or how it contributes to organisational success. This confusion is perhaps hardly surprising given there is still a lack of consensus among public affairs scholars and professionals themselves about the meaning of the term 'public affairs' (Fleisher and Blair 1999; McGrath et al. 2010). Indeed Harris and Moss (2001) suggested that despite the growth in numbers of public affairs professions and in resources invested in public affairs activities, the term 'public affairs' 'remains one that is surrounded by ambiguity and misunderstanding. In short, public affairs remains a function in search of a clear identity' (p.102).

The scope of public affairs

Although traditionally public affairs tends to be seen as the organisational function that focuses particularly on managing organisational relationships with government, government bodies and other political stakeholders, it is also increasingly seen to have a broader remit that

Box 20.1

Public policy

The preferred definition of public policy for our purpose is:

Public policy is a purposive and consistent course of action produced as a response to a perceived problem of a constituency, formulated by a specific political process, and adopted, implemented and enforced by a public agency.

Box 20.2

The Public Affairs Council (PAC)

The PAC was established in 1954 at the urging of the then-President Dwight D. Eisenhower to provide unique information, training and other resources to its members to support their effective participation in government, community and public relations activities at all levels. The Council has more than 600 member companies and associations that work together towards the goal of enhancing the value and professionalism of the public affairs practice, and providing thoughtful leadership as corporate citizens. (See http://pac.org/)

encompasses communication and other relational activities directed towards a cross-section of organisational stakeholders. From this latter perspective, public affairs can been seen to embrace a number of outward-facing communications functions, including media relations, issues management and community relations (see later discussion of Figure 20.1). Here, for example, writing from a European perspective, Pedler (2002: 4) has suggested that:

Public affairs may be defined as the management skill that internalises the effects of the environment in which an organisation operates and externalises actions to influence that environment.

A similar view was expressed by Post (1982: 30) who suggested that: 'the critical role of the public affairs unit is to serve as a *window out* of the corporation, enabling management to act in the external environment, and a *window in* through which society influences corporate policy and practice'. This two-way perspective of public affairs can be seen to mirror in many ways the 'two-way symmetrical' model of public relations that Grunig and his co-researchers (1992, 2002) have argued strongly represents the most

effective and 'excellent' model of public relations practice. In the case of public affairs, the emphasis is ideally about balancing the organisation's and external stakeholders' interests, particularly where these respective interests coalesce around issues that have some public policy dimension.

This notion of public affairs serving as an 'intermediary' and interpretive function between business and governments is reflected in the underlying mission of perhaps the most prominent industry association in the field of public affairs, the Washington-based Public Affairs Council, whose mission is to 'help the business community have a more effective voice in dealing with government'. However, as its mission statement suggests, public affairs is seen to embrace a broader remit than simply government relations.

Thus, in reviewing academic and professional definitions of the (corporate) public affairs function, what emerges is a broad continuum of views polarised between two dominant positions (see Figure 20.1). At one extreme lie relatively

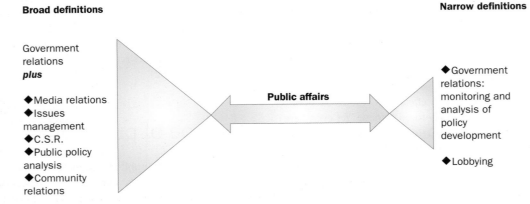

Figure 20.1 Broad and narrow definitions of public affairs

narrow politically orientated perspectives of public affairs, which treat public affairs as synonymous with 'political lobbying'. At the other extreme are interpretations of public affairs that position it as fulfilling a broader communications role, albeit focused around the nexus of politics, public policy and organisational/business concerns/issues. This perspective recognises the intermediary role of public affairs, often sitting alongside and inextricably linked to other communications activities that serve to connect business and not-for-profit organisations to 'government' in all its various forms or guises (see Figure 20.2 later on). From this perspective, the public affairs function's responsibility among these communications functions focuses on enabling organisations to deal with those external public policy and regulatory challenges that might impact (favourably or unfavourably) on the realisation of their goals. It may involve handling a broad array of corporate stakeholder relationships and the issues associated with them. One more or less common central element of both perspectives of the corporate public affairs function is the recognition of the central importance for what is generally termed the 'issue management' function (Hainsworth and Meng 1988; Heath 2002) as providing the underlying analysis for determining the public affairs agenda and focus for all strategic public affairs planning. We will examine the central importance of the issue management function and process in relation to public affairs later in this chaper, and a fuller discussion of issue management can be found earlier in Chapter 16 of this book.

The existence of what appears to be the two principal arms of public affairs – the government relations/lobbying perspective and a broader community relations/corporate reputation/responsibility perspective – essentially frame what can be seen to constitute the lingua franca 'of public affairs – a dialogue at both a societal and government level'. By implication, those working in the public affairs field increasingly are required not only to be proficient communicators but to have a sound appreciation of how the political parties work, how policies are developed and how parties may be influenced, run campaigns and are funded. Moreover, the type of issues and challenges that normally

> ### Think about 20.1
>
> ## Government business interaction
>
> Taking any one industry, such as automobile manufacture or construction, try putting together a list of all the key government departments whose work might affect that industry and try to build a contact list of the most important ministers, MPs, or MEPs, etc. whose support would be needed or helpful in campaigning for changes in any regulation affecting that industry.

fall within the public affairs domain generally require far more complex and sophisticated solutions than those required when tackling market-related communications campaigns (Harris and Moss 2001, p.108).

Thus perhaps the simplest way to describe the field of public affairs is as an **intermediary** function focused around political and social environmental intelligence gathering, linked to advising and supporting organisations in building and maintaining their relationships with key stakeholder groups in their business environment, specifically in terms of handling the type of socio-political issues that might affect the realisation of the organisation's strategic goals. Here public affairs acts both reactively as well as proactively, scanning, analysing the issues arising within the environment and helping management determine the most appropriate strategies for the organisation to pursue with respect to specific issues. In short, the public affairs role can be likened to that of a 'ship's pilot', enabling organisations to 'navigate' successfully through the potentially tricky environmental 'waters' that may stand between it and its strategic goals. In terms of operationalising this role, perhaps the most well-known and equally most controversial tool employed by public affairs is that of **lobbying** in all its various guises, whether this takes place at the state, national, or local levels, or even working on an international basis.

> ### Explore 20.1
>
> ## Political/regulatory influence
>
> Consider the number of laws and by-laws that any business, charity or voluntary organisation may have to comply with or take into account when setting up operations. Think about the consequences of ignoring such legislation.

Lobbying

Put simply, lobbying is any action designed to influence the actions of the institutions of government. That means it covers all parts of central and local government and other public bodies, both in the UK and internationally (Miller 2000: 4). In terms of its scope, therefore, lobbying can include attempts to influence legislation, regulatory and policy decisions and negotiations on public sector contracts or grants. However, despite the increasing attention

The British Gurkha Welfare Society (BGWS) is the largest welfare organisation supporting Gurkhas in the UK and Nepal. Founded in 2004, the BGWS has been one of the leading campaigners on issues of Gurkha welfare, including settlement and pension rights.

The Gurkhas were brought fully into the public consciousness in 2009, when a high-profile media-led campaign, headed by the actress Joanna Lumley, overturned the policy of the then-Government and secured settlement rights for Gurkhas who had retired before 1997 – opening the door for these veterans to relocate to the UK. In addition to the high-profile programme of media relations, the campaign also comprised a massive grass roots programme involving hundreds of thousands of people who signed Gurkha Justice petitions, lobbied their MPs, campaigned and attended rallies and marches.

At midday on 21 May, the then Home Secretary Jacqui Smith made the announcement to the House of Commons that the Government had recognised the case advanced by the Gurkha Justice Campaign and that all ex-Gurkhas who have served more than four years in the British Army will have the right to settle in the UK if they wish. After such a long fight, with huge ups and downs, this was a superb result.

---

paid to, and critical scrutiny of, lobbying in recent years (notably as a result of the considerable scandal surrounding the clandestine payment of MPs for their support and influence within Parliament in the UK), the process of lobbying remains an obscure practice and no definitive definition can be said to exist (Zetter 2008).

Here it is important to distinguish between the essential *purpose* of lobbying, which does appear to be broadly understood, and the *methods or processes* used by lobbyists to achieve the desired outcome, which are generally less well understood. The former is about, on one hand, monitoring and analysing government thinking and strategies, and, on the other hand, representing and championing a particular company, industry or organisation's views to government or government bodies, and securing a favourable political outcome (whether in terms of legislative action, regulation or other public policy change). Thus, in short, lobbying is essentially a form of two-way asymmetrical or persuasive communication activity. Much of the concern that continues to surround the practice of lobbying stems from the 'mystique' and rather 'cloak and dagger' image of the various lobbying tactics that are seen to be used to gain access to, and influence with, sections of government. Indeed such tactics are often portrayed as offering those with the greatest power and wealth an undue influence within government circles – an accusation that has led to increasing calls for the regulation of political lobbyists. A further examination of lobbying tactics is provided below. Here, of course, it should be stressed that lobbying is essentially a legitimate activity – a means by which various stakeholder groups can attempt to ensure that their voices are heard within the public policy arena, and hence it is important to the democratic process per se.

Picture 20.1 The Gurkhas were brought fully into the public consciousness in 2009, when a high-profile media-led campaign, headed by the actress Joanna Lumley, overturned the policy of the then-Government and secured settlement rights for Gurkhas
(*source*: Tim Graham/Getty Images)

Lobbying practices

Perhaps, traditionally, lobbying has been associated with mass protest and representations to government by disaffected groups – for example, Trade Union rallies against public sector pay cuts, or the recent mass student protest in the

UK about the raising of university tuition fees. Similarly, the British Gurkha lobbying campaign outlined above contained an element of mass rally and protest to challenge government policy. However, while such protests and rallies do undoubtedly capture public, and hence government attention, their effectiveness is often due to their magnification through the coverage such rallies may receive in the media – both traditional mass media and increasingly also social media. Indeed, in today's increasingly media-driven society, it is the ability of such protest activity to capture the media's attention and hence to put the issue of concern on the 'public's agenda' that is crucial to building momentum and putting pressure on government for change. Thus a well-orchestrated media relations and social media campaign has and continues to be a crucial element of virtually all lobbying and broader public affairs strategies.

In essence, however, lobbying is about persuasive argument – the presentation of cogent and compelling arguments to appropriate decision makers and their key advisors, whether this be in the form of one-to-one meetings, presentations to appropriate committees or in written reports/documentation or a combination of all of these different methods. These forms of direct communications with appropriate, influential decision makers and advisors are often where much of the hard work is done in shaping or reshaping government thinking and proposals on issues or on legislation. Here the release of what might be quite sensitive information to the media relating to the issues in hand needs to be carefully handled in order not to upset what might be quite delicate 'negotiations' over the matter in hand. In essence, governments do not like to be seen to be backing down or caving in under external pressure, and hence often the lobbying strategy may involve giving government the opportunity to be seen to be engaging and responding positively to representations from industry or other bodies – 'a win-win scenario'.

This discussion leads to two further key principles of successful public affairs/lobbying, or for that matter any other communications campaigns, namely:

1. **Timing is nearly always crucial:** there is a natural life cycle with all decision-making processes, and especially government decision making, that will be partly determined by the particular cycle of government (when do the particular chambers of government sit, where is the incumbent government in its planned cycle of legislation, etc.). One of the keys to any successful lobbying campaign is to get the issue in question onto the government's agenda. Thus, for some major issues that require a significant change in legislation or social change, there may need to be an ongoing medium- to longer-term strategy that may extend over a number of years in order to reach a position that is acceptable to all interested parties – e.g., changing the

---

Explore 20.2

Influencers and decision makers

Try to construct a detailed structural 'map' of the government structures and departments that would oversee a major infrastructure project, such as a new regional airport or new train line in your region of your country. Consider who would be involved in such a decision and what time-scales might be involved in bringing it to fruition.

---

laws on the sale of tobacco products and alcohol in the UK, or animal welfare legislation relating to dog ownership and registration.

2. **Targeting is absolutely vital:** here it is essential to understand the structure and operation of the government or government bodies you are trying to influence – where does the influence lie, who are the 'power brokers' (formal and informal), who are the gatekeepers and who knows their way around the system? Here authors such as Miller (2000) and Nugent (2003) offer valuable insights into the working of government in the UK and European Union. There are also a number of official and unofficial websites offering quite comprehensive information about the structure and working of government (e.g., in the UK, websites such as www.direct.gov.uk; www.parliament.uk). Similar information sources can be found that cover government structures and government processes in countries around the world – e.g., the University of Keele's Politics Department maintains a comprehensive database of information about governments in Latin America, http://www.keele.ac.uk/depts/por/labase.htm#lawide, or information about the US government can be found from its official website: www.usa.gov/

A legitimate activity?

Clearly a central concern with lobbying, wherever it is practised, is the underlying concern that it may lead to undue and inappropriate influence on government decisions and legislation that favours the interests of one party or organisation at the expense of others and/or the 'public good'. Such concerns have been heightened in recent years as a result of a number of scandals and media exposés of corruption and illegal payment to politicians or influential officials to secure favourable decisions or contracts. The so-called 'cash for questions' scandal in the UK led to the establishment of the Nolan Committee in 1994 to investigate and set out basic standard for the behaviour of MPs, civil servants and others holding public office – see Boxes 20.3 and 20.4.

Box 20.3

Nolan Committee standards in public life

Nolan principles that should govern the behaviours of all holders of public office:

- Selflessness
- Integrity
- Objectivity
- Openness
- Honesty
- Leadership.

Building on these concerns about the conduct of civil servants and politicians when faced with perhaps a well-prepared and well-resourced lobbying strategy, guidelines have been drawn up that are intended to remind those engaged in the work of government about their primary duty to serve the state and citizens, rather than the vested interests of particular businesses or industry sectors (see Boxes 20.5a and 20.5b).

Box 20.4

Implications for lobbyists in the UK political system

The Nolan Committee said in their first report, 'it is the right of everyone to lobby Parliament and ministers, and it is for public institutions to develop ways of controlling the reaction to approaches from professional lobbyists in such a way as to give due weight to their case while always taking care to consider the public interest'.

The Government's approach, reflecting the approach of the Nolan Committee, is not to ban contacts between civil servants and lobbyists but to insist that wherever and whenever they take place they should be conducted in accordance with the Civil Service Code, and the principles of public life set out by the Nolan Committee. This means that civil servants can meet lobbyists, formally and informally, where this is justified by the needs of government.

Box 20.5a

Guidance for civil servants: contact with lobbyists

All civil servants, including special advisers, are employed by the Crown and paid by the taxpayer to serve the government of the day in a manner that upholds the highest standards of propriety in public life.

Basic principles

1. The basic principles are set out in the Civil Service Code. They are demanding. But it is worth remembering that they are reflected in every department's Management Code, and that any breach may give rise to disciplinary proceedings.

2. Civil servants should conduct themselves with integrity and honesty. They should not deceive or knowingly mislead Parliament or the public. They should not misuse their official position or information acquired in the course of their official duties to further their private interests or the private interests of others. They should not receive benefits of any kind, which others might reasonably see as compromising their personal judgement or integrity. They should not without authority disclose official information that has been communicated in confidence in Government or received in confidence from others.

3. The principles of public life, set down by the Nolan Committee in its first report in 1995, are also relevant – in particular:

- **Selflessness**: holders of public office should take decisions solely in terms of the public interest; they should not do so in order to gain financial or other material benefits for themselves, their family, or their friends.

- **Integrity**: holders of public office should not place themselves under any financial or other obligation to outside individuals or organisations that might influence them in the performance of their official duties.

- **Honesty**: holders of public office have a duty to declare any private interests relating to their public duties and to take steps to resolve any conflicts arising in a way that protects the public interest.

Box 20.5b

Guidance for civil servants: practical considerations

These basic principles apply to all contacts between civil servants and people outside government, be they businessmen, trades unionists, journalists or campaigners of any kind. What the principles mean in practice will depend on the circumstances of each case. It is not possible exhaustively to cover every situation that may arise, but the main points to have in mind in dealings with professional lobbyists, given the nature of their work, is as follows. Some things are completely unacceptable. For instance:

■ DO NOT leak confidential or sensitive material, especially market-sensitive material, to a lobbyist.

■ DO NOT deliberately help a lobbyist to attract business by arranging for clients to have privileged access to ministers or undue influence over policy. These would be serious disciplinary offences and trigger procedures under which you would be liable to dismissal. Much more common are situations where dealings with a lobbyist are acceptable provided that they are handled with care. These are grey areas where common sense has to be used. Here, again, breaking the basic rules may lead to disciplinary action.

■ DO NOT say or do anything that could be represented as granting a lobbyist preferential or premature access to information, parliamentary or governmental, that you have received because of your official position.

■ DO CONSIDER whether meeting one group making representations on a particular issue should be balanced by offering other groups a similar opportunity to make representations.

■ DO NOT accept gifts or other benefits from a lobbyist that are offered to you because of your official position and could place you, or reasonably be considered to place you, under an obligation to the donor.

■ DO NOT give the impression to a lobbyist that any particular advice, idea or information from their clients could or will be decisive in the decision-making process. Decisions are for ministers, who will want to weigh up all the evidence and all the advice they receive before they judge the public interest.

■ DO NOT do anything that might breach Parliamentary privilege or offend against the conventions of Parliament. Remember that the papers and reports of Select Committees are the property of the Committees and subject to Parliamentary privilege. If in doubt whether particular papers are in the public domain, seek guidance from the Clerk of the Select Committee.

■ DO NOT use your knowledge about what is going on inside Government to impress your contacts in the lobbyist world. What may seem simple gossip to you may make money for someone else, or amount to improper help.

■ DO NOT use your position to help a lobbyist get a benefit to which he or she is not entitled.

■ DO NOT offer, or give the impression of offering, a lobbyist preferential access to ministers or their officials. Where you think someone can contribute some interesting ideas, you should tell those concerned and let them decide for themselves.

■ DO always declare to your department any personal or family business interests that may at some time create an actual or potential conflict of interest with the work of your department, and comply with any instructions from the department designed to eliminate the conflict.

■ BE CAREFUL about accepting hospitality from a lobbyist.

These guidelines must of course be interpreted with common sense. If, for instance, you have a friend who is a lobbyist, you do not have to sever your friendship and stop meeting them socially. If you are married to one, you do not have to get divorced! But do make sure that the ground rules are understood, that you make proper arrangements to deal with any conflict of interest and that you do not get tempted into doing something that would lay you open to criticism or be misunderstood.

Source: http://webarchive.nationalarchives.gov.uk

Regulation of lobbying

In June 2007, the Public Administration Select Committee (PASC) announced its inquiry into the lobbying industry in the UK. As part of the Committee's ongoing investigations, the three founding industry members of what was to become the UK Public Affairs Council provided oral evidence to the Committee's later inquiry in July of that year. The Committee published its report, 'Lobbying: access and influence in Whitehall', in December 2008, in which it recommended that a public register of lobbyists be created.

Under the stewardship of Sir Philip Mawer, former Parliamentary Commissioner for Standards and independent advisor to the then Prime Minister Gordon Brown, a body comprising the APPC, CIPR and PRCA was formed to begin implementing the Committee's recommendation for a public register.

The first meeting of the UK Public Affairs Council took place in July 2010, with the three industry bodies being joined by three independent members, including the Chairman Elizabeth France CBE. That month, Deputy Prime Minister Nick Clegg announced that the Government intended to legislate for a statutory register of lobbyists. To date, progress has been relatively patchy in terms of getting all lobbyists to sign up to the register on a voluntary basis, and of course the 'jury is still out' on whether formal registration of lobbyists would be effective in eliminating some of the more nefarious and unacceptable activities of what is generally acknowledged to be a small minority of practitioners.

International perspectives on public affairs and lobbying

Reviewing the treatment of public affairs and its sub-discipline, lobbying, within a broad cross-section of academic and specialist professional literature, it is evident that until comparatively recently the vast majority of the work has focused largely on examining public affairs in either the UK or US context (see McGrath et al. 2010), as well as more recently in a wider European context (e.g., Pedler and Van Schendelen 1994; Pedler 2002). This predominantly 'Western perspective' of public affairs has been disseminated and embraced on an international scale, at least in terms of the basic understanding of what the public affairs role should be and how it is organised and practised. In addition to dissemination of Western ideas via a range of literature, the Western perspective of public affairs has been spread through the expansion of Western-owned public affairs consultancies and corporate networks into other parts of the world. However, despite this apparent Western hegemony of ideas in the field of public affairs, it would be wrong to suggest that public affairs takes the same form in organisations across the world irrespective of the local economic, social and political environment. Indeed, this author's own research in the field of international corporate public affairs has revealed significant variations in how public affairs is understood, organised and practised, even across the different offices of the same global operating companies – see Box 20.6.

It is almost certainly the case nowadays that most major international corporations have recognised the need for some form of public affairs function, whether provided via an in-house team, by means of external consultants or a combination of the two. However, there does not appear to be any uniform structure or formula for how the public

Box 20.6

Public affairs management: an exploratory study

Research aims

This study set out to explore how the public affairs function may be structured, organised and managed in the international/global business context. The study also sought to examine how public affairs is perceived and what role it plays in relation to senior management in a global business context.

Method

The study comprised an initial multi-site case study based in the geographically dispersed regional public affairs offices of a large global consumer products company. This multi-site case study was supplemented by a further set of in-depth interviews with public affairs directors, drawn from a cross-section of international companies. In total, the study comprised some 25 in-depth interviews with senior public affairs professionals.

Findings

Only a summary of the key findings of this research can be presented here. For an expanded version of the paper see the reference* at the bottom of the box.

Size, structure and scope of the public affairs function

- Multi-site case study company – 165 staff in total, spread across a network of offices globally.

- Marked variations in size, structure and scope of communications/public affairs function in different parts of the world, both within the multi-site company and across the rest of the sample – see Table 20.1.

box 20.6 (continued)

Company	Sector	Department	Size	Structure/composition
A	Consumer goods	Public affairs	165 globally spread across some 14 regional/country offices Corporate centre comprises 8–10 practitioners. Other offices range in size from 8–10 to 1–2 practitioners supported by other communications/business functions	Specialist public affairs function in major government centres, particularly in London, Brussels and Washington. More diffuse responsibilities in other locations spanning: Corporate communications Media relations CSR Regional business communications support
B	Consumer food Producer	Public affairs	3 plus admin	Specialist European public affairs function based in Brussels
C	Beer, spirits and wines	Corporate relations	220 spread across 19 communications 'hubs' around the world plus smaller global functional teams at HQ	Corporate communications Brand communications Media relations Employee communications Public affairs and policy CSR Alcohol policy
D	International banking	Corporate affairs	20 based in head office and regional offices	Subdivided into stakeholder relations CSR Political analysis Regulatory and legal oversight
E	Industrial chemicals and technology	Corporate communication	250– worldwide including 30–35 in the European office, mapped onto major business markets	Based around corporate communications Business communications Geographic/country communications
F	Insurance	Communications public affairs	8 with 1 specialist public affairs person	Corporate communications Issue management Government and regulatory
G	Energy and utilities	Corporate affairs	38 based in the head office plus local business communications managers	Corporate reputation and internal communications Media relations Public affairs and EU policy Regional affairs CSR
H	Energy	External corporate affairs	3 people but support from legal and regulatory specialists	Communications Issues management Public affairs Legal and regulatory

Table 20.1 Communication/public affairs functional size and structure

box 20.6 (continued)

Company	Sector	Department	Size	Structure/composition
I	Brewing and distribution	Public affairs	5 handling European public affairs supported by similar teams based in N. America and Asia	Specialist public affairs function Government relations and lobbying
J	Water and power utility	Group communications	30 with 3 working specifically in public affairs	Media relations Customer communications Internal communications Public affairs Education
K	Petrochemicals	Policy and external relations	12 in global issues and regulation plus local teams supporting different business divisions in handling local/regional issues	Part of policy and external relations team Handles all global reputation issues
L	Healthcare	Public affairs	1 public affairs advisor	Specialist advisor to CEO on public affairs

Table 20.1 (*continued*)

- A raw comparison of functional numbers can be very misleading, since it can cloak significant variations in experience and expertise amongst communications/public affairs staff.

- The most experienced staff tend to be found in offices based around the main centres of government – London, Brussels, Washington, etc.

Functional titles and responsibilities

- All the organisations examined in this study exhibited some broad similarities in terms of the range of functional responsibilities performed by their communications/public affairs departments.

- There was also something of a polarisation between departments that were narrowly focused around a government relations/lobbying role and those that were far less specialised, playing a broader corporate communications/public affairs role.

- A range of functional titles was found, from 'corporate communications' to simply 'communications' and, more specifically and narrowly, 'public affairs'. In some cases, the departmental/functional title did reflect the scope of responsibilities performed; in other cases less so.

Practitioner expertise

- Background and range of expertise found varied across the sample as a whole, as well as between offices within the same organisation.

- The degree of specialised experience (knowledge of government working, lobbying, issue management) possessed by practitioners was notably greater in most of the Western centres of government.

- In more remote regions, the emphasis was on a broad range of communications/public affairs skills, as smaller, less specialised teams were required to handle whatever communications challenges might crop up.

Reporting relationships and lines of authority

- In most cases the communications/public affairs functions appeared to report directly to the CEO or the senior management team.

- For multinational/global companies reporting was often to a regional chairperson or regional senior management team.

- There was evidence of some conflict between corporate centres and regional management over priorities and strategies.

Senior management relationships

- In the majority of cases it was claimed that, at the more senior levels of management, the importance and value of public affairs was recognised, but that

box 20.6 (continued)

senior management might not always fully understand what the public affairs function does.

- The role and value of public affairs to the company was generally less well understood or appreciated at the middle and lower levels of management within other functions.

Public affairs strategy development

- In most cases, central corporate public affairs functions claimed to have overall responsibility for determining the broad public affairs agenda, strategy and goals, and for setting the direction for the function as a whole.

- In large multinational/global companies responsibility for day-to-day public affairs operations is devolved to regional or country level.

- There was evidence of some tensions in global companies between corporate centres and regional operating companies in terms of who determines public affairs strategic priorities.

Factors affecting the operation of public affairs

- The evidence suggests two broad categories of factors affecting the configuration and management of corporate public affairs: (i) 'people-related', 'organisational-systems/values-related'; and (ii) 'local operational context-related' factors.

- Perhaps the most potent positive influence identified was the company's reputation and long-standing position and track record of success in many of its markets around the world.

- More negative factors included the limited resources available to many regional offices, the politically complex operating environment that a number of the regional operating companies faced and tensions created by the dual lines of reporting to regional/national company chairmen and to the corporate head office.

- In terms of people-related factors, positive influences included the available expertise of many of the senior public affairs practitioners, who could be deployed to support regional or national offices that might lack sufficiently experienced public affairs personnel to handle particular issues as they arose.

- More negative influences included the varied level of public affairs experience found among the practitioners in some regions of the world and the lack of specific training to upgrade their knowledge and skills.

- Some interviewees also pointed to something of a 'silo' mentality within the regional offices, which militated against closer integration of the public affairs function as a whole.

In summary, perhaps the overriding conclusion to emerge is that effective corporate public affairs, like any other function, comes down to the quality of people employed. In a number of cases it emerged that central cost pressures and restructuring had adversely impacted on staffing levels and the depth of experienced personnel available. The following comment from a senior public affairs practitioner at a large international industrial chemical company reflected well some of these views:

Companies still make the mistake that they put junior people into the (public affairs) role, and I think what you need to do is to consider the environment in which you let people loose – the political environment means you need to understand your company, your products well, but you also need to understand the political environment in which decisions are made and you need them . . . that typically is something which you don't go into, either straight out of school, or even new to the company. And . . . there is no way around experience in that area.

A full version of this research is due to be published in the Journal of Public Affairs (2012) 12(1).

---

affairs function should be best organised, let alone managed. Drawing parallels with research into international/global public relations practice (e.g., see Sriramesh and Vercic 2009), it is perhaps only to be expected that there might be differences, perhaps some quite marked, in the way in which public affairs is understood, organised and practised in different parts of the world (see also Wakefield 2011). Here Sriramesh and Vercic's analytical framework for examining international/global variations in public relations arguably can also provide a useful starting point

in analysing and perhaps predicting the likely variations in public affairs practice. This framework focuses on the importance of the environmental context in determining how public relations (or, for our purposes, public affairs) is understood and practised. In particular they highlighted the significance of the socio-economic, political and media environments as constraining and influencing factors on both the historical development of public relations, as well as on contemporary practice. Arguably these same contextual variables are likely to have an equally formative influence on how public affairs has developed and is understood and practised today. Perhaps most importantly, the political system and structures in any country/society will very much frame and shape how far it is possible for public affairs practitioners to function in the type of conventional role that they have typically played in Western democracies. To take a somewhat extreme example, it is very difficult to see public affairs functioning in its conventional role and manner in autocratic command and control regimes, such as have prevailed in North Korea or Burma. Yet public affairs practitioners have adapted and found ways to work effectively with the newly emerged states that formed after the break up of the Soviet Union in the early 1990s, e.g. in Russia, Ukraine, etc. albeit that the nature of the political systems and climate in these newly formed countries dictated that the approaches taken to corporate public affairs may be very different to those that might be adopted in most Western regimes.

Focusing on the issue of globalisation and its implications for communications/public relations practice, Wakefield (2011) suggests that the most effective approach for globally-based organisations may lie in applying the principles of 'glocalisation' to all functional strategies, including global communications and public affairs management. Essentially the 'glocalisation' approach attempts to apply centrally determined core strategies while also enabling locally based practitioners the freedom to adapt and tailor their public affairs approach to the local prevailing setting and priorities. This approach recognises where compromise and a 'softly-softly' approach may yield better longer-term results than an unbending, standardised approach. Indeed, in some of the more difficult political climates around the world it is generally acknowledged that the work of the public affairs function is often critical to gaining access for companies to trade and do business in what might be quite heavily regulated or government-controlled markets. In such cases, public affairs expertise is needed to help steer the organisation through what can be very difficult and politically sensitive market channels. Further insights into working in an international context, both in terms of public relations and public affairs, are provided earlier in the text.

Public affairs management

There has been a growing base of academic and professional literature focused on the area of public affairs over the past decade or more (see, for example, the *Journal of Public Affairs*), yet despite growing interest in defining public affairs, examining the role and scope of public affairs and examining the elements of public affairs practice, relatively little attention has been paid to the question of determining how the public affairs function is or should be managed, and equally what does 'best practice' look like and how should it be achieved. Here, for example, in the study of global public affairs summarised earlier (see Box 20.6), one of the underlying initial interests of organisations engaged in the research was to explore the characteristics of 'best practice' in global public affairs. It soon became apparent, however, that such a quest for any *universal* principles of 'best practice' in public affairs was likely to prove something of a 'futile quest'. In effect, what emerged was that the most effective forms of practice were likely to prove very situational and reflect very much the systems, values, culture and prevailing management 'worldviews' characterising each organisation, and thereby shaping priorities and the approach taken to public affairs.

Think about 20.3   Best practice concept in public affairs

The study of international public affairs summarised in Box 20.6 illustrates the problems of attempting to identify the characteristics of 'best practice' in any functional area. One of the organisations participating in the study had been through a major restructuring exercise, alongside a change of senior management, which had led to significant reductions in staffing across all functions, including public affairs. This restructuring inevitably impacted on how the function operated, both on an international global basis and at each regional level, as reductions in head count impacted to differing degrees across the organisation's offices. The one lesson that emerged from this study was that any attempt to achieve 'best practice' or the most effective practice clearly depends on the adequacy and quality of the personnel working in the function. Where there is significant pressure on head count and cost reduction, it may be incompatible, at least in the short term, with efforts to focus attention on defining and achieving what might constitute functional 'best practice'. Of course, in principle, staffing and cost reduction are not inconsistent with efficiencies and hence more effective practice – they may, in fact, lie at the heart of improved performance – but developing such a recognition and ingraining it into the way that the organisation and its functions operate is inevitably a challenging and, for some organisations, painful process.

Explore 20.3

Best practice in other disciplines

Conduct a search of the literature in a number of professional areas, such as accountancy, medicine, engineering, etc., to identify whether and how the concept of 'best practice' is understood and what criteria, if any, have been identified to 'measure' best practice.

Box 20.7

The 'classical models' of management

Classical perspective of management treats management as a logical, rational activity that can be broken down into a number of discrete but related tasks. One of the best known such models is that advanced by Gulick and Urwick (1937), which defined seven core elements of management – *planning, organising, staffing, directing, coordinating, reporting* and *budgeting* – that became known in management circles by the acronym POSDCORB.

MACIE: a functional management framework

It is somewhat ironic that while most definitions of public relations and corporate communications or, for that matter, public affairs position these functions as essentially 'managerial' in character, talking, for example, about 'the management of communication between an organisation and its publics', or 'managing the interface between organisations and government' few actually define the managerial processes and responsibilities involved in any detail. Indeed, there is a lack of any clear framework for analysing the component elements of the management process, or management stages involved in managing the various forms of internal and external communication on behalf of an organisation. Indeed, as Moss (Moss et al. 2005, 2007; Moss and Desanto 2011) has pointed out, communications/public relations scholars have generally failed to acknowledge and draw on the extensive body of management literature when discussing the management role within the function. Thus, for example, in defining the manager's role in public relations there is little recognition of the evolving debate between the 'classical' models of management as advanced by scholars such as Gulick and Urwick (1937) and Fayol (1949), which defined management in terms of a set of basic tasks or elements of management responsibility (see Box 20.7), and the subsequent behavioural critique of this classical school, which recognises the need to distinguish between management *tasks and responsibilities* and managerial *behaviours* (Mintzberg 1973, 1990; Hales 1986); in short, distinguishing between *what* tasks or roles managers are responsible for carrying out, and *how* they go about performing them.

In attempting to explore the managerial dimension of public relations in more detail, Moss et al. (2000, 2005, 2007) sought to define a number of core dimensions of communication management, as well as offering a strong critique of the existing definitions of the public relations manager role. Building on this work, more recently Moss

Think about 20.4

What managers do

Think about people you know who work in a managerial-type job and what they do on a day-to-day basis. What sort of responsibilities do they have, what skills do they seem to need to demonstrate and, if you compare a number of 'managers', do they all have the same type of responsibilities?

and Desanto (2011) have suggested a simple yet powerful framework for examining and analysing the key elements of the management process that arguably can be applied to all communication functions including public affairs. The four stages, or elements, in this management process arguably encompass what can be seen as the key tasks and responsibilities that communication/public affairs managers perform in most organisational settings – namely *analysing* the situation they face, *making choices* about how best to respond, *implementing* the chosen set of actions and *evaluating* the outcomes. Moreover, this four-stage process can be seen to apply to both strategically important decisions and actions as well as to dealing with more routine operational matters. What this framework does not identify *explicitly*, however, are the specific managerial *behaviours* associated with performance of key tasks at each of these stages. However, managerial *behaviour* and managerial *work* are not always so easily separated and, in fact, can be seen as 'two-sides of the same coin', representing the 'what' and the 'how' of managerial work. This four-stage communications management framework (which

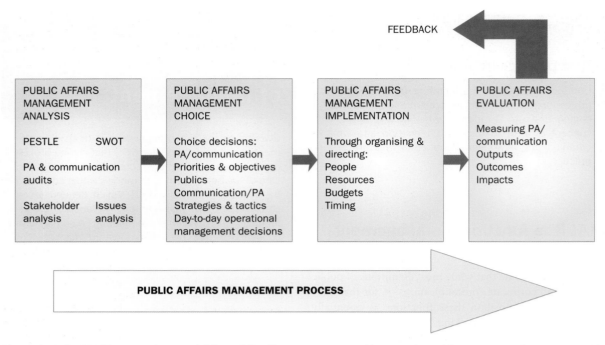

Figure 20.2 'MACIE' framework: a model for public affairs management (*source*: adapted from Moss and Desanto 2011)

includes public relations and public affairs) is designated by the acronym (C)-MACIE:

■ (Communications) management analysis

■ (Communications) management choice

■ (Communications) management implementation

■ (Communications) management evaluation

This framework adapted for public affairs purposes is illustrated in Figure 20.2, and each element or stage of the process as they relate to the area of public affairs is explained briefly next.

Public affairs management analysis

The first element in this framework, *communication/public affairs management analysis*, represents the essential first step in the communication management process – namely analysing the particular situation facing the organisation and determining the issues and challenges that need to be tackled. At the more strategic level, such analysis is concerned with the essential work of continually scanning, analysing and interpreting data from the organisation's external and internal environments in order to identify and understand and, where possible, anticipate the forces shaping the current (and future) situation the organisation faces, particularly in terms of its relationship with key stakeholder groups, the issues that affect these relationships and the implications for the organisation's communication/

public affairs strategies. At the day-to-day operational level, such analysis involves examining the more immediate challenges that might be faced, identifying how best to husband and utilise resources, how to deploy people and manage available budgets, etc.

In terms of analysis tools, many of the techniques that both public affairs and broader-based communications professionals can use to help scan, assess and interpret the nature of the environments in which their organisations operate and identify the communications issues and challenges they face, are common across a range of functional disciplines, such as PESTLE, SWOT and stakeholder and issues analysis. A summary of the purpose and methods associated with each of these key analysis techniques is provided in Figure 20.3. You have also already encountered a number of these analysis tools earlier in Chaper 8 and you might find it useful to revisit these sections to remind yourself about these techniques at this stage.

Of all the analysis techniques, *issue analysis* is a particularly critical element of the public affairs analysis and planning process and is examined further below. Here, Mini case study 20.2 illustrates the importance of understanding how changes, in this case in government policy, might create serious issues and challenges for an organisation or whole industry's operations. This initial context analysis should not only look outward, assessing the external environment and external issues, but should also review past communications activity and internal resources and

Mini case study 20.2
Turning the lights out on solar power installations

As part of its climate change strategy, the UK Government's Department of Energy and Climate Change (DECC) launched a Feed-in Tariff subsidy scheme, whereby households installing solar panels to help meet their electricity consumption were able to receive a specially enhanced subsidy payment for surplus electricity generated from the solar panels that they would sell back into the local grid. The scheme generated widespread interest across the UK on the back of an extensive advertising and public relations campaign. The number of solar energy installers also expanded rapidly to meet the demand and exploit the market opportunity. Then, in December 2011, the DECC announced a cut to Feed-in Tariff subsidies that would apply to any installation after 12 December that year. Environmental campaign group Friends of the Earth (FoE) and two solar companies – Solarcentury and HomeSun – challenged this announcement because the change was made before the end of a consultation period for the solar scheme.

The High Court then ruled in December 2011 that the change was 'legally flawed' but the DECC launched an appeal to have this ruling overturned. The appeal leaves households who have installed solar panels after this date with no guarantee of the rate they will receive for generating energy.

The change in the scheme means that the amount paid for solar panel-generated electricity was reduced from 43.3p per kWh to 21p – slashing the revenue that can be earned, on average, by households from £1,100 to £500.

The uncertainty over the proposed change of policy with respect to the level of feed-in subsidy effectively 'torpedoed' any further growth in the household solar panel market, and threatened to bring about the demise of a number of firms that had expanded rapidly into what had promised to be a very attractive new market.

Put yourself in the position of the public affairs advisor appointed to advise the solar energy industry, and specifically solar panel installers, about how they should respond to the DECC's proposed cut in feed-in Tariff. What are the key issues on which to build a campaign and which stakeholder groups should the campaign engage with?

Read more: http://www.thisismoney.co.uk/money/bills/article-2082270/Government-launches-appeal-High-Court-ruling-deemed-cut-solar-panel-feed-tariff-subsidies-legally-flawed.html#ixzz1inkqMfKo

Explore 20.4

Environmental analysis

Taking an organisation with which you are familiar, conduct a thorough external environment analysis using the techniques discussed and identify what you see are the key communications/public affairs challenges that the organisation needs to address.

capabilities to enable the subsequent identification and choice of the most appropriate communications/public affairs strategies and tactics. Here the use of a *communications audit* can provide the necessary data to conduct this type of internal capability review.

As suggested above, as well as earlier in the chapter, of the various environmental analysis techniques available, it is '*issue analysis*' that generally has the greatest relevance and importance for public affairs, in terms of teasing out those problematic consequences of stakeholder-organisational

Picture 20.2 Solar energy is an important government policy agenda issue for many countries. What are the key issues on which to build a campaign and which stakeholder groups should the campaign engage with? (*source*: Shutterstock.com/Elena Elisseeva)

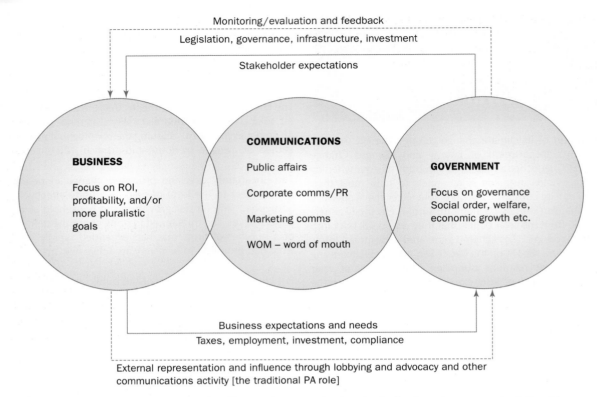

Figure 20.3 The intermediary role of public affairs and communications in the business/government relationship

relationships, which in turn may be shaped by environment trends and events. Indeed issue management is normally recognised as an integral part of the public affairs management framework and is crucial to its success (Hainsworth and Meng 1988; Heath 2002). Here, in particular, public affairs takes the classical view of issue management that focuses on defining the key *public policy issues* that may impact on the organisation's current operations and future strategy. Public policy issues are those that arise out of the nexus and interaction of business, government and citizens – see Figure 20.3. Here the issue life cycle concept is often used to help track the momentum of issues and identify their escalation towards what can be a crisis point. Further discussion of issue management process as a means of mapping and analysing issues that are relevant to any specific organisation can be found earlier in the text.

Public affairs management choice

The work of communication/public affairs analysis prepares the way for what is often seen as the core task of management, namely exercising *management choice* with respect to the appraisal and selection of alternative strategy options, or decisions about what operational actions should be undertaken. For communications/public affairs

managers, these choices centre around decisions about which challenges/issues they should focus attention on, which stakeholders will need to be targeted, what communication/public affairs strategies should be adopted and what specific tactics should be used. Equally, at the communications department level, management choice may involve decisions about how to allocate responsibilities among staff, how resources should be utilised and what tasks should be prioritised, to name but a few of the numerous 'choice decisions' that managers face every week, if not every day.

Decisions particularly about the choice of alternative communications/public affairs strategies invariably involve consultation and approval of senior management. Indeed, as essentially a support function, the role of the public affairs function is to support and facilitate the achievement of the organisation's broader corporate goals and strategies, and hence communications/public affairs management decisions will normally take a lead from these higher-level decisions.

Choice tools, or techniques, are the methods that managers can draw upon to help determine the best options for the organisation to pursue. Although it is beyond the scope of this chapter to explore in detail some of the more sophisticated choice/decision-making tools available, it is worth highlighting some of the more commonly used techniques that can be deployed in this context. Of course, ultimately, choice decisions usually come down to a 'judgement call' by the senior professionals charged with decision-making responsibility. However, many larger organisations nowadays have access to relatively sophisticated computer systems that are capable of collecting, sifting and analysing large quantities of data, and conducting probability and risk analysis on the likely outcome of different future scenarios. Clearly, such analysis can perhaps take some of the 'guess work' out of decisions about future courses of action. However, such systems are only mathematical modelling processes, and predicting the vagaries of human behaviour and accounting for the often 'boundedly' rational behaviour of individuals and/or groups can make any such systematic reductionist approaches problematic, particularly when it comes to predicting future scenarios that depend on human actions and behaviour. Some of the more commonly used choice decision tools include:

- *Ranking methods*: alternative options are assessed against an agreed set of predetermined criteria that are identified as important to the organisation, such as cost or investment considerations, fit with resource capabilities, or even ethical considerations.

- *Scenario building*: the idea is to match alternative options against a range of possible future scenarios in order to assess the best fit, given alternative future situations. Of course, the challenge here is to 'second guess' future developments, whether they be at an industry level or perhaps, more problematically, at a societal level, and how such developments might manifest themselves in terms of stakeholder behaviour.

- *Decision tree analysis:* another method of assessing alternative courses of action, but here preferred options emerge progressively by introducing requirements of preferred conditions that need to be met, such as, for example, levels of acceptable risk. Here the construction of a 'decision-tree diagram' is often used as a visual aid to such decision making.

- *Risk analysis:* an approach that often works alongside choice techniques in terms of attempts to assess the degree of hazard or adverse consequence associated with alternative courses of action, weighed against the potential rewards. Statistical 'probabilistic risk assessment' methods have been developed to try to assess the level of risk associated with specific projects, but the value and accuracy of such measures depends very much on the adequacy and accuracy of the input data, the magnitude or severity of the adverse consequences of each event and the likelihood of occurrence of that event. Of course, the application of such probabilistic analysis is more suited to physical engineering and process projects than to predicting the consequences of alternative patterns of human behaviours. In the latter case, however, risk assessment can be undertaken but is often based on collective judgements made by panels of experts and experienced managers from the field in question.

Public affairs management implementation

Much of the discussion of the communication/public affairs management process tends to focus on the analysis and strategic and operational decision-making (choice) stages of the process, rather than on implementation. However, how communications/public affairs departments manage the *implementation* of their policies/strategies and programmes is arguably no less important to achieving their intended outcome, since even the most well-designed strategies and programmes can fail through poorly managed implementation. It is generally recognised that the key to successful implementation of communications/

Think about 20.5   **Public affairs accountability**

Perhaps one of the most controversial aspects of public affairs work relates to the expenditure on activities designed to help build and sustain key relationships with politicians, civil servants, etc. How such expenditure on corporate hospitality and other relationship building activities is budgeted and accounted may be very difficult to assess. Moreover, the professional standards and mores of doing business in the USA or UK may be very different from what is the acceptable norm in other parts of the world. Consider the challenge for public affairs when confronted with doing business in a country where, effectively, 'bribes' and 'under the counter' payment are treated as an acceptable part of doing business. Essentially such issues, while perhaps more relevant to a discussion of professional ethics, equally impinge on the questions of effective implementation of programmes. How would you advise your senior public affairs management team to behave if faced with such a situation?

public affairs policies and programmes lies in the effective management of *people* and *resources* involved in their delivery.

Arguably communications/public affairs functions and professionals have historically had a relatively poor track record in terms of many aspects of effective people management and, more particularly, budgetary management. However, such criticisms have perhaps been much more relevant to the consultancy sector than to in-house communications/public affairs departments. Both areas of people management and budgetary/financial management are ones that have not necessarily been recognised as core areas of professional competence associated with communications/public affairs. However, with increasing investment in communications/public affairs activity, notably on the part of large corporate and multinational corporations in particular, communications/public affairs functions are expected to demonstrate the same level of professionalism and accountability for the use of resources and management of people that is expected of all other corporate functions.

Public affairs management evaluation

The final element of this public affairs management framework focuses on *evaluation* of the outcomes of the communications/public affairs function's strategies and programmes. The issue of effective evaluation has long been something of an 'Achilles heel' for all areas of communications, including public affairs. However, at least in principle, evaluation should not prove an overly complicated task, but the difficulty has always been in identifying, isolating and measuring the *impact* of communications/public affairs programmes. Here the aim is to establish, firstly, the extent to which the immediate programme and longer-term policy objectives have been achieved and, secondly, the significance of external and internal factors affecting the programme outcomes. As suggested above, organisational objectives and targets have increasingly become more diverse, reflecting the need to balance different stakeholder expectations of organisations – recognising that financial performance may have to be set against other environmental, social and even political considerations affecting an organisation's longer-term position and success. Where organisations have accepted the need for this type of 'balanced scorecard approach' to objective and target setting (e.g., Kaplan and Norton 1992), it follows that any evaluation of performance and outcomes will need to use an appropriate set of quantitative and qualitative performance measures. While this discussion of balanced scorecards and more pluralistic organisational objectives and performance measures has focused mainly on the areas of broader corporate and business policy and strategy making, the arguments can be applied equally to

the area of communications/public affairs policies and programmes. Indeed, communications/public affairs practitioners are generally seen as advocates and champions of a broader stakeholder perspective of organisational and business strategy and policy-making. Thus, it is perhaps only logical to expect them to be advocates of a balanced scorecard approach to the evaluation of their work, reflecting the potentially varied range of ways in which activities can contribute to organisational success.

Thus while in principle there would appear to be broad agreement about what is required in terms of communications/public affairs evaluation, in practice, identifying appropriate measures and carrying out the evaluation of the outcomes of designated programmes has proved highly problematic, particularly in terms of isolating and measuring the specific communications/public affairs effects. Here the debates about communications evaluation have tended to crystallise around the distinction between 'process' and 'impact' measurement (Dozier 1984; Grunig and Hunt 1984; Broom and Dozier 1990; Macnamara 1992). Although this debate has focused on the evaluation of public relations programmes rather than public affairs, arguably many of the measurement techniques (both process and impact measures) can be seen to be more or less applicable to public affairs. There are, of course, some more obviously relevant impact measures for public affairs, particularly where the function's goal relates to the change or modification or passing of a specific piece of legislation or regulation. In such cases, any measurement of the media coverage generated can only reveal part of the story of activity directed at bringing about legislative modification or change. It is only the achievement of the legislative change itself that can be said to represent a full measure of the public affairs programme's impact/success. A fuller examination of the debates about approaches to communications/public relations evaluation was provided earlier in Chapter 9 and it may be worth revisiting this chapter to refresh your memory about the theme of what constitutes effective evaluation.

Explore 20.5

How campaigns are evaluated

Review the public affairs campaigns that you have come across/read about over the past few months in *PRWeek*, *Public Affairs News* or the *Journal of Public Affairs*, etc., and identify what forms of evaluation are being used to assess the success of the reported campaigns.

Summary

Public affairs has become an increasingly important corporate/organisational function in many of today's more turbulent, increasingly globalised and politicised business environments. In this section we have explored how public affairs is understood and defined, highlighting the polarised nature of how public affairs tends to be viewed and understood. Traditional views of public affairs position it as essentially a specialised government relations/lobbying function, whereas public affairs has, in many cases, assumed the mantle of overseeing a broad cross-section of communications-related sub-functions, such as issue management, community relations and CSR. However, lobbying activity in its various forms, directed at government and government departments at all levels, remains the day-to-day 'bread and butter' work of the public affairs function. With the internationalisation of most markets and the opening up of a number of previously closed trading areas, public affairs is playing an increasingly important role in liaising with relevant government and regulatory bodies in some of the new countries keen to develop trade with the UK.

Bibliography

Argenti, P. (2009). *Corporate Communication: International edition*. New York, NY: Irwin McGraw-Hill.

Broom, G.M. and D.M. Dozier (1990). *Using Research in Public Relations: Applications to program managment*. Englewood Cliffs, NJ: Prentice Hall.

Cornelissen, J. (2008). *Corporate Communications: A guide to theory and practice*, second edition. London: Sage.

Dozier, D.M. (1984). 'Program evaluation and roles of practitioners'. *Public Relations Review* **10**(2): 13–21.

Dozier, D.M. (ed.) (1992). 'The organizational roles of communicators and public relations practitioners' in *Excellence In Public Relations and Communications Management*. Hillsdale, NJ: Lawrence Erlbaum Associates, Inc.

Fayol, H. (1949). *General and Industrial Management*. London: Pitman.

Fleisher, C.S. and N.M. Blair (1999). 'Tracing the parallel evolution of public affairs and public relations: an examination of practice, scholarship and teaching'. *Journal of Communication Management* **3**(3): 276–292.

Griffin, J.J. and P. Dunn (2004). 'Corporate public affairs: commitment, resources, and structure'. *Business & Society* **43**(2): 196–220.

Grunig, J.E. and L.A. Grunig (1992). 'Models of public relations and communication' in *Excellence in Public Relations and Communication Management*. J.E. Grunig (ed.). Hillsdale, NJ: Lawrence Erlbaum Associates.

Grunig, J.E., L.A. Grunig and D.M. Dozier (2006). 'The excellence theory 1'. *Public Relations Theory* **II** (19).

Grunig, J.E. and T. Hunt (1984). *Managing Public Relations*. Orlando, FL: Harcourt Brace Jovanovich.

Gulick, L. and L. Urwick (1937) (eds). *Papers on the Science of Administration*. New York, NY: Institute of Public Administration.

Hainsworth, B. and M. Meng (1988). 'How corporations define issue management'. *Public Relations Review* **14**(4): 18–30.

Hales, C. (1986). 'What do managers do? A critical review of the evidence'. *Journal of Management Studies* **23**(1): 88–115.

Harris, P. and D. Moss (2001). 'Editorial: In search of public affairs: a function in search of an identity'. *Journal of Public Affairs* **1**(2): 102–110.

Heath, R.L. (1994). *Management of Corporate Communication: From interpersonal contacts to external affairs*. Abingdon: Routledge.

Heath, R.L. (2002). 'Issues management: its past, present and future'. *Journal of Public Affairs* **2**(4): 209–214.

Hillman, A.J. (2002). 'Public affairs, issue management and political strategy: methodological issues that count – a different view'. *Journal of Public Affairs* **1**(4) & **2**(1): 356–361.

Kaplan, R. and D. Norton (1992). 'The balanced scorecard: measures that drive performance'. *Harvard Business Review* **70**(1): 71–79.

McGrath, C., D. Moss and P. Harris (2010). 'The evolving discipline of public affairs'. *Journal of Public Affairs* **10**(4): 335–352.

Mcnamara, J. (1992). 'Evaluation of public relations; the Achilles heel of the PR profession'. *International Public Relations Review* **15**(4): 17–31.

Meznar, M.B. and D. Nigh (1995). 'Buffer or bridge? Environmental and organizational determinants of public affairs activities in American firms'. *Academy of Management Journal*, **38**(4): 975–996.

Miller, C. (2000). *Politico's Guide to Political Lobbying*. London: Politico's Publishing.

Mintzberg, H. (1973). *The Nature of Managerial Work*. New York, NY: Harper & Row.

Mintzberg, H. (1990). 'The design school: reconsidering the basic premises of strategic management. *Strategic Management Journal* 11(3): 171–195.

Mintzberg, H. (2009). *Managing*. Harlow: FT, Prentice Hall.

Moss, D.A. and B. Desanto (eds) (2011). *Public Relations: A managerial perspective*. London: Sage.

Moss, D.A., G. Warnaby et al. (2000). 'Public relations practitioner role enactment at the senior management level within UK companies'. *Journal of Public Relations Research* 12(4): 227–308.

Moss, D.A., A.J. Newman and B. Desanto (2005). 'What do communication managers do? Defining and refining the core elements of management in the public relations/communications context'. *Journalism & Mass Communication Quarterly* 82(4): 873–890.

Moss, D.A., B. Desanto and A.J. Newman (2007). 'Building an understanding of the main elements of management in the communication/public relations context: a study of U.S. practitioner practices'. *Journalism & Mass Communication Quarterly* 84(3): 439–454.

Moss, D.A., C. McGrath, J. Tonge and P. Harris (2012). 'Exploring the management of the corporate public affairs function in a dynamic global environment'. *Journal of Public Affairs* 12(1): 47–60.

Moss, D., G. Warnaby and A. J. Newman (2000). 'Public Relations practitioner role enactment at the senior management level within UK companies'. *Journal of Public Relations Research* 12(4): 277–307.

Nugent, N. (2003). *The Government and Politics of the European Union*. Durham NC: Duke University Press.

Pedler, R.H. (ed.) (2002). *European Union Lobbying: Changes in the arena*. Houndmills: Palgrave.

Pedler, R.H. and M.P.C.M. Van Schendelen (eds) (1994). *Lobbying the European Union: Companies, trade associations and issue groups*. Aldershot: Dartmouth.

Post, J. (1982). 'Public affairs: its role' in *The Public Affairs Handbook*. J.S. Nagelschmidt (ed.). New York, NY: Amacom.

Reil, C.V. (1995). *Principles of Corporate Communication*. Hemel Hempstead: Prentice Hall.

Showalter, A. and C.S. Fleisher (2005). 'The tools and techniques of public affairs' in *The Handbook of Public Affairs*. P. Harris and C.S. Fleisher (eds). London: Sage.

Sriramesh, K. and D. Vercic (eds) (2009). *The Global Public Relations Handbook: Theory, research and practice*. Mahwah: NJ, Lawrence Erlbaum Associates.

Wakefield, R. (2011). 'Managing global public relations' in *Public Relations: A managerial perspective*. D.A. Moss and B. Desanto (eds). London: Sage.

Watts, D. and C. Pilkington (2005). *Britain in the European Union*. Manchester: Manchester University Press.

Zetter, L. (2008). *Lobbying: The art of political persuasion*. Petersfield: Harriman House.

Websites

The Daily Telegraph: www.dailytelegraph.co.uk
The Guardian: www.guardianunlimited.co.uk
Parliament: www.Parliament.uk

CHAPTER 21

Public relations in the world of finance

Learning outcomes

By the end of this chapter you should be able to:

- identify some of the different PR activities in global financial centres
- distinguish the range of interests represented by PR in financial markets
- understand some of the challenges of communicating finance to different stakeholders
- appreciate the skills and training that are beneficial to PR practitioners in this sector.

Structure

- Public relations for global financial centres: the context
- Public relations for wholesale financial markets
- Public relations in retail financial markets
- Media in financial centres
- The global financial crisis

Introduction

So much of daily life depends on the wheels of finance to keep things going. Many of us have, for example, become used to withdrawing money from a cash machine whenever we need it, without thinking about how that service is organised. It is increasingly normal to have student debt, credit card debt or a mortgage on our homes. Many of us are investors in company shares, bonds, property or other assets without even knowing it, because we do so through a life insurance policy or pension scheme. Our daily lives have become increasingly financialised as we seek to get ahead in a globalised world (Martin 2002).

The wheels of finance are also crucial in helping businesses to invest in infrastructure, to expand and enter new markets. Finance has enabled major commercial developments in green energy, such as solar panels, wind farms and hybrid cars, together with one-of-a-kind projects on a grand scale – the launch of the world's largest telescope, the James Webb space telescope, and the expansion of the Panama Canal. Governments need finance too – they borrow money to facilitate trade with other governments, to invest in social housing, hospitals and highways and to manage the flow of money in the economy. It is an understanding of this reality that makes public relations for the world of finance such a fascinating activity.

Much of the arranging and issuing of finance takes place in global financial centres, such as London and New York – the world's largest financial centres. Smaller, more niche financial centres compete as tax 'havens', including Geneva, Luxembourg, the Cayman Islands and the Isle of Man. The Asia/Pacific region now has five financial centres ranked among the 'top ten' – more than Europe or the Americas (Z/Yen Group 2012). Hong Kong and Tokyo are integral to the movement of money around the world, together with Chicago, Frankfurt, Paris, Toronto and Zurich (see Table 21.1). It is in the largest, most global of these financial centres that public relations has evolved into a range of activities representing financial markets.

Picture 21.1 Frankfurt – home of the German stock exchange and the European Central Bank – is one of the world's leading financial centres (*source*: Siegfried Layda/Getty Images)

	Broad and deep	Relatively broad	Relatively deep	Emerging
Global	**Global leaders**	**Global diversified**	**Global specialists**	**Global contenders**
	Chicago	Amsterdam	Beijing	Luxembourg
	Frankfurt	Dublin		Moscow
	Hong Kong	Seoul		
	London	Shanghai		
	New York	Singapore		
	Paris			
	Tokyo			
	Toronto			
	Zurich			
Transnational	**Established transnational**	**Transnational diversified**	**Transnational specialists**	**Transnational contenders**
	Copenhagen	Boston	Athens	Bahrain
	Geneva	Istanbul	Dubai	British Virgin Islands
	Madrid	Kuala Lumpur	Edinburgh	Cayman Islands
	Montreal	Washington DC	Glasgow	Gibraltar
	Munich		Mumbai	Guernsey
	Sydney		Qatar	Isle of Man
	Vancouver		Shenzhen	Jersey
Local	**Established players**	**Local diversified**	**Local specialists**	**Evolving centres**
	Brussels	Bangkok	Abu Dhabi	Buenos Aires
	Calgary	Warsaw	Bahamas	Jakarta
	Helsinki		Budapest	Johannesburg
	Lisbon		Hamilton	Manila
	Melbourne		Malta	Mauritius
	Mexico City		Monaco	Osaka
	Milan		Oslo	Taipei
	Prague		Reykjavik	Wellington
	Rome		Rio de Janeiro	
	San Francisco		Riyadh	
	Sao Paulo		St Petersburg	
	Stockholm		Tallinn	
	Vienna			

Table 21.1 Financial centre profiles (*source*: Global Financial Centres 12 published by the Z/Yen Group in September 2012)

Public relations for global financial centres: the context

Public relations as a specialist activity in major financial centres came into its own after many Western economies deregulated and liberalised in the 1980s, releasing money to move more freely around the globe. In these locations, financial markets expanded rapidly in size, complexity and distribution channels as more companies turned to the capital markets for finance, issuing bonds or shares, merging with or acquiring other companies. For more than twenty years, developed and most developing countries experienced faster growth in their financial sectors than in their actual economies.

In this fast-changing environment, public relations became an important means of building credibility in and shaping attitudes toward financial markets. PR enabled various groups of financial experts to compete by promoting their differentiation. PR practitioners were then enlisted to build compelling narratives about all sorts of financial products and services that offer safety and protection from risk, and that meet the needs of the future. Above all, PR helped to position investment as the discovery of hidden financial opportunities, thus supporting the value of financial instruments and the growth of financial markets. Such PR activity is not without controversy, as will be discussed later on in the chapter. For now, it is worth acknowledging that in many countries, financial services contribute to a substantial portion of domestic productivity, while the world of finance is responsible for a significant share of the money spent on PR activity.

Today, there are many different roles for public relations within financial centres. Some PR practitioners represent publicly quoted companies to the markets as part of their overall communications role. Others are the sole PR representative within a financial institution or professional services firm. Still others belong to small in-house PR teams, or are part of large teams where each PR practitioner represents a single financial product line or business area. Some practitioners work for PR agencies representing *both* listed companies and financial institutions, or specialising in one or the other group.

In addition to the range of PR roles, there are a number of different specialisms within financial sector communication – from the practitioners focused on public affairs and lobbying on behalf of financial services to those engaged in business-to-business (B2B) activity or in consumer finance, and, finally, those focused on investor relations and financial PR. Of the various specialisms, financial PR is arguably the best-known, coming into its own when financial markets opened up in the 1980s. Financial PR addresses the communication needs of

Explore 21.1

Financial public relations

Financial PR practitioners help to promote the exciting ways that money can be used to aid businesses to start up, grow and enter new markets; below are some of the activities they advise on. What can you discover about these terms?

- Bond issues
- Company results
- Initial public offering
- Proxy battle
- M&A

Feedback

Once you have learned a bit about M&A, look for business stories about Ryanair's attempt at a hostile takeover of Aer Lingus in 2012. Was Ryanair successful? Which PR firms were involved? What were the messages communicated by the two companies and their stakeholders?

companies accessing finance from capital markets through mergers and acquisitions (M&A), initial public offerings (IPOs) and the marketing of shares and bond issues (see Explore 21.1). Of all the PR activity in financial markets, financial PR is seen as the most quantifiable, because of the immediate impact it can have on a company's share price.

As more and more financial institutions opened their doors, PR practitioners began to represent all sorts of financial providers, including investment banks, asset managers, private equity firms, retail banks, credit card companies, 'supermarket banks', insurance companies, building societies, wealth managers, stockbrokers, mortgage specialists and financial advisers. As the rules of marketing professional services were modified, practitioners also represented the professional services firms that offer financial services expertise, such as law firms, accountancy firms, actuarial firms, management consultants and other intermediaries.

While there is no precise data available on the number of PR professionals representing financial markets, the UK – home to London, the world's largest financial centre (Z/Yen 2012), as well as smaller centres such as Edinburgh, Belfast and Leeds – has some 8 per cent of all in-house practitioners working in financial services, while 25 per cent of agency practitioners reported that they were likely

Box 21.1

In the spotlight

A financial services PR practitioner in Zurich, Kilian Borter

'As one of the world's most important financial centres, Switzerland is the subject of constant media attention, both nationally and internationally. Against the backdrop of fiscal transparency initiatives worldwide, and European countries trying to recover assets held by their nationals offshore as they seek to tackle their sovereign debt problems, this focus is even keener today than in the past.

'Being a small country, Switzerland has always been very internationally orientated. It is broadly accepted that the impact of economic, financial and political aspects are not limited by its national borders, and neither are the factors influencing them. There is a strong interdependence with neighbouring countries, the European Union and the other important financial centres worldwide. Hence, everything a PR professional in the financial industry does is international in nature. There is also an important political dimension, as the international

pressure on Swiss bank client confidentiality has prompted political discussions of this issue and how to deal with international tax issues. High bonuses for board members and management are also the subject of heated public debate.

'This creates an extremely interesting and challenging environment for PR professionals. More than ever, all communication activities have to take into account the potential political reaction, while at the same time keeping constant tabs on moves and comments by politicians that could trigger new disputes or debate on the national or international level. Switzerland has also been negotiating new tax treaties with countries such as the UK, Germany, France and the US, which are attracting public interest in these countries.

'The Swiss financial centre is, therefore, firmly in the spotlight of both national and international media alike. What does this mean for financial services PR professionals in Switzerland?

'On the one hand, daily working life has become more challenging. With the advent of online media, everything has become faster and internal information has more than ever become intertwined with external communication. The range of expertise required to deal with these challenges has changed, and PR specialists now need to have greater knowledge of other markets, legal and compliance risks, political aspects and regulatory changes. Last, but not least, banks are having to contend with high pressure on their margins, necessitating more efficient organisation and changes to business models. These are all aspects that have to be communicated internally and externally. While integrated communication was for a long time merely an expression used to impress, it has now become a real need. PR professionals now have to take a broader view, and address a wider range of stakeholders than just the media and internal audiences.

'That said, all these aspects make for a much more interesting working environment, one where the need for well-qualified PR expertise is beyond dispute. Be it internally within companies or as external consultants, the standing of PR professionals has never been higher.'

(*Photo source*: Kilian Borter)

to do most of their work with the financial services sector (CIPR 2010). Some of these PR practitioners focus more on wholesale financial markets (the factory floor of financial services), while others may spend more time working with clients and organisations in retail financial markets (the shop window).

Public relations in wholesale financial markets

Wholesale financial markets are rather like the 'factory floor' of global finance. Here, finance takes place on a large

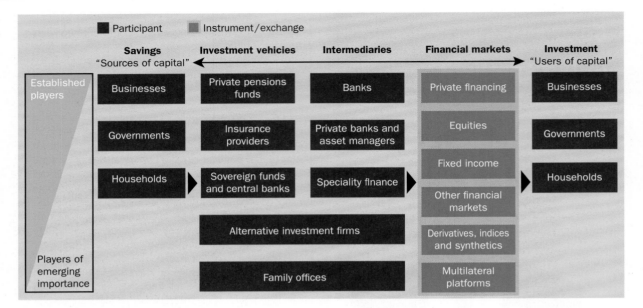

Figure 21.1 Established and emerging players in wholesale financial markets (*source*: World Economic Forum 2009)

scale – mathematicians and physicists devise complex models to forecast future financial performance – large transactions are conceived, new and innovative financial products are engineered. Here, central banks issue bank notes, monitor currency, manage inflation and act as lender-of-last-resort to other banks. Here, too, is where companies make a market for and trade in large blocks of company shares, in government and company loans, in commodities such as wheat, corn or soya, gold, oil or diamonds, together with derivatives of all these investments. In wholesale financial markets, arrangements are made to assist companies with export or trade financing, or to help countries borrow large amounts of money. Here is where pensions and investment funds worth billions are managed, and insurance and reinsurance policies are sought for potential risks and disasters.

PR represents a host of established and emerging players in wholesale financial markets (see Figure 21.1), where communications needs vary. The most high-profile activity is financial PR – those PR practitioners who promote company results, prepare for share issues, mergers and acquisitions, and garner investor perceptions of company and market activity. Financial PR is high-profile because it is often well-compensated, particularly when offering strategic and crisis communications support for large multinationals and blue chip companies, as well as for billion-dollar cross-border transactions. While financial PR practitioners often focus on wholesale markets, some aspects of their work require them to communicate directly with consumers – when representing a new company share issue, for example, or when promoting company results.

By contrast, there are many PR practitioners working in wholesale financial markets who are not engaged in financial PR. They may, instead, represent the financial institutions that provide specialist, outsourced services to *other* financial institutions, or that serve companies in the wider economy. These PR practitioners may specialise in corporate communications and/or B2B communications, in wholesale market roles that include representing investment bankers targeting corporate clients, money market funds targeting treasury departments or asset managers targeting pension schemes.

One of the most important tools for PR practitioners working in wholesale financial markets is 'thought leadership', a term used rather loosely to describe the 'intellectual firepower' (Brocklebank-Fowler 2008: 8) assembled and published in communications material. Thought leadership is an important means by which firms in wholesale markets assert their certainty, skill and expertise in a way that sets them apart from the competition. In its simplest form, thought leadership can refer to the technical articles contributed to specialist trade publications, explaining how a product, service or legislation works. It can also include the speeches and presentations made by industry experts at conferences and events. More accurately, thought leadership describes lengthier, thoughtful documents, or 'white papers', promoting an organisation's views on government policy or industry issues. In various scenarios, a PR practitioner may be commissioned to write thought leadership material, assist in editing and/or packaging completed thought leadership to promote with stakeholders and the media. By promoting thought leadership, PR can help an accountancy firm, an investment bank, a management consultant or other financial expert to establish greater authority and differentiation in wholesale financial markets.

Picture 21.2 Financial services white papers by KPMG, the global professional services network (*source*: KPMG)

Mini case study 21.1
Thought leadership: 'creating the BRICs'

The term 'BRICs' – the acronym referring to Brazil, Russia, India and China – is now part of the lexicon, in part due to PR activity in financial markets. BRICs was originally coined as an investment term by the asset management business of Goldman Sachs, the global investment bank. In 2001, Goldman Sachs published the first in a series of reports to demonstrate its thought leadership on new global growth opportunities to be found in emerging markets. These reports were subsequently promoted to Goldman Sachs' clients and prospects through PR and marketing activity.

When the first report, *Building Better Global Economic BRICs*, was published in November 2001, reactions to the unprecedented attack of 11 September that year had already fomented misgivings and uncertainty among US policy-makers and business interests toward the rest of the world. Goldman Sachs economist, Jim O'Neill, set out to persuade clients that they needed to look further than the US if they wanted to invest in economic growth. 11 September became central to the report's warning that the world's economic disturbances since the late 1990s – as well as its biggest changes – had largely involved countries outside the G7 nations. In 2003, Goldman Sachs published a fol-low-up report, *Dreaming with the BRICs*. In this second report, the firm cemented the financial case for its BRICs thesis by painting a clear, explicit picture for investors of what the world would look like in the next 50 years.

Source: Bourne 2012

Public relations in retail financial markets

Connecting with savers and investors

Retail financial markets are the 'shop window' of the financial world. The 'shop window' connects ordinary people with finance in many different ways – as consumers and taxpayers, savers and investors, employees and holiday-makers and as homeowners and pensioners. In highly competitive financial markets, financial institutions have to work hard to communicate with customers to keep existing business, and to cross-sell new products and services to existing customers. The size of a country's retail financial market correlates with levels of affluence, so it is not surprising that many of the narratives PR produces for retail finance link to aspirations such as buying a home, planning a family, saving for a university education, taking a dream holiday, insuring against emergencies and saving for retirement. It is these narratives that drive PR activity in retail financial markets, more so than the products that enable these aspirations, such as bank accounts, general

Think about 21.1

First aid for financial jargon?

Could you be the PR 'super hero' who one day translates the arcane terms used in everyday finance into straightforward, compelling language? One veteran PR practitioner describes the ongoing challenge of differentiating between 'pensions' and 'annuities' in communication:

'What I was not prepared for, on entering the UK life sector . . . was the sheer lack of interest anyone has in the pension industry . . . those who would benefit from understanding annuities, don't; while those who do, do not need them in the first place . . . I began to realise that the problem may be semantics. Everyone I know thinks they understand pensions . . . long-term savings for the time you no longer earn money from employment. The problem is that they also think that the money they receive each month in retirement is also called a pension. As one friend recently put it, *it was a car when I drove it into the garage, why is it a tractor when I take it out again?'*

Source: Fulton 2010

insurance, personal loans, mortgage loans, credit cards and more sophisticated, long-term financial products such as pensions and investments.

PR for retail financial markets is influenced by technological, geographic and cultural realities as well as individual attitudes to finance. In some countries, increased connectivity, transaction speed and efficiency of e-commerce has enabled new market players to set up online-only businesses. In these countries, Internet penetration is very high, enabling many people to do their banking online or on their mobile phones, and to shop for financial products on the Internet. Other people have very restricted physical access to finance because they live in isolated rural areas with poor transport and technology links. In certain countries, traditional financial institutions such as community banks, credit unions and friendly societies continue to thrive as mass market providers. Elsewhere, by contrast, non-traditional providers, such as supermarkets and department stores, are now successfully retailing loans, insurance and other financial services.

PR practitioners in retail financial markets also need to be aware that customers have different attitudes to financial products and services. These attitudes can be shaped by many factors including personality, family background and socio-economic status. Certain individuals and groups of people also have strong ethical and religious beliefs about finance, which has led to the development of special products tailored to these beliefs (see Think about 21.2).

Think about 21.2   'It's a good day for gold'

Picture 21.3 Gold prices in India are influenced each year by the Akshaya Tritiya festival (*source*: Shutterstock. com/FikMik)

Early one April morning, Indian television anchorman Udayan Mukherjee opened his live market show, *Bazaar Morning Call* on CNBC-TV 18, with this cheery announcement: 'It's a good day for gold!' Mukherjee was acknowledging the annual festival of Akshaya Tritiya,

considered an auspicious day in Hindu mythology for buying precious metals and making investments. By the end of the day, the gold price in India had reached record highs driven by heavy buying to mark the festival.

Akshaya Tritiya is widely celebrated in Indian communities, irrespective of religious faith and social groupings – any ventures initiated on the day are expected to grow and bring prosperity. The effect that this festival can have on gold prices is a reminder to PR practitioners working in financial markets that it is important to understand cultural realities and belief systems as well as financial rules and regulations, for both can affect behaviour in financial markets.

Feedback

How many other countries or cultures can you think of that have specific beliefs, special days or festivals that might influence the way people invest? How would you take this into account when planning an annual PR programme for an investment firm?

One of the most important communication considerations for a PR practitioner in retail financial markets is that financial products and services are intangible. It can be hard to compare complicated products, which are structured and priced in different ways. It can also be hard to assess risk and uncertainty when buying long-term savings products as it may be years before customers know if their purchase will deliver on its promises. For this reason, much of the PR in retail financial markets focuses on three 'e's – choice **editing**, third-party **endorsement** and financial **education**.

The first 'e' – choice **editing** – is a necessary service in highly competitive retail financial markets where there is overwhelming choice. In these markets, savers and investors often turn to 'choice editors' (Henley Centre 2005) to help them decide what to buy. PR practitioners often develop campaigns that help to differentiate financial brands. This way, potential customers can discern the different names when leafing through personal finance pages or when watching and listening to money programmes on TV or radio, or surfing the Internet. For most consumers, preferred choice editors are family, friends and 'people like us' (Edelman 2011). Social media has dramatically changed the power of choice editing: in 2007, for example, HSBC faced a Facebook-led revolt by angry students whose interest-free overdrafts had been scrapped. In this environment, it is even more vital for PR programmes to generate case studies reflecting real customers' genuine experiences with a financial product or service. These case studies may appear on websites, via social media, in magazine features, company brochures, on money programmes or in the personal finance press. In certain markets, PR practitioners also liaise with price comparison websites that have established themselves as professional choice editors – 'one-stop' shops where consumers can take advantage of powerful databases to learn all they need to know about available products and services, at a glance.

Box 21.2

What skills and education do you need for PR in financial markets?

While some practitioners move into PR after working in banking, financial journalism or other parts of financial services, many do not. Whatever your background, you will be required to understand aspects of financial markets well in order to explain them to your relevant stakeholders.

Read avidly
The business and financial media are a useful place to start learning how finance works. For any PR practitioner just starting out in financial markets, global newspapers such as *The Economist*, the *Financial Times* and *The Wall Street Journal* are useful sources, as are television channels such as Bloomberg, CNBC and specialist financial programmes on other channels. There are also a plethora of websites and other sources that you may find helpful.

Study broadly
For those still at university, courses in economics and economics history can be very useful foundations for understanding how finance works. If you haven't studied for years, there are many easy-to-read books on economics and on globalisation, including Niall Ferguson's *Ascent of Money*, which was also made into a TV documentary series by Channel 4 in the UK.

Attend training courses
Once you are on the job, in-house PR roles often provide training opportunities in your company's specialist field. PR agency practitioners may also have access to training budgets. In some countries, PR professional bodies have specialist financial divisions that occasionally provide training and seminars. However, it is often more productive to find specialist training providers offering financial courses tailored to the needs of non-financial professionals.

Become financially literate
Financial literacy will be important in establishing your credibility and will help you to do your job well. Some practitioners must understand balance sheets and company accounts thoroughly. Others need to understand the basic formulae used to calculate pension products, together with bond yields and interest rates. Some PR practitioners gain further credibility by earning specialist qualifications, opting to become qualified financial advisers by studying for the Investment Management Certificate (IMC), becoming Chartered Financial Analysts (CFA) or even Chartered Management Accountants (CMA).

Know the relevant rules of your market
Whether you represent a life insurer, a general insurer, a bank, building society, hedge fund, investment manager, a stock broker or a listed company, you must know the appropriate rules and regulations of the market in which you operate. In addition, if you are employed in an in-house role you may be required to pass tests on anti-money laundering and anti-fraud measures, and/or to understand rules on staff share dealing before you are allowed to represent your organisation.

Third-party **endorsement** – obtaining credibility for a financial brand from an outside source (Ehrlich and Fanelli 2004) – is a second activity supported by PR in retail financial markets (and is equally important in wholesale markets too). Third-party endorsement goes a step further than choice editing as it is effectively a recommendation or 'seal of approval' from authoritative experts or well-known, trusted individuals. PR practitioners may aim to get third-party endorsement from respected journalists, commentators or independent experts who are in a position to make positive remarks about a financial product or service or a company's shares. Third-party endorsement can also be achieved when a financial brand, product or service receives commendations in respected industry surveys, awards and league tables. PR practitioners sometimes get involved in writing and submitting award entries and applications for organisations wishing to be considered among the 'best' brands in surveys and rankings.

Financial **education** is the third 'e' of PR activity in retail financial markets; it involves explaining how financial products and services work, clarifying associated risks and simplifying complex terms. Although financial institutions have a vested interest in educating consumers, much of the financial education in financial centres is carried out by government departments, regulators and non-governmental organisations (NGOs), which have a broader remit to improve financial capability. Through international forums such as the Global Partnership for Financial Inclusion (gpfi.org), launched by the G20 countries in 2010, many countries now have a national strategy for financial education and capability. Agencies associated with such initiatives use PR activity to promote financial education via websites, radio and television, workshops, school and workplace programmes.

Media in financial centres

The explosion in financial services that took place across many Western economies in the 1980s helped drive the growth of specialist financial media in the larger financial centres. Some of these media organisations have very recognisable names and global reach, others are national media houses with strong business and finance coverage, while a third group consists of specialist financial titles. In the first category are the global business and financial media organisations that cater to more financially-educated publics – from *CNBC* to *Bloomberg*, *Reuters* and *Dow Jones*, to the *Financial Times* and *The Wall Street Journal* and their associated websites. These media houses have their headquarters in the US and Europe, but they disseminate news to even the smallest financial markets. They also wield substantial influence over market players,

for example helping to drive share prices up and down, or giving greater visibility to bond market trading, which is not well-covered in the general business media.

The second category of financial media organisations tend to be regional or national in focus. In Europe, news outlets such as *L'Agefi*, *Börsen Zeitung*, *Diario Economico*, *Les Echos*, *Expansión*, *Het Financieele Dagblad*, *Finanz und Wirtschaft* and *Il Sole 24 Ore* are among the important contacts for PR practitioners operating in continental financial centres; in the Asia-Pacific region, important outlets include the *Australian Financial Review*, *The Financial Express* (India), *Khaleej Times* and the *South China Morning Post*, to name just a few. Asia-Pacific is a rapidly evolving area for financial media: China, for example, has now admitted certain global media organisations, such as *Reuters* (which has translated its name into the Chinese characters for 'penetrating', 'thorough' and 'transparent') (Schlesinger 2009), together with Chinese outlets such as Xinhua.

Some regional and national titles have journalists who cover finance as part of a broader remit to cover business news. Consequently, they may avoid forensic coverage of finance so as to avoid boring their audience (Doyle 2006; Hilton 2008). Editors may encourage storylines centred around personalities, events and intrigues – for example, bankers' bonuses. National media may also make business and financial news accessible by using expert commentators to explain and interpret financial news in an interesting manner, sometimes stirring up public controversy as a consequence (Doyle 2006). Dedicated money programmes on TV and radio, and supplementary sections in newspapers, act as 'choice editors' (FSA & Henley Centre 2005), helping consumers to navigate the range of personal finance opportunities on offer. Some media houses and individual journalists and columnists are quite influential, able to sway customers to surrender insurance policies or funds or to avoid financial products or company shares altogether. Other journalists adopt a campaigning stance, helping 'mum and dad shareholders' – the least powerful players in financial markets – to avoid taking precarious risks in order to make money with their life savings (Pixley 2005).

A third and final media segment in financial markets is the specialist financial trade press. These specialist media titles include scores of weekly and monthly magazines targeting financial professionals. Specialist magazines are generally funded by advertising – employment and career ads seeking to attract the world's best financial talent, ads for products and services and ads showcasing firms' performance and achievements. Specialist titles cover every financial topic imaginable – from investment, life insurance and pensions to banking, mortgage products and credit cards; from private equity and corporate finance to commodities and real estate; and from financial technology to debt and equity capital markets. Specialist titles

Press release headline	Organisation
'Triodos Bank comments on the FSA's complaints data'	Triodos Bank
'Contact HMRC – or your tax credits might stop'	Low Incomes Tax Reform Group
'Andrew Beal gives his outlook for the Asian economies and how they will continue to offer good value and long-term returns'	Henderson Managed Investment Trusts and Investment Companies
'Investors reminded of the effectiveness of regular saving this ISA season'	Invesco Perpetual
'ONS figures on energy bill no surprise'	uSwitch
'LV= offers enhanced allocation on flexible guarantee bond'	LV=
'Zurich welcomes Supreme Court decision on asbestos liability'	Zurich Financial Services
'Credit card holders to get a different kind of statement hitting their doormat this year'	UK Cards Association
'Audit reforms are needed but there should be a measured approach'	Investment Management Association
'Levy deadlines and failure scores'	Pension Protection Fund
'Financial stretch leaves Brits lagging decades behind their life plans, Skipton survey reveals'	Skipton Building Society
'Which? comment on FSA complaints data'	Which?
'OFT launches consultation on Competition Act procedures guidance'	Office of Fair Trading
'Illegal car sales on the increase'	Finance & Leasing Association
'Business, Innovation and Skills Committee report on debt management'	Debt Managers Standards Association
'March madness: annual surge in accidental damage claims as DIY season starts'	Churchill Insurance
'Nationwide launches new 75-day saver rate'	Nationwide Building Society
'TD customers focus on Gulf and take to Range'	TD Direct Investing
'Nationwide launches new issue of MySave Online Plus'	Nationwide Building Society
'Riots lifted lid on plight of forgotten families'	Family Action
'Tax campaigners criticise withdrawal of paper filing options for VAT returns'	Low Incomes Tax Reform Group
'FSA publishes six-monthly firm complaints data for the second half of 2011'	Financial Services Authority
'Ticking timebomb – nearly 1 in 7 UK households stuck on interest-only mortgages with no plan to pay off the debt'	Unbiased.co.uk
'UK growth worse than expected for final three months of 2011'	Schroders
'A current 2% discount on the 5% entry charge is available on all new ISA investments and transfers with Invesco Perpetual'	Invesco Perpetual
'Over one in three education workers have no idea how much they are currently due to retire on'	MoneyVista
'Latest white paper talks about the importance of culture, leadership and communication when developing wellbeing strategies'	Simplyhealth
'Barclays Stockbrokers sees increase in funds traded in an ISA'	Barclays Wealth
'Wesleyan shows continued growth in 2011'	Wesleyan Assurance Society
'Retired nation is sitting on £96.41 billion of personal debts'	MGM Advantage
'Stereotypical spenders? Male and female credit card usage revealed'	Santander

Table 21.2 A day of press releases in UK financial services (*source*: Headlinemoney.co.uk, table of press releases from March 2012.)

take a more in-depth and informed approach to financial stories than the generalist media, and will often champion a particular set of industry interests; hedge fund publications, for example, often tackle the prospect of increased hedge fund regulation across international jurisdictions.

The expansion of financial media to cover increased competition in financial markets has forced journalists to produce more copy with fewer resources. Financial journalists have therefore built a symbiotic relationship with PR practitioners to fill the resource gap, with the result that the financial media often appear to have higher levels of PR content than in other sectors (Davis 2007). Journalists and PR practitioners build relationships with each other through face-to-face meetings and telephone discussions, with PR practitioners providing story ideas and access to spokespeople. Prominent PR tools include press releases and other announcements, along with backgrounders, fact sheets, research, commentary, case studies, biographies and photographs. PR practitioners also organise events with journalists in mind, including company results presentations, product launches, briefings, press trips and site visits, as well as off-site corporate entertaining.

However, changes in media ownership – mergers and downsizing – have influenced the way that PR practitioners interact with the financial media. Increasingly, journalists have less time to meet face to face, and changing technology has also meant that journalists and PR practitioners interact more and more through websites and social media. In the UK, home to several financial centres, websites such as Business4Media and Headlinemoney.co.uk bring journalists and PR practitioners together to post news items or request case studies and contacts. Headlinemoney is an online information resource used extensively by the UK's money media, including financial journalists, in-house PR practitioners and PR firms. PR practitioners post company stories and other information on the site for journalists to access. Journalists, meanwhile, post requests for personal finance case studies, seeking, for example, homeowners who have 'locked into' a fixed-rate mortgage, or pensioners whose retirement products are performing below expectation.

The global financial crisis

Since the process of deregulation began reducing government power in Western financial markets in the 1980s, there have been a series of high-profile financial crises resulting in a loss of public trust in financial services. The implications of these successive crises for public relations are two-fold. Firstly, there is the question of whether PR played a role in helping these crises to evolve – this question is still to be meaningfully debated. One author

describes this glaring oversight as the 'elephant in the room' (Callaghan 2003). Veteran practitioner George Pitcher goes further, placing blame squarely at the feet of the public relations industry as 'the silver-tongued mountebank that has sold a perceived value as a fundamental value for a generation' (2008: 69). Pitcher singles out financial PR as complicit in contributing to a message that was 'only ever about boom and to hell with the bust' (2008: 69). Instead of debating its potential role in triggering crises, the PR profession has generally responded to financial crises by moving forward and 'setting things to rights' (PRSA 2003; Nicholas 2004). Typically, this takes the form of PR campaigns mounted to 'rebuild trust' in respective areas of finance. Such approaches raise a second question: is it either rational or ethical to rebuild trust in the financial sector before its weaknesses have been corrected? With the advent of the global financial crisis this question has become more salient than ever (see also Chapter 12 for a discussion on PR ethics).

In 2007, a global credit crunch – a freeze of lending in capital markets – helped trigger the global financial crisis in the following year. The crisis progressed in different phases, exposing endemic weaknesses within the global financial system, with attendant implications for PR in financial markets. For communicators operating on the 'factory floor', or wholesale financial markets, there remains the taxing issue of complexity associated with new and innovative products with daunting names such as Collateralised Debt Obligations (CDOs). Debt, credit and the derivatives market were relatively hidden from the public's view for a long time – what financial editor Gillian Tett (2009: 6) refers to as 'the iceberg problem', whereby mainstream media refrained from covering these markets because they were too technical and too dull. PR practitioners struggled to find journalists willing to talk about debt capital markets, and debt market players were content to avoid the limelight. Attempts to restore trust in these markets must surely require a wholesale translation of the language of capital markets, with PR at the forefront in communicating the technical aspects of finance.

For PR practitioners in retail financial markets, an important issue arising from the global financial crisis concerns the reputation of the banking sector – a reputation damaged by its role in helping to trigger the crisis through an inappropriate appetite for high-risk products and hardly mitigated by the banking sector's apparent refusal to mend its ways, despite hefty taxpayer bailouts in many countries. Negative public perception of banks and other financial institutions therefore tops the list of challenges faced by PR practitioners in affected markets (Makovsky & Company 2012). Various organisations have focused PR activity on addressing reputational issues in financial markets. At the national level, trade bodies

Picture 21.4 The Occupy movement has been at the vanguard of activism against financial capitalism (*source*: AFP/Getty Images)

such as London-based TheCityUK are working to educate opinion formers and the public about financial services' economic role and contribution. At the global level, various international institutions are redefining global financial architecture and engaging in PR activity to inform stakeholders of their progress. (See Explore 21.2.)

Perhaps the most crucial issue for PR in financial markets, arising from the global financial crisis, is the issue of global inequality. Globalisation was once heralded as the 'new knight to fight poverty' (Koku and Acquaye 2011: 354), yet after decades of market freedom, an astounding volume of wealth is now controlled by a small proportion of the world's citizens, many of whom are successful bankers, hedge fund managers and other financial professionals. A complex global debate has emerged, with PR playing a visible role in promoting different viewpoints; since the summer of 2011, the Occupy movement has been at the vanguard of activism against financial capitalism. The movement has crystallised in many cities around the world, with diverse groups participating in protests strategically organised under the Occupy banner. The many Occupy groups engage in PR activity to varying degrees. In another corner of this debate are groups that argue that an important way to achieve equality is to enable *more* people

Explore 21.2

Official voices of global finance?

Visit the websites of the following institutions and explore their media centres. Can you determine what are their key messages? Are those messages easy to discern, simple to understand? Who are their primary stakeholders? How do their various missions overlap?

Bank for International Settlements – http://www.bis.org/list/press_releases/index.htm

Financial Stability Board – http://www.financialstability board.org/list/fsb_press_releases/index.htm

International Monetary Fund – http://www.imf.org/external/news/default.aspx?pr

Global Financial Markets Association – http://www.gfma.org/news/?newsType=Press+Releases

World Federation of Exchanges – http://www.world-exchanges.org/news-views/press-releases

to access financial services. Ninety per cent of people in developing countries lack access to financial services from institutions, either for credit or savings – further fuelling a 'vicious cycle of poverty' (Hinson 2011: 320). NGOs such as Accion (accion.org) actively employ PR to promote financial inclusion. Interestingly, this same agenda has been adopted and promoted by financial institutions aiming to sell products and services in developing markets.

Summary

This chapter has provided a broad view of the ways that public relations is conducted in financial markets, on behalf of many special interests – some opposing, some overlapping. It is also an area of PR that will continue to experience change in the coming years as new financial centres emerge, and as technology and increased regulation continue to transform financial communication. For students and researchers in the field of PR, this opens up many interesting avenues for research, exploring areas such as the 'geographies' of PR in emerging financial centres. Too few studies deconstruct the work done by PR practitioners in financial markets: for example, there is potential to analyse the changing narratives of pilloried institutions such as banks since the global financial crisis. Aspiring researchers might uncover more hidden forms of PR activity, such as financial lobbying. It is equally important to explore the use of PR by less well-resourced organisations such as consumer groups and community finance. Meanwhile, financial markets offer varied career opportunities and PR specialisms for those keen to enter the world of finance. The ever-changing nature of financial markets is undoubtedly part of its appeal for those who take up the challenge of communicating about finance and its role in shaping the way we live.

Bibliography

Bourne, C. (2012). 'Producing trust in country financial narratives' in *Discourses of Trust*. C.N. Candlin and J. Crichton (eds). Basingstoke: Palgrave-Macmillan.

Brocklebank-Fowler, S. (2008). *Differentiation Wins the Day*. London: PR Week.

Callaghan, T. (2003). *Repent Professional Sins: Letter to the Editor*. Public Relations Strategist.

CIPR (2010). *State of the PR Profession Benchmarking Survey*. London: Chartered Institute of Public Relations.

Davis, A. (2007). 'The economic inefficiencies of market liberalisation: the case of financial information in the London Stock Exchange'. *Global Media and Communication* 3(2): 157–178.

Doyle, G. (2006). 'Financial news journalism: a post-Enron analysis of approaches towards economic and financial news production in the UK'. *Journalism* 7(4): 433–452.

Edelman (2011). *2011 Edelman Trust Barometer: Eleventh global opinion leaders' study*. New York, NY: Edelman.

Ehrlich, E. and D. Fanelli (2004). *The Financial Services Marketing Handbook: Tactics and techniques that produce results*. Princeton, NJ: Bloomberg Press.

FSA & Henley Centre (2005). 'Consumer Paper 35: towards understanding consumers' needs'. In Financial Services Authority, *Consumer Paper*. London: FSA.

Fulton, S. (2010). 'Personal view: one candle'. *CorpComms: The Magazine for the Corporate Communicator*, February: 46–47.

Henley Centre (2005). 'Consumer Paper 35: towards understanding consumers' needs'. London: FSA.

Hilton, A. (2008). 'Business news not taken seriously'. *PRWeek*, 12 December: 9.

Hinson, R.E. (2011). 'Banking the poor: the role of mobiles'. *Journal of Financial Services Marketing* 15(4): 320–333.

Koku, P.S. and H.E. Acquaye (2011). 'Who is responsible for rehabilitating the poor? The case for church-based financial services for the poor'. *Journal of Financial Services Marketing* 15(4): 346–356.

Makovsky & Company (2012). '2012 Makovsky Wall Street Reputation Study'. New York, NY: Makovsky PR.

Martin, R. (2002). *Financialization of Daily Life*. Philadelphia, PA: Temple University Press.

Nicholas, K. (2004). 'Financial services are passing the buck'. *PRWeek* 22.

Pitcher, G. (2008). 'Financial PR is no scapegoat'. *Profile: Chartered Institute of Public Relations*, December/January: 69.

Pixley, J. (2005). *Emotions in Finance: Distrust and uncertainty in global markets*. Cambridge, UK: Cambridge University Press.

PRSA (2003). 'A discussion on public trust'. *Public Relations Tactics*: 31–33.

Schlesinger, D. (2009). 'Transparency and the role of the media in China'. Paper presented at the Sinhua World Media Summit. http://blogs.reuters.com/reuters-editors/2009/10/08/transparency-and-the-role-of-media-in-china/

Tett, G. (2009). 'Icebergs and ideologies: how information flows fuelled the financial crisis'. *Anthropology News*, October: 6.

World Economic Forum (2009). 'The future of the Global Finance System: A near-term outlook and long-term scenarios'. World Economic Forum: Geneva, Switzerland.

Z/Yen Group (2012). *The Global Financial Centres Index 11*. London.

CHAPTER 22

Judy Strachan and Neil Kelley

Integrated marketing communications

Learning outcomes

By the end of this chapter you should be able to:

- define and discuss integrated marketing communications issues
- evaluate the importance of integrated marketing communications to organisations and their publics
- identify the key principles and methods used to integrate marketing communications activities
- apply this understanding to realistic and meaningful scenarios
- recognise integrated marketing communications activities through case examples
- apply key principles of integrated marketing communications to real-life scenarios.

Structure

- Definitions of integrated marketing communications (IMC)
- The marketing communications toolbox
- Segmentation, targeting and positioning (STP)
- Branding and integrated marketing communications
- Agency perspectives
- Planning for integration of the marketing communications mix

Introduction

As consumers, we all engage with and use a wide range of products (both goods and services) that a variety of organisations market to us. You'll have your own favourite brands, which you use on a regular basis, and have brands you aspire to own and use. Other people's favourite brands may be very different, but we all tend to feel more drawn to some brands than others. How does this happen? How do we develop a sense of a brand image that makes a brand 'for us' or 'not for us'?

The information we use to develop our sense of what an organisation, brand or product stands for comes from a variety of sources, but a major influence is how the marketers of the brand have communicated with us. When we think of marketers communicating with consumers we usually think of advertising, and advertising does have a strong influence. But there's more to communicating with consumers, and potential consumers, than advertising. Marketers have a range of communication methods they can use. Which ones they decide upon for a particular campaign depends on the brand and the people they believe form the market for that brand (the target market). Making

effective choices of which tools to use, how to use them and when to use them is the basis of integrated marketing communications (IMC) – a way of planning for, integrating, coordinating and evaluating the use of different ways to communicate with the target market, which results in a highly effective and cost-efficient package of communications (a campaign).

So what has this to do with public relations? In marketing terms, PR can be seen as one of the ways a brand or organisation can communicate with its target market. PR is, of course, used for lots of other purposes, but it is a widely used 'tool' of marketing communications. As a consumer you'll be familiar with lots of the other marketing communications tools as you're on the receiving end: you see advertising on the television, in magazines and on the backs of buses; you might be sent text messages or emails by brands you use; you go to sporting events or music festivals that are sponsored by brands; you're given special discount coupons to use when shopping; and much, much more. All of these things will have been planned as part of an integrated marketing communications strategy.

In this chapter, we take a closer look at integrated marketing communications – which we'll refer to by its acronym IMC – giving a more detailed and academic definition; describing the many different channels of communication that make up the IMC 'toolbox'; analysing the important concepts of segmentation, targeting and positioning; taking a look at why the concept of the brand is so vital; seeing how the suppliers of services to marketers, such as advertising agencies and PR agencies, handle the integration aspect of communications; and, finally, discussing the strategic planning process that supports the whole process of IMC. All of this is then pulled together in the closing Case study 22.1 of the IMC campaign for Dove.

As a future PR practitioner you may be involved in PR activities that are part of your organisation's or client's overall marketing communications strategy. Having knowledge of the IMC process and when and how PR fits in will be of great importance. In the world of marketing communications, it's not enough to just think of advertising; nor is it enough to just think of PR. All marketers need to think IMC.

Definitions of integrated marketing communications (IMC)

All organisations use marketing communications to get their message across to their consumer publics – or their 'target market' and 'target audiences', to use the language of marketing. As Shimp (2010: 7) says, marketing communications is a 'critical aspect of companies' overall marketing missions and a major determinant of their success or failure'. From the perspective of the managers of an organisation's marketing, what is needed, however, is not an ad hoc and almost random collection of messages going out, and that say different things. It's essential that every communication

is designed to support a brand – often referred to as consumer 'touch points' and portrays the brand in a way that is holistic, synergistic and consistent with the brand's image and values. This requires careful planning and coordination, and is why the concept of IMC was born.

IMC is a process. It is a series of intentional touch points that take place over time, but for every touch point to be as effective and efficient as possible, every detail needs to be planned. There must be an overall strategy for the IMC campaign, with clearly set objectives, before any activity can be implemented at a tactical level. Planning a brand's communications so that they fit into an overall IMC strategy is therefore a major part of marketing directors' and marketing managers' jobs.

Once the strategy and objectives have been agreed, the next task is to work out which particular touch point

Think about 22.1 You as a brand consumer

You are probably reading this text as part of your public relations studies. But as a consumer you're on the receiving end of a variety of marketing communications. Think about all the ways the brands you use communicate with you. Which ways do you prefer? What appeals to you most? What does it take to make you pay attention, and even stop and read? Make some notes and discuss with your fellow students.

---

activities need to be created and implemented, and ensure that their production is managed so that the combined and synergistic message all touch points co-create fully supports the desired brand image. (See Explore 22.1.)

There is a wide range of activities (or tools of the marketing communications mix) that can be used, and an important part of IMC planning is ensuring that the most effective tools are chosen for a particular campaign. It's certainly *not* a case of trying to use as many different tools as possible, as this can spread a budget too far and make the whole campaign ineffective, but it is also rare for a campaign to be highly effective by using only one method of communication. The skill lies in knowing which tools will be most effective when combined together into a campaign.

An academic definition of IMC has been provided by Shimp (2010: 10):

IMC is a communications process that entails the planning, creation, integration and implementation of diverse forms of marketing communications that are delivered over time to a brand's targeted customers and

prospects. The goal of IMC is ultimately to influence or directly affect the behaviour of the targeted audience. IMC considers all touch points, or sources of contact, that a customer/prospect has with the brand as potential delivery channels for messages and makes use of all communications methods that are relevant to customers/prospects.

A different kind of definition, provided by Jim Taylor of agency G2 Worldwide (*Campaign* 2010: 4), is that IMC 'is about message and media and it is driven from the planning process. It involves strategy and creative thinking'. Simply using a variety of marketing communications activities, or tools, therefore doesn't make for IMC: the result can too easily be an ad hoc collection of activities that fail to support each other and leave consumers confused about what the brand or the company is saying. It is strategic thinking and planning that ensure only the best tools are chosen for a particular campaign, and that the tools selected work together in a synergistic and mutually supportive way to deliver a strong, meaningful and consistent message to the consumer. (See Think about 22.1.)

Explore 22.1

Which touch points?

Use your experience as a consumer of one of your favourite brands, and therefore a receiver of marketing communications messages aimed at you, to notice and find out how many different ways that brand is creating touch points for you to experience. Do they advertise on television, in magazines, on the Internet, via outdoor posters? Do they have a web page, and are on they on Facebook and Twitter? Do they ever send anything to you by text, email or post? Do they sponsor anything? Do they get media coverage that might have resulted from sending out a press release? What else might they be doing? Then study what you find and see how well you think it works together and is integrated: does it all seem to be part of an IMC campaign? (See also Table 22.2.)

Advertising source	Spend (£UK)	
Television	4,261 million	(4.2 billion)
Internet	4,064 million	(4.0 billion)
Newspapers	3,202 million	(3.2 billion)
Magazines	1,066 million	(1 billion)
Outdoor	873 million	
Radio	519 million	
Cinema	182 million	
Total advertising spend	**14,167 million**	**(14.1 billion)**

But this doesn't include *all* marketing communications so the spend by marketers on communications is considerably higher.

Table 22.1 UK advertising spend by media 2010 (£UK) (*source*: World Advertising Research Centre (WARC))

Mini case study 22.1
Cadbury's Gorilla

The Cadbury Gorilla campaign was unleashed in 2007 and became the most viewed and most popular commercial of the year. It went on to win several prestigious industry awards, including the IPA's Effectiveness Award 2007. The 'big idea' was that 'all communications should be as effortlessly enjoyable as eating the bar itself' (Fallon, Cadbury's advertising agency). The star of the commercial was the actor Garon Michael, who had been inside an ape suit in several films, including 2001's *Planet of the Apes*.

But the campaign wasn't just a short piece of film. The full campaign used the following marketing communications tools or channels, some of them planned right from the beginning and some of them added as the campaign gained momentum and became such a favourite with consumers:

■ Primetime television 90-second slot with the ad launched during *Big Brother*

■ Outdoor billboards and posters
■ Charity sponsorship via the 'Great Gorilla Run' in London
■ Online activity including competitions, games, downloads
■ Online presence on YouTube, Facebook and Twitter
■ Glass and a Half Full Productions' website with spoof ads made by the public
■ Cinema advertising
■ 'Advertising Avenue' attraction at Cadbury World
■ Media coverage and PR activity.

The campaign has been an international sensation and has become much-loved by the general public. It has won many prestigious advertising awards, including IPA, D&AD, Clio, Cannes and One Show. And, along the way, it has persuaded people to buy an awful lot of Cadbury chocolate! Sales of Cadbury Dairy Milk increased by 5.9 per cent year on year in the month the gorilla ad was released, reversing a previous pattern of declining sales volume.

Sources: Cadbury, IPA Effectiveness Awards 2008, Campaign

The marketing communications toolbox

For most consumers, the word 'advertising' is used to refer to a wide range of what marketers call 'marketing communications'. Advertising has a more precise definition than consumers often give it. So there is much more to marketing communications than advertising – just as you now already know that there is a great deal more to PR than sending out press releases. Advertising is just one of the tools in the marketing communications toolbox, albeit an important tool that often, but not always, accounts for the majority of a marketing communications budget. (See Table 22.1.)

So how else do brands communicate with their consumers, both users and potential users, in addition to advertising? You already know that PR can be used with a marketing purpose, and this chapter introduces you to all the other ways brands communicate with, and therefore build a relationship with, their target market.

Table 22.2 lists the different communications tools that marketers can use and integrate in order to create an integrated programme of touch points between their brands and their target markets. (See also Mini case study 22.1.)

These are all touch points: brand encounters, brand conversations, even moments of truth, as they have variously

been called. Notice the common theme here – the emphasis is on *the consumer* and their role: how consumers use touch points to engage with a brand, and create their own meaning and feelings to attach to the brand. And, in practice, they often overlap: for example, you can have a direct response advertisement in a magazine, a press release about the sponsorship of an event, a competition run on Facebook, or an email inviting people to an exhibition.

What's important about IMC, however, is that tools are chosen because they will work best for the brand, the campaign, the target audience and the budget. It's not about using as many as possible – too many and the budget is stretched too far and cannot create the required impact. As Nick Emmel of advertising agency Dare (Campaign 2010: 3) says, 'It is tempting to do all these things because they are there – when a press ad would have worked just as well . . . Consumers don't always want to interact with your brand on multiple levels and sometimes a single idea communication in one channel is enough.'

On the other hand, it's rare for only one channel or tool to be used, as too few components to an IMC and the message may miss important members of the target audience. Light (2004) argues that: 'The days of mass media advertising are over. Any single ad . . . is not a summary of our strategy. It's not representative of the brand message. We don't need one big execution of a big idea. We need one

Media advertising	Place advertising	Direct response advertising
■ Television	■ Posters	■ Direct mail
■ Radio	■ Billboards	■ Telephone
■ Magazines	■ Transportation (bus, train, tube, etc.)	■ Text messaging
■ Newspapers	■ Ambient	■ Email
■ Cinema		
■ Product placement		
In-store & point-of-sale	**Sponsorship & events**	**Personal selling**
■ Store signage	■ Sports sponsorship	■ Sales people
■ In-store signs and displays	■ Arts and festivals sponsorship	■ Customer service
■ Shopping trolleys	■ Charity sponsorship	■ Demonstrations
■ In-store events	■ Events	■ Presentations
■ Packaging design	■ Stunts	■ Exhibitions and fairs
■ Merchandising		
Promotions	**Online/digital**	**PR & journalism**
■ Special price offers	■ Social media	■ Press releases
■ Coupons and discount codes	■ Websites and forums	■ Media and trade events
■ Samples	■ Viral and buzz	■ Advertorials
■ Competitions and lotteries	■ Blogs	■ In-house magazines
■ Gifts and bonus packs	■ Gaming	■ Newsletters

Table 22.2 Touch points: the IMC toolbox (*source*: adapted from Keller et al. 2008 and Shimp 2010)

big idea that can be used in a multidimensional, multi-layered and multifaceted way.'

So what can all these communications activities in the toolbox do?

1. **Media advertising:** traditionally, advertising is defined as paid-for and non-personal messages transmitted through the media to a mass audience, from an identifiable advertiser or source with the purpose of persuading and/or informing. Media advertising includes the obvious things we know as advertising. So any marketing communications that are carried by a mass medium and paid for by the brand being promoted are classified as advertising.

2. **Place advertising:** paid-for messages put onto billboards and poster sites, on the sides and backs of buses, at underground, train and bus stations and at airports. Sometimes also called 'Out Of Home' (OOH) advertising.

3. **Direct response:** messages aimed at known consumers and addressed to them personally, usually sent by phone, email or post. Also includes advertising designed to persuade interested consumers to make personal contact with the advertiser by phone, mail or via a website.

4. **In-store and point-of-sale:** any communications taking place in a retail location. In-store communications can be posters and signage, three-dimensional displays and products put on special display in supermarkets, such as dump bins and gondola ends. The packaging of the product itself also has an important role to play in building a brand image.

5. **Sponsorship and events:** we're all familiar with football players and stadia being adorned with the logos of their sponsors. Music festivals are frequently linked with a sponsor, such as Carling's relationship with the Leeds Festival. Costa Coffee sponsor the Costa Book Awards, Jack Wills sponsor polo and sponsorship of a variety of sports, culture and music events forms a major part of Red Bull's marketing strategy.

6. **Personal selling:** sales people are engaging in marketing communications when they engage you in discussion, whether that's in a retail store, on the telephone or in your own home. Stands at exhibitions, shows and trade fairs involve conversations between people representing the brand and consumers. Anyone involved in customer service is providing a consumer touch point that has an impact on how someone perceives the brand.

7. **Sales promotions:** promotional activity tends to aim at a short-term result by providing consumers with a reason to 'act now', hence the emphasis is on an immediate and sales-orientated response. There are numerous ways to give consumers a money-off offer: having a sale, making a BOGOF (buy one get one free) or 3-for-2 (buy three and pay only for two) offer or giving out discount coupons and codes all have the same result – the consumer can buy the product for a lower price for a limited time. Other promotions offer free product: giving out samples, increasing the pack size for a limited time or giving away a free gift with purchase. Most promotional activity will, however, use one of the other categories of marketing communications tools to get the message to the consumer. Retailers might advertise a sale in a local newspaper, there might be a discount coupon to cut out in a magazine advertisement, or point-of-sale displays and posters may be created to highlight the offer.

8. **Online/digital:** this has taken on an increasingly significant role in IMC and there are now a number of digital media that can be used to communicate with consumers. Communications are predominantly delivered via online platforms, such as corporate websites, e-commerce stores, email and social networks, using the relevant technology such as computers, mobile phones and tablets. However, the influence of digital has begun to have a wider impact on many of the other communication tools, such as group buying and voucher codes in relation to sales promotion and, while not solely used as a communications tool, the success of the 'app' has led organisations to produce branded interactive content to engage with consumers.

There has, however, been a change in how marketers approach the choosing of the tools at their disposal. The

Picture 22.1 Zara, the international fashion design and retail brand, makes heavy use of store displays as one alternative to advertising (see Mini case study 22.3.) (*source*: Picture Net/Getty Images)

impact of technology over the last two decades has been phenomenal. New ways of reaching consumers have become available via the Internet and using mobile phones, and the introduction of smart phones and the app has created yet another way to engage and communicate with mass markets. In the UK, we now have access to an at times bewildering array of digital television channels, instead of the five analogue channels that were our only choices for many years (and going back further in time, the choice was simply two: BBC and ITV). Newspapers can now be read online instead of in print. All these changes mean consumers are now much more in control of what they access, when and how.

As Hughes and Fill (2007) have noted, these changes have created a shift in emphasis from *promoting to* consumers to *communicating with* consumers. There is now much more attention paid to how to create a two-way flow of communication with consumers who are active participants, rather than the now outdated view of passive

Think about 22.2

Communicating with teenagers

Teenagers and young adults – and particularly male teenagers – can be difficult consumer groups to reach, mainly due to not using a lot of mass media such as television, newspapers and magazines. But teenagers are not all alike. Think about how a marketer could reach a particular teenage audience. Which tools of the IMC toolbox would work best with which teenagers and young adults?

Think about 22.3

Which tools work with your mum?

Go through Table 22.2 and think about the different tools and how they can work differently for different people. Which tools seem to work for your mother (or any other older adult) and which ones work for you? Why is there a difference?

Mini case study 22.2
The campaign goes global

The concept of IMC allows multinational organisations to run truly global campaigns that have a local flavour embedded into each country's version; or, as contemporary jargon calls it, run a 'glocal' campaign.

The 'Hello I'm a Mac' campaign that ran in the UK, designed to persuade consumers to perceive the Apple Mac as preferable to, and much cooler than, a PC, starred David Mitchell and Robert Webb, already well known to audiences – and especially to the target audience for an Apple Mac campaign – for their comedy shows. But the campaign ran in a number of countries, and each one used a different pairing of celebrities that gave a local cultural twist to the Apple Mac versus PC idea.

In this campaign, a big idea was adapted to link into each country's cultural identity, turning a global campaign into a series of localised campaigns.

Mini case study 22.3
The no-advertising campaign

Zara, the international fashion design and retail brand, doesn't use media advertising except for local store-opening campaigns. But they make heavy use of the following, which they see as the most effective ways to communicate with their target audience:

- Store location
- Store window displays
- Interior design
- In-store displays
- Customer service
- Word of mouth
- PR

consumers who simply absorb the messages aimed at them. You only have to read the trade journals *Campaign*, *Marketing* and *Marketing Week* to realise that the talk these days is of consumer *engagement and participation*.

IMC, when planned for and executed well, is a highly effective and efficient way to reach the right consumers at the right time, and that encourages engagement and participation with brand communications in a way that ultimately benefits both consumers and brand owners. (See Think abouts 22.2 and 22.3 and Mini case study 22.2.)

Segmentation, targeting and positioning (STP)

For IMC to be successful, it has to be seen as a *strategic* process. As Fill (2011: 91) emphasises, taking a strategic perspective means making 'key decisions (about) the overall direction of the programme and target audiences, the fit with marketing and corporate strategy, the key message and desired positioning the brand is to occupy in the market, and the resources necessary to deliver the position and satisfy the overall goals'. Three key decisions to be made at the strategy stage are how to segment the market, which of those segments to target in a particular campaign and how the brand is to be positioned within the communications that will form the campaign. Making these key decisions is known as the STP process – **s**egmentation, **t**argeting and **p**ositioning.

Segmentation

No campaign can ever hope to be all things to all people. Segmentation involves dividing a market into groups that are distinctive, readily identifiable and reachable. Details of which segment(s) a campaign needs to appeal to and persuade then become an important part of the brief that goes to those responsible for coming up with the 'big idea' for the campaign.

The most common ways for marketers to segment mass markets are by:

1. *Demographics:* measurable characteristics of people, such as age, gender, occupation, income, education and socio-economic status (class).

2. *Geographics:* where people are located can have an impact on their consumer behaviour.

3. *Geodemographics:* refers to the particular location, and often type of housing, where people live. ACORN and Mosaic are commercially available classifications of geographic information overlaid with demographic information.

4. *Psychographics:* segments consumers by their preferences with regard to their lifestyle, interests, opinions, attitudes and personality.

5. *Behaviouristics:* categorises people by their consumer (buyer) behaviour, such as usage patterns, buying habits and spending priorities.

Segmenting consumer markets by brand usage and loyalty is also often used. Rossiter and Bellman (2005: 83) devised a way to categorise consumers by their relationship with a brand, dividing consumers into:

■ *Loyal brand users:* they may be loyal because they love the brand or they may be loyal out of habit and inertia, but they are the most important segment.

■ *Favourable brand switchers:* consumers who are willing to try new brands or often switch brands but on the whole tend to be favourable towards our brand.

■ *Other brand switchers:* again, are willing to try new brands or often switch brands but tend to favour a competing brand over ours.

■ *Other brand loyals:* have a favourite brand to which they are loyal, but it isn't ours. Can be difficult to persuade them to switch, even on a trial basis.

■ *(Potential) new category users:* consumers who have just entered the market for the category to which our brand belongs. Are open to trialling brands and can respond well to offers.

Which segment(s) an IMC campaign needs to be aimed at depends on the objectives of the campaign and is very much a strategic decision backed by the outcomes of market research and linked to the achievement of corporate and marketing objectives.

Targeting

Once the segments an IMC campaign needs to focus on have been determined, the actual target groups for the campaign can be isolated. Aiming at known and predetermined targets is essential if the communication messages that are to be created and implemented are to fulfil the campaign's objectives, as trying to be all things to all people usually results in bland messages that fail to have the desired impact.

It's important, however, to select targets that are reachable in practice. Fill (2011: 95) provides a useful summary of what to take into account when making targeting decisions. The target(s) chosen must be:

■ *Measurable:* easy to identify and measure

■ *Substantial:* provide a large enough pool of consumers

■ *Accessible:* must be able to be reached through marketing communications

■ *Differentiable:* must be clearly different from other target groups

■ *Actionable:* the IMC must be capable of actually reaching them.

As Hackley (2010: 85–86) points out, 'get it wrong, and all the effort is wasted. If the defined audience is too narrow then opportunities for consumer engagement will be lost . . . If the target group definition is too wide, then the impact may be lost or the campaign might be scheduled on a medium which the real targets don't use.' (See Explore 22.2.)

Positioning

Positioning is about how consumers in the market for the category think and feel about a brand in comparison to its competitors. Once a market segment and target for a campaign has been decided, the task is to work out how the brand needs to be positioned within the ensuing communications. A positioning statement needs to be written from the consumer's point of view and answer the important question, 'what's in it for me?'. What does the brand do for consumers, how does it benefit them, what emotional pay-off does it provide, and how does it differ from competing brands are important questions that marketing managers must be able to answer clearly, precisely and succinctly.

So positioning is about what goes on in the heads and hearts of consumers that makes them see one brand as different to another, even when the actual products are not all that different. Think about how soap powder, shampoos and toothpaste are given a competitive advantage that consumers believe in, even though their functional benefit is much the same. (See Think about 22.4.)

Successful brands have a consistent positioning over a long time, and consumers readily associate them with their positioning. Volvo has always been positioned as safe, Kellogg's Special K with keeping a trim figure and Primark for cheap, disposable fashion.

A useful way of categorising positioning stances is provided by Ouwersloot and Duncan (2008):

■ *Category positioning:* where a brand defines, creates or owns a category. Think of Heinz and baked beans ('Beanz Meanz Heinz'), Kleenex for tissues and Hoover for vacuum cleaners (although this is changing – see the next category).

■ *Unique product feature positioning:* based on something tangible or intangible that is genuinely unique about the brand. Price is used as a positioning stance

Think about 22.4   Positioning as competitive differential

Think about two brands that belong to the same product category, such as two different fashion stores or two different supermarkets. How do you think they might be positioning themselves so as to present themselves as different to their competitors?

by Primark in the category of fashion retail and by Aldi in the supermarket category. Dyson has been able to use unique product feature positioning by focusing on its bagless vacuum cleaner technology.

- *Image positioning:* creates differentiation on the basis of a created (or symbolic) association. Is often based on a deliberately created strong association that cannot be applied to competitors – think of ComparetheMarket.com and its association with meerkats.

- *Benefit positioning:* based on fulfilling a consumer need or desire. This can be a tangible need, as used by Toilet Duck, which focuses on the real benefit of its bottle design, or intangible such as the Lynx positioning focus on the symbolic desire of making young men irresistible to women.

Being able to write a highly useful and accurate positioning statement is a key skill of strategic marketing as it is how the brand is to be positioned to the targeted audience that drives the creative work that is subsequently produced. Some practitioners have taken the concept a lot further in recent years and considered the impact of everything the organisation does, how it acts and behaves, as being influential in their positioning. Graham Hales (2011: 140), Managing Director of Interbrand UK, puts forward that 'organisations need to align their brand (position) with all aspects of their operations, stretching across products and services, human resources practices, corporate behaviour, environments and communications'.

Explore 22.2

Analysing the target audience

Look in a magazine and study an advertisement. Then go online and find that magazine's Advertising Rate Card, which will provide details of who reads that particular magazine. Using this information and the content of the advertisement, what can you say about *who* is the target audience and *how* the brand is positioned?

Branding and integrated marketing communications

The idea of the brand – as opposed to the product or service being marketed, or the company doing the marketing – is now a major underpinning concept of marketing and IMC. As Moor (2007: 3) explains, 'the term branding has only come to prominence during the last 15 years. It was during the 1990s, in particular, that a previously diffuse set of practices – product design, retail design, point-of-purchase marketing, among others – became consolidated into an integrated approach to marketing and business strategy known as branding'.

There have been numerous attempts to define the term 'brand', with mixed results. The American Marketing Association (2012) online dictionary states a brand is a 'name, sign, symbol, or design, or a combination of them, intended to identify the goods or services of one seller or group of sellers and to differentiate them from those of the competition'. The problem with this definition is that it ignores the fact that a consumer's relationship with a brand is also about associations, beliefs, values and emotions that make the brand represent more than the sum of its part. Is a brand just a distinguishing symbol such as a logo?

Picture 22.2 Shopping for beauty products. Dove's Campaign for Real Beauty has been one of the more enduring IMC campaigns of recent years (*source*: Guido Mieth/Getty Images)

Rank	Previous rank	Brand	Region/Country	Sector	Brand value ($m)	Change in brand value
1	1	CocaCola	United States	Beverages	71,861	2%
2	2	IBM	United States	Business services	69,905	8%
3	3	Microsoft	United States	Computer software	59,087	−3%
4	4	Google	United States	Internet services	55,317	27%
5	5	GE	United States	Diversified	42,808	0%
6	6	McDonald's	United States	Restaurants	35,593	6%
7	7	intel	United States	Electronics	35,217	10%
8	17	Apple	United States	Electronics	33,492	58%
9	9	Disney	United States	Media	29,018	1%
10	10	hp	United States	Electronics	28,479	6%
11	11	Toyota	Japan	Automotive	27,764	6%
12	12	Mercedes Benz	Germany	Automotive	27,445	9%
13	14	cisco	United States	Business services	25,309	9%
14	8	NOKIA	Finland	Electronics	25,071	−15%
15	15	BMW	Germany	Automotive	24,554	10%
16	13	Gillette	United States	FMCG	23,997	3%
17	19	SAMSUNG	South Korea	Electronics	23,430	20%
18	16	Louis Vuitton	France	Luxury	23,172	6%
19	20	Honda	Japan	Automotive	19,431	5%
20	22	ORACLE	United States	Business services	17,262	16%

Table 22.3 The world's top 20 brands (*source*: Interbrand 2011)

De Chernatony et al. (2011: 28) define a brand as 'the result of a carefully conceived array of activities across the whole spectrum of the marketing mix, directed towards making the buyer recognise relevant added values that are unique when compared with competing products'. So the idea of brand adds value for the buyer (the consumer) and makes the brand appear different to competing brands. But what are those added values? Keller et al. (2008: 39) define them as 'other dimensions that differentiate it in some way from other products designed to satisfy the same need' and goes on to say that those differences 'may be rational and tangible or more symbolic, emotional and intangible'. Think about your own brand choices – is the brand of perfume you like wearing or the car you drive based purely on their functional benefit to you? Or are your preferences also to do with your emotional reaction to the brand and what it symbolises for you?

By including the idea of the symbolic value of a brand for the consumer, however, the image of the brand becomes something created by the consumer. Brand owners will, of course, work hard to try to engineer a positive brand image in the consumers that comprise their target market, but they're not fully in control as brand image is something that happens inside the minds, or hearts and heads, of consumers. But what will influence consumers in their creation of a brand image is how the brand has been communicated to them – which is why IMC and its strategically coordinated approach to consumer touch points is so important to the successful marketing of a brand.

Dahlen et al. (2010: 2) put the case for today's marketers needing to 'build a brand narrative – tell a brand story. That means having a big idea that is a platform for creating, involving and sustaining customer engagement'. Grant (2005: 12) claims that 'a brand is a cluster of strategic cultural ideas with an intention behind them'. And Hackley (2010: 20) argues that 'marketing communications do not simply portray brands; they *constitute* those brands in the sense that the meaning of the brand cannot be properly understood in separation from the consumer perceptions of its brand name, logo, advertising, media editorial, its portrayal in entertainment shows, peer comment and the other communications associated with it'.

Take a look at the list of the world's Top 20 brands by brand value (See Table 22.3). How many do you recognise? How often have you seen marketing communications from most of them? What kind of brand image do you have for the ones you know well?

How brands create added value for consumers has been broken down into its components by Feldwick (2002). He argues that the concept of the brand offers consumers:

- a recognisable and trustworthy badge of origin and authenticity
- a promise of performance and reliability
- a heightened pleasure, confidence and enjoyment
- transformation and intensification of experience
- a relationship due to the brand having a personality
- a social dimension that allows us to make a statement about ourselves.

Mini case study 22.4
The integrated brand campaign

The L'Oreal brand covers a number of product ranges: hair care, skin care, etc. Although each range has it own IMC campaign, there are links between them that serve to promote an overall L'Oreal brand strategy that results in a brand story that is independent of a particular produce range. The links are:

- 'Because you're worth it' tag line
- Use of celebrities known for their beauty and glamour
- Close-up photos of celebrities' faces (often retouched!)
- Heavy use of women's magazines, with ads for several different product ranges often appearing in the same issue.

Together, these form the added value that a brand provides, above and beyond a product's mere functionality, and all these aspects of what a brand offers consumers underpins today's successful IMC campaigns. (See Mini case study 22.4.)

Agency perspectives

'Clients need their agencies to offer an integrated communications solution which offers value and impact by using different communications channels in a single campaign . . . (But) with the flux of change in the advertising environment, advertising agencies cannot be expected to be the experts in every communication channel' (Hackley 2010: 7). IMC make obvious sense, but implementing true IMC can be a challenge for marketers. Ultimately, of course, it is for the marketer – as brand owner, brand custodian and holder of the budget – to be the 'conductor' who directs and supervises the activities of everyone involved in the planning, creation and implementation of a campaign. But when that involves a number of different agencies, who are experts in their specialist field but may not be particularly expert in other communications channels, 'orchestration' can be challenging and difficult to achieve. Such orchestration is often the responsibility of brand managers working with their marketing director.

But getting marketers and their agencies to agree on what constitutes IMC and who should 'run the show' isn't easy. Suzanne Bidlake, the Associate Editor of *Campaign* (2010: 3), comments that 'views on what integration means, how it affects agency structures, what type of agency is best to lead it and what is the smartest way to apply it to a client's business vary markedly'. If a brand manager uses the services of a creative advertising agency, a media planning and buying agency, a public relations agency, a direct marketing agency, a digital agency and a sales promotion agency, how can they ensure each agency produces work that is faithful to the brand but also coordinates with the work produced by the other agencies so that everything forms part of a true IMC? With difficulty! The emerging trend, however, is for the client to take a much more central role than in the past. Clients such as Diageo, Heineken and Unilever now employ their own planners (*Campaign* 2010: 5) in order to develop brand strategies, rather than depending on the input of their agencies. So although agencies will remain essential to marketers, they are increasingly being seen as providers of specialist expertise in a particular aspect of marketing communications, with the integration element the responsibility of an in-house brand custodian. That brand custodian needs to be particularly skilled in planning.

Author:	Dahlen et al. (2010)	Fill (2011)	Hackley (2010)	De Pelsmaker et al. (2007)
Analysis	Current brand evaluation	Context analysis	Brand research	Situation analysis and marketing objectives
	Analysis		Target audience	Target audience
Planning	Marketing communications objectives	Communications goals and positioning	Communications objectives	Communications objectives
	Planning	3Ps of comms strategy	Strategy, creative approach and media plan	Tools, techniques, channels and media
	Application	Coordination of communications mix	Action plan and tactics	Budgets
			Budget estimates	
Implementation	Implementation	Implementation		
Control	Evaluation	Control and evaluation	Effectiveness	Measurement

Table 22.4 Comparison of IMC planning frameworks

Planning for integration of the marketing communications mix

In order to deliver a successful integrated marketing communications campaign it is essential that everyone involved in its creation, delivery and measurement follow a logical, structured planning process. Table 22.4 considers four IMC planning frameworks put forward by academic authors. They all relate to the Analyse, Plan, Implement and Control (APIC) planning process framework put forward by Kotler et al. (2008) and have significant similarities with some subtle differences.

A simple way to see the planning process is to ask a series of questions:

■ Where are we?

■ What does 'where we are' mean?

■ Where do we want to be?

■ What STP factors and budget need to govern IMC activities?

■ What does the IMC need to say to the target audience?

■ How can the target audience be best reached?

■ How does this turn into creative ideas?

■ How do we measure the effectiveness of the resulting IMC?

Dahlen et al. (2010: 6) emphasise that IMC needs a holistic approach. This means ensuring that the planning process results in a campaign that has:

■ A dominant, coherent big idea (is creative)

■ A single voice (is single-minded)

■ Consistent appeal and appearance (is consistent)

■ Combined value-added effect (is synergistic)

■ Cross-media presence (is multifaceted).

A detailed and carefully thought through plan will then be used to brief each of the specialists involved in creating elements of the IMC to ensure that all elements combine and work together in a synergistic way.

Case study 22.1

Dove and the 'Campaign for Real Beauty'

Dove's 'Campaign for Real Beauty' has been one of the more enduring IMC campaigns of recent years. Beginning in 2003, it has now been around for a decade.

Dove as a brand dates from the 1950s, when it became the brand name attached to a facial and body cleansing bar produced to ease the suffering of burns victims during the Korean war. Today, the Dove brand is owned by Unilever, and Dove is the UK's top-selling cleansing bar. In 2010, 45 per cent of the UK population bought at least one Dove product from their range of facial cleansers, body washes, deodorants and antiperspirants, bath foams, body moisturisers, shampoos, hair conditioners, hair treatments and lip balm.

The development of a highly coordinated IMC strategy for the overall Dove brand has been instrumental in positioning Dove as an effective, good-value and much-loved brand that now dominates the personal care market. Since 2004, when Dove's 'Campaign for Real Beauty' was launched, the brand and its communications agencies have won prestigious awards for their IMC work including IPA Effectiveness, EFFIE and Cannes. The campaign has been handled by a number of different agencies over the years, including Ogilvy and Mather and Mother for UK advertising, and JCPR and Lexis for PR.

The beginnings of a communications colossus

The 'big idea' – or the creative platform on which the entire 'Campaign for Real Beauty' has been based – is to

Picture 22.3 Dove's 'big idea' is to redefine the notion of female beauty (*source*: Gregor Hocevar/Getty Images)

redefine the notion of female beauty. Ogilvy and Mather came up with the concept of providing consumers with what they called 'documentary evidence' instead of advertising evidence, using a range of marketing communications channels.

The campaign began with outdoor billboard sites and transport advertising before expanding into print and television. The creative approach involved six real women (with a different six being chosen for each country where the campaign was run), all wearing white underwear and photographed against a white background. Dove made a point of letting consumers know, through PR and their website, that the women in the ads were *not* professional models, and that the photographs used had *not* been retouched in any way. Brand management and their agencies agreed that the strategy used should defy traditional media approaches to beauty in light of the 'size zero' debate and photographic retouching controversies.

A series of print ads were then run using a tick box approach. Pictures of real women – with wrinkles, grey hair, freckles and other features not usually associated with traditional concepts of beauty – were run next to two tick boxes asking consumers questions such as 'grey?' or 'gorgeous?'. These ads carried the URL for the 'Campaign for Real Beauty' website, encouraging consumers to find out more and participate.

These two advertising components, combined with a website, were the basis of the campaign that is still running. It was based on a strategy of promoting the idea that 'real beauty' lies outside the norms portrayed in the media by creating supportive relationships with women in a product category that is often seen as having a negative impact on women's psyche, to the detriment of their self-esteem.

Integration at work

Initially, magazines, posters and the website were the primary tools used to communicate the message of the 'Campaign for Real Beauty'. Integration of these elements ensured the same message and creative appeal appeared in different media channels, so that a consistent and recognisable campaign was the result. The advertising and online content was supported by PR, with the women featured in the ads appearing on daytime television and in the national press (see *Daily Mail* feature of 4 May 2004), talking about not the Dove brand but the 'real beauty' focus of the campaign. In turn, the PR activity drove consumers to the website and created increased awareness of the advertising.

case study 22.1 (continued)

Other elements of this long-running IMC include:

- Sales promotion linked with ASDA
- Send off to Dove to receive free samples
- Dove 'Self-Esteem Fund' started in 2006
- Internal communications to support the campaign
- 'Dove Evolution' video/viral.

The creative approach was integrated across channels by being a major focus of the Dove website (www.Dove.co.uk with similar websites for other countries, such as www.Dove.us for the USA). The 'Campaign for Real Beauty' part of the website not only promotes the Dove range of products, but includes information, a forum where consumers can participate and chat to each other, videos, a section for younger girls focusing on self-esteem issues and a section for mums, teachers and mentors of young girls.

All the elements of IMC provide a consistent message and show a consistent brand identity. The result is that consumers are helped to develop a positive brand image for Dove, which has translated into sales success and increased market share.

Questions

- What different activities from the marketing communications toolbox do Dove use, and how do the activities link together to form an IMC?
- How have Dove segmented the consumer market, which groups of consumers do they segment and how do they position their brand?
- Which IMC activities do you believe would work well for a different brand of your choice?

Now refer to Think about 22.5.

Sources: Unilever (2011), Ogilvy and Mather, YouTube, *The Guardian, Daily Mail*

Think about 22.5   Dove's future campaign

This case study illustrates most of the points made in this chapter. It shows how IMC that are carefully planned from a strategic focus can take a 'big idea' and turn it into a long-running and highly successful campaign. But all plans need to be flexible and take into account changes within society. Where do you think Dove should take their 'Campaign for Real Beauty' in the future?

Summary

In this section, we have discussed how integrated marketing communications (IMC) is the way in which today's most successful brands present themselves to their target market, and is the framework within which anyone working in any area of marketing communications is now operating.

We've looked at how to define IMC, and examined the wide variety of activities that make up the marketing communications toolbox that become various touch points for consumers. Then we looked at the role of segmentation, targeting and positioning (STP) in producing an IMC strategy, and the importance of the concept of branding. Finally, we discussed IMC from an agency perspective, as this is proving to be an area fraught with difficulties.

Your career in public relations will no doubt see you working, at some stage, for a brand that has decided PR is an essential component of an IMC. Understanding how your specialist input needs to integrate with all the other components is now vital if you want to do the best work possible for your employer and your clients.

Bibliography

American Marketing Association (2012). 'AMA Dictionary'. www.marketingpowere.com accessed July 2012.

Campaign (2010). *What Next in Integration?* 3 December.

Dahlen, M., F. Lange and T. Smith (2010). *Marketing Communciations: A brand narrative approach*. Chichester: John Wiley & Sons.

De Chernatony, L., M. McDonald and E. Wallace (2011). *Creating Powerful Brands*. Oxford: Butterworth-Heinemann.

De Pelsmacker, P., M. Geuens and J. Van den Bergh (2007). *Marketing Communications: A European perspective*. Harlow: Pearson Education.

Feldwick (2002). 'What is a Brand?'. WARC Monograph. www.warc.com.

Fill, C. (2011). *Essentials of Marketing Communications*. Harlow: Pearson Education.

Grant, J. (2005). *The Brand Innovation Manifesto: How to build brands, redefine markets and defy conventions*. Chichester: John Wiley.

Hackley, C. (2010). *Advertising and Promotion: An integrated marketing communications approach*. London: Sage.

Hales, G. (2011). 'Branding' in *The Marketing Century*. J. Kourdi (ed.). Chichester: John Wiley & Sons.

Hughes, G. and C. Fill (2007). 'Redefining the nature and format of the marketing communications mix.' *Marketing Review* 7(1): 45–57.

Interbrand (2011). '2011 ranking of the top 100 brands'. www.interbrand.com accessed December 2011.

Keller, K.L., T. Aperia and M. Georgson (2008). *Strategic Brand Management: A European perspective*. Harlow: Pearson Education.

Kotler, P., G. Armstrong, V. Wong and J. Saunders (2008). *Principles of Marketing*, fifth European edition. Harlow: Prentice Hall.

Light, L. (2004). 'AdWatch: Outlook 2004' conference. New York, NY.

Moor, L. (2007). *The Rise of Brands*. Oxford: Berg.

Ouwersloot, H. and T. Duncan (2008). *Integrated Marketing Communications*. Berkshire: McGraw Hill Education.

Rossiter, J. and S. Bellman (2005). *Marketing Communications: Theory and applications*. London: Prentice Hall.

Shimp, T. (2010). *Integrated Marketing Communications in Advertising and Promotion*. USA: Cengage Learning.

Unilever (2011). 'Dove'. www.unilever.co.uk/brands/personalcarebrands/dove.aspx accessed October 2011.

CHAPTER 23

Ryan Bowd, Iain Sheldon and Ralph Tench

Sponsorship

Learning outcomes

By the end of this chapter you should be able to:

■ define what sponsorship means
■ recognise different types of sponsorship activity
■ understand what these different types of sponsorship can do and how they work
■ understand the types of sponsorship and the role different audiences and parties play in the process of leveraging a sponsorship
■ understand the ways by which sponsorship can be enacted and developed
■ critically evaluate sponsorship as an effective communication tool.

Structure

■ Sponsorship: an overview (facts and figures)
■ Definitions of sponsorship
■ Why is it so popular and how does sponsorship work?
■ Developing a sponsorship strategy
■ Activation strategies: six In-depth case studies
■ The role of PR
■ Measuring success (evaluation and control)

Introduction

Sponsorship is ever-present in our society – it underpins and enables key sporting, art, societal, industrial and political events. Key shared global experiences, such as the Olympics, football (soccer), rugby and cricket world cups, moments such as Austrian Felix Baumgartner's world record parachute jump (in 2012 he broke the speed of sound at an estimated 1,342.8 km/h jumping from the stratosphere), down to the smallest art gallery show or local children's football team trip to a tournament, are all made possible by sponsorship of various forms.

The word is ubiquitously linked to financial assistance; however, more appropriately, it can be simply described as an exchange relationship whereby one entity (company, individual, government, etc.) supports another entity (company, team, individual, league, venue, event, etc.) that controls a 'sponsorship property' via financial or 'value in kind' (VIK) support in return for a series of 'sponsorship rights' and 'sponsorship category'. This might be GE's sponsorship of the Olympic Games, O2's sponsorship of the England Rugby Football Team, Emirates' sponsorship of the new cable car in London, England or Veolia's sponsorship of the Natural History Museum and BBC's Wildlife Photographer of the Year awards.

Like other specialist areas of communication, sponsorship has some key terms and language that are important to understand when talking about the practice. Box 23.1 describes some of the key terms that will enable you to understand and engage in the language of sponsorship.

There are a variety of reasons why an organisation may get involved with sponsoring, and this chapter will explore many of these possibilities. Figure 23.1 identifies eight grouped reasons for an organisation to get involved in sponsorship and also identifies where some of the discussions on these topics lie outside this text. These eight reasons are:

1. To support products and services (Veoila's sponsorship of the Wildlife Photographer of the year competition internationally, that supports its commitment to responsible business.).

Box 23.1

Key terms for sponsorship

'Sponsorship property'

A term historically used to describe the entity that can be sponsored. Typically, sponsorship properties have been:

- Awards (Man Booker prize for literature in the UK or Veoila's Wildlife Photographer of the Year)
- Content/programming (such as books, magazines, newspapers, television shows, programme slots, movies, music videos, YouTube, Facebook or other digital content)
- Events (political party conferences, awards, celebrations, launches, sporting games or tournaments, arts or cultural events, expeditions, or record attempts and other 'firsts')
- Individuals (adventurers, explorers, musicians, writers, artists, chefs and athletes; from local emerging talent to global superstars)
- Objects (buildings, planes, trains, boats, statues, *objet d'art*)
- Organisations/groups (from museums, art galleries, schools and universities to bands and professional associations)

- Sporting leagues (such as National Basketball League, National Football League, Premiership Football, Major League Baseball and more)
- Systems (transport [train, metro or light rail], waterways, roads, etc.)
- Teams (from mainstream to niche sports, from the grassroots of sports [local youth team] to the biggest teams on the planet, such as Manchester United and Real Madrid football [soccer] clubs and the New York Yankees in baseball and the LA Lakers basketball team)
- Venues (such as stadia and arenas).

But any 'rights' that are for sale or can be agreed could be classified as such. The entity that controls a sponsorship property is described as the 'rights holder'.

'Value in kind (VIK)'

'The use of goods or services in exchange for sponsorship rights'. These goods and services can take the form of provision of physical products, such as clothing, equipment or food and drink products (IEG Sponsorship Report 2008). An example of this could be a sports nutrition company's sponsorship of a sports team, such as Gatorade's sponsorship of NFL American football teams in the United States.

box 23.1 (continued)

Service value in kind sponsorships can range from traditional consumer service sectors, such as accommodation, catering or travel, through to corporate services such as cleaning, accounting and legal and consulting services such as PR itself. As an example, most London 2012 Olympic supplier or provider sponsorships were based around a required service for the Games; these include Holiday Inns (Intercontinental Hotel Group) running the Olympic Athlete Village, Freshfield's provision of legal support or Deloitte's accounting support of the Olympic Games.

Additionally, value in kind could simply be the provision of staff time to carry out roles required by an organisation, such as marshalling at a sporting event.

'Sponsorship category'

'Sponsorship category' is a term used to describe the area of exclusivity a sponsor has with respect to a sponsorship property. Categories are designed to protect the sponsor and also enable the sponsorship property 'rights holder' to sell multiple sponsorships without there being a perceived clash. A sponsor will expect to be 'the only company within its product or service category associated with the sponsored property' to protect its ability to derive value from the sponsorship (IEG Sponsorship Report 2009). There are no hard or fixed categories for a sponsorship property; they tend to develop logically to match the available 'rights'. Title sponsors of a property, i.e. those with what is referred to as naming rights, tend to get both that category and their own product and service category. It is also not uncommon for a sponsor to secure multiple categories.

As an example, the Virgin Active London Triathlon (the world's largest with 13,500 participants in 2012) had the following partners with the following categories (authors' interpretation):

■ Title sponsor and health club: Virgin Active Health Club

■ Timing and watch categories: Timex

■ Sports hydration: Gatorade

■ Sports nutrition (foods): Maxifuel

■ Wetsuit and clothing: Speedo

■ Shoes: Skechers

■ Accommodation: Crowne Plaza

■ Retailer: TRI UK

■ Official photography: Marathon Photos

■ Official charities: Cancer Research UK and Wellchild

■ Fundraising: Virgin Money Giving

■ Media partners: Triathlon Plus and Tri247.com

From this we see that the rights holder has managed to create a diverse list of categories, which in some cases has allowed them to work with two competitive brands in Gatorade and Maxifuel (which for one reason or the other have decided to coexist) and in some cases even sees multiple organisations sharing one category.

'Rights holder'

This is the individual, organisation or business that owns or has licensed the sponsorship property and its rights.

'Sponsorship rights'

'Sponsorship rights' or the 'rights' is a term used to describe what a sponsor gets in return for their financial or value in kind support of a sponsorship property. These rights are usually assigned in a legally binding contract, along with the sponsor's category or categories being defined. These may include, but are not limited to;

■ **Naming rights**: often called 'title sponsorship' rights, where a sponsor has the right for the sponsorship property to be named after them. Examples include the O2 (North Greenwich Arena) in London, England, or the Barclay's Centre in Brooklyn, New York.

■ **Branding rights**: the rights for a sponsor to have branding on, at or around the sponsorship property, such as branding on the pitch sides of sporting events.

■ **Hospitality rights**: the rights for a sponsor to conduct hospitality around, at or on a sponsorship property.

■ **Image and name rights**: the rights for a sponsor to use the sponsorship property's name or image(s) in their own communications, such as the rights of a company such as Nike to use the images of the famous athletes they work with in their advertising, PR, marketing and online.

■ **Staff, customer and stakeholder engagement rights**: these are the rights that allow the stakeholders of a sponsor to engage with the property. These could be an athlete or team providing access, coaching, insight or unique experiences for a sponsor's audiences. An example of this might be an F1 team offering a driving experience for customers and staff of its sponsor, or a Tour De France cycling team taking someone, such as a key business influencer of an organisation, in the team car during a stage.

Explore 23.1   Partnership benefits

With a plethora of sponsorships available in the market, it is crucial for public relations (PR) practitioners to recognise and answer the following questions. You can also think about how you would answer them for a given sponsorship you know about or are interested in:

1. Why should we sponsor?
2. What are our (corporate/organisation) goals and objectives?
3. How does the property fit with our brand company?
4. What are the opportunities and what are the threats to working with the sponsorship property?
5. How will we measure our investment and its return?
6. How will we decide if we are to do it again?

This support sometimes is through brand linkage or it can be through direct sales delivery. Many sponsors are able to track the direct sales increase from their involvement.

2. To build on media interest (some events make news on their own, such as individual challenges like Felix Baumgartner's high-altitude parachute world record, sponsored by Red Bull).

3. To reinforce or articulate the corporate identity – the brand. Sometimes it is useful to reaffirm the brand identity by sponsoring something that has positive associations for customers and other stakeholders (see Mini case study 23.1). Other times something is required that will project an existing or new attribute to stakeholders, and the best way to do this is to borrow or leverage a clearly visible attribute from a third party.

4. To build goodwill. This can be done through cause-related marketing initiatives and community activity, such as GE Capital's Community Triathlon masterclass (see Case study 23.6).

5. As part of an integrated campaign to raise awareness in specific stakeholder groups ranging from customers and the media to key retailers (see Case study 23.4).

6. In place of advertising. Tobacco company Philip Morris International (currently with Ferrari) and contraceptives company Durex (previously with Hispania Racing) both sponsor(ed) Formula 1 to get around advertising/marketing regulations in various markets.

7. Staff engagement. Using sponsorships as a vehicle to build staff engagement with an organisation and brand affinity and understanding (see Case study 23.5).

8. Lobbying. Sponsorship can be used as a lobbying tool, either through hospitality moments that enable engagement (though, as an example, in some countries (such as the UK) laws have been enacted to try to minimise this) or affinity through showing a mutual interest or an investment in something that the organisation being lobbied is interested in or passionate about.

In this chapter we will discuss sponsorship in its broadest sense but with a focus on the commercial application of the practice, and a heavy but non-exclusive case discussion of sport sponsorship. Sponsorship of – and investment in – more community-based initiatives is further explored elsewhere in the text.

Mini case study 23.1
Shell Guide

The first *Shell Guide to the English Countryside*, aimed at weekend motorists, was published in June 1934 and offers an excellent example of how sponsorship can work.

Legend has it that the editor John Betjeman (later Poet Laureate) worked next door to the publicity manager of Shell-Mex Ltd., Jack Beddington, and the two men shared a love of the English countryside. They produced a trial guide, for a mere £20, and presented it to Shell, which then agreed to support the project financially.

The idea of a comprehensive country guide series exclusively associated with the corporate name and logo proved to be a success story for the oil company. The guidebooks were not only to become a distinct compendium of the English countryside, they also were hugely successful and thus prestigious communication for their sponsor. The financial liaison continued until the mid-1980s and the guides still create goodwill among nostalgic readers and collectors. Today the Shell brand name is an integral part of all major motor sport events. With the help of the sponsorship of social, ecological, scientific and cultural events, the motor oil company continues to project its image as a good corporate citizen.

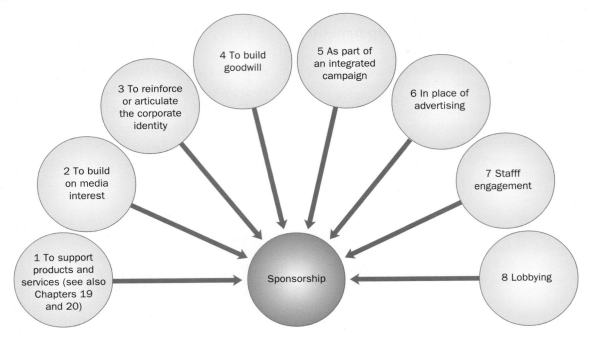

Figure 23.1 Reasons for sponsoring (*source*: Bowd et al. 2013)

Picture 23.1 Austrian Felix Baumgartner and his 2012 altitude parachute jump (*source*: Red Bull Handout/Red Bull Content Pool/Corbis)

Sponsorship: an overview (facts and figures)

With the multitude of reasons for an organisation to engage in sponsorship, its growth as a diverse communication tool has been exponential over the past decades. The sponsorship industry has grown from a modest $6 million in the early 1970s into a $48.6 billion business today, with Germany, Japan, the UK and the USA being the lead markets and India and Brazil among the emerging key markets (IEG Sponsorship Report 2012a). Figure 23.2 illustrates overall growth of sport sponsorship globally by region; an examination of the figures illustrates that sport accounts for the lion's share of global spend (Sport Business International 2010).

In the future, it is expected that sponsorship growth will continue globally, but that this growth will be around 4 to 5 per cent per annum, with emerging markets such as China, Asia and South America (encouraged by the Rio 2016 Olympics) driving the growth at a greater rate than the more established European and North American markets (IEG Sponsorship Report 2012a).

Though not currently experiencing the highest rate of growth, by far the biggest sponsorship market globally is the USA. The IEG Sponsorship Report (2003) estimated the market size to be about £8 billion and in 2011 this had

Total sponsorship revenues by region ($m)

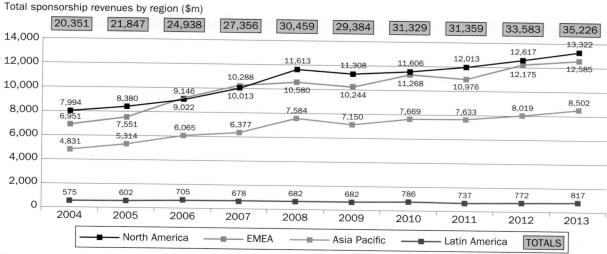

Source: PricewaterhouseCoopers LLP (UK), Wilkofsky Associates

Figure 23.2 Total (sport) sponsorship revenues by region (*source*: Sport Business International 2010)

2011 rank	Amount	Company	2003 top 10 ranking
1	$340m–$345m	PepsiCo, Inc.	1
2	$265m–$270m	The Coca-Cola Co.	4
3	$255m–$260m	Anheuser-Busch InBev	2
4	$215m–$220m	Nike, Inc.	5
5	$175m–$180m	AT&T, Inc.	6
6	$170m–$175m	General motors Co.	3
7	$150m–$155m	Toyota motor Sales USA, Inc.	Outside top 10
8	$135m–$140m	millerCoors LLC	6
9	$135m–$140m	Ford motor Co.	8
10	$135m–$140m	Adidas North America, Inc.	Outside top 10

Table 23.1 Top 10 US sponsors (*sources*: IEG Sponsorship Report 2012b)

grown to about $18.11 billion (IEG Sponsorship Report 2012a). This growing industry is fuelled not only by moderate budget increases from established sponsors but also from first-time investors. In the light of increased competition and new technologies that allow an advert-free media environment, US companies are looking into alternative promotion possibilities. As such there has been an increasing fragmentation in the North American sponsorship market, with a larger number of minor deals by small firms replacing major sponsor deals. That said, it is still the multinationals that dominate the industry, as is shown in Table 23.1, and have done for the last decade, with there being great consistency among the top 10.

Even more impressively, all this growth takes place in an environment of increased sponsorship literacy (see Think abouts 23.1 and 23.2).

Think about 23.1   Technology's impact on advertising

Consider some of the technological developments that are affecting traditional marketing techniques and encouraging alternative approaches to communication, such as sponsorship.

Feedback

In this context of developing technology, consider innovations such as TiVo and other set-top or TV-integrated programme recorders that digitally record TV programmes and therefore make it possible to cut out any commercial breaks in the programmes you watch.

Also consider other forms of on-demand content, such as YouTube and social networks such as Facebook, and how 3G/4G-enabled tablets and smart phones are able to minimise the effectiveness of advertising and marketing channels through their different interfaces.

Think about 23.2   An age of sponsorship literacy?

As far back as 2004 a study by Mediaedge (see Figure 23.3 later on) examined particular target groups to discover whether some sponsorship activities could be more effective than others. Fifteen to twenty-four year olds seemed especially receptive to sponsorship messages, whereas the support of good causes (CRM, community and societal sponsorship) cut through the information clutter of all age groups. However, in 2004 there was not the same prevalence of consumer awareness of sponsorship activities as now and, one could say, acceptance of the need for sponsorship. As an example, the James Bond film *Skyfall* came under some criticism for the prevalence of sponsorship in the film, particularly Heineken's drink sponsorship that saw the Bond character switch from his classic Vodka Martini to that particular beer as his drink of choice in an estimated $45 million deal (Moviefone 2012). With respect to this criticism, the film's lead actor, Daniel Craig (who plays Bond), commented: 'This movie costs a lot of money to make, it costs nearly as much again if not more to promote, so we go where we can. The great thing is that Bond is a drinker, he always has been, it's part of who he is, rightly or wrongly, you can make your own judgement about it, having a beer is no bad thing, in the movie it just happens to be Heineken' (Moviefone 2012). Do you think this had a detrimental effect on the movie? Also, can you think of other situations where the consumer literacy of sponsorships could either be negative or positive for a brand?

Feedback

In this case, as the Bond franchise is so inextricably linked with products such as the Omega watch, cars including Aston Martin and BMW and phones such as Nokia, one could see that the consumer will accept Daniel Craig's defence, coupled with Heineken's clever leveraging of their sponsorship that they are staying true to the spirit of the classic film franchise (www.heineken.com/gb/jamesbond/start/crack-the-case.aspx). Therefore it is unlikely that Heineken did not benefit from this activity. Consumers or audiences may reject sponsorships when they feel that the sponsor has no right to be in the space and that their activation is not true to the 'sponsorship property's' brand or values. As an example, in 2003 Cadbury created a cause-related marketing campaign to provide sports equipment for schools, through the collection of vouchers on Cadbury's packaging. In this case the chocolate manufacturer and the athletes they sponsored to endorse the programme came under huge criticism for what was perceived as a brand whose products lead to obesity using sport and sponsorships in sport in a way that would only perpetuate obesity (*The Guardian* 2003). Interestingly, and insightfully, Cadbury learnt from this and repositioned their involvement in sport as the official treat to the London 2012 Olympic and Paralympic Games – to high levels of consumer and stakeholder approval – thus articulating an understanding of where their products and brand could sit alongside the values of the sponsorship property.

Definitions of sponsorship

With its huge growth and wide reasons for sponsorship engagement, it would be prudent (before continuing) to examine the different definitions and perspectives on sponsorship itself. Previously some of the key sponsorship lexicon has included terms such as: sponsorship property, sponsorship right, sponsorship category, and kinds of sponsorship, among others; however, what exactly is a 'sponsorship' and a 'sponsor' have not been fully defined.

From all of this, if you were asked to explain what sponsorship is, you would probably say that it refers to any form of financial or in-kind support for a specific person, event or institution – with or without a service in return. You may also describe the term using your own experience of observing a major sporting event as an example (see Think about 23.1.)

Maecenatism

As a starting point for reflection, a historical perspective helps to shed light on the origins of the concept of sponsorship. Corporate contributions to culture, sport or social events have a long tradition, which can be traced back to Gaius C. Maecenas (70 BC–8 BC). As a material supporter of contemporary poets such as Horace and Virgil, his name is remembered as a generous patron of fine arts. Despite the noble image still associated with his name, the Roman diplomat and counsellor to Octavian (later Emperor Augustus) exercised patronage as a political means end strategy. If applied to Figure 23.1 this could be interpreted as 'sponsorship as lobbying'. That is, Maecenas used the communication channel of his times publicly to praise the reign of his friend Octavian.

Nevertheless, 'Maecenatism' today stands for the altruistically motivated support of culture and communities, where the support idea and not the association with a specific patron/organisation is to the fore; in other words, where the receiver not the donor is the main purpose or focus.

Charitable donations

Closely connected to the concept of Maecenatism is the act of charitable donations. As an expression of charity it is again the altruistic (concern for other people) motive that dominates the support process. Social considerations play an important role, and in its original meaning no immediate advantages such as image promotion or the representation of the donor as a 'good' citizen are being sought. Another significant aspect of charitable donations is that control is not assumed over the beneficiary or over the use of the funds. Despite this blueprint, charitable donations do present the opportunity for raising an organisation's public profile. Think, for example, about the naming of donors in TV charity shows such as Comic Relief and Sport Relief in the United Kingdom, or the American TV channel PBS and its various telethons, or the financial support of political parties. (See Think about 23.3 and Explore 23.2.)

> ### Think about 23.3
>
> ## Sponsorship of events you know
>
> Think about the main sponsor of your favourite sports personality or team and the way this sponsorship is promoted. You recognise sponsorship when you see it, don't you? On second thoughts, however, you may have come across its broader colloquial use: students might refer to their parental financial help as 'sponsoring'; interest groups donate money for political campaigns in Germany, for example (political parties around the world usually have to disclose any donation of more than a certain threshold amount – in the UK this is a figure of £7,500 [$12,000]); and trusts support social projects (Electoral Commission 2012).
>
> ### Feedback
>
> Although these are all examples of sponsorship, they do not adequately reflect its full scope, nor do they distinguish between related concepts such as Maecenatism, charitable donations or corporate philanthropy.

> ### Explore 23.2
>
> ## How a campaign can evolve
>
> The bi-annual BBC television-broadcasted (in the UK) Comic Relief appeal is a major event, which reaches out to the public for donations. The appeal's 'corporate partners' include major UK brands such as Sainsbury's and British Airways. Find out how companies can benefit from being associated with the charity by going to www.comicrelief.com/partners/corporate-partners/long-terms-partners

Corporate philanthropy

The dual purpose of corporate social responsibility and market orientation is reflected in the term 'corporate philanthropy'. More than the no-profit, no-win paradigm of charity donations, corporate philanthropy embraces more directly the idea of competitive advantages (Porter and Kramer 2002). By linking corporate giving to business-related objectives, focused charitable investments can be more strategic than unplanned, one-off donations. It allows donations to become part of a proactive communication approach aimed at commercial capitalisation. Contrary to the concepts described earlier, the spender sees to it that the philanthropic activities are closely connected to the corporation (or its objectives). In return for

Think about 23.4

Making donations

The next time you come across a charity appeal, ask yourself what motivates you to make – or refuse – a donation.

Feedback

In the corporate world, the art of giving is not only benevolent in nature, in many cases more tangible reasons, such as taxation laws, may drive corporate donations. Regardless of the intentions, charitable donations can be seen as a development of Maecenatism and in general describe a unidirectional, or one-way, relationship. Commercial advantages or expectations, such as corporate visibility or goodwill, here play a minor role, as unlike in a sponsorship they are not leveraged beyond what the receiver of the donation promotes.

Mini case study 23.2
Red Products (RED)™

(RED)™ Products is a unique cause-related marketing initiative. In this case, it was initiated not by a corporate organisation but by the supporters of a cause – specifically the joint desire of U2 rock star and activist Bono and philanthropist Robert Shriver to fight the AIDS disease in Africa. The (RED)™ is licensed to companies who create red products where a portion of the profits of each sale go to a charitable partner (www.theglobalfund.org), who then carries out the 'brand' mission.

Brands benefit by tapping into the consumer's desire 'to do good' and create an additional reason for their product to be chosen over a competitor's. This unique model has seen engagement from brands including Apple, American Express, Beats by Dr Dre, Nike and Starbucks. For more information visit: www.joinred.com/aboutred/how-red-works/

the financial or in-kind support the corporation may publicise these efforts. A historical example of this was the *Shell Guides to the English Countryside*, discussed in Case study 23.1. A modern example of corporate philanthropy at work in the United States is the work of the bank JP Morgan Chase & Co. in celebrating Dr Martin Luther King, Jr and preserving his legacy by carrying out a vast amount of philanthropic initiatives in a cohesive programme (JP Morgan Chase & Co. Sponsorships; JP Morgan Chase & Co. MLK).

Cause-related marketing (CRM)

In contrast to the concepts previously described, cause-related marketing relates solely to profit objectives. Companies financially contribute to good-cause events, movements or organisations in return for exposure and association. The main focus of support is image exploitation and the hope for enhanced corporate reputation. Unlike the concept of corporate philanthropy, cause-related marketing is transaction-based and clearly not driven by altruistic motives. Target groups for cause-related marketing include not only present and potential customers, but it can also prove effective in reactivating employee motivation as well as attracting future candidates. Building on a reciprocal partnership, the integration of communication and promotion are of vital importance. In the build up to the 2012 London Olympic Games the UK saw a plethora of sport-related cause-related marketing initiatives, with brands looking to capitalise on the nation's affinity for sport. One such example was the highly commended Jaguar Academy of Sport that supported

75 young athletes over the three years leading up to London 2012. The programme provided financial and sport 'educational' support via the UK's leading elite sport development charity, SportsAid, with the help of British sports stars. One academy athlete, Jade Jones, went on to win gold in Taekwondo. Jaguar has leveraged the academy in various PR and external and internal marketing initiatives. Another very different CRM programme is outlined in Mini case study 23.2 (see Chapter 15).

Sponsoring

'Sponsoring' is derived from the Latin word *spondere* (or 'promise solemnly'), hence its use as formula for prayer (*sponderis*) in a Christian context. The derivative word 'sponsor' was used for 'godparent', which is also the original English meaning. A sponsor is defined by the *Collins English Dictionary* (2012) in the following ways:

1. 'a person or group that provides funds for an activity, esp:

   a. a commercial organisation that pays all or part of the cost of putting on a concert, sporting event, etc.

   b. a person who donates money to a charity when the person requesting the donation has performed a specified activity as part of an organised fundraising effort.'

2. 'a person or business firm that pays the costs of a radio or television programme in return for advertising time'

3. 'a legislator who presents and supports a bill, motion, etc.'

Think about 23.5

Definitions of a sponsor

Which of the Collins definitions of a sponsor do you think is closest to the concept discussed in this chapter?

Feedback

The first and second definitions are closest to the concept we are discussing. However, broadcasting is not the only media space that is paid for by a sponsor.

4. '*also called*: godparent:

   a. an authorised witness who makes the required promises on behalf of a person to be baptised and thereafter assumes responsibility for his Christian upbringing

   b. a person who presents a candidate for confirmation'

5. 'a person who undertakes responsibility for the actions, statements, obligations, etc. of another, as during a period of apprenticeship; a guarantor.'

Alternatively, business knowledge site Investopedia defines corporate sponsorship more specifically as: 'A form of marketing in which a corporation pays for all or some of the costs associated with a project or program in exchange for recognition. Corporations may have their logos and brand names displayed alongside that of the organisation undertaking the project or program, with specific mention that the corporation has provided funding. Corporate sponsorships are commonly associated with non-profit groups, who generally would not be able to fund operations and activities without outside financial assistance. It is not the same as philanthropy.'

These definitions reveal three broad dimensions to sponsorship in a marketing and PR construct:

1. it entails motives for the support by the sponsor and the rights holder;

2. there is a relationship formed between spender (sponsor) and receiver (rights holder); and

3. it generates publicity for the sponsor and potentially the sponsorship property or its rights holder

A fourth dimension

However, the authors would contend that these definitions are lacking one key aspect in order for marketers and PR practitioners to derive maximum success: the opportunity to derive additional value for the organisation with varied stakeholders. This is what the sponsor is increasingly paying for: the *opportunity* to use that sponsorship. In the same way that you as an individual will only derive full benefit from your gym membership by actually committing to using the gym, a sponsor will only get full value from their sponsorship by committing to actively *use* the rights they have bought.

Figure 23.3 shows graphically the important elements of sponsorship, some of which have already been covered, others we will take a more detailed look at. The figure

Figure 23.3 What is sponsorship? (*source*: Bowd et al.)

compares the scope of sponsorship with related sponsorship-support techniques.

In this instance, sponsorship brings with it a more *process-orientated* view that includes planning, implementing and control mechanisms. So definitions that see sponsorship as merely 'an investment in cash or kind in an activity in return for access to the exploitable commercial potential associated with this activity' do not go far enough, as aforementioned (De Pelsmacker et al. 2004). Although the study of support in return for services is of interest to PR practitioners, sponsoring involves quite a bit more.

As such, one could propose a definition of organisational/corporate sponsorship that is: 'A planned organisational/corporate-focused activity aimed at facilitating the achievement of a goal or objective that sees the provision of financial or in-kind support via a sponsorship rights holder for a sponsorship property from within a certain sector through the utilisation and leveraging of the ensuing sponsorship rights by the sponsor through marketing, PR and communications activities.'

Why is it so popular and how does sponsorship work?

With this holistic viewpoint of sponsorship is, and perspective on the exponential growth, let us now discuss why it is so popular and what sponsorship can achieve for an organisation with respect to their goals in terms of commercial, psychological or organisational benefits.

Though increasingly professional and strategic in orientation, sponsorship remains a multifaceted tool. It reaches from high-profile media presence to the support of a local youth football club. Equally sponsorship can manifest in diverse societal arenas such as sport, education or arts and deliver divergent communication goals such as contact with audience (psychological benefit) or a specified market share increase (commercial benefit). Depending on the scope and importance of the investment made in the sponsorship, sponsorship can affect multiple things, a few of which include:

1. Passion marketing
2. Image transfer
3. Integrated communications
4. Multiple stakeholders communications
5. Direct sales.

Passion marketing

Sponsorship is widely regarded as a cheap alternative to advertising. This often goes hand in hand with the common misconception that sponsorship activity is merely logo exposure. If sponsorship involved no more than brand presence, it would very likely be useless as a communication tool. After all, multimillion investments, such as Gatorade's US nine-figure investment in the American NFL league or significant investment with British Cycling in the UK, have to be commercially justified. This raises the question about the capabilities and efficiency of sponsorship. Today's 'experiential economies' call for passionate brand communication – and this is exactly the added value sponsorship can provide (Pine and Gilmore 1998). Depending on the perceived relevance to the audience, sponsorship can convey memorable emotions and experiences more effectively than any other communication channel. With this power of association, sponsorships deliver marketing communications in a compelling manner to a highly receptive audience. The O2 campaign highlighted in Case study 23.1 in the 'Activation strategies' part of this section is a good example of a campaign tapping into the passions of an audience.

Image transfer

One of the main purposes of sponsorship is to favourably affect consumers' attitudes towards, and beliefs about, a brand or corporation. As attitudes can be good predictors of (consumer) behaviour and represent an overall evaluation of associations linked to an object, the formation and change of attitudes is of interest to the marketer (see also Chapter 18). What makes sponsorship a unique persuasive tool is its association potential. Sponsorship generally has positive connotations among audiences. It also does not rely on elaborate cognitive information (thought) processing – its emotional appeal makes it easy for the consumer to understand. The sponsorship entity sets the stage for inducing emotions such as joy, hope, excitement, fear, anger, etc. Marketing messages are presented in this context in the hope that consumers will experience these emotions. Research evidence suggests that it is not only the situational experience that influences behaviour, but also the overall attitude towards an event (Cooper 2003). A positive evaluation of something (event, person, team, etc.) will create positive feelings, which may then be transferred to the brand. This means that it is important to monitor opportunities carefully to ensure a good match between the sponsorship and the attitudes of the target audience. See Case study 23.2 on Mark Bayliss and 23.3 on British Airways London 2012 Olympic sponsorships to see how, in to two very different situations, image transfer was leveraged in a sponsorship.

Integrated communications

Sponsorship, unlike a consumer advertising campaign, can form the basis of a holistic multi-stakeholder integrated communications campaign, delivering benefits as well as organisational objectives. They can be manifest across multiple forms of internal and external communications. The ASICS (Case study 23.4) and the GE Capital (Case study 23.6) case studies provide good examples of how a sponsorship can form the basis of integrated communications involving content, PR, advertising, point of sale, experiences, internal engagement and more.

Multiple stakeholders communications

Beyond the function of communication with potential customers, sponsorship can aim to create additional results with other stakeholders. At the organisational level, employee motivation and identification can be supported by sponsorship activities. Research also suggests that there is a correlation between image and employment attractiveness, so that personnel marketing/recruiting might also benefit from these activities. Establishing goodwill with external groups, such as financial institutions, shareholders or investors, is an additional target variable of sponsorship. This is also true for the relationship with distributors, sales personnel and business partners. In some cases, sponsorship activities may also be used to develop relationships with decision makers in governmental institutions. Such stakeholder relationships are often enhanced through sponsorship activities such as VIP events and corporate hospitality see the aforementioned ASICS and GE Capital cases, along with the Intercontinental Hotel Group case (Case study 23.5).

Direct sales

Beyond the ability to facilitate passion marketing, image transfer, integrated communications and stakeholder communications, sponsorship can also be a conduit to enabling direct sales. That is, sales not generated through the effects of a brand built through image transfer or as a result of association with one's passion but through the direct network of the sponsorship property/rights holder or their inherent power to open doors. Sponsors are usually unwilling to specifically divulge the direct results of these relationships, as it may affect their renegotiations for sponsorship renewals in a manner that may raise the cost going forward.

Taking Olympic sponsorships as an example, many of the worldwide sponsors of the Olympics, known as The Olympic Partners (TOP), and partners and suppliers of individual Organising Committees for the Olympic Games (OCOG) engage in the sponsorship for, among other reasons, its ability to help deliver sales – sales derived through either selling products and services into the organisations tasked with delivering the games, other partners or via the sporting and civil infrastructure of the individual host nations as they scale up and down for each games. Additionally, sales are derived by using Olympic-themed incentive programmes to generate increased sales via the sales forces or resellers who hope to 'win' tickets through excelling in their performance beyond normal targets. For some Olympic sponsors this can create return on investment many times the value of their sponsorship in each cycle before they even start to market their relationship in traditional ways.

Direct sales are not limited to large sponsorships. As an example, the hotel industry has used partnership sponsorship deals with sports bodies or events to deliver guaranteed or incremental business for decades. Mass-participation sporting events (from major global marathons to regional or local runs or triathlons) often have a hotel sponsor whose motivation to sponsor is down to direct sales they can achieve. These sales are achieved by communicating directly with participants at the time of their registration to inform them of preferential rates or incentives in order to secure booking before the athlete consumers shop around. Additionally, hotel deals in sport often occur with the major leagues or governing bodies, not necessarily for the consumer sales but the sales that can be achieved via those organisations' business-to-business networks, which tend to include extensive networks of small clubs, suppliers, businesses, and other sponsors. This model can also be seen to apply in the areas of arts and tourism, among other sectors.

A further example of this is currently being enjoyed by sponsors of the Sky Pro Cycling Team, whose rider Bradley Wiggins won the 2012 Tour De France. Cycling equipment brands linked to the team are in the most part enjoying much greater success at securing listings with retailers, in what has been called by industry experts the 'Team Sky' effect – where the brand pull of the team means that consumers want to use whatever the team is using through an

---

Think about 23.6

Future of sponsorship

With the plethora of properties that can be sponsored, and sectors where sponsorship exists, what do you think will be the next trends and sectors for sponsorship?

Feedback

As discussed throughout this chapter, the future, in theory, could be anything. Many media pundits expect sponsored journalism and content to be an area of growth; however, this will be just one of many unique areas.

Box 23.2

Mainstream sectors for sponsorship

- Arts (film festivals, music festivals, orchestras, galleries and exhibitions, such as those sponsored by various organisations at the Guggenheim in New York).

- Broadcasting (television programmes, series of programmes, films and content, such as (in the UK) Sainsbury's and BT's sponsorship of the 2012 Paralympic broadcasts).

- Charity (events, appeals and work on social issues, such as the previously mentioned Comic Relief appeal and Red Products initiative).

- Culture (local initiatives and events, such as celebrations or festivals; e.g., New Year's Eve in Times Square in New York, which in 2012 was sponsored by Nivea and multiple other sponsors, or winter ice rinks in the UK, including major outdoor rinks in London sponsored by Tiffany's at Somerset House and Starbucks at the Natural History Museum).

- Ecology/environment (recycling and conservation programmes, such as Sky's [UK and European satellite television provider] Rain Forest Rescue Programme with the World Wildlife Fund).

- Education (for example, book series, individual academic posts, chairs, or full faculties such as in the US where corporate foundation sponsorship of business schools is common place, such as the Marriott School of Management at Brigham Young University).

- Industries/business/trades (sponsorship of research initiatives, industry events, associations and awards, such as the *PRWeek* Awards in the UK whose sponsors include major polling and services suppliers to the public relations industry).

- Sport (from athletes to teams and major tournaments, and big sporting events such as the Olympics with its multiple sponsorship opportunities; see Case studies 23.1–23.6 for in-depth examples).

- Venues and infrastructure (from libraries and arenas to transport infrastructure in cities, such as the Barclays Bank-sponsored cycle (bike) hire scheme in London, or the Emirates airline cable car in London).

Box 23.3

Venues and infrastructure – emerging areas of sponsorship

The sponsorship of venues, such as sports stadia, is nothing new, especially in the United States; however, traditionally this has been a naming rights exercise for branding and hospitality purposes.

A great example of this is the O2 Arena in London, England. O2 are a British mobile (cell) phone and communications company that use the arena sponsorship as both a huge brand driver, through the naming rights and the coverage it derives, but also use access to the events to deliver 'priority tickets' to their customers. Driving not only brand awareness and understanding

but providing a further point of differentiation for their existing and potential customers with the exclusive early access to tickets, along with their own complimentary hospitality area, it provides opportunities to see the biggest names in music and sport (whom they don't directly sponsor).

This model of sponsorship has exploded throughout Europe and the United States since the success that O2 and the arena have mutually enjoyed since the venue launched in 2007.

A more recent emerging trend is the use of sponsorship to fund public infrastructure projects, whether these be transport projects such as the aforementioned London cycle hire scheme or cable car, or the sponsorship of metro stations in India on the Gurgaon Rapid Metro, where station-naming rights have been secured by companies such as Vodafone.

Additionally, as an example in the UK, sponsorship in the public sector has grown to include the creation of 'academy schools' and other private finance initiatives.

innate belief it is the best, due to the strength of the team's attributes. As an example, one of the team's sponsors saw apromotion featuring the team help it to double its number of retail listings.

What can be sponsored?

Sponsorship's ability to deliver such a wide range of significant organisational results is a key driving force in the previously discussed growth of the sector, along with its subsequent cultural omnipresence throughout the globe.

This has led to an evolution of the market which means that the properties that are being (or can be) sponsored now encompass almost anything. This is highlighted in the discussion of 'sponsorship properties', this can include; awards, content, events, individual objects, organisation/groups, venues, sporting leagues, systems, teams, venues and more.

Likewise, whereas previously sponsorship properties were limited primarily to sport, the arts, charitable and education, these now include a broad spectrum of sectors,

as is demonstrated in Box 23.2, which provides an overview of the sectors where sponsorship is commonplace, as well as some key emerging sectors such as venues and infrastructure.

Figure 23.4 shows four graphs that illustrate within sport, the arts, broadcast and other sectors how the global spend in sponsorship in 2011 was divided (for reported deals).

If economic conditions are difficult there will be more opportunities for clever organisations to engage in sponsorship to their benefit. Recently, the US luxury jeweller, Tiffany's, through their foundation led a programme in the UK restoring some of the iconic fountains and drinking fountains in the Royal Parks of London. The programme, called 'Tiffany's Across The Water', generated positive press coverage and also created several key events, where they could host stakeholders and help 'embed' the brand as a cornerstone of British culture.

Other unique examples in this space included the US fast-food company KFC when they offered to sponsor pothole repair in major US cities in 2009.

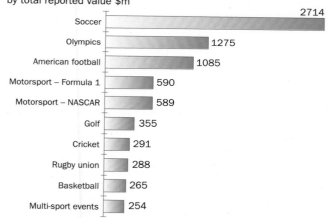

Top 10 sponsored sports 2011
by total reported value $m

Soccer	2714
Olympics	1275
American football	1085
Motorsport – Formula 1	590
Motorsport – NASCAR	589
Golf	355
Cricket	291
Rugby union	288
Basketball	265
Multi-sport events	254

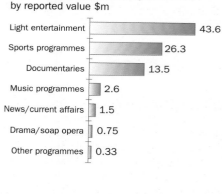

Top broadcast sponsorship genres 2011
by reported value $m

Light entertainment	43.6
Sports programmes	26.3
Documentaries	13.5
Music programmes	2.6
News/current affairs	1.5
Drama/soap opera	0.75
Other programmes	0.33

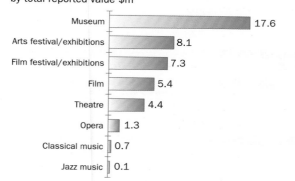

Top 10 sponsored arts & culture activities 2011
by total reported value $m

Museum	17.6
Arts festival/exhibitions	8.1
Film festival/exhibitions	7.3
Film	5.4
Theatre	4.4
Opera	1.3
Classical music	0.7
Jazz music	0.1

Top activities non sport, arts, broadcast 2011
by reported value $m

Conservation/environment	40.6
City/community celebrations	9.5
Other	9.1
Education	3.4
Trade fairs	0.75
Conferences	0.48
Charities/causes	0.43

Figure 23.4 Breakdown of spend by sport, arts, broadcast and other (*source*: IFM Sports Marketing Surveys 2012)

Developing a sponsorship strategy

So how does an organisation arrive at its sponsorship strategy? Sponsorship involves more than the support of an event, such as the FIFA World Championship, the PGA (golf) Masters series or the local volleyball club, in return for logo exposure. The activities covered in our definition highlight much of the approach, scale and scope of today's sponsorship environment. They also indicate the necessary professionalism that comes with the understanding of sponsorship as part of an integrated communication and relationship strategy. In the spirit of Maecenatism, not long ago 'gut decisions' on who and what to sponsor were commonplace (this was sometimes known as 'the chairman's

Box 23.4

The importance for rights holders to think about potential sponsor objectives and goals

In the world of sponsorship, it is important for the rights holder to think about the needs of both existing or potential sponsors and their individual situations, in order to maximise their revenue. Often the importance of this thought process is more important the less 'traditionally' high-profile or mainstream the entity is to sponsor; thus the likes of Formula 1, NBA, NFL, MLB, Premier League Football, Olympics, etc., though hugely expensive to sponsors, may find it significantly easier to sell in their sponsorships than a smaller rights holder.

The authors of this chapter working in practice are often approached by organisations and individuals selling sponsorships with little thought of what are the needs and wants of the organisations they would like to sponsor, or truly what is their value and their reach. Case study 23.2 provides a clear discussion of how a rights holder who thinks about the goals and objectives of an organisation can benefit.

Think about 23.7 — Ensuring you choose the right property

When selecting a sponsorship property it is vital that practitioners think not only about a property's ability to deliver against the goals and objectives of the organisation, as discussed previously, but also about any potential risk associated with the sponsorship. It is important to weigh up the risk of any associated sponsorship and calculate the risk versus return cost. In the realm of sport this could be things like the effects on a sponsor if an athlete or team has been found to cheat, for example. Take a moment and think about what effects a title sponsor of a mass-participation sporting event might suffer if there was an operational issue with an event.

delivery of race packs prior to the event, and the organiser's perceived failure by participants to respond to queries on the event's official Facebook page, saw Nike come under attack via social media (see Picture 23.2.). As the title sponsor they were perceived to have a greater degree of control on the operation of the events and, as such, paid the price for it with respect to their brand reputation. Detailed research into the event's past would have shown perceived basic logistical failings that have at times negatively affected some sponsors, but allowed those who pre-emptively took action or had plans in place to shine through.

Feedback

The operational issue effects that a title sponsor could suffer from with an event will obviously depend on a whole series of factors, the main one being the perceived severity of the issues and the organiser/rights holder's response, with the most severe being due to someone's death as a result of negligence. As an example, though not one involving a fatality, the Gorkana Group's (media contact database, cuttings and measurement group) blog, Measure Matters, outlines the case in 2012 of the British 10K – a running event in the UK that was title-sponsored by Nike. Problems in the event organiser's

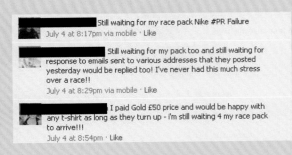

Picture 23.2 'Measurement Matters' blog 2012

discretion' or 'chairman's wife syndrome', as sponsorship of one's favourite team or of the opera or society events secured grace and favour with these organisations). Despite its strategic importance and the increased professionalism of sponsorship, many decisions follow management preferences rather than calculated communication objectives. In contrast to 'gut decisions' leading to hit-and-miss activities, modern sponsorship thinking is planned and decisive.

Opportunity analysis, scenario planning, alternative target generation, strategy selection, budget and time horizon decisions, implementation, integration in marketing mix, communication channel coordination, evaluation and control mechanisms are all examples of a systematic and process-based view of sponsoring (see the Glossary at the end of the book for definitions of these terms). These terms also explain how sponsorship can be systematically integrated into strategic marketing. Here the word *systematic* means that sponsorship should not be a question of trial and error, but should follow a management process with specified communication goals. This implies account-

ability and controllability, because otherwise any financial or in-kind commitment would be highly risky. As we will see later, the development of evaluation tools is, due to the nature of sponsoring, a major challenge to PR and corporate communication departments.

An organisation or corporation that takes sponsoring as a communication tool into consideration faces a range of challenges in planning, implementing and controlling the activities. This is the area of responsibility of sponsorship management. Figure 23.5 shows phases of the planning process of sponsoring. There are numerous models, both academic and professional, in existence, most of which share three commonalities; international sponsorship consultancy IMG refer to these as the *Discover, Design* and *Delivery* phases.

Insight and analysis phase (discover)

Starting with the phase of analysis and prognosis, sponsorship management deals first of all with the collection and

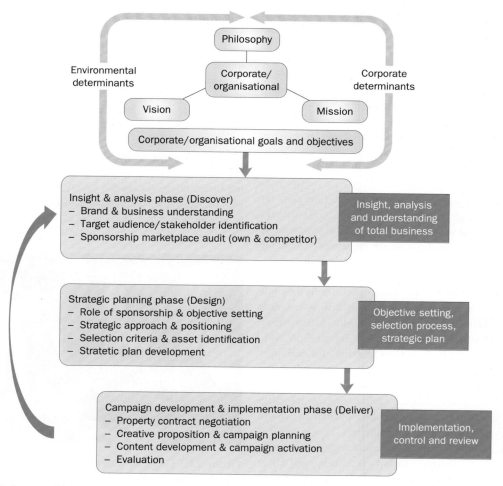

Figure 23.5 Sponsorship management as a planning process (*source*: modified from Tench and Yeomans 2009)

evaluation of information. This is important so as to understand not only the brand DNA and marketing objectives, but also to try and understand the core business practices, the key operational aspects that sponsorship can impact through employee and trade relationships, direct and indirect sales and promotional opportunities or indeed provision of services in value in kind for example. Alongside this, understanding the target audience and their interests along with what competitors are doing are all important considerations that need to be taken into the next phase, to enable the creation of a clear sponsorship approach that meets the needs of the brand or business, and increasingly both.

Strategic planning phase (design)

With an understanding of the brand, the business and the marketing space within which it operates, the strategic planning phase can begin. This phase is focused on some key elements; target audience(s) (consumer, trade customer, stakeholders); geography (local, regional, international); core objectives (short, medium and long-term); key messaging (what – if anything – will be communicated?); and any business elements to include (showcasing of business services/technology for example). This information when considered together enables a clear articulation of the primary role of sponsorship. This is an important first step as it fundamentally informs the rest of the process, and enables the establishment of some key objectives and core criteria for evaluating different types of sponsorship and eventually sponsorship properties. It's also an important step in enabling the business to simply inform staff and key internal stakeholders why they sponsor and what its role is for the organisation.

It might for example be primarily about driving brand awareness or brand status, in which case properties with strong media exposure (Premiership football shirt deals for example) and high levels of prestige (Olympics, FIFA World Cup, etc.) should be sought, with a clear perspective on target audience of course. However, it may be more important for the business to be able to demonstrate what they do and to showcase their expertise, using sponsorship to translate a complex message into one more simply understood. This is the route taken by some of the leading technology businesses, such as IBM with their SlamTracker™ (Wimbledon, French Open, US Open and Australian Open) or SAP (Tennis, Golf, NFL, etc.) with their 2013 Runs Better Campaign, for example.

It is also important at this stage to understand the role of sponsorship within the broader communications mix. As Cornwell and Maignan (2001) argue, sponsorship activities may not, in themselves, be sufficient to achieve specific objectives for all target audiences. This is why it is important that sponsorship activities are reinforced through complementary communication activities. As these cross-marketing operations may include sales promotion, advertising or special product offers (among others), total

expenditure may easily exceed the sponsorship budget. It is also important to note that the coordination of communication activities towards a common goal increasingly takes an integrative sponsorship perspective.

Campaign development and implementation phase/(deliver)

The process-orientated view also highlights the dual nature of sponsorship: not only does the selection of a strategic programme and its coordination need to be addressed, but also how to put this strategy into practice. It is easy to underestimate the complexity and importance of implementing sponsorship plans. Activities are as good as the weakest link in the sponsoring process and a good plan does not necessarily translate into a successful campaign. Sponsoring is sensitive to trends and sudden changes. Football teams can be relegated, events can be mismanaged, celebrities can be arrested – any of these may lead to negative publicity or inability to exercise the rights to their maximum for the sponsor. (The O2 example in Case study 23.1 is a great example of how to create a campaign that it is not wholly dependent on a team's results.)

Furthermore, a sponsorship campaign calls for cooperation between several internal and external departments. Therefore, a manager should be involved in all phases of sponsoring and responsible for the planning as well as the implementation. Since implementation is a key determinant of success, many specialised agencies have evolved – such as IMG; additionally, major corporations such as BMW or Microsoft have their own departments that coordinate all sponsorship activities.

The following Case studies (23.1–23.6) highlight various approaches to planning, programme creation and implementation, along with highlighting their evaluation with respect to passion marketing, image transfer, integrated communications and direct sales.

Picture 23.3 Gregg Wallace Judges England's Rugby World Cup Stars for the launch of Get Up for England in 2011 (*source*: Iain Sheldon/IMG)

Activation strategies: six in-depth case studies (23.1–23.6)

Case study 23.1

The importance of a single-minded approach in developing an integrated campaign

O2: England team sponsorship and the 2011 Rugby World Cup in New Zealand

Strategic planning

O2 is a British mobile (cell) telephone and communication network, and the main (shirt) sponsor of the England rugby union team and a partner of the Rugby Football Union (RFU). The challenge was to provide O2 customers with a 'Priority' added-value experience, around a tournament that was 12,000 miles and a 12-hour time difference away and where O2 had no tournament rights or visibility (with the O2 logo stripped off the team shirt due to World Cup tournament rules to protect their own sponsors).

The strategy was influenced by some key insights:

- Performance wasn't expected (correctly) to be good, so a classic 'passion' campaign could backfire quickly.

- But, as England's main sponsor, O2's positioning needed to support the team.

- Matches would start as fans were getting out of bed, so they would mainly be watching at home.

This led to the campaign thought (and eventual campaign line) to help the fans 'Get Up For England', both emotionally and literally.

Development of the plan

The core concept was to deliver O2 England fans a 'breakfast supporters' pack', with a unique breakfast pie delivered to customers' homes and providing them with all they needed to support England.

This focused approach reaped benefits in the implementation phase, with the need to create awareness peaks to drive sign-up for ordering around England's matches (the breakfast packs had to be ordered a week before each match), supplemented by on-going 'breakfast' messaging.

The resultant campaign included:

- Media relations launch activity: *MasterChef* (British and international television series) style pie cook off, with four teams of England players hosted by TV chef Gregg Wallace (one of the British *MasterChef* hosts) and generating 41 items of coverage.

- Television 'above the line' campaign (ATL) – 'The pre-match boost': England supporter does a 'Priority walk' from his bed to the lounge, supported by England players and their coach Martin Johnson, who dress and feed him on the way to the lounge to sit down and watch the game in front of the TV and support them (www.youtube.com/watch?v=7W9W4FrH5mw).

- PR and media support throughout the tournament: a series of stories were placed in national and rugby press throughout the World Cup to support the campaign. These were supplemented with a national radio 'breakfast' media partnership with TalkSport radio (Official Rugby World Cup broadcaster) and a print media partnership with the UK-based *Sport* magazine.

- Digital: 'Get Up For England' wake-up mobile 'app', with alarm call messages from the team and special editions of O2 *Inside Line* inside the camp video programme (a behind the scenes online documentary series about the England rugby team).

Summary

The success of this campaign relied on a clear understanding of the Rugby World Cup regulations and close liaison with the RFU, one wrong step from O2 could see the England team expelled from the tournament.

At all stages O2 and their agencies presented their ideas to the RFU, providing them with a final proposal and marketing plan to ensure they were happy with the plan from a regulatory standpoint, as well as to gain buy-in and support from the management team and players.

O2 also worked with fellow RFU partners Greene King (a British ale/beer company), who provided the beer for the breakfast supporter packs.

The number of different elements involved (pie production, packaging, order and delivery system, etc.) meant a major focus on managing the approvals process aligned with budget management. The pressure of a rolling order system as England progressed added further complications to this final element.

case study 23.1 (continued)

'Finally, clear KPIs and an evaluation system were put in place prior to the campaign, to ensure clear tracking of key elements. Some of the results from the campaign for O2 included:

- +22 per cent increase in top box 'the only network I would choose' consideration

- 88,000 new O2 customers signed up for Priority during RWC 2011

- Cumulative TV/print/radio reach of 8.8 million

- Online: 9.76 million media impressions, with 1.67 per cent click through rate (CTR)

- O2 was the most spontaneously recalled rugby sponsor during the Rugby World Cup in England.

'Additionally, the campaign won the "Best Integrated Sport Marketing Campaign Award" at the 2012 Sports Industry Awards in the UK.'

Think about 23.8 — Identifying success factors

In the O2 case study, O2 and their communications agencies had to do a lot more than just arrange the sponsorship, carry out media relations, digital communications and advertising to leverage the campaign. What other elements were key to the campaign success?

Feedback

Beyond the normal communications/marketing mix, the O2 campaign required;

- A detailed understanding of tournament marketing rules and the legal implications to the England Rugby Team and RFU

- An extensive programme of winning the support of the RFU and its team (players and management) to engage and provide the unique content for this campaign

- An extensive reach-out and logistics programme with suppliers to ensure the programme delivered on its promises. A failure to deliver packs caused by a breakdown at any layer of the system (technical, manufacturing or delivery) would have caused embarrassment to O2 and harmed customer relationships.

Case study 23.2

Packaging, packaging, packaging: how Mark Bayliss sold himself for the Enduroman Arch to Arc challenge

In late 2009, early 2010, Mark Bayliss, a director of a UK based transport company, set himself the goal of tackling the gruelling Enduroman Arch to Arc triathlon in September 2012. This challenge involves an 87-mile run from Marble Arch in London, England, to Dover on the English coast, followed by a Channel swim from Dover to Calais, France, finishing with an epic 181-mile bike ride from Calais to the Arc de Triomphe in Paris.

As Mark prepared for this challenge, he was doing everything required of an athlete to ensure he would be ready. Included with his focused training, Mark tackled a Channel swim, the *Marathon des Sables* and many additional swimming challenges in training. Throughout this two things happened: (1) costs started to mount (the fee for the Arch to Arc attempt is $8,000 USD); and (2) he decided to be the first person to do the swim section of the Arch to Arc without a wetsuit and go for a new record time. Following a conversation in late 2011 with a friend who is a leading sports marketing consultant, Mark made a decision to try and recruit sponsors. The sponsors would help with both the costs of taking on this challenge but also ensure he maximised his performance.

As a starting point, a reasonable list of what he actually needed was developed in early 2012:

- Financial support (any, but $5,000–$10,000 USD would make a significant difference)

→

case study 23.2 (continued)

- A time-trial bike, fitted and equipped for the specific needs of the event
- Footwear and clothing
- Nutritional products
- Science (sports) support.

Though this list may not seem initially challenging, for an individual without a significant profile within his own sport (with the exception of the most dedicated endurance/distance athletes) or outside, it was a lot to ask. As such, the next step was to develop the following questions, and responses:

What were the key elements we had that would/could appeal to sponsors?	We decided on three key elements that would appeal to sponsors. 1. Sports equipment/science companies would want to demonstrate the technical superiority of their product and services through enabling Mark to accomplish this challenge. 2. Utilising Mark's personal brand, attributes of commitment, dedication, determination. Further, what can be achieved when you plan and prepare; a true demonstration of the power of the human spirit, etc. to develop their brand image or proposition by either borrowing or using their products, to highlight or mirror the company's own attributes. 3. A unique story to provide a point of differentiation from the plethora of Olympic-focused sponsorship campaigns but one that still reflected the attributes of what had become a UK obsession in talking about both 'Great Britons' and the legacy of the games outside of the Olympics (London 2012).
Who would potentially have the resources available to sponsor in 2012, with the Olympics happening in London that year and most of the traditional spenders in sports having already allocated their budgets?	It was decided that it would be logical to target companies who were either not Olympic sponsors but in their competitive set, or those companies involved in sport whose products were focused at a high-end demographic of affluent but aspirational and committed athletes.
What did Mark have to offer, if not an existing profile or brand?	1. A track record of accomplishing true tests of the human spirit (Channel swim, *Marathon des Sables*, etc.). 2. A very unique challenge; though 10 people had accomplished the challenge previously, none had properly articulated or communicated the accomplishment. 3. The fact that even if he did not break the 10-year-old world record he would, at the minimum, achieve a world first.

The answers to these questions were coupled with the realisation that the majority of the companies that Mark would be targeting would be time-poor and need Mark to deliver a guaranteed set of results. The following package was developed with the focus on one significant title partner (cash and product/services) and multiple supplier-level partners of products and services only.

The package for the title and suppliers delivered:

- Sponsorship of Mark, including branding but more importantly ambassadorial time for speaking, public appearances, media work or even assistance in product development and feedback.

- Photography and video content, provided by award-winning documentary maker and published sports photographer, that the sponsor could use for their own purposes, as desired.

- Three guaranteed significant features in a leading triathlon magazine (done via a 'soft' media partnership) and other features pre-secured on his training/ preparation.

- Strong personal digital platform (www.teambayliss.co.uk website, blog and Twitter).

case study 23.2 (continued)

Picture 23.4 How to gain sponsorship from a niche sporting activity and an 'unknown' athlete (*source*: Ryan Bowd)

- Support pre- and post-challenge from a world-class, award-winning sports PR agency (subject to title sponsor) or, at the minimum, support from an award-winning PR practitioner (in own time).

- Budget for a digital campaign to seed and place the content pre and post the challenge.

- A charitable element with an Olympic feel, as Mark was raising money for SportsAid – a UK charity that provides funding to potential future athletes to help them with training and competition costs.

This package for a title sponsor was taken to market at a rate of just over $42,000, of which Mark would receive only $8,000. To minimise the risk to any title sponsor, it was clearly communicated that release of funds (payments) would be proportional to the key moments where value through media and digital (social) media coverage would be achieved. These were: the announcement of the challenge attempt; the week before the start; and the time post a successful completion.

With this clear understanding of what would be delivered and how their investment would be protected, potential sponsors were approached and a shortlist of interested parties was quickly defined. In the end the title sponsorship was taken by UK-based sports company inov-8. The company was looking for ways to share its brand with committed athletes across a wider spectrum of sporting areas. Additionally, high-end US company Parlee was secured to provide the bike, and Gatorade (along with the Gatorade Sports Science Institute) provided the nutrition and science support. Furthermore, a series of other, smaller supplier partners were secured to provide various pieces of key equipment. In the end a total of over $50,000 of support in cash and value in kind was generated to enable Mark's challenge attempt; a challenge that saw Mark start on 5 September, 2012 in London and complete 73 hours 39 minutes and

12 seconds later in Paris, breaking the existing record by roughly 8 hours and setting a world first.

Additionally, the package of support provided to sponsors resulted in;

Coverage summary

- 79 pieces of coverage
- Total circulation of 11,517,784
- Coverage secured in UK, USA, France, South Africa, New Zealand and Spain

Twitter coverage summary

- 371 tweets sent during the record attempt, reaching 436,213 target audience members

Facebook

- inov-8 Facebook page gained over 500 likes during the record attempt
- Challenge posts were shared by inov-8 South Africa, inov-8 Singapore and inov-8 Czech and Slovakia; this was a first for the brand to see such engagement by other market teams

Mark Bayliss (Teambayliss.co.uk) website

- Mark Bayliss website was re-branded for inov-8 during the challenge period and received 72,612 unique visits – an average of 4,271 a day

Digital advertising campaign

- Google campaign run in UK, Ireland, USA, Denmark, France and Italy
- Total ad impressions 1,953,630
- CTR 0.2 (over 0.1 is considered good for a Google campaign) . . .

. . . and specific Parlee and Gatorade coverage that discussed what their products and teams did to enable and support the challenge.

In the end, Mark, as the 'rights holder', not only generated the sponsorship income he required but delivered for his sponsors a package that means he is well positioned to be able to generate income going forward for future challenges.

Furthermore, inov-8, prior to the challenge starting, could already see the benefits of the concept and model for their brand and future-proofed their investment by branding it as a challenge series, with this as the first athlete within it, so that they could roll the model out going forward with other committed athletes if successful.

Picture 23.5 The challenge facing Mark Bayliss was more than just physical, he needed sponsorship too (*source*: Ryan Bowd)

case study 23.3 (continued)

Campaign roll-out

The campaign was phased to build towards Games time, using the three key elements to create distinct, yet ultimately linked, elements:

1. Great Britons (2010/11): mentoring Great British talent in three distinct arenas:

   ■ Food with Heston Blumenthal that manifested in a BA pop-up restaurant pre the Games in London, and menus on certain planes to London designed by up-and-coming chef Simon Hulstone

   ■ Art with Tracey Emin that manifested in the Golden Dove Plane designed by Pascal Anson

   ■ Film with Richard E. Grant that manifested in the film *Boy* scripted by Prasanna Puwanarajah.

2. Celebrating BA expertise (2011)

   ■ Above the line (ATL) campaign celebrating BA skills in an Olympic theme

   ■ 'They Will Fly' (100 days to go).

   It had always been felt important to find a route for BA to physically support the team. Using insight from Olympic athletes, BA's travel agency partner created a new service tailored specifically to athletes' unique and unusual needs while training and competing around the world.

   BA signed key relationships with national governing bodies (NGBs) and leading individual athletes to deliver this, which was ultimately brought to life through the 'They Will Fly' ATL campaign. This support was genuine and felt to make a real difference by those they supported. 'The support provided by British Airways to the UK Athletics team goes beyond the traditional sponsorship model into the territory of a genuine partnership, where they actively contribute to our complex logistical operation of moving hundreds of British athletes and their equipment around the globe each year which undoubtedly has a positive impact on their performance' (Niels de Vos, CEO, UK Athletics). This part of the campaign

was viewed to be such a success in itself that it won Best Sponsorship of a Team at the 2012 Sports Industry Awards in the UK.

3. Support Team GB – create a home advantage and stay home (May–July 2012)

   With the Games imminent, the final element of the campaign began. This rather 'unusual' campaign for an airline was the output of all the agencies collaborating together and understandably required extensive sell-in to the broader business. In many ways, the decision to proceed with a campaign that essentially told people not to fly during the Olympic and Paralympic Games was a testimony to the success of the campaign to date in re-building pride, faith and confidence in the BA brand. It manifested itself in two predominant ways:

   ■ #HomeAdvantage: the campaign used sponsorship assets to communicate a message to Team GB supporters to create a home advantage for their athletes

   ■ 'Don't Fly. Support Team GB': secondly it actively encouraged people to stay in the UK for the Games and support the team, and then not until post the games did it encourage people to take a holiday in celebration.

Summary

A key element to the success of the BA Olympic programme was the ability to align the BA brand strategy and objectives against some key business needs, particularly internal.

This required a concentrated investment in internal stakeholder engagement and education, getting the business on board with the core campaign elements. This was allied with an extensive approvals process and compliance monitoring to ensure key deadlines were reached and the continued delivery of an extensive marketing programme for both external and internal audiences.

Think about 23.10   Aligning interested parties

In the BA case study numerous parties had to be aligned in order to be about such an integrated campaign. Who do you think would have needed to be aligned? Find a colleague and examine your lists and discuss.

Feedback

In the BA case those who needed to be aligned included internal audiences from all areas of communications,

HR and management at multiple levels through to the CEO and Chairman of the Board. Externally, all BA communications agencies needed to be aligned but one could also see that various financial and other audiences would need to be aligned prior to any service company advocating their consumer to 'not use their service'.

Case study 23.4

ASICS Smarter Rugby: driving the trade relationship and ultimately sales through a sponsorship campaign

For many consumer retail brands, the trade opportunity sponsorship delivers is a vital element, providing them with unique materials to help them establish, retain or improve their in-store fixture.

In 2010, ASICS in the UK had a great rugby product, a great reputation for excellence from their running shoes, but needed an effective means to transfer that into a retail offering to drive uptake of their rugby boots in the highly competitive specialist rugby trade.

Strategic Idea: Smarter Rugby

Traditionally sports shoes marketing focuses on 'heroing' the stars of the game, with the leading manufacturers vying for the signature of the leading players to wear their boots, which they then utilise in both advertising and point of sale.

ASICS decided, out of both brand position and a stark economic reality that in rugby they didn't have the sales to justify the cost of signing the game's biggest stars, to take a different approach, creating a strategy to deliver a point of difference to retailers, as well as talking directly to their consumers.

'Smarter Rugby' was based on inherent trust in the product (many players wear ASICS running shoes in training), aligned with the natural thirst for knowledge to improve their game among amateur players. The output was 'Smarter Rugby', led by advocacy and core content rather than relying on traditional player ambassador deals.

ASICS UK signed an exclusive deal with a core 'trusted advocate', Sir Ian McGeechan ('Geech') – the legendary British Lions coach – to create a series of unique and insightful training video:

- YouTube channel with regular Geech training content
- Retail POS and exclusive video content for major online retailers

- Trade engagement programme with 'meet Geech' launch event and tiered support programme
- Value in kind (VIK) partnerships with key media, supported by a broader PR campaign (e.g., *Times, Rugby World*, rugbydump.com).

This holistic approach of PR, advertising, experience and content, coupled with in-store activity, helped ASICS to make huge steps forward in their business between 2010 and 2011 with the key trade. Key highlights included:

- Rugby retailer sell-in increased 188 per cent YOY (year on year)
- Rugby gross margin increased 4.3 per cent
- Digital traffic (ASICS website) increased 88 per cent
- 170,000 + YouTube views.

Picture 23.6 Sir Ian McGeechan ('Geech'), the legendary British Lions coach, supported the ASICS sponsorship campaign (*source*: Ryan Bowd)

Think about 23.11   Choosing ambassadors

In the ASICS rugby case, the performance shoe manufacturer sponsorship approach utilised a legend of UK rugby, Sir Ian McGeechan, to help them build their retail sales, rather than a superstar of the sport or an upcoming young player. Why was this so effective at this stage in their brand's development in the sport, when of the 1 million plus rugby players in the UK only around 160,000 of them are adults, to whom Geech would be personally relevant?

Feedback

This approach was effective, as initially the audience that ASICS needed to win over was not the consumer, but the retailers who control the consumers' access to products. For this audience Geech was not only a hero (as most are past players and current fans) but also credible, as he had never worked with a brand in this way, and due to his level of integrity the retailers knew he would only work with a brand whose product quality matched all its claims. Secondly, when it came to retail, the campaign may not have had pulling power with youngsters in the way an icon of the sport would have but it did resonate highly with fathers, many of whom fund the boot purchase.

Explore 23.4   Building a sponsorship strategy

In the ASICS rugby case, how would you have evolved the sponsorship programme and campaign in future years to support the 'Smarter Rugby' proposition? Note you are still restricted by a budget that does not allow you to invest in icons of the sport.

Feedback

To widen the appeal of ASICS and the campaign beyond the retailers' audience and older adults, you could sign young up-and-coming stars in the sport, prior to them making their national teams (England, Scotland and Wales teams), and have them work with Geech to produce content relevant to individual players' positions on the field, rather than the game as a whole. These new ambassadors would both deepen the content pool and provide player imagery and be stars among the younger players who really follow the game.

Case study 23.5

Intercontinental Hotel Group: driving employee engagement through London 2012

Sponsorship is entered into for many reasons and increasingly companies are looking internally for the impact of their sponsorship programmes, sometimes to the exclusion of any outward-facing benefits. The 2012 London Olympics was potentially a watershed for this type of sponsorship activation and certainly for IHG (Intercontinental Hotel Group), who were a provider to the Games through their Holiday Inn brand. IHG increased employee engagement and subsequent pride in the company (and increased productivity) – all key drivers for their sponsorship programme.

Creating unforgettable experiences for employees

Some sponsorships (in this case Olympic) deliver few opportunities for large companies to create opportunities for direct interaction for staff – ticket numbers (and similar benefits) are relatively minimal, especially as IHG were only a Tier 3 partner (supplier/provider) to the 2012 Olympics.

The answer for IHG was to bring the Olympic Games to life for staff through athlete-led experiences: creating a team of 50 potential Team GB athletes (33 of whom were selected for the Games) through an innovative negotiation approach – delivering free hotel rooms for athletes and their coaches/family in return for their time with staff and customer engagement and PR, with top-ups for advertising and wider marketing rights.

This programme delivered:

- 37 Olympic masterclasses covering . . .
- 20 Olympic sports involving . . .
- 62 Olympians and coaches who met . . .

case study 23.5 (continued)

■ 2,500+ staff from . . .

■ 77 hotels.

Delivering . . . in more ways than one

Within six months employees' awareness of the sponsorship increased from 49 per cent to 73 per cent, matched by engagement levels.

The programme delivered an average Net Promotor Score (Bain and Company) of 97 . . . and, unexpectedly, created part-time jobs for 15 athletes within IHG. IHG were able to maximise the activity by creating parallel 'pop-up' Olympic experiences for IHG Loyalty Programme and Facebook followers, and driving strong PR coverage – a lesson in 'sweating your assets'.

Definition: Net Promoter Score

'The Net Promoter Score and System is defined as: know the score.

'The Net Promoter Score (or NPS®) is based on the fundamental perspective that every company's customers can be divided into three categories: Promoters, Passives

and Detractors. By asking one simple question – How likely is it that you would recommend (your company) to a friend or colleague? – organisations can track these stakeholder groups and get a clear measure of their company's performance through the customers' eyes. Customers respond on a 0–10 point rating scale and are categorised as follows:

1. Promoters (score 9–10) are loyal enthusiasts who will keep buying and refer others, fuelling growth.

2. Passives (score 7–8) are satisfied but unenthusiastic customers who are vulnerable to competitive offerings.

3. Detractors (score 0–6) are unhappy customers who can damage your brand and impede growth through negative word of mouth.

To calculate a company's NPS, they take the percentage of customers who are Promoters and subtract the percentage who are Detractors.'

Source: modified from www.netpromoter.com/why-net-promoter/know/2012

Picture 23.7 British Olympians, such as former World Champion and record Tour de France stage winner Mark Cavendish, took part in staff masterclasses as part of IHG's sponsorship to drive employee engagement (*source*: IHG)

Think about 23.12   No money deals

In the IHG case study the 50 Olympic/Paralympic athletes were remunerated for their time through free hotel rooms for their personal use, or use by their friends, family and coaches, in exchange for a reasonable amount of rights.

The amount of room nights varied by athlete and was dependent on the athlete's profile (i.e., payment was commensurate with status).

This 'value in kind' (VIK) approach to sponsorship worked as the athletes received something of real use to them, something that they would normally have to pay commercial rates for, so they valued the nights at face value in exchange for their time. For IHG it meant that they were able to work with more athletes than they would have if paying cash, as they were able to benefit from the internal rate on rooms between the parent

company and hotels (i.e., X dollars of room nights for IHG meant X times, say, 2 or 3 dollars' worth of athletes).

From this case example how do you think IHG managed to convince the agents who take cash commissions on deals to allow these relationships to happen?

Feedback

Agents and their companies have a similar need to the athletes, i.e. accommodation for 'business' reasons. As such, IHG remunerated the agents, who normally receive 20 per cent commission from athletes, with hotel room nights to a value roughly equivalent of 20 per cent of the room nights the athletes received. In order to make this attractive, IHG worked with a limited amount of agents in order to maximise the benefit and incentive to allow their athletes to engage in the programme.

Explore 23.5   Activating athletes at their 'level'

In the IHG case study the athletes involved in the programme existed at three predominant levels of profile: existing Olympic legends (with medals from previous games); likely medallist for 2012 (athletes who had medalled at recent World or European championship); and up and coming athletes. In most cases athletes' masterclass days involved a mix of employee, customer and media engagement.

Try planning an activity schedule for each level of athlete above and think about how you might structure it.

Feedback

The higher profile the athlete, the more likely their appeal reaches beyond their sport and into the mainstream world and media. The less profiled the athlete, the more important their sport is over themselves and the more focused the media needs to be to the sport (sport-specific media) or the athlete's microcosms (i.e., their local paper, etc.).

The role of PR

As one will have probably deduced from the preceding case studies, public relations' role in sponsorship is clearly present in value generation through media relations. But its role is ever more prevalent, as the public relations or communications teams are often running the whole or significant parts of the strategic sponsorship management process. As sponsorships have moved away from basic branding or badging exercises to in-depth programmes of value generation, with multiple objectives in relation to varied stakeholder groups, the PR or corporate/organisation communications function of the stakeholder

communications role has evolved and come to the fore. This evolution of more active engaging of stakeholders is an emergent trend in sponsorship, especially in sport, and one that will continue to change and shape the scope and function of PR (Sport Business 2008). Case study 23.6 provides a good example of the breadth of this active engagement with respect to internal and external stakeholder communications and the use of sponsorship through events, community relations, media relations, use of content and more to deliver value. This programme was designed by a PR practitioner at GE Capital's UK sponsorship agency at the time and is a good example of the changing role.

Case study 23.6

GE Capital and GB triathletes Helen and Marc Jenkins

Utilising an employee sponsorship to engage employees, clients, key stakeholders and the community and garnering brand exposure through media relations and coverage.

GE Capital* needed a solution to help leverage GE's sponsorship of the Olympics and British Triathlon Federation, which formed the parent company's London 2012 sponsorship platform* to engage their employees, key business influencers (KBIs) and clients. GE Capital's dilemma was that they were exempt from GE's Olympic sponsorship so needed something to instil the Olympic values within their target groups. The solution was to sponsor two GB triathletes, Helen and Marc Jenkins, who had a resounding story that resonated in so many ways to the recent situation of the GE Capital business. Both had been through a recent career slump and were on a resurgent revival back to winning ways. Through these athletes GE Capital were able to engage their employees and clients through a well-executed campaign that has continued to run since May 2010.

About Marc:

- 2004 Olympian
- Retired in 2007 after a serious health scare
- Returned to competition in 2010, re-entered the top 100 athletes in the world in 2011
- Coaching his wife Helen towards London 2012.

About Helen:

- 2008 and 2011 ITU World Champion
- 2008 Olympian
- 2012 Team GB athlete and strong contender to medal.

The sponsorship and campaign objectives:

- Engage UK employees with the Olympics
- Increase physical activity among employees in line with GE's health initiative 'Healthahead'
- Engage clients in a non-business environment
- Inspire employees with Olympic philosophies
- Relate sport to everyday business

- Encourage business development and idea generation
- Create better team dynamic and peer-to-peer recognition
- Increase brand awareness in relevant industry areas through PR and branding.

In 2011, GE Capital used their involvement in triathlon as a platform to encourage employees and clients to participate in physical activity, set achievable targets for the year and grow both individually and as a team. This was achieved in the following ways.

Hyde Park Triathlon – August 2011

GE Capital used the 2011 Hyde Park Triathlon to encourage employees and clients to take part in a three-person 'team relay' race on the exact course where the Olympics would be held one year later.

In the build up to the event, all participants were driven to a specific micro-site that provided race information, expert training guides, accommodation tips and other integral information to help them maximise their performance on the day. To create a unity and increase the brand presence, all 350 participants were given a GE Capital branded bike/run top to compete in.

The day was neatly integrated back to Helen's Olympic qualification race, with all employees encouraged to watch her compete and go on to win!

Masterclass events

To prepare for Hyde Park, the Jenkins couple hosted masterclasses in Birmingham and London that allowed employees and clients to participate in the three-hour sessions, which included:

- Introduction to triathlon
- Specialist training in all three disciplines
- Q&A
- Branded kit.

Community relations

At the London masterclass, Capital invited 20 inner-city 11–14 year-olds from community group SAZ (Sports-Action-Zone) to learn a sport they wouldn't normally have access to. The five-hour session included:

- Introduction to triathlon
- Specialist coaching in all disciplines
- Open-water swim practice
- Olympics talk
- Nutritional advice
- Branded kit.

case study 23.6 (continued)

Local and national media were invited to also attend the day, generating over 30 pieces of coverage both in print and online.

Training tips

The Jenkins created 10 training guides and 13 videos providing tips and regimes, distributed to employees and clients and available online through Facebook. By the end of 2011 these video clips had received over 100,000 views on YouTube.

Coaching courses

Through the GE Team sponsorship employees and clients have the opportunity to gain level 1–3 Triathlon Coaching qualifications through the BTF.

Business challenge

Using a purpose-built online incentive programme, all UK employees were invited to participate in the 'Triathlon Challenge'. Employees won virtual medals, which were accrued over the year, converting into a position on a leaderboard. Participants were asked to 'upload' medals (gold-silver-bronze), which were assessed by senior management. The three areas to win medals were:

1. Swim: peer-to-peer recognition – nominate colleagues for going above and beyond their daily role

2. Bike: business recommendations – suggesting ways the business can improve

3. Run: healthy pledges – employees encouraged to commit to healthy pledges, from bronze (e.g., drinking a litre of water a day) through to gold (e.g., running 10k for charity). Once achieved, they could redeem their medal.

Roundtable/conferences/public speaking

The Jenkins attended six events to speak to clients and employees. Sessions included informal roundtable discussions and client/employee conferences. Topics included:

■ Overcoming adversity and getting back to winning ways

■ Links between goal and objective-setting in sport and business

■ Olympic stories

■ Reacting to the situation and being prepared in case of failure.

Branding

The sponsorship of the Jenkins gives prime position on their race kit, prominent at all races as well as any media the pair do. With Helen racing all over the world and continually finishing on the podium this has created excellent PR opportunities and visual branding across hundreds of different medias, both online and in print.

Results

This holistic campaign delivered increased staff engagement, both within the business and community and in terms of their own health and wellbeing, while also engaging clients, key stakeholders and the community. The outputs of this initially employee-focused programme were then leveraged to deliver a vast and significant amount of brand media coverage.

Participation levels:

■ 45 teams took part at Hyde Park – 135 employees and clients

■ Increased participation – 135 per cent on 2010 activity at the London Triathlon

■ 74 employees and clients took part in a masterclass event

■ 14 employees and clients have undergone at least a level 1 coaching course.

Triathlon challenge:

■ 55 per cent of UK employees logged in

■ 410 healthy pledges made

■ 295 pledge redemptions

■ 68 peer-to-peer nominations

■ 113 business recommendations. (In 2009, without this system in place, senior management received 16 recommendations, so this is an increase of nearly 860 per cent.)

Roundtable/conferences/public speaking

■ 500 employees and clients attended a motivational speech by Marc

■ 80 per cent of survey respondents (72 people) rated Marc's speech 9/10+ for content and delivery

case study 23.6 (continued)

- 200 employees attended a talk from Marc at a quarterly all-employee event in the Sale offices

- 92 per cent of survey respondents (54 people) found Marc's speech engaging and informative and relevant to their working role

- 65 employees have attended one of three roundtable events in London hosted by Marc and Helen

- Objectives achieved: engage employees, customers, clients and KBIs/reiterate business strategy.

GE Capital media coverage

- Branded coverage in over 30 countries – national sport and triathlon media

- Branded TV coverage of athletes or sponsorships with over 200 million unique impressions reaching an audience of over 54 million actual viewers

- Over 500+ print national, sport and specialist sport pieces of coverage (branded and content) in the UK

- 972,000 Google search results for 'Helen Jenkins GE Capital' – up 1,000 per cent on 2010 results

- Branded training videos on YouTube received over 100,000 views

- 470 downloads of training guides from Facebook.

*GE Capital are the financial businesses within GE in the UK

Source: Simon Hearn

Explore 23.6   Building a sponsorship strategy

Put yourself in the position of a sponsorship consultant responsible for organising a major music festival for international music in Berlin. This festival is part of an internationally renowned series, however, so far no sponsor has been found to support it.

You are asked to devise a sponsorship strategy for this particular event, which must include:

- defining potential sponsors
- developing key selling points
- thinking about ways of contacting potential sponsors
- planning media coverage.

Feedback

If a sponsorship property is not selling, chances are it is either overpriced or not supplying potential sponsors with what they need. The starting point in such a situation is to start to examine in-depth what the event truly can or could offer (if augmented or altered) sponsors, and what kinds of sponsors would respond to this offering. Additionally, it is important to benchmark the proposed cost of the relationships against other sponsorship properties in the market able to deliver the same benefits (this might not just be direct competitors such as events but could be organisations, etc.).

Once this process is completed, you may find it is necessary to alter or augment the rights offering/sponsor support, change the types of organisations being approached or reduce the costs. The Mark Bayliss case study (23.2) provides a good model for approaching selling rights.

Picture 23.8 Helen Jenkins, Olympic and former world ITU triathlon champion, was sponsored by GE Capital to support employee engagement

Measuring success (evaluation and control)

Evaluating the effectiveness of sponsorship is of paramount importance. However, in practice, sponsorship activities are not conducted in a controlled environment, so that measurement becomes an uphill battle. Constraints include, for example, where many communication tools and channels are used, so, in an integrated campaign, it may not be possible to identify the particular contribution of sponsorship to the overall outcomes. Also, spill-over effects from prior activities, uncontrollable media coverage (the

channel is the message) or unspecified target objectives make a clear evaluation next to impossible. This also explains the reluctance of many managers to invest in sponsorship activities despite the opportunities. Attempts to evaluate effectiveness range from contact points (how many times did the logo appear on TV?) and cost ratio (cost per relevant consumer?) to opportunity analysis (advertising cost equivalent?) and scorecard approaches (how does sponsorship investment rate on various dimensions?) (Ukman 1996; Anderson 2003; Walliser 2003).

Depending on the sponsorship goals, *evaluation methods* rely on the modern marketing research instruments shown in Box 23.5.

Box 23.5

Marketing research instruments to measure sponsorship

The measurement methods for sponsorship should, as much as possible, match those utilised by the business for its other communications and business activities. This provides managers with an ability to measure a level of impact, and understanding of the success of a programme (or otherwise).

In normal circumstances the key measures should be as follows:

- Brand visibility (logo exposure, media coverage, etc.)
- Brand equity (image, attitudinal shifts, etc.)
- Brand loyalty
- Purchase intent (direct and indirect sales, purchase funnel impact)
- Engagement (social activity, experiential interaction)
- Employee satisfaction measures.

For a better control of sponsorship effects, tracking studies are increasingly deployed, in which data are collected at time intervals (multiple time-series design). Even though advanced research methods are used, it must be noted that there is no conclusive evidence of a relationship of common diagnostic measurements (e.g. image) and commercial results. Nevertheless, from a management point of view, it is the return on investment (ROI) that justifies a sponsorship engagement. So, ultimately, market share and sales increase (or maintaining market share and sales) will decide further activities. However, we must keep in mind that sponsorship activities only develop their full strategic potential as follows:

- through clearly defined goals
- over a longer time period
- within a communication bundle.

Managers must clearly define what they expect from their sponsoring investment, including a breakdown into specific sub-goals. This process approach guarantees permanent monitoring of sponsorship activities. As an integrative tool a sponsorship audit must at the same time reflect the interrelatedness – and dynamics – of the overall communication strategy.

Summary

As highlighted throughout, sponsorship has experienced unprecedented growth for a communications and marketing tool over the past decades, and the practice has evolved and changed significantly. When properly carried out it can deliver significant results for an organisation, both towards intangibles such as brand and reputation and through to tangibles such as stakeholder reach and direct financial returns. These changes have not gone unnoticed by major players in the global communications industry. Sponsorship agencies, advertising agencies, media planning companies and research institutes have a communication expertise that they now need to extend to the sponsorship field. Under the roof of communications services groups, there is a trend towards establishing sponsorship departments. Many media planning agencies, for example, link up with niche sponsorship, sport, art or cultural agencies to expand their service portfolio. Sponsorship has grown up and, as a modern communication tool, faces new challenges.

What does the future hold for sponsorship? With its exponential growth it could go anywhere. Sport Business, in 2008, stated that the trends for sports sponsorship were going to be greater active engagement in leveraging sponsorships, greater focus on reaching the next generation, sustainability, the convergence of media and sport itself and a threat of regulation preventing some of the biggest players from soft drinks (such as PepsiCo), fast food and other sectors viewed to be involved in contributing to society's ill – such as obesity or pollution – from being able to use sponsorship. These are still key issues for the future of sponsorship for all practitioners to consider. Only time will tell where this area of the communications mix, that was only a short time ago in its relative modern day infancy, will go as it becomes a key elder statesman.

Bibliography

Anderson, L. (2003). 'The sponsorship scorecard'. *B&T* 12 December: 13–14.

Bruhn, M. and C. Homburg (2001). *Gabler Marketing Lexikon.* Wiesbaden: Gabler Verlag.

Collins English Dictionary (2012). 'Definition of sponsorship'. www.collinsdictionary.com/dictionary/english/sponsorship accessed 12 October 2012.

Cooper, A. (2003). 'The changing sponsorship scene'. *Admap* 144, November.

Cornwell, B. and I. Maignan (2001). 'An international review of sponsorship research'. *Journal of Advertising* **27**(1): 1–21.

De Pelsmacker, P., M. Geuens and J. Van den Berg (2004). 'Sponsorship' in *Marketing Communications.* Harlow: Prentice Hall.

Electoral Commission (2012). 'Overview of donations to political parties'. www.electoralcommission.org.uk/guidance/resources-for-those-we-regulate/parties/donations-and-loans accessed 12 October 2012.

IEG (2000). *IEG Sponsorship Report – Outline.* Chicago, IL: IEG.

IEG Sponsorship Report (2008). 'Negotiating in-kind value and category exclusivity'. www.sponsorship.com/IEGSR/2008/11/03/Negotiating-In-kind-Value-And-Category-Exclusivity.aspx accessed 12 October 2012.

IEG Sponsorship Report (2009). 'Fun with category exclusivity'. www.sponsorship.com/About-IEG/Sponsorship-Blogs/Carrie-Urban-Kapraun/July-2009/Fun-with-Category-Exclusivity.aspx accessed 12 October 2012.

IEG Sponsorship Report (2012a). 'Economic uncertainty to slow sponsorship growth in 2012'. www.sponsorship.com/About-IEG/Press-Room/Economic-Uncertainty-To-Slow-Sponsorship-Growth-In.aspx accessed 12 October 2012.

IEG Sponsorship Report (2012b). 'Following the money: sponsorship's top spenders of 2011'. www.sponsorship.com/IEGSR/2012/05/28/Following-The-Money--Sponsorship-s-Top-Spenders-of.aspx accessed 12 October 2012.

IFM Sports Marketing Surveys (2012). *The World Sports Monitor Annual Review 2011.* United Kingdom.

Investopedia.com (2012). 'Corporate sponsorship'. www.investopedia.com/terms/c/corporate-sponsorship.asp accessed online 12 October 2012.

marketingmagazine.co.uk (2012). 'Marketing Society Awards for Excellence 2012: cause-related marketing'. www.brandrepublic.com/features/1135807/ accessed 20 October 2012.

Mawson, C. (2004). 'A history of the Shell county guides'. www.shellguides.freeserve.co.uk/history.htm.

Measurement Matters Blog (2012). 'Crisis and social media – a match made in heaven?'. www.gorkana.com/measurement-matters/measurement-matters/brand-reputation/crisis-and-social-media-a-match-made-in-heaven/ accessed 24 October 2012.

Meenaghan, T. (1998). 'Current developments and future directions in sponsorship'. *International Journal of Advertising* **17**(1): 3–28.

Moviefone (2012). 'Daniel Craig defends *Skyfall* Heineken sponsorship: "The movie cost a lot of money to make"'. http://news.moviefone.com/2012/04/16/daniel-craig-skyfall-heineken-sponsor_n_1429567.html accessed 24 October 2012.

MSNBC 'Tapping into shoppers' do-gooder spirit www.nbcnews.com/id/.../ns/.../retailers-tap-do-gooder-spirit accessed 31 May 2013.

New York Times (2010). 'For New Year's Eve, the tie-ins erupt'. www.nytimes.com/2010/12/14/business/media/14adco.html?_r=0 accessed 23 October 2012.

Pine, J. and J. Gilmore (1998). 'Welcome to the experience economy'. *Harvard Business Review* **76**(4): 97–105.

Porter, M. and M. Kramer (2002). 'The competitive advantage of corporate philanthropy'. *Harvard Business Review* **80**(12): 56–69.

Sport Business (2008). *The Future of Sports Marketing.* London.

Sport Business International (2010). *Sport Business In Numbers, Volume 4.* London.

Tench, R. and L. Yeomans (2009). *Exploring Public Relations.* London: FT Prentice Hall.

The Guardian (2003). 'Cadbury condemned over school sports sweetener'. www.guardian.co.uk/politics/2003/mar/30/schoolsports.schools accessed online 10 October 2012.

The Guardian (2012). 'Red Bull and Felix Baumgartner take sponsorship to new height'. www.guardian.co.uk/sport/blog/2012/oct/15/red-bull-felix-baumgartner-sponsorship accessed 15 October 2012.

Ukman, L. (1996). 'Defining objectives is key to measuring sponsorship return'. *Marketing News* **30**(18), 26 August: 5–6.

Walliser, B. (2003). 'An international review of sponsorship research'. *International Journal of Advertising* **22**(1): 5–40.

Websites

O2: www.o2.co.uk

ASICS Smarter Rugby: www.asics.co.uk/rugby/

Barclays cycle hire scheme: www.tfl.gov.uk/roadusers/cycling/14808.aspx

Comic Relief: www.comicrelief.com

Deloitte: www.deloitte.co.uk/london2012/index.cfm

Emirates airline: www.emiratesairline.co.uk

Freshfields: www.freshfields.com/en/united_kingdom/london_2012/Work/

Guggenheim: www.guggenheim.org/new-york/support/corporate/supporters

Gurgaon Metro: www.rapidmetrogurgaon.com/Advertizewithus.aspx

Holiday Inn: www.holidayinn.com/hotels/gb/en/global/offers/olympics_welcome

IMG Consulting: www.imgworld.com/services/consulting.aspx

inov-8: www.inov-8.com

Intercontinental Hotel Group: www.ichotelsgroup.com

JP Morgan Chase & Co. MLK: www.jpmorganchase.com/MLK

JP Morgan Chase & Co. Sponsorships: www.jpmorganchase.com/corporate/Corporate-Responsibility/sponsorships.htm

KFC potholes sponsorship: www.kfc.com/about/newsroom/032509.asp

London Triathlon: www.thelondontriathlon.co.uk

Mark Bayliss: www.teambayliss.co.uk

MLB: www.mlb.com

Natural History Museum ice rink: www.nhm.ac.uk/visit-us/whats-on/ice-rink/index.html

NBA: www.nba.com

NFL: www.nfl.com

PBS: www.pbs.org

Premier League: www.premierleague.com

PRWeek Awards: www.prweekawards.com

Rugby Football Union (England Rugby Team): www.rfu.com

Skyfall (James Bond movie): www.skyfall-movie.com

Sky Rainforest Rescue: www.wwf.org.uk/skyrainforestrescue

Somerset House ice rink: www.somersethouse.org.uk/ice-rink

SportsAid: www.sportsaid.org.uk

Sports Industry Awards: www.sportindustry.biz/awards

Sport Relief: www.sportrelief.com

Team Sky: www.teamsky.com

The O2 Arena: www.theo2.co.uk

Tiffany's Across the Water: www.supporttheroyalparks.org/explore/tiffany_fountains/drinking_fountain_restoration

PART 4

Sectoral considerations

This part of the text comprises chapters that are not conventionally included within a public relations (PR) text – yet their link to PR seems too important for them to be left out. The discussions and debates contained within each section highlight the link to PR, but also point out differences in worldview or approach.

The first chapter argues that corporate communication is often PR with a different label, but at the same time there is a conscious effort to define corporate communication as 'reputation management' – a term rarely found in the PR literature but more often found in management and marketing. The second chapter demonstrates that campaigning on behalf of NGOs or pressure groups is also PR when viewed as a process, yet there are special characteristics that make campaigning different from conventional PR. The next chapter considers the challenging environment for and different facets of health communication, while the following chapter identifies that while the dominant paradigm for the arts, leisure and entertainment sectors is marketing, it is PR that is helping to move these sectors forward in reaching fragmented audiences. The next chapter is an extension of some of the issues highlighted in the previous section but focuses on a highly visible part of communications – the role of PR in the support and promotion of celebrity cultures and individuals. Finally, the last chapter looks to the future, addressing key issues emerging from recent research among practitioners that will be of major importance to the profession.

CHAPTER 24

Emma Wood

Corporate communication

Learning outcomes

By the end of this chapter you should be able to:

■ define and describe how corporate communication is conceptualised and practiced, recognising the implications of different perspectives (whether it is about 'reflecting diversity' as opposed to 'integration and consistency', for example)

■ identify the influence of different ways of conceptualising corporate communication (from a marketing as opposed to a PR or organisational communication mindset) when reviewing public relations literature or practice and understand the implications of this

■ select effective frameworks for analysing the purpose and practice of corporate communication – using concepts of legitimacy and social capital – to identify key objectives and principles

■ understand that the ability to practice corporate communication in particular ways is affected by how the function is placed within (or integrated into) organisational structures.

Structure

■ Defining the term 'corporate communication'
■ The purpose of corporate communication (or frameworks for practice)
■ Corporate communication in practice
■ The organisational context: how corporate communication fits into organisational structures

Introduction

The news media, and particularly business journalists, often refer to 'large corporates', 'corporate environments' and worldwide 'corporations'. So what do we mean by the term 'corporate' and, more importantly, how do we define corporate communication?

Just as the term 'public relations' is used to signify anything from the antics of publicists to the maxim of mutual understanding, so a debate rages about the definition of 'corporate communication'.

It is a contested term – and the contest here is between functionalist scholars (often writing from a *marketing* or *management* perspective), who claim that corporate communication is about **integrating all communication to ensure the consistency of messages** (referred to as 'managing and orchestrating all internal and external communications' by van Riel and Fombrun 2007, for example), and critical scholars (often writing from an *organisational communication* perspective), who argue that communication cannot be controlled in this way and should be about **facilitating diversity and listening to 'the multiple voices of individuals'** (Christensen and Cornelissen 2011: 405).

These perspectives dominate polar ends of a broad spectrum, so this chapter will take what's valuable from both functionalist (or managerial) and critical perspectives and aim to: define the term; help the reader understand the aims or purpose of corporate communication (the frameworks which underpin practice); explore how to practice corporate communication and consider the organisational context – how organisations should be structured to facilitate effective corporate communication practice.

Defining the term 'corporate communication'

On the whole, definitions of corporate communication are often unclear, vague, or even missing in the conventional literature. Many textbooks, thus, take the notion of corporate communications for granted and define it only indirectly by listing the different types of activities it encompasses (Christensen and Cornelissen 2011: 385).

Perhaps authors prefer to avoid penning 'definitive' definitions of corporate communication because the conceptual terrain is contested and diverse. There are no real boundaries around what functions corporate communicators are responsible for, or, indeed, what they judge to be their goal or role in an organisation, as can be seen in Tables 24.1 and 24.2, which report results from the 2011 CCI Corporate Communication Practices and Trends Study benchmarking key elements of public relations practice in the USA among the Fortune 1,000 (America's 1,000 largest corporations ranked by *Fortune* magazine).

Any definition needs to reflect the philosophical underpinning of the concept but also what, in practical terms, practitioners aim to achieve on behalf of the organisations they work for. To avoid the accusation of being vague or of avoiding the difficult task of defining the concept and practice, the following is presented as a definition that hopefully embraces the philosophical ambitions of *organisational communication* and the practical outcomes engendered by a *managerial* perspective.

Corporate communication means engaging with stakeholders to establish and communicate *meaningful* (Christensen et al. 2008b) values to encourage the organisation (and organisational members) to *behave* in a way that is consistent (but not homogeneous) with these values in order to build *social capital* and establish *legitimacy*. The aim is to secure stakeholder support (measurable as outcomes such as local communities being open to corporate plans, employees feeling highly motivated, top performers seeking employment with an organisation, investors wanting to invest and legislators not jumping to introduce punitive legislation *as well as* potential consumers being more open to promotional messages aimed at persuading them to purchase goods or use services).

The purpose of corporate communication (or frameworks for practice)

Corporate communication as establishing and maintaining legitimacy

'Legitimacy is a generalized perception or assumption that the actions of an entity are desirable, proper, or appropriate within some socially constructed system of norms, values, beliefs and definitions' (Suchman 1992: 574). Weber is widely

Percentage of respondents who agree that they perform the following functions	%
Communication strategy	100.0%
Media relations	98.0%
Public relations	98.0%
Crisis communication	94.1%
Communication policy	94.1%
Executive communication	92.2%
Reputation management	88.2%
Intranet	88.2%
Internal communication	88.2%
Social media	83.3%
Internet communication	80.4%
Issues management	78.4%
Annual report	70.6%
Corporate identity	69.2%
Community relations	62.7%
Mission statement	60.8%
Corporate culture	56.9%
Corporate citizenship	56.9%
Brand strategy	45.1%
Marketing communications	41.2%
Advertising	35.3%
Government relations	21.6%
Investor relations	15.7%
Technical communication	11.8%
Training and development	9.8%
Ethics	7.8%
Labour relations	2.0%

Table 24.1 Key corporate communication functions and budget responsibilities (*source*: Corporate Communication International 2011)

1. Manager of company's reputation
2. Counsel to the CEO and the corporation
3. Manager of the company's image
4. Manager of employee relations (internal communication)
5. Advocate or 'engineer of public opinion'
6. Driver of company publicity
7. Source of public information about the company
8. Branding and brand perception steward
9. Member of the strategic planning leadership team
10. Manager of relationships (non-customer constituencies)
11. Support for marketing and sales
12. Manager of relationships (all key constituencies)
13. Corporate philanthropy (citizenship) champion

Table 24.2 Role that best describes corporate communication function (ranked) (*source*: Corporate Communication International 2011)

credited as defining legitimacy as an important sociological concept, predominantly focusing on the legitimacy of political and social institutions – but Suchman's definition has informed much of the organisational literature on legitimacy where it is a central concept within organisa-

tional theory (Meyer and Rowan 1977; Scott 1998 in Waeraas 2009). Increasingly, however, the concept is also being used to analyse public relations activity and, in some cases, to define the practice itself (Mettzler 2001; Waeraas 2009). Waeraas states that: 'We may assert that public relations is involved not only in acquiring legitimacy and making sure that the organization has the voluntary support of its stakeholders, but also in protecting the organization's legitimacy itself . . . then we may easily argue that public relations is all about obtaining and preserving legitimacy' (p.309).

It could be argued that this definition does not embrace the aim of much *public relations* practice, which goes beyond establishing legitimacy and aims to provoke or encourage specific behaviours – in particular to persuade consumers to buy products or services or to support causes. Establishing and sustaining legitimacy does, however, seem to perfectly describe the aim of *corporate communication*, which isn't immediately focused on consumer activity but is focused on establishing the levels of trust and respect that will result in stakeholders granting a 'license to operate' – in other words building and maintaining legitimacy for organisations.

As we exist in an increasingly unstable and changing society it becomes more difficult and also more important for organisations to establish legitimacy. Habermas

(1973/1976) has famously pointed to a crisis in legitimation – an erosion in trust of, and support for, political institutions and even nation states. Bearing in mind that we are currently living through what some would call unprecedented levels of uncertainty in the corporate sector (in the midst of a global financial crisis), it is not far fetched to claim that not only do political and state institutions face a legitimation crisis – but corporate bodies do too. Whereas a few decades ago professionals such as bank managers and doctors and the organisations that employed them were viewed as sacrosanct, more recent corporate and other crises have eroded that 'taken for granted' trust, resulting in a 'death of deference'. This means that organisations now have to earn legitimacy rather than expect or assume it. Surely then, earning legitimacy is the primary job of the corporate communication specialist?

Explore 24.1

How corporate communicators establish and maintain the legitimacy of their organisations

In 2011, Apple topped the *Fortune* list of the world's most admired companies for the fourth year in a row. This can clearly be seen as an indication of its legitimacy – think of four reasons why Apple is a legitimate organisation with a good reputation.

Feedback

Is it because:

■ It is perceived as always obeying law and hasn't been involved in any scandals?

■ It is a huge company and one of the very first producers of home computers and therefore is seen as an authority based on tradition?

■ It's a 'cool' company and associated with the late Steve Jobs, a very charismatic leader?

Each of these reasons relates to the principles on which Weber (1922/1968 in Waeraas 2009: 304) claims legitimacy may be based. Readers interested in following these principles to guide corporate communication practice aimed at legitimating the organisations they represent would do well to read Waeraas (2009).

■ It is always in the media – with its executives routinely used as sources of expert opinions?

Routine media exposure can result in an accumulation of 'institutional legitimacy' and media capital (Davis 2003; Davis and Seymour 2010) or cultural capital (Bourdieu 1986).

Corporate communication as developing social capital

It's interesting to consider the accumulation of media or cultural capital (discussed above) as a way of establishing and maintaining legitimacy for an organisation or individual. And this leads on to a consideration of what other resources corporate communicators can draw on in order to do their jobs effectively.

Ihlen (2009) analyses the forms of resources (or capital) conceptualised by Bourdieu and presents a reworked typology interpreted in relation to the public relations practitioner. Out of these, *social capital* and *symbolic capital* are particularly important to the corporate communicator. Symbolic capital resonates very much with the concept of legitimation already discussed, and social capital is a valuable resource in building trust, relationships and reputation – all of which are key outcomes of corporate communication practice.

The concept of social capital is significant in current political thinking and policy making in the UK, with the introduction of a happiness or wellbeing index (which already operates in France and Canada) as an addition to measuring GDP. The concept of social capital is central to the development of this (and to policy making about community capacity building). Thinking further afield, it's useful to consider the definition of social capital adopted by the Office for Economic Co-operation and Development (OECD), which states:

> *Social capital is defined as the norms and social relations embedded in the social structures of societies that enable people to co-ordinate action to achieve desired goals.*

The term 'social capital' has found its way into economic analysis only recently, although various elements of the concept have been present under different names for a long time . . . Economists have added the focus on the contribution of social capital to economic growth. There is still no consensus, however, on which aspects of interaction and organisation merit the label of social capital, nor on how to measure it and how to determine empirically its contribution to economic growth and development (OECD 2011).

As the concept is emerging as an influence on policy making internationally, it's clearly important for corporate communicators to understand it and be able to demonstrate how their organisations contribute to building social capital within the communities in which they operate.

Putnam's (2000: 19) conceptualisation of social capital as 'connections among individuals – social networks and the norms of reciprocity and trustworthiness that arise from them' is possibly the most familiar – he writes about the disintegration of this type of community cohesion in contemporary America (Putnam 1996, 2000, 2002). So, for corporate bodies, social capital can refer to the impact that organisations may have on sustaining cohesive societies (through employment creation, community relations and corporate social responsibility activities and so on) but, as the OECD recognises (OECD 2011), the concept can be defined in different ways. And an alternative interpretation – propounded by Bourdieu (1986) – is also useful to corporate communicators. This definition is nuanced in a way that is more pragmatic in highlighting the strategic benefits to be accrued for people and organisations with high levels of social capital. Bourdieu's view is that such benefits can be accrued by building relationships as a member of a network, which Ilhen (2009: 74) translates for public relations as investment in 'strengthening connections with politicians, journalists, activist groups bureaucrats, researchers and other organisations'.

Effective corporate communicators then must be able to demonstrate how their organisations contribute to building social capital within communities (perhaps through CSR, community engagement and establishing dialogue with a variety of stakeholder groups as part of organisational decision making) in order to demonstrate value to society. But also, they must be able to develop relationships within broad networks of appropriate actors to accrue social capital as defined by Bourdieu (1986) and Ilhen (2009). Both activities are aimed at enhancing visibility, developing relationships and a trustworthy reputation in order to establish and maintain legitimacy and an organisation's license to operate.

So – how do you build social capital and establish legitimacy?

Corporate communication in practice

Defining corporate communication as the communication of *corporate* values, as opposed to the promotion of *consumer* products or services, means marketing communication is aimed at consumers, and corporate communication is communication aimed at engaging with other publics and stakeholders. This approach (and, in particular, notions of establishing legitimacy and building social capital) links corporate communication in practice to concepts of managing *corporate reputation*, *corporate image* and *relationship management*. For example, in the case of the Fairtrade Foundation, its *corporate* communication strategy may be aimed at developing strong relationships with partners and employees and building its reputation as an organisation that contributes to sustainable develop-

ment by offering better trading conditions to, and securing the rights of, marginalised producers and workers. In contrast, its *consumer* or *marketing* communication would focus on promoting the benefits of various Fairtrade certified products to customers and potential customers.

So, consumer communication is focused on selling a service or product, and contrasts with corporate communication, which is focused on a broader range of stakeholders and is aimed at building positive relationships and reputation. In the case of the Fairtrade Foundation, it is clear how its reputation and relationships facilitate more effective selling of its products. But effective corporate communication is not just linked to creating a favourable sales environment; it can contribute to business strategy in many other ways, as shown in Box 24.1.

Typically, then, corporate communication conceptualised in this way refers to communication (or relationship building) with political, community, financial, media, competitor, supplier and internal publics (but not consumers).

Defining corporate values

A key issue for public relations is to ensure that communication doesn't just focus on packaging the organisation in a way that appeals to *consumers* but involves two-way communication (hopefully dialogue) with a *diverse range of stakeholders*, many of whom may have conflicting needs, or interests: which is why some commentators feel that the function should be organised separately from marketing, as discussed later in the chapter. Difficulties can emerge, then, in determining clear, consistent communication for an organisation, which is important in relation to reputation and creating a clear identity, without excluding or alienating some stakeholder groups. This can't be achieved by a branding exercise, which involves *imposing* corporate key messages and ensuring organisational members adhere to them. It can be helped, though, by *involving* a whole range of stakeholder groups in the process of identifying key values and demonstrating how these can help focus communications emanating from different parts of an organisation.

This has usefully been conceptualised as identifying 'common starting points' (CSPs) (van Riel 1995), which are central values developed by communications staff from research into an organisation's desired corporate identity and image. Examples of CSPs include reliability, innovation, quality, profit making and synergy (ibid.). CSPs function as 'wavelengths' or 'parameters' to guide communication activity. The concept of CSPs fosters a notion of an organic process of developing and communicating organisational images rather than a top-down approach, which limits staff to static, agreed perceptions. As Leitch and Motion

Box 24.1

How corporate communication, which is conceptualised as managing corporate reputation (establishing legitimacy)* or relationship management (building and maintaining social capital), contributes to business strategy

Anyco is a toy manufacturer with a strategic aim of expanding its factory (located in a suburb of a large city, adjoining an area of natural beauty). Its reputation as a good employer and conscientious neighbour, coupled with strong relationships with a range of stakeholders, may have the following results:

- stop the local community from objecting to planning permission

- make politicians more confident in granting planning permission

- engage environmental groups in measures to protect local wildlife

- involve the media in communicating a positive case for the expansion

- encourage suppliers to supply increased orders efficiently and with care for the local community (using the roads at times that do not coincide with local children going to school, for example)

- ensure employees feel involved in the expansion and remain committed to Anyco

- attract the best prospective employees to apply for jobs

- persuade shareholders and others to invest in the project.

Although the expansion will eventually help Anyco produce and sell more products, it can clearly be seen that communication designed to build a strong reputation and relationships in this context is not aimed at persuading consumers to buy products or services. So, when commentators talk about corporate communication being aimed at a broader spectrum of stakeholders than marketing or promotional communications, this is the type of approach they mean. This example also illustrates a range of *corporate communication objectives* (which again differ from those associated with marketing or consumer communication).

The concepts of legitimacy and social capital are rarely explicated in most functionalist public relations writing, whereas the concepts of reputation and relationship management often are. These ideas are certainly not interchangeable but there are interesting relationships between them. For further discussion of this see Deephouse and Suchman (2008) and Deephouse and Carter (2005), who explain that 'legitimacy emphasizes the social acceptance resulting from adherence to social norms and expectations whereas reputation emphasizes comparisons among organizations'.

(1999: 195) explain: 'An organisation may present multiple images to its various publics provided that these images are consistent, not with each other, but with the organisation's CSPs.' They have developed the concept to include the identification of common end points (CEPs), or communication goals, and the idea is that by understanding or internalising both of these, organisational members can be free to communicate in a way that suits them in all the various and unpredictable interactions with stakeholders (multiple identity enactments or MIEs) (Motion and Leitch 2002) because they will always be guided by their knowledge of the CSPs and CEPs. However, Christensen et al. (2008a, 2008b) warn that approaches such as these, while seeming to be about facilitating multiplicity or diversity, can actually be controlling. The key to their criticism

of ways of identifying and establishing central values is that these processes can be top down and 'tend to reinforce a vertical and thus hierarchical communication structure and ignore or downplay the importance of horizontal communication exchanges' (Christensen et al. 2008a: 439). To avoid this they advocate common process rules, or CPR.

The key to all this is the understanding that organisations are not homogeneous but multifaceted and populated by lots of individuals in different work groups. The modern organisation also looks to build partnerships with external stakeholder groups and integrate them into the organisation too. So the process of identifying shared values must engage and involve the diverse range of stakeholders, and not just senior management views. A key corporate communication task is to engage to identify the

Case study 24.1
Illustrating CSPs and CEPs

Queen Margaret University (QMU) in Edinburgh teaches a whole range of degree courses, and its academics are involved in many different types of research – ranging from research by health professionals into how to manage pain to research in the drama school into the role of the pantomime dame. Clearly, then, the way in which such disparate areas will communicate with both internal and external stakeholders will be very different – and it would be inappropriate to impose a homogeneous approach on everyone. At the same time, though, it's important that people have a clear image or idea of what QMU is and does – so how should the corporate communication team guide communication to achieve a consistent image or reputation?

The answer is to identify shared values and common starting points (CSPs), which in this case focus everyone's activities on 'relevance', 'addressing society's needs' and 'developing knowledge which touches people's everyday lives'.

So at QMU the institution details that its shared values are:

- development of academic excellence in service to the community;

- social responsibility towards all of the communities we serve, demonstrating respect, care, social justice, equality and fairness;

- concern for the environment and sustainable use of natural resources; and

- commitment to continuous improvement in all we do.

And the common end points (CEPs) include:

- We will be known for delivering **inter-professional** education and research that has the well-being of the person in mind at all times; this will be achieved through **inter-disciplinary** working and research.

- Our **inter-professional** education and research will allow us to work within and across academic and practice areas, cross-fertilising thinking and facilitating the development of joined-up solutions. Our inter-disciplinary approach will help encourage professional groups to work better together for the benefit of others.

- The education and research that we provide will be **industry-relevant**, guided by the needs of society for high quality and socially responsible industry, the professions we serve, the local community and society as a whole.

values and then ensure everyone knows how these can be embedded into all aspects of organisational communication (including use of symbols and behaviour).

Many organisations involve teams of people engaging with stakeholders in different ways. For example, investment management companies may need to demonstrate their ability to take risks and embrace cutting edge developments to growing companies seeking their venture capital, while simultaneously demonstrating to their rich private clients that their money is in safe, stable hands. Or a city council may have to demonstrate that it will listen to and engage with its local communities and service providers while also having to demonstrate that it can make tough budget decisions.

The first job for any corporate communicator, then, is to identify these key shared values, which resonate with diverse stakeholders and encapsulate what an organisation stands for.

Identifying shared values

This process should first involve research to identify values *currently* emerging through organisational communication and then research to determine if these are coherent (tell a

corporate story about what type of organisation it is) and are consistent with what a range of stakeholders believe to be the values of the organisation they are involved with.

The most obvious way to identify values currently being communicated is to conduct a content and discourse analysis of things like mission statements, websites, promotional brochures, annual reports and social media, and so on. But only focusing on these 'controlled' communications doesn't take account of many of the ways in which an organisation communicates – Leitch and Motion's (2002) multiple identity enactments. In particular, it could exclude communication that happens at the subtle (but very important) level of culture. So an interesting way to audit or identify organisational values in an inclusive (rather than top-down) way is to use Johnson et al.'s (2011) tool to audit the culture of organisations. Culture is seen to influence 'the way we do things round here' – the 'taken for granted assumptions, or paradigm, of an organisation' (Johnson et al. 2011: 176).

The values that inform 'the way we do things around here' can be identified from a careful analysis of aspects of the culture web. See Johnson et al. (2011: 179) for an application of the cultural web to a law firm in the UK and a whole range of appropriate research questions investigating areas such as: the type of behaviour encouraged by particular routines; core beliefs reflected by stories; ways in which power is distributed in the organisation; and the status symbols favoured.

Once values *currently being communicated* via stories told, corporate materials produced, symbols highlighted and so on are identified, it's then time to engage a diverse range of external as well as internal stakeholders to focus on identifying what shared values, common starting points and common end points *should be communicated*. It's important to avoid this being a top-down approach, or an empty consultation exercise where values identified by senior managers are presented to stakeholders to agree so that an 'engagement' box can be ticked in a tool kit approach to corporate communication. And a significant body of knowledge points to dialogue theory and dialogic and deliberative approaches (see Kapein and van Tulder 2003; Anderson et al. 2004; Deetz and Simpson 2004; Heath 2007; de Bussy 2010) as being the best way to achieve engagement with stakeholders. (Indeed, views are emerging that point to the importance of this approach to public relations: (Kent and Taylor 2002; Heath et al.

2006; Bruning et al. 2008; Pieczka 2011.) In this approach, very specific facilitation techniques need to be employed in order to achieve real dialogue – which depends on participants suspending assumptions, not being judgmental and creating a 'safe space' for discussions to take place. For more information about dialogic techniques see the QMU Centre for Dialogue (http://www.qmu.ac.uk/mcpa/cdial/default.htm).

Communicating corporate values

Having engaged a range of stakeholders in identifying shared values, common starting points and common end points, it's important to ensure that everyone understands them and that they influence the way everyone communicates with stakeholders (see Figure 24.1 for ways in which corporate communicators communicate). An important part of this is to practice two-way communication and make sure corporate values influence corporate strategies.

Corporate strategy gurus Johnson et al. explain that: 'Strategy is the long-term direction of an organisation' (2011: 4), although an earlier definition may be more

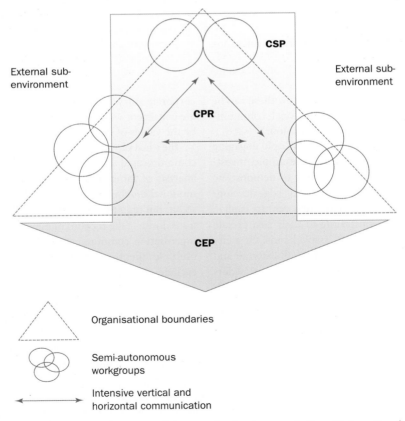

Figure 24.1 The balance between centralisation and decentralisation in organisational integration (*source*: Christensen et al. 2008: 440)

helpful: 'strategy is the *direction* and *scope* of an organisation over the *long term*: which achieves advantage for the organisation through its configuration of *resources* within a changing environment, to meet the needs of *markets* and to fulfill *stakeholder* expectations.' (Johnson and Scholes 2002: 10). (See Figure 24.2.)

In simplistic terms, organisations are usually run by a chief executive and a board of directors or executive committee, depending on the type of organisation it is (whether it is in the public or private sector, etc.). This dominant coalition (Grunig 1992; Grunig et al. 2002) formulates the corporate strategic plan, which sets out what the organisation aims to achieve (often over a five-year period) as well as the values and philosophy to which it will adhere. This could be considered to be stage one of the planning process. (See Figure 24.3.)

However, as well as being a member of the executive board, each director is also responsible for directing the management of a specific division/department/business unit (the use of alternative labels in the literature is seemingly endless, so for the purposes of this text the term 'division' will be used). The names of some typical divisions are included in the various structure diagrams elsewhere in this chapter.

The director and the management team of the division will then analyse the overall corporate strategic plan and identify ways in which their division's activities can contribute to achieving these overarching aims. This takes us to stage two of the planning process, when each division sets its own five-year plan. For example, the corporate communication senior management team identifies how *communication* can help achieve specific organisational strategic aims and objectives and sets a communication plan to direct and focus future communication effort.

And finally, stage three in the planning process occurs at an operational level when the management team works with the 'technicians', or communication team responsible for implementing the plans, to identify and schedule the activities that, it is to be hoped, will achieve the divisional and, eventually, the corporate objectives.

Clearly, this is a vastly simplified model of an approach to strategic planning. Its purpose is to demonstrate the way in which corporate communication can be tied to overall corporate strategy but in no way attempts to represent the literature in this field. It should also be noted that although this appears to be a hierarchical, 'top-down' and linear process, in reality it could be much more inclusive and organic. For an effective guide to corporate strategy, see Johnson et al. (2011). See also Case study 24.2.

Linking communication activities to the overall organisational plan is often deemed vital in ensuring communication is taken seriously at the highest levels (i.e., viewed as strategic and central to organisational success). 'Practitioners must not focus on pushing communication higher up senior management's agenda, but rather connect communication to what is already at the top of that agenda' (Quirke in Steyn 2003).

It could also be argued that really strategic communication would have already been involved in setting the senior management agenda.

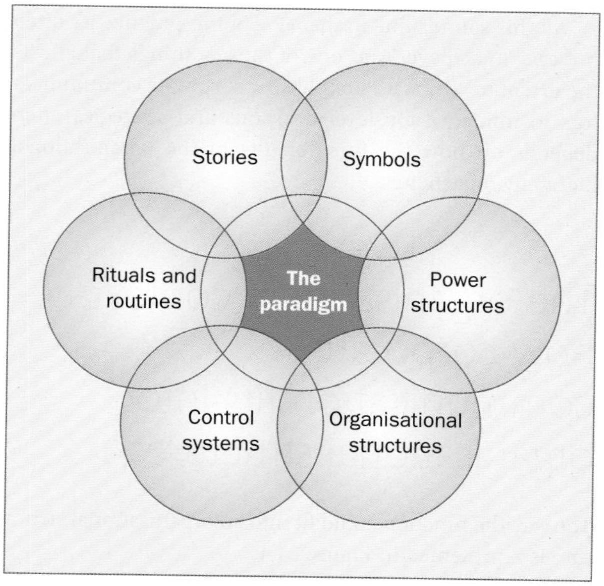

Figure 24.2 A cultural web (*source*: Johnson et al. 2011: 176)

Stage 1

Dominant coalition create corporate strategy embodied in corporate mission and values and five-year plan (influenced by commercial and other imperatives including stakeholder expectations, government policy and other issues prevalent in its particular environment)

Stage 2

Corporate communication director and communication managers identify ways in which communication can help achieve overall corporate objectives.
Expressed as aims and objectives in a communication strategy

Stage 3

Communication managers work with communication 'technicians' (e.g. writers) to develop tactics that will deliver communication objectives (expressed as tactics in the communications plan)

Figure 24.3 Three stages of strategic planning

Case study 24.2

'Anytown University College' (AUC)

An example of how communication aims and objectives relate to overall strategic aims

Stage 1
One of AUC's overall strategic aims is to achieve full university status.

Stage 2
One of the criteria for achieving university status is having 4,000 students (AUC currently has 3,000 students).

The UK Government caps the number of European Union (EU) undergraduate students AUC can recruit, so the vice-principals recognise that one of the things AUC needs to do to become a university is to recruit more *postgraduate* and *overseas* students. So the communication director considers how communication can help achieve this and sets a communication aim of increasing enquiries from suitable overseas and postgraduate students (note that the aim here is not to recruit more students – that is not achievable by public relations alone, as enrolling a student depends on many factors outside the control of the public relations department, so the aim is focused only on what *communication* can achieve).

Stage 3
The public relations team recognises that the website is an important communication channel and sets an objective geared towards ensuring that at least 90 per cent of postgraduate and overseas students considering applying to AUC are able easily to access information that is useful and pertinent to them via the website.

How corporate communication influences corporate decision making

One of the key characteristics of Grunig and colleagues' (2002) 'Excellent' public relations programmes is the public relations director holding a powerful role 'in or with the **dominant coalition**'.

Correspondingly, then, one of the key aspects of the corporate communication role would be the extent to which the 'communication czar' (Grunig et al. 2002) is involved in influencing and shaping the *overall business strategy*, rather than just being involved in the 'second layer' of decision making (about how communication can help achieve predetermined company goals).

So, if corporate communication is the area that 'oversees' communication, it would seem that this is the area that can balance the needs of stakeholders with those of the organisation. It is the corporate communicator's role, then, to determine whether most resources are shared among a broad range of stakeholders or only channelled towards the powerful (the customer, shareholder or politician). For further debates on this see discussions about stakeholder mapping and CSR earlier in the text.

All this sounds fine in theory – but in practice it's often not easy to achieve. And one of the key things that affects the extent to which it's possible for corporate communicators to influence top-level decisions and strategies often depends on how the function fits in the organisational hierarchy or structure.

Definition: The *dominant coalition* is 'the group of individuals within the organisation who have the power to determine its mission and goals. They are the top managers who "run" the organisation. In the process, they often make decisions that are good enough to allow the organisation to survive but designed primarily to maintain the status quo and keep the current dominant coalition in power' (Grunig et al. 2002: 141). It is not a term most practitioners would recognise – in practice, terms such as 'board of directors' or 'senior management' would be used, but the inference is the same.

The organisational context: how corporate communication fits into organisational structures

The way the function could fit into an organisational structure is represented in Figure 24.4.

In this way the director of corporate communication will be part of the 'dominant coalition' and be able to influence organisational decision making from a corporate

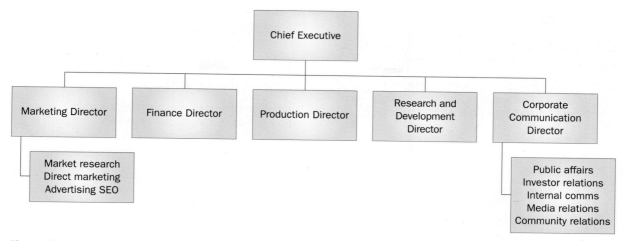

Figure 24.4 How corporate communication and marketing can fit into an organisational structure

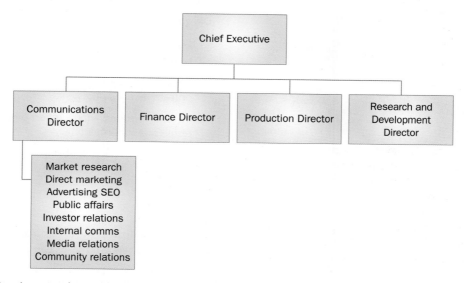

Figure 24.5 How integrated communication fits in an organisation

communication perspective (i.e., thinking through impacts on a wide range of stakeholders and in relation to building legitimacy and social capital). However, the corporate communication function can be incorporated differently – not as a separate corporate communication division but as an *integrated communications* division (integrated with marketing), and not reporting through a specialist director of corporate communication but through a director of integrated communications, as represented in Figure 24.5.

Both the structures outlined in Figures 24.4 and 24.5 represent a *centralised* approach to communication, where all communication is channelled through a single department, which delivers clear benefits here in terms of facilitating consistency.

Clearly, geography and knowledge of local culture is also a significant variable related to the ideal positioning of the communication department within the organisational structure. For example, can a centralised communication department really effectively represent geographically disparate locations?

The Confederation of British Industry (CBI), for example, has a press office at its London headquarters where other corporate public relations functions, such as lobbying and public affairs, take place. However, it also has people with responsibility for local public relations in its regional (and other national) offices (see Picture 24.1). And, of course, understanding the culture and complexity of specific areas becomes even more important when practising internationally. (See Explore 24.2.)

CBI offices

To ensure that the CBI remains close to and responsive to its members, wherever they are located, we have offices in 12 distinct geographical areas. We are also able to monitor and influence European legislation through our Brussels office, and American legislation through our staff based in Washington DC

In each area, the CBI's local director and a small team ensure that members have opportunities to be involved in consultations on policy and to hear from CBI policy experts, local MPs and ministers on how government

Picture 24.1 CBI location map (*source*: adapted from CBI, offices location map, http://www.cbi.org.uk)

Defining corporate communication as integrated communication

Much has been made in the literature of the ideas of *integrated communication*, where all communication functions are integrated into the same department and guided by the same strategic communication plan led by what Grunig et al. (2002: 302) refer to as 'a communication czar, pope or chief reputation officer'.

Although this approach to corporate communication is often referred to as integrated communication, true integration is rare (Grunig 2002; Hutton 2010). It is far more likely that one area (corporate or consumer) has been subsumed into the other and therefore exists in a

---

Explore 24.2

How corporate communication departments work

Whether integrated within the organisational structure or not, corporate public relations supports or works in conjunction with other departments. List ways in which a corporate communication department could work with:

1. marketing
2. human resources/personnel
3. finance
4. management.

Feedback

Did you suggest the following?

1. Media relations before or during a new product launch.
2. Employee engagement events or communication or team meeting notes.
3. Investor relations, annual report preparation and results announcements.
4. Issue management, lobbying, community relations and crisis management.

---

department dominated by a particular (and possibly restrictive) worldview. And so, as Christensen et al. (2009: 212) argue, the push for integrated communication isn't just about ensuring consistency but is also about power: 'the power to define the limits of integration and by extension select the signs that represent the organization and reject the ones that do not'. As has already been explored, effective corporate communication must be about two-way communication and engaging *with stakeholders* rather than being about communicating nicely packaged coherent branding messages *at audiences*. Of these two different approaches, the first is usually associated with public relations/organisational communication and the latter with a marketing approach. This is significant then if, when communication is integrated, those in control or directing activities are from marketing rather than a public relations or organisational communication background. This process (the takeover of corporate as well as marketing communication) is often referred to as *encroachment*.

The key issue is: which paradigm (consumer or corporate) dominates the communication approach? If all

Explore 24.3   Structuring corporate communication

List all the advantages of having a single communication department that directs communication with all stakeholders.

What are the advantages of a decentralised approach, where instead of a single department, communication specialists are employed in different divisions or units throughout the organisation, or stakeholders can contact anyone in the organisation for comment?

What are the advantages and disadvantages of using public relations and/or specialist communications consultancies instead of in-house employees?

Feedback

In thinking about *centralisation*, have you considered issues such as: having more control over information released about the organisation; being able to direct media requests to appropriate (and trained) spokespeople; being able to ensure all information is newsworthy or of value; and checking consistency of corporate messages? The disadvantage of a centralised approach may well be that too much control could appear to be suspicious (trying to block free access to information), slow down the process by which stakeholders (particularly the media) can get information and negate the value of local knowledge or relationships.

communication activity is represented at board level by a single individual, like Grunig's (2002) communication czar (otherwise known as the communication director, *or* chief communication officer), it is likely that they are either from a marketing background *or* from a corporate communication/public relations background, but not both. It could be argued, therefore, that their mindset will frame their approach to communication. The crucial question is this: is it a *marketing* mindset, in which case a *consumer*

paradigm may dominate and public relations will be confined to the rather narrow focus of consumer PR? Or is it a *public relations* mindset, in which case communications will encroach on marketing and a broader *stakeholder* perspective will direct communication activity – meaning a full range of stakeholders including employees, community, political publics and suppliers will be prioritised alongside consumers? (See Box 24.2 and Explore 24.2.)

Box 24.2

Controversy and debate

Marketing encroachment of public relations – does mind-set matter?

Kitchen and Schultz (2001) seem to epitomise the *marketing-centred* way of conceptualising corporate communication: their perspective is informed by the idea that 'the corporation, in our view, has become a brand that also needs to be "marketed", or, put another way, *communicated* for in our view, most marketing is communication and most communication is essentially marketing' (Kitchen and Schultz 2001: 5). This approach informs their conceptualisation of corporate communication as an umbrella 'raised as a protective nurturing device held over the strategic business units and individual brands within its portfolio' (Kitchen and Schultz 2001: 11). (See Figure 24.6.)

'What we mean by "raising the corporate umbrella" is that senior executives, led by the CEO, need to conceive

and present the organisation in such a way that it not only protects and nurtures all the individual brands and customer relationships within its portfolio, but that the organisation stands for something other than an anonymous faceless profit-taking corporate entity.' (Kitchen and Schultz 2001: 5)

There is a clear resonance here with a public relations-centric conceptualisation of corporate communication (particularly in the aim of communicating a 'more than profit-taking' identity), but it is interesting to note the gaps and differences. In particular, Kitchen and Schultz specify an organisation protecting and nurturing 'individual brands and *customer* relationships'. No mention of the broader range of *stakeholders* deemed essential by public relations. Looking at the spokes of the Kitchen and Schultz umbrella – 'employees' and 'partners' are represented, but the local community, government, suppliers and activist groups (or NGOs) are significantly absent.

Contrast this with a public relations-centred conceptualisation, as represented by Grunig and Hunt's (1984) application of the Esman model of external linkages of organisations (Figure 24.6).

→

box 24.2 (continued)

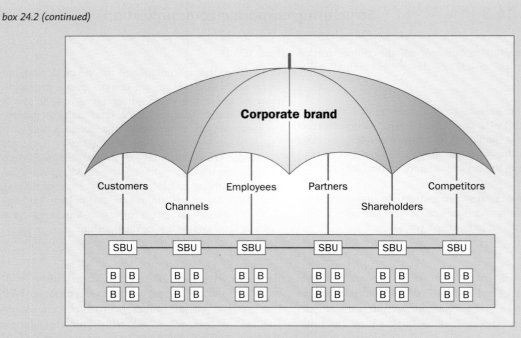

Figure 24.6 Raising the corporate umbrella (*source*: Kitchen and Schultz 2001: 11)

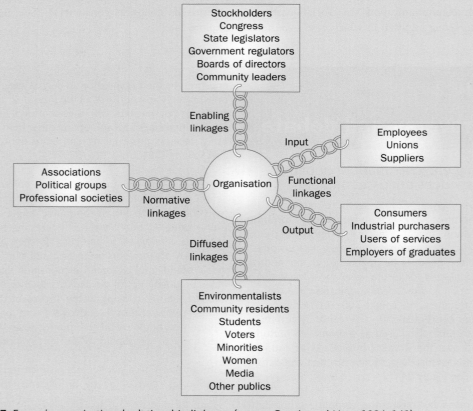

Figure 24.7 Esman's organisational relationship linkages (*source*: Grunig and Hunt 1984: 141)

box 24.2 (continued)

In what can be termed a *marketing-centred approach* to corporate communication, which is evident throughout much of the literature, significant stakeholders, such as politicians and local communities, are routinely absent and corporate communication (and public relations) is represented as promotion of a product or service.

This is one of the strongest reasons for public relations scholars to reject the notion of integrated communication: 'The organization is best served by the inherent diversity of perspectives provided by marketing and public relations when those functions remain distinct, co-ordinated yet *not integrated*' (Grunig et al. 2002: 264).

From the other side of the divide (or perhaps on the fence), some marketing academics consider the basis of public relation's rejection of the marketing paradigm as being flawed. Hutton (2010: 516), for example, believes that 'some PR scholars fail to understand what marketing involves and thus when describing the relationship between marketing and public relations make a number of claims that would be considered nonsense by sophisticated marketing practitioners'.

So, there are some clear distinctions to be made between marketing and public relations but there are also areas of shared ground within the separate paradigms. Cheney and Christensen note these as being primarily linked to the conception of communication as a *two-way process* by both disciplines: 'public relations and marketing have come to conceive of their communication with the external world as an on-going dialogue' (Cheney and Christensen 2001: 237). (See Table 24.3.)

Clearly, then, just as approaches to public relations differ across sectors and according to practitioners' expertise and background, so do approaches to marketing. Thus Hutton attacks public relations theorists for being inflexible in prescribing a 'best' structural relationship between marketing and public relations, regardless of context – an approach he deems to be 'false and not in keeping with a true management orientation, which would argue that form should vary according to situation and objectives' (Hutton 2010: 513).

	Marketing	Public relations
Traditional differences		
Target group	Markets/customers/consumers	Politics/stakeholders
Principal goal	Attracting and satisfying customers through the exchange of goods and values	Establishing and maintaining positive and beneficial relations between various groups
Shared perspectives		
General image of organisation	An open and externally influenced system	
Communication ideal	Communication as an on-going dialogue with the external world	
Prescription for management	Organisational flexibility and responsiveness vis-á-vis external wishes and demands	

Table 24.3 Differences and similarities between marketing and public relations (*source*: Cheney and Christensen 2001: 238)

Summary

This chapter has considered the frameworks that help us understand the purpose of corporate communication (establishing and maintaining legitimacy and social capital); how corporate communicators can approach practise (identifying and communicating shared values); and how the organisational context can affect practise. This should help practitioners to make clear and informed choices about how they do their jobs and everyone else to evaluate the impact of their practise – both in terms of success in setting and meeting oragisational goals and in relation to the broader society in which it takes place.

Bibliography

Anderson, R., L.A. Baxter and K.N. Cissna (2004). 'Texts and contexts of dialogue' in *Dialogue. Theorizing Difference in Communication Studies*. R. Anderson, L.A. Baxter and K.N. Cissna (eds). Thousand Oaks, CA: Sage Publications.

Bourdieu, P. (1986). 'Forms of capital' in *Handbook of Theory and Research for the Sociology of Education*. J.C. Richards (ed.). New York, NY: Greenwood Press.

Bruning, S.D., M. Dials and A. Shirka (2008). 'Using dialogue to build organization-public relationships, engage publics, and positively affect organizational outcomes'. *Public Relations Review* **34**(1): 25–31.

Cheney, C.G. and L.T. Christensen (2001). 'Organizational identity: linkages between internal and external organizational communication' in *The New Handbook of Organizational Communication*. F.M. Jablin and L.L. Putnam (eds). Thousand Oaks, CA: Sage.

Christensen, L.T. and J.P. Cornelissen (2011). 'Bridging corporate and organizational communication: review, development and a look to the future'. *Management Communication Quarterly* **25**(3): 383–414.

Christensen, L.T., M. Morsing and G. Cheney (2008). *Corporate Communications: Convention, complexity and critique*. Thousand Oaks, CA: Sage.

Christensen, L.T., J. Cornelissen and A.F. Firat (2009). 'New tensions and challenges in integrated communications'. *Corporate Communication: An International Journal* **14**(2): 207–219.

Corporate Communication International (CCI) at Fairleigh Dickinson University (2011). 'CCI corporate communication practices and trends study 2011: Final report'. www.corporatecomm.org/pdf/report2011.pdf accessed 10 November 2011.

Davis, A. (2003). 'Public relations and news sources' in *News, Public Relations and Power*. S. Cottle (ed.). London: Sage.

Davis, A. and E. Seymour (2010). 'Generating forms of media capital inside and outside the political field: the strange case of David Cameron' in *Media, Culture and Society* **32**(5): 1–20.

De Bussy, N. (2010). 'Dialogue as a basis for stakeholder engagement: defining and measuring core competencies' in *The Sage Handbook of Public Relations*. R.L. Heath (ed.). Los Angeles, CA: Sage Publications.

Deephouse, D.L. and S.M. Carter (2005). 'An examination of differences between organizational legitimacy and organizational reputation'. *Journal of Management Studies* **42**: 329–360.

Deephouse, D.L. and M.C. Suchman (2008). 'Legitimacy in organizational institutionalism' in *The Sage Handbook of Organizational Institutionalism*. R. Greenwood, C. Oliver, K. Sahlin and R. Suddaby (eds). Thousand Oaks, CA: Sage.

Deetz, S. and J. Simpson (2004). 'Critical organizational dialogue: open formation and the demand of "otherness"' in *Dialogue: Theorizing difference in communication studies*. R. Anderson, L. Baxter and K. Cissna (eds). Thousand Oaks, CA: Sage.

Ehling, W.P., J. White and J.E. Grunig (1992). 'Public relations and marketing practices' in *Excellence in Public Relations and Communications Management*. J.E. Grunig (ed.). Hillsdale, NJ: Lawrence Erlbaum Associates, Inc.

Fombrun, C.J. and C.B.M. Van Riel (2004). *Fame and Fortune: How successful companies build winning reputations*. Upper Saddle River, NJ: Pearson Education.

Frankental, P. (2001). 'Corporate social responsibility – a PR invention'? *Corporate Communications: An International Journal* **6**(1): 18–23.

Friedman, A.L. and S. Miles (2002). 'Developing stakeholder theory'. *Journal of Management Studies* **39**(1): 1–22.

Grunig, J.E. (ed.) (1992). *Excellence in Public Relations and Communication Management*. Hillsdale, NJ: Lawrence Erlbaum Associates, Inc.

Grunig, J.E. and T.E. Hunt (1984). *Managing Public Relations*. New York, NY: Holt, Rinehart & Winston.

Grunig, L., J.E. Grunig and D.M. Dozier (2002). *Excellent Public Relations and Effective Organizations: A study of communication management in three countries*. Abingdon: Routledge.

Habermas, J. (1973/1976). *Legitimation Crisis*. London: Heinneman.

Heath, R.G. (2007). 'Rethinking community collaboration through a dialogic lens: creativity, democracy, and diversity in community organizing'. *Management Communication Quarterly* **21**: 145.

Heath, R.L. (ed.) (2001). *Handbook of Public Relations*. Thousand Oaks, CA: Sage.

Heath, R., B. Pearce, J. Shotter, J. Taykor, A. Kersten, T. Zorn, J. Roper and J. Motion (2006). 'The process of dialogue: participation and legitimation'. *Management Communication Quarterly* **19**(3): 341–373.

Hutton, J.G. (2010). 'Defining the relationship between public relations and marketing: public relations' most important challenge' in *Handbook of Public Relations*. R.L. Heath (ed.). Thousand Oaks, CA: Sage.

Hutton, J.G., M.B. Goodman, J.B. Alexander and C.M. Genest (2001). 'Reputation management: the new face of corporate public relations?' *Public Relations Review* **27**: 247–261.

Ihlen, O. (2009). 'On Bourdieu, public relations in field struggles' in *Public Relations and Social Theory*. O. Ihlen, B. Van Ruler and M. Fredriksson (eds). New York, NY: Routledge.

Jablin, F.M. and L.L. Putnam (eds) (2001). *The New Handbook of Organizational Communication*. Thousand Oaks, CA: Sage.

Johnson, G. and K. Scholes (2002). *Exploring Corporate Strategy*, 6th edition. Harlow: Prentice Hall.

Johnson, G., R. Whittington and K. Scholes (2011). *Exploring Strategy*, 9th edition. Harlow: Prentice Hall.

Kapein, M. and R. van Tulder (2003). 'Toward effective stakeholder dialogue'. *Business and Society Review* **108**(2): 203–224.

Kent, M.L. and M. Taylor (2002). 'Toward a dialogic theory of public relations'. *Public Relations Review* **28**: 21–37.

Kitchen, P. and D. Schultz (eds) (2001). *Raising the Corporate Umbrella: Corporate communication in the 21st century*. London: Macmillan.

Ledingham, J.A. and S.D. Bruning (eds) (2000). *Public Relations as Relationship Management: A relational approach to the study and practice of public relations*. Mahwah, NJ: Lawrence Erlbaum Associates, Inc.

Leitch, S. and J. Motion (1999). Multiplicity in corporate identity strategy. *Corporate Communications: An International Journal* **4**(4): 192–200.

Leitch, S. and D. Neilson (2001). 'Bringing publics into public relations' in *Handbook of Public Relations*. R.L. Heath (ed.). Thousand Oaks, CA, London and New Delhi: Sage.

Mettzler, M.S. (2001). 'The centrality of organizational legitimacy to public relations practice' in *Handbook of Public Relations*. R.L. Heath (ed.). London: Sage.

Motion, J. and S. Leitch (2002). The technologies of corporate identity. *International Studies of Management and Organization* **32**(3): 45–64.

OECD (2011). 'A definition of social capital measures'. http://stats.oecd.org/glossary/detail.asp?ID=3560 accessed 10 September 2011.

Pieczka, M. (2011). 'Public relations as dialogic expertise?' *Journal of Communication Management* **15**(2): 108–124.

Putnam, R.D. (1996). 'Tuning in, tuning out: the strange disappearance of social capital in America'. *PS: Political Science and Politics* **28**: 665–683.

Putnam, R.D. (2000). *Bowling Alone: The collapse and revival of American community*. New York, NY, London: Simon & Schuster.

Putnam, R.D. (2002). *Democracies in Flux: The evolution of social capital in contemporary society*. New York, NY: Oxford University Press.

Riel, C.V. (1995). *Principles of Corporate Communication*. Hemel Hempstead: Prentice Hall.

Steyn, B. (2003). 'From strategy to corporate communication strategy: a conceptualisation'. *Journal of Communication Management* **8**(2): 168–183.

Suchman, M.C. (1992). 'Managing legitimacy: strategic and institutional approaches'. *Academy of Management Review* **20**(3): 571–610.

Van Riel, C.B.M. (2003). 'Defining corporate communication' in *Corporate Communication: A strategic approach to building reputation*. P.S. Bronn and R. Wiig (eds). Oslo: Gyldendal Akademisk.

Van Riel, C.B.M. and C. Fombrun (2007). *Essentials of Corporate Communication*. Abingdon: Routledge.

Waeraas, A. (2009). 'On Weber. Legitimacy and legitimation in public relations' in *Public Relations and Social Theory: Key figures and concepts*. O. Ihlen, B. Van Ruler and M. Fredriksson (eds). London: Routledge.

CHAPTER 25

Nilam Ashra-McGrath

Non-government organisations and pressure groups

Learning outcomes

By the end of this chapter you should be able to:

- contextualise the work of NGOs within a broader international development arena
- recognise the importance of donor relations
- recognise the communication issues for smaller NGOs
- critically assess some NGO websites and images used for fundraising.

Structure

- What is an NGO?
- Fishes and ponds: the international development context
- What has changed for communicators in NGOs?
- Common communication issues facing NGOs
- Relationships with donors
- Donors and communication in small NGOs
- PR and its link to fundraising
- The power of the website
- Advocacy and campaigning
- Getting donations
- Brand, reputation and identity
- NGOs as corporations and superbrands

Introduction

Non-government organisations (NGOs) and pressure groups are set up to operate independently from governments. Their aim is to change socio-economic and environmental circumstances for communities of people. These communities are bound together either by a single issue or cause (for example, increasing the working rights of those with disabilities), or by geographical boundaries (for example, disaster response programmes), or by sections of society and cultures to which people feel they belong (for example, women or minority groups). This sense of belonging is an important emotion that NGOs seek to tap into to gain support and funding for their work, and it lays the foundation for much communication work within the NGO sector. This chapter explores the common communication issues faced by NGOs, large and small, and how aspects such as PR, marketing and fundraising can be linked to relationships with donors and large funding agencies. Finally, Case study 25.1 examines the PR work of an NGO.

What is an NGO?

Non-government organisations (NGOs) come in many shapes and sizes and exist across many sectors: education, health, community cohesion, social welfare, sports, arts, human rights and justice, disaster response, environment, religion, politics, research, gender, disability, governance – the list is endless. They contribute to civil society, and the World Bank defines civil society as 'the wide array of non-governmental and not-for-profit organizations that have a presence in public life, expressing the interests and values of their members or others, based on ethical, cultural, political, scientific, religious or philanthropic considerations' (The World Bank Group 2011). Civil society can therefore be viewed as 'the arena in which people come together to pursue the interests they hold in common' (Edwards 1998: 2). Civil society has a strong relationship with the state: as state services decline, become diluted or are withdrawn, civil society organisations begin to fill the void, and one such organisation 'which flourishes in – and emerges from – this [void] is the non-governmental organisation – the NGO' (Gray et al. 2006: 324).

The definitions in Box 25.1 suggest that NGOs cover a lot of ground. They can be large or small, local or global, and focus on single or multiple issues. They can also work in many sectors. (see Think about 25.1)

Pressure groups are a little more difficult to define. Pressure groups are given this label because of the pressure they place on governments and corporations to change aspects of their behaviours, policies or laws. The 'pressure' aspect of the group is actually the *aim* of the NGO (Stoker and Wilson 1991) and relates to a specific part of its vision or mission – for example, to campaign for policy changes on behalf of vulnerable

> **Definition:** A *'pressure group'* is 'any group which tries to influence public policy without seeking the responsibility of government' (Moran 1989: 121, cited in Stoker and Wilson 1991: 21).

> # Box 25.1
>
> # Definitions of an NGO
>
> *'Also referred to as voluntary agencies. These are private organizations of a charitable, research or educational nature that are concerned with a range of social, economic and environmental issues . . . They may act on an international, national or local scale. Some raise money from the public and from government to help fund development projects . . . others attempt to educate the public and campaign on major issues or to lobby governments and international agencies to change public policies.'*
>
> *Source*: Crump and Ellwood (1998: 186)
>
> *'[NGOs] can represent the interests of the weak and marginalized groups as intermediaries, or build social capital among these groups to enable them to command more responsiveness from government agencies directly.'*
>
> *Source*: Brinkerhoff and Brinkerhoff (2002: 6)

Think about 25.1 — NGOs and sectors

Like corporations, the work of NGOs can be confined to one sector or can overlap many sectors. Below is a list of sectors in which NGOs work. Can you think of examples of a local, national or international NGO that works in each of these sectors?

- **Education:** for example, a local reading skills group aimed at adults
- **Health:** for example, Médecins Sans Frontières, which works in more than one country
- **Social policy and social cohesion:** for example, local youth work projects
- **Sports:** for example, the UK-based Sport Relief
- **Arts:** for example, local and national museums and galleries

- **Human rights:** for example, Amnesty International, which works in more than one country
- **Environment:** for example, local allotment or recycling groups
- **Disaster response:** for example, Merlin, which works in more than one country
- **Religion:** for example, Tearfund, which works in more than one country
- **Gender equality:** for example, ActionAid, which works in more than one country
- **Business and micro-enterprise:** for example, Grameen Bank, which works in Bangladesh.

---

or marginalised groups. Pressure groups aim to either 'defend the sectional interests of their members' (e.g., trade unions) or act as 'promotional groups concerned with the interests of others' (e.g., a childrens' charity) (Stoker and Wilson 1991: 22). (see Think about 25.2)

High-profile pressure groups, such as Greenpeace, that aim to change aspects of corporate behaviour or government law often use techniques that are dramatic, innovative or disruptive to corporations and governments, gaining maximum media exposure in the process. This requires a particular type of communication expertise, namely the ability to campaign effectively. Pressure groups are known for their activism and micro-activism (Lombard 2011), which can even become a 'lifestyle choice' – for example, when individuals move from one demonstration to another (Blood 2004).

Think about 25.2

Pressure groups

Can you think of an NGO that is known solely as a pressure group? What are they campaigning for? Is there a particular law or corporate policy that they are trying to change?

In addition to NGOs and pressure groups covering many sectors at any one time, they can also be known by different acronyms that help to categorise an NGO even further. Box 25.2 lists some of the many acronyms that categorise different types of non-profit organisations.

Box 25.2

An NGO by any other name . . .

Acronyms for non-profit organisations, along with their defining characteristics, include:

CBO: community-based organisation

- Formally represent sectoral interests of the community
- Self-administered groups that generate some income

- Can be unions, associations, cooperatives or small-scale enterprises
- Important part of civil society.

GRO: grassroots organisation

- Work to improve and develop their own communities.

PO: people's organisation

- Overlaps with CBO
- Represents member interests
- Leaders are accountable to members
- Substantially self-reliant.

box 25.2 (continued)

QUANGO: quasi-autonomous non-government organisation

- Semi-public body financed by government
- Management team, often appointed by government.

NGO: non-government organisation

- Independent national bodies
- Deal with issues of that country or within a particular sector
- Concentrate on service delivery, training and advocacy.

VO: voluntary organisation

- Pursue a social mission
- Driven by shared values.

INGO: international non-government organisation

- Overseas organisations working in developing countries
- Some are privately run.

Other names for the NGO sector include the *voluntary sector* or the *third sector*. NGOs are also known as *charities*.

Source: adapted from Bennett and Gibbs 1996 and Sukuki 1998

Fishes and ponds: the international development context

NGOs are broadly viewed as being part of the (international) development sector. The function of NGOs has shifted since the 1980s from providing direct services to incorporating more sophisticated welfare support programmes, advocacy and political lobbying (Blood 2004: 128). The nature of the sector is such that NGOs 'can represent almost every possible policy position, even those that are mutually contradictory' (Blood 2004: 126). For example, NGOs exist to campaign for and against climate change, or for and against the rights of smokers in public spaces. Given that NGOs can represent almost anything and anyone, this makes for a crowded market, with some NGOs feeling like small fish in a big pond while other NGOs monopolise the space. In communication terms, this has led to a dramatic change in the role of communication within the NGO sector, as they have to be sophisticated in making their voice heard. Additionally, the wider NGO sector is now under just as much scrutiny as their corporate counterparts, with financial transparency being particularly important to an NGO's legitimacy and its reputation among stakeholders (Burger and Owens 2010). (see Explore 25.1)

Explore 25.1

Issues of transparency

Let's think about how transparency is viewed by NGOs and by corporations. Visit the following two websites:

1. Corporate Watch – www.corporatewatch.org.uk

   What reason does Corporate Watch give for monitoring corporations? What opinion do they have of the use of PR in the corporate world? Can you find examples from your wider reading to counter their opinion?

2. NGO Watch – www.globalgovernancewatch.org/ ngo_watch/

   What reason does NGO Watch give for monitoring the transparency of NGOs? Can you find examples from your wider reading that illustrate transparency issues in NGOs?

What has changed for communicators in NGOs?

According to Maxwell (2009), the development sector faces three challenges: (1) *coverage*, (2) *capacity* and (3) *communications*. *Coverage* refers to the scope of work being undertaken within the sector, and *capacity* refers to the resources within developing and developed countries that are needed to increase the coverage and impact of development programmes. *Communications* refers specifically to the use of new technology. The Internet has markedly changed how development issues are communicated, and the use of new technology is seen as 'an essential vehicle for policy influence' (Maxwell 2009: 789). Activism, in particular,

Oxfam's web presence

Let's look at how a website and social media tools can help an NGO communicate with its stakeholders. Begin by taking a look at the website for Oxfam International at www.oxfam.org and answer the following questions:

■ What type of information can you access that will, first, help you learn about development issues, and, second, help you get involved in their campaigns?

■ What social media tools do they use on their international website?

■ Now see if Oxfam have a website for your country or global region. What additional information can you get from these country/region-specific pages?

Feedback

The type of sophisticated web and social media presence we see with Oxfam helps them maintain a strong voice within the development sector. Ultimately, it makes them accessible and transparent.

has taken on a new lease of life, with technology offering activists (such as the 2011 Occupy Movement) flexibility and spontaneity (Lombard 2011). The increased use of new technology has also encouraged a new level of transparency and engagement among NGOs, as it has spawned 'new [online] knowledge networks' (Maxwell 2009), forcing campaigners, development workers and policy makers to account for their actions and justify their stance in a very public way. An online search of NGOs in different countries shows that knowledge networks are crucial if NGOs are to maintain a voice in a crowded market. It is rare to find an NGO website that does not share links, resources based on its own research, policy papers, responses to government initiatives, views from beneficiaries, case studies, and the like. The Internet has made it easier for NGOs to show their impact by placing 'outputs' and evidence of their work online, and in doing so, they ensure that they are part of a wider development discourse. (see Explore 25.2)

Common communication issues facing NGOs

Communication performs similar functions in NGOs as it does in corporations, and the technical competencies of

communication practitioners in both sectors are identical. On the face of it, the issues within the NGO and corporate sectors appear to be the same: financial sustainability, leadership and management, change in focus, organisational growth and decline, reputation and media coverage, engagement with stakeholders, quality of service and accountability. However, the treatment of some of these issues differs. For example, *financial sustainability* is largely determined by an NGO's ability to secure grants and donations, and generate income from additional brand merchandise and trading. (Oxfam now generates income through specialist second-hand bookstores that it has established in towns throughout the UK.) *Reputation and media coverage* for corporations is about creating brand awareness and gaining a competitive advantage, whereas with NGOs it is primarily the *cause or issue* that is promoted, along with the suggestion that we can make a difference to the cause by giving a small amount of money. However, branding is still important for NGOs, and larger NGOs can become powerful brands in their own right (see section on NGOs as 'superbrands'). For example, Amnesty International is a powerful brand and its involvement on a campaign carries with it a level of associated power. In such cases, the brand of the NGO embodies the cause or issue and communication practitioners will capitalise on this brand where necessary.

Where corporations have *shareholders* to whom they are accountable, NGOs are accountable to *stakeholders*, and these include (at any one time) volunteers, board members, paid staff, beneficiaries of their work, donors (individuals and grant-giving bodies) and government agencies. Finally, where corporations value the 'bottom-line' and profits, NGOs place value on the change that they can bring about – change that aims to raise living standards, increase sustainable livelihoods and increase access to health, utilities, education and social services for their beneficiaries. The communication function of an NGO therefore has a very different focus to a communication function in a corporation, with social welfare, justice and empowerment (Kilby 2006) underpinning many of the messages that they craft.

Relationships with donors

NGOs' relationships with donors and grant-giving bodies are complex, and it doesn't help the communication process that at any one time NGOs can have reporting requirements to trusts, corporations, venture capitalists, government agencies, larger NGOs and individual donors. Donors have their own agenda for giving money, and some have enough power to sway the NGO into working in a particular way, or to take on a project that does not necessarily 'tally' with their organisational mission (Juma 2004). This 'clash of interests and norms' (2004: 236) can lead to the work of the NGO becoming diluted, to potential conflicts of interest (Drucker 1990), or to the NGO compromising their values (Juma 2004). In the longer term, this may lead to a loss of financial and other support, as well as damage to their reputation.

One of the most important communication roles within the NGO is therefore dealing with donor needs, establishing a long-term relationship and maintaining a high level of trust in that relationship (Morgan and Hunt 1994). A high level of trust in successful donor relationships can secure financial and emotional commitment to the NGO's cause. MacMillan et al. (2005) state that communication is the easiest factor to change when trying to improve trust in a relationship. '[NGOs] cannot easily change their values, but they can use strategies to improve their communication with funders' (MacMillan et al. 2005: 815). The four strategies NGOs can adopt are:

1. informing funders about the groups with which they work;

2. keeping funders informed about forthcoming events, and their use of funds, through networking events that allow them to experience the NGOs' services first hand;

3. seeking information about funders' needs and motivations; and

4. approaching staff in the funding organisation who are responsive, knowledgeable and passionate about the NGOs and their services.

Source: adapted from MacMillan et al. 2005: 815

Donors may give because they get material and non-material benefits from their relationship with NGOs (MacMillan et al. 2005: 809). Material benefits come by learning from the NGO and by any positive publicity they might receive from being in that relationship (2005: 809). Non-material benefits include trusting that the NGO is making best use of the funding and that it is having a clear and positive impact (2005: 809). The role of the communication practitioner (or donor relations officer) is therefore to broadly emphasise both the material and non-material benefits of that relationship to the donor. In practical terms, this means ensuring internal and external reporting requirements are met, and helping to disseminate the results of the NGO's work to all stakeholders. Ultimately, donor relations amounts to a form of external relations, which 'have always been important for non-profit organizations, since [non-profit organizations] rely on external sources for resources (funding, volunteers, members and board members) and legitimacy' (Balser and McClusky 2005: 311). (see Think about 25.3)

Is the two-way symmetrical model useful in this context?

Yes, and no, is the answer. Yes, it is useful in that the two-way symmetrical model of communication allows for 'compromise' between stakeholders (Balser and McClusky 2005: 297). The model presents a negotiating area for donor relations to develop in a mutually beneficial way, offering the potential of a 'win-win' scenario in the process (Dozier et al. 1995: 48). However, we can also say that the model is not useful because it presents a static version of a single relationship, whereas NGOs deal with multiple stakeholders at any given time. It also fails to account for the varying agendas of each of the stakeholders, and the associated conditions placed on the NGO in return for funding (Villanger 2004).

However, it is not as black and white as that. The communications practitioner situated within the NGO may be compelled to find 'a compromise around an issue in which true differences exist between parties' (Dozier et al. 1995: 48), suggesting that dilemmas, ethical or otherwise, sometimes exist. In such cases, 'it is possible to be both co-operative and competitive in the same campaign' (Aitken-Turff and Jackson 2006: 86). This type of approach is called 'mixed motive' public relations (Murphy 1991, cited in Grunig et al. 1995), where 'each side in a stakeholder relationship retains a strong sense of its own self-interests, yet each is motivated to cooperate to attain at least some resolution of the conflict. They may be on opposite sides of an issue, but it is in their best interests to cooperate with each other' (Plowman 2007: 87).

Think about 25.3

Donor expectations

Managing the expectations of your donors is an important role. Think about how you would keep donors informed about the work of an NGO. How would you do this if one of your donors is overseas? How would your strategy change if one of your donors is local? How would you treat individual donors?

Donors and communication in small NGOs

While larger NGOs have marketing, public affairs, donor relations and fundraising teams to help mobilise resources, smaller NGOs and community-based organisations (CBOs) aren't as fortunate, and donors play a role in this. The lack of internal communication, PR and publicity activity within smaller NGOs relates directly to the nature of funding. The focus on field work or projects means that staff activity remains centred on ensuring specific social, environmental and economic outcomes 'in the field'. Publicity and raising awareness is therefore seen as a secondary activity by both donors and smaller NGOs and CBOs in favour of project-related activities (Ashra 2002). This is particularly detrimental to those organisations that have 'raising awareness' as part of their mission. The low priority given to campaigning or communicating organisational mission can lead to negative public perceptions, as NGOs and CBOs are not seen to be actively campaigning for anything. Internally, the aim to raise awareness may be viewed as 'too grand' due to the lack of staff training or capacity, and lack of time (Ashra 2002).

Research shows that continual exposure to the organisation's key messages attracts donations by the public (Frumkin and Kim 2001) and campaigns are more likely to be successful if the NGO offers publics an opportunity to act on the message (McQuail 1987). Examples of this include the fundraising campaigns of the Disasters Emergency Committee, or 'Christian Aid Week.' However, such work requires specialist skills in internal communication, PR and campaigning, which rarely exist within small organisations, as it requires a dedicated person for which core funding is seldom available. Where there are few technical skills to write a press release, lobby effectively, publicise specialist events and gain media coverage, the result is sometimes muddled, leading to some commonly held myths about communication, such as 'all you need is a leaflet' or 'it's all about external publicity' (Ashra 2005), which leaves out important internal communication issues. The lack of capacity in small NGOs and CBOs, combined with the lack of funding available for dedicated publicity and awareness-raising roles, means that either the vital communication role does not exist in many smaller organisations (Ashra 2002), or that communications and PR remains a peripheral activity (Ashra 2008). (see Think about 25.4 and Box 25.3)

Think about 25.4

Communications on a small budget

Look around your local community and identify a small charity. What methods do they use to publicise themselves? List three new methods that would help them communicate on a small budget.

Box 25.3

Thoughts from an NGO communications practitioner

'My experience in public relations is mostly within Canadian NGOs where there are mostly small, or even very small, communication teams. In that context, public relations means, for me, many things, starting with public engagement. Then again, public engagement means to me engaging the Canadian population into international development by encouraging them to become a donator or a volunteer in Canada or abroad. PR often includes, as well, communication tasks such as programming, writing press releases, articles for the website or the newsletters, organising events, managing the virtual communities on social media, etc. So, to me, public relations, as long as it's related to NGOs, includes many tasks and, since the resources are often very low, I think that the main difficulty is to set the priorities!'

Source: Johanne Veilleux, Independent Communications Advisor, Canadian NGO Sector

PR and its link to fundraising

The fundraising teams in NGOs are sophisticated machines. They work closely with marketing to target carefully selected groups into donating time, money and other resources (for example, pro bono training or legal services). Research shows that in a corporate environment, marketing departments often 'encroach' on the remit of PR departments, and may end up taking over (Lauzen 1991). A similar relationship has been shown to exist in non-profit organisations, where the fundraising department encroaches on the PR function (Kelly 1993). One of the factors of encroachment appears to be fundraising's ability to secure 'bottom-line' contributions to the NGO, versus PR's 'storytelling' contribution (1993: 356), suggesting that the link to the economic contribution of a department determines their status within the organisation. This is exacerbated when an NGO undergoes a period of change or turbulence, as it relies on fundraising to ensure its financial sustainability, which in turn redefines PR as a 'secondary' function (1993: 356). For larger NGOs, their fundraising teams (as opposed to the one or two people fundraising in smaller NGOs) are able to tap into diverse income streams, ranging from 'private memberships, donations, legacies, commercial activities, commercial sponsorship . . . grants from private foundations [and] governments' (Blood 2004: 122). Smaller NGOs, by comparison, have the issue of resource deficit – i.e., a limited skill set to carry out sophisticated fundraising activities beyond asking for donations from the public. There is hope, however, through the clever use of technology, but technology (for example, an interactive website or social media presence) has to be used as part of a strategic plan, and implemented by a communications professional (rather than by development workers, as sometimes happens). A sophisticated and carefully thought out web presence therefore offers much hope to smaller NGOs.

What about the role of marketing?

Traditional marketing techniques can still play a role in fundraising. 'Cause-related marketing', or CRM (Bennett and Sargeant 2005: 798), is one technique that appears to offer a 'win-win' scenario for the NGO and for businesses, and could be cited as an excellent example of the two-way symmetrical model in practise (Dozier et al. 1995). CRM happens when 'a business promotes or assists [an NGO] by publicising that a proportion of its profits or sales will be devoted to that cause' (Bennett and Sargeant 2005: 798). By entering into this type of agreement, the NGO brand and the business brand are clearly and visibly linked on packaging, advertising and any online presence (Bennett and Sargeant 2005). They also become linked in the public's mind, leading to brand and reputation enhancement for both parties. (Now read Mini case study 25.1)

Mini case study 25.1

A snapshot of corporate fundraising and cause-related marketing

Terrence Higgins Trust's corporate fundraising team work with a range of companies that either donate money or fundraise for the charity. Typically, the income generated by the team is restricted and used to fund specific services. Their high-value partnerships tend to be more strategic and are good for both the partner organisation and for the charity. For example, Barclays is a long-term sponsor of the organisation's activities, particularly with African communities in the UK. Barclays' support of African communities in the UK is an extension of their support for employees across their African operations, where they have implemented an HIV/AIDS policy and health and wellbeing programme. Then there are the smaller partnerships that involve securing lower-level corporate donations. This would involve partnering on cause-related marketing campaigns, where a company donates a percentage of the profits generated from the sale of individual items. For example, in the past, the charity has partnered with the skin and haircare company Kiehl's on an exclusive hand cream. The corporate team also work to secure gifts in kind, which can include a range of products, time or services for the charity.

Source: with thanks to Terrence Higgins Trust

The power of the website

NGOs with limited resources can use the Internet to their advantage (Naude et al. 2004). By using a website to engage with potential and existing donors, their beneficiaries and sections of the public, they can save an extraordinary amount of money (Long and Chiagouris 2006) while giving voice to their purpose and the issues they are aiming to tackle. They can take part in broader debates with governments and their beneficiaries (Long and Chiagouris 2006) and use tools that were previously not available to them – for example, conducting surveys (Naude 2004) and sending out email alerts and bulletins, as well as responding to government proposals in a professional manner. As stated earlier, the NGO market is a crowded one and websites are now the first port of call for anyone looking to learn more about an NGO and its work. For this reason, it's important that they are accessible and interactive (Kent et al. 2003). However, there are factors that impede the design and use of a good website, namely the 'lack of technical knowledge, a lack of time, money and manpower' (Naude et al. 2004: 90), and these factors exist in smaller NGOs and CBOs.

Two-way symmetrical communication features heavily on the more interactive websites, and Naude et al. (2004) suggest that older NGOs are more likely to rely on the traditional, one-way mass communication model that imparts information to the masses. This suggests that newer, smaller or more technology-savvy NGOs are in a good position to lead by example. (see Explore 25.3 and Box 25.4)

Explore 25.3

Looking at two-way communication on NGO websites

Pick one local, one national and one international NGO website to explore. Do they meet the principles described in Box 25.4? Which websites meet most of the criteria? Is there another technique that NGOs could use on their websites that is not included in the five principles?

Box 25.4

Five principles of two-way communication for websites

There are five principles of two-way symmetrical communication for NGO websites:

1. **The digital/dialogue feedback loop** – include real-time discussions, places to post comments, contact information and staff, volunteer and member biographies.

2. **Usefulness of information** – make sure the content is of general use and can be used in press packs and news briefings; allow people to sign up for information.

3. **Generation of return visits** – make the site attractive, update the information regularly and include easily downloadable specialist information.

4. **Intuitiveness/ease of the interface** – make sure it's well organised and structured, and cut out all the unnecessary 'bells and whistles'.

5. **Conservation of visitors** – do not distract from the message by using sponsors or advertising.

Source: Kent and Taylor 1998 and Kent et al. 2003

Advocacy and campaigning

As stated earlier, applying pressure to corporations and governments can be an aim of the NGO and, if it is their sole function, then campaigning and advocacy is at the core of their work. Campaigners use facts to research and substantiate their position. Accuracy is paramount, as inaccurate or skewed arguments can damage campaigns. Mark Lattimer (2000) suggests that campaigners source

their facts rigorously and not ignore anything that contradicts the argument they are trying to put forward, but instead use it to contextualise their position. Campaigners work in a volatile environment that is ever changing and subject to continual opposition (Lattimer 2000: 360). For this reason, campaigners have to remain alert to the media ploys used by those trying to discredit them, for example using 'dirt briefings', where the quality of the NGO's research is questioned, or a hidden agenda is implied (Lattimer 2000: 151).

Explore 25.4

Campaigning and advocacy

Kalayaan is a UK charity that provides advice, advocacy and support services to migrant domestic workers. It was a Guardian Charity Award Winner in 2010, singled out for combining 'both [a] professional service with campaigning and influencing public policy' (*The Guardian* 2010). Its services include advice (immigration, employment, healthcare), information and guidance, English language training, IT classes, support and advocacy during legal cases, research and events. Have a look at its website (www.kalayaan.org.uk) and think about:

- Who are their allies and supporters?
- What have these relationships led to?
- What techniques do they use to campaign? How does this differ, if at all, from the campaigns of larger organisations, such as Oxfam?

Feedback

Their techniques and approaches differ from the larger NGOs because they are a 'single-issue' charity. This means that although their services range from giving advice through to teaching English, they are all aimed at protecting the rights of one group – migrant domestic workers based in the UK. Can you think of any other single-issue charities that are effective campaigners in their field?

Lattimer (2000) claims that techniques such as petitions and rallies have little effect unless you have influence over the small group of people who actually write the policies and who are in a position to change the law. This is why establishing good relationships with policy makers is crucial to a successful campaign. (see Explore 25.4)

Getting donations

In the US, an 11-year study of 2,359 non-profit organisations concluded that 'aggressive communication of mission is a more potent driver of contribution than maintaining efficient operations' (Frumkin and Kim 2001: 272), suggesting that communicating purpose is essential if an NGO is to remain financially sustainable via donations. However, there is a danger that if an NGO spends most of its time fundraising, then this could lead to 'goal deflection' (Brinkerhoff and Brinkerhoff 2002), which is a failure that

is characteristic of the NGO sector and the funding regimes upon which it relies.

Donations are therefore key to the survival of NGOs, and fundraising is a role that is embedded within the broader communication remit. In Box 25.5 Cheung and Chan (2000) offer a useful blueprint for how NGOs can engage with publics meaningfully to attract donations without damaging the livelihoods and dignity of the people they are there to help. In particular, they cite the need to promote 'people's self-efficacy' programmes, such as skills training, or activities that increase 'confidence in one's ability and skill to perform a certain act' (2000: 243). Promoting the positive impact of an NGO's self-efficacy programmes encourages trust and ongoing financial commitment.

Box 25.5

How to encourage donations

- Emphasise the ordinary person's ability to contribute (for example, suggesting small amounts such as £1 or $2)
- Position yourself as accessible and welcome to any public donation, regardless of the amount
- Show the process you have used to support your targeted groups and the impact of your work
- Let your target groups speak about how they have benefited from the NGO's support
- Show how all your programmes fit together to improve the quality of life for your target groups
- Encourage authority figures (not necessarily celebrities) to highlight the importance of the issues you are trying to tackle
- Continually evaluate your programmes and make this information accessible to any of your donors.

Source: adapted from Cheung and Chan 2000: 251

Explore 25.5

Looking at ways to donate on NGO websites

Revisit some of the NGO websites you have viewed throughout this chapter so far. Do they meet the principles outlined in Box 25.5?

Brand, reputation and identity

Large or small, all NGOs will encounter branding issues as they move through the organisational lifecycle. Research shows that appearing to spend too much money on 'glossy fundraising brochures' is a common branding issue for NGOs (Bennett and Gabriel 2003; Griffiths 2005), as is competing for a limited amount of financial support from governments and foundations. This ultimately places pressure on good branding to help distinguish your NGO from the others in a competitive market (Griffiths 2005).

NGOs, like corporations, need good reputations if they are to survive any negative publicity and maintain trust with their donors (Bennett and Sargeant 2005), but they need 'both a salient image and a sound reputation' (Bennett and Sargeant 2005: 800). The issue with crafting a reputation is that reputations are based on 'value judgements' that 'evolve over time', whereas images have immediate connotations attached to them, which may be 'old-fashioned or . . . inappropriate' (Bennett and Sargeant 2005: 800). The advantages of a good reputation are that it positions the NGO in a 'preferred status over other organizations . . . [it] can justify support for the organization . . . [and] it enhances their value' in the sector (Padanyi and Gainer 2003: 252). Reputation is linked to identity, and for an NGO identities 'navigate its course of action and shape strategy for the future' (Young 2001: 155). This means that identities, of which the vision and mission are part, often define communications plans, and the plan is instrumental in conveying the impact of NGO activities. However, smaller NGOs lacking the necessary communication skill set are at a disadvantage because they are in danger of not planning their use of different media in a strategic way (Naude et al. 2004). Consider NGOs and reputation in Mini case study 25.2.

NGOs as corporations and superbrands

'It would appear that NGOs have managed to harness the advantages of capitalism – resource and managerial efficiency, focus and competitive diversity – without (so far) creating organisations so large and powerful that the public begins instinctively to fear them' (Blood 2004: 124).

Larger NGOs now operate like 'superbrands' (Wootliff and Deri 2001) or 'political corporations' (Blood 2004). This means that they have resources at their disposal to implement sophisticated communication plans. Robert Blood of the NGO tracking website SIGWatch (www.sigwatch.com) argues that they 'are the political equivalent of private corporations' (2004: 130) in the way they adapt the traditional

Mini case study 25.2
International NGOs come under the spotlight

The reputation of international NGOs was put under the spotlight in 2001, in the aftermath of a devastating earthquake in Gujarat State, Western India. The earthquake claimed approximately 20,000 lives and injured 1.6 million people (Rawat 2002: 58). There was a rush by international NGOs to be on the scene with support, but a number of reports were critical of NGOs for '[pursuing] their own interests' (Disasters Emergency Committee 2001a: 11). The use of imagery during fundraising in the UK came under particular scrutiny. With regards to transparency and being accountable to beneficiaries and people who donated, the Disasters Emergency Committee (DEC) evaluation 'detected a tendency amongst some aid agency staff in the UK to regard public sympathy as a commodity to be exploited rather than a perception to be developed' (Disasters Emergency Committee 2001a: 13). This leaves a question mark over the tone used in prior and subsequent emergency appeals, particularly in how the dignity of those affected by natural disasters is portrayed. The evaluation went on to state that 'the image of an old man with hands raised in supplication used in the original appeal and the "Thank-you" parade in the Nick Ross follow-up film were not examples of best practice' (Disasters Emergency Committee 2001a: 14). The core issue was the use of some images that did not portray communities as 'dignified', but instead as victims and dependent on Western aid entirely. However, HelpAge India's booklet was singled out as an example of how the communities affected were portrayed in a dignified manner, showing 'a pair of happy-looking (and only moderately old) musicians on its front cover, and (has) as its main (and spectacular) illustration a very dignified shoemaker with the caption in very small letters – "providing livelihoods"' (Disasters Emergency Committee 2001b: 44). The broader issues here were about how international NGOs did not display sensitivity when choosing images, which later damaged their reputation. As Dogra (2007) states, 'there is still a choice which is deliberately exercised by the NGO when it selects one image over another and uses it publicly' (2007: 170).

corporate structure to suit their needs. In PR terms, they are able to 'operate like brands, building "issues" and capturing new ones just as corporations build consumer brands and leverage them to open new markets' (2004: 122). They can also allocate their resources across the globe as and when needed – for example, dispatching healthcare workers, shelter and medicines in the wake of natural disasters – often making them more flexible than governments and corporations. This quick response is a unique feature of how they have subverted the corporate model to suit their need, and in the process have established a political status that is influential (*The Economist* 2003). As such, these 'superbrands,' with their bank of resources, are adept at developing relationships and maintaining the trust of donors and the public by using imagery and clear messaging to appeal to others on an emotional level (Wootliff and Deri 2001). However, they are not exempt from criticism and can come under heavy scrutiny by corporations and NGO 'watchers' who encourage transparency. In the past, international NGOs responding to disasters across the globe have come under fire for their portrayal of people suffering in the aftermath. (see Explore 25.6)

Explore 25.6

Choosing images for NGO campaigns

Look at these four pictures and assess which of these would be appropriate to use as part of a campaign to raise funds for a homeless charity. What are the pros and cons of using each picture? What do your decisions and choices suggest about homeless people? Would you crop these images for any reason? Discuss your choices with others.

(i) Homeless sleeping along the Victoria Embankment of the River Thames. (*source*: Eric Nathan/Loop Images/Corbis)

(iii) Resident of a homeless shelter. (*source*: Bob Sacha/Corbis)

(ii) Men eating at a homeless shelter. (*source*: Ted Spiegal/Corbis)

(iv) Destitute young man in a corner of a room. (*source*: Bob Thomas/Corbis)

Case study 25.1

Communications at Terrence Higgins Trust

Terrence HIGGINS TrUST

Terry Higgins was one of the first people in the UK to die of AIDS, aged 37, in 1982. The Terry Higgins Trust was set up in 1982, by his partner and friends, who wanted to prevent others from suffering in the same way as Terry. By naming the trust after Terry, they hoped to humanise and personalise AIDS in a very public way. It was a further two years before the Terrence Higgins Trust took shape with a constitution, bank account, board of directors and, finally, charitable status. Since the mid-1980s, the charity has undergone further transformations in its size, network, aims and services. This has led to some internal, external and strategic communication issues along the way.

External issues: dealing with the media

As so much about HIV was unknown in the early days of the epidemic, there was a real sense of panic in the media and not all coverage was helpful – for example, with headlines like 'I'd shoot my son if he had AIDS, says vicar' (*The Sun* 1985). The charity therefore worked hard to counter this type of opinion and focused on informing a wide audience about this mysterious new disease that was devastating parts of the gay community.

In the mid-1990s, effective antiretroviral drug treatments began transforming HIV from a terminal illness to a manageable condition. People in the UK were no longer dying from AIDS in the same numbers as they had been,

and as the condition slid down the priority list for public health and government funding, the media followed suit, leading to a decline in public awareness about HIV.

The messages Terrence Higgins Trust promotes today – use a condom, go for regular HIV testing – are as important now as they were at the beginning of the epidemic, but journalists are always after a new angle. This means that the main challenge now is securing media coverage around HIV prevention work by finding new and innovative ways to communicate old messages. The charity's media activity tends to fluctuate from one project to the next, and might involve, for example, creating targeted advertising campaigns, building information websites, running support groups or coordinating outreach programmes in bars, clubs, saunas and cruising grounds.

Internal issues: communicating within a growing organisation

In 1999, Terrence Higgins Trust merged with other, smaller organisations throughout the UK, expanding its organisation and range of services considerably. One of the charity's strategies was to send a press release to local media outlining any changes in services and to ensure service users were aware of what was happening. It also provided an excellent opportunity for the press office to start working with new staff, build relationships, outline how the press office worked and gauge what level of media work regional offices had engaged in. For smaller organisations, this may have been the first time they had a dedicated PR person working for them, so it was important to communicate the benefits of what would come from raising their regional profile.

Currently, this means that the press office gives PR support to 30 regional centres across England, Scotland and Wales. Some centres are very keyed-in to media work and are proactive in contacting the press office each week with stories and suggestions. Others are less proactive and sometimes need a little encouragement. The press officer contacts each of the centres at least once a month to ask whether they have any projects or events coming up they might like to inform the media about, or whether there are any existing services that need a little push. Not every centre will have something, but it's a useful way of making sure regional centres feel supported by a central office.

Training is important at Terrence Higgins Trust, and they run media training courses twice a year, in which eight individuals from across the organisation learn how to give effective broadcast interviews (no staff member is permitted to speak to the media unless they've taken

case study 25.1 (continued)

this course). Having these trained spokespeople in each regional centre is a great asset to the charity's media plans, particularly as offering a 'local voice' will often make the difference as to whether a broadcaster will use the charity's spokesperson or someone from another organisation.

Responsibilities for strategic issues

Having an overall strategy has become increasingly important since the charity's growth. The organisation operates such a variety of projects that it's crucial there are strong structures in place to ensure that the communication function runs smoothly. Overall responsibility for the communications strategy sits with the Head of Media – with the Communications Director providing a strategic steer and feeding in insight from high-level meetings. The press office is generally given a free rein in planning PR activities. As they're only a small department (see Box 25.6 below), there are opportunities for the Press Officer to act as strategic lead on particular pieces of work – for example, creating the current strategy documents for gay men and African communities.

Strategic issues: donors and funding

When it comes to funder agreements, this really does vary. Occasionally funders stipulate they require a full communications strategy as part of an initial bid, although generally a couple of paragraphs outlining the strength of the charity's media profile is enough. These relationships are managed by a dedicated team within the fundraising department. If the organisation is launching a project that has been funded by a certain organisation, they will always mention the funding body in press materials (unless they request to remain anonymous), and send material for sign-off before distribution. Some funders, particularly those supporting large projects, also like to include a supportive quote and boilerplate in the press release. The press office will often provide the fundraising team with a coverage report to include in evaluation documents for funders.

Strategic issues: fundraising

The charity uses a number of fundraising techniques – online donations, fundraising challenges, shop and give, payroll giving and corporate donations – and all of these techniques are effective in different ways. One structure that brings in consistently high levels of income to the charity is the Gala Events programme. It runs four regular events throughout the year (Lighthouse Gala Auction, Cocktail Club, Gala Dinner and Supper Club), and encourages its high net-worth donors to attend. The Gala Auction, for example, regularly brings in over £200,000 in income. From a PR point of view, the celebrity attendance at these events helps them secure coverage in areas of the media that the charity's brand wouldn't otherwise reach (e.g., showbiz sections, diary pages, etc.).

Source: with thanks to the Terrence Higgins Trust

Box 25.6

Life is a busy press office

Will Harris, Press Officer at Terrence Higgins Trust, gives an insight into what it takes to work in the NGO sector.

'Anyone who thinks the NGO sector is boring can think again. I cut my teeth agency side, working on some of the UK's most exciting brands, but it was only on joining Terrence Higgins Trust that I started to understand what true job satisfaction really feels like. At Terrence Higgins Trust we have 300 staff members, 1,000 volunteers, and a press office of two. That's two people to support all the charity's proactive projects – including HIV prevention campaigns, fundraising drives and events, and the work of thirty regional centres across England, Scotland and Wales – as well as manning full reactive and internal comms functions. We're responsible for a big brand, and expectations are high.

'Somehow, though, the enjoyment you get from working on a national news issue like HIV – whether it's participating in high-level media briefings at Downing Street, supporting people living with the condition through broadcast interviews, or cajoling a coterie of agony aunts into dressing gowns for a photo opp – far outweighs the pressure of trying to generate media stories with next to no budget.

'A good PR can thrive in this environment, but you need to be creative and adaptable, with rock-solid planning and organisational skills. A talent for securing pro bono support from your agency friends helps too!'

Source: with thanks to the Terrence Higgins Trust

Summary

NGOs work in many sectors. Some have more sophist-icated communication plans than others, and some lack the capacity or understanding of communication techniques to do anything other than react to events happening around them. In this chapter, we have defined NGOs and outlined the international development context within which they broadly work. We have also outlined the common communication issues experienced by NGO communication practitioners, with an emphasis on donor relations, fundraising and advocacy.

NGOs work in a competitive market and they have to distinguish themselves from others in their sector and work hard to carve out a niche for themselves. They do, in fact, face the same issues as corporations, and are increasingly being scrutinised for their trans-parency, how they undertake projects and how they spend donated money and resources. They face the same internal issues about income generation and power and politics, but their work is fundamentally different because they are not working towards a profit; yet some, such as Oxfam, have trading companies to generate income for their project work. What is clear is that NGOs need sophisticated and focused communication plans, yet the sector still suffers from thinking that communica-tions is a technical skill that does not sit as one of the core functions of an organisation; this is more apparent in smaller NGOs.

Bibliography

Aitken-Turff, F. and N. Jackson (2006). 'A mixed motive approach to lobbying: applying game theory to analyse the impact of cooperation and conflict on perceived lob-bying success'. *Journal of Public Affairs* **6**: 84–101.

Ashra, N. (2002). 'An Evaluation of the Participatory Organ-isational Appraisal Process (POAP) using Two Voluntary Organisations in Bradford District'. Unpublished MSc thesis, University of Bradford.

Ashra, N. (2005). 'All you need is a leaflet: 5 myths of com-munication for community based organisations.' *Third Sector Magazine*: 14 September.

Ashra, N. (2008). 'Inside stories: Making sense of the daily lives of communication practitioners'. PhD thesis, University of Leeds.

Balser, D. and J. McClusky (2005). 'Managing stakeholder relationships and nonprofit organization effectiveness'. *Nonprofit Management and Leadership* **15**(3): 295–316.

Bennett, J. and S. Gibbs (1996). *NGO Funding Strategies: An introduction for Southern and Eastern NGOs*. Oxford: INTRAC.

Bennett, R. and H. Gabriel (2003). 'Image and reputational characteristics of UK charitable organizations: an empiri-cal study'. *Corporate Reputation Review* **6**(3): 276–289.

Bennett, R. and A. Sargeant (2005). 'The non-profit marketing landscape: guest editors' introduction to a special section'. *Journal of Business Research* **58**(6): 797–805.

Blood, R. (2004). 'Should NGOs be viewed as political corpo-rations'? *Journal of Communication Management* **9**(2): 120–133.

Brinkerhoff, J.M. and D.W. Brinkerhoff (2002). 'Government-nonprofit relations in comparative perspective: evolution, themes and new directions'. *Public Administration and Development* **22**: 3–18.

Burger, R. and T. Owens (2010). 'Promoting transparency in the NGO sector: Examining the availability and reliability of self-reported data'. *World Development* **38**(9): 1263–1277.

Cheung, C.-K. and C.-M. Chan (2000). 'Social-cognitive factors of donating money to charity, with special attention to an international relief organization'. *Evaluation and Program Planning* **23**(2): 241–253.

Crump, A. and W. Ellwood (1998). *The A to Z of World Development*. Oxford: New Internationalist.

Disasters Emergency Committee, Humanitarian Initiatives UK, Disaster Mitigation Institute and MANGO (2001a). 'Inde-pendent Evaluation: The DEC Response to the Earthquake in Gujarat. January–October 2001'. Volume One. *Executive Summary*. London: Disasters Emergency Committee.

Disasters Emergency Committee, Humanitarian Initiatives UK, Disaster Mitigation Institute and MANGO (2001b). 'Independent Evaluation of Expenditure of DEC India Earthquake Appeal Funds. January – October 2001'. Volume Two. *Full Evaluation Report*. London: Disasters Emergency Committee.

Dogra, N. (2007). ' "Reading NGOs visually" – implications of visual images for NGO management'. *Journal of Inter-national Development* **19**: 161–171.

Dozier, D.M., L.A. Grunig and J.E. Grunig (1995). *Manager's Guide to Excellence in Public Relations and Communi-cation Management*. Mahwah, NJ: Lawrence Erlbaum Associates, Inc.

Drucker, P. (1990). *Managing the Non-profit Organization*. Oxford: Butterworth-Heinemann.

Edwards, M. (1998). 'Nailing the jelly to the wall: civil society and international development.' www.futurepositive.org/edwards.php accessed 29 May 2012.

Etherington, S. (2010). 'Video: Kalayaan. Charity awards winner'. www.guardian.co.uk/charity-awards/2010-winner-kalayaan

Frumkin, P. and M.T. Kim (2001). 'Strategic positioning and the financing of nonprofit organizations: is efficiency rewarded in the contributions marketplace?' *Public Administration Review* **61**(3): 266–275.

Gray, R., J. Bebbington and D. Collison (2006). 'NGOs, civil society and accountability: making the people accountable to capital.' *Accounting, Auditing and Accountability Journal* **19**(3): 319–348.

Griffiths, M. (2005). 'Building and rebuilding charity brands: the role of creative agencies'. *International Journal of Nonprofit Voluntary Sector Marketing* **10**(2): 121–132.

Grunig, J.E., L.A. Grunig, K. Sriramesh, Y.H. Huang and A. Lyra (1995). 'Models of public relations in an international setting'. *Journal of Public Relations Research* **7**(3): 163–186.

Jenkinson, A., S. Branko and K. Bishop (2005). 'Optimising communications for charity brand management'. *International Journal of Nonprofit Voluntary Sector Marketing* **10**(2): 79–92.

Juma, M.K. (2004). 'The compromised brokers: NGOs and displaced populations in East Africa' in *Human Rights, The Rule of Law, and Development in Africa*. T. Zeleza and P.J. McConnaughay (eds). Philadelphia: University of Pennsylvania Press.

Kelly, K.S. (1993). 'Public relations and fund-raising encroachment: losing control in the non-profit sector'. *Public Relations Review* **19**(4): 321–334.

Kent, M.L. and M. Taylor (1998). 'Building dialogic relationships through the World Wide Web'. *Public Relations Review* **24**(3).

Kent, M.L., M. Taylor and W.J. White (2003). 'The relationship between Web site design, and organizational responsiveness to stakeholders'. *Public Relations Review* **29**(1): 63–77.

Kilby, P. (2006). 'Accountability for empowerment: Dilemmas facing non-government organizations'. *World Development* **34**(6): 951–963.

Lattimer, M. (2000). *The Campaigning Handbook*, 2nd edition. London: Directory of Social Change.

Lauzen, M.M. (1991). 'Imperialism and encroachment in public relations'. *Public Relations Review* **17**(3): 245–255.

Lombard, D. (2011). 'Case study: occupy the London Stock Exchange.' *Third Sector Magazine*: 15 November.

Long, M.M. and L. Chiagouris (2006). 'The role of credibility in shaping attitudes toward nonprofit websites'. *International Journal of Nonprofit Voluntary Sector Marketing* **11**(3): 239–249.

MacMillan, K., K. Money, A. Money and S. Downing (2005). 'Relationship marketing in the not-for-profit sector: an extension and application of the commitment-trust theory'. *Journal of Business Research* **58**(6): 806–818.

Maxwell, S. (2009). 'Where next for development studies? Coverage, capacity and communications'. *Journal of International Development* **21**(6): 787–791.

McQuail, D. (1987). *Mass Communication Theory: An introduction*. London: Sage Publications.

Morgan, R.M. and S.D. Hunt (1994). 'The commitment-trust theory of relationship marketing'. *Journal of Marketing* **58**(3).

Naude, A.M.E., J.D. Froneman and R.A. Atwood (2004). 'The use of the internet by ten South African non-governmental organizations – a public relations perspective'. *Public Relations Review* **30**.

Padyani, P. and B. Gainer (2003). 'Peer reputation in the nonprofit sector: its role in nonprofit sector management'. *Corporate Reputation Review* **6**(3): 252–265.

Plowman, K.P. (2007). 'Public relations, conflict resolution, and mediation' in *The Future of Excellence in Public Relations and Communication Management: Challenges for the Next Generation*. E. Toth (ed.). Mahwah, NJ: Lawrence Erlbaum Associates.

Rawat, A. (2002). 'Part three: older persons in emergencies: a case study of HelpAge India' in *Ageing in Asia and the Pacific: Emerging Issues and Successful Practices*. Social Policy Paper No.10. Bangkok: United Nations Economic and Social Commission for Asia and the Pacific.

Sargeant. A. (2005). *Marketing Management for Nonprofit Organizations*, 2nd edition. New York, NY: Oxford University Press.

Stoker, G. and D. Wilson (1991). 'The lost world of British local pressure groups'. *Public Policy and Administration* **6**(2): 20–34.

Sukuki, N. (1998). *Inside NGOs: Learning to manage conflicts between headquarters and field offices*. London: Intermediate Technology Publications.

The Economist (2003). 'Non-government organizations and business: living with the enemy'. 9 August.

The Guardian (2010). 'Guardian Charity Awards honour "remarkable" winners'. URL: http://www.guardian.co.uk/society/2010/dec/02/guardian-charity-award-winners?intcmp=239 accessed 22 December 2011.

The Sun (1985). 'I'd shoot my son if he had AIDS, says vicar.' 14 October.

The World Bank Group (2011). http://web.worldbank.org/WBSITE/EXTERNAL/TOPICS/CSO/0,,contentMDK:20

101499~menuPK:244752~pagePK:220503~piPK:220476~theSitePK:228717,00.html accessed 29 May 2012.

Villanger, E. (2004). 'Company influence on foreign aid disbursement: Is conditionality credible when donors have mixed motives?' *Southern Economic Journal* **71**(2): 334–351.

Wootliff, J. and C. Deri (2001). 'NGOs: the new super brands'. *Corporate Reputation Review* **4**(2).

Young, D.R. (2001). 'Organizational identity in nonprofit organizations: strategic and structural implications'. *Nonprofit Management and Leadership* **12**(2): 139–157.

Websites

Corporate Watch: www.corporatewatch.org.uk

Disasters Emergency Committee: www.dec.org.uk

NGO Watch: www.globalgovernancewatch.org/ngo_watch

HelpAge India: www.helpageindia.org

Kalayaan: www.kalayaan.org.uk

Oxfam International: www.oxfam.org

SIGWatch: wwwsigwatch.com

Terrence Higgins Trust: www.tht.org.uk

Strategic communication and social marketing in healthcare organisations

Learning outcomes

By the end of this chapter you should able to:

- consider and explore further the different facets of health communication
- analyse the challenging environment in which healthcare organisations operate
- discuss the strategic preoccupations and priorities of healthcare communicators
- critically evaluate social marketing and other aspects of practice
- reflect on the usefulness of concepts such as wicked problems.

Structure

- Communication as a core systems asset
- Confronting 'wickedness' in health
- Social marketing: the battle between good and evil
- Internal challenges and communication

Introduction

Health communication is a large and diverse field of practice. As an academic area of study it has spawned its own industry of books, journals and conferences. This is hardly surprising given that health issues pervade the media we consume and the conversations we conduct. How to finance the health of the nation is a dominant public policy narrative throughout the world. Poor health and lives cut unnecessarily short frame many of the inequalities that exist within and across societies (Wilkinson and Pickett 2009). Debates about medical research divide opinion. Government campaigns never tire of telling us what we should eat, drink and do with our time. Our vanities and insecurities are goaded by a private sector that exploits a desire to look fit and healthy. Celebrity culture champions perverted distortions of youth over the natural process of ageing. Clinicians are still publicly lauded and admired in a world where trust in others has eroded dramatically (Edelman 2011). The hospital remains an iconic setting for much of our popular entertainment (such as TV dramas),

while an inherent fascination with health and well-being underscores the language that permeates our everyday interactions with others. International greetings such as *how are you*, *como esta usted* and *ca va* initiate the conversations we have with both close and casual acquaintances.

At the heart of these different perspectives is a kaleidoscope of communication issues that reflect a complex world of work and generate a rich agenda of study. The subjects explored include how politicians present health policy, patient communication, how people share information about different illnesses, behaviour change and social marketing, engagement between healthcare professionals, public involvement, the impact of the mass media, crisis communication, ethics and the role of the Internet. These and related issues are also debated in other academic fields such as psychology, public policy, sociology and international relations. Such linkages and subject matter result in an eclectic and challenging area of research and practice.

This chapter examines this terrain from an organisational perspective. Its focus is the hospitals, doctors' surgeries, dental clinics, care homes, government departments, international agencies and other organisations responsible for administering healthcare. Such an emphasis provides an opportunity to discuss the particular challenges confronting communicators operating in this sector – therefore shining a light on a demanding, multidimensional role.

Ties that bind

The study of communication in a healthcare environment is intriguing because it involves a consideration of organisations operating in the private, public and third sectors. Some are financed from tax revenues; other organisations rely on social or private insurance to bankroll their activities. Healthcare services are also funded and run by charities and other non-governmental organisations (NGOs).

Explore 26.1   Health issues around you

During the course of a week make a note of the different communicative contexts in which health issues emerge. For example:

- Monitor a range of international, national and local media. What health stories were covered? How would you categorise these? Were they political, scientific, consumer or celebrity stories? Can you detect any differences between the types of stories that are being covered in each media?

- What marketing activity did you notice with a health message? Do not confine your observations to campaigns that are linked explicitly to health and well being. Consider activity that also uses health connotations to promote a particular product or service. How was this achieved? Who was behind

this marketing activity? What do you think was the purpose of the campaign?

- Were you part of any conversations that discussed health issues? Where did these conversations take place? What prompted the discussion? Was it a news story, a personal experience or something else?

Feedback

Health issues straddle a range of societal agendas. They are the province of governments, organisations and individuals. This diversity of interest is reflected in the way health is discussed in the media we consume. It is also a staple of day-to-day conversation. Furthermore, it's interesting to note how different cultures respond to health issues and the impact this has on public discourse.

Think about 26.1

Healthcare in your region

- How are the healthcare organisations in your area funded?

- Is the money they spend on communication scrutinised by stakeholders such as the media or politicians?

- How do they communicate with you? Do they develop proactive campaigns? Do you only hear from them when they are responding to a crisis? Are they visible in the local community beyond their own premises?

- Do you think their communication activity is effective and appropriate, given how they are funded?

Feedback

In the United Kingdom publicly funded health organisations are criticised for spending money on communication. Health communicators have been characterised by journalists as *spin doctors*, more concerned with defending the reputation of the organisation than engaging with the public. Communicators are seen as a legitimate target given that the health system is funded by taxpayers.

Furthermore, rather than relying on just one funding model most societies are characterised by a mixed market of financial and service provision. This creates a diverse range of systems and organisational structures across the world. (see Think about 26.1 and Explore 26.1.)

Given this hybrid landscape, is it possible to consider generically the communication challenges faced by a range of organisations operating in different social, economic and political contexts? Do they face similar issues regardless of their financial model and location? This chapter argues that the concept of *wicked* problems (Rittel and Webber 1973) can be used to highlight areas of common ground. Such a perspective is not unique to healthcare organisations but does serve as a useful lens through which to view communication in this context. The idea of wicked problems links together different types of organisation and reinforces the strategic role of communication. Their resolution requires healthcare organisations to have a wide-ranging communicative capacity, and this supports an important proposition that underpins the text.

Communication as a core systems asset

For communication to make a full contribution to the effectiveness and success of the modern healthcare organisation it has to be seen as offering more than message delivery, expertise on channel use or contributing to building brand or reputation. The effectiveness of the communication function depends on a more developed understanding of its role. 'Communication' no longer satisfactorily captures the scope of the practitioner's activities. The role is concerned with analysis, understanding and the management and evaluation of key relationships in order to achieve results within and through them, such as improvements to service quality, collaboration, productivity and so on.

In practical terms, managed communication adds value to healthcare organisations by providing a range of scientifically based interventions including:

- issue monitoring, including management and resolution capability

- analysis of key internal and external relationships based on research expertise

- partnership engagement and working

- market research and competitor intelligence

- public opinion polling

- scenario planning

- crisis and risk planning, management and communication

- brand building and management

- change management and internal communication

- messaging, content and presentation

- evaluation and managing of reputation

- evaluation of outward and inward communication programmes to pre-defined outcomes, including social marketing initiatives

- development of strategies for reliable and scientifically valid feedback

- media relations expertise

- analysis and development of organisational culture and climate.

This range of activities highlights that health communication is not only done to facilitate the management of the organisation but is central to the delivery of the core business. It also requires the communicator to move seamlessly between reactive, proactive and interactive roles, depending on the relationship with the stakeholders involved. Communication is far more than the deployment of a set of communication skills and techniques. It needs to be regarded as a core systems asset concerned with building the reputational and relational capital of the healthcare organisations in order to promote, protect and deliver health services.

Confronting 'wickedness' in health

Healthcare organisations are surrounded by 'wicked' problems, whether they operate in the public, private or third sectors. Rittel and Webber (1973) developed the first systematic conceptualisation of **wicked problems**

and applied this new thinking in a planning context. They were motivated by the realisation that many public policy challenges cannot be addressed by adopting a traditional and linear problem-solving approach. Their insights were applied to other areas of social planning by scholars such as Roberts (2000, 2002), while Conklin (2006) built on this work by developing the idea of wickedness for the private sector. Rittel and Webber noted originally that ten attributes make a problem wicked, but Conklin distils this thinking into six key characteristics (see Box 26.1).

> **Definition:** *'Wicked problems'* are problems that are unstructured and difficult to define, cut across many stakeholders and are relentless (Weber and Khademian 2008). These characteristics require fluid problem solving, the application of many different perspectives, collaboration and long-term commitment.

Box 26.1

Six key characteristics of wicked problems (Conklin 2006)

1. You don't understand the problem until you have developed a solution.

Another way of looking at this statement is that a proposed solution only serves to expose new aspects of the problem. To help illustrate this conundrum, imagine that you are a communication professional in a team commissioned to tackle the problem of obesity in a local community. You may come to the conclusion that regular exercise is one solution that will help people who are obese to lose weight. This leads, unfortunately, to another problem. How do you persuade a disparate group of people to change their behaviour and commit to a regular programme of exercise? This realisation requires further adjustments to the potential solution as a new set of challenges emerges. It requires you to step back and view the problem afresh.

This insight also highlights that there can be no definitive articulation of a *wicked* problem. They are inherently hard to define as they are likely to be caused by a range

of factors and forces. If you return to the previous scenario, how or why does somebody become obese? Such a condition could be caused by a range of physiological and social-economic factors. Defining the problem will also be influenced by who you ask. Different stakeholders will have different views about what the problem is, as well as what an acceptable solution might be. This leads to the conclusion that an understanding of the context that frames a *wicked* problem is crucial.

2. Wicked problems have a no stopping rule.

Given there is no definitive definition of a wicked problem there can never be a definitive solution. Conklin (2006) notes that the problem-solving process ends when the players in the process run out of resources, such as time, money, or energy, rather than when some optimal or 'final and correct' solution emerges. If we return to a health context, consider whether it is possible for social issues such as obesity or HIV to ever be 'solved'? Do they not require ongoing action and commitment on the part of healthcare organisations, governments and individual citizens?

3. Solutions to wicked problems are not right or wrong.

This is yet another fuzzy area of wicked problems, given their intricate character. Solutions are relative (better or

box 26.1 (continued)

worse than what we have already), rather than simply right or wrong. This means that evaluating a solution to a wicked problem is not an objective process. Solutions are instead assessed in a social context where a range of legitimate stakeholders will bring a host of different perspectives, values and goals. It is suggested here that this can be termed a 'parallax view of evaluation': that is, the same thing can look different when observed from different viewpoints.

4. Every wicked problem is essentially unique and novel.

Given a complex context of factors and conditions, no two wicked problems are the same. Off-the-shelf solutions are, therefore, not appropriate. Salvation instead lies in tailored, custom-made solutions. One community's successful response to obesity may be due, for example, to an inspirational local resident who has galvanised the people around them. The same initiative might not generate the same positive results in another area lacking such a charismatic and determined individual. Furthermore, if that person were to try to replicate their success in another community they might lack the credibility and networks that made their original intervention effective.

5. Every solution to a wicked problem is a 'one-shot operation'.

This characteristic highlights that every attempt at a solution has consequences. It was discussed earlier that you cannot learn about the problem without trying solutions. According to Rittel and Webber (1973), every solution you try is expensive and has lasting unintended consequences that are likely to spawn new wicked problems. As a communicator you may devise a public health campaign that successfully encourages people to stop smoking. An unintended consequence of this might be that they begin to eat more and put on weight. This then creates a new obesity problem in your community.

6. Wicked problems have no given alternative solutions.

According to Conklin (2006) this characteristic calls for both creativity and judgement. The enigmatic nature of wicked problems suggests a feast or famine in terms of solutions. A range of remedies may be possible, or none at all. Alternatively, some solutions may never be thought of by the team confronting the wicked problem. This means it is a matter of creativity to devise potential solutions and a matter of judgement to determine those that should be developed and implemented.

A chronic challenge

A problem is not required to possess all six characteristics in order for it to be considered wicked. What is important about the typology that has been discussed is that it illuminates the intractable nature of many of the issues faced by organisations. This underlines the reasons behind Rittel and Webber's original frustration with traditional problem-solving techniques. It also begins to show how many of the societal and internal challenges facing healthcare organisations can be framed as wicked problems. For example, tackling poor health today is as much about addressing the lifestyle choices that people make as the number of clinicians working in hospitals.

According to the World Health Organisation (2005), chronic conditions such as cancer, cardiovascular illness and diabetes now make up one half of the world's burden of disease. The WHO estimates that by 2015 deaths from these diseases will have increased to 41 million. These chronic conditions are related to individual behaviours such as diet, smoking and exercise rather than infectious diseases. A study by Cancer Research UK (2011) revealed that tobacco, obesity, alcohol and what people eat are behind

more than 100,000 cancers in the United Kingdom. This is the equivalent of one third of all cancers diagnosed in the country each year.

Similar challenges also beset the developing world. Epidemics remain the major contributor of poor health in developing countries, but Kaneda (2006) notes that the challenge here is to also 'reorient health sectors towards managing chronic diseases'. In India, the world's second-largest producer and consumer of tobacco, cardiovascular disease mortality is projected to account for one-third of all deaths by 2015 (Reddy and Yusuf 1998, cited in Kaneda 2006).

Social marketing: the battle between good and evil

Social marketing can be viewed as one organisational response designed to tackle the wicked problems associated with encouraging healthy lifestyle choices. The subtitle of Hastings' (2007) book on the subject captures the essence of this beautifully: *Why should the devil have all*

> **Definition:** *'Social marketing'* is the application of commercial marketing techniques to the analysis, planning, execution and evaluation of programmes designed to influence the voluntary behaviour of target audiences in order to improve their personal welfare and that of society (Andreasen 1995).

the best tunes? In a healthcare context, **social marketing** is a weapon that is used increasingly by organisations in the war to combat the impact of chronic diseases. It also places the communicator at the heart of this battle between good and evil.

The stakes are high and the weight of expectation placed on social marketing-inspired approaches is enormous. McKie and Toledano (2008), despite their passionate exposition of social marketing's potential, also note it lacks the necessary academic hinterland to increase or maintain the recognition it has earned so far. They credit Kotler and Zaltman (1971) as the originators of the term 'social marketing' but also note the additional tides and currents that have influenced its development from the 1960s onwards as other academics considered the application of marketing methods to tackle social problems. It is necessary, however, to look even further back in history to the world of practice rather than academia in order to detect the first stirrings of what might be termed a social marketing approach. Government information campaigns in the first half of the twentieth century, as well as the development of organisations such as the Central Office of Information in the UK, prompted the development of a discipline with progressive social designs (Gregory 2011).

Social marketing generates plenty of interest and excitement in academic and professional circles because of its concern with the use of marketing strategies and techniques to create a social rather than a commercial dividend. Marketing approaches are used in the private sector to generate company profit. In contrast, social marketing is a discipline that is concerned with the generation of positive social impacts. These might include persuading citizens to recycle their rubbish to reduce the amount of waste being buried in landfill sites, encouraging people to drive more responsibly to cut the number of road deaths, or getting them to eat more fruit and vegetables so they can live longer.

This orientation does not mean that social marketing can lack a financial motivation. Many social marketing initiatives in the health sector are driven by a desire to save money. Chronic conditions linked to behaviours, such as diet and smoking, are a huge drain on health systems. On its website, the Department of Health (2011)

in the UK notes that 'weight problems cost the wider economy in the region of £16 billion and this will rise to £50 billion per year by 2050 if left unchecked'. Similarly, the social aftermath of crime, teenage pregnancy, traffic accidents, drug use and other systemic problems have a collective as well as individual dimension that can be calculated in monetary terms. As an aside, it should also be noted that social marketing activity is often executed by private sector communication agencies rather than in-house, public sector practitioners. For these agencies, their participation is based upon a commercial rather than a social contract.

A health warning

Social marketing's focus on behaviour can lead to an individualistic, psychological approach to change. Viewed from this perspective, problems are addressed by altering people's mindset and attitude – therefore prompting a change in behaviour. An emphasis on insight that can help trigger individual behaviour change becomes the Holy Grail pursued by organisations seeking to address a range of social dilemmas. If it is unchecked this perspective can overstate an individual's ability to change his or her behaviour. Much of what governs human behaviour in a health context is based upon socialisation, culture and genetics (Wright et al. 2008). Viewing the world in any other way might be best termed naïve and at worst irresponsible. It places responsibility for a range of societal issues in the hands of the individual. This over-exaggerates self-efficacy – that is, the belief in an individual's ability to exert personal control over a situation.

The battle against tobacco addiction underlines graphically why certain health issues cannot be left to the individual. Waxman (2011), a Professor of Oncology at Imperial College London, illustrates the point forcefully:

> *Twenty-five years ago, about half the population smoked. Now that figure is 20 per cent. That shift would not have happened without powerful government intervention that took on the tobacco companies (and ignored the lamentations of the pension funds). Changing lifestyles not only needed information campaigns; it required mandatory and gory warnings on packets, an ever-increasing vice tax on cigarettes, advertising bans and forcing smokers out of pubs and offices and on to the streets with their habit.*

This argument also contains its own difficulties. Viewed from another vantage point, both the call for government intervention in the form of legislation and the activation of social marketing campaigns can be viewed as a contemporary expression of the omnipotent, paternalistic state.

Picture 26.1 This 'coughing' bus stop led to a controversial local news story – but word of mouth helped raise awareness of the symptoms of lung cancer (*source*: Crown Copyright/Yorks and Humber Strategic Health Authority)

Implicit in this desire to change peoples' behaviour is the notion that government knows what's good for its citizens. A mixture of legislation and an arsenal of persuasive techniques are then used to bring the individual around to its way of thinking.

Waxman (2011) acknowledges this argument but turns to the issue of food to counter it. He notes that some will regard the banning of advertisements for high fat foods or taxing the use of saturated fats as an attack on their personal freedom. He contends, however, that 'the people with the least ability to make informed choices are the poor, who happen also to be more likely to smoke or to be fat. Food is a class issue and it must be easier for the poorest in our country to eat well' (Waxman 2011).

Anchored in safe water

This debate underlines the need for any social marketing activity to be embedded within a wider strategic communication process. This will allow the organisation to consider this activity in the context of its broader purpose, values and societal responsibilities. Such a process

is inherently stakeholder-orientated and therefore provides an opportunity for the organisation to consider the implications of its social marketing activities from a range of different perspectives. Organisations responsible for delivering healthcare provide a service that is regarded as an inalienable right held in common by all citizens. This requires them to demonstrate an acute level of social sensitivity and highlights the particular importance of contextual intelligence in a healthcare environment.

The context that envelops an organisation determines the norms and values that govern its behaviour. L'Etang (2008) notes that culture is especially important in this regard as it 'shapes our understanding and sense making facilities and determines what is taken for granted or assumed in a particular environment'. What is deemed appropriate and acceptable is situational: communicators do not face a fixed landscape but one that changes over time and across different cultures.

Healthcare organisations therefore need to connect with their key stakeholders in order to understand their needs, to appropriately tailor services to those needs and to maintain broad public support. For communicators this requires the collection and interpretation of information that helps them to maintain their organisation's overall license to operate. According to Steyn (2003) it is the process that allows the organisation to consider 'the qualitative aspects of the business (the opinions, judgement, even feelings of stakeholders) and the environment it faces . . . it is problem solving in unstructured situations, being able to recognise changing situations'.

An effective and ethical healthcare communication function provides management with evidence-based analysis of the ongoing issues and relationships that may have an impact. Relevant insights are then fed into the organisation's decision-making process through a range of formal and informal channels, such as conversations with senior managers, presentations to the board, emails that highlight key insights and suggest appropriate action, policy papers and the provision of data as part of the organisation's annual corporate planning process. Social marketing is a discipline that needs to be governed and regulated by this wider strategic communication perspective. At its heart is a persuasive, transactional model that should be deployed with caution as it contains both the strengths and weaknesses of a marketing approach.

Implementation challenges in social marketing

Marketing is a strategic management discipline. According to Kotler (2000), 'it is the process of planning and executing the conception, pricing, promotion and distribution of

Picture 26.2 Tackling obesity in the UK – intervention programmes by Carnegie Weight Management (MoreLife)

ideas, goods, services to create exchanges that satisfy individual and organisational goals'. This might involve a range of activities, including the generation of customer insight, product or service design, channel management and logistics, retail strategies, as well as promotion (Brassington and Pettitt 2003). The role of communication techniques in this process is usually at the promotional stage.

Managers implementing social marketing programmes must also adopt a similarly holistic approach. It is no use promoting a smoking cessation service to local people unless it has been designed with their needs in mind. Even the most targeted and creative promotional campaigns cannot on their own secure the long-term success of a social marketing initiative if other parts of the jigsaw are not in place. A focus on service-users, delivery partners, suppliers and employees is therefore crucial to the social marketing process. The communication team should play a vital role in developing, delivering and evaluating success in this area. Such an orientation means that as well as public and patient insight informing organisational decision making, it also influences local priorities, product and service design. It can also identify the levers by which behavioural change may be achieved.

Armed with this data the communication function, working with appropriate colleagues, can shape the agenda for discussion. In addition, communicators can facilitate complex discussions with stakeholders who may have

conflicting and competing priorities and ensure the perspectives of all stakeholders are considered. The communication function can also contribute to the market intelligence that delineates the size of the market and information on competitor activity: a vital component of decision making. The concept of 'the competition' in social marketing is particularly important, as Schlosser (2002) makes clear in *Fast Food Nation*. At the same time as an organisation might be trying to persuade people to eat more healthily, some of the world's largest companies are marshalling huge marketing budgets with the opposite objective in mind. 'The competition' can also be framed in terms of competing demands on peoples' time. A call for children to take more exercise will have to be considered against other attractions such as computer games and television. (see Think about 26.2.)

Think about 26.2

Social marketing effectiveness

What do you think of the social marketing programme described in Case study 26.1? Did it manage to tackle the challenges it set out to?

Case study 26.1

NHS Peterborough: tackling childhood obesity and promoting healthy lifestyles

Background

Obesity is regarded by the UK Government as a significant and preventable health challenge. Peterborough, a city in the east of England, has a rising prevalence of childhood obesity.

As part of the National Child Measurement Programme (NCMP), school nurses in the town annually measure height and weight for all Reception Year children (aged 4–5 years) and Year 6 pupils (aged 10–11 years). Preliminary results from the 2008/2009 study showed that:

- One in seven (13.8 per cent) reception-age children were overweight and almost one in ten (9.2 per cent) obese.

- Of Year 6 pupils almost one in seven (14.3 per cent) were overweight, and one in five (19.8 per cent) were obese.

Peterborough was failing to achieve national and regional targets to halt the year-on-year rise in obesity by 2010 and to meet the goal of reversing the trend and returning to 2000 prevalence levels by 2020.

NHS Peterborough, the organisation responsible for providing primary healthcare services in the city, decided to fund a social marketing programme to tackle the problem. It commissioned three consultancy partners to develop and implement the programme: Blue Marble, Purebrand Public Sector and Carnegie Weight Management (now More-Life).

Programme aims

- To reduce rates of obese/overweight children (Reception and Year 6);

- to increase the measurement rate across the city as part of the National Child Measurement Programme;

- to promote healthy lifestyles and healthy weight activity and services in the city.

Partners

The programme brought together a range of partners from across the city. These included representatives from local services linked to education, the environment, health, sports and leisure, as well as the media and families from within the community.

Strategy

The three consultancies worked with NHS Peterborough's Public Health Team to:

- engage with key partners and services in the city to analyse the prevalence of obesity and develop a new delivery programme (management consultants Blue Marble);

- undertake a local area study to inform service delivery, planning and to support communication activity (marketing consultancy Purebrand Public Sector);

- deliver child weight management services across the city (programme delivery partner Carnegie Weight Management).

Implementation

- A ten-week Childhood Obesity Solutions Centre process was created. This initiative brought together partners from across the city to work through and develop appropriate solutions in response to the challenge of rising childhood obesity. The process of engaging key stakeholders – from partnership boards, to local practitioners on the front line and end users from the community – was intended to stimulate collective accountability and responsibility. The aim was to 'develop a shared solution to a shared problem'. For the first time, staff from various agencies across the partnership developed solutions together through a series of workshops and focus groups.

- The Solutions Centre process generated a requirement for a local area study. This was to support the planning, delivery and communication of new health services linked to obesity, in particular an effective weight management programme. It involved:

  - Workshops (with community health workers, community health trainers, community volunteers and young families).

  - Visits to key wards and interviews and consultations with key community stakeholders.

  - Interviews and consultation with both local authority and NHS staff involved in delivering initiatives targeting specific health outcomes.

  - Working with Carnegie Weight Management, the weight management delivery partner, and utilising their previous experience and expertise to inform the research process.

case study 26.1 (continued)

- Staging an engagement event to inform organisations and partner agencies from within the referral network about the project and to stimulate referrals to future weight management programmes being delivered by Carnegie Weight Management.

- Engaging with key clinical and other stakeholders in promoting and generating referrals for the Carnegie Weight Management programme.

- Delivery of the Carnegie Weight Management Clubs in the city. Carnegie monitor and report on weight loss, as well as any behaviour and lifestyle changes among the programme's participants.

- Carnegie Weight Management made its programme available to families with very young children (aged 2+) for the first time. This allowed NHS Peterborough to work with parents to promote healthy habits at an early stage of family life.

Results

Outcomes achieved:

- Childhood obesity levels in reception-aged children fell from 12.6 per cent to 9.2 per cent.

- More families and children accessed healthy living services and obesity prevention interventions due to the stakeholder engagement strategy.

- 37 families and their children participated in the two Carnegie programmes. 65 registered for future autumn programmes.

- 87 enquiries were received for participation in future Carnegie Clubs.

- 100 per cent of the respondents following the briefing event to launch the project and stimulate referrals said they found the event useful; 100 per cent stated that they would recommend the programme to other members of staff to promote the service. When asked how likely they were to refer others on to the programme, 95 per cent said they were very likely or likely to.

- Positive media coverage generated in local press, TV and radio. Media activity reached an estimated 643,000 people in the Cambridgeshire area.

Benefits delivered by the programme:

- Cross-partnership involvement in developing solutions
- New interventions coordinated between partners
- Multi-agency solutions created across all age ranges
- Cross-agency commissioning and re-focusing of funds
- More effective pooling and targeting of resources
- Improved referrals on the programmes.

Internal challenges and communication

Many of the issues leaders confront *within* healthcare organisations can also be characterised as wicked problems. In addition to the challenges linked to chronic conditions, many countries are also grappling with the healthcare implications of an ageing population. This challenge is not just confined to developed countries. Kinsella and Velkoff (2001) estimate that between 2000 and 2030 the number of people aged 65 or older in developing nations is expected to rise from 249 million to 690 million. Figures from the United Nations (2011) are a reminder of the shocking inequalities that still exist in the world due to epidemics. In 2009 more than 8 million children under five died, global deaths from malaria equalled 781,000 and an estimated 2.6 million people were newly infected by HIV. At the same time as the list of health issues confronting societies grows, the global economic crisis has squeezed the financial

resources available to confront these challenges. As a result, healthcare organisations find themselves pitched in the middle of a perfect storm.

This situation requires organisations to rethink how they operate. What services do they provide in the future? How do they ensure that the right people receive treatment, at the right time? How do they reach the most vulnerable in society? How can they do more for less? How can healthcare managers and clinicians work together more effectively to improve patient care? How do they create a culture of innovation among employees to meet these challenges? These are the sort of questions that confront healthcare organisations in the second decade of the twenty-first century. (See Mini case study 26.1.)

The importance of collaboration

The characteristics of wicked problems highlighted earlier suggest that top-down solutions to these sort of internal

Mini case study 26.1
The NHS: turbulence, challenge and change

Since its inception more than 60 years ago, the UK National Health Service (NHS) has become the world's largest publicly funded health system. With 1.5 million staff, this complex system is also the fourth largest employer in the world.

The Government White Paper, *Equity and Excellence: Liberating the NHS*, has initiated the most profound change in the NHS since its formation. The change for the NHS is said to be driven by three key principles:

1. Putting patients at the heart of the NHS. This will mean a transformation of the relationship between the NHS, public and patients, who will be newly empowered by the provision of information and able to exercise choice. The decision of 'no decision about me without me' is central to this aspiration.

2. Ensuring local organisations and clinical professionals lead the health service. This involves making services more directly accountable to patients and communities, but also requires cutting bureaucracy and encouraging innovation.

3. A focus on clinical outcomes. This means a move away from targets and processes to high-quality care outcomes.

To be successful this complex reform programme will require a change in culture, behaviours, relationships and ways of working. An ethos of service, customer orientation and improved clinical outcomes will need to permeate the whole of the NHS. This has profound implications for communicators working in the system at the same time that communicative capacity in the NHS has been cut by 40 per cent.

challenges are inappropriate. A more collaborative method is needed. This involves engaging with all relevant stakeholders to formulate a common, agreed approach. The people who are affected become participants in the process. They are not just asked for their views but are actively involved in shaping the outcome. It recognises that involving patients in their own health choices is critical to health outcomes, as is engaging employees in a process of collective learning. This is clearly not the right approach if leaders are trying to legitimise a decision that has already taken place behind closed doors and which participants are misled into thinking they can affect. The scope for change must be part of the process.

These insights illustrate why collaborative leaders focus on the process of decision making rather than any particular outcome. When faced with wicked problems they have little time for formal power, but function instead as first among equals in a process that encourages their peers to take ownership of a problem (Hackman and Johnson 2009). This supports Conklin's (2006) conclusion that the resolution of wicked problems must be a social, communicative process. This moves the key to success in organisations away from the creation of an optimal strategy to a more skilful strategy process. The communication team should be at the heart of this effort to ensure that a strategic stakeholder engagement process opens up decision making and change to those who will add value.

Summary

The chapter began by noting the ubiquitous nature of health issues in society. This illustrated some of the influences behind the diverse agenda of health communication research, as well as locating the subject of communication within healthcare organisations in a wider context. The discussion was then shaped by two ideas: the first suggests that healthcare organisations are increasingly concerned with the resolution of wicked problems; the second relates to communication being regarded as a system asset rather than just a technical function.

Social marketing was then framed as one organisational response to a set of external wicked problems that confront healthcare organisations. This led to a discussion of a range of issues and challenges linked to such an approach. The importance of anchoring social marketing programmes within a wider strategic communication framework was highlighted as a necessary antidote to some of the ailments that were identified. The importance of contextual intelligence was underlined, as was the role played by the strategic communicator in organisational decision making by helping to bring social, ethical and economic concerns into alignment. An in-depth social marketing case study provided an opportunity to consider the practical challenges that face communicators in this difficult area. Wicked problems that are internal to healthcare organisations were discussed in the final section, and this brought ideas of collaborative leadership and active employee engagement to the fore.

Bibliography

Andreasen, A.R. (1995). *Marketing Social Change: Changing behaviour to promote health, social development, and the environment*. San Francisco, CA: Jossey-Bass.

Brassington, F. and S. Pettitt (2003). *Principles of Marketing*. Harlow: Pearson.

Cancer Research UK (2011). 'The causes of cancer you can control'. http://scienceblog.cancerresearchUK.org/2011/12/07/the-cause-of-cancer-you-can-control/ accessed 11 December 2011.

Conklin, J. (2006). *Dialogue Mapping: Building shared understanding of wicked problems*. New York, NY: Wiley.

Department of Health (2011). 'Obesity general information'. www.dh.gov.uk/eu/ublichealth/Obesity/DH_078098 accessed 12 December 2011.

Edelman (2011). 'Trust barometer'. http://edelman.com/trust/2011 accessed 20 December 2011.

Elkington, J. (1998). *Cannibals with Forks: The triple bottom line for 21st century business*. Gabriola Island: New Society Publishers.

Gregory, A. (2011). 'Government and the dance with communications: coming full circle in the 21st century'. International History of Public Relations Conference, Bournemouth, UK. July 2011.

Hackman, M.Z. and C.E. Johnson (2009). *Leadership: A communication perspective*. Long Grove: Waveland Press.

Hastings, G. (2007). *Social Marketing: Why should the devil have all the best tunes?* Oxford: Butterworth-Heinemann.

Kaneda, T. (2006). 'Healthcare challenges for developing countries with aging populations'. www.prb.org/Articles/2006/Health-care-challenges-for-developing-countries-with-aging-populatons.aspx accessed 12 December 2011.

Kinsella, K. and V.A. Velkoff (2001). *An Aging World*. Washington, DC: US Census Bureau.

Kotler, P. (2000). *Marketing Management: The millennium edition*. New Jersey: Prentice Hall.

Kotler, P. and G. Zaltman (1971). 'Social marketing: an approach to planned social change'. *Journal of Marketing* **35**: 3–12.

L'Etang, J. (2008). *Public Relations: Concepts, practice and critique*. London: Sage.

McKie, D. and M. Toledano (2008). 'Dangerous liaison or perfect match? Public relations and social marketing'. *Public Relations Review* **34**: 318–324.

Reddy, K.S. and S. Yusuf (1998). 'Emerging epidemic of cardiovascular disease in developing countries'. *Circulation* **97**: 596–601.

Rittel, H. and M. Webber (1973). 'Dilemmas in a general theory of planning'. *Policy Sciences* **4**: 155–159.

Roberts, N.C. (2000). 'Wicked problems and network approaches to resolution'. *International Public Management Review* **1**(1): 1–19.

Roberts, N.C. (2002). *The Transformative Power of Dialogue*. Boston, MA: JAI Press.

Schlosser, E. (2002). *Fast Food Nation: The dark side of the all-American meal*. New York, NY: Harper Collins.

Steyn, B. (2003). 'From strategy to corporate communication strategy: a conceptualisation'. *Journal of Communication Management* **8**(2): 168–183.

United Nations (2011). 'The Millennium Goals Report 2011'. http://un.org/millenniumgoals/pdf/(2011) accessed 18 November 2011.

Waxman, J. (2011). 'To avoid cancer, let the state dictate your diet'. *The Times*, 9 December: 36.

Weber, E.P. and A.M. Khademian (2008). 'Wicked problems, knowledge challenges and collaborative capacity builders in network settings'. *Public Administration Review* March/April.

Wilkinson, R. and K. Pickett (2009). *The Spirit Level*. London: Allen Lane.

World Health Organisation (2005). *Preventing Chronic Disease: A vital investment*. Geneva: World Health Organisation.

Wright, K.B., L. Sparks and H.D. O'Hair (2008). *Health Communication in the 21st Century*. Oxford: Blackwell.

CHAPTER 27

Shirley Beresford and Wendy Carthew

Arts, leisure and entertainment marketing and communications

Learning outcomes

By the end of this chapter you should be able to:

- critically analyse the practice of communications in key sectors of creative arts industries in the public, private and voluntary sectors
- examine the application of marketing and communications theory to arts industries
- understand the role of public relations and marketing in arts and entertainment sectors
- consider trends in the creative industries and their communications needs.

Structure

- A *very* brief overview of definitions of 'the arts'
- Some key concepts and themes: audience development
- Role of public relations in the creative industries
- Trends and directions

Introduction

Arts and leisure marketing and communications operate in a globally dynamic and challenging environment. The role of communications in supporting, developing and enhancing the arts to audiences across the world, and its ability to respond with innovative and creative solutions, places new demands on the PR and marketing professional. Customer and audience needs continue to grow, increasing levels of expectation on those developing the artistic or cultural product or service and those charged with the communications surrounding it. Boundaries between art forms and communications methods, tools and techniques are converging and hybrid forms of arts and marketing have emerged.

Arts, cultural industries and entertainment enhance our lives. They are a source of emotional engagement, creativity and fun. They can challenge, stimulate, shock and excite. The huge creative output of artists, producers and entertainers needs to be managed sensitively if they are to present their artistic forms to a receptive public. It is the task of the communications professional working in these diverse areas to understand the creative product, the aspirations of the creative producers and to have a keen sense of the customers' desires and expectations from an arts or leisure experience.

Before the world economic crisis, overall growth within the arts, cultural industries and entertainment sectors was a worldwide trend, with an increasing need for public relations (PR) and marketing communications experts to understand the dynamics of this increasingly fragmented and competitive environment. The arts play a powerful role in society, and many governments are involved in their encouragement and regulation as vehicles for social inclusion, economic regeneration and prosperity. Further, the rapid growth of social media and interactive and mobile technology is increasingly recognised as of major importance to new creative activity, especially for the young, which has implications for broader social and educational policy. Increasingly in the UK, and indeed in other Western industrialised countries, governments lead public policy, legislation and funding through organisations, such as the Arts Council of Great Britain or The Sports Council of England and Wales.

The fundamental communications planning processes used by individual artists or cultural producers and arts and cultural management must be employed with a demonstrable understanding of contemporary societal trends. These include the unfolding impact of new economic realities, increasing globalisation, the perceived threat of terrorism, fragmentation and proliferation of the media, the growth of cultural tourism and consumerism in new markets, new technology-driven marketing and PR techniques and tools and celebrity culture.

Importantly, the strategic role of public relations in the arts and cultural industries has never been so important for the future health of these sectors. Reputation management and corporate communications are vital to the very survival of many arts and cultural organisations as they face the same serious economic and social challenges as any other area of society.

PR, corporate communications and marketing practitioners working in the arts and entertainment sectors have to be increasingly aware of these trends and developments to maximise the creative opportunities for communications planning. Until the impact of recent global financial uncertainties, employment in the creative industries has grown steadily and there has been increasing government awareness in the UK and Europe of the financial as well as social benefits to the economy of these sectors. The response from communications professionals has been increasingly to call for greater integration and understanding of communications in this new technological and social environment.

This chapter aims to introduce students to the specialist areas of communications in the arts and entertainment sectors from a practitioner perspective. A short industry overview of a selection of arts areas is provided, together with a discussion of key concepts and definitions in arts marketing and communications. The role of communications and the strategies and tactics required by arts and entertainment organisations are explored, with the help of a variety of contemporary case studies. Trends and issues affecting communications in this sector are then discussed, such as the growing impact of new technologies and the breakdown in barriers between practitioner activities as a result.

A *very* brief overview of definitions of 'the arts'

Arts, culture and the creative industries have many definitions and can be viewed from the perspectives of governments, academics and, of course, artists themselves. Before considering definitions of arts marketing and communications it is useful to have some appreciation of some of the context in which public relations and communications operate in practice.

In the UK, the government's Department of Culture Media and Sport (DCMS) defines the creative industries as: 'Those industries which have their origin in individual creativity, skill and talent and which have a potential for wealth and job creation through the generation and exploitation of intellectual property.' While there is no official government definition of 'culture', the following

Box 27.1

The creative industries in the UK

- Creative industries contributed 2.9 per cent of the UK's gross value added in 2009; this is an increase from 2.8 per cent in 2008.

- 1.5 million people are employed in the creative industries or in creative roles in other industries – 5.1 per cent of the UK's employment.

- Exports of services by the creative industries accounted for 10.6 per cent of the UK's exports of services.

- There were an estimated 106,700 businesses in the creative industries on the Inter-Departmental Business Register (IDBR) in 2011; this represents 5.1 per cent of all companies on the IDBR.

Source: http://www.culture.gov.uk/what_we_do/ Creative_industries/#Creative Creative Industries December 2011

activities provide an illustrative guide that is useful in understanding the diversity of these areas. They include:

- performing arts and visual arts, craft and fashion
- media, film, television, video
- museums, artefacts, archives and design
- libraries, literature, writing and publishing
- built heritage, architecture, landscape and archaeology
- sports events, facilities and sports development
- parks, open spaces, wildlife habitats and countryside recreation
- children's playgrounds and play activities
- tourism, festivals and attractions
- informal leisure pursuits (www.culture.gov.uk).

The UK Government, like many others, raises money for the arts from taxes and from a National Lottery, which was introduced in 1994. Box 27.2 shows how much revenue has been raised for arts, leisure and entertainment from the Lottery; Box 27.3 shows how different areas of the arts have benefited from Lottery funding.

Box 27.2

UK lottery funding in 2012

Since 1994, more than £27 billion has been raised for good causes, funding over 370,000 projects in the arts, sport, heritage, charity, voluntary, health, education and environmental sectors.

In the period up to March 2012, around 28 per cent of total National Lottery revenue was expected to go to the good causes and be distributed as follows:

- Health, education, environment and charitable causes – 50 per cent
- Sports – 16.67 per cent
- Arts – 16.67 per cent
- Heritage – 16.67 per cent.

Source: http://www.national-lottery.co.uk/player/p/ goodcausesandwinners/wherethemoneygoes.ftl

Box 27.3

The Arts Council for England – funding

Between 2008 and 2011, the Arts Council for England invested £1.3 billion of regular funding in around 880 arts organisations across England, including the Royal Opera House, Birmingham Royal Ballet, Punchdrunk, BALTIC and Southbank Centre.

In 2011/2012, regular funding for the arts in England by art form:

Music	£95.9m
Visual arts	£41.49m
Theatre/drama	£100.1m
Combined arts	£39.37m
Dance	£35.6m
Literature	£5.6m
Non-specific art form	£6.8m
Total	£324.9m

Source: http://www.artscouncil.org.uk/funding/past-funding-programmes/regular-funding-for-organisations/

However, as the impact of the global financial crisis fully unfolds, the pressure on these funding arrangements for the future are increasing, and hard cash is decreasing in real terms. In the UK, the arts has seen the abolition of arts and marketing organisations at national, regional and local levels, and the emergence of debates by communications practitioners on alternative structures and governance to address marketing and communications demands.

Arts and cultural industries reframed

Traditional categorisation of the arts is usually described in terms of visual, music, film, heritage and performance areas. However, arts policy and practice in the UK and elsewhere has increasingly adopted a more comprehensive approach to the arts – one that is open to current emerging and challenging technological trends in arts practice, and in breaking down the boundaries between art forms and other disciplines.

It is important to remember that this is a huge field of activity. The arts and cultural industries can operate as big global business or within an 'arts for arts sake' ethos; for example, a music event could be a classical opera at La Scala, Milan, or a gig in the back room of a bar. Drama might mean a Broadway show in New York or a mime act street performer. Tickets might cost hundreds of pounds or the event might be free. The variety of arts encompasses the privately and publicly funded, the celebrity-driven to the artistically obscure. Despite challenging global economic conditions, it appears that the consumption and demand for performance, exhibitions, shows and events is still buoyant at both an amateur and professional level.

According to Anderson (1991), Barrere and Santagata (1999) and Parsons (1987), calling the arts an 'industry' has resulted in considerable academic debate, with some believing that it is no more than an industrial product, while others view it from a semiotic perspective where the art work possesses an aesthetic sign that is culturally defined. (See later in the section on concepts of culture for more on this debate.)

Clearly, definitions are problematic for the art world, and for the PR and marketing practitioner working within it. However, the growth of the arts market itself in the twenty-first century cannot be questioned, as can be seen by the figures given in Box 27.4. Fillis (2004) argues that arts PR and marketing put the artist and the product at the forefront of planning, unlike conventional marketing activities that are centred on the consumer, and this poses a unique challenge to the communications professional.

Box 27.4

Top global art exhibitions 2010 by daily attendance (and total)

- 12,116 (292,526) Hasegawa Tohaku, Tokyo National Museum, Tokyo
- 10,757 (777,551) Post-Impressionism: from the Musée d'Orsay, National Art Center, Tokyo
- 9,290 (2,926,232) Designing the Lincoln Memorial, National Gallery of Art Washington
- 9,098 (244,347) Hasegawa Tohaku, Kyoto National Museum, Kyoto
- 8,436 (595,346) Van Gogh: the Adventure of Becoming an Artist, National Art Center, Tokyo
- 8,073 (749,638) The Original Copy: Photography of Sculpture, Museum of Modern Art, New York
- 7,873 (755,850) Harmony and Integrity: Yongzheng Emperor, National Palace Museum, Taipei
- 7,380 (703,256) Picasso in the Metropolitan Museum of Art, Metropolitan Museum of Art, New York
- 7,120 (561,471) Marina Abramovic: the Artist is Present, Museum of Modern Art, New York
- 7,011 (644,975) Falnama: the Book of Omens, Freer and Sackler Galleries, Washington
- 6,971 (602,524) Matisse: Radical Invention, 1913–17, Museum of Modern Art, New York
- 6,859 (535,000) 29th Bienal de São Paulo, Pavilhão Ciccillo Matarazzo, São Paulo
- 6,825 (445,598) Islam, Centro Cultural Banco do Brasil, Rio
- 6,802 (477,106) Regina Silveira: Shadow Line, Centro Cultural Banco do Brasil, Rio
- 6,716 (313,756) Rebecca Horn, Centro Cultural Banco do Brasil, Rio
- 6,630 (682,867) India: the Art of the Temple, Shanghai Museum, Shanghai
- 6,469 (616,411) Hans Memling, Galleria degli Uffizi, Florence

Source: The Art Newspaper no. 223, April 2011

Consequently, marketing gurus such as Kotler are now calling for, and fostering, more creative ways of interpreting marketing and PR in the arts and deriving more meaningful theory.

Audiences' and consumers' views of the differences between entertainment and leisure and the arts and cultural industries are increasingly blurred as a result of the number of important societal changes – most significantly the rise of digital media and social networking. Communications professionals in these areas are finding that the distinctions drawn between sectors are being challenged, and new opportunities to merge types of activity and experience produce a new creative dynamic.

The concept of leisure reflects time and money spent on activities and pursuits away from the workplace. According to Torkildsen (2000), the world of leisure has changed and expanded substantially in the last ten years as a result of economic and social changes and new technologies. Changes in government policies, the growth of tourism and service sector economies and the booming success of commercial leisure industries have all had an unprecedented effect on the growing expectations of people for healthier or alternative lifestyles, leisure, fashion, services and choice.

The term 'leisure' now typically encompasses:

- gambling
- eating out/restaurants (food and beverage market)
- travel (theme parks/attractions)
- sport (professional and amateur)
- shopping
- interactive electronic entertainment (games such as Sony PlayStation/XBox/Gameboy)
- traditional pastimes (professional and amateur).

These activities do not, however, operate in isolation from arts and cultural activity. The wider and more total experiences of consumers and audiences interplay with arts and culture. A thriving restaurant area in a city is positioned close to performing arts venues; electronic gaming is now recognised as producing some of the very best visual artists; couture fashion and fine art often coexist as producers of individual art pieces sold at auction for record prices; and the London 2012 Cultural Olympiad provides an example of how sport and the arts can produce and commission exciting new work by young and up and coming artists in many arts fields. (See Mini case study 27.1.)

Mini case study 27.1
Arts and sport – hybrid arts marketing

imove – Cultural Olympiad for Yorkshire and the Humber

imove celebrates human movement through outstanding arts projects, many combining arts and sport, across the Yorkshire and Humberside region in the run-up to the London 2012 Olympic and Paralympic Games. imove is funded by Legacy Trust UK and Arts Council England. The Legacy Trust UK is a charity set up to create a cultural and sporting legacy from the London 2012 Olympic and Paralympic Games across the UK.

imove brings together the best creative talent from the region to produce a programme of events designed to inspire the public in the run-up to the London 2012 Games. Over the twelve months leading up to the Olympics, more than 100 events will take place across the region encompassing many art forms including dance, drama, music and photography, and all sports from cricket to synchronised swimming. Locations and venues include some of the region's most iconic landscapes, as well as theatres, galleries and sports venues.

According to its creative director, Tessa Gordziejko, "imove is Yorkshire's special part of the creative explosion across the UK as we prepare to welcome the London 2012 Olympic and Paralympic Games to our capital. While athletes from all around the globe travel to London, we celebrate human movement across Yorkshire and Humberside. imove is shaped by many of our region's outstanding artists and creative producers in places where the physical and creative can play together – whether dancing on the street, finding expressive power from a North Sea swim, making a musical tale of cycling heroism or discovering how to fly without leaving the ground. London 2012 has been a catalyst for artists to work in completely new ways."

Source: imove *What's On Guide* www.imoveand.com September 2011; http://www.imoveand.com/about-imove/

Think about 27.1

Cultural Olympiad – imove

- What do you think are the main communications aims and objectives of the Cultural Olympiad? What PR strategy and tactics would you use to promote a project like imove regionally?

- What might have been the main communications problems or barriers to success during 2012 itself?

- How could PR be used strategically to highlight the importance of a coordinated project such as imove beyond 2012?

- How would you measure the impact of the imove project? And why would those measures be appropriate to the funders, partners, artists, audiences and participants involved?

Definitions and concepts of culture

Defining culture is an impossibly huge task, however it is vital for PR practitioners in the arts and cultural industries to appreciate some key concepts to assist in framing their role and activity.

McQuail (2005: 113) suggests that culture has the following characteristics:

- collectively formed and held
- open to symbolic expression
- ordered and differently valued
- systematically patterned
- dynamic and changing
- spatially located
- communicable over time and space.

This makes it clear that culture is about a shared experience, which uses symbols to express different values and that can be communicated across distances or at different times. For communications practitioners in the arts these qualities are very important to understand and embrace.

O'Sullivan et al. (1994) say that culture is the 'social production and reproduction of sense, meaning and consciousness. The sphere of meaning, which unifies the spheres of production (economics) and social relations (politics)' (1994: 68). They also make it clear that there are many interpretations of culture, depending on the

viewpoint of the different theorists. In the past, people used to talk of 'high' culture, meaning opera and classical theatre, and 'low' culture, meaning popular entertainment, like soap operas on TV. Today, there are many different interpretations of culture, including the following concepts.

Cultural studies

This school of thought concentrates on how culture reflects power divisions in society (O'Sullivan et al. 1994). For example, it might examine the representation of black people, women or people with disabilities in soap operas or Hollywood movies. It will ask: whether villains are often Arabic in US films; whether women get powerful roles or are just cast to make the male lead look good; and how people with physical or mental challenges are portrayed. This approach was developed in the 1960s, building on the work of Hoggart and Williams, who challenged the class assumptions behind the terms 'high' and 'low' culture. Much of the work has taken place in the Birmingham School, under Stuart Hall. Its scholars draw on other academic disciplines and schools of thought, such as Marxism, feminism, psychoanalysis, linguistics and others. It has provided hugely influential tools for studying the media, in particular, but can be applied to all artistic and creative outputs: the key question is not the intent of the creator but the social and political values, especially power relations, embodied in the work.

Semiotics

This approach studies the meanings that can be decoded from signs – words and images – used in communication, and was first developed by the linguist de Saussure at the turn of the twentieth century, then extended in the 1960s by Barthes (O'Sullivan et al. 1994). Like cultural studies, it is also less interested in the intentions of communicators than in the meaning embedded in their 'texts', which can be anything from movies, books or sculptures to promotional videos or T-shirts. The focus is on the way that the reader or viewer 'decodes' the message, regardless of what was intended. It has been particularly applied to the meanings that can be read into aspects of popular culture.

Post-modernism

This term has come to mean a great many things across a wide range of cultural activities, including film, literature and fashion. It tends to reject historical analysis and theories that seek to unify experience (O'Sullivan et al. 1994).

Instead, it emphasises the fragmentation of modern life, the brevity of experience and even the triviality of art. Here the creator is a major part of the performance – for example, when a narrator in a book or an actor in a play addresses the reader/camera directly. But, at the same time, the reader/viewer is encouraged to construct their own meanings from an assembly of ingredients, in a spirit of play rather than reverence. It does away with a sense of historical 'progress' (which was central to modernism), instead suggesting that there is a timeless free-for-all and styles from different eras can be put together to make a building, a play or a movie. There is a sense that reality can be and is constructed by viewers/readers/consumers of culture, not the producers (Strinati 1995). It has been very influential in film, visual arts – including architecture – and fashion in particular (think Tarantino, Damien Hirst and Vivien Westwood, for example).

This brief outline illustrates some of the ways in which culture can be studied. There is always a debate about what art means to society, whether it is intended to uplift or entertain, whether it should be good for us and how much it reflects back the society we live in.

Definitions of arts marketing – academic developments

'Arts marketing' as an academic discipline has grown rapidly in the last five years. The establishment of *Arts Marketing: An International Journal*, launched in 2011, is testament to this. The world's first academic journal dedicated to the rapidly growing field of arts marketing, its content is multi- and interdisciplinary and concerns itself with a variety of relationships between arts and marketing in their broadest sense (Dennis et al. 2011). This mirrors the practice of PR, marketing and communications in arts communities and commerce.

Arts marketing has developed within organisations such as the Academy of Marketing, which hosts the second-largest Special Interest Group dedicated to Arts, Heritage, Non-Profit and Social Marketing, and which runs an Annual International Colloquium. Arts marketing has attracted academic interest from those in areas outside marketing, such as arts management, cultural economy, cultural studies, museology and celebrity.

Usefully, O'Reilly's (2011) scoping study begins to define the territory for arts marketing, which includes cultural economics, cultural policy and management, arts consumption and the specialist activities of arts areas such as film, visual, music and performing arts. Strategic public relations, corporate communications and persuasive communications in the arts and cultural industries are illustrated in case studies in this chapter.

Some key concepts and themes: audience development

As we have seen previously in the text, practitioners and academic authors talk about PR as being a platform for building or managing relationships and about 'creating and maintaining goodwill and understanding between organisations and their publics and stakeholders'.

Elsewhere in the text PR is discussed as more of a persuasive communications instrument or philosophy. These perspectives view PR activity as less of a two-way process and far less than an equal conversation between equally powerful parties. The role of public relations in the practice of 'audience developmen in the arts and entertainment sectors is often viewed as one of the most important areas of activity for many arts organisations' communications, engagement and outreach functions. Maitland (2000) defines audience development as 'a planned process which involves building a relationship between an individual and the arts'. This relationship is viewed as central to the work of communications teams or specialist practitioners working in the creative industries. Similarly, audience development is also defined as 'sustaining and expanding existing or regular audiences or visitors, creating new attenders and participants and enhancing their enjoyment, understanding, skills and confidence across art forms' (Rogers 1998).

Audience development, co-creation, audience engagement, participation and public engagement (the terminology differs in a variety of arts areas) are increasingly part and parcel of creating great art experience (Walmsley and Franks 2011), and public relations and communications plays a vital role in this process – connecting audiences and art forms. 'Audience includes attendees, visitors, readers, listeners, viewers, participants, learners and people who purchase works of art.' (ACE 2006)

Arts Council England (2010) proposes that 'as an ethos audience development places the audience at the heart of everything the organisation does'. This can mean that all aspects of the arts organisation and its activity, including marketing, programming, customer care, education, commissioning and distribution, place the audience at the centre of its thinking. This has clear parallels with PR and marketing management philosophies.

Most authors and government bodies broadly agree that audience development is about access. For non-profit and publicly subsidised music, dance, theatre, heritage or visual arts organisations, the strong imperative for audience development is to demonstrate the value of the taxpayer's investment – ideally with a return on increased audience numbers, repeat business, depth of experience, good reviews and, crucially, the breaking down of barriers or blocks to the public's connection to the arts. Public relations tools and techniques can be used to break down these barriers to attendance, whether financial, psychological, social or emotional, and to help the artist or organisation reach out to new communities or to help existing audiences enjoy and participate in fresh and exciting ways. The special, niche role of PR in audience development is to find and manage the messages and channels to enable this process to exist. PR can help to maintain and develop relationships and create a depth of understanding between arts organisations and their audiences over short- and longer-term communications campaigns and programmes. PR can support the process of audience development by attempting to persuade new or existing audiences to attend unfamiliar events or art forms, increasing frequency of attendance, encouraging lapsed attenders back to the arts, enticing audiences to engage in making donations or volunteering to support the arts organisation, and consulting on programming or the co-creation of projects.

The objectives of PR for audience development can be to connect different communities in innovative ways via a range of real-time communications platforms, including Twitter, YouTube and Facebook. (See Case study 27.1 – Frankenstein's Wedding.)

There are parallels with the development of social marketing employed in sectors such as health in the UK and US. Audience development can be viewed as having similar practices and ethos as social marketing in that the objective of the activity is often to encourage behavioural change and to be viewed as operating for a societal good.

'The aim of arts marketing is to bring an appropriate number of people, drawn from the widest number of social backgrounds, economic conditions and age, into an appropriate form of contact with "the artist" and in doing so, arrive at the best financial outcome compatible with the achievement of that aim.' (Diggle 1994) For those areas of the arts within the non-profit environment, arts organisations seek to expand the potential for the arts experience – 'the product is a changed human life' (Drucker 1990). Not-for-profit or subsidised arts organisations in the UK, for example, work on a threefold set of strategic priorities. They must respond to the artistic urge and safeguard artistic integrity, remain financially viable and, because they use taxpayers' monies, have a moral and social responsibility to ensure maximum access and equality of opportunity for all (Fraser et al. 2004).

Co-creation, collaboration and communications

Co-creation is seen as a popular contemporary development in arts production, and communication again plays a vital role in the development of trust and deeper relationships between audiences and artists. Co-creation, or co-production, can mean that artists work with audiences (either new or existing) to create something totally new together. This can have many different artistic manifestations, including crowd-sourced films, user-generated online content for museums and galleries, a collective or collaborative experience in theatre or performing arts spaces, exhibitions or events.

There are many mechanisms for collaboration and co-creation, and technology and social media have impacted this significantly in recent years. Unlike some audience development activity, co-creation and co-production suggests a more proactive approach to the artistic experience with real involvement in the process of creation. Inevitably this needs close communications with audiences as the relationship develops and can achieve quite unexpected results as the process is collectively conceived and delivered, for and in a community. (See Mini case study 27.1.)

Despite reservations in some quarters about the cosmetic nature of some collaborations, or the accepted limits of possible mass engagement, authenticity is viewed as crucial to success. The message tone and delivery, and the perceived genuine nature of the relationship between artists and publics and stakeholders, are the important underpinnings for the success of various creative projects and their legitimacy. Public relations activity therefore needs to be sensitive and responsive to enable this process of trust and respect to develop effectively. Perhaps these contemporary creative dialogues are an example of Grunig's ideal of win-win two-way symmetric communication processes?

Experiential marketing and cultural tourism

For the cultural industries and tourism sector, marketing and communications theory and practice has developed and adapted to include thinking around the experience economy and experiential marketing (Pine and Gilmore 1998). Schmitt (1999) argues that experiential marketing views consumers as rational and emotional human beings who are concerned with achieving pleasurable experiences. Different types of experience are identified and can be used to formulate marketing and communications strategy. The ultimate goal of experiential marketing is to create holistic experiences: sensory experiences (SENSE); affective experience (FEEL); creative cognitive experiences (THINK); physical experiences, behaviours and lifestyles (ACT); and social-identity experiences that result from relating to a reference group or culture (RELATE). These experiences are implemented via 'experience providers' (EXPros), such as communications, visual identity, product presence,

Case study 27.1

Community arts – 'Frankenstein's Wedding . . . Live in Leeds'

'Frankenstein's Wedding . . . Live in Leeds' was a BBC live drama, music and dance event that took place in March 2011 at Kirkstall Abbey and was broadcast on BBC Three. The audience played a real role as wedding guests for the fictional nuptials of scientist Victor Frankestein (Andrew Gower) and his beloved Elizabeth Lavaneza (Lacey Turner) in the live TV production.

A spectacular moment in 'Frankenstein's Wedding . . . Live in Leeds' was an audience mass wedding dance. Local free dance workshops took place in advance for audience members to learn the dance routine for a mass audience dance moment.

Participants were advised to dress up as a wedding guests ('glamour and warmth, suits and frocks in silver, gold, black and white') and to take part in the dance and other moments of audience participation.

The dance workshops were run by the Leeds-based Phoenix Dance Theatre, a BBC partner for 'Frankenstein's Wedding . . . Live in Leeds'. Phoenix Dance Theatre was responsible for the choreography for the main event and worked with key regional partners to run dance workshops in advance.

Two types of workshops took place. Lead Dancer Workshops were for people with dance experience. This group led the audience around them in the dance at the main event. Public Workshops were for people with little or no dance experience. At the main event these dancers were grouped together.

The workshops lasted two hours and participants were trained by a professional dancer. All workshop dance participants received a ticket giving them free entry to the event.

The workshops were open to anyone 16 years or over with a good general level of fitness. All 16–17 year-olds needed consent from parents and guardians to attend a workshop and the main performance. Phoenix Dance Theatre operated an inclusive policy in relation to access: the dance was adapted for wheelchair users and people with other disabilities. Places were allocated on a first come, first served basis.

Lead dancers were positioned among the general audience so they could help lead people around. Public Workshop dancers were in a group of other people who had learned the dance. Dance rehearsals took place before the performance started to give participants a chance to practise.

The event received mixed reviews, with *The Guardian*'s John Baron blogging: 'As an experiment in televisual drama, I think the jury's very much out – on the TV brave-ometer, it was pretty much off the scale. But as a testament to all that's good about Leeds and its people – and for raising the city's profile – it's been a terrific success and raised the profile of the city.'

Sources: http://news.bbc.co.uk/local/leeds/hi/people_and_places/nature/newsid_9219000/9219777.stm
www.phoenixdancetheatre.co.uk/frankenstein

Posted by John Baron Monday 21 March 2011: http://www.guardian.co.uk/leeds/2011/mar/21/opinion-frankenstein-s-wedding-leeds-did-itself-proud

Here's how people tweeted the experience:

#frankensteinswedding

- Just watched the #frankensteinswedding mass dance back on iPlayer, looks incredible!!
- Frankensteinswedding was an ambitious project but it was pulled off quite well. As ever, #laceyturner was amazing.
- Had fun last night at #frankensteinswedding. Thank you #BBC for this freebie. PS – Top respect to the actress in the birthing chamber!
- The crowd dancing scene was just absolutely both moving and amazing. My favourite part in #frankensteinswedding. #looknorth are the Pro's.
- Can't get over how good #frankensteinswedding was last night with @katwee_, very cold but we had sooo much fun, thanks @BBC
- was a Big event last night. Cold but quite incredible. Live tv as a live event I'm still not 100 per cent sure about though.
- Great crowd participation – go for it Leeds!
- Got cold feet at Frankenstein's Wedding.
- #frankensteinswedding a bit rubbish – freezing, dodgy singing and mostly pre records or out of sight so basically watching tv in a field.
- #Frankensteinswedding was fab although a bit cold down at Kirkstall Abbey! Thanks to all involved for putting on such a great performance!
- Just starting to feel my feet again from #frankensteinswedding bbbrrrrr cold! But so worth it!

digital media, etc. The theoretical ideas of experiential marketing are apparent in the rhetoric of cultural tourism strategies and policies in the UK.

While experiential marketing has become a trend in retailing, branding and events marketing, its application and extension to arts and culture is increasingly apparent. Discussion of the experience economy is increasingly relevant to the management and marketing of destinations (arts and cultural). This may include the design, co-creation and delivery of memorable experiences involving stake-holders in the experience creation. Pine and Gilmore (1998) noted that 'an aesthetic experience must be true to itself and come off as real to its guest/visitors'. Authenticity, therefore, is an important factor for experiential marketing and can been seen as vital to the value and success of the artistic venture.

Convergence – citizen journalists and critics

The effect of the YouTube/Facebook social media genera-tion on arts and entertainment consumption cannot be overstated. Interactive mobile technologies have effected major changes in audience experience and expectation of the arts and entertainment sectors over the last five years. The diversification of digital media, proliferation of media platforms and channels, 24/7 news and the expansion of access to global players by the viewing public have all transformed attitudes to the experience of consuming arts and entertainment products. Despite legal and piracy issues around media subscriptions and copyright, the contempor-ary arts consumer is more likely to be able to access these products and services instantly and, as a result, audience demands are growing in terms of speed, choice and expect-ation of real-time conversation, comment and debate.

With the advent of Twitter, Facebook and the like, for many their social expectations are that every experience must and can be interactive, and produce some level of dialogue. When this expectation is not met online, any organisation can find themselves with communications issues, problems and indeed crises. Increasingly, the active role of PR in the arts and entertainment industries is to attempt to manage that dialogue via these communica-tions channels.

Communications practices in arts sectors

Film marketing and public relations

Film encompasses both commercial and art house movies. Film production is international, with strong manufac-turing activity in Europe, India and South America, for example. However, film distribution and commercial movie success is largely dominated by the USA, particularly in terms of financial box office success. This is understand-able as it defines itself firmly as a commercial as well as artistic industry. The main stages of activity in the US film industry are vertically integrated (that is, the main com-panies own all the stages of film production, from the studios where the films are made to the cinema chains that show the finished product) including development, production, post-production, distribution and exhibition (Kerrigan 2010). This integration does appear to create a commercially successful model and, while European films do enjoy some success, the USA still dominates the European box office.

In Europe and the USA, both film and TV companies are using market research more effectively at every stage of the movie or TV programme lifecycle. Producers recog-nise the importance of defining the target audiences they seek to reach at the very earliest stages of creative develop-ment. Most US-dominated publicity remains aimed at the 18–24-year-old segment, where the largest audience lies (75 per cent of the film audience in the USA is under the age of 39) (Wilcox et al. 2002). Durie et al. (2000) define film marketing as 'any activity that assists a film in reaching its target audience at any time throughout its life and by extension, its earning potential' (2000: 5). Public relations activity is central to the generation of stories and narratives for film fans and critics. From script to screen, PR's role is to create, generate and maintain stories and interaction with audiences, especially with the objective of generating positive word of mouth around a film's star performers, director, special effects, story or genre. While one of the key aims of PR and marketing activity is to generate interest in a film to ensure audiences go to see it in the first week of its release, there is a growing recogni-tion that, after release, this word of mouth is the most powerful endorsement tool. Anderson (1998) defines word of mouth as 'informal communications between private parties concerning evaluation of goods and services'. Electronic word of mouth and online virtual communities are now important aspects of any film PR campaign. For example, continued online discussion around interpreta-tions and meanings in the *mise-en-scène* of Ridley Scott's film *Prometheus* in 2012 (the extension of the *Alien* film franchise) generated potential repeat viewings of the movie, and a continued deeper consumer relationship to the pro-duct beyond the opening week.

Beyond the Hollywood blockbuster, the emergence of user-generated, co-created films are an example of how long-term relationships using online communications has developed creative projects with global financial success and artistic recognition. (See Case study 27.2.)

Case study 27.2

Life in a Day – crowdsourced documentary film

On 24 July 2010, thousands of people around the world uploaded videos of their day to YouTube to take part in *Life in a Day*. This historic cinematic experiment was designed to create a documentary film that serves as a time capsule to show future generations what it was like to be alive on that day.

Life in a Day is a crowdsourced documentary film comprising an arranged series of video clips selected from 4,500 hours' of footage captured in 80,000 YouTube contributions from 192 countries, giving glimpses of people's lives from around the world on 24 July 2010. The completed film debuted at the Sundance Film Festival on 27 January 2011 and the premiere was streamed live on YouTube.

The film was the result of a partnership among YouTube, Ridley Scott Associates and LG electronics, announced on 6 July 2010. People were invited to upload their videos recorded on 24 July 2010 to YouTube, and then Ridley Scott produced the film and edited the videos into a film with director Kevin Macdonald and film editor Joe Walker, consisting of footage from some of the contributors. All chosen footage authors are credited as co-directors.

Director Kevin Macdonald told *The Wall Street Journal* that the project was initially conceived as a way to commemorate the fifth birthday of YouTube, and that he wanted to 'take the humble YouTube video . . . and elevate it into art'. Editor Joe Walker said that, as he understood it, the concept for the crowdsourced documentary came from Ridley Scott's production company 'Scott Free U.K.' and from YouTube, while Macdonald explained more specifically that 'the inspiration for me was a British group from the 1930s called the Mass Observation movement. They asked hundreds of people all over Britain to write diaries recording the details of their lives on one day a month and answer a few simple questions . . . These diaries were then organized into books and articles with the intention of giving voice to people who weren't part of the "elite" and to show the intricacy and strangeness of the seemingly mundane.'

About 75 per cent of the film's content came from people contacted through YouTube, traditional advertising, TV shows and newspapers; the remaining 25 per cent came from cameras sent out to the developing world.

Film editor Joe Walker told *Wired* magazine's Angela Watercutter that the film 'couldn't have been made without technology. Ten years ago it would've been impossible.' Macdonald explained that YouTube 'allowed us to tap into a pre-existing community of people around the world and to have a means of distributing information about the film and then receiving people's "dailies". It just wouldn't have been organizationally or financially feasible to undertake this kind of project pre-YouTube.'

The filmmaking team 'used YouTube's ability to collect all of this material and then we had this sort of sweatshop of people, all multilingual film students, to sift through this material. It couldn't have been done any other way. Nobody had ever done a film like this before, so we had to sort of make it up as we went along.'

Walker, whose team edited the whole film over seven weeks, remarked to Adam Sternbergh of *The New York Times* that 'The analogy is like being told to make Salisbury Cathedral, and then being introduced to a field full of rubble. You have to start looking for buttresses and things that connect together.' Walker indicated that a team of roughly two dozen researchers, chosen both for a cinematic eye and proficiency with languages, watched, logged, tagged and rated each clip on a scale of one to five stars. Walker remarked that 'the vast amount of material was two stars', and that he and director Kevin Macdonald reviewed the four-star and five-star rated clips.

In addition to the star rating system, the editing team also organised the 80,000 clips according to countries, themes and video quality as part of the selection process, and had 60 different frame rates to convert to make the result cinematically acceptable.

Sources: http://www.guardian.co.uk/film/2011/jun/07/ life-in-a-day-macdonald?INTCMP=SRCH

http://blogs.wsj.com/speakeasy/2011/07/22/life-in-a-day-director-kevin-macdonald-aims-to-elevate-youtube-videos-into-art/?KEYWORDS=kevin+macdonald+a+day+in+the+life

http://www.wired.com/underwire/2011/07/ life-in-a-day-interviews/all/1

http://www.youtube.com/movie?v=JaFVr_cJJIY&ob=av1n&feature=mv_sr

Think about 27.2

Crowdsourcing

- What are the ethical considerations for marketing a crowdsourced film project?

- What are the communications challenges for this approach to film production, distribution and promotion?

- Is crowdsourcing a one-off idea, or an ongoing trend in film making due to technological changes in film distribution and social media?

- How could success or value be measured for a project like this?

Media relations in film

Film studios, production companies, networks and celebrity publicists all apply the principle of a steady output of information and stories, a 'drip-drip-drip' approach to publicity around a new movie (Wilcox et al. 2002). This PR technique enables the key players in the industry process to maximise media attention both before and after production and public showing of the movie itself. These opportunities for story generation can include the following:

- initial signing up of a film director to a studio or project idea

- script evolution

- assigning a cinematographer or writer

- 'work in progress', including insights into the making of the film, e.g. locations, technical issues, developments by the creative team

- actors and stars signing up to the project

- actors and stars not getting the role!

- quotes and interviews from directors, producers, actors during and after production

- controversial debate generated by social or political issues in a film

- technology – interactivity with audiences during the creative process, e.g. on official and unofficial websites.

Previews, exclusives and award ceremonies are all PR tools and techniques employed during the process to reach the target publics of film critics, industry stakeholders and the audiences. Promotional activity reaches a crescendo with the premiere or launch night of the movie. This presents another opportunity to generate interest in the film,

although it is also essential to maintain the profile of the movie for a sustained period after this time.

Online media PR campaigns will integrate with target print, broadcast and radio with story opportunities over potentially a two- to three-year period (depending on the scale or size of the production or franchise). Film products are now launched online or in other formats, providing again re-promotion to new audiences. Action and adventure films translate well into electronic interactive games. For example, the *Lord of the Rings* trilogy and Marvel movies such as *Spiderman* have become Sony PlayStation, XBox and Gameboy games across different platforms and genres. So consumer spend is increased and sales revenue from games can sometimes exceed the box office film ticket sales.

Music marketing and PR

New business models have fundamentally transformed the consumption of popular music (Walmsley and Franks 2011), but also traditional genres of classical and jazz music. The move to digital with iTunes, iPods, laptops, tablets and other mobile devices has subverted structured pricing and distribution. Illegal and legal downloading and file sharing of music has changed consumption patterns. Copyright and secondary ticketing are just a few issues that the sector faces. Major record labels and high-street music stores have struggled with many of these changes. Innovations such as the pay-what-you-like model, where artists release work free in collaboration with media partners, has grown, resulting in positive PR and increased touring sales. Relationships between audiences and producers have changed as a result of these rapid changes in communications technology; however, brands and brand management remains an important strategic communications dimension for major artists. Fans' perceptions of these music brands come from the communications management of social media, publicity, concerts, promotional videos and merchandising. For many artists and music TV talent shows, the core product has become the live performance rather than the track or single. Music festivals, therefore, have remained buoyant in the market with strong brands emerging and wider participation of a mix of young, older and family audiences. Festivals remain very much part of the experience economy as fans turn attendance into statements about self and social identity (O'Reilly 2011). Attendance at major festivals has become a right of passage for teenagers as well as expressions of the recapturing of youth for an older generation. Unique and powerful brand partnerships have arisen in the sector, where mass volunteering opportunities have emerged with UK universities (see Mini case study 27.2).

Picture 27.1 Reading and Leeds, Latitude and Hove represent festivals with strong branding and innovative volunteering relationships with UK universities

Mini case study 27.2
Strategic partnerships – Festival Republic

'During the 2012 festival season, over 200 students, staff and alumni volunteered at Hove, Latitude and Leeds Festivals through Leeds Metropolitan University's partnership with Festival Republic.

'Volunteers worked on a variety of projects, including stage management, filming, running campsite DJ parties, performing and providing information to festival-goers.

'In addition, a handful of students were lucky enough to work as interns with Festival Republic, one of their contractors or with our staff team on-site. These are really hard-to-find placements, enabling Leeds Metropolitan

students and alumni to be one step ahead of the competition, as well as providing an excellent work experience opportunity.

'The festival placements tie in to a wide range of courses and enable some students to gain credit for the work they do, as well as making vital contacts and learning more about the festival industry.

'Leeds Metropolitan University has been working in partnership with Festival Republic (organisers of Leeds and Reading Festivals, Latitude Festival, Hove Festival in Norway and operational management for Glastonbury Festival) since 2007, providing exciting opportunities for students and staff to develop experience and skills in a festival setting, contributing significantly to the work of Festival Republic and enhancing research in festivals and creative performance.'

Source: http://www.leedsmet.ac.uk/festivalvolunteering/
index_about.htm accessed 18 July 2012

Visual arts marketing

Fillis (2004) suggests that creative arts marketing puts the artist and the product at the forefront of planning, unlike conventional marketing activities centred around the customer. The contemporary visual arts (CVA) market has certainly seen the rise of the celebrity artist in the UK and the development of high-profile arts fairs and exhibitions where the cross-overs between showbusiness, fashion and art have collided in a truly global way. International centres include London, New York and, increasingly, South America and Russia. Supply and distribution in the CVA centres around public galleries and artist-led independent producers, art fairs and exhibitions (for example, Venice Biennale), websites (such as AXIS – the UK's national database of the contemporary arts), open studios and retailers, degree shows, commercial auction houses and dealers. The Art Eco-System Model illustrates the complexity of relationships and hints at some of the communications dynamics between parties. Demand and buyers in the arts market can be segmented into groups of existing buyers, such as serious collectors and connoisseurs, or potential buyers, such as young aesthetes and arts school friends (ACE Report 2002; Morris et al. 2004). Dealers, agents, galleries, intermediaries and critics play their role in the building of artist brands and reputations. Many researchers in the field acknowledge the power of word of mouth and networking in the process of endorsement of artists' work, and international PR is vital to that process. (See Case study 27.1 Frankenstein's Wedding.)

Communications in performing arts

For contemporary and historical plays, stage versions and adapations, musicals, variety, dance, ballet, opera and new theatrical developments, the needs of the performing arts audiences must be understood by communications practitioners. The motivations for theatre audiences can be around social hedonism, intellectual enrichment, the arousal of emotions and pure entertainment (Bouder-Pailer 1999). Audience development is, therefore, a crucial concept for marketers. Building frequency of attendance, developing audiences' understanding of the art forms they are seeing and listening to and ultimately creating loyalty and enthusiasm are key objectives. Membership schemes, subscriber and patron benefits and friends societies all support these aims.

The economic impact of UK theatres in London and the regions has been measured and recognised by governmental arts bodies. Commercial and not-for-profit theatres and venues generate spend not just from performances but also from the direct and indirect contributions to local economies (AVS – Additional Visitor Spend). By attracting audiences into a performance space, people will spend on eating out, transport and local services. This helps to sustain jobs and acts as a force for economic and social regeneration (Wyndham Report 1998).

New communications developments in co-creation, engagement and participation are explored in the case studies (see Case study 27.2 Life in a day).

Role of public relations in the creative industries

As seen in previous chapters, PR can be defined as a promotional tool or tactical range of techniques, operating as part of the marketing mix, or can alternatively be defined as a strategic management philosophy. This chapter illustrates the operation of public relations and communications activity from both these viewpoints.

It is the task of the communicator to understand, connect with and attract audiences for the creative professionals working in these areas. The communications strategies employed for this task use the full range of PR and marketing communications tools, with the additional requirement that the practitioner needs to be very familiar with niche promotional channels available to each area and the importance of social and digital media. Importantly, an appreciation of the notions of culture sharpen the practitioner's ability to respond to these challenges and the examples of best practice in this text reflect that.

The creative demand on the PR profession is increasing. In highly 'artistically' focused industries such as these, communications techniques and tools must be competitively innovative and dynamic. It is essential to embrace the latest technologies and overcome long-standing barriers between different sectoral and cultural traditions to create unique creative platforms for PR campaigns. For example, sport stars support artistic ventures, artists endorse travel organisations, celebrities add glamour to more traditional ventures. The PR professional needs to be aware and ahead of fashionable trends in these demanding and quixotic sectors.

Increasingly in PR practice, professionals find the boundaries between arts, leisure and entertainment PR blurred. When is a PR agency dealing with an entertainment client or an arts client? Is Tracey Emin or Damien Hirst an artist or a celebrity, or are they indeed both? The challenge for PR is the profession's creative ability to absorb these fast-moving fashionable industry trends and identify and exploit cross-over opportunities. The broad public appetite for this type of synthesis across

Mini case study 27.3

Interactive community co-created performance

The Passion in Port Talbot, Wales, 22–24 April 2011

More than 1,000 local residents took part in this National Theatre Wales production, *The Passion* – a re-working of biblical passion plays – over the Easter weekend in 2011. Hollywood actor Michael Sheen returned to his home town of Port Talbot, south Wales, to co-direct and star as a Christ-like character in the 72-hour non-stop production that took place on the streets of the town. It involved a core cast of 15 professional actors, but the bulk of the cast was made up of volunteers from Port Talbot, including choirs, youth theatres and voluntary groups.

The open-air play began at 5.30 in the morning on Good Friday with a seafront scene, inspired by John the Baptist's baptism of Jesus, which was watched by hundreds who had heard about it by word of mouth. By the time the first main part of the play was performed on Aberavon Beach at 3.00pm, organisers estimated up to 6,000 people had gathered to watch. On Saturday, there were sequences in Llewelyn Street, the Castle Street underpass, Aberfan Shopping Centre, the seaside social and labour club in Sandfields and nearby Abbeyville Court.

A trial was performed on Civic Square before a procession from Station Road, with the final scene, the crucifixion, taking place on Aberavon beach on Easter Sunday.

The production, written by Welsh poet and novelist Owen Sheers, was the last and largest of a series of National Theatre Wales 'moving productions' to promote its first year programme. John McGrath, artistic director of National Theatre Wales, said at the time, 'It's exceeded everybody's expectations – it's caught the mood of the moment. It's absolutely fantastic – the whole town understood it and got the bug. It's created a real sense of pride among the people of this town.'

Sources: http://www.bbc.co.uk/news/uk-wales-south-west-wales-13149673; http://www.bbc.co.uk/news/uk-wales-south-west-wales-12326895

industries, art forms, leisure activities and entertainment appears voracious. (See Mini case study 27.3 and Think about 27.3.)

Implications for PR planning – objectives, strategies and tactics

Most of the PR work conducted by practitioners in the arts and entertainment field is similar to that practised in other fields. However, there are particular factors that affect PR and the arts and these are now outlined.

Publics for arts organisations

In the arts and entertainment sectors, Kotler and Scheff (1997) identify *input publics* (playwrights, composers), who supply resources that are converted by *internal publics* (performers, staff, board of directors, volunteers) into useful services or offers (performances, educational programmes) that are carried out by *intermediate publics* (PR agencies, advertising agencies, critics) to consuming publics (audiences, activists, media) (see Figure 27.1, see also Explore 27.1). This model is now also expanded by the surrounding digital and online communities who

Think about 27.3

Audience development

What are the strengths, weaknesses, opportunities and threats associated with a community-based approach to performance?

Why are audience development approaches to performing arts considered important to theatre companies/performing arts organisations?

What are the tools and techniques available for audience development with community engagement projects?

Find examples of SMART aims and objectives for audience development activity for a co-produced theatre project.

What sorts of stories would the media/social media be interested in around the project?

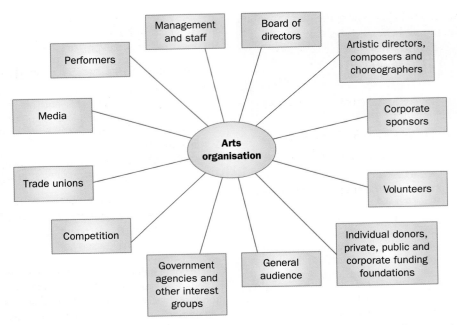

Figure 27.1 A model of an arts organisation's publics (*source:* adapted from *Standing Room Only: Strategies for Marketing the Performing Arts*, Harvard Business School Press, Boston, MA (Kotler, P. and Scheff, J. 1997). Reprinted by permission of Harvard Business School Press Copyright © 1997 by the Harvard Business School Publishing Corporation, all rights reserved)

Explore 27.1   A record company

Select a record company or individual artist brand. Look at its website and social media profiles. See if you can draw a map of its key publics along the lines of Figure 27.1. Which publics do you think are most influential? Do you think this may have changed in recent years?

Feedback

Consumer patterns of behaviour are changing rapidly as a result of new technologies and increased accessibility to the arts and entertainment sectors. Online booking, flexible subscription ticket schemes, direct marketing, a 'virtual' presence for events and activities online and integrated PR and marketing campaigns have brought a change in consumer patterns of access to these sectors' offers. Experiential marketing, cultural tourism and hedonistic arts experiences are new concepts in the arts. New audiences are developing as a result of these patterns of consumption.

create dialogue and conversation around the arts organisation and between and across its active and passive publics.

Generating conversation for the arts

One of the primary goals of many arts, leisure or entertainment organisations is to sell tickets to events. PR campaigns provide publicity build-up to inform fans, viewers, participants, critics, readers or listeners that an event will occur, and stimulate the desire to purchase tickets and attend (Wilcox et al. 1998). Successful PR searches

for fresh, targeted news angles to maximise on, and offline media coverage across integrated marketing communications (see also Chapter 22).

Media partnerships have proved highly successful in generating conversation and dialogue around an arts organisation and its events, performances and exhibitions (see Case study 27.4).

At the core of effective PR and marketing communication in arts and entertainment sectors is a clear understanding of the target audience and consumer behaviour. PR professionals are required to understand the motives, preferences and behaviours of their organisation's current and potential audiences (Kotler and Scheff 1997: 69). (Consumer behaviour is discussed in Chapters 18 and 22.) Key factors influencing consumer behaviour can be summarised as:

- macro-environmental trends (social, political, economic and technological)
- cultural factors (nationality, subcultures, social class)
- social factors (reference groups, opinion leaders, innovativeness)
- psychological factors (personality, beliefs and attitudes, motivation)
- personal factors (occupation, economic circumstances, family, lifecycle stage).

(Adapted from Kotler and Scheff 1997: 69.)

Identifying and selecting target audiences and positioning the offer to the 'consumer', whether in the arts, leisure or entertainment sectors, is crucial to successful PR

Think about 27.4

Sponsorship and branding in the arts

- What is the role and impact of sponsorship in the contemporary visual arts (CVA)? See Case study 27.3.
- Can a regional CVA event, such as the Northern Art Prize, compete in international markets?
- How can the involvement of audience voting enhance the experience of the event? What role does branding play in the CVAs?

---

planning and campaigns. An example of the way in which careful targeting, branding and an appreciation of the consumers' needs have been identified clearly is the successful commercial art event Frieze Art (see Case study 27.4).

Case study 27.3

Branding – the Northern Art Prize and Frieze Art Fair

The Young British Artists (YBA) and Brit Art movement was a name given to a group of contemporary conceptual artists, painters and sculptors and installation artists based almost exclusively in London, many of whom attended Goldsmiths College in the late 1980s. Artists such as Damien Hirst, Tracey Emin and The Chapman Brothers have since become international art celebrities, and galleries such as White Cube, The Saatchi and Tate Modern and international art fairs such as Frieze have made Britain (i.e. London) the recognised international home of cutting edge modern art.

At a time when public funding of the visual arts was very limited under a conservative government, a core group of artists led by Damien Hirst organised an exhibition called Freeze (1988). A cheap alternative warehouse space established the artist-run/artist-as-curator approach to exhibiting. These events resonated with the 'Acid House' music scene which, although producing little press exposure, got the Brit Art movement started. Quickly, Charles Saatchi, contemporary art collector and co-founder of the Saatchi and Saatchi

advertising agency, promoted the YBA's exhibitions and became their main collector. By the mid 1990s Saatchi was the acknowledged main sponsor of Brit Art – a name he invented for a series of shows that became the iconic work of British art in the late 20th century. Brit Art was the symbol of contemporary art worldwide and his highly professional communications skills and resources ensured strong media coverage and international marketing of the art product itself. Moreover, the 'celebrity artist' was promoted to new heights in a media-hungry environment.

In turn, Brit Art revitalised a whole generation of contemporary art galleries, spaces and events. Frieze International Art Fair, and an explosion of new or revitalised publications, such as *Art Monthly*, *Art Review* and *Modern Painters*, all contributed to marketing the art being produced over the period.

The 'Sensation Show' at the Royal Academy in 1997 and Tracey Emin's Turner Prize in 1999 finally positioned Brit Art as 'establishment' to many art critics such as Roger Scrutin and Jonathan Jones. Although the opening of the Tate Modern in 2000 did not provide any major accolade for the YBAs, their clear inclusion was another affirmation that their status was not really open to question. More recent criticism of the Brit Art/Tate Modern legacy is developed by writers such as Waldemar Januszczak (*Times* Online, 'The Tate: pompous, arrogant and past it?' 8 February 2009).

→

mini case study 27.3 (continued)

To many the post-Brit Art bubble may have burst with Sotherby's sale of Damien Hirst's diamond-encrusted skull, a piece called 'For the Love of God'. Its sale price was £50m, but rumour surrounds the actual sale itself and the media coverage is shrouded in contradictory reports. It appears the skull has yet to be sold, despite PR boasting record prices. Media coverage of the Sotheby's sale told of 'a new record for a sale dedicated to one artist of £111m' (BBC, 16 September 2008). At Frieze Art Fair in autumn 2008, again record prices in the contemporary art market were being talked about. Attendances by the art-buying publics at auctions and art fairs of contemporary art (Brit Art and now new global markets) were still very buoyant in 2008. But as the full extent of the global financial crisis developed between 2008 and 2009, the CAM (contemporary art market) has been sensitive to changes; it remains outwardly confident, although clearly the focus of its purchasing appears to be on the move. Januszczak reports that the Middle East and Russia is where new contemporary artists and art markets are emerging (*Times Online* 2009). In 2011, interest in contemporary visual arts shows no sign of waning, according to the Royal Academy of Arts' magazine (Autumn 2011): 'Frieze Art Fair has set London abuzz every autumn for almost ten years and, despite the economic climate, there's no sign of that changing.'

As a result of this massive shift in the economic and social importance of contemporary art in British society (almost exclusively based in London), the UK regional response in the form of the Northern Art Prize (NAP) is an interesting development.

The Northern Art Prize

The Northern Art Prize celebrates contemporary visual artists based in the North of England. Founded in 2007, it has established itself as an important award – recognised nationally as a relevant profiler of artists working in the North East, North West and Yorkshire regions.

Each year NAP asks 12 arts professionals from across the North of England, representing both urban and rural areas, organisations and freelancers, to nominate two artists to be put forward for the prize. Nominated artists can be of any age, any nationality and working in any media as long as they are based in the North. The nominated artists are invited to submit examples of their work and four selectors drawn from national arts organisations or established artists use this information to select a shortlist of four. The nominators and selectors change each year.

The shortlisted artists work with Sarah Brown, Curator at Leeds Art Gallery, to put together an exhibition of recent and new works. The selectors return to view the exhibition and choose a winner. The prize provides a significant financial reward to the winning artist, who receives £16,500, with the other shortlisted artists receiving £1,500.

The NAP is sponsored by five Leeds-based organisations, including Logistik, Leeds City Council and ARUP.

Sources: http://www.northernartprize.org.uk/about
http://news.bbc.co.uk/1/hi/entertainment/7619720.stm

Case study 27.4

Media partnerships in arts marketing – The BBC Proms

The Proms, more formally known as The BBC Proms, or The Henry Wood Promenade Concerts presented by the BBC, is an eight-week summer season of daily orchestral classical music concerts and other events held annually, predominantly in the Royal Albert Hall in London. Founded in 1895, each season currently consists of more than 70 concerts in the Albert Hall, a series of chamber concerts at Cadogan Hall, additional Proms in the Park events across the United Kingdom on the last night and associated educational and children's events. In 2009 the total number of concerts reached 100 for the first time. In the context of classical music festivals, Jiří Bělohlávek, Chief Conductor, London Symphony Orchestra, has described the Proms as 'the world's largest and most democratic musical festival'.

Origins and Sir Henry Wood

Promenade concerts had existed in London's pleasure gardens since the mid eighteenth century, but in 1895 impresario Robert Newman arranged the first series of indoor promenade concerts, in the Queen's Hall in

mini case study 27.4 (continued)

Langham Place. Newman's idea was to encourage an audience for concert hall music who, though not normally attending classical concerts, would be attracted by the low ticket prices and more informal atmosphere. In addition to promenading, eating, drinking and smoking were all allowed. He stated his goal as follows:

'I am going to run nightly concerts and train the public by easy stages. Popular at first, gradually raising the standard until I have created a public for classical and modern music.'

Newman continued to work in the artistic planning of these promenade concerts until his sudden death in November 1926. With time, Sir Henry Wood became the name that was most closely associated with the concerts. As conductor from the first concerts, Wood was largely responsible for expanding the repertoire heard in later concerts, such that by the 1920s the concerts had grown from being made up of largely more popular, less demanding works, to presenting music by contemporary composers such as Claude Debussy, Richard Strauss and Ralph Vaughan Williams.

BBC involvement

In 1927, the BBC took over the Proms, and for three years the concerts were given by 'Sir Henry Wood and his Symphony Orchestra', until the BBC Symphony Orchestra was formed in 1930 and became the main orchestra for the concerts. The Proms now reached a far wider audience, and although some feared that broadcasting would reduce audience numbers, Wood emphasised its role in achieving his aim 'of truly democratising the message of music, and making its beneficent effect universal'.

Wood continued his work with the Proms until his death in 1944. In the post-war period, major names in the classical world took over conducting and leadership roles, including charismatic figures such as Sir Adrian Boult and Sir Malcolm Sargent.

In the 1960s, the Proms repertory expanded both forwards in time, to encompass then contemporary and avant-garde composers such as Boulez, Peter Maxwell Davies, Ligeti, Stockhausen and Tippett, as well as backwards to include music by past composers such as Purcell, Monteverdi, Byrd and Palestrina, as well as less-often performed works of Johann Sebastian Bach and Joseph Haydn. From the 1960s, the number of guest orchestras at the Proms also began to increase, with the first major international conductors (Leopold Stokowski, Georg Solti) and the first foreign orchestras, including the Moscow Radio Symphony Orchestra. Since that time, almost every major international orchestra, conductor and soloist has performed at the Proms.

Since 1990

The Proms now present newly commissioned music alongside pieces more central to the repertoire and early music. Innovations continue, with pre-Prom talks, lunchtime chamber concerts, children's Proms and Proms in the Park either appearing or being featured more heavily over the past few years. In the UK, all concerts are broadcast on BBC Radio 3, an increasing number are televised on BBC Four with some also shown on BBC One and BBC Two. The theme tune played at the beginning of each programme broadcast on television is an extract from the end of the 'Red' movement of Arthur Bliss's *A Colour Symphony*. It is also possible to hear the concerts live from the BBC Proms website. 'The Last Night' is also broadcast in many countries around the world.

Although the scope of the Proms has increased enormously since 1895, Henry Wood's concept for the season remains largely unaltered: to present the widest possible range of music, performed to the highest standards, to large audiences.

And promenading in the Royal Albert Hall's arena continues to be a central feature, lending the Proms its unique, informal atmosphere. Promming tickets cost the same for all concerts (£5 as of 2012), providing a considerably cheaper option for the more popular events. Since the tickets cannot be bought in advance (although there are season tickets and weekend passes available), they provide a way of getting in to otherwise sold-out concerts.

Sources: http://en.wikipedia.org/wiki/The_Proms
http://www.bbc.co.uk/proms/features/history
http://www.bbc.co.uk/proms
http://en.wikipedia.org/wiki/BBC_Electric_Proms

Think about 27.5

Media partnerships

- What is distinctive about the positioning and branding of events such as the Proms?

- Are promenaders also performers? And why could this be important to the arts experience?

- In what ways could social media enhance the experience of engagement with the performance? Are there any limitations of social media?

- Sir Henry Wood and the partnership with the BBC popularised The Proms and it now reaches a wide audience (although some feared back in 1930s that broadcasting would reduce audience numbers). Wood emphasised its role in achieving his aim 'of truly democratising the message of music (classical), and making its beneficent effect universal'. Is his ethos and philosophy still relevant? And why?

Trends and directions

As a multi- and interdisciplinary area, arts marketing and communications faces the same serious economic and social challenges as other areas of society. Some of the trends and issues, including the use of celebrity, hourly developments and changes in media and channel technologies, are briefly explored.

Role of celebrity

Celebrity remains a powerful concept in arts and entertainment marketing; its media impact is all pervading.

In the arts and entertainment sectors celebrity status is now accorded to most international artists, musicians and performers of all kinds. Moreover, the nature of celebrity has changed: whereas once it derived from excellence in an arts or leisure activity, now appearing on reality TV shows or enjoying the success of a global viral video qualifies many for celebrity status.

Arts, leisure and entertainment celebrities are increasingly used to support and enhance consumer 'brands'. Successful celebrity product placement and sponsorship tie-ins have flourished in these sectors. Nessman (2008) has contributed to the debate and discussion in this area with academic research and educational courses under the label of 'personal communication management'. Matching a 'brand personality' to a celebrity brand, however, can have its problems and pitfalls, and for every successful joint venture there are numerous failures. Moreover, the media are increasingly interested in 'news', however trivial, concerning a celebrity – a trend associated with the commercialisation of mass media (McQuail 2005). Again, this can be a mixed blessing: the front page may carry the desired picture of the star making an award to your charity – or falling down drunk outside a nightclub. (See Think about 27.6 Use of celebrities.)

Pringle (2004) identifies a number of key trends in celebrity that will impact on the arts and entertainment sectors, in particular: the use of charismatic stars of minority sports; leisure and arts pursuits brought into the mainstream; and the cross-over between cultures and continents. Obviously, many arts, leisure and entertainment activities already involve celebrities, who may help generate media coverage. Indeed, the Hollywood 'star' system reflects not just the popularity of certain actors but their ability to bring in audiences regardless of the quality of the film.

It may seem as though the concept of 'celebrity' plays an increasing role in communications activity in the arts,

Think about 27.6   ### Use of celebrities

Consider the advantages and disadvantages of using the stars (lead actors) of a film or TV programme to promote the entertainment product itself. What are the qualities that celebrities and stars bring to a PR campaign? Is the star always the main attraction for audiences? What else attracts audiences to view a film or TV programme and what are the implications for the PR professional?

Feedback

While stars and celebrities are expected (and often, indeed, legally contracted) to play their part in PR and marketing campaigns to support the launch of a new television or film production, their ability to act as spokespeople can be uneven in terms of successful communications with audiences. Interviews with stars are often carefully scripted to include the key messages about the film or TV product that the production companies wish to convey. However, 'unscripted', 'off-message' or plain ill-informed or incorrect remarks to interviewers in the mass media can result in devastatingly negative results. High-profile celebrities with perceived temperamental qualities can be more of a liability to the promotion of the movie or TV programme than a bonus. While a star can add glamour to a PR campaign, the risks and costs of relying on this vehicle of communication can be massive.

leisure and entertainment industries. Clearly, celebrity has indeed been a driving force behind high-profile work in the promotion of these sectors for many years. The sheer visibility of celebrity in communications in the late twentieth and early twenty-first centuries inevitably tends to push us to the conclusion that without its presence in society these sectors would falter.

However, for every film featuring mega-stars such as Brad Pitt, there are thousands of film and television actors working in local, regional and national productions. For every professional Broadway theatre show there are small-scale village hall entertainments by amateur companies. For every international blockbuster book, translated into dozens of languages, there are independent publishers of poetry and verse appealing only to minority audiences. For every 'international celebrity' visual artist, such as Tracey Emin, there are thousands of creative people active in the production of creative work. In emerging co-produced works the impact of joining both amateur artists and celebrity producers, actors or directors is seen to effect audiences' views of success and value.

Communications expertise, education and new business models

Clearly, not all arts organisations or individuals have the same sets of communications skills and competencies. Communications and marketing expertise in arts and cultural industries range from the award-winning professional in-house teams of major museums to the zero-funded local artist, the enthusiast or amateur to the professionally qualified. The opportunities for PR, communications and marketing education in these sectors continues to have massive potential, especially as the need for new approaches to funding, entrepreneurship and philanthropy grow as austerity and competition bites. Leadership for arts and entertainment organisations in these areas also requires strong communications understanding and resource. As new business models are created, evolve and transform the arts and cultural environment (Walmsley and Franks 2011), so too the need for new thinking in communications and marketing to enable arts organisations to compete and fulfill the most basic organisational function. The financial viability of many arts organisations at this time is of fundamental concern and the role of PR, marketing and importantly strategic corporate communications is probably ever more relevant to basic survival. Public and community affairs, reputation management, stakeholder engagement and CSR are increasingly important aspects to successful communications operations in the arts and cultural industries (see Case study 27.5). Where communications is positioned in organisational structures, how communications is commissioned, organised, planned and executed, and how governance for communications is addressed, are major challenges ahead for practice. Cultural leadership and the role of strategic communications within it is a dynamic area of development.

Case study 27.5
Strategic public relations – stakeholder and reputation management

The British Museum – The Elgin Marbles and 'A History of the World in 100 Objects'

During the first decade of the nineteenth century, the agents of Lord Thomas Elgin (British Ambassador to Constantinople 1799–1803) removed ancient sculptures from Greece's capital city of Athens. The pride of this collection was a large amount of fifth-century BC sculpture taken from the Parthenon, the temple to the goddess Athena, which stood on the Acropolis hill in the centre of the city.

The Parthenon sculpture included about a half (some 75 metres) of the sculpted frieze that once ran all round the building, plus 17 life-sized marble figures from its gable ends (or pediments) and 15 of the 92 metopes, or sculpted panels, originally displayed high up above its columns.

These actions were controversial from the very beginning. Even before all the sculptures – soon known as the Elgin Marbles – went on display in the British Museum in London (following their purchase from Lord Elgin by the British Government), Lord Byron attacked Elgin in stinging verses, lamenting (in 'Childe Harold's Pilgrimage') how the antiquities of Greece had been 'defac'd by British hands'.

Since then, there has been a never-ending international debate about Elgin's removal of the sculptures, and whether they should be returned to Athens.

Source: Beard, M. (2011) *Lord Elgin – Saviour or Vandal?* http://www.bbc.co.uk/history/ancient/greeks/parthenon_debate_01.shtml

The debate

In early 2004, The British Museum had done little proactive communications to communicate why the

case study 27.5 (continued)

sculptures should remain on its premises. Very little visible lobbying for the marbles to stay in the British Museum had taken place. Meanwhile the pressure mounted. The Greek Government and supporters such as the UK's Committee for the Reunification (previously Restitution) of the Parthenon Marbles to Greece lobbied the European Union for the reinstatement to take place before the Olympic Games in Athens in 2004 – a symbolic moment for both countries – but it did not transpire.

Campaigners calling for their return to Greece argue that these priceless ancient sculptures and artefacts from the ancient classical times would be best appreciated in their original setting – the Parthenon in Athens – and that both are intrinsically linked. The Greek Government has campaigned for the return of the Marbles since 1829, after independence from the Turkish Empire.

According to campaigners, the Parthenon Marbles, as they prefer to call them, belong to Greece. They are willing to negotiate a deal whereby the Marbles are on long-term loan to Greece, and kept in a special museum that will be an outstation of the British Museum, referring to St Petersburg's branch of the Hermitage Museum in London's Somerset house and New York's Guggenheim Museum, which has branches in Bilbao and Venice. In anticipation of the Marbles' return, Greek authorities commissioned a new $55m Acropolis Museum in 2000 which was completed in 2007.

Sources: http://www.theacropolismuseum.gr/default. php?pname=History&la=2; http://www.parthenonuk.com/

In 2012, the British Museum states on its website:

'The British Museum exists to tell the story of cultural achievement throughout the world, from the dawn of human history over two million years ago until the present day. The Museum is a unique resource for the world: the breadth and depth of its collection allows the world public to re-examine cultural identities and explore the complex network of interconnected world cultures. Within the context of this unparalleled collection, the Parthenon sculptures are an important representation of ancient Athenian civilisation.

'Each year millions of visitors, free of charge, admire the artistry of the sculptures and gain insights on how ancient Greece influenced, and was influenced by, the other civilisations that it encountered.

'The Trustees of the British Museum warmly welcome the opening of the New Acropolis Museum, which will allow the Parthenon sculptures that are in Athens to be appreciated against the backdrop of ancient Greek and

Athenian history. The new museum, however, does not alter the Trustees' view that the sculptures are part of everyone's shared heritage and transcend cultural boundaries. The Trustees remain convinced that the current division allows different and complementary stories to be told about the surviving sculptures, highlighting their significance for world culture and affirming the universal legacy of Ancient Greece.'

http://www.britishmuseum.org/about_us/news_and_press/
statements/parthenon_sculptures.aspx
http://www.britishmuseum.org/explore/highlights/article_
index/p/the_parthenon_stewardship.aspx

The museum movement

Over the last 200 years the sculptures have come to 'belong' in the British Museum and are now historically rooted there as well as in Athens. Not only were they an important part of British nineteenth-century culture (inspiring Keats and others, and prompting replicas of themselves across the country), but they are also integral to the whole idea of the Universal Museum and the way museums over the last two centuries have come to display and interpret human culture.

The museum movement depended on collection, on moving objects from their original location, and on allowing them to be understood in relation to different traditions of art and cultural forms. In the British Museum, the Elgin Marbles gain from being seen next to Assyrian or Egyptian sculpture, at the same time as they lose from not being 'at home in Greece'.

This is what causes the irresolvable conflict – it has turned out that there is more than one place that can legitimately call itself 'home' to the Elgin Marbles

Adapted source: Beard, M. (2011) *Lord Elgin –
Saviour or Vandal?*
http://www.bbc.co.uk/history/ancient/
greeks/parthenon_debate_01.shtml

'A History of the World in 100 Objects'

'A History of the World' was a 2010 partnership between the BBC and the British Museum, involving schools, museums and audiences across the UK.

At the heart of the project was the BBC Radio 4 series *A History of the World in 100 Objects*: 100 15-minute programmes, each focusing on an object from the British Museum's collection (including the Parthenon Marbles) and written and narrated by Neil MacGregor, Director of the British Museum.

case study 27.5 (continued)

The programmes told a history of two million years of humanity through the objects we have made, starting with the earliest object in the museum's collection.

Source: http://www.bbc.co.uk/ahistoryoftheworld/about/

To realise the project, the British Museum, the BBC and more than 550 museums across the UK came together to serve the public in an ambitious partnership that captured the imaginations of millions across the globe.

The project was judged so successful and groundbreaking that it was awarded the 2011 Art Fund Prize of £100,000 for its excellence, originality and imagination.

Michael Portillo, Chair of the Judges, said: 'We were particularly impressed by the truly global scope of the British Museum's project, which combined intellectual rigour and open heartedness, and went far beyond the boundaries of the museum's walls. Above all, we felt that this project, which showed a truly pioneering use of digital media, has led the way for museums to interact with their audiences in new and different ways. Without changing the core of the British Museum's purpose, people have and are continuing to engage with objects in an innovative way as a consequence of this project.'

http://www.artfundprize.org.uk/art-fund-prize-winner-announced.php

Source: CIPR Case Study 2004

Explore 27.2   Co-creation

Select a co-created arts event, production, performance or film from an online search.

■ How would you plan your communications to widen the appeal of these arts and encourage participation?

■ How would you suggest using social media and social networks to engage an audience before, during and after an event like this?

■ Suggest how the marketing and communications of arts events like this one could be evaluated or measured.

Explore 27.3   Questions for further research

Consider the following questions in the context of your own country of origin. Try to draw out comparisons with other countries. What are the potential differences or similarities? How do you account for these? What social, political, economic or technological factors impact on these questions? Can PR and marketing theory be applied to answering some of these questions? Do you think new theoretical models and concepts are required in arts, leisure and entertainment PR and marketing in the future? How could this specialised and adapted communications theory assist these sectors?

1. How can an arts, leisure or entertainment organisations attract and develop new audiences or members?

2. How can arts or leisure organisations increase the frequency of attendance of their current members/ audience?

3. How can an arts or entertainment organisation, such as a theatre or a film production company, create offerings, products and messages to which its target audience will enthusiastically respond without, at the same time, compromising its 'artistic' integrity?

4. Why should artistic directors, artists, managing directors and board members take communications seriously and make it a central part of an organisation's decision-making and leadership process?

5. How can arts, leisure or entertainment organisations work in partnership with each other to achieve their goals more effectively and efficiently than they could do on their own?

6. In such dynamic environments as the arts and entertainment sectors, can organisations develop long-range strategic communications plans?

Think about 27.7

■ For international museums and galleries, national pride and right of ownership are complex on both sides – are the legal arguments of the British Museum relevant to a post-imperial age?

■ Returning the Marbles would set the precedent for other claims for the repatriation of artefacts considered as cultural theft. The British Museum's collection, along with those of other internationally renowned cultural institutions such as the Louvre in France, Rijksmuseum in Amsterdam, the Metropolitan in New York and museums in Hong Kong, would similarly be called into question.

■ How does the British Museum's positioning statement and BBC partnership for 'A History of the World in 100 Objects' enhance its argument for keeping the Parthenon Marbles?

Summary

This chapter has outlined key elements of a variety of different activities in the culture industries, providing facts and figures to illustrate the current status of these activities. It has also provided a wide range of case studies to offer more in-depth analysis of how different issues are impacting on given arts and entertainment organisations.

As well as looking at the practical aspects of the culture industries, the section briefly discussed some relevant theories that explore the concepts.

The practice of PR in these sectors was examined, particularly where it differs from PR in other sectors, as well as the demands of arts organisations and their need for strategic and tactical PR skills.

Finally, the section looked at how changing technologies and relationships are affecting communications in arts and cultural organisations.

Bibliography

American Heritage® Dictionary of the English Language (2006). 4th edition. Houghton Mifflin Company.

Anderson, P. (1991). 'Constructing the arts industry'. *Culture and Policy* 3(2): 51–63.

Arts Council England (2004). Grants to the Arts – Audience development and marketing. London: Arts Council.

Arts Council England (2010). 'Audience development and marketing'. www.artscouncil.org.uk/information-sheet/audience-development-and-marketing-grants-for-the-arts accessed 4 July 2012.

Barrere, C. and W. Santagata (1999). 'Defining art from the Brancusi trail to the economics of artistic semiotic goods'. *International Journal of Art Management* 1(2): 28–38.

Beresford, S. (2005). Unpublished research, interview with Tim Hincks. Leeds: Leeds Metropolitan University.

Beresford, S. (2011). Unpublished research, Northern Art Prize. Leeds: Leeds Metropolitan University.

Bouder-Pailer (1999). 'A model for measuring the goals of theatre attendance'. *International Journal of Arts Management* 1(2): 4–15.

Buck, L. (2004). 'Market Matters: The dynamics of the contemporary art market'. Arts Council of England Publication.

Dennis, N., G. Larsen and M. Macaulay (2011). 'Editorial: terraforming arts marketing 2011'. *Arts Marketing: An International Journal* 1(1): 5–8.

Diggle, K. (1994). *Arts Marketing*. London: Rhinegold.

Drucker, P. (1990). *Managing the Non-Profit Organisation*. Harper Collins.

Durie, J., A. Pham and N. Watson (2000). *Marketing and Selling your Film Around the World*. Los Angeles, CA: Silman-James Press.

EAO (2003). 'Focus 2003: world film market trends' in *Arts Marketing*. F. Kerrigan, P. Fraser and M. Ozbilgin (eds). London: Butterworth-Heinemann.

Fill, C. (2004). *Integrated Marketing Communication*. Harlow: Pearson Education.

Fillis, I. (2004). 'The theory and practice of visual arts marketing' in *Arts Marketing*. F. Kerrigan, P. Fraser and M. Ozbilgin (eds). London: Butterworth-Heinemann.

Hill, E., C. O'Sullivan and T. O'Sullivan (2003). *Creative Arts Marketing*, 2nd edition. Oxford: Butterworth-Heinemann.

Kerrigan, F. (2002). 'Does structure matter? An analysis of the interplay between company structure and the marketing process in the film industry'. Paper presented at the Academy of Marketing Conference, University of Nottingham Business School.

Kerrigan, F. (2010). *Film Marketing*. London: Butterworth-Heinemann.

Kerrigan, F., P. Fraser and M. Ozbilgin (2004). *Arts Marketing*. London: Butterworth-Heinemann.

Kotler, P. and J. Scheff (1997). *Standing Room Only: Strategies for marketing the performing arts*. Boston, MA: Harvard Business School Press.

Maitland, H. (2000). *A Guide to Audience Development*, 2nd edition. Arts Council of England.

McQuail, D. (2005). *McQuail's Mass Communication Theory*. Newbury Park, CA: Sage.

Morris, G., J. Hargreaves and A. McIntrye (2004). *Taste Buds: How to cultivate the art market*. Arts Council of England.

Nessman, K. (2008). 'Personal communication management: how to position people effectively'. EUPRERA Conference, Milan, 16–18 October, www.euprera.org.

O'Keefe, D. (2002). *Persuasion Theory and Research*, 2nd edition. London: Sage.

O'Reilly, D. (2011). 'Mapping the arts marketing literature'. *Arts Marketing: An International Journal* **1**: 26–37.

O'Sullivan, T., J. Hartley, D. Saunders, M. Montgomery and J. Fiske (1994). *Key Concepts in Communication and Cultural Studies*. London: Routledge.

Parsons, P. (1987). *Shooting the Pianist: The role of government in the arts*. Sydney: Current Press.

Phillips, D. (2001). *Online Public Relations*. Institute of Public Relations, PR in Practice Series. London: Kogan Page.

Pine, B.J. and J.H. Gilmore (1998). *The Experience Economy*. Boston, MA: Harvard Business School.

Pringle, H. (2004). *Celebrity Sells*. Chichester: John Wiley & Sons.

Rogers, R. (1998). *Audience Development: Collaborations between education and marketing*. London: Arts Council.

Schmitt, B. (1999). *Experiential Marketing*. New York, NY: The Free Press.

Strinati, D. (1995). *An Introduction to Theories of Popular Culture*. London: Routledge.

Torkildsen, G. (2000). *Leisure and Recreation Management*, 4th edition. London: E & FN Spon.

Travers, T. (1998). The Wyndham Report (1998) Society of London Theatres MORI.

Veal, A.J. (2002). *Leisure and Tourism Policy and Planning*, 2nd edition. Oxford: CABI Publishing.

Walmsley, B. and A. Franks (2011). *Key Issues in the Arts and Entertainment Industry*. Oxford: Goodfellow Publishers.

Wilcox, D.L., P.H. Ault and W.K. Agee (2002). *Public Relations Strategies and Tactics*, 7th edition. New York, NY: Addison-Wesley.

Websites

Academy of Marketing Special Interest Group, Arts, Heritage, Non-Profit and Social Marketing: http://www.academyofmarketing.org/arts-heritage-nonprofit-social-marketing-sig/
Arts Marketing Association: www.ama.co.uk
Arts Council: www.artscouncil.org.uk
BBC: www.bbc.co.uk
Chartered Institute of Marketing: www.cim.co.uk
Chartered Institute of Public Relations: www.cipr.co.uk
Department for Culture, Media and Sport: www.culture.gov.uk
imove: www.imoveand.com

CHAPTER 28

Elliot Pill

Celebrity culture and public relations

Learning outcomes

By the end of this chapter you should be able to:

- define celebrity culture
- discuss how celebrity PR is distinct from other forms of PR
- understand how the celebrity industry has developed
- analyse the impact celebrities have on consumers
- understand how celebrity image is managed and controlled
- analyse emerging models of celebrity PR firms.

Structure

- Growth of celebrity culture
- Celebrities classified
- The personality market
- Celebrity production: the publicists
- Celebrity economy: why celebrities are good for the bottom line
- Celebrity infamy and public relations
- Celebrity, privacy and public relations
- Critique of celebrity

Introduction

This chapter discusses the development of celebrity PR and assesses the impact of celebrity culture on society. It seeks to analyse why celebrities are so appealing and appalling in equal measure and looks at the skill set of the 'celebrity creators' and publicists who build the celebrity brand to differentiate the persona from other celebrity brands. The chapter also takes into consideration the position celebrity culture adopts in our cultural economy and discusses its growth within the landscape of popular culture.

It is also important to critique and discuss the close relationship between publicists and their clients and media owners who act as producer and director, building a soap opera story together and identifying the 'characters' or celebrities to take leading roles. This extends the recent UK debate around celebrity and privacy and the newspaper 'hacking' scandal, as formally investigated by the Leveson Inquiry, which sought to investigate the role of the media and police in hacking phone messaging services to gain illegal access to private information in order to build sensational news stories.

But first, let us define and understand how celebrity culture has developed and how a new star system was created to describe people who gained public attention.

Growth of celebrity culture

A celebrity is a well-recognised person who commands a high degree of public and media attention, or a person who is 'known for being known' (Boorstin 1961). Celebrity culture is a growing element of 'promotional culture' (Wernick 1991), which, in turn, is the ideological process of understanding the way advertising, marketing and public relations shape cultural formation in society. Wernick (1991) shows how advertising copy and other promotional texts have a significant impact on cultural formation through the dissemination of cultural values. The resulting promotional culture has, in turn, transformed the form and character of communication. For example, it would have once been unthinkable for universities in the UK to see themselves as part of a competitive marketplace; now, universities are increasingly ranked and judged, not only on their academic performance but on the way they communicate their 'brand' through websites, open days and famous alumni.

In the 1960s, the pop art creator Andy Warhol popularised the term 'superstar'. In his 1975 book, *The Philosophy of Andy Warhol*, he described a friend named Ingrid who developed a new last name to brand her talent. Warhol wrote: 'She called herself Ingrid Superstar. I'm positive Ingrid invented that word. At least, I invite anyone with "superstar" clippings that predate Ingrid's to show them to me. The more parties we went to, the more they wrote her name in the papers, "Ingrid Superstar", and "superstar" was starting its media run' (Warhol 1975). Before we discuss celebrity and public relations in a modern-day context, it is important to define and describe the creation of a celebrity system, understand some core techniques and get a sense of the academic discourses and research within the field.

Pseudo-events and 'star' making

In the early 1900s film companies began promoting film personalities by releasing stories about these actors to fan magazines and newspapers. This was the beginning of what Boorstin describes as the 'pseudo result', which was a direct outcome of the graphic revolution in the late 1800s. In his 1961 book, *The Image: A guide to pseudo-events in America*, Boorstin described an activity that exists for the sole purpose of the media and that involves the creation of a form of news that serves no other function in real life. Without media coverage nothing actually occurs at the event, and therefore these events are only considered real after they are viewed through news, advertisements, television or other media.

A press conference is a classic example of a 'pseudo-event', where an organisation or publicist will call a conference of invited journalists to a venue organised by the host to hear news shaped and packaged for the audience to mediate to specific audiences, such as fans. This promotional strategy was deliberately formed to build brand loyalty for the film company's actors and films and create a differentiation to fans. By the 1920s, Hollywood image makers, as they had now become known, began to create manufactured news that delivered a steady stream of pseudo-information to reinforce the branded persona of the 'star'. This served to maintain the on-screen image in an off-screen environment, thereby extending the commercial appeal of the celebrity. Such examples would be famous 'still' pictures from classic Hollywood films for Marilyn Monroe, John Wayne, Grace Kelly and Marlon Brando. A star system was being formed, and academic interest into the study of celebrity emerged.

Seminal texts on stardom have been developed by Boorstin (1971), Alberoni (1972) and Dyer (1979), which examined in various forms the representations of stars

Box 28.1

Pseudo-event creation: the 'photo op'

A 'photo op', short for photograph opportunity, is an opportunity to take a memorable and effective photograph of a politician, celebrity, or event that creates an impression in the mind of the viewer. It is an element of the created news culture borne out of the Hollywood star-making era in the early 1900s. The term was thought to be created by the political staff of the controversial US President Richard Nixon, who was advised to get people in 'for a picture'. Those pictures would then be used to create a positive image for the President in American and international media.

While initially creative and effective, the photo op has acquired a negative connotation, referring to a carefully planned pseudo-event. It is associated with politicians, business leaders and celebrities performing tasks such as planting trees, handing over a giant cheque, attending dinners and award ceremonies. These pictures are pre-planned and serve no other purpose than creating a positive image for the photo op creators.

An example of where photo ops are used to good effect can be seen on the 'red carpet', where celebrities pose to promote and launch new films. It can also be seen in sport, where global sport brands such as Manchester United FC or Barcelona FC want to publicise the arrival of a new star footballer. Another classic use of the photo op was of Victoria Beckham at the press conference by LA Galaxy to announce the arrival of her husband, David. Attending the conference, Victoria wore a striking colourful dress with big black sunglasses to ape the look of English socialite Holly Golightly in the film *Breakfast at Tiffany's*. She attained much of the press coverage and announced her arrival in the US as well as her husband's. The photo op, then, remains a tactical tool in the armoury of the celebrity publicist to shape reputation and protect image but is essentially a manufactured, worthless form of news and gossip, as highlighted in Boorstin's work.

Explore 28.1

Learning about your celebrity universe

In small groups, discuss the following to get a sense of individual perspective on celebrity impact. During your discussions write down some of the key points and identify common themes and attitudes towards celebrities.

- Analyse the way organisations use celebrities to market their products.
- Would celebrity endorsement entice you to buy a product?
- If so, why?
- Who would you describe as true, global celebrities and why?
- Do you see any negative impact of celebrity culture on society?

affecting and impacting all facets of social life and closely connected to widespread economic, political, technological and cultural developments. Indeed, L'Etang (2008) quite rightly asks the question why celebrity cultural studies has taken so long to establish itself within the framework of promotional culture research, as it has such an impact on the formation of lifestyles. (see Box 28.1 and Explore 28.1.)

Celebrities classified

With the growth of Western promotional culture in the 1950s and 1960s spawning a new generation of celebrities, a clear celebrity sub-culture was forming and academics quickly set about researching the impact celebrities had on society. But it wasn't until the late 1990s that academics attempted to classify celebrities in trying to understand how celebrities are created. Chris Rojek (2001) has developed a five-section model (see Box 28.2) to name the type of celebrity actors in the stardom universe. The model is useful in that it maps the vast change that has taken place in the development and impact of celebrity culture.

What are the factors that have influenced today's celebrity culture? Rojek (2001) maintains that celebrity creation and culture is the consequence of the democratisation of society, the decline in organised religion and the commodification of everyday life. But as we have already

with the Hollywood system. More recently, academics have broadened that agenda to analyse celebrity from a cultural studies perspective. Gamson (1994), Marshall (1997), Giles (2000), Turner et al. (2000), Rojek (2001), Turner (2004) and L'Etang (2008) have all found a pervasive celebrity culture

networks, is also at play. He maintains the larger and more complex the social network, the more difficult visibility is and, as social media expands, gaining visibility is an accomplishment in itself.

Ascribed celebrity

This is celebrity status acquired through lineage or inheritance. These celebrities could be members of a royal family, politicians or business people. Interestingly, their children also fall into this category, producing a sort of celebrity lineage. An example from business and cross-gender would be Bernie Ecclestone and his daughter, Tamara, and from sport, David and Victoria Beckham and their children, Brooklyn, Romeo, Cruz and Harper Seven (see Mini case study 28.1).

Achieved celebrity

This is celebrity status achieved by being exceptional at something, popular and of note. Achieved celebrity is a

---

Box 28.2

Rojek (2001) classified celebrity as:

1. Ascribed
2. Achieved
3. Attributed
4. Celetoid
5. Celeactors

---

discussed, celebrity culture isn't new: it has just been taken to new heights with changing media consumption, globalised, interconnected cultural markets and the rise of the global media brand of the masses – the Internet. Murray Milner (2005) broadens Rojek's position. He argues that a shrinking sense of self, caused by globalised social

---

Mini case study 28.1

Celebrity economy in practice: Posh and Becks – global 'ascribed' celebrity icons

A modern global celebrity phenomenon is David and Victoria Beckham and family, or 'Posh and Becks' as they are branded by the world's media. The couple have four children, Brooklyn, Romeo, Cruz and Harper Seven: each can be described as 'ascribed' celebrities.

David Beckham shot to fame as a member of the famous Manchester United football team in the late 1990s. He went on to play for Real Madrid and to captain England in the World Cup, and is now in the twilight of his football career at Paris Saint-Germain.

He married Victoria Beckham, a member of the pop band The Spice Girls. The band was manufactured and put together by music entrepreneur, Simon Fuller. The Spice Girls became a global phenomenon, breaking all records for sales and number one hits with a brand banner of 'girl power'. Victoria's character was 'Posh Spice'. The

UK press instantly loved the couple and realised that front-cover pictures of the famous duo would sell copies. This was classic infotainment fodder, with the couple adopted by the UK tabloid press as a front-page replacement for the late Princess Diana who died in a Paris car crash being pursued by press photographers.

'Posh and Becks' became the new UK royalty and lived in a house dubbed 'Beckingham Palace', a side swipe at the House of Windsor's Buckingham Palace in central London. The UK was also undergoing huge political and social change, with Tony Blair being elected as the first socialist Prime Minister in many years, and his style and leadership signalled a new era in the cultural history of the UK.

David Beckham was marketed like a silent movie star at the beginning of his career and early years in the celebrity spotlight. It was all about the look and not the words in an attempt to build a brand purely on image and his success on the football pitch. He gained sponsorship deals with adidas, Vodafone, Gillette, Police eyewear and Emporio Armani. He now has his own perfume while his wife, Victoria, has her own fashion label. This combination of on- and off-football field earnings has made Beckham the richest footballer in the world. According to *Forbes* magazine, in 2012 he earned $40million from salary, bonuses and commercial endorsements. In second and third place were Cristiano Ronaldo ($38million) and Lionel Messi ($28million).

meritocratic celebrity status acquired through a specific talent or individual skill. Examples would be: footballer Wayne Rooney; round-the-world sailor Ellen MacArthur; businessman Lord Alan Sugar; and singer and entertainer Beyonce Knowles.

Attributed celebrity

This is celebrity status created from repetitive media exposure. Examples would be television and radio presenters, such as Jeremy Kyle, Alan Carr, Jonathan Ross and Oprah Winfrey.

Celetoid

This describes celebrities who command media attention because of scandals, pseudo-events or appearances on reality TV shows, such as *Big Brother, I'm a Celebrity . . . Get Me Out Of Here, X Factor* and *Strictly Come Dancing*. The

Picture 28.1 Kim Kardashian: a 'celetoid'?
(*source*: Getty Images)

celebrity status is generally short-lived but many do extend their celetoid celebrity status by taking part in a number of reality television shows. Indeed, celetoid celebrities such as Katie Price and Peter Andre and the Kardashians have developed their own reality television shows, where they are the stars and viewers and fans get an up-close and personal view of their lifestyles.

Other celetoid celebrities create media dramas, do raunchy photo shoots in 'lads' mags' and create their own pseudo-events and gossip to stay in the media spotlight. The current celetoid phenomenon is for 'normality' reality television shows such as *The Only Way Is Essex* and *Made in Chelsea* to spawn new stars who appear in reality shows such as *I'm a Celebrity . . . Get Me Out of Here* in order to extend their celetoid status.

Celeactors

These are fictional characters that achieve media attention and become cultural reference points, and include the Disney icons Sleeping Beauty and Snow White and, more recently, the ogre Shrek in the film of the same name. (Now refer to Explore 28.2.)

The personality market

Nessmann's concept of the personality market builds on Rojek's findings. Nessmann (2008) placed celebrity types into a universe and coined the term, the *personality market*. He put forward a four-dimensional model of the interplay between different actors in the celebrity bubble and broadens the debate. Nessmann identified four linked elements in the making of the personality market and they are described in Figure 28.1.

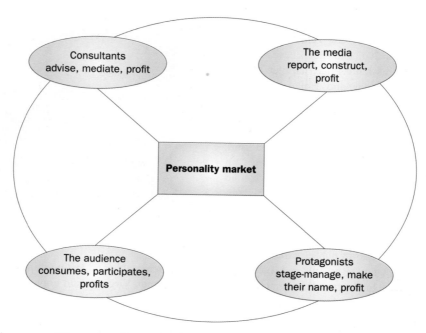

Figure 28.1 Four key areas of the personality market (*source*: Nessmann 2008)

The protagonists (celebrities)

The spectrum of protagonists ranges from largely unknown individuals to prominent figures from various fields. They are all pushing their way into the media and profit by making themselves better known, thus guaranteeing popularity, power, influence or financial success.

The media (print, broadcast, digital)

The media include more reports on the protagonists and profit from increased circulation, sales figures, listening and viewing figures and Internet hits.

The audience

The group classified as the audience consumes these 'stories', takes part in what is going on, identifies with the celebrities and profits by satisfying their voyeuristic needs.

The consultants

These are marketing or PR consultants who mediate between the protagonists, the media and the audience; they publish books, hold seminars and profit by charging fees for their time.

Celebrity production: the publicists

Having examined different types of celebrity and the universe in which they exist, let us now examine the role of the publicists (the 'consultant' in Nessmann's model) in producing celebrity image and managing reputation. Celebrity PR is often seen as the 'Cinderella' specialist area of the PR service portfolio, something that isn't serious, offers a bit of fun, is tactical and lightweight. The reality couldn't be further from the truth, with key figures commanding significant power in their ability to shape editorial news pages and agendas and create 'stars' overnight.

The celebrity publicist Max Clifford, through his agency Max Clifford Associates (MCA), wields unparalleled power in breaking celebrity stories. He also has equal power in his ability to keep bad news out of the media. He claims to have broken more tabloid front-page stories in the UK than any other journalist. It would be hard to argue against this claim with the demand for gossip evidenced through soap opera-style stories gracing newspapers and digital portals around the world. Interestingly, Clifford maintains that his business today has changed due to the rise of digital media and the decrease in the ability to apply privacy law internationally. Mr Clifford says his business is more to do with protecting clients and keeping them out of the media spotlight, rather than promoting clients to gain as much 'media spotlight' time as they can.

Claire Powell, Managing Director of Can Associates, is another example of the modern-day celebrity publicist. Her firm was established in 2002 and clients have included 'celetoid' celebrities such as Katie Price, Jennifer Ellison, Kerry Katona, Nell McAndrew and Hollywood acting legends, Ursula Andress and Melanie Griffiths. Can Associates is also behind the production of pop star Peter Andre's highly successful reality television programme series. Like reality television celebrity pioneers The Osbournes, Andre and Can Associates offer fans and viewers an intimate insight into the life of a modern-day celetoid celebrity. The celebrity production power described is supported in research by Rein et al. (2006), who found that PR was the dominant marketing service contributing to the construction of celebrity.

Other services offered by celebrity publicists include media interview coaching, presentation techniques and voice training. They also offer financial management advice and online brand management. Powell's Can Associates additionally offer clients plastic surgery under a different brand name.

So, clearly, celebrity association can be good for business and building brand image and maintaining a relevant public image. We now need to discuss why celebrities are used by business to enhance reputation and create visibility.

Celebrity economy: why celebrities are good for the bottom line

Consumers and 'buyers' of products and services are heavily influenced in their purchase decisions by celebrity endorsement. If it wasn't so, commercial organisations would not spend the vast sums of marketing budgets they do linking their message to celebrity status. It is believed that when an endorser (celebrity) is used to promote a product or service to an audience, that audience takes more notice of the product and therefore stands out in a busy brand crowd and creates a sense of trust. An example would be the use of the world's most famous athlete, Usain Bolt, to 'front' Virgin media's broadband communication campaign in the run-up to the 2012 Olympics in London.

In the advertising campaign, Bolt is seen sporting a grey beard to replicate the trademark facial hair of Virgin celebrity business boss, Sir Richard Branson. In the advert, Bolt introduces himself as Sir Richard Branson and tells the audience he is 'fast' – the inference being the Virgin broadband service is 'fast' and should be trusted. The communications campaign allows the Virgin brand to stand out from the crowd in a hyper-competitive market place and

Picture 28.2 Tiger Woods is good for the bottom line (*source*: Getty Images)

form a memorable and lasting impression in the mind of the consumer. Virgin would hope that their brand will be at the front of consumers' minds when making their broadband purchase decisions.

In the US, Srinivasan et al. (2010) found that celebrity endorsement significantly affected the bottom-line profits of organisations that used celebrities to endorse products. They specifically looked at the golf market and analysed the sales of golf balls and celebrity endorsement. They found that in endorsing Tiger Woods, Nike's golf ball division reaped additional profits of $60 million through the acquisition of 4.5 million new customers. Indeed, the whole golf ball market increased in value as a result of the well-publicised endorsement.

In India, a celebrity endorsement survey of 2,019 people across 12 cities and small towns by the India Market Research Bureau (IMRB) and a PR company, IPAN, revealed that 86 per cent of those surveyed said they remembered ads with celebrities in them and 22 per cent of people actually believed that the celebrities used the product they endorsed (Mahajan-Bansal 2008). IMRB said that factors such as quality, price, word of mouth and experience is what makes people buy. However, in the same survey it is revealed that people do recall the brands endorsed by celebrities and therefore one could argue that brand recall would lead to buying the endorsed product.

It is further argued that celebrity association builds a relationship between the product and the audience and therefore higher prices can be charged due to a perception that the endorsed product is somehow 'better' than a rival product. This added-value marketing outcome allows marketers to use celebrities to enhance the brand value and therefore create greater price and profit margins over their competitors.

The inherent brand personality of the celebrity is matched by the marketer to the product, as seen by the Virgin and Usain Bolt example, in order to differentiate one brand from another and subliminally play on the consumers' subconscious desire to be associated with a particular product because it bestows a certain social status. Other examples would be pop star Kylie Minogue and her association with the Lexus hybrid car brand and Alfa Romeo's Giulietta car endorsed by Hollywood film star Uma Thurman.

And while, clearly, celebrities are good for the bottom line, any association has its risks and, to some marketers, celebrity endorsement is a very high-risk brand strategy. So let us now look at the downside of celebrity association and celebrity infamy.

Celebrity infamy and public relations

While there is no doubt that vast fortunes can be built by celebrities, those fortunes and reputations can be lost in an instant as they operate in an aggressive media environment out to create the next big headline. In that process many celebrities, whatever their status, come crashing down to earth with a big bang from which they struggle to survive. Indeed, work by former UK television personality, Dr Pamela Stephenson, examined the psychological effects of fame and its consequences for celebrities and what being in the spotlight felt like. In a 2012 television documentary, *The Fame Report*, Dr Stephenson interviewed a range of famous people including her husband, comedian and actor, Billy Connolly, actor Alan Cummings and Hollywood Oscar-winner Tatum O'Neil. She discovered that, to many famous people, being in the spotlight was a form of trauma from which they could never escape. She describes the attainment of fame as a hollow victory for those seeking love, sex and money. A classic tale of celebrity infamy and fame as trauma involved the world's highest-paid sportsman, Tiger Woods (see Mini case study 28.2). Celebrity infamy leads us onto our next section of discussion and investigation: the extent to which celebrities have a right to privacy.

Mini case study 28.2

Celebrity infamy and the bottom line: Eldrick 'Tiger' Woods

His global reputation as the world's greatest ever golf player and sporting role model of the digital age evaporated in November 2009 when Eldrick 'Tiger' Woods admitted to a string of extramarital affairs. Woods' sporting childhood was dominated by his military-man father, Earl. He had spotted his golfing potential and set about shaping his son into a world-class golfer. Tiger's status was further enhanced when IMG (International Management Group), one of the world's leading sports marketing organisations set up by the late Mark McCormack following the success of one of his first clients, Arnold Palmer, took over player management.

IMG set about building a range of corporate sponsorship deals for Woods off the golf course, while he concentrated on success on the golf course. This growing status and power allowed Woods and IMG to create a wall of privacy around his personal life, where he was protected from the media and protected from the fans. However, that wall of privacy was removed on 25 November 2009 when the *National Enquirer* magazine in the US ran a story that Woods had been having an affair with nightclub promoter, Rachel Uchital. On 27 November, Woods crashed his car into a tree outside his Florida home following an argument with his wife, Elin Nordegren.

Following a number of other allegations, Woods and IMG tried to take a hold of the unfolding crisis. Woods apologised via his website to his fans and announced an 'indefinite hiatus' from professional golf. He further made a press conference-style address to his friends, which was broadcast live to a global audience, in which he apologised for his behaviour and asked for forgiveness.

From a PR practitioner point of view, the key to crisis management, according to leading crisis communications expert Mike Regester, is to 'tell the truth, tell it all and tell it fast'. This is certainly true in today's media landscape, where privacy is difficult to maintain and fans feel they have a right to see 'inside' the lifestyles of the rich and famous and demand 'warts and all' honesty. In short, audiences demand authenticity. Also, from a PR practitioner perspective, there was a clear lack of judgement or appreciation for the media and fan environment in which Woods found himself. Woods and IMG maintained a wall of silence, even while thousands of negative comments were being pasted on Tiger Woods' official website in the aftermath of the news being published in the *National Enquirer*. The people (fans) who respected him most were telling him what they wanted to hear, but both the celebrity and his management team and reputation managers failed to act quickly. And when they did finally communicate 'the truth' via a staged press conference, Woods, to many, came across as emotionally cold and insincere.

Woods and his management team failed to meet any of Regester's crisis communications 'musts' and never filled

mini case study 28.2 (continued)

the vacuum of communication craved by fans, the media and sponsors. As a result, his reputation and initial brand value dropped through the floor, although sponsors reacted in different ways. Accenture, a global software company and one of Woods' main sponsors, withdrew their support, as did others. Nike, however, remained loyal and even broadcast a controversial advert of a pensive Woods looking at the camera with the words of his late father, Earl, seemingly talking to his son. Nike was criticised for trying to create empathy for a character with whom the public had fallen out of love.

It is possible to understand the extent of Nike's support from a business perspective when research shows that the company, in the wake of the scandal, lost an estimated $1.3 million in profit and 105,000 customers and the rest of the golf industry lost $6.2 million in profit. Indeed, Nike were better off supporting Woods through the scandal than breaking the ten-year sponsorship contract, as Nike's profit during the crisis period was $1.6 million greater with Woods than without him. In 2010 Woods earned $90.5m. This made him the highest-earning professional sportsman in the world. So, while as tragic and traumatic as Woods' fall from grace was, perhaps there is something in the saying, 'there is no such thing as bad publicity'.

Source: based on Chung et al. 2011

Celebrity, privacy and public relations

Clearly, many celebrities have significant media power and possess the ability to shield their private lives from public attention, but in the digital media landscape and the clamour for celebrity gossip, this privacy has been eroded and celebrities have been fighting back. Indeed, there is an emerging strand to the public relations industry specialising in 'litigation PR'. These firms advise clients of the potential media impact of any legal process or dispute on celebrity reputation. A litigation PR service may include the following:

- Media risk assessment
- Dispute profiling
- Political PR strategies
- Settlement PR
- Trial PR handling
- Aftermath management.

This interplay and relationship between the media, litigation PR firms, celebrities, publicists, police and politicians was discussed in the UK in 2012 in the form of a judicial inquiry by Lord Justice Leveson. At the centre of the investigation was the specific relationship between media owners, editors, journalists and police, sparked by the illegal technique of hacking the phones of the rich, influential and famous to gain access to private information in order to publish sensational news stories. As a result, the media tycoon Rupert Murdoch closed the biggest-selling tabloid newspaper in the UK, the *News of the World*, amid allegations of celebrity phone hacking, and appeared before a select committee at the House of Commons with his son, James, to answer questions of illegal newspaper practice (see earlier in the text for more on this case study and its implications for journalism).

At the inquiry, J.K. Rowling, the author of the Harry Potter books, talked about the time her young daughter returned from school and she found a letter addressed to her in her daughter's bag asking for an interview; while actress Sienna Miller (Miller 2011: 5) told the court:

I am still angry that for a long period of time the News of the World *made my life hell in the pursuit of stories about me. They damaged a lot of my relationships, they made me nervous and paranoid and all because they thought personal details about my private life, as opposed to my professional acting career, would sell papers and make them money. All those involved should be held to account so that this cannot happen again.*

On the flip side of this argument for media restraint is the use of injunctions, coined 'super injunctions', by wealthy celebrities to stop newspapers printing allegations about their private lives that they would not wish the public and fans to know. The value of these injunctions is now questioned by celebrities when users of popular social network sites publish the names of the people who have filed for a super injunction without fear of prosecution. This is due to the fact that UK law is difficult to apply to international social networks and the individuals who use them.

So this debate continues apace, with the clashing agendas of the many players in this celebrity universe. Some celebrities want more privacy and believe it to be a right, while other celebrities make their money out of ensuring they have no privacy at all. At the centre of the issue is the publicist or litigation PR practitioner – shaping media agendas and providing the wealthy with significant armoury to control personal privacy. (see Think about 28.1.)

Critique of celebrity

Many see the cult of celebrity as a scourge of modern life. Cintra Wilson (BBC 2001) argues that people had a lot of reverence for people with talent, but now there are a lot of celebrities who are famous for doing essentially worthless things and that people live vicarious lives through celebrities who are rich and beautiful. She maintains:

Like, basically, if you're a completely edgeless pastry of a person then the largest cross-section of people who don't have very good taste are going to really like you. The sort of perfect looking person and perfect sounding person and somebody who nobody laughs at and everybody loves and oh they are rich and they live this fabulous life and they become completely faceless to me. They have no soul, they have no message.

Ian Hargreaves, a former editor of the *Independent* newspaper and Professor of Digital Economy at Cardiff University, says: 'Even if you buy the proposition that celebrities are a healing balm for the fragmented societies or a vehicle for the valid public representation of private concerns, you would want to ask some pretty searching questions about the power structure of the celebrity economy. If celebrities are so important, then we need to interrogate much harder the system which manufactures them' (BBC 2001).

That investigation is only now taking place, and the debate on the celebrity economy and its impact on culture is a theme that will endure – particularly as emerging consumer economies such as China, India and Russia embrace broader forms of celebrity entertainment. (see Case study 28.1.)

Case study 28.1

Celebrity culture and PR in China

China has undergone significant social, economic and political reform and a unique celebrity culture has emerged. This culture draws much on the pre-digital, Western-centric view of celebrity as either ascribed or an achieved-type status; meaning you are famous because of your lineage or because you have a particular talent.

While reality, celetoid-type celebrities are emerging in China, its political and social systems control the type of information produced and consumed by citizens. For example, culturally, the term VIP (very important person) is used by publicists and event managers in China to describe a range of guests at events who are treated differently to normal citizens. Within this group of VIPs would be a high proportion of politicians as well as pop stars, businessmen and actors. In China, politicians form a part of its emerging celebrity culture, while in countries such as the United States and the United Kingdom, politicians toy uncomfortably with mainstream popular celebrity culture.

Indeed, before 1978, the year the Chinese government embraced social change and reform, the only celebrities in Chinese society were politicians, with Chairman Mao Zedong as the 'superstar' who had founded the People's Republic of China in 1949. Interestingly, even translating the term 'celebrity' into Chinese (mandarin) is problematic as there are a number of meanings, from superstar to hero to great person to successful person to political leader. What can also be taken out of the meaning is that the term 'celebrity' in a Chinese context refers to a person who has gained public attention but more through infamy than demonstrating a unique skill or talent. From a Western perspective this would be similar to a Z-list celebrity description; someone known, but not widely recognised. China's cultural emphasis on wisdom, tradition and education has tended to make 'stars' out of people who use thoughts, words and deeds in attracting public attention rather than the rampant hedonistic trend of celetoid celebrity in Western culture. But that is changing.

'Chinese people, not the party, are able to choose whomever they worship as icons with no restraint. Replacing the cult of personality that the Communist party created around Mao, the Chinese are now embracing a new cult, that of fame and celebrity' (Leicester 2008). And that cult of worship is not restricted to Chinese celebrities. Mark Rowswell, a Canadian actor and comic, is one of the most recognised faces in China. The Chinese refer to him as 'Dashan', which means 'big mountain'. Fluent in Mandarin, Rowswell has been a big

case study 28.1 (continued)

hit with Chinese audiences since 1988, though he and fellow 'celebrities' did have problems trying to mix their fame with commercial endorsements as the government strictly controlled personality endorsements.

Today the market has completely changed, with celebrities making good livings through performing and endorsing products in the press, on television and in outdoor posters (Plafker 2008). This growth is supported and directed by both home-grown PR consultancies and international PR brands. Indeed, a whole new entertainment and celebrity media culture is developing via multimedia platforms. Web portals such as Sina.com show that the most well-followed blogs belong to Chinese pop and movie stars. CCTV-3's talk show *YiShuRenSheng* and Hunan TV's *Luyu Yue* are hugely popular and feature interviews with Chinese celebrities.

So there is both a distinct and familiar celebrity culture emerging in China and one that, one could argue, mirrors a US-centric style of celebrity worship. An example of this would be the 2006 opening of China's Madame Tussaud's Wax Museum in Shanghai. Here, alongside waxworks of rich and famous 'foreigners', sit home-grown talents such as Jackie Chan, pop singer Andy Lau and Yao Ming (Plafker 2008). Further, the latest Chinese reality talent show was won by a British student, Jess Leaverland. Jess, aged 21, won China's *Min Xing Chang Fan* ('I want to sing to the stars') in 2011. The show is a similar format to the UK's *X Factor*. Leaverland has signed a multi-million pound contract with Decca Records to sing in Mandarin. Ms Leaverland said: 'I really thought they would want a Chinese person to win.'

Source: Pill E. (unpublished)

Summary

Public relations practitioners continue to have a strong influence on celebrity production, and that influence will continue to grow as celebrity culture develops in economies such as India, China, Latin America and Russia. In this chapter we have seen how the 'star' system emerged and how it was shaped to form a core part of promotional culture through a range of techniques aimed at creating different forms of news. Academic discussions have largely developed around classifying celebrities and analysing the production of fame.

From a practitioner viewpoint, the emerging role is that of the publicist not solely focused on promotion but taking a broader strategic role within celebrity management.

We see publicists identifying emerging talent, shaping the talent, producing media and managing celebrity reputation. This emerging model gives total control to the publicists in developing the interaction between celebrity clients and fans. This is particularly important today, where the social media network environment has reformed our views of what is and isn't privacy.

To that end, celebrities are fighting back to regain a right to personal privacy and debating of their celebrity persona what is and isn't for public consumption. It will be fascinating to track the way the industry of celebrity production develops across the next five years in response to the changing media environment, and this field will continue to provide a rich source of research for academics.

Bibliography

Alberoni, F. (1972). 'The powerless elite: theory and sociological research on the phenomenon of Stars' in *Sociology of Mass Communications*. D. McQuail (ed.). Baltimore, MD: Penguin.

Atunes, A. (2012). 'The world's highest paid celebrity couples'. www.forbes.com/sites/andersonantunes/2012/08/06the-worlds-highest-paid-celebrity-couples-2/ accessed 24 September 2012.

BBC (2001). 'Transcript. BBC Current Affairs, Radio 4 "Shooting Stars,"' broadcast 22 March 2001, presented by Ian Hargreaves, produced by Michael Blastland and edited by Nicola Meyrick.

Bernays, E. (1923). *Crystallizing Public Opinion*. New York, NY: Boni and Liveright.

Bernays, E. (1928). *Propaganda*. New York, NY: Liveright.

Bernays, E. (1955). *The Engineering of Consent*. Norman, OK: University of Oklahoma Press.

Boorstin, D.J. (1961). *The Image: A guide to pseudo-events in America*. Harmondsworth: Penguin Books.

Boorstin, D.J. (2006). 'From hero to celebrity: the human pseudo-event' in *The Celebrity Culture Reader*. P.D. Marshall (ed.). Oxford: Routledge.

Braudy, L. (1997). *The Frenzy of Renown: Fame and its history*. New York, NY: Vintage Books.

Cashmore, E. (2006). *Celebrity Culture*. London: Routledge.

Chung, K.Y.C., T. Derdenger and K. Srinivasan (2011). 'Economic value of celebrity endorsements: Tiger Woods' impact on sales of Nike golf balls'. Tepper School of Business, Carnegie Mellon University, Pittsburg, PA. www.econ.ucla.edu/workshops/papers/IO/CelebrityEndorsements.pdf accessed 2 March 2012.

Curtin, P. and T.K. Gaither (2005). 'Privileging identity, difference and power: the circuit of culture as a basis for public relations theory'. *Journal of Public Relations Research* **17**(2): 91–115.

Curtin, P. and T.K. Gaither (2007). *International Public Relations: Negotiating culture, identity and power*. Thousand Oaks, CA: Sage.

Edwards, L. and E.M. Hodges (2011). *Public Relations, Society and Culture*. Oxford: Routledge.

Epstein, J. (2005). 'The culture of celebrity: let us now praise famous airheads'. *The Weekly Standard* **11**(5): 1–3. www.weeklystandard.com/Content/Public/Articles/000/000/006/187rmfyj.asp accessed 9 September 2012.

Ewans, A. and G.D. Wilson (1999). *Fame: The psychology of stardom*. London: Vision.

Ewen, S. (1996). *PR! A Social History of Spin*. New York, NY: Basic Books.

Festinger, L. (1957). *The Theory of Cognitive Dissonance*. New York, NY: Harper Row.

Gamson, J. (1994). *Claims to Fame: Celebrity in contemporary America*. Los Angeles, CA: University of California Press.

Giles, D.C. (2000). *Illusions of Immortality: A psychology of fame and celebrity*. Basingstoke: MacMillan.

Halpern, J. (2007). *Fame Junkies: The hidden truth behind America's favourite addiction*. New York, NY: Houghton Mifflin.

Inglis, F. (2009). *A Short History of Celebrity*. Princeton, NJ: Princeton University Press.

Leicester, J. (2008). 'China's new celebrity culture'. www.usatoday.com/news/world/2008-06-08-435069282_x.htm accessed 6 August 2008.

L'Etang, J. (2008). *Public Relations Concepts, Practice and Critique*. London: Sage.

Lu, X.P. (2008). *Elite China Luxury Consumer Behavior in China*. Singapore: John Wiley & Sons (Asia).

Mahaban-Bansal, N. (2008). 'Does celeb ad blitz really push up sales?' http://articles.timesofindia.indiatimes.com/2008-03-28/india-business/27755211_1_celebrity-endorsements-soap-brand-small-towns accessed 7 November 2012.

Marhsall, P. (1997). *Understanding Celebrity*. London: Sage.

Marshall, P. (2006). *The Celebrity Culture Reader*. Oxford: Routledge.

Miller, S. (2011). 'The Leveson Inquiry. Witness statement of Sienna Miller'. www.levesoninquiry.org.uk/wp-content/uploads/2011/11/Witness-Statement-of-Sienna-Miller.pdf accessed 7 November 2012.

Milner, M. (2005). 'Celebrity culture as a status system'. *The Hedgehog Review: Critical Reflections on Contemporary Culture* 7(1): 66–77.

Nalapat, A. and A. Parker (2005). 'Sport, celebrity and popular culture: Sachin Tendulker, cricket and Indian nationalisms'. *International Review for the Sociology of Sport* **40**(4): 433–446.

Nessmann, K. (2008). 'Personal communication management; how to position people effectively'. Paper presented at EUPRERA 2008 congress, 'Growing PR: Institutionalizing Public Relations and Corporate Communications', 16–18 October, Milan, Italy.

Plafker, T, (2008). 'There is another boom in China: culture of celebrity grows apace'. www.nytimes.com/2008/06/27/world/asia/27iht-rchinceleb.2.14041563.html?pagewanted=2 accessed 27 June 2008.

Rein, I., P. Kotler, M. Hasskin and M. Stoller (2006). *High Visibility: Transforming your personal and professional brand*, 3rd edition. New York, NY: McGraw-Hill.

Rojek, C. (2001). *Celebrity*. London: Reakton.

Schickel, R. (2000). *Intimate Strangers: The culture of celebrity in America*. Chicago, IL: Ivan R. Dee.

Stephenson, P. (2012). 'The Fame Report'. A redstripe production for Channel Four, aired 17 April 2012.

Turner, G. (2004). *Understanding Celebrity*. London: Sage.

Warhol, A. (1975). *The Philosophy of Andy Warhol: From a-b and back again*. New York, NY: Harcourt Brace & Jovanovich.

Wernick, A. (1991). *Promotional Culture: Advertising, ideology and symbolic expression*. London: Sage.

Wilson, C. (2001). *A Massive Swelling: Celebrity re-examined as a grotesque crippling disease and other cultural revelations*. London: Penguin Group.

Websites

The Fame Report: http://www.channel4.com/programmes/pamela-stephenson-the-fame-report/episode-guide/series-1/episode-1

CHAPTER 29

Ralph Tench and Liz Yeomans

What next? Future issues for public relations

Learning outcomes

By the end of this chapter you should be able to:

■ discuss some of the key themes emerging from the book
■ consider trends in public relations theory and practice
■ identify possible areas for research and further study.

Structure

■ Campaigning and pressure groups
■ Internationalisation of public relations
■ Publics
■ Public relations' identity
■ Issues
■ Technology
■ Practitioner roles and professionalism in public relations
■ Specialisation of public relations practice
■ Media fragmentation
■ Education
■ Future trends and issues for public relations

Introduction

As we write this chapter we are conscious of setting ourselves the most difficult, if not impossible, brief (challenge) – predicting the future for the practice. What next for public relations? Well, one thing is certain – how we look and operate as a 'community of practitioners' (Tywoniak 2007) today will not be the same as tomorrow. The sector, and indeed society, is transforming at a rapid rate (Institute for the Future 2011). As academics, students and practitioners we can only observe, monitor, measure and reflect on these changes to endeavour to improve the role and function of public relations in a modern society. This chapter provides a summary of what we believe are some of the key themes and trends for public relations research and practice that emerge both from the content of this book and contemporary research among practitioners in Europe (European Communication Monitor 2007–2013; ECOPSI 2013).

These themes and trends are by no means comprehensive, nor are they isolated; they are linked because they reflect the wider issues in the social, political, economic and technological environment. The purpose of identifying these themes is to pose questions for further class discussion and initial bases of investigation for students planning a dissertation or thesis.

Campaigning and pressure groups

Nearly one-fifth of the world's 37,000 non-governmental organisations (NGOs) were formed in the 1990s (McGann and Johnston 2006). The activities of NGOs as campaigning and pressure groups are on the increase in the developed world in response to a wide range of global issues concerned with the effects of human consumption and resources: the food we eat; the energy we use; the environment we inhabit and the ways in which resources are distributed among nations and societies; as well as the ways in which human rights are dealt with. Many of these issues are coming to prominence via technology, notably through the widespread use of social media by citizens and consumers, global news channels providing 24/7 news and the interaction between these elements to galvanise public opinion and present challenges for governments and corporations alike. The future is likely to see a further rise in NGOs as their ability to act swiftly and mobilise public support contrasts markedly with the apparent slow-moving forces of government and corporations. (See Think about 29.1.)

Think about 29.1

Campaigning organisations and pressure groups

1. Why is 'public relations' more often associated with governments and corporations, whereas pressure groups 'campaign'? Are there any real differences in approaches, strategies and tactics, from what you have learned? Think about this question from the point of view of (a) a large corporation that you are familiar with and (b) a large campaigning organisation that you support.

2. Is it possible to be both passionate about a cause and a public relations professional?

3. In demonstrating their commitment to social responsibility, should public relations agencies be required to work pro bono (literally 'for the good', involving little or no fee) for a campaigning organisation or pressure group?

Internationalisation of public relations

Public relations has become a global phenomenon. Business is increasingly globalised, markets are more and more interlinked and so are the communications issues for companies, organisations and governments. No organisation operating across international borders can function effectively without knowledge of other cultures, media systems and communication practices. While international public relations may be more readily associated with multinational corporations (MNCs), such as Microsoft, Philips or Tesco, it is not just a concern for commercial organisations operating in global markets. In attempts to encourage positive worldwide opinion to support favourable trading conditions, economic investment and tourism, public relations techniques are adopted by organisations of all kinds including 'unpopular' political regimes and previously unknown nations.

Public relations has made the first steps towards professionalisation on a global scale, although it is likely to take many more years to achieve a globally recognised status. Evidence of global growth in public relations is regularly reported, with emerging economies demonstrating the fastest growth in public relations. Recognition and appreciation of cultural diversity is the next step and this will need to become part of both practice and theory development. As discussed earlier, we live in a multicultural world and public relations practitioners are in the business of intercultural mediation. Wherever we live, we are exposed to other cultures. Public relations, if interpreted as the management of communication and relationships, is directly concerned with the management of cultural differences. It is in this way that Dejan Verčič's chapter argues for the potential for public relations practitioners to act and perform like 'intercultural interpreters'.

As well as practitioner associations, organisations, networks and meeting groups have formed in national and international contexts over the past few years to support in principle the ongoing development of public relations (EUPRERA, the Global Alliance, the World Public Relations Forum, AMEC, etc.). These organisations take up the campaigning cause of issues of relevance and importance for the practice. For example, the Second World Public Relations Festival in 2005 chose 'diversity' as its main theme, adopting a manifesto about how organisations should strive to communicate 'for diversity, with diversity and in diversity' (World Public Relations Forum 2005). In the future, the public relations industry will need to demonstrate its own commitment to diversity in a more dynamic and effective way. (See Think about 29.2.)

Think about 29.2

Internationalisation of public relations

1. According to opinion polls, trust in leaders of organisations and politicians appears to be in decline in the developed world. Research among UK communication directors (*PRWeek* 2012) confirms that maintaining public trust is the biggest challenge for corporations. Will the internationalisation of public relations contribute to building trust among a global community?

2. What can the public relations profession do to 'recognise and appreciate' diversity in practice? What will this mean in practical terms?

3. How can the public relations industry demonstrate its own 'social responsibility'? To whom is it responsible?

Another example of coordinated practitioner interest is in the work to build shared understanding about evaluating the impact of public relations. Evaluating the impact and measuring the effect of communications campaigns is one of the hardest parts of explaining and justifying what public relations is and how it can contribute and add value to organisations and society. (see Box 29.1.) The Barcelona

Box 29.1

Do organisational leaders listen to communication advisers?

People look to leaders of all kinds – politicians, leaders of business and leaders of public service organisations – to involve them in decision making, to make the right decisions and to communicate those decisions effectively. In times of difficulty, such as the recent economic crisis in Europe and the US, people expect leaders to take charge and solve problems. However, not only has there been a growing cynicism towards leaders – politicians especially – in their ability to lead effectively, but there is also an expectation that leaders will fail to achieve their goals (Ketchum 2012). A lack of trustworthiness in leaders is

the main issue, a factor that is strongly linked to the way in which leaders both demonstrate and communicate authentic leadership in their actions and words to earn and maintain public trust (Ketchum 2012; *PRWeek* 2012).

However, while communication professionals lay claim to the role of advising organisational leaders on their communication with stakeholders and the general public, research suggests that leaders may be under-utilising professional communications advice. In the 2012 European Communication Monitor survey, more than 80 per cent of practitioners in Europe report top management's lack of understanding of communication practice; furthermore, up to 16 per cent of practitioners' productive time at work may be spent coaching, training and educating members of the organisation or clients (Zerfass et al. 2012). In summary, most practitioners face a continuous challenge in proving the value of communication with organisational leaders, while leaders are under increasing scrutiny from the public to demonstrate their integrity in difficult times.

Principles are a set of guidelines intended to help public relations practitioners to articulate consistently how to measure the impact of PR campaigns. The Principles were developed in 2010 when over 200 communications and measurement specialists from more than 30 countries met in the European city. The Barcelona Principles are described as 'a new declaration of standards and practices to guide measurement and evaluation of public relations'.

The Barcelona Principles have been subsequently debated at follow up conferences and they have received mixed responses, with many practitioners endorsing and supporting them while academics have been more challenging and questioning of the impact and effect they have had, both on practice and on moving the discipline forward. In summary, the Barcelona Principles are not particularly imaginative or innovative but they do provide some simple guidelines and rules for engagement on the much-debated issue of measurement and evaluation. What is positive is that they provide a clear and transparent set of basic standards and best practices. As Paul Noble indicates in his chapter, the Barcelona Principles have also made an impact in helping the practice to move away from the use of advertising value equivalents (AVEs) and also place measurement at the centre of developing a communications strategy.

Publics

The notion of 'a public' is central to public relations, yet there is a growing debate in the literature about the meaning of the term. The term 'public' is commonly used in many academic disciplines and usually refers to everyone in the population (e.g. 'general public'), but the use of 'public' in public relations often refers to carefully defined 'target groups' of the organisation. Public relations theory is criticised for defining publics from the organisation's point of view: that 'publics' exist only because the organisation says so. Critics point out that taking this instrumental view of publics denies publics their self-identity and agency in setting their own objectives. Meanwhile, other academic commentators (e.g., Kruckeberg and Vujnovic 2010) argue that with the rise of unpredictable activist publics on the Internet, greater consideration should be given to 'the general public' when organisations communicate.

Throughout this text, we have seen evidence in practice that 'publics' are asserting more power. Campaigning groups are taking an active interest in organisations and their goals, while other groups such as consumers are consciously turning away from corporate and consumer messages that are not 'tuned in' to their particular interests or

needs. At the same time, public sector organisations are trying to get nearer to publics by stressing concepts of 'choice' in public access to information and services, and participation and involvement in policy decision making. (See Explore 29.1 and Think about 29.3.)

Public relations' identity

Public relations emerged during the last half of the twentieth century. It is, therefore, a relatively new phenomenon as both a management function and as an academic discipline. The identity problem starts with the term 'public relations': this in itself is regarded as an Anglo-American construct and direct translations into other languages cannot always be found. Elsewhere, as in the case of Europe, 'communication management' is a preferred term. Definitions of public relations – its role and purpose – is a further area of debate: there is no agreed definition, although preferred definitions abound.

Public relations (as evidenced in the scope of this text) lays claims to a wide range of activities – from lobbying to sponsorship – yet those involved in these somewhat

Explore 29.1

How publics are viewed

Compare three retail organisations' annual reports (by downloading from their websites) and examine the language that is used to discuss consumers, employees or other publics such as the local community. Note the variation in the terms used and their connotations. Consider how each organisation views its publics. Which organisation appears to consider its publics as powerful and active? What theories can you use to explain the different approaches?

Think about 29.3

Publics

1. Referring to theoretical discussions, what is 'a public'? Is it simply a defined target group of an organisation? Or does 'a public' have its own identity?

2. How will the development of the Internet influence the concept of 'a public'?

Think about 29.4

Future identity of public relations

1. Why does identity matter? Does it matter that public relations is defined in different ways (e.g., 'relationship management' or 'reputation management'), given other labels such as 'corporate communication' and may denote varying activities across organisations?

   ■ Consider the arguments for and against public relations as an academic discipline – are the available theories adequate in defining the field?

   ■ Consider the arguments for and against public relations as a discrete management function – can it be differentiated from other functions?

2. Looking at the arguments in this text concerning the identity and reputation of the profession, will 'public relations' be a commonly used term in ten or even five years' time?

3. Is the specialisation of public relations practice a safeguard for professional identity, or merely further evidence that public relations cannot easily be defined?

Think about 29.5

Issue management

1. What global issues are likely to become prominent over the next five years?

2. As the opportunities for people to access information increase (e.g., through freedom of information legislation, databases and discussion forums on the Internet), what type of skills should a public relations practitioner develop?

3. Is it possible to 'manage' a whole range of issues for a large organisation? Drawing on theory and practice, how should issue management be organised in the future?

disparate areas may not describe themselves as public relations practitioners at all. And when we consult the international literature, 'public relations' is a term used to denote other activities, including 'guest relations' and interpersonal contact (as in China).

Without a clear identity, the practice has been subject to encroachment from marketing, human resources, management consultancy and (as in the USA) the legal profession. Having discussed the problems of a lack of identity for public relations, the growth in the number of public relations qualifications means that academics will continue their attempts to define the field and professional bodies will continue to pursue their goals of professional recognition. (See Think about 29.4.)

Issues

As we have already seen in this text, issues arising from the social, political, technological and economic environments have increasingly become a concern for governments and organisations, due to the wider availability of information on the Internet and the number of activist groups that are

prepared to protest about the perceived risks arising from the issue, either vocally or through direct action. Furthermore, issues are global, fast-moving and potentially hard-hitting as the 'euro-zone' currency crisis that emerged in 2010 has demonstrated. Financial austerity measures adopted by economies in the European Union to tackle rising government debts have adversely affected economies, both within the EU and outside it.

Issues affect all organisations, not just big governments and multinational organisations. In a risk-averse society, the linked issues of obesity and the fat content of food can affect the stakeholder relationships of a small business processing food products or a school catering service – unless either organisation takes action to manage the issue and reduce the perceived risk to consumers. (See Think about 29.5.)

Technology

For public relations practice the impact of technology focuses on information and communication technologies (ICT). Technology has transformed the way we communicate in recent years and this has had specific effects on the practice of public relations.

Since 2009, when the last edition of this text was published, the growth in popularity of social media has presented new challenges and opportunities for PR practitioners. As discussed in many of the chapters in the current edition, social media use by citizens and consumers not only has implications for the current and future knowledge and skills of PR but also implications for the PR-communication model within an interactive, online environment.

'Digital' PR firms specialising in online communication have gained competitive advantage in the short term but mainstream PR firms and in-house practitioners are incorporating (if somewhat cautiously) the rapidly-evolving social media network tools into their communication strategies. However, while some digital PR experts encourage practitioners to embrace the challenges of Web 3.0 – 'the semantic network' (e.g., Sheldrake 2012), other commentators worry about online security and risk, and the lack of industry standards and codes of conduct (e.g., Morris and Goldsworthy 2012). These areas, no doubt, will be the subjects of further debate as much as the opportunities provided by technological innovation.

Meanwhile, companies such as Microsoft and Apple permeate nearly every country of the world through product dissemination. However, there are common assumptions about technology's spread and people's access to it that can lead to what is called the 'digital divide'. This is the exclusion of certain social and demographic groupings from technology's reach – in some developing countries this is the majority of the population. Therefore it is important to recognise that some publics may not share the somewhat privileged technological perspective of the professional communicator. This is one of many future issues that students, academics and practitioners of public relations should be aware of and manage. (See Think about 29.6.)

Practitioner roles and professionalism in public relations

Public relations practitioners are quite rightly subject to frequent public scrutiny. As this book has demonstrated, the role has a wide range of activities and influences in contemporary society. To demonstrate this, consider just the chapter headings in the contents – the specialist areas such as media relations, internal communication, financial public relations, issue management and public affairs.

Discussion within this book has also been about the social responsibilities of organisations in society (Chapters 4 and 15), as well as the behaviour of the practitioners themselves. Debates, for example, surround the description of public relations practitioners as 'ethical guardians'. As with journalism, there is a major debate evolving about the ethics of the discipline as well as the behaviour of its practitioners, including maintaining good behaviour online – an issue highlighted in Neil Washbourne's and Jo Fawkes' chapters (3 and 12). The text cites examples of good and bad ethical practice at both corporate and individual level. As students and academics we need to maintain these debates and this focus on what is a complex and challenging area. (See Think about 29.7.)

Think about 29.6

Technology's future impact on public relations

1. Consider the theoretical and practical implications of the digital divide on public relations in your own country. Are some social groups effectively excluded from important debates affecting their lives as a result of limited access to technology?

2. Technology is increasingly being used in the political electoral process around the world. What effect will these types of intervention have on the future of political communications?

3. What are some of the ethical considerations communications specialists should make with regard to technology and public relations? What should a social media code of conduct include?

Think about 29.7

Role of the public relations practitioner

1. What is a public relations practitioner? This straightforward question is still not simply answered. More work is required to explain the role, its origins and definition.

2. What is a profession? This is an old sociological debate and one that now includes analysis of public relations practice. Some work has been done but more is required.

3. Why is relatively little known about the position of ethnic minorities within the public relations profession? An ESRC-funded project in the UK reported on the experiences of black minority ethnic practitioners, but more work is needed.

Box 29.2

Communication management – current trends and issues

The ECOPSI EU-funded research project (Tench et al. 2013a, b and c)

It's a common cliché that once learnt you never forget how to ride a bike. Learning to do so is a combination of skills and knowledge that enable most of us to safely and competently navigate the streets from childhood to old age. Therefore 'competence' is a word we use frequently to describe our abilities to do a variety of tasks, from day-to-day activities such as driving a car to technical sports pursuits such as sailing or skiing – but what does competence mean when we talk about our professional capabilities? Is it simply a case of once learnt we never forget and don't need to work to maintain and develop the competence? Much is written about competencies for different disciplines and fields, particularly psychology and human resource management. But this debate is also highly relevant for the communications industry(ies) as we try to maintain our grip on what it is we do in an ever-changing world, but also keep on top of the training and development needs and provision to support the practice.

Similar questions have been raised by professional associations in the USA (PRSA), as well as in the Netherlands through Logeion (2012), and have involved recent published reports. Among academics – again working with practitioners – there is some interesting work in New Zealand by Jeffrey and Brunton (2011) from Massey University into competencies. In addition there's the ongoing longitudinal European Communication Monitor (Zerfass et al. 2008, 2009, 2010, 2011, 2012), which has this year focused a significant proportion of its data collection on the skills, training and development needs of practitioners.

It is in this context that a team of European academics have been working on what is possibly the largest EU-funded public relations/communications sponsored research project to date. This is the ECOPSI (European Communication Skills and Innovation Programme www. ecopsi.org.uk) – a project that is based on the foundation work of the European Communication Monitor. Its principal focus is on developing the current understanding and future skills and competence needs of communication practitioners across Europe. The aim is to influence both theory and practice with this project by building

knowledge, understanding and practical outputs that will support entrants and established practitioners in understanding their skills and competences, as well as opportunities for development. As such the focus is clear:

- Understanding the practice
- Understanding the skills and competence needs (for today and the future)
- Supporting the European community in diagnosing and providing potential direction for access to training and development
- Disseminating and ensuring open access (networks and online portals) to skills development resource(s).

The ECOPSI project is, therefore, interested in the professional skills and competencies of communication practitioners in Europe. The programme aims to map and understand these capabilities in order to support the professional development of the community going forward. The initial desk research and data collection from the project reaffirmed that communications roles are complex and potentially diverse across Europe. The project also suggests that, unlike learning to ride a bike, being a competent practitioner does require ongoing training and development to ensure practitioners don't lose their skills or those skills lose their relevance in a modern, changing society.

Picture 29.1 It's a common cliché that once learnt you never forget how to ride a bike. Is this the same for learning the skills and knowledge to be a competent public relations practitioner? (Tench et al. 2013c). (*source*: Steven May Alamy Images)

Think about 29.8

Future of specialisms in public relations

Will specialist practice areas evolve to such a degree that they no longer form the underpinning of the practice? In other words, will they live as separate or distinct disciplines with different labels and terms of reference?

Feedback

Consider the social media manager. Is this a role for the future? Will it exist or will the role, activities and expectations of the social media manager be subsumed within the job description for PR managers?

Think about 29.9

The media landscape over the next few years

As the media outlets change and diversify, can practitioners maintain their commitment to keeping all stakeholders informed?

Specialisation of public relations practice

Public relations is big. This text reflects this blunt statement. The range of subjects covered, the disciplines that feed into the literature and the named practices are diverse and include: politics, psychology, philosophy, management theory, communications, cultural theory, sociology, strategy and, of course, public relations itself. If you also review what people do, whether by looking at job adverts or the activities of consultants, it is similarly diverse. Part 3 of the book provides discussions of the theory and practice of some of these specialist areas of practice. Within some of these areas practitioners are engaged in nothing else but working in that defined area. In others, the specialist skills may form a large but not an exclusive component of the practitioners' day-to-day life. So where are these specialisms going? Will they continue to refine, getting ever more focused in what they do with dedicated knowledge and underpinning, which require specific vocational and academic training?

Media fragmentation

The media have been viewed as a powerful force in society for over a century. Their role in society, politics, business and even armed conflict has been acknowledged and frequently subject to in-depth research. The academic interest has focused on behavioural influences, whether these be encouraging us to vote in a particular way, buy specific products or to internalise the views and opinions of political leaders and institutions.

In this text we have also explored how the media landscape has evolved with the globalisation of media ownership, including the recent controversy concerning the failed takeover of British Sky Broadcasting (BSkyB) by Rupert Murdoch's News Corporation. Further developments include the continued introduction of new media formats and technological developments and changes in audience loyalties linked to this evolution (such as more choice for the receiver). (See Think about 29.9.)

Education

It would be surprising in an academic text if education were not raised as a core future concern. However, for public relations this is particularly true. As discussed earlier, education in public relations is still relatively young. Research in the USA (PRSA 1999, 2006) and the UK (Tench and Fawkes 2005) demonstrates that education in the discipline is still evolving. The body of knowledge is increasingly being defined and clarified but this work is not yet complete. Tench and Deflagbe (2008) argue that public relations (PR) education is responding to the challenges of the globalisation of communication and economies – but slowly and unevenly. They identify that problems defining the field are multiplied when the different cultural perspectives on public relations itself come into play. Even within Europe the term has varying connotations, reflecting cultural associations with 'the public sphere'. Several scholars express concern that the lack of a central concept for PR is weakening its hold in the marketplace. These debates in the literature reflect tensions between academics and between academics and practitioners, and illustrate some of the problems facing the project of a global curriculum (see earlier for a discussion on the role of the practitioner and the intercultural and multicultural issues for public relations).

Consideration should be given to who is coming into the practice and, specifically, on new entrants' demographics. For instance, are they male or female, where are they from, what age do they enter, what social and educational backgrounds do they come from and what skills do they enter with?

Role of education in influencing the future of public relations practice

1. Consider the arguments for and against a future profession that is wholly defined by entry qualifications.

2. Will a more educated profession (i.e., in terms of public relations knowledge) ensure more ethical practice?

3. Should public relations research and education only focus on improving the practice?

Debates continue about the skills required for public relations and whether they are – or should be – intellectual, practical or personal. Is public relations education about training technicians or strategic thinkers? These are important and challenging issues for students to research and explore. (See Think about 29.10.)

Future trends and issues for public relations

Firstly let's look at the findings from the largest transnational study of communication management, the European Communication Monitor. (see Box 29.3.) This research was initiated in 2007 and has been conducted on an annual basis since then. It is intended to be an annual snapshot of communication management in Europe (see www.communicationmonitor.eu).

The European Communication Monitor 2007–2015

Background of the survey

The annual European Communication Monitor (Zerfass et al. 2008–2012) is the most comprehensive empirical survey of communication management worldwide, with 2,185 participating professionals from 42 countries in 2012. The research is conducted by a group of professors from 11 universities across Europe within the framework of the European Public Relations Education and Research Association (EUPRERA). Partners include the European Association of Communication Directors (EACD) and *Communication Director Magazine*, as well as Ketchum Pleon – a leading European public relations agency that is sponsoring the project from this year onwards. The questionnaire used for the survey covered 19 sections and 30 questions, based on a research model that has been revised and expanded from the previous editions. In order to fulfil the highest empirical standards, only 2,185 fully completed replies (of 4,107 responses) by participants who were identified as part of the profession were evaluated and analysed using SPSS and a variety of statistical tests, such as Pearson's chi-square, Spearman's and Kendall's rank correlation, ANOVA/Scheffé post-hoc and T-tests.

A look at the demographics shows that 71.7 per cent of the respondents work on the first or second level of the communication hierarchy as heads of communication, unit leaders or agency CEOs. The average age is 41.5 years and nearly 68 per cent have worked in communications for more than ten years. Based on this, it can be claimed that the results are founded on statements of those who take responsibility for the profession today and who will shape its future in Europe. The distribution of gender (57.6 per cent female, 42.4 per cent male) and the regions (29.6 per cent Northern Europe, 30.5 per cent Western Europe, 10.7 per cent Eastern Europe, 29.2 per cent Southern Europe) reflects the diversity of the profession. Once again, the survey shows that several countries and types of organisations follow different paths of development. While this article reports on the overall trends, detailed analyses for various groups can be found in the full report, available at www.communicationmonitor.eu.

Overview of findings 2012

According to the 2012 findings, the practice of professional communication is marked by contradictions. For example, shaping the same and consistent image for all stakeholders, a core idea of integrated communications, is less popular than the concept of 'polyphony', meaning a simultaneous and sequential stimulation of several perceptions to address different stakeholders. Mobile applications on the social web are seen as important tools, but there are large gaps between their perceived importance and real implementation in most European organisations. Ethical challenges are more prevalent

box 29.3 (continued)

than ever in the field, but current codes of ethics are seldom used, and rated as outdated by many professionals. And there is still a large gap between the skills and knowledge that need to be developed and the training offered by employers.

So what does this mean for communication practitioners, potential recruits to the industry and students studying the discipline? Based on a deep analysis of the data, the researchers have identified five key insights that might stimulate the ongoing debate about strategies to advance communication's influence and power in organisations in the coming years.

Multiple images

The complexity of communication is increasing. Organisations are interacting with more stakeholders through more media in more directions. Of the respondents, 82 per cent say that their organisation, compared to five years ago, has more 'touchpoints' with its publics. According to comparative data from the GAP VII study, conducted by the Annenberg School of Communication (Swerling et al. 2012), the situation is even more extreme in the United States: the figure there is almost 93 per cent. Three out of four European communication professionals agree that the corporate or organisational voice is created by all organisational members interacting with stakeholders. So it is not surprising that the idea of shaping a consistent image for all stakeholders is supported by fewer respondents than the alternative concept of polyphony (Christensen and Cornelissen 2011), meaning that several perceptions are stimulated simultaneously and sequentially in different stakeholder relationships. This approach challenges traditional concepts of integrated communications. It asks for new strategies to create flexible identities with a common core and overlapping, ambiguous domains. Clearly, today's methods of reputation measurement, which champion solid images and can seldom deal with shades of reality construction, are not equipped to cope with this development. The tools need to be redesigned to fit the new paradigm of liquid realities.

Proving value

Data from different sections of the monitor can be combined to identify the key challenges for communication professionals in Europe in these times of turbulence. It is all about understanding business needs, implementing strategic orientation and proving efficiency and effectiveness of communication activities. On the level of organisations and their attitude towards communication, a lack of understanding of communication practice within the top management (reported by 84 per cent of respondents) and difficulties of the profession itself to prove the impact of communication activities on organ-

Picture 29.2 The European Communication Monitor reveals a large gap between the perceived importance of social media tools for communication and the actual rate of implementation in European organisations (*source*: Iain Masterton/Alamy Images)

isational goals (75 per cent) are the main barriers for further professionalisation. On the functional level (i.e., within the realm of communication departments), linkages between business strategy and communication as well as a better support of top-management decision making are identified as major issues that have not been resolved until now. On the individual level, practitioners report that their competencies in need of further development are mainly management skills and management knowledge (46 and 42 per cent, respectively) as well as business knowledge and business skills (39 and 33 per cent). Combining these insights, a clear picture emerges: communication professionals should strive to make communication a business partner, helping others in the organisation and top management to reach their goals. This requires more competencies in fields that are – as other results of the survey show – seldom part of the training offered by organisations nowadays. While there is a plethora of training in communication skills (more than

box 29.3 (continued)

actually needed, according to the respondents), a large gap between needs and offerings exists in the areas of developing management knowledge (current affairs, societal and political trends, legal, ethical) as well as in business knowledge (markets, products, competitors) and management skills (decision making, planning, leading, etc.).

Going mobile

The monitor reveals a large gap between the perceived importance of social media tools for communication and the actual rate of implementation in European organisations. Most obviously, mobile applications have entered the top three ranks of important social media platforms, but at the same time the backlog of implementation is higher than in any other field. Online communities or social networks are considered by far the most important social media tool available. With more than 75 per cent support by respondents, they are leading the list of important social media tools, followed by online videos (67 per cent), mobile applications such as

apps and mobile webs (65 per cent), micro blogs such as Twitter (56 per cent) and weblogs (45 per cent). However, less than 56 per cent of the communication departments actually use online communities in their communication – a gap of more than 20 per cent compared to the importance this tool is given by practitioners. The biggest difference between importance (65 per cent) and implementation (31 per cent) is found for mobile applications – a gap of almost 35 points.

A cross-matrix analysis shows that mobile applications, weblogs and photo sharing are considered the most important opportunities in social media communication (see Figure 29.1). All communication managers report rather moderate skills for using digital technologies for internal and external communication, regardless of their gender. Despite this, only every second respondent thinks that training is useful. Informal approaches to enhance those skills are clearly favoured. Eight out of ten European professionals think that the best way to learn

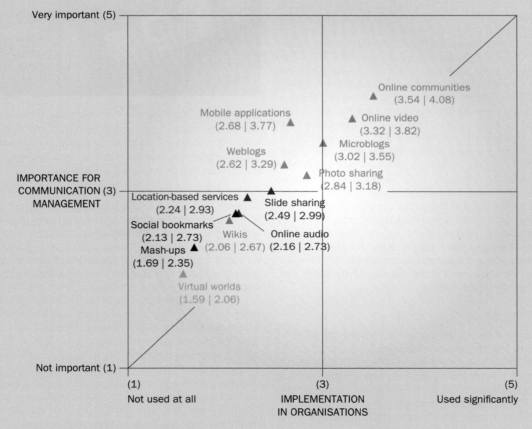

n = 1,925 communication professionals

Figure 29.1 Importance and implementation of social media tools (*source*: Zerfass et al. (2012). European Communication Monitor 2012. Challenges and Competencies for Strategic Communication. Results of an Empirical Survey in 42 Countries. Brussels: EACD/EUPRERA, p. 66)

box 29.3 (continued)

about online tools is to use them as part of the regular work, as well as privately. Although social media has been much discussed in the profession for many years, by now only two channels (online communities and online videos) are rated as very important, or at least as important, by a majority of the respondents. This shows that there is still a long way to go. Evaluating the potential of social media and investing in platforms and digital competencies stay at the top of the agenda for communication professionals.

More reflection

Changes in the environment are requiring communication professionals in Europe to reconceptualise and reorganise what they do. Although the majority of productive time still goes to operational communication (talking to colleagues and media, writing texts, monitoring, organising events, etc.) this does not account for more than 37 per cent of a typical week (see Figure 29.2). Managing activities related to planning, organising, leading staff, evaluating strategies, justifying spending and preparing for crises takes 29 per cent of the time. Reflective communication management, aligning communication, the organisation/client and its stakeholders, takes 19 per cent and coaching, training and educating members of the organisation or a client takes almost 15 per cent. As expected, there are significant correlations with the position of a communicator in the organisational hierarchy, with the influence of the communication function (having more influence on top management correlates with more reflection and less operations) and with sectors – all businesses (private companies, joint stock companies and consultancies) allow for more reflexive management than non-profit and governmental organisations.

Media relations professionals perform the largest portion of operational work, while practitioners engaged in governmental relations, public affairs and lobbying spend more time on reflective activities. Results from the European Communication Monitor 2012 prove for the first time what has been elaborated in theory before (van Ruler and Verčič 2005): communication managers should not only communicate on their own, but strive to enable others in the organisation to communicate and build an architecture of listening that will contribute to the alignment of an organisation's mission and the expectations of stakeholders. In a nutshell, this means that communicators should increasingly look to stop communicating themselves and start enabling others to do so.

Ethical challenges

Six out of ten communication professionals in Europe report that they have encountered ethical challenges within the last 12 months – i.e. situations in which activities might be legally acceptable, but problematic from a moral point of view (see Figure 29.3). One third of the respondents have actually experienced several of those challenges. Professionals working in governmental relations, lobbying, public affairs and in online communication and social media are more exposed than colleagues working in other areas. The survey shows that ethical issues are much more relevant than five years ago, driven by compliance and transparency rules, the increase in social media and – to a lesser extent – by the international character of communication today. Despite these challenges, the majority of European communication practitioners has never used a professional code of ethics such as the Code of Athens to solve moral problems. Only a minority of 29 per cent has ever applied

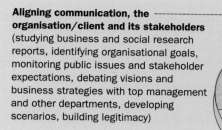

Aligning communication, the organisation/client and its stakeholders (studying business and social research reports, identifying organisational goals, monitoring public issues and stakeholder expectations, debating visions and business strategies with top management and other departments, developing scenarios, building legitimacy)

Coaching, training and educating members of the organisation or clients (on the vision, mission and other communication related issues as well as upgrading their communicative competence, preparing them for communicating with the media, stakeholders etc.)

Operational communication (talking to colleagues and journalists, writing press releases and print/online texts, producing communication media, monitoring results of activities, organising events etc.)

Managing communication activities and co-workers (planning, organising, leading staff, budgeting, evaluating processes and strategies, justifying communication spending, preparing for crises)

37.0% 19.3% 14.7% 29.0%

n = 2,185 communication professionals; figures display median for each item

Figure 29.2 How communication managers spend their productive time at work (*source*: Zerfass et al. (2012). European Communication Monitor 2012. Challenges and Competencies for Strategic Communication. Results of an Empirical Survey in 42 Countries. Brussels: EACD/EUPRERA, p. 46)

box 29.3 (continued)

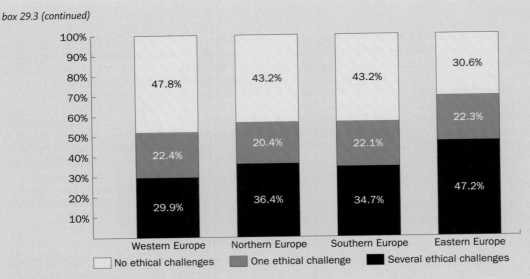

n = 2,137 communication professionals in 43 countries

Figure 29.3 Ethical challenges experienced within the last 12 months (*source*: Zerfass et al. (2012). European Communication Monitor 2012. Challenges and Competencies for Strategic Communication. Results of an Empirical Survey in 42 Countries. Brussels: EACD/EUPRERA, p. 22)

such a code. While 32 per cent of the respondents think that current codes of ethics are outdated, an overwhelming majority (93 per cent) find that the communication profession needs such rules. According to the monitor, professional associations on the national or international level are most eligible to provide such a code. This can be interpreted as a call for action to provide up-to-date guidelines made to fit the digital age in Europe. Obviously, this is not only a question of moral reasoning and norms, but also of institutions and processes that have to be installed to make such codes vivid and sustainable.

Perspectives

In times of economic uncertainty and ever more fragmented publics, communication professionals face hard times. Growing demands from partners within the organisation and external stakeholders have to be dealt with. However, resources are limited and new options do not mean that established ones are not needed any more. In order to deal with these issues, traditional modes of benchmarking and gradual adjustment might not now be sufficient. New rules of the game ask for new structures, strategies and tactics, as well as for courage to guide the change. This can be high-risk, but it is also the path to a more advanced vision for the profession and those who lead it.

Summary of key findings from the ECM 2012

There are a number of interesting findings from this survey that are relevant to students and practitioners. For example:

■ Traditional approaches to integrated communications are challenged by the concept of 'polyphony', which recognises that communication can not be controlled and every member of the organisation contributes to shaping communicative identities.

■ Ethical challenges are more prevalent than ever in communication management. While today's codes of conduct are obviously not viable any more, most practitioners are striving for new guidelines that help to do business in an effective and acceptable way.

■ Professional development and training needs more attention. There are large gaps between current development needs of communication professionals and training opportunities offered by organisations. However, when recruiting young professionals most organisations rely on university level education in communication management.

■ A new vision for the communication function emerges. Instead of thinking of themselves as professional communicators, i.e., those who publish and explain what others have decided, communicators may try to fulfil the roles of enablers and consultants – i.e., those who are experts in public opinion, understanding media channels and content production while working in a communicative organisation where everybody is a spokesperson and speaks out.

(*source*: Zerfass et al. (2012). European Communication Monitor 2012. Challenges and Competencies for Strategic Communication. Results of an Empirical Survey in 42 Countries. Brussels: EACD/EUPRERA, p. 66)

Summary

This chapter provides a summary of what we believe are some of the key themes and trends for PR research and practice. These themes and trends emerge from the content of this text and the evolving world of communications and PR practice, which it attempts to understand. These themes and trends are by no means comprehensive, nor are they isolated: they are linked because they reflect the wider issues in the social, political and technological environment that has been discussed. By identifying and highlighting these themes our aim is to pose questions for further class discussion and present initial bases of investigation for students planning a dissertation or thesis. You will and should, however, continue to innovate and look for the gaps in this enquiry that suit you. Use your interests, insights and enthusiasm to choose topics for research and exploration that you will find exciting and hopefully fulfilling, while also contributing to the growing knowledge and understanding of PR and its practice. Good luck.

Bibliography

Bartlett, J., S. Tywoniak and C. Hatcher (2007). 'Public relations professional practice and the institutionalisation of CSR.' *Journal of Communication Management* **11**(4): 281–299.

BVC, Dutch Professional Association for Communication (2002). *Job Profile Descriptions in Communication Management*, 3rd revised edition. The Hague: BVC & VVO.

Christensen, L.T. and J. Cornelissen (2011). 'Bridging corporate and organizational communication: review, development and a look into the future'. *Management Communication Quarterly* **25**: 383–414.

Institute for the Future (2011). 'Future Works Skills 2020'. University of Phoenix Research Institute. http://innovation.itu.int/wp-content/uploads/2012/01/future-work-skills-333x440.jpg accessed 7 October 2012.

Jeffrey, L.M. and M.A. Brunton (2011). 'Developing a framework for communication management competencies'. *Journal of Vocational Education and Training* **63**(1): 57–75.

Ketchum (2012). 'Ketchum Leadership Communication Monitor'. www.ketchum.com/leadership-communication-monitor accessed 4 October 2012.

Kruckeberg, D. and M. Vujnovic (2010). 'The death of the concept of publics (plural) in 21st century public relations'. *International Journal of Strategic Communication* **4**(2): 117–125.

Lewis, J., A. Williams, B. Franklin, J. Thomas and N. Mosdell (2008). 'The quality and independence of British journalism'. Cardiff School of Journalism, Media and Cultural Studies. www.mediastandardstrust.org/resources/mediaresearch/researchdetails.aspx?sid=12914, accessed 12 October 2008.

Logeion (2012). 'Beroepsniveauprofielen' [Job level profiles]. www.logeion.nl/beroepsniveauprofielen

London Stock Exchange (2005). www.londonstockexchange.com

Loomis, B. (2003). 'Doing well, doing good and (shhh!) having fun: a supply-side approach to lobbying'. Paper presented at the American Political Science Association, Philadelphia.

McGann, J. and M. Johnston (2006). 'The power shift and the NGO credibility crisis', *The International Journal of Not-for-Profit Law* **8**(2), www.icnl.org/knowledge/ijnl/vol8iss2/art_4.htm accessed 23 October 2008.

Morris, T. and S. Goldsworthy (2008). *PR – A Persuasive Industry? Spin, public relations and the shaping of the modern media*. Basingstoke: Palgrave Macmillan.

Morris, T. and S. Goldsworthy (2011). *PR Today: The Authoritative Guide to Public Relations*. Palgrave Macmillan.

PRSA (Public Relations Society of America) (1999). (National Commission on Public Relations Education). 'A Port of Entry – Public relations education for the 21st century'. New York: PRSA.

PRSA (Public Relations Society of America) (2006). 'Education for the 21st Century. The Professional Bond'. *Public Relation Education and the Practice*. www.compred.org/report/2006. Report of the Commission edited by J. VanSlyke Turk, November 2006.

PRWeek (2008). 'Global growth patterns'. *PRWeek*: 25 July.

PRWeek (2012). 'Six trends that define 2012 for the comms director'. *PRWeek*: 7 September.

Sha, B-L. (2011). '2010 practice analysis: professional competencies and work categories in public relations today'. *Public Relations Review* **37**(3): 187–196.

Sheldrake, P. (2012). 'Here comes Web 3.0 and the internet of things' in *Share This: The social media handbook for PR professionals*. D. Waddington (ed.). Wiley: Chartered Institute of Public Relations.

Swerling, J., J. Gregory, J. Schuh, T. Goff, J. Gould, X.C. Gu, K. Palmer and A. Mchargue (2008). *Fifth Annual Public Relations Generally Accepted Practices (GAP) Study (GAP V)*. Los Angeles, CA: University of Southern California.

Swerling, J., K. Thorson and B. Tenderich (2012). *GAP VII: Seventh Communication and Public Relations Generally Accepted Practices Study – Full Report*. Los Angeles, CA.

Tench, R. and D. Deflagbe (2008). '*Towards a Global Curriculum: A summary of literature concerning public relations education, professionalism and globalisation*'. Report for the Global Alliance of Public Relations and Communication Management, Leeds Metropolitan University, UK.

Tench, R. and J. Fawkes (2005). 'Mind the gap – exploring attitudes to PR education between academics and employers'. Paper presented at the Alan Rawel Education Public Relations Conference, University of Lincoln.

Tench, R. and H. Juma (2013). 'Do you measure up?'. *Communication Director* **2**: 22–25.

Tench, R., A. Moreno, A. Okay, D. Vercic, P. Verhoeven and A. Zerfass (2013a). ECOPSI (European Communication Practitioner Skills and Innovation programme). www.ecopsi.org.uk

Tench, R., A. Zerfass, P. Verhoeven, A. Moreno, A. Okay and D. Vercic (2013b). ECOPSI Benchmarking Report (Full). May 2013. Leeds, UK: Leeds Metropolitan University.

Tench, R., A. Zerfass, P. Verhoeven, D. Verčič, A. Moreno and A. Okay (2013c). Communication Management Competencies for European Practitioners. (Book). Leeds, UK: Leeds Metropolitan University.

Tywoniak, S. (2007). 'Knowledge in four dimensions'. *Organisation* **14**: 53–76, cited in Bartlett, J., S. Tywoniak and C. Hatcher (2007). 'Public relations professional practice and the institutionalisation of CSR.' *Journal of Communication Management* **11**(4): 281–299.

Van Ruler, B. and D. Verčič (eds) (2004). *Public Relations and Communication management in Europe. A nation-by-nation introduction to public relations theory and practice*. Berlin/New York, NY: Mouton De Gruyter.

Van Ruler, B. and D. Verčič (2005). 'Reflective communication management: future ways for public relations research'. *Communication Yearbook* **29**: 239–273.

Wang, J. (2008). *Corporate Communication Practices and Trends at the Dawn of the New Millennium: A China study 2008*. New York, NY: Baruch College/CUNY.

World Public Relations Forum (2005). www.wprf.org accessed 22 June 2005.

Zerfass, A., A. Moreno, R. Tench, D. Verčič and P. Verhoeven (2008). 'European Communication Monitor 2008. Trends in Communication Management and Public Relations – Results and Implications'. Brussels, Leipzig: EUPRERA/University of Leipzig. Available at: www.communicationmonitor.eu

Zerfass, A., A. Moreno, R. Tench, D. Verčič and P. Verhoeven (2009). 'European Communication Monitor 2009. Trends in Communication Management and Public Relations – Results of a Survey in 34 Countries'. Brussels, Leipzig. EUPRERA/University of Leipzig. Available at: www.communicationmonitor.eu

Zerfass, A., A. Moreno, R. Tench, D. Verčič and P. Verhoeven (2010). 'European Communication Monitor 2010. Status Quo and Challenges for Communication Management in Europe. Results of an Empirical Study in 46 Countries'. Brussels, Leipzig: EUPRERA/University of Leipzig. Available at: www.communicationmonitor.eu

Zerfass, A., P. Verhoeven, R. Tench, A. Moreno and D. Verčič (2011). 'European Communication Monitor 2011. Empirical Insights into Strategic Communication in Europe. Results of an Empirical Survey in 43 Countries'. Brussels, Leipzig: EUPRERA/University of Leipzig. Available at: www.communicationmonitor.eu

Zerfass, A., D. Verčič, P. Verhoeven, A. Moreno and R. Tench (2012). 'European Communication Monitor 2012. Challenges and Competencies for Strategic Communication. Results of an Empirical Survey in 42 Countries'. Brussels, Leipzig: EUPRERA/University of Leipzig. Available at: www.communicationmonitor.eu

Websites

ECOPSI (European Communication Professional Skills and Innovation): www.leedsmet.ac.uk/ecopsi
European Communication Monitor (ECM): www.communicationmonitor.eu
Ketchum: www.ketchum.com

Glossary

9/11 *9/11* has become the worldwide shorthand reflecting the date 11 September 2001, when international terrorists crashed planes into the World Trade Center and the Pentagon in the USA. (Americans write the date month first, day second.)

Advertising A form of promotional activity that uses a totally controllable message to inform and persuade a large number of people with a single communication. The message is invariably paid for.

Advertising value equivalent (AVE) A very crude measure of media relations performance that is still cited and relates to a measurement of the column inches or centimetres devoted to the client or the product, and a calculation of the equivalent cost had that space been paid for as advertising.

Advertorial Bought space in a publication that is used to print an article written in the editorial style of the journal to portray a similar 'feel' of objectivity to the editorial pages.

Agenda setting (by media) Sometimes referred to as 'the ability to tell the public what issues are important', this is a theory developed by McCombs and Shaw (1972) that the media direct public attention to particular issues that fit news priorities and, in doing so, influence public opinion.

Aggregate public A group of individuals who make up an audience for a television programme but who do not necessarily interact and influence each other.

Aggregate view The sum total of individual opinions of the population governed by the democratic state. One example of such an issue is banning smoking in public places. In the UK the views of the majority of the population, tested over time through polls, appeared to be in favour of a ban, and this was ultimately introduced in 2007.

AGM Annual General Meeting.

AIM Alternative and Investment Market.

Alternative target generation Thinking through alternative target audiences.

Attitudes 'When we talk about *attitudes*, we are talking about what a person has learned in the process of becoming a member of a family, a member of a group and of society that makes him react to his social world in a consistent and characteristic way, instead of a transitory and haphazard way. We are talking about the fact that he is no longer neutral in sizing up the world around him: he is attracted or repelled, for or against, favourable or unfavourable' (Sherif 1967: 2).

Axiom A statement, proposition or idea that people accept as self-evidently true, even though the proposition itself may be unproven.

Baseline A starting point from which any changes can be calculated.

Belief Commitment to something, resulting from an intellectual acceptance of its validity.

Benchmark An external or previous reference point that provides a useful comparison.

Bogof An abbreviated term used in sales promotion for selling two products for the price of one: 'buy one, get one free'.

Brainstorming When a group of colleagues get together to discuss an issue and come up with different ideas collectively.

Brand A label that seeks to add perceived value to a consumer product by generating loyalty or preference.

Broadsheets Large-format newspapers, sometimes referred to as 'serious' or 'quality' newspapers.

Business ethics Trevino and Nelson (1995) define this as 'the principles, norms and standards of conduct governing an individual or group'.

Business-to-business (B2B) The sale of a product to a manufacturer, a government body, a retailer, a not-for-profit institution – indeed any organisation or individual – for a purpose other than personal consumption.

Capitalism An economic system based on privately owned businesses producing and distributing goods, the key features of which are a free, competitive market and making a profit from the sale of goods and services.

Categorical imperative   A test that can be applied to see if it conforms to the moral law. If the action could be made into a universal law, which would be regarded as acceptable if applied to everyone faced with the same situation, then it would be regarded as ethical.

CEO   Chief Executive Officer.

CESR   Committee of European Regulators.

Chancellor of the Exchequer   The title held by the British Cabinet minister who is responsible for all economic and financial matters.

Circulation   How many copies of a magazine are distributed.

City (The)   All those stakeholders and publics that make up the financial community. Traditionally in the UK these organisations and individuals were based in the 'City of London' – the historic square mile financial district. In the United States the equivalent would be Wall Street.

Cognitivism   Used by philosophers to define the view that there are actual and objective moral truths and absolutes (that is, we can make firm statements one way or another, about whether something is good or bad, right or wrong).

Collective view   Issues that emerge through rational discussion in the population. One example of such an issue is the general agreement among opinion formers (for example, health professionals) that obesity in young children is caused through poor nutrition and a lack of exercise.

Commercial pluralism   The condition where market and business values, ideas and practices prevail over substantial challenges from non-business or anti-business groups.

Commoditisation   The process whereby a new product or service – for example, a technological device such as the washing machine – becomes an everyday item of purchase.

Communications messages   All those messages sent and received either intentionally or unintentionally that provide information about products, services and organisations. They may result from specific marketing communications activities such as advertising or direct mail or indirectly, for example, as a result of people talking about brands or seeing brands being consumed. Intentionally sent messages will usually be positive and controlled; those resulting from word-of-mouth situations may be critical or negative and uncontrolled.

Communitarianism   A concept defined by Etzioni in his 1995 book that supports building community structures so that people take a shared responsibility for what happens to them. People should take a collective, mutually supportive responsibility for each other through local community institutions.

Company propaganda   A negative term used by some journalists to describe positive statements presented by an organisation about its beliefs and practices.

Concentrated media ownership   Sections of the press, radio and television that are concentrated into a few companies or corporations.

Connotative   All the associations connected with a word (feelings, attitudes) that go beyond the denotative meaning.

Content analysis   A method of quantifying the content of textual material.

Convergence   The process of technologies coming together from different directions. The mobile telephone is the product of the convergence between telecommunications (sending/receiving messages) and computers (processing information). Once in existence, the phone can also be used to combine (converge) further technologies – taking photographs using the mobile phone, for example.

Copy   A term used generically by the communications industries to describe written text for news releases, adverts, advertorials, editorials, articles and in-house newsletter articles, etc.

Corporate culture   An organisation's values and practices that underpin its operations; they can be managed to produce better business outcomes.

Corporate philanthropy   An aspect of corporate citizenship – 'giving something back to the community' by improving quality of life for local communities and for employees.

CPD (continuing professional development)   Acknowledgement in all professions (law, medicine, accountancy, PR, etc.) of the role of continued learning and updating throughout the career.

Cross-cultural communication   Communication between people from different cultures. Intracultural communication is communication between members of the same culture, including racial, ethnic and other co-cultures.

Cub reporter   Junior or trainee reporter/journalist.

Cultural norm   A pattern of behaviour that is considered acceptable and legitimate by members of society.

Culture   The property of a group – a group's shared collective meaning system through which its values, attitudes, beliefs, customs and thoughts are understood. It is a product of the members' social interaction while also determining how group members communicate.

Dearing Report   A report by Sir Ron Dearing, in the UK, into the whole of UK higher education (HE), which came up with specific recommendations for the sector as it moved towards the millennium. Many of his proposals were applauded and adopted by HE institutions.

De-listing When an organisation either withdraws its shares from an exchange and becomes a privately owned company or is removed from an exchange for some form of regulatory reason, it is 'de-listed'.

Demographics External differences between people – for example, race, age, gender, location, occupational status, group membership.

Denotative The dictionary definition of a word that is the specific, generally agreed-on definition.

Direct mail Electronic and posted communications sent to individuals' text phone, email, work and home postal addresses.

Discourse Particular ways of making sense of the world, communicated, sustained and justified through language and social institutions.

Dominant coalition The group of powerful individuals within an organisation who control its direction, determining its mission and goals. It is believed that though the decisions they make are good for the organisation's survival, their primary aim is maintaining the status quo, thereby keeping the existing dominant coalition in control. It is not a term most practitioners would recognise – in practice, terms such as 'board of directors' or 'senior management' would be used, but the inference is the same.

Downsizing The term used to describe the reduction in the number of employees working for an organisation in either full- or part-time positions.

Econometric consultancies Consultancies that specialise in areas including forecasting and effectiveness measurement and that make increasingly significant contributions to marketing communication planning and evaluation as clients seek performance-measurement criteria.

Editorial Written text in a journal, magazine or newspaper that has been written either by a journalist/reporter or submitted by a public relations practitioner and then reviewed/edited before printing by the editor or sub-editor of the publication. An 'editorial' is the opposite of 'advertising', which is bought (paid-for) space in a publication. An editorial is perceived as having greater impact because it is endorsed by the publication.

Elitists Those who argue that real political power is effectively concentrated in the hands of an elite few (perhaps an ethnic group or educated minority or big business), who dominate the decision-making process.

Entrepreneur Someone who looks for opportunities to start new projects, reach new markets, lead in a creative way. Entrepreneurial organisations are often led by a charismatic leader, tend to be authoritarian and proactive, take the initiative and are prepared to take risks.

Ethics Systematic frameworks that codify moral principles. The term may also be used to mean the extension of good management. (See **Morals**; **Values**.)

Exclusives Stories that are made available to one newspaper about issues and people (for example, an interview with Princess Diana's former butler). 'Exclusives' are often supplied by public relations consultancies on behalf of their clients.

Experiential economies A term coined by the authors Pine and Gilmore (1998) that refers to the progression of economic value through experiences.

Financial Regulation of Donations The legal requirement in the UK that any donation over £200 has to be recorded in a company's end-of-year annual report and accounts (the financial statement to shareholders).

Fmcg products Products known as *fmcg* are typically those we buy from supermarkets and convenience stores – branded products from manufacturers such as Heinz, Kellogg's, Procter & Gamble – baked beans, breakfast cereals, shampoos, etc.

Formative evaluation An evaluation that takes place during a public relations programme or campaign. (See **Goal-free evaluation**; **Summative evaluation**).

Free market The idea that businesses – in this case media organisations – operate competitively without government interference to provide a service that the market wants.

Freelancers Journalists who work for themselves, independent of particular media groups. They are self-employed and work on short-term contracts or on a temporary basis for different media employers. They are often given one-off assignments or commissions by media organisations or they might develop a story and take it to the media outlet.

FSA Financial Services Authority.

G8 countries These are Canada, France, Germany, Italy, Japan, Russia, the UK and the USA. Every year, the heads of state or government of these industrial democracies meet to deal with major economic and political issues.

Game theory This theory is based on observations about negotiation and compromise that demonstrate that many conflicts are based on the zero-sum principle, whereby for someone to win, their opponent has to lose. Win–win outcomes are the result of compromise and mutually satisfactory negotiation.

Goal-free evaluation The examination of a programme or campaign after any intervention in terms of the situation and not of existing goals or objectives. (See **Formative evaluation**; **Summative evaluation**.)

Heterophily The difference between speaker and audience.

High footfall retail centre A shopping centre that attracts a large number of passing shoppers.

Homophily The similarity between speaker and audience.

Image transfer potential The ability of consumers to transfer positive feelings experienced at a sports or arts event, for example, to the brand that sponsored that event.

Implementation The phase where a sponsorship plan, for example, becomes a reality and is put into action.

Impressions See **OTS (Opportunities to see)**.

Inclusivity see **Transformational**.

Interactional see **Transformational**.

Intercultural communication Communication between people whose cultural perceptions and symbol systems are distinct enough to alter the communication event.

International communication The cultural, economic, political, social and technical analysis of communication patterns and effects across and between nation-states. It focuses on global aspects of media and communication systems and technologies.

International public relations The planned communication activity of a (multinational) organisation, government or an international institution to create a positive and receptive environment through interactions in the target country, which facilitates the organisation (or government) to achieve its business (or policy) objectives without harming the interests of the host publics.

IPO Initial Placing Offer.

IR Investor relations.

Kiss and tell When someone recounts or goes public through the media about a sexual relationship they have had, usually with a politician, a celebrity or a person in the public eye.

Liberal democracy A political system based on free elections, multiple political parties, political decision making made through an elected government and an independent system of justice that is responsible for law enforcement.

Listed A business whose shares are traded on a stock exchange.

Lobbying The influencing of public policy making through the private means of meeting MPs, ministers, civil servants, councillors or local government officials.

Malevolence The quality or state of being malevolent; malicious behaviour.

Marketing The management process responsible for identifying, anticipating and satisfying customer requirements profitably.

Marketing mix The term used to define the four key elements of an organisation's marketing programme: product, price, place and promotion.

Marketing refusenik The term created to describe consumers who are sceptical about marketing claims and make a conscious effort to ignore mass-message communication.

Marxists *Marxists* accept the analysis of Karl Marx (1818–1883) that political power reflects economic power. Thus the masses cannot have real power when income and wealth are highly concentrated in the hands of the few (for example, in capitalist economies).

Media Any medium interface or channel that allows communications messages to flow between senders and receivers, in both directions.

Media effects The effects that the media has on audiences as a result of the audiences being exposed to the media and its content.

Media neutrality *Media neutrality* advocates a shift away from what might be called 'traditional' forms of media, such as TV for branded goods, towards other media, including direct mail, sponsorship and PR. It also promotes a more even allocation of resources across media channels rather than the domination of one major medium. This allows for wider distribution of communications messages to identified target audiences whose media consumption habits are becoming more fragmented. An important aspect of this process is the growth in online advertising through search engines such as Google and Yahoo, as well as the impact of the so-called social media (for example, MySpace, Facebook and Bebo), both as advertising platforms and community networks generating informal communications, via word of mouth, relating to brands. Campaigns targeted at the so-called 'Facebook generation' of dynamic and young consumers involve the development of interactive audio and video slots and are aimed at 'blogs, mashups, wikis and podcasts'. This kind of new media terminology is rapidly becoming commonplace in the development of integrated marketing communications campaigns.

Media pluralism   *Media pluralism* means that there are differing and independent voices, representing a range of political opinions and cultural standpoints, operating within the media.

Metanarrative   An attempt to make sense of the larger picture, or the wider social environment. Critical theorists and postmodernists suggest organisations and individuals use metanarratives as overarching explanations of the way the world works. They believe reliance on these 'stories' can prevent closer examination of reality.

Metric   A quantitative measure for evaluating public relations programmes.

Mianzi   This refers to face or face work – that is, the process of impression management, or presenting oneself in an advantageous light, in order to expand or enhance human networks.

Modernism   In PR, this means an approach that legitimises the discourse of management and organisations as given and superior. Modernist PR attempts to reduce or eliminate crises, control publics and contribute to organisational effectiveness, and is usually measured in financial terms.

Moral panic   As defined by Cohen (1972), this refers to 'the intensity of feeling expressed by a large number of people about a specific group of people who appear to threaten the social order at a given time'. This occurs when an 'episode, condition, person or group of persons' is 'defined as a threat to societal values and interests' by 'stylized and stereotypical' representation by the media, and condemnation by those 'in power' (for example, politicians and the church).

Morals   Personal values or principles that guide behaviour. (See, **Ethics**; **Values**.)

Muckraking   Unearthing and publicising misconduct by well-known or high-ranking people or organisations.

Multilevel governance   A term that captures the complexity of modern government, which involves many layers or levels. 'Governance' emphasises the process of governing rather than the institutions of government. The term includes all those who contribute to public policy and the delivery of public services.

NAFTA   North American Free Trade Agreement.

Neoliberals   *Neoliberals* believe democracy and free-market capitalism are mutually dependent and that both are threatened by the growth of state intervention and bureaucracy (the rule of public officials in their own interests).

Niche audiences   Groups with shared interests who are traditionally hard to reach. Radio programmes that target Asian youths, retired people or jazz fans, for example, allow advertisers to reach a better-defined audience than mainstream broadcasters.

Non-cognitivism   *Non-cognitivism* states that morality is purely subjective or is bound up with the specific cultural context of individuals. Non-cognitivists say that there are no moral absolutes, only beliefs, attitudes and opinions.

Non-governmental organisations (NGOs)   Groups without governmental affiliation that have a particular interest in a subject: for example, charities and campaign groups.

Objective   A clearly defined end-point that the public relations programme is designed to achieve.

Operationalisation   The process of defining a fuzzy concept (knowledge, attitudes, behaviour) and showing how this concept is to be measured.

Opportunity analysis   The process of identifying opportunities for sponsorship.

Organisational culture   The expression of attitudes within an individual organisation. This term encapsulates the values and beliefs, and patterns of behaviour and language, that are the norm for that group of people, providing a framework of meaning for the organisation.

Organisational identity   The sum total of proactive, reactive and unintentional activities and messages of organisations.

Organisational image   The impression gained by an individual of an organisation at one moment in time. Organisational image can differ from individual to individual and also throughout time.

Organisational public relations   These affect an entire organisation, not just one (or a few) of its parts in isolation. Organisational public relations are proactive, and strategies are deployed and managed to reduce the gap between how the various internal and external publics of an organisation view it and how the organisation would like to be viewed by those publics.

Organisational reputation   This consists of the sum total of images an individual has accumulated over a period of time that lead an individual to form an opinion about an organisation.

OTS (Opportunities to see)   The total number of times, potentially, that a public could be exposed to a message – known in the USA as 'impressions'.

Outcome   The ultimate impact of public relations activity.

Output   The immediate product of public relations activity.

Oxygen of publicity   This phrase was first used by Margaret Thatcher in a speech to the American Bar Association (London, 15 July 1985), when referring to the need to 'starve the terrorist and the hijacker of the oxygen of publicity on which they depend'. The image springs from the way that oxygen increases the intensity of a fire – in other words, publicity fans the flames of a cause.

PA   The Press Association.

Paternalism   When an elite group of people, often experts, make decisions in a 'fatherly' manner on behalf of the general public, about what is 'good' or appropriate for them.

Path to purchase   This describes the stages a consumer takes in the journey from initial need and product awareness to purchase and consumption.

Philanthropy   Defined in the *Concise Oxford Dictionary* as 'a love of humankind; practical benevolence, especially charity on a large scale'.

Pickup systems   These are a key element of crisis preparedness when it is essential to have systems in place to identify potential crisis situations in advance and to provide up-to-date information on how the company is perceived during a crisis. Many agencies provide news-monitoring services; others monitor content in Internet chat rooms, giving real-time updates of what is being said. An effective pickup system, of course, also needs dedicated resources within the company to act on the intelligence available, and a defined communication tree of developing issues.

Piloting   Testing a questionnaire among a few people from the target population to be investigated.

Pluralism   The social and political condition whereby differing values, behaviours and material interests coexist, with different organisations and groups representing them. All these groups have political and economic rights. Civic and commercial pluralism are these differences expressed outside and inside markets.

Pluralists   *Pluralists* suggest that power and influence are widely dispersed in modern democracies, not just by the right to vote and checks and balances in the political system, but more particularly through the activities and effective influence of countless freely competing pressure groups.

Postmodernism in public relations   There are no absolute truths and PR departments/companies can generate perceived truths among publics through their role as creators of organisational discourse. Postmodernist PR recognises that the language used in PR also generates, sustains and shapes power relations in society.

Pressure group   Any organised group that seeks to exert influence on government (at any level) to influence particular policies or decisions.

Price-sensitive information   If information is price sensitive, it is confidential information that the stock market is unaware of and, were it known, would cause the share price of a company to rise or fall.

Proactive   To control a situation, issue or crisis, rather than responding to something after it happens. (See **Reactive**.)

PRSA   Public Relations Society of America.

Psychographics   Attributes relating to internal differences between personalities – e.g. anxious, approval-seeking, high self-esteem, etc.

Psychological contract   The perceptions of the employee and employer regarding their mutual obligations towards each other.

Public affairs   A public relations specialism that seeks to influence public policy making via lobbying and/or through the media.

Public diplomacy   The process by which a government communicates with foreign publics in an attempt to foster an understanding of its nation's ideas and ideals, its institutions and culture, as well as its national goals and current policies.

Public goods   These are goods required by everybody but which no one, individually, has an incentive to produce. Examples of these are energy conservation and the problems of pollution.

Public relations   This has been defined as 'about reputation – the result of what you do, what you say and what others say about you. Public relations practice is the planned and sustained effort to establish and maintain goodwill and mutual understanding between an organisation and its publics.' (Chartered Institute of Public Relations 2005: www.cipr.co.uk)

Public service   The idea that broadcast media have a responsibility to provide a service to inform, educate and entertain the public. Implicit in this idea is that minority interests are catered for.

Qualitative research   A field of enquiry that aims to identify, and carry out an in-depth exploration of, phenomena such as reasons, attitudes, etc. (See **Quantitative research**.)

Quango   An acronym standing for 'quasi-autonomous non-governmental organisation'. In practice, quangos are appointed (rather than elected) public bodies. Examples in the UK include the Health and Safety Commission, Learning and Skills Councils and Primary Care Trusts.

Quantitative research A field of enquiry that aims to quantify variables such as attitudes or behaviours and point out correlations between them. Results can be generalised, which means research that generates findings can be applied to a wider public or situation. (See **Qualitative research**.)

Reactive Responding to an issue or crisis rather than creating or controlling it: for example, a public relations activity being driven by the demands of others rather than the plans of the communicators. Sometimes communicators need to be reactive – that is, be able to respond quickly to situations. (See **Proactive**.)

Readership The actual numbers reached by written communications. Note that more people read trade journals because they are based in an office with one subscription, which is shared: for example, the *Architects' Journal* is circulated around the team in an architects' practice, often with comments on relevant or interesting features/ articles.

Reform journalism Practised by journalists who oppose, for example, the exploitation of workers for the sake of profit and press for social change to curb the negative effects of enterprise.

Refusenik Originally a citizen of the former Soviet Union, especially a Jewish citizen, who was not allowed by the government to emigrate. Now the term refers to somebody who refuses to cooperate with something.

Renqing A set of social norms based on the exchange of gifts and support, by which one must abide to get along well with others in Chinese society.

Representative democracy A system of democracy whereby people are allowed to vote for somebody to represent them in government. In the UK, this happens at local level in council elections and at national level in the House of Commons.

Return on investment (ROI) The positive value or contribution that can be achieved by making an investment in a particular business activity. In marketing communications terms, this might include the sales resulting from specific, identifiable and measurable communications activities. For example, £5 million sales directly attributable to a direct mail campaign costing £1 million provides a £4 million return on the communication investment. Although described here in financial terms, the 'return' might also be assessed more subjectively by measuring increased brand awareness or improved corporate image resulting from a range of communications activities.

Rhetoric The study of language and how it is used to create shared meanings.

Risk management The business technique of anticipating, minimising and preventing accidental loss through taking precautionary measures.

RNS Regulatory News Service.

Sales promotion Short-term or temporary inducements – for example, price cuts or two-for-one offers – designed to encourage consumers to use a product or service.

Sampling Deriving a small sub-group of the research population, frequently designed to be representative.

Scenario planning Involves playing out different outcomes of a sponsorship, anticipating what could happen.

SEC Securities and Exchange Commission (US).

Semiotics The study of language, symbols and images and how they are created by audiences or used to generate relevant meaning.

Senior practitioners People who occupy a formal senior management position in their organisations, or people who hold a skilled role that requires several years' of experience to gain the competence necessary to do the job.

Setting the agenda see **Agenda setting**.

Soap opera A broadcast drama, serialised in many episodes, which generally deals with domestic themes. The name originates from the USA where these types of programmes were sponsored by soap powder manufacturers targeting householders.

Social marketing The application of commercial marketing techniques to the analysis, planning, execution and evaluation of programmes designed to influence the voluntary behaviour of target audiences in order to improve their personal welfare and that of society (Andreasen 1995).

Sponsorship The provision of money, services, knowhow or in-kind support by corporations or organisations to individuals, groups or institutions involved in sports, charities, education or broadcasting, or in cultural and ecological activities. Activities are chosen for sponsorship based on their ability to project the right commercial and psychological message that fits in with the specific corporate goals of a sponsor.

Sponsorship property The venue, event, activity, cause, team or individual that is the subject of sponsorship.

Stakeholder Someone who has an interest (stake) in the organisation, which may be direct or indirect interest as well as active or passive, known or unknown, recognised or unrecognised.

Stand-out To give prominence to a brand, product or service through a marketing campaign.

Stock market index Wikipedia defines a *stock market index* as: 'a listing of stocks, and a statistic reflecting the composite value of its components. It is used as a tool to represent the characteristics of its component stocks, all of which bear some commonality such as trading on the same stock market exchange, belonging to the same industry, or having similar market capitalizations. Many indices compiled by news or financial services firms are used to benchmark the performance of portfolios such as mutual funds. Stock market indices may be classed in many ways. A broad-base index represents the performance of a whole stock market – and, by proxy, reflects investor sentiment on the state of the economy. The most regularly quoted market indices are broad-based indices including the largest listed companies on a nation's largest stock exchange, such as the American Dow Jones Industrial Average and S&P 500 Index, the British FTSE 100 and the Japanese Nikkei 225' (Wikipedia 2008).

Strategy selection Term used for selecting a sponsorship strategy.

Summative evaluation Evaluation carried out at the end of the programme of activity. (See **Formative evaluation**; **Goal-free evaluation**).

Systems theory The theory that describes how organisations work in terms of interlocking and interdependent systems of communication, production, etc. It embraces both the internal and external environments.

Tabloidisation This occurs when a 'quality' broadsheet attempts to broaden its appeal to popular interests – for example, through a greater focus on 'human interest' stories and celebrity gossip.

Tabloids Small-format newspapers, sometimes referred to as the 'popular press', often written in a sensationalist style and containing a large number of photographs.

Team briefing A method of communication whereby a line manager briefs their team – usually on a regular basis – about company policy and on day-to-day issues related to the completion of team tasks. Team briefings are often structured to allow for staff feedback and questions.

Terrestrial channels Television channels that broadcast from the UK and not via satellite. Terrestrial channels are subject to greater regulation than satellite channels.

Think-tank An organisation made up of experts who undertake research and provide advice to governments.

Tipping point The moment when the spread of a debate, idea, or message reaches critical point and ultimately leads to change. This phrase emerged from Gladwell's influential book, *The Tipping Point: How little things can make a big difference* (2000).

Transformational, interactional and inclusive Styles of management and leadership, employing negotiation and adjustment rather than hierarchy or command to make decisions.

Triple bottom-line reporting A phrase increasingly used to describe the economic, environmental and social aspects that are being defined and considered by business. These are sometimes called the three Ps – profit, plant and people.

Typology Classifying and dividing things according to 'type': for example, in a PR context, working out the key elements that distinguish one kind of PR practitioner, or activity, from another.

UKLA UK Listings Authority (a division of the FSA).

Upward communication A system of communication that allows employees to feed back their views to their team leaders or line managers, and where line managers in turn feed back these views to senior management.

Values The business practice of identifying an organisation's corporate vision – where it wants to go and how it wants to be perceived through its core values. (Go to the Internet and look up value and mission statements for corporations.)

Vision and values The business practice of identifying an organisation's corporate vision – where it wants to go and how it wants to be perceived through its core values.

Wannabe Negative slang for a person who aspires to be well known in the media or to be perceived as successful in a pursuit that is in the public eye (sport, arts, popular music, etc.), although lacking the necessary qualifications and/or talent.

Watchdog A term used to describe a body that monitors behaviour and activities in different sections of society to protect the consumer or citizen.

Weblog A website in the form of a diary, containing time-stamped articles and frequently linking to sources and other sites of interest. Weblogs usually reflect the views of one person or a small group of individuals and are read generally by a limited number of people on the Internet but are capable of attracting large readerships through references on other websites. Webloggers are the individuals who run weblog journals on the world wide web.

Whistleblower Someone who goes outside the normal reporting procedures to alert internal senior managers or external sources to wrongdoing, unethical behaviour or malpractice in the organisation. For example, employees who tell the public about financial mismanagement or theft inside an organisation, or government employees who leak evidence of wrongdoing such as arms sales to particular regimes, or government actions that contravene policy or legal frameworks.

Wicked problems   Problems that are unstructured and difficult to define, cutting across many stakeholders (Weber and Khademian 2008). These characteristics require fluid problem solving, the application of many different perspectives, collaboration and long-term commitment.

Wire service   A news-gathering organisation that distributes syndicated copy (information) electronically, as by teletype or the Internet, usually to subscribers.

World Trade Organisation (WTO)   This comprises 148 countries, and is the 'only global international organization dealing with the rules of trade between nations' (www.wto.org). The WTO is based in Geneva, Switzerland, and administers trade agreements, acts as a forum for trade negotiations and handles international trade disputes.

Index